INTERNATIONAL LAW

Cavendish
Publishing
Limited

London • Sydney

INTERNATIONAL LAW

John O'Brien

Lecturer in Law, University of Hertfordshire

Cavendish
Publishing
Limited

London • Sydney

First published in Great Britain 2001 by Cavendish Publishing Limited, The Glass House, Wharton Street, London WC1X 9PX, United Kingdom

Telephone: +44 (0)20 7278 8000   Facsimile: +44 (0)20 7278 8080

Email: info@cavendishpublishing.com

Website: www.cavendishpublishing.com

O'Brien, John
International law
1 International law
I Title
341

ISBN 185941 630 6

Printed and bound in Great Britain

This edition is dedicated to Louise and Joseph

INTRODUCTION

This is a text which attempts to set out the principles of public international law within a reasonable compass and in a manner which will be intelligible to the law student and also to those following courses in international relations.

In producing a general text on public international law a degree of choice has to be exercised. An attempt has been made both to outline matters of general principle but also to embrace specialist areas of concern such as the environment, human rights and economic co-operation. In the modern world there are a wide variety of opinions as to the nature of of international law. This volume proceeds on the assumption that in contemporary society, when problems arise between states, evidence can be received, facts found and legal rules determined. The extent to which those rules are applied or enforced will of course depend on the circumstances of the case.

This text appears at a time when international institutions are trying to absorb the changes precipitated by the end of the Cold War and the collapse of the Soviet Union. In Europe any euphoria or complacency that arose after 1989 has rapidly receded as evidence has come to light of the tragic events that accompanied the dissolution of the Socialist Federal Republic of Yugoslavia. In the last decade Europe has witnessed conduct of violence and brutality on a scale unprecedented since 1945. On another continent events in Rwanda after 1990 have raised difficult questions about how the international community can respond promptly enough to ensure minimum standards of conduct.

It is arguable that today the international community faces four distinct challenges. First, there is the problem of poverty, under-investment and economic disadvantage that blights lives in so many different states. Secondly, there is the need to curb aggression and to promote the peaceful settlement of disputes whilst also restraining the proliferation of weapons. Thirdly, the requirement exists to maintain and develop a respected corpus of international human rights law. Fourthly, there is the pressing task of developing measures of international environmental protection which themselves do not unduly restrict economic growth. None of these challenges is anything other than daunting; none can be attempted without states co-operating together. All four tasks will require leadership, statesmanship, understanding and co-operation. Increasingly the role of international law and international organisations has been to provide both a mechanism for rational discussion and a vehicle to facilitate co-operation.

A number of friends and colleagues have helped in the production of the text. Some commented on work in progress; others shared their practical knowledge and experience. I am indebted to Yutaka Aria, Lucy Canning, Marina D'Engelbronner, Ilaine Foster, Peter Marsh, Hersha Pandya, Mary Percival, Catherine Rendell, Harjit Singh, David Slee, Colleen South, Diana Tribe and Charles Wild. It is proper that I should record my thanks to Jacqui Coleman and Eppey Gunn for their considerable help and advice in matters of word processing. However, I alone am responsible for the errors, omissions and infelicities that remain.

I have attempted to state the law as at 31 March 2001 although it has proved possible to take account of certain later developments when correcting proofs.

Finally I should like to thank Jo Reddy, Cara Annett, Ruth Massey and the editorial staff at Cavendish Publishing for their patience, good humour and efficiency in organising the production of this edition.

John O'Brien
London
August 2001

CONTENTS

TABLE OF CASES

TABLE OF INTERNATIONAL LEGISLATION

Treaties and Conventions

Declarations

International documents

OVERSEAS LEGISLATION

Australia

Africa

Canada

China

Columbia

Cuba

Cyprus

TABLE OF ABBREVIATIONS

AC	Law Reports, Appeal Cases (United Kingdom)
AD	Annual Digest of Public International Law Cases (vols 1–15 (1919–48)), thereafter continued as the International Law Reports
Adv Op	Advisory Opinion
All ER	All England Law Reports
AFDI	Annuaire Francais de Droit International
AFJICL	African Journal of International and Comparative Law
AG	Aktiengesellschaft/public company (Germany)
AJCL	American Journal of Comparative Law
AJIL	American Journal of International Law
ALR	Australian Law Reports
ASIL	American Society of International Law
AYIL	Australian Yearbook of International Law
BFSP	British and Foreign State Papers
BGH	Bundesgerichtshof (Germany) Federal Court of Justice
BVerfG	Bundesverfassungsgericht (Germany) Federal Constitutional Court
BYIL	British Yearbook of International Law
CEDAW	Convention on the Elimination of All Forms of Discrimination against Women (1979)
CFC	Geneva Convention on Fishing and the Conservation of the Living Resources of the High Seas (1958)
CFCs	chlorofluorocarbons
Ch	Law Reports, Chancery Division (United Kingdom)
CILJ	Cornell International Law Journal
Clunet	Journal du Droit International Privé (Clunet)
CLJ	Cambridge Law Journal
CLP	Current Legal Problems
CMLRev	Common Market Law Review
CMLR	Common Market Law Reports
Cmnd	Command Papers (United Kingdom)

CoLR	Columbia Law Review
Cranch	Cranch Reports, United States Supreme Court
Crim LR	Criminal Law Review (United Kingdom)
CSC	Geneva Convention on the Continental Shelf (1958)
CSCE	Conference on Security and Co-operation in Europe
CYIL	Canadian Yearbook of International Law
DLR	Dominion Law Reports
DUSPIL	Digest of United States Practice in International Law
EC	European Community
ECHR	European Convention on Human Rights and Fundamental Freedoms
ECJ	European Court of Justice
ECOSOC	United Nations Economic and Social Council
ECOWAS	Economic Community of West African States
ECR	European Court Reports
ECSC	European Coal and Steel Community
EEC	European Economic Community
EEZ	Exclusive Economic Zone
EFZ	Exclusive Fishing Zone
EHRR	European Human Rights Reports
EJIL	European Journal of International Law
ELR	European Law Review
ER	English Reports
ESA	European Space Agency
EU	European Union
EURATOM	European Atomic Energy Community
Ex D	Law Reports, Exchequer Reports (United Kingdom)
Fam	Law Reports, Family Division (United Kingdom)
FAO	United Nations Food and Agriculture Organisation

FCO	Foreign and Commonwealth Office
F 2d	Federal Reporter (Second Series) (United States)
FTA	Canada-United States Free Trade Agreement
GA	General Assembly (United Nations)
GAOR	General Assembly Official Reports
GA Res	General Assembly Resolution
GATT	General Agreement on Tariffs and Trade
GATS	General Agreement on Trade in Services
GJIL	Georgia Journal of International Law
GYIL	German Yearbook of International Law
HILJ	Harvard International Law Journal
HLR	Harvard Law Review
HR	Hague Academy of International Law Recueil Des Cours de l'Academie de droit international de La Haye Collected Courses of the Hague Academy of International Law
HRC	Human Rights Committee
HRJ	Human Rights Journal
HRLJ	Human Rights Law Journal
HRQ	Human Rights Quarterly
HSC	Geneva Convention on the High Seas (1958)
IBRD	International Bank for Reconstruction and Development (World Bank)
ICAO	International Civil Aviation Organisation
ICCPR	International Covenant on Civil and Political Rights (1966)
ICESCR	International Covenant on Economic, Social and Cultural Rights (1966)
ICJ	International Court of Justice/International Court of Justice Reports
ICLQ	International and Comparative Law Quarterly
ICRC	International Committee of the Red Cross
IDA	International Development Association
IFC	International Finance Corporation

IFOR	Implementation Force in (former) Yugoslavia
IJIL	Indian Journal of International Law
ILA	International Law Association
ILC	International Law Commission
ILC Ybk	International Law Commission Yearbook
ILM	International Legal Materials
ILO	International Labour Organisation
ILR	International Law Reports (from 1948 and following on from the Annual Digest and Reports of Public International Law cases)
ILQ	International Law Quarterly
IMO	International Maritime Organisation
IMF	International Monetary Fund
IR	Irish Reports
Iran-US CTR	Iran-United States Claims Tribunal Reports
ITU	International Telecommunication Union
JBL	Journal of Business Law
JSL	Journal of Space Law
JWTL	Journal of World Trade Law
KB	Law Reports, King's Bench (United Kingdom)
LAS	League of Arab States
LNTS	League of Nations Treaty Series
LOSC	United Nations Convention on the Law of the Sea (1982)
LQR	Law Quarterly Review
LS	Legal Studies
MARPOL	International Convention for the Prevention of Pollution from Ships (1973)
MIJL	Michigan Journal of International Law
MIGA	Multilateral Investment Guarantee Agency

MLR	Modern Law Review
Moore Int Arb	Moore, History and Digest of the International Arbitrations to which the United States has been a Party, 6 vols (Washington DC)
NATO	North Atlantic Treaty Organisation
NGOs	Non-governmental organisations
NLJ	New Law Journal
NILR	Netherlands International Law Review
NQHR	Netherlands Quarterly of Human Rights
NYIL	Netherlands Yearbook of International Law
NZLR	New Zealand Law Reports
OAS	Organisation of American States
OAU	Organisation of African Unity
OCSE	Organisation for Co-operation and Security in Europe
OECD	Organisation for Economic Co-operation and Development
OEEC	Organisation for European Economic Co-operation
OPEC	Organisation of Petroleum Exporting Countries
P	Law Reports, Probate, Divorce and Admiralty Division of the High Court (United Kingdom) (1891–1972)
PCA	Permanent Court of Arbitration
PCIJ	Permanent Court of Justice
PCIJ, Ser A	Permanent Court of Justice Collection of Judgments (1922–30)
PCIJ, Ser A/B	Permanent Court of Justice, Collection of Judgments Orders and Advisory Opinions (1931–40)
PCIJ, Ser B	Permanent Court of Justice, Collection of Advisory Opinions (1922–30)
PD	Law Reports Probate Divorce and Admiralty Division of the High Court (United Kingdom) (1875–90)
PL	Public Law (United Kingdom)
PLO	Palestine Liberation Organisation

QB	Law Reports, Queens Bench Division of the High Court (United Kingdom)
Restatement	American Law Institute, *Restatement of the Law: The Foreign Relations of the United States,* 3rd edn, 2 vols (1987)
RDILC	Revue de droit international et de legislation comparée
RIAA	United Nations Reports of International Arbitral Awards
RPF	Rwandese Patriotic Front
SALR	South African Law Reports
SALJ	South African Law Journal
SAYIL	South African Yearbook of International Law
SC	United Nations Security Council
SDR	Special Drawing Rights
SIA	State Immunity Act 1978 (United Kingdom)
SJIL	Stanford Journal of International Law
TGS	Transactions of the Grotius Society
TRIMs	Trade Related Investment Measures
TRIPS	Trade Related Intellectual Property Rights
TSC	Geneva Convention on the Territorial Sea and the Contiguous Zone (1958)
UDHR	Universal Declaration on Human Rights (1948)
UKMIL	United Kingdom Materials in International Law
UKTS	United Kingdom Treaty Series
UN	United Nations
UNCC	United Nations Compensation Commission
UNCED	United Nations Conference on Environment and Development
UNCHR	United Nations Centre of Human Rights
UNCITRAL	United Nations Commission on International Trade Law
UNCLOS I	First United Nations Conference on the Law of the Sea (1958)
UNCLOS II	Second United Nations Conference on the Law of the Sea (1960)
UNCLOS III	Third United Nations Conference on the Law of the Sea (1973–82)

UNCTAD	United Nations Conference on Trade and Development
UNEP	United Nations Environment Programme
UNESCO	United Nations Educational, Scientific and Cultural Organisation
UNTS	United Nations Treaty Series
UNYB	United Nations Yearbook
UPU	Universal Postal Union
US	United States Reports (Supreme Court)
USTS	United States Treaty Series
Va JIL	Virginia Journal of International Law
VCIO	Vienna Convention on the Law of Treaties between States and International Organisations (1986)
VCSST	Vienna Convention on the Succession of States in Respect of Treaties (1978)
VCT	Vienna Convention on the Law of Treaties (1969)
WEU	Western European Union
WHA	World Health Assembly
WHO	World Health Organisation
Wis ILJ	Wisconsin International Law Journal
WLR	Weekly Law Reports (United Kingdom)
WTO	World Trade Organisation
YBIL	Yearbook of International Law
YBWA	Yearbook of World Affairs
YJIL	Yale Journal of International Law
YLJ	Yale Law Journal
Zao RV	Zeitschrift für ausländisches öffentliches Recht und Volkerrecht
ZLW	Zeitschrift für Luft und Weltraumrecht
ZVR	Zeitschrift für Volkerrecht

GLOSSARY

ab initio:	from the beginning
actio popularis:	a legal action brought on behalf of a number of citizens
amicus curiae:	an individual allowed to present arguments relevant to a case before a tribunal or court but not representing the interests of any of the parties to the proceedings
animus:	intention
animus revertendi:	the intention of returning
casus belli:	an act provoking or justifying war
compromis:	an agreement between states to submit an issue to a tribunal or court
consuetudo:	established usage
culpa:	the term used in civil law jurisdictions to show a lack of reasonable care
de facto:	as a fact
de jure:	as of right
de lege ferenda:	the law as it should be
dicta:	statements in a court judgment not directed to the central issues in the case
dolus:	the intention to inflict harm
erga omnes:	valid against 'all the world'
ex aqueo et bono:	a judgment of the International Court of Justice based not on strict rules of international law but on those principles that seem appropriate to the Court
in casu:	in the instant case
in limine:	at the outset without the need to consider other matters
in statu nascendi:	in the state of being born
inter se:	between the parties to a specific transaction
jure gestionis:	acts *jure gestionis* are state acts of a commercial character
jure imperii:	acts *jure imperii* are state acts of a sovereign or governmental character
lex causae:	the law governing an issue

lex domicilii:	the law of a person's domicile
lex fori:	the law of the country whose court is dealing with the matter
lex loci delicti commissi:	the law of the place where a tort is committed
lex situs:	the law of the place where the property is situated
locus regit actum:	the law of the place where an act takes place governs that act
locus standi:	the existence of a sufficient legal interest in the matter in issue
modus vivendi:	a way of co-existing
ne bis in idem:	no person should be proceeded against twice in respect of the same matter
onus probandi:	the burden of proof
opinio juris:	a requirement in the formation of a rule of customary international law; the belief that a practice is mandatory rather than habitual
opinio juris sive necessitas:	acknowledgment that a rule is binding either because it is the law or because it is necessary so to do
pacta sunt servanda:	the principle in customary international law that treaties are binding on the parties
par in parem non habet imperium:	the principle that one sovereign state cannot sit in judgment on another sovereign state by reason of their legal equality. An equal has no authority over an equal
prima facie:	in principle
public international law:	international law: the term used to distinguish it from the conflict of laws or private international law
qua:	in the capacity of
ratio decidendi:	the propositions of law arising from a case
ratione materiae:	by reason of the subject matter
ratione personae:	by reason of the status or dignity of the person
ratione temporis:	by reason of time
rebus sic stantibus:	the implication of a clause or term in a treaty that the obligations come to an end with a change of circumstances

res communis:	territory not open to acquisition by any state but to be enjoyed by all members of the international community
res extra commercium:	things outside commerce; territory which is not subject to national appropriation but is open to use by all
res inter alios acta:	a matter affecting third parties
res judicata:	a matter on which a court has already reached a binding decision, the implication being that the same matter cannot be re-litigated between the same parties
sensu lato;	in its broad meaning
sensu stricto:	in its narrow meaning
stare decisis:	the principle that a tribunal should follow its own previous decisions and those of superior tribunals
sui generis:	of its own kind
sui juris:	of full age and capacity
terra nullius:	territory which does not belong to any state or people and is thus capable of acquisition by 'occupation'
travaux preparatoires:	preparatory work in respect of the conclusion of a treaty
ultra vires:	outside the lawful powers of a person or agent
uti possidetis:	the principle that the frontiers of a independent state should follow those of the prior colonial territory

CHAPTER 1

THE NATURE AND HISTORY OF PUBLIC INTERNATIONAL LAW

1 INTRODUCTION

Public International Law (sometimes known as the Law of Nations) is that system of law which is primarily concerned with the relations between states. Although the full title of the subject is 'Public International Law' many today simply refer to the discipline as 'International Law'; however such an abbreviated title can lead to confusion with the related but distinct subject of Private International Law. It is widely accepted that Public International Law has grown steadily both in volume and importance since the 16th century. At the beginning of the 20th century it could be confidently asserted by one leading authority[1] that Public International Law was concerned only with the relations between states; however it is accepted today that the subject extends to rights and duties pertaining to international organisations,[2] companies[3] and individuals.[4] Nevertheless many of these developments are of comparatively recent origin so that one can still safely assert that Public International Law is primarily concerned with the relations between states.

As previously indicated it is usual to refer to that branch of law that governs the relations between states as Public International Law. However, until the 19th century it was common to employ the expression 'the Law of Nations' and while the expression 'Public International Law' is widely used by scholars and judges some have sought to use other expressions such as 'the common law of mankind'[5] or 'transnational law'.[6] The expression 'Public International Law' appears to have been first used by the English philosopher Jeremy Bentham at the end of the 18th century.[7] From the beginning of the 19th century it has been usual to draw a distinction between Public and Private International Law. The expression 'Private International Law' would appear to have first been employed by Joseph Story in 1834[8] and the subject itself comprises those rules that apply when a domestic court is confronted with a claim that concerns a foreign element. A simple example would be where an English court is concerned with a bequest made by a French citizen who died domiciled in Italy or where two English persons on holiday in

---

1   LH Oppenheim (1858–1919) in *International Law*, 1st edn, 1905. For the influence of Oppenheim, see later in Chapter 5.

2   'Reparations for injuries suffered in the service of the United Nations' (1949) ICJ 174; 16 ILR 318.

3   *Barcelona Traction, Light and Power Company* case (1970) ICJ 3; 46 ILR 178.

4   The obvious example being the development of a distinct international human rights law in the period following the Second World War and in particular since the Universal Declaration on Human Rights (1948). The development of this particular aspect will be outlined in the chapter devoted to human rights (Chapter 15).

5   CW Jenks (1909–73), *The Common Law of Mankind*, 1958.

6   PC Jessup (1897–1986), *Transnational Law*, 1956.

7   Jeremy Bentham (1748–1832) in 1780 in his *Introduction to the Principles of Morals and Legislation*. Bentham followed Hobbes and Puffendorf in questioning whether International Law was indeed law. This approach was adopted by his follower John Austin (1790–1859) and is discussed below.

8   Joseph Story (1779–1845) (Judge, US Supreme Court 1811–1845), *Commentaries on the Conflict of Laws*, 1st edn, 1834.

Spain are involved in a road accident that injures a German motorist and an Italian pedestrian. In the first case, concerning succession to property, there is clearly a number of foreign elements and the second, a case of an alleged tort, raises questions as to which court should have jurisdiction and which law should be applied. These are examples of the practical problems that fall to be resolved within the scope of Private International Law. It is sometimes asserted that Private International Law comprises three elements, namely: (i) which court should exercise jurisdiction; (ii) which law should be applied; and (iii) to what extent will country A recognise and enforce judgments given by the courts of country B. Clearly the subject is concerned with rights arising in private law and enforceable by individuals against each other. Although the title 'Private International Law' is used widely in the United Kingdom the subject is more usually referred to as the 'conflict of laws'.[9] In the United States it is common to use the expression 'the conflict of laws' rather than 'Private International Law'[10] thus enabling Public International Law to be referred to simply as 'International Law'.

Certain subjects such as the topic of jurisdiction may arise in both Public International Law and Private International Law. It is not unusual for a piece of litigation to give rise to problems in both areas.[11] However, an important distinction between the two subjects is that, while Public International Law is said to comprise a single system, there can be as many forms of Private International Law as there are municipal systems. To return to the example cited above, a German court might well apply a different rule in respect of a bequest made by a French citizen dying domiciled in Germany. But in Public International Law if a German court and an English court were seeking to establish the width of the territorial sea of either country they would be guided by the same relevant international conventions and the same prior judgments of the International Court of Justice.[12]

2 THE HISTORY OF PUBLIC INTERNATIONAL LAW

Public International Law cannot be properly understood without some knowledge of its history. The accepted view amongst scholars is that the subject began to emerge in Western Europe in the 16th century and that this emergence is associated with the evolution of the modern nation state. Partly this was a by product of the development of constitutional law as men began to reflect on the nature of sovereignty[13] and the

---

9   This may be partly due to the fact that AV Dicey (1835–1922) chose the title 'The Conflict of Laws' for his treatise in 1896; this has remained the pre-eminent work on the subject since that date. Prior to that date, the subject was probably more generally referred to as Private International Law. It is noteworthy that the first distinctly English text on the subject was by John Westlake (1828–1913) and appeared in 1858 as A Treatise on Private International Law and in rewritten form under the same title in 1880.

10 The expression 'private international law' widely used in Western Europe; although even in the United Kingdom both expressions are used as evidence by the enactment of the Private International Law (Miscellaneous Provisions) Act 1995.

11 For an example of litigation giving rise to problems in both areas, see Kuwait Airways Corporation v Iraqi Airways Company [1995] 1 WLR 1147 and subsequent proceedings.

12 The relevant international conventions being the Geneva Convention on the Territorial Sea and Contiguous Zone (1958) and the Law of the Sea Convention (1982).

13 Until 1700 most of the writers on the subject would have considered themselves to be theologians, philosophers or political scientists rather than lawyers.

responsibilities that a ruler owed to his subjects and to his fellow rulers. Many writers have argued that little guidance can be obtained from the period prior to 1500 since the medieval king even if secure internally owed external allegiance to either the Pope or the holy Roman Emperor.The broad structure of Public International Law reflects developments in Europe in the period after 1600;[14] indeed some writers see the period 1600 until 1914 as the period during which the classic rules of Public International Law were developed.[15]

Thus as a preliminary observation one can note that Public International Law is a subject that is the product of slow historical evolution and that something approaching a recognisable system of the Law of Nations came into existence in the 16th century and that the subject has grown in scope and volume since that date. However many of the matters that are now the concern of Public International Law can be traced back as far as ancient Greece.

Before examining the history in detail one should note at the outset that scholars of International Law have identified two theoretical bases for the subject. In general terms, the first school of thought asserts that one can deduce a series of principles superior to municipal or domestic law and these principles should govern the relations between nations. Such thinking involves a two stage process: (i) the assertion that human reason can be employed to deduce certain ethical standards; and (ii) that the deduction of these ethical standards may be aided by divine revelation or by the exercise of secular ethical theories. This school of thought is normally referred to as the natural law school. It is probably true that all writers on Public International Law prior to Grotius (1583–1645) considered themselves to be within the natural law tradition;[16] in the most general terms these writers sought to describe a system of law superior to municipal law.

The second school of thought which emerged in the 17th century was that of positivism. Positivism was based on the empirical tradition in philosophy that emerged during the Enlightenment and was particularly associated with the epistemology of John Locke.[17] The positivists approached International Law by asking who were the relevant legal persons, how did they behave and what rules did they accept as binding upon themselves. One of the legacies of the 16th century had been the identification of sovereignty as the essential precondition of the nation state; it was therefore a short step in the 17th century to assert that International Law comprised those minimum rules that individual states would accept. Thus, to a strict positivist International Law was no more than the minimum rules that individual states would accept.

A number of qualifications require to be made to these initial observations. The first is that International Law has not only been moulded by writers and judges but it has also

---

14 It might be thought that excessive emphasis is being placed on Europe, but it has to be borne in mind that, even as late as 1900, the only significant non-European powers were Japan and the United States.

15 It is arguable, therefore, that the classic period came to an end with the First World War and that one should then distinguish the periods (i) 1919–45; (ii) 1945–89; (iii) the post-Cold War period originating either with the assumption of power by President Gorbachev in 1985 or the collapse of the Soviet backed regimes in Eastern Europe after 1989.

16 Hugo Grotius (1583–1645) sometimes referred to as the founder of modern International Law. His views are set out in *De Jure Belli ac Pacis* (1625) and *Mare Liberum* (1609) and his contribution is discussed further below.

17 John Locke (1632–1704), in particular his *Essay concerning Human Understanding*, 1690.

been influenced by institutional changes. As will be seen later the role of international organisations has modified considerably the nature of International Law. Secondly it should be borne in mind that while the history of the subject since 1600 is testimony to the rise of positivism it should also be borne in mind that natural law thinking has emerged as an important influence in the years since 1945.

A third qualification concerns geography; as indicated above the broad history of International Law shows a subject that emerged in Western Europe in the years after 1600. The dominance of Europe is best indicated by reflecting that as recently as 1900 the only significant independent states outside Europe were Japan and the United States. This lead to a further important factor namely the increase in the number of independent states. The 20th century has witnessed a considerable increase in the number of states; indeed since 1945 the membership of the United Nations has more than tripled. Many of these states are the products of decolonisation and thus the International Community now contains many states that do not share the history of the legal systems of Western Europe. At the same time the world family now includes a large number of states at a low level of economic development.

A further important consideration is that International Law has been profoundly influenced by events; in municipal law, the constitutional law of a particular country is to an extent a reflection of the history of that country, so too with International Law. The present institutional structures and the law itself have been profoundly influenced by the two major armed conflicts of the 20th century and the lessons that statesmen drew from those experiences. If the United States had not emerged as the major world power after 1945, and if President Roosevelt[18] had been less energetic, it is unlikely that the United Nations Charter (1945) would have emerged in the form that it did in San Francisco in June 1945. In brief, the influence of political, military and economic factors upon International Law should not be underestimated.

With these broad considerations in mind it is proposed to take matters in the following order: (i) the period until 1500; (ii) the 16th century; (iii) the 17th century; (iv) the 18th century; (v) the period from 1800 until 1914; (vi) the establishment of the League of Nations system; (vii) the inter-war years (1919–39); (vii) the establishment of the United Nations system; (viii) the new system from 1945.

(a) The period until 1500

The consensus amongst scholars is that a recognisable *corpus* of International Law is no more than 500 years old. It is generally agreed that the subject as a distinct discipline began to to emerge in Europe in the years following 1500 as the concept of the self-sufficient state began to develop. The fact that the subject emerged from within Europe had the consequence that the subject came to be influenced by European conceptions of the sovereign nature, independence and equality of states. Many of the concepts of European political theory remain at the root of modern International Law.

---

18 Franklin Roosevelt (1882–1945) (President 1933–April 1945). The work on the preliminary drafts of the United Nations Charter had proceeded to a 'Draft Constitution' as early as June 1943 under the direction of the Secretary of State, Cordell Hull (1871–1955) (Secretary of State 1933–44).

However, even though the subject does not begin to emerge until 1500 it is necessary[19] to say a little of developments prior to that date. Records exist of the making of treaties and the sending of ambassadors from at least the time of ancient Egypt. The Code of Hammurabi[20] included provisions for the release of hostages on payment of ransom. The laws of the Hittites made reference to the requirement of a formal declaration of war and the establishment of peace by treaty. Indeed the conflict between Egypt and the Hittites in 1269 BC was brought to an end by a peace treaty. Around 1100 BC, Ramases II of Egypt concluded an agreement with the King of the Hittites pledging peace and brotherhood.

Later Cyrus, King of the Persians,[21] provided that enemy wounded should be treated in the same manner as his own soldiers. In so far as records exist, the subject itself is concerned with rights and duties pertaining to waging war and making peace.

Historians examining the records of the Greek city states have found evidence pertaining to the conduct of relations and declarations of war. These practices were clearly thought of as religious or moral rather than narrowly legal but they do indicate that the individual city states might as an entity conduct relations with other such entities. The history of Alexander the Great's[22] battles against the Persians reveal a willingness to avoid damage to certain property and include reference to the status of envoys and the exchange of prisoners of war. That these concerns were not restricted to Europe is indicated by the fact that the Indian epic *Mahabharata*[23] contains reference to the duty owed to an adversary incapable of further combat.

There has been some dispute as to the influence, if any, of the Roman Empire upon the development of International Law. In the sphere of armed conflict, the Romans were prepared to recognise the status of prisoners of war and acknowledged the need for formal declarations of war. During the Empire, relations between Rome and its various peoples were considered as legal relations. However these were not relations between sovereign independent entities. The more important long term influence of Roman law is that following the Reception,[24] when theologians and philosophers came to write about problems of international order in the 15th century, it was Roman law that provided the concepts and precedents capable of being applied to the relations between states.

---

19 See, on the history, A Nussbaum, *A Concise History of the Law of Nations*, 2nd rev edn, 1954.

20 Hammurabi, King of Babylon (1728 BC–1686 BC).

21 Cyrus the Great (died 529 BC) who established the Persian Empire and conquered Asia Minor adding Babylonia (including Syria and Palestine) to his Empire.

22 Alexander the Great (356 BC–323 BC).

23 *Mahabharata* (c 400 BC).

24 The reception is best viewed as an evolutionary trend whereby Roman law began to influence legal teaching in Western Europe. Beginning with Inerius (c 1055–1130) in Bologna and his analysis of Justinian's *Digest*, the movement was taken up by the commentators or post-glossators such as Bartolus (1314–57) and his pupil Baldus (1327–1400). Bartolus, who is sometimes viewed as the first writer on Private International Law, adopted Roman law to the problems posed by different jurisdictions in Italy. The teaching of Roman law came to be centred in the universities of Northern Italy, Southern France (Montpellier, Arles, Toulouse) and in Germany. Historians point to the importance of the Supreme Court of the Holy Roman Empire (*Reichskammergericht*) deciding in 1495 that half its judges had to be trained in Roman law. This practice had been adopted by other territories of the Empire, such as the Duchy of Burgundy and the Low Countries. It was therefore inevitable that Grotius (1583–1645) should be influenced by Roman law concepts when expounding the Law of Nations.

During the early medieval period there were a number of factors that restrained a distinct Law of Nations. First, Europe was said to represent a unity under the spiritual guidance of the Pope and the military restraint of the Holy Roman Emperor. The concept of the unity of Christendom prevented the growth of distinct states and a separate law governing their relations. Secondly, the feudal structure of Western Europe created a hierarchical structure that inhibited the development of autonomous states. In so far as natural law thinkers reflected upon any supranational law, they tended to concentrate upon the universality of natural law or canon law. At the same time, in those situations where trade was involved, states did make some concessions to a wider world. In England, a Law Merchant was established and applied to foreign traders in maritime disputes.

However, the medieval world of seeming spiritual and political unity would be fractured by a number of changes that began to emerge that would, in time, lead to: (i) the emergence of distinct states; (ii) the development of political theories as to the nature of government; and (iii) the development of a distinct Law of Nations. Although the allegiance of most people was local and the modern state was many years away, some historians have pointed to 1500 as a period when the unity of the medieval world had begun to fracture and the conditions began to emerge that would make a distinct Law of Nations possible. Among these factors were: (i) the emergence of monarchies in England France and Spain within distinct and broadly accepted boundaries; (ii) the development of the concept that the monarch alone was entitled to the legal use of force; (iii) the development of trade and the discovery of the New World;[25] (iv) the discovery of printing;[26] (v) the Renaissance in learning; and (v) the challenge to established authority represented by the Reformation.

(b) The 16th century

The early years of the 16th century witnessed a degree of ferment and intellectual debate that would fracture the unity of Christendom. In retrospect, one can detect four distinct themes that run through the century: (i) questions of religious belief and organisation; (ii) the relationship between religion and the ruler of a particular territory; (iii) the source of the power of a ruler and his relationship with his subjects; and (iv) the question as to how a ruler should conduct himself with his fellow rulers. In respect of the first matter, the effect of the Reformation was to weaken papal authority and to lead to the emergence of a

---

25   Although Christopher Columbus would not reach the West Indies until 1492 and Amerigo Vespucci discovered Brazil in 1499, the Portuguese had been engaged in exploration since 1450 and they concluded a treaty with Spain in 1479. Such endeavours were made possible by improvements in ship design and navigation during this period.

26   Normally credited to Johannes Gutenberg of Mainz in 1455; by 1475, William Caxton had, in England, produced a translation of the Bible. The discovery of printing enabled classical authors to become available to a wider audience just at the time when unity of Christianity was coming under attack.

form of nation state in England[27] while the Diet of Augsburg of 1555[28] recognised the religious and territorial division of Germany.

However, from the perspective of a developing International Law it is strongly arguable that the most important matter was the third element namely the increasing emphasis by writers and theorists as to the source of secular power. One of the first to ponder such questions was the Florentine diplomat Niccolo Machiavelli (1469–1527). Best known for *Il Principe* (1513), Machiavelli[29] perceived that the spiritual unity of Europe under the Pope and the political unity provided by the holy Roman Empire had been fractured. The state, he argued, was a self-standing entity. In *Il Principe* (1513) he reflected on how the Prince might retain power within the state and how he might conduct himself vis à vis his fellow rulers.

The problem of the location of political power began to be explored by writers. Martin Luther had favoured separate jurisdictions for spiritual and secular power[30] but his fellow reformer Jean Calvin had indicated that both should co-operate in a common enterprise.[31]

However, the most enduring impact was made by Jean Bodin[32] who published *Les Six Livres de la Republique* in 1576; Bodin held that sovereignty or supreme law making power was an essential characteristic of the ordered state. The location of sovereignty within the state was an important insight and it lead to at least five lines of future enquiry: (i) it was taken up by Thomas Hobbes[33] in the following century to develop a distinct political philosophy; (ii) it was drawn upon later by the English jurist John Austin[34] to develop, within municipal law, a theory of positivism; (iii) it was drawn upon by Grotius[35] in his early writings on Public International Law; (iv) it was impliedly adopted by Ulrich Huber in the first major text on Private International Law;[36] (vi) in the 18th century it would lead to distinctions between political sovereignty and legislative sovereignty. However, all these developments, in political theory, while they would influence International Law, remained in the future. It is important to say a little about the

---

27 There can be little doubt that the climate of debate was changed by the availability of printing; the printing of the 95 theses of Martin Luther (1483–1546) in 1517 expanded his influence and the translation and printing of the Bible permitted protestant clergymen to emphasise the content of an earlier form of Christianity. For the influence of Martin Luther, see Heiko Oberman, *Man Between God and the Devil*, 1989.

28 Which recognised the division of Germany and provided that each state should follow the religion of its particular ruler.

29 Machiavelli, who worked as a diplomat and undertook a number of missions, also produced *The Discourses* (written 1513–19); *The Art of War* (1520); *Florentine History* (1527). It is a matter of speculation as to whether the humiliations Machiavelli endured as a diplomat for Florence influenced the content of his political theory; see JR Hale, *Machiavelli and Renaissance Italy*, 1961.

30 *On Secular Authority*, 1523.

31 Jean Calvin (1509–64). The first edition of his *Institution of Christian Religion* appeared in 1536.

32 Jean Bodin (1530–96). Claimed by some to be the first work on political economy.

33 Thomas Hobbes (1588–1679), whose best known work, *Leviathan*, was published in 1651.

34 John Austin (1790–1859), who saw the nature of law as being the commands of a sovereign power backed by sanctions. Austin was to have considerable influence on the general perception of Public International Law; these matters are discussed further below.

35 Hugo Grotius (1583–1645), regarded today as the founder of modern Public International Law.

36 Ulrich Huber (1634–94). In his *De Conflictu Legum* (1689) he advanced as his first proposition that the laws of each state have authority within its frontiers. Such a formulation linked three concepts: (i) the state; (ii) sovereignty; and (iii) the territory.

early 16th century writers on International Law who drew upon a different strand of thinking.

The earliest writers on the Law of Nations[37] tend to be described as naturalists. One of the problems is that there were differences between them and the expression 'natural law' can be employed in a number of senses. In this context the expression might mean (i) a perfect law deducible by reason; (ii) the conditions *sine quibus non* for the existence of law; or (iii) the fundamental rights that men enjoy in the state of nature prior to the establishment of the state. The concept of a law of nature can be traced back to the ancient Greeks, although by this time the doctrine was particularly associated with the philosophy of Thomas Aquinas. Many of the early writers were Spanish or Portuguese, which was not surprising having regard to the fact that these were the countries most active in the work of exploration. Moreover, many of the writers had a background in theology or moral philosophy, so that it was a natural step to seek to apply Thomist philosophy to an emerging Law of Nations. The writers who comprise this grouping are Vittoria (1480–1546),[38] Brunus (1491–1563), Beli (1502–75), Fernandez Vasquez de Mechaca (1512–69), Ayala (1548–84), Suarez[39] (1548–1617) and Gentili[40] (1552–1608). These writers tended to concentrate on the circumstances of a just war, the right to use force and the freedom of the seas.

Particular attention should be devoted to Francisco de Vittoria who, in posthumously published lectures,[41] argued against the claim of the Pope and the holy Roman Emperor to exercise temporal jurisdiction over other princes. Vittoria saw the Law of Nations (or *jus gentium*[42] as he chose to describe it) as being founded on natural law, and in principle it governed not only relations with other states but also with non-European people. Similar sentiments can be found expressed in the work of Francisco Suarez. Suarez, who also held a chair in Theology, considered the Law of Nations to be founded upon natural law and he directed his attention to the contemporary problems of the legitimacy of the use of force, the freedom of the seas and the status of non-European peoples.[43]

In retrospect the most influential writer of the century was Alberico Gentili. Gentili was an Italian Protestant who became Regius Professor of Civil Law at Oxford in 1587.

---

37 This phrase or *droit de gens* tended to be used until well into the 19th century, although the expression 'International Law' used by Jeremy Bentham from 1780.

38 Francisco de Vittoria (1480–1546) was a Dominican friar and Professor of Theology at the University of Salamanca.

39 Francisco Suarez (1548–1617) Spanish Jesuit scholar and Professor of Theology; his *De Legibus ac deo Legislatore* (Treatise on Law and God the Legislator) (1612) he reflected on the circumstances in which the use of force was justified. In the posthumously published *De Fide* (1621), he rejected the view that conquered people were subject to a natural condition of servitude.

40 Alberico Gentili (1552–1608), Italian Protestant, who became Regius Professor of Civil Law at Oxford in 1587. His *De Jure Belli libri tres* (1598), which dealt with the right to wage war and freedom of the seas, was relied upon by Grotius in his subsequent work. See A Van der Mole, *Alberico Gentili and the Development of International Law*, 2nd edn, 1968; T Meron, 'Common rights of mankind in Gentili, Grotius and Suarez' (1991) 85 AJIL 110.

41 The lectures were delivered in Salamanca in 1539 but were not printed until 1557 as *De Indis et de Jure Belli Relectiones*.

42 The phrase *jus gentium* had originally been used to describe that part of the private law of Rome which was supposed to be common to Rome and other people; after Vittoria and Grotius, the phrase came to mean the law governing relations between one people and another.

43 Some of the views expressed subsequently in *De Triplici Vertute Theologica, Fide, Spe et Charitate* (The Three Theological Virtues, Faith, Hope and Charity) (1621).

His major work *De Jure Belli Libri Tres* appeared in 1598[44] and emphasised the secular aspect of natural law. Gentili devoted attention to the making of treaties, the use of force, the right of slaves and the freedom of the seas. There is little doubt that his work was heavily drawn upon by Grotius and there is a case for saying that he has not received sufficient recognition as the first writer to put the Law of Nations on a secular basis, so much so that some have argued that he should share with Grotius the title of the founder of International Law.[45]

Reviewing the situation in the year 1600, it is clear that the Reformation had fractured the unity of Western Europe and the individual ruler and his sovereignty was now a subject of analysis. Of the early writers on the Law of Nations, two features stand out: first, they has tended to base the subject on natural law or on analogies drawn from classical authors; secondly, they had been content to deal with the problems that seemed then to possess a contemporary relevance, such as the limits to the use of force, the acquisition of territory or the status of non-European peoples.

(c) The 17th century

The 17th century marks a transition between the divine based natural law theories of the previous century and the secular positivism of the 18th century. The most significant writer of the century was the man who is sometimes described as the founder of modern International Law. Dutch by birth, Hugo Grotius (1583–1645) was a true Renaissance polymath who mastered law, history, theology and mathematics; at various times, Grotius was a diplomat lawyer and scholar. His fame rests on his two main publications, *Mare Liberum* (1609) which argued for the freedom of the seas and *De Jure Belli ac Pacis* (1625). Grotius remained in the natural law tradition but he sought to found the Law of Nations upon a secular form of natural law. Grotius argued that human beings were both competitive and had a desire for harmony or society. A secular form of natural law would demonstrate how states could live together without conflict; this secular natural law was not the product of divine revelation but of sober reflection on the human condition.

By the use of reason, individuals could determine that rules should operate to govern relations between rulers; these rules were not the concern of theology. Indeed, Grotius argued that, even if there were no God, a secular form of natural law would be required to regulate relations between states; this was a bold claim in a century bedevilled by religious conflict. After Grotius, the Law of Nations would be founded on a mixture of secular natural law and positivism. In considering the writings of Grotius, three qualifications need to be made: first, much had been said before by other writers; secondly, some of the views expressed by Grotius were favourable to the trading interests of the Dutch East India Company and were contrary to the claims of Spanish or Portuguese interests who were anxious to limit the freedom of the seas and the access to territory; and thirdly, the writings of Grotius were influential because his works were studied in the universities and by diplomats. Many of the subjects treated by Grotius such

---

44 The first part had appeared in 1588, the second and third in 1589. On Gentili, see T Meron, 'Common rights of mankind in Gentili, Grotius and Suarez' (1991) 85 AJIL 110.

45 A view expressed by TE Holland in his inaugural lecture in 1874.

as the legitimacy of force or the freedom of the seas had been treated elsewhere but none had sought to set out such a comprehensive treatment founded on such wide ranging scholarship.

It is a matter of much debate as to whether Grotius should be accorded the title of the 'founder of International Law'. Some have argued that he was overly influenced by the interests of the Dutch East India Company, while others have contended that he was anxious to restore the unity of Christendom that had been fractured by the Reformation.[46] It may be that a man is recognised as the founder of a particular discipline because his work is published at an opportune time and that, although his views have been expressed previously by others, he has brought such opinions together to constitute a coherent whole and then those views have been accepted by subsequent generations. In an influential article, Professor Lauterpacht[47] argued that, even if what Grotius had written was not original, he had brought together many independent streams of thought and expressed matters in a particularly scholarly manner. Secondly, Professor Lauterpacht argued that there can be found in *De Jure Belli ac Pacis* (1625) textual support for a number of ideas that have subsequently gained general acceptance. Among these would be: (i) the principle that international relations are subject to the rule of law and that this exists independent of theology; (ii) that a secular natural law had a role as a source of International Law; (iii) that the social nature of man was the basis of the law of nature; (iv) that the basic unit of international relations was the state; (v) that the principle of *raison d'etat* was not acceptable as foundation of the Law of Nations; (vi) that one of the principal tasks of the writer on the subject was to differentiate between the just and the unjust war; and (vii) that one of the tasks of the subject is to promote peace or, as would be said today, it is to promote the peaceful settlement of disputes.

Probably the reason why Grotius has been accepted as the founder of the Law of Nations is that he was possessed of such a level of erudition that, even though a Protestant of Lutheran leaning, he had a detailed knowledge of the natural law thinking of Catholic theologians and he attempted to apply this to the post-Reformation world. Although admitted as a lawyer, he was knowledgeable in classics, theology and history and knew enough of practical diplomacy to avoid the exclusively theoretical. Drawing upon the natural law teaching that extended back to Aquinas, he was able to represent it in a secular fashion in a manner calculated to win acceptance in the post-Reformation world of independent states.

The most significant political event of the century in Europe was the Peace of Westphalia (1648). In effect this brought to an end the period of religious wars and restricted the power of the Papacy and the Holy Roman Emperor. The Peace of Westphalia was significant in that those German princes capable of conducting relations were separately represented. Europe was no longer subject to a unified Church or a lay Emperor; Protestant states in Germany and those beyond would be free to regulate worship within their own territories and more importantly to conduct their own external

---

46 On Grotius, see M Shaw, *International Law*, 4th edn, 1997, p 21; RW Lee, 'Hugo Grotius' (1946) 62 LQR 53; H Lauterpacht, 'The Grotian tradition in international law' (1946) 23 BYIL 1.

47 H Lauterpacht (1897–1960) (Professor of International Law 1937–55) (Judge ICJ 1955–60); H Lauterpacht (1946) 23 BYIL 1 'The Grotian tradition in international law'.

relations. The policy of France's Cardinal Richelieu (1585–1642) had been to create semi-autonomous states within Germany and to restrict the expansion of Hapsburg power.[48] By endorsing the principle of *cujus regio, ejus religio*, the Peace of Westphalia had paved the way for the development of the Law of Nations as a set of rules devised by foreign princes to regulate dealings with each other. Grotius himself had acted as a diplomat for the Netherlands and Sweden and had negotiated with Richelieu. Although Grotius died before the Peace of Westphalia, he had anticipated it; by advocating a Europe of orderly relations between independent states freed from the hegemonial power of the Hapsburgs, Grotius had opened the way for the new European society in a manner consistent with the interests of the protestant states of Europe. It is not without relevance that Grotius had a background in law and diplomacy unlike many of the writers of the previous century who had a background in theology and were more inclined to see a unity in Christendom. The Peace of Westphalia (1648) made it impossible to return to a universal Europe under a single holy Roman Emperor; instead stability was to be sought by separate states attempting to achieve a balance of power.

Two other writers on International Law during the century testified to the evolving nature of the subject. Samuel Pufendorf (1632–94) in his *De Jure Nature et Gentium* in 1672 viewed the Law of Nations as founded on universal natural rights and considered war lawful in only strictly limited circumstances where natural law had been violated. The work was only of limited value, first because it was too abstract and theoretical and, secondly, because the author failed properly to take account of evidence of state practice and the increasing importance of relations founded on treaties.[49]

A completely different approach was advanced by Richard Zouche (1590–1661) who, like Gentili, was Professor of Civil Law at Oxford. Zouche[50] rejected natural law and concentrated upon how sovereign rulers behaved. This emphasis upon actual conduct rather than a theory of natural law has lead some to claim Zouche as the first writer of the positivist school. In retrospect, it is clear that Gentili, Grotius and Zouche had the legal and diplomatic backgrounds similar to future writers on International Law. The era of International Law as part of theology was passing. However, it is important to note the indirect influence of two of the most important philosophers of the century.

Thomas Hobbes (1588–1679) had witnessed the Civil War in England (1642–49), the execution of a monarch and the Thirty Years War (1618–48) and reflected upon the misery caused by revolution, war and the employment of armed force. In his principal work, *Leviathan* (1651), Hobbes argued that the sorry condition of man within the state of nature made it necessary to establish civil society under a contractual relationship with a

---

48 Cardinal Richelieu (1585–1642) (First Minister of France 1624–42) had sought to establish French supremacy in Europe by breaking Hapsburg power. This he accomplished by establishing coalitions with Sweden and the German Protestant princes against Austria; from 1635, France had participated in the Thirty Years' War. The effect of such coalitions was to further fracture the political unity that had existed in Europe; it also illustrated the principle that one state might be able to secure a balance of power in Europe by constructing coalitions of like minded states.

49 Samuel Pufendorf had been Professor of Philosophy at the University of Heidelberg and, although he had worked in the service of Sweden, his work owed more to the former than the latter.

50 Richard Zouche was Regius Professor of Civil Law (1620–61) and, like Gentili, he had experience of the Admiralty courts, serving as an Admiralty judge from 1641. In his *Juris et Juducii, sive Juris inter gentes ... explicatio* (1650), Zouche preferred to write of *juris inter gentes* rather than *jus gentium* and he devoted considerable attention to the actual conduct of states.

sovereign power. He emphasised that any study of individual states must concentrate upon the location of sovereign power within that state. Although his analysis tended towards absolutism, Hobbes stressed that sovereign power derived not from divine right or natural law but from the contractual relationship with the subject. Although the emphasis on absolutism was to be repugnant to future generations, Hobbes was within the tradition of Bodin in stressing the importance of secular power within a sovereign state. According to Hobbes only the sovereign could make war or declare peace and only the sovereign could make laws.[51]

Of more far reaching impact was the work of a fellow Englishman, John Locke (1632–1704) and it is arguable that no philosopher has had greater impact on the related subjects of constitutional law and International Law. In the *Two Treatises of Government* (1690), Locke contended that governments were necessary evils in civil society and that ideally they were based on a form of social contract that existed to preserve fundamental rights. By rejecting divine right and emphasising the consent of the governed, Locke's ideas would be influential in the years after 1760 when the American colonists began to resist the rule of George III. Locke agreed with Hobbes that it was the uncertainty of the state of nature that caused men to establish civil society; however, he emphasised that government was only legitimate if founded on consent. Both writers held the view that the state was legitimated by the need to avoid war and general disorder.[52] This analysis of the contractual nature of government and the need for governments to be subject to certain legal controls would, in the 18th century, influence those who sought republican government within the terms of a written constitution.[53] Locke argued that the state existed for the benefit of its citizens, that it was founded on consent and that the power of the state was limited and should be exercised for the benefit of its citizens.

In relation to the Law of Nations, the opinions expressed in John Locke's other well known work proved more directly relevant. In his *Essay Concerning Human Understanding* (1690), Locke advanced the view that human knowledge was founded upon sensation and reflection. The emphasis upon empirical knowledge[54] was at the basis of the 18th century movement known as the Enlightenment. Applied to the Law of Nations, the empiricist would prefer to found his conclusions upon the actual and expressed conduct of states rather than on principles to be deduced with the aid of divine revelation or secular reason.[55] The emphasis on empiricism in the Law of Nations was reflected in those writers that are described as positivists. Although the expression 'positivism' has many different meanings that vary according to the context, in the sphere of International Law positivism as a school began to develop after 1700 and viewed the Law of Nations

---

51 On Thoman Hobbes, see RS Peters Hobbes (1956); CB Macpherson, *The Political Theory of Possessive Individualism*, 1964; Leviathan edited and with an introduction by CB Macpherson (1985).

52 On John Locke, see Maurice Cranston; John Locke: *A Biography*, 1957; John Dunn: *Locke*, 1984; John W Yolton, *Locke: An Introduction*, 1985.

53 The influence of John Locke is clear in the Preamble to the United States Declaration of Independence (July 1776).

54 In contrast to the view advanced by Rene Descartes (1596–1650) that individuals were each endowed with innate ideas whose validity was authenticated by God.

55 The influence of Locke in this area was considerable; the first book specifically on the law of evidence in England by Jeffrey Gilbert (1674–1726) was dedicated to and founded upon the epistemology of John Locke.

as: (i) comprising independent states; (ii) regulating the relations between independent states; and (iii) examining the actual conduct of those states as expressed in treaties or as manifested over a period of time. The positivist would tend to stress the regulatory nature of International Law rather than fundamental ethical principles.

For the historian, it is clear that the 17th century had been a formative period for International Law. Europe had divided into distinct states and that division had been validated in the Peace of Westphalia (1648). Secondly, the concept of the sovereignty of the individual state had come to be accepted. Thirdly, statesmen had come to accept a Law of Nations of a regulatory character that served to determine the relations between independent sovereigns based on actual conduct rather than immutable ethical principles.

(d) The 18th century

Developments in the Law of Nations in the 18th century took place against the background of the Enlightenment. Although the precise limits of the period are the subject of debate, it is generally accepted that the spirit of the Enlightenment endured until at least 1740, when it assumed a less optimistic demeanour under the influence of colonial wars. It is recognised that the Enlightenment was a wide and ill defined movement, but it is also evident that the period was characterised by a way of thinking that was empirical, optimistic and founded upon reason.[56]

The movement itself embraced many disciplines including history, law, science, government and philosophy; it was also arguably a movement founded on the culture of the generalist[57] rather than the specialist. The emphasis was on the duty of the educated man to think matters out for himself. Against this background it was open to any educated man to form a view as to how states should conduct their relations.

Although the century witnessed the gradual rise of positivism at the expense of traditional theories of natural law, the period also saw the development of theories of natural rights from which the modern law on human rights may be traced. Both Hobbes and Locke had argued that governments were necessary to ensure that, in civil society unlike in the law of nature, certain fundamental rights of man might be protected. By the standards of the 17th century, these fundamental rights would be classified as pertaining to life, liberty and property.[58] Thus, although traditional natural law was in decline in the 18th century, there was an increasing emphasis on the natural or fundamental rights of man and these concepts were to play a role in both the French Revolution and the constitutional settlement established in the United States after the War of Independence.

---

56 See A Cobban, *A History of Modern France*, 1957, Vol 1; N Hampson, *The Enlightenment*, 1968.

57 An example being Voltaire (1694–1778) (pen name of François Marie Arouet), who acquired a reputation as a dramatist, poet, historian and man of letters. Of more direct relevance to the Law of Nations was Christian Wolff (1679–1754) who, in addition to writing on the subject, produced books on logic, ethics, politics and mathematics.

58 The concept of natural rights was set out in the Declaration of Independence of July 1776 which includes the passage: 'That to secure these rights, Governments are instituted among men.' The movement towards constitutional guarantees of basic or natural rights is evidenced by the Declaration of the Rights of Man (France 1789) or the Bill of Rights (1791). See, on the general background, Bernard Bailyn, *The Ideological Origins of the American Revolution*, 1967; RR Palmer, *Age of the Democratic Revolution*, 2 vols: 1959, 1964.

In the political sphere, the attempt by Louis XIV to establish the dominance of France in Europe had been frustrated by a coalition of powers brought together not by considerations of religion or dynasty but *raisons d'etat*. The resulting Treaty of Utrecht (1713) had, in its preamble, contained a clear warning as to the danger of violent conflict between states and, by that stage, the cost to a Royal Treasury of sustained war was already clear. With the modernisation of Russia by Peter the Great,[59] five powers would dominate Europe in the 18th century – France, Austria, Great Britain, Prussia and Russia. Two themes dominated 18th century statecraft to a degree that had not been present previously. The first factor was that the conduct of states was dominated by self-interest. The Enlightenment was the Age of Reason and statesmen calculated according to national self-interest and not according to religion, race or dynastic loyalty. Secondly, the experience with the Hapsburgs in the 17th century and later with Louis XIV[60] had persuaded diplomats that peace in Europe was most likely to be achieved by respect for the Law of Nations and by the promotion of policies designed to achieve a balance of power.[61] Already the Law of Nations was viewed as a horizontal system regulating the relations of sovereigns and distinct from the vertical systems pertaining in domestic law. The Law of Nations continued to focus on its traditional areas of concern, namely: (i) the circumstances in which force was justified; (ii) the rules relating to the conduct of diplomacy; and (iii) the law of the sea; the subject itself came to be dominated by writers, although increasingly the writers tended to have some experience of diplomatic work. During the 18th century, three writers in particular played a significant role in the development of the Law of Nations.[62]

Cornelis van Bynkershoek (1673–1743) served as a judge of the Supreme Court in The Netherlands and produced three works covering various aspects of the Law of Nations.[63] Van Bynkershoek is often viewed as one of the first positivist writers in that he placed reliance upon conduct, custom and treaties rather than the principles of natural law. As

---

59 Peter I (1672–1725), Tsar of Russia from 1689; after conquering territory on the Baltic coast from Sweden, he established the capital at St Petersburg. Russian territory was extended by wars with Sweden (1700–21) and Persia (1722–23).

60 In a series of unsuccessful expansionist wars, Louis XIV had attempted to dominate Europe. These wars, fought in the years 1667–68, 1672–78, 1688–97 and 1701–13 (the War of Spanish Succession), had ended with the death of Louis XIV in 1715. Ranged against Louis had been The Netherlands, Britain and Sweden. One of the important legacies of the conflicts had been the realisation that the Law of Nations by itself was not sufficient to secure peace in Europe. Writers would come to the conclusion that peace required a balance of power within Europe.

61 The balance of power was designed to establish an equilibrium in Europe and prevent one state dominating another. It is is clear that writers such as Vattel considered the concept of the balance of power to be a central component of the Law of Nations. The willingness of states to change sides was well illustrated in the 18th century. In the War of Austrian Succession, Prussia was in alliance with France, Spain, Bavaria and Saxony (which changed sides in 1743) while Great Britain sided with Austria. In the Seven Years' War (1756–63), the parties were reversed as Austria sided with Russia, France, Saxony and Sweden while Great Britain and Hanover supported Prussia.

62 Cornelis van Bynkershoek (1673–1743); Christian Wolff (1679–1754); Emmerich de Vattel (1714–67), although regard should also be paid to two German Professors of Law Moser (1701–95) and von Martens (1756–1821). Georg Friedrich von Martens was best known for *Précis du droit des gens modernes de L'Europe* (1789), while Johann Jacob Moser followed a broadly positivist approach in *Versuch der neuesten europaischen Volkerrechts in Frieden und Krieggszeiten* (1777–80), building upon his earlier work in *Grundsatze des jetzt üblichen Volkerrechts in Friedenzeiten* (1750) and *Grundsatze des jetzt üblichen Volkerrechts in Krieggszeiten* (1752).

63 *De Dominio Maris Dissertatio* (1702) (The Law of the Sea – in which he dealt with the question of the width of the territorial sea); *De Foro Legatorum* (1720) (The Status of Ambassadors); *Quaestiones juris publiciii* (1737) (rules derived from treaty and international custom).

works on the Law of Nations came to be written by diplomats and legal practitioners it was inevitable that more attention would be devoted to the actual conduct of states.

The second writer of importance was Christian Wolff (1679–1754); Wolff was a Professor of Philosophy and had been greatly influenced by Leibniz, so much so that it is sensible to say a little first of GW Leibniz (1646–1716).[64] Leibniz was a mathematician and philosopher by training and he argued that legal study consisted of the logical deduction of rules from general principles; he had written on the subject of sovereignty and had analysed the nature of diplomatic immunity. Leibniz followed Grotius in arguing that a law of nature would be deducible without God and he was scathing of the attempts of Pufendorf to found the law of nature on divine revelation. Leibniz's writing had been influenced by the reaction to the wars of Louis XIV and he drew attention to the distinction between a natural law of nations founded on reason and a voluntary law of nations founded on agreement.[65]

Christian Wolff shared with Leibniz a training in mathematics and philosophy and, like his master he wrote on a very wide range of subjects that would now be regarded as distinct academic disciplines.[66] Wolff followed Leibniz in seeking to ground the Law of Nations in the form of a number of logical propositions; he argued that individual nations were subject to the rules of a single society (*societas* or *civitas*) and that such rules comprised those that the individual nations could agree upon.[67] There has been much debate as to whether Wolff was advocating a republican super state or a form of federation.[68] It is arguable that Wolff was a writer in the tradition of Bartolus (1314–57), as one viewing civil society being founded on a hierarchy of associations each with its own distinct purpose. However, it is also clear that the work of Wolff would only have a limited impact, both because it was founded on theory and logical deduction but also because it paid little regard to the actual conduct of states. Moreover, it was clear that, by the middle of the 18th century, the Enlightenment emphasis on empirical knowledge had the consequence that works on the Law of Nations would have to pay some regard to actual state conduct.

The most influential writer on the Law of Nations in the 18th century was Emerich de Vattel (1714–67), a Swiss lawyer whose *Le Droit des Gens* (1758) emphasised the actual practice and conduct of states.[69] Although Vattel had studied philosophy and had written a work on Leibniz, he rejected the analysis of Wolff as too theoretical for the actual world of the 18th century. Vattel defined the Law of Nations as 'the science of those rights which exist between nations and states, and of the obligations corresponding to these rights'.

---

64 GW Leibniz (1646–1716) produced a *Treatise on Sovereignty* (1677) that drew upon Bodin and Hobbes, and a *Codex Juris Gentium Diplomatici* (1693); Leibniz produced works of distinction in mathematics, history and philosophy.

65 JW Jones, 'Leibniz as international lawyer' (1945) 22 BYIL 1.

66 Wolff was Professor of Mathematics and Philosophy at Halle 1706–23 and again after 1740; he spent the years 1723–40 at Marburg following concern that his views on natural law gave only a limited place to divine revelation.

67 *Jus gentium methodo scientifica pertractatum* (1749) translated in 1764 as *The Law of Nations According to Scientific Method*.

68 N Onuf, '*Civitas Maxima*: Wolff, Vattel and the fate of Republicanism' (1994) 88 AJIL 280.

69 *Le Droit des Gens ou principles de la loi naturelle* (1758); Vattel had originated in Prussia and went on to play a role in the public life of Saxony. He had previously produced a work on the philosophy of Leibniz; see *Défense du Système Leibnitien*, 1741.

In contrast to Wolff, Vattel considered each state to be sovereign and he rejected any *civitas maxima*. Vattel considered each state to be sovereign, equal and independent and he placed particular emphasis on actual state practice. He contended that the Law of Nations comprised: (i) the texts of writers as evidence of state practice; (ii) treaties as evidence of actual consent by states; and (iii) custom as evidence of the tacit consent of states.

There are aspects of Vattel's work that resemble a modern text on international relations. For example, he accepted that states were, in theory, equal but, in practice, varied in size and power. Thus, he argued, it was necessary for statesmen to build alliances by treaty to ensure that a balance or equilibrium was maintained in Europe. In emphasising the equality of states, Vattel's views would be attractive to the United States in the years after Independence, when it sought to establish itself as a distinct force in international affairs.[70] One other reason for the influence of Vattel's work may have been that he advocated both the freedom of the seas and the balance of power within Europe. These were policies that were supported by Great Britain, which would emerge as a dominant power in 19th century. In respect of the doctrine of the balance of power, Britain had adopted the earlier policy of Cardinal Richelieu; King William III had assembled a coalition[71] to prevent Louis XIV dominating Europe and this policy was followed throughout the 19th century.[72] As a small island off the coast of Europe, Great Britain was anxious to ensure that no single power dominated[73] the continent of Europe.

The work of Vattel which appeared immediately before the stability of the European order was shattered by the War of American Independence (1776–83) and the events of the French Revolution. The Enlightenment had lead to an emphasis on empirical knowledge and this had tended to undermine ideas of natural law. The closing decades of the century witnessed significant political events as men struggled against royal absolutism and the Founding Fathers sought to establish a government founded upon the consent of the governed. These developments would influence the Law of Nations by diminishing natural law at the expense of positivism.

Just as the leaders of the American Revolution drew upon writers such as Locke who were long dead, the rise of positivism in the 19th century can be traced back through a line of writers who had paved the way (Zouche, Bynkershoek, Vattel). The events arising out of the American Revolution were also to affect the Law of Nations. Writers such as Thomas Paine[74] argued not only for popular republican government, but also for entrenched rights and an end to slavery and colonialism. The Law of Nations would now

---

70 In the years after the establishment of the Union (1789), the United States was drawn into a number of naval disputes arising from the conduct of the Napoleonic War. Both James Madison (Secretary of State 1801–09) and Henry Wheaton drew upon Vattel to demonstrate sources of International Law. See J Madison, *An Examination of the British Doctrine*, 1805 and H Wheaton, *Elements of International Law*, 1836.

71 Which between 1688 and 1713 included Sweden, Savoy, Spain, Austria and the Dutch Republic.

72 As Great Britain formed alliances in the wars of 1740–48 and 1756–63.

73 In practical terms, this meant striking a balance between the interests of the Hapsburgs and the Bourbons.

74 Thomas Paine (1737–1809), although born in England, espoused the case of democratic republican government founded upon a conception of individual rights, his views are set out in three principal publications: *Common Sense*, 1776; *Rights of Man*, 1792; and *The Age of Reason*, 1794.

have to adapt to the presence of a significant non-European power operating a republican form of government based on a degree of popular consent.[75] Although it was not fully realised at the time, the impact of popular theories of government would mean that the 18th century concept of the Law of Nations as the rules of a sovereign's club could not be easily re-instated.

That the old order of the 18th century was coming under pressure was recognised by the most distinguished philosopher of the time. Immanuel Kant (1724–1804) reflected on the turbulent political events in the last decades of the century. In *Perpetual Peace* (1795),[76] Kant argued that what mattered was not the identity of a ruler but whether a state was stable and just. Recognising the waste caused by war and the preparations made to deter war under the doctrine of the balance of power, Kant favoured the most powerful states (operating under constitutions) coming together in a Covenant to preserve peace. He envisaged that greater use could be made of compulsory negotiations and the reallocation of territory by agreement.

Teaching at the University of Konigsberg, Kant had witnessed at first hand the competition for domination in the Baltic, however the idea of permanent and collective effort to secure peace has a surprisingly modern ring and was to be taken further in the 19th century. At the end of the century, the notion was beginning to emerge that governments were dependent on the will of the people of the territory and, in time, this would be carried further in the principle that the foreign policy of a state would have to pay some regard to the opinions of the people of that state. To an extent, developments in constitutional law were beginning to influence the operation of the Law of Nations.

(e) The 19th century

The 19th century did not witness a prolonged military conflict in Western Europe[77] but it did testify to profound and rapid social change; population growth, trading disputes, industrialisation and class conflict all gave rise to problems within municipal law. Although universal suffrage was yet to be introduced in many European countries,[78] the general trend was towards an extension of the franchise and, in government, it was increasingly the case that aristocratic foreign ministers might be obliged to share power with bourgeois businessmen. In matters of foreign policy, it would be increasingly necessary for a Foreign Minister to consider the nuances of popular opinion within his

---

75 When the revolutionary French Government took power in 1792, Thomas Jefferson (Secretary of State 1789–93) instructed the United States envoy in Paris to deal with it because it had been 'formed by the will of the nation substantially declared'. This contrasted with the European approach in the 18th century where legitimacy arose not by popular consent but under a hereditary ruler or by virtue of a treaty of alliance.

76 *Zum ewigen Freiden*, 1795. Kant was of course influenced by the events of the revolutionary wars (from 1793) but was also aware of the writings of both Leibniz and Christian Wolff on the subject of international order. See R Walker, *Kant*, 1978; E Cassirer, *Kant's Life and Thought* (trans J Haden), 1981.

77 The conflicts tended to be brief in duration, eg, the Crimean War (1853–56); the campaign in Italy (1859); the Austro Prussian War (1866); the Franco Prussian War (1870–71).

78 In the United Kingdom, it was not until 1918 when the Representation of the People Act 1918 conferred the vote on all males above the age of 21 and all females above the age of 30.

own state.[79] As the population moved from the land to the town, the role of government increased and, for the first time, foreign policy priorities would have to compete for funds with those of a domestic character.[80] In examining the events of the 19th century in relation to the evolution of International Law, one can detect a number of themes.

The first theme that can be discerned early in the century was the increasing realisation that international relations required to be managed. After the turbulence of the revolutionary wars and the struggle to defeat Napoleon, the major powers sought at the Congress of Vienna (1814–15) to construct a system of international relations that would minimise the risk of domestic revolution or future conflict. However, no permanent organisation was put in place and each of the powers had different ideas as to the purpose of co-operation. As Metternich had realised, any conflict between major states might well produce social consequences that could not be confined to a single country; the Congress redrew the map of Europe and provided for closer consultation between the great powers but, beyond this, there was little common agreement. So much so that, by 1820, Castlereagh was able to assert that the suppression of popular movements in Spain, Naples or South America was not a matter of common interest to the major powers.[81]

A second theme that can be detected is that some attention had to be paid to the interests of individuals; at the outset of the century, this manifested itself in the campaign against the slave trade,[82] while towards the end of the period the Treaty of Berlin (1878) provided for a degree of protection for minorities within the Ottomann Empire. At the same time, politicians sought to draw attention to the abuses of human rights within other countries.[83]

A third theme that can be discerned is the pressure caused by a change in perception as to the nature of Europe: travel improved as railways were constructed and more powerful ships left the drawing board. In the third quarter of the century, improvements in printing and journalism served to increase awareness of conduct in other states; the reflection that the world was becoming smaller began to assert itself towards the end of the century and statesmen began to calculate that the probable cost of conflict made it necessary to construct defensive alliances between states.

---

79 Illustrated in the United Kingdom by the careers of Robert Cecil, Third Marquess of Salisbury, who acted as Foreign Secretary for much of his period as Prime Minister 1885–86, 1886–92, 1895–1902, and Joseph Chamberlain (1836–1914) who, as a former Mayor of Birmingham, was anxious to follow a foreign policy that was popular with the domestic electorate.

80 The reason given for the resignation of Lord Randolph Churchill as Chancellor of the Exchequer in 1886 was he was unable to secure a reduction in the War Office budget so as to increase the local government grant.

81 See Harold Nicolson, *The Congress of Vienna* (c 1946), 1989. On the litigation arising from the revolutions in South America and its legal implications, see G Marston, 'The personality of the foreign state in English law' (1997) 56 CLJ 374.

82 Slavery had been illegal in England since at least the judgment in *Somersett's Case* (1772) 20 St Trials 1. Due to the efforts of William Wilberforce (1759–1833) legislation was carried abolishing the slave trade as far as Britain was concerned in 1807, followed by its abolition throughout the Empire in 1833. The French outlawed the trade in 1815 and Spain and Portugal followed in 1820.

83 That the conduct of foreign policy might be a matter of political debate emerged during the Midlothian campaign of WE Gladstone (1809–98) in 1880, probably the first attempt by a national political figure to take his case directly to the newly enfranchised electorate. Gladstone devoted considerable attention to the foreign policy of the government of Benjamin Disraeli (1874–80).

Industrialisation might produce a higher standard of living but it also made possible the production of more lethal weapons. The Law of Nations had, from at least the 16th century, sought to answer two basic questions: (a) in what circumstance should a state resort to force (*jus ad bellum*)?; and (b) are there any limits to the manner in which a state might seek to conduct military operations (*jus in bello*)? These problems had surfaced before the 19th century,[84] but it was during the century that concrete steps were taken to develop humanitarian law. Henri Dunant, a Swiss citizen, was so moved by the suffering at the Battle of Solferino (1859)[85] that he resolved to do something to provide a permanent system of humanitarian relief. His published work resulted in the establishment of a *Comité International et Permanent de Secours aux Blessés Militaires* (1863) which adopted the emblem of the Red Coss in the same year. The following year, the first Geneva Convention was adopted.[86] At the same time, in the United States the high numbers of losses on both sides in the Civil War (1861–65)[87] not only prompted the Lieber Code but would prepare the ground for those who, later in the century, would promote conciliation or arbitration as a method of settling international disputes. In respect of the *jus in bello*, concern as to the nature of conflict led Tsar Nicholas II of Russia to summon a conference at the Hague in 1899; this meeting and the subsequent Convention[88] represented the first serious attempt to regulate the conduct of modern warfare. The International Humanitarian Law of the 20th century has its roots in these 19th century initiatives.

Although the 19th century is viewed as the period in which nationalism represented the dominant force, this assertion must be accepted with a degree of qualification. Even in the era of Cavour and Bismarck,[89] one can find evidence that states recognised that certain problems would be required to be dealt with on an international basis. As communications improved, railways, wireless and waterways all required some form of international organisation. The Congress of Vienna (1815) established a Rhine Commission and vested in it wide ranging powers; a commission for the Danube followed in 1856. At the same time, international commissions were established for the Elbe (1821), the Druro (1835) and the Po (1849). Technological change prompted co-operation; the development of wireless telegraphy prompted the establishment of the International Telegraph Union in 1865 and this was followed by the Universal Postal Union in 1874. Developments in governmental co-operation existed alongside

---

84 It is said that during the Thirty Years' War, Gustavus Adolphus carried a copy of *De Jure Belli ac Pacis*; see CV Wedgwood, *The Thirty Year War*, 1938. At Fontenoy (1745), Louis XV ordered similar treatment for both French and enemy wounded, indicating that the wounded were not to be regarded as enemies. Both Vattel and Rousseau argued for humane treatment of the wounded.

85 A battle fought as part of Napoleon III's campaign against Austria.

86 Geneva Convention for the Amelioration of Condition of Wounded Armies in the Field (1864).

87 620,000 would die in the course of the war.

88 In fact, the Hague Conference of 1899 resulted in three conventions, namely (i) On the Pacific Settlement of Disputes; (ii) On the Regulation and Customs of War on Land; and (iii) On Maritime War (Protection of Wounded, Sick and Shipwrecked). There is no reason to doubt the sincerity of the motives of Tsar Nicholas II; however, other Russian officials appear to have been concerned more that industrialised states would have an advantage in any future conflict.

89 Otto von Bismarck (1815–98), as Prime Minister of Prussia after 1862, had engaged in expansionist wars against Denmark (1863–64), Austria (1866) and France (1870–71) to secure the unification of Germany but, after 1871, sought to manage international relations by a series of alliances designed to preserve the newly established *status quo*.

developments in the private sphere amongst which was the establishment of the International Law Association in 1873.[90]

The trend towards co-operation in Europe was offset by difficulties abroad. Towards the end of the century, European powers began to expand by the acquisition of territory in Africa; although the precise motivation for the 'scramble for Africa' is a matter of some controversy,[91] it was of course clear that foreign adventures could produce disputes about the acquisition of territory or the recognition of local boundaries that would require resolution.[92] At the same time, the major European powers found that a positive and patriotic foreign policy was likely to win votes at home and to counter the claims of emerging liberal and social democratic parties who were pressing for increasing government expenditure on social reform.

Many of the specific areas of contemporary International Law have their roots in decisions or procedures initiated in the 19th century or even slightly before. Cases involving points arising under the Law of Nations had been coming before the English courts since the middle of the 18th century;[93] however, the Napoleonic War did begin to throw up problems of International Law within the municipal court system and judgments were given that in some instances remain good law today.[94] At a later date, the revolutions in Latin America and the struggle for political liberty in mid-century Europe would give rise to delicate problems for municipal courts.[95] Although the century was dominated by European powers, the voice of the United States was increasingly being heard and could not be taken for granted.[96]

However, political philosophy continued to influence the subject. One of the most important philosophers of the century was GW Hegel (1770–1831) and his writings were

---

90 For the distinction between private international bodies and public international initiatives, see DW Bowett, *The Law of International Institutions*, 4th edn, 1982.

91 See J Gallagher and R Robinson, *Africa and the Victorians*, 1961. Writers have argued that it was based on (i) a desire for raw materials; (ii) possible new markets; (iii) defence needs. For the traditional Marxist position, see VI Lenin (1870–1924), *Imperialism as the Highest Form of Capitalism*, 1916.

92 This was held in check while foreign policy in Europe was dominated by Chancellor Bismarck (1870–90), who was anxious to preserve peace and the gains of Germany after 1870; with the dismissal of Bismarck in 1890, power passed into the hands of an immature erratic and intellectually limited Kaiser Wilhelm II and a succession of increasingly mediocre Chancellors.

93 *Buvot v Barbuit* (1737) Cas Temp Talb 281; *Triquet v Bath* (1764) 3 Burr 1478 (Lord Mansfield); *Heathfield v Chilton* (1767) 4 Burr 2015.

94 See, for example, on the question of recognition, *City of Berne v The Bank of England* (1804) 9 Ves Jun 347; *Dolder v The Bank of England* (1805) 10 Ves Jun 352; *Dolder v Lord Huntingfield* (1805) 11 Ves Jun 283. The Law on Sovereign Immunity influenced by the judgment of Marshall CJ in *The Schooner Exchange v McFaddon* (1812) 7 Cranch 116.

95 *Thompson v Powles* (1828) 2 Sim 194; *Taylor v Barclay* (1828) 2 Sim 214; *Emperor of Austria v Day and Kossuth* (1861) 3 De GF & J 217; 30 LJ Ch 690.

96 The Jay Treaty (1794) and the Treaty of Ghent (1814) are but early examples of the desire of the United States to place international relations on a legal basis; this trend continued with the Alabama Arbitration (1872) and would reach its fruition with the demands of Woodrow Wilson in 19i9 to establish agreed procedures to restrain conflict. Although Francis Wharton became legal adviser to the State Department in 1885, the American Society for International law would not be founded until 1907. An early example of the tendency is to be found in the letter sent by Daniel Webster as Secretary of State in the *Caroline* case (1841) indicating the circumstances in which the use of force in self defence was justified.

to have a significant effect on the subject. In a series of books,[97] Hegel argued that the study of history would indicate a broad trend of historical development or progression and that society itself was never static. Having lived through the humiliation of Prussia during the Napoleonic Wars, this view was certainly not without contemporary relevance. As Professor of Philosophy at the University of Berlin after 1818, Hegel[98] was to influence 19th century Marxist thought and there is some evidence of his impact upon 20th century existentialism. Although Hegelian philosophy has been variously described as shallow and obscure, one possible interpretation was that history revealed the development of different forms of human association and that the highest form of human association was the nation state. Although Hegel's writing gave rise to various schools of thought, one possible construction of human history was that it would progress until reaching its culmination in an efficient well ordered state.[99] At a time when self-confidence in Germany had been damaged by a series of French victories, such a political philosophy found a ready audience amongst those seeking to reform the Prussian state. A second legacy of Hegelian thought was to regard the nation state as the highest form of political organisation; this would be a very convenient viewpoint for those who favoured a Law of Nations founded simply on the consent of sovereign states. To this extent Hegelian thought tended to accentuate the movement towards positivism in International Law.

A second theme in 19th century Europe was the rise of the nation state; the dynastic Empires were in slow retreat and the creation of new independent states in Europe posed problems of relations between new entities. Partly this was a response to the ideas of the French Revolution, partly it was a reaction to the conduct of occupying French forces and to some extent, as in Italy, it was a protest against foreign rule. At the same time, nationalism was an attractive theme for a professional and business class seeking to oust aristocratic foreign rule. The century witnessed the steady increase in distinct nation states in Europe[100] and this was matched by a similar growth in Latin America as the Spanish Empire collapsed following a series of unilateral declarations by its constituent parts.[101]

A fundamental aspect of these political developments was the slow emergence of the principle that the people of a territory were entitled to determine their future free of foreign rule. Ambitious politicians such as Cavour and Bismarck were able to harness these social forces to their own particular ends.

Another important development worthy of note was the development of International Law as a subject of serious study within Universities. Textbooks began to

---

97   *The Phenomenology of Mind* (1807); *The Science of Logic* (1812–16) and *The Philosophy of Right* (1821).
98   P Singer, *Hegel*, 1983; C Taylor, *Hegel*, 1975.
99   The influence of the state in the work of Hegel had undoubtedly been influenced by the events of the Napoleonic War and the perceived weakness of Prussia and other German states. Hegel was familiar with and influenced by the work of JG Fichte (1762–1814) who had taught at the University of Berlin since 1799 and had issued an appeal in 1808 (*Reden an die deutsche Nation*: Addresses to the German Nation) which urged German self-awakening and resistance to French occupation.
100 Greece (1821); Belgium (1830); Italy (1859); Germany (1870).
101 United Provinces of Rio de la Plata (1816), Chile (1817), Columbia (including Venezuela and Ecuador) in 1819, Mexico and Peru in 1821.

appear in both Europe and America with the object of replacing Vattel as the standard treatment of the subject.[102] In England, the expansion of legal education in the second half of the century lead to the establishment of distinct teaching posts in the subject[103] and Foreign Ministries began to employ staff to advise on the legal implications of particular transactions.[104] Gradually, the subject came to be influenced by the texts of University Professors and the articles contributed by the legal and diplomatic staff of Foreign Ministries. In England, where the level of legal education had been behind that in Europe, the expansion of University legal study in the second half of the century lead both to the establishment of distinct teaching posts in the subject[105] and to a reduction in the influence of the civilian lawyers at Doctors' Commons.[106]

In the wider world, internal rebellions and a number of wars at the end of the century would raise questions of International Law in municipal courts and prompt thought as to how international disputes might be the subject of peaceful resolution.[107] The initiative of Tsar Nicholas II in summoning the Hague Conference in 1899 was prompted by concern as to the too ready recourse to force; the conference provided for the promotion of international commissions of inquiry as a means of resolving disputes and this system was carried further by the Hague Convention of 1907.[108] At the same time, the second half of the century witnessed a steady increase in the employment of international arbitration as a method of resolving disputes.[109]

(f) The 20th century

In the year 1900, it was strongly arguable that Japan and the United States were the only significant non-European powers. One of the most important features of the century was the steady increase both in the number of states and the level of interdependence. At the same time, the century was to witness a pace of technological change never before

---

102 Henry Wheaton (1785–1845), *Elements of International Law*, 1836; *History of the Law of Nations in Europe and America*, 1841. At the same time, Joseph Story produced the first edition of his *Commentaries on the Conflict of Laws*, 1834.

103 Travers Twiss (1809–1897) held a chair in the subject at London University from 1852–55.

104 Francis Wharton (1820–89), who became Chief of the Legal Division of the Department of State in 1885, produced *A Treatise on the Conflict of Laws*, 1872 and *A Digest of the International Law of the United States*, 1886; in the latter task he was assisted by JB Moore (1860–1947), who also worked in the State Department and who, after a lengthy period as Professor of International Law at Columbia (1891–1924), would become a Judge of the PCIJ in 1921.

105 The most influential lawyer being John Westlake (1828–1913) whose *International Law: Peace*, 1904, and *War*, 1907, would not endure as long as Lassa Oppenheim's *International Law*, 1st edn, 1905.

106 See A McNair, 'The debt of International Law in Britain to the civil law and civilians' (1954) 39 TGS 183. In England, the Foreign Office was advised on International Law matters by a member of Doctors' Commons known as the Queen's Advocate. This office was held by Travers Twiss until 1872. In 1886, the first Legal Adviser was appointed (Mr Edward Davidson) but he did not receive an assistant until Cecil Hurst was appointed in 1902. For the evolution of a distinct legal department, see GG Fitzmaurice and FA Vallat (1968) 17 ICLQ 267.

107 The Boer War (1899–1902); The Boxer Rebellion (China 1900); The Spanish American War (1898); Russo-Japanese War (1904–05). On litigation in England, see *Cook v Sprigg* [1899] AC 572; *R v Lynch* [1903] 1 KB 444; *West Rand Mining Co v The King* [1905] 2 KB 391.

108 Commission of Inquiry into the Dogger Bank Incident (November 1904).

109 Bering Sea Arbitration (*Great Britain v United States*) (1893); JB Moore, *International Arbitrations*, Vol 1 p 935; North Atlantic Coast Fisheries Arbitration (*Great Britain v United States*) (1910) 11 RIAA 173.

encountered in human history. By the end of the century, one of the principal problems arising in International Law would be the disparity in wealth and income between affluent states and those that were less fortunate.

The experience of the First World War (1914–18) prompted a reconsideration of the methods employed in international relations. The overall objective after the conflict was to produce a Europe in which the risk of future conflict would be minimised. The League of Nations system sought to build upon the the various methods of peaceful resolution that had been developed by the end of the 19th century. This rethinking was prompted by a number of distinct but converging considerations:

(i)   The First World War had caused a loss of human life greater than in any other previous war;[110] the nature of the conflict, the nature of the hostilities and the increasing role of science and technology would mean that the costs of any future conflict would fall upon an entire nation.[111] In simple terms, the experience of the First World War had been to convince many that the cost of conflict in the future would always be too high in terms of human life and material resources.

(ii) A feeling developed that the war itself had resulted not from the aggression of a single state but had been caused by misunderstandings that had arisen when older methods of international relations had been found wanting.

(iii) The final two years of the First World War had witnessed the full participation of the United States and, in the aftermath, of victory Woodrow Wilson[112] resolved to re-order international relations to ensure that the principles of collective security and the rule of law should play a greater role in the resolution of problems between states.

To achieve these ends, the Treaty of Versailles provided the Covenant for the League of Nations which would contain provisions designed to restrict the recourse to force;[113] at the same time the post-war treaties with newly independent states would contain guarantees of minority protection.[114] Consistently with this desire to improve human rights, the mandate system placed clear duties on the mandatory to improve the welfare of those subject to the mandate.

At Versailles, a Committee of Jurists was established to draft a statute that would serve as the constitution for the Permanent Court of International Justice. The Committee (The Root-Phillimore Committee) reported in 1920 and the Permanent Court of International Justice began sitting at the Hague in 1922. The structure set in place would endure until 1939 and would serve as the basis upon which to construct a new system after 1945.

---

110 France and Germany lost a million and a half men each; the British Empire lost nearly a million; Great Britain alone, three quarters of a million.

111 A sentiment expressed in England in *Attorney General v De Keyser's Royal Hotel* [1920] AC 508.

112 Woodrow Wilson (1856–1924). As President of the United States (1913–21), Wilson endeavoured to apply the concept of the rule of law to international relations. He was frustrated by his inability to persuade the United States Senate that the Treaty of Versailles should be ratified. Wilson was the first American President to assume a central role in international diplomacy.

113 The operative Articles of the Covenant of the League being Articles 12–15. Under Art 12, signatories agreed to submit any dispute 'likely to lead to rupture' 'to arbitration or judicial settlement or enquiry by the (League) Council'. The Article also provided for a three month waiting period before recourse to war.

114 Poland (Versailles 1919); Czechoslovakia and Yugoslavia (St Germain-en-Laye 1919); Romania (Trianon 1920); Greece (Sèvres 1920).

Although the League of Nations experience was to culminate in the Second World War, the period between 1919 and 1939 did witness some significant achievements, amongst which was the gradual acceptance of the desirability of some form of collective security and a recognition of the need for international disputes to be resolved peacefully, if at all possible. The level of losses in the First World War had a profound effect on statesmen thereafter; most major European states would now elect their governments on a system of universal suffrage so that public opinion was now an important factor in the conduct of foreign affairs. However, the failure of the United States to ratify the Treaty of Versailles ensured that the United States would not become a member of the League of Nations; the absence of such a significant power was to make the resolution of international disputes more difficult.[115] But peaceful methods of resolving disputes prompted by Secretary Bryan[116] came to be more widely employed in the period after 1920, so much so that, by 1940, nearly 200 treaties had been signed involving some method of conciliation.

The Covenant of the League of Nations had reflected the initial objectives of the Hague Conferences[117] and the 14 points of Woodrow Wilson, by making disarmament a central aspect of concern.[118] However, the arrival of Adolf Hitler in power in January 1933, and the subsequent conduct of Benito Mussolini, meant that it was difficult to make any progress in this area. The Japanese invasion of Manchuria in 1931 produced only a tentative response by the League and lead to the withdrawal of Japan from membership in 1933.[119] Shortly after, the invasion of Abyssinia by Italy in 1935 produced a limited effort at sanctions but these were not sufficient to prevent Italy withdrawing from the League in 1937.[120] At the time, although the Spanish Civil war was in essence a civil war it did attract foreign involvement and once again the League proved powerless to restrain the course of the conflict.

The outbreak of the Second World War in September 1939 lead to the effective collapse of existing international machinery and the League of Nations was simply a

---

115 The failure of the United States Senate to permit ratification was partly due to the isolationist tendencies of the republicans led by Henry Cabot Lodge, but also because Woodrow Wilson's influence diminished following a stroke in 1919; as with other American Presidents in the 20th century, he found difficulty in imposing his will during a second term.

116 William Jennings Bryan (1860–1925) (Secretary of State 1913–15) promoted the idea of treaties including provision for the peaceful resolution of disputes. The American Society of International Law had been founded in 1907 and there is no doubt that Wilson, as a former Professor of Jurisprudence, felt that the risk of conflict would be reduced by strengthening the rule of law in the conduct of international disputes.

117 Tsar Nicholas II had been motivated in calling the Hague Conference of 1899 by concern as to the cost and capacity of modern armaments. Concern with the level of armaments was a consistent theme in the years prior to the First World War. The first Nobel Prize was awarded in 1901. In the same year, the young Winston Churchill would warn the House of Commons that 'when the resources of science and civilisation sweep away everything that might mitigate their fury, a European war can only end in the ruin of the vanquished and scarcely less fatal dislocation and exhaustion of the conquerors. Democracy is more vindictive than Cabinets. The war of peoples will be more terrible than those of kings'.

118 See Art 8 of the Covenant of the League. The 14 points were those war aims of the United States set out by President Wilson in January 1918 and included disarmament and involved the construction of international relations on different principles to those pertaining prior to 1914.

119 Although the United States was not a member, Secretary of State Stimson attended the League Council meetings on Manchuria in 1932. This was perhaps the first recognition that certain international crises could not be resolved without the active participation of the United States.

120 The invasion itself lead to interesting litigation in England on the effect of de jure and de facto recognition; see Haile Selassie v Cable & Wireless Ltd [1938] 1 Ch 545; [1938] 1 Ch 839; [1939] 1 Ch 182.

spectator to unfolding events. However, it was clear that after hostilities some form of new international structure would be required to keep the peace. In May 1940, the Permanent Court of International Justice moved from the Hague to Geneva and those judges who could return to their own country did so.[121]

It is sensible to trace the events that lead to the establishment of the post-war structures. Much of the impetus came from President Roosevelt and his Secretary of State Cordell Hull,[122] who wished to establish an effective system of international dispute resolution. That such a system could come into effect in 1945 owed much to the intensive preparatory efforts undertaken during the years of the Second World War; the important steps in the process were as follows:

(i) *The Inter Allied Declaration* (12 June 1941)

Representatives of Great Britain and her Dominions issued this declaration pledging themselves to establish a post-war world founded on peace and security.

(ii) *The Atlantic Charter* (August 1941)

Winston Churchill,[123] Franklin Roosevelt met off Newfoundland to agree the broad principles that should govern any post war international machinery.

(iii) *The United Nations Declaration* (1 January 1942)

Representatives of 26 states met in Washington DC to approve the principles of the Atlantic Charter and also to consent to the establishment of a new international organisation that would be provisionally called 'the United Nations'.

(iv) *The London Committee* (20 May 1943)

A committee met in London to consider the possibility of a new International Court of Justice; the committee met on 19 occasions and produced its report on 10 February 1944.[124]

(v) *The Moscow Declaration* (30 October 1943)

Representatives of the United States, Britain, China and the Soviet Union signed the Moscow Declaration on General Security indicating their approval of the concept of an international body charged with the responsibility for the maintenance of peace.

(vi) *Tehran* (November 1943)

President Roosevelt, Prime Minister Churchill and General Secretary Stalin met in Tehran to review the course of the conflict; the leaders agreed in principle that a new international body would be established to preserve world peace.

---

121 The final days of the PCIJ are related by Geoffrey Marston in 'The London Committee and the Statute of the International Court of Justice', in Vaughan Lowe and Malgosia Fitzmaurice (eds), *Fifty Years of the International Court of Justice*, 1996.

122 Franklin Delano Roosevelt (1882–1945), President of the United States (1933–45); Cordell Hull (1871–1955), Secretary of State 1933–44, sometimes described as the 'Father of the United Nations', Nobel Peace Prize 1945.

123 Winston Churchill (1874–1965), Prime Minister of the United Kingdom 1940–45; 1951–55.

124 See Geoffrey Marston 'The London Committee and the Statute of International Court of Justice', in Lowe and Fitzmaurice (eds), *Fifty Years of the International Court of Justice*, 1996.

(vii)*Bretton Woods* (1–21 July 1944)

The Bretton Woods conference in New Hampshire. The United States witnessed the establishment of the International Monetary Fund (IMF) and the International Bank for Reconstruction and Development (the World Bank).[125]

(viii)*The Dumbarton Oaks Conference* (21 August– October 1944)

The State Department had been working on a number of drafts for a United Nations Charter since at least 1943;[126] after a final draft had been approved by President Roosevelt, it was put to a conference at Dumbarton Oaks, a country house outside Washington DC. The American plan was entitled 'Tentative United States Proposals for a General International Organisation' and contained within it a division of responsibilities between the Security Council and the General Assembly. The terms of the proposal were approved and made public in October 1944.

(ix) *The Yalta Conference* (4–11 February 1945)

An ailing President Roosevelt met with Joseph Stalin and Winston Churchill to settle the structure of the new post-war institutions; the constitution and powers of the Security Council were agreed. It was decided that a conference should take place at San Francisco and that a Commission of Jurists should be established to produce a Statute for the proposed International Court of Justice.[127] On 12 April 1945, President Roosevelt died; the first decision of his successor, Harry S Truman,[128] was to order that the projected San Francisco conference should proceed as planned.

(x) *The San Francisco Conference* (April 25–26 June 1945)

President Truman opened the conference in the San Francisco Opera house on 25 April 1945; the conference concluded with the signing of the United Nations Charter on 26 June 1945. At the same time the draft statute for the International Court of Justice was approved.

The United Nations Charter came into force on 24 October 1945.[129] The first meeting of the General Assembly took place in London on 10 January 1946.[130] On 18 April 1946 the last session of the League of Nations Assembly was held for the purpose of dissolving both the League and the Permanent Court of International Justice (PCIJ). On that same day, the International Court of Justice sat for the first time.

---

125 The United Kingdom being represented by JM Keynes (1883–1946), on which see DE Moggridge, *John Maynard Keynes: An Economist's Biography*, 1992; R Skidelsky, *John Maynard Keynes: Fighting for Britain* (1937–45), 2000.

126 See Ruth B Russell, *A History of the United Nations Charter: The Role of the United States 1940–1945*, 1958.

127 The Committee of Jurists met in Washington on 9 April 1945 to begin work on the draft; the United Kingdom being represented by Gerald Fitzmaurice (1900–82) (judge of the ICJ 1960–73) together with William Malkin and Maurice Bathurst. The committee reported to the San Francisco conference on 25 April 1945.

128 Harry S Truman (1884–1972), President of the United States (1945–53). In the first months of office, President Truman would be concerned with three events that would have considerable impact on the development of International Law: (a) the establishment of the United Nations; (b) the decision to authorise the use of atomic weapons in August 1945; and (c) the Truman Declaration in respect of the Law of the Sea in September 1945.

129 When the ratifications required under Art 110 of the UN Charter had been received.

130 During which, intensive lobbying took place on the question of the site of the Permanent Headquarters.

The General Assembly established a Permanent Headquarters Commission which then voted to establish a temporary headquarters in New York City. At the outset, the temporary headquarters comprised a number of buildings made available by the United States government. However, the acquisition of the East River site in 1946[131] enabled a permanent headquarters to be open for the Seventh Session of the General Assembly in October 1952.[132] The location of the Headquarters in the United States and not Europe was a reflection of the economic and military power of the host nation but also an acknowledgment of the efforts of both President Wilson and President Roosevelt to lead the United States away from isolation towards full participation in international affairs.

As an international organisation, the United Nations was designed to play a central role in the post-war world. One of its principal objectives was to 'establish conditions under which justice and respect for the obligations arising from treaties and other sources of International Law can be maintained'.[133] In broad terms, the objectives of the organisation were set out in Art 1 and might be summarised as having four main aspects: (a) to maintain international peace and security; (b) to develop friendly relations among nations; (c) to achieve international co-operation in solving international problems; and (d) to be a centre for harmonising the actions of nations in the attainment of common ends. That the United Nations Charter was to be a fundamental document was made clear by Art 103 which provided that its terms should prevail over any other treaty obligations entered into by a member state.

The detailed provisions of the United Nations Charter will be considered at a later stage but, at this point, a number of general points need to be made. First, in any problem of International Law a distinction will have to be drawn between the position prior to the Charter and the impact of any provisions within the Charter.[134] Secondly, the United Nations was designed to usher in a form of collective security that would enable international relations to be managed; although the League had failed to prevent World War II, the conviction remained that international peace was best preserved by some form of collective security. Thirdly, the arrangements under the Charter reflected the power structure in 1945; 50 states signed the Charter in San Francisco in 1945 but by 1980 the number of members of the United Nations had increased beyond 150. Fourthly, the Charter was drawn up at a time when governments were learning of the abuses by Germany and Japan during the Second World War; in consequence the Charter contained detailed references to human rights and thus represented a movement away from the extreme positivism of the 19th century. Fifthly, one of the lessons of the Second World War had been the need for international co-operation to secure victory; the Charter followed this general approach in stressing the need for international co-operation not only to preserve peace but also to address common economic and social problems.

---

131 Made possible after a gift by JD Rockefeller Jr (1874–1960), who directed the affairs of the Rockefeller Foundation which had been founded by JD Rockeller (1839–1937) in 1913.

132 See Trygve Lie, *In the Cause of Peace*, 1954; Trygve Lie (1896–1968) served as Secretary General of the United Nations from 1946–53 when he resigned following Soviet criticism of his handling of the Korean War.

133 See Preamble to the United Nations Charter (1945).

134 This is particularly important in the context of debates as to whether any use of force outside the terms of the United Nations Charter is consistent with international law: on this see below.

Having traced the general outline of the development of International Law until 1945, it is now proposed to examine a number of matters of theoretical interest. I will then consider the development of International Law in the years after 1945 in Chapter 2.

3 IS INTERNATIONAL LAW REALLY LAW?

One of the most debated questions by writers is as to whether International Law is really law. To some extent, this depends on the definition one attributes to the word 'law'; obviously, if the word is given a very wide definition then anything can come within its ambit. This controversy is of long standing; questions as to the exact nature of International Law are to be found in the works of Hobbes, Pufendorf and Bentham.

Secondly, since classical International Law proceeded on the basis of the sovereignty of the individual state, it was natural for writers to question the extent to which obligations in the Law of Nations could have the same binding force as the laws that governed the relationship between the ruler and his subjects. Thirdly, there were those who argued that the Law of Nations was little more than the the traditions of comity that one ruler owed to another sovereign ruler. It is perhaps not surprising that questions as to the Law of Nations are associated with the Anglo-Saxon tradition of empirical philosophy which laid stress both upon the acquisition of knowledge through experience and also upon the precise analysis of concepts.[135] Fourthly, although some writers have been sceptical as to the legal nature of the Law of Nations, it has not prevented them from supporting International Law as a vehicle for the peaceful settlement of disputes. An example is afforded by the approach of Jeremy Bentham (1748–1832) who argued that individual laws emanated from a sovereign power and yet devoted time to drawing up a code of International Law and urged the case for an international court which would adjudicate on disputes between states and whose judgments would be enforced by the sanction of world opinion.[136]

Those who dispute the legal nature of International Law point to a number of pieces of evidence to sustain their case:

(i) *The lack of institutions*: It has been accepted in constitutional law since the 18th century that it is possible to differentiate the functions of government into the legislative, executive and judicial. Some writers argue that it is then necessary to ensure that these functions are exercised by different individuals to avoid tyranny.[137] In the context of International Law, it is not possible to locate a permanent supreme legislative body. The General Assembly of the United Nations is not such a body and was never intended to be so; the Security Council has power by resolution to regulate the conduct of disputes between states (see Chapter VI and Chapter VII of the United Nations Charter), but these powers are limited to specific threats to peace and can only be made within the specific terms of the Charter.[138] In respect of the Security

---

135 See Stephen Priest, *The British Empiricists*, 1990.

136 See John Dinwiddy, *Bentham*, 1989.

137 The principle of the separation of powers developed by John Locke in the *Second Treatise of Civil Government*, 1690, but more closely associated with Montesquieu in *L'Esprit des Lois*, 1748.

138 An issue arising in the *Lockerbie* case (*Libyan Arab Jamahiriya v United Kingdom and United States*) (1992) ICJ 3.

Council, some writers have pointed to the seeming paralysis of the institution in the years of the Cold War when the veto or threat of veto by one or other major power could prevent action being taken. Since the arrival in power of Mikhail Gorbachev in 1985 and the subsequent collapse of Soviet power in Eastern Europe, this has ceased to be such a practical obstacle. However, even in those limited circumstances when the Security Council is prepared to pass a resolution, it does not have the state organs to implement its will and is beholden to member states to provide the resources to implement its resolutions. In contrast, in an efficient and well organised state, a legislature will not only be able to pass a law but also be capable of raising the revenue through taxation to provide the resources to implement that law.

In the context of the judicial branch, it is pointed out that an international court only dates from 1920 and, as it does not possess compulsory jurisdiction, even a dispute that is capable of legal analysis may not be referred to the court.[139]

(ii) *The command theory*: A second objection to International Law is that it does not meet the definition of 'law' propounded by 19th century analytical positivists. Often described as the 'Austinian question' this school of thought is most closely associated with John Austin (1790–1859),[140] although it can be traced back much further. Austin held that for a rule to be regarded as a legal rule it must take the form of a command[141] by a sovereign power backed by sanctions in the event of breach. Such an approach assumes that a legal system is vertical and based on coercion. In propounding such a definition of law, Austin sought to draw a distinction between legal rules and ethical rules. Manifestly a system of International Law horizontal in nature and founded upon co-operation between autonomous sovereign states does not come within the strict terms of Austin's narrow definition of law.

Although there are many meanings of the term 'positivism',[142] two that have gained widespread acceptance are: (a) the theory that laws are commands; and (b) the view that a clear distinction should be drawn between law as it 'is' and law as it 'ought' to be. Both these views were advanced by Austin.

First, in answer to Austin, it is necessary to draw a distinction between municipal law and International Law. Municipal law is essentially a vertical system where the citizen or subject is ultimately subordinate to the will of the state government. International law is a system of rules operating in an international society of over 175 members and each is, in theory, independent and sovereign; such a system is inevitably horizontal and decentralised. It therefore follows that the international legal system is unique and not strictly comparable to any municipal law system.

---

139 Examples would be the question of the precise border between Iraq and Kuwait, the Falkland Islands, Kashmir, territorial disputes within the former Yugoslavia.
140 Austin's views appeared in *The Province of Jurisprudence Determined*, 1832, and in the posthumously published *Lectures in Jurisprudence*, 1861.
141 The idea of law as a command criticised by HLA Hart in *The Concept of Law*, 1961, where the learned author pointed out that a command is normally directed to particular persons in specific circumstances in contrast to a statute which applied generally and bound also those who drafted it.
142 In one sense, we have come across it earlier when used to describe those jurists who consider International Law to be no more than those minimum rules accepted by states. On the many meanings of the expression, see HLA Hart, 'Positivism and the separation of law and morals' (1958) 71 HLR 593; WL Morison, 'Some myths about positivism' (1960) YLJ 212.

Moreover, it is strongly arguable that Austin oversimplified the role of law within a municipal legal system.[143] There are a large number of laws within the municipal sphere that cannot be categorised as imperative commands; indeed Austin admitted that, even within the domestic sphere, there were a considerable number of exceptions (for example, limitation legislation, repealing legislation, declaratory legislation) that could not be categorised as imperative commands. The fact that Austin was prepared to admit exceptions within the domestic sphere serves to weaken the force of his argument when it is applied to the sphere of International Law.

Austin was writing at a time when customary International Law was the dominant source of International Law;[144] he had no experience of the codifying multilateral treaty and could not have foreseen a 20th century in which problems could not be dealt with by a single state. While there may not be a single supreme legislative body, the mechanism for the creation of mutlilateral law making treaties has a considerable degree of formalism. Fourthly, many of the written constitutions drawn up since the 18th century expressly provide that sources of International Law shall be regarded as law and shall be treated as the law of the land;[145] so that Austin's opinions have not enjoyed a widespread degree of support amongst constitutional draftsmen. Fifthly, there is little indication that Austin's opinions influenced the judiciary; from the beginning of the 19th century there are judgments of the highest authority indicating that a municipal court will have to take into account any rule of International Law.[146] Sixthly, all the contemporary evidence indicates that those who work for foreign ministries consider the rules of International Law to constitute legal rules rather than a moral code.[147] Further, the Austinian theory is open to the objection that it is difficult to find a constitution in which there is a single sovereign; the doctrine of the separation of powers is designed to prevent such a situation arising and in many constitutions there will be more than one law making authority. It is also worthy of note that Austin viewed himself as continuing the utilitarian approach of Jeremy Bentham and, as has been indicated above, the latter saw a role for International Law in promoting the peaceful settlement of disputes. Moreover, it is arguable that Austin paid insufficient attention to those primitive communities in which law existed without there being a clear Austinian sovereign.[148]

---

143 It is difficult to imagine how Austin would have explained the expansion of judicial review in administrative law that has been a feature of English law and other legal systems in the years since 1945. It has often been remarked that Austin thought of law in terms of the normal 19th century criminal statute.

144 As will be seen below, one of the difficulties with customary International Law was that the rules were often vague and uncertain and overly dependent on the opinion of learned jurists.

145 United States Constitution (1787), Art VI, para 2; France: the Constitution of the Fifth Republic (1958), Art 55; Italy: the Constitution of 1947, Art 10.

146 See Marshall CJ in *The Schooner Exchange v McFaddon* (1812) 7 Cranch 116 (United States Supreme Court); Gray J in *The Paquette Habana* (1900)175 US 677, p 700, observed 'International Law is part of our law, and must be ascertained and administered by the Courts of Justice of appropriate jurisdiction, as often as questions of right depending upon it are duly presented for their determination'.

147 A point made by F Pollock in his *Oxford Lectures*, 1890, and stressed by JL Brierly in *The Outlook for International Law*, 1944. The observations of Pollock are of some interest because in 1890 the Foreign Office had no more than one full time legal adviser.

148 A point made by Henry Maine (1822–88) in his *Early History of Institutions*, 1875.

However, while the general views of John Austin cannot be accepted since they depend on a highly artificial definition of law, it has to be admitted that Austin made a very valuable contribution in directing attention to: (a) the need for rules to be clear and precise; and (b) the need to distinguish between matters of law and matters of ethics.

(iii) *Effectiveness*: There are those who argue that, even if International Law can be regarded as law, it is so ineffective as to be meaningless. Nothing could be further from the truth. First, on a daily basis agreements are executed between states and are for the most part observed. As Louis Henkin observed in 1979, 'almost all nations observe almost all principles of International Law and almost all of their obligations almost all of the time'.[149] Much of this work is transacted in private between the legal departments of foreign ministries and does not attract much public attention. In contrast, whenever there is a serious breach of International Law it tends to attract press attention and the public may form the view that International Law is ineffective.[150] Such treatment contrasts with that accorded to municipal law; in most advanced states, the statute books will contain numerous provisions relating to motor vehicles; every day motorists exceed the speed limit or drive carelessly yet no commentator claims that the laws should be set aside as ineffective.

Secondly, far from being ineffective, the horizontal nature of International Law tends to place the emphasis on mutual respect and co-operation. Since the early part of the 19th century, it has become increasingly clear that there are many problems that an individual state cannot resolve by itself and co-operation with other states is both necessary and desirable. International Law acts as a vehicle to promote international co-operation between states.[151] At the present time there are increasing concerns about environmental protection; this is one of the areas of International Law that is growing more quickly than others.[152]

(iv) Another jurist whose writings examined the precise nature of International Law was Hans Kelsen (1881–1973). Kelsen[153] asserted that a legal system was made up of series of laws or norms that existed to regulate human conduct. He believed that a legal system could be analysed without reference to political, social or economic

---

149 Louis Henkin, *How Nations Behave*, 2nd edn, 1979, p 47.

150 The very serious breaches of International Law often requiring the use of force tend to attract a disproportionate degree of attention, eg, the Falkland Island invasion (1982); the invasion of Kuwait (1982), and tend to distract attention from the daily instances of co-operation between individual states.

151 Such co-operation can be traced back to the Congress of Vienna (1815) and the establishment of the Commission on the Rhine which provided for the participation of each littoral state.

152 See Chapter 17 for the increasing number of multilateral environmental treaties included in the last quarter of a century.

153 On Kelsen, see 'The pure theory of law' (1934) 50 LQR 474; (1935) 51 LQR 517; *Peace Through Law*, 1944; *General Theory of Law and State*, 1946; and *The Pure Theory of Law* (trans M Knight), 1967; JW Jones (1935) 16 BYIL 5; J Stone (1963) 26 MLR 34.

elements and thus his theory became known as the 'pure' theory of law.[154] Kelsen[155] asserted that laws were but 'ought' propositions and that the validity of a law should be judged by reference to a prior law. Thus, he viewed a legal system as hierarchical and to some extent this can be applied to municipal law. So where X is fined by a court for breach of a statutory instrument, the validity of the fine depends on the delegated legislation which itself is legitimised by the primary legislation. In the United Kingdom, the validity of the primary legislation depends on the principle of the legislative supremacy of the Crown in Parliament. At the apex of the structure there will be the fundamental norm or *Grundnorm*, although the *Grundnorm* will differ from state to state; in a country with a written constitution, the *Grundnorm* will be the proposition that the constitution ought to be obeyed, while in a totalitarian state it might be the will of the supreme ruler.

It is a little difficult to envisage how this analysis can be applied to the structure of International Law. Kelsen himself recognised that some qualification would be necessary. First, he held a monist position, considering International Law to be superior to national law. Secondly, he acknowledged that the International Law laboured under the disadvantage of primitive legislative institutions. Thirdly, the theory depended on the location of the ultimate norm or *Grundnorm*; Kelsen considered that the basic source was customary International Law so that the *Grundnorm* was the proposition that states ought to behave as they have customarily behaved; however, this is not satisfactory because it involves stating that states which obey rules ought to obey those rules thus enabling an 'is' to give rise to an 'ought' which was at variance with Kelsen's original theory that the validity of a norm could only be derived from a prior norm. So that it has been remarked that while Kelsen's analysis may operate within municipal law it is of limited usefulness in International Law because one cannot satisfactorily locate a basic norm.[156]

---

154 Even this was in dispute because the *Grundnorm* itself might depend on political or sociological factors.

155 Kelsen's thought has a varied pedigree and the precise category into which he falls is a matter of some debate: (i) he is often described as a positivist in the tradition of Austin in that he considered law was a distinct form of rules of ethics and he drew a distinction between *lex lata* and *de lege ferenda*; (ii) he is sometimes described as a neo-Kantian either (a) because he sought to give law a scientific basis akin to the physical sciences; or (b) because he stressed that laws were determined by antecedent laws; (c) because he held that our perceptions are shaped by *a priori* preconceptions including those of causation; (iii) he is directly in line with David Hume (1711–76) in stressing the distinction between the 'is' and the 'ought'; (iv) in relation to International Law, he has some affinity with early natural law thinkers; (v) some have argued that, in the context of International Law, he placed too much emphasis on logic and not enough on experience, so much so that Professor Friedmann in his *Legal Theory* (1944) wondered whether, according to his own premises, Kelsen should have denied International Law the character of a legal system.

156 The validity of Kelsen's analysis in the context of International Law is questioned by R Dias, *Jurisprudence*, 5th edn, 1985, and J Stone, *Legal System and Lawyers' Reasonings*, 1964. There is some evidence that Kelsen only considered the application of his theory to International Law as something of an afterthought. Professor Stone considered the application of the theory to be flawed in the case of International Law because of the failure to locate a *Grundnorm* while Professor Lauterpacht (former pupil of Kelsen) considered the theory to be a reversion to natural law thinking. Since many states do not accept a monist view of the subject, the theory was unlikely to attract widespread support. For debate as to the ultimate norm, see J Stone, 'Mystery and mystique in the basic norm' (1963) 26 MLR 34; H Kelsen, 'Professor Stone and the pure theory of law' (1965) 17 Stanford Law Review. For rejection in the municipal law context see *Jilani v Government of Punjab Pak LD* (1972) SC 139.

(v) International law has been described as a primitive form of legal order by the jurist HLA Hart (1907–92). In his book *The Concept of Law* (1961), Professor Hart argued that an advanced legal system required the coming together of primary and secondary rules supported by a rule of recognition. The purpose of the primary rules was to impose duties and such rules could be found in primitive legal systems; however, an advanced legal system required the operation of secondary rules which contained powers to create, modify and adjudicate upon primary rules. According to Professor Hart, the international legal order is a primitive legal system because its institutional limitations have prevented the development of a system of secondary rules. As evidence of this, he cited the absence of both a supreme legislature and a court with compulsory jurisdiction operating without a clear fundamental rule or rule of recognition. However, Professor Hart acknowledged that the system could be described as a legal order rather than a collection of social rules because: (i) rules did exist as to how states ought to behave; (ii) appeals were commonly made to precedents and treatises; (iii) the system itself operated with a degree of ethical neutrality; and (iv) the system was capable of change by treaty.

It has to be admitted that some of the controversy concerning Austin, Kelsen and Hart depends on how one defines the word 'law'; if one gives the word a very narrow definition, then it is possible to exclude International Law from its ambit.

Professor Hart makes the point that a society that relies on primary rules alone will be a primitive legal society, thus he argues that a rule of recognition is necessary to identify the primary rules; to an extent, this function is performed by the Statute of the International Court of Justice. Secondary rules of change are needed to prevent the paralysis that would arise with simply primary rules; to a limited extent treaties operate as rules of change. It is also asserted that any sophisticated legal system requires rules of adjudication; in this context it has to be admitted that the number of methods of peaceful dispute resolution has greatly increased in the 20th century with many treaties containing extensive compulsory forms of adjudication.

(vi) An objection sometimes made to International Law is that it is determined by the self-interest of individual states. Thus, it is argued that state A may act if its vital interests are threatened but not otherwise. Such writers point to the conduct of the United States in organising the bombing of Lybia in 1986 or liberating Kuwait in 1990–91, while showing considerable reluctance to involve itself in the disintegration of Yugoslavia. Such persons further argue that the votes cast in the Security Council are determined by how individual states view their own particular interest. In this context, some point to the tendency of particular powers to share the same approach.

A number of points should be made. First, any democratically elected government can only act in a manner that is acceptable to the majority of its electorate; it would be surprising if it were otherwise, if it has attained power on the basis that it will conduct a particular form of foreign policy. Secondly, this objection is not confined to International Law; in municipal law, power is attained by political parties that are themselves coalitions of social and economic groupings; a political party seeks power on the basis of a manifesto designed to appeal to particular social groups and, having attained power, it legislates to give effect to those objectives be they lower taxation or higher public spending. The legislatures of the world are made up of politicians who have been elected to promote various social and class interests. Thirdly, many international obligations involve the commitment of resources; the government of an individual state can only act in a manner that is broadly in sympathy with the concerns of its electorate. Since 1918, when foreign policy passed out of the hands of hereditary rulers, democratically elected governments can only conduct a foreign policy that is broadly in line with the wishes of its electorate.

(vii) Some writers argue that the controversy as to the legal nature of International Law simply proceeds from linguistic confusion and from a failure to appreciate that Austin's traditional definition was not the only possible definition of the term 'law'.[157] Some writers complain that International Law places excessive reliance on states to the detriment of individuals, but that would seem to be an argument as to scope rather than existence.[158] In recent years, some have argued that International Law is not 'law' because it is inextricably linked with ethical and political considerations, but this is an argument that applies to many municipal rules.[159] In contrast, municipal law and International Law do have a common feature in that they both depend on an underlying acceptance by the community.[160]

(viii) *Ubi societas, ubi jus.* Some writers argue that it serves little purpose to propound a definition of law and then to ask whether International Law does or does not meet that definition. Given that the analyses of Austin, Kelsen and Hart have not been completely accepted in respect of municipal law there is much, it is argued, that can be achieved by simply looking at the evidence. First, it is argued that no society has operated successfully for any length of time without legal rules to balance the competing interests in that society. Law is thus both a social fact and a social necessity. Secondly, it is argued that International Law arose because individual rulers needed some form of code to regulate their relations so that, in the modern world of over 150 autonomous states, law is needed to regulate and promote a degree of co-operation between these states, not least in addressing common problems. Thus, in the modern world where isolation is not a serious option and co-operation is the norm, it is claimed that law is simply a social necessity. Thirdly, it is argued that those who are concerned with international relations, such as diplomats and politicians, accept the existence of a body of rules known as International Law and have assented to the various references to it in the United Nations Charter (1945). According to this view, International Law exists because practitioners not only need it but perceive that its existence is beneficial. Fourthly, although such an explanation may be regarded as sociological, it does have a legal pedigree. As the Law of Nations evolved in the 18th century one of the principal contentions was that the sovereignty was linked to territory, so that the ruler of state X was only sovereign within that territory; such a premise naturally gave rise to questions as to the status of the ruler of X outside his own territory so that where sovereignty ended the Law of Nations began. Thus, it is

---

157 G Williams, 'International law and the controversy concerning the word "law"' (1945) 22 BYIL 146.

158 P Allott, *Eunomia: New Order for a New World*, 1990.

159 M Koskenniemi, *From Apology to Utopia: The Structure of International Legal Argument*, 1989, Helsinki.

160 DW Greig, *International Law*, 2nd edn, 1976.

argued that Public International Law and Private International Law grew up because of the territorial limitations on sovereignty.

Those who take this approach included John Westlake,[161] who argued that every society had a legal system and that International Law existed if one could demonstrate that international society existed; Westlake (1828–1913) was confident that international society existed and today, with such a large number of international organisations, there can be no doubt on that point.

Finally, in International Law there are some areas that are more clearly established than others; for example, the rules on the Law of the Sea can now be stated with reasonable certainty but the principles governing state succession are less than clear. However, this is not a valid argument against the existence of international rules, merely a plea for clarity. Moreover, such a problem also arises in domestic law; in most municipal legal systems it is probably quite simple to ascertain the constituent elements of the offence of theft,[162] but the relevant principles of the rule against perpetuities[163] may not be so succinctly stated. In any legal system some rules will be more clearly established than others.

4 THE ENFORCEMENT OF INTERNATIONAL LAW

A criticism made by some of International Law is that the system appears devoid of proper means of enforcement. In municipal law, if a citizen of a state steals property then he will be arrested, taken before a court and punished. In the last analysis, the full weight of the state's law enforcement machinery can be brought to bear. It is certainly true that the view is commonly expressed that International Law lacks sanctions; it is arguable that this is a legacy of the 1930s when the system of collective security was seen to break down and it is noticeable that such sentiments tend to be expressed when there has been a serious breach of International Law attracting widespread publicity. However, as noted above, the vast majority of states obey International Law most of the time. Nevertheless it is important to examine further the suggestion that International Law is deficient in methods of enforcement.

First, as will be seen later, it is evident that problems within International Law are capable of legal analysis and methods of enforcement do arise. International law has a considerable number of methods of dispute resolution; most of these methods involve examining the evidence and finding the facts in a manner not unlike those operating in municipal law.[164] Secondly, it is important to note that a system of laws may be respected not on account of vigorous methods of enforcement but because the relevant rules are viewed as necessary to the smooth functioning of the community. Compliance is based on

---

161 L Oppenheim, *Collected Papers of John Westlake*, 1914, Chapter 1.

162 In England and Wales, reference would be made to the Theft Act 1968.

163 In England and Wales, it is necessary to have some knowledge of the common law rules because the Perpetuities and Accumulations Act 1964 only applies to instruments taking effect after 15 July 1964.

164 Methods of dispute resolution will be dealt with later but it should be noted here that the conventional methods are: (i) mediation; (ii) inquiry; (iii) conciliation; (iv) arbitration; (v) judicial resolution in municipal courts or before the ICJ; (vi) through the offices of the United Nations.

acceptance rather than the severity of the sanctions. To take a simple example: in many European countries, a motorist will be obliged to stop at a particular traffic indicator; compliance is based not on the severity of the sanctions (normally a modest fine) but on the realisation that such a requirement is conducive to a safe road traffic system. In like terms, it is arguable that states observe International Law because its content is founded upon reason and the rules are necessary for the smooth functioning of the international community. It is also a matter of record that within municipal law systems it is common for writers to question whether the sanction or penalty for a particular criminal act is sufficient to deter future acts; indeed, criticism of the level of compensation in the civil courts is often also the subject of comment. So International Law cannot reasonably expect to be immune from scrutiny as to its sanctions and methods of enforcement.

Thirdly, as will be seen later, many writers argue that some rules of International Law are enforced by becoming part of a national legal system through an act of incorporation;[165] in these circumstances the sanctions available do not differ greatly from those available in respect of municipal law. Fourthly, a serious breach of International Law will cause a state to suffer in its dealings with other states. The invasion of the Falkland Islands in 1982 certainly did not improve Argentina's relations with the United Kingdom or with those states who considered that the conduct was unlawful; likewise, the conduct of France in respect of the *Rainbow Warrior* in 1985 harmed its relations with New Zealand. The invasion of Kuwait by Iraq in 1990 resulted in widespread condemnation and many states indicated their reluctance to deal with a state that had flouted its treaty obligations. Thus unlawful conduct by state A directed against state B may may result in action by states D, E and F.

Fifthly, at the international level, the Security Council may take enforcement action in the event of serious breaches of the United Nations Charter; this matter will be explored further later. However, it should be noted at this stage that the measures taken by the Security Council may involve the use of force (Korea (1950), Iraq (1990), (1998)), or some form of economic sanctions[166] (Southern Rhodesia (1966), South Africa (1977)), or indeed restrictions on travel (Lybia (1992)) or trade (Sierra Leone (1998)).

In an interdependent world, a breach of International Law may result in specific action being taken by individual countries. The invasion of the United States Embassy in Tehran in 1979 resulted in the freezing of Iranian assets in the United Kingdom, the United States and other countries. It is not unusual for individual states to take such action even though the state subject to the offending act may also begin legal proceedings as well.[167]

Seventhly, an individual state may take action to suspend rights and privileges enjoyed by the offending state; this may take the form of suspending diplomatic relations[168] or downgrading the level of representation. In appropriate cases, treaty obligations may be suspended.

---

165 JB Scott, 'The legal nature of international law' (1907) 1 AJIL 831.

166 The role of economic sanctions and the effect on third parties has been the subject of recent consideration, see J Carver and J Hulsmann, 'The role of Article 50 of the United Nations Charter in the search for international peace and security' (2000) 49 ICLQ 528.

167 See 'United States Diplomatic and Consular Staff in Tehran' (1979) ICJ 7; (1980) ICJ 3.

168 For diplomatic relations see below; diplomatic relations do not cease when all the staff are withdrawn. In the years 1987–89, the United Kingdom withdrew all diplomatic staff from Iran but continued a form of diplomatic relations.

In the wider world no state can hope to enjoy economic prosperity without entering into relations with neighbouring states.[169] In the world since 1945, a considerable number of treaties have been drawn up to promote social and economic co-operation. Most treaties include some method of compulsory dispute resolution.[170] In addition, many states participate in international organisations and the constituting treaty provides for suspension of a state in the event that it offends against International Law.[171]

Since 1920 there has been an International Court capable of hearing disputes between states; this institution will be explored in detail later but it should be noted that it does not have compulsory jurisdiction and it only hears a small number of cases each year.

In most systems of municipal law the individual is entitled to use reasonable or proportionate force in defence of self, family or property.[172] In like terms, in International Law it has long been recognised that a state is entitled to employ force in strictly limited circumstances when all other methods of peaceful resolution have been exhausted. The circumstances in which force can be lawfully employed and whether any use of force can be lawful outside the terms of the United Nations Charter[173] is a matter that will be dealt with later. Suffice it to observe at this juncture that one of the earliest concerns of the Law of Nations was as to when force could be lawfully employed.

As has been indicated above, International Law has a number of methods of dispute resolution and a variety of sanctions in the event of breaches. However, there are two other points that require to be made. Since 1945, the number of individual states has increased more than threefold; some states are prosperous, others very poor and lacking in natural resources. Since 1945, the establishment of international organisations designed to promote social and economic progress has given even the poorest state a vested interest in observing the rules of the international community. Secondly, it is becoming clear that the greatest sanction to ensure observance of International Law is the force of public opinion. In a state that operates a free press, regular elections and freedom of expression there will usually be considerable pressure on the executive branch of government to ensure respect for International Law. There may be a dispute as to the precise requirements of International Law, but democratically elected governments will be anxious to ensure that International Law is respected.[174] It is a matter of record that the most serious breaches of International Law since 1918 have tended to follow from the conduct of states that did not enjoy a democratically elected government subject to a

---

169 The last to attempt it was Albania under Enver Hoxha (1908–85) but during his period of supreme rule the country remained one of the poorest in Europe.

170 The treaty may include a number of methods as is the case under the Law of the Sea Convention (1982).

171 For example, Israel was suspended from the International Atomic Energy Authority after its attack on an Iraqi nuclear reactor near Baghdad.

172 Criminal Law Act 1967, s 3; Criminal Damage Act 1971, s 5; *R v Duffy* [1967] 1 QB 63; *R v Julien* [1969] 2 All ER 856; *Palmer v R* [1971] 1 All ER 1077; *R v Williams* (1984) 78 Cr App R 276, CA.

173 See in particular Art 2(4) and Art 51 of the United Nations Charter (1945).

174 See, for example, discussion in the United Kingdom in April 1982 in respect of the Falkland Islands or the wide debate in the United States from August 1990 to February 1991 in respect of the invasion of Kuwait. A more recent example is afforded by the Kosovo campaign of spring 1999 where the existence of a right of humanitarian action outside the express sanction of a Security Council resolution was questioned.

tradition of freedom of expression.[175] This is a particular concern where attempts are being made to enforce newer areas of International Law such as respect for human rights.

Thus the broad conclusion must be that International Law now comprises a number of methods of enforcement; these methods differ from municipal law because the subjects are autonomous sovereign states and, while the techniques may be less than perfect, they can be seen to be evolving in accordance with developments within the international community. As in municipal law, if traditional methods of peaceful resolution fail then force may need to be employed by those acting on behalf of the wider international community.

---

175 Examples being Germany (not a functioning democracy after 1933) Japan and the Soviet Union in the 1930s; in recent years Argentina (1982). Iraq (1990) were ruled by forms of military power.

CHAPTER 2

INTERNATIONAL LAW AND THE MODERN WORLD

1 THE INCREASED SCOPE OF INTERNATIONAL LAW

Victory for the Allied Powers in 1945 had been achieved at a considerable cost; the major European states would need to embark on large programmes of social reconstruction. Although it was not immediately apparent, the post-1945 world would be dominated by the United States and the Soviet Union. European influence would be limited and the defeat of Japan was so comprehensive that potential aggression from that state was no longer a cause of concern. The United Nations had been born of a mixture of both American idealism and realism; the decision to locate the headquarters in New York reflected the new post-war realities. Within months of the signing of the Charter, events only served to emphasise the need for improved methods of co-operation; the employment of nuclear weapons in August 1945[1] and the reaction to the Truman Declaration of September 1945[2] indicated the need to foster improved methods of international understanding and co-operation. The end of the conflict had left the United States as the dominant industrial power, possessing nuclear weapons and being one of the few states with a constitutional structure intact and whose governing class had not been discredited. The only other major power capable of giving a lead in the reconstruction of international order was the United Kingdom, but it had been exhausted by the effort of victory and viewed its long term interests as being best served by co-operation with its major ally rather than by launching any distinctly European initiatives. International order was to be restored by the efforts of the United States.

Although much of the planning had been done prior to 1945, Franklin Roosevelt had had to grapple with the isolationist trend in American life. However, the experience of the League of Nations convinced both President Roosevelt[3] and President Truman that international order would require to be based on rules. Just as the United States had been held together by the constitution of 1787, so it was hoped that international society could coalesce around certain agreed rules. These rules would draw upon principles of American constitutional law, such as democracy and the rule of law, together with principles of decolonisation, the peaceful settlement of disputes, and a degree of free trade and open markets. International society would be managed through the United Nations and the task of economic reconstruction would fall to those institutions

---

1   The nature of the devastation prompted demands to limit such technology and to continue with the disarmament objectives of the League of Nations. The last effect was to persuade statesmen that the cost of any further major European conflict would simply be too high. This was later to have the effect of tempting the Soviet Union to intervene in minor disputes in other parts of the world.

2   The Truman Declaration of that month was concerned with the continental shelf and waters adjacent to the United States; it marks the beginning of the modern law of the sea. The difficulty was that unilateral action by the United States was followed by extensive maritime claims by other states leading to a degree of uncertainty as to the precise law of the sea. See Chapter 13.

3   The death of President Roosevelt on 12 April 1945 meant that it fell to President Truman to give effect to plans drawn up during the Second World War.

established after the Bretton Woods Conference of July 1944.[4] The general objective was well expressed by President Truman at San Francisco in June 1945,[5] when he observed that 'The United Nations Charter is dedicated to the achievement and observance of human rights and fundamental freedoms. Unless we can attain these objectives for all men and women everywhere – without regard to race, language or religion – we cannot have permanent peace and security'.

However, the desire to build an international order modelled on American constitutional law had to yield to events. While American influence could be employed to reform Japanese political life, it could not prevent the ascent to power of communist forces in China after 1949 and it was powerless to restrain excesses of Soviet influence in Eastern Europe. The realisation that Western Europe depended on the United States for its defence lead to the signing of the North Atlantic Treaty in 1949 and thereafter there was a tendency to view the world as divided between the American led western democracies founded on the rule of law and market economies as against those states which were subject to Communist party rule; the view that communist regimes were minded to expand served to lead to distrust and made co-operation in the Security Council very difficult in the 1950s. It also contributed to high levels of tension in 1956 in respect of the invasion of Hungary and later such suspicion manifested itself in the form of the Cuban Missile Crisis of 1962.[6]

First, although decolonisation would begin immediately after 1945, many writers are minded to view the subsequent half century as divided into a number of distinct periods. The initial period extended down to 1960 when the United Nations and General Assembly were dominated by those powers that had been victorious in the Second World War. Secondly, it is possible to point to the period after 1960 when the General Assembly had increased in size and began to reflect the influence of newly decolonised states. Thirdly, one can point to the period after 1985[7] when political change in the Soviet Union, and then in Eastern Europe, led to a reduction in tension and it made it possible for the Security Council to operate with less fear of the veto; it also allowed action to be taken against rogue states. These are, of course, only broad categories but they serve to emphasise that international law had to develop after 1945 against a background not only of an unprecedented increase in the number of states but also one of ideological conflict between competing blocs.

However, in reviewing the evolution of international society after 1945, while it is sensible to acknowledge the difficulties posed by ideological conflicts between states,[8] it is also important to recognise that there were a number of factors emerging that would contribute to the broadening of the scope of international law. First, technical change

---

4   The International Bank for Reconstruction and Development (IBRD) (the World Bank), designed to promote reconstruction by facilitating capital investment, and its close relative, the International Monetary Fund (IMF), designed to promote international trade through exchange rate stability.

5   In closing the San Francisco conference; these remarks were to be legally relevant because the United Nations Charter contained a number of references to the maintenance of human rights.

6   See Q Wright, 'The Cuban quarantine' (1963) 57 AJIL 546.

7   1985 marks the arrival in power of Mikhail Gorbachev; the collapse of Soviet power in Eastern Europe is normally dated from 1988–89.

8   Difficulties with the Soviet Union would prompt the resignation of the first Secretary General of the United Nations. Trygve Lie would describe the office as 'the most impossible job on this earth'.

would lead to the exploration of both outer space and the sea bed; to prevent an undignified scramble to assert rights it was necessary to put in place an international regulatory regime. Secondly, improvements in communications emphasised and served to accentuate the interdependence of the modern world in areas such as civil aviation and telecommunications. Thirdly, as statesmen reflected on the lessons to be drawn from the conflict of 1939–45, it became evident that international institutions would have to be developed to permit more detailed diplomatic exchanges and to avoid the threat to peace posed by the possible proliferation of nuclear weapons. The role of the international institutions was recognised in the Advisory Opinion of the International Court of Justice in 1949 in the *Reparation for Injuries* case.[9] After 1949, regional organisation to promote co-operation or military alliances would lead to a proliferation of international organisations. Fourthly, the process of decolonisation would increase the number of states but it was evident that many were economically backward, operating with an immature political culture. In these circumstances, regional and international organisations would be required to concentrate on work of humanitarian assistance. Fifthly, the conflict of 1939–45 was a watershed in the century. Modern technology in the form of newsreels would inform a scarcely believing world of the genocide perpetrated during the years after 1938. The establishment of an international tribunal at Nuremberg contributed to a steady growth in interest in matters of human rights. The judgment of the tribunal was endorsed by the General Assembly[10] and within a couple of years the Universal Declaration on Human Rights (1948) would set out certain basic principles. The law on human rights which would emerge is directly traceable to the events of 1933–45 and the conviction began to develop that, in certain circumstances, the manner in which a state treated its own nationals was a concern of the wider international community.

After 1945, there were three basic economic models that a developed state might adopt. The first was the free market model which would require a regime of free trade to be implemented by treaty. The conviction grew that open trade was likely to lead not only to economic growth through larger markets but also to a reduced risk of conflict. In Western Europe, the establishment of the Benelux Union in 1948 was built on in the Treaty of Paris in 1950. Seven years later, six European states would sign the Treaty of Rome and establish the European Economic Community. Secondly, the social democratic governments that took office after 1945 were influenced by Keynesian economics[11] and sought to avoid mass unemployment by international co-operation, both to promote economic growth and to counter the effect of trade cycles.[12] Thirdly, those governments influenced by Marxist thinking favoured trading activities being conducted by state

---

9   *Reparation for Injuries Suffered in the Service of the United Nations* (1949) ICJ 174; 16 ILR 318.

10 GA Res 95 (I), GAOR Res 1st Session (1946), p 188.

11 Maynard Keynes (1883–1946) had been a member of the delegation at Versailles and played an important role at the Bretton Wood Conference. He was influential in promoting the view that economic co-operation at an international level was as important in securing peace as that of conventional diplomatic exchanges. For a review of his work in establishing the post-war institutions, see D Moggridge, *Maynard Keynes* (1992); for an account of his early years and his reflections on Versailles, see Robert Skidelsky, *John Maynard Keynes*, Vol I, 1983; Vol II, 1992; and Vol III, 2000. In the years 1939–45, Keynes played an important role, not only raising funds to continue the war but he played a significant part with Harry Dexter White in establishing the post-war international organisations that operate today.

12 It is of interest that some social democratic thinkers stressed the protection of the environment as an objective, see CAR Crossland, *The Future of Socialism*, 1956.

bodies and this prompted developments in traditional concepts of immunity as the courts in Western nations sought to draw a distinction between sovereign functions and trading activities.[13]

Although one of the central objectives of the United Nations Charter was to promote the peaceful settlement of disputes, it was clear that in an increasingly interdependent world one of the roles of international law would be to facilitate co-operation between states in those areas where the state could not act alone. This prompted the establishment of the International Law Commission in 1947 charged by the General Assembly with the progressive development of international law and its codification. The far reaching work of this specialist body is to be found in a number of multilateral law making treaties.[14] The Commission[15] comprises 34 members from Africa, Asia, America and Europe who serve for a five year period and who are appointed from lists furnished by national governments. Much of the work of the International Law Commission consists of preparing the first drafts for international law making treaties. In some instances, drafts produced by the International Law Commission may serve as evidence of rules of customary law.

2 DECOLONISATION

The colonial Empires acquired by European powers had grown up in the years since 1500 when improvements in navigation made expansion into the new world possible. Some colonies had been lost early on; the revolt of the American colonies after 1776 and the liberation of Latin America in the years after 1815 indicated the difficulties that a European power would experience in seeking to retain possessions far from Europe. Attitudes to overseas possessions varied; the British had been content to accord Dominion status to Australia and Canada but after 1919 the political debate tended to focus upon India.

The Congress of Berlin in 1878 had required the Ottoman rulers to pay regard to the interests of their minorities and, in 1885, the same European powers indicated that colonies were to be held on trust. However, at the end of the century liberal intellectuals began to contend that colonies were being acquired as a means to export capital and as a solution to the problems of under consumption. JA Hobson's *Imperialism*, published in 1902, had linked colonial expansion to structural problems in the capitalist system.[16] Such

---

13 This is considered in detail in the chapter concerned with immunity from jurisdiction. For a contemporary case indicating judicial reservations as to the scope of immunity see *Krajina v Tass Agency* [1949] 2 All ER 274.

14 The Geneva Conventions of 1958 on the Territorial Sea, High Seas, and Continental Shelf; Vienna Convention on Diplomatic Relations (1961); Vienna Convention on the Law of Consular Relations (1963).

15 See I Sinclair, *The International Law Commission*, 1987; B Graeforth, 'The International Law Commission tomorrow: improving its organisation and methods of work' (1991) 85 AJIL 597.

16 JA Hobson had, before 1902, advanced a theory of under consumption. He argued that the products of industry could not be all consumed by the rich and could not be afforded by the poor. In his work *Imperialism* in 1902 he argued both that capital would tend to be exported and that competitive imperialism would tend to lead to war. Hobson's theories of under consumption would influence Maynard Keynes when he came to write his *General Theory of Employment, Interest and Money*, 1936.

works tended to detract from the appeal of colonies abroad. At the end of the 18th century a wider electoral suffrage in many Western European countries was creating demands for social reform; such measures could only be paid for by curtailing defence and other expenditures. Some argued that colonialism had played its part in the outbreak of the First World War and this questionable analysis was extended by VI Lenin in his *Imperialism: The Highest Stage of Capitalism*.[17] Although this view was not accepted by all,[18] and there was much evidence to contradict it, by 1919 much liberal intellectual opinion favoured some form of self-determination on the basis of language and cultural ties; such an approach was also endorsed by Woodrow Wilson. The danger that self-determination might simply create a new set of minorities was not always appreciated. Thus, in the Covenant of the League of Nations the duties owed in respect of mandated territory were clearly spelled out. Article 22 indicated that such territory and its peoples should form 'a sacred trust of civilisation'. The duties on the Mandatory required it to raise the standard of living of the people so as to prepare the territory for independent statehood. The same general obligation was continued in the United Nations Trusteeship system.[19] The duties towards mandated territories and the granting of Dominion status indicated that some European powers realised that decolonisation was inevitable. By the mid-1920s both Australia[20] and Canada[21] had acquired full internal autonomy and the power to conduct external relations.

The duration and intensity of conflict in the Second World War was to place a heavy strain on European states and after that date decolonisation began in earnest. As regards the United Kingdom, the effort of securing victory had exhausted national resources and future revenues would be needed for social reform at home.[22] The administration of Clement Attlee acted to grant independence to India[23] and this process of decolonisation was then followed by subsequent administrations in the 1950s. In the case of the United Kingdom, the Suez debacle prompted a re-assessment of objectives[24] and applications to join the European Economic Community followed shortly thereafter.

The return of De Gaulle[25] to power in 1958 lead to a re-assessment of French foreign policy and the role of France in the world. Acting with considerable speed, De Gaulle had

---

17 *Imperialism: The Highest Stage of Capitalism*, 1917.

18 In his *Zur Soziologie des Imperialismus* (Imperialism and Social Classes), 1919, Joseph Schumpeteer pointed out that capitalism appears to prosper in conditions of peace and free trade and that colonialism could be explained on the basis of the mistaken self interest of a ruling class.

19 Articles 73–76 of the United Nations Charter (1945).

20 See Commonwealth of Australia Act 1900.

21 British North America Act 1867; the position clarified further in the Statute of Westminster 1931.

22 The economic difficulties encountered by the United Kingdom after 1940 are set out in detail in Robert Skidelsky's *John Maynard Keynes: Fighting for Britain (1937–1946)*, 2000.

23 Clemant Attlee (Deputy Prime Minster 1940–45; Prime Minster 1945–51). Attlee had served on the Simon Commission in 1928–29 and had first hand knowledge of the Indian problem which, in the 1920s, he regarded as 'particularly intractable and nearly insoluble'. In retirement he was to consider the granting of independence to India as the achievement of which he was most proud: see Francis Beckett, *Clem Attlee: A Biography*, 1997.

24 The long term effect of Suez being to emphasise the financial cost of foreign obligations as well as the need for the United Kingdom to reassess its foreign policy priorities. Negotiations for entry into the EEC began in 1961 although entry would not take place until 1973.

25 Charles de Gaulle (1890–1970) had served as head of the provisional government in 1944 before resigning in 1946 over the constitution of the Fourth Republic. He served as the first President of the Fifth Republic (1958–69).

by 1960 secured the effective independence of those territories in French West Africa,[26] but had underwritten such a transition by varying forms of association with France. At the same time, De Gaulle moved to extricate France from Algeria where it had been the colonial power since 1830. Such action was taken following a sober reappraisal of the role of France and the need for it to focus upon assisting Germany in seeking to mould the European Community which had come into existence in 1958. However, such an approach to decolonisation was in line with the demands of international law. On 14 December 1960, the General Assembly passed the Declaration on the Granting of Independence to Colonial Countries and Peoples[27] which required that:

> ... immediate steps shall be taken in Trust and non self-governing Territories, or in all other Territories which have not yet attained independence, to transfer all powers to the people of those Territories without any conditions whatsoever ... The inadequacy of political, economic, social or educational preparedness should never serve as a pretext for delaying independence.

The experience of Suez and the emerging forms of European co-operation prompted the United Kingdom to reconsider its role in the world. In theory the British Empire had always been based on the principle that colonies would be guided towards self-government but the administration of Harold Macmillan[28] decided to expedite the process. Pressures to implement social reforms required strict control of defence spending; the circle could be squared by reducing foreign commitments. Macmillan followed the path of De Gaulle, outlining his philosophy in the 'Winds of Change' speech in 1960.[29] In 1961, preparatory work began on an application for membership of the European Community. Although the formal application of 1963 would fail decolonisation proceeded apace. The United Kingdom therefore followed France in seeking an exit from Africa. The hope was that economic and cultural ties would remain and that the newly independent states would adopt democratic constitutional structures and participate in the work of the United Nations. Although there were difficulties in the case of Southern Rhodesia[30] the pattern followed that of France. The presence of a non-democratic regime in Portugal had the consequence that decolonisation of Portuguese colonies was delayed until after the 1974 revolution.[31]

In retrospect, decolonisation was inevitable but what was surprising is the speed of disengagement. In 1945 colonial rule extended across a considerable part of the globe; after 1965 it was largely gone.[32] European states lacked the will or the resources to stay and domestic electorates demanded increases in welfare spending that could only be

---

26 The territories of the then Ivory Coast, Malagasy, Senegal, Niger, Cameroon, Gabon, Chad.

27 Resolution 1514 (XV) 14 December 1960.

28 Harold Macmillan (1894–1986) (Prime Minister 1957–63).

29 Delivered in Cape Town on 3 February 1960.

30 See Southern Rhodesia Act 1965; Southern Rhodesia Act 1979; Zimbabwe Act 1979. For a discussion of the constitutional position, see *Madzimbamuto v Lardner Burke* [1969] 1 AC 645.

31 Mozambique became independent in 1975; Frelimo forces had struggled for independence from Portugal since 1962; in Angola the struggle for independence from Portugal began in 1961 but was plagued by differences between the left leaning MPLA and the right leaning UNITA. Independence from Portugal was achieved in 1975.

32 Eg, India (1947), Pakistan (1947), Burma (1948), Ghana (1957), Cyprus (1960), Nigeria (1960), Tanganyika/Tanzania (1962), Uganda (1962), Malaysia (1963), Kenya (1963), Northern Rhodesia/Zambia (1964).

afforded by tight control of external obligations. Negotiations for independence were normally conducted with small elites who tended to be more optimistic than the facts warranted about the prospects on independence. The consequence was that many small states were poor and laboured under problems of a limited infrastructure; in Africa, ethnic tensions produced unstable governments and, in some cases, constitutionalism gave way to military rule.

Thus, in the 1960s international law was having to operate in a greatly changed environment. The main contours were an ideological struggle between the Soviet Union and the United States, the relative decline of Europe and an increase in the number of third world states, many of whom were plagued by problems of poverty, illiteracy and lack of investment. International law, which might still have been viewed as Eurocentric in 1900, now had to accommodate a much larger number of states ranging from the very prosperous to the near bankrupt. Such diversity was without precedent and raised the problem of how to reconcile such interests.

A sign of the changing international scene was the Afro-Asian conference summoned by President Sukarno[33] to Bandung in April 1955. The gathering was attended by 23 states from Asia and four from Africa. The conference was called at a time when there was a degree of euphoria amongst newly independent states and a reluctance to acknowledge how intractable some of the problems of underdevelopment would prove to be. The conference contained a demand for African and Asian countries to refrain from siding with either grouping in the Cold War.

Although, of course, the increase in the number of states augmented the membership of the General Assembly and thereby superficially increased the influence of newly decolonised states, this may have been a mirage. In the case of Africa and, to a lesser extent, in Asia, the domestic problems of such states were considerable; with high levels of illiteracy and poverty, many were plagued by underdevelopment and political instability. In Africa, several passed from constitutional rule to *de facto* military dictatorship. Those that sought to increase the gross domestic product by some form of socialist planning were at first able to rely on support from the Soviet Union but, after the death of Leonid Brezhnev in 1982, those holding power in Moscow became more concerned with their own internal problems. The experience of such states contrasts with Western Europe and the United States, where the years after 1945 witnessed a steady increase in domestic prosperity. A period of peace allowed considerable progress to be made in the areas of education, transport, health provision and welfare. The most radical transformation was in Germany where the country defeated and occupied in 1945 was, under the leadership of Konrad Adenauer,[34] able to play a significant role in the establishment of the European Community as provided for in the Treaty of Rome in 1957.

The effect of such post-war developments was that although international society contained a greater number of states the diversity in social and economic conditions was without precedent. In some states, constitutional government under the rule of law

---

33   Achmed Sukarno (1901–70), President of Indonesia (1945–67).
34   Konrad Adenauer (1876–1967) Chancellor of West Germany (1949–63). The *Wirtshaftswunder* of the Adenauer-Erhard period is a matter of record, But it is also sensible to reflect on French success. Notwithstanding the political difficulties of the Fourth Republic (1946–58), industrial production tripled in the period 1952–72.

provided the conditions for the economic growth that permitted steady increases in standards of health, housing, education, transport and leisure. In other states, the absence of political stability and problems of under investment caused continuing problems of poverty, illiteracy and premature death. Thus, the task of the United Nations and of international law has been to construct those institutions and rules that will permit beneficial co-operation between the affluent world and the poorer states. After 1945 the emphasis in international law has been to facilitate measures of co-operation.

3 THEORIES AS TO THE NATURE OF INTERNATIONAL LAW

One of the consequences of the abuses perpetrated during the Second World War was a revival of interest in natural law thinking. The conduct of the rulers of Germany in the period 1933–45 served to demonstrate the dangers of those schools of extreme positivism which placed no limitations on state sovereignty. In the aftermath of the Holocaust it[35] was obvious that the international community should seek to maintain minimum standards of state conduct. Such objectives are set out in the United Nations Charter (1945) and the Universal Declaration of Human Rights (1948). At the same time, many states produced new constitutional documents designed either to confer basic guarantees of human rights or to provide that established rules of international law should be incorporated into municipal law.[36] On the international plane, the revival of the natural law tradition is to be found in the expansion of the law on human rights and, in the related sphere of private international law, the same guiding principles is to be detected in the reluctance of municipal courts to acknowledge and enforce foreign laws objectionable on ethical grounds.[37] Natural law thinking is also identifiable in the provisions of the United Nations Charter (1945) designed to restrain aggression and to restrict the use of force. Of all the horrors arising in the Second World War, the systematic destruction of the Jewish population in Europe was the gravest. Thus, the natural law emphasis on minimum international standards is to be found not only in the judgment of the Nuremberg tribunal but also in the Genocide Convention (1948) and the Convention Relating to the Status of Refugees (1951). Moreover, the natural law emphasis on the peaceful settlement of disputes and the avoidance of armed conflict was particularly pertinent when, after 1945,[38] the world had become aware of the likely cost of a nuclear conflict. It is therefore possible to view the years after 1945 as giving greater emphasis to

---

35 Although the precise figure will never be known, it is accepted by most historians that the figure of innocent victims was in the region of 6 million; see *Attorney General of Israel v Eichman* (1961) 36 ILR 5. Historical research indicates that six million of Europe's eight million Jews perished. For a detailed treatment, see Martin Gilbert, *The Holocaust*, 1986.

36 The most obvious example being the provisions as to basic rights in the German Constitution of 1949 which, by Art 19, may not be encroached upon. Article 25 provides for general rules of public international law to be part of federal law and to take precedence. This was not a fresh start as Art 4 of the 1919 Weimar Constitution had carried a like provision.

37 *Oppenheimer v Cattermole* [1976] AC 249.

38 Although nuclear weapons were not used against Japan until August 1945, several weeks after the signing of the United Nations Charter; the preparatory work on the United Nations Charter had taken place in the years 1943–45, at the same time that research on nuclear weapons was being conducted. President Roosevelt was, of course, aware that the nature of such weapons made it imperative that the United Nations framework was robust enough to restrain international conflict.

arguments based upon natural law and natural rights, in particular in the attempts to develop an international law of human rights.

While decolonisation and the tension of the Cold War would influence the development of international law, the impact of theory should not be underestimated. Positivism had dominated the subject since the 18th century; it was a theory that accorded with the rationalist and optimistic spirit of the enlightenment and in the 19th century it was congenial to the practitioners of *Realpolitik* such as Cavour and Bismarck who sought to avoid any restraints on state conduct. However, positivist theories would themselves influence the teaching, if not the practice, of international law.

One of the most influential writers was Hans Kelsen (1881–1973), who drew upon Immanuel Kant's theory of knowledge to put forward his own analysis of legal systems. Kant had argued that knowledge was not merely an aggregate of sense impressions but depended on the categories and concepts imposed by human beings themselves. Kelsen[39] asserted that law and a legal system should be subject to a similar analysis. Law, he held, should be analysed by reference to its constituent elements without reference to extraneous political, cultural or social phenomena. A legal system under such a 'pure' analysis was but a hierarchy of norms or ought propositions where each norm is validated by reference to a prior norm until one reaches the fundamental norm or *Grundnorm*. The *Grundnorm* would not be the constitution itself but the constitutional evolution which validates it. In relation to international law, Kelsen adopted a monist approach and tended to the view that the *Grundnorm* was based on the principle of customary law that *pacta sunt servanda*. He viewed law as a unified area of knowledge and once it was conceded that international law comprised legal rules binding upon states, it followed that it must be part of a single system. Kelsen viewed international law as being based on a hierarchy of custom, treaty and judicial and arbitral decisions.

The difficulties with this approach are considerable. First, the monist theory is certainly not accepted by most states and appears to have been adopted to fit Kelsen's general theory into the scheme of international law. Secondly, the uncertain nature of customary law makes it an unsuitable choice for a *Grundnorm* and the principle of *pacta sunt servanda* lacks the requisite element of effectiveness. Thirdly, any attempt to analyse international law without reference to historical, social or economic conditions must be open to serious question. Although Kelsen's analysis of international law has attracted considerable textbook comment, there is no evidence of it being relied upon in international tribunals and treatment in municipal courts has been equivocal at best.[40]

While the relevance of Kelsen's thought to international law has been deemed questionable, considerable attention has been paid to the analysis of the philosopher and jurist HLA Hart whose *The Concept of Law* was published in 1961; this volume was widely read and precipitated a considerable volume of scholarly comment. Professor Hart[41] was

---

39 For Hans Kelsen, see 'Pure theory of law' (1934) 50 LQR 485; (1935) 51 LQR 517; *General Theory of Law and State* (trans A Wedberg), 1949; *Pure Theory of Law* (trans M Knight), 1967. For comment on Kelsen, see Jones (1935) 16 BYIL 5; Harris (1971) CLJ 103; Harris (1977) 36 CLJ 353; Paulson (1980) 39 CLJ 172.

40 See *The State v Dosso* (1958) Pak LD SC 533; *Jilani v The Government of Punjab* (1972) Pak LD SC 139; *Madzimbamuto v Lardner Burke* (1968) 2 SA 284.

41 HLA Hart (1907–92), philosopher and jurist. The most influential legal philosopher in England after 1945 and Professor of Jurisprudence at Oxford University 1954–69.

a writer in the Benthamite tradition who contended strongly for the separation of law and morals but also, as a linguistic philosopher, was concerned to emphasise how language was actually used. Hart viewed a legal system as being concerned to render certain forms of conduct 'non optional or obligatory'. He considered a legal system to depend on the interaction of primary and secondary rules. The function of primary rules is to regulate behaviour while the function of secondary rules is to permit the changing of primary rules and to provide means of adjudication. In an advanced society, there will be a rule of recognition that permits the identification of primary rules, while a primitive legal system will be characterised simply by primary rules. This theoretical construct has not passed without criticism, in particular as to whether it makes sufficient allowance for the differences between rule making institutions.[42]

Professor Hart devoted particular attention to the nature of international law. He viewed international law as a primitive legal system which, being devoid of a legislature and without a rule of recognition or primary norm, was but simply a collection of primary rules, although the author was careful to distinguish between claims made under international law and moral claims.[43] Professor Hart conceded that obligations arose under the United Nations Charter (1945) and that the judgments of the International Court of Justice were normally respected,[44] but he asserted that international law was distinct from a developed municipal legal system in lacking secondary rules of adjudication and a rule of recognition. Although, it should be observed that Professor Hart thought that international law was subject to evolution and might develop into a system closer to an advanced system of municipal law.[45]

To the extent that the analyses of Kelsen and Hart were intended to apply regardless of the system or its culture; both represent modified forms of positivism. These analyses have been subject to criticism, on the ground that they place too great an emphasis on rules and thus attach too little importance to the principles and rights that judges, bound by precedent, seek to sustain or the policies and goals that legislatures seek to develop.[46] However, given the evolving and different nature of international law, Professor Hart is surely correct to indicate that it may yet evolve in a manner analogous to a developed system of municipal law.

Those seeking support for positivism as an influential theory in the present century often refer to the judgment of the Permanent Court of International Court of Justice in the *Lotus* case[47] where the court observed 'the rules of law binding upon States ... emanate from their own free will ... restrictions upon the independence of States cannot therefore be presumed'. Moreover, after 1945, Marxist governments tended to adopt a positivist approach, as did newly independent states who often advanced positivist arguments to stress the role of treaties and to diminish the position of customary international law.

---

42 See J Raz, 'The institutional nature of law' (1975) 38 MLR 489. See, also, R Summers (1963) 98 Duke Law Journal 629; MS Blackman (1977) 94 SALJ 415.

43 See *The Concept of Law*, 2nd edn, 1994, p 227.

44 *Ibid*, p 232.

45 *Ibid*, p 237.

46 Notably by Ronald Dworkin in *Taking Rights Seriously*, 1977; *A Matter of Principle*, 1986; *Law's Empire*, 1986; *Freedom's Law*, 1996. On this writer generally, see Stephen Guest, *Ronald Dworkin*, 2nd edn, 1997.

47 The *Lotus* case (1927) PCIJ, Ser A, No 10, p 18.

Positivism as a theory has always been favoured by those states seeking freedom of action in all spheres save those where voluntary restraints have been accepted.

One of the most significant developments in the 19th century was the emergence of sociology as a distinct academic discipline. Although this subject may have many different schools,[48] a consistent theme has been the desire to emphasise the study of law and legal institutions in relation to society as a whole. Such an approach might be political, reformist or revolutionary but the usual technique was to analyse law against the society in which it operates. Thus, the Marxist view of the evolutionary and determinist nature of social change directly influenced the approach of the Soviet Union to questions of international law. One of the consequences of the sociological approach has been that there came to be an increasing emphasis on empirical evidence rather than formal theories. Although it is possible to trace the sociological approach back to Jeremy Bentham, the figure most associated with the movement is Roscoe Pound.[49] Pound argued that the formation, interpretation and application of law should take account of social facts; such an approach could only be based on an objective interpretation of empirical evidence.[50] The objective was a society that was efficient and biased towards the elimination of waste; the task of the lawyer and administrator was seen as analogous to that of the engineer. The importance of this approach was that it first took root in the the United States, the state which would dominate international society after 1919; secondly, the movement coincided with the writings of those jurists held to belong to the realist school.

American realism has been described as a combination of the positivist and the sociological approach. It may be an exaggeration to speak of the movement as a school and it might simply be regarded as a gloss upon the sociological school; thus the sociological approach would examine how the law reacted to other social forces, while the realists tended to analyse how the legal system worked in practice. Realism was said to draw on the extra judicial writings of Oliver Wendell Holmes Jr,[51] although it would be unwise to categorise that learned judge as belonging to the school. Other writers in the United States who followed such an approach would be Jerome Frank[52] and Karl Llewelyn.[53] Related to these forms of legal realism is the realism to be detected amongst scholars of international relations who view international conduct as grounded in the self-

---

48   It is sometimes argued that one can distinguish (i) the political sociology of Montesquieu (1689–1755) and De Tocqueville (1805–59); (ii) those sociologists grouped around Auguste Comte (1798–1857), who probably first coined the term 'sociology' in 1830. Comte, who had trained as a mathematician, placed emphasis on scientific research, industrial application and an ethical system based on reason; (iii) those sociologists who followed the evolutionary, determinist and utopian thought of Karl Marx (1818–83). The seizure of power by VI Lenin resulted in a state government dedicated to pursue a Marxist approach in the conduct of international relations.

49   Roscoe Pound (1870–1964): see 'The scope and purpose of sociological jurisprudence' (1911) 24 HLR 591; (1912) 25 HLR 140, p 489; 'A survey of social interests' (1944) 57 HLR 1.

50   See, also, J Stone, 'The golden age of Pound' (1962) 4 Sydney Law Review 1.

51   Oliver Wendell Holmes Jr (1841–1935). Before becoming a Supreme Court Judge in 1902, Holmes had taught at the Harvard Law School alongside John Chipman Gray (1839–1915) another writer within the realist school. For the career of Holmes and his influence on younger lawyers see GE White, Justice Oliver Wendell Holmes, 1993.

52   Jerome Frank (1889–1957), Law and the Modern Min, 1949.

53   Karl Llewelyn (1893–1962), 'Some realism about realism' (1931) 44 HLR 1222; The Bramble Bush, 1930; The Common Law Tradition, 1960; see also W Twining, Karl Llewelyn and the Realist Movement, 1973.

interest of particular nation states.[54] Both the legal realist and the scholar of international relations tended to focus on the actual conduct of states.

The influence of such approaches in the United States was to move the terms of the discussion away from formal theories towards actual conduct. Such a method could easily be applied to international law and had an obvious affinity with the developing discipline of international relations.[55] The increasing number of regional and international organisations provided subjects for such analysis.

The influence of the American realist movement was at first domestic but, in the 1950s, as the Cold War deepened and concern about possible nuclear conflict grew, the influence of realism extended to international affairs where writers asked whether relations between the United States and the Soviet Union were determined by international law or by some other principle. One approach to this was the so called New Haven school, whose leading proponent was Professor Myers S McDougal.[56] This school, based at the Yale Law School, New Haven, Connecticut, tended to view that international law was no more than a process of decision making whereby law was but a factor amongst a number of elements in contributing to the resolution of problems on the international plane. Scholars of the New Haven school stress both the role of values and the processes by which policy decisions are made. In theory, the school rejects natural law as too subjective and positivism as being unconcerned with human dignity. However, it is arguable that the school is a mixture of both classical theories, in that it embraces the concern of the natural lawyer with values and it acknowledges the concern of the positivist with formal methods of decision making. In its emphasis on context it draws on the interdisciplinary tradition in the United States and has some affinity with the related discipline of international relations.[57]

This approach is subject to a number of reservations. First, it downgrades the role of law in the process and probably underestimates the need for the requisite degree of certainty. Secondly, it is one thing to argue that, in certain important matters, strict compliance with legal forms may not be the only consideration,[58] it is quite another to argue that rules generally are but one factor amongst many. Thirdly, although the school originates in the United States, it is not borne out by the conduct of the Department of State which tends to assert the importance of the maintenance of rules voluntarily assumed.[59] Fourthly, some later writers seen as adopting this approach have tended to respond to these criticisms by placing a greater emphasis on legal rules.[60] Fifthly, while

---

54 H Morgenthau, *Politics Among Nations: The Struggle for Power and* Peace, 5th edn, 1973.

55 In the years prior to 1945, those studying international relations tended to have been trained in the disciplines of classics, history or law; after 1945. the subject began to emerge as a discipline in its own right. See PA Reynolds, *An Introduction to International Relations*, 1st edn, 1970; 3rd edn, 1994. It was not until as late as 1919 that a chair in the subject was first established at a United Kingdom university. In the period since 1945, the subject has grown steadily in importance and has tended to focus on the study of the work of international and regional organisations.

56 Of Yale University.

57 R Falk, 'Casting the spell: the New Haven school of international law' (1995) 104 YLJ 1991.

58 An example being NATO operations against Kosovo in March 1999, where some expressed concern as to the absence of a prior Security Council Resolution.

59 See the traditional United States assertion that states participating in the General Agreement on Tariffs and Trade (GATT) should meet the letter and spirit of the rules.

60 Eg, Professor Falk in *Human Rights and State Sovereignty*, 1981; *On Human Governance*, 1995.

such an approach may have value in explaining conduct on the international plane, it is of limited utility when a judge in a municipal court is seeking to ascertain and apply a rule of public international law. Sixthly, some writers have questioned whether the approach of the school is either too subjective[61] or too vague[62] or too much a cultural product of the Cold War.[63] It is not without significance that this approach began to emerge in the decade after 1945 when scholars in the United States began to reflect on how United States foreign policy should react to the ideological opposition of communist states. American political thought has tended to be divided between those who argue[64] that the United States should seek to extend its constitutional traditions to other states and those who argue that the United States should simply provide a model for other states to follow if they are minded to.

In addition to the policy based approach of Professor McDougal, other writers have sought to explain international law as being grounded on considerations of 'fairness' or 'legitimacy'[65] or considerations of humanity.[66] Some writers view international law as a mode of justifying international conduct,[67] while others see the system as grounded in self-interest where most states will consider the advantages of obedience to outweigh the disadvantages of non-compliance.[68] In this context, the writings of Thomas M Franck have attracted a considerable degree of interest. Professor Franck has asked the question 'Why do states observe rules of international law?' He then argues that if a rule is viewed as legitimate, then it is likely to be observed; the greater the degree of legitimacy, the more likely the observance. It is argued that the legitimacy of a rule is capable of determination on the basis of particular evidentiary criteria. The learned writer takes his argument further in arguing that legitimacy and justice are two elements of the aspect of fairness which he views as a central element in international law.[69] The liberal democratic approach of Professor Franck brings together the concerns of both constitutional law and international law. The individual citizen consents to the institutions of the state while the

---

61 O Young, 'International law and social science: the contributions of Myers S McDougall' (1972) 66 AJIL 60.

62 G Dorsey, 'The McDougall-Lasswell proposal to build a world public order' (1988) 82 AJIL 41.

63 See the different views on nuclear testing in the 1950s: E Margolis, 'The hydrogen bomb experiments and international law' (1955) 64 YLJ 629 and M McDougal and N Schlei, 'The hydrogen bomb tests in perspective: lawful measures for security' (1955) 64 YLJ 648.

64 The traditional divide in United States political life between those favouring the export of American constitutional traditions and those of a more isolationist approach is traceable back to the debates between Woodrow Wilson and Theodore Roosevelt. The history of the debate is set out in detail by Henry Kissinger in *Diplomacy*, 1994, New York.The division of opinion is of importance today because it is linked with the question of how far the United States (or any other state) should go in seeking to sustain the observance of human rights.

65 Thomas M Franck, *The Power of Legitimacy among Nations*, 1990; *Fairness in International Law and Institutions*, 1995; 'Legitimacy in the international system' (1988) 82 AJIL 705. This writer sees a relationship between the degree of legitimacy of a rule and the pressure upon a state to comply.

66 P Allott, *Eunomia: New Order for a New World*, 1990; 'Reconstituting humanity – new international law' (1992) 3 EJIL 219.

67 M Koskenniemi, *From Apology to Utopia: The Structure of International Legal Argument*, 1989.

68 L Henkin, *How Nations Behave*, 2nd edn, 1979. In this context, it cannot be said that states such as Lybia, Iraq, South Africa (in respect of the apartheid period), Indonesia (in respect of East Timor) derived any benefit from defiance of the wishes of the international community.

69 See TM Franck, 'Fairness in the international legal and institutional system' (1993) 240(III) HR 9-498.

state itself consents to the basic principles of international law. Thus, international law is sustained by a form of liberal social contract involving both citizen and state.

One of the schools of thought that has emerged in the last two decades is that of the critical legal studies movement. Deriving from the United States in the unsettled period of the early 1970s,[70] the critical legal studies movement follows the American realists in emphasising actual conduct, but it rejects the liberal outlook of that movement and, in particular, the assumption that legal reasoning is distinct from the society that it serves. The movement follows Marxist thought in examining the economic interests served by a particular legal rule. So that the principle of freedom of contract is viewed not an essential element within liberal society,[71] but as a doctrine designed to promote the interests of private capital. The movement itself is hostile to black letter formal legal rules and places emphasis on an extreme degree of scepticism. Broadly, the movement tends to the view that, at best, law tends to favour the *status quo* and, at worst, it may serve to confer legitimacy on unjust social structures. Scholars of the critical legal studies movement stress the political, social and cultural background of a legal system; the possibility of a distinct legal system with an objectively determined rule is denied. Writers such as Koskenniemi[72] urge public international lawyers to focus less on the technical analysis of rules and more on seeking justice within a particular context. In short, such writers seek to minimise the importance of general rules and stress the importance of an analysis of the context in which the dispute arises.

The critical legal studies movement asserts that law plays an important role in moulding social change and so the movement might be viewed as part of the general post modernist view that it is ideas rather than the economic base that constitute modern society. However, economic considerations are not ignored; one of its most influential writers, Roberto Unger, has placed considerable emphasis on providing greater access to capital in contemporary society.[73] In the context of international law, writers[74] have tended to focus on the role of law in promoting conflict resolution and have emphasised the conduct of the individual participants. Such writers reject a universal definition of law and regard international difficulties as forms of social conflict to be resolved by political means. It has to be recognised that while such views may have had some impact on the teaching of international law they are very much at the margin if not *de lege ferenda* and thus have had little impact in practice.

---

70 Coinciding with the protests in the United States as to the conduct of the Vietnam War and the polarised nature of the American political process in the years 1972–74, which culminated in the enforced resignation of President Nixon in August 1974. The election of President Carter in November 1976 resulted in a greater emphasis being placed on human rights questions in the conduct of American Foreign Policy.

71 The traditional statement being that of Sir George Jessel MR in *Printing and Numerical Registering Co v Sampson* (1875) LR 19 Eq 462, p 465. George Jessel had served as a Liberal MP and Solicitor General in the first administration of WE Gladstone (1868–74).

72 M Koskenniemi, *From Apology to Utopia: The Structure of International Legal Argument*, 1989.

73 RM Unger, *The Critical Legal Studies Movement*, 1983; 'Legal analysis as institutional imagination' (1996) 59 MLR 11.

74 D Kennedy, 'A new stream of international law scholarship' (1988) 7 Wis ILJ 6; A Carty, *The Decay of International Law*, 1986; 'Critical international law: recent trends in the theory of international law' (1991) 2 EJIL 66; M Koskenniemi, *From Apology to Utopia: The Structure of International Legal Argument*, 1989; 'The politics of international law' (1990) 1 EJIL 4; G Dencho, 'Politics or rule of law: deconstruction and legitimacy in international law' (1993) 4 EJIL 1.

A school of thought that has developed in the last two decades is that of the feminist analysis of international law.[75] In essence, feminism is viewed as 'a mode of analysis, a method of approaching life and politics, a way of asking questions and seeking for answers';[76] in the specific context of international law, criticism has tended to focus on male domination of state elites. To an extent, this is a problem that is being remedied as women are beginning to hold a greater number of governmental positions in both the United States and Western Europe.[77] However, it is argued that women are disproportionately affected by abuses of human rights in third world countries. It is difficult to obtain precise statistics on such matters but such persons will benefit by the general movement to improve human rights that has been part of international law since 1945. While most Western European states have some form of equal pay[78] and sex discrimination legislation, feminists have directed attention to the commercial exploitation of women in third world countries. The principle of sex equality is alluded to in the preamble to the United Nations Charter and specific reference is made in Art 1(3) and Art 8. Moreover, some feminist writers point to the under representation of women in international organisations; to an extent this problem is in the process of being resolved as increasingly women take advantage of the educational opportunities and the level of female participation in public life increases in each state.[79]

Amongst writers of the feminist school, there are a number of approaches. Some, such as liberal feminists, stress the need for non-discrimination and equality of opportunity,[80] while cultural feminists point to the male domination within the international legal

---

75 For a general survey, see Hilaire Barnett, *Introduction to Feminist Jurisprudence*, 1998. On the specific aspect of international law, see Hilary Charlesworth, Christine Chenkin and Shelley Wright, 'Feminist approaches to international law' (1991) 85 AJIL 613. For a detailed exposition, see H Charlesworth and C Chinkin, *The Boundaries of International Law: A Feminist Analysis*, 2000.

76 Nancy Harstock in *Feminist Theory and the Development of Revolutionary Strategy*, in ZR Eisenstein (ed), *Capitalist Patriarchy and the Case for a Socialist Feminism*, 1979. See, also, Nancy Harstock, *Money, Sex and Power: Toward a Feminist Historical Materialism*, 1983.

77 A conspicuous example being Madeleine Albright who served as United States Ambassador to the United Nations before assuming the office of Secretary of State in 1997.

78 Equal Pay Act 1970; Sex Discrimination Acts 1975, 1986. An example of the early emphasis by Western Europe on equality of the sexes is to be found in Art 119 of the Treaty of Rome (1957).

79 It is interesting to observe the increasing numbers of women serving as members of legislatures or as government ministers. Sometimes this is a result of a left leaning progressive regime, such as after the election of François Mitterand in France in 1981 or Bill Clinton in the United States in 1992. In the United Kingdom, Margaret Thatcher became the first woman Prime Minister in May 1979. The election of Tony Blair as Prime Minster in 1997 coincided with record numbers of women being elected to the House of Commons. The number of female cabinet ministers increased steadily under both John Major (1990–97) and Tony Blair. In 1995, the United Kingdom provided the first female judge to the International Court of Justice. No woman has yet served as United Kingdom Foreign Secretary, although several have served in the Foreign and Commonwealth Office as junior ministers. No woman has yet served as United Nations Secretary General, although Mary Robinson (former President of Ireland) was a serious candidate in 1996. Women have, of course, served as European Commissioners, of whom the best known is Edith Cresson, a former Prime Minster of France.

80 L Finley 'Transcending equality theory: a way out of the maternity and workplace debate' (1986) 86 Columbia Law Review 1118.

order.[81] In contrast, radical feminists, such as Catherine MacKinnon,[82] stress the need for legal action as a method of remedying wrongs against women. Such writers, however, tend to come from affluent developed countries and it is noticeable that different opinions are expressed by those writers described as third world feminists, who are concerned with problems of economic and racial exploitation, illiteracy and poverty. Although there are differences of approach, it is possible to see in all the viewpoints a common humanitarian concern and a desire to use national and international institutions to achieve a measure of social justice and equality for women. However, it is accepted by most[83] that the problems faced by women in the poorest countries are often the most severe, often lacking food, health care or educational opportunity.

Feminist writers further argue that international law has failed to curb practices that undermine the human rights of women in third world countries; they point to the continuance of forced sterilisation, trafficking in women, interference in family life and the practice of female circumcision. Feminist writers allege that international bodies are reluctant to confront cultural and religious traditions that subordinate the role of women. Attention has also been directed by feminist writers to the limited educational opportunities available for women and the commercial exploitation of women and children. On the international plane, the Convention on the Elimination of All Forms of Discrimination against Women (1979) has attracted a considerable number of accessions but many instruments have been accompanied by reservations designed to preserve religious or cultural requirements. The allegation made by some feminist writers is that respect for state sovereignty allows the continuance of practices that discriminate against women. This is particularly frustrating for American feminist writers who have placed emphasis on using constitutional law and liberal interpretation to improve the legal position of women.[84]

Although many of the analyses of international law since 1945 have tended to seek to relate the legal rules to the social facts, much depends on the actual facts under consideration. There are a number of writers who stress that, in the final analysis, the continued operation of international society depends on the capacity and willingness of dominant states to deploy social, economic and military power. Such writers accept that, for the most part, international law is observed by states out of motives of self-interest. As the United States was the dominant power after 1945, it is perhaps not surprising such an approach has found favour there. Such writers accept that while international law can regulate day to day activities and serves as a basis for co-operation, there will be a limited

---

81 C Gilligan, *In a Different Voice: Psychological Theory and Women's Development*, 1992.

82 C Mackinnon, *Feminism Unmodified: Discourses on Life and Law*, 1987, Cambridge, Mass: Harvard University Press.

83 See C Johnson-Odim, 'Common themes, different contexts', in C Mohanty, A Russo and L Torres (eds), *Third World Women and the Politics of Feminism*, 1991.

84 Thus being in line with the tendency in the United States for social and ethical disputes to be translated into matters of constitutional interpretation. See Catherine Mackinnon, *Towards a Feminist Theory of the State*, 1989. This of course is possible in the United States where the Constitution in the First Amendment requires 'wholesale neutrality' between church and state. (See *School of Abington Township v Schempp* (1963).)

number of situations in which compliance can only be obtained by the willingness to deploy economic and military power.[85]

All such analyses are concerned with the traditional question, 'What is the theoretical basis of international law and why do states observe it?'. It is unlikely that one can reach agreement on this question and, as Oscar Schachter[86] noted, there are such a wide number of theoretical justifications for the existence of International Law. One aspect that requires comment is the revival in natural law thinking. In the years after 1945 it is possible to detect such a movement. The reasons are not difficult to determine. The loss of life and the systematic genocide of the years 1939–45 enacted in the heart of Europe had a profound effect on statesmen seeking to build the post-war world. Further, the employment of nuclear weapons in 1945 prompted a movement to internationally agreed minimum standards of conduct. Although there had been conflicts in the past resulting in great loss of life, technical advances in film and photography enabled the wider public to learn directly of the abuses of state power that led to Auschwitz, Belsen, Birkenau and Treblinka. Moreover, public opinion was able to make a connection between political extremism and abusive conduct. The conclusion that many drew was that there had to be limits to the positivist emphasis on state sovereignty which appeared to permit the ethically unacceptable under a cloak of legality. Positivism had flourished with the optimism of the Enlightenment and the scientific advances of the 19th century. Such optimism ended in 1914 and the subsequent history of the 20th century was characterised by consistent abuses of state power. The modern revival in natural law thinking and the emphasis on observance of human rights is founded upon a reaction to past abuses of state power.

4 MARXIST APPROACHES[87]

The seizure of power by the Bolshevik party in 1917 resulted in a European government being under the control of a political organisation dedicated to promoting the philosophy of Karl Marx (1818–83) and Friedrich Engels (1820–95). Although Karl Marx had spent a short period of time as an undergraduate in law,[88] his later writings were not marked by

---

85 R Aron, *Paix et Guerre entre des Nations*, 1984. H Morgenthau, *Politics Among Nations*, 6th edn, 1985; H Kissinger, *Diplomacy*, 1994.

86 Hamilton Fish Professor Emeritus of International Law at Columbia University. In an article in (1968) 8 Va JIL 300, the learned writer noted that one could formulate more than 12 justifications, namely: (i) the consent of states; (ii) customary practice; (iii) a sense of 'rightness' or conscience; (iv) natural law or natural reason; (v) social necessity; (vi) the will of the international community; (vii) direct intuition; (viii) common purpose; (ix) effectiveness; (x) sanctions; (xi) systematic goals; (xii) shared expectations as to authority; (xiii) rules of recognition.

87 See generally, GI Tunkin, *Theory of International Law*, 1970 (trans London: 1974); GI Tunkin (ed) *International Law*, 1986; 'Co-existence and international law' (1958) 95 HR 1; 'The legal nature of the United Nations' (1966) 119 HR 1; 'International law and the international system' (1975) 147 HR 1; 'Politics, law and force in the interstate system' (1989) 219 HR 227; 'The contemporary Soviet theory of international law' (1978) CLP 177. For the traditional Marxist position, see VI Lenin, *State and Revolution*, 1916.

88 He spent a year at the University of Bonn studying law (or rather *not* studying law) before transferring to the University of Berlin to study philosophy. For the man, see I Berlin, *Karl Marx: His Life and Environment*, 1978; David McLellan, *Karl Marx: His Life and Thought*, 1973; P Singer, *Marx*, 1980.

a great deal of attention to legal matters. In the preface to his *Contribution to the Critique of Political Economy* (1859), Marx had viewed law and the legal system (together with religion, philosophy and aesthetics) as being part of the social superstructure resting upon an economic base. With the expansion of the Soviet Union and the absorption of Eastern Europe, by 1950 nearly one-half of the world's population was under a regime that, at least in theory, adopted a Marxist philosophy. In these circumstances it is sensible to say a little about such states.

Traditional Marxist thought had viewed legislation not as eminating from the autonomous will of the legislature but being dictated by the interests of the economically superior class. Later writers would assert that oppression arose when a ruling group imposed its views and values on other groups within society; law was viewed as an instrument of oppression.[89]

International Law has traditionally centred around the concept of the state. However, Engels had asserted that the state was likely to 'whither away'.[90] On seizing power in 1917, VI Lenin had modified this approach by asserting that the *corpus* of the state would remain intact until the proletarian revolution had rendered it redundant. In this transitional period, the question arose as to which laws should apply either internally or internationally. Although Marxist thought had rejected the Diceyan notion of the rule of law as a mask concealing the interests of bourgeois industrial power, some doctrine was needed to preserve the situation during the transitional period.

In respect of legal developments, it is possible to draw a distinction between events between 1920 and 1936 and developments subsequent to that date. During the first period, Soviet economic policy fluctuated between the period of war communism, the period of the New Economic Policy and the later period of the five year plans. In the early years, it was necessary to compromise with private ownership and some form of legal theory was needed. This was provided by EB Pashukanis (1893–1937),[91] who argued that law was divorced from the interests of the state and was grounded in a desire to reduce those conflicts between individuals that would somehow disappear when class antagonisms were eliminated. He further held that law would 'whither away', as indeed at a later date would the state. Pashukanis had sought to advance a legal theory that was in general conformity with Marxist teaching but met the pragmatic requirements of the transitional period. Pashukanis argued that bourgeois forms of municipal law or of international law could be employed until the historically inevitable accomplishment of world socialism was effected by proletarian revolution. Although there were elements of this that deviated from classic Marxist thought, this was a heroic attempt to reconcile theory with reality.

---

89 Engels, in particular recognising the role of the ideological superstructure: see Anti Duhring at pp 308–09 (English edn, 1942).

90 See F Engels, *Origin of the Family, Private Property and the State*, 1884, advanced the ideas: (i) of the state being under the direction of those who controlled the means of production; (ii) appeared to link patriarchy with the development of private property. Engels had reflected on urban poverty in *The Condition of the Working Class in England* (1845) and had participated in the drafting of The Communist Manifesto (1848). Engels was influenced by positivism and Darwinian thinking. Although there are differences between Marx and Engels, it should be noted: (i) Engels regarded the two as holding identical views; (ii) both held the view that the state would wither away but this would not mean an end of government.

91 EB Pashukanis, *Allgemeine Staatslehre und Marxismus* (German edn, 1927).

By 1936, if not earlier, it was clear that there was unlikely to be an upsurge of revolutionary activity within Europe. Secondly, the re-establishment of capitalist states after 1919, and the failure of revolutionary movements in other countries, had given way to the emergence of National Socialist governments. The international climate had ceased to be so tranquil after 1933 with the accession of Adolf Hitler to power in Germany and the instability caused by continuing high levels of unemployment and rapid re-armament. In these circumstances, the new Soviet Constitution of 1936 had placed emphasis on building a strong centralised state to resist capitalist encirclement. The emphasis of Pahukanis on law as a medium of conflict resolution in a transitional period was now far less important, as efforts were made to outlaw private capital and private enterprise. Law was now to be employed as a method of social domination and control in the service of the Communist Party. The views of Pashukanis that law would in time 'whither away' were no longer acceptable and he perished in the purges of 1936–38; these purges and show trials in which large numbers of innocent person died owed much to the efforts of the public prosecutor Andrei Vyshinsky[92] and it was his views that came to dominate Soviet legal thinking both domestically and internationally.

Just as domestic legal thinking reflected economic imperatives, so the same relationship can be detected in the approach to international law. In the immediate period after 1917, Pahukanis had argued that international law was a class based system and that the Soviet Union would need to compromise until the inevitable victory of the forces of international socialism. After the Soviet Union had been recognised by other European states[93] and then by the United States, a modification of attitude can be detected. Following the eclipse of Pashukanis, legal policy fell into the hands of Andrei Vyshinsky who started from the theoretical position that the Soviet Union was only bound by those rules that it had expressly consented to. Given that the policy was now to build socialism in a single country, Vyshinsky stressed the sovereign equality of states and the principle of non-interference. Beyond this, it would not be sensible to attribute to Andrei Vyshinsky any coherent theory of International Law. He viewed all law as a form of party discipline and considered the task of the legal system as 'an application of the law as a political expression of the Party and the Government'; in respect of the judicial function, he felt that 'the judge must be a political worker, rapidly and precisely applying the directives of the Party and the Government'.[94] Pashukanis had followed the traditional Marxist position that law was a product of economic relations of production and exchange. Vyshinsky viewed law as an instrument to effect the dictatorship of the party and his conduct of the Moscow trials indicated that he viewed the judicial branch as an

---

92 Andrei Vyshinsky (1883–1954) served as a commissor of justice and prosecutor at the treason trials of 1936–1938; he later succeeded VM Molotov, in 1949, and served as Foreign Minister until 1953. Vyshinsky bore a heavy personal responsibility for the brutal conduct of the Moscow trials in the period 1936 until 1938, when large numbers of defendants were tortured into providing false confessions. Vyshinsky appears to have modelled his conduct on Fouquier Tinville during the period of Robespierre's Terror. For a time, Vyshinsky represented the Soviet Union at the United Nations and, in a bizarre incident, was actually entertained to dinner by the judges during the Nuremberg Trials.

93 The Soviet Government was accorded *de facto* recognition by the United Kingdom in 1921 and *de jure* recognition; the United States accorded recognition under the Litvinov Agreement of 1933. For municipal case law turning on recognition, see *Luther v Sagor* (1921) 3 KB 532; *United States v Belmont* (1937) 301 US 324.

94 A Vyshinsky, *Judicial Organisation in the USSR*, 1937.

instrument of executive power. It was not until 1956 that it could be openly acknowledged that the legal system in the 1930s had given rise to serious abuses and injustice.

The need to obtain the help of the Soviet Union in securing victory over Nazi Germany served to minimise differences. During the war years, the Soviet Union participated in the wartime conferences and, on victory, acquired a permanent seat in the Security Council. Whatever the theoretical objections to International Law, the provision of veto powers for permanent members gave the Soviet Union a privileged position within the United Nations structure. Full participation in international affairs was now on offer.

This offer was not accepted. The years after 1945 witnessed an increase in tension partly caused by the level of Soviet military spending and partly by the attitude adopted to client states in Eastern Europe; the Cold War had the effect of freezing international relations on ideological lines. However, scholars in the Soviet Union increasingly tended to the view that international law constituted a single system in a society in which capitalist and socialist states could co-exist peacefully;[95] it was argued that the role of international law was to provide rules to promote co-operation and thus, by reducing conflict, served to sustain the overriding principle of peaceful co-existence.[96] Indeed, by the late 1950s, Soviet scholars were ready to discuss the question as to when a rule of customary international law might be of universal application.[97]

The influence of the Soviet Union was bolstered by its position as a nuclear power, permanent membership of the Security Council and its theoretical leadership of the socialist/communist bloc. In the 1950s, weaknesses in Soviet society were not as clear as they were later to become. The nature of superpower rivalry tended to increase the role of international law because it led to a proliferation of international and regional organisations such as NATO, the Warsaw Pact and COMECON.

After the arrival in power of Nikita Khrushchev,[98] the principal Soviet foreign policy[99] theme was that of peaceful co-existence; this principle carried with it the associated doctrines of respect for state sovereignty and non-interference in the domestic affairs of other states. Although the attitude of the Soviet government might sometimes be described as unco-operative and, occasionally, a violation of International Law, attempts were made to justify conduct if only to preserve good relations with socialist parties in Western Europe.[100] The interventions in Hungary (1956) and Czechoslovakia (1968) were justified by reference to the desire to sustain a socialist system of government.

---

95 GI Tunkin, 'Co-existence and international law' (1958) 95(III) HR 1-82.

96 Professor Kozhevnikov in *International Law*, 1961; see, also, GI Tunkin, 'The contemporary Soviet theory of international law' (1978) CLP 177.

97 GI Tunkin, 'Co-existence and international law' (1958) 95(III) HR 1, p 18.

98 Nikita Khrushchev (1894–1971) General Secretary of Communist Party 1953–64. His resignation in 1964 was forced by mishandling of relations with China and the Cuban Missile crisis (1962).

99 Consistency in Soviet Foreign Policy was partly due to the long tenure of Andrei Gromyko (1909–89) who served as Foreign Minister from 1957 until 1985; the negative and defensive nature of his stewardship is illustrated by the fact that, when serving as the representative at the United Nations in the years 1946–49, he exercised the Soviet veto more than 25 times.

100 See J Hazard, 'Codifying peaceful co-existence' (1961) 55 AJIL 111.

The doctrine[101] was propounded that the Soviet Union was entitled to intervene in the affairs of those states within its Eastern European sphere of influence to protect the socialist system from capitalist subversion.[102] It was argued that the ethical superiority of socialism justified this approach; such an explanation carried little conviction in Western Europe, particularly as many of the interventions appeared to be motivated by a desire to restrain the exercise of basic civil liberties.

However, the general emphasis of the Soviet approach to international law founded upon state sovereignty and autonomy was attractive to those newly independent African states seeking to resist western influence and attempting to build an economy on collective or socialist lines. Soviet foreign policy, which tended to avoid direct confrontation with the United States,[103] was content to seek influence and promote its objectives by entering into alliances with newly independent African states. In some cases, the desire for influence was accompanied by the use of force. The installation of a friendly regime in Afghanistan in 1979 was secured by the employment of considerable numbers of Soviet troops. Such action was in clear violation of the United Nations Charter and would have been condemned by the Security Council had the Soviet Union not vetoed the resolution.[104]

The appointment of Mikhail Gorbachev as General Secretary of the Communist Party in 1985 represented an important generational change. Adopting flexible policies of *perestroika* (restructuring) and *glasnost* (openness), Gorbachev drew upon his previous experience in economic affairs[105] to promote internal reform and a measure of civil liberty.

Gorbachev and his Foreign Minister Edward Shevardnadze[106] realised that the Soviet Union would require western assistance to raise domestic living standards. As with other states, foreign policy had to change to facilitate national objectives. Soviet foreign policy, in seeking a better relationship with the West, moved towards a policy of detente, disarmament and respect for International Law. The emphasis was on solving problems

---

101 The doctrine came to be referred to as the 'Brezhnev doctrine' after Leonid Brezhnev (1906–82) who was a protégé of Stalin and had joined the Politburo in 1952; he became ceremonial President of the USSR in 1960 and in 1964 ousted Krushchev and assumed full power as General Secretary of the Communist Party. Although technically the ruler of the Soviet Union until his death in 1982, serious illness after 1976 leaves it open to question as to how far he was responsible for acts in breach of international law, such as the invasion of Afghanistan in 1979. During his period of rule, economic problems increased and Brezhnev became associated with policies of stagnation, conservatism and corruption.

102 See E McWhinney and K Grzybowski, 'Soviet theory of international law for the seventies' (1983) 77 AJIL 862.

103 Save in respect of the Cuban Missile Crisis of 1962.

104 On 7 January 1980.

105 Two themes in Gorbachev's policies were traceable to his earlier career. As a young man he had studied law at Moscow University and, perhaps in consequence, sought to promote the rule of law within the Soviet Union and in the sphere of international relations. More relevantly, he needed to secure a measure of arms control to allow rebuilding of the Soviet Economy. This would require treaty negotiations with the United States and agreements for verification and compliance. Secondly, Gorbachev had been a member of the Politburo since 1980 and had direct personal experience of the problems posed by inefficiency and corruption within the economy.

106 Edward Shevardnadze (b 1928) had succeeded Andrei Gromyko as Foreign Minister in 1985. As with President Gorbachev, he regarded it as important to improve international relations in order to pursue reform of the Soviet Economy.

of common interest through the structures of the United Nations. As President Gorbachev tried to reform the Soviet Union and construct a society based on the rule of law with an independent judiciary, so foreign policy began to emphasise the importance of the United Nations as an institution for resolving problems of common concern.[107] The accident at the Chernobyl nuclear reactor in 1986 seemed to demonstrate clearly the need for an improved level of international co-operation.

The collapse of Soviet rule in Eastern Europe in 1989 and the efforts by the Moscow leadership to seek a better working relationship with the West marked the effective end of the Cold War. The disintegration of the Soviet Union in 1991 seemed to offer the prospect of a more stable environment. However, much of this optimism was misplaced. Although it became common to talk of a New World Order, this seemed to be of little direct relevance. The phrase 'New World Order' seemed to refer to a situation in which the Security Council could play a greater role in ordering international affairs.[108] However, the disappearance of communist rule led to the emergence of ethnic and religious conflict in the former republics of the Soviet Union and later, after 1992, in the former Republic of Yugoslavia.

The United Nations Charter (1945) had been remarkably successful in curbing direct conflict between states but it was not best suited to restrain the outbreak of civil wars and, even if the Security Council could agree on a course of action, it was often unable to persuade states to contribute the necessary armed forces. The ideological divisions of the Cold War had ended in Eastern Europe only to be replaced by a much more volatile situation, as was illustrated by the disintegration of the Federal Republic of Yugoslavia in the years 1992–95.

There can be little doubt that one consequence of the end of the Cold War was an excessive degree of optimism as to what might be possible. Some thought that, with superpower rivalry a thing of the past, the Security Council would be able to function free of the ideological veto and thus constitute a surer instrument of international order. It was also hoped that regional problems in the Middle East or Africa might prove easier to resolve by direct negotiation; this has not proved to be the case. The first problem was that, while the Security Council might pass resolutions in respect of particular problems, actual enforcement depended on the willingness of states to contribute military forces; in many instances there was a tendency to desist unless the United States gave a firm indication that it would provide resources. Secondly, it was evident that in some cases the particular goal was unclear and when objectives were frustrated recriminations tended to increase. Thirdly, some of the difficulties that faced the United Nations in the New Word Order were intractable problems of ethnic tensions in situations of *de facto* civil war.[109] In such circumstances, many states were reluctant to provide resources for effective United Nations intervention. Fourthly, the effectiveness of United Nations action often depended

---

107 R Quigley, '*Perestroika* and International Law' (1988) 82 AJIL 788; R Mullerson, 'Sources of international law: new tendencies in Soviet thinking' (1989) 83 AJIL 494; W Reisman, 'International law after the Cold War' (1990) 84 AJIL 859.

108 It was symbolised by the efforts of US President, George Bush and Secretary of State, James Baker to build a coalition of states to conduct the Gulf War (August 1990–February 1991)

109 For example, the practical difficulties encountered by the United Nations in giving effect to Security Council resolutions in Somalia (1992–93), Rwanda (1994) and Bosnia (1992–95). See Boutros Boutros Ghali, *Unvanquished: A US-UN Saga*, 1999.

on the willingness of the United States, as the sole remaining superpower, to assist; in the 1990s it became clear that the conduct of United States foreign policy was made more difficult by the need to accommodate various groupings within the United States Congress,[110] some of whom held isolationist views.

Although direct rivalry between the superpower blocks ended in 1989, international society has had to grapple with a number of difficult problems posed by ethnic conflict, regional tension[111] and civil wars. Flagrant defiance of the United Nations Charter has been reversed by force[112] but in more complex situations, such as the disintegration of Yugoslavia, a clear international approach was often difficult to detect. The number of states has grown steadily to over 185 but many labour under problems of poverty, illiteracy and under investment.

5 THE DEVELOPING WORLD

As indicated above, the number of states has increased steadily since 1945 and much of the increase has been due to decolonisation. The entitlement to independence was recognised in the General Assembly Declaration on the Granting of Independence to Colonial Countries and Peoples (1960)[113] and, thereafter, the pace of decolonisation increased. Many newly independent states tended to view with suspicion 19th century concepts of international law that had permitted imperialism and exploitation; such states tended to be sceptical of rules of customary international law, preferring to accept obligations arising only under treaty. In some cases, resentment against a prior colonial power or a desire to establish a collective economy lead to a movement towards Marxism and the Soviet Union. However, after 1982 the Soviet Union had other priorities leaving newly independent states with little choice but to co-operate within existing international organisations. Such states have for some years had a majority in the General Assembly and are specifically provided for in the rules pertaining to membership of the Security Council, the International Court of Justice and the International Law Commission; in many cases such states have required assistance from the the International Monetary Fund or the World Bank.

It would be wrong to view all such states as being subject to like problems; some possess oil or other natural resources, some enjoy constitutional stability and high levels of foreign investment, while others are land locked and afflicted by poverty and internal dissent. A large number of decolonised states are to be found in Africa and such states

---

110 For the relations between the United States and the United Nations in a period where only one superpower existed see Warren Christopher, *In the Stream of History*, 1998; Boutros Boutros Ghali, *Unvanquished: A US-UN Saga*, 1999; Michael Dobbs, *Madeleine Albright: A Twentieth Century Odyssey*, 1999; Henry Holt, Ann Blackman, *Seasons of Her Life: A Biography of Madeleine Korbel Albright*, 1998.

111 Although the emphasis since 1945 has been on international disarmament; one of the problems posed in the last two decades has been that of the proliferation of nuclear technology.

112 In the Falklands Conflict (1982) and the Gulf Conflict (1990–91). The subsequent military action in Kosovo in 1999 raised the question as to whether international law recognised a right of international humanitarian intervention.

113 General Assembly Resolution 1514 (XV), 14 December 1960.

collectively express their views through the Organisation of African Unity, established in 1963.

In general, developing states tend to accept the basic rubric of international law, if only because the subject proceeds on the basis of the sovereign equality of states. Particular areas of international law tend to attract the attention of specific states. Those states threatened with secession tend to stress the principle of territorial integrity.[114] Many developing states express resentment at the role of international economic organisations or reject customary rules pertaining to the compensation of foreign investors.[115] Most stress the entitlement of each state to determine its own social and economic system. Some states invoke principles of state sovereignty[116] to resist probing on matters of human rights.[117] Other states are concerned with sovereignty over natural resources or rights in respect of the sea; indeed the precise contents of the United Nations Law of the Sea Convention (1982)[118] owes much to the desire to accommodate the concerns of developing states.

Finally, while developing states may object to particular aspects of international law all are members of the United Nations and thus bound by the terms of the United Nations Charter (1945). Moreover, in many instances, access to economic assistance by international organisations is contingent on observance of international norms. In short, the developing state has an interest in subscribing to the general principles of international law, particularly if it wishes to stimulate economic growth by attracting foreign investment.

6 CONCLUDING OBSERVATIONS

Attention above has been directed to those theories that seek to explain the nature and scope of international law. It is sensible to conclude by making limited reference to those principles that international civil society seeks to sustain. Since 1945, the United Nations Charter has set twin objectives of the peaceful settlement of disputes[119] and the promotion of social progress and better standards of life.[120] In the last two decades scholars[121] have argued that these objectives might best be attained the the promotion of

---

114 See Chapter 7 on territory.
115 See Chapter 19 on international economic law.
116 See Chapter 5 on the subjects of international law.
117 A particular example being afforded by the reaction of the government of Nigeria in the late 1990s to external criticism of its conduct.
118 For the Law of the Sea and the concerns of developing states, see Chapter 13.
119 See Preamble and Art 33 of United Nations Charter.
120 See Preamble and Arts 13 and 55 of United Nations Charter.
121 See T Franck, 'The emerging right to democratic governance' (1992) 86 AJIL 46; T Franck, *Fairness in International Law and Institutions*, 1995; C Crena, 'Universal democracy: an international legal right or the pipe dream of the west?' (1995) 27 New York Journal of International Law and Politics 289; G Fox, 'The right to political participation in international law', 'National sovereignty revisited: perspectives on the emerging norm of democracy in international law (1992) Proceedings of the American Society of International Law 249. This is not the view of all; see T Carothers, 'Empirical perspectives on the emerging norm of democracy in international law' (1992) Proceedings of the American Society of International Law 261.

the norm of democratic government It is argued that by promoting democratic constitutional government within the rule of law together with observance of human rights is likely to best achieve the objectives of the United Nations Charter. The general view of many states[122] is that by establishing such internal constitutional safeguards it is more likely that the state will be able to secure foreign investment and less likely that such a state will seek to threaten its neighbours. By the promotion of constitutional law, it is argued, international law is likely to prosper.

---

122 It is argued by some that while full democracy may not be attainable immediately, the United Nations should seek to ensure, at the minimum, non corrupt government. It is certainly arguable that a contract made abroad to bribe a government official will not be enforced in England as contrary to public policy in accordance with traditional principles of private international law; see *Lemenda Trading Company Limited v African Middle East Petroleum Company Ltd* [1988] QB 448.

CHAPTER 3

THE SOURCES OF INTERNATIONAL LAW[1]

1 INTRODUCTION

In any legal system there must be some accepted criteria by which 'laws' are established. To put the matter another way, there must be clear sources of law. In the normal municipal system one might begin by studying the written constitution of the state. In most developed states[2] it is usually possible to identify the legislative, executive and judicial branches and, having done so, one can then ascertain the precise sources of municipal law.[3] In the United Kingdom, one might refer to primary legislation enacted in the form of bills passing through Parliament and followed by the Royal Assent. Reference might also be made to those clear statements of legal principle that can be deduced from the decided cases in the appellate courts and which the doctrine of precedent requires to be followed by the lower courts.[4] Since 1973, any lawyer in the United Kingdom will also be required to consider the relevance of any European primary or secondary legislation or, indeed, any material rulings of the European Court of Justice.[5] In short, there are clear sources of law and in many cases a lawyer will be able to advise confidently, on the basis of such materials, as to the conclusion that a municipal judge is likely to reach in a particular case. Indeed, in many states today there will be a written constitution that sets out such matters in considerable detail.

In international law, partly because of the horizontal nature of the subject, the position is[6] less straightforward. However, in the last 50 years it has been accepted that Art 38 of the Statute of the International Court of Justice provides the most convenient summary of the sources of international law and reads as follows:

(1) The Court, whose function is to decide in accordance with international law such disputes as are submitted to it, shall apply:

---

1   See generally, M Akehurst, *Modern Introduction to International Law* (Malanczuk (ed)), 7th edn, 1977, p 35; I Brownlie, *Principles of Public International Law*, 5th edn, 1990, p 1; M Dixon, *Textbook on International Law*, 4th edn, 2000, p 21; M Shaw, *International Law*, 4th edn, 1997; IA Shearer, *Starke's International Law*, 11th edn, 1994, p 28; R Jennings and A Watts, *Oppenheim's International Law*, 9th edn, 1992, p 22; JL Brierly, 'Le fondement du caractere obligatoire du droit international' (1928) 23 HR 463; P Weil, 'Towards relative normativity in international law' (1983) 77 AJIL 413; W Czaplinski, 'Sources of law in the *Nicaragua* case' (1989) 38 ICLQ 151.

2   Even if there is no written constitution and no formal separation of the branches of government, as is the case in the United Kingdom.

3   See, for example, United States Constitution (1787) indicating the location of the legislative power in Art 1, ss 1 and 7.

4   An example being *Woolmington v DPP* [1935] AC 462 which sets out the burden and standard of proof in criminal trials.

5   Having regard to the principle of the supremacy of European Community law as enunciated in cases such as Case 26/62 *NV Algemene Transport en Expeditie Onderneming Van Gend en Loos v Nederlandse Administratie der Belastingen* [1963] ECR 1; [1963] CMLR 105; Case 6/64 *Costa v Ente Nazionale per l'Energia Elettrica (ENEL)* [1964] ECR 585; CMLR 425.

6   Although the Article refers to disputes, no distinction is drawn between contentious and advisory proceedings.

(a) international conventions, whether general or particular, establishing rules expressly recognised by the contesting States;

(b) international custom, as evidence of a general practice accepted as law;

(c) the general principles of law recognised by civilised nations;

(d) subject to the provisions of Article 59, judicial decisions and the teachings of the most highly qualified publicists of the various nations, as a subsidiary means for the determination of rules of law.

(2) This provision shall not prejudice the power of the Court to decide a case *ex aequo et bono*, if the parties agree thereto. [7]

The provisions of the present Art 38 of the statute re-enact in large part the provisions of Art 38 of the Statute of the Permanent Court of International Justice,[8] save for the addition of the words indicating that the Court's function is 'to decide in accordance with international law such disputes as are submitted to it'. Whatever the reservations that may have been expressed at the time, the sources were based upon those that had been employed in international arbitrations in the 19th century; the sources themselves were followed in a number of arbitrations in the inter-war years.[9]

The expression 'sources of law' has a wide variety of meanings. Writers refer to 'formal sources', 'material sources', 'evidentiary sources' and 'intangible sources'; the differing use of language has caused some confusion. The distinction between a formal source and a material source is often employed in constitutional law. According to Salmond: 'A formal source is that from which a rule of law derives its force and validity ... The material sources, on the other hand, are those from which is derived the matter, not the validity, of the law. The material source supplies the substance of the rule to which the formal source gives the force and nature of law.'[10]

It is to be observed that Art 38 does not actually contain the word 'source' but the Article has been taken since 1920 as stating the relevant sources. In respect of formal sources, it is said that a formal source is a procedure and method for creating binding legal rules.[11] It has been said that a formal source represents the mechanism through

---

7   The provisions of the present Statute of the International Court of Justice resulted directly from the Commission of Jurists meeting in Washington in 1944 and 1945 and Commission IV of the United Nations Conference on International Organisation meeting in San Francisco in 1945. However, preparatory work on producing a statute was undertaken by the Informal Inter Allied Committee on the Future of the Permanent Court of International Justice (sometimes known as 'the London Committee'). For a detailed account, see Geoffrey Marston, 'The London Committee and the Statute of the International Court of Justice', in AV Lowe and M Fitzmaurice (eds), *Fifty Years of the International Court of Justice*, 1996.

8   The Covenant of the League of Nations had provided for the establishment of a Permanent Court of International Justice (see Art 14) and an Advisory Committee of Jurists had met in June and July 1920 to prepare a Statute; the Committee was chaired by Baron Descamps and a significant role was played by Elihu Root and Lord Phillimore. For reflections on the work, see Lord Phillimore (1920) 6 TGS 89. The idea that there should be a court at all owed much to the urging of Sir Cecil Hurst (1870–1963), a member of the British delegation at Versailles and later a judge of the court (1929–40).

9   *The Nautilus* case (1928) 2 RIAA 1011; the *Cysne* case (1930) 2 RIAA 1035; *Case Regarding the Interpretation of Article 11 of the London Protocol* (1926) 2 RIAA 755.

10   JW Salmond, *Jurisprudence*, 7th edn, 1924, para 44.

11   See HLA Hart, *The Concept of Law*, 1961.

which the law comes into being,[12] while a material source indicates where the legal rules come from, that is, where the rules are located. One writer has argued that formal sources constitute what the law is, while material sources identify where the law may be found.[13] If one applied the distinction to the United Kingdom, it might be said that the principle of the legislative supremacy of Parliament constitutes a formal source, while an individual Act of Parliament constitutes a material source. Whether such distinctions can be drawn in practice is open to doubt. Brownlie argues that such distinctions drawn from constitutional law are not appropriate, given the nature of international society.[14] Other writers assert that Art 38(1)(a), (b) and (c) constitute formal sources.[15] It must be questionable whether differences of nomenclature are important because the International Court of Justice has not devoted any attention to the controversy and has tended to avoid theorising as to the sources of international law.[16] Indeed, there is no indication that the original draftsmen in 1920 were concerned with anything more than identifying agreed sources.[17]

A problem arises as to whether the list of sources is exhaustive. The short answer is in the negative. Article 38(1)(c) was included in 1920 to enable the Court to draw analogies from municipal law when the other sources did not enable the Court to reach a settled conclusion. The 1920 committee had been influenced by the practice in some civil law countries where judges were entitled to resort to general principles in situations where a Code did not provide clear guidance. There are also a number of sources[18] that the Court has been prepared to consider that are not listed within Art 38; these will be outlined at the conclusion of the chapter after those matters expressly listed have been considered.

A related question has arisen as to whether the sources are hierarchical. The answer to this is in the negative. The matter was discussed in 1920 and an attempt to include the words 'in the undermentioned order' in Art 38 was rejected by the committee so that the Article in its final form included no express reference to hierarchy. It is sometimes argued that there are two general principles of international law that may be preyed in aid. The first is that a later rule normally has preference over an earlier rule (*lex posterior derogat juri priori*) and the second principle that a specific rule may derogate from a general rule (*lex specialis derogat legem generalis*). Such presumptions would tend to favour the later treaty at the expense of the earlier customary rule; however, such preference does not always arise and in many cases a treaty has been drawn up because the meaning and scope of the prior customary rule is uncertain. However, a treaty can come to an end through

---

12   I Detter, *The International Legal Order*, 1994.

13   R Wallace, *International Law*, 2nd edn, 1994.

14   I Brownlie, *Principles of International Law*, 4th edn, 1990, pp 1–3.

15   G Schwarzenberger, *International Law*, Vol 1, 3rd edn, 1957, pp 26–27; R Wallace, *International Law*, 2nd edn, 1992, p 8. The viewpoint of other authors is of interest. Akehurst's *Modern Introduction to International Law*, 7th edn, 1997, does not express a view on the distinction. M Shaw, *International Law*, 4th edn, 1997, is sceptical. The editor of *Starke's International Law*, 11th edn, 1994, considers the sources to be material sources.

16   *Gulf of Maine* case (1984) ICJ 246, p 299.

17   Lord Phillimore (1920) 6 TGS 89 (where the learned judge indicates that the task was to reach agreement on sources not to embark on any classification of such sources).

18   Examples under this heading would be (a) the rules of international organisations; (b) rules of equity; (c) the so called 'soft law' sources.

desuetude – a situation in which a treaty is ignored by one or more party with the acquiescence of the others. Such a situation often takes the form of the emergence of a new rule of customary law, conflicting with the prior treaty provision.

It is argued by some writers that Art 38(1)(c) is subordinate to Art 38(1)(a) and Art 38(1)(b), since the purpose of general principles is to fill gaps in treaty and customary law. Such an analysis would appear to be in line with the intentions of the 1920 Committee of Jurists.[19] It is more clearly established that Art 38(1)(d) is a subordinate source, since the express words refer to judicial decisions and learned writings as being 'subsidiary means for the determination of rules of law'. The relationship between treaty provisions and rules of customary international law is dealt with below. However, as a matter of general impression, while there is no expressly stated hierarchy of sources in the event of a direct conflict a treaty provision (unless it violated a rule of *jus cogens*[20]) would prevail over a customary rule.

It is now proposed to examine each of the relevant sources of international law; it is intended to begin with custom as the oldest source rather than to proceed in the order set out in Art 38 of the Statute of the International Court of Justice.

2 CUSTOM

(a) Introduction

In primitive society, rules of conduct evolve and are observed by force of social pressure. Such rules of conduct may be referred to as 'usages' or 'customs'. A practical distinction can be made between a 'usage' and a 'custom'. Usage represents the preliminary stage and a custom may be said to arise when the practice has become general. Although the precise process is a matter of debate amongst legal historians, it is clear that the common law system of law developed in England after the Norman Conquest by building upon prior customs. Indeed the first two books on the common law expressly refer to the role of custom.[21]

Thus, in the earliest times, the development of municipal law was significantly influenced by rules based upon custom. Although today many textbooks include custom as a source of municipal law, the role of custom within common law systems is minor when set against that of legislation and judicial precedent.

At the same time, custom did not merely influence the development of municipal law; in ancient Greece the conduct of relations between city states was governed by custom. At a later date, in the Italy of the early Middle Ages, the relations between the various city states and republics was also governed by custom. Thus, when Europe began, in the 16th

---

19   Lord Phillimore (1920) 6 TGS 89.

20   On *jus cogens*, see below.

21   *Tractatus de Legibus et Consuetudinibus Angliae Tempore Regis Henrrici Secundus* (known as Glanvill) probably by Ranulf de Glanvill c 1187–89; *De Legibus et Consuetudinibus Angliae* (1250–56) by Henry de Bracton, probably a judge of the King's Bench.

century, to divide into distinct nation states, it was logical that the earliest rules governing relations between rulers should be expressed in the form of customary rules.[22]

Manifestly, such rules only extended at that time to those areas of particular concern, namely questions of war and peace, problems of diplomatic representation and competing claims in respect of the high seas. Until the beginning of the 20th century, rules of customary international law comprised the substantial part of the Law of Nations and the precise content of the rule owed much to the interpretation of municipal courts and prize courts.[23] The relevant principle was that the general consent of states might create rules of general application. This principle had developed in the 18th century as statesmen began to formulate the rules that should govern the relations between sovereign states.[24] Against this background, it was logical for the draftsmen in 1920 to include customary law as one of the sources for the newly established Permanent Court of International Justice. The precise words of Art 38(1)(b) read 'international custom, as evidence of a general practice accepted as law'. It has been assumed since 1920 that a rule of customary international law will only exist if a twofold test is met, namely: (i) evidence of the actual conduct of states (sometimes referred to as the evidence of material fact); and (ii) evidence of the subjective belief that such conduct or behaviour constitutes 'law' – this is sometimes alluded to as the psychological requirement or the *opinio juris sive necessitatis*.[25] Before turning to the specific elements, a number of general comments require to be made. First, the value of customary law is the subject of controversy; some writers hold that it represents a sensible flexible system most appropriate for a decentralised international community, while others contend that the rules are vague and too slow moving for a rapidly changing international environment. Secondly, it has been argued that one must be careful to distinguish rules that create rights from those that impose obligations and that the evidentiary requirements for each may be different. Thirdly, while it is normal to consider the requirements under the twofold test, other formulations have been put forward.[26] Fourthly, it is important to draw a distinction between those situations in which a general rule of customary international law is alleged and those where a regional or local rule is in issue.

However, it is now proposed to examine the first broad requirement, namely the material fact.

---

22 Although, from the outset, a problem would arise as to whether a customary rule could be stated with sufficient clarity and precision to be acknowledged before a municipal court; see *West Rand Central Gold Mining Company v R* [1905] 2 KB 391.

23 See, for example, *The Schooner Exchange v M'Faddon* (1812) 7 Cranch 116; a judgment of the United States Supreme Court which was influential in developing the law of sovereign immunity.

24 Such rules might be said to be the rules pertain to the club of European nations.

25 It is argued by some that the second requirement of *opinio juris* can be traced back to the German historical school of Savigny and Ranke, who viewed the *opinio juris* as the legal consciousness of a *Volk* or a people; see Anthony Carty, *The Decay of International Law?*, 1986, pp 30–39.

26 In 1950, Professor Hudson argued in a paper for the ILC that a rule of customary international law would be established if it could be demonstrated: (a) that there was a concordant practice by a number of states with reference to a situation falling within the domain of international relations; (b) continuation or repetition of the practice over a considerable period of time; (c) a conception that the practice is required by, or consistent with, prevailing international law; (d) general acquiescence in the practice by other states. Cited in I MacGibbon, 'Customary international law and acquiesence' (1957) 33 BYIL 115, p 125.

(b) The material fact

If the existence of a rule of customary international law is founded upon state practice, then the first question that arises is as to the nature and forms of evidence that are admissible to demonstrate such state practice. First, each state is represented by a government and in principle acts or statements of all three branches of government are admissible as evidence of state practice. Thus, executive decisions, legislative enactments and municipal judicial decisions are all, in principle, admissible. In the modern world, statements are made by governments to the press, to legislative assemblies and to various international organisations. Much will depend on the context as to the weight that should be given to such announcements and it is arguable that a distinction should be made as to communications with other governments and statements made for domestic consumption. Correspondence between foreign ministries may constitute evidence of practice, although not all states publish such documents.[27]

It is clear that conduct in relation to international organisations may constitute evidence of state practice and, in this context, guidance can be obtained from law officers' opinions, diplomatic correspondence and draft replies to the International Court of Justice.

Some have asserted that a distinction can be drawn between a state act and a mere claim; the latter, it is argued, is but an assertion that is not enforced and thus cannot constitute evidence of state practice.[28] However, this viewpoint would appear to be a minority view[29] and claims have been advanced as evidence of state practice in several leading cases before the International Court of Justice.[30]

Assuming that evidence of state practice can be established, the question arises as to whether there is a minimum duration of state practice that will be required to demonstrate the existence of a rule of customary international law. In many municipal law systems, a minimum period of time is necessary to establish property rights.[31] The International Court of Justice has not specified a particular duration, although the time element may be important in determining weight. In the *Asylum* case,[32] the International Court of Justice indicated that a customary rule must be founded upon 'a constant and uniform usage'. A reason for this is partly the need for flexibility and partly because, since 1945, certain areas of international law have changed rapidly within a single generation.[33] However, duration is not unimportant and while in the *North Sea Continental Shelf* case[34]

---

27 The most detailed compilations being those of the United States, in particular, JB Moore, *Digest of International Law*, 1906, 8 Vols; GH Hackworth, *Digest of International Law*, 1940–44, 8 Vols; MM Whiteman, *Digest of International Law*, 1963–73, 15 Vols.

28 See the dissenting opinion of Judge Reed in the *Anglo Norwegian Fisheries* case (1951) ICJ 116, p 191; (1951) 18 ILR 86, p 132; see, also, A D'Amato, *The Concept of Custom in International Law*, 1971.

29 H Thirlway, *International Customary Law and Codification*, 1972.

30 *Asylum (Columbia v Peru)* case (1950) ICJ 266; *Rights of US Nationals in Morocco* case (1952) ICJ 176; *North Sea Continental Shelf* case (1969) ICJ 3.

31 The requirement at common law that an easement be enjoyed from 1189 or the specific time periods indicated in the Prescription Act 1832.

32 *Asylum (Columbia v Peru)* case (1950) ICJ 206, p 277.

33 The examples being the law of the sea, the law of outer space and international law as concerned with the environment.

34 *North Sea Continental Shelf* case (1969) ICJ 3.

the International Court of Justice did not regard a short duration as an insuperable barrier, it observed that if a customary rule was to be founded on a brief duration then state practice had to be extensive and virtually uniform.

Related to duration is the question of consistency. It would seem that minor inconsistencies in the observance of the rule will not negate clear evidence of state practice. It has been argued that a single instance will not be sufficient evidence of state practice[35] and a rule cannot be grounded in a practice that is subject to 'uncertainty and contradiction';[36] however, minor inconsistencies will not prevent a rule arising. The position is illustrated by the *Asylum* case[37] where the facts were as follows.

Haya de la Torre, a Peruvian citizen, was sought by Peru after an unsuccessful revolt. He was granted asylum by Columbia at its embassy in Lima. Peru refused a request to grant safe conduct out of the country. Columbia brought an action claiming that it was entitled to classify the offence as political rather than criminal (as Peru maintained) and in which case asylum and safe passage out of the country could be maintained.

In seeking to substantiate a rule, Columbia referred to a large number of cases in which asylum and right of passage had been sought or granted. The International Court of Justice held that no rule could be deduced because the evidence disclosed uncertainty and contradiction rather than any 'constant and uniform usage'.[38]

A broadly similar approach was expressed in *Nicaragua v United States (The Merits)*[39] where the International Court of Justice observed:

> In order to deduce the existence of customary rules, the Court deems it sufficient that the conduct of states should in general, be consistent with such rules, and that instances of state conduct inconsistent with a given rule should generally have been treated as breaches of that rule, not as indications of the recognition of a new rule.

In a world of over 150 states, the question arises as to how many states are required to demonstrate such a degree of generality of practice. First, while practice should be general, this is not required to be universal. Secondly, generality is relative to the subject matter; if the subject matter in issue is a rule relating to the Law of the Sea then the conduct of major maritime states will be of considerable importance while the views of landlocked states may carry less weight. In the case of outer space law or practice relating to nuclear weapons, then the conduct of those states possessed of the requisite technology will assume a greater importance than the conduct of those states who do not participate in such activities.

(c) The nature of state practice

As indicated above, much will depend on the volume of evidence that can be produced as to the nature of state practice; on the international plane, a state is represented by its

---

35 *Lübeck v Mecklenberg-Schwerin* (1927–28) ADPIL No 3.
36 *Asylum (Columbia v Peru)* case (1950) ICJ 266, pp 276–77.
37 *Ibid*.
38 The other issues in the case being: (i) whether a rule of customary international law could exist simply on a regional level; and (ii) whether any such rule was binding on Peru.
39 *Nicaragua v United States (The Merits)* (1986) ICJ 14.

government so that the acts of each of its branches may be relied upon. It is sensible to examine the elements of state practice in greater detail.

(i) *Diplomatic relations between states*

Official statements by foreign ministers, the opinions of legal advisers and bilateral treaties all constitute evidence of state practice. Similarly statements by Ambassadors or diplomatic representatives fall within this category. It is doubtful whether any distinction can be drawn between oral and written statements.

(ii) *The practice of international organisations*

Since much activity between states is conducted through the auspices of international organisations, it is not in dispute that the cumulative conduct of an international organisation may constitute evidence of state practice. In the Advisory Opinion on the status of the United Nations, the International Court of Justice examined the conduct of the organisation before concluding that it enjoyed international personality.[40] An international organisation may enjoy law making power and this is a matter to be taken into account in considering the nature of state practice.[41] Moreover, particular attention may be paid to Resolutions of the General Assembly of the United Nations; this matter is dealt with later in the chapter.

(iii) *State laws and decisions of municipal courts*

In seeking evidence of state practice it is legitimate to examine the judgments of municipal courts and the enactments of individual legislatures. An example is afforded by the judgment of the United States Supreme Court in *The Scotia*[42] where the facts were as follows.

In 1863, the British Government adopted certain regulations in respect of maritime collisions. In 1864, the United States Congress adopted similar regulations and later other maritime states followed. At a later date the *Scotia* (a British vessel) was in collision with the *Berkshire* (an American vessel). The question was whether the *Berkshire* was liable for not displaying lights. To determine this question, the Court was obliged to consider whether the matter was governed by the general maritime law existing before the regulations of 1863.

The United States Supreme Court held that liability was to be determined under the new rules of customary international law that had arisen by virtue of the widespread acceptance of the British regulations. The Court noted that this was not a case of giving extra territorial effect to the British regulations nor of regarding them as general maritime laws 'but it is a recognition of the historical fact that, by common consent of mankind, these rules have been acquiesced in as of general obligation. Of that fact we may take judicial notice'. In principle, a rule of customary international law may be deduced by comparing legislative enactments to determine whether there is a degree of uniformity of practice.[43]

---

40 Advisory Opinion on Reparation for Injuries Suffered in the Service of the United Nations (1949) ICJ 174.
41 Namibia (SW Africa) Advisory Opinion (1971) ICJ 16.
42 *The Scotia* (1871) 14 Wallace 170.
43 A recent example is afforded by the case of *R v Bow Street Metropolitan Magistrate ex p Pinochet Ugarte (No 1)* [1998] 3 WLR 1456 where the dissenting minority (Lord Lloyd and Lord Slynn) examined municipal court decisions to determine whether there was any agreed practice as to the circumstances in which sovereign immunity might be set aside.

(iv) State claims and state acts

As indicated above, there is some dispute as to whether a state claim as well as a state act may constitute evidence of state practice. Some writers argue that a claim is not evidence of state practice because its evidentiary value is limited until it is known whether the state resolves upon enforcement action.[44] The judicial authority for this approach is limited.[45] It may indeed be the case that the remarks made in the *Anglo Norwegian Fisheries* case should be read as applying to abstract claims in respect of territorial waters. Some writers have argued that a claim may be evidence of state practice if it is made in a concrete situation and not merely in the abstract.[46] It would seem that a claim should be admissible as evidence of state practice but its weight will depend on the circumstances of the claim.[47] Moreover there are a considerable number of cases in which claims have been advanced as evidence of state practice before the International Court of Justice.[48] However, as a matter of principle, if the basis of state practice is conduct then such conduct should include both acts and assertions. Moreover, in the *Fisheries Jurisdiction (Merits)* case,[49] 10 of the 14 judges were prepared to accept the legality of a 12 mile exclusive fishing zone on the basis of evidence of claims without considering whether such claims were consistently enforced.

(d) Opinio juris

The words of Art 38(1)(b) refer to 'international custom, as evidence of a general practice accepted as law'. If state A wishes to rely upon a rule of customary international law, then it will not be sufficient to demonstrate that it is grounded in state practice; it will be necessary to show that observance is dictated by the view that such conduct is obligatory as a matter of law. This psychological element is sometimes referred to as the *opinio juris sive necessitatis*.

It has to be admitted that this aspect is not without its difficulty. While many accept that the doctrine is required to distinguish habit from custom there is little agreement about its evolution. D'Amato[50] considers that the employment of the concept in international law is attributable to Geny,[51] while others look to the historical school of legal theory.[52] There is also some division of opinion as to how the doctrine should

---

44 See A D'Amato, *The Concept of Custom in International Law*, 1971.

45 See *Anglo Norwegian Fisheries* case (1951) ICJ 116 (see dissenting speech of Judge Read).

46 H Thirlway, *International Customary Law and Codification*, 1972.

47 It may be that Judge Read in the *Anglo Norwegian Fisheries* case was concerned with the situation after the Truman Declaration (1945) when some states began to make claims to a territorial sea of 200 nautical miles, contrary to the practice of established maritime states and at variance with efforts to obtain international codification.

48 *Asylum (Columbia v Peru)* (1950) ICJ 266; *The Rights of US Nationals in Morocco* case (1952) ICJ 176; *North Sea Continental Shelf* case (1969) ICJ 3.

49 *Fisheries Jurisdiction (Merits)* case (1974) ICJ 3.

50 A D'Amato, *The Concept of Custom in International Law*, 1971.

51 F Geny, *Methode d'interpretation et sources en droit prive positif*, 1899, para 110.

52 See A Carty, *The Decay of International Law?*, 1986, who traces the doctrine back to Savigny; in contrast, C Parry, in *The Sources and Evidences of International Law*, 1965, attributes the concept to William Blackstone.

operate. Positivists view the *opinio juris* as founded on the will and consent of numerous States, while others have argued that the *opinio juris* is founded upon the obligatory recognition of a pre-existing right.[53]

The purpose of the doctrine of *opinio juris* is to demonstrate that the right or obligation comprising the rule is not a mere matter of usage or practice. The need for such a second element is alluded to in a number of cases before the International Court of Justice[54] and indeed before national tribunals. In the case of *West Rand Gold Mining Co v R*,[55] Lord Alverstone LCJ observed that a rule of customary international law must be 'of such a nature, and has been so widely and generally accepted, that it can hardly be supposed that any civilised State would repudiate it'.

It would seem that the correct approach is to examine the evidence of state practice and to consider whether the correct inference to be drawn is that the practice is dictated by a sense of legal obligation. In some cases where the evidence of state practice is long and unambiguous, then strict proof will not be required. However, if a state is obliged to demonstrate a customary rule, then it will be necessary to demonstrate the *opinio juris*. Thus, in the *Lotus* case,[56] the PCIJ found that France was required to demonstrate that the practice of states other than the Flag state abstaining from claiming jurisdiction was an abstention founded on a sense of legal obligation. In the *North Sea Continental Shelf* case,[57] where one of the issues was whether a rule of customary international law providing for delimiting the Continental Shelf had developed after the Geneva Convention of 1958, the International Court of Justice observed:

> Although the passage of only a short period of time is not necessarily, or of itself, a bar to the formation of a new rule of customary international law on the basis of what was originally a purely conventional rule, an indispensable requirement would be that within the period in question, short though it might be, State practice, including that of States whose interests are specially affected, it should have been both extensive and virtually uniform in the sense of the provision invoked, and should moreover have occurred in such a way as to show a general recognition that a rule of law or legal obligation is involved.

A similar approach was followed in *Nicaragua v United States (The Merits)*,[58] where the Court noted that:

> ... as was observed in the *North Sea Continental Shelf* cases, for a new customary rule to be formed, not only must the acts concerned 'amount to a settled practice' but they must be accompanied by the *opinio juris necessitatis*. Either the States taking such action or other States in a position to react to it, must have behaved so that their conduct is 'evidence of a belief that this practice is rendered obligatory by the existence of a rule of law requiring it.

---

53 I MacGibbon, 'Customary international law and acquiescence' (1957) 33 BYIL 115; TO Elias, 'The nature of the subjective element in customary international law' (1995) 44 ICLQ 501.

54 *The Lotus* (1927) PCIJ, Ser A, No 10; 4 ILR 153; the *Asylum* case (1950) ICJ 266; 17 ILR 280; *Case concerning the Rights of Nationals of the United States of America in Morocco* (1952) ICJ 199; 19 ILR 255; the *North Sea Continental Shelf* case (1969) ICJ 3; 41 ILR 29; *Nicaragua v United States (The Merits)* (1986) ICJ 14; 76 ILR 349.

55 [1905] 2 KB 391.

56 *The Lotus* (1927) PCIJ, Ser A, No 10.

57 *North Sea Continental Shelf* case (1969) ICJ 3.

58 *Nicaragua v United States (The Merits)* (1986) ICJ 14.

The need for such a belief, ie, the existence of a subjective element, is implicit in the very notion of the *opinio juris sive necessitatis*'.[59]

The doctrine of *opinio juris* has attracted a considerable degree of comment. It is argued by some that a distinction should be drawn between customary rules that are of a permissive nature and those rules that impose duties.[60] In respect of a permissive rule, it is arguable that it is sufficient to demonstrate that other states have acted in a particular manner and that those states affected have not protested that the conduct was unlawful. In respect of rules that impose duties, it is necessary to demonstrate that other states regard such acts as obligatory and that failure to observe such conduct has been considered unlawful by other states. Those who argue that it is important to analyse the nature of the precise rule point to the case of the *Lotus*[61] where the facts were as follows.

A French merchant vessel (the *Lotus*) was in collision on the high seas with a Turkish ship (*Boz-Kourt*) as a result of the alleged negligence of one Lieutenant Demons, the officer on watch on the *Lotus*. In consequence, eight Turkish nationals lost their lives and the *Boz-Kourt* was sunk. When the *Lotus* returned to Istanbul, the French officer was arrested and tried. At a later date, France and Turkey agreed to submit the question of jurisdiction to the PCIJ. Turkey argued that it was entitled to try the officer. France argued that there was a clear rule of customary international law conferring jurisdiction on the courts of the Flag state and that Turkey was under a duty to refrain from criminal proceedings.

In rejecting the submissions of France and upholding the jurisdiction of Turkey, the PCIJ reasoned: (i) that as international law was premised on state sovereignty, then jurisdiction should be presumed unless contrary to international law;[62] (ii) that while few states in the position of Turkey had so acted, there had not been any protests by affected states; (iii) although most states in Turkey's position had refrained from acting, there was no evidence that they had done so out of a sense of legal obligation. One of the reasons that the Court gave for rejecting the French view as to the nature of customary law was that, even if the evidence established that other states had not prosecuted in the past, 'only if such abstention were based on their being conscious of a duty to abstain would it be possible to speak of an international custom'.[63] The court thereby indicating that evidence of both fact and sense of legal obligation would be required to establish a customary rule.

A theoretical difficulty arises as to how customary law changes if the requirement of *opinio juris* means that conduct must already be law before it can become law. Or, to put the matter another way, the conduct must be considered as law before it can become law. This has led some writers to question the need for *opinio juris*;[64] however, the need for

---

59 (1986) ICJ 14, pp 108–09, citing (1969) ICJ 44; 76 ILR 349, p 442, citing 41 ILR 73.

60 See Michael Akehurst, 'Custom as a source of international law' (1974–75) 47 BYIL 1.

61 *The Lotus* (1927) PCIJ, Ser A, No 10, p 18; 4 ILR 153; see WE Beckett (1927) 8 BYIL 108; JL Brierly (1928) 44 LQR 154.

62 It is widely accepted today that it is for the state (ie, Turkey) to show jurisdiction under international law. See *Anglo Norwegian Fisheries* case (1951) ICJ 116; the *Nottebohm* case (1955) ICJ 4; See also Geneva Convention on the High Seas (1958), Art 11(1); Law of the Sea Convention (1982), Art 97. The case is discussed further below in Chapter 8 on jurisdiction.

63 PCIJ, Ser A, No 10, p 28; 4 ILR 159.

64 P Guggenheim, *Traité de droit international public*, 1953, Vol 1, pp 46–48.

opinio juris has been consistently reaffirmed by the International Court of Justice,[65] which is not surprising since it is necessary to have some device that enables a court to determine where courtesy and habit end and rules begin.

Customary law represents the oldest form of international law and its supporters argue that being founded upon state conduct and consent it is more flexible than might appear. An example often taken is the development of the law relating to territorial waters after 1945. At that time, it was probably the case that states were permitted to claim a maritime belt of three nautical miles; in the period after 1950 many states began to make claims up to 12 nautical miles. These claims were accepted by other states and gradually a new customary rule founded on state conduct displaced the earlier customary rule.[66]

Those writers who have pointed to the theoretical difficulties posed by *opinio juris* cannot point to judicial decisions in their favour. Nevertheless, they argue that the requirement of *opinio juris* should be redefined as requiring a belief that conduct is required by an extra legal norm. Kelsen argued, in 1945, that *opinio juris* should not be restricted to where conduct is required by law, but that it should be 'sufficient that the states consider themselves bound by any norm whatever'. While in like form, Thirlway considered that the requirement of *opinio juris* should be satisfied if the 'practice was potentially law'. However, the difficulty with such an approach is the absence of judicial authority; indeed, the jurisprudence of the International Court of Justice has consistently stressed the need to differentiate ethical and legal obligations.[67]

(e) Acquiescence and the problem of the protesting state

At a time when a particular practice is developing that may crystallise into a rule of customary international law a state may react in three possible ways: (i) by doing nothing (that is, complete silence or acquiescence); or (ii) by objecting to the practice from the outset (that is, the persistent or initial objector); or (iii) by objecting at a later date when the rule has arisen (that is, the subsequent objector).

The wording of Art 38(1)(b) reads 'international custom, as evidence of a general practice accepted as law'. It is argued that the effect of this formulation is to create a presumption that all states, whether or not they have participated in the practice are presumed to have assented to the rule unless they can demonstrate that they have the status of a persistent objector.

It would seem that where there has been consistent practice by a number of states, then silence by others may be interpreted as acquiescence in the development of a rule of customary international law. In such circumstances, acceptance of the rule is established by acquiescence. This will particularly be the case where the state in question has no direct interest in a matter that constitutes the basis of the rule. Thus, if state A has no

---

65 *North Sea Continental Shelf* case (1969) ICJ 3; *Nicaragua v United States* (1986) ICJ 14 (a case that also raised the question as to whether the conduct of a state is consequent upon a treaty obligation).

66 *Fisheries Jurisdiction* cases (1974) ICJ 3, pp 23–26.

67 *South West Africa Case (Second Phase)* (1966) ICJ 3.

interest in the development of outer space, then it will normally be bound by any customary rule that develops amongst the states interested in this area.

However the position is different where the state has objected to a particular practice at the time when the rule is in the process of formation. Such a state is sometimes described as a 'persistent' or 'initial' objector. It is important that the objection is clear and unequivocal from the outset and that the state does not at any subsequent stage seek to rely upon the rule for its own advantage. A state cannot both disavow and affirm. The matter was discussed in some detail in the *Anglo Norwegian Fisheries* case,[68] where one of the arguments advanced by the United Kingdom was that there was a rule of customary international law that established a 10 mile limit in respect of baselines drawn across the mouth of bays. The United Kingdom failed to demonstrate such a rule on the evidence, but the majority of the court ruled that this rule would not have been enforceable (that is, opposable to) against Norway because:

> In any event, the ten mile rule would appear to be inapplicable against Norway in as much as she has always opposed any attempt to apply it to the Norwegian coast.[69]

So that even if general practice has resulted in a rule of customary international law, which is in principle binding on all states, then such a rule would not be binding on those states that can demonstrate the status of a persistent objector. The rationale for this is that one of the justifications for customary international law is that it is founded upon the consent (express or implied) of individual states; a persistent objector is indicating, at the outset, the absence of consent. It would seem from the *Anglo Norwegian Fisheries* case that the status of the persistent objector will cease if at any time that state sought for its own purposes to rely on the rule which it had previously contested. The one exception to this pertains to the evolution of rules constituting the *jus cogens*; having regard to the importance of this matter these are outlined below.

(f) Regional and bilateral relations

The *Asylum* case[70] indicated that, in principle, a customary rule could exist within a region or a particular locality. On the facts, the International Court of Justice found that such a custom had not been established on the evidence and, in any event, Peru had always objected. This approach was approved in the *Case concerning the Rights of Nationals of the United States of America in Morocco*,[71] It has been argued that these two cases support the view that a high standard of proof will lie upon the state alleging a local or a regional custom.[72]

---

68 (1951) ICJ 116; the details of the case are discussed more fully in Chapter 13 on the law of the sea; see DH Johnson (1952) 1 ICLQ 145; M Hudson (1952) 46 AJIL 23; J Evenson (1952) 46 AJIL 609.

69 (1951) ICJ 116, p 131.

70 *Asylum (Columbia v Peru)* case (1950) ICJ 3.

71 (1952) ICJ 200.

72 See A D'Amato, 'The concept of special custom in international law' (1969) 63 AJIL 211, where the learned author argues that a special custom was subject to distinct rules under the Roman law of *desuetudo* and was also so regarded by common lawyers such as William Blackstone in his *Commentaries*.

Further, it would seem that a local customary rule can arise in respect of only two states. Thus, in the *Rights of Passage over Indian Territory* case,[73] Portugal's rights over Indian territory were upheld even though India objected that no customary rule could exist between two states. However, it would appear that in the case of a regional custom not only is a high degree of proof placed upon state A but it will also be necessary to demonstrate that state B has consented because the nature of a special custom is that it involves a departure from an otherwise general rule.[74]

(g) Proof of a rule of customary international law

A municipal court will often take judicial notice of the provisions of its own law. In the context of international law a rule of customary international law may arise before a municipal court, an international arbitration or the International Court of Justice. In these circumstances state A will have to demonstrate: (i) that the two elements of the rule indicated above can be established; and (ii) that the rule is enforceable against state B. To this extent there is an *onus probandi* upon state A.

It has to be admitted that rules of customary international law have acquired a reputation for vagueness and uncertainty not least amongst judges in municipal courts. It is therefore important that the rule should be capable of being formulated with a degree of precision particularly if it is being relied upon in a municipal court. [75] It is also clear that it is a rule that is required to be established and such a rule is distinct from the opinions of textbook writers. In *West Rand Central Gold Mining Company v R,*[76] Lord Alverstone LCJ required that the proposition or rule be widely and generally accepted and he cautioned that: 'The mere opinions of jurists, however eminent or learned, that it ought to be recognised, are not themselves sufficient.'

(h) 'Instant' customary international law

A particular problem arises as to whether it is possible for a rule of customary international law to develop without extensive evidence of state practice. In the *North Sea Continental Shelf* cases,[77] the International Court had indicated that there was no particular duration required as evidence of state practice. Some writers such as Bin Cheng have gone further and asked whether a customary rule can exist without evidence of state practice. It is argued that in the modern world with the faster tempo of life it is unrealistic to wait for extensive evidence of prolonged practice. The essence of custom, it is argued, comprises the *opinio generalis juris generalis* and that if the time element is not critical then why should the *opinio juris* not be deduced form non-binding resolutions. In 1965, Dr Cheng posed the question as to whether United Nations General Assembly Resolutions

---

73   *Rights of Passage Case (Portugal v India)* (1960) ICJ 6.

74   *Asylum (Columbia v Peru)* case (1950) ICJ 3; *United States Nationals in Morocco* (1952) ICJ 200; see also G Fitzmaurice (1953) 30 BYIL 1, pp 68–69; A D'Amato (1969) 63 AJIL 211.

75   *R v Keyn* (1876) 2 Ex D 63; *West Rand Central Gold Mining Company v R* [1905] 2 KB 391; *R v Secretary of State for the Home Department ex p Thakrar* [1974] 1 QB 684, p 709, for sceptical remarks by Lawton LJ.

76   [1905] 2 KB 391.

77   (1969) ICJ 3.

were not examples of 'instant' international customary law.[78] However, there are a number of reasons why one should proceed with caution. First, there is no clear case of the International Court of Justice that endorses the concept of 'instant' customary international law. Secondly, even though the concept of duration was minimised in the *North Sea Continental* cases, the Court made it clear that the shorter the duration the more extensive state practice would be required. Thirdly, it might be argued that the debate in question should be confined to those General Assembly Resolutions that concern outer space where particular considerations apply and repeated acts of state practice are unlikely. Fourthly, it has been argued that the important question is the legal status of a General Assembly Resolution and that confusion has arisen by trying to place such Resolutions within the category of treaty or custom. Fifthly, a problem arises if customary international law is instant in that states that might have objected to the evolution of a rule would have no opportunity to do so. Sixthly, it is arguable that instant customary international law is only suitable when sudden technological advance and common interest makes it desirable for a number of states to proceed without evidence of state practice.[79] Seventhly, there is some evidence of the rejection of any doctrine of instant customary international law in the *Nicaragua* case where the Court observed:

> The mere fact that States declare their recognition of certain rules is not sufficient for the Court to consider these as being part of customary international law ... Bound as it is by Article 38 of its Statute ... the Court must satisfy itself that the existence of the rule in the *opinio juris* of States is confirmed by practice.[80]

Moreover, there is some evidence that the original article that stimulated the debate as to 'instant' customary law did not intend to assert that, normally, General Assembly resolutions are automatically instant customary international law – indeed there is good reason to believe that the original article was misinterpreted.[81]

3 TREATIES[82]

Article 38(1)(a) of the Statute of the International Court of Justice requires the court to apply 'international conventions, whether general or particular, establishing rules expressly recognised by the contesting states'.

Treaties have played a significant role in the development of international law at least since the Peace of Westphalia (1648) and it will be necessary to deal with the subject in detail later. At this stage the limited purpose is to outline the role of treaties as a source of

---

78 See B Cheng, 'United Nations resolutions on outer space: "instant" international customary law?' (1965) 5 IJIL 23.

79 An example cited by Professor Brierly in 1950 would be the speedy decision of states in 1914 to determine the question of sovereignty over airspace.

80 *Nicaragua (The Merits)* case (1986) ICJ 14, p 97.

81 For an interesting review of the controversy, see B Cheng, *Studies in International Space Law*, 1997, pp 191–205.

82 See generally on the topic, AD McNair, *The Law of Treaties*, 1961; I Detter, *Essays on the Law of Treaties*, 1967; TO Elias, *The Modern Law of Treaties*, 1974; A Aust, *Modern Treaty Law and Practice*, 2000.

international law; the rules relating to the formation of treaties are discussed in Chapter 11 below.

Before doing so, it is necessary to say a word about nomenclature; the expression 'treaty' comprises a large number of instruments that may use different names.[83] In the broadest terms a treaty is an agreement between parties on the international plane. The definition provided by Art 2(1)(a) of the Vienna Convention on the Law of Treaties (1969) is that the word 'treaty' 'means an international agreement concluded between states in written form and governed by international law, whether embodied in a single instrument or in two or more related instruments and whatever its particular designation'. As a possible source, a treaty has a particular advantage over custom in that it is able to set out rules clearly and in detail, in contrast to the sometimes vague and general propositions of customary international law. A treaty will normally involve a state in giving express consent and it is thus less objectionable to newer states who object to rules of customary international law formulated in a prior era. For these reasons, there is no doubt that the law of treaties has grown in volume and importance in the years since 1945.

Another important point is that since 1945 the entire international order is centred upon a particular treaty, the United Nations Charter (1945), which provides that in the event of conflict between obligations under the Charter and obligations 'under any other international agreement' obligations under the Charter shall prevail.[84]

As a source of law the treaty is founded on certain accepted principles which may be summarised as follows:

(a) The treaty arises from the express consent of a state. Such consent may be expressed by one of the accepted methods (signature, ratification, accession). Being based on consent the general principle is that only the parties to a treaty are bound by its terms. There are a number of exceptions to this general principle. It is recognised that there is a distinct category of 'dispositive treaties' that create an objective legal regime binding upon third states. Examples of such treaties would be those that govern international waterways (for example, Permanent Neutrality and Operation of the Panama Canal Treaty 1978) or those that determine boundaries.[85]

(b) A state that consents to a treaty is bound by the terms of the treaty in its dealings with other parties to the treaty. As is sometimes said the treaty governs the relations of the parties *inter se*. As a general principle the state signing a treaty will not be affected in its dealings with a non-signatory state. However, this latter principle has to be qualified because a treaty may be held to have codified or constituted customary international law.

---

83 The names employed include Convention, Protocol, Agreement, Arrangement, Statute, Covenant, Declaration, General Act, Final Act, Pact, Charter – the meaning of these terms will be dealt with further in Chapter 11.

84 See United Nations Charter (1945), Art 103.

85 See *Case concerning Kasikili/Sedudu Island (Botswana/Namibia)* (ICJ) 13 December 1999; for a discussion, see M Shaw (2000) 49 ICLQ 964.

(c) Where a treaty codifies customary international law,[86] then those states that sign the treaty are bound by the treaty in accordance with normal principles.

(d) Where a treaty codifies customary international law, then non-parties may be bound not under the treaty but because the obligations arise in customary international law. The substance of the obligation may be the same for a party or a non-party but the source of that obligation is different. The existence of identical rules in international treaty law and customary law was recognised in the *North Sea Continental Shelf* cases[87] and in the *Nicaragua* case.[88] In the latter case, the International Court of Justice observed 'it will therefore be clear that customary international law continues to exist and to apply separately from international treaty law, even where the two categories of law have an identical obligation'.[89] The existence of such 'parallel obligations' had the consequence in the *Nicaragua* case[90] that the ICJ had jurisdiction to examine conformity with rules of customary international law even when it was excluded by the relevant American reservation from considering compliance with obligations arising under treaty. The Court specifically rejected an argument of the United States that a norm of customary international law relating to self-defence had been 'subsumed' by Art 51 of the United Nations Charter.

(e) Many multilateral conventions are drawn up under the auspices of International Law Commission and combine elements of the codification of customary international law together with provisions that seek to further the progressive development of that law:

(i) In such cases treaty parties are bound by all the obligations arising under the treaty but non-parties will only be bound by those provisions that may be said to constitute customary international law.

(ii) The question whether a treaty provision crystallises as a new principle or rule of customary law depends on: (a) whether the treaty provision is 'of a fundamentally norm creating character such as could be regarded as forming the basis of a general rule of law';[91] and (b) whether there is evidence of consistent state practice in line with the treaty provision.[92] Thus, in 1982 the International Court of Justice[93] was prepared to accept that the concept of the Exclusive Economic Zone stipulated in the Law of the Sea Convention[94] had crystallised to such an extent that it might be regarded as part of customary international law. As indicated above the customary norm and the treaty norm retain distinct identities even if they seem identical in content.[95]

---

86 For general consideration of the codifying effect of some of the provisions of the Vienna Convention on the Law of Treaties (1969), see *Namibia* case (1971) ICJ 16; *Fisheries Jurisdiction* case (1974) ICJ 3; *Territorial Dispute* case (*Libya v Chad*) (1994) ICJ 6; *Danube Dam* case (*Hungary v Slovakia*) (1998) 37 ILM 162.

87 *North Sea Continental Shelf* case (1969) ICJ 3.

88 *Nicaragua (Merits)* case (1986) ICJ 14; 76 ILR 349.

89 *Ibid*, p 96; p 430.

90 *Nicaragua (Merits)* case (1986) ICJ 14.

91 *North Sea Continental Shelf* case (1969) ICJ 3.

92 *Ibid*.

93 *Tunisia/Lybia Continental Shelf* case (1982) ICJ 18.

94 The Law of the Sea Convention did not itself enter into force until November 1994.

95 *Nicaragua v United States (The Merits)* (1986) ICJ 14, pp 92–96.

All treaties contain obligations for the states that are parties to them. However, a distinction is often drawn between 'law making' treaties and the 'treaty contract'. The 'law making' treaty will purport to lay down general rules, will be multilateral in character and the observance of the rules will not dissolve other treaty obligations. In essence such a treaty will contain general rules designed for future and continuing observance. Because the international community has no legislature the multilateral law making treaty is employed to stipulate common rules. Many of the best known international agreements fall within this category.[96]

One distinguished writer[97] argued that, in international law, the treaty is best viewed as a vehicle to perform a number of functions that in municipal law might be dealt with separately – such functions being: (i) domestic legislation; (ii) the law of contract and conveyance; and (iii) the law relating to memoranda of association in municipal company law. However, this analogy cannot be pursued too far if only because legislation of a municipal legislature will apply to all citizens within the territory, whereas a law making treaty will apply only to those states that indicate agreement. Beyond concentrating the mind on the wide variety of tasks undertaken by treaty, the analogy is only of limited value.

In contrast to 'law making treaties' (*traités-lois*), one can also identify the 'treaty contracts' (*traités-contrats*), namely treaties which resemble contracts. An example of this latter form would be the situation whereby state A agreed to advance money to state B.

It has been asserted by some writers that only law making treaties are sources of law. Such writers argue that, unless a treaty lays down rules of general application to operate in the future, then it cannot constitute a source *strictu sensu*. There are a number of difficulties with this viewpoint. First, a treaty may contain provisions that are of a contractual and law making nature so that classification of the two distinct forms is difficult in practice.[98] Secondly, even a simple bilateral treaty may be of a law making nature.[99] Thirdly, a treaty contract will at the minimum create legal obligations between the parties. Fourthly, even though Art 38 does not include the word 'source', it is clear that the International Court of Justice is directed to consider international conventions 'whether general or particular'. Fifthly, the substantive law of treaties does not draw a distinction between the two types of treaty since classification is often in practice very difficult. In these circumstances, the sensible conclusion is to consider both forms as sources of legal obligation.

One of the most significant changes in International Law has been the growth in the volume of treaties. The evidence is set out in the United Nations Treaty Series and the United Kingdom Treaty Series. Indeed since 1945 over 30,000 treaties have been registered with the United Nations under the terms of Art 102 of the United Nations Charter. The growth in the volume of treaties is a reflection of important changes within international

---

96 Convention on the Prevention and Punishment of the Crime of Genocide (1948); Vienna Convention on Diplomatic Relations (1961); United Nations Convention on the Law of the Sea (1982).

97 See Michael Akehurst, *A Modern Introduction to International Law*, 6th edn, 1987, although the writer did argue that the analogy was only of limited value.

98 Continental jurists distinguish between *Vereinbarungen* and *Vertrage*.

99 See the Hay-Pauncefote Treaty of 1901 providing a regime for Panama Canal.

law itself. It is sensible to reflect on why this development has occurred. First, the world today contains more sovereign states. Co-operation in areas of common interest (civil aviation, telecommunications, the environment) has lead to the need to specify detailed rules in treaty form. Secondly as the rules of customary law are often vague many states are only prepared to respect those rules to which they have expressly consented being suspicious of the 'Eurocentric' nature of customary law. This was particularly the case with those states that viewed international law from a Marxist Leninist perspective or those newly independent states who considered themselves bound only where they had given express consent. Thirdly, the pace of technological change has been such that detailed rules drafted in 1955 might not be appropriate in 1975; in these circumstances, the flexibility of a treaty based regime is clearly seen to have advantages.

So one of the most significant trends since 1945 has been the growth in the number of bi-lateral and multilateral treaties designed not only to set in place legal frameworks but also to promote co-operation in an interdependent world.

4 THE RELATIONSHIP BETWEEN TREATY PROVISIONS AND RULES OF CUSTOMARY INTERNATIONAL LAW

(a) Law

A question that sometimes arises is as to the relationship between a treaty provision and a rule of customary international law. In all cases the matter will have to be examined chronologically but, subject to that requirement, the following represents state of the law:

(i) A treaty is a voluntary agreement which in principle binds only those states that are party to it. There are a number of exceptions to this rule and they will be considered later. Subject to these exceptions, the treaty creates obligations for the parties *inter se.*

(ii) It is an accepted rule of customary international law that treaty obligations should in principle be respected (*pacta sunt servanda*).

(iii) Difficulties can arise in respect of obligations arising in customary international law and obligations arising under a treaty.

(iv) There are three possible effects that a treaty might have on a rule of customary international law:

(a) it may codify a pre existing rule of customary international law;

(b) it may crystallise a rule of custom *in statu nascendi;*

(c) it may serve to generate a rule of customary international law in the future.

(v) If a rule of customary international law exists a later treaty may have the effect of codifying these rules. An example is afforded by the Vienna Convention on Diplomatic Relations (1961). Those states that are parties to the treaty will bound by its terms under the normal principles of treaty obligations. However, a state that is not a party to the treaty will not be bound under that treaty but will be subject to any established rule of customary international law. The actual obligation may be the same but the source of the obligation will be different.

(vi) If a rule of customary international law exists and it is then followed by a treaty provision that conflicts with it, then between parties to the treaty the provisions of the treaty will apply.[100] This is because either: (a) the treaty is an express act creating legal obligation; or (b) in accordance with the *maxim lex posteriori derogat juri priori*;[101] or (c) in accordance with the principle *lex specialis derogat legem generalis*.[102]

(vii) In some cases the treaty is intended not merely to codify customary international law but to promote its development. An example of such a multilateral treaty would be the Vienna Convention on the Law of Treaties (1969). In such circumstances state parties will be bound by all the provisions of the treaty. In respect of non-parties, it will be important to determine whether state practice develops in line with the provisions of the treaty. If this indeed proves to be the case, then non-parties will be governed by any new rules of customary law.

(viii) A difficult problem arises where customary international develops in a manner contrary to a prior treaty. In respect of non-parties, then they will be governed by new customary rule. In respect of parties to the treaty, it would seem that they will be governed by the treaty provisions and that subsequent customary international law will only modify prior treaty obligations in the most exceptional circumstances.[103]

(ix) In the event of conflicting treaty provisions, then normal rules of interpretation apply so a new treaty will, in general, replace an old treaty[104] and a general rule will be displaced by a special rule.

There are a number of cases where the International Court of Justice has been required to consider the relationship between treaty provisions and customary law. In the *North Sea Continental Shelf* cases the question arose between Germany, Holland and Denmark as to the principle governing the delimitation of the Continental Shelf under the North Sea. Article 6 of the Geneva Convention on the Continental Shelf (1958) had specified that, in the absence of agreement, the method employed should be that of equidistance from the nearest point of the baselines from which the territorial sea was measured. Such a method would have given a relatively small Continental Shelf to Germany because of the concave nature of its coastline. The problem arose because Germany had signed, but not ratified, the Geneva Convention on the Continental Shelf (1958). In consequence, Holland and Denmark argued that the equidistance principle set out in Art 6 was binding on Germany either as a pre-existing rule of customary international law or because Art 6 had the effect of creating a new rule of customary international law. The Court rejected the contention that Art 6 reflected an existing rule of customary international law and then considered the second argument. The Court held that a treaty provision could have the effect of generating a rule of customary international law but this inference could only be made where the provision was of a norm creating nature and that the subsequent conduct of states was both extensive and virtually uniform. In reviewing such conduct, particular weight was to be accorded by states affected by the provision. Thus, the Court found that

---

100 Save in respect of matters arising under the *jus cogens*; this is discussed later in the chapter.
101 The later law takes priority over the earlier law.
102 The specific law derogates from the general law.
103 *North Atlantic Coast Fisheries Arbitration (United States v Great Britain)* (1910) 11 RIAA 167.
104 See Art 30 of the Vienna Convention on the Law of Treaties (1969).

the provision did not in this instance generate a rule of customary international law binding on Germany.

In the subsequent *Tunisia-Libya Continental Shelf* case,[105] the International Court of Justice was prepared to accept that the principle of the EEZ set out in the Law of the Sea Convention (1982) was also to be regarded as part of customary law. At a later date, both the Chamber[106] and the Court[107] have been prepared to draw upon the Law of the Sea Convention (1982) to establish the customary law status of the EEZ even though the Convention was not in force.[108]

The principle set out in the *North Sea Continental Shelf* cases[109] that treaty provisions might generate rules of customary international law was followed by the Court in *Nicaragua v United States (The Merits)*,[110] where the Court was prepared to find that Art 2(4) of the United Nations Charter, together with subsequent General Assembly Resolutions, had the effect of generating a rule of customary law similar in content to Art 2(4) but existing parallel to it.

There are two other matters that arise concerning the relationship between treaty provisions and customary law, namely the doctrine of *jus cogens* and the operation of Art 103 of the United Nations Charter. Both these matters will be considered at the conclusion of the chapter.

5 GENERAL PRINCIPLES OF LAW

Article 38(1)(c) of the Statute of the International Court of Justice requires the Court to apply 'the general principles of law recognised by civilised nations'. This is an original provision of the Statute of the Permanent Court of International Justice and was prompted by the work of the Advisory Committee of Jurists. The problem the Committee had experienced was that there might be a situation arising in which neither treaty rules nor customary law would provide an answer to the case in point – that is, the problem of *non liquet*. In these circumstances, certain continental jurists mindful of the experience with Codes wished to give the court a wide residual jurisdiction to do abstract justice.

To meet these concerns, Lord Phillimore and the Hon Elihu Root proposed the clause that became Art 38(1)(c) being a provision that was known in previous arbitrations and would meet the problem of *'non liquet'* without being dangerously vague and open ended.

Some jurists (for example, Verdross)[111] have argued that the purpose of the provision in Art 38(1)(c) is to incorporate natural law into international law. The problem is that this is not borne out by the *travaux preparatoires* and the subsequent history of the provision.

---

105 *Tunisia-Libya Continental Shelf* case (1982) ICJ 18.

106 *Gulf of Maine* case (1984) ICJ 246.

107 *Libya-Malta Continental Shelf* case (1985) ICJ 13.

108 It did not come into force until November 1994.

109 *North Sea Continental Shelf* case (1969) ICJ 3.

110 *Nicaragua v United States (The Merits)* (1986) ICJ 14.

111 Hague *Recueil* (1935 II) 204–06.

Other jurists such as Guggenheim argue that it adds little to Art 38(1)(a) and 38(1)(b) on the basis that national law cannot be part of international law save as when it has been expressly adopted in state treaties and state practice.[112] However, the majority view holds that the purpose of the provision was to enable the court to take principles recognised in national law and to apply them in appropriate situations if their application appears relevant to the resolution of an international dispute. [113] This viewpoint seems to be in line with the objectives of Lord Phillimore and Elihu Root and is supported by leading textbook opinion,[114] although it should be noted that some hold the view that the purpose of Art 38(1)(c) is to allow the judges to extend international law by analogy, by inferring certain general principles from specific rules by means of inductive reasoning. This narrow view is not borne out by actual practice. There is much to be said for the view that the inclusion of the provision was prompted by the tendency in some civil codes to include a provision whereby the judge is directed to apply the general principles of law in order to fill any lacunae in the domestic law.[115]

While there had been some progress in the 19th century towards the peaceful settlement of disputes, the view in 1920 was that a viable system of judicial settlements was in its embryonic stages and it might be necessary to adopt principles employed by Prize Courts, arbitral commissions and municipal courts in appropriate cases. The reference to civilised nations has a rather dated feel today, but it served to indicate that legal principles found in some of the world's major legal systems might be employed by the court, even if those principles were not known in less advanced legal systems. Even today, where the world is divided into more than 180 states, many municipal legal systems are members of one or other of the world's major legal families – for example, there is a certain degree of harmony between legal systems in Commonwealth countries and North America while the legal systems of many Latin American states have much in common having regard to their shared colonial history. However, this was not an unprecedented decision; in the 16th and 17th century, writers such as Suarez and Grotius had not hesitated to borrow concepts from Roman law or canon law.

In examining the evidence in the case law, it is clear that in appropriate situations the International Court of Justice may refer to established legal doctrines drawn from municipal law. In the earlier case law, the Permanent Court of International Justice had laid some stress on rights arising in private law. In the *German Settlers in Poland* case,[116] the Court drew attention to the importance of respect for private law rights while, several years later in the *Chorzow Factory* case,[117] which concerned the seizure of a factory the court noted that 'it is a general conception of law that every violation of an engagement involves an obligation to make a reparation' and, in passing, it made reference to the principle of *res judicata*. In the same decade, the court referred to 'the general principle of

---

112 P Guggenheim, *Traité de droit international public*, 1967, Vol 1, p 152.

113 Waldock 106 Hague *Recueil* (1962 II) 54.

114 See LH Oppenheim (1858–1919) in *International Law*, 1st edn, 1905, Vol 1, p 29; the view is also expressed by I Brownlie, *Principles of Public International Law*, 5th edn, 1998, p 16.

115 HC Gutteridge, 'The meaning of the scope of Article 38(1)(c) of the Statute of the International Court of Justice' (1952) 38 TGS 125.

116 *German Settlers in Poland* (1923) PCIJ, Ser B, No 6.

117 *Chorzow Factory (Indemnity)* case (1928) PCIJ, Ser A, No 17.

subrogation' in the *Mavrommatis Palestine Concessions* case[118] and in the *Eastern Carelia* case,[119] the Court referred to 'the independence of states' as a 'fundamental principle of international law'. So, from the outset, the Court has been prepared to draw upon principles from both municipal and international law.

It is not surprising that this should be so since many members of the Court will have had experience as lawyers litigating claims before municipal courts. It is a matter of record that a case coming before a municipal court raising questions of international law will also give rise to problems of municipal law.[120] In general terms, a judge will have qualified as a municipal lawyer before specialising in international law. It is to be expected that such a judge will in appropriate cases draw upon principles arising in municipal law.

In some cases, the Court has refused to apply a particular principle. In the *Serbian Loans* case,[121] where the Court was required to determine a dispute between French bondholders and the Serbian government, the Court declined to apply the equitable principle of estoppel partly on the basis that the substantive issue was to be governed by Serbian law as the *lex causae*. As with the European Court of Justice, the Court has been much concerned with questions of procedural justice and evidence, as these are matters fundamental to any proper system of judicial adjudication. Thus in the *Corfu Channel* case,[122] the Court, in reflecting upon the role of circumstantial evidence, observed that 'this indirect evidence is admitted in all systems of law and its use is recognised in international decisions' and, in the same case, it alluded to principles of international law by noting 'certain general and well recognised principles, namely: elementary considerations of humanity, even more exacting in peace than in war; the principle of the freedom of maritime communication; and every state's obligation not to allow knowingly its territory to be used for acts contrary to the rights of other states'.[123]

The reliance upon general principles is, of course, a source of concern for the extreme positivist who views international law as founded on the consent of states; however, the history of the subject indicates a willingness by writers to borrow from other sources where appropriate. However, reliance on principles drawn from municipal law must be subject to a degree of restraint and a cautionary note was sounded by Judge McNair in the case of the *International Status of South West Africa*,[124] where he asked:

> To what extent is it useful or necessary to examine what may at first sight appear to be relevant analogies in private law systems and draw help and inspiration from them? International law has recruited and continues to recruit many of its rules from private systems of law. Article 38(1)(c) of the Statute of the Court bears witness to that this process

---

118 *Mavrommatis Palestine Concessions* case *(Jurisdiction)* (1924) PCIJ, Ser A, No 2.

119 *Eastern Carelia* case (1923) PCIJ, Ser B, No 5.

120 A recent example being the 'Pinochet saga' which, while raising obvious points of international law, has also given rise to questions of constitutional law and private international law; see *R v Bow Street Metropolitan Magistrate ex p Pinochet Ugarte (No 1)* [1998] 3 WLR 1456.

121 *Serbian Loans* case (1929) PCIJ, Ser A, Nos 20–21.

122 *Corfu Channel* case *(UK v Albania) (The Merits)* (1949) ICJ 4, p 18; 16 ILR 155, p 157.

123 *Ibid*, p 22.

124 *International Status of South West Africa* case (1950) ICJ 128.

is still active, and it will be noted that this article authorises the court 'to apply ... (c) the general principles of law recognised by civilised nations'.

The way in which international law borrows from this source is not by means of importing private law institutions 'lock stock and barrel' ready made and fully equipped with a set of rules. It would be difficult to reconcile such a process with the application of 'the general principles of law'. In my opinion, the true view of the duty of international tribunals in this matter is to regard any features or terminology which are reminiscent of the rules and institutions of private law as an indication of policy and principles rather than as directly importing these institutions.

As the learned judge indicated there is much to be said for proceeding cautiously where principles drawn from municipal law are in issue. A principle that may be appropriate in the relations between private persons may not be practical to govern the relations between sovereign states. However, some principles are inextricably linked with the judicial function itself and these will be appropriate regardless of whether the litigation is municipal or international. One such principle is that of finality in litigation. Thus, in the *Administrative Tribunal* case,[125] the Court was prepared to endorse the principle of *res judicata* while in the *Northern Cameroons* case[126] it indicated that its jurisdiction to grant a declaratory judgment would only be exercised where it had some practical purpose in relation to concrete facts.

One doctrine that has given rise to debate is the principle of estoppel. In the *Serbian Loans* case,[127] the Court found the doctrine inapplicable on the facts, but shortly after, in the *Eastern Greenland* case,[128] the principle was invoked to prevent Norway disputing Danish sovereignty after it had previously acknowledged the same in treaty negotiations. The basic principle of the doctrine of estoppel is that of preventing a party from denying a state of affairs he has previously asserted.[129] The doctrine is particularly suitable in respect of disputes about territory so that in the *Temple* case,[130] Thailand was precluded from denying title to the area round the Temple of Preah Vihear because, in the past, Thailand had accepted French sovereignty over the area; while in the *North Sea Continental Shelf* cases,[131] the Court appeared to indicate that for a state to be able to rely upon estoppel it would be necessary not only to show a representation but also a detrimental change of position. The need for strict evidentiary requirements was confirmed in the *ELSI* case,[132] where the Chamber of the International Court noted 'the

---

125 *Administrative Tribunal* case (1954) ICJ 54.

126 *Northern Cameroons* case (1963) ICJ 15.

127 *Serbian Loans* case (1929) PCIJ, Ser A, Nos 20–21.

128 *Eastern Greenland* case (1933) PCIJ, Ser A/B, No 53.

129 Although the doctrine has a long history, there can be little doubt that it has acquired greater prominence in common law jurisdictions following the *obiter* remarks of Denning J (as he then was) in *Central London Property Trust Ltd v High Trees House Ltd* [1947] KB 130, which ushered in a flood of case law. See (1947) 63 LQR 278; (1948) 64 LQR 28. For reflections on the doctrine a generation later, see *Crabb v Arun District Council* [1976] Ch 179.

130 *Temple of Preah Vihear* case (1962) ICJ 6; see DH Johnson, 'The case concerning the *Temple of Preah Vihear*' (1962) 11 ICLQ 1183.

131 *North Sea Continental Shelf* cases (1969) ICJ 3.

132 *Elettronica Sicula SpA (ELSI)* case (*United States v Italy*) (1989) ICJ 15; See M Dixon, 'The *ELSI* case' (1992) 41 ICLQ 701.

obvious difficulties in constructing an estoppel from a mere failure to mention a matter at a particular point in somewhat desultory diplomatic exchanges'.

While it is clear that estoppel emerged as a principle of domestic law, the position is less clear with the principle of *pacta sunt servanda* which has been recognised in both municipal law[133] and on the international plane.[134] Similarly, while most municipal legal systems stress respect for acquired property, this principle has been endorsed in international law.[135] In some situations, it is difficult to determine whether the principle arises in international law or municipal law or in both. An example is afforded by the principle of acting in good faith; in most municipal law systems the absence of good faith may be a ground for refusing discretionary relief.[136] There is some evidence of the principle of acting in good faith existing on the international plane. Indeed, the principle of *pacta sunt servanda* which is the foundation of the law of treaties is itself based on the principle of acting in good faith.[137] The principle is set out in Art 2(2) of the United Nations Charter (1945) which reads 'all Members, in order to ensure to all of them the rights and benefits resulting form membership, shall fulfil in good faith the obligations assumed by them in accordance with the present Charter', and the principle is also expressly stated in the Preamble to the Declaration Concerning Friendly Relations and Co-operation among states which was adopted by the General Assembly in Resolution 2625(XXV) in October 1970. The Preamble notes 'that the faithful observance of the principles of international law concerning friendly relations and co-operation among states and the fulfilment in good faith of the obligations assumed by states, in accordance with the Charter, is of the greatest importance for the maintenance of international peace and security and for the implementation of the other purposes of the United Nations'. The emphasis on acting in good faith was stressed by the International Court of Justice in the *Nuclear Tests* cases[138] where the Court noted that: 'One of the basic principles governing the creation and performance of legal obligations, whatever their source, is the principle of good faith. Trust and confidence are inherent in international co-operation ...' However, it is also clear that principle of good faith applies to the creation and performance of legal obligations but is not, in itself, a source of obligation where none would otherwise exist.[139]

It is also clear that there may be litigation on the international plane where concepts drawn form municipal law are central to the case and will have to be accommodated. In the *Barcelona Traction* case,[140] Belgium brought a claim on behalf of its nationals who comprised the majority of shareholders in the Barcelona Traction, Light and Power

---

133 The traditional position in English law being robustly stated by Sir George Jessel MR in the well known case of *Printing and Numerical Registering Co v Sampson* (1875) LR 19 Eq 462.

134 Vienna Convention on the Law of Treaties (1969), Art 26.

135 *German Interests in Polish Upper Silesia* case (1926) PCIJ, Ser A, No 7, p 22.

136 As illustrated at common law by the maxim *ex turpi causa non oritur actio* and also in the equitable maxim that he who comes to equity must come with clean hands: *Loughran v Loughran* (1934) 292 US 216, p 229, *per* Brandeis J; Z Chafee (1949) Mich Law Rev 877, p 1065.

137 *Nuclear Test* cases (*Australia v France* and *New Zealand v France*) (1974) ICJ 253, p 267.

138 *Ibid.*

139 *Border and Transborder Armed Actions* case (*Nicaragua v Honduras*) (1988) ICJ 105.

140 *Barcelona Traction, Light and Power Company Limited* case (*Belgium v Spain*) (*Second Phase*) (1970) ICJ 3.

Company Limited, a company incorporated in Canada. In rejecting the claim of Belgium, it was necessary for the Court to consider the nature of corporate personality and the distinction between wrongs done to a company and wrongs committed against individual shareholders. Further, it was necessary for the Court to consider the distinction between a company in receivership and a company in liquidation. Before the point of international law could be adjudicated upon, it was necessary to analyse relationships arising under municipal law since 'a distinction must be drawn between a direct infringement of the shareholder's rights, and difficulties or financial losses to which he may be exposed as a result of the situation of the company'.

Thus the sensible conclusion must be that Art 38(1)(c) permits the Court to apply principles drawn from either municipal law or international law where the facts so merit.

6 EQUITY AND INTERNATIONAL LAW[141]

In addition to the references to 'General Principles of Law' in Art 38(1)(c), there has been much discussion as to whether an international tribunal or the International Court of Justice may apply equitable principles in the resolution of disputes. Equity is not a separate source of law; it comes within the provisions of Art 38(1)(c) and is a mechanism for mitigating what the law would otherwise require. Because of its prominence it requires to be considered separately.

It is certainly true that there have been many passing references in the case law[142] to equity and equitable principles, but it has to be recognised that equitable rules exist to achieve justice where that is not possible under the general law, so that the object of invoking equitable principles is to achieve justice between the parties. The most celebrated remarks about the role of equity were made by Judge Hudson in the *Diversion of the Water from the Meuse* case,[143] where the learned judge noted that: 'What are known as principles of equity have long been considered to constitute a part of international law, and as such they have often been applied by international tribunals,' and, in a later part of his ruling, he observed that: 'It must be concluded, therefore, that under Art 38 of the Statute, if not independently of that Article, the Court has some freedom to consider principles of equity as part of the international law which it must apply.' The same approach was followed by the arbitrators in the *Rann of Kutch Arbitration* in 1968.[144]

Not only have equitable principles been invoked as part of substantive law, they have been drawn upon in determining remedies. In the *North Sea Continental Shelf* cases,[145] the final determination by the International Court of Justice required delimitation to be 'in

---

141 B Cheng, 'Justice and equity in international law' (1955) 8 CLP 185; M Akehurst, 'Equity and general principles of law' (1976) 25 ICLQ 80; RY Jennings, 'Equity and equitable principles' (1986) ASDI 38; AV Lowe, 'The role of equity in international law' (1992) 12 AYIL 54.

142 *Diversion of Water from the Meuse* (1937) PCIJ, Ser A/B, No 70; 8 ILR 444; *Rann of Kutch Arbitration* (1968) 50 ILR 2; *North Sea Continental Shelf* case (1969) ICJ 3; 41 ILR 29; *Tunisia/Libya Continental Shelf* case (1982) ICJ 18; 67 ILR 4; *Gulf of Maine* case (1984) ICJ 246; *Libya-Malta Continental Shelf* case (1985) ICJ 13; *Frontier Dispute* case (*Burkina Faso v Mali*) (1985) ICJ 554.

143 PCIJ, Ser A/B, No 70, pp 73, 77; 8 ILR 444, p 450.

144 *Rann of Kutch Arbitration* (1968) 50 ILR 2.

145 (1969) ICJ 3; 41 ILR 83. For equitable delimitation of the Continental Shelf, see now Art 83(1).

accordance with equitable principles'. It is certainly true that equitable principles may be of some value in cases of territorial disputes[146]or where problems arise as to delimitation of maritime belts.[147]

However, a degree of caution is required. The future of the International Court of Justice depends on it being seen to apply existing legal rules and principles to established facts. Equity must therefore be seen as part of the substantive law and not as a vehicle for the judge to decide the case on the basis of his own individual preferences. Thus, a clear distinction has been drawn between the relevant equitable principles and the power that the Court enjoys under Art 38(2) to decide a case *ex aequo et bono*, if the parties so agree.[148] It has been argued that on the international plane the concept of equity may be in issue in three distinct situations: (i) where the court is asked to adapt the law to the facts of the individual case (equity *infra legem*); (ii) where the court is asked to fill gaps in the law (equity *praeter legem*); and (iii) where the court seeks to rely on equity as a ground for refusing to apply an unjust law (equity *contra legem*).[149] It is widely recognised that equity is easier to describe than to define. But even if the expression is taken in its popular sense of justice or morality, there are considerable difficulties in applying it in litigation on the international plane. At the municipal level where the emphasis is on judicial discretion the approach of the court may vary, although such variations are controlled by the operation of the doctrine of judicial precedent. In international society where the value systems are much wider and more diverse than in municipal society, difficulties can arise unless some restraint is shown. What is equitable to a prosperous country in Western Europe may seem oppressive to a poor country in Africa. One has only to reflect on the controversies that surround the question of the appropriate level of compensation to be paid for taking the assets of a foreign investor. So, if equitable principles are to be applied, then it must be with a degree of caution and much will depend on whether the parties to the case share the same value system. So, it might be possible to apply traditional equitable principles in a dispute between the United States and the United Kingdom but in the case of a dispute between the United States and a poor country in the third world, a proper degree of caution is called for.

Although applying equity depends to some extent on subscribing to a similar ethical system, the International Court is regularly urged to apply equitable principles in cases coming before it. Most writers date this from the *North Sea Continental Shelf* cases (1969) and it is probably true that the majority of cases have concerned either: (i) the delimiting of maritime boundaries; or (ii) disputes as to territorial boundaries. In cases of maritime delimitation, the Court (and its Chamber) have been particularly ready to emphasise the importance of achieving an equitable result by employing equitable criteria.[150] This willingness to adopt equitable principles in the area of maritime delimitation is also to be found in the Law of the Sea Convention (1982) in Arts 59 and 74, while Art 83 provides

---

146 *Frontier Dispute* case *(Burkina Faso v Mali)* (1986) ICJ 554.

147 *Fisheries Jurisdiction* case *(United Kingdom v Iceland)* (1974) ICJ 3.

148 *Rann of Kutch Arbitration* (1968) 50 ILR 2; *AMCO Asia Corporation v The Republic of Indonesia* (1985) 89 ILR 365; *Frontier Dispute* case *(Burkina Faso v Mali)* (1986) ICJ 554.

149 M Akehurst (1976) 25 ICLQ 801.

150 *North Sea Continental Shelf* case (1969) ICJ 3; *Tunisia-Libya Continental Shelf* case (1982) ICJ 18; *Gulf of Maine* case (1984) ICJ 246; *Libya-Malta Continental Shelf* case (1985) ICJ 13; *Denmark v Norway: Maritime Boundary in the Area between Greenland and Jan Mayen Island* (1993) ICJ 38. These cases will be discussed in detail in Chapter 13 on the law of the sea.

for the delimitation of the continental shelf between states with opposite or adjacent coasts 'in order to achieve an equitable solution'.

The same degree of willingness has been exhibited in cases concerning boundary disputes; however, the limits to such a process were indicated by the Chamber of the Court in the *Burkina Faso v Mali* case[151] where it was noted:

> ... that the Chamber cannot decide *ex aequo et bono* in this case. Since the Parties have not entrusted it with the task of carrying out an adjustment of their respective interests, it must also dismiss any possibility of resorting to equity *contra legem*. Nor will the Chamber apply equity *praeter legem*. On the other hand, it will have regard to equity *infra legem*, that is, that form of equity which constitutes a method of interpretation of the law in force, and is one of its attributes. As the Court has observed 'It is not a matter of finding simply an equitable solution, but an equitable solution derived from the applicable law.' [*Fisheries Jurisdiction* case (1974) ICJ 3.]

Within a couple of years the Chamber of the Court held in the *Case Concerning the Land, Island and Maritime Frontier Dispute*[152] that where the line of a *uti possidetis juris* boundary could not be defined in a particular area then it was permissible to fall back on equity *infra legem*.

In summary, the recent jurisprudence would appear to indicate a number of propositions: (i) that the role of equity has developed in cases of boundary disputes and maritime delimitation; (ii) that the equity in question is equity *infra legem*; and (iii) that the exercise of any such equity should be distinguished from the power to decide *ex aequo et bono* under Art 38(2);[153] and (iv) that beyond these distinct circumstances equitable rules have to be approached with a degree of caution because the application of equity is premised on an agreed value system.[154]

7 JUDICIAL DECISIONS

The words of Art 38(1)(d) of the Statute of the International Court of Justice require 'judicial decisions' to be applied 'as subsidiary means for the determination of rules of law'. This provision is expressly subject to Art 59 which reads: 'The decision of the Court has no binding force except between the parties and in respect of that particular case.'

It is arguable that in 1920 the Advisory Committee of Jurists were anxious to prevent a strict system of precedent developing so that states C and D might be bound by a prior judgment given affecting states A and B. First, the object appears to have been to give the

---

151 *Frontier Dispute* case (*Burkina Faso v Republic of Mali*) (1986) ICJ 554.

152 *Case concerning the Land, Island and Maritime Frontier Dispute (El Salvador v Honduras, Nicaragua Intervening)* (1992) ICJ 355; M Shaw (1993) 42 ICLQ 929.

153 Under Art 38(2), socio-economic and political considerations might be relevant: see *Gulf of Maine* case (1984) ICJ 246.

154 See P Weil, 'L'equité dans la jurisprudence de la Cour Internationale de Justice' and B Kwiatowska, 'Equitable maritime boundary delimitation', in AV Lowe and M Fitzmaurice (eds), *Fifty Years of the International Court of Justice*, 1996. See also two important contributions by Sir Robert Jennings, 'Equity and equitable principles' (1986) 42 Annuaire suisse de droit international 27–38 and 'The principles governing maritime boundaries', in K Hailbronner, G Ress and T Stein (eds), *Staat und Volkerrechtsordnung, Festschrift für Karl Doehring*, 1989.

Court the freedom to resolve cases as and when they arose. However, every system of law requires the application of settled principles to established facts. Nothing would be more damaging for the reputation of the Court if its judgments lacked any degree of consistency. Secondly, it would be impossible for legal advisers in foreign ministries to give advice with confidence if a prior judgment of the International Court was not likely to be followed. Indeed legal texts would have little value if authorities were liable to be frequently departed from. The orderly development of international law requires some respect for existing principles and authorities. For this reason, writers have tried to place some limits on the meaning of Art 59. Hersch Lauterpacht[155] argued that one purpose of Art 59 was to protect the state that did not appear in proceedings; so that proceedings between states A and B should not affect state C and that the meaning of Art 59 was to be determined by reference to Art 63 of the Statute.

WE Beckett[156] pointed out that the wording of Art 59 concerns 'decisions of the Court' and thus does not extend to the legal principles propounded. It is trite law that the doctrine of precedent operates upon the relevant legal principles and, although the Court has observed that: 'The object of (Art 59) is simply to prevent legal principles accepted by the Court in a particular case from being binding on other States or in other disputes,'[157] this must be regarded with a degree of caution. The practical reality is that the Court often refers[158] to past judgments, and advisers and practitioners advance arguments to the Court by reference to the judgments in past cases. It would seem, therefore, that the practical advantage of Art 59 is to confirm the position that a decision of the Court between states A and B will, in principle, not affect state C.[159]

From the outset, the judgments of the International Court of Justice in both contentious and advisory matters have been important in the clarification and progressive development of international law. The *Reparations* case[160] lead to a re-evaluation of the legal standing of international organisations, while the *Genocide* case[161] contributed to a change in the rules in the law of treaties concerning reservations. While it is arguable that Advisory Opinions have proved more influential, the judgment in the *Anglo Norwegian Fisheries* case[162] led to changes in the methods of drawing baselines in the Geneva Convention on the Territorial Sea 1958, while the *Nottebohm* case[163] contributed to a clarification of the principles pertaining to state responsibility. A

---

155 H Lauterpacht (1931) 12 BYIL 60.

156 WE Beckett 39 Hague *Recueil* (1932 I) 135. At the time, Beckett was serving as Second Legal Adviser in the Foreign Office. For a review of his general approach to questions of international law and the difference between the PCIJ and the ICJ, see G Fitzmaurice and F Vallat, 'An appreciation' (1968) 17 ICLQ 267.

157 *German Interests in Polish Upper Silesia* (1926) PCIJ, Ser A, No 7, p 19.

158 *North Sea Continental Shelf* cases (1969) ICJ 3 (referring to *The Lotus* case (1927) PCIJ, Ser A, No 10 and *The Anglo Norwegian Fisheries* case (1951) ICJ 116); the *Western Sahara* case (1975) ICJ 12 (citing *Advisory Opinion on Namibia* (1971) ICJ 16); the *Nicaragua* case (*The Merits*) (1986) ICJ 14 (citing the *North Sea Continental Shelf* case (1969) ICJ 3).

159 *Ceratin Phosphate Lands in Nauru* case (*Nauru v Australia, Preliminary Objections*) (1993) 32 ILM 46.

160 *Reparations for Injuries Suffered in the Service of the United Nations* (1949) ICJ 174.

161 Reservations to the Convention on the Prevention and Punishment of the Crime of Genocide (1951) ICJ 15.

162 *Anglo Norwegian Fisheries* case (1951) ICJ 116; See Geneva Convention on the Territorial Sea (1958), Art 4.

163 *Nottebohm* case (*Second Phase*) (1955) ICJ 4.

judgment that is viewed as unsatisfactory may be displaced by subsequent changes in treaty provision. However, there can be little doubt that judgments of the International Court of Justice occupy a central place in the evolution of international law and enjoy a degree of influence that the founders of 1920 could not have anticipated.

The expression 'judicial decisions' extends beyond the judgments of the International Court of Justice and extends to judicial determinations at national and regional level and also to arbitral awards such as those made by the Permanent Court of Arbitration. One particular contemporary problem is the proliferation of intermediate judicial bodies such as: (i) regional courts;[164] (ii) courts designed to supervise the operation of regional human rights treaties;[165] (iii) the forthcoming international criminal court; (iv) the Tribunal for the Law of the Sea;[166] (v) *ad hoc* international tribunals. At present, there is no system of references to the International Court of Justice so that these bodies operate independently and within the terms of their individual jurisdictions. The value of their decisions will depend on the quality of the judgment and the distinction of individual judges.

Judgments of national courts fall within Art 38(1)(d). There are a number of municipal judgments that have been influential in particular areas of international law.[167] However, a degree of caution must be taken in examining domestic judgments because the municipal court will also be concerned with its own domestic rules.[168] As will be seen later, there are a considerable number of areas of international law where it is likely that if litigation arises it is more likely to do so in the municipal court. Subjects such as recognition of states, extradition, state immunity and the law of prize are all likely to give rise to litigation in municipal courts. Indeed, it is not unusual for a court in state A, when considering a question of international law, to be influenced by the approach of domestic courts in other states.[169] It is sometimes argued that there is particular value in the judgments of those courts operating in a federal structure; this must be open to question because normally such a court will have to pay first regard to the terms of the written constitution of the state.[170]

In international law, the expression 'judicial decision' extends to awards made by arbitrators. Arbitration as a method of peacefully resolving disputes began to emerge in

---

164 An example being the European Court of Justice established under Art 169 of the Treaty of Rome (1957).

165 Perhaps the best known being the European Court of Human Rights but also includes the Inter American Court of Human Rights. In respect of human rights enforcement, see Chapters 15 and 16.

166 Established under Art 287 of the Law of the Sea Convention (1982) and Annex VI.

167 Examples would be certain judgments of the United States Supreme Court, eg, *Schooner Exchange v M'Faddon* (1812) 7 Cranch 116; *Thirty Hogshead of Sugar, Bentzon v Boyle* (1815) 9 Cranch 191; *The Scotia* (1871) 14 Wallace 170; *The Paquete Habana* (1900) 175 US 677. Another example would be the influence exerted on the law of prize by Lord Sowell (1745–1836) who served as an Admiralty judge (1798–1827).

168 An example is afforded by the case of *R v Bow Street Magistrates ex p Pinochet Ugarte (No 3)* [2000] 1 AC 147, where the House of Lords was required to devote considerable attention to the State Immunity Act 1978 and the Extradition Act 1989. The value of any municipal judgment may be influenced by whether the individual state adopted a monist or a dualist approach to international law. On this aspect see Chapter 4.

169 Noted by Marshall CJ in the United States Supreme Court in *Thirty Hogshead of Sugar, Bentzon v Boyle* (1815) 9 Cranch 191, p 198.

170 Save, possibly, where a federal court is considering boundaries between constituent units; see *Iowa v Illinois* (1893) 147 US 1; *Vermont v New Hampshire* (1933) 289 US 593.

the 19th century and the *Alabama Claims Arbitration* (1872) is normally viewed as an important step forward.[171] Several important arbitrations followed in the period until 1914, either establishing important points of international law or confirming arbitration as a legitimate method of dispute resolution.[172] Since that date, there have been a considerable number of arbitrations that have proved important in clarifying and developing international law.[173] However, in each case the weight to be accorded to the particular award will depend on the quality of the reasoning and the distinction of the individual arbitrator.

8 THE WRITINGS OF PUBLICISTS

Article 38(1)(d) refers as a subsidiary source for determining rules of law 'the teachings of the most highly qualified publicists of the various nations'. Originally, the views of writers and teachers played a significant role in the development of international law and tribunals would wish to be informed of the views of Grotius, Pufendorf, Bynkershoek and Vattel. In the 17th and 18th centuries the works of such writers would be consulted and their statements of opinion might be taken as representing the law. However, in the 19th century this influence declined, partly because writers tended to concentrate on matters of general principle which would be of limited value when specific matters were in issue. The increase in the number of treaty provisions and customary rules tended to curtail such influence. In the 19th century, the textbook would be used to obtain a description of the relevant rules rather to follow the opinion of a distinguished author.[174] Finally, there was a growing realisation that a writer might be influenced by political and cultural connections with a particular state.

---

171 See JB Moore, *International Arbitrations*, 1898, Vol 1, p 653. The *Alabama Arbitration* was established following the Treaty of Washington (May 1871) and concerned United States claims in respect of damage caused to Federal ships during the American Civil War (1861–65) by a vessel built in Liverpool on behalf of the Confederate States. The award made to the United States ($15.5 million) and the manner in which the arbitration was conducted was not well received by public opinion and enabled Benjamin Disraeli to attack WE Gladstone at the General Election of 1874 for failing properly to protect legitimate national interests. See Robert Blake, *Disraeli*, 1966.

172 See *Bering Sea Arbitration (United States v United Kingdom)* (1893) (1898) 1 Moore Int Arbitrations 935; *North Atlantic Fisheries Arbitration* (1910) *(United Kingdom v United States)* 11 RIAA 173. An amusing account of the personalities in this arbitration (who included Elihu Root and Robert Finlay) is provided by Raymond Asquith (1878–1916) (junior counsel) in John Joliffe (ed), *Raymond Asquith: Life and Letters*, 1980.

173 *Tinoco Arbitration (Great Britain v Costa Rica)* (1923) 1 RIAA 369 (Arbitrator Taft CJ: recognition of Governments); *The Island of Palmas Arbitration (Netherlands v United States)* (1928) 2 RIAA 829; 4 ILR 3 (Arbitrator Huber – exhaustive discussion of the principles concerning the acquisition of territory); *Trail Smelter Arbitration (United States v Canada)* (1938/1941) 3 RIAA 1905 (principles of international environmental law).

174 A point made by Lord Alverstone LCJ in *West Rand Mining Company v The Crown* [1905] 2 KB 391.

Thus, if a writer exerted a dominant influence it was normally because he had become the recognised specialist in a particular area of international law.[175]

However, in the absence of a supranational legislature, the legal textbook provides an important vehicle for establishing the basic principles of international law and setting them out in a coherent fashion. When a case involving international law comes before a municipal court, then a judge[176] will certainly wish to consult leading textbooks.[177] In the case of the International Court of Justice, there has been a reluctance to cite writers in majority opinions, but this is not so in dissenting and separate opinions,[178] although, of course, it is common for parties to refer to writers in pleadings and written arguments before the Court.

Another forum in which writers play a part is in debates in the Security Council. On those occasions when a debate is held to review the conduct of a particular state, it is not unusual for the various parties to justify their action by reference to the published works of well known authorities.[179] Strictly speaking, this is not as a source of law but the works of the writer are being drawn upon to advance a particular interpretation of a specific source. Moreover, it is quite common for the views of writers to be cited in diplomatic correspondence, as parties seek to establish the general principle that should govern a particular issue. Perhaps the cardinal reason for the decline in the influence of the individual writer is that the Foreign Ministries of most Governments have their own legal departments and their own 'in-house' body of expertise. In these circumstances, it is more likely that an individual writer will be influential in a particular area rather than across the entire terrain of international law.

It is probably correct to view the process today as one of ongoing discussion and debate between practitioners and writers. The dominant journals on international law are noteworthy for attracting contributions from practitioners, teachers and writers. The volume of material today is such that no one individual could exercise the influence that Vattel exerted in the 18th century. It is, however, well recognised that the textbook on international law performs a valuable function. As Gray J observed in the United States Supreme Court: 'Such works are resorted to by judicial tribunals, not for the speculations

---

175 Eg, Professor Gilbert Gidel, who influenced the development of the modern law of the sea following his *Le Droit international de la mer* (3 vols 1932–34).

176 See the citation of writers in *R v Keyn (The Franconia)* (1876) 2 Ex D 63; the *Eichmann* case (1961) 36 ILR 5 (District Court of Jerusalem); (1962) 36 ILR 277 (Supreme Court of Israel). See Green (1960) 23 MLR 507; Fawcett (1962) 38 BYIL 181. A number of writers were cited by the House of Lords in *R v Bow Street Metropolitan Stipendiary Magistrate ex p Pinochet Ugarte (No 1)* [1998] 3 WLR 1456.

177 In the present century, the leading textbook has probably been Lassa Oppenheim's *International Law*, 1st edn, 1905. For a review by John Westlake, see (1905) 21 LQR 432. For a history of this text see Mark Janis, 'The new Oppenheim and its theory of international law' (1996) 16 OJLS 329. Three of the subsequent editors have served as judges of the International Court of Justice, ie, Arnold McNair (1945–55), Hersch Lauterpacht (1955–60) and Robert Jennings (1982–95).

178 *Asylum (Columbia v Peru)* case (1950) ICJ 266, p 335; *Genocide* case (1951) ICJ 15, p 32; *Aerial Incident* case (1959) ICJ 127, p 174; *Temple of Preah Vihear* case (1962) ICJ 6, p 39.

179 In the June 1981 debate in the Security Council following the Israeli bombing of an Iraqi nuclear reactor at Osarik, near Baghdad, the question arose as to the nature of any right of anticipatory self defence under Art 51 of the United Nations Charter. The Israeli representative drew upon the works of Professor Waldock, Professor Katzenbach and Professor Bowett.

of their authors concerning what the law ought to be, but for trustworthy evidence of what the law really is.'[180] If a municipal court is confronted with a problem on which there is no relevant treaty provision and customary rules are unclear, then the evidence of writers is admitted.[181] Thus, in the Privy Council case of *In Re Piracy Gentium*,[182] Viscount Sankey LC was prepared to review leading writers from the time of Grotius before concluding that actual robbery was not an essential ingredient of the crime piracy *jure gentium*.

It is sometimes argued that writers are liable to be influenced by their own national interest. This fear has been exaggerated. As Clive Parry has noted,[183] international lawyers tend to have been municipal lawyers first and will doubtless be influenced by national legal traditions but, beyond that, there is far less tendency for writers on international law to have been actively involved in political activity than was the case in the time of Grotius or Vattel.[184]

9 ETHICAL PRINCIPLES AND CONSIDERATIONS OF HUMANITY

The problems that arise in respect of ethical principles and considerations of humanity are threefold: (i) such principles vary with the viewpoint of the individual judge; (ii) to some extent, such principles are already reflected in existing legal rules; and (iii) the preambles to many international conventions[185] contain reference to general ethical principles and thus such principles may be subject to the traditional canons of treaty interpretation. To the extent that international law grew out of reflection by philosophers and theologians on the duties of rulers and states, it is not surprising that the case law should include references to ethical principles and considerations of humanity.

An early reference in the post-war world arose in the *Corfu Channel* case,[186] where the court referred to 'elementary considerations of humanity'. While such considerations will not always prevail,[187] there is an increasing readiness to allude to such considerations in giving judgment. This may partly be because of the threats to humanity posed by environmental pollution,[188] terrorist acts, the proliferation of nuclear weapons,[189] or the

---

180 *The Paquette Habana* (1900) 175 US 677, p 700.
181 *New Jersey v Delaware* (1934) 291 US 361; *Banco Nacional de Cuba v Sabbatino* (1964) 376 US 398; see KR Simmonds (1965) 14 ICLQ 452.
182 *In Re Piracy Jure Gentium* [1934] AC 586.
183 Clive Parry, *The Sources and Evidences of Public International Law*, 1965.
184 The remarks made by Arbitrator Huber in the *Spanish Zones of Morocco Claims* (1925) 2 RIAA 615, p 640 would seem to be overstated.
185 See Preamble to the United Nations Charter (1945). In the regional sphere, it is noteworthy how often the European Court of Justice makes reference to the principles set out in the Treaty of Rome (1957) which themselves refer to the United Nations Charter.
186 *Corfu Channel* case (*UK v Albania*) (*The Merits*) (1949) ICJ 4. (The expression was used to indicate the duty of the coastal state to warn of the presence of mines.)
187 See *South West Africa* case (*Second Phase*) (1966) ICJ 6 (but see the dissenting opinion of Judge Tanaka).
188 *Nuclear Tests* case (1995) ICJ 290 (see separate opinions of Judge Koroma, p 342 and Judge Weeramantry, p 368). See R Volterra, 'The *Nuclear Tests* case: avoiding the meta juridical' (1996) 55 CLJ 3.
189 'Legality of the threat of nuclear weapons' (1996) ICJ 226; AV Lowe, 'Shock verdict: nuclear war may or may not be unlawful' (1996) 55 CLJ 415.

difficult problems posed by claims to self-determination.[190] In the period since 1945, the general law of human rights has assumed a growing importance within international law and more emphasis has been placed on general obligations under the United Nations Charter in the context rights to self-determination and matters of discrimination.[191]

However, it is important for an tribunal determining a matter of international law to preserve the distinction between matters *de lege lata* and matters *de lege ferenda*.

10 SOFT LAW[192]

In recent years, considerable attention has focused on those instruments that might be described as 'soft law'. The expression 'soft law' is intended to indicate that the instrument is not in fact 'law' but its importance within international society is such that it is worthy of attention. Soft law can indicate those values and guidelines that may in future emerge as international law. Alternatively 'soft law' may mean those instruments which do not specify concrete legal rights in respect of the legal persons to whom they are addressed. There is a danger that such documents may be so vague as to be meaningless. Essentially the category of 'soft law' inhabits the middle ground between binding legal norms and irrelevant political assertions. The category of 'soft law' is said to comprise certain declarations and recommendations of international organisations as well as resolutions of international conferences. In essence, soft law instruments are concluded by states to combine collective regulation and restraint, but also to permit flexibility and freedom to manoeuvre where events or changing circumstances so require.[193]

Some writers see the development of 'soft law' as the inevitable consequence of an underdeveloped international legal system seeking to cope with problems of growing complexity;[194] others point to the role of 'soft law' in overcoming deadlock in a world often characterised by ideological division.[195] Some have objected to the confusion that can arise by including the word 'law' in respect of something that lacks binding legal character and have regretted the blurring of the distinction between *lex lata* and *de lege ferenda*.[196]

Examples of 'soft law' are afforded by the Helsinki Final Act 1975, the Bonn Declaration on International Terrorism 1978 and the Rio Declaration of the United Nations Conference on Environment and Development 1992. However, the international community is never static and a document having the initial status of 'soft law' may

---

190 *East Timor (Portugal v Australia)* case (1995) ICJ 90 (see dissenting opinion of Judge Weeramantry, p 158); AV Lowe, 'The International Court in a timorous mood' (1995) 54 CLJ 484.

191 These matters will be dealt with under human rights; see Chapters 15 and 16.

192 See generally, I Seidl-Hohenveldern, 'International economic "soft law"' (1979) 163 HR 165; P Weil, 'Towards relative normativity in international law' (1983) 77 AJIL 413; J Gold, 'Strengthening the soft international law of exchange arrangements' (1983) 77 AJIL 443; C Chinkin, 'The challenge of soft law: development and change in international law' (1989) 38 ICLQ 350.

193 See C Chinkin, 'The challenge of soft law: development and challenge in international law' (1989) 38 ICLQ 850.

194 See P Weil, 'Towards relative normativity in international law' (1983) 77 AJIL 413.

195 *Op cit*, Seidl-Hohenveldern, fn 192.

196 DJ Harris, *Cases and Materials on International Law*, 1988, London: Sweet & Maxwell.

develop into forming accepted rules of customary international law[197] or a 'soft law' source may provide the basis for a later treaty.[198]

While it is, of course, important to preserve the distinction between *lex lata* and *de lege ferenda*, the role of 'soft law' is important in structuring international conduct; states may be unwilling to enter into specific legal commitments but may be prepared to indicate consent to general principles as to their future conduct. The fact that a document cannot be enforced before an international tribunal does not mean that it cannot have effect in shaping conduct in international society; indeed, it might be argued that soft law plays a role not dissimilar to that of the constitutional convention in municipal law.[199]

11 OTHER POSSIBLE SOURCES OF INTERNATIONAL LAW

The General Assembly was not established as a law making body. Indeed, operating on the basis of one vote for each state if it had been a legislative body, then a small proportion of the world would have been able to legislate for the majority. The intention was to follow the example of the League of Nations and to stipulate that the General Assembly would operate in an advisory capacity while law making power would reside in the Security Council. The purpose of the body was deliberative and it was never the original intention of the founders of the United Nations that the General Assembly should have power to enact legal obligations directly binding on member states.

However, under the United Nations Charter there are a number of internal matters in which a vote of the General Assembly will have legal effect. Matters such as the setting of the budget, the election of the Security Council and the appointment of judges are all of legal effect and will be considered at the appropriate place. These are all resolutions of internal effect and are not our present concern.

The question arises as to the external legal effect of General Assembly resolutions. One course would be to say that under the Charter the majority of such resolutions do not have direct legal effect. However, such a negative approach has proved unpopular with some writers, particularly those who are impatient with the slow process of establishing rules of customary international law. There has, therefore, been an attempt to reposition General Assembly resolutions within the context of treaties and customary law. A resolution is not a treaty and this approach has not proved fruitful, especially when General Assembly resolutions have been passed with a Treaty annexed.[200]

There has been a tendency to try and fit General Assembly resolutions within the scheme of customary international law. Some General Assembly Resolutions clearly

---

197 It is arguable that the Universal Declaration on Human Rights (1948) had the status of 'soft law' when it was adopted, but now any of its provisions constitute accepted rules of customary international law.

198 The United Nations Declaration on Torture (1975) GA Res 3452 formed the basis for the later Convention Against Torture and Other Cruel, Inhuman or Degrading Treatment or Punishment (1984).

199 For discussion of the role of constitutional conventions in municipal law, see *Madzimbamuto v Lardner-Burke* [1969] AC 645; *Attorney General v Johnathan Cape Ltd* [1976] QB 752; *Reference Re Amendment of the Constitution of Canada* (1982) 125 DLR (3d) 1.

200 Resolution 2222(XXI) with the Treaty of Principles Governing the Activities of States in the Exploration and Use of Outer Space, annexed 19 December 1966.

cannot have this effect. If a Resolution is passed calling for future action to prevent a possible threat to the environment, then such a resolution is simply a call to action exhorting future common effort. As a matter of interpretation, it is not an assertion as to the state of the law. If the Resolution sets out a general principle of law and 160 states vote for it, then it is arguable that this is evidence of state practice and thus of customary international law. However, the weight of such evidence will depend not only on the number of states voting against but also the clarity of the Resolution itself. Unless the Resolution actually asserts that X is the law then the evidentiary value will be limited.

Much will depend on the circumstances and character of the Resolution. One writer[201] has drawn a distinction between: (i) decisions;[202] (ii) recommendations;[203] and (iii) declarations. It is the latter that are said to have a possible law making quality. In some instances, it may be possible to argue that the resolution is declaratory of existing customary international law.[204] Moreover, there will be those situations where the resolution is adopted unanimously where it may be possible to argue that the effect is to crystallise a rule of customary international law. [205] Thirdly, it might be argued that the effect of a resolution is to set aside an existing rule of customary international law although such would require the clearest evidence. It would seem that the effect of a resolution will always be a matter of context, content and circumstances and this was the view alluded to by the International Court of Justice in the 1996 Advisory Opinion on the Legality of the Threat or Use of Nuclear Weapons when they observed:[206]

> General Assembly resolutions, even if not binding may sometimes have normative value. They can, in certain circumstances, provide evidence important for establishing the existence of a rule or the emergence of an *opinio juris*. To establish whether this is true of a given General Assembly resolution, it is necessary to look at its content and the conditions of its adoption; it is also necessary to see whether an *opinio juris* exists as to its normative character. Or a series of resolutions may show the gradual evolution of the *opinio juris* required for the establishment of a new rule.

12 RELATED MATTERS

There are a number of matters that while not sources of international law can be conveniently mentioned at this juncture.

(a) Codification

The expression 'codification' may be used in the narrow sense of 'setting down in comprehensive and ordered form the rules of existing law'.[207] Codification has always

---

201 BF Sloan, 'General Assembly Resolutions revisited' (1987) 58 BYIL 93.
202 Under Art 17 of the UN Charter.
203 Under Art 10 of the UN Charter.
204 Declaration on Principles of International Law concerning Friendly Relations and Co-operation among States (1970) (XXV) (Resolution 2625).
205 Declaration on the Granting of Independence to Colonial Territories and Peoples (1960) (XV) (Resolution 1514).
206 (1996) 35 ILM 809, 826; (1996) ICJ 226.
207 The definition adopted by I Brownlie in *Principles of International Law*, 4th edn, 1990, p 30, and 5th edn, 1998, p 30.

been a process central to civil law jurisdictions. Interest in codification increased in the United Kingdom after the Judicature Acts 1873–75 and much effort was expended on the codification of municipal law in the period prior to 1914.[208]

In the international sphere, interest in codification began at the turn of the century following a number of international conferences.[209] The experience of the First World War prompted thought as to how co-operation might be improved. The advisory committee of jurists which drew up the Statute of the Permanent Court of International Justice in 1920 recommended that efforts be made to promote codification. In 1927, the League of Nations resolved upon a conference to be held in the Hague to consider codification of a number of areas of law. The conference met in 1930 but no agreement was reached.[210]

Article 13 of the Charter of the United Nations provides that the General Assembly shall be active in 'encouraging the progressive development of international law and its codification'. In 1947, the General Assembly voted to establish the International Law Commission.[211] This body comprises 34 members drawn from America, Africa, Asia and Europe. The normal practice is for the International Law Commission to prepare draft articles and then to circulate the papers for comment; when a degree of agreement has been reached, then an international conference will be called and attempts made to secure approval for a treaty. Many post-war law making treaties have resulted from the efforts of the International Law Commission.[212]

The work of the International Law Commission is important, not only because it may lead to a law making treaty, but also because its drafts may serve as evidence of the state of customary law or it may result in such a change of practice as to create new customary law.[213]

(b) Comity

Much of the literature on international law contains references to the concept of 'comity'. The expression has a long history and may be used in a number of different senses. It may

---

208 Bills of Exchange Act 1882; Partnership Act 1890; Marine Insurance Act 1906.

209 See Hague Peace Conferences 1899 and 1907, resulting in the Hague Convention on the Peaceful Settlement of Disputes 1899 as revised in 1907. The first conference had been called by Tsar Nicholas II who had been alarmed by the growth in armaments expenditure and wished to clarify the rules relating to state conduct.

210 See M Hudson (1926) 20 AJIL 656; A McNair (1928) 13 TGS 129; J Reeves (1930) 24 AJIL 52.

211 HW Briggs, *The International Law Commission*, 1965; I Sinclair, *The International Law Commission*, 1987; R Jennings, 'The progressive development of international law and its codification' (1947) 24 BYIL 301; H Lauterpacht (1955) 49 AJIL 16; S Rosenne, 'The International Law Commission 1949–1959' (1960) 36 BYIL 104; R Jennings, 'Recent developments in the International Law Commission' (1964) 13 ICLQ 385.

212 Geneva Convention on the High Seas (1958); Vienna Convention on Diplomatic Relations (1961); Vienna Convention on Consular Relations (1963); Vienna Convention on the Law of Treaties (1969).

213 B Graefrath, 'The International Law Commission tomorrow: improving its organisation and methods of work' (1991) 85 AJIL 597.

be used: (i) as a synonym for international law;[214] or (ii) as simply meaning courtesy in dealing with fellow sovereigns;[215] (iii) it may be employed as the intellectual justification for private international law;[216] (iv) it may be employed as indicating a requirement of public policy;[217] or (v) it may be used as the justification for a particular rule of public international law.[218]

Manifestly, 'comity' is not itself a source. However, the concept is often alluded to in municipal courts when cases of international law arise such as: (i) where a question arises as to sovereign immunity;[219] (ii) where a problem arises as to the legislative acts of a foreign state;[220] or (iii) where a problem arises as to which state should claim jurisdiction or (iv) as a reason for enforcing the public laws of another state. In respect of 'comity', the case law indicates that the meaning of the expression will vary according to the context in which it is employed.

(c) Private international law/the conflict of laws

As the discussion of comity indicates, there is a close relationship between public international law and private international law (often known in the common law world as the conflict of laws). One hundred years ago it would have been said that public international law was concerned with relations between states while private international law was concerned with the problems that arise between individuals and foreign legal systems. Because a case may involve both disciplines it is sensible to draw a number of distinctions.

(i) Public international law is universal in character so that a basic rule should be broadly the same in a court in Germany, the United Kingdom or the United States.

(ii) Private international law is part of national law and governs cases with a foreign element. Being part of municipal law it is subject to domestic conceptions of public policy.[221]

(iii) Private international law is concerned with rights and duties arising between individuals and companies in cases involving a foreign element.

(iv) A significant part of public international law is concerned with relations between states while private international law is concerned with the relationship between jurisdictions or common law districts. Thus, to take an example, the United States

---

214 Probably employed in this sense by Brett LJ in *The Parlement Belge* (1880) 5 PD 197, *per* Brett LJ (as he then was) in the course of a judgment in which he referred to Vattel and Wheaton.

215 In the sense of 'comity of nations' – a meaning much favoured by English judges in the 19th century.

216 As used by Ulric Huber (1636–94) in *De Conflictu Leguum*, 1689, and by Joseph Story (1779–1845) in his *Commentaries on the Conflict of Laws*, 1st edn, 1834, and meaning that private international law is founded on respect for the laws of fellow sovereigns.

217 *Hilton v Guyot* (1895) 159 US 113; *Foster v Driscoll* (1929) 1 KB 470 (where a contract was made to export whisky to the United States in defiance of then then laws on prohibition).

218 *Re AB* (1941) 1 KB 454 (Lord Caldecote LCJ in a case concerning diplomatic immunity); *Krajina v Tass Agency* (1949) 2 All ER 274 (Cohen LJ in a case concerning the nature of state immunity).

219 *The Christina* [1938] AC 485.

220 *Luther v Sagor* [1921] 3 KB 532.

221 *Dynamit AG v Rio Tinto Co* [1918] AC 260.

exists as a state on the international plane and is so regarded in public international law. However, problems might arise as to whether a divorce acquired in California or Texas should be recognised in France or Scotland. The relationship between law districts is governed by the relevant rules of private international law that each municipal law system will possess. It is sometimes said that private international law concerns itself with three questions: (a) does the court of England/France/Scotland have jurisdiction in a particular case; (b) if so, what law should it apply? and (iii) should a judgment given by a court in Texas be recognised and enforced in England/France/Scotland?

It is important to be aware of the nature of private international law because a case coming before a municipal court may raise problems of both public and private international law.[222]

13 HIERARCHY OF SOURCES AND *JUS COGENS*[223]

A matter that naturally arises is whether Art 38 embraces a hierarchy of sources. Article 38(1)(d) is expressly stated to be in a subordinate position. Historically, the role of Art 38(1)(c) is to provide an answer when Arts 38(1)(a) and 38(1)(b) provide no real answer.

A difficulty that arises is as to the relationship between Art 38(1)(a) and Art 38(1)(b). In the event of conflict, a number of presumptions arise. In principle, the later rule will normally prevail over the earlier rule (*lex posterior derogat juri priori*) and a specific rule will normally prevail over a general rule (*lex specialis derogat legem generalis*) The situations in which such a conflict arises are likely to be limited because in the modern world the function of law making treaties is normally to replace or codify customary international law. Although in each specific case it will be for the International Court of Justice to analyse chronologically the evolution of both the customary rule and the treaty provision.

A second matter that requires attention is the principle of *jus cogens*. The basic meaning of the concept of '*jus cogens*' is that of certain fundamental rules of customary international law that are incapable of being modified or derogated from by treaty. The concept is therefore one of non-derogation; the principle derives from those natural law thinkers who argued that treaty provisions were void if they violated the moral law. As an idea, it has some similarity with the concept of public policy that exists in areas of municipal law and plays a significant role in private international law. In the modern world, the concept has been linked to ideas about the common heritage of mankind and it is argued that rules within the *jus cogens* are not subject to the principles concerning persistent objectors in customary international law.[224] In recent years, the concept has attracted more attention because of the two references in the Vienna Convention on the Law of Treaties (1969). Article 53 reads as follows:

---

222 See *Arab Monetary Fund v Hashim (No 3)* [1991] 2 AC 114 (international organisation acquiring personality under the law of foreign state). See, also, *R v Bow Street Magistrate ex p Pinochet Ugarte (No 1)* [1998] 3 WLR 1456, where private international law questions arose as to the principle of non-justiciability.

223 See G Christensen, 'The World Court and *jus cogens*' (1987) 81 AJIL 93.

224 J Charney, 'Universal international law' (1993) 87 AJIL 529.

A treaty is void if, at the time of its conclusion, it conflicts with a peremptory norm of general international law. For the purposes of the present Convention, a peremptory norm of general international law is a norm accepted and recognised by the international community of States as a whole as a norm from which no derogation is permitted and which can be modified only by a subsequent norm of general international law having the same character.

The purpose of the provision is to regulate the relationship between existing *jus cogens* rules and those treaty provisions which at the time of conclusion are in conflict with such rules.

Attention should also be given to Art 64 which is concerned with the situation where a rule of *jus cogens* emerges and is in conflict with an existing treaty provision. The text of Art 64 reads:

If a new peremptory norm of general international law emerges, any existing treaty which is in conflict with that norm becomes void and terminates.

In respect of *jus cogens*, two problems arise, namely: (i) which rules are within the ambit of *jus cogens*?; and (ii) the question as to how rules of *jus cogens* are created. In respect of the first question, there is certainly not complete agreement but it would seem that rules relating to genocide, aggression, torture, slavery and racial discrimination are within the scope of *jus cogens*. The second question, which is linked to the first, concerns how such rules are created. On this, there are a variety of opinions; some writers favour custom while others argue for treaty provisions. Some deny that such rules cannot be founded on natural law, while others would be prepared to deduce rules of *jus cogens* from general principles of law. The concept of such rules was noted by the International Court of Justice in the *North Sea Continental Shelf* cases[225] and in the *Barcelona Traction (Second Phase)* case,[226] the Court drew a distinction between obligations that a state might owe vis à vis another state and obligations existing 'towards the international community as a whole'. The Court observed:

Such obligations derive, for example in contemporary international law, from the outlawing of acts of aggression, and of genocide, as also form the principles and rules concerning the basic rights of the human person, including protection from slavery and racial discrimination.

While in the *Nicaragua* case (*The Merits*)[227] the Court quoted with approval the following statement by the International Law Commission that:

... the law of the Charter concerning the prohibition of the use of force in itself constitutes a conspicuous example of a rule of international law having the character of *jus cogens*.

There is probably a minimum level of agreement that rules of *jus cogens* have to be derived from custom or treaty law. In this context, an interesting question arises as to the relationship with Art 103 of the United Nations Charter. It will be recalled that Art 103

---

225 *North Sea Continental Shelf* cases (1969) ICJ 3, p 42, para 72.

226 *Barcelona Traction (Second Phase)* (1970) ICJ 3, p 32.

227 *Nicaragua* case (*The Merits*) (1986) ICJ 14, p 100, para 190. It is noteworthy that in the Advisory Opinion in the *Legality of Nuclear Weapons* case (1996) ICJ 226, the ICJ did not consider it necessary to consider whether principles of international humanitarian law are part of the *jus cogens* under Art 53.

provides that the provisions of the Charter should prevail over conflicting treaty obligation. The matter was dealt with by Judge Lauterpacht[228] in his 1993 Opinion on a request for provisional measures in the *Case Concerning the Application of the Convention on the Prevention and Punishment of the Crime of Genocide,*[229] where the learned judge observed:

> The concept of *jus cogens* operates as a concept superior to both customary international law and treaty. The relief which Art 103 of the Charter may give the Security Council in case of conflict between one of its decisions and an operative treaty obligation cannot – as a matter of simple hierarchy of norms – extend to a conflict between a Security Council resolution and *jus cogens*. Indeed, one only has to state the opposite proposition thus – that a Security Council resolution may even require participation in genocide – for its unacceptability to be apparent.

While this statement is undoubtedly correct it is equally the case that a Security Council resolution that violated a rule of *jus cogens* might also be *ultra vires* the Charter.

---

228 Sitting as an *ad hoc* judge.
229 (1993) ICJ 325.

CHAPTER 4

INTERNATIONAL LAW AND MUNICIPAL LAW[1]

1 INTRODUCTION

One of the most important topics in public international law is the relationship with the rules of municipal law. Although litigation may take place between individual states before the International Court of Justice, the number of such cases will be limited. Many cases will come before municipal courts giving rise to issues of international law.[2] Indeed, in some areas of public international law, nearly all the relevant case law derives from the municipal courts. Examples might be questions such as whether the courts of state A had jurisdiction to try an individual for a particular offence[3] or whether X is immune from the jurisdiction of the courts of state B,[4] or whether the courts of state C should recognise certain individuals as comprising the government of state D.[5]

It is possible to view the subject as comprised of three central questions, namely: (i) the status of rules of municipal law before international tribunals; (ii) the circumstances in which a rules of public international law will be applied by a municipal court; and (iii) the question as to what is to happen if a rule of municipal law is in conflict with a rule of international law? To put the matter another way, the first and second problems turn on the theoretical question as to whether international law and municipal law are part of a single legal order (monism), or whether they comprise two distinct systems of law (dualism). The third aspect turns upon the question as to what is to happen if there is a conflict in a situation where a case has been brought either before an international tribunal or before a municipal court. Many of the disputes are of a practical and rather mundane nature; for example, fishermen charged under municipal law with unlawful fishing in territorial waters might seek to argue either that the conduct was legitimate under international law or that the waters were not territorial but part of the high seas. So that, in certain instances, a rule of international law might be raised as defence to a charge before a municipal court.[6]

---

1   See generally, M Akehurst, A *Modern Introduction to International Law* (P Malanczuk (ed)), 7th edn, 1997, pp 63–75; I Brownlie, *Principles of Public International Law*, 5th edn, 1998, pp 31–57; Jennings, RY and Watts, AD, *Oppenheim's International Law*, 9th edn, 1992, Vol 1, pp 52–87; M Dixon, *Textbook of International Law*, 4th edn, 2000, pp 82–104; M Shaw, *International Law*, 4th edn, 1997, pp 99–136; I Shearer, *Starke's International Law*, 11th edn, 1994, pp 63–83; A Cassese, 'Modern constitutions and international law' (1985) 192 HR 331; I Sinclair, 'The interpretation of treaties before municipal courts' (1963) 12 ICLQ 508; J Collier, 'Is international law part of the law of England?' (1989) 38 ICLQ 924.

2   As Mr Justice Powell observed in the United States Supreme Court, 'Until international tribunals command a wider constituency, the courts of various countries afford the best means for the development of a respected body of international law': see *First National City Bank v Banco Nacional de Cuba* (1972) 425 US 682, pp 774–75.

3   *Attorney General of Israel v Eichmann* (1961) 36 ILR 5 on appeal; (1962) 36 ILR 277.

4   *R v Bow Street Metropolitan Stipendiary Magistrate ex p Pinochet Ugarte* [2000] 1 AC 147.

5   *Republic of Somalia v Woodhouse, Drake & Carey (Suisse) SA* [1993] QB 54.

6   As in the celebrated 19th century case of *R v Keyn* (1876) 2 Ex D 63, where the Court of Crown Cases Reserved was required to determine whether the Central Criminal Court had jurisdiction to try a German national for manslaughter arising from an incident two and a half miles from Dover Beach.

In respect of municipal law, one means the domestic law of an individual sovereign state. Whether any particular rule constitutes a rule of municipal law is a matter to be determined by the constitutional arrangements of that state. Questions may arise as to the territorial ambit of such law or indeed whether the law of state A should be recognised and applied in the courts of state B. In general terms, municipal law will comprise both primary and secondary legislation together with the principles to be deduced from the judicial decisions of the superior appellate courts. As a matter of language, municipal law may be referred to as domestic law, internal law, national law or state law.

For the purpose of English law, the municipal law of any other country is a question of fact; such factual questions are not the subject of judicial notice and must be proved by expert evidence.[7] The enactment of s 4 of the Civil Evidence Act 1972 has prevented the need for the evidence of foreign law from being repeated in each case.

The relationship between municipal law and international law has been influenced by a number of theoretical issues and it is sensible to say a little about these first.

2 THE RELATIONSHIP BETWEEN INTERNATIONAL LAW AND MUNICIPAL LAW

Historically, there have been two theoretical doctrines that have sought to illuminate the relation between municipal law and international law. These two doctrines are referred to as monism and dualism; both doctrines assume that each legal system (that is, municipal and international law) operates within a common field and that there must be a conflict as to which is to prevail. In the period since 1945, other writers have sought to portray the controversy as unreal and attempted to focus on the actual conduct of municipal courts.

The doctrine of monism represents the older of the two doctrines. Monism holds that both legal systems are part of a single legal structure. The earliest writers on international law tended to be theologians or civil lawyers who viewed international law as being founded upon natural law principles. It was inevitable that such writers should regard international law as part of a single system. Originally, the monist held that the prince and his municipal law was subordinate to a higher law of nations; the idea that the law of nations was a higher law, with legislative power delegated to the state, persisted within monist thought. Thus, the monist considers international law and municipal law to operate within a common field and to be concerned with the same subject matter; it is then argued that, if there is a conflict between the two, then the rules of international law should prevail. A number of writers can be identified as tending towards this viewpoint.[8]

In contrast, the doctrine of dualism is closely associated with the positivist approach to international law. From at least the beginning of the 18th century, the positivist asserted that the international community comprised a number of sovereign, independent and

---

7   See R Fentiman (1992) 108 LQR 142; see, also, R Fentiman, *Foreign Law in English Courts*, 1998. The European Communities Act 1972, s 3(2), provides for the taking of judicial notice by the English courts of Community treaties and the judgments of the European Court of Justice. It is also to be noted that the House of Lords takes cognisance of the law of Scotland and the Privy Council takes cognisance of the laws of the British Commonwealth: *Elliot v Joicey* [1935] AC 209.

8   Hans Kelsen (1881–1973); Hersch Lauterpacht (1897–1960) (Judge of International Court 1955–60).

equal states who consented to a limited number of rules which governed relations within the international community. This analysis placed the individual state and its will at the centre of the argument. Whereas the monist might stress the importance of the individual and his inalienable rights, the positivist asserted that only the state constituted a legal person for the purposes of the Law of Nations. From this viewpoint, the dualist proceeded to argue that international law and municipal law were but two separate systems. The former regulated the relations between states, while the latter was concerned with the relationship between the state and its citizens. The dualist then argued that, as they were two distinct systems, international law only operated in the municipal sphere to the extent that there had been a specific act of adoption by the sovereign state. In the event of a conflict between the two, it was argued that the municipal court should give effect to municipal law.

Dualism therefore was closely associated with a positivist analysis of international law and it increased in importance in the 19th century as philosophers such as Hegel[9] sought to place the state at the centre of their political theory. The doctrine was particularly appropriate in 19th century Europe when nationalist aspirations became a motivating force in foreign policy. To the statesman of the age of *Realpolitik*, such as Cavour and Bismarck, it would certainly have been inconvenient if state conduct had to be answerable to any higher authority. Thus, positivism and its close relation, dualism, tended to be attractive doctrines in 19th century Europe. In England, there was less emphasis on theoretical debates about dualism and monism, partly because of the pragmatic traditions of English law and partly because the doctrine of the legislative supremacy of Parliament had been settled in the Bill of Rights of 1689. The United Kingdom had been a unitary national state since the 17th century and the English constitution, if it had been influenced by political philosophy, then it looked to Locke and notions of limited government rather than to Hegel. Thus, many of the writers asserting a dualist position tended to have a civil law background. The most celebrated exponents are Triepel,[10] Strupp[11] and Anzilotti.[12] According to Triepel, the fundamental differences between municipal law and international law are twofold: first, the subjects of municipal law are individuals while the subjects of international law are states solely and exclusively;[13] and secondly, that the source of municipal law is the will of the state while the source of international law is the common will of states.[14]

The distinction between the two systems was explored by Anzilotti, who contended that each system was founded on a fundamental principle or norm. Municipal law,

---

9   GW Hegel (1770–1831).

10 H Triepel, *Volkerrecht und Landesrecht*, 1899, Berlin.

11 K Strupp, 'Les règles générales du droit de la paix' (1934) 47 HR 257–596.

12 Dionisio Anzilotti (1867–1950) (Judge of PCIJ 1921–30), *Corso di Diritto Internazionale*, 3rd edn, 1928, Vol 1.

13 To some extent, this was not much different to views expressed in the common law world. Thus, John Westlake (1828–1913) could observe in his chapters on the *Principles of International Law*, 1894, that 'international law is the body of rules prevailing between states' while, slightly later, LH Oppenheim (1858–1919) noted in his *International Law*, 1st edn, 1905, that 'states solely and exclusively are the subjects of international law'.

14 Perhaps it is not surprising that jurists in the newly established German Empire (1871) and the recently unified Kingdom of Italy should place emphasis on the role of the state. The Anglo American common law tradition had placed emphasis on the need for a limited government and co-operation between states to ensure a balance of power in Europe.

Anzilotti contended, was founded on the principle that state legislation was to be obeyed while international law was founded on the principle that agreements between states were to be respected; that is, *pacta sunt servanda*. At a later date, in the case of *The Electricity Company of Sofia and Bulgaria*,[15] Anzilotti observed:

> It is clear that, in the same legal system, there cannot at the same time exist two legal rules relating to the same facts and attaching to these facts contradictory consequences ... In cases of this kind, either the contradiction is only apparent and the two rules are really co-ordinated so that each has its own sphere of application and does not encroach on the sphere of application of the other, or else one prevails over the other, that is, is applicable to the exclusion of the other.

Anzilotti therefore favours dualism, in the sense that he accepts two legal systems, but he recognises that the systems deal with two different subject matters, that is, each has its own sphere of application.

In addition to those writers who argue from a dualist standpoint, it is useful to reflect on the actual practice of municipal courts. In a municipal court, the judge will be familiar with the conventional sources of municipal law, such as statutes and precedents; in contrast, when a problem of international law arises, then the judge will be expected to deal with less familiar sources such as treaty provisions and rules of customary international law.

In contrast to those who propound a monist or a dualist view of the relation between municipal and international law, attention in recent years has focused upon a third view that holds that, since municipal law and international operate within a different sphere, then the controversy is unreal. This approach derives from the lectures delivered by Sir Gerald Fitzmaurice at the Hague Academy in 1957 who observed:[16]

> A radical view of the whole subject may be propounded to the effect that the entire monist-dualist controversy is unreal, artificial and strictly beside the point because it assumes something that has to exist for there to be any controversy at all – and which in fact does not exist – namely a common field in which the two legal orders under discussion both simultaneously have their spheres of activity.

According to Fitzmaurice, the two systems cannot conflict because there is no common field of activity. International law he contends operates on the international plane while in the municipal court the domestic law is paramount. It may be that there could be a conflict of obligations but, according to Fitzmaurice, the conflict would be resolved as would a problem in private international law. If there were a conflict between French law and English law, then the rules of English private international law would determine which was to prevail. In cases of a conflict between national law and international law then, Fitzmaurice argues, the national law would remain valid even though its enforcement might expose the state to liability on the international plane. Fitzmaurice was writing in 1957 and he was aware that the relationship between English law and international law was subject to well established rules. Since that date, problems have

---

15 *Electricity Company of Sofia and Bulgaria* (1939) PCIJ, Ser A/B, No 79 .

16 Gerald Fitzmaurice (1900–82) (Legal Adviser, Foreign Office 1953–60) (Judge, ICJ 1960–173). See G Fitzmaurice, 'The general principles of international law considered from the standpoint of the rule of law' (1957) 92 HR 1.

arisen under the European Convention on Human Rights (1950) where an English court has given a judgment and then the substance of the law has been found not to comply with the international obligations of the United Kingdom. In those circumstances, legislation has been introduced to bring English law into line with international obligations.

Views similar to those of Fitzmaurice are also advanced by Rousseau,[17] who places emphasis on international law as a system of co-ordination. Fitzmaurice and Rousseau point to the fact that, in contemporary life, conflicts do not arise and that attention should be directed to the actual practice of the courts.

In the United Kingdom, it is highly unlikely that any such conflict will arise. The expansion in international law since 1945 has been in the form of treaty obligations. As will be seen later, that is a matter governed by well established constitutional rules that reflect a generally dualist approach to international obligations. Fitzmaurice was writing in 1957 and rightly pointed to the actual practice of the courts. Since that date there have been cases in England where an English court has given a judgment and then at a later date the state of the law has been found not to meet the international obligations of the United Kingdom. The normal procedure has been for legislation to be introduced to bring domestic law into line with international obligations.

3 MUNICIPAL LAW BEFORE INTERNATIONAL COURTS AND TRIBUNALS

As noted earlier, it is clear that, in appropriate circumstances, the judgments of a national court may constitute a 'source' of international law.[18] Equally the case law indicates that it will be necessary, in many instances, for an international tribunal to consider the provisions of municipal law[19] and the relevant concepts of domestic legal systems.[20] It is submitted that the two principal questions that give rise to difficulty are:

(i) is the international tribunal required to determine the dispute according to municipal law or international law or both; and

(ii) if the international tribunal is required to determine the dispute in accordance with international law then are statements as to municipal law simply questions of fact.

The central question that arises is as to the extent that a state may prey in aid a provision of municipal law on the international plane. The general rule is that a state may not rely upon a provision municipal law to excuse a breach of international obligations. In the context of treaties, this is made abundantly clear by Art 27 of the Vienna Convention on the Law of Treaties (1969) which reads, in part: 'A party may not invoke the provisions of its internal law as justification for its failure to perform a treaty.'

---

17 C Rousseau, *Droit International Public*, 1953; '*Principes de droit international public*' (1958) 93 HR 369.
18 *The Schooner Exchange v McFaddon* (1812) 7 Cranch 116 ; *The Paquete Habana* (1900) 175 US 677.
19 *The Nottebohm* case (1955) ICJ 5.
20 *Barcelona Traction, Light & Power Co (Second Phase)* (1970) ICJ 3.

Where the international tribunal[21] has been charged with determining a matter according to international law it is clear that obligations arising under international law prevail over the terms of municipal law.[22] Moreover, disabilities under domestic law cannot be regarded as an excuse for non-performance of international obligations.[23] In like terms the European Court of Justice has adopted the same approach under Art 169 of the Treaty of Rome[24] where individual states seek to advance the state of municipal law as a reason for non-compliance with European law.

The principle that a state cannot rely on a provision of its own municipal law to excuse a breach of an international obligation has a long history. In the *Alabama Claims Arbitration* (1872),[25] the United Kingdom was unable to rely on the absence of restraint in its own domestic law when a vessel built at Liverpool for the Confederate forces damaged federal shipping during the American Civil War (1861–65) and thus violated the status of the United Kingdom as a neutral.

There will indeed be those cases where evidence of municipal law is placed before an international tribunal as part of the basic factual material in the dispute; that factual material will need to be absorbed before questions of international law can be determined.[26] There may indeed be cases before an international tribunal where the court is required to answer according to national law. [27] Evidence of national law may be important in determining the conduct of a state[28] and whether that conduct is consistent with international law.[29] However, the fact that an act is unlawful under municipal law does not necessarily render it unlawful under international law.[30]

There may be situations, particularly in regard to concession agreements between a state and a private corporation, where the agreement not only stipulates that disputes should be subject to arbitration but there will be a form of choice of law clause that

---

21 It is, of course, possible for an international tribunal to be charged with determining a case under municipal law ; see the *Serbian Loans* case (1929) PCIJ, Ser A, No 20.

22 *Applicability of the Obligation to Arbitrate* case (1988) ICJ 12, p 34; 82 ILR 225, p 252.

23 *Case concerning Questions of Interpretation and Application of the 1971 Montreal Convention arising from the Aerial Incident at Lockerbie* (1992) ICJ 3, p 22; 94 ILR 478, p 515.

24 Now Art 226 of the Treaty of Amsterdam. The general purpose of the original provision was to enable the European Commission to bring before the European Court of Justice those states that had not met their obligations under European Law. It was quite common for the state in default to allege difficulties under its own domestic law. See Case 39/72, *Commission v Italy* [1973] ECR 101; CMLR 439; Case 167/73, *Commission v French Republic* [1974] ECR 359; 2 CMLR 216; Case 28/81 *Commission v Italy* [1981] ECR 2577.

25 See JB Moore, *History and Digest of International Arbitrations to which the United States has been a Party*, 1898, Vol 1, pp 495, 653. The award was important in the development of the system of arbitration as a method of the peaceful settlement of disputes. However, the arbitration was made more difficult in that case by a failure to give clear instructions to the arbitrators on the matter of compensation.

26 *Certain German Interests in Polish Upper Silesia* case (1926) PCIJ, Ser A, No 7; *Anglo Norwegian Fisheries* case (1951) ICJ 116 (where it was necessary to absorb the history of the municipal law of Norway).

27 *Serbian Loans* case (1929) PCIJ, Ser A, No 20. The PCIJ was concerned with a dispute between French bondholders and the Serb-Croat Government. The Court, having to determine the loan obligations, was required to consider the private international law choice of law question as to whether French or Serbian law should apply to each of the contractual obligations.

28 *Brazilian Loans* case (*France v Brazil*) (1929) PCIJ, Ser A, No 21.

29 *Certain German Interests in Polish Upper Silesia* case (1926) PCIJ, Ser A, No 7.

30 *Elettronica Sicula SpA (ELSI)* (1989) ICJ 15, p 73; 84 ILR 311, p 379.

provides that the arbitrators are to decide according to the national law of the state and the relevant rules of international law.

On a practical level, the concern of each state will be to ensure that its municipal law is in line with its international obligations; a state will be anxious to ensure that its domestic law is in accordance with any United Nations Security Council Resolutions.[31] In recent years, a state will need to ensure that its domestic legislation is in line with the provisions of any regional human rights treaty.[32] Subject to these caveats,the position was well expressed in the *Finnish Ships Arbitration*,[33] where the arbitrators noted:

> As to the manner in which its municipal law is framed, the state has under international law, a complete liberty of action, and its municipal law is a domestic matter in which no other state is entitled to concern itself, provided that the municipal law is such as to give effect to all the international obligations of the state.

4 INTERNATIONAL LAW BEFORE MUNICIPAL COURTS

The status and treatment of international law will differ from state to state. The starting point for any discussion will be the constitutional arrangements of the particular state. In most states, there will be a written constitution, often contained in a single document, and that fundamental text may well refer to how international law is to be treated by the courts of that state.

It is important at this stage to say a little about the terms 'incorporation' and 'transformation'. The doctrine of incorporation holds that a rule of international law will automatically become part of municipal law without any express act of adoption. It is asserted that adoption will operate unless there is some clear provision of statute or precedent that indicates otherwise. In such a situation, a treaty signed and ratified by state A would become binding on the citizens of that state A without any legislation being passed. In some states, the written constitution of the state will provide that rules of international law should automatically become part of municipal law.

In contrast, the doctrine of transformation holds that the rules of international law do not become part of municipal law unless and until there has been an express act of adoption. The rule of international law must be 'transformed' into domestic law. To take an obvious example: if state A entered into a treaty, that instrument would not be given effect to in the courts of state A unless domestic legislation had been enacted to 'transform' it into municipal law.

The doctrine of incorporation holds that international law is automatically part of municipal law while the doctrine of transformation requires a positive act on the part of the state. It is sometimes argued that the two doctrines combine with the related doctrines

---

31 Effected in England under the terms of the United Nations Act 1946.

32 In the United Kingdom there has been the need to ensure that domestic law remains in compliance with the terms of the European Convention on Human Rights (1950) See *Sunday Times Ltd v The United Kingdom* (1979) 2 EHRR 245 and the sequel in the form of the Contempt of Court Act 1981; *Malone v Metropolitan Police Commissioner* [1979] Ch 344; (1984) 7 EHRR 14 and the sequel in the Interception of Communications Act 1985. The Convention now having the force of law in the United Kingdom since the coming into effect of the Human Rights Act 1998.

33 *Finnish Ships Arbitration* (1934) 3 RIAA 1484.

of monism and dualism. The monist holds that international law and municipal law are part of a single system so that incorporation is the logical consequence of this view. In contrast the dualist holds that the two distinct systems of law so it is logical to argue that a rule of international law will not operate within domestic law unless it is transformed into that system.

It is proposed to examine the practice in the United Kingdom and the United States before turning to practice in other states.

(a)   The United Kingdom

It is a matter of common knowledge that the United Kingdom constitution is not to be found in a single document but in a variety of sources. Such sources derive from the 17th century when the Civil War (1642–47) and the ousting of James II (1685–88) enabled Parliament to stipulate the terms of the constitutional settlement in the Bill of Rights of 1689. Since that time, the doctrine of the legislative supremacy of Parliament has been the fundamental doctrine of the English constitution. In respect of public international law, the United Kingdom has drawn a distinction between rules of customary international law and treaty provisions.

Rules of customary international law

In respect of customary rules, the approach of the United Kingdom has been to regard such rules as part of the common law of England providing they are not inconsistent with prior or subsequent statutory provision.

This approach can be traced back to the 18th century and was espoused by William Blackstone (1723–80) when he observed that:[34]

> ... the law of nations, wherever any question arises which is properly the object of jurisdiction is here adopted in its full extent by the common law, and it is held to be a part of the law of the land.

An early judicial reference occurs in *Triquet v Bath*,[35] where Lord Mansfield observed that 'the Law of Nations, in its full extent, was part of the law of England'. The case itself concerned the question whether a domestic servant to the Bavarian Minister to England could claim diplomatic immunity. In giving judgment, Lord Mansfield expressed the view that the Law of Nations had been regarded as part of the law of England by other common law and equity judges such as Lord Talbot,[36] Lord Hardwicke and Lord Chief Justice Holt.

The 18th century approach was that the rules of the Law of Nations would be accepted as part of the law of England provided that they were not contrary to either

---

34   *Commentaries on the Laws of England*, Vol IV, p 55.

35   *Triquet v Bath* (1764) 3 Burr 1478; See also *Heathfield v Chilton* (1767) 4 Burr 2015; *Viveash v Becker* (1814) 3 M & S 284.

36   *Buvoit v Barbuit* (1737) Cas temp Talb 281, where Lord Talbot LC had used the words 'that the law of Nations, in its fullest extent, was part of the law of England'.

statute law or the doctrine of precedent.[37] At this stage the rules of customary law were very limited in scope[38] and being restricted to Western Europe they were rules that the United Kingdom had played a considerable part in formulating.

From the mid-18th century, cases involving points of international law began to arise periodically in the English courts.[39] The Napoleonic wars and the subsequent liberation movements in Latin America generated a considerable volume of litigation in London. In the latter case, much of the litigation arose because of commercial dealings with the unrecognised governments of newly emerging states. During this period, a number of distinguished equity and common law judges expressed the view that the rules of customary law were part of the law of England. Both Lord Eldon LC in *Dolder v Huntingfield*[40] and Lord Ellenborough CJKB in *Woolf v Oxholm*[41] assumed that the rules of customary law were part of the law of England. A generation later, similar views were expressed by Abbott CJ in *Novello v Toogood*[42] and by Best CJ in *De Wutz v Hendricks*.[43] In the latter case, where the court refused to enforce a contract of loan designed to aid the Greeks in revolt against Ottoman rule, Best CJ observed:

> It occurred to me at the trial that it was contrary to the law of nations (which in all cases of international law is adopted into the municipal code of every civilised country) for persons in England to enter into engagements to raise money to support the subjects of a government in amity with our own, in hostilities against their governments.[44]

So that it was evident by mid-century that certain rules of customary international law would be applied by an English court provided that they did not conflict with statutory provisions or the emerging doctrine of precedent.

A sensitivity to questions of international law can be detected in mid-century particularly in relation to questions pertaining to sovereign immunity.[45] At this point, it would probably have been said that English law adopted the incorporation doctrine.

---

37 It was not until the restructuring of the court system after 1873 that the doctrine of precedent became so important, as the House of Lords became the final court of appeal. See *Beamish v Beamish* (1861) 9 HLC 274; *London Street Tramways v London County Council* [1894] AC 489.

38 Concerned with questions such as sovereign and diplomatic immunity, the law of the sea and the law of war.

39 There had been some cases arising from the American War of Independence (1776–83): *Wright v Nutt* (1789) 1 H Bl 137; *Folliot v Ogden* (1789) 1 H Bl 123; *Ogden v Folliot* (1790) 3 TR 726 (where Lord Loughborough was concerned with a matter within the province of private international law, namely whether the English court should recognise the legislative acts of a New York legislature).

40 The influence of Lord Eldon (LC 1801–06, 1807–27) in this area of law was considerable; see *City of Berne v Bank of England* (1804) 9 Ves Jun 347.

41 *Woolf v Oxholm* (1817) 6 M & S 92, pp 100–06.

42 *Novello v Toogood* (1823) 1 B & C 554.

43 *De Wutz v Hendricks* (1824) 2 Bing 314.

44 In strict terms, this would be regarded today as a case in private international law since it raised the question as to whether a contract should not be enforced in England because it prejudiced the relations of the United Kingdom with a foreign state. See, also, *Foster v Driscoll* [1929] 1 KB 470. Such cases turn on English law conceptions of public policy.

45 *Duke of Brunswick v King of Hanover* (1844) 6 Beav 1, (1848) 2 HLC 1; *Emperor of Austria v Day & Kossuth* (1861) 2 Giff 628; 30 LJ Ch 690 (Stuart VC) affirmed, (1861) 3 De GF & J 217; *The Charkieh* (1873) LR 8 QB 197 ('the questions raised relate to international law which is recognised by the municipal law of this country').

A question then arose as to whether adherence to the incorporation doctrine was unsettled by the judgment in *R v Keyn (The Franconia)*.[46] The facts of the case were as follows.

A German vessel, *The Franconia,* collided with and sank an English vessel within three miles of the English coast; loss of life resulted. The German captain was indicted and convicted of the manslaughter of an English passenger at the Central Criminal Court. The question for the Court of Crown Cases Reserved was whether the court had jurisdiction to try the offence.

The case itself is not a model of clarity. It was originally argued before six judges who being divided then adjourned to allow the case to be reargued before 14 judges who later delivered 13 judgments. [47]

By a majority, the Court of Crown Cases Reserved considered that the Central Criminal Court lacked jurisdiction to try the offence. At the time some writers considered that the judgment placed doubt on the principle that rules of customary international law were automatically incorporated into English law. This is a misreading of the case and there is nothing in the judgments that warrants such an inference.[48] The questions properly formulated might be expressed as follows: (i) did customary international law permit a maritime belt of three nautical miles?; (ii) if so, did that carry with it the right to exercise criminal jurisdiction?; (iii) if so was that criminal jurisdiction exercised at common law?; (iv) if not, should such criminal jurisdiction be exercised in the absence of statute. The conclusion of the majority did not cast doubt on the incorporation doctrine.

The question of the status of customary international law was reviewed in the subsequent case of the *West Rand Mining Co v R*,[49] where the facts were as follows.

The plaintiffs owned gold that was taken over by the Transvaal Republic. the territory of which was conquered during the Boer War (1899–1902), and the plaintiffs alleged that the Crown was liable for the gold. It was argued: (i) that a rule of customary international law existed that a conquering state was liable for the contractual obligations of a conquered state; (ii) that customary international law was part of the law of England; (iii) that such a principle had been previously recognised in English case law.

The High Court dismissed the application of the plaintiffs. In a much quoted judgment, Lord Alverstone LCJ explained:

It is quite true that whatever has received the common consent of civilised nations must have received the assent of our country, and that to which we have assented along with other nations in general may properly be called international law, and as such will be acknowledged and applied by our municipal tribunals when legitimate occasion arises for those tribunals to decide questions to which doctrines of international law may be relevant. But any doctrine so invoked must be one really accepted as binding between nations, and

---

46 *R v Keyn (The Franconia)* (1876) 2 Ex D 63.
47 Archibald J died after the argument (June 1876) but before judgment was delivered (November 1876).
48 As Lord Alverstone LCJ pointed out in *West Rand Central Gold Mining Co v R* [1905] 2 KB 391, p 408.
49 *Ibid* (Lord Alverstone LCJ, Wills and Kennedy JJ).

the international law sought to applied must, like anything else, be proved by satisfactory evidence.[50]

It is clear that the Divisional Court approved the incorporation doctrine in respect of rules of customary international law and any doubt caused by *R v Keyn* was silenced by the express approval given to the case. Lord Alverstone LCJ made it clear that while customary law was to be proved by evidence of actual conduct, the mere opinion of text book writers would not be sufficient. So the *West Rand*[51] case established that a rule of customary international law would be applied if it can be demonstrated upon evidence. The question, however, arose as to what was to happen if the rule conflicted with a provision of domestic law; that difficulty fell to be considered in the case of *Mortensen v Peters;*[52] the facts of the case were as follows.

A Danish captain was prosecuted under a bylaw for fishing in the Moray Firth. The vessel was in the area stipulated by the bylaw but beyond the three mile limit sanctioned by international law. The Danish captain was convicted and he appealed to the High Court of Justiciary.

In dismissing the appeal, the High Court of Justiciary emphasised that any rule of customary international law would have to yield to the clear words of any Act of Parliament.[53]

So that, by 1914 at the latest, the case law established that a rule of customary international law would be incorporated, save in those case where it conflicted with a provision of primary legislation. In the next two decades, the case law coming before English courts was consistent with this approach.[54] A classic statement of the position was made by Lord Atkin in *Chung Chi Cheung v R* where the learned judge observed:[55]

> The Courts acknowledge the existence of a body of rules which nations accept among themselves. On any judicial issue they seek to ascertain what the relevant rules is, and having found it, they will treat it as incorporated into domestic law, so far as it is not inconsistent with rules enacted by Statutes or finally declared by their tribunals.

His Lordship was indicating that any rule required to be proved by appropriate evidence. Often this will involve historical research. Thus, in the case of *Re Piracy Jure Gentium,*[56] the Privy Council were prepared to consider the writings of Grotius, Hall, Moore and Wheaton, in addition to the common law authorities of Coke, Blackstone, Hale and Hawkins. In the subsequent case of *The Cristina,*[57] Lord Macmillan indicated that

---

50 [1905] 2 KB 391, pp 406–07.

51 It is of some interest that R Finlay QC appeared in the case; he would become the first United Kingdom judge in the PCIJ.

52 *Mortensen v Peters* (1906) 8 F (J) 93.

53 The operative legislation being the Herring Fishery (Scotland) Act 1889 and the Sea Fisheries Regulation (Scotland) Act 1895.

54 *Commercial and Estates Co of Egypt v Board of Trade* [1925] 1 KB 271; 2 ILR 423; *The Fagernes* (1927) P 311; *Re Piracy Jure Gentium* [1934] AC 556, p 588; *The Christina* [1938] AC 485; *The Arantzazu Mendi* [1939] AC 256.

55 *Chung Chi Cheung v R* [1939] AC 160 (PC); 9 ILR 264.

56 *Re Piracy Jure Gentium* [1934] AC 556 (PC) (Viscount Sankey LC, Lords Atkin, Macmillan, Tomlin and Wright).

57 *The Cristina* [1938] AC 485.

evidence of customary law would be sought in 'authoritative textbooks, practice and judicial decisions'.

However, while it is clear that an English court will consult a variety of sources, it is also clear that the evidence must go as far as to establish the existence of the rule; it is not sufficient merely to show textbook opinion. A sceptical note was sounded by Lawton LJ when, in reflecting on customary international law in *R v Secretary of State for the Home Department ex p Thakrar*,[58] the learned judge observed:

> In this sphere of jurisprudence there has been no Moses to bring the Law of Nations down from Mount Sinai. As with Mosaic law, there have been many learned doctors to comment on it, but without a Moses there is something lacking ... But when anyone in the United Kingdom seeks to enforce against the Crown what he alleges is a right arising under public international law, the courts have to decide what is the nature and extent of the right and whether there are any limitations imposed on it by statute.

The difficulty for an English court will be to ascertain whether there is sufficient evidence to demonstrate: (i) that a customary rule exists; (ii) that it can be formulated with precision; and (iii) that it has been accepted by the United Kingdom and a considerable number of states. As Lord Atkin had expressed the matter in *Chung Chi Cheung v The King*:

> It must be always remembered that, so far, at any rate, as the courts of this country are concerned, international law has validity save in so far as its principles are accepted and adopted by our own domestic law.[59]

Subsequent case law in the English courts has proceeded on the basis that rules of customary international law will be incorporated and form part of the common law.[60]

On the assumption that incorporation is the correct principle, difficulties can arise with the doctrine of precedent. Since 1898[61] at the latest, the English courts have adhered to a strict doctrine of precedent. Problems can therefore arise if the Court of Appeal decides in 1936 that X represents a rule of customary international law and the same question arises in 1976 when the rule of customary international law may have changed. Is the notional Court of Appeal in 1976 bound by the ruling in 1936 or should it give effect to the newly established rule of customary international law? This was particularly a problem after 1945 when customary rules on sovereign immunity were subject to change.

In *Thai-Europe Tapioca Service Ltd v Government of Pakistan*,[62] a strong Court of Appeal held that once a rule of international law had been incorporated into English law by a decision of a competent court, the principle of *stare decisis* applies. However this approach was rejected by a differently constituted Court of Appeal in *Trendtex Trading Corporation v*

---

58 *R v Secretary of State for the Home Department ex p Thakrar* [1974] 1 QB 684, p 709.

59 Cited with approval by Lord Denning MR in *ibid*, p 701.

60 See *R v Bow Street Magistrates ex p Pinochet (No 1)* [1998] 3 WLR 1456; *R v Bow Street Magistrates ex p Pinochet (No 3)* [1999] 2 WLR 272.

61 *London Street Tramways v London County Council* [1898] AC 489.

62 *Thai Europe Tapioca Service Ltd v Government of Pakistan* [1975] 1 WLR 1485 (Denning MR, Scarman LJ, Lawton LJ). Interestingly, Lord Denning MR did not express a view on this point: [1975] 3 All ER 961; 64 ILR 81.

Central Bank of Nigeria;[63] the case itself turned on the narrow issue as to whether the Central Bank of Nigeria was entitled to claim sovereign immunity. Lord Denning MR and Shaw LJ rejected the application of the principle of *stare decisis*. As Shaw LJ observed: '... the true principle as to the application of international law is that the English courts must at any given time discover what the prevailing international law rule is and apply that rule.' In this context, it is important to remember that much of the case law in the post-war period concerned the extent to which a defence of sovereign immunity could be claimed in respect of commercial activities. Some English judges were anxious to ensure that English case law reflected the general movement towards restrictive immunity; such a movement was not possible if the English court remained bound by the doctrine of precedent.[64]

That the incorporation doctrine represents the dominant view is evidenced by the Court of Appeal judgments in *Maclaine Watson v The Department of Trade*.[65] Both Nourse LJ and Kerr LJ accepted that a rule of customary international law, properly formulated, would become part of English law, although the two judges differed as to the precise formulation of the rule. Further support for the incorporation view is to be found in the various judgments in *R v Bow Street Metropolitan Magistrate ex p Pinochet Ugarte (Nos 1 and 3)*, where several of the judges referred to 'the requirements of customary international law, which are observed and enforced by our courts as part of the common law';[66] further, the case contains support for the view that rules of customary international law are not subject to the doctrine of *stare decisis*.[67]

So the position in English law as regards rules of customary international law may be summarised thus: (a) a rule customary international law will be applied as part of the common law;[68] (b) that such a rule will have to be formulated with precision and proved by evidence;[69] (c) that any such rule is not subject to the doctrine of *stare decisis*;[70] (d) that such a rule will not be applied in the face of conflicting primary legislation.[71]

The status of treaties

Rules of customary international tend to develop gradually and normally depend on the actual conduct of a number of states. In contrast, treaties may be negotiated speedily and they are often influenced by the conduct of the executive branch of government. The

---

63 *Trendtex Trading Corporation v Central Bank of Nigeria* [1977] 1 QB 529; 1 All ER 881; 2 WLR 356 (Lord Denning MR, Shaw and Stephenson LJJ).

64 *Rahimtoola v Nazim of Hyderabad* [1958] AC 379; *Thai-Europe Tapioca Service Ltd v Government of Pakistan* [1975] 1 WLR 1485; *Trendtex Trading Corporation v Central Bank of Nigeria* [1977] QB 529; *The Philippine Admiral* [1977] AC 373.

65 *Maclaine Watson v The Department of Trade* [1988] Ch 1 (Millett J); [1989] Ch 253 (Kerr LJ, Nourse LJ, Ralph Gibson LJ); [1990] 2 AC 418 (House of Lords, where the claim was said to turn on treaty rights).

66 *R v Bow Street Metropolitan Stipendiary Magistrate ex p Pinochet (No 1)* [1998] 3 WLR 1456; *(No 3)* [1999] 2 WLR 272; the phrase itself derives from the dissenting speech of Lord Lloyd of Berwick at [1998] 3 WLR 1456, p 1482.

67 See [1998] 3 WLR 1456, p 1471, *per* Lord Slynn of Hadley.

68 *Maclaine Watson v The Department of Trade* [1989] Ch 253.

69 *West Rand Central Gold Mining Co v R* [1905] 2 KB 391.

70 *Trendtex Trading Corporation v Central Bank of Nigeria* [1977] QB 529.

71 *R v Secretary of State for the Home Department ex p Thakrar* [1974] QB 684.

difference between the two sources became more acute as the volume of treaties began to grow in the 19th century. However, by that date, the doctrine of the legislative supremacy of Parliament had already been established. One of the legacies of the Civil War (1642–49) and the Bill of Rights (1689) had been the acceptance that only Parliament could legislate. In general, treaties are negotiated, signed and ratified under the terms of the exercise of the royal prerogative in foreign affairs.[72] However, if such a treaty were to operate automatically in England, then it would mean that the executive branch could change the law without reference to Parliament.

Thus, it is well established that treaties that seek to: (i) modify common law or statute; (ii) change the rights of British subjects; (iii) cede territory; (iv) vest additional powers in the crown; or (v) impose additional financial obligations upon subjects, then such treaties must receive Parliamentary assent. Where implementing legislation is required, then the terms of the enactment must be unambiguous.[73]

One of the clearest examples of the principle arose in the years after 1970, when it became common for litigants in England to refer a judge to the provisions of the European Convention on Human Rights and Fundamental Freedoms (1950). The court would be obliged to point out that the document had the status of an unincorporated treaty and thus could not be a source of legal rights and duties;[74] although some judges were influenced by the relevant jurisprudence in seeking to fill gaps in the common law, this stopped short of developing new rights.

The United Kingdom therefore takes a dualist approach to treaty obligations. This is partly explained by history and partly because treaty obligations arise from the act of the executive branch alone. The principle that an unincorporated treaty cannot be the source of legal rights was established beyond doubt in the *Parlement Belge*[75] where the relevant facts were as follows.

A British tug was in collision with the *Parlement Belge*, a vessel belonging to the King of Belgium which was used for taking cargo. The owners of the tug brought an action against the *Parlement Belge* and her freight. The Attorney General intervened asserting that an 1876 agreement with Belgium provided for immunity in respect of commercial vessels on the same basis as warships.

Phillimore J ruled that while immunity might arise under the rules of customary international law, no such immunity could be created or extended by treaty unless that treaty was itself given effect to in domestic law. The view that an unincorporated treaty could not change domestic law was reiterated by Lord Atkin in *Attorney General for Canada v Attorney General for Ontario*,[76] where he observed that 'the making of a treaty is

---

72 *R v Foreign Secretary ex p Rees Mogg* [1994] QB 552; G Marshall [1993] PL 402; R Rawlings (1994) PL 254.

73 *Republic of Italy v Hambros Bank* [1950] Ch 314.

74 *Malone v Metropolitan Police Commissioner* [1979] Ch 344; (1984) 7 EHRR 14; *AG v Guardian Newspapers Ltd (No 2)* [1990] 1 AC 109; *R v Secretary of State for the Home Department ex p Brind* [1991] 1 AC 696; *Derbyshire County Council v Times Newspapers Ltd* [1992] 1 QB 777 (CA); [1993] AC 534. This would, of course, not now be the position after the coming into effect of the Human Rights Act 1998.

75 The judgment of Phillimore J (1879) 4 PD 129 was set aside by the Court of Appeal (Brett LJ, Baggallay LJ, James LJ) (1880) 5 PD 197 on other grounds.

76 *Attorney General for Canada v Attorney General for Ontario* [1937] AC 326.

an executive act, while the performance of its obligations, if they entail alteration of domestic law, requires legislative action'. The subsequent case law supports this broad statement.[77] The traditional approach of English courts was recently stated by Lord Templeman in *JH Rayner Ltd v The Department of Trade*:[78]

> A treaty is a contract between the governments of two or more sovereign states. International law regulates the relations between sovereign states and determines the validity, the interpretation and the enforcement of treaties. A treaty to which Her Majesty's Government is a party does not alter the laws of the United Kingdom. A treaty may be incorporated into and alter the laws of the United Kingdom by means of legislation. Except to the extent that a treaty becomes incorporated into the laws of the United Kingdom by statute, the courts of the United Kingdom have no power to enforce treaty rights and obligations at the behest of a sovereign government or at the behest of a private individual.[79]

In the same case,[80] Lord Oliver stressed the non-justiciability of untransformed treaties and held that the court should not pay regard to an untransformed treaty to determine the substantive legal rights of the parties. This approach follows logically from the status of the untransformed treaty. The *Tin Council* case[81] centred upon the legal personality in municipal law of an organisation established by international treaty and is discussed further in Chapter 23. The case itself was followed shortly after by *Arab Monetary Fund v Hashim (No 3)*,[82] which concerned the entitlement of the Arab Monetary Fund to sue in England; the Arab Monetary Fund was an international organisation established under an untransformed treaty. The House of Lords in restoring the first instance judgment of Hoffmann J allowed the Arab Monetary Fund to sue in England, on the basis that the rules of private international law allowed English law to recognise the granting of legal personality to the Arab Monetary Fund by the laws of another foreign state.[83]

In *Arab Monetary Fund v Hashim (No 3)*,[84] the conflict of laws solution required the recognition of international organisations incorporated under the municipal law of another state. However, this did not resolve the question of what would happen if the international organisation arising under an untransformed treaty was subject to different treatment in other sovereign states. In *Westland Helicopters Ltd v Arab Organisation for Industrialisation*,[85] this problem fell to be considered, The Arab Organisation for

---

77 *Republic of Italy v Hambros Bank Ltd* [1950] Ch 314; *James Buchanan & Co Ltd v Babco Forwarding and Shipping (UK) Ltd* [1978] AC 141; *Malone v Metropolitan Police Commissioner* [1979] Ch 344; *Fothergill v Monarch Airlines Ltd* [1981] AC 251; *R v Secretary of State for the Home Department ex p Brind* [1991] 1 AC 696; *Derbyshire County Council v Times Newspapers Ltd* [1993] AC 534.

78 *JH Rayner Ltd v Department of Trade* [1990] 2 AC 418.

79 [1990] 2 AC 418, at p 476, *per* Lord Templeman.

80 *JH Rayner Ltd v Department of Trade* [1990] 2 AC 418.

81 *JH Rayner Ltd v Department of Trade* [1990] 2 AC 418. (In this case, the House of Lords was prepared to find that personality in municipal law arose because of a statutory instrument made under the International Organisations Act 1968.)

82 *Arab Monetary Fund v Hashim (No 3)* [1991] 2 AC 114 (the case is discussed further in Chapter 23).

83 The Arab Monetary Fund had been granted legal personality under the laws of the United Arab Emirates. In the *Tin Council* case, the United Kingdom had been a party to the untransformed treaty and a statutory instrument had been made under the International Organisations Act 1968. In the *Arab Monetary Fund* case, the United Kingdom had not been a party to the treaty and no statutory instrument had been made.

84 [1991] 2 AC 114.

85 *Westland Helicopters Ltd v Arab Organisation for Industrialisation* [1995] QB 283.

Industrialisation (AOI) had been established as an international organisation in a regional treaty in 1975; however, in 1979 several of the state parties withdrew and the AOI was continued by subsequent provisions made under Egyptian municipal law. At a later date, a judgment creditor under an international arbitration obtained garnishee orders against bank deposits of the AOI; at that point, the AOI as constituted under Egyptian law sought to set aside the garnishee orders. It was argued, following *Hashim*, that as the AOI had been incorporated under Egyptian law it should be so recognised in England. This was rejected by Coleman J, who ruled that the incorporation within a sovereign state of an international organisation that arose under an untransformed treaty did not prevent the proper law of the agreement being public international law. Further, the learned judge argued that questions of breach of the original treaty or the continuation of the organisation were questions of public international law pertaining to the conduct of sovereign states and thus non-justiciable before a municipal court. Consequently, as the reconstituted AOI could not show itself to be the original organisation, then it had no entitlement to seek to set aside the garnishee orders.

These three cases[86] indicate the difficulties that can arise in respect of the untransformed treaty. In the *Tin Council* case,[87] legal personality arose by virtue of a statutory instrument made in municipal law; in *Arab Montary Fund v Hashim (No 3)*,[88] legal personality arose by recognition of the legislative act of another sovereign state; in *Westland v Arab Organisation for Industrialisation*, an international organisation arising under an untransformed treaty did not cease to be subject to international law simply because it had been incorporated within the municipal law of a single state.

Having regard to the importance of democratic scrutiny, it is the practice of the United Kingdom government to lay before Parliament copies of all treaties which it has signed or intends to accede to. Under the terms of the Ponsonby rule which pertains to treaties that have been signed but require ratification to come into effect, the executive notifies Parliament of the treaty and will not ratify it (save in cases of emergency) until 21 working days have elapsed.[89]

While ratification of treaties is effected under the prerogative, some legislative restraints exist. The European Parliamentary Elections Act 1978 stipulates that no treaty providing for an increase in the powers of the European Parliament shall be ratified by the executive without first being approved by Act of Parliament.[90]

Where legislation has been enacted, there is a well established presumption of statutory construction that the enactment is to be interpreted as far as possible to give

---

86 Ie, *JH Rayner Ltd v Department of Trade* [1990] 2 AC 418; *Arab Monetary Fund v Hashim (No 3)* [1991] 2 AC 114; *Westland Helicopters Ltd v Arab Organisation for Industrialisation* [1995] QB 283.

87 *JH Rayner Ltd v Department of Trade* [1990] 2 AC 418.

88 *Arab Monetary Fund v Hashim (No 3)* [1991] 2 AC 114.

89 HC Deb 1 April 1924 cols 2001–04. The practice is named after a Mr Arthur Ponsonby who served as Under Secretary of State for Foreign Affairs. In order to improve the mechanism of scrutiny, on 16 December 1996 the Under Secretary for Foreign Affairs informed the House of Commons that from 1 January 1997 every international agreement laid under the Ponsonby Rule would be accompanied by an explanatory memorandum, the purpose of which would be to bring more clearly to the attention of Parliament the main features of the treaty in question.

90 European Parliamentary Elections Act 1978, s 6; see *R v Secretary of State for Foreign Affairs ex p Rees Mogg* [1994] QB 552.

effect to international obligations. However, there are limits to this principle; as Diplock LJ observed in *Salomon v Commissioners of Customs and Excise*:[91]

> If the terms of the legislation are clear and unambiguous, they must be given effect to, whether or not they carry out Her Majesty's treaty obligations, for the sovereign power of the Queen in Parliament extends to breaking treaties ... and any remedy for such a breach of an international obligation lies in a forum other than Her Majesty's own courts. But if the terms of the legislation are not clear but are reasonably capable of more than one meaning, the treaty itself becomes relevant, for there is a *prima facie* presumption that Parliament does not intend to act in breach of international law, including therein specific treaty obligations; and if one of the meanings which can reasonably be ascribed to the legislation is consonant with the treaty obligations and another or others are not, the meaning, which is consonant is to be preferred ...

Thus, in cases where the enactment is unambiguous the statute will prevail over the treaty.[92] However, where more than one interpretation is possible, then the court will normally seek to find an interpretation consistent with international law.[93] This desire to act in conformity with international law means that the courts are prepared to consult *travaux preparatoires*.[94] In recent years, it has been noticeable that English courts will be particularly vigilant where the statute gives effect to a treaty that is intended to establish an international legal order;[95] in such circumstances, the English judge will expect to be referred to foreign case law interpreting the same provisions.[96]

(b)   The United States

Although the United Kingdom and the United States share a number of historical, cultural, legal and linguistic links, it has to be borne in mind that the United States is a federal state operating under the terms of a written constitution.[97] Thus, while the two countries broadly adopt the same approach to questions of international law, there are a number of important differences.[98]

---

91   [1967] 2 QB 116, p 143.

92   *Republic of Italy v Hambros Bank Ltd* [1950] Ch 314; *Collco Dealings Ltd v IRC* [1962] AC 1; *The Banco* (1971) P 137.

93   *Salomon v Commissioners of Customs & Excise* [1967] 2 QB 116; *Corocraft Ltd v Pan American Airways Inc* [1969] 1 QB 616; *Fothergill v Monarch Airlines Ltd* [1981] AC 251.

94   *James Buchanan & Co Ltd v Babco Forwarding and Shipping (UK) Ltd* [1978] AC 141.

95   *Sidhu v British Airways plc* [1997] 2 WLR 26 (Warsaw Conventions 1929, 1955).

96   *Re H (Minors) (Abduction: Acquiesence)* [1998] AC 72; [1997] 2 WLR 26 (where Lord Browne-Wilkinson stressed the importance of uniformity of interpretation in cases arising under the Hague Convention on the Civil Aspects of International Child Abduction (1980), given effect to under the Child Abduction and Custody Act 1985). As the learned judge pointed out, if national courts applied different criteria then the whole purpose of the Convention would be undermined.

97   Unlike the United Kingdom, which is a unitary state without a single written document operating under a constitution drawn from a number of sources.

98   Of course, both are common law countries who support the principle of the rule of law in the conduct of international relations. Of more practical importance is that both played a significant part in the establishment of the United Nations (1945) and are permanent members of the Security Council.

From the outset of the American Republic, both the executive and the judicial branches of government paid particular regard to the Law of Nations.[99] References to the Law of Nations are to be found in judgment of Marshall CJ in *The Schooner Exchange v McFaddon*,[100] while the classic exposition as to the general approach is to be found in the judgment of Gray J in *The Paquette Habana*,[101] where the learned judge observed:

> International law is part of our law, and must be ascertained and administered by the Courts of Justice of appropriate jurisdiction, as often as questions of right depending upon it are duly presented for their determination. For this purpose, where there is no treaty and no controlling executive or legislative act or judicial decision, resort must be had to the customs and usages of civilised nations ...

Thus, the conventional view was that rules of international law were deemed part of national law and thus binding on both federal and state courts. However, a rule of customary international law will yield to a direct congressional act,[102] although it is normally presumed that legislation will have been passed with the intention of complying with international law unless the contrary has been expressly stated.[103]

From the outset, the United States position in respect of customary international law was one of incorporation and federal courts tended to follow their own previous judgments. This did begin to cause difficulties in the area of sovereign immunity when the trend in customary international law began to move in favour of the doctrine of restrictive immunity.[104]

However, a rule of customary law will not prevail over express words in congressional legislation. In *Tag v Rogers*,[105] the Court of Appeals observed that 'there is no power in this Court to declare null and void a statute adopted by Congress ... merely on the ground that such a provision violates a principle of international law'. A generation later, the Court of Appeals noted that 'no enactment of Congress can be challenged on the ground that it violates customary international law'.[106]

In the last 20 years, there have been a number of cases brought before the United States courts where a party has alleged abuse of human rights by a foreign government. In such circumstances, the plaintiffs might seek to rely on rules of customary international law. In some circumstances, this might involve probing allegations of tortious acts

---

99   As instanced by James Madison (Secretary of State (1801–09; President 1809–17), who had studied Vattel and wrote a pamphlet on an aspect of international law while serving as Secretary of State under Thomas Jefferson; Madison had, of course, drawn on European political theory when drawing up the United States Constitution (1787). The establishment of the Republic and its early adherence to the Law of Nations served to broaden the European basis of the subject. Some research has now been done on the question on the effect of borrowing both European political theory and also the Law of Nations; see N Onuf 'Civitas Maxima: Wolff, Vattel and the fate of republicanism' (1994) 88 AJIL 280.

100 *The Schooner Exchange v McFaddon* (1812) 7 Cranch 116.

101 *The Paquette Habana* (1900) 175 US 677, p 700.

102 *Committee of United States Citizens Living in Nicaragua v Reagan* (1988) 859 F 2d 929.

103 *Murray v Schooner Charming Betsy* (1804) 6 US (2 Cranch) 64; *Schroeder v Bissell* (1925) 5 F 2d 838; *Cook v United States* (1933) 288 US 102; *Weinberger v Rossi* (1982) 456 US 25.

104 *Beirzzi Bros v The SS Pesaro* (1925) 271 US 562; (1925–26) 3 AD 186 following *The Schooner Exchange v Mcfaddon* (1812).

105 *Tag v Rogers* (1959) 267 F 2d 664, p 666; 28 ILR 467.

106 *Committee of United States Citizens Living in Nicaragua v Reagan* (1988) 859 F 2d 929, p 939.

committed abroad. Thus, in *Filartiga v Pena Irala*,[107] the Court of Appeals held that torture committed in Paraguay constituted a breach of customary international law sufficient to confer jurisdiction on the domestic courts of the United States. At a subsequent hearing, the District Court held that the relevant law to be applied was that of the law of nations not that of Paraguay.[108]

While there has been an increasing tendency to bring claims against foreign governments in the court of the United States, many such actions have been met by a defence of sovereign immunity.[109] Thus, in the United States it can be said that a rule of customary international law will be applied unless it violates the express terms of a congressional enactment.

However, there are some differences in approach concerning treaties. In the United Kingdom, treaties are negotiated, signed and ratified by the executive as part of the Crown prerogative in foreign affairs. At no point is the consent of Parliament required.[110] In contrast the United States Constitution stipulates that a treaty is negotiated by the executive but can only be ratified by the President if two-thirds of the Senate agree.[111] The Constitution also provides, in respect of treaties, that 'all Treaties made, or which shall be made, under the Authority of the United States, shall be the supreme Law of the Land and the Judges in every state shall be bound thereby'.[112] It was decided early in the history of the Republic that a treaty took precedence over state law.[113]

The Constitution places treaty provisions and federal law on an equal footing. However, the treaty must be one that can be described as 'self-executing'. The distinction between a self-executing treaty and one that is not self-executing is that the former require no legislative act, while the latter cannot be given effect to before domestic courts in the absence of municipal legislation. The distinction between the two forms has provided a fertile source of litigation in the courts.

In *Eyde v Robertson*,[114] it was argued that an Act of Congress was invalid because it conflicted with an earlier United States treaty; the argument was rejected on the facts. However, Miller J in giving judgment noted that 'A treaty is primarily a compact between independent Nations ...', but that the Court had to recognise those treaties which 'contain provisions which confer certain rights upon the citizens or subjects of one of the Nations residing in the territorial limits of the other, which partake of the nature of municipal law,

---

107 *Filartiga v Pena-Irala* (1980) 630 F 2d 876; 77 ILR 169. The Second Circuit of the Court of Appeals held that torture conducted in Paraguay constituted a breach of the Law of Nations and thus the United States court had jurisdiction under the Alien Tort Claims Act of 1789 which provides that 'district courts shall have original jurisdiction of any civil action by an alien for a tort only committed in violation of the law of nations'.

108 See, also, *Amerada Hess v Argentine Republic* (1989) F 2d 421; 79 ILR 1.

109 *Siderman de Blake v Republic* (1992) 965 F 2d 699 (held by the 9th Circuit Court of Appeals that although prohibition again torture had acquired the status of *jus cogens* in international law, it did not deprive the defendant state of immunity under the Foreign State Immunities Act 1976). No doubt this judgment must now be reconsidered following the judgment in *R v Bow Street Metropolitan Stipendiary Magistrate ex p Pinochet Ugarte (No 3)* [1999] 2 WLR 827.

110 Save as provided under the Ponsonby rule (1924), see *supra*.

111 United States Constitution (1787), Art II, s 2.

112 *Ibid*, Art VI, s 2.

113 *Ware v Hylton* (1796) 3 US 199; *Clark v Allen* (1947) 331 US 503.

114 *Eyde v Robertson* (1884) 112 US 580.

and which are capable of enforcement as between private parties in the courts of the country'. The learned judge was referring to the distinction between the self-executing and the non-self-executing treaty. It is generally accepted that this distinction is traceable to the judgment of Marshall CJ in *Foster v Neilson*[115] in 1829, although the phrase 'self-executing' was not used in a Supreme Court judgment until 1887.[116] A modern exposition of the distinction was expounded by Gibson CJ in the Supreme Court of California in *Sei Fuji v State of California*.[117] The facts of the case were as follows.

A Japanese citizen had purchased property in California. State legislation provided such property would be forfeit and pass to the state. The plaintiff argued that the state legislation violated the terms of the United Nations Charter; this raised the question of the status of the treaty. The Court ruled that the treaty was not self-executing but decided in favour of the plaintiff on other grounds.

In the course of giving judgment Gibson CJ observed that in order for a treaty provision to be self-executing the position was that:

> In order for a treaty provision to be operative without the aid of implementing legislation and to have the force and effect of a statute, it must appear that the framers of the treaty intended to prescribe a rule, that standing alone would be enforceable in the courts.

If the treaty is both self-executing and within the Constitution, it will prevail over state law,[118] customary law,[119] a prior but not a subsequent Act of Congress.[120]

The separation of powers within the United States Constitution and the provision for different electoral cycles means that the executive branch might be without a majority in the legislature; the practice grew up of seeking to employ the device of the 'executive agreement'. The lengthy Presidency of Franklin D Roosevelt[121] led to the growth in the use of executive agreements which, while binding the United States internationally, do not require a two-thirds majority in the Senate. The legal status of such agreements[122] was upheld by the United Sates Supreme Court in two cases arising from the Litvinov Agreement of 1933.[123]

---

115 *Foster v Neilson* (1829) 27 US (2 Pet) 253; it is clear that the controversy as to the status of went back to the birth of the Republic: see *Ware v Hylton* (1796) 3 US (3 Dall) 273 (Iredelll J); *United States v Schooner Peggy* (1801) 5 US (1 Cranch) 103 (Marshall CJ).

116 *Bartram v Robertson* (1887) 122 US 116 (Field J); *Whitney v Robertson* (1888) 124 US 190 (Field J). The actual phrase used by Marshall CJ in 1829 had been to the effect that a treaty 'is carried into execution ... whenever it operates of itself'; see, also, *United States v Percheman* (1833) 32 US (7 Pet) 51; the history of the matter is traced in some detail by JJ Paust in 'Self-executing treaties' (1988) 82 AJIL 760; see, also, CM Vasquez, 'The four doctrines of self-executing treaties' (1995) 89 AJIL 695.

117 (1952) 38 Cal (2d) 718.

118 (1796) 3 US 199.

119 *Tag v Rogers* (1959) 267 F 2d 644.

120 *The Cherokee Tobacco* (1870) 78 US 616; *Whitney v Robertson* (1888) 124 US 190.

121 Franklin D Roosevelt (1882–1945) served from March 1933 until his death in April 1945. His Presidency witnessed the strengthening of the executive branch (sometimes described as the 'Imperial Presidency'), a feature that lasted until the Vietnam War and the events of 1972–74 when Congress became more assertive.

122 Although executive agreements have a long history; one was employed pursuant to an Act of Congress to admit Texas in 1845 after the Senate had rejected a treaty of admission in 1844. President Roosevelt used executive agreements to aid allies in the Second World War.

123 *United States v Belmont* (1937) 301 US 324, 8 ILR 34; *United States v Pink* (1942) 315 US 203, 10 ILR 48.

This exercise of federal power attracted the attention of Congress; in 1952, Senator John Bricker lead an attempt to amend the Constitution to restrict the treaty making power and to make all executive agreements subject to congressional control. In February 1954, a milder version of the 'Bricker Amendment' failed by one vote to secure the necessary two thirds majority in the Senate.

On other occasions, tensions have arisen because the two branches of government have entertained different views as to the conduct of foreign affairs. In *Diggs v Schultz*,[124] the Court of Appeals was required to uphold a congressional enactment even though it placed the United States in breach of a Security Council resolution.

The United States Constitution embraces not only the principle of the separation of powers, but also seeks to maintain reserve powers in favour of the component parts. There has been concern that the federal government might seek to utilise the treaty making power as a form of indirect legislation and as a means of avoiding constitutional limitations. This concern was accentuated by the judgment in *Missouri v Holland*,[125] where the Supreme Court upheld the Migratory Bird Treaty Act 1918, which gave effect to a treaty shortly after federal legislation in the same area had been declared *ultra vires* in lower federal courts, although Holmes J did note that the decision did not mean that there were 'no qualifications to the treaty making power'. Since then, treaties are scrutinised so as not to undermine the constitutional rights of the individual states.[126]

(c) Other states

The manner in which international law is regarded will depend on the constitution of the particular country. Some states follow the British approach and may state this expressly in their written constitution. In all states, the precise constitutional arrangements will reflect the history of that country and, where there have been abuses in the past,[127] the written constitution may make express reference to international law. That reference may take a number of forms: (i) that the executive branch shall respect certain fundamental rights internally; (ii) that the executive branch shall conduct itself externally in accordance with international law; or (iii) the constitution may make separate provision in respect of treaty provisions and rules of customary international law.

In each country it will be a question of studying the precise constitutional arrangements but, at the risk of over simplification, a number of general points can be made.

(i) A considerable number of states follow the English tradition and provide that rules of customary international law will be applied and are deemed to be consistent with national law, unless the contrary is demonstrated, in which case municipal laws will

---

124 *Diggs v Schultz* (1972) 470 F 2d 461; 60 ILR 393.
125 *Missouri v Holland* (1920) 252 US 416.
126 *Reid v Covert* (1957) 24 ILR 549 (in which the Supreme Court held certain treaty provisions to be unconstitutional); *Seery v United States* (1955) 22 ILR 398; *Geisser v United States* (1975) 61 ILR 443.
127 As would be the case with Art 4 of the German Constitution of 1919 or Art 25 of the Basic Law of the Federal Republic 1949.

prevail; this will be the position in those countries that have inherited a system of English common law, such as many Commonwealth countries or Israel.[128]

(ii) The traditional position in Commonwealth countries in respect of treaties was that the making of such a treaty was an executive act and that implementation depended on legislative action. The traditional position had been stated by Lord Atkin in the *Attorney General for Canada v Attorney General for Ontario*[129] to the effect that treaty obligations did not form part of domestic law unless incorporated into municipal law by statute. Such a doctrine recognises the responsibility of the executive branch to negotiate treaties and the monopoly power of the legislature to change the law. Such a doctrine is consistent with traditional principles of the separation of powers and the need for legal changes to have been validated by democratically elected representatives.

(iii) Some states with a common law tradition have a written constitution that expressly refers to international law. Article 29 of the Constitution of Eire requires the executive branch to observe the rules of international law in its dealings with other states, but also provides that treaties will not become part of domestic law save as approved by the Oireachtas (Parliament). Article 15(2) of the Constitution provides that only Parliament can make laws. Thus, for a treaty to be given effect in an Irish court implementing legislation is required.[130]

In contrast, the constitution of India, while requiring the executive branch to respect international law, requires legislation to give effect to treaty obligations. In the event of conflict with a statute, then the domestic enactment will prevail; however, the courts have recognised the need to interpret statutes so as to give effect to international law if at all possible.[131]

The common law tradition is preserved in Canada, where legislative action will be required to give effect to treaty obligations and the clear words of a statute will prevail over the terms of a treaty.[132] The position is similar in Australia, where effect will be given to rules of customary international law,[133] but legislative action is necessary to give effect to a treaty.[134] Indeed, in 1995 the High Court of Australia rather surprisingly held that ratification of an unincorporated treaty could give rise to a 'legitimate expectation' that the executive branch would act in conformity with the

---

128 *Silberwacht v Attorney General* (1953) 20 ILR 153; *Stampfer v Attorney General* (1956) 23 ILR 284; *Attorney General of Israel v Eichmann* (1962) 36 ILR 5.

129 *Attorney General for Canada v Attorney General for Ontario* [1937] AC 326; 8 ILR 41.

130 *Re O'Laighleis* (1957) 24 ILR 57; *Re Woods* (1967) 53 ILR 552; *Crotty v An Taiseach* (1987) 93 ILR 480; [1987] 2 CMLR 666; see Lang [1987] 24 CMLR 709.

131 See Art 51 of the Constitution; *Birma v State* (1950) 17 ILR 5; *Union of India v Jain and Others* (1954) 21 ILR 256; *Sharma v State of West Bengal* (1954) 21 ILR 272; *Maharaja Bikram Kishore of Tripura v Province of Assam* (1955) 22 ILR 64.

132 *Croft v Dunphy* (1933) 1 DLR 225; [1933] AC 156; *Francis v R* (1956) 23 ILR 459; *Swait v Board of Trustees of Maritime Transportation Unions* (1966) 43 ILR 1; *Mastini v Bell Telephone Co of Canada* (1971) 60 ILR 389.

133 But see I Shearer, 'The internationalisation of Australian law' (1995) 17 Sydney Law Review 121.

134 *Bluett v Fadden* (1956) 23 ILR 477; *Chin Yin Ten v Little* (1976) 69 ILR 76; *Simsek v Macphee* (1982) 148 CLR 636; *Chung Kheng Lin v Minister for Immigration* (1992) 176 CLR 1; *Minister of State for Immigration and Ethnic Affairs v Ah Hin Teoh* (1995) 128 ALR 353; see A Lester [1996] PL 187; R Piotrowicz [1996] PL 190.

treaty in the absence of indications to the contrary. The Australian government quickly issued a statement to prevent such an expectation arising.[135] The Australian approach is followed in New Zealand, where a treaty purporting to change the law will require legislative action.[136] Further, New Zealand follows the position in Pakistan, where the principle, that statutes are, if possible, to be interpreted in accordance with international law, is applied by the courts.[137] However, this contrasts with Cyprus, where treaties concluded in a particular manner shall have the force of law;[138] such provisions are more far reaching than is normally the case in common law countries.

(iv) In Western Europe, many states operate under legal systems within the civil law world and are to a limited extent traceable back to Roman law. Many states in Western Europe also drew up new constitutional arrangements after 1945;[139] in some cases, the clear object was to ensure that future governments respected citizens internally and obeyed international law in their external dealings. The most obvious example is Germany,[140] where Art 25 of the 1949 Basic Law provides that: 'The general rules of public international law shall be an integral part of the federal law. They shall take precedence over the laws and shall directly create rights and duties for the inhabitants of the federal territory.' However, this provision has to be read with Art 59, which requires that treaties that affect political relations or those that affect federal law shall be the subject of municipal legislation. Thus, rules of customary international law will take effect under Art 25; but treaty provisions will need to comply with Art 59. Any treaty and its implementing legislation is open to challenge before the *Bundesverfassungsgericht* on the ground that the provisions violate the Basic Law. There have been a number of challenges some of which arising from membership of the European Union.[141]

France has been subject to two written constitutions since 1945. The preamble to both the 1946 constitution and the 1958 constitution refer to the rules of public international law and these references have been taken by French courts as referring to the rules of public international law. The 1958 constitution contains a number of

---

135 See statement of Attorney General and Minister of Foreign Affairs 10 May 1995; for comment see M Allars (1996) 17 Sydney Law Review 204.

136 *Hoani te Heubeu Tukino v Aotea District Maori Land Board* [1941] AC 308; *Ashby v Minister of Immigration* (1981) 1 NZLR 222; *Falema'i Lesa v Attorney General of New Zealand* [1983] 2 AC 20.

137 *Imperial Tobacco Company of India v Commissioner of Income Tax,South Zone, Karachi* (1958) 27 ILR 103.

138 Cyprus Constitution (1960), Art 169(3).

139 It is well established that a state will only draw up a new written constitution after some particularly serious event such as: (i) internal revolution; (ii) acquisition of self government; (iii) collapse of a regime due to war.

140 It should be noted that Art 4 of the Weimar Constitution of 1919 made reference to international law by providing that 'the universally recognised rules of international law are valid as binding constituent parts of the German Federal law'.

141 *Assessment of Aliens for War Taxation* case (1965) 43 ILR 3; *Acquisition of German Nationality* case (1966) 57 ILR 306; *Parking Privileges for Diplomats* case (1971) 70 ILR 396; *Re Treaty on the Basis of Relations between the Federal Republic of Germany and the German Democratic Republic* 1972 (1973) 78 ILR 150; *Re Unification Treaty Constitutionality* case (1989) 94 ILR 42. See, also, Case 11/70 *Internationale Handelsgesellschaft mbH v Einfuhr und Vorratsstelle für Getreide und Füttermittel* [1972] CMLR 255.

references to treaties. Article 53 requires certain types of treaty to be ratified or and approved by law. In a distinctly dualist tone, Art 54 indicates that the *Conseil Constitutionnel* may declare a treaty to be at variance with the Constitution, in which case, it may only come into force internally if the Constitution is amended. Article 55[142] provides that a treaty duly ratified or approved shall on publication have authority superior to laws but only where there is evidence of reciprocity.

In like terms the Italian Constitution of 1948 makes express reference to international law. Article 10 provides that the Italian legal system shall give effect to the general principles of international law; this is normally taken to mean the rules of customary international law. Article 80 provides that treaties which involve a change in domestic law shall not be ratified until implementing legislation has been enacted.[143]

(v) One noticeable feature since 1945 has been that, in those situations where there has been the collapse of an entire political system, those drawing up the new constitution have often made express reference to international law in the hope of confining any future government to internationally agreed norms. Article 98 (2) of the Japanese Constitution of 1946 provides that: 'The Treaties concluded by Japan and established laws of nations shall be faithfully observed.' The jurisprudence since 1946 has been to interpret this as requiring courts in Japan to give effect both to customary law and international treaty obligations.[144]

The collapse of the Soviet Union and the system of Marxist Leninism that sustained it resulted in the drawing up of the constitution of the Russian Federation in 1993. This basic law provides that treaties are to be negotiated, signed and ratified by the President and that the Constitutional Court may determine whether treaties are in conformity with the Constitution. The Soviet Union had always tended towards a dualist position and Art 15(4) of the 1993 Constitution stipulates that: '... the generally recognised principles and norms of international law and the international treaties of the Russian Federation shall constitute part of its legal system. If an international treaty of the Russian Federation establishes other rules than those stipulated by the law, the rules of the international treaty shall apply.'[145]

A similar advance is to be found in South Africa; the constitutions of 1910, 1961 and 1983 had made no reference to international law. This was perhaps hardly surprising because, since 1948, South Africa was the subject of criticism from the United Nations.

---

142 These provisions are traceable to Arts 26 and 28 of the 1946 Constitution. Some of the case law has arisen by virtue of obligations under European law: see *Re European Communities Amendment Treaty* (1970) 52 ILR 418: *Re Direct Elections to European Assembly* (1976) 74 ILR 527; *Re Nicolo* [1990] 1 CMLR 173; *Re Treaty on European Union* (1992) 93 ILR 337.

143 *Combes de Lestrade v Ministry of Finance* (1955) 22 ILR 882; *Re Masini* (1957) 24 ILR 11; *Treasury Ministry v Di Raffaele* (1974) 77 ILR 562; *Re Cuillier, Ciamborrani and Vallon* (1979) 78 ILR 93.

144 Y Iwasawa, 'The relationship between international law and national law: Japanese experiences' (1993) 64 BYIL 333.

145 Margolis (1955) 4 ICLQ 116; Ginsburgs (1965) 59 AJIL 523; Blishchenko (1975) 69 AJIL 819; Danilenko (1994) 88 AJIL 451. Manifestly, there is no state that has undergone a greater change in its approach to international law; the approach of the Soviet Union was to subordinate international law to the requirements of Marxist doctrine. The desire of the Russian Federation is to play a role within the wider community and thus there is a greater emphasis on the rules and procedures of the international community.

Political change in the country resulted in a less hostile attitude. The interim constitution of 1993 provided that rules of customary law should be given effect save where they were at variance with the constitution or domestic legislation.[146] The constitution of 1996 contains extensive reference to international law. Following upon the 1993 provisions, it is stipulated that customary international law is to be given effect to unless it is contrary to domestic law or the constitution.[147] The constitution provides for treaties to be given effect to following implementing legislation and the courts are directed to interpret domestic legislation, so far as is possible, in accordance with the principles of international law.[148]

(vi) In reviewing the evidence of state practice, it is manifest that most states make some reference to the status of international law within the terms of a written constitution. Many constitutions provide that customary rules will have effect, unless they are in direct conflict with domestic law; in contrast, most states provide that treaty provisions that purport to change domestic law will require some form of legislative approval. In so far as it is a matter of theory, the evidence of state practice would seem to support the positivist view that the enforceability of international law internally will depend on the conduct of the individual state. Secondly, such a practice is in conformity with traditional theories of democratic government that require the consent of elected representative before additional burdens are placed upon citizens.

5 JUSTICIABILITY, ACT OF STATE AND OTHER DOCTRINES

A matter that deserves attention at this juncture is the concept of justiciability. A matter is justiciable if it can be the subject to legal analysis and adjudication. When a matter comes before a municipal court, it might be asserted that it is non-justiciable. It is often argued that a matter is non-justiciable because it would involve passing a judgment on the acts and conduct of a foreign government within its own territory.[149] The doctrine is normally viewed as one of private international law, but it often arises in cases concerning public international law;[150] however, the whole area has become bedevilled by a confusion of terminology and it is important to distinguish five factual situations:

(a) There are those cases where the central problem is whether the courts of state A possess jurisdiction over the parties and in respect of the matter.[151]

---

146 Interim Constitution (1993), s 231(4).

147 Article 232, 1996 Constitution.

148 Articles 231 and 233, 1996 Constitution.

149 See FA Mann, 'The sacrosanctity of foreign acts of state' (1943) 59 LQR 42, p 155; M Zander, 'The act of state doctrine' (1959) 53 AJIL 826; M Singer 'The act of state doctrine in the United Kingdom: an analysis with comparisons to United States practice' (1981) 75 AJIL 283.

150 In *R v Bow Street Metropolitan Stipendiary Magistrate ex p Pinochet Ugarte (No 1)* [1998] 3 WLR 1456. Lord Lloyd of Berwick would have dismissed the application on grounds of non-justiciability.

151 Different rules will apply according to whether the matter is a criminal case or a civil action. In broad terms, criminal actions will be determined by the operative rules of public international law while civil actions in the United Kingdom will be determined by the rules of private international law. The question of jurisdiction is dealt with in Chapter 8.

(b) There are those cases where the courts of state A possess jurisdiction but that it might be expedient to decline jurisdiction on some particular ground such as *forum non conveniens*[152] or *lis alibi pendens*.[153]

(c) There are those cases where in principle the court of state A enjoys jurisdiction but it is argued that an individual defendant enjoys immunity from jurisdiction.[154]

(d) There are those cases where the courts of state A may be asked to rule on the conduct of the government of state B (the doctrine of non-justiciability[155]). The doctrine holds that the courts of state A should refrain from passing judgment on the governmental acts of state B committed within its own territory.

(e) There are those cases in the United Kingdom arising within the sphere of constitutional law, where the executive branch of government may be able to raise as a defence the principle of act of state when the plaintiff is alleging infringement with his private legal rights.[156]

It is proposed to say a little at this stage about the matters set out in paragraph (d) supra while other matters will be dealt with at the appropriate place.[157]

That an English court will refrain from adjudicating upon the acts of a foreign government derives from the House of Lords judgment in the *Duke of Brunswick v King of Hanover*,[158] where the court refused to set aside a guardianship document executed by the Duke of Brunswick. In giving judgment Lord Cottenham LC noted:

> If it is true, the bill states that the instrument was contrary to the laws of Hanover and Brunswick but, notwithstanding that it is so stated, still if it is a sovereign act, then, whether it be according to law or not according to law we cannot enquire into it.

Although there are a number of possible explanations for the decision, it was taken as establishing that an English court could not 'sit in judgment upon the act of a sovereign ... done in the exercise of his authority vested in him as sovereign'.[159] The principle that such a rule of judicial restraint exists has been accepted in England in subsequent case

---

152 An area that has developed considerably in the last 20 years; see *The Atlantic Star* [1974] AC 436; *MacShannon v Rockware Glass Ltd* [1978] AC 795; *Spiliada Maritime Corporation v Cansulex Ltd* [1987] AC 460; *Connelly v RTZ Corporation plc* [1998] AC 854; *Lubbe and others v Cape plc* [2000] 1 WLR 182.

153 *The Abidin Daver* [1984] AC 398.

154 As indeed was argued without success in *R v Bow Street Metropolitan Stipendiary Magistrate ex p Pinochet Ugarte (No 1)* [1998] 3 WLR 1456, but not in *(No 3)* [1999] 2 WLR 272.

155 It is described as the doctrine of non justiciability in the United Kingdom but in the United States the doctrine is referred to as 'act of state'; in the United Kingdom, the expression 'act of foreign state' sometimes employed. However, it should be noted that when the expression 'act of state' is employed in the United Kingdom it refers to situation (e) above.

156 *Entick v Carrington* (1765) 19 St Tr 1030; *Buron v Denman* (1848) 2 Ex 167; *Walker v Baird* [1892] AC 491; *Johnstone v Pedlar* [1921] 2 AC 262; *Nissan v Attorney General* [1970] AC 179. The circumstances in which such a plea can be raised are very limited, but the situation where the conduct of the executive branch is in issue is distinct from a problem arising from the conduct of a foreign government.

157 Matters indicated in (a) and (b) will be dealt with in the chapter concerned with jurisdiction, matters arising under (c) will be dealt with in the chapter concerned with immunity from jurisdiction. Matters arising under (e) belong within the sphere of constitutional law.

158 (1844) 6 Beav 1; aff'd (1848) 2 HLC 1.

159 (1848) 2 HL Cas 1, p 17, *per* Lord Cottenham LC.

law.[160] The difficulty arises if such a principle of judicial restraint has the effect of frustrating the application of a relevant rule of customary international law.

The principle that the courts of state A should, in certain circumstances, refrain from judging the governmental acts of state B was adopted in the United States in the celebrated case of *Underhill v Hernandez*,[161] where the facts were as follows.

The plaintiff was an American citizen resident in Venezuela. The defendant was a general in command of the revolutionary forces which afterwards prevailed. The plaintiffs brought proceedings against the defendant in New York alleging wrongful imprisonment.

In rejecting the claim, Fuller CJ observed in a much cited *dictum*:

> Every sovereign state is bound to respect the independence of every other sovereign state, and the courts of one country will not sit in judgment on the acts of another done within its own territory. Redress of grievances by reason of such acts must be obtained through the means open to be availed of by sovereign powers as between themselves.[162]

The principle propounded in *Underhill v Hernandez* has been applied in subsequent case law in the United States,[163] although it is not every case of involving foreign affairs where the principle pertains.[164] Much will depend on the precise question that is before the court; direct attempts to question the foreign policy of the United States will not be countenanced although the court will determine the matter if it simply turns on private rights in a particular incident.[165]

The American courts have experienced difficulty with cases involving the taking of property by foreign governments. The general rule in private international law is that title to property is determined by the *lex situs*. However, difficulties arise if property is taken by a government in state A without paying compensation as recognised in international law. If, at a later date, proceedings take place in the United States, should a court recognise the title to the property on the grounds that the principle in *Underhill v Hernandez* so requires or should it hold the transfer of title to be a breach of international law? By a majority of 8 to 1, the Supreme Court in *Banco Nacional de Cuba v Sabbatino*[166] decided that the principle enunciated in *Underhill v Hernandez* prevented the questioning of the taking of property by a foreign government, even though such taking might be in breach of public international law. Although federal legislation was introduced to modify

---

160 *Buck v Attorney General* [1965] Ch 745 (Diplock LJ); *Butes Gas Oil Co v Hammer (No 3)* [1982] AC 888 (Lord Wilberforce); *R v Bow Street Magistrate ex p Pinochet Ugarte (No 1)* [1998] 3 WLR 1456.

161 *Underhill v Hernandez* (1897) 168 US 250.

162 *Ibid*, p 252.

163 *Greenham Woman against Cruise Missiles v Reagan* (1984) 591 F Supp 1332; 99 ILR 44 (court cannot review agreement with friendly state to deploy cruise missiles on its territory).

164 *Baker v Carr* (1962) 369 US 186, p 211 (the case itself concerned the equitable apportionment of voters among legislative districts in Tennessee).

165 *Linder v Portocarrero* (1992) 963 F 2d 332; 99 ILR 54 (murder of United States citizen working for the Nicaraguan government could be determined without involving findings as to the nature of United States foreign policy in Nicaragua).

166 *Banco Nacional de Cuba v Sabbatino* (1964) 376 US 398; 35 ILR 2 (White J dissented rejecting the presumption of non-review in cases where breaches of public international law were in issue).

the results of the decision,[167] it was followed in a subsequent case.[168] Problems arose as to whether the federal legislation restricting the act of state doctrine applied to property both within and beyond the United States. The reaction to the *Sabbatino* decision had been hostile, as writers pointed out that it involved an American court directing a United States citizen to surrender property in the United States to a foreign state in respect of an act of that state that was contrary to international law and was executed because he was a United States citizen. Further, such an act would, if undertaken, in the United States have been a violation of the 5th and 14th Amendments of the United States Constitution.

In such circumstances, there has been a reluctance to apply the act of state doctrine where to do so would involve the United States court validating acts that not only violated international law but were unconstitutional under the United States Constitution. Although the judgment in *Sabbatino* has not been overruled, recent case law has drawn on an exception to the act of state doctrine[169] to enable the court not to apply it where there is evidence from the executive branch that failure to apply it would not damage the conduct of foreign affairs.[170] The *Sabbatino* judgment illustrates the danger of too inflexible an application of the act of state doctrine; although not formally overruled, the courts are likely to be more cautious and to seek exceptions in appropriate cases.[171]

6 EXECUTIVE CERTIFICATES

The English courts have traditionally adopted the practice of consulting the executive branch to obtain conclusive rulings in certain matters of foreign affairs. Examples would be questions as to the identity of a head of state,[172] the existence of a state,[173] the extent of territorial jurisdiction,[174] or whether a state of war existed with the United Kingdom.[175] The reason for this approach stemmed partly from a conviction that the executive and the judiciary should speak with one voice and partly because certain matters of fact were particularly within the knowledge of the executive branch and not readily proved by admissible evidence.[176] The use of the procedure can be traced back a

---

167 Foreign Assistance Act 1964.

168 *First National City Bank v Banco Nacional de Cuba* (1972) 406 US 479; (1972) 66 ILR 102.

169 Deriving from *Bernstein v VanHeyghen Frères Société Anonyme v NV Nederlandishe-Amerikanische Stoomvaart-Maatschappij* (1947) 163 2d 246 (2d Circ) cert denied (1947) 332 US 772.

170 Thus, in *Banco Nacional de Cuba v First National City Bank* (1972) 406 US 479, the Legal Adviser to the State Department informed the Supreme Court that failure to apply the act of state doctrine would not interfere in the Executive's conduct of foreign affairs. In the case of *Alfred Dunhill v Republic of Cuba* (1976) 425 US 682, the Legal Adviser invited the Court to overrule *Sabbatino* and observed that if 'acts of state would thereafter be subject to adjudication in American courts under international law we would not anticipate embarrassment to the conduct of foreign policy of the United States'.

171 See M Zander, 'The act of state doctrine' (1959) 53 AJIL 826; M Singer, 'The act of state doctrine in the United Kingdom' (1981) 75 AJIL 283; M Halberstam, '*Sabbatino* resurrected' (1985) 79 AJIL 68.

172 *Mighell v Sultan of Johore* [1894] 1 QB 149; for background see M Nash, 'From Sultan to Senator' (1999) 149 NLJ 182.

173 *Duff Development Co Ltd v Government of Kelanton* [1924] AC 797; *Carl Zeiss Stiftung v Rayner & Keeler Ltd (No 2)* [1967] 1 AC 853.

174 *The Fagernes* (1927) P 311 (Atkin, Lawrence, Bankes LJJ).

175 *R v Bottrill ex p Keuchenmeister* [1947] KB 41.

176 *The Arantzazu Mendi* [1939] AC 256, p 264 (Lord Atkin) *Carl Zeiss Stiftung v Rayner & Keeler Ltd (No 2)* [1967] 1 AC 853, p 961 (Lord Wilberforce).

long way,[177] although it was authoritatively recognised by the House of Lords in *Duff Development Co Ltd v Government of Kelanton*.[178] The facts of the case were as follows.

The Government of Kelanton applied for an order blocking the enforcement of an arbitration award on the ground that Kelanton was an independent sovereign state. The Secretary of State indicated that Kelanton was an independent state; the House of Lords held that this answer was conclusive.

Lord Cave expressed the matter thus:

> It has been for some time the practice of our Courts when such a question is raised, to take judicial notice of the sovereignty of a state, and for that purpose (in any case of uncertainty) to seek information from a Secretary of State; and when information is so obtained the Court does not permit it to be questioned by the parties.[179]

The effect of the certificate will depend on the statutory provisions under which it has been issued.[180] Thus, in *R v Secretary of State for Foreign and Commonwealth Affairs ex p Trawnik*,[181] the Divisional Court ruled that a certificate issued under s 40(3) of the Crown Proceedings Act 1947 was conclusive as to whether the alleged liability of the Crown arose other than in respect of Her Majesty's Government in the United Kingdom and that such a certificate would not be reviewable unless it were a 'nullity'.

One matter that should be mentioned at this stage is that the decision of the United Kingdom government in 1980 to refrain from the formal recognition of foreign governments has lead to a modification in the role of executive certificates in this context. This matter will be dealt with in the chapter on recognition.[182]

The limited point to be noted at this stage is that there are a number of matters concerning foreign affairs where an English court may be required to rely on the facts stated in the executive certificate.

Questions of foreign affairs that come before the courts in the United States may result in the judge seeking guidance from the Department of State. Any such guidance or suggestion tends to be more detailed than that made available in England. While difficulties have arisen in the context of claims to sovereign immunity the general

---

177 *Taylor v Barclay* (1828) 2 Sim 213; *Mighell v Sultan of Johore* [1894] 1 QB 149; *The Fagernes* [1927] P 311; *Duff Development Co Ltd v Government of Kelanton* [1924] AC 797; *Engleke v Musmann* [1928] AC 41; *R v Bottril ex p Keuchenmeister* [1947] KB 41.

178 [1924] AC 797.

179 *Duff Development Co Ltd v Government of Kelanton* [1924] AC 797, p 805, *per* Viscount Cave; the relevant Secretary was Winston Churchill (1874–1965) serving as Secretary of State for the Colonies.

180 See Diplomatic Privileges Act 1964, s 7; State Immunity Act 1978, s 21, which reads 'a certificate by or behalf of the Secretary of State shall be conclusive evidence on any question'. Examples of statutory provisions are Foreign Marriage Act 1892, s 16; Foreign Jurisdiction Act 1890, s 4; Trading with the Enemy Act 1939, s 15(2); Fugitive Offenders Act 1967, s 4(4); Criminal Law Act 1977, s 9; Internationally Protected Persons Act 1978, s 1(5); Deep Sea Mining (Temporary Provisions) Act 1981, s 17.

181 *R v Secretary of State for Foreign and Commonwealth Affairs ex p Trawnik* (1985) *The Times*, 18 April. For related proceedings, see *Trawnik v Lennox* [1985] 1 WLR 532 (Megarry VC); [1985] 1 WLR 544 (CA); *R v Foreign Secretary ex p Trawnik* (1986) *The Times*, 21 February.

182 See *Republic of Somalia v Woodhouse,Drake and Carey (Suisse) SA* [1993] QB 54; 94 ILR 608 (Hobhouse J); C Warbrick, 'Executive certificates in foreign affairs: prospects for review and control' (1986) 35 ICLQ 138; E Wilmhurst, 'Executive certificates in foreign affairs: the United Kingdom' (1986) 35 ICLQ 157.

tendency of the courts is to follow such guidance.[183] In times of difficulty then considerable latitude is allowed to the executive since 'flexibility, not uniformity, must be the controlling factor in times of strained international relations'.[184]

---

183 *The Novemar* (1938) 303 US 68, 9 ILR 176; *Mexico v Hoffmann* (1945) 324 US 30; 12 ILR 143; *National City Bank of New York v China* (1955) 348 US 356; 22 ILR 210.
184 *Rich v Naviera Vacuba* (1961) 197 F Supp 710, p 724; 32 ILR 127 (difficulties with Cuba).

CHAPTER 5

THE SUBJECTS OF INTERNATIONAL LAW[1]

1 THE NATURE OF LEGAL PERSONALITY

In any legal system the nature of legal personality is of central importance. Possession of legal personality indicates that the entity may enjoy legal rights and litigate to enforce those rights; the entity in question will also be subject to legal obligations. In municipal law an individual above a certain age and of sound mind will have legal personality to sue and be sued. That individual enjoys legal personality and is subject to legal rights and duties. In like terms it was established in the 19th century that the corporation aggregate was a legal entity distinct from its own members and could itself sue and be sued.[2] In municipal law the question as to whether an entity enjoys legal personality will depend on analysing the basic constitutional document and drawing the appropriate inferences. A finding of legal personality will lead to different conclusions according to the entity in question; the acts capable of being performed by an individual differ from those that a corporation may itself perform.[3] However, in municipal law it is broadly accepted that legal personality indicates that the entity may be subject to legal rights and duties. Some municipal legal systems draw a distinction between subjectivity and personality or capacity so that a minor may be a subject but not possess full personality or capacity.

Such distinctions are not normally employed in international law; the terms 'legal subject' and 'legal person' are normally employed interchangeably; legal personality indicates that the entity may be capable of possessing international rights and duties. The influence of positivism in the classical era of international law[4] was far reaching; the positivist tended to the view that the only legitimate legal person on the international plane was the state; indeed this is reflected in the traditional eighteenth century name of the subject, namely, 'the Law of Nations'. The position could not have been expressed more clearly than by Lassa Oppenheim[5] who observed in 1912: 'Since the Law of Nations is based on the common consent of individual states, and not of individual human beings,

---

1   See generally G Schwarzenberger, *International Law*, 3rd edn, 1957, Vol 1, p 89; N Mugerwa, 'Subjects of international law', in M Sorensen (ed), *Manual of Public International Law*, 1968, p 247; R Jennings and A Watts, *Oppenheim's International Law*, Vol 1, 9th edn, 1992, Chapter 2; M Akehurst, *Modern Introduction to International Law*, 7th edn, 1997, pp 75–106; I Brownlie, *Principles of Public International Law*, 5th edn, 1998, Part II, pp 57–83; J Crawford, *The Creation of States in International Law*, 1979; I Shearer, *Starke's International Law*, 11th edn, 1994, pp 85–116; P Guggenheim, *'Les états comme sujets de droit des gen'*, in *Les principes de droit international public* (1952) 80 HR 1-190; J Crawford, 'The criteria for statehood in international law' (1977) 48 BYIL 93; J Andrews, 'The concept of statehood and the acquisition of territory in the 19th century' (1978) 94 LQR 408.

2   *Salomon v A Salomon & Co Ltd* [1897] AC 22; *Macaura v Northern Assurance Co Ltd* [1925] AC 619; *Lee v Lee's Air Farming Ltd* [1961] AC 12 (PC).

3   At the outset, the corporation being subject to the full rigour of the *ultra vires* doctrine, see *Ashbury Carriage Co v Riche* (1874) LR 7 HL 653; *Cotman v Brougham* [1918] AC 514.

4   The classical period normally taken by writers to be the period prior to 1914.

5   Lassa Oppenheim (1858–1919) (Whewell Professor of International Law 1908–19).

states solely and exclusively are the subjects of international law.'[6] The view that states were the sole subjects of international law was traceable to the dualist approach which dominated in the years prior to 1914.[7]

While states remain the most important subjects of international law one feature of developments since 1945 has been the recognition of other legal persons. In principle it is for international law to determine firstly whether an entity has legal personality and secondly the scope of that personality.

In reviewing developments since 1945 a number of general themes emerge. First, there are simply more states. Decolonisation has resulted in a threefold increase in the number of states and all states need to co-operate in an increasingly interdependent world. Secondly, to ensure a high degree of co-operation there has been a proliferation in the number of regional and international organisations[8] and this change has been recognised by the International Court of Justice.[9] Thirdly, it is a matter of common ground that the position of the individual has been transformed not only with the emphasis on the prohibition of international criminal conduct but also because of the varying rules as to *locus standi* contained in regional human rights instruments. Fourthly, the international stage has witnessed increasing levels of activity by non-governmental organisations and public companies.

There are thus a wide variety of actors upon the international stage and whether a particular entity is acknowledged as a legal person is partly a question of meeting certain criteria and partly a question of whether there is sufficient will within the international community to accord acceptance; the first element is one of law, the second is one of practical experience.

On the assumption that a particular entity is accorded personality are there any specifically legal consequences? First, the entity will be subject to obligations arising under international law. Secondly, the entity will have *locus standi* to enforce rights arising under international law before an international or a municipal tribunal. Thirdly, in appropriate cases the entity will have capacity to enter into agreements themselves creating rights and duties. Fourthly, in appropriate cases the entity may be able to claim immunity from jurisdiction in particular legal proceedings.

With these general considerations in mind it is necessary to examine in turn each of the candidates for legal personality.

---

6   LH Oppenheim, *International Law*, Vol 1 (Peace), 2nd edn, 1912, p 19; similar sentiments had been expressed in the first edition in 1905.

7   Thus John Westlake could observe in his chapters on the *Principles of International Law*, 1894, that 'international law is the body of rules prevailing between states'.

8   Although the number of such organisations had been developing slowly since the Congress of Vienna in 1815; see DW Bowett, *The Law of International Institutions*, 4th edn, 1982; C Archer, *International Organisations*, 2nd edn, 1992.

9   *Advisory Opinion on the Reparation for Injuries Suffered in the Service of the United Nations* (1949) ICJ 174.

2 THE STATE AS AN INTERNATIONAL LEGAL PERSON

The rise of positivism in the 18th century placed the state as the basic political unit at the centre of international diplomacy. The Law of Nations comprised those rules governing relations between states and the rulers of those states. From the outset the state has been at the centre of international society.[10] Even today only the state may seek membership of the United Nations or participate in litigation before the International Court. Only the state commands the permanently organised armed forces and it is normally only the state that can mobilise the large resources needed to relieve suffering and afford humanitarian relief. One of the consequences of the increase in the number of states has been the great differences in military and economic power between the wealthiest and the less fortunate. These considerations make it important to review the circumstances under which an entity might be viewed as a state.

(a) Creation

Whether a state exists for the purpose of international law is partly a question of law and partly a question of fact. The task requires that the evidence is found, the facts established and then those facts should be tested against internationally recognised criteria for statehood. Today it is generally accepted that the legal criteria for statehood are those set out in Art 1 of the Montevideo Convention on the Rights and Duties of States (1933) which reads:

> The State as a person of international law should possess the following qualifications: (a) a permanent population; (b) a defined territory; (c) a Government; and (d) a capacity to enter into relations with other States.[11]

The first three criteria were acknowledged in 19th century Europe,[12] while the fourth criterion derives from Latin American writers.

A defined territory

Territory is the essence of statehood. In principle the state must enjoy sovereignty over a defined area – thus, the principle of territorial sovereignty is one of the fundamental principles of international law.[13] Thus, within a defined area the state will possess sovereignty and may prevent any other state acting without its consent. Sovereignty carries with it the right to exercise jurisdiction and this jurisdiction may be in one of a

---

10 At least since the 16th century, when a recognisable form of international law began to emerge.

11 These criteria might be contrasted with the definition propounded by the Arbitration Commission of the European Conference on Yugoslavia in Opinion No 1 which asserted that 'a state is commonly defined as a community which consists of a territory and a population subject to an organised political authority'; the Commission was established pursuant to the declaration of 27 August 1991 of the European Community. The definition propounded in the Montevideo Convention is not water tight and it is open to argument as to whether Katanga in 1960 and Biafra in 1967 might have met the criteria.

12 G Jellinek, *Allgemeine Staatslehre*, 3rd edn, 1914.

13 Often a state will rely on the principle of territorial sovereignty when others seek to criticise its internal conduct (eg, China in response to criticisms relating to its record on human rights).

number of forms.[14] The matter was well expressed by Judge Huber when sitting as an arbitrator in *The Island of Palmas Arbitration*,[15] where he observed:

> Territorial sovereignty ... involves the exclusive right to display the activities of a State. This right has as a corollary a duty; the obligation to protect within the territory the rights of other States, in particular their right to integrity and inviolability in peace and war, together with the rights which each States may claim for its nationals in foreign territory.

Normally the territory will be subject to internationally agreed boundary lines; in some instances the state will comprise a single legal system in other cases there may be a number.[16] Existence as a state is not diminished by the fact that the boundaries may be in dispute; many states are subject to border disputes[17] and agreed borders are not a precondition for statehood. While in theory borders should be agreed and accepted by third parties, in many cases they are not and so the International Court of Justice could observe in the *North Sea Continental Shelf* cases[18] that: 'There is, for instance, no rule that the land frontiers of a State must be fully delimited and defined, and often in various places and for long periods they are not.' Thus, a state must control a recognisable area of territory;[19] the fact that the precise borders may be in dispute is a question of boundaries not of status.

Sometimes an entity may be considered a state before any of its borders have been fully determined.[20] In principle, territory includes airspace above the land, although there is no consensus on the upper limit. Theoretically, territory includes the earth beneath as far as the centre of the globe. In appropriate cases, the concept of territory includes the territorial sea adjacent to the coast for a distance of twelve nautical miles.[21]

Population

A second requirement is that there should be a stable population. The evidence must disclose a degree of permanence so that nomadic tribes without any settled territorial links will not be sufficient;[22] however, where such tribes move through territory with a permanent population then statehood is possible.[23] While the absence of a permanent

---

14 Ie, it will correspond to the legislative, executive and judicial roles of government.

15 *Island of Palmas Arbitration* (1928) 2 RIAA 829, p 839. See PC Jessup, 'The Palmas Island Arbitration' (1928) 22 AJIL 735.

16 So in the United Kingdom there are separate legal systems for England and Wales, Northern Ireland and Scotland. In the United States there are 50 distinct legal systems.

17 Eg, Israel at various times since 1948; Iraq/Kuwait ; Denmark/Greenland; Pakistan/India.

18 *North Sea Continental Shelf* cases (1969) ICJ 3, p 32; 41 ILR 29, p 62.

19 For this reason, 'the State of Palestine' declared at the Algiers Conference of November 1988, was not a state because there was no evidence of control of territory. However, the territory does not have to be linked as is indicated by the division of Pakistan prior to 1971 and the secession of Bangladesh.

20 Israel in 1948. Albania was recognised by many states prior to 1914, even though the borders were in dispute.

21 Law of the Sea Convention (1982), Art 3.

22 Western Sahara (Advisory Opinion) (1975) ICJ 3; see J Andrews (1978) 94 LQR 408.

23 As might be said to be the case in the Republic of Somalia.

population is fatal there is no requirement as to a minimum number. Thus Nauru, which became an independent state in 1968, only had a population of 8,000 in its 1983 census.[24]

While it is agreed that there is no minimum number for statehood, it should be noted that difficult problems can arise to whether the same test should apply in respect of claims self-determination. At the other end of the spectrum there is no maximum population so that China with a population of over one billion is considered as a single state.

There is no requirement that the population should have any common features so that differences of colour, creed, culture, language, religion and ethnic origin are acceptable. Where a state consists of a people with the same language culture and history it is usual to refer to such a state as a nation state. The composition of the population may require that constitutional law within the state makes appropriate provision for the rights of minorities. Moreover in each case it will be important to determine whether peoples of different cultures are living voluntarily within the same state or whether they are being held together by force.[25]

The state itself will have a view on who constitutes its permanent population and this will be reflected in its citizenship laws; subject to a number of caveats, international law allows the state to stipulate its own conditions for citizenship. The state will exercise jurisdiction over those persons who are physically present within its borders and will claim a degree of personal jurisdiction in respect of certain acts committed by its nationals abroad.

Control by a government

There must be a degree of effective government control over the territory in question.[26] A state is a political entity and there must be an element of control by government. However, once a state is established its existence will not be terminated by a civil war[27] or by political instability, frequent revolutions,[28] or by attempts at secession.[29] Indeed, defeat in war and occupation by a victorious army will not lead to extinction as a state; thus, Germany and Japan did not cease to be states in 1945. In respect of secessionist movements, the general practice is to withhold recognition from such groups although in 1968 some states did accord recognition to Biafra.[30]

---

24 Thus, the Vatican City enters into diplomatic relations even though it has a population of about 1,000; it is not, however, a member of the United Nations and many of its functions are discharged by Italy.

25 Belgium and the United States being examples of the former, while the former Soviet Union was an unfortunate example of the latter.

26 See International Committee of Jurists Report (1920) on the Republic of Finland in 1918.

27 Lebanon remained a state in the 1970s although plagued by civil war.

28 In the *Sambiaggio Claim* (1903) 10 RIAA 499, the Umpire rejected the argument that Venezuela should not be regarded as a state because of political instability and frequent revolutions.

29 Only a small number of states recognised Biafra in 1967–69; the remainder continued to regard Nigeria as a state.

30 No recognition was accorded to the Confederate States in the American Civil War (1861–65). The recognition of Slovenia, Croatia and Bosnia-Herzegovina has attracted some comment; see M Weller, 'The international response to the dissolution of the Socialist Federal Republic of Yugoslavia' (1992) 86 AJIL 569.

It is important that the government should itself be sovereign in that it is not dependent on the instructions of another state. Manifestly, in the modern world it is common for states to seek to influence each other but what is in issue here is whether state A has entered into a binding legal agreement to follow the instructions of state B, or has allowed state B to exercise important governmental functions. An example is afforded by the conduct of the South African government in establishing the Homelands of Transkei, Ciskei Venda and Bophuthatswana; it is arguable that the entire exercise was contrary to international law in that it was designed to promote the unlawful policy of apartheid. Setting that aside for a moment recognition was denied because there was insufficient evidence of operational or financial independence from South Africa. Thus, the Homelands were not recognised as independent states by the United Nations, the Organisation of African Unity or by the United Kingdom[31] and have now been reabsorbed within South Africa.[32]

The need for a government to be possess effective internal control is a matter to be determined by the evidence; in the modern world it is often a question of degree and the evidence may provide conflicting indications.[33] The emphasis is upon internal control, not the ethical conduct of the government; different considerations may arise when considering abuses of human rights or the principle of self-determination, but where the existence of a state is in issue it is the effectiveness of the internal control that is important.[34] The fact that the government may have come to power through unsavoury means is *nihil ad rem*.[35] Even if a government has acted in defiance of United Nations, authority it will still be regarded as in internal control and as the appropriate representative of the state.[36] In cases where there is a civil war,[37] then the general policy is to continue to recognise the existence of the state and not to recognise those seeking to secede.[38]

---

31 The legal status of Ciskei was analysed in *Gur Corporation v Trust Bank of South Africa Ltd* [1987] QB 599; 75 ILR 675.

32 The effect of the 1993 Constitution was to repeal the relevant Homeland legislation and to reabsorb the four 'independent states' within South Africa.

33 For example, it is strongly arguable that Somalia did not, in the early 1990s, have a government with effective control and it might be said, after 1979, that the government in Afghanistan was not truly independent of Soviet control.

34 Although there was evidence of serious abuses of human rights in Germany 1933–45, it was not suggested that the government did not have internal control.

35 The matter was expressed with a certain world weariness by Warren Christopher (Deputy Secretary of State 1977–81; Secretary of State 1993–97) when he observed: 'We maintain diplomatic relations with many governments of which we do not necessarily approve. The reality is that, in this day and age, coups and other unscheduled changes of government are not exceptional developments. Withholding diplomatic relations from these regimes, after they have obtained effective control, penalises us.' (Speech, 11 June 1997.)

36 Eg, negotiations with the government of Iraq in the period 1990–99.

37 An example being the Belgian Congo in 1960 which attained independence and was admitted to the United Nations but whose central government had little control. See CC O'Brien, *To Katanga and Back, A United Nations Case History*, 1962.

38 This was, of course, the policy with the civil war in Spain (1936–39) or in Nigeria (1967–70); however, a different policy was followed in respect of the Federal Republic of Yugoslavia. This matter is discussed in Chapter 6.

The capacity to enter into relations with other states

The fourth requirement that the state has capacity in its external dealings is a requirement drawn from Latin America, although it has as well found favour in the United States.[39] It is arguable that this criterion will be applicable in the case of the few remaining colonies, protectorates and territories subject to trusteeship. It is, however, arguable whether this is a distinct criterion. If the government has internal control then capacity to conduct external relations is a consequence not a criterion of statehood. If it does not have internal control then it will lack the capacity to give effect to international obligations.

The object of this criterion is to act as a barrier to the acknowledgment of satellite states. An example is afforded by Manchuria. In 1931, the Japanese conquered Manchuria and the following year proclaimed the new independent state of Manchukuo. When the matter was placed before the League of Nations the League decided to send a commission of enquiry under Lord Lytton which noted that the administration was in the hands of Japanese officials. In the light of the report the League concluded that Manchukuo was under the control of Japan and thus not entitled to recognition.[40]

The criteria listed above are not employed on every occasion and in some circumstances the recognition of a state involves a delicate exercise in political judgment. The subject will be explored further in the chapter devoted to recognition. Consideration will also be given there to the problems posed by the disintegration of the Federal Republic of Yugoslavia.

(b) Protectorates and protected states

In the 19th century it was the practice for certain European powers to create protectorates over undeveloped areas of Africa;[41] this was normally achieved by a treaty with a local or tribal ruler. The effect of such an agreement was that the local ruler retained control of internal affairs but the protecting state would conduct external relations on its behalf. The concept of the protectorate applied not only in Africa[42] but elsewhere and its effects continued beyond 1945.

Prior to the establishment of the protectorate, the territory did not have international personality and once the protectorate ceased then the territory became a state in its own right. As indicated above, the effect of the protectorate was to permit the protecting state to determine the conduct of external relations although sometimes the exact legal status of a protectorate was less than clear cut.[43] The system of protectorates was therefore a

---

39 See Third Restatement of the American Law Institute.

40 The role of the United Kingdom in the affair and the conduct of John Simon (Foreign Secretary 1931–35) is discussed in David Dutton's *Simon: A Political Biography of Sir John Simon*, 1992, Chapter 5.

41 Eg, Swaziland, Northern Rhodesia, Kenya, Uganda, Nyasaland.

42 Eg, Kuwait became a British protectorate in 1899; sometimes such a arrangement was said to create a 'vassal state'. See the relations between China and Tibet governed by treaties in 1904, 1914, 1951 and 1954.

43 On the status of protectorates, see *Ex p Sekgome* [1910] 2 KB 576; *Sobhuza II v Miller* [1926] AC 518 (PC); *Nyali Ltd v Attorney General* [1956] 1 QB 1; [1957] AC 253; *Ex p Mwenya* [1960] 1 QB 241; *R v Amihya* (1964) 53 ILR 102.

product of the colonial system and in the fullness of time most became independent states endowed with full legal personality.

In contrast a protected state is a state that already enjoys international personality but has entered into an arrangement whereby another state exercises certain functions on its behalf. In normal conditions such an arrangement will not be readily construed as depriving the protected state of international personality. Clearly everything will depend on the interpretation of the precise agreement.[44] An example would be the Treaty of Fez of 1912 whereby France agreed to exercise certain sovereign powers on behalf Morocco; such an arrangement did not deprive Morocco of international personality.[45]

There are few protected states remaining but an example might be Bhutan which although becoming a member of the United Nations in 1971 is bound by treaty 'to be guided by India in the conduct of its external relations'.

However, a state will not be regarded as protected if it voluntarily delegates certain of its functions to another state. An example is afforded by the case of Liechtenstein, which had been refused admission to the League of Nations because it delegated certain of its sovereign functions. Liechtenstein became a party to the statute of the International Court of Justice and was a party to the celebrated *Nottebohm* litigation.[46] In 1990, it became a member of the United Nations. Similarly a state whose independence contains provisions to guarantee future conduct will not be regarded as protected.[47]

(c) Federal states

Traditional constitutional law recognises that there are a number of forms in which a state can exist. First, it may be a unitary state, such as the United Kingdom, in which all power is ultimately held at the centre.[48] Secondly, it may be a federal state in which there is a formal distribution of powers between the centre and the constituent parts.[49] Thirdly, there may be a confederation where a number of states come together in a loose association with few powers held at the centre. In the final analysis, it is a matter for each state to determine the model that is suitable for it; in a state that comprises a number of languages and ethnic groupings over a broad territory a federal solution may be preferable to a unitary state. To determine whether a state is federal or unitary is a

---

44 *Rights of United States Nationals in Morocco* [1952] ICJ 185.

45 See *Nationality Decrees in Tunis and Morocco* case (1923) PCIJ, Ser B, No 4, where the Court observed that the 'extent of the powers of a protecting State in the territory of a protected state depends, first, upon the treaties between the protecting state and the protected state establishing the Protectorate, and, secondly, upon the conditions under which the Protectorate has been recognised by third powers as against whom there is an intention to rely on the provisions of these Treaties'. See, also, *Rights of Nationals of the United States in Morocco* case (*France v United States*) (1952) ICJ 176.

46 Liechtenstein became a party to the statute in 1949 and thus was able to operate the provisions of the Optional Clause against Guatemala. See *Nottebohm* case (1953) ICJ 122; (1955) ICJ 4.

47 Cyprus became independent in 1960, subject to a Treaty of Guarantee which allowed the guarantors to intervene to protect the *status quo*.

48 Thus, in respect of devolution schemes for Scotland, Wales and Northern Ireland, this is an example of delegating central government power without relinquishing sovereignty. See Scotland Act 1998; Government of Wales Act 1998; Northern Ireland Act 1998.

49 The precise distribution being set out in a written constitutional document as in the United States or Germany with a supreme judicial body charged with ensuring that the distribution is respected.

question of constitutional law to be resolved by interpreting the basic constitutional documents.

From the perspective of international law, a federal state can give rise to a number of problems. First, there is the problem if parts of the federation wish to secede; is that a problem that can be regarded as purely internal? Secondly, to what extent should international law recognise a right of self-determination on the part of the constituent parts? As events in Yugoslavia have demonstrated there are sometimes few easy answers to these questions and much is a matter of degree and appreciation.

The first question that arises is as to who is to conduct external relations on behalf of the federal state? Normally, that will be set out in the federal constitution. So that Art 1, s 10 of the United States Constitution (1787) places the responsibility for the conduct of external relations on the federal government.[50] It may be that the constitution permits a particular unit to enter into agreement with another state on a matter of local interest such as the maintenance of common facilities.[51]

There have been instances where international law has disregarded the federal structure of a state. Thus, in 1945 the Soviet Union was able to secure the admission of Byelorussia and the Ukraine as members of the General Assembly even though they were at that time simply constituent parts of the Soviet Union. The effect was to give the grouping three votes but was considered a small price to pay for involving the Soviet Union within the United Nations.

A more difficult problem has arisen with federal states in respect of the negotiation of treaties. It may be that a federal state negotiates certain treaty obligations on the international plane but the component unit has executive or legislative authority in the same area; this can give rise to problems if the state or province takes a different view from the central government.

(d) Recognition

One of the most important questions that arise in respect of states are the those turning on recognition. Recognition is the name given to the process by which a particular factual situation is accorded certain legal consequences. The subject itself has been dominated by theories. Broadly, the constitutive theory holds that it is the fact of recognition that confers legal status upon the state. In contrast, the declaratory theory holds that what matters is whether certain criteria for statehood have been met and when they have then the state exists. Any recognition is, thus, an acknowledgment of an existing state of affairs. This area of law has been complicated by the practice in the past of recognising both governments and states. The second difficulty is that recognition has consequences both on the international plane and in municipal law; a typical problem that might arise is as to whether state A can bring a legal action before the courts of state B. Having regard to a number of related problems, the subject of recognition is considered in Chapter 6.

---

50 The responsibility discharged by the Department of State since Thomas Jefferson became the first Secretary of State in 1789; Arts 24 and 73 of the German Constitution confer power on the Federal Government in matters of foreign affairs.

51 See Art 24(1)(a), German Constitution; in the United States local agreements have been made with Canadian provinces for the maintenance of facilities such as roads and bridges with the approval of the federal government.

(e) Determination of statehood

A state may come to an end by absorption, merger or annexation.[52] The disappearance of a state has to be contrasted with the disappearance of a government; a government may come to an end for a variety of reasons including civil war but this will not lead to the extinction of the state. Thus, even if the authority of the government is undermined during a civil war the state is deemed to continue.

The arrival in power of Mikhail Gorbachev in 1985 resulted in a series of changes that have considerably modified state boundaries in Western Europe. The most significant was the decision of the regions in the German Democratic Republic (DDR) to join with the Federal Republic of Germany (BRD) with effect from October 1990. Such an absorption was precipitated by the collapse of the Marxist Leninist system and the imminent bankruptcy of the German Democratic Republic.[53] It is arguable that this was a form of absorption even though it took the form of accession.

The liberation of Eastern Europe from Soviet influence has resulted in other consensual changes. On 1 January 1993, the Czech and Slovak Federal Republic dissolved and two new states emerged in the form of the Czech Republic and Slovakia. Technically this is an example of voluntary dissolution.

Within the former Soviet Union the changes have been far reaching. The Baltic States announced their independence in 1990 and this was recognised by the Soviet Union.[54]

At the same time the Republics of the Soviet Union indicated their wish to become sovereign states. In December 1991 the Alma Ata Declaration recorded the extinction of the Union of Soviet Socialist Republics and the creation of the Commonwealth of Independent States (CIS). At the same time it was recognised that the Russian Federation would succeed to the rights and obligations of the USSR including the entitlement to a permanent seat on the United Nations Security Council. Whether this is a form of managed dismemberment or simple disintegration the lesson is clear; when a large federation begins to break up the military and economic changes may be so rapid that the role of the constitutional lawyer is limited to providing a legal framework for changes that have already been wrought.

It is proposed to deal with the history of the Socialist Federal Republic of Yugoslavia at the appropriate place; however it should be noted that after 1945 the federal state comprised six republics (that is, Bosnia-Herzegovina, Slovenia, Croatia, Serbia, Montenegro and Macedonia). Beginning with the declaration of independence by

---

52   This will not be an issue today, since any annexation coupled with the use of force will be unlawful under the United Nations Charter (1945). The matter is well illustrated by the invasion of Kuwait by Iraq in August 1990. After the initial invasion, Iraq purported to annex Kuwait but such annexation was declared unlawful in a number of Security Council resolutions.

53   The State Treaty on Unification was signed on 31 August 1990 and provided for unification on 3 October 1990 by means of the accession of the German Democratic Republic under the terms of the then Art 23 of the *Grundgesetz* which was itself then repealed by Art 4(2) of the Unification Treaty. Article 146 of the *Grundgesetz* has been modified to read: 'This basic law, which following the achievement of the unity and freedom of Germany is valid for the entire German people ...'

54   This procedure was slightly unusual because the absorption of Estonia, Latvia and Lithuania in 1940 was regarded by Western Europe as simple annexation and both the United Kingdom and the United States had refused to recognise the territory as *de jure* part of the Soviet Union. In 1991 the Soviet Union recognised their independence.

Croatia and Slovenia in June 1991 the Socialist Federal Republic of Yugoslavia (SFRY) has simply disintegrated with military events running ahead of constitutional schemes. In short this has been an example of dissolution of a federal state without agreement. By 1995 Security Council Resolution 1022 could indicate that the Socialist Federal Republic of Yugoslavia 'has ceased to exist'.

In contrast, there are occasionally cases of voluntary merger; an example is afforded by the decision of North and South Yemen to come together in a single state named the Republic of Yemen.[55]

3 THE FUNDAMENTAL RIGHTS AND DUTIES OF A STATE

On the assumption that a state exists certain legal consequences flow; in broad terms they can be expressed as: (i) the doctrine of the equality of states; (ii) the principle of independence of states; (iii) the principle of non-interference; (iv) the principle of peaceful co-existence; (v) the principle of self-preservation or self-defence. To some extent, these principles overlap and are but consequences of each other however in the interests of clarity it is sensible to take each of them separately.

(a) The doctrine of equality of states

The natural lawyer tended to assert the notion of the equality of man before a Supreme Being so that it was logical for the natural lawyer to consider all states as theoretically equal within the sphere of the Law of Nations. Customary law in its positivist phase was founded upon the common consent of sovereign communities; so that it was a logical consequence that each was equal to the other as regards their legal personality. However, this equality was restricted to a narrow legal equality; in the sense that each state was equally answerable within the Law of Nations for its acts and the consequences of those acts. At no time have states been equal in economic or political power and there is a natural tendency for the stronger state to seek to exercise pressure upon the weaker. Although the number of states has grown considerably since 1945 the differences between states have increased dramatically, with some states possessing considerable economic, military and political power while others lack the means to feed or educate their own population.

The United Nations Charter (1945) is premised on the legal equality of states so that in the preamble it refers to 'the equal rights of men and women and of nations large and small' while Art 2(1) expressly asserts that: 'The Organisation is based on the principle of the sovereign equality of all its Members.' To a limited extent this is reflected in the rule that within the General Assembly each state has one vote. A quarter of a century later in the Declaration on Principles of International Law (1970),[56] it is expressly asserted that:

---

55   Ie, in 1990. For the text of the Agreement on the Establishment of the Republic of Yemen, see (1991) 30 ILM 820.

56   To be more precise, the Declaration on Principles of International Law concerning friendly relations and co-operation among states in accordance with the Charter of the United Nations (1970).

All States enjoy sovereign equality. They have equal rights and duties and are equal members of the international community, notwithstanding differences of an economic, social, political or other nature.

In particular, sovereign equality includes the following elements:

(a) States are juridically equal.

(b) Each State enjoys the rights inherent in full sovereignty.

(c) Each State has the duty to respect the personality of other States.

(d) The territorial integrity and political independence of the State are inviolable.

(e) Each State has the right freely to choose and develop its political, social, economic and cultural systems.

(f) Each State has the duty to comply fully and in good faith with its international obligations and to live in peace with other states.

There are of course a number of contrary indications. First, Art 23 of the United Nations Charter provides that certain states will be permanent members of the Security Council while others will become members only by election. Secondly, some states wield considerable economic, political and military power so that they will be major financial contributors to international organisations and their concerns will need to be addressed in promoting reform of international law.[57] Thirdly, on those occasions when an international agency needs to take any form of enforcement action such as the provision of humanitarian relief it will be reliant on the good will of the most powerful states.

Thus, it would seem that the concept of equality indicates that each state will be answerable in international law for its conduct. It is arguable that a number of consequences flow from the equality which might be expressed as follows: (i) that each state is independent; (ii) that states are entitled to jurisdiction within their own territory and must in principle abstain from interference in the affairs of other states; (iii) that state A will normally be immune from the jurisdiction of the courts of state B; and (iv) that in principle states are free to participate or not in international organisations.

(b) Independence

A significant aspect of statehood is independence; it is arguable that this concept is linked with that of the sovereign equality of states. It has been argued that independence is but a consequence of sovereignty. Be that as it may, independence normally indicates: (i) the right of the state to exercise jurisdiction over its territory and population; (ii) the duty not to intervene in the affairs of other states; and (iii) the right to exercise some forms of self-defence. To an extent it is clear that sovereignty implies independence and independence implies jurisdiction.

---

57 An example would be the concern of the United Nations to meet the concerns of the United States in respect of the Law of the Sea Convention (1982) prior to it entering into force in November 1994.

Independence is traditionally defined as freedom from the subjection of others. Judge Huber in the *Island of Palmas Arbitration*[58] observed: 'Sovereignty in the relations between States signifies independence. Independence in regard to a portion of the globe is the right to exercise therein, to the exclusion of any other State, the functions of a State ... '

While independence is an aspect of statehood, it is also clear that it is for international law to determine the limits of such independence; it is not a matter to be determined by the unilateral declaration of a particular state. The conventional view is that limitations on independence will not be lightly assumed; in the *Lotus* case[59] the Permanent Court of International Justice observed:

> International law governs relations between independent States. The rules of law binding upon States therefore emanate from their own free will as expressed in conventions or by usages generally accepted as expressing principles of law and established in order to regulate the relations between these co-existing independent communities or with a view to the achievement of common aims. Restrictions upon the independence of States cannot therefore be presumed.

It is possible for a state to voluntarily accept restrictions upon its independence; an example is afforded by the Austro German Customs Union case that came before the Permanent Court of Justice.[60] The facts were simple in the extreme. In 1919, Austria had agreed under Art 88 of The Treaty of St Germain to abstain from any act that might compromise her independence; this obligation was repeated and to some extent broadened in the Geneva Protocol of 1922. At a later date, it was proposed that Austria and Germany should establish a customs union; an advisory opinion of the Permanent Court was sought as to whether this was compatible with the prior treaty obligations of Austria. The Court concluded in the negative but in an interesting dissenting opinion Judge Anzilotti observed that independence should not be lost by a voluntary submission to limitation of action but would be forfeited where state A sought to place itself under the legal control of State B.

Existing international instruments place an important emphasis upon independence. Article 2(7) of the United Nations Charter (1945) reads in part: 'Nothing contained in the present Charter shall authorise the United Nations to intervene in matters which are essentially within the domestic jurisdiction of any State or shall require such Members to submit such matters to settlement under the present Charter ...' A similar sentiment appears in the Declaration on Principles of International Law (1970)[61] which asserts that:

> No State or group of States has the right to intervene, directly or indirectly, for any reason whatever, in the internal or external affairs of any other State.

The problem then arises as to what is an 'essentially domestic matter' and who is to make that determination. In the 1950s and 1960s Western colonial powers tended to view difficulties with colonies as domestic but this argument did not prevail with the United Nations General Assembly. In the particular case of apartheid South Africa continued to

---

58 (1928) 2 RIAA 829, p 838.
59 *The Lotus* (1927) PCIJ, Ser A, No 10.
60 (1931) PCIJ, Ser A/B, No 41; 6 ILR 26.
61 Ie, the Declaration on Principles of International Law concerning Friendly Relations and Co-operation among states in accordance with the Charter of the United Nations (1970).

contend that the nature of civil liberties was an internal or domestic matter; the United Nations did not accept this contention.

Although a state may in principle act within its own territory there are some obvious limitations dictated by the need to respect the rights of others. In the *Corfu Channel* case, the International Court of Justice noted 'every State's obligation not to allow knowingly its territory to be used for acts contrary to the rights of other States'.[62] There is no agreed list of limitations but most would accept there is a duty not to cause environmental damage,[63] not to subvert another government,[64] not to abuse human rights,[65] and not to conduct police operations without permission on the territory of another state.[66]

(c) Jurisdiction and immunity from jurisdiction

As indicated above it is generally agreed that one of the attributes of statehood is the right to exercise jurisdiction within the territory and over the population. This matter will be dealt with separately in Chapter 8.

A related consequence is said to be that state A and its officials will normally be immune from the jurisdiction of the courts of state B in respect of official acts. This matter too will be dealt with separately in Chapter 9.

(d) Self-defence

It was normally accepted that in customary law a state had a right in the final analysis to take measures to defend itself against attack, Today this is also regulated by the related provisions of Art 2(4) and Art 51 of the United Charter (1945). These provisions give rise to complex issues as to when force may lawfully be employed and are therefore postponed for consideration in Chapter 21.

(e) Peaceful co-existence

Classical international law developed in the period prior to 1914 and regulated the dealings of like minded Western European states together with the United States whose legal system and culture drew upon the common law tradition of Locke and Blackstone. Since that time the landscape has changed considerably. The accession to power of the Bolsheviks in 1917 allowed a Marxist Leninist regime to emerge that had radically different ideas about international society. Although not all Marxist thinking about international society can be described as coherent the more extreme versions did posit a conflict between capitalist states and socialist states; indeed classic Marxist thought

---

62 *Corfu Channel (The Merits)* (1949) ICJ 4, p 22.

63 *Trail Smelter Arbitration* (1938–41) 3 RIAA 1905.

64 *Nicaragua v United States (The Merits)* (1986) ICJ 14.

65 Either by virtue of particular regional human rights treaties to which the state may be a party or by virtue of the general provisions on human rights contained within the United Nations Charter.

66 See SC Res 138 of June 1960 concerning the abduction of Adolf Eichmann from Argentina. It was accepted that the conduct did represent a *prima facie* violation of the territorial sovereignty of Argentina.

viewed the state not as a permanent unit of international society but as an entity that in time would whither away. Marxist thought traditionally viewed economic power as the dominant force in society. Political institutions and the legal system that is established were viewed merely as the 'superstructure' which existed to give effect to the will of the class which controlled the means of production distribution and exchange. Until the Bolsheviks obtained power in 1917 it was not necessary to reconcile the Law of Nations with Marxist thought. However, after 1917 the first instinct was to maintain that there were two systems of international law one for the capitalist world and one for the socialist world but by the 1930s writers had come to accept that there was a single form of international law.

The intervention by foreign forces in Russia after the Revolution in 1917 had tended to influence communists that war between capitalist and socialist states was inevitable and that any such conflict would result in the spread of Marxist communism to former capitalist states. The need for allied co-operation in the Second World War and the granting of a permanent seat in the Security Council to the Soviet Union meant that objections to international law had to be conducted from within its own institutions.

Marxist thought tended to be hostile to rule of customary international law as being the product of the dominant bourgeois states of 19th century. The Western European emphasis had tended to be upon free trade, democracy and free enterprise within the rule of law; even if the Marxist theory of international law was not fully worked out it was certainly clear that it was in conflict with Western European assumptions not least in its wish to spread revolutionary socialism to other states.

After 1945 the position became more complicated as newly independent states swelled numbers within the General Assembly. Such states rejected any attempts to limit their sovereignty and asserted the right to proceed with a social and economic system of their own choosing. Many such states were poor and there was a natural tendency to place emphasis on a planned economy with limitations on foreign companies; such states sought to achieve economic growth through central direction and controls on foreign investment. In short, international society had now to accommodate different social systems. At the same time the conflict of 1939–45 had demonstrated that international law had to find a means to accommodate tensions in a nuclear age. The doctrine of peaceful co-existence began to emerge against this background.

After earlier attempts,[67] the Sino-Indian Treaty of 1954 set out five principles of peaceful co-existence and this was restated in the Bandung Conference of 1955. Shortly after, in 1956, the new General Secretary of the Soviet Union Nikita Krushchev[68] in seeking to distance himself from the legacy of Josef Stalin argued that war between capitalist and communist states was not inevitable and that communism would triumph peacefully both because of its ethical superiority and also its ability to deliver higher living standards for the common man. Thus, the USSR embarked on a policy of competing with capitalist states in the space programme. Krushchev followed a policy of

---

67 In 1949 the International Law Commission produced a draft Declaration of Rights and Duties of States and was alluded to in a number of General Assembly Resolutions: 1949 (IV) 375; 1951 (VI) 596, without being taken any further.

68 Nikita Krushchev (1894–1971) (General Secretary of the Communist Party 1953–64).

peaceful co-existence[69] in international affairs subject to the reservation of a right to intervene in those countries in Eastern Europe where Soviet influence was threatened.[70] The doctrine of peaceful co-existence was as much a political doctrine as a legal principle but it drew upon traditional strands in international law and reworked them to meet the anxieties of the Cold War and the nuclear age. In essence the doctrine required respect for territorial integrity and sovereignty, non-aggression, and non-interference in internal affairs based on the principle of the equality of status. In the years after 1956, the USSR claimed that they were entitled to exercise control within those countries within their sphere of influence in Eastern Europe.[71] Thus, the doctrine itself was not new in that it drew upon traditional principles of international law and it had some similarity with the 19th century concepts of spheres of influence. In respect of problems between East and West the doctrine was designed to reduce tension and allow each to operate within its own sphere.

In respect of third world countries the doctrine had the advantage that each would be allowed to choose its own social system free from interference. This was reflected in some regional instruments. Thus, Art 13 of the Charter of the Organisation of American States (1948) indicates the right of each state 'to develop its cultural, political and economic life freely and naturally' and elements of the principle of peaceful co-existence are to be found in the Charter of the Organisation of African Unity (1963) and the preamble to the Declaration of Principles of International Law (1970). The latter document represented an attempt to present the principle of peaceful co-existence in a more coherent legal form deprived of the political rhetoric. The preamble in effect states seven principles which may be summarised thus:

(i)   States shall refrain in international relations from the threat or use of force.

(ii) States shall settle their international disputes by peaceful means.

(iii) States recognise a duty not to intervene in matters within the jurisdiction

      of another state.

(iv) States recognise a duty to co-operate with one another in accordance with the United Nations Charter.

(v)   States recognise the principle of equal rights and self-determination of peoples.

(vi) States recognise the principle of sovereign equality.

(vii) States agree to fulfil in good faith the obligations assumed under the Charter.

Thus, by 1970 the principle of peaceful co-existence had been given a more concrete form and the subsequent change in Soviet Foreign policy under Mikhail Gorbachev lead to a

---

69 Made easier by the fact that Andrei Gromyko (1909–89) served as Foreign Minister from 1957–85; Gromyko had participated in the Tehran, Yalta and Potsdam conferences and previously served as Ambassador to the United States.

70 Thus explaining the decision to intervene in Hungary in October 1956 and the installation of the regime of Janos Kadar.

71 Thus, the principle was stretched to accommodate the so called Brezhnev Doctrine which argued that the Soviet Union was entitled to intervene in any state in Eastern Europe in which the system of state socialism was threatened. This doctrine was relied upon to intervene in Czechoslovakia in 1968 and oust the liberal regime of Alexander Dubcek. The doctrine itself being named after Leonid Brezhnev (1906–82) (General Secretary of Communist Party of USSR 1964–82).

greater willingness to work within existing international institutions.[72] It is therefore doubtful today as to what the phrase 'peaceful co-existence' adds to obligations arising under other international instruments.

4 INDIVIDUALS

In the 17th century, when the Law of Nations was seen as founded on natural law principles, it was logical to view individuals as endowed with legal personality. However, the rise of positivism in the 18th century placed the state at the centre of international law; only the state was endowed with legal personality and the subject itself was concerned with the rights and duties of states. It might have been said that treaties that provided protection for slaves constituted an exception as indeed did the provisions in customary international that provided for universal jurisdiction in respect of pirates.[73] Thus, at the turn of the century Lassa Oppenheim could write: 'States solely and exclusively are the subjects of international law.'[74]

However, there is no doubt that the position has changed in the course of the present century. Certain jurists such as Kelsen argued that as the state is but an abstract agglomeration of individuals then the duties imposed on the State are duties binding on the individuals within that state. According to Kelsen, international law and state law both bind individuals but the former does so by operating through the concept of the state while the latter does it directly.[75] Support for a less traditional approach is to be found in the judgment of the Permanent Court of International Justice in the *Danzig Railway Officials* case,[76] where the Court held that a treaty could in certain circumstances confer rights directly on individuals and that there was nothing in international law to prevent individuals from acquiring rights directly under a treaty provided it was the intention of the parties. The principle that certain provisions of a treaty may be invoked by individuals in national courts is a central doctrine of European Union law today.[77]

The 20th century has witnessed a change in the attitude to conflict. In the 16th or 17th century the defeated party might be obliged to hand over territory but the ruler would retain his thrown. In the 20th century the conflicts fought have engaged entire nations and resulted in unparalleled loss of human life. In these circumstances the demand arose that those who offended against international order should be held personally to account and that there should be no defence by virtue of office held. Although attempts to indict Kaiser Wilhelm I were not pursued the concept of personal responsibility was raised. The Nuremberg Tribunal (1945) was premised on the personal responsibility of individuals and Art 7 of the Charter made it clear that there would be no immunity by virtue of office.

---

72 As exemplified by the policy of *detente* followed by the Soviet Foreign Minister Eduard Shevardnadze after 1985.

73 See *Re Piracy Jure Gentium* [1934] AC 586.

74 LH Oppenheim, *International Law*, 1st edn, 1905.

75 H Kelsen, '*Les rapports de système entre le droit interne et le droit international public*' (1926) 14 HR 227.

76 *Advisory Opinion on the Jurisdiction of the Courts of Danzig* (1928) PCIJ, Ser B, No 15.

77 Case 26/62 *Van Gend en Loos v Nederlandse Administratie der Belastingen* [1963] ECR 1; Case 6/64 *Costa v ENEL* [1964] ECR 1.

The counts charged in the indictment were all directed against individuals and the judgment of the tribunal made it clear that the holding of state office was not a barrier to personal responsibility. In giving judgment, the Nuremberg Tribunal had noted:

> Crimes against international law are committed by men, not by abstract entities, and only by punishing individuals who commit such crimes can the provisions of international law be enforced.[78]

The principle that individuals will be answerable for breaches of duties imposed by international law has been maintained by the International Tribunal for the Persecution of Persons Responsible for Serious Violations of International Law Committed in the Territory of the former Yugoslavia (1993) and the International Tribunal for Rwanda (1994). Further the agreement to proceed to an International Criminal Court reached in 1998 is designed to ensure that individuals answer for a wide variety international crimes. International instruments produced have paid attention to individual responsibility. Article IV of the Genocide Convention (1948) indicates that persons shall be punished regardless of 'whether they are constitutionally responsible rulers, public officials or private individuals'. In more recent times, Security Council Resolution 674 of 29 October 1990 reminded Iraqi leaders of their personal responsibility for acts contrary to international law committed within Kuwait.[79]

It is sensible to reflect on why there has been such a steady shift towards personal responsibility. First, it is clear that the First World War had a profound effect on the European outlook; the very heavy loss of life caused by ever more lethal armaments prompted governing classes in European states to conclude that the price demanded by war was simply too high and that an international legal order should be put in place to restrain aggression. This coincided with the rise of socialist parties in European countries that placed emphasis on the ideal of international co-operation.

Secondly, international law now provides numerous methods for the peaceful resolution of disputes so that it is argued that there can be no justification for indiscriminate violence against the people of another state. Thirdly, a general view has grown that respect for international law does depend to some extent on the requirement that those who commit gross violations are held personally to account. Fourthly, there can be little doubt that technical change has enabled the various media to transmit detailed accounts of such violations Thus, causing public opinion to demand that something is done to bring wrongdoers to account.[80]

In addition to imposing duties on individuals international law has been active in promoting legal rights. It remains the case that the International Court of Justice only has contentious jurisdiction in respect of states but nevertheless the development of

---

78 Official Record, Vol 1 Official Documents, p 223 ; see also 1948 Tokyo International Tribunal.

79 In the Kosovo Crisis of April–June 1999, Serbian leaders were repeatedly warned about their personal responsibility for abuses of human rights.

80 Clearly the televising of conflict can influence public opinion. Newsreel accounts of the concentration camps of the Second World War played a significant part in informing the public. Attitudes to the Vietnam War were influenced by television. The conflict in Yugoslavia has been the subject of continued television coverage. The difficulties that can arise when public opinion demands 'something has to be done' are discussed by Douglas Hurd in *The Search for Peace: A Century of Diplomacy*, 1997, London: Little, Brown.

international and regional human rights instruments[81] has enabled individuals to pursue cases before international tribunals and it is a central doctrine of European Union law that treaty provisions are capable of conferring rights directly upon European citizens. It is certainly true that the operation of human rights law and European law does require the consent of individual states but the fact remains that more and more cases are brought by individuals before international and regional tribunals.

The willingness to allow individuals to bring cases before international tribunals is traceable back to the First World War[82] and it has been followed recently in the Iran-United States Claims Tribunal and the International Centre for the Settlement of Investment Disputes (ICSID).[83] Indeed, the United Nations Compensation Commission (UNCC) established after the Gulf War actually provides that individual applicants are to have priority.

Clearly, the position of the individual is a matter of context but the position has changed considerably since the first edition of Oppenheim in 1905 and the general principle is well stated by the learned editors of the present edition who observe in respect of the individual that: 'International law is no longer – if it ever was – concerned solely with states.'[84] In many instances international law may have created the right but it is vested in a particular state and it is enjoyed by an individual by operation of implementing national law.

5 CORPORATIONS

One of the features of the modern industrial age has been the accumulation of capital by large corporate enterprises. A corporation may be based in state A but might operate in many other states either directly or through wholly owned subsidiaries. Such enterprises are described as transnational or multinational enterprises. Most are highly reputable organisations whose technical skills have made a considerable contribution to improving standards of living; however problems do arise where an individual state has to deal with an entity that possesses such economic and political power. Many poorer states may be troubled by the political and economic power such enterprises command; while wealthier states are often concerned with the levels of foreign investment.

The first problem that can arise concerning corporations concerns that of *locus standi*. An illustration is afforded by the *Barcelona Traction* case.[85] In this case the facts were straightforward.

A company was established under Canadian law in 1911 in connection with the development of electricity supplies in Spain. In 1948 the company was declared bankrupt

---

81 The expansion in human rights law since 1945, both at the international and the regional level, is a matter well evidenced in treaty law.

82 The Mixed Arbitral Tribunals established under the Treaty of Versailles and the Upper Silesia Mixed Tribunal established under the Polish German Convention of 1922.

83 The International Centre for the Settlement of Investment Disputes (ICSID) was established in 1965 by the International Bank for Reconstruction and Development (World Bank).

84 R Jennings and A Watts, *Oppenheim's International Law*, 9th edn, 1992, Vol I (Peace), p 846.

85 *Barcelona Traction Light and Power Co (Second Phase)* (1970) ICJ 3.

by the Spanish authorities and steps were taken that proved damaging to the company. At first the Canadian government intervened but then withdrew. Nearly 90% of the shares were held by Belgian citizens. Thus, Belgium brought an action against Spain. Spain argued that Belgium lacked *locus standi*.

The International Court of Justice rejected Belgium's claim[86] and ruled that as the damage had been suffered by the company rather than the shareholders the international claim should have been brought by Canada. The case indicates that in certain circumstances an international tribunal will be required to recognise the well established municipal rule that a company has a legal personality distinct from that of its own members.

A second problem that can sometimes arise in the modern world is as to whether the courts of a particular state have jurisdiction over the acts of a multinational company. In strict terms this is a matter for the relevant rules of private international law. An illustration may suffice. Suppose a plaintiff brings an action against company A before the courts of state X in respect of breaches of duty alleged to have been committed by company B (a wholly owned subsidiary of company A) when operating in state Y. Manifestly a question arises as to whether the courts of state X should accept or decline jurisdiction.[87] It should be noted at this stage that the operations of multi national companies may give rise to considerable problems of private international law.

A third problem that may arise concerning corporations is where a company enters into some form of contractual relationship with a state or state entity as part of a concession. In such a case the relevant law will be one of contract and question will arise as to the choice of law and the means of resolving the dispute. In many situations the relevant law will have been expressly chosen and arbitration may have been selected as mode of resolving the dispute. Probably no actual question of public international law will arise.

A fourth problem that can arise in respect of a corporation is where a corporation has operated in a particular state and then at a later date the government of that state seeks to nationalise or in some other way seek to expropriate corporate assets. In such a case difficult questions may arise as to the legality of the action and the appropriate level of compensation. These problems are concerns of public international law and will be dealt with in due course when considering the principles of state responsibility.

A fifth problem that can arise is as to the conduct of a multinational enterprises. Suppose an enterprise is based in state A but conducts its operations in state B should the wages it pays be equivalent to the norm in state B or should it be what is fair and just in all the circumstances.[88]

---

86 *Barcelona Traction Light and Power Co (Second Phase)* (1970) ICJ 3; for earlier proceedings, see *Barcelona Traction, Light and Power Co (Preliminary Objections)* (1964) ICJ 6.

87 These were in essence the facts of *Connelly v RTZ Corporation plc* [1998] AC 854 where, because of exceptional features, the House of Lords allowed litigation to proceed to trial in England. See also, *Lubbe and Others v Cape plc* [2000] 1 WLR 1545.

88 See United Nations Draft Code of Conduct on Transnational Corporations (1978) 17 ILM 453, subsequently revised; ILO Tripartite Declaration on Principles Concerning Multinational Enterprises and Social Policy (1978) 17 ILM 453; OECD Guidelines for Multinational Enterprises (1976) 15 ILM 969.

In essence, a public company does not enjoy international legal personality as such but in some cases it may wield greater economic power than many states. Rather, such transnational companies are important international actors even if they do not enjoy full personality.

6 INSURGENTS AND NATIONAL LIBERATION MOVEMENTS

The position of insurgents has long been recognised in international law. Under customary international law the state will not normally be responsible for the acts of insurgents. The position is reaffirmed in the International Law Commission's Draft Article on State Responsibility (1996) whereby Arts 14 and 15 indicate that the acts of the insurgent will not become an act of government save that the insurgents will be retrospectively liable if they subsequently assume responsibilities of government.

The distinction between a group of insurgents and a national liberation movement is not always easy to draw. In general a national liberation movement will be seeking not only possession of territory but will be striving to wrest the power of government from colonial, alien or discriminatory forces. Thus, it is arguable that if a group is simply seeking to replace individual A with individual B as Head of State then the requirements for a national liberation movement have not been met.

It is often difficult for states to agree as to whether a particular group constitutes a national liberation movement and some states may refuse recognition because of disapproval of the methods employed. In some instances national liberation movements have been granted observer status at the United Nations but this has not been without difficulty.[89] A number of writers have argued that the liberation movement has a temporary status in international law; some liberation movements are successful in which case a state is created having full personality in international law[90] or the movement simply fails.[91] The practical reality of contemporary politics is that in certain situations a state will be obliged to negotiate with a liberation movement, however much it may disapprove of its methods, as part of the general scheme of conflict resolution. In any post-colonial situation, a lasting peace is normally obtainable by including all relevant parties in the negotiations.

7 MINORITIES

States normally comprise a wide variety of ethnic, social, religious and linguistic groupings. The essence of a minority is that the concept embraces a group numerically inferior whose members are nationals of the state but who exhibit both ethnic, religious and linguistic traditions and a settled determination to preserve those traditions.

---

89 Obligation to Arbitrate on UN Headquarters Agreement (1988) ICJ 12.
90 Namibia, Angola, Algeria, Zimbabwe.
91 In the case of Biafra. On Biafra, see Ijalaye, 'Was Biafra ever a state in international law?' (1971) 65 AJIL 551; F Forsyth, The Biafra Story, 1969.

In a modern state, it is normal for legislation to be passed to prevent discrimination against particular sections of the population.[92] Secondly, it is a matter of common knowledge that the most difficult problems since 1945 have been conflicts within a single state rather than the invasion of one state by another; often such conflicts have arisen because of tension between a majority and a minority population.

In some instances, the position of the minority is protected under treaty[93] and the modern movement in human rights law can be traced back to the efforts of the Congress of Berlin (1878) to protect minorities within the Ottoman Empire.

Although it cannot be claimed that minorities have a distinct international personality, such grouping do raise a number of practical difficulties in the operation of the international society. First, there is the difficult question as to whether a right of self-determination exists; this matter will be considered below. Secondly, there is the question as to when a mother country (state A) may intervene to protect a minority in state B.[94] Thirdly, difficulties can arise when a minority seeks to secede; in such instances it is rare for the secessionists to be able to obtain more than a limited number of recognitions.[95] Because of the difficulties that can be caused by secession the emphasis since 1945 has been to endeavour to persuade majorities to accord minimum human rights to those minorities within their borders.[96]

8 NATIVE PEOPLES

At first blush it is difficult to comprehend any sensible distinction between a minority group and native or indigenous peoples. In recent years considerable attention has focused upon indigenous or native peoples. Examples would be the Aborigines in Australia, the Maori in New Zealand and the Indians (Native Americans) in America. The essence of such groups is a degree of continuity with a pre-invasion or pre-colonial past.[97] However, it is doubtful whether such groups can have a distinct international personality and most of the problems relating to such groups will have to be resolved domestically within the context of the individual state. It has been calculated that at least 40 states contain groupings of indigenous peoples.

The general aspirational approach of international law is reflected in Principle 22 of the Rio Declaration on Environment and Development (1992) which states, in respect of native people, that indigenous people and their communities, and other local

---

92 In the United Kingdom, one can point to the Race Relations Acts 1965, 1968, 1976; the Sex Discrimination Act 1975; Disability Discrimination Act 1995. For a discussion of the expression 'ethnic group' in the domestic context of Race Relations legislation, see *Mandla v Dowell Lee* [1983] 2 AC 548.

93 See Treaties of Versailles, Neuilly, Trianon and St Germain 1919; Treaty of Upper Silesia 1922; *Polish Nationals in Danzig* case (1931) PCIJ, Ser A/B, No 44.

94 Czechoslovakia (1938); more recently, the efforts by Albania to assist the non Serb population in Kosovo.

95 Eg, Biafra (1967–70).

96 In this context it is sensible to bear in mind that the original wish of Western European leaders in 1990–91 was to try to preserve the structure of the Federal Republic of Yugoslavia.

97 As so defined by JR Martinex Cobo, the United Nations Special Rapporteur who produced a Study on the Problem of Discrimination against Indigenous Populations in 1983.

communities, have a vital role in environmental management and development because of their knowledge and traditional practices. States should recognise and duly support their identity, culture and interests and enable their effective participation in the achievement of sustainable development.

Further recognition was accorded by the production of Draft United Nations Declaration on the Rights of Indigenous Peoples adopted by the United Nations Commission of Human Rights in 1994.

However, the relations with such groups must be normally be matters of the domestic law of the individual state.[98] It is a matter of conjecture as to why there has been such an emphasis on the rights of indigenous persons in recent years. A number of reasons might be advanced. First, with the development of social history much attention has been placed upon the precise circumstances in which modern states were established. Secondly, the increasing interest may be seen as part of the wider human rights movement. Thirdly, there have been the efforts of bodies such as the Unrepresented Nations and Peoples Organisations (UNPO) an NGO working from the Hague. Fourthly, the interest may be part of wider environmental concerns as emphasis is placed on the disruption to existing cultures caused by economic growth.

9 MANDATED AND TRUST TERRITORY

The conclusion of the First World War gave rise to the problem as to what was to be done with certain colonial territory of Germany and Turkey. The solution to this problem was set out in the mandate scheme the essential elements of which was stipulated in Art 22(1) and Art 22(2) of the Covenant of the League of Nations which read as follows:

22(1) To those colonies which as a consequence of the late war have ceased to be under the sovereignty of the States which formerly governed them and which are inhabited by peoples not yet able to stand by themselves under the strenuous conditions of the modern world, there should be applied the principle that the well being and development of such peoples form a sacred trust of civilisation and that securities for the performance of this trust should be embodied in this Covenant.

22(2) The best method of giving practical effect to this principle is that the tutelage of such peoples should be entrusted to advanced nations who by reason of their resources, their experience or their geographical position can best undertake this responsibility, and who are willing to accept it, and that this tutelage should be exercised by them as Mandatories on behalf of the League.[99]

---

98 For the United States, see *Fletcher v Peck* (1810) 6 Cranch 87; 2 Peters 308; *Johnson and Graham's Lessee v M'Intosh* (1823) 8 Wheaton 543; *Cherokee Nation v State of Georgia* (1831) 5 Peters 1. In respect of New Zealand, see Treaty of Waitangi (1840); *Hoani Te Heuheu Tukino v Aotea District Maori Land Board* [1941] AC 308. In respect of Canada, see *R v Secretary of State for Foreign Affairs ex p Indian Association of Alberta* [1982] QB 892. In respect of tribal rights, see *Re Southern Rhodesia* [1919] AC 211.

99 This was of course in line with the basic objective of Woodrow Wilson to secure progress towards self-determination.

The character of the mandate was to differ according to the degree of social and economic development of the people. This mandated territory would be classified as class A, class B, or class C according to the levels of economic development.

At the conclusion of the Second World War, the mandate system was replaced by the trusteeship system whose main elements were set out in Chapter XII (Arts 75–85) and Chapter XIII (Arts 86–91). The general objective was that prior mandated territories would, by agreement, be transferred to within the trusteeship system. One of the difficulties of the mandate system had been a degree of uncertainty as to where sovereignty resided and a number of answers were proposed.[100]

The legal implications of the mandate system were examined in a series of cases concerning South West Africa. South West Africa had been created as a Type C mandate by the League of Nations under the Union of South Africa. When the Charter of the United Nations was drawn up, South Africa refused to transfer the territory to the trusteeship system. In 1950, in an Advisory Opinion, the International Court of Justice ruled that South Africa could not be obliged to transfer the territory.[101] However, the Court further ruled that South Africa remained bound by the terms of the mandate and that any change in the status of the territory required the consent of the United Nations as the successor in title to the League of Nations.[102] South Africa contended that the mandate had lapsed and refused to co-operate with the United Nations. In consequence the General Assembly established a Commission to monitor the development of the mandate in accordance with the advisory opinion of 1950. It was necessary in 1955 to seek a further advisory opinion as to the manner in which the supervisory function was to be exercised[103] and, in 1956, the International Court of Justice was required to determine whether petitioners from the mandated territories could be heard.[104]

In 1960, Ethiopia and Liberia as former members of the League brought proceedings against South Africa alleging that it was in breach of the terms of the mandate. In 1962, at the preliminary objections stage, the court decided that it had jurisdiction to determine the merits of the dispute.[105] However, at the second phase, the Court decided, by the casting vote of its President, that Ethiopia and Liberia did not have *locus standi* in a matter concerning legal obligations under the mandate.[106]

The 1966 judgment was viewed as excessively technical and lead the General Assembly to take a more direct interest in the problem. In 1966, a General Assembly

---

100 Sovereignty might be said to reside: (a) in the mandatory; (b) in the mandatory and the Council of the League; (c) in the principal allied powers; (d) in the League; (e) in the inhabitants of the mandated area; (f) sovereignty might be in abeyance.

101 *International Status of South West Africa* case (1950) ICJ 132.

102 The position became more acute after the National Party attained power in 1948 and Dr Hendrik Verwoerd (Minister of National Affairs 1950–58; Prime Minister 1958–66) began to introduce legislation to sustain the system of apartheid. Such a system was clearly at variance with the obligations under the original Art 22.

103 *South West Africa (Voting Procedure)* case (1955) ICJ 67.

104 *South West Africa (Hearing of Petitioners)* case (1956) ICJ 23.

105 *South West Africa (Preliminary Objections)* case (1962) ICJ 319.

106 *South West Africa (Second Phase)* case (1966) ICJ 6; the composition of the court had changed between the two hearings. The result of the litigation was greeted with dismay amongst third world states.

Resolution declared South Africa to be in breach of the terms of the mandate.[107] In 1967, the General Assembly established a United Nations Council for South West Africa (later to become the Council for Namibia) with the object of administering the territory until independence.[108] In 1968, the General Assembly changed the name of the territory to Namibia. Throughout this period, South Africa refused to co-operate with a number of General Assembly and Security Council Resolutions,[109] so that, in 1970, the Security Council declared South Africa's continued presence in Namibia to be unlawful.[110]

Thereupon, the Security Council requested an opinion of the International Court of Justice as to the legal consequences of the continued presence of South Africa in Namibia. In giving judgment, the Court held that South Africa was acting unlawfully and was legally obliged to withdraw.[111] From 1972, the South West Africa People's Organisation (SWAPO) was allowed to participate as an observer in General Assembly discussions on Namibia and in 1976 the Security Council called for free elections in Namibia[112] and in 1985 condemned the attempt by South Africa to establish an interim government. Following complex negotiations beginning in 1988, and in consequence of a more flexible foreign policy by South Africa, independence for Namibia was secured on 21 March 1990.

10 CONDOMINIUM

Condominium is the name given to the situation when two or more states exercise sovereignty jointly over a territory. Examples are afforded by the condominium exercised over the Sudan by Great Britain and Egypt from 1898 until 1956 and that exercised over the New Hebrides by France and Great Britain from 1914 until 1980.[113] In some instances, the condominium is exercised not over land but in respect of a gulf or a bay. Sometimes, the device of a condominium is the appropriate vehicle prior to the granting of independence.[114]

The essence of condominium is the exercise of sovereignty by more than one state; it represents an exception to the normal rule of single sovereignty over the same territory. Thus, the announcement on 6 June 1945 by Great Britain, United States, Russia and France of a declaration of supreme authority over Germany did not constitute a condominium because there was no assumption of sovereignty.

An example of condominium is provided by the pluristatal bay – that is, the bay that is bordered by two or more states. In the *Gulf of Fonseca* case (1917) heard by the former

---

107 GA Res 2145 (XXI) (1967).

108 GA Res 2248 (XXI) (1967).

109 GA Res 2325 (XXII) (1967); GA Res 2372 (XXII) (1968); SC Res 245 (1968); SC Res 246 (1968).

110 SC Res 276 (1970).

111 Legal Consequences for States of the Continued Presence of South Africa in Namibia (South West Africa). Notwithstanding SC Res 276 (1971) ICJ 16.

112 SC Res 385 (1976).

113 New Hebrides became independent as the state of Vanuatu in 1980; see New Hebrides Act 1980; see, also, DP O'Connell, 'The condominium of the New Hebrides' (1972) 43 BYIL 71.

114 Eg, the islands of Canton and Endenbury subject to joint control by United States and United Kingdom became independent as part of Kiribati in 1979. See Kiribati Act 1979.

Central American Court of Justice,[115] the court ruled that the Gulf of Fonseca was a historic bay and subject to the joint sovereignty of the three riparian states of El Salvador, Honduras and Nicaragua. The status of the Gulf was raised again in the case concerning El Salvador and Honduras that came before a chamber of the International Court of Justice;[116] the Court noted that a condominium normally arose by express agreement between states but it could arise as the legal consequence of state succession. Thus, the Gulf of Fonseca which is nearly nineteen miles across at its mouth was held to be an historic bay and subject to joint sovereignty save in respect of the three mile limit.

11 SELF-DETERMINATION IN INTERNATIONAL LAW[117]

In general terms, the principle of self-determination refers to the right of persons living in a particular territory to determine the political and legal status of that territory.[118] This aspect of international law is linked to the theory in constitutional law of representative government: the view that those who govern draw their legitimacy from the consent of the people of the territory. In the 19th century, when the Ottoman Empire was in the process of disintegration, it became the practice to seek to guarantee minority rights.[119] The principle of self-determination developed from this desire to protect the position of minorities.

The principle of self-determination is linked to strains in constitutional law that are traceable back to the English Civil War and the political philosophy of John Locke; this political philosophy was adopted by parties during both the American War of Independence and the French Revolution. In essence, the philosophy places stress upon the desirability of popular representative government within a nation state; this can also be expressed by saying that the government of a territory draws its legitimacy from the will of the population. At the end of the 19th century, this approach was placed in the shadows during the period of colonial expansion but it had been recorded in writing in the American Constitution (1787) and it is not coincidental that the principle of self-determination began to emerge at the same time as the United States assumed a major role in world affairs. During the First World War, the principle was alluded to as a justification for the conflict and it was impliedly advanced by Woodrow Wilson in his statement of war aims made in January 1918;[120] the vision was held out of a peace settlement based upon ethnically identifiable peoples who would govern themselves.

---

115 *El Salvador v Honduras* (1917) 11 AJIL 510.

116 *Land, Island and Maritime Frontier Dispute* case (1992) ICJ 351; M Shaw (1993) 42 ICLQ 9292.

117 A Cobban, *Nation State and National Self-determination*, 1969; LC Green, 'Self-determination and the settlement of the Arab-Israeli conflict' (1971) 65 AJIL 40; M Pomerance, 'The United States and self-determination' (1976) 70 AJIL 1; A Whelan, 'Wilsonian self-determination and the Versailles Settlement' (1994) 43 ILCQ 99; R McCorquodale, 'Self-determination: a human rights approach' (1994) 43 ICLQ 857; H Quane 'The United States and the evolving right to self-determination' (1998) 47 ICLQ 537.

118 The definition is that of Michael Akehurst as set out in *A Modern Introduction to International Law*, 6th edn, 1987.

119 As, for example, under the Treaty of Berlin (1878) whereby Bulgaria, Montenegro, Serbia, Romania and Turkey all assumed obligations to respect religious freedom.

120 The statement of war aims made on 8 January 1918 came to be known as the 14 points.

The idealistic Woodrow Wilson[121] sought at Versailles in 1919 to establish a settlement in Europe based on: (i) the principle of the rule of law in the resolution of international disputes; (ii) pursuant to this principle disputed areas and boundaries would be settled by plebiscite; (iii) that where possible identifiable peoples would be given statehood; (iv) that those ethnic groups too small or too dispersed would be accorded minority protection.[122]

The difficulty with the application of the principle was to decide which peoples were sufficiently numerate and proximate to constitute the 'self'; as Sir Ivor Jennings was to observe later 'the people cannot decide until someone decides who are the people.[123] In other words, it is clear that difficulties can arise as to the identity of the 'peoples' and the territory to which the principle applies. However, the principle tended in the German direction of the *Volk*; the idea that a state was founded not on agreed boundaries and institutions but on the ethnic identity or homogeneity of its peoples. From the outset, it was clear that such a principle would have to be applied with caution and restraint. Indeed Wilson's Secretary of State, Lansing, observed, in 1921: 'Without a definite unit which is practical, application of this principle is dangerous to peace and stability.'[124]

Before 1919 it was probably the case that no legal right to self-determination could arise unless it arose under a treaty.[125] Although the principle of self-determination is separate and distinct, it has to be read against the general background in the 1920s and 1930s, when statesmen were seeking to build peace and security by restrictions on the use of force.[126]

Self-determination was part of the general framework because it was thought that there could be no lasting peace and security unless there was a measure of justice.

After 1945 the principle of self-determination assumed a greater degree of importance as pressure grew for the granting of independence to peoples subject to colonial rule. The United Nations Charter (1945) referred to the principle of self-determination in Art 1 and Art 55 and a General Assembly Resolution of December 1952[127] urged that 'the States members of the United Nations shall uphold the principle of self-determination of all peoples and nations'. The objective during this period was to stress self-determination from colonial rule but to do nothing to precipitate pre independence secession movements. This dual track approach appears in the General Assembly's Declaration on the Granting of Independence to Colonial Countries and Peoples (1960);[128] para 2 refers to the right of self-determination, while para 4 refers to the need to respect the integrity of

---

121 Woodrow Wilson (1856–1924) (28th President of the United States 1913–21). Wilson had qualified as a lawyer but had also held a chair in political science before becoming President of Princeton University in 1902.

122 For a more worldly view of the peace conference, see H Nicholson, *Peacemaking*, 1919.

123 WI Jennings, *The Approach to Self Government*, 1956, pp 55–56.

124 7 April 1921 in an article in *The Saturday Evening Post*.

125 Eg, The Treaty of Versailles (1919) provided for a plebiscite in Upper Silesia to determine whether it wished to join with Poland or Germany.

126 The Peace of Paris (1928) (The Kellogg-Briand Pact 1928); the Stimson Doctrine of Non-Recognition (January 1932).

127 GA Res 637 A (VII).

128 GA Res 1514 (XV).

national territory.[129] In 1970, when the General Assembly adopted the Declaration on the Principles of International Law concerning Friendly Relations,[130] there were a number of references to the principle of self-determination but the document noted that nothing should be done 'to dismember or impair ... the territorial integrity or political unity of sovereign and independent states'.

Up until 1970, the principle could be applied simply in colonial situations to require the colonial power to grant independence. The difficulties began to arise after 1970, when it was sought to extend the principle to neo colonial or non-colonial situations. In such situations, application would need to be restrained and each case turned on matters of fact and degree.[131] The difficulty of applying the principle in many situations,[132] has lead to attempts to analyse further what the principle demands. It is now clear that what the principle requires will vary from one situation to another. First, in some situations such as pre-independence it may involve consultation with the people of a territory. Secondly, in some situations it may demand constitutional guarantees of democracy and non-discrimination. In essence, the principle has to be applied flexibly according to the facts of each individual situation.[133] Thirdly, there has been a readiness to admit that a simple reference to a 'people' and 'territory' will not be sufficient and there is a growing body of opinion that favours considering questions of self-determination alongside questions of human rights and recognition.[134] Thus, the Badinter Commission in considering the competing claims in Yugoslavia ruled that the rights of Serbs living in Bosnia-Herzegovina had to be taken into account before any possible right of self-determination by the Bosnians could be given effect to.[135] This is in conformity with the requirements of international human rights instruments that indicate that the principle of self-

---

129 The experience of the Belgian Congo (1960) and Nigeria (1967–70) indicated that great caution was required in seeking to apply the principle of self-determination.This had been recognised earlier in the decade. Article III of the Charter of the Organisation of African Unity (1963) requires 'respect for the sovereignty and territorial integrity of each state and for its inalienable right of independent existence'.

130 GA Res 2625 (XXV) (1970).

131 The principle was invoked in respect of the black majority in South Africa during the apartheid system (broadly, 1948–94); the principle has been raised in respect of the Palestinians and attempts to find a lasting peace settlement in the Middle East. The dissolution of Yugoslavia (1990–99) has witnessed various groupings preying in aid the principle. A further example arises in respect of dealing with Eritrea.

132 As UN Secretary General Boutros Boutros-Ghali observed in his Agenda for Peace: '... if every ethnic, religious or linguistic group claimed Statehood, there would be no limit to fragmentation,and peace, security and economic well-being for all would become much more difficult to achieve,' reproduced in A Roberts and B Kingsbury, *United Nations, Divided World*, 2nd edn, 1993.

133 For an interesting discussion as to whether there is a 'right' at all, and for an analysis of whether the scheme of W N Hohfeld can be applied, see Anthony Whelan, 'Wilsonian self-determination and the Versailles Settlement' (1994) 43 ICLQ 99.

134 The argument being that the principle of self-determination must be flexible enough to accommodate other requirements of international law in particular to ensure that the human rights of all parties are protected. The conduct of the various parties in the dissolution of Yugoslavia indicates the wisdom of this approach. See R McCorquodale,'Self -determination: A human rights approach' (1994) 43 ICLQ 857.

135 Opinion No 2 (11 January 1992) 3 EJIL 183–184.

determination is not an absolute value and must be applied with sensitivity and flexibility.[136]

Actual judicial decisions on the principle of self-determination have been limited; the principle was raised and accepted in both the *Namibia*[137] and the *Western Sahara*[138] advisory opinions; both involved post colonial situations and not surprisingly the principle received judicial support. More recently the issue has arisen indirectly. One of the arguments raised by Portugal in the *East Timor* case[139] was as to whether the agreement between Indonesia and Australia infringed the right of the people of East Timor to determine their own future. While acknowledging the principle of self-determination the Court held itself unable to accept jurisdiction because it would involve ruling on the conduct of another state without its consent.

Of course, the principle of self-determination is fraught with difficulty when any attempt is made to extend it beyond the narrow colonial context; this is particularly so in the case of established states. An example is afforded by the separatist tendencies within the province of Quebec. *In re Reference by the Governor in Council concerning certain questions relating to the secession of Quebec from Canada*[140] the Canadian Supreme Court was required to rule on whether any right of self-determination arising in international law gave Quebec the right unilaterally to secede from Canada. In rejecting the existence of any such right the Court ruled:

(i) that international law recognises a distinction between internal self-determination[141] and external self-determination;

(ii) that any right of external self-determination arises in strictly limited circumstances;

(iii) that international law does not specifically grant component parts of sovereign states the legal right to secede unilaterally from the 'parent' state;

(iv) that international law supports the general principle of the territorial integrity of existing states;

(v) that any right to external self-determination could only arise:

    (a) in the colonial context;

    (b) where there has been alien subjugation; or

    (c) where the right of internal self-determination is denied.

---

136 See Art 1(3) of the ICCPR the identical provision in Art 1(3) of the ICESCR both indicate that the right to self-determination must be 'in conformity with the provisions of the Charter of the United Nations'.

137 The Legal Consequences for States of the Continued Presence of South Africa in Namibia (1971) ICJ 16.

138 *Western Sahara* case (1975) ICJ 12.

139 *East Timor* case (*Portugal v Australia*) (1995) ICJ 90; see AV Lowe (1995) 54 CLJ 484.

140 *In re Reference by the Governor in Council concerning certain questions relating to the secession of Quebec from Canada* (1998) 161 DLR (4th) 385. (In the case the Court had to consider whether any right of unilateral secession arose: (i) under the Constitution; or (ii) by virtue of international law. The Court answered both questions in the negative.)

141 By this is meant the entitlement of a people to pursue its political, economic, social and cultural development within the framework of an existing state – which is, of course, another way of alluding to the protection of minorities.

Thus, even if the population of Quebec could be characterised as a 'people' it was clear that as the people of Quebec had full rights to participate in civil and political life[142] no right of external self-determination could be said to exist.

12 INTERNATIONAL TERRITORY

The phrase international territory is often employed but it has little precise meaning other than to indicate that a particular piece of territory is subject to an international regime of control. The phrase is sometimes employed to indicate territory subject to trusteeship.

In such situations it is important to identify where sovereignty resides. Thus, where one state exercises a degree of sovereignty that in law is vested in another it is not correct to refer to the territory as 'international'. Thus, it would not apply in respect of Cyprus from 1878 to 1914 when the then Turkish island of Cyprus was under British administration. When Cyprus acquired independence in 1960 a number of international guarantees were put in place but this did not detract form the fact that sovereignty was vested in the state and that international guarantees did not detract form that fact.

More recently when NATO forces entered Kosovo in June 1999 this was regulated by a Security Council resolution and the territory itself remained as part of the sovereign territory of Serbia even though subject to international control. Thus, in many instances when the phrase 'international territory' is employed it indicates that at a particular time it might be subject to a degree of multinational control even though sovereignty is unaffected.

13 INTERNATIONAL ORGANISATIONS[143]

Since the 19th century, there has been a steady growth in the number and scope of international organisations. An international organisation indicates an organisation established by states under treaty as distinct from a private international union or a non-governmental organisation; the latter resulting from the initiatives of individuals or private corporations. The growth and development of international organisations can be traced back to the Congress of Vienna (1815) and the establishment of the Rhine Commission. The reasons for such a development are not hard to seek; states have increasingly come to realise that there are a wide variety of tasks that can only be accomplished by co-operating together and such co-operation has to be organised on a permanent basis. The international organisation exists to ensure that such a level of co-operation is achieved.

---

142 As was noted in evidence for close to 40 of the past 50 years the Prime Minister of Canada has been a Quebecer. In the last 50 years, Quebecers had at various times held all the major political, judicial and defence positions within the federal government. Quebec had not been subject to any form of attack on its physical existence or integrity and its fundamental rights had been respected. It was therefore not possible to say that the people of Quebec were oppressed.

143 See, generally, DW Bowett, *The Law of International Institutions*, 4th edn, 1982; C Archer, *International Organisations*, 2nd edn, 1992.

Although the United Nations is probably the best known organisation and *sui generis*, an increasing role is played by regional organisations. The principal regional forms are: the Organisation of American States (OAS), the Organisation of Central American States (ODECA), the Organisation of African Unity (OAU), the Association of South East Asian Nations (ASEAN) and the Arab League.

It has been well settled since the *Reparation for Injuries* case[144] that an international organisation can enjoy international legal personality. As the Court itself observed:

> ... fifty states, representing the vast majority of the members of the international community, have the power, in conformity with international law, to bring into being an entity possessing objective international personality and not merely personality recognised by them alone, together with the capacity to bring international claims.[145]

However, the essential question in most cases is not the possession of legal personality but the precise legal powers enjoyed by the organisation. Manifestly the legal powers enjoyed by the International Labour Organisation (ILO) will be different from those that govern the World Health Organisation (WHO). In such circumstances it will be necessary, as in municipal law, to determine the extent of those powers by inspection of the basic constitutional documents.[146]

Having noted the role of international organisations and their possession of legal personality a number of other aspects arise. These matters will be considered in Chapter 23.

14 CONCLUSIONS

It is evident that states remain the central legal persons. The nature of international society makes this inevitable. However, the number of international legal persons has steadily increased in the years since 1945. There are at least six reasons for this development. First, the number of states has increased nearly fourfold since 1945. Secondly, in the *Reparation for Injuries* case,[147] the court indicated that in appropriate cases new international persons could be created. Thirdly, the development of human rights law with its emphasis upon regional human rights treaties has served to emphasise the position of the individual.

Fourthly, the movement towards establishing international crimes has had the effect of placing the emphasis upon individual rights and duties. Fifthly, the number of international organisations has increased steadily in the period since 1945. Sixthly, a considerable number of international tribunals are confronted with claims made by a variety of legal persons such as companies and non-governmental organisations.

---

144 *Reparation for Injuries Suffered in the Service of the United Nations* (1949) ICJ 174; 16 ILR 318.

145 (1949) ICJ 174 , p 178; 16 ILR 318, p 321.

146 Legality of the Use by a State of Nuclear Weapons in Armed Conflict (1996) ICJ 66.

147 *Reparations for Injuries Suffered in the Service of the United Nations* case (1949) ICJ Rep 174;16 ILR 318.

CHAPTER 6

RECOGNITION OF STATES AND GOVERNMENTS[1]

1 INTRODUCTION

One of the most significant characteristics of international society is the pace of change. International society is never static. States come into existence,[2] merge[3] or dissolve;[4] likewise governments are elected, are ousted and in some cases return to power. Some mechanism has to exist whereby states and governments acknowledge the existence of other states and governments. That mechanism is provided by the process of recognition. In a world of over 180 states there will always be some states and governments that are subject to turmoil and dissent. Recognition is a statement by one international legal person acknowledging the existence of another entity as a legal subject. Recognition is normally an act of government and although subject to legal criteria it will be influenced by political considerations such as approval or disapproval of the regime in question. Thus, the United States withheld recognition from the communist regime in Peking after 1949 even though there could be no real doubt that it exercised effective control throughout the territory. Similarly, many Arab states withheld recognition from the state of Israel after 1949 because of disapproval even though the permanence of the government was not in dispute.

In respect of recognition there are a number of broad points that need to be absorbed at the outset. First, there is not a single principle that can reconcile in perfect harmony all past case law because the topic has been significantly influenced by political considerations. Secondly, recognition has effects on both the international plane and in municipal law. Thirdly, much of the relevant case law on the subject tends to arise in municipal courts in the context of commercial disputes. Fourthly, a distinction needs to be drawn between those cases turning on recognition of a state and those solely concerned with recognition of a government. Fifthly, matters relating to recognition are never static, a decision properly given at first instance may have to be reversed on appeal because the executive branch has had a change of view.[5] Sixthly, a distinction can be drawn between the act or process of recognition and the consequences of recognition. Seventhly,

---

1   See generally RY Jennings and AD Watts, *Oppenheim's International Law*, 9th edn, 1992, Vol 1, pp 126–204: H Lauterpacht, *Recognition in International Law*, 1948; TC Chen, *The International Law of Recognition*, 1951; IA Shearer, *Starke's International Law*, 11th edn, 1994, pp 117–43; I Brownlie, *Principles of Public International Law*, 5th edn, 1998, pp 85–105; H Kelse, 'Recognition in international law – theoretical observations' (1941) 35 AJIL 605; PM Brown 'The effects of recognition' (1942) 36 AJIL 106; E Borchard, 'Recognition and non-recognition' (1942) 36 AJIL 108H; M Blix, 'Contemporary aspects of recognition' (1970) HR 587; CR Symmons, 'United Kingdom abolition of the doctrine of recognition' [1981] PL 249; I Brownlie, 'Recognition in theory and practice' (1982) 53 BYIL 197; MJ Petersen, 'Recognition of governments should not be abolished' (1983) 77 AJIL 31; M Weller, 'The international response to the dissolution of the Socialist Federal Republic of Yugoslavia' (1992) 86 AJIL 569.

2   Eg, the emergence of separate states form within the borders of the former Yugoslavia.

3   The merger of North and South Yemen to form the Republic of Yemen in May 1990; the reunification of Germany in 1990.

4   The dissolution of Czechoslovakia in January 1993 to form two distinct states.

5   See *AM Luther v James Sagor & Co* [1921] 1 KB 453 (Roche J); 1 ILR 47; reversed by Court of Appeal [1921] 3 KB 532; 1 ILR 49 (Bankes, Warrington and Scrutton LJJ).

recognition is a subject in which complete agreement has not been forthcoming. As Hans Kelsen observed in 1941: 'The problem of recognition of states and governments has neither in theory nor in practice been solved satisfactorily. Hardly any other question is more controversial, or leads in the practice of states to such paradoxical situations.'[6] Another distinguished writer believed that the reason was that the subject of recognition was a 'subject of enormous complexity, principally because it is an amalgam of political and legal elements in a degree which is unusual even for international law'.[7] Indeed the division of opinion is such that some question the future role of recognition; thus Baxter J writing in 1978[8] could observe that recognition was 'an institution of law that causes more problems than it solves' and 'must be rejected and replaced by working arrangements that are flexible and realistic'. However, others see recognition as serving distinct functions within the international legal system such as: '... ensuring that only regimes clearly deserving such status are accepted as governments of states, assuring new governments that others will respect their status, and informing courts, government agencies, and nationals of recognising states that a particular regime is in fact the government of another state.'[9]

With these divisions of opinion in mind it is necessary to turn now to the substance of the matter.

2 RECOGNITION OF STATES ON THE INTERNATIONAL PLANE

Recognition indicates the willingness to deal with the another state as a legal person on the international plane. Such recognition may be express or implied. The recognition of states has to be distinguished from the recognition of governments.

Recognition may be accorded by a single state or by a number of states; in the latter case it is referred to as collective recognition. The subject of recognition has been the subject of two doctrines. The constitutive theory[10] holds that it is the act of recognition by other states that has the effect of creating the new state. This theory gives rise to a number of problems. First, the question arises as to what is the status of the state pending recognition. Secondly, what is to happen if only a limited number of states choose to recognise. Is it possible to refer to partial recognition or partial personality? Further, difficulties can arise when states that have chosen not to recognise state A then challenge breaches of international law by that same state. The theory holds that it is the act of recognition by other states that creates the state and confers upon it legal personality; however this approach may be at variance with the facts on the ground and has some affinity with the 18th century notion that a ruler had to wait until he was admitted to the select circle of fellow European rulers. The theory received some support in the period

---

6   Hans Kelsen, 'Recognition in international law – theoretical observations' (1941) 35 AJIL 605.
7   Cited by Josef Kunz in 'Critical remarks on Lauterpacht's *Recognition in International Law*' (1950) 44 AJIL 713.
8   Richard Baxter, Foreword to *LT Galloway, Recognising Foreign Governments, The Practice of the United States*, 1978, p xi.
9   MJ Peterson, 'Recognition of governments should not be abolished' (1983) 77 AJIL 31.
10 Subscribed to at various times by Anzilotti, Kelsen and Lauterpacht. Although for criticism that it gives a greater role to law than the political realities admit, see Josef Kunz (1950) 44 AJIL 713.

during which Metternich dominated European politics[11] and revolutionary governments would not be acknowledged by fellow rulers until they had been recognised. The essence of the theory is that the legal personality of the state is contingent not on the factual situation pertaining but on the will of other states. Taken to its logical extreme the theory holds that the unrecognised state cannot be the subject of rights and duties in international law. Such a position is not tenable in the interdependent world of the late 20th century. Notwithstanding the practical difficulties associated with the theory it has attracted a degree of academic support although this support has often been based on both a right to recognise and a duty to recognise. One of the attempts to strengthen the constitutive theory was made by Professor Lauterpacht, who argued that when the conditions of statehood established in international law had been met, then there was a duty to recognise.[12]

While the constitutive theory is correct in emphasising the right of each state to determine with whom it conducts bilateral relations it is highly arguable that if the act of recognition is a legal act (as this school claims) then determination should be based on the objective evaluation of established facts. However, the theory permits the subjective and politically influenced appreciation by others. Thus, it has been claimed by some that the theory confuses the capacity to enter into bilateral relations with capacity to act as an international legal person. Thus, if one takes the case of the Soviet Union; the government was not recognised by the United States until 1933 but it is clear that it had been effective for more than a decade and its laws had been given effect to not only in municipal courts but also within courts that were within the common law tradition.[13] Thus, it might be said that while the fact of non-recognition prevented full bilateral relations with the United States it did not prevent the Soviet Union being regarded as a full legal person by other states.

Those who support the constitutive theory point to the effect of recognition on the status of East Germany after 1949. Subsequent to that date methods had been found to avoid regarding East Germany as a legal nonentity.[14] Moreover, the case law does not support the constitutive theory. In the *Tinoco Arbitration*,[15] Great Britain made a number of claims against Costa Rica arising from the conduct of the Tinoco government. The point was raised by Costa Rica that the government had not been recognised by a number of states including Great Britain. However, Taft CJ[16] acting as arbitrator ruled that this was not material; what was in issue was whether the government met certain objective criteria of which the most important was effective control of the country. He ruled that Great Britain was entitled to pursue claims on the international plane on behalf of its citizens against a government which it had not itself recognised but which had been recognised by other states as the *de facto* government. Taft CJ further ruled that the number of recognitions would only be material if the fact of effective control had been in dispute.

---

11 Klemens Metternich (1773–1859) (Austrian Foreign Minister 1809–48).
12 See below.
13 See *Princess Paley Olga v Weisz* [1929] 1 KB 718.
14 Contrast *International Registration of Trade Mark (Germany)* case (1949) 28 ILR and *Carl Zeiss Stiftung v Rayner & Keeler (No 2)* [1967] 1 AC 853.
15 *Tinoco Arbitration (Great Britain v Costa Rica)* (1923) 1 RIAA 369.
16 William Howard Taft (1857–1930) (Secretary of State for War 1904–08; President of the United States 1909–13; Chief Justice United States Supreme Court 1921–30).

The second theory is the declaratory or evidentiary theory which holds that statehood exists prior to the act of recognition and that the act of recognition is simply a formal acknowledgment of existing facts. It is argued that such a theory is in line with the positivist approach since it places the emphasis on the conduct of the individual state. The declaratory theory tends to the view that the act of recognition is essentially a matter of politics not law and that only the consequences of recognition are legitimately within the sphere of international law. The evidence tends to favour the declaratory theory. First, a state may well argue that another 'state' is bound by the rules of international law even though that 'state' has not been accorded recognition. Secondly, the declaratory theory places the emphasis on the emergence of evidence and the establishment of facts and as such corresponds with the nature of events. Thirdly, the declaratory theory is in line with experience in other areas of law. Quite often events happen, technologies change and legal forms are invented to accommodate to these changes; in like terms the declaratory theory stresses the formal acknowledgment of established facts. Fourthly, the experience of history indicates that recognition is often withheld for political reasons. It is highly doubtful whether a strictly legal process could be subject to so many political variables. Fifthly, the pragmatic approach of municipal courts is to focus on the date that a state came into existence and the rule that recognition normally has a retroactive effect is consistent with the declaratory theory rather than the constitutive theory. Thus, the balance of the argument tends to favour the view that the act of recognition acknowledges rather than creates statehood.[17]

The position today is that most writers accept the declaratory theory and support is to be found in a number of international instruments. Thus, Art 3 of the Montevideo Convention on Rights and Duties of States (1933) reads:

> The political existence of the State is independent of recognition by the other States. Even before recognition the State has the right to defend its integrity and independence, to provide for its conservation and prosperity, and consequently to organise itself as it sees fit, to legislate upon its interests, administer its services, and to define the jurisdiction and competence of its courts. The exercise of these rights has no other limitation than the exercise of the rights of other States according to international law.

Three years later, in 1936, the Institut de Droit International observed that:

> ... the existence of the new state with all the legal effects connected with that existence is not affected by the refusal of one or more states to recognise.[18]

This approach is also reflected in Art 9 of the Charter of the Organisation of American States (1948) which reads:

> ... the political existence of the state is independent of recognition by other states. Even before being recognised the state has the right to defend its integrity and independence.[19]

---

17 If one examines some of the constitutional changes required by the Arbitration Commission in respect of the states of the former Yugoslavia, the assumption is that the state already exists but will not be acknowledged until it performs certain governmental acts.

18 (1936) 39 *Annuaire de L'Institut de Droit International* 300.

19 Sometimes described as the Bogota Charter of the Organisation of American States (1948). Article 9 became Art 12 in the 1967 amendment. Latin American countries tended to adopt a non technical approach to questions of recognition, preferring to place emphasis on the need to preserve diplomatic relations. This may be linked to the degree of political instability in the region.

Modern support for the declaratory theory is to be found in Opinion No 1 of the European Community Arbitration Commission on Yugoslavia where the Commission posed the question in respect of republics that sought to secede from the Federal Republic of Yugoslavia and then noted:

> ... the answer to the question should be based on the principles of public international law which serve to define the conditions on which an entity constitutes a State; that in this respect, the existence or disappearance of the State is a question of fact;that the effects of recognition by other States are purely declaratory.[20]

Therefore, the modern view must be that the effect of the act of recognition is declaratory. However, it is sometimes argued that there is a constitutive element to the process. For example if a problem arises in the municipal court of state A about the existence of a state or government that court will often be prepared to look at whether other states have formally recognised the entity; thus, a number of recognitions can have a cumulative effect in municipal law.[21] Indeed, this was acknowledged by the Arbitration Commission on Yugoslavia who observed in Opinion No 8 in the context of the recognitions accorded to constituent parts of the former Yugoslavia that 'while recognition of a state by other states has only declarative value, such recognition along with membership of international organisations, bears witness to these states' conviction that the political entity so recognised[22] is a reality and confers on it certain rights and obligations under international law'.

Thus, whatever the merits of the doctrinal disputes the evidence today indicates that the majority of states regard the act of recognition of being of declaratory effect; the criteria for such recognition may be based upon the Montevideo Convention (1933) or some modification thereof.

All the evidence indicates that individual states are careful about their discretion to recognise another state. The United Kingdom has traditionally taken a pragmatic position and the matter was set out by the Minister of State at the Foreign Office in 1986 in the context of the non-recognition of Bophuthatswana where it was stated:

> The normal criteria which the Government apply for recognition as a State are that it should have, and seem likely to continue to have, a clearly defined territory with a population, a Government who are able of themselves to exercise effective control of that territory, and independence in their external relations. Other factors, including some United Nations resolutions, may also be relevant.[23]

Similarly the United State has taken a robust attitude to recognition considering it to be a matter solely for the United States to determine. Thus, when the United States decided to make an early grant of recognition to the state of Israel, Warren Austin observed in the Security Council:

---

20 Arbitration Commission, EC Conference on Yugoslavia, 29 November 1991; 92 ILR 162.
21 *Democratic Republic of East Timor v State of The Netherlands* 87 ILR 73. See, also, *Republic of Somalia v Woodhouse Drake & Carey* [1993] QB 54, where Hobhouse J considered the number of international recognitions to be a relevant factor.
22 Opinion No 8 dated 4 July 1992; the opinion concludes that 'the process of dissolution of the Socialist Federal Republic of Yugoslavia is now complete'.
23 *Hansard*, HC Deb, Vol 102 (written answer), col 977, 23 October 1986.

I should regard it as highly improper for me to admit that any country on earth can question the sovereignty of the United States of America in the exercise of that high political act of recognition of the *de facto* status of a state. Moreover, I would not admit here by implication or by direct answer, that there exists a tribunal of justice or of any other kind, anywhere, that can pass judgment upon the legality or the validity of that act of my country.[24]

A more recent statement was given by the United States Department of State in 1976 where it was stated:

In the view of the United States, international law does not require a state to recognise another entity as a state: it is a matter for the judgment of each state whether the entity merits recognition as a state. In reaching this judgment, the United States has traditionally looked to the establishment of certain facts. These facts include effective control over clearly defined territory and population;and organised governmental administration of that territory;and a capacity to act effectively to conduct foreign relations and to fulfil international obligations. The United States has also taken into account whether the entity in question has attracted the recognition of the international community of states.[25]

While each state will follow its own traditions in the matter of recognition there is a growing tendency in the Western world to promote the process of collective recognition particularly amongst those states that are members of the European Union. In these circumstances other criteria may be adopted and these are discussed below.

In respect of the recognition of a state it would seem that it will still be a matter for the court to seek evidence from the executive branch as to whether a particular state has been recognised.[26]

3 RECOGNITION OF GOVERNMENTS ON THE INTERNATIONAL PLANE

Recognition of a government is distinct from recognition of a state. Recognition of a state will involve examining the evidence to determine whether certain criteria have been met.[27] In the case of recognition of governments, the concern is with those administrations that have secured power by violent or unconstitutional means. No problem arises when one administration is voted out of office and another takes its place; thus, no question of recognition arose in January 1993 when Bill Clinton was sworn in as President of the United States and George Bush departed from office. Such a process was dictated by the election result of November 1992 and the relevant provisions of the United States Constitution; indeed it is arguable that democratic constitutional government is contingent on periodic changes in office of political party.

---

24   SCOR 3rd Year, p 16.

25   (1978) 72 AJIL 337.

26   *Gur Corporation v Trust Bank of Africa Ltd* (1987) 1 QB 599; 75 ILR 675, where the letter from the Foreign Office drew a distinction between questions of recognition of a state and questions of recognition of a government; on the latter aspect, see below.

27   This may be the criteria under the Montevideo Convention (1933) or, as in the case of the Republics within Yugoslavia, it may be certain specific criteria.

However, where a regime has taken office unconstitutionally two approaches are possible. A state may ask whether certain objective criteria have been established by evidence; for example, does the administration possess effective control over the territory.[28] Alternatively, the state might ask itself whether the regime is politically compatible or can be relied upon to behave in a certain manner, for example, respect basic human rights. The first approach might be described as objective while the latter might be described as subjective. In the early 20th century the United Kingdom tended towards the former approach.

The practice of the recognition of governments has a long history; in the 19th century governments of the Holy Alliance under the influence of Prince Metternich[29] refused to acknowledge those governments that had acquired power through radical or revolutionary action. However, the attitude of the United Kingdom was more pragmatic[30] tending to concentrate upon whether the government was in effective control of territory or not; this was partly due to a tendency to support liberal reform movements in Europe which was also reflected in liberal laws on political asylum and it also stemmed from the fact that England was not subject to absolute monarchical rule unlike Austria, Prussia and Russia.

In the early part of the present century, five Central American Republics agreed by treaty in 1907 and 1923 to follow what became known as the Tobar Doctrine; under these treaty arrangements, the states pledged that recognition would be denied to a government taking power by revolutionary action which did not thereafter seek constitutional legitimacy.[31]

Such an approach may have been unrealistic in the light of the political instability in the region[32] and produced a reaction in the form of the Estrada Doctrine. Señor Estrada, the Foreign Minister of Mexico, urged in 1930 that emphasis should be placed not on the act of recognition but on the maintenance of diplomatic relations. Recognition was to be rejected because: (i) what was important was the maintenance of diplomatic relations; and (ii) that failure to recognise constituted an unjustified interference in domestic affairs. Thus, the Mexican government indicated that in future it would not recognise governments; the only question that would be asked was whether the new administration had effective control over territory. Some have questioned whether such a doctrine

---

28 The traditional United Kingdom approach on the formal recognition of governments was set out by the Foreign Secretary Herbert Morrison in 1951 when he stated that 'the conditions under international law for the recognition of a new regime as the *de facto* Government of a state are that the new regime has in fact effective control over most of the state's territory and that this control seems likely to continue. The conditions for the recognition of a new regime as the *de jure* Government of a State are that the new regime should not merely have effective control over most of the State's territory, but that it should, in fact, be firmly established'.

29 Klemens Metternich (1779–1859) (Austrian Foreign Minister 1809–48).

30 However, recognition was denied to the first French Republic established in September 1792, when the monarchy was formally abolished; the trial and execution of Louis XVI in January 1793 was followed by a declaration of war with Great Britain. In 1903, recognition was denied to the new government of Serbia following the assassination of the King and Queen.

31 Dr Tobar was the Minister of Foreign Relations of Ecuador; at a later date both Salvador and Costa Rica denounced the treaties.

32 For case law in England arising from political instability in Latin America, see *Lynch v Provisional Government of Paraguay* (1871) 2 P & D 268; *Republic of Peru v Peruvian Guano Company* (1887) 36 Ch D 497; *Republic of Peru v Dreyfus Bros Co* (1888) 38 Ch D 348; *Republica de Guatemala v Nunez* [1927] 1 KB 669.

preserves a proper distinction between recognition and the maintenance of diplomatic relations. However, be that as it may there has been a steady drift towards some form of the Estrada Doctrine. By the mid-1960s there had been a steady move towards this approach; France and Belgium adopted this approach from 1965 and were followed by the United States in 1977. The decision of the United Kingdom in 1980 to adopt this approach was subsequently followed in Canada, New Zealand and Australia.

That the criteria that a state may adopt for recognition may change over time is nowhere better illustrated that by examining the position of the United States. In the early years of the Republic, the first Secretary of State, Thomas Jefferson, stressed the element of popular consent as the test for recognition of governments.[33] At a later date Lincoln's Secretary of State William Seward[34] stressed the need for a new regime to honour its international obligations while Rutherford Hayes[35] looked for evidence of popular support. In the present century Woodrow Wilson placed stress upon democracy and free elections.[36]

The difficulty with imposing tests for recognition was that the United States found that recognition was often equated with approval and severe embarrassment could be caused if a new regime indulged in extreme conduct. However, if there was no recognition and limited diplomatic contact then experience indicated that the United States was unable to influence any new regime to behave in a responsible manner. Thirdly, in the 20th century the influence of public opinion could not be discounted in the formation of foreign policy. The United States therefore began to move slowly in the direction of the Estrada Doctrine. The new policy was announced during the term of office of President Carter;[37] the statement issued in 1977 in reflecting on the past observed:

> One result of such complex recognition criteria was to create the impression among other nations that the United States approved of those governments it recognised and disapproved of those from which it withheld recognition ... In recent years United States practice has been to de-emphasise and avoid the use of recognition in cases of changes of governments and to concern ourselves with the question whether we wish to have diplomatic relations with the new governments.

> The Administration's policy is that establishment of relations does not involve approval or disapproval but merely demonstrates a willingness on our part to conduct our affairs with the other government directly.

The justification for such a change of policy was that the United States found it to its advantage to continue diplomatic contacts even with those regimes it disapproved of; in essence the only test would be whether the new government had effective control over

---

33 Thomas Jefferson (Secretary of State 1789–93) was addressing the American Minister in Paris on the subject of the recognition of the republican regime of September 1792; Jefferson had, of course, served as Minister in Paris (1785–89) and knew many of the personalities involved.

34 William Seward (Secretary of State 1861–69).

35 Rutherford Hayes (President 1877–81).

36 Woodrow Wilson (President 1913–21); such a view was in line with the efforts of his first Secretary of State (William Jennings Bryan, 1913–15) to promote methods for the peaceful resolution of disputes between states.

37 This is significant because the general emphasis of foreign policy under President Carter had been wherever possible to promote awareness of human rights.

the territory. The general philosophy was explained by Deputy Secretary of State Warren Christopher[38] when he observed in 1977:

> We maintain diplomatic relations with many governments of which we do not necessarily approve. The reality is that, in this day and age, coups and other unscheduled changes of government are not exceptional developments. Withholding diplomatic relations from these regimes, after they have obtained effective control, penalises us. It means that we forsake much of the chance to influence the attitudes and conduct of a new regime ... Isolation may well bring out the worst in a new government.

From the 19th century, the United Kingdom had tended to adopt a pragmatic approach to recognition of governments. *De facto* recognition would be accorded if the new regime appeared to have effective control over the territory.[39] However, there were exceptions to this policy where there had been a violent seizure of power or there was a continued dependence on foreign troops.[40] The traditional United Kingdom position had been set out by the then Foreign Secretary in March 1951 where he observed:

> ... the conditions under international law for the recognition of a new regime as the *de facto* Government of a State are that the new regime has in fact effective control over most of the State's territory and that this control seems likely to continue. The conditions for the recognition of a new regime as the *de jure* Government of a State are that the new regime should not merely have effective control over most of the State's territory, but that it should, in fact, be firmly established. His Majesty's Government consider that recognition should be accorded when the conditions specified by international law are, in fact, fulfilled and that recognition should not be given when these conditions are not fulfilled. The recognition of a Government *de jure* or *de facto* should not depend on whether the character of the regime is such as to command His Majesty's Government's approval.[41]

Although this policy was confirmed in 1957,[42] 1967,[43] 1970[44] and June 1979,[45] a number of difficult cases[46] caused the United Kingdom Government to review past practice; the review concentrated upon the practice of other countries and the danger that recognition

---

38 Warren Christopher served as Deputy Secretary of State (1977–81) and Secretary of State (1993–97). For an explanation of the objectives of United States Foreign Policy, see Warren Christopher, *In the Stream of History*, 1998, Stanford UP, California.

39 Thus, the United Kingdom recognised the Soviet Government in 1921 but the United States did not until 1933.

40 This explained the refusal as late as October 1979 to recognise the Heng Samrin government in Cambodia because. although it had control of the greater part of the territory. it was being aided by military forces from Vietnam. This had the embarrassing consequence that the regime of Pol Pot continued to be recognised until December 1979, even though subject to very serious allegations of abuses of human rights. See C Warbrick (1981) 30 ICLQ 568; C Symmons [1981] PL 249.

41 Mr Herbert Morrison, *Hansard*, HC Deb, Vol 485, cols 2410–11; 21 March 1951.

42 HL Deb, Vol 204, col 755 '*de facto* recognition does not constitute a judgment on the legality of the Government concerned; still less does it imply approval of it'.

43 HC Deb, Vol 742, col 6–7.

44 HC Deb, Vol 799, col 23.

45 HC Deb, Vol 968, col 917.

46 The Kadar Government in Hungary in 1957; the coup by Jerry Rawlings in Ghana resulting in allegations of summary executions (1979); the complex situation in Cambodia where the regime of Pol Pot continued to be recognised; see C Symmons [1981] PL 249.

was too often interpreted as approval. Thus, in April 1980 the Foreign Secretary[47] announced that:

> We have therefore concluded that there are practical advantages in following the policy of many other countries in not according recognition to Governments. Like them, we shall continue to decide the nature of our dealings with regimes which come to power unconstitutionally in the light of our assessment of whether they are able of themselves to exercise effective control of the territory of the State concerned.

At the time of the announcement a number of writers expressed concern as to how the courts would now respond to the new policy of the executive branch.[48] Since 1980 there have only been a limited number of cases but the new policy seems to have caused few practical difficulties. In *Gur Corporation v Trust Bank of Africa Ltd*,[49] which concerned recognition of a state the Court of Appeal were able to allow the state to participate in the litigation without departing from existing precedents. In the subsequent case of *Republic of Somalia v Woodhouse, Drake & Carey (Suisse) SA*,[50] where the central issue was whether a particular party could be described as the government of Somalia Hobhouse J was able to formulate a test to determine whether a particular entity could be described as a government. This test has been followed in the subsequent case of *Sierra Leone Telecommunications Co Ltd v Barclays Bank plc*[51] and will be considered below in respect of effects in municipal law.

4 *DE FACTO* AND *DE JURE* RECOGNITION

The subject of recognition embraces not only recognition of states and governments but is complicated further by distinctions between *de facto* recognition and *de jure* recognition. Thus, it was said that recognition might be *de facto* or *de jure*. In principle, the distinction between the two forms related to recognition of governments rather than states and is thus unlikely to be prominent after 1980. Prior to 1980, it was possible to have grants of *de jure* and *de facto* recognition to different regimes in respect of substantially the same territory.[52] A regime that possessed a grant of recognition might claim immunity when property claims were made against it and might seek to initiate proceedings or demand recognition of its legislative decrees.[53] These overlapping claims made it particularly difficult for municipal courts to determine property disputes; a claim allowed at first instance might be reversed on appeal simply because a new grant of *de facto* recognition had been made.[54] The problem was compounded by the fact that grants of recognition tended to operate retrospectively.[55]

---

47 Lord Carrington (Foreign Secretary 1979–82); an identical statement was made to the House of Commons by his deputy Sir Ian Gilmour; see HL Deb, Vol 408, cols 1121–22; HC Deb, Vol 983, cols 277–79.
48 C Warbrick (1981) 30 ICLQ 568; C Symmons [1981] PL 249; Talmon (1992) 63 BYIL 231.
49 *Gur Corporation v Trust Bank of Africa Ltd* [1987] 1 QB 599; 75 ILR 675.
50 [1993] QB 54 (Hobhouse J).
51 [1998] 2 All ER 821.
52 *The Cristina* [1938] AC 485; *The Arantzazu Mendi* [1939] AC 256.
53 *Banco de Bilbao v Sancha* [1938] 2 KB 176.
54 *Haile Selassie v Cable and Wireless Ltd (No 2)* [1939] 1 Ch 182.
55 *Luther v Sagor* [1921] 1 KB 456; 3 KB 532. On the retroactive effect of a grant, see below.

Recognition *de jure* was the superior level of recognition; it indicated that there were no doubts about the status of the government or its prospects. It is sometimes asserted that a grant of *de jure* recognition is irrevocable. In contrast *de facto* recognition was accorded when a government had effective control over territory but there was some evidence that justified caution as to the long term prospects. To an extent *de facto* recognition represents a reserving of judgment until the position is clearer.

Although the position is unlikely to be the same after 1980, the authorities indicate that the courts in the United Kingdom experienced difficulty in three situations: (i) the position of the Soviet Union after 1917; (ii) the fluctuating fortunes during the Spanish War; and (iii) the litigation arising from the Italian invasion of Abyssinia. In all three cases, conflict was continuing on the ground so that legal grants of recognition changed in accordance with the unfolding of events.[56]

In respect of the Soviet Union, the United Kingdom accorded *de facto* recognition[57] to the Soviet government in April 1921 so that the Court of Appeal in *Luther v Sagor*[58] were able to reverse the first instance judgment of Roche J, given in December 1920, on the basis that the effect of the grant of recognition was to operate retrospectively to the time of the seizure of power by the Bolsheviks in October 1917.

During the Spanish Civil War (1936–39), the United Kingdom recognised the Republican government as the *de jure* government but accorded *de facto* recognition to the forces of General Franco as they began to take over the country. This resulted in considerable litigation in the English courts.[59] Thus, in *Banco de Bilbao v Sancha*[60] it was held that directions given by a *de jure* government at a time when it no longer had control over territory would be disregarded. The same problem of competing authority arose in *The Arantzazu Mendi* case,[61] where the facts were as follows. The vessel the *Arantzazu Mendi* was registered in Bilbao and requisitioned by the Nationalist government. The vessel arrived in London where the Republican government sought to take possession; the Nationalist government sought to set aside the writ on grounds of sovereign immunity. At first instance, Bucknill J sought guidance from the Foreign Office who indicated that while the Republican government was recognised *de jure* the Nationalist government were recognised *de facto* in respect of the area in question. Thus, the Nationalist government was entitled to immunity and Bucknill J set aside the writ for possession.[62] This decision was upheld by the Court of Appeal[63] and the House of Lords.[64]

---

56 See A McNair, 'The law relating to the Civil War in Spain' (1937) 53 LQR 471; H Lauterpacht, 'Recognition of insurgents as a *de facto* government' (1940) 3 MLR 1.
57 *De jure* recognition was not granted until 1924 partly because of concerns as to whether the Soviet Government would honour international obligations.
58 *Luther v Sagor* [1921] 1 KB 456 (Roche J); [1921] 3 KB 532 (Scrutton, Warrington and Bankes LJJ). This important case is discussed further, below.
59 *Banco de Bilbao v Sancha* [1938] 2 KB 176 (Lewes J; Greer, Clauson and Mackinnon LJJ); *The Cristina* [1938] AC 485; *The Arantzazu Mendi* [1938] P 233 (Bucknill J); [1939] P 37 (CA); AC 256.
60 [1938] 2 KB 176.
61 [1939] AC 256.
62 *The Arantzazu Mendi* [1938] P 233.
63 *The Arantzazu Mendi* [1939] P 37 (CA).
64 *The Arantzazu Mendi* [1939] AC 256 (Lords Atkin, Wright, Macmillan, Russell, Thankerton).

Meanwhile, problems arose in respect of the Italian invasion of Abyssinia. The invading Italian forces were accorded *de facto* control in 1936 and *de jure* control in 1938; at the same time, litigation arose before the English courts. Thus, in *Bank of Ethiopia v National Bank of Egypt and Ligouri,*[65] the court gave effect to Italian decrees in Abyssinia on the basis that the United Kingdom government had recognised Italy as being in *de facto* control.

Another case arising out of the invasion was that of *Haile Selassie v Cable and Wireless Ltd,*[66] where the facts were as follows.

In 1935, the plaintiff as Emperor of Ethiopia entered into a contract with the defendant for the payment of certain monies under a wireless telegraph contract. In May 1936, Italian forces proclaimed the annexation of Abyssinia and the plaintiff left the country. In December 1936, the United Kingdom recognised the King of Italy as *de facto* sovereign. In January 1937, the plaintiff began proceedings to reclaim the sums of money due under the contract. An objection to the jurisdiction of the court was overruled by the Court of Appeal.[67] When the matter came on for trial, Bennett J held that the plaintiff as *de jure* sovereign could succeed. After the trial, the United Kingdom decided to recognise Italy as the *de jure* sovereign. The Court of Appeal allowed the appeal ruling that the *de jure* recognition being retroactive until at least the date of *de facto* recognition (December 1936) and as this was prior to the date of the issue of the writ (January 1937) the plaintiff had no *locus standi* to claim.[68]

The case law in England in the 1920s and 1930s indicates the difficulties that a municipal court may face when dealing with property disputes against a background of overlapping grants of recognition. The regime that was able to claim some form of recognition was able to assert sovereign immunity and to demand that its legislative decrees were respected.[69]

Having regard to the change of policy on the recognition of governments in 1980, it must be doubtful whether such problems will arise in the future. It is probably true that a grant of *de facto* recognition does not normally extend to the exchange of diplomatic relations. Likewise where a state enjoys *de jure* recognition action may be taken to preserve property rights in the recognising state. Two important cases on the relationship between the concepts of *de facto* and *de jure* recognition will be considered below.[70]

---

65 [1937] Ch 513.

66 *Haile Selassie v Cable and Wireless Ltd (No 1)* [1938] 1 Ch 545 (Bennett J); 1 Ch 839 (CA) (Greene MR, Scott, Clauson LJJ) followed by *Haile Selassie v Cable and Wireless Ltd (No 2)* [1939] 1 Ch 182 (Bennett J, July 1938); 1 Ch 194 (CA) (Greene MR, Scott LJ, Clauson LJ, December 1938).

67 *Haile Selassie v Cable and Wireless Ltd (No 1)* [1938] 1 Ch 545 (Bennett J); 1 Ch 839 (CA) (Greene MR, Scott, Clauson LJJ).

68 *Haile Selassie v Cable and Wireless Ltd (No 2)* [1939] 1 Ch 182 (Bennett J, July 1938) (CA) (Greene MR, Scott, Clauson LJJ, December 1938).

69 In respect of property such decrees will not be accorded extra territorial effect, see *Lecouturier v Rey* [1910] AC 262; *Re Russian Bank for Foreign Trade* [1933] Ch 745; *Lorentzen v Lydden & Co* [1942] 2 KB 202; *Bank voor Handel en Scheepvaart NV v Slatford* [1953] 1 QB 248.

70 *Gydnia Ameryka Linie v Boguslawski* [1953] AC 11; *Civil Air Transport Inc v Central Air Transport Corp* [1953] AC 70.

5 IS THERE A LEGAL DUTY TO RECOGNISE?

Some writers who have tended towards the constitutive theory have argued that there is a legal duty upon other states to recognise. This view is open to objection in that it is at variance with actual state practice; most states take the view that the decision to accord recognition or not is one for their discretion. This legal duty was asserted by supporters of the constitutive theory but its final result approximates the constitutive theory to the declaratory theory.

Lauterpacht,[71] writing in 1947, argued that because there was no central international authority once certain conditions had been complied with then there is a legal duty by other states to accord recognition. This was seen more as an attempt to rationalise the operation of the constitutive theory rather than a statement of actual conduct. The objections half a century later seem considerable. First, most states regard the act of recognition as a political act. Secondly, most regard it as a matter of political discretion rather than legal duty. Thirdly, there is no evidence that states have shown any willingness to surrender to international law their liberty to decide upon the recognition of states and governments. This is illustrated by the decision of the United States and the United Kingdom to change policy in 1977 and 1980 respectively. Fourthly, all the evidence points to the declaratory theory being dominant. Fifthly, if such a legal duty arose who is to enforce it? If recognition is a matter of customary international law and thus founded on state conduct, no legal duty can arise unless founded in state conduct; as states view that matter as one of political discretion it is difficult to see how such a duty can arise.

Perhaps the circle can be squared by observing that while state A may not be under a legal duty to issue an express formal declaration of recognition in respect of state B; once state B is in existence (and possibly a member of the United Nations) then while there is no legal duty to recognise there is a duty to accord minimum courtesies to a fellow state. Thus, Arab states were obliged to respect the territory of Israel after 1949 and the United States was obliged to follow accepted norms of international law in respect of the government in Beijing.

6 IMPLIED RECOGNITION[72]

In normal situations recognition, will be an express act either by letter, declaration, or treaty[73] leaving no room for ambiguity. However, recognition may be implied in a limited number of circumstances but the evidence has to disclose an unequivocal intention to establish relations with a new state or government. While in each case the evidence has to

---

71 H Lauterpacht, *Recognition in International Law*, 1947; H Lauterpacht (1897–1960) (Whewell Professor of International Law 1937–55; Judge, ICJ 1955–60). It is interesting that, while most reviewers at the time praised the scholarship and presentation of the subject by Professor Lauterpacht, a number did express reservations about this aspect of the work, see J Kunz (1950) 44 AJIL 713; EJ Cohn (1948) 64 LQR 404.

72 H Lauterpacht (1944) 21 BYIL 123.

73 Eg, the United Kingdom and Burma agreed by treaty on 17 October 1947 that the United Kingdom recognised 'the Republic of Burma as a fully independent state'.

be carefully examined, it is possible that the following acts might constitute implied recognition of a state or government:

(i) the formal establishment of diplomatic relations;

(ii) the issue of a consular exequator;

(iii) the signing of a bi-lateral treaty between two states designed to comprehensively regulate relations;[74]

(iv) the sponsoring or voting for the admission of a state as a member of an international organisation.

It would seem that the following acts will not of themselves constitute implied recognition:

(i) the maintenance of unofficial contacts;

(ii) the initiation of negotiations;[75]

(iii) the exchange of trade missions with a unrecognised state;

(iv) the fact that one state becomes a party to a multi lateral treaty to which an unrecognised state is a party;

(v) by the presence of a state at an international conference at which the unrecognised state is present;

(vi) by the admission of an unrecognised state to an international organisation in respect of those states opposing admission;

(vii) by presenting an international claim against an unrecognised state;

(viii) by paying compensation to an unrecognised state;

(ix) by the retention of a diplomatic presence during an unsettled time;[76]

(x) by acts undertaken by a state as depository of a treaty.[77]

It is possible that an act by a state will be subject to an explanation;thus the United Kingdom decision to vote for Macedonia as a member of the United Nations was regarded as constituting admission of that state. [78]

7 COLLECTIVE RECOGNITION

Whereas recognition is normally accorded expressly by a single state there may be practical advantages in the process of collective recognition. Following the Advisory Opinion of the International Court of Justice in Conditions of Membership in the United

---

74 France recognised the United States in 1778 by a Treaty of Amity and Commerce.

75 The United States negotiated with Communist China at the Indo China conference of 1954 to safeguard the interests of captured airmen but it indicated that this was not to be taken as any form of recognition.

76 Eg, the continuance of the British Embassy in Kabul in 1979 even though the Afghanistan government was not recognised.

77 Belgium as depository dealing with the accession of the German Democratic Republic to the Universal Postal Union.

78 HC Debs, Vol 223, cols 241 (written answer, 22 April 1993).

Nations,[79] it is clear that statehood is a requirement for admission. Thus, collective recognition may arise when a number of states act expressly to recognise or impliedly where a number of states vote for a particular state to be admitted as a member of the United Nations. However, while admission may raise a presumption of statehood those states that vote against are obliged to accord that state the minimum duties under international law even if they themselves are unwilling to enter into bilateral relations.

The most prominent example of collective action arises in the context of European Union Law where member states seek to reach a minimum level of agreement on the conduct of foreign policy. Thus, when it became clear that Yugoslavia was on the point of disintegration the Council of Ministers of the EC adopted on 16 December 1991 Guidelines on the Recognition of New States in Eastern Europe and in the Soviet Union. The object was to set out agreed criteria for recognition which in broad terms were as follows:

(i) respect for the provisions of the United Nations Charter (1945) and the commitments subscribed to in the Final Act of Helsinki[80] and in the Charter of Paris, especially with regard to the rule of law, democracy and human rights;

(ii) guarantees for the rights of ethnic and national groups and minorities in accordance with the commitments subscribed to in the framework of the CSCE;[81]

(iii) respect for the inviolability of all frontiers which can only be changed by peaceful means and by common agreement;

(iv) acceptance of all relevant commitments with regard to disarmament and nuclear non-proliferation as well as security and regional stability;

(v) commitment to settle by agreement, including where appropriate by recourse to arbitration, all questions concerning state succession and regional disputes;

(vi) the Declaration concluded by observing that the European Community and its Member States would not recognise entities founded upon acts of aggression.

The requirements were devoted to the specific situation of Eastern Europe and the Soviet Union but it does indicate a willingness to go beyond the limited criteria set out in the Montevideo Convention. The requirements have not proved difficult for the former republics of the Soviet Union.[82]

In regard to the problems posed by the dissolution of Yugoslavia, the EC member states had established a Conference on Yugoslavia with the object of assisting the parties to find a negotiated settlement. In order to secure proper resolution of legal questions the Conference established an Arbitration Commission comprising judges drawn from EC member states and chaired by Judge Badinter of France. In the period between November 1991 and July 1992 the Commission delivered a number of rulings on matters relating to recognition. Among the general conclusions were:

---

79 (1948) ICJ 57.
80 Final Act of the Conference on Security and Co-operation in Europe, Helsinki, 1975 (1975) 14 ILM 1292.
81 Conference on Security and Co-operation in Europe; an ongoing process established under the Helsinki Final Act 1975.
82 See 21 December 1991, Alma Ata Declaration.

(i)   that the Socialist Federal Republic of Yugoslavia was in the process of dissolution;[83]

(ii) that the Socialist Republic of Yugoslavia was no longer in existence;[84]

(iii) that the Federal Republic of Yugoslavia (Serbia and Montenegro) could not claim to be the successor state to the Socialist Federal Republic of Yugoslavia;[85]

(iv) that the applications of Bosnia-Herzegovina, Croatia, Macedonia and Slovenia for recognition as independent states should be granted,[86] save in respect of the full consultation of the people by referendum[87] and in the second of the passage of certain constitutional guarantees.[88]

(v) that all existing frontiers should be respected in line with the principles stated in the United Nations Charter (1970), in the Declaration on Principles of International Law concerning Friendly Relations and Co-operation among states in accordance with the Charter of the United Nations (General Assembly Resolution 2625 (XXV).[89]

It has to be admitted that the situation was not satisfactory with events on the ground likely to render rulings academic; indeed the Commission acknowledged this being mindful of the fact that its 'answer to the question before it will necessarily be given in the context of a fluid and changing situation'.[90] This is not the place to reflect on the lessons of the dissolution of Yugoslavia save to observe that the Arbitration Commission sought to set out the relevant principles of international law at a time when various parties were seeking to obtain territory by military action.

8 DOCTRINES OF NON-RECOGNITION

The subject of recognition has attracted a number of doctrines. One that deserves attention is the Stimson[91] doctrine of non-recognition. In broad terms, the doctrine holds that a state will not recognise the acquisition of territory or the establishment of a state founded on the unlawful use of force. The doctrine stems from the efforts of the League of Nations in the 1930s to restrain aggression. In 1931, Japanese forces invaded and occupied

---

83   Opinion No 1 (November 1991) 92 ILR 162.

84   Opinion No 8 (July 1992) 92 ILR 199.

85   *Ibid.*

86   Opinion Nos 4–7 (1992) 92 ILR 173.

87   The referendum was held in Bosnia-Herzegovina on 29 February 1992 and 1 March 1992 – the Serb population boycotted the referendum. Nearly all those voting voted for independence. Bosnia-Herzegovina was recognised by the EC and its member states in April 1992 as was Macedonia. Slovenia and Croatia had been recognised by EC and member states in January 1992.

88   Germany had recognised Croatia as early as December 1991; Croatia agreed to introduce the constitutional guarantees required.

89   Opinion No 3 (11 January 1992) 92 ILR 170.

90   Opinion No 3 (11 January 1992) 92 ILR 170; it is worthy of note that Bosnia-Herzegovina, Croatia, Slovenia and Macedonia have all become Members of the United Nations. However, the Federal Republic of Yugoslavia (Serbia and Macedonia) was not allowed to continue the membership of the Socialist Federal Republic of Yugoslavia and was required to apply for membership in its own right.

91   Henry Stimson (1867–1950) served as War Secretary under President Taft (1911–13) then as Secretary of State under President Hoover (1929–33) and again as War Secretary under President Roosevelt.

the Chinese province of Manchuria and moved to establish a puppet state of Manchukuo. China placed the matter before the Council of the league in accordance with Art 11 of the Covenant. While the League debated what action to take Henry Stimson wrote to the Chinese and Japanese Governments informing them that:

> The United States cannot admit the legality of any situation *de facto* nor does it intend to recognise any treaty or agreement between those Governments, or agents thereof, which may impair the treaty rights of the United States ... and it does not intend to recognise any situation, treaty or agreement which may be brought about by means contrary to the covenants and obligations of the Treaty of Paris of August 27 1928.

Stimson was outlining the national policy of the United States which since Woodrow Wilson had been directed to the peaceful resolution of territorial disputes. The reference to the Treaty of Paris was a reference to the General Treaty of 1928 for the Renunciation of War (known as the Kellogg-Briand Pact); this treaty had been signed by the United States as well as China and Japan. The policy of non-recognition in respect of acts of force was taken further by the Resolution adopted by the League of Nations Assembly on 11 March 1932 where it provided that:

> It is incumbent upon Members of the League of Nations not to recognise any situation. treaty or agreement which may be brought about by means contrary to the Covenant of the League of Nations or the Pact of Paris.

Although there was little success in restraining aggression in the late 1930s,[92] one legacy of the Second World War was that territory taken by force would be returned and the prohibition on the use of force contained in Art 2(4) of the Charter of the United Nations made it inevitable that seizures of territory by force would not attract recognition.[93] Similarly, the Declaration of Principles of International Law (1970) expressly states that: 'No territorial acquisition resulting from the threat or use of force shall be recognised as legal.' A number of other international instruments contain express prohibitions on the use of force and some provide for non-recognition.[94]

There have been a number of occasions since 1945 where the Security Council has condemned the use of force and indicated that no territorial gains can result therefrom.[95]

In the case of the declaration of independence by Southern Rhodesia in November 1965, the Security Council called on states not to recognise nor to assist the regime of Mr Ian Smith;[96] in consequence, the regime was only able to maintain limited diplomatic links with Portugal and South Africa. In like terms, resolutions have been passed in

---

92   Thus, the Italian annexation of Ethiopia was accepted and many western powers accorded *de facto* recognition to the Soviet annexation of the Baltic states of Lithuania, Estonia and Latvia.

93   On 9 August 1990 the Security Council unanimously adopted Resolution 662 which declared that the Iraqi annexation of Kuwait was null and void and called upon states not to recognise the annexation.

94   Article 11 of the Montevideo Convention on the Rights and Duties of States (1933); Art 17 of the Bogota Charter of the Organisation of American States (1948); Art 11 of the Draft Declaration on the Rights and Duites of States (prepared by ILC 1949); Art 52 of the Vienna Convention on the Law of Treaties (1969).

95   See SC Res 242 (1967) inadmissibility of territorial acquisition by war; SC Res 476 (1980)and SC Res 478 (1980) changes in the status of Jerusalem; SC Res 491 (1981) extension of laws to the Golan Heights to be without international effect.

96   SC Res 216 (1965); SC Res 217 (1965); SC Res 277 (1970); SC Res 288 (1970) economic sanctions being imposed see SC Res 221 (1961); SC Res 232 (1966); SC Res 253 (1968).

relation to the Turkish invasion of Cyprus[97] and the attempts to establish an independent state.[98]

The issue of non-recognition has arisen before the International Court of Justice; in the Advisory Opinion on Namibia,[99] the Court indicated that, as the presence of South Africa in Namibia was unlawful, it followed that states were obliged to refrain from any action that might imply recognition of that presence. The legality or otherwise of Indonesian rule in East Timor could not be the subject of determination because of the refusal of the International Court of Justice to accept jurisdiction.[100]

It would seem that the doctrine of non-recognition is important in the modern world; if territory is seized by force then it is likely that the Security Council will as a first step declare the seizure to be unlawful and not to be recognised.

9 PRECIPITATE OR PREMATURE RECOGNITION

When a state decides to make a grant of recognition will in most cases be a matter of individual discretion; a judgment will have to be made as to whether the relevant criteria have been met. History reveals however that sometimes recognition is granted to achieve a political objective when the basic criterion of effective independent existence has not been made out. Under Art 2(7) of the United Nations Charter there is an obligation to respect the internal affairs of another state. Thus, in cases of secession there is a reluctance to recognise a secessionist or liberation movement; thus, in 1968, Biafra[101] was only able to attract a limited number of symbolic recognitions and in 1998 little enthusiasm was displayed for espousing the case of an independent Kosovo.

However, it is certainly open to argument that in the case of the dissolution of Yugoslavia precipitate recognition might have made a difficult situation worse. Manifestly Yugoslavia was an unusual situation with several groupings seeking at the same time to secede from a federal state. Nevertheless, the decision of the German government to recognise Croatia in December 1991 appeared to disregard: (a) the fact that Croatia did not control a large part of its territory; (b) that the human rights and constitutional guarantees required in the EC Declaration on Yugoslavia[102] were not yet in place. Similarly, the decision by the EC and its member states to recognise Bosnia-Herzegovina in April 1992 ignored the fact[103] that: (a) the considerable abstention from the referendum in March 1992 was a cause of concern; and (b) that the new government would not be in effective control of a considerable part of its territory. It is arguable that, in the entire episode, Western powers were using the device of recognition to secure good

---

97 SC Res 353 (1974) called for respect for the independence of Cyprus and an end to foreign intervention.

98 SC Res 541 (1983) described the Turkish 'Republic of North Cyprus' as unlawful; and this was repeated in SC Res 550 (1984).

99 (1971) ICJ 16.

100 *East Timor* case *(Portugal v Australia)* (1995) ICJ 90.

101 D Ijalaye, 'Was Biafra at any time a state in international law?' (1971) 65 AJIL 51.

102 EC Declaration on Yugoslavia (1991) 62 BYIL 559.

103 See M Weller, 'The international response to the dissolution of the Socialist Federal Republic of Yugoslavia' (1992) 86 AJIL 569.

behaviour while others on the ground were using military force to achieve different objectives. Normally, a grant of recognition is made when the situation has settled and the facts have become clear; that was not the case in Yugoslavia in 1992 and was not so until at least 1995.

The experience in Yugoslavia may have been prompted by the fact that in some situations in the past premature recognition has been granted to ensure a political objective. Thus, in 1903 the United States immediately recognised the secession of Panama from Columbia and in May 1948 it recognised the state of Israel before its border had finally been settled. In December 1971, India recognised Bangladesh even though the Pakistani forces occupied a considerable part of the then East Pakistan. In two of these situations, the choice was between the secessionists and the parent government and recognition might have been seen as helping to tilt the balance. However, in Yugoslavia the complex problem of ethnic groupings crossing traditional boundaries lead to a less certain outcome.

Just as recognition may be premature there are a number of situations where recognition has been delayed because of political difficulties in so doing.[104] In this context it should be borne in mind that while the executive branch of government grants recognition it cannot normally do so without the support of its legislature and public opinion.

10 WITHDRAWAL OF RECOGNITION

Recognition may be expressly or impliedly withdrawn. *De facto* recognition has of its nature a more transitional element and does not entail the same consequences. Some of the most difficult case law in the municipal courts has arisen when there is some form of overlap between *de facto* and *de jure* recognition. The express granting of *de jure* recognition impliedly withdraws a prior grant in respect of the same territory. Thus, the decision in November 1938 to accord *de jure* recognition to the King of Italy in respect of the conquest of Abyssinia impliedly withdrew the recognition of the Emperor of Ethiopia.[105] In 1940, this recognition was withdrawn as the fighting developed.

Normally the granting of *de jure* recognition will expressly or impliedly withdraw a prior grant in respect of the same territory. Thus, the decision of the United Kingdom in July 1945 to recognise the Provisional Polish Government in Poland had the effect of withdrawing recognition from the government in exile in London.[106] Similarly, the decision to grant *de jure* recognition to the Communist government in Beijing in January 1950 had the effect of withdrawing recognition from the Nationalist Government. Thus, when the United States recognised China in 1979 this had the effect of withdrawing

---

104 Israel was not recognised by Egypt until 1979 and not by Jordan until 1995. Bangladesh was not recognised by Pakistan until 1974. The United Kingdom did not recognise the German Democratic Republic until 1973. The United States recognised the government of the People's Republic of China in January 1979 and withdrew its recognition of the Nationalist Government in Formosa.

105 *Haile Selassie v Cable and Wireless Limited (No 2)* [1939] 1 Ch 182.

106 *Gydnia Ameryka Linie Zeglugowe Spolka Akcyjna v Boguslawski* [1953] AC 11.

recognition from the government in Taiwan save where there had been specific domestic legislation in the United States.

If the government of State A enjoys *de jure* recognition and a grant of *de facto* recognition is made to a different group in respect of part of the territory then laws made by that *de facto* regime will be given effect to.[107]

It is possible for a grant of recognition to be withdrawn and not to be followed by any subsequent grant. Thus, the decision in December 1979 to withdraw recognition from the Pol Pot government in Cambodia was not followed by any grant of recognition to the Hang Samrin regime.[108]

The withdrawal of recognition is not likely to be such a problem after the decision in 1980 not to make a formal grant of recognition of governments. However, a distinction will continue to be drawn between matters of recognition and matters of diplomatic relations.[109]

11 THE LEGAL EFFECTS OF RECOGNITION WITHIN THE UNITED KINGDOM

Cases on aspects of recognition have been coming before the English courts since at least the early part of the 19th century. Having regard to the change of policy by the executive branch in 1980, it is sensible to examine the case law in chronological form. Some of the problems that troubled the courts prior to 1980 are unlikely to arise in similar form in the future. It is important to note that many of the cases concerning recognition give rise to problems about property rights and may also give rise to questions of immunity from jurisdiction.

(a) The case law prior to 1980

The traditional view of the English courts was that an unrecognised entity (or government) did not have *locus standi* to sue in England[110] and could not raise a defence of sovereign immunity.[111] Whether an entity was recognised or not depended on the inferences to be drawn from information supplied by the Secretary of State for Foreign Affairs. After some hesitation it came to be accepted that statements of fact in a foreign

---

107 *Banco de Bilbao v Sancha* [1938] 2 KB 176; *The Arantzazu Mendi* [1939] AC 256.

108 Because at the time it was seem as reliant on Vietnamese troops who remained in the country. See C Warbrick, 'Kampuchea: representation and recognition' (1981) 31 ICLQ 234.

109 The United Kingdom has at various times broken off diplomatic relations with certain states normally because of serious breaches of international law. Eg, Albania 1946; Lybia 1984 (over the events outside the Libyan People's Bureau); Syria 1986–90 (following a criminal trial in London in respect of an attempt to blow up an El Al airliner); Argentina 1982–90 (following the Falklands War) and Iran (the Salmon Rushdie affair); Iraq and North Korea.

110 *City of Berne v Bank of England* (1804) 9 Ves Jun 347; *Dolder v Bank of England* (1805) 10 Ves Jun 352; See articles by PL Bushe Fox (1931) 12 BYIL 63; (1932) 13 BYIL 39.

111 *The Annette and The Dora* [1919] P 105.

Office certificate were conclusive.[112] Thus, a revolutionary group controlling the City of Berne was not allowed to sue to recover funds belonging to the previous administrators of the city[113] while an unrecognised Provisional Government was not able to claim immunity from the arrest of a vessel.[114]

The English case law has tended to follow the pattern of political events; thus cases arose from the Napoleonic wars and the liberation movements in Latin America in the 1820s. In the present century the events of the Russian Revolution,[115] the Spanish Civil War[116] and the Italian invasion of Abyssinia[117] have resulted in litigation before the municipal courts. After 1945 problems arose in respect of the status of the German Democratic Republic[118] and other entities emerging at the conclusion of the Second World War.[119]

Locus standi

As indicated above, it is normally only the recognised government that has *locus standi* to sue in an English court.[120] Thus, in *Haile Selassie v Cable and Wireless Ltd (No 2)*[121] the retroactive effect of the grant of *de jure* recognition to the King of Italy deprived the Emperor of Ethiopia of *locus standi* to sue and thus the Court of Appeal were compelled to allow the appeal from Bennett J. This view of the law was accepted as correct in the later case of *Carl Zeiss Stiftung v Rayner & Keeler (No 2).*[122] However, in that case the House of Lords reversed the Court of Appeal and allowed proceedings to be brought by the Plaintiffs even though they were under the administrative control of an unrecognised entity (ie the German Democratic Republic). This result was achieved by holding the unrecognised entity to be acting as the agent of the *de jure* sovereign power (that is, the Soviet Union). This agency or 'county council' solution avoided the practical difficulties of the strict application of the rule. This line of reasoning was followed by a later Court of Appeal in *Gur Corporation v Trust Bank of Africa Ltd*[123] where the court was prepared to regard the unrecognised State of Ciskei as the agent of South Africa, a *de jure* sovereign.

---

112 *Jones v Garcia de Rio* (1823) T & R 297; *Thompson v Powles* (1828) 2 Sim 194; *Taylor v Barclay* (1828) 2 Sim 213; *The Charkieh* (1873) LR 4 A & E 59; *Mighell v Sultan of Johore* (1894) 1 QB 149; *Duff Development Co Ltd v Kelanton* [1924] AC 797.

113 *City of Berne v Bank of England* (1804) 9 Ves Jun 347; *Dolder v Bank of England* (1805) 10 Ves Jun 352.

114 *The Annette and The Dora* [1919] P 105 (Hill J).

115 *The Gagara* [1919] P 95 (CA); *The Annette and The Dora* [1919] P 105; *AM Luther Ltd v James Sagor & Co Ltd* [1921] 1 KB 456; [1921] 3 KB 532; *Princess Paley Olga v Weisz* [1929] 1 KB 718.

116 *Banco de Bilbao v Sancha* [1938] 2 KB 176; *The Cristina* [1938] AC 485; *The Arantzazu Mendi* [1939] AC 256.

117 *Bank of Ethiopia v National Bank of Egypt and Ligouri* [1937] Ch 513; *Haile Selassie v Cable and Wireless Ltd* [1938] 1 Ch 545 (Benett J); [1938] 1 Ch 839; *Haile Selassie v Cable and Wireless Limited (No 2)* [1939] 1 Ch 182.

118 *Carl Zeiss Stiftung v Rayner & Keeler (No 2)* [1967] AC 853.

119 *Gydnia Ameryka Linie v Boguslawski* [1953] AC 11; 19 ILR 72.

120 *City of Berne v Bank of England* (1804) 9 Ves Jun 347.

121 *Haile Selassie v Cable and Wireless Ltd (No 2)* [1939] 1 Ch 182.

122 *Carl Zeiss Stiftung v Rayner & Keeler Ltd (No 2)* [1967] AC 853; 43 ILR 23.

123 *Gur Corporation v Trust Bank of Africa Ltd* [1987] QB 599; [1986] 3 WLR 583; see J Crawford (1986) 57 BYIL 405.

The retroactive effect of a grant

It is normally said that the effect of a grant of recognition is retroactive and this principle derives from the important case of *Luther v Sagor*[124] where the facts were as follows.

The plaintiffs owned a sawmill in Russia which was subject to a nationalisation decree by the new Soviet Government in 1919. In 1920, agents of that Government purported to sell certain wood to the defendant company;the wood had formerly belonged to the plaintiffs. The defendant company brought the wood to England. The plaintiffs sought a declaration that they were entitled to the property.

The question for Roche J at first instance was whether the defendants had acquired good title. The learned judge held that the legislative decree was without effect as it emanated from an unrecognised government; that being the case a declaration was granted.[125] Subsequent to the hearing but prior to the appeal the United Kingdom granted recognition *de facto* to the Soviet Government. The Court of Appeal held in allowing the appeal that the effect of the grant of recognition was retrospective[126] so that the legislative decree must be respected and the defendants acquired good title. According to the court the grant would be retrospective to the point at which the Bolshevik government took power.[127] Although the implications of the decision would have to be worked out in subsequent case law, the case appeared to establish the following four propositions: (i) that the legislative and administrative acts of an unrecognised entity would be a nullity; (ii) that effect would be given to the legislative acts of a recognised government; (iii) that the effect of a grant of recognition would normally be retrospective; and (iv) that the law governing the transfer of title to property was that of the *lex situs*.

The problems that can arise in the context of conflicting grants and the operation of retroactive effect is illustrated by two cases that came before the courts within a short period of time of each other. In *Gdynia Ameryka Linie v Boguslawski*,[128] the facts were as follows.

The Polish Government in exile in London was the recognised government of Poland. A new government took office in Poland on 28 June 1945; in accordance with the meeting at Yalta it was the intention of the United Kingdom to recognise this government. Recognition was granted on 5 July 1945. In the period between the two relevant dates, the London government entered into certain agreements to pay compensation to Polish seamen in the form of severance pay. Mr Boguslawski sued to recover his arrears of pay

---

124 *AM Luther & Co v James Sagor & Co* [1921] 1 KB 456 (Roche J); [1921] 3 KB 532 (Bankes, Scrutton, Warrington LJJ).

125 Roche J gave judgment in December 1920; *de facto* recognition was granted in April 1921 and documentary evidence of this fact was available at the time of the appeal hearing. In accordance with traditional principles of the law of evidence, the Court of Appeal was justified in receiving fresh evidence that was not available at the time of the original hearing.

126 Bankes LJ followed the Supreme Court cases of *Williams v Bruffy* 96 US 176; *Underhill v Hernandez* (1897) 168 US 250; *Oetjen v Central Leather Co* (1918) 246 US 297.

127 Ie, after the October Revolution of 1917 when VI Lenin (1870–1924) replaced the government of Alexander Kerensky (1881-1970).

128 *Gydnia Ameryka Linie v Boguslawski* [1953] AC 11 (Lords Porter, Oaksey, Morton, Reid and Tucker) on appeal from [1951] 1 KB 162 (CA) (Bucknill, Denning, Cohen LJJ), affirming Finnemore J.

and the defendants argued that the actions of the London government were invalidated by the retroactive effect of the grant of recognition. Finnemore J and the Court of Appeal found for the plaintiff. This ruling was upheld by the House of Lords.

Lord Porter in giving judgment in the House of Lords held that even if the grant of recognition was retrospective it could only operate within its proper sphere namely in those matters in which the new government had *de facto* control. As the dealing with the fleet in England was not one of those matters the plaintiff was entitled to succeed. Thus, in *Luther v Sagor*[129] the principle of retroactivity validated the title because the property was within the jurisdiction while in the *Boguslawski* case[130] the retroactivity of recognition could not invalidate the actions of the old government because the dealings took place outside the area of *de facto* control of the new government.

The second case that raised a not dissimilar problem was that of *Civil Air Transport Incorporated v Central Air Transport Corporation*[131] where the salient facts were as follows.

Aircraft belonging to the Nationalist Government of China were flown to Hong Kong and purchased by the plaintiffs, an American corporation, on 12 December 1949 at a time when the Nationalist Government was still recognised as the *de jure* Government of China. On 5 January 1950, the United Kingdom recognised the Communist rulers in Beijing as the *de jure* government of China.[132] At a later date, the plaintiffs sought a declaration that they owned the aeroplanes; the claim was dismissed by the Chief Justice of Hong Kong and the Full Court. The plaintiffs appealed to the Privy Council who allowed the appeal.

In allowing the appeal and giving judgment on behalf of the Privy Council, Viscount Simon indicated that the principle of retroactivity of recognition had to be approached with caution. First, he observed that 'retroactivity of recognition operates to validate acts of a *de facto* government which has subsequently become the new *de jure* government, and not to invalidate the acts of a *de jure* government'.[133] In the *Civil Air Transport* case, the sale to the plaintiffs took place at a time when the Nationalist government was recognised *de jure* and in principle the any title could not be impeached by a foreign tribunal. Secondly, the subsequent granting of *de jure* recognition to the Communist government could not operate retrospectively to invalidate or annul a transaction made by the prior *de jure* government in respect of assets that were still under its control at the operative date. Thus, the case law indicates that while recognition may operate retroactively it will not operate to invalidate the acts of a *de jure* government in respect of assets under its control.

The acts of a recognised government

As a general principle the legislative and executive acts of a recognised government in respect of property within its own territory will be acknowledged and given effect to in

---

129 [1921] 3 KB 532.
130 [1953] AC 11.
131 *Civil Air Transport Incorporated v Central Air Transport Corporation* [1953] AC 70.
132 It being argued that this grant operated retroactively to 1 October 1949, the date on which the Communist rulers assumed *de facto* control in Beijing.
133 [1953] AC 70, p 93.

an English court.[134] There are a number of exceptions to this broad statement arising under the rules of English private international law. Thus, effect will not be given to foreign revenue laws,[135] nor to foreign penal laws;[136] indeed, it would seem that the act of a foreign government in flagrant defiance of public international law may not be given effect to as offending English public policy.[137] However, notwithstanding the limited exceptions recognition is important because the legislative and executive acts of an unrecognised entity will not be given effect to. Thus, in *Adams v Adams*[138] Simon P refused to give effect to a judicial divorce granted in *Southern Rhodesia* because the judge had been appointed under the unlawful and unrecognised regime of Mr Ian Smith.

Holding the acts of an unrecognised government to be a nullity has the singular disadvantage that it may cause injustice to the private rights of innocent parties who have acted in good faith. In the case of *Carl Zeiss Stiftung v Rayner and Keeler (No 2)*[139] Lord Wilberforce indicated that, in normal matters of private rights, acknowledgment should not be based on whether the government is recognised but by the application of the relevant choice of law rules. In the Court of Appeal hearing in *Hesperides Hotels v Aegean Holidays Ltd*,[140] Lord Denning MR appeared to take the same view when he observed:

> If it were necessary to ... I would unhesitatingly hold that the courts of this country can recognise the laws or acts of a body which is in effective control of a territory even though it has not been recognised by Her Majesty's Government *de jure* or *de facto*; at any rate, in regard to the laws which regulate the day to day affairs of people, such as their marriages, their divorces, their leases, their occupations, and so forth; and furthermore that the courts can receive evidence of the state of affairs so as to see whether the body is in effective control or not.[141]

The legislative acts of a *de facto* regime will be recognised in so far as they extend to territory within its control. Some writers assert that this appears to follow from *The Arantzazu Mendi*,[142] where the facts were as follows.

The Arantzazu Mendi was a private vessel registered at Bilbao. In the summer of 1937 the area was captured by the Nationalist forces. The Republican government then issued an order requisitioning all vessels. This was followed by a similar order from the

---

134 *Luther v Sagor* [1921] 3 KB 532; *Princess Olga Paley v Weisz* [1929] 1 KB 718.

135 *Government of India v Taylor* [1955] AC 491.

136 *Huntington v Attrill* [1893] AC 150; *AG of New Zealand v Ortiz* [1984] AC 1.

137 *Kuwait Airways Corporation v Iraqi Airways Co* (1998) (Mance J) confirmed by CA December 2000 (not yet reported).

138 *Adams v Adams* [1971] P 188. Today the wife would have been able to seek a divorce in England following the Domicile and Matrimonial Proceedings Act 1973.

139 [1967] 1 AC 853; see DW Greig (1967) 83 LQR 96; FA Mann (1967) 16 ICLQ 760.

140 [1978] QB 205, p 218. The matter was not raised in the House of Lords [1979] AC 508; see J Merrills (1979) 28 ICLQ 523; M Shaw (1978) 94 LQR 500; D Lloyd Jones (1978) 37 CLJ 48.

141 [1978] QB 205, p 218.

142 *The Arantzazu Mendi* [1939] AC 256. It would seem that Lord Atkin in the House of Lords approached the case as one of immunity and not recognition of the legislative decrees of a government. English law has traditionally been reluctant to enforce extra territorial decrees of a government be it *de facto* or *de jure*; see *Lecouturier v Rey* [1910] AC 262. The argument that decree is enforceable by virtue of nationality was rejected in *Re Russian Bank for Foreign Trade* [1933] Ch 475; see, also, *Lorentzen v Lydden & Co* [1942] 2 KB 202; *Bank voor Handel en Scheepvaart NV v Slatford* [1953] 1 QB 248.

Nationalist forces in April 1938. When the vessel arrived in the Thames the officers of the vessel opted for the Nationalist side. An action by Republican elements to gain possession of the vessel was dismissed by Bucknill J, the Court of Appeal[143] and the House of Lords.

It is arguable that the case could have been decided on one of two bases: (i) that the decree of the Nationalist government should be given effect to as an entity with *de facto* control; or (ii) that in the circumstances the *de facto* government enjoyed immunity from suit. It would seem that only the second of the two arguments is valid since, at the time of the decree, it is not clear whether the vessel was within any territory under the control of the *de facto* government.[144] Since the Master and officers were prepared to hold for the Nationalist government, the House of Lords[145] dismissed the possession proceedings on the basis that they were an attempt to implead the Government of a foreign state. It would seem that the principle that the legislative acts of a *de facto* government in respect of property situate within its territory will be recognised emerges more clearly from *Bank of Ethiopia v National Bank of Egypt and Ligouri*[146] and *Bank de Bilbao v Sancha*.[147]

The availability of a plea of sovereign immunity

As will be seen later a recognised government, *de facto*[148] or *de jure*, will in certain circumstances be able to raise plea of sovereign immunity; although the scope of such a plea is narrower than it was,[149] it cannot be raised by an entity that is not recognised.[150] Thus, no such plea could be raised in *The Annette*[151] but it could be raised by a *de facto* government as in *The Gagara*[152] or *The Arantzazu Mendi*[153] and by a *de jure* government as in *The Cristina*.[154] In more recent times, the plea was accepted in part in *Kuwait Airways Corporation v Iraqi Airways Company*.[155] Thus, the question of recognition in a municipal court is relevant both to *locus standi* as a plaintiff and to the possible plea of sovereign immunity as a defendant.

(b) Litigation since 1980

The change of policy by the executive branch in 1980 has meant that while the judge may be supplied with factual information it will be for the court to draw its own inferences. There have been only a limited number of cases where recognition has been directly in

---

143 [1939] P 37.
144 In fact, at the time the Republican authorities issued a decree the vessel was on the high seas and at the time the Nationalist authorities issued a decree she was at port in London and, thus, within the internal waters of the United Kingdom.
145 [1939] AC 256.
146 [1937] Ch 513 (Clauson J).
147 [1938] 2 KB 176 (CA) (Greer, Mackinnon and Clauson LJJ).
148 *The Arantzazu Mendi* [1939] AC 256.
149 A narrowing of the plea resulting from the State Immunity Act 1978.
150 *The Annette* [1919] P 105.
151 *Ibid* (Hill J).
152 *The Gagara* [1919] P 95 (CA) (*de facto* recognition of Estonian National Council).
153 *The Arantzazu Mendi* [1939] AC 256 (*de facto* recognition of Nationalist forces in Spanish Civil War).
154 *The Cristina* [1938] AC 485 (*de jure* recognition of Republican government).
155 [1995] 1 WLR 1147.

issue. In *Gur Corporation v Trust Bank of Africa*,[156] the question was whether Ciskei could be allowed to be joined as a third party in a commercial dispute. Ciskei had been established as a homeland state by the South African government in the Status of Ciskei Act 1981. Before the Court of Appeal, the Foreign Office certificate indicated that while Ciskei was not recognised as an independent state the practice was to make representations about Ciskei to the South African government. In an interesting reserved judgment Sir John Donaldson MR indicated that there were some differences between the Foreign Office certificate in the *Carl Zeiss* case[157] and that presently before the court. In the *Carl Zeiss* case, the certificate had expressly said that the USSR was still *de jure* entitled to exercise sovereign control over East Germany whereas the later certificate was silent on the question. The learned judge however concluded that the available evidence indicated that Ciskei was exercising delegated authority as a subordinate body of South Africa as the *de jure* sovereign state. Thus, the appeal from Steyn J[158] was allowed. As the approach of the court indicated the question was one of recognition of a state rather than a government and the result seems sensible on the facts and consistent with prior case law.[159]

The second case to come before the courts was that of the *Republic of Somalia v Woodhouse Drake & Carey Suisse SA*[160] where the facts were as follows.

In 1991, the Republic of Somalia purchased a cargo of rice for delivery at Mogadishu. The captain decided it was too dangerous to deliver the cargo so that the High Court in London ordered the cargo to be sold and the proceeds to be paid into court. In 1991 an international conference had nominated Mr M as President of Somalia and he had appointed Mr Q as his Prime Minister. The question for Hobhouse J was whether the proceeds of sale should be paid out to the solicitors acting for the interim government of Mr Q.

In giving judgment, Hobhouse J held that the question of who was entitled to the proceeds of sale depended on who could be described as the government of Somalia; in particular whether the interim government of Mr Q met that requirement. The learned judge proposed that in municipal law the position could be expressed thus:

> ... the factors to be taken into account in deciding whether a government exists as the government of a state are: (a) whether it is the constitutional government of the state; (b) the degree, nature and stability of administrative control, if any, that it of itself exercises over the territory of the state; (c) whether Her Majesty's Government has any dealings with it and if so what is the nature of those dealings; and (d) in marginal cases, the extent of international recognition that it has as the government of the state.

On the evidence the learned judge found that the interim government did not meet this test. This fourfold test would seem to be a sensible method of approach that is likely to be followed in the future. According to one commentator 'the advance this judgment makes

156 *Gur Corporation v Trust Bank of Africa Ltd* [1987] QB 599 (Steyn J, Donaldson MR, Nourse and Glidewell LJJ).

157 *Carl Zeiss Stiftung v Rayner & Keeler Ltd (No 2)* [1967] 1 AC 853.

158 Who, at first instance, had concluded that there was no evidence to conclude that the Republic of South Africa was still exercising authority in Ciskei and that Ciskei had no *locus standi*.

159 Beck (1987) 36 ICLQ 350; Crawford (1986) 57 BYIL 405; Mann (1987) 36 ICLQ 348.

160 [1993] QB 54 (Hobhouse J).

is to prise away the question who is the government for international, political purposes from the question of who it is for domestic legal purposes. The judgment allows the question of who is the government to be approached in relation to the purpose for which the question is being asked'.[161]

The usefulness of the 'Hobhouse formula' was recognised in the subsequent case of *Sierra Leone Telecommunications Co Ltd v Barclays Bank plc*[162] where the facts were as follows.

Sierra Leone Telecommunications Co Ltd (Sierratel) was a company incorporated in Sierra Leone and wholly owned by the government of Sierra Leone which controlled its dealings. Sierratel held a US dollar account at Barclays Bank in Knightsbridge, London. The relevant bank mandate had been drawn up in July 1996 and provided for four signatories.

In May 1997, the democratically elected government of President Kabbah was ousted in a military coup and replaced by a junta. The ministers in the government of President Kabbah fled to the Republic of Guinea. From the time of the coup the British government had continued to deal with President Kabbah and had been active in demanding the restoration of democratic government. The military regime was condemned by the Commonwealth, the Organisation of African Unity and the European Community. In December 1997 the London Bank received a letter purportedly from Sierratel in Freetown which stated that the original bank mandate be suspended. It was not in dispute that the governing law in respect of the bank mandate was English law, and it was also accepted that questions of the corporate capacity of Sierratel were to be determined under the law of Sierra Leone. The London Bank was thus faced with a conflict between the wishes of the original signatories to the mandate and the instructions now emanating from the head office of Sierratel. The Sierra Leone High Commissioner in London (who remained loyal to the regime of President Kabbah) began proceedings seeking a declaration that the London Bank account remained subject to the original mandate of July 1996.

In granting the declaration, Cresswell J held that the question turned on whether the military junta was the recognised government of Sierra Leone. The learned judge held that this was to determined by applying the fourfold criteria propounded in the *Republic of Somalia* case.[163] In applying these criteria, it was obvious that the military junta was not the government[164] so that the plaintiff was entitled to the declaration sought, namely that the account was subject to the original bank mandate.

Thus, it would seem that in future cases coming before the English courts where the status of a government is in issue it is likely that the test propounded in the Republic of Somalia case will be applied.

---

161 C Warbrick, 'Recognition of governments' (1993) 56 MLR 92.

162 *Sierra Leone Telecommunications Co Ltd v Barclays Bank plc* [1998] 2 All ER 821 (Cresswell J).

163 [1993] QB 54 (Hobhouse J).

164 The application of the principles could not have been simpler: (i) The British Government was continuing to deal with President Kabbah and had been active in seeking the restoration of his democratic regime; (ii) that the military regime did not have control beyond Freetown; and (iii) the military regime had been condemned by the Commonwealth and the Organisation of African Unity; (iv) that United Nations sanctions against the regime had been given the force of law by delegated legislation in the United Kingdom.

In respect of post-1980 litigation mention should be made of the judgment in *Arab Monetary Fund v Hashim (No 3)*,[165] which raised the question of the recognition of the acts of another sovereign state. The facts of the case were as follows.

Proceedings were brought in the Chancery Division of the High Court in London by the Arab Monetary Fund against Dr Hashim and certain other defendants, seeking the return of substantial sums of money. The Arab Monetary Fund was an international organisation established by treaty, however, the United Kingdom was not a party and no order had been made under the International Organisations Act 1968. The Fund had been incorporated under the laws of the United Arab Emirates, a sovereign state with which the United Kingdom enjoyed full diplomatic relations. Certain of the defendants moved to strike the action out on the grounds that it was not an entity under English law. At first instance, Hoffmann J ruled that the plaintiffs could sue as they possessed juridical personality under the law of the United Arab Emirates and this was entitled to recognition in England under the rules of the conflict of laws. The appeal of the defendants was allowed by the majority in the Court of Appeal. The appeal of the plaintiffs was allowed by the House of Lords and the order of Hoffmann J was restored.

In essence, the case concerned the legal personality of the plaintiff fund and the question that arose for decision was whether its personality arose under an unincorporated non-justiciable treaty or did personality arise by virtue of its status under the law of a friendly foreign state. The House of Lords adopted the latter approach holding that the Courts of the United Kingdom would recognise a corporate body created by the laws of a foreign state recognised by the crown.[166]

Following upon the case, the Foreign Corporations Act 1991 has been enacted. Section 1 of the legislation provides that where a corporation has been incorporated in a territory with a settled court system, then that body will have legal personality under English law, even though the state itself may not be recognised by the United Kingdom.

12 THE LEGAL EFFECTS OF RECOGNITION IN THE UNITED STATES

Attitudes in the United States to the problems of recognition have influenced judges in the United Kingdom. Thus, in the leading case of *Luther v Sagor*,[167] Bankes LJ cited with

---

165 *Arab Monetary Fund v Hashim (No 3)* [1991] 2 AC 114 (Lords Templeman, Bridge, Lowry, Ackner, Griffiths) on appeal from [199] 2 All ER 769 (CA) (Lord Donaldson MR, Nourse LJ, Bingham LJ dissenting) allowing an appeal from Hoffmann J [1990] 1 All ER 685.

166 It should be noted that Lord Lowry dissented in the House of Lords. In the Court of Appeal the majority (Donaldson MR, Nourse LJ) were of the opinion that the earlier case of *JH Rayner (Mincing Lane) Ltd v Department of Trade* [1990] 2 AC 418 compelled them to find that an entity arising under an unincorporated treaty could not sue without an Order in Council having been made. As Lord Templeman observed in the House of Lords: 'The *Tin Council* case left untouched the principle that the recognition of a foreign state is a matter for the Crown and the principle that if a foreign state is recognised by the Crown, the courts of the United Kingdom will recognise the corporate bodies created by that state.' See G Marston, 'The origin of the personality of international organisations in United Kingdom law' (1991) 40 ICLQ 403; FA Mann, 'International organisations as national corporations' (1991) 107 LQR 357.

167 *Luther v Sagor & Co* [1921] 3 KB 532.

approval the Supreme Court judgment in *Oetjen v Central Leather Co*[168] where in the context of retroactivity the court had observed:

> When a government which originates in revolution or revolt is recognised by the political department of our government as the *de jure* government of the country in which it is established, such recognition is retroactive in effect and validates all the actions and conduct of the government so recognised from the commencement of its existence.[169]

It is arguable that *Oetjen* was concerned with the effect of a *de jure* recognition validating acts prior to the grant of *de facto* recognition which was not the situation before the court in *Luther v Sagor*. However, the general willingness to look for guidance from the United States can be seen again in the House of Lords judgment in *Carl Zeiss Stiftung v Rayner & Keeler (No 2)*[170] where both Lord Reid and Lord Wilberforce noted with approval the willingness of courts in the United States to acknowledge day to day acts taking place in the territory of an unrecognised entity.[171]

The United States had to grapple with problems of recognition from the middle of the 19th century. Following outbreak of the American Civil War (1861–65) questions arose as to whether acts taking place within the Confederate States should be accorded recognition. The common sense solution was to recognise acts that were not contrary to the federal government or the Constitution.[172] It is probably the case that recognition which is *de jure* is retroactive. The emphasis on *de facto* recognition is now less important because of the decision by the executive branch in 1977 to decline to recognise governments. In matters of foreign policy, the practice is to seek guidance from the Department of State.

Difficulties have arisen as to whether a grant of *de jure* recognition can operate retrospectively and extend to matters arising outside the area of which the regime had *de facto* control.[173] Early Supreme Court authority indicated in the negative[174] and this was supported by the Circuit Court of Appeals in *Lehigh Valley Rail Co v Russia*.[175] However, there are two cases[176] where the Supreme Court has been prepared to impliedly uphold the acts of an unrecognised regime acting outside its jurisdiction. However, both these decisions concerned the Litvinov Agreement of 1933 which was designed to promote a comprehensive settlement of outstanding issues with the USSR as a prelude to recognition. Moreover, some of the reasoning indicates a wish to uphold the status of treaties under United States law and the desire 'to validate so far as this country is

---

168 *Oetjen v Central Leather Co* (1918) 246 US 297.

169 (1918) 246 US 297, pp 302–03.

170 [1967] 1 AC 853.

171 A consistent feature of Lord Wilberforce's distinguished judicial career being his willingness to explore practice other common law jurisdictions. See *Chaplin v Boys* [1971] AC 356; *National Carriers Ltd v Panalpina (Northern) Ltd* [1981] AC 675. It is open to argument that courts in the United States are more familiar with recognition problems because questions of the conflict of laws play so much greater part in a state with over 50 distinct jurisdictions.

172 *Texas v White* (1868) 74 US 700. This pragmatic approach being followed in *United States v Insurance Cos* (1874) 89 US 99 (concerning companies established by the legislature of the state of Georgia while it remained part of the Confederacy).

173 This was of course the problem in *Gydnia Ameryka Linie v Boguslawski* [1953] AC 11.

174 *Kennett v Chambers* (1852) 56 US 38.

175 *Lehigh Valley Rail Co v Russia* (1927) 21 F (2d) 396.

176 *United States v Belmont* (1937) 301 US 324; 8 ILR 34; *United States v Pink* (1942) 315 US 203; 10 ILR 48.

concerned all the acts of the Soviet Government here involved from the commencement of its existence'.[177]

Although the United States held to the view that an unrecognised state or government could not sue in its courts, the long period during which the government of the Soviet Union[178] was refused recognition lead to a willingness by the courts to be more flexible; there was a tendency to approach matters on a case by case basis and to be indulgent if a favourable decision was not at variance with the executive certificate, the interests of justice or the fundamental principles of the constitution. Such an approach was justified because it was clear that the refusal to recognise had been based on broader political considerations rather than the absence of effective territorial control. Thus, Cardozo J in *Sokoloff v National City Bank of New York*[179] was prepared to accept that the acts of an unrecognised entity might be acknowledged provided there was 'no violence to principles of justice or public policy'. The learned judge held that the consequences of non-recognition should not be allowed to extend beyond the bounds of 'common sense and fairness'. Thus, in *Wulfsohn v RSFSR*,[180] when the plaintiff alluded to the Soviet Republic the court was prepared to assume its existence.

The evolving case law indicated that the attitude of the court was likely to be influenced by the tone of the executive certificate and the precise legal point at issue. Thus, in *Salimoff v Standard Oil Co of New York*[181] which concerned the nationalisation of assets and the passing of title the court was prepared to accept the existence of the Soviet Government and proceeded to apply the normal rule of private international law that the acquisition of title is governed by the *lex situs*.

Where a State Department certificate or communication indicates that a particular course is contrary to the requirements of United States foreign policy, it will be respected and normally followed by the courts. Thus, in both *The Maret*[182] and *Latvian State Cargo Lines v McGrath*,[183] the court declined to recognise Soviet decrees made following the annexation of the Baltic states. As such conduct had not been recognised and fell clearly within the Stimson doctrine of non-recognition this is an example of the executive and judicial branches acting with one voice.

A distinction might also be discerned between those cases where the issue of recognition is central and those where it is incidental or simply raised as a doubtful defence to avoid a normal commercial obligation. Thus, in *Upright v Mercury Business Machines*[184] a bill of exchange was drawn upon the defendant and then assigned by 'a

---

177 *United States v Belmont* (1937) 301 US 324, p 330.

178 Ie, from 1917 until 1933; in contrast the United Kingdom had accorded *de facto* recognition in 1921 and *de jure* in 1924.

179 *Sokoloff v National City Bank of New York* (1924) 239 NY 158; 2 ILR 44. The case itself being heard in the New York Court of Appeals, Cardozo J did not reach the Supreme Court until he was nominated to succeed Holmes J in 1932.

180 (1923) 138 NE 24; 2 ILR.

181 *Salimoff v Standard Oil Co* (1933) 186 NE 679; 7 ILR 22 ; 262 NY 220. In that case, Pound CJ posed the question: 'What is the Soviet Russia, a band of robbers or a government?'

182 *The Maret* (1944) 145 F 2d 431; 7 ILR 29. As the ship in question was in a United States port, it is also possible to explain the case as being one where recognition has been denied to nationalising decrees made outside the jurisdiction of a *de jure* government.

183 *Latvian State Cargo Lines v McGrath* (1951) 188 F (2d) 1000; 18 ILR.

184 *Upright v Mercury Business Machines* (1961) 213 NYS (2d) 417; 32 ILR 65.

state controlled enterprise of the German Democratic Republic'; the defendant when sued by the plaintiff argued that, as the assignor could not sue, the assignee could be in no better position. The Appellate Division of the Court of New York rejected this argument holding that such a defence could not prevail where a governmental entity had such a clear *de facto* existence.[185]

Where an entity has been created with the object of overcoming a procedural bar then the court will not be so accommodating. In *Kunstsammlungen zu Weimar v Elicofon*[186] the plaintiff KZW had been an agency of the East German government until 1969. After that date it became a separate entity formed simply to avoid the barriers posed by non-recognition; the court refused to accept this stratagem holding that this would undermine the executive branch policy of non-recognition of the German Democratic Republic. In contrast in those cases where the executive statement is supportive of the unrecognised entity then the courts are willing to accept such an indication.[187] Indeed, in *National Petrochemical Co of Iran v The M/T Stolt Sheaf*[188] a United States Court of Appeals held that having regard to the limited emphasis now accorded to the recognition of governments the unrecognised entity should be permitted to sue provided that the executive branch did not object.

The flexible approach of the United States courts means that it is difficult to reconcile harmoniously all the cases involving problems of recognition. However, a number of general principles do seem clear. First, there is a general desire to proceed on a case by case basis. Secondly, the approach will vary according to the nature of the case. Thirdly, an executive certificate if clearly hostile will be followed.[189] Fourthly, if the executive is favourable or declines to express an opinion then non-recognition will not be fatal.[190] Fifthly, much depends on whether the issue of recognition arises in the context of *locus standi* or is merely incidental.[191] Sixthly, in cases where non-recognition is raised as an incidental defence in circumstances where there have been commercial dealings then the defence is unlikely to succeed.[192] Seventhly, acts of an unrecognised entity will be acknowledged if they operate within state territory in accordance with the rules of private international law favouring the *lex situs*,[193] but not if they extend beyond state frontiers.[194]

185 *Upright v Mercury Business Machines* (1961) 213 NYS (2d) 417; 32 ILR 65.
186 *Kunstsammlungen zu Weimar v Elicofon* (1972) 358 F Supp 747; 61 ILR 143.
187 *Transportes Aeros de Angola v Ronair* (1982) 544 F Supp 858; 94 ILR 202.
188 (1988) 860 F 2d 551.
189 *The Maret* (1944) 145 F 2d 431; 12 ILR 29.
190 *Salimoff v Standard Oli Co of New York* (1933) 262 NY 220; 7 ILR 22; *National Petrochemical Co of Iran v The M/T Stolt Sheaf* (1988) 860 F 2d 551.
191 *Upright v Mercury Business Machines* (1961) 213 NYS (2d) 417; 32 ILR 65.
192 *Ibid.*
193 *Salimoff v Standard Oil Co of New York* (1933) 262 NY 220; 7 ILR 22.
194 *The Maret* (1944) 145 F 2d 431; 12 ILR 29.

CHAPTER 7

TERRITORY[1]

1 INTRODUCTION

As has been indicated earlier, international law is founded upon the political unit of the state. The essential characteristic of the state is that it enjoys sovereign power; that sovereignty will be both internal in respect of its own territory and external in the form of its identity and equality as an international legal person.

It follows that a state must possess territory[2] and that territory may be vast as in the case of the United States or very small as demonstrated by the principality of Liechtenstein or the state of Nauru. This internal sovereignty is founded upon the territory possessed by the state and the possession of that sovereignty entitles the state to enjoy jurisdiction. It follows that there is a close connection in international law between the concepts of 'the state', 'sovereignty', 'territory' and 'jurisdiction'. Thus from a narrow legal perspective 'territory' is a matter of central concern to international law.

A wider historical perspective indicates that the effective power of a state is linked to its population and resources; both these indicia are linked to the territory which the state controls. It is a melancholy fact of human history that more conflicts have been started and more lives lost in disputes about territory than about any other single cause.[3] Some territorial disputes may take the form of civil wars or disputes between states but the underlying cause is often a conflicting claim to territory. In municipal law one of the central concerns of real property law is to formulate rules for the acquisition of title to property because property is a source of wealth and often the occasion of dispute. Likewise any system of international law would be inadequate if it did not have rules as to how title to territory might be acquired; such rules are necessary if only to minimise the risk of conflicts over territory. As Phillip Allott expressed the matter in 1990:[4]

> Endless international and internal conflicts, costing the lives of countless human beings, have centred on the desire of this or that state-society to control this or that area of the earth's surface to the exclusion of this or that state-society.

---

1   See generally, RY Jennings and AD Watts, *Oppenheim's International Law*, 9th edn, 1992, Chapter 5; RY Jennings, *The Acquisition of Territory in International Law*, 1963; J Crawford, *The Creation of States in International Law*, 1979; MN Shaw, *Title to Territory in Africa: International Legal Issues*, 1986; W Schoenborn, 'La nature juridique du territoire' (1929) 30 HR 81; S Bstid, 'Les problèmes territoriaux dans la jurisprudence de la Cour internationale de Justice' (1962) 107 HR 361; JG Starke, 'The acquisition of title to territory by newly emerged states' (1965–66) 41 BYIL 411.

2   Thus it is said, 'A state without territory is not possible'. See H Lauterpacht, *Oppenheim's International Law*, 8th edn, 1955, Vol I, p 451; see also RY Jennings and AD Watts, *Oppenheim's International Law*, 9th edn, 1992, p 563.

3   In recent years, there has been the Falklands Conflict (1982) precipitated by a dispute about territory; in 1990 the Gulf Conflict was caused in part by the territorial claims of Iraq over Kuwait. In the civil war in Yugoslavia a desire to acquire particular territory contributed to the duration of the conflict.

4   P Allott, *Eunomia: New Order for a New World*, 1990, p 330.

Therefore the concept of territorial sovereignty has always been central to international society and this is reflected in the provisions of Art 2(4) and Art 2(7) of the United Nations Charter (1945) and in the first principle of the Declaration on Principles of International Law Concerning Friendly Relations and Co-operation Among States (1970).

In classic international law the doctrine of territorial sovereignty was employed to justify the principle that the actions that a state took within its own borders were not the concern of other states. In the 20th century the principle of absolute territorial sovereignty has come under challenge from two broad movements. First, in many areas international co-operation is necessary so that a state may be obliged to restrain conduct within its own territory that might be injurious to the interests of other states.[5] Secondly, the movement in international law designed to prevent abuses of human rights has the consequence that the state might be answerable for conduct committed within its own territory. Indeed, there is a clear conflict between the old form of international law founded on territorial sovereignty and the new model based on respect for minimum international standards.

However problems concerning territory are as old as international law itself. Indeed one of the reasons for the development of international law was to restrain European monarchs wasting human lives by seeking to seize territory by force.[6] The rules concerning the acquisition of territory grew up in Western Europe in the years since 1600 and have been heavily influenced by Roman Law as the dominant legal system then prevailing.

As indicated earlier, in the municipal sphere property law is one of the most important elements of civil law. In England, the law of real property and its close relative the law of trespass represents one of the oldest forms of civil law. In an agricultural economy income from the land was the principal source of wealth. Real property law remains in essence hierarchical with estates in land held from the Crown and inferior interests being carved out of the fee simple absolute in possession. In most states, the history of real property reflects the history of the nation. In England, the feudal origins of the subject are well known; in the 15th century the development of the trust and the strict settlement indicated that forms of property rights would evolve according to social and economic circumstances. In the 17th and 18th century new property rights began emerge in the form of patents,[7] copyright[8] and later trade marks.[9] While the 19th century case law tended to reflect the *laissez-faire* philosophy of the age, by the end of the century certain property rights had acquired statutory protection.[10] After 1945, the introduction of a legislative scheme based upon compulsory planning control served to transform the entire subject.[11]

---

5   Examples being in the area of the environment and matters pertaining to civil aviation.
6   As indicated in Chapter One, international law is traceable to the efforts of Spanish and Portuguese theologians in the 15th century who asked the question as to when the use of force was legitimate.
7   Statute of Monopolies (1623).
8   Copyright Act 1709.
9   See Trade Marks Registration Act 1875.
10 For legislative change, see Increase of Rent and Mortgage Interest (War Restrictions) Act 1915 and Agricultural Holdings Act 1923. Also noticeable are the efforts of the courts to protect the weaker party in property transactions see *Samuel v Jarrah Timber and Wood Paving Corporation Ltd* [1904] AC 323.
11 Town and Country Planning Act 1947.

In any advanced state matters of property will be central to the legal system and where compulsory registration of title exists[12] then definite answers may be given to even the most intractable property dispute. Indeed in most societies property law will exist alongside the related subjects of housing law, planning law and environmental law.

It has to be admitted that in international law cases on rights over territory are likely to be horizontal disputes between two or three states rather than the complex vertical disputes that might exist in municipal law such as between the mortgagee, landlord, tenant and licensee. Secondly, in domestic property law the presence of statutory codes often means that a court is able to come to a clear and absolute answer while in international law the tribunal may simply be reduced to ruling that state A has a better right to territory X than state B. Thus in the *Eastern Greenland* case,[13] the Permanent Court of International Justice noted that:

> It is impossible to read the records of the decisions in cases as to territorial sovereignty without observing that in many cases the tribunal has been satisfied with very little in the actual exercise of sovereign rights, provided that the other State could not make out a superior claim.

Thus, in many case the tribunal is concerned to rule on the relative merits of each case. Thirdly, in international law the consequences of a change of title to territory involve not only a change of sovereignty, but will also entail changes in citizenship laws, the legal system and often the language spoken. In municipal law, if X sells a property to Y then they remain the parties principally affected; in international law the entire people of the territory will be affected. Fourth, municipal law and international law have a common feature in that in both chronology is of supreme importance. In international law, territorial disputes have to be analysed chronologically examining the unfolding evidence and drawing the appropriate inferences. Most leading judgments and arbitral awards resemble a detailed historical survey.

2 THE CONCEPT OF TERRITORIAL SOVEREIGNTY

As a matter of principle the expression 'territorial sovereignty' denotes the enjoyment of rights over territory. The classic exposition is that of Judge Huber sitting as Arbitrator in the Island of Palmas Arbitration,[14] where he observed:

> Sovereignty in the relations between States signifies independence. Independence in regard to a portion of the globe is the right to exercise therein, to the exclusion of any other State, the functions of a State ... Territorial sovereignty, as has already been said, involves the exclusive right to display the activities of a State. This right has as corollary a duty: the obligation to protect within the territory the rights of other States, in particular their right to integrity and inviolability in peace and in war, together with the rights which each State may claim for its nationals in foreign territory.

---

12 Introduced on a progressive and compulsory basis in England and Wales by the Land Registration Act 1925.
13 *Legal Status of Eastern Greenland* (1933) PCIJ, Ser A/B, No 53.
14 *The Island of Palmas Arbitration (Netherlands v United States)* (1928) 2 RIAA 829.

Territorial sovereignty depends on a state being able to demonstrate title to territory. In municipal law it is often provided that only certain documents may constitute evidence of title; in international law the approach is much more liberal with a tribunal being prepared to examine evidence of both acts and documents to determine which party has the better right to exercise territorial sovereignty. Most contested cases require the tribunal both to undertake a chronological survey of the territory and to analyse the effect of various state acts.

Apart from a number of exceptional situations, to be noted below, one can draw a fourfold distinction in matters of sovereignty:

(1) Territory subject to the sovereignty of a single state (for example, California is subject to the sovereignty of the United States).

(2) Territory with its own status and thus not subject to the sovereignty of a single state. (for example, mandate or trust territory).[15]

(3) The *res nullius* – the land capable of being acquired by a state but not as yet subject to territorial sovereignty.

(4) The *res communis*, consisting of the high seas and outer space, which is not capable of being placed under the sovereignty of any single state. This matter will be examined in detail later.

Much of the jurisprudence concerning territory has been developed in the context of litigation between states; the types of territorial disputes might be summarised thus:

(1) The classic border/boundary dispute where state A and state B and possibly state C are at variance as to the precise point at which a border/boundary should be drawn.[16]

(2) Those disputes where state A and state B claim sovereignty over the same territory (sometimes a remote and thinly populated island).[17]

(3) Those disputes where the legitimacy of a particular community is in issue.[18]

In principle the territory of a state will comprise its land mass, its internal waters and its territorial sea. It is normally the case that in respect of each piece of territory there can only be a single sovereign state.

Exceptional situations may arise. First, the condominium, where two or more states agree to exercise sovereignty jointly over territory. Secondly, it is also possible to have a situation of indeterminate sovereignty where one sovereign power has renounced sovereignty but the subsequent position is clouded by competing claims. An example would be Formosa where the Japanese have abandoned any claim to sovereignty but the territory while clearly not *terra nullius* is subject to dispute between the Communist

---

15 *Status of South West Africa* case (1950) ICJ 128.

16 *Chamizal Arbitration* (1911) 5 AJIL 782; *Frontier Land Case (Belgium v Netherlands)* (1959) ICJ 209; *Frontier Dispute* case *(Burkina Faso v Mali)* (1985) ICJ 6; (1986) ICJ 545. The disputes outstanding between Iraq and Kuwait, India and Pakistan and Somalia and Kenya.

17 *Island of Palmas Arbitration* (1928) 2 RIAA 82; *Clipperton Island Arbitration* (1932) 26 AJIL 390; *Minquiers and Ecrehos* case (1953) ICJ 47.

18 The attitude of some Arab states towards Israel after 1949; the attitude of Argentina in respect of the Falkland Islands.

regime in Beijing and the Nationalist regime. Thirdly, one can note the concept of reversionary sovereignty. An example is afforded by the treaty of 1918 between France and Monaco which provided for the independence of Monaco under the royal family of that state. Fourthly, it is possible for sovereignty to exist in state A but to be exercised by state B. Examples would include the Turkish island of Cyprus which was administered by the British from 1878–1914 or the Turkish province of Bosnia-Herzegovina which was administered by Austria Hungary from 1878 until 1908.

There are a number of other situations that require special mention but they will be outlined at the conclusion of the chapter.

3 THE ACQUISITION OF TERRITORY IN INTERNATIONAL LAW[19]

There are five classic methods by which territory might be acquired in international law. They are: (1) accretion; (2) cession; (3) occupation; (4) prescription; (5) conquest. It will be necessary to say a little about each individually but it should be noted that the methods are not mutually exclusive and a particular dispute may give rise to problems in more than one category. The methods themselves are linked to concepts drawn both from Roman law and from Western European conceptions of sovereignty. Thus, a territory occupied by primitive peoples in the 17th century might be regarded at that time as *terra nullius* because the people and its ruler had not been admitted by recognition to the select circle of European rulers. The further back the chronology is traced the greater will be the influence of Western European forms of legal thought. Secondly, in many cases it will be necessary for the tribunal to settle upon a critical date after which no further evidence will be relevant or admissible. Thus, in the *Island of Palmas Arbitration*[20] it was accepted by the parties that the critical date was 10 December 1898, being the date on which Spain had purported to cede its rights under treaty of cession to the United States. In the more recent *Taba Arbitration*[21] which concerned a boundary dispute in Sinai between Egypt and Israel the critical date was fixed at 23 September 1923, being the date of the entry into force of the Mandate. Thirdly, as will be seen below, the operation of all five categories may be complicated by the application of the principles of acquiescence, recognition and estoppel. The broad categories have to be applied sensitively according to the facts of each individual case. Fourthly, in many cases the task of the tribunal may be complicated by disputes as to the burden and standard of proof.

It is hardly surprising that international law has paid particular attention to the topic of the acquisition of territory since the growth of international law was partly prompted by, and contemporaneous with, the expansion of Europe into the New World in the 15th and 16th centuries. As indicated above, the methods by which title can be acquired are drawn from Roman law. Lawyers traditionally draw a distinction between original title where there was no transfer from a previous sovereign and derivative title where there was such a transfer. Accretion and occupation are clearly examples of the former while

---

19 R Jennings, *The Acquisition of Territory in International Law*, 1963; H Waldock (1948) 25 BYIL 311; D Johnson (1950) 27 BYIL 332; (1955) CLJ 215; G Schwarzenberger (1957) 51 AJIL 308.

20 *The Island of Palmas Arbitration* (1928) 2 RIAA 829.

21 *Taba Arbitration* (*Egypt v Israel*) (1988) 80 ILR 226.

cession illustrates the latter. Annexation and prescription are less easy to categorise since each is based on the extinction of the title of a former sovereign rather than on its non-existence.

The possession of territory is of supreme importance in international law because *prima facie* it carries with it the right to exercise jurisdiction.[22] With these general considerations in mind, it is sensible to turn to specific categories.

(a) Accretion

Accretion is the name given to the increase in land through new formations. Alternatively, accretion can be defined as an increase in land through the operation of nature. In principle a state has the right to sovereignty over any additions or formations made to its territory.[23] Such accretions may be artificial or natural. In considering operations of nature, a distinction is drawn between accretion and avulsion. Where there has been a gradual movement, then the process is known as accretion but where there has been a sudden act of nature then the process is known as avulsion. Thus, if an island were to emerge in territorial waters as a result of volcanic action then this would be an example of avulsion. An instance is afforded by the creation of Surtsey in 1963 as a result of volcanic activity within Icelandic territorial waters.[24]

Although accretion and avulsion are both examples of the operation of nature, the distinction is important when considering the position of rivers that serve as boundaries between states. Where a river is not navigable, then the boundary will be the mid line of the river. Where the river is navigable, then the boundary will be the mid line of the 'thalweg' or principal navigation channel. Where a boundary river undergoes a sudden change of course (avulsion) then the boundary will continue to be the mid line of the former main channel. However, where the physical change is gradual (accretion) then the boundary will reflect the physical changed. Thus, the distinction between accretion and avulsion is of significance in the context of disputes over river boundaries.

The number of cases in international law on the question of river boundaries has been limited but there has been some interesting litigation coming before the United States Supreme Court arising from boundary disputes between states.[25] In the *Chamizal Arbitration*,[26] a question arose as to the sovereignty of a tract of land following the movement southwards of the Rio Grande. The arbitrators considered that the part of land that resulted from the accretion was subject to the sovereignty of the United States but not the part that resulted from a sudden flood. An example of the international rules being applied in the domestic context is afforded by *Louisiana v Mississippi*,[27] where the dispute

---

22 As will be seen in Chapter 8, although international law recognises a number of bases on which jurisdiction might be exercised the oldest and the most clearly established is that the act took place within the territory of the state.

23 See *Southern Centre of Theosophy v State of South Australia* [1982] AC 706.

24 See also Written Answer in Parliament on 17 July 1986, p 478, HL Deb 1005, concerning the emergence of an island within the territorial sea of Iwo Jima following an under sea volcano that had erupted six months earlier.

25 *Arkansas v Tennessee* (1918) 246 US 158; *Louisiana v Mississippi* (1931) 282 US 458.

26 *Chamizal Arbitration (United States v Mexico)* (1911) 5 AJIL 782.

27 *Louisiana v Mississippi* (1931) 282 US 458.

centred on the boundary between two states. In giving judgment the court held that the gradual erosion of soil from the Mississippi bank to the Louisiana bank in the years 1823–1912 passed title to Louisiana but a sudden change of course in the years 1912–13 did not divest Louisiana of the territory already acquired by accretion.

(b) Cession

Cession involves the transfer of territory from one state to another; this is normally accomplished by treaty. Cession is therefore an example of derivative title. Territory may be ceded amicably.[28] Sometimes, cession may take place through an intermediary such as when Austria ceded Lombardy to France in 1859, who in turn ceded the province to Sardinia as part of the scheme of Napoleon III to promote Italian unification. In 18th century Europe, it was not unknown for territory to be passed as part of a dynastic marriage contract. In general, the principle is that ceded territory carries with it rights and obligations arising in international law.[29] An example of cession arising before an international tribunal is afforded by the *Island of Palmas* case.[30] In that case, the United States claimed that it had acquired sovereignty by cession from Spain under the terms of the Treaty of Paris of December 1898. However, the Arbitrator Judge Huber found that at the time of the purported transfer title lay not with Spain but with The Netherlands. Thus, as Spain did not have good title, the United States could be in no better position.

It would seem that for cession to be effected there must be both an agreement and an actual taking of possession. Thus would seem to emerge from the *Iloila* case[31] where the facts were as follows.

A claim was made to a British American Tribunal in respect of damage to the property of British subjects at Iloila in the Philippines which arose on 11 February 1899. The Treaty of Paris had been signed on 10 December 1898 and provided that following the exchange of ratifications Spain would evacuate the islands in favour of the United States. However, on 24 December 1899, Spanish forces were compelled to withdraw by local insurgents. On 10 February 1899, American forces captured Iloila but then the insurgents carried out the threat to burn the town. The tribunal held that as ratifications were not exchanged until 11 April 1899 *de jure* sovereignty did not pass until that date.

It would seem that where three states are parties to the cession then the intermediary need not enter into possession. Thus, where state X cedes to state Y and state Y then cedes to state Z it is not material that state Y does not enter into possession.[32]

---

28 The sale of Alaska to the United States by Russia in 1867 for $7.2 m. The sale of islands constituting Danish West Indies (St Thomas, St John, St Croix) for $25 m in 1916.

29 *Cook v Sprigg* [1899] AC 572.

30 *Island of Palmas* case (*Netherlands v United States*) (1928) 2 RIAA 829.

31 *Iloila* case (*United Kingdom v United States*) (1925) 4 RIAA 158.

32 Cited by the arbitrators in the *Columbia-Venezuela boundary dispute* (1922) 1 RIAA 224; it is arguable that the cession of Venice by Austria to France and then to Italy in 1866 falls within the same category.

The authorities indicate that the cession of land will carry with it the right to sovereignty over any territorial sea and adjacent airspace.[33] Difficulties may however arise where a state purports to cede by treaty territory that is described as inalienable in its basic constitutional documents; in such circumstances it is arguable that competence might be questionable since it might be said that the act concerned a rule of its internal law of fundamental importance.[34]

(c) Occupation

In international law the concept of 'occupation' has a narrow and clearly defined meaning. In essence, occupation is an original method of acquiring title over territory which is not subject to any sovereign power (that is, *terra nullius*). There is an overlap with prescription because, in many cases, it will be difficult to demonstrate the absence of a sovereign power. However, occupation is a distinct method of acquisition with its own criteria. In principle, a claim based on occupation must demonstrate: (a) that prior to the acts of occupation the territory was *terra nullius*; (b) that the occupation was for and on behalf of a state rather than individuals; (c) that there must have been an effective taking of possession; and (d) that there must have been an intention to occupy as sovereign.

Before occupation can be legally effective the territory must be *terra nullius*; this may arise either because there was no sovereign or because of abandonment by the previous sovereign. In the modern world it is rare to find territory that can be described as *terra nullius*. In the 19th century, some European lawyers took the view that tribal or non-European powers did not constitute states and thus the territory could be described as *terra nullius*. However, in Africa and Asia in many instances this difficulty was avoided by colonial powers by securing a treaty of concession or protection from a local ruler. Such an approach has now to be read in the light of the advisory opinion in the Western Sahara case,[35] where the International Court held that territory occupied by tribes or peoples with some form of social and political organisation should not be regarded as *terra nullius*.

In respect of the requirement of acting on behalf of a state this is a question of evidence but if the individuals are acting on behalf of a branch of government (for example, navy, army etc) then this is clearly sufficient. In respect of the taking of possession, the position was clearly set out in the Clipperton Island Arbitration:[36]

> It is beyond doubt that ... besides the *animus occupandi*, the actual, and not the nominal, taking of possession is a necessary condition of occupation. This taking of possession consists in the act, or series of acts, by which the occupying State reduces to its possession the territory in question and takes steps to exercise exclusive authority there. Strictly speaking, and in ordinary cases, that only takes place when the State establishes in the territory itself an organisation capable of making its laws respected. But ... there may be cases where it is unnecessary to have recourse to this method. Thus, if a territory, by virtue of the fact that it was completely uninhabited, is, from the first moment when the

---

33 *Grisbardana* case (1909) 2 RIAA 147; the contrary opinion expressed by Bynkershoek (*De Domino Maris*, Chapter 5) must be subject to qualification in the light of developments in the law of maritime zones; see, also, *Beagle Channel* case (1977) 52 ILR 93.

34 See Vienna Convention on the Law of Treaties (1969), Art 46.

35 *Western Sahara* case (1975) ICJ 12; (1975) 59 ILR 14.

36 *Clipperton Island Arbitration* (1931) 2 RIAA 1105; (1932) 26 AJIL 390; (1932) 6 ILR.

occupying state makes its appearance there, at the absolute and undisputed disposition of that state, from that moment the taking of possession must be considered as accomplished and the occupation is thereby completed.

Thus, what constitutes effective occupation is a matter of fact and degree and will vary according to the location, the nature of the terrain and the presence or absence of competing states. It is easier to establish effective control over barren uninhabited territory than it is over territory where there are various armed factions. The relative nature of the exercise was candidly acknowledged by the Permanent Court of International Justice in the *Eastern Greenlands* case[37] where it observed:

> Another circumstance which must be taken into account ... is the extent to which the sovereignty is also claimed by some other Power. In most of the cases involving claims to territorial sovereignty which have come before an international tribunal, there have been two competing claims to sovereignty, and the tribunal has had to decide which of the two is the stronger ... in many cases the tribunal has been satisfied with very little in the way of actual exercise of sovereign rights, provided that the other State could not make out a superior claim. This is particularly true in the case of claims to sovereignty over areas in thinly populated or unsettled countries.

The cases in this area often on involve a chronological survey extending back to the point of discovery. Today, discovery of itself confers no title but in the 16th century it was arguable that it conferred an inchoate title which had to be followed by effective displays of sovereignty. Thus, in the *Island of Palmas* case,[38] the initial discovery by Spain was displaced by the subsequent acts of sovereignty by The Netherlands. In the *Clipperton Island Arbitration*,[39] where the conflict was between France and Mexico the Arbitrator found that the execution of a geographical survey, the landing of some men, and a proclamation of sovereignty in Honolulu was sufficient to found title. However, this finding was influenced by the isolated and uninhabited nature of the island. In the *Eastern Greenland* case,[40] Denmark was able to resist any suggestion that the territory was *terra nullius* by pointing to its acts of sovereignty such as the granting of concessions, its colonies in other parts of Greenland, and the various favourable documentary references in treaty provisions. In the *Miniquiers and Ecrehos* case,[41] the International Court of Justice was influenced by various local acts of administration and references in legislative acts to declare in favour of the claims of the United Kingdom.

While there can be no comprehensive list of acts of effective occupation and a broad approach to the question is justified, it is clear from the cases that the effective occupation must be coupled with an intention to occupy as sovereign. Thus, it might be said that there is a threefold requirement: (a) acts of effective occupation; (b) an *animus occupandi*; and (c) an *animus occupandi* as sovereign. This third element appears in a number of cases and is designed to exclude the random acts of individuals. As Judge McNair observed in

---

37 *Eastern Greenland* case (1933) PCIJ, Ser A/B, No 53, p 46.
38 *Island of Palmas* case (*Netherlands v United States*) (1928) 2 RIAA 829.
39 *Clipperton Island Arbitration* (1931) 2 RIAA 1105; (1932) 26 AJIL 390; (1932) 6 AD Case No 50.
40 *Eastern Greenland* case (1933) PCIJ, Ser A/B, No 53, p 46.
41 *Minquiers and Ecrehos* case (1953) ICJ 47.

the *Anglo Norwegian Fisheries* case,[42] 'the independent activity of private individuals is of little value unless it can be shown that they have acted in pursuance of ... some ... authority received from their Governments or that in some other way their Governments have asserted jurisdiction through them'. The modern tendency is to approach each case with a degree of discrimination as to the nature of the territory. This was observed in the *Rann of Kutch Arbitration*,[43] where the tribunal noted the importance of bearing in mind when assessing acts of sovereignty that in an agricultural economy there was a less clear cut distinction between public and private ownership.

(d) Prescription[44]

Prescription like occupation is based on effective control over territory; however it differs from occupation as a method of establishing title over territory as it applies where the territory is not *terra nullius*. As in municipal law it is the legitimisation of title by passage of time in circumstances where the original acquisition may have been doubtful or unlawful. It is based on the presumed grant or acquiescence of a former sovereign. It is founded on the principle that international stability requires 'a state of things which actually exists and has existed for a long time should be changed as little as possible'.[45] Prescription is therefore based on the two fold practical considerations of the passage of time and the implied acquiescence of the dispossessed sovereign. There is thus some similarity with the concept of limitation of actions in real property law in that after a certain period of time action by the true owner become time barred or the title is itself extinguished.

Cases on prescription arise, directly or indirectly, in a number of forms. First, there are those cases based simply on immemorial possession where the original title is uncertain. In such cases title is based on undisturbed continuous possession. As the eighth edition of *Oppenheim* observed, prescription was 'the acquisition of sovereignty over a territory through a continuous and undisturbed exercise of sovereignty over it during such a period as is necessary to create under the influence of historical development the general conviction that the present condition of things is in conformity with international order'.[46] Secondly, there are those cases where it is arguable that prescription is the basis of the title but it is not expressly stated. Thus, in the *Island of Palmas* case[47] it is clear that there must have been a point at which the Spanish title ceased and The Netherlands acquired title by prescription but it was not expressly stated in the award.

In respect of the criteria for a claim based on prescription there are four elements that arise for consideration: (i) a display of sovereign authority; (ii) the absence of recognition of sovereignty in another state; (iii) peaceful and uninterrupted possession; (iv) the

---

42 *Anglo Norwegian Fisheries* case (1951) ICJ 116.
43 *Rann of Kutch Arbitration* (1968) 50 ILR 2; 17 RIAA 553.
44 D Johnson, 'Acquisitive prescription in international law' (1950) 27 BYIL 332; R Pinto, 'La prescription en droit international' (1955) 87 HR 387.
45 See *The Grisbardana* case (1909) 2 RIAA 147.
46 Such a definition repeated in RY Jennings and AD Watts, *Oppenheim's International Law*, 9th edn, 1992, p 706.
47 *Island of Palmas* case (*Netherlands v United States*) (1928) 2 RIAA 829.

absence of objection. In respect of the first element, it is simply a question of examining the relevant evidence of governmental acts.[48] The second element is a question of fact, but the absence of recognition of another may be powerful evidence. The third and fourth elements are related in that there cannot be peaceful possession unless there is an absence of objection. Thus, in the *Chamizal Arbitration*,[49] one of the points made was the United States might have acquired title to a disputed tract of land near the Rio Grande by peaceful possession. This was rejected by the tribunal on the basis that title had not been uninterrupted because of the consistent diplomatic protests by Mexico. It is clear that the protests must be sustained and made in the appropriate form; it will not be sufficient to 'go through the motions'. It would seem that the protests must be made at the level of the appropriate regional or international tribunal. Thus in the *Minquiers and Ecrehos Islands* case,[50] the United Kingdom argued that French protests against English legislation were ineffective to displace acquiescence because they did not demand arbitration; indeed the judgments in the case appear to indicate that where state A and state B have an agreement to settle disputes by arbitration then protests will only have weight where these procedures are invoked. In the recent *Kasikili/Sedudu Island* case (*Botswana v Namibia*)[51] the two states agreed that for a claim based on prescription to succeed it was necessary to demonstrate: (i) that possession had to be exercised in the character of a sovereign; (ii) that possession must be peaceful and uninterrupted; (iii) that possession must be public; and (iv) that possession must endure for a length of time.

It is doubtful whether any particular length of time can be stipulated for a claim based on prescription to be advanced;[52] everything depends on the precise facts of the case and it is doubtful whether analogies drawn from Roman law or the law of real property are helpful. The doctrine of prescription, or 'acquisitive prescription' as it is sometimes described, is not without its difficulties. Some jurists have doubted its validity and in the case that is most preyed in aid the doctrine is not expressly referred to.[53]

The doctrine of prescription has been subject to a rival in recent years. The jurist Charles de Visscher has advanced the doctrine of historical consolidation (or consolidation) as a mode of acquisition of title.[54] According to this doctrine however unlawful the taking of possession and whatever the degree of subsequent protest there will come a time when the condition of things should not be disturbed. The justification for this approach is that it promotes peace and order. Such authority as there is derives from some remarks contained in the *Anglo Norwegian Fisheries* case.[55] However, a considerable degree of caution is required in adopting this approach. First, any form of

---

48 As in the *Minquiers and Ecrehos* case (1953) ICJ 47.

49 *Chamizal Arbitration* (1911) (*United States v Mexico*) (1911) 5 AJIL 782.

50 *Minquiers and Ecrehos Islands* case (1953) ICJ 47.

51 *Kasikili/Sedudu Island* case (*Botswana v Namibia*) ICJ, 13 December 1999. In the circumstances, Namibia was not able to sustain a title based on prescription. See M Shaw, 'Case concerning Kasikili/Sedudu Island (*Botswana v Namibia*)' (2000) 49 ICLQ 964.

52 In the *Boundary Arbitration between Great Britain and Venezuela* in 1899, the Arbitrators were instructed to accept a title based on adverse possession or prescription of a period of 50 years.

53 *Island of Palmas* case (*Netherlands v United States*) (1928) 2 RIAA 829.

54 C De Visscher, *Theory and Reality in Public International Law* (1953) (English translation by Corbett (1960)).

55 *Anglo Norwegian Fisheries* case (1951) ICJ 116, p 138.

consolidation is based upon the taking of possession so that the *modus operandi* is no different. Secondly, the remarks in the *Anglo Norwegian Fisheries* case were simply addressed to the Norwegian system of fixing maritime baselines at a time when the rules of customary international law were uncertain. Thirdly, as the particular extract was expressed in the conditional tense it is difficult to infer that it represents *lex lata*.[56] Fourthly, the extract indicates that the remarks were confined to the particular circumstances of the Norwegian decrees.

If the doctrine simply asserts that one must face political realities then the evidence indicates that everything depends on the circumstances of the case. Difficult problems of reconciling law and practice can arise where territory is taken by force. In the instance of the invasion of Goa by India in December 1961, even though the conduct was a breach of the United Nations Charter the subsequent acquiescence and recognition by the international community and the absence of censure by the Security Council had the effect of validating the title.[57] It is arguable that, in such an instance, writers such as Jennings[58] and Shaw are correct in asserting that title is validated by the subsequent acquiescence or recognition by other states. However, in the modern world the attitude of the Security Council will be crucial. Thus, when Israel acquired territory in Jordan and Egypt following the war of June 1967 the Security Council moved to assert that the acquisition of territory by force was inadmissible.[59]

A further difficulty that arises with claims based upon prescription is whether such a claim can only succeed when accompanied by positive evidence of acquiescence or whether such a claim will prevail in the absence of clear protest.

(e) Conquest and annexation[60]

This method of the acquisition of territory has been described as being only of academic interest today. Prior to the First World War, it was not unusual for territory to change hands following the use of force. Conquest by itself was not sufficient for that simply constituted occupancy by a belligerent force. Difficulties did arise over the distinction between military occupation and annexation.[61] In order to confer an effective title, there had to be both physical occupation together with an intention to occupy as sovereign. This was normally effected by a formal declaration of annexation although in some instances this would be accomplished by a formal ceding of the territory by the vanquished state.[62]

---

56 The extract reads: 'Since ... these ... constitute ... the application of a well defined and uniform system, it is indeed this system itself which would reap the benefit of general toleration, the basis of an historical consolidation which would make it enforceable against all States.'

57 The invasion was opposed by Adlai Stevenson (1900–65) (the United States Ambassador to the United Nations) but a censure resolution was vetoed by Russia.

58 RY Jennings, *Acquisition of Territorial Sovereignty*, 1963; MN Shaw, 'Title to territory in Africa' (1986) International Legal Issues.

59 SC Res 242 November 1967.

60 Q Wright, 'The Stimson Note of January 7 1932' (1932) 26 AJIL 342; AD McNair, 'The Stimson doctrine of non-recognition' (1933) 14 BYIL 65.

61 See *US v Hayward* (1814) 2 Gall 485 (Story J).

62 An example being the ceding of Alsace Lorraine to Germany by France in 1871.

The loss of human life in World War I prompted a change in the attitude to conflict. European statesmen acting under the influence of the United States sought to limit the circumstances in which force might be employed and efforts were made to encourage the peaceful settlement of disputes. The Covenant of the League of Nations (1919) contained detailed provisions both to deter the use of force and to promote the peaceful settlement of disputes.[63] The loss of human life and the economic disruption caused by conflict meant that the price of war was simply too high for any rational state.

This general theme was continued in the Kellogg-Briand Pact of 1928[64] in which war was outlawed as an instrument of national policy. Shortly after the acceptance of the Stimson Doctrine of Non-Recognition (1932) was propounded indicating that territory acquired by force would not be recognised. Although some seizures were accorded recognition in the 1930s,[65] the German annexations were rendered invalid after 1945 and the judgment of the Nuremberg War Crimes Tribunal (1946) contained a clear condemnation of the acquisition of territory by force. The post-war settlement set out in the United Nations Charter (1945) contained express provisions against the use of force. Such prohibition is impliedly stated in the Preamble and Art 1(1) of the Charter and the matter is expressly dealt with in the clear words of Art 2(4) which reads:

> All Members shall refrain in their international relations from the threat or use of force against the territorial integrity or political independence of any State, or in any manner inconsistent with the Purposes of the United Nations.

The application of this principle will vary according to the precise circumstances. Thus in the context of the Middle East Security Council Resolution 242[66] refers to 'the inadmissibility of the acquisition of territory by war'. In the Declaration of Principles of International Law adopted by the General Assembly in 1970 it is clearly stated:

> The territory of a State shall not be the object of military occupation resulting from the use of force in contravention of the provisions of the Charter. The territory of a State shall not be the object of acquisition by another State resulting from the threat or the use of force. No territorial acquisition resulting from the threat or use of force shall be recognised as legal.

Against this background it is sensible to examine the likely sequence of events should territory be seized by force. In the modern world if state A attempts to seize the territory of state B then it is likely that state B or its allies will seek a meeting of the Security Council which would then probably pass a resolution declaring any purported annexation null and void and calling on all states to refrain from recognition. In August 1990 when Iraq purported to annex Kuwait, Security Council Resolution 662 provided that:

> Annexation of Kuwait by Iraq under any form and whatever pretext has no legal validity, and is considered null and void.

Any such resolution would probably be followed in the first instance by economic sanctions. In the case of Iraq the unlawful conduct was reversed by the use of force.

---

63   The provisions being contained in Arts 10–16 of the Covenant of the League of Nations; efforts in this area had been proceeding slowly prior to 1914, in the form of the work of the Hague Conferences.

64   The Treaty of Paris 1928 or the General Treaty for the Renunciation of War.

65   As indicated by the granting of recognition in respect of the Italian invasion of Abyssinia.

66   November 1967.

Another contemporary problem of the use of force concerns the Middle East. Following the war of 1967 Israel held territory in the Sinai Peninsular. East Jerusalem, the Gaza Strip and the Golan Heights. This territory had formerly been part of Egypt, Jordan and Syria. In November 1967 in Resolution 242 the Security Council affirmed the principle of 'the inadmissibility of the acquisition of territory by war'. In 1979, the territory in Sinai was returned following the peace agreement between Israel and Egypt.

A third example in the contemporary world was the Indian invasion of Goa in December 1961; although debate in the Security Council was hostile to India[67] no resolution was actually passed because of the veto of the USSR. India retained control of Goa from 1961 until 1974 when its seizure was recognised by the post-Salazar regime in Portugal. It is certainly arguable that this is a rare instance in the post-1945 world of territory being seized by force.

Twenty years later, when Argentinean forces seized the Falkland Islands, the response of the Security Council in Resolution 502 was to demand an immediate withdrawal of troops from the Islands.

The experience since 1945 has been that the invasion of state A by state B is less of a problem than the difficulties arising in civil wars. However if such an invasion by one state is undertaken then it is likely to be met by immediate condemnation by the Security Council. To this extent the clear prohibitions in the United Nations Charter have produced an improvement in the conduct of states.

(f) Self-determination

The concept of self-determination is not strictly a principle applicable to the acquisition of territory however disputes about territory often focus on questions of self-determination by the relevant peoples of the territory (this matter is discussed in Chapter 5, section 11).

(g) Judicial decisions

The role of judicial and arbitral bodies in determining territorial disputes should not be underestimated. Of course such tribunals reach their judgment by reference to the principles cited above but until they reach a determination the question of sovereignty remains uncertain. Thus the *Island of Palmas* case,[68] *Clipperton Island Arbitration*,[69] *Eastern Greenland* case,[70] *Minquiers and Ecrehos* case[71] and the *Frontier Dispute* case,[72] all resolved disputes about entitlement to exercise sovereignty. Titles that were in dispute were rendered certain by operation of the judicial and arbitral process.[73]

---

67 The argument in the Security Council being put by the United States representative Adlai Stevenson that the merits of the dispute could not be preyed in aid to justify a clear breach of Art 2(4); some other states being prepared to give India the benefit of the doubt because of the nature of the Portuguese regime and the need to promote decolonisation.

68 *Island of Palmas Arbitration* (1928) 2 RIAA 82.

69 *Clipperton Islands Arbitration* (1932) 26 AJIL 390.

70 *Eastern Greenland* case (1933) PCIJ, Ser A/B, No 53.

71 *Minquiers and Ecrehos* case (1953) ICJ 47.

72 *Frontier Dispute* case (*Burkina Faso v Mali*) (1985) ICJ 6; (1986) ICJ 554.

73 See *El Salvador/Honduras* (1992) ICJ 351; *Libya v Chad* (1994) ICJ 6; *Dubai/Sharjah* 91 ILR 543; *Eritrea/Yemen (First Phase on Territorial Sovereignty)* 114 ILR 1.

4 RECOGNITION, ACQUIESCENCE AND ESTOPPEL

Recognition, acquiescence and estoppel are not themselves methods of acquiring title to territory but they do play a role in the resolution of disputes. Recognition represents the approval of states other than those in dispute about territory. In the *Eastern Greenland* case,[74] the Permanent Court of International Justice alluded to the fact that treaties with a number of states had indicated an acceptance of Denmark's sovereignty over Greenland. In like terms it can be argued that India's seizure of Goa in 1961 was validated by the subsequent recognitions granted by other states and most crucially by the recognition by Portugal itself in 1974. In the context of the acquisition of territory the concept of recognition applies to the attitude of other states while acquiescence refers to the attitude of the 'losing state' that is, the state that might be expected to protest but does not in fact do so.[75] In essence it is a matter of evidence from which an inference may be drawn.

Closely related is the doctrine of estoppel. The doctrine of estoppel derives from the Court of Equity and in the context of international law it means that in certain circumstances it will be impossible for a state to go back on its previous acts or statements. In municipal law the essence of estoppel is the making of representations by one party and the subsequent acting in reliance or to detriment by the other.[76] The attitude of international law is not particularly consistent in this area and it is open to argument whether it is enough to establish reliance on the conduct of another or whether it is necessary to show both the making of representations and the acting to detriment. Thus, in the *Gulf of Maine* case, the International Court of Justice noted that 'the element of detriment ... distinguishes estoppel *strictu sensu* from acquiescence'.[77] It is always difficult for a litigant to go back upon his previous statements or acts and the question arises as to whether this is precluded as a matter of law or simply as a matter of evidence. In the leading case on estoppel, the *Temple of Preah Vihear* case,[78] the facts were as follows.

The dispute between Thailand (formerly Siam) and Cambodia concerned the precise border between the two states. The border had been subject to a 1904 treaty between Siam and France (as the sovereign power over French Indo China which included Cambodia). A boundary commission was established under the treaty. Siam called for a map which showed the temple in Cambodian territory. Siam then called for further copies of the map without making any protest. At a later date, a Thai prince attended a reception with the French flag flying over the temple.

Although the case raised a number of issues, including that of treaty interpretation, the International Court considered that Thailand was estopped from objecting to Cambodian title because it was estopped by past acts of acquiescence.[79] Similarly in the *Eastern Greenland* case,[80] the Permanent Court of International Justice regarded Norway's

---

74 *Eastern Greenland* case (1933) PCIJ, Ser A/B, No 53.
75 The *Lybia v Chad* case (1994) ICJ 6; 100 ILR 1, where the court remarked that one party had after 11 years not challenged particular treaty boundaries.
76 *Ramsden v Dyson* (1865) LR 1 HL 129; *Willmott v Barber* (1880) 15 Ch D 96; *Crabb v Arun DC* [1976] Ch 179.
77 *Gulf of Maine* case (1984) ICJ 286.
78 *Temple of Preah Vihear* case (1962) ICJ 6; (1962) 33 ILR 48.
79 DH Johnson (1962) 11 ICLQ 1183.
80 *Eastern Greenland* case (1933) PCIJ, Ser A/B, No 53.

acquiescence in treaties with Denmark, which included references to Greenland, as raising an estoppel in respect of any claim to the territory.

Thus, although recognition, acquiescence or estoppel are not themselves grounds on which title may be claimed they may be preyed in aid as defences where a claim is made by another state.

5 INTERTEMPORAL LAW

The rules as to the acquisition of territory have changed over the centuries. At one time title acquired by conquest and annexation was acceptable; that is of course not true today. This raises the problem as to the law one applies on a particular date.[81] The general view is that the law that should be applied is that applicable at the date of the alleged acquisition. This is justified on the ground that save in exceptional circumstances laws should not operate retrospectively. However, the concept has to be read in the light of the *Island of Palmas* case.[82] The facts in the case were remarkably straightforward.

The Island was discovered by Spain in the 16th century. However, at a later date the Dutch began to exercise effective control. In 1898 Spain purported to cede the Island to the United States. After 1906, the United States discovered the Dutch flag flying over the island. The question of title was submitted to Max Huber, then President of the Permanent Court of International Justice. The Arbitrator found in favour of The Netherlands.

It emerged from the award given by Max Huber that acts should be judged in the light of the contemporary law but also that such rights once acquired might be lost if not maintained in accordance with changes brought about by the development of international law.[83] Thus the right Spain acquired by discovery might be lost if were not supported by subsequent acts. The rights Spain acquired might be described as an inchoate title in which case it could not prevail over the continuous and peaceful display of authority by another state. If, however, discovery did confer an absolute title it could be lost if it was not followed by subsequent acts of sovereignty. The doctrine of intertemporal law therefore has two elements. As one distinguished writer has expressed it, 'one requires that there must be acquisition of title by discovery or in some other acceptable manner, and the other that this abstract or inchoate title must be followed by manifestation of authority by the sovereign effective enough to warrant the inference of full and continual possession at the time the dispute arises'.[84] Or, to put the matter another way, the doctrine of intertemporal law judges the creation of the right in accordance with the then contemporary law but holds that such a right will cease to exist if it is not followed by subsequent effective acts of sovereignty.

---

81 This is of course not the same concept as that of the 'critical date', on which see below.

82 *Island of Palmas* case (*Netherlands v United States*) (1928) 2 RIAA 829.

83 On the question of discovery, see FA Von der Heydte, 'Discovery, symbolic annexation and virtual effectiveness in international law' (1935) 29 AJIL 448.

84 TO Elias, 'The doctrine of intertemporal law' (1980) 74 AJIL 285.

Although the second element of the doctrine was criticised at the time by Philip Jessup[85] who feared that it might lead to states actually losing territory to which they had previously gained title the general thrust that the law should not operate retrospectively was in line with past case law[86] and has been preyed in aid on subsequent occasions.[87] Although most would accept that 'a juridical fact must be appreciated in the light of the law contemporary with it, and not with the law in force at the time when a dispute in regard to it arises or falls to be settled', states sometimes seek to avoid this principle. In 1961, when the Security Council debated the Indian invasion of Goa one of the arguments advanced by India was that the Portuguese title acquired by conquest in the 16th century would not be a valid method of acquiring title in the 20th century. There is a natural tendency for states to seek to specify the date most favourable to themselves and while the principle of intertemporal law should be applied sensitively according to the facts of each case the doctrine of the rule of law normally precludes retrospective measures so that to this extent there is much to be said for the approach in the *Island of Palmas* case.[88]

6 THE CRITICAL DATE

The concept of the critical date may be important in some arbitrations. In simple terms, it is the date beyond which no evidence of title will be admissible. Thus, in the *Island of Palmas* case the claim by the United States was based on cession by Spain in December 1898; as the United States could be in no better position than Spain then the critical date was fixed at 10 December 1898, being the date of the Treaty of Paris between Spain and the United States. The fixing of the critical date will determine the nature of the evidence that can be admitted and also the particular grounds that the parties can advance.

7 UTI POSSIDETIS

The doctrine of *uti possidetis* derives from the 19th century, when it was determined that the administrative boundaries of the Spanish Empire in Latin and Central America should form the international boundaries of the newly independent states. The policy has also been followed in post-colonial Africa where the colonial frontiers were taken as the starting point for the boundaries of the newly independent states. In due course, this policy was adopted by the Organisation of African Unity.[89] The object of such a policy was to prevent damaging boundary disputes when the colonial power withdrew. The problem, particularly in Africa, was that colonial borders were arbitrary and were often not in line with ethnic or tribal divisions and such an approach tended to lead to attempts at secession, as in the Belgium Congo or Nigeria. The approach was seen as placing administrative convenience ahead of ethnic and cultural identity.

---

85 P Jessup, 'The *Palmas Island Arbitration*' (1928) 22 AJIL 735.
86 *Grisbadarna* case (1909) Hague Ct Rep (Scott) 121; (1910) 4 AJIL 226; (1909) 2 RIAA 147.
87 *Minquiers and Ecrehos* case (1953) ICJ 47; *Aegean Sea Continental Shelf (Greece v Turkey)* (1978) ICJ 1.
88 *Re Island of Palmas Arbitration* (1928) 2 RIAA 829; (1928) 22 AJIL 875.
89 Adopted by the Organisation of African Unity in the Cairo Resolution, 21 July 1964.

The principle of *uti possidetis* has probably now attained the status of a rule of customary international law, not only in respect of South America but generally in post-colonial situations. Thus in the *Frontier Dispute* case (*Burkina Faso v Republic of Mali*),[90] the Chamber of the International Court of Justice appeared to endorse *uti possidetis* as a general principle alluding to the 'intangibility of frontiers inherited from colonisation'.[91]

Nevertheless, the principle is not a special rule which pertains solely to one specific geographical location. It is a general principle, which is logically connected with the phenomenon of obtaining independence, wherever it occurs. Its obvious purpose is 'to prevent the independence and stability of new states being endangered by fratricidal struggles provoked by the challenging of frontiers following the withdrawal of the administering power'.[92] This principle was subsequently followed by the ICJ Chamber in the case of *El Salvador v Honduras*,[93] where it was stressed that '*uti possidetis* is essentially a retrospective principle, investing as international boundaries administrative limits intended originally for quite other purposes'.[94]

However, while there are sound reasons for the application of the principle in the straightforward situation of the withdrawal of a colonial power, it is certainly open to argument as to whether the principle should be so applied in the complex situation of the dissolution of the former Yugoslavia where the federal state itself had only recently been carved out of the territories of the former Ottoman Empire. In any event, the Arbitration Commission on Yugoslavia observed in Opinion No 2:[95]

> The Commission considers that international law as it currently stands does not spell out all the implications of the right to self determination. However, it is well established that, whatever the circumstances, the right to self-determination must not involve changes to existing frontiers at the time of independence (*uti possidetis juris*) except where the States concerned agree otherwise.

The implication of this being that the Serbian population in Bosnia while entitled to full human rights protection was bound by the boundaries of the former Bosnia-Herzegovina. This was carried further in Opinion No 3 where the EC Commission[96] observed that:

> Except where otherwise agreed, the former boundaries become frontiers protected by international law. This conclusion follows from the respect for the territorial *status quo*, and in particular from the principle of *uti possidetis*.

It must be open to argument as to whether a principle developed to manage a post-colonial problem should automatically have prevailed over the principle of self-determination in the complex and fluid situation pertaining in the former Yugoslavia.

---

90 *Frontier Dispute* case (*Burkina Faso v Mali*) (1986) ICJ 554; 80 ILR 459.

91 *Ibid*, p 557; p 462.

92 *Ibid*, p 565; p 469.

93 *Land, Island and Maritime Frontier Dispute (El Salvador v Honduras) (Merits)* case (1992) ICJ 351; 97 ILR 266.

94 (1992) ICJ 351, p 388; 97 ILR 266, p 301. For general discussion of the case, see M Shaw, '*Case concerning the Land, Island and Maritime Frontier Dispute*' (1993) 42 ICLQ 929.

95 The EC Arbitration Commission on Yugoslavia (Chairman, R Badinter) (1992) 92 ILR 167.

96 *Ibid*.

8 CONTIGUITY

Contiguity or geographical contiguity as it is sometimes called is not a method or mode by which title to territory may be acquired under international law. However, it is a concept that is raised in many disputes about territory and its general significance should not be underestimated. First, in the law of the sea the principle of geographical contiguity will be important in determining disputes about entitlement to a territorial sea or a continental shelf.

Secondly, while contiguity is not a method by which title may be acquired it is a factor that can arise and determine the manner in which a state presents its case. Disputes about territory raise popular passions and it is not unknown for a state to argue its case both on legal grounds but also on wider political grounds. As Professor Jennings has noted, this may serve to convince a state that it has a stronger case than the legal merits allow.[97] In some instances, arguments about geographical contiguity are advanced alongside submissions based on historical continuity. Any suggestion that contiguity could be a method of acquiring title was rejected by Arbitrator Huber in the *Island of Palmas* case,[98] where he observed:

> ... it is impossible to show the existence of a rule of positive international law to the effect that island situated outside territorial waters should belong to a state from the mere fact that its territory forms the *terra firma* (nearest continent or island of considerable size) ...

> ... Nor is this principle of contiguity admissible as a legal method of deciding questions of territorial sovereignty; for it is wholly lacking in precision and would in its application lead to arbitrary results.

However, the principle of contiguity may be important in raising a presumption of effective occupation; thus in the *Eastern Greenland* case,[99] the Permanent Court of International Justice was prepared to take into account the factor of contiguity in concluding that Denmark enjoyed sovereignty over Greenland when the actual area of settlement was limited. In this sense contiguity may be preyed in aid as a method of interpreting other evidence.

Thirdly, arguments based on geographical contiguity may be raised in the context of submissions based on historical continuity. It is arguable that a number of the most difficult territorial disputes in the modern world give rise to these features. To an extent, these arguments are present in the disputes involving the status of Gibraltar (in the claim by Spain), in the Falkland Islands (in the claim by Argentina) and in Northern Ireland (in the claim by the Republic of Ireland); in all three, the claimant relies upon geographical contiguity and a version of history while the other party preys in aid other arguments including those based on the principle of self-determination. Further, it is worthy of note that Iraq's claims against Kuwait in the 1960s and in 1990 were based on arguments deriving from history and geographical continuity although of course such arguments cannot be the basis of an unlawful use of force.

---

97 RY Jennings, *The Acquisition of Territory in International Law*, 1962.
98 *Island of Palmas* case (1928) 2 RIAA 829.
99 *Eastern Greenland* case (1933) PCIJ, Ser A/B, No 53.

9 RIGHTS OF FOREIGN STATES OVER TERRITORY

It is an accepted principle of international law that state A will have exclusive sovereignty over its own territory. However there may be a limited number of situations where a foreign state (that is, state B) will have rights over the territory of another (that is, state A). It is proposed to examine a number of such situations.

(a) Leases

A right over the territory of another would be that of the lease, such as where state A (that is, the grantor) makes a grant of identifiable territory for a particular duration to state B (that is, the grantee). An example would be the leases granted by China in 1898 in favour of France, Germany and Britain, the best known being the lease of the 'New Territories' which was attached to and administered with the colony of Hong Kong.[100] The advantage of the lease to European colonial powers was that it would enable control to be taken of strategic points of territory without the expense and commitments associated with annexation; this was particularly the case in respect of territory beyond Europe.[101] It is normally the case that the effect of the lease is to pass sovereignty for the duration of the lease to the grantee; at the expiration of the lease sovereignty reverts to the original sovereign grantor. A further example would be the treaty concluded in 1903 whereby Panama granted a ten mile strip of territory in favour of the United States. One aspect of this transaction that was unusual was that the grant was made 'in perpetuity' rather than for a definite term. The Hay-Varilla treaty of 1903 had provided guarantees by the United States of the Independence of Panama as well as stipulating rules for the projected canal. The treaty was revised in 1936 and 1955 but this did not prevent concern about the impact of the 1903 treaty on the sovereign rights of Panama. In 1977 the Panama Canal Treaties provided for the return to Panama of sovereignty over the Canal Zone together with provision for the United States to maintain and operate in the zone until the conclusion of the treaty on 31 December 1999.

Although a lease will normally provide for the transfer of sovereignty such a situation should be distinguished from two other types of arrangement. First, there may be situations where state A agrees to administer the territory of state B; thus in 1878 the Treaty of Berlin provided for British administration of the Turkish island of Cyprus. Under this arrangement which persisted until 1914 sovereignty did not pass but remained with the Ottoman Empire.[102] A second distinction can be made in the cases of military bases. Such agreements are sometimes described as 'leases' and everything will turn on the precise terms of the agreement as to where sovereignty resides. In agreements made by the United Kingdom with the United States in respect of military bases in

---

100 The Anglo Chinese Agreement of 1984 and the Hong Kong Act 1985 provided for the termination of British sovereignty on 1 July 1997. The 19th century had witnessed three treaties: (1) The Treaty of Nanking 1842, whereby Hong Kong was ceded in perpetuity; (2) the Convention of Peking in 1860, whereby the southern part of the Kowloon peninsular and Stonecutters Island were ceded in perpetuity; and (3) the Convention of 1898, whereby the New Territories were leased for 99 years from 1 July 1898.

101 In 1898, a weak Chinese regime leased Port Arthur to Russia, and Kuang-chou Wan to France.

102 The island was annexed by Britain in 1915.

England, it was normal to agree to pass to the grantee 'all the rights, powers and authority ... necessary for the establishment use, operation and defence' of the areas granted. Manifestly, it was not intended to pass sovereignty which would be inappropriate in the context of a mere airfield and in any event in the United Kingdom such cession would have to sanctioned by Act of Parliament.

(b) Servitudes

In principle, an international servitude exists where the territory of state A is subject to rights in favour of another state. Broadly, the state enjoying the benefit may be able to do certain acts such as remove water, exercise a right of passage or even station troops. The concept of the servitude derives from the Roman law of property. Such a concept has formed the basis of the modern law of easements in the common law world where the dominant landowner (A) enjoys certain benefits over the land of the servient landowner (B). In general when the dominant land is sold then A will be able to pass the benefit to C and when the servient land is sold then the burden may pass from B to D subject to the requirements as to registration of third party rights.[103] However, a number of writers have questioned the employment of the word 'servitude' and questioned whether such rights on the international plane have any connection with easements in the municipal law. A servitude may arise by treaty or by local custom however international tribunals are most reluctant to find limitations on the sovereign territory of a state. There are a number of cases where the concept has been discussed but careful attention has to be paid to the precise facts in each case. It is now established that a servitude can exist in international law,[104] but it can probably only arise by express grant.[105] In certain circumstances, the servitude may 'run with the land'.[106] It would seem that a servitude may be extinguished by express or implied agreement.[107]

10 PARTICULAR SITUATIONS

It is proposed to examine a number of situations giving rise to particular problems; not all of these problems are resolved at the time of writing.

(a) The Arctic

The physical geography of the North Pole is such that most of the area comprises ice not over land but above a frozen sea. There are some islands that are subject to specific

---

103 The requirements for an easement to exist in England were set out by Lord Evershed MR in *Re Ellenborough Park* [1956] Ch 131. It is widely assumed that the first edition of *Gale on Easements* in 1839 was based on the Roman law of servitudes.

104 *Rights of Passage over Indian Territory* case (1960) ICJ 6.

105 *North Atlantic Fisheries Arbitration* case (1910) 11 RIAA 167.

106 See *Oppenheim's International Law*, 9th edn, 1992, p 674. The learned authors take as an example the case of the Alsatian town of Huningen which under the Peace Treaty of 1815 was not to be fortified so as to secure the interest of the Swiss canton of Basle. This agreement imposing restrictions was held to run when the town passed to German hands in 1871 and when it returned to France in 1918.

107 *Free Zones of Upper Savoy and the District of Gex* (1932) PCIJ, Ser A/B, No 46.

territorial claims. Denmark has traditionally claimed Greenland and its associated islands while Norway has exercised sovereignty over Spitzbergen for most of the 20th century.

In respect of the frozen ice pack some states have made claims to sovereignty founded upon the sector principle (for example, Canada and Russia). Under this principle land territory facing the Arctic is thought to constitute the basis for claiming sovereignty over all territory in the north and within a sector between the eastward and westward meridians of longitude at each end of the land territory and extending northward until they reach the North Pole. The sector principle owes something to both previous ideas of spheres of influence and to the principle of contiguity.

In contrast other Arctic states such as the United States, Norway or Finland have abstained from such claims. Indeed they have argued that as the area is but frozen sea then in principle it is subject to the same regime as pertains to the high seas.

It is arguable that the status of the Arctic is unsettled and in some respects uncertain. There is no comprehensive treaty regime and that omission may be explained by the seeming absence of mineral resources. However, as the area linked the Soviet Union and the United States it always had considerable military significance because of the capacity of nuclear powered submarines to patrol and spy in isolated waters. With the dissolution of the Soviet Union and the relative decline of Russia as a naval power this aspect is perhaps less significant today.

(b) The Antarctic

The Antarctic represents nearly a 20th of the world's surface and it has been calculated that it comprises over half the supply of freshwater. In terms of physical geography it comprises a land mass covered by ice; the land mass under the ice is known to include valuable mineral deposits. This factor alone contributes to the level of state interest. The area of Antarctica is broadly considered to constitute the territory southwards of latitude 60 S. The minerals available may extend beyond coal and gas to oil and precious metals. The first question is whether any such exploitation should be founded an traditional claims of state sovereignty or should it be based on some collective system.

Originally seven states made claims to sovereignty over Antarctica (Argentina, Australia, Chile, France, New Zealand, Norway and the United Kingdom). These claims were based on arguments of contiguity or sometimes on the sector principle but none of these claims was subject to detailed impartial examination.

During the 1950s tension arose between some of these states and the United Kingdom sought to bring Argentina and Chile before the International Court of Justice but the case was struck out for want of jurisdiction. It became clear that progress could only be made on the basis of an agreed treaty regime. To this end the Washington Treaty on Antarctica was drawn up in 1959 and entered into force in 1961.[108] The original contracting parties were Argentina, Australia, Belgium, Chile, France, Japan, New Zealand, Norway, South Africa, the Soviet Union, United Kingdom and United States. Since 1961, when the treaty came into force, the number of parties has increased to over 40.[109] The treaty provides

---

108 For the United Kingdom, see Antarctica Treaty Act 1967.
109 See E Hambro, 'Some notes on the future of the Antarctic Treaty collaboration' (1974) 68 AJIL 217.

that regular meetings should take place between the parties and such meetings may produce binding recommendations (Art 9). Full participation in the meetings is reserved to the original contracting parties and those states who produce evidence of substantial scientific research in the area.

The first object of the treaty is to provide that Antarctica shall only be used for peaceful purposes (Art 1(1)) and that all forms of military measures are prohibited save where military personnel are engaged in scientific research (Art 1(2)). The treaty prohibits the employment of nuclear weapons or the disposal of nuclear waste (Art 5). The essence of the treaty is to be found in Art 4(2) which provides that while claims are not deemed abandoned:

> No acts or activities taking place while the present Treaty is in force shall constitute a basis for asserting, supporting or denying a claim to territorial sovereignty in Antarctica or create any rights of sovereignty in Antarctica. No new claim, or enlargement of an existing claim, to territorial sovereignty in Antarctica shall be asserted while the present Treaty is in force.

The purpose of this provision is to freeze all territorial claims and to put on one side issues of sovereignty in the interests of collective co-operation. The treaty provides for regular meetings of the consultative parties which may result in binding recommendations and this method of proceeding has lead to a number of internationally agreed instruments.[110]

The Antarctic Treaty did not include any express provisions as to the exploitation of mineral resources. Thus in November 1988 the Convention on the Regulation of Antarctic Mineral Resource Activities[111] was opened for signature. In essence the Convention provided that exploitation would be regulated by a permit system with appropriate safeguards designed to ensure environmental protection. The Convention sought to regulate the processes of prospecting, exploration and development. The operation would involve four institutions, a Commission, a Scientific, Technical and Environmental Advisory Committee, Regulatory Committees and also provision for Special Meetings of Parties. The Convention was in line with the view of the United States and the United Kingdom that as exploration was inevitable it was better to produce agreed rules comprising proper environmental safeguards.

However opinion against any form of mining was strengthening. In 1988 a General Assembly Resolution expressed concern at the absence of a total ban[112] and in 1989 at the Paris meeting of the Consultative Parties under the 1959 Treaty France and Australia proposed that the mining ban should be total and the area designated as a 'wilderness reserve'. This initiative resulted in the production in October 1991 of the Protocol on

---

110 1972 Convention for the Conservation of Antarctic Seals – in force 1978, 16 parties including the United Kingdom. 1980 Convention for the Conservation of Antarctic Marine Living Resources – in force 1982, 27 parties including the United Kingdom. See M Howard, 'The Convention on the Conservation of Antarctic Marine Living Resources: a five year review' (1989) 38 ICLQ 104.

111 For the legislation in the United Kingdom, see Antarctic Minerals Act 1989. See generally, C Joyner, 'The Antarctic minerals negotiating process'(1987) 81 AJIL 888. For a general review, AD Watts, 'The Convention on the Regulation of Antarctic Mineral Resource Activities 1988 (1990) 39 ICLQ 169; ID Hendry, 'The Antarctic Minerals Act 1989' (1990) 39 ICLQ 183; S Blay, 'New trends in the protection of the Antarctic environment' (1992) 86 AJIL 37; C Redgwell, 'Environmental protection in Antarctica: the 1991 Protocol' (1994) 43 ICLQ 599. The 1988 Convention did not come into force because international opinion began to favour a complete ban on mineral exploitation.

112 GA Res 43/83.

Environmental Protection to the Antarctic Treaty which designated Antarctica as 'a natural reserve, devoted to peace and science' (Art 2). After setting out certain principles on environmental protection, Art 7 provides that 'activity relating to mineral resources other than scientific research, shall be prohibited'; however, this provision has to be read with Art 25 which provides that the prohibition on such activity shall remain in force unless there is a legal regime introduced under the special procedure of the Antarctic Treaty or by means of a review conference held 50 years after the operation of the Protocol. The effect of this is that all mining is prohibited for a period of 50 years with an option to continue thereafter in the absence of any new binding legal regime.[113] Under the terms of Art 23, the Protocol will enter into force 30 days after ratification by all states who were Antarctic Treaty Consultative States in October 1991. In these circumstances, it is unlikely that the 1988 Convention founded on licensed exploration will enter into force and will be replaced by the 1991 Protocol with its emphasis upon a total ban. The 1991 Protocol does not affect sovereignty rights held in abeyance under Art IV[114] of the Antarctic Treaty. There is every prospect of the 1991 Protocol coming into force.[115]

(c) The Falkland Islands[116]

One of the most difficult territorial disputes in the last two decades has been the dispute between the United Kingdom and Argentina as to the sovereignty over the Falkland Islands (or Las Malvinas as they are described in Argentina). An examination of the complex history of the territory indicates why some territorial disputes are difficult to analyse and even more difficult to resolve.

The Falkland Islands appear to have been first discovered by the navigator Esteban Gomez who sailed with Magellan in 1520. Early British accounts place the first sighting in 1592 by the mariner John Davis. It would seem to be agreed that the first landing was made in 1690 by Captain John Strong RN, who named the islands after Viscount Falkland then Treasurer of the Navy; however, the islands remained unoccupied and no acts of sovereignty can be detected for some time thereafter.

In 1764, the French established a settlement at Port Louis on East Falkland while, in 1765, the British landed at Saunders island, a mile off West Falkland, and in 1766 established a settlement on West Falkland at Port Egmont. It would seem that in 1767 the French ceded their settlement to Spain. (and it was renamed Port Soledad). The British settlement was expelled by Spain in 1770, but returned by agreement in 1771, and in 1774 appears to have been withdrawn because of financial difficulties. Although the terms of this incident are subject to dispute, the settlers left behind a Union flag and a plaque affirming possession in the name of George III (1760–1820). There is no evidence of the

---

113 1991 Protocol Art 25(5)(a).

114 The 1991 Protocol contains reference to a change in the territorial status of Antarctica since, under Art 2 of the Protocol, the parties 'designate Antarctica as a natural reserve, devoted to peace and science'.

115 For the United Kingdom, see Antarctic Act 1994. The 1991 Protocol requires ratification by all 26 consultative parties. The United Kingdom has ratified.

116 J Goebel, *The Struggle for the Falklands*, 1st edn, 1927, 2nd edn, 1982; T Franck (1983) 77 AJIL 109; M Reisman (1983) 93 YLJ 287; M Hastings and S Jenkins, *The Battle for the Falklands*, 1983; *Report on the Falkland Islands*, House of Commons Select Committee (1985) Cmnd 9447.

Spanish settlement being extended to West Falkland and none of the British settlement being extended to East Falkland.

The Spanish settlement and garrison were withdrawn in 1811, partly because of difficulties in South America and partly because of the Napoleonic War. In 1816, the United Provinces of the River Plate (Argentina) declared their independence from Spain and in 1820 sent a Colonel Jewett to take possession of the islands, this fact being advertised in the London *Times* in August 1821. Argentina appointed a governor who never visited the islands and then made a grant of grazing rights in 1823. It was not until 1825 that Argentina was recognised by Great Britain. In 1829 the appointment of one Louis Vernet as Military Commander of the Islands resulted in a protest from Great Britain.

In 1831 Vernet seized three American sailing ships for unlawful sealing. In retaliation, an American corvette sailed to the islands and destroyed the settlement on East Falkland. It was reported that the islands were 'free of all government'. In 1832 Argentina appointed another Governor but he was murdered by mutinous soldiers shortly after his arrival. At the end of 1832, the British appointed a Captain Onslow to 'exercise British rights of sovereignty'. In January 1833, Captain Onslow arrived at Port Soledad on East Falkland and persuaded the remaining Argentinean troops to leave. The extent of force used is a matter of dispute. Since that date the island remained in British possession. The Argentinean Government protested on a regular basis and in particular in 1833, 1834, 1841, 1842, and 1849 and in 1884, 1888 and 1908. An attempt by Britain to bring the matter before the international Court of justice in 1955 failed because neither Argentina nor Chile would accept the jurisdiction of the court.

At various times questions have been raised as to the nature of the British title to the Falklands. In the absence of an authoritative ruling by a judicial body, one can only examine the available evidence. First, it is argued that a distinction should be drawn between events pre-1833 and events post-1833. Secondly, it is arguable that the events of 1833 might serve to found a claim based on conquest and annexation. However, when Argentina raised the matter in the 1930s it was difficult for the United Kingdom to openly endorse such a basis even though, in 1833, conquest and annexation was an acceptable method for acquiring territory. The emphasis based upon prescription is open to question because of the acts of Argentina after 1816 and the nature of subsequent protests. Thirdly, it is open to argument that the prescription claim is validated by the fact that for a long period Argentina did not protest at all (1849–84; 1888–1908). Fourthly, it is now clear that the British case is placed both on uninterrupted occupation since 1833 and the principle of self-determination. Fifthly, it is noteworthy that the international community has accepted the United Kingdom's sovereignty over the Falkland Islands and has been prepared to conclude multilateral treaties on that basis and have accepted the United Kingdom as the relevant maritime power. Sixthly, following the invasion by Argentina in April 1982, the terms of Security Council Resolution 502 demanded an immediate withdrawal of Argentinean armed forces. In contrast, the Argentinean claim is based partly on the doctrine of *uti possidetis* as at 1816 and partly on the basis that no prescriptive title has arisen because of continued and sustained protest.

Having regard to the confused history, it is difficult to come to a settled conclusion. The balance of the evidence would seem to indicate that the United Kingdom case is based on: (i) conquest and annexation in or about 1833; (ii) peaceful sustained acts of occupation and sovereignty since that date; (iii) acquiescence by members of the international community since that date; and (iv) the expressed wishes of the people.

The invasion of the Falkland Islands in 1982 was clearly contrary to the United Nations Charter (1945) and was reversed by force. Diplomatic relations were resumed[117] in 1990, without prejudice to sovereignty claims, and co-operation between the United Kingdom and Argentina is effected through the South Atlantic Fisheries Commission and the South West Atlantic Hydrocarbons Commission.

---

117 M Evans, 'The restoration of diplomatic relations between Argentina and the United Kingdom' (1991) 40 ICLQ 473.

CHAPTER 8

JURISDICTION[1]

1 INTRODUCTION

As has been indicated elsewhere, the state is the basic political unit in international society. The essential characteristic of the state is that it enjoys sovereignty or supreme power internally and that externally it is equal to all and thus legally inferior to no other state.

In examining domestic or internal sovereignty one can identify three distinct aspects: (i) the power of the state or government to make laws within its own territory in respect of persons, property or events (sometimes called the prescriptive or legislative jurisdiction); (ii) the power of the state to ensure compliance with such law (sometimes called the executive or enforcement jurisdiction); and (iii) the power of the courts of a state to hear and determine actions and causes (sometimes described as judicial jurisdiction).

Jurisdiction therefore concerns the power of the state to act and is a consequence of the principle of state sovereignty. In broad terms jurisdictional questions can arise in respect of the activities of the legislative, executive and judicial branches of government. It is a matter of common knowledge that jurisdictional problems can arise everyday in the normal workings of the municipal courts. It may be a problem as to whether an action should be heard in court A or court B or it may be somewhat more complicated such as whether particular relief is available in a specific court or whether the court does possess jurisdiction but should decline to exercise it for some public policy reason. In most cases a court will be required to determine whether it possesses jurisdiction before considering the merits of a particular case.[2]

Taking a number of simple examples might serve as an illustration. A Frenchman on holiday in England might be prosecuted for exceeding the speed limit on an English road. Such a prosecution is justified because the Road Traffic legislation is designed to control conduct of all users of motor vehicles on English roads regardless of nationality. It would be argued by some private international lawyers that the Frenchman has agreed to submit himself to English laws on road safety by using his vehicle on English roads. To take second example: suppose an Italian citizen came to England and robbed a bank before returning to Italy. There is no doubt that the Theft Act 1968 enables such a prosecution to be brought because the robbery took place in England but the individual in question

---

1 See RY Jennings and AD Watts, *Oppenheim's International Law*, p 456; RY Jennings, 'Extra-territorial jurisdiction and the United States anti-trust laws' (1957) 33 BYIL 146; FA Mann, 'The doctrine of jurisdiction in international law' (1964) 111 HR 1; M Akehurst, 'Jurisdiction in international law' (1972–73) 46 BYIL 145; DW Bowett, 'Jurisdiction: changing problems of authority over activities and resources' (1982) 53 BYIL 1; FA Mann, 'The doctrine of international jurisdiction revisited after twenty years' (1984) 186 HR 9; AV Lowe, 'Problems of extra-territorial jurisdiction: economic sovereignty and the search for a solution' (1985) 34 ICLQ 724; L Henkin, 'International law: politics, values and functions, general course on public international law' (1989) 216 HR 9, p 277–330; PM Roth, 'Reasonable extra-territoriality' (1992) 41 ICLQ 245.

2 Of course it is not unknown for the ICJ or indeed a municipal court to decline to rule on jurisdiction unless it has become fully acquainted with the merits of the case.

cannot be arrested by an English policeman in Rome because that is territory beyond the United Kingdom and thus, in principle, outside the jurisdiction of the state. If the individual is to stand trial in England then the co-operation of the Italian authorities will be necessary. Thus, while a state may legislate in respect of persons, property and acts in its own territory enforcement jurisdiction often depends on the co-operation of others.

At first blush one can detect two basic principles. First, state A is in principle entitled to legislate in respect of persons, acts and events within its own territory. Secondly, state A will only be able to take enforcement action in the territory of state B with the consent of state B.

As a general rule, a state is concerned with acts that take place within its own territory or affect its territory or are committed by its citizens abroad. For this reason, a state may claim jurisdiction to try its citizens in respect of certain acts that they commit abroad. European countries which adopt nationality as a connecting factor in the conflict of laws tend to claim jurisdiction over their nationals for offences committed abroad. The English tradition is only to seek to try its nationals over very serious offences committed abroad such as murder, treason or bigamy.[3] It is perfectly sensible for England to take the view that it has no interest in trying an English citizen for driving too quickly along the streets of Turin.

Questions of jurisdiction often give rise to popular attention although sometimes the true question is not one of jurisdiction. For example, an Englishman might go abroad and be prosecuted for a particular act. Popular attention might focus on the mode of criminal proceedings or the sentence imposed. These are not truly questions of jurisdiction; the court of state X has jurisdiction to try the Englishman because the crime has been alleged to have been committed within that state. It may be that the rules of criminal procedure does not meet relevant international standard or are different to English criminal procedure but these are different questions. Even more difficult are problems related to legislative jurisdiction where individuals who been prosecuted abroad for activities that are perfectly lawful when committed in their own country.[4]

It is arguable that, in considering jurisdiction, three areas of law overlap. Public international law purports to set out certain general principles as to when a state may claim and exercise jurisdiction (for example, the United Kingdom or the United States). However, within that state there may a number of distinct legal systems (as in the United States or the United Kingdom) so it will be a matter for the appropriate rules of constitutional law to determine which court is to determine the matter. This is particularly a problem in a federal state but it may also arise in a unitary state where there is more than one legal system. Thirdly, if the case concerns a foreign element the court in question will have to apply its own rules of private international law to determine whether jurisdiction exists. Such jurisdiction may in some instances be founded upon fleeting presence but in other cases there may be a requirement that the defendant is domiciled within the jurisdiction.

---

3   See Offences Against the Person Act 1861, ss 9, 57; Official Secrets Act 1911; Official Secrets Act 1989.

4   For example, prosecutions of Europeans abroad for offences relating to alcohol.

Everything will depend on which municipal court hears the matter and much will turn on the nature of the case. In some situations a state is anxious to attract litigants for financial reasons and operates an open door policy; in other situations a state may be anxious that certain disputes should only be heard in state A if the parties have some nexus with that state. It is a fact of the modern age that a judicial system has to paid for out of public funds and no state is anxious to have its court lists full of disputes that concern matters of little direct concern to that state or its citizens. In any event it is sensible to bear in mind that any dispute about jurisdiction may involve rules of either constitutional law or private international law as well as of public international law.

Having regard to the wider international aspect it is well established that while state A is sovereign within its own territory it is under a corresponding duty to refrain form interfering in the domestic affairs of another state. This principle is set out in Art 2(7) of the United Nations Charter which reads:

> Nothing contained in the present Charter shall authorise the United Nations to intervene in matters which are essentially within the domestic jurisdiction of any State or shall require the Members to submit such matters to settlement under the present Charter ...

To take a simple example it would not be appropriate or sensible for the United Kingdom government to openly support a particular candidate in a United States Presidential Election as such a decision is a matter for the electorate within the United States. It is now clear that whether a matter is one of domestic jurisdiction or not is a matter for international law to determine.[5] It is also clear that the international community has since 1945 narrowed and restricted the circumstances in which a state is able to assert that a matter is within its domestic jurisdiction. This trend began in the late 1940s and early 1950s, when European colonial powers were unable to rely on Art 2(7) to limit the growing call for decolonisation. After 1961, the international community was unwilling to allow South Africa to rely on Art 2(7) to silence criticism of its apartheid policies. However, as the movement towards an international law on human rights began to gather pace after 1945 it was clear that an individual state could not be allowed to argue that serious abuses were a only a matter of domestic concern. Fourthly, in an interdependent world the conduct of state A may have profound effects on state B. To take an obvious example if state A allows an unlawful drugs business to operate the social consequences may be felt on the streets of its immediate neighbours. Fitfully, the important cultural change since 1945 is that a state should be able to defend its conduct on the merits in open debate; to seek to hide behind Art 2(7) is not unlike the obviously guilty man who seeks to challenge the jurisdiction of the court with a number of technical objections knowing that he has no defence on the merits.

In respect of legislative jurisdiction a number of points fall to be made. First, a state will, in principle, legislate in respect of matters arising within its own territory; indeed there is a principle of statutory construction that Parliament does not intend to legislate in

---

5   *Nationality Decrees in Tunis and Morocco* case (1923) PCIJ, Ser B, No 4; (1923) 2 ILR 349; *Anglo Norwegian Fisheries* case (1951) ICJ 116; *The Nottebohm* case (1955) ICJ 4, p 20; (1955) 22 ILR 349, p 357.

respect of the territory of another state unless the clearest wording has been used.[6] International law accepts that a state may in certain circumstances impose penalties on its citizens for acts committed abroad and it may rely on various concepts (for example, nationality, domicile, habitual residence, temporary residence) to impose taxation.

Secondly, difficult questions can arise as to whether the courts of state A will recognise and enforce the legislative acts of state B. In broad terms, this is a question to be resolved by the rules of private international law of state A. If the legislative act is restricted to property within state B it will probably be recognised even if the decree has confiscatory elements.[7] However, if a foreign legislative decree is extra-territorial it will probably not be enforced even if it is directed to the property of nationals held abroad;[8] the rationale being that legislative jurisdiction coincides with sovereignty and such sovereignty cannot be exercised over the territory of another sovereign. In England, it is well established that neither foreign penal laws[9] nor foreign revenue laws[10] will be enforced. Lord Denning MR, in giving judgment in the Court of Appeal in *AG of New Zealand v Ortiz*,[11] held that there was a third category of laws that would not be enforced which the learned judge described as 'other public laws' and within this might come foreign legislation of extra-territorial effect together with legislation that offends English rules as to public policy. It should be borne in mind that there is a distinction between enforcement and recognition so that in certain circumstances English law may be prepared to allow a foreign state to obtain evidence in matters of taxation.[12]

It is equally clear that there are some foreign laws that would not be enforced in England because they violate principles of English public policy. To take a simple example; suppose state X were to confiscate without compensation all the property of persons of a particular ethnic grouping. It would be argued that such conduct was a violation of the principles of public international law in respect of treatment of aliens. However, such a law might not be enforced in England because it offended a head of English public policy which is automatically part of English private international law.[13]

In respect of executive jurisdiction the principle is that executive and law enforcement agencies only operate within their own territory and if they venture abroad they are

---

6   Or, to put the proposition another way, there is presumption that Parliament did not intend to commit a breach of international law; see *Corocraft Ltd v Pan American Airways Inc* [1969] 1 QB 616; *James Buchanan & Co Ltd v Babco Forwarding and Shipping (UK) Ltd* [1978] AC 141; *Fothergill v Monarch Airlines Ltd* [1981] AC 251.

7   *Luther v Sagor* [1921] 3 KB 532; *Princess Olga Paley v Weisz* [1929] 1 KB 718.

8   *Re Russian Bank for Foreign Trade* [1933] Ch 745.

9   *Huntington v Attrill* (1893) AC 150; *Banco de Vizcaya v Don Alfonso de Borbon y Austria* [1935] 1 KB 140; *Frankfurter v WL Exner Ltd* [1947] Ch 629.

10 *Government of India v Taylor* [1955] AC 491.

11 *Attorney General of New Zealand v Ortiz* [1984] AC 1, p 20.

12 *Re State of Norway's Application (Nos 1 and 2)* [1990] 1 AC 723.

13 *Dynamit AG v Rio Tinto Co Ltd* [1918] AC 260 (*per* Lord Parker); *Oppenheimer v Cattermole* [1976] AC 249; *Williams and Humbert v W and H Trade Marks (Jersey) Ltd* [1986] AC 368; FA Mann (1986) 102 LQR 191; (1987) 103 LQR 26; (1988) 104 LQR 346. On the subject of the recognition and enforcement of foreign law, see Peter North and James Fawcett, *Cheshire and North: Private International Law*, 13th edn, 1999, London: Butterworths, Chapter 8; J O'Brien, *Smith's Conflict of Laws*, 2nd edn, 1999, Chapter 9.

obliged to seek permission of that other sovereign state.[14] It follows that the security forces of state A should not act in state B without the permission of state B.[15] The best known example arose in 1960 when individuals who were probably Israeli agents seized the wanted war criminal Adolf Eichmann and brought him to Israel to stand trial. The Security Council recognised in June 1960 in Security Council Resolution 138 that such conduct had violated the territorial sovereignty of Argentina although within a matter of months the two states reached an agreement to regard the matter as closed. A variant on the problem is where the United Nations itself indicates its clear disapproval of the conduct of the executive arm of government within its own territory.[16]

The third aspect of the subject comprises judicial jurisdiction and arises when an individual X appears before a municipal court and argues that particular court has no jurisdiction to determine the matter. It is sometimes said that where objection is taken to the jurisdiction of the court it may be based on one of three grounds: (i) *ratione materiae* – that objection is taken by reason of the nature of the matter; (ii) *ratione temporis* – that objection is taken as to time: that the court has no jurisdiction in respect of an act at a particular time; and (iii) *ratione personae* – that the court has no jurisdiction by reason of the status of the person. In respect of an objection *ratione materiae* it is clear that there is some overlap with the rules of private international law, in particular that there may be certain matters that are not justiciable before a municipal court.[17] A distinction also has to be drawn between those cases where it is accepted that the court has jurisdiction,[18] but it is argued that it should decline jurisdiction in favour of some more appropriate jurisdiction[19] and those cases where it is argued that the court does not possess jurisdiction at all. Before turning to such matters, it is necessary to say a little about the distinction between criminal and civil proceedings.

2 CRIMINAL AND CIVIL PROCEEDINGS

The legal system of most states preserves at least in part a distinction between criminal proceedings and civil proceedings. In England, such proceedings are in general conducted in different courts although members of the judiciary may act in both forms. In some legal systems, it is possible to include a claim for civil compensation in the context

---

14 Thus the Security Guards of a foreign Head of State (eg, the President of the United States) seek permission to carry firearms on the territory of another state.An example of conducting operations by agreement is afforded by the Anglo French arrangements for conducting security checks on the Channel Tunnel.

15 An obvious example in the modern world being when state B asks another state to send specialist counter terrorist advisers to help its own forces. For obvious reasons, the details of such requests are not normally the subject of public discussion.

16 In this context, one can include Security Council Resolutions 1168 and 1199 relating to Kosovo.

17 Sometimes described as the 'act of state doctrine' deriving from *Duke of Brunswick v King of Hanover* (1848) 2 HLC 1; *Buck v Attorney General* [1965] Ch 745; *Buttes Oil v Hammer* [1982] AC 888, relied upon by the minority in *R v Bow Street Magistrate ex p Pinochet Ugarte (No 1)* [1998] 3 WLR 1456 (Lords Lloyd and Slynn).

18 For relevant principles in England see *Spiliada Maritime Corporation v Cansulex Ltd* [1987] AC 460.

19 *Connelly v RTZ Corporation plc* [1998] AC 854.

of criminal proceedings.[20] However, it is true that in the final analysis the enforcement of civil remedies depends on the willingness to employ criminal sanctions, for example, the possibility of committal to prison for defiance of a civil injunction. With these qualifications noted, it is generally the case that most systems of municipal law draw a distinction between civil proceedings where the object is generally compensation and criminal proceedings where public duties and punishment may be in issue.

It is a fact of modern life that most states guard jealously their power to bring criminal proceedings; serious criminal acts attract popular attention and electorates demand that a government brings alleged wrongdoers before its courts. This is particularly the case when a serious criminal act appears to be a direct challenge to the legitimacy of a government.

Civil claims do not raise similar passions beyond the interests of the parties immediately involved. Because of the particular nature of criminal proceedings it is not surprising that to avoid unedifying squabbles between states public international law has developed a number of principles that indicate when a state may claim jurisdiction in criminal matters.

The position as regards civil proceedings is more complex. First, it is generally agreed that civil proceedings involving a foreign element are regulated by private international law and everyday attempts are made by municipal courts not to trespass on the jurisdiction of courts in other countries. In broad terms, the world divides into those countries that have a legal system derived from Roman Law (that is, the so called 'civil law countries') and those such as the United Kingdom or the United States who belong to the common law family. Each has a different approach to jurisdiction. The common law countries tended to regard jurisdiction as a matter of procedure; indeed it has been argued English law lacked any theory of jurisdiction. In contrast civil law countries tended to found jurisdiction on a particular concept that established a nexus for example, domicile, habitual residence or possession of assets.

In England civil proceedings were started by the service of a writ and even if X were only on a fleeting visit jurisdiction would be assumed if it could be shown that he had been properly served with the writ; this would apply even in the case of the briefest visit[21] so that jurisdiction could be based on fleeting presence. So by serving a writ on X while he was in England for a brief visit, jurisdiction could be established and X would then have to go to court and seek to set the writ aside on grounds of *forum non conveniens*. This was not easy to do as the English courts tended towards an 'open door' policy. In addition the English courts would allow a writ to be served on an individual abroad if certain conditions were met.[22]

In contrast in civil law countries jurisdiction was established if the plaintiff could establish that the defendant had some nexus with the jurisdiction. The form of this nexus

---

20 *Raulin v Fischer* [1911] 2 KB 92 (Hamilton J) (where the judge was prepared to sever the civil and criminal aspects of the judgment for the purpose of enforcement proceedings in England).

21 *Colt Industries Inc v Sarlie* [1966] 1 WLR 440 (Frenchman staying at London hotel for one night); *Maharanee of Baroda v Daniel Wildenstein* [1972] 2 QB 283 (defendant in England to attend Royal Ascot).

22 Under the terms of RSC Ord 11 deriving from the Common Law Procedure Act 1852.

might differ according to the case so that the courts of X[23] might have jurisdiction: (i) if the contract was made in X; (ii) the tort arose in X; (iii) the defendant was domiciled or habitually resident in X; or (iv) the defendant has property situate in X. Before the advent of civil aviation, forum shopping and contingency fee systems the common law tradition and the civil law approach could happily co-exist.

One of the objects of the Treaty of Rome (1957)[24] was to enable a judgment obtained in state A to be enforced before the courts of state B. However, it was realised shortly after 1957 that no state would agree to such an arrangement unless they could be satisfied that the original court had properly assumed jurisdiction. Thus, it was necessary to provide for uniform bases of civil jurisdiction in order to achieve the greater objective of the free circulation of judgments. This was achieved in the Brussels Convention on Jurisdiction and Judgments in Civil and Commercial Matters (1968) which became part of English law on 1 January 1987 when the relevant parts of the Civil Jurisdiction and Judgments Act 1982 were brought into effect. At the same time, to ensure conformity with European obligations a scheme was introduced to allocate jurisdiction within the United Kingdom.[25] At a later date, a scheme was given effect to in the Lugano Convention (1988) by which jurisdiction in the remaining EFTA countries was brought within the terms of the Brussels Convention.[26]

The cumulative effect of these developments is that for many states in Western Europe detailed rules on civil jurisdiction are set out in a number of international conventions that have been given effect to in domestic law. To a considerable extent, the rules on the conflict of laws in respect of civil jurisdiction have been harmonised. However, the question arises as to how this affects public international law. First, it is arguable that the rules a country stipulates as part of its private international law should conform to the broad principles of public international law. Secondly, in the present instance the detailed international conventions reflect an agreed international understanding as to the principles on which civil jurisdiction may be exercised. Thirdly, it is probably true that while rules on civil jurisdiction operate within the sphere of the conflict of laws the scope and application of such rules is determined by the basic principles of public international law. To take a simple example: one of the general principles of the Brussels Convention (1968) is that an individual should, subject to some alternative provisions, be sued in the courts of the state in which he is domiciled.[27] Given the meaning of 'domicile' in the European context, this is not so dissimilar from the territorial principle as propounded in public international law.

In these circumstances, the sensible conclusion must be that the relevant principles of public international law concerning jurisdiction directly influence the content of municipal criminal jurisdiction but in civil matters they operate by determining the scope and application of the relevant rules of private international law. With these qualifications

---

23 X may be an individual state but it may also be a distinct law district such as Scotland, Northern Ireland and England and Wales.
24 Article 220.
25 Civil Jurisdiction and Judgments Act 1982, s 16, Sched 4; for the operation of the scheme, see *Kleinwort Benson Ltd v Glasgow City Council* [1999] 1 AC 153; [1997] 3 WLR 923.
26 Given effect to in England by the Civil Jurisdiction and Judgments Act 1991.
27 Brussels Convention (1968), Art 2.

noted it is important to turn to the relevant principles upon which public international law acknowledges that a state may exercise jurisdiction.

3 PRINCIPLES OF JURISDICTION

As noted above a number of principles may be invoked to justify assuming jurisdiction; such principles are most relevant to judicial jurisdiction but they may also be material when problems of prescriptive and enforcement jurisdiction arise.

(a) Territorial jurisdiction

One of the oldest doctrines of international law is that a state is sovereign within its own territory so that in principle a state will be able to prosecute in respect of acts and omissions arising within its own territory. This is certainly practical in that a state will have a vested interest in the maintenance of law and order within its own territory; it is consistent with both wider international law and traditional political theory in stressing that the first duty of any government is to maintain law and order within its own territory.

Secondly, the oral witnesses and the physical evidence are likely to be within the territory; indeed, so may be the alleged wrongdoer. Thus, in the much discussed *Lockerbie* case (1988) one practical reason for asserting the jurisdiction of Scotland was that the physical evidence was located within that jurisdiction. Thus, a French citizen who commits a murder in London is likely to be prosecuted and tried before an English court; if he should return to France then it would be open to the English prosecuting authorities to seek his extradition. The broad rationale was clearly put by Lord Macmillan in *The Cristina*[28] where he observed:

> It is an essential attribute of the sovereignty of this realm, as of all sovereign independent States, that it should possess jurisdiction over all persons and things within its territorial limits and in all causes civil and criminal arising within these limits.

The English common law placed considerable emphasis on presence within the jurisdiction using it as the basis to establish civil jurisdiction however fleeting the presence. Certainly when an act begins and is completed within a single territory then the territorial principle is grounded in tradition and practicality. The territorial principle is the oldest principle of jurisdiction. Thus, in 1891 Lord Halsbury LC was able to declare:

> All crime is local. The jurisdiction over the crime belongs to the country where the crime is committed, and, except over her own subjects, Her Majesty and the Imperial Legislature have no power whatsoever.[29]

For the purpose of determining territory one includes: (i) the maritime belt of territorial waters; (ii) ships bearing the flag of the state; and (iii) internal ports. These matters will be considered in Chapter 13 on the law of the sea.

---

28 *Compania Naviera Vascongado v SS Cristina* [1938] AC 485, pp 496–97.
29 *Macleod v Attorney General for New South Wales* [1891] AC 455.

The territorial principle together with relevant extensions for the Law of the Sea[30] was sufficient in the 19th century but problems began to arise in the new era of civil aviation, rapid communications and international trade. In such circumstances, an agreement can be made in state A, preparatory acts undertaken in state B and the crime completed in state C. Sometimes the states where the preparatory acts took place were reluctant to uphold a conviction if the preparatory acts were directed towards an object that might not be criminal in that state. Thus in *Board of Trade v Owen*,[31] the House of Lords ruled that there could not be a prosecution for conspiracy to commit a crime abroad unless the contemplated act was one for which an indictment would lie in England. The difficulty was whether the accused should be tried by the courts of the state in which he did the physical acts (that is, the initiatory theory) or by the courts of the state in which consequences of the accused's physical acts took effect (that is, the terminatory theory of jurisdiction). However, if all the requisite acts have been completed in state A then jurisdiction will arise. Thus, in *Treacy v DPP*[32] the House of Lords upheld a conviction for blackmail under s 21 of the Theft Act 1968 where letter and its unwarranted demand with menaces was directed to a person living in Germany. Indeed, as Lord Diplock argued in *Treacy* there was much to be said for regarding such problems as ones turning not on jurisdiction but on the characteristics and components of each individual offence.

To avoid cases where the defendant would argue that the court lacked jurisdiction the territorial principle was modified by some states into: (i) the subjective territorial principle; and (ii) the objective territorial principle. According to the subjective territorial principle, a state would have jurisdiction to prosecute a crime initiated in its own territory but completed abroad. In contrast under the objective territorial principle state A would have jurisdiction to try criminal offences where the acts were initiated in the territory of another state but had either been completed in state A or produced harmful consequences in state A. If one takes the conventional example of a man standing on the territory of state A but close to the border with state B who fires a gun and kills a man in state B then in such an instance it is arguable that state A could claim jurisdiction on the subjective territorial principle and state B could claim jurisdiction by invoking the objective territorial principle.

The leading case in which the territorial principle has been discussed is that of *The Lotus*.[33] The case itself is sometimes said to be an authority that favours the objective territorial principle. However, it is not the clearest case, the judgment is not unanimous and some of the reasoning if not subject to question has been rendered redundant by subsequent events. In brief, the facts were as follows.

---

30 Territory will include the territorial sea and, in some cases, the contiguous zone; it will also extend to the high seas where the the state is the Flag state of the vessel.

31 *Board of Trade v Owen* [1957] AC 602 (see the submissions of Neil Lawson QC and Sebag Shaw (as they then were), pp 610–11).

32 *Treacy v DPP* [1971] AC 537 (Lord Diplock thought such cases should turn on the constituent elements of the crime rather than on jurisdiction while Lord Reid observed, 'The present state of the law is, in my view, far from satisfactory ... If a person in this country does all he can to ensure that a crime is committed abroad so that he can reap the benefit here,I can see nothing contrary to legal principle in our law holding him guilty of a crime').

33 *The Lotus* [1927] PCIJ, Ser A, No 10.

A French steamer, *The Lotus,* was involved in a collision on the High Seas with a Turkish collier the Boz-Kourt. The latter vessel sank; eight Turkish nationals died. When the French steamer proceeded to Constantinople the captain and the officer of the watch were arrested and put on trial by the Turkish courts for manslaughter. The Turkish courts rejected a submission of no jurisdiction; the officer of the watch was convicted and sentenced to 80 days imprisonment. At a later date, France and Turkey agreed to submit the question of jurisdiction to the Court at the Hague.

An interesting preliminary question arose as to whether it was incumbent upon France to demonstrate that Turkey did not possess jurisdiction or was the burden upon Turkey to show that it did. To put the matter another way does a state enjoy jurisdiction unless and until a rule of international law indicates otherwise or should the starting point be that the state does not enjoy jurisdiction unless it can be shown that such jurisdiction is consistent with accepted principles of international law. Although a wide variety of matters were canvassed in argument the majority of the court: (i) rejected the contention of France that there was a rule of customary international law that the state of the flag had exclusive jurisdiction over the conduct of individuals on a vessel on the High Seas; (ii) accepted the argument by Turkey that the Turkish vessel could be regarded as an extension of Turkish territory and thus jurisdiction could be assumed under the objective territorial principle; (iii) asserted that a state was entitled to exercise jurisdiction within its own territory unless and until it could be shown to be prohibited under international law; (iv) that such a principle was consistent with the broad understanding that international law was founded on the agreement of sovereign independent states; (v) while only a few states in the position of Turkey had chosen to prosecute the absence of protest in such cases indicated that there was no rule of customary international law prohibiting such conduct; (vi) while many states had refrained from prosecuting there was no evidence that they had done so out of a sense of legal obligation.[34]

The judgment was criticised at the time[35] and subsequently as being too positivist in tone placing the state at the centre of international law and assuming that state conduct is valid unless manifestly and expressly prohibited. Today most writers would assert that state X only has jurisdiction if it can be shown to be consistent with international law. Secondly, the value of the case is diminished by the number and distinction of the dissenting judgments. Thirdly, the French submission as to jurisdiction is now accepted as part of international law. Article 11(1) of the Geneva Convention on the High Seas (1958) reads:

> In the event of a collision or of any other incident of navigation concerning a ship on the high seas, involving the penal or disciplinary responsibility of the master or of any other person in the service of the ship, no penal or disciplinary proceedings may be instituted against such persons except before the judicial or administrative authorities either of the flag State or of the State of which of which such person is a national.

---

34 The case was decided by the casting vote of the President the judges being equally divided. For Huber (President) de Butamante, Oda, Anzilottii, Pessoa and *ad hoc* Judge Feizi-Daim. Dissenting, Lord Finlay, Nyholm, Moore, Loder, Weiss, Altimira.

35 JL Brierly (1928) 44 LQR 154.

This provision is reproduced in Art 97(1) of the Law of the Sea Convention (1982); thus, this aspect of the *Lotus* judgment has been superseded by events.[36] It is clear that the judgment of the majority supports the objective territorial principle and probably also the passive personality principle however on the latter aspect Judge Moore dissented arguing that it was inconsistent with international law.

While jurisdiction is in principle territorial, it is open to individual states to reach agreement for the sharing of territorial jurisdiction. An example is afforded by the Anglo French co-operation in respect of the Channel Tunnel (that is, the Fixed Link). The detailed Protocol concerning frontier controls and policing, co-operation in criminal justice, public safety and mutual assistance relating to the Channel Fixed Link contains specific provisions relating to priority as to jurisdiction and the rules to be applied within the Fixed Link where it cannot be determined where the offence was committed or where it was initiated in one state and completed in another.[37] It is not unusual for rules as to territorial jurisdiction to be modified by international treaty.[38] In the Second World War the United Kingdom had the problem of several governments in exile and a number of visiting forces. The Allied Forces Act 1940 extended the Visiting Forces (British Commonwealth) Act 1933 to provide that visiting forces should be governed by their own military law,[39] while the United States of America (Visiting Forces) Act 1942 applied the same principle to United States servicemen resident in the United Kingdom.

A matter that has become increasingly important in recent years is whether a meaningful distinction can be drawn between the objective territorial principle (where the consequences taking place in the second jurisdiction are a constituent part of the offence) and the so called 'effects doctrine' where this is not the case. The 'effects doctrine' has been relied upon in anti-trust and restrictive practice enforcement in both the United States and in Europe; it is considered below.

Much of the litigation coming before English courts[40] has tended to focus on what may be described as cross-border crimes. Although it is not possible to reconcile harmoniously all the case law it would seem that if the consequences of the initial act form part of the constituent elements of the offence then jurisdiction will be claimed under the objective territorial principle; thus jurisdiction will be claimed if some of the essential elements of the crime take place in England or where some elements of the

---

36 See, also, Art 6 of the High Seas Convention (1958) and Art 92 of the Law of the Sea Convention (1982).

37 For the 1986 Treaty between France and the United Kingdom signed on 12 February 1986 and entering into force on 29 July 1987, see Cmnd 9745. For an earlier review of the legal problem arising, see G Marston (1974–75) 47 BYIL 290. For the relevant domestic legislation, see Channel Tunnel Act 1987.

38 Examples would be the 1903 and 1977 Treaties between Panama and the United States concerning the canal; the 1951 NATO Status of Forces Agreement concerning jurisdiction of NATO forces based in other NATO states. More recently the Israel-Jordan Treaty of Peace 1994 contains provisions for shared jurisdiction.

39 See *Re Amand (No 1)* [1941] 2 KB 239; *Re Amand (No 2)* [1942] 1 KB 445; see FA Mann (1943) 59 LQR 57; Oppenheimer (1942) 36 AJIL 589.

40 The United Kingdom has, from the 19th century, been a strong supporter of the territorial system: (a) because in criminal law matters it is for the people of the relevant territory to determine the rules they wish live under; (b) it is practical in that English criminal procedure places considerable reliance on the testing of oral testimony by cross-examination. That is best achieved in the relevant territory.

offence can be deemed to have taken place in England. The emphasis of the English court was to lay less stress on international law and more on an analysis of the constituent elements of the crime.[41] In so far as a consistent approach could be divined in the case law, the attitude of the English courts had been: (i) to adhere to the territorial principle; (ii) to lay stress upon the specific elements of each crime under municipal law; (iii) to favour the terminatory theory rather than the initiatory theory; (iv) to draw a distinction between 'conduct crimes' and 'result crimes'. In respect of the terminatory theory, the approach was to discover where the last constituent element of the offence took place and to accept jurisdiction if this took place within territorial limits. The distinction between 'conduct crimes' and 'result crimes' was founded on an analysis of the constituent elements of the offence. A conduct crime was said to be one founded on actual behaviour while a result crime required the actual conduct of the offender to be followed by a particular result. Thus, in *Treacy*[42] blackmail was categorised as a conduct crime and as the acts took place in England jurisdiction was asserted. In respect of a result crime jurisdiction would arise in England 'if any part of the proscribed result takes place in England'.[43] However, during the 1970s there was a movement away from such technical classification to simply assuming jurisdiction if a substantial measure of the activities took place in England.

In reviewing the trend of English case law La Forest J in the Supreme Court of Canada[44] observed:

> ... the English courts have decisively begun to move away from definitional obsessions and technical formulations aimed at finding a single situs of a crime by locating where the gist of the crime occurred or where it was completed. Rather, they now appear to seek by an examination of relevant policies to apply the English criminal law where a substantial measure of the activities constituting a crime take place in England, and restrict its application in such circumstances solely in cases where it can seriously be argued on a reasonable view that these activities should, on the basis of international comity, be dealt with by another country.

This broad summary of the more flexible attitude of the English courts was adopted with approval by Lord Griffiths when delivering the judgment of the Privy Council in *Somchai Liangsiriprasert v The United States*.[45]

However, while there is a desire to be flexible where some of the relevant criminal acts take place in England the courts are slow indeed to assume that legislation is other than territorial; there is a well recognised assumption that other countries should be left to order their own affairs within their own boundaries and an English judge would require

---

41 On municipal case law, see *R v Barnard* (1858) 1 F & F 240; *R v Warburton* (1870) 1 CCR 274; *R v Ellis* [1899] 1 QB 230; *R v Mackenzie* (1910) 6 Cr App Rep 64; *Board of Trade v Owen* [1957] AC 602; *Treacy v DPP* [1971] AC 757; *DPP v Doot* [1973] AC 807; *R v El-Hakkaoui* [1975] 1 WLR 396; *DPP v Markus* [1976] AC 35; *DPP v Stonehouse* [1978] AC 55; *R v Berry* [1985] 1 AC 246.

42 *Treacy v DPP* [1971] AC 757.

43 *Secretary of State for Trade v Markus* [1976] AC 35, p 61, *per* Lord Diplock. Thus, it was sometimes said that murder was a result crime requiring both physical acts by the wrongdoer and resulting death.

44 *Libman v The Queen* (1985) 21 CCC (3d) 206.

45 [1991] 1 AC 225 (a case involving a request by the United States for extradition from Hong Kong which was the subject of appeal to the Privy Council).

clear and express words to displace this basic presumption.[46] There is also the question of perspective: it is one thing for a judge to assume that the legislature does not intend to legislate for other countries it is quite another to find that an English court does not have jurisdiction when the defendant has already been convicted on the merits and where some of the acts have taken place in England.[47]

It has to be conceded that the problem of transnational and international crime was less than satisfactory under English law. The statutory presumption against extra-territorial jurisdiction and the common law emphasis on the terminatory theory lead to be the view that there might be a 'gap' in jurisdiction in cases where an act of deception was made in England but the obtaining occurred abroad.[48] Thus, the Law Commission were asked to review the area and produced a report in 1989.[49] This was followed by legislation in the Criminal Justice Act 1993. The legislation provided that, in respect of a large number of offences listed in s 1, jurisdiction would be based not on the terminatory or 'last act' theory[50] but instead 'if any of the events which are relevant events in relation to the offence occurred in England and Wales'.[51] Further, the legislation makes it an offence under English law, subject to certain conditions, to conspire or attempt in England to commit certain offences abroad.

A further concern in recent years has been the need to curb the activities of the so called 'child sex tourism industry'. In essence individuals in developed countries would travel to poor and developing parts of the world to engage in abusive sexual acts with young children.[52] Had such acts been committed in their own country they would have attracted severe criminal penalties. In principle the United Nations Convention on the Rights of the Child (1989) commits states to act to restrain such conduct.[53] Sometimes poorer states have found it difficult to police such practices so some developed states have passed extra-territorial legislation[54] to punish such conduct. In the United Kingdom there has been a strong preference for the territorial basis of criminal jurisdiction so that in the Sexual Offences (Conspiracy and Incitement) Act 1996,[55] it was made a criminal

---

46 *Air India v Wiggins* [1980] 1 WLR 815; *Holmes v Bangladesh Biman Corporation* [1989] AC 1112.
47 This will often be the case in England where the evidence will have been heard at first instance and the question of jurisdiction will arise in the appellate courts in the form of an appeal against conviction.
48 *R v Harden* [1963] 1 QB 8.
49 Law Commission, *Jurisdiction over Offences of Fraud and Dishonesty with a Foreign Element*, No 180, 1989.
50 *R v Sansom* [1991] 2 QB 130.
51 Criminal Justice Act 1993, s 2(3).
52 Young children in the Phillipines, Sri Lanka and Thailand being particularly at risk.
53 In particular, Art 32, United Nations Convention on the Rights of the Child (1996).
54 Legislation having been enacted in the United States, Australia and New Zealand.
55 The bill being introduced by a Private Member, Mr John Marshall MP; the resulting debate persuaded the Home Secretary to announce on 1 February 1996 that he would establish an interdepartmental review to consider the question of extra-territorial criminal legislation. The results of the Review were reported to Parliament on 23 July 1996. In brief, the Review came down against any general extension in respect of the conduct of British citizens abroad, save where stringent criteria might be met, namely: (i) the offence is serious; (ii) witnesses and evidence is available in the United Kingdom; (iii) there is international agreement that such conduct is reprehensible; (iv) action is needed because of the vulnerability of the victim; (v) there is a danger that no action will be taken to deal with the offence.

offence to conspire in England and Wales to commit certain sexual acts against children abroad;[56] the legislation also made incitement of such acts a criminal offence.[57]

(b) Nationality

It is normally a matter for each state to determine its rules of citizenship.[58] International law has traditionally accepted that a state may exercise jurisdiction over its nationals for crimes committed abroad (that is, the active nationality principle). This approach is followed in the United Kingdom and the United States although such prosecutions are normally for breaches of domestic law not the law of another state. Traditionally the United Kingdom will not enforce the penal laws of another state.[59] A wide jurisdiction founded upon nationality is more usual in civil law countries[60] where nationality has a greater role in determining the personal law than in common law countries where the traditional personal nexus is that of domicile. The United Kingdom only seeks to prosecute its nationals for serious offences committed abroad, such as murder, manslaughter, bigamy or treason.[61]

In general international law does not regulate the granting of nationality by a state and the matter is regarded as one within the domestic jurisdiction of the individual state. Thus, in the *Nationality Decrees in Tunis and Morocco* case the Permanent Court of International Justice observed:[62]

> ... whether a certain matter is or is not solely within the jurisdiction of a state is an essentially relative question, it depends on the development of international relations. Thus, in the present state of international law, questions of nationality are, in the opinion of this court, in principle within the reserved domain.

Similar sentiments were expressed in 1930 in Art 1 of the Hague Convention on the Conflict of Nationality Laws where it is stated that:

> ... it is for each state to determine under its own laws who are its nationals. This law shall be recognised by other states in so far as it is consistent with international conventions, international custom and the principles of law generally recognised with regard to nationality.

---

56   Sexual Offences (Conspiracy and Incitement) Act 1996, s 1.

57   *Ibid*, s 2.

58   It is sometimes important to distinguish between citizenship (a concept of municipal law) and nationality (a concept of international law). International law is concerned with nationality, the nexus between the person and the state.

59   *Huntingdon v Attrill* [1893] AC 150; *Attorney General of New Zealand v Ortiz* [1984] AC 1.

60   It is noteworthy that while some European countries take a wide extra-territorial jurisdiction in respect of their own nationals such countries often have constitutional provisions to prevent the extradition of their own nationals. In contrast, the United Kingdom is prepared to extradite its own nationals and has extradition arrangements with over 100 states. (See United Kingdom Interdepartmental Review of extra-territorial jurisdiction presented to House of Commons, 23 July 1996.)

61   For the United Kingdom, see Offences Against the Person Act 1861, s 9 (murder and manslaughter); s 57 (bigamy); Official Secrets Act 1911, s 10; Official Secrets Act 1989, s 15; War Crimes Act 1991; Antarctica Act 1994, s 21; *R v Casement* [1916] 1 KB 98 (treason).

62   (1923) PCIJ, Ser B, No 4; (1923) 2 ILR 349.

In general, nationality will depend on some form of link with the state. This may be on the basis of descent from parents who are nationals (*jus sanguinis*) or the fact of having been born within the territory.[63] Municipal legislation may draw a distinction between legitimate and illegitimate births. In some municipal systems it is provided that the illegitimate child shall take the nationality of the mother.

In the modern world the law on nationality is linked to questions of immigration control although in some states the immigration legislation has preceded the detailed nationality legislation. Questions of nationality may be important in matters of extradition because some states provide that their own nationals shall not be extradited. Thirdly, in civil countries the concept of nationality will govern questions of the validity of marriage or of testamentary dispositions. However, in the United Kingdom questions pertaining to the personal law will tend to be governed by the concept of domicile which is favoured in common law countries and reflects the different legal systems that often comprise the state. Fourthly, most states provide that aliens may acquire nationality through naturalisation by means of a period of lawful residence. Fifthly, in the United Kingdom matters of immigration control and nationality are the subject of detailed provisions in municipal law and where these are clear and unambiguous they will be given effect to.[64]

One of the abiding concerns of international law has been that of statelessness, hence Art 24.3 of the International Covenant on Civil and Political Rights (1966) provides that each child should have the right to acquire a nationality and this is confirmed by Art 7.1 of the United Nations Convention on the Rights of the Child (1989) which reads: 'The child shall be registered immediately after birth and shall have the right from birth to a name, the right to acquire a nationality and, as far as possible, the right to know and be cared for by his or her parents.'

A common source of difficulty concerning nationality arises in respect of marriage. Difficulties could arise where a state provides that a woman would lose her nationality when marrying a foreigner. Article 15.2 of the Universal Declaration of Human Rights (1948) provided that nobody should be arbitrarily deprived of their nationality. In 1957 the General Assembly adopted the Convention on the Nationality of Married Women. Article 1 of the Convention provides that contracting parties accept that a woman would not lose her nationality upon marriage to an alien. This is confirmed by Art 9 of the Convention on the Elimination of All Forms of Discrimination against Women (1979) which requires state parties to grant equal rights with men to acquire change or retain their nationality, and to ensure in particular that neither marriage to an alien nor change of nationality by the husband during marriage shall automatically change the nationality of the wife, render her stateless or force upon her the nationality of the husband.

---

63 Birth within the United Kingdom is not enough; broadly, the parents must be married and one a British citizen; see British Nationality Act 1981, s 50. The legislation provides for the acquisition of citizenship by adoption: s 1(5).

64 Nationality legislation being contained in the British Nationality Act 1981 and in a small number of matters the British Nationality At 1948. The system of immigration control can be traced through the Aliens Act 1905; Aliens Restriction Act 1914; British Nationality and Status of Aliens Act 1914; Commonwealth Immigrants Act 1962; Commonwealth Immigrants Act 1968; Immigration Act 1971. For the proposition that where municipal law is clear then it will prevail, see *R v Secretary of State for the Home Department ex p Thakrar* [1974] QB 684; (1974) 59 ILR 450.

In respect of the obtaining of nationality, the effect of marriage will differ from state to state. Some states will provide for the automatic acquisition of the husband's nationality upon marriage; others provide for freedom from immigration control and less onerous terms for naturalisation;[65] some provide that marriage has no effect on nationality.

Problems of nationality may arise in respect of ships and aircraft. Article 91 of the Law of the Sea Convention (1982) provides that a ship will have the nationality of the flag which it is entitled to fly. It will be a matter for each individual state to stipulate a regime for registration, the granting of nationality and the right to fly its flag. Although there has been a requirement of a genuine link since Art 5 of the 1958 Convention on the High Seas this appears to have had little influence on state practice. In respect of aircraft, Art 17 of the Chicago Convention on International Civil Aviation (1944) provides that an aircraft will have the nationality of the state in which it is registered however the conditions for registration are a matter for municipal law.

Although the United Kingdom traditionally only makes limited use of the nationality principle an interesting development arose with the enactment of the War Crimes Act 1991. Section 1 of the legislation enabled trials to take place in the United Kingdom in respect of conduct committed between September 1939 and June 1945 by persons who were not then United Kingdom nationals but had become so before or after March 1990. The wisdom of this legislation, having regard to the evidentiary difficulties, was the subject of some comment.[66]

(c) The protective principle (sometimes known as competence réele)

It has been accepted for over 100 years that a state may prosecute an alien for acts committed abroad that are directed at the existence and social fabric of a society. The difficulty arises not as to the existence of the principle but as to its scope. Is it restricted to acts against the organs of government or does it extend to mere financial crimes? In *Re Urios*,[67] the Cour de Cassation considered that it extended to maintaining contact with the enemies of the state in wartime and this broad principle is now reflected in Art 694 of the French Code de procedure penal. In the common law world the principle was alluded to in the case of *Joyce v DPP*,[68] although a number of other points of constitutional law also contributed to the final outcome. The facts in brief form were as follows.

William Joyce was born in the United States in 1906 and came to England in 1921; he was a natural born citizen of the United States. In 1933 he fraudulently acquired a British passport by alleging that he had been born in Ireland. In 1939, he left England and began to work as a radio announcer in Germany. In 1940 he claimed to have acquired German

---

65   See British Nationality Act 1981, s 6 and Sched 1 where the regime is less stringent when a person is married to a British citizen.

66   AT Richardson (1992) 55 MLR 73. It must be doubtful whether the legislation was in spirit retrospective having regard to the terms of Art 7.2 of the European Convention on Human Rights and Fundamental Freedoms. The legislation was enacted under the terms of the Parliament Act 1911.

67   *In re Urios* (1922) ILR 107 (Spaniard who while in Spain maintained contact the the enemies of France during the course of the First World War – charged under Art 7 of the then Code d'instruction criminelle).

68   *Joyce v DPP* [1946] AC 347.

nationality. In 1945 he was arrested and charged with treason. He was convicted at trial before a jury at the Central Criminal Court and his appeal was dismissed by the Court of Criminal Appeal and the House of Lords.[69]

In giving judgment in the House of Lords Lord Jowitt LC noted that treason could be committed outside the realm[70] and went on to observe that 'no principle of comity demands that a state should ignore the crime of treason committed against it outside its territory. On the contrary a proper regard for its own security requires that all those who commit that crime, whether they commit it within or without the realm should be amenable to its laws'.

At a later date, this extract was taken by the District Court of Jerusalem in *Attorney General of the Government of Israel v Eichmann* as establishing support for the protective principle. In the *Eichmann* case,[71] it was not possible for Israel to rely on the territorial principle or the nationality principle because although the victims were Jewish they were nationals of other states and at the relevant time the state of Israel did not exist. In a detailed judgment the court explained that the basis of the protective principle was the concept of the 'linking point' (that is, *Anknuepfungspunkte*) between the accused and the state in respect of acts which concern that particular state more than they concern other states.[72]

There had been a number of cases in the United States demonstrating some support for the protective principle in a wide range of circumstances.[73] However, a clearer move can be seen from the middle of the 1980s as attempts were made to secure jurisdiction over those causing loss of life abroad. After the *Achille Lauro* incident, Congress enacted the Diplomatic Security and Anti-Terrorism Act 1986 which had the effect of conferring jurisdiction on United States courts in respect of the killing of a United States national abroad where the intention was to coerce, intimidate or retaliate against a government or civilian population. The legislation was within the protective principle in proceeding on the basis that terrorist acts are directed against the state. However, the legislation is only to be employed in the clearest cases and no prosecution can be mounted unless the Attorney General certifies that the act in question falls within the requirements of the legislation.

---

69 *Joyce v DPP* [1946] AC 347. The judgment in the Court of Criminal Appeal is reported at (1945) WN 220; (1945) 173 LT 377. The case proceeded on the basis that a conviction for treason depended on an individual owing allegiance to the Crown. The prosecution case was that the acquisition of the passport had the effect of both conferring protection and creating the duty of allegiance. The acquisition of German nationality would not be recognised in time of war, see *R v Lynch* [1903] 1 KB 444. See, also, H Lauterpacht (1947) 9 CLJ 330.

70 *R v Casement* [1917] 1 KB 99.

71 For the background to the case, see H Arendt, *Eichmann in Jerusalem*, 1963.

72 (1961) 36 ILR 5; The judgment of the Supreme Court is reported at (1962) 36 ILR 277. For comment, see Fawcett (1962) 38 BYIL 181; Green (1962) 38 BYIL 457; Green (1962) 23 MLR 507.

73 See *United States v Rocha* (1960) 182 F Supp 479; (1961) 288 F 2d 545 (attempt to breach immigration laws); *United States v Pizzarusso* (1968) 388 F 2d 8 (violation of immigration laws); *United States v Layton* (1981) 509 F Supp 212 (murder of United States congressman in Guyana while on official duties).

(d) The passive personality principle

The principles listed above have attracted a wide degree of acceptance as the basis upon which to found jurisdiction. More controversial is the passive personality principle. This head of jurisdiction holds that a state is entitled to found jurisdiction on the basis of the nationality of the actual or potential victim. Thus, the courts of state A might try a citizen of state C for the murder of one of its citizens committed in state B. The principle acquired prominence first in the *Cutting* case (1886)[74] where Cutting, an American national, published defamatory statements in Texas concerning a Mexican citizen. This was a criminal offence under Mexican Law and at a later date Cutting was arrested while in Mexico and put on trial; Mexico claimed to exercise jurisdiction under the passive personality principle. Such conduct prompted a diplomatic protest by the United States and Cutting was eventually released when the victim of the tort declined to continue with the legal action. To that extent the case ended without a settled conclusion although it tended to harden the view of common law countries against such a basis of jurisdiction.

The principle was subject to criticism by the minority in the *Lotus* case;[75] the majority did not find it necessary to rely on the principle after having invoked the objective territorial principle. Several years later, the Harvard Research Draft Convention on Jurisdiction with Respect to Crime (1935) did not include the principle and the accompanying commentary indicated that state practice was at best inconclusive.

However, with the increase in foreign tourism after 1945 there is evidence of a change in state practice. There have been incidents where the citizens of state A might be murdered in state B by individuals from state C in circumstances where state B was unable or unwilling to bring the wrongdoers to justice. In such circumstances state A might seek to try such individuals before its own criminal courts. Thus, there are references to the principle as a basis of jurisdiction in a number of international conventions designed to restrain terrorism or other abusive conduct.[76] Traditionally the principle has been invoked by civil law countries such as Mexico, Italy and Brazil[77] but it has now been endorsed the United States as a response to attacks on its citizens abroad.[78]

The United States relied on the principle in seeking the extradition from Italy of the leader of the group responsible for the seizing of the *Achille Lauro* in 1985; the only link with the United States being the murder of a United States citizen. The same principle was relied upon by the United States Court of Appeals, District of Columbia in *United States v Yunis (No 2)*[79] to justify the trial of a Lebanese citizen for the hijacking of a Royal Jordanian Aircraft on which United States citizens were travelling. The court rejected any

---

74 *Moore's Digest of International Law*, 1906, Vol II, p 228.

75 The *Lotus* case (1927) PCIJ, Ser A, No 10.

76 See Art 4(b) of the Tokyo Convention on Offences and Certain Other Acts Committed on Board Aircraft (1963); Art 9 of the International Convention against the Taking of Hostages (1979); Art 5(1)(c) of the Convention against Torture and Other Cruel, Inhuman or Degrading Treatment or Punishment (1984).

77 In so far as the extradition request in *Re Pinochet* (1998–2000) alleged the murder of Spanish citizens in Chile by persons who had never held Spanish citizenship this was an instance of reliance on the passive personality principle by the Spanish prosecuting authorities.

78 In cases where the individual is attacked in his capacity as a representative of the state (eg, as Ambassador) then the protective principle may be invoked.

79 *United States v Yunis (No 2)* (1988) 82 ILR 344; see also 88 ILR 176.

limitation on the principle to those cases where there had been a deliberate attempt to target particular nationalities. In both such cases the principle of universal jurisdiction might also have been relied upon. The principle has subsequently been relied upon in the United States to justify the trial of a Mexican citizen for the murder of an American law enforcement officer in Mexico,[80] and the Third Restatement of United States Foreign Relations Law refers to the 'increasing acceptance of the principle'. There is little doubt that the United States has moved away from its opposition to the principle[81] and seeks to apply this head of jurisdiction in cases of terrorism.

(e) Universal jurisdiction

The basis of universal jurisdiction is that each state has jurisdiction on the principle that the act in question is offensive to the international community as a whole. A distinction has to be drawn between a crime that attracts universal jurisdiction and an international crime. In customary international law there were two categories of crime that might be regarded as universal crimes, namely piracy and crimes against humanity or war crimes. The essence of such offences is that jurisdiction exists regardless of where the act takes place or the nationality of the wrongdoer; jurisdiction is founded upon the nature of the act.

It is important to say a little about each of these.

Piracy[82]

Piracy (or piracy, *jure gentium*) has been recognised as a crime against the international community for several centuries. It was accepted in customary international law that each state had the right to catch and try those engaged in piratical activity either on the high seas or within state territory.[83] It is important that the acts in question should constitute piracy in international law not simply in municipal law. The accepted definition was formulated in Art 15 of the Geneva Convention on the High Seas (1958) and is as follows:

Piracy consists of any of the following acts:

(1) Any illegal acts of violence, detention or any act of depredation, committed for private ends by the crew or the passengers of a private ship or a private aircraft, and directed:

   (a) on the high seas, against another ship or aircraft, or against persons or property on board such ship or aircraft;

   (b) against a ship, aircraft, persons or property in a place outside the jurisdiction of any State.

---

80 *United States v Alvarez Machain* (1992) 95 ILR 355; see for comment, M Halberstam (1992) 86 AJIL 736; MJ Glennon (1992) 86 AJIL 746.

81 For domestic legislation, see 1984 Comprehensive Crime Control Act; 1986 Omnibus Diplomatic Security and Anti-Terrorism Act.

82 For an interesting social history of the subject, see David Cording, *Life Among the Pirates: The Romance and the Reality*, 1995; see, also, DH Johnson, 'Piracy in modern international law' (1957) 43 TGS 63; GE White, 'The Marshall Court and international law: the piracy cases' (1989) 83 AJIL 727.

83 Hugo Grotius argued that the pirate was not a national because he has placed himself beyond the protection of any state; he was to be considered *'hostis humani generis'* and so justiciable by any state anywhere. See *De Jure Belli ac Pacis*, Vol 2, cap 20.

The stipulation that piracy[84] must in international law be directed for private ends leaves difficulties in respect of those cases coming before the municipal courts that concern the position of insurgents operating against an existing government of a state.[85] In any event, this definition has been accepted and is reproduced in Art 101 of the Law of the Sea Convention (1982). The elements of the offence were considered in detail by the Privy Council upon a special reference from Hong Kong in the case of *Re Piracy Jure Gentium*.[86] The precise question at issue was whether actual robbery was required for the offence of piracy or whether a frustrated attempt was sufficient. In a lengthy review of English legislation originating in 1536 and of the relevant literature Viscount Sankey LC in giving judgment on behalf of the Privy Council concluded that actual robbery was not required.

War crimes and crimes against humanity

It has been accepted that war crimes and crimes against humanity are universal crimes that are subject to the jurisdiction of any state. This development is a creature of the twentieth century. Article 6 of the Charter establishing the Nuremberg International Military Tribunal (1945) draws a distinction between a war crime and a crime against humanity and this distinction is alluded to in the subsequent judgment of the tribunal. In 1946 the General Assembly indicated that it affirmed 'the principles of international law recognised by the Charter of the Nuremberg Tribunal and the judgment of the Tribunal'.[87] It is arguable that the two categories apply to many of the same acts but the classification of crimes against humanity extends beyond acts committed during an armed conflict.

The traditional understanding that war crimes and crimes against humanity are subject to universal jurisdiction is reinforced by the provisions of the four Geneva Conventions of 1949 which place an obligation on state parties to punish grave breaches of the Conventions.[88]

An example of such a jurisdiction being assumed by a municipal courts is afforded by the case of *Attorney General of Israel v Eichmann*,[89] where the District Court of Jerusalem asserted that these crimes were such grave offences against the law of nations as to be subject to universal jurisdiction. The fact that the acts were committed prior to the

---

84 At common law, the general understanding was that a pirate was one who committed robbery on the high seas (see Act of Henry VIII (1536 c 15); It was important to distinguish the pirate from the privateer (an armed vessel who was authorised to attack and seize the vessels of other nations). In general, pirates operating in the Mediterranean were known as Corsairs, while those operating in the Caribbean were often described as Buccaneers (from the French *boucaner* to smoke dry or cure) because of their manner of cooking meat.

85 *The Magellan Pirates* (1853) 1 Sp Ecc & Ad 81; *The Ambrose Light* (1885) 25 F 409.

86 *Re Piracy Jure Gentium* [1934] AC 586 (PC) (judgment delivered by Viscount Sankey, but panel included Lord Macmillan, Lord Atkin, Lord Wright and Lord Tomlin).

87 General Assembly Resolution 95(I).

88 This matter is discussed further in Chapter 24; see Geneva Convention I (For the Amelioration of the Condition of the Wounded and Sick in Armed Forces in the Field), Art 50; Geneva Convention II (For the Amelioration of the Condition of Wounded Sick and Shipwrecked Members of Armed Forces at Sea), Art 51; Geneva Convention III (Relative to the Treatment of Prisoners of War), Art 129; Geneva Convention IV (Relative to the Protection of Civilian Persons in Time of War), Art 147.

89 *Attorney General of Israel v Eichmann* (1961) 36 ILR 5; on appeal (1962) 36 ILR 277.

establishment of the state of Israel and against non-nationals was of no relevance and could not detract from the principle of universal jurisdiction in cases 'which struck at the whole of mankind'. There is no doubt that genocide comes within the scope of crimes against humanity although in the Statute of the International Tribunal in respect of Yugoslavia a distinction is drawn between genocide[90] and the wider category of crimes against humanity[91] and war crimes.[92] In 1968 the General Assembly had adopted a Convention on the Non-Applicability of Statutory Limitations to War Crimes and Crimes Against Humanity indicating clearly that war crimes constituted a particular class of crime under international law susceptible of universal jurisdiction. In 1954 the International Law Commission included genocide and other acts against humanity in its Draft Code of Offences against the Peace and Security of Mankind and this treatment was extended in the 1991 Draft Code.[93]

It is sometimes argued that there are a number of other crimes which should properly be regarded as subject to universal jurisdiction; the candidates include hijacking, drug trafficking, apartheid, slavery; however it is doubtful whether such crimes were so regarded under customary international law. Such crimes in the last half century been subject to a degree of international co-operation and by various treaty regimes they are subject to extended rules as to jurisdiction (that is, not depending on territory or nationality) so much so that they have been labelled variously as 'international crimes' or 'quasi universal crimes'.[94] The developments in this area are linked with the evolution of an international law of human rights founded on the concept of the 'international crime'.

However, there does seem to be value in maintaining a distinction between those crimes that were subject to universal jurisdiction in customary international law and those that are regarded as international crimes under various treaty arrangements. In this context there is much force in the point made by Lord Slynn in his dissenting judgment in *R v Bow Street Magistrate ex p Pinochet Ugarte (No 1)* where the learned judge observed:[95]

> It does not seem to me that it has been shown that there is any state practice or general consensus let alone a widely supported convention that all crimes against international law should be justiciable in national courts on the basis of universality of jurisdiction.

A similar note of caution was sounded by Lord Browne-Wilkinson in *R v Bow Street Magistrate ex p Pinochet Ugarte (No 3)* when the learned judge observed:

> Apart from the law of piracy, the concept of personal liability under international law for international crimes is of comparatively modern growth. The traditional subjects of international law are states not human beings. But consequent upon the war crime trials after the 1939–1945 World War, the international community came to recognise that there

---

90 Statute of the Tribunal, Art 6.

91 *Ibid*, Art 7.

92 *Ibid*, Art 8.

93 In 1991 the International Law Commission provisionally adopted a Draft Code of Crimes Against the Peace and Security of Mankind.

94 For example, in *DPP v Doot* [1973] AC 807 Lord Wilberforce indicated that he thought drugs related offences fell within that category while in *United States v Yunis* (1988) 681 F Supp 896; (1988) 82 ILR 344 the United States court was of the opinion that hostage taking should be subject to like treatment.

95 *R v Bow Street Metropolitan Magistrate ex p Pinochet Ugarte (No 1)* [2000] 1 AC 61; [1998] 3 WLR 1456, p 1473.

could be criminal liability under international law for a class of crimes such as war crimes and crimes against humanity.[96]

In these circumstances it does seem sensible to preserve a distinction between the two crimes that might be regarded as truly subject to universal jurisdiction in customary international law and a wider category of international crimes that have emerged in the last quarter of a century as attempts have been made to construct an international law of human rights.

Criminal conduct subject to extended jurisdiction by treaty

In addition to the two crimes regarded as subject to universal jurisdiction in customary international law considerable efforts have been made to provide for the extension of state jurisdiction by treaty where the acts in question offend the international community as a whole. Examples are to be found in provisions such as Art 6 of the Genocide Convention (1948),[97] which provides for the assumption of jurisdiction by states in respect of genocide, or Art 4 of the Convention against Torture and Other Cruel or Degrading Treatment (1984)[98] which provides that torture shall be made an offence in municipal law and that jurisdiction is extended under the terms of Art 5 to situations where the acts have taken place beyond state territory.

There are thus a wide range of offences which while not strictly crimes of universal jurisdiction have attracted the attention of international law. These international conventions have a number of features in common. First, there will be an agreed definition of the offence. Secondly, each state will agree to make it a criminal offence punishable by severe penalties. Thirdly, the treaty will normally provide for an extended basis of jurisdiction. Fourthly, the treaty will often provide that in the event of non-prosecution the state will extradite to a requesting state. In some instances, the convention may provide that the offence in question shall not be a political offence for the purpose of extradition law. In a dualist state, much will therefore depend on the willingness of the legislature to introduce implementing legislation. Normally the treaty will be followed by implementing legislation and that legislation will often provide for an extended basis of jurisdiction. Thus, in the United Kingdom the Genocide Convention (1948),[99] the Convention on the Protection and Punishment of Crimes against Internationally Protected Persons Including Diplomatic Agents (1973)[100] and the International Convention against the Taking of Hostages (1979)[101] have all been implemented by the legislature.

---

96 *R v Bow Street Metropolitan Magistrate ex p Pinochet Ugarte (No 3)* [2000] 1 AC 147; [1999] 2 WLR 827, p 840.

97 See Genocide Act 1969.

98 See Criminal Justice Act 1988.

99 See Genocide Act 1969. (It is of some interest that in the hearing in the Divisional Court of the Queen's Bench Division in the *Pinochet* litigation' Lord Bingham LCJ devoted some attention to how the Genocide Convention (1948) had been implemented.)

100 For the United Kingdom, see Internationally Protected Persons Act 1978. For the Convention, see Rozakis (1974) 23 ICLQ 32; Wood (1974) 23 ICLQ 791.

101 For the United Kingdom, see Taking of Hostages Act 1982.

Some writers argue that such treaty regimes have created a class of international crimes. this must be open to question. What has taken place is that a large number of states have agreed that certain acts should be punished in all states and that traditional concepts of jurisdiction should be extended to see that wrongdoers do not escape punishment and that in all cases the principle *dedere aut punire* should apply. However, the criminal offence is created under municipal law and much will depend on the willingness of the state to ratify and the terms in which it implements. Thus, in *R v Bow Street Metropolitan Magistrate ex p Pinochet Ugarte*[102] the House of Lords ruled that extra-territorial torture was not a criminal offence under English Law until the International Convention against Torture (1984) had been implemented by the Criminal Justice Act 1988. This is particularly the case where extradition is in issue and the double criminality rule has to be complied with.

4 PROBLEMS WITH REGARD TO CIVIL AVIATION[103]

Developments in civil aviation and the increase in criminal activity directed against aircraft have resulted in the need to introduce specific regimes designed to clarify and extend jurisdiction in respect of such unlawful acts. In broad terms, the problems arise in respect attacks on aircraft on the ground, offences committed in flight, acts of hijacking and wrongs directed against aircraft passengers. The serious threat posed both to human life and the viability of international civil aviation has resulted in a heightened level of international co-operation between states. Such efforts at co-operation began in the 1960s but became more important in the 1970s with the increase in terrorist activity directed against aircraft.

The first tangible effort is to be found in the Tokyo Convention on Offences and Certain Other Acts Committed on Board Aircraft (1963).[104] The purpose of the Convention was to ensure that those who committed criminal acts in flight[105] would not be able to escape prosecution.[106] Secondly, the Convention was designed to set out clearly the power of the aircraft commander to maintain order and discipline on board.[107] Thirdly, the Convention does not apply to aircraft used in military, customs or police operations. Fourthly, while Art 3 provides that the state of registration should assume jurisdiction this provision is to be read with Art 16 which provides that acts committed on board aircraft shall be treated for the purpose of extradition as taking place not only where it occurred but also in the state of registration. In so far as the Convention addressed the problem of hijacking it provided that where there had been a wrongful

---

102 *R v Bow Street Metropolitan Magistrate ex p Pinochet Ugarte (No 1)* [2000] 1 AC 61; *(No 3)* [2000] 1 AC 147.

103 See Chapter 14 below for a discussion as to the general principles of the law relating to airspace.

104 Opened for signature 14 September 1963.

105 'In Flight' was to be interpreted as being from the moment when power is applied for the purpose of take off until the moment when the landing run ends (Art 1.3).

106 By providing that the state of registration should assume jurisdiction (Art 3).

107 Articles 5–10 set out clear powers for the aircraft commander to take necessary action to maintain discipline and order and for the handing over to a competent authority any person involved in stipulated misconduct.

assumption of control, contracting states were under a duty to ensure that the aircraft was returned to lawful control and that the crew and passengers were to be allowed to proceed on their journey as soon as practicable;[108] any person involved in such conduct was to be detained pending criminal proceedings or extradition.[109]

By the end of the 1960s the upsurge in radical political action in some European states[110] had served to make the problem of aircraft hijacking a serious menace to air safety. Such incidents tended to attract considerable publicity.[111] To this end, the Hague Convention for the Suppression of the Unlawful Seizure of Aircraft was opened for signature on 16 December 1970.[112] The limited object of the Convention[113] was to deal with the problem of hijacking; it was intended that other unlawful acts would be dealt with in a later instrument. The Convention itself did not employ the term 'hijacking' but defined the ingredients of the offence in Art 1.[114] In Art 2 each contracting state agreed to make the offence punishable by severe penalties. In respect of prosecution, Art 4 required Contracting states to assume jurisdiction:

(a) when the offence is committed on board an aircraft registered in that State;

(b) when the hijacked aircraft lands in the territory of a contracting state with the alleged hijacker still on board;[115]

(c) when the offence is committed on board an aircraft leased without crew to a lessee who has his principal place of business or, if the lessee has no such place of business, his permanent residence, in that State.

Under the terms of the Convention if a hijacker is located within the territory then a contracting state is obliged to take him into custody[116] and Art 7 provides that such a state shall prosecute or extradite. By Art 8 the offence of hijacking is deemed to be an extraditable offence in extradition treaties between contracting states. The Hague

---

108 Article 11(1) and (2).

109 Article 13(2).

110 Some of which was associated with protest against the Vietnam War or the role of corporations in contemporary society; for a discussion of the phenomenon and the reaction to affluence in post-war European society, see Jillian Becker, *Hitler's Children: The Story of the Baader Meinhof Gang*, 1978.

111 It is, of course, relevant that in September 1970 the Dawson's Field Hijacking had taken place when three civil airliners were hijacked to Dawson's Field in Jordan and then blown up. Shortly, after, hijacking was expressly condemned in a General Assembly Resolution FA Res 2645 (25th Session).

112 In force in 1971; now 151 parties including the United Kingdom. Legislative effect being given by the Hijacking Act 1971 which imposes a maximum life sentence. In the United States, the Anti-Hijacking Act 1974 carries the death penalty if death results from the act.

113 For the United Kingdom see Hijacking Act 1971.

114 Article 1 reads: 'Any person who on board an aircraft in flight (a) unlawfully, by force or threat thereof, or by any other form of intimidation, seizes, or exercises control of, that aircraft, or attempts to perform any such act ... commits an offence.'

115 This would apply to the circumstances in *R v Abdul-Hussain* [1999] Crim LR 570, where the Court of Appeal (Rose LJ, Rougier J, Johnson J) were considering the case where an aircraft on a flight from Sudan to Jordan was hijacked to Stanstead Airport in the United Kingdom. The appeal raised the question as to when (if at all) a hijacker could raise a defence of duress; the defendant alleged that they were at risk of being sent back to Iraq from Sudan.

116 Article 6 of the Hague Convention.

Convention extended and clarified the definition of the concept 'in flight'[117] in contrast to that set out in the earlier Tokyo Convention.

As indicated above, the period of the late 1960s and early 1970s witnessed an upsurge in the number of acts perpetrated against civil aviation. Many of these acts fell short of actual hijacking so that it was necessary for Hague Convention to be supplemented by the Montreal Convention for the Suppression of Unlawful Acts against the Safety of Civil Aviation.[118] The scope of the Montreal Convention[119] is indicated by the wide terms of Art 1 which is directed to the various forms of acts that might be directed against an aircraft in flight. The Convention applies to acts committed while the aircraft is in service as well as in flight.[120] The Convention provides that each contracting state shall make such acts punishable by severe penalties. Under Art 5 of the Convention contracting states undertake to establish jurisdiction in respect of various types of offences (for example, if the offence is committed within the territory of that country or in respect of an aircraft registered there). In general, the provisions of the earlier Conventions regarding the taking into custody and the obligation to prosecute or extradite are reproduced. There is growing evidence that acts against civil aircraft if not universal crimes are the subject of a wide jurisdictional scope and are subject of universal condemnation by states. The Montreal Convention was itself subject of a Protocol signed in 1988 which provides for common action in respect of unlawful acts directed against aircraft.

The practical problem arises when a particular state refuses to co-operate by prosecuting or extraditing hijackers. In some instances there have been bilateral agreements in other cases there have been joint declarations. In 1978 and 1988, the seven chief industrial nations indicated that flights to and from a particular state would cease where there had been a refusal to prosecute or extradite. In some instances states chose to give into demands[121] while others have decided upon direct action in particular

---

117 Article 3 of the Hague Convention reads: 'For the purpose of this Convention, an aircraft is considered to be in flight at any time from the moment when all its external doors are closed following embarkation until the moment when any such door is opened for disembarkation. In the case of a force landing, the flight shall be deemed to continue until the competent authorities take over responsibility for the aircraft and for persons and property on board.'

118 Opened for signature 23 September 1971.

119 In force in 1973; for implementation in the United Kingdom, see Protection of Aircraft Act 1973.

120 Article 2(a) adopts the same definition for 'in flight' as the prior Hague Convention. Article 2(b) provides that 'an aircraft is considered to be in service form the beginning of the pre flight preparation of the aircraft by ground personnel or by the crew for a specific flight until twenty four hours after any landing'.

121 In September 1977 the Japanese Government decided to give in to demands by hijackers of the Japanese Red Army.

instances.[122] There have indeed been a number of incidents where military aircraft have been used to arrest hijackers.[123]

5 EXTRADITION[124]

One of the commonest causes of problems as to jurisdiction arises in extradition proceedings. Extradition is the process by which state A requests state B to return an individual suspected of certain criminal offences in order that he may be tried before the courts of state A. The process of extradition developed in the nineteenth century on the basis of treaty obligations; it is generally asserted that there is no obligation to extradite arising in customary international law.[125]

Although each specific case will depend on the particular terms of the treaty there are a number of common themes that arise in extradition law. First, there is the requirement of double criminality,[126] namely, that the offence should be a crime in both the requesting state and the extraditing state at the date when the act is committed.[127] Secondly, there is the principle of speciality which requires that the offender extradited should only be tried for those offences for which formed the basis of the extradition order. Thirdly, many extradition treaties provide that there shall be no extradition in respect of political offences. This is a legacy of the 19th century emphasis on granting asylum to liberal politicians struggling against despotic regimes. However, in this context there has been an attempt to narrow this exception both by statute and in the case law so as to permit the

---

122 The two most celebrated incidents being: (a) In June 1976 An Air France airliner bound for Paris from Tel Aviv was hijacked to Entebbe in Uganda. By this stage both Israel and Uganda had ratified the 1970 Hague Convention. However, there was some evidence that Uganda had co-operated with the hijackers. In the subsequent Security Council debate, Israel relied on both the right to self-defence and the duty to protect its own nationals. In this particular instance (later known as the 'Raid on Entebbe'), Israel acted alone. (b) An example of internationally approved direct action arose in October 1977 when a Lufthansa Boeing 737 on a flight from Majorca to Frankfurt was hijacked to Mogadishu in Somalia by associates of the Red Army Faction. Chancellor Helmut Schmidt (in consultation with various Security Council Members) ordered the *Grenzschutz Gruppe Neun* (GSG 9) to storm the plane rather than submit to the demands of the hijackers. A number of foreign governments offered to assist.

123 In October 1985 United States fighter aircraft persuaded an Egyptian civil aircraft which was carrying the hijackers of of the *Achille Lauro* to land in Sicily.

124 See A Jones, *Jones on Extradition*, 1989; I Stanbrook and C Stanbrook, *The Law and Practice of Extradition*, 1980; G Gilbert, *Aspects of Extradition Law*, 1991.

125 See the *Lockerbie* case (1992) ICJ 3; 94 ILR 478.

126 *Governor of Canada v Aronson* [1990] 1 AC 579.

127 *R v Bow Street Stipendiary Magistrate ex p Pinochet Ugarte (No 3)* [2000] 1 AC 147; [1999] 2 WLR 827 (where in respect of many of the charges this was not the. For earlier case law, see *Re Arton (No 1)* [1896] 1 QB 108; *Government of Denmark v Nielsen* [1984] AC 606; *United States Government v McCaffery* [1984] 2 All ER 570; a double criminality test applied under the Fugitive Offenders Act 1967, see *R v Governor of Pentonville Prison ex p Sinclair* [1991] 2 AC 64.

extradition of those suspected of terrorist offences.[128] Fourthly, many municipal legal systems provide that extradition is only to be ordered by the court when the requesting state has produced *prima facie* evidence of a criminal offence.[129] Fifthly, although this is a matter for constitutional law many states provide for a division of roles between the executive branch and the judicial branch. The requesting state will normally have to satisfy the judicial branch[130] that there is case to warrant extradition but it will be for the executive branch to determine whether the extradition actually proceeds.[131] Sixthly, some states provide that there can be no extradition of their own nationals although these may be states which also claim a wide jurisdiction on the basis of nationality.[132]

In respect of the United Kingdom there had been a long series of legislation dating back to the Extradition Act 1870. The legal system recognised three categories: (i) extradition arrangements with Commonwealth countries;[133] (ii) extradition arrangements with the remainder of the world;[134] (iii) the particular arrangements that operate with respect to the Republic of Ireland.[135]

In the 1980s it became clear that such arrangements were not working well and that extradition from the United Kingdom was becoming too difficult. After a detailed review of the law,[136] changes were introduced in the Criminal Justice Act 1988 and were

---

128 Clearly such an exception is not appropriate when the requesting state is a liberal democratic state with an independent judiciary and a well established system of civil liberty. For the political exception see Extradition Act 1989, s 6; *Re Castioni* [1891] QB 149; *Re Meunier* [1894] 2 QB 415 (anarchists in Paris); *Re Arton (No 1)* [1896] 1 QB 108; *Schtraks v Government of Israel* [1964] AC 556 (child stealing in Israel); *Cheng v Governor of Pentonville Prison* (1973) AC 931 (the act must be directed against the requesting state, not a third state). Case law now to be read in the light of *T v Home Secretary* [1996] AC 742 (attack on airport killing civilians not a political crime); *R v Home Secretary ex p Finivest SpA* [1997] 1 All ER 942.

129 The duty will vary according to the treaty; see Extradition Act 1989, s 9. For the full requirement see *R v Ashford Remand Centre ex p Postlethwaite* [1988] AC 924. For the position under the 1989 Act, Sched 1, see *R v Governor of Pentonville Prison ex p Alves* [1993] AC 284. Whether there is an obligation to determine the existence of a *prima facie* case will depend on the particular extradition arrangements in force, see Extradition Act 1989, s 9(4), (8) and Sched 1, see *R v Governor of Pentonville Prison ex p Alves* [1993] AC 284.

130 In many states extradition matters are handled from the outset by a senior judicial figure. In England proceedings will normally start before a stipendiary magistrate at Bow Street followed by a habeas corpus application to the High Court with direct appeal to House of Lords under the Administration of Justice Act 1960. The unwisdom of the direct appeal was illustrated in *R v Bow Street Metropolitan Magistrate ex p Pinochet Ugarte (No 1)* [2000] 1 AC 61.

131 The executive branch being able to take into account evidence that might not be admissible in court and considerations such as the health of the subject and wider questions of public policy. In the United Kingdom this function is performed by the Home Secretary normally at the conclusion of extradition hearings in the courts. One of the unusual features of the Pinochet litigation was the attempt to seek judicial review prior to the extradition proceedings commencing.

132 See Art 16(2) of the *Grundgesetz* of the Federal Republic of Germany; see also Art 3(1) of the French Extradition Law of 1927.

133 Governed by the Fugitive Offenders Acts 1881 and 1967; rather confusingly described as rendition since the wrongdoer was being returned to another part of the Crown's dominion.

134 Governed by Extradition Acts 1870–1935.

135 The Backing of Warrants (Republic of Ireland) Act 1965; see *Keane v Governor of Brixton Prison* [1972] AC 204; *R v Governor of Winson Green Prison ex p Littlejohn* [1975] 2 All ER 208.

136 *A Review of the Law and Practice of Extradition in the United Kingdom*, Home Office, 1982, Cmnd 9421, 1985; Cmnd 9658, 1986.

consolidated in the Extradition Act 1989. One of the objects of the legislation was to harmonise arrangements between Commonwealth and non-Commonwealth countries.

Secondly, those treaties negotiated under the 1870 Extradition Act could not be amended unilaterally but would be subject to the terms of Schedule 1 to the Extradition Act 1989. New treaties will be negotiated under the terms of the 1989 legislation. Thirdly, one of the objects of the legislation was to enable the United Kingdom to ratify the European Convention on Extradition; with the enactment of the 1989 legislation extradition to 24 European states now takes effect under the Convention. In 1990 a modified scheme of extradition was agreed between Commonwealth countries and this now takes effect under the same legislation. Although efforts have been made to simplify the procedure a state can be caught by conflicting obligations[137] and this may give rise to problems in the United Kingdom when cases are brought under the Human Rights Act 1998.[138]

6 EXERCISING JURISDICTION OVER PERSONS APPREHENDED IN BREACH OF INTERNATIONAL LAW[139]

Problems can arise if a person appears before the courts of state A and he alleges that he has been brought into that court by unlawful means. In normal circumstances such an individual will appear before the courts after he has been subject to lawful extradition procedures. In considering this problem a number of factual situations require to be distinguished: (i) where state A has an extradition treaty with state B but prefers instead to employ direct action within state B; (ii) where there is no extradition[140] treaty and state A employs direct action within state B; (iii) where state A and state B do have an extradition treaty but instead collude to avoid its impact, for example, by the simple expedient of deportation.

The question that arises is whether unlawful apprehension should deprive a court of jurisdiction. The initial common law approach in England[141] and in the United States[142] was that the unlawfulness of the apprehension should not affect the jurisdiction. The attitude of the United Kingdom courts had been that if a person was lawfully in custody within the United Kingdom the court had no power to inquire how he was brought here.

---

137 For problems arising for the United Kingdom in respect of treaty obligations under the European Convention on Human Rights (1950) as well as extradition obligations vis à vis the United States, see *Soering v United Kingdom* (1989) 11 EHRR 439.

138 The difficulty will arise because a person present in the jurisdiction is *prima facie* entitled to the protection of the European Convention on Human Rights (1950). For an illustration, see *Soering v United Kingdom* (1989) 11 EHRR 439.

139 For literature, see F Morgenstern, 'Jurisdiction in seizures effected in violation of international law' (1952) 29 BYIL 256; P O'Higgins, 'Unlawful seizure and irregular extradition' (1960) 36 BYIL 279; A Lowenfeld, 'US law enforcement abroad: the constitution and international law' (1989) 83 AJIL 880; A Lowenfeld, 'The constitution and international law, continued' (1990) 84 AJIL 444; A Lowenfeld, 'Kidnapping by government order: a follow up' (1990) 84 AJIL 712; A Lowenfeld, 'Still more on kidnapping' (1991) 85 AJIL 655.

140 As was indeed the case in the seizure of Adolf Eichmann in June 1960.

141 *Ex p Scott* (1829) 9 B & C 466.

142 *Ker v Illinois* (1886) 119 US 436; *Frisbie v Collins* (1942) 342 US 519.

The traditional position was expressed with characteristic robustness by Lord Goddard LCJ in *ex p Elliot*[143] where he observed:

> If a person is arrested abroad and he is brought before a court in this country charged with an offence which that court has jurisdiction to hear, it is no answer for him to say, he being then in lawful custody in this country 'I was arrested contrary to the laws of the State of A or the State of B where I was actually arrested'. He is in custody before the court which has jurisdiction to try him. What is it suggested that the court can do? The court cannot dismiss the charge at once without its being heard. He is charged with an offence against English law, the law applicable to the case.[144]

The same approach was followed a generation later by the Divisional Court in *R v Plymouth Justices ex p Driver*,[145] where the court held that it was no part of its duty to inquire how a person had been brought within the jurisdiction. This approach was not restricted to the United Kingdom and was followed in Palestine,[146] in France[147] and cited with approval in by the District Court of Jerusalem in the *Eichmann* case.[148] However, there are now signs that this approach must be reassessed in the light of the House of Lords judgment in *R v Horseferry Road Magistrates' Court ex p Bennett*.[149] In essence, the facts of the case were as follows.

Bennett, a New Zealander, who was wanted in England for fraud was located in South Africa. At first the South African authorities decided to deport him to New Zealand but at Johannesburg he was placed on a plane to London.

The House of Lords ruled that the criminal proceedings could not proceed. In a forceful speech Lord Griffiths argued that the extradition procedures were used to maintain the rule of law in international affairs and that by including judicial involvement they were designed to protect the legitimate interests of the accused. The learned judge argued that in cases where extradition was available the doctrine of abuse of process could be relied upon where there had been a deliberate flouting of such procedures. In contrast to the *Eichmann* case there had been no flouting of South African sovereignty and an extradition treaty was available. The House of Lords was influenced by developments in other jurisdictions including New Zealand and South Africa[150] and by a desire to ensure that collusive police agreements do not undermine the judicial protection accorded by extradition proceedings. However, it is probably the case that the principle propounded in *Bennett*[151] can only be relied upon in the United Kingdom

---

143 *R v O/C Depot Battallion RASC, Colchester ex p Elliot* [1949] 1 All ER 373.

144 It is arguable that this is consistent with the former attitude in civil matters that the presence of the defendant in the jurisdiction was enough to found jurisdiction. Indeed, the same judge argued that that there were only very limited circumstances in which a court could exclude unlawfully obtained but relevant evidence: see *Kuruma v The Queen* [1955] AC 197 (PC).

145 [1986] 1 QB 95; 77 ILR 351.

146 *Afouneh v Attorney General* (1942) 10 ILR 327.

147 *Re Argoud* (1964) 45 ILR 90 (forcible abduction).

148 (1961) 36 ILR 5.

149 [1994] 1 AC 42.

150 *R v Hartley* (1978) 2 NZLR 199 (Australian police put defendant on plane after call from New Zealand police); *S v Ebrahim* (1991) (2) SA 553 (abduction from Swaziland by South African forces to stand trial for treason).

151 [1994] 1 AC 42.

courts if it can be shown that United Kingdom officials participated[152] in breaches of international law.

However, not all states take the same view. In the United States the rule for many years was that a court should not decline jurisdiction and was not deprived of jurisdiction because of some irregularity or illegality in the mode of apprehension.[153] However, this has been qualified in some cases by the indication that jurisdiction should not be accepted where there has been fraud or force[154] but it would seem that such misconduct must fall within the category of 'torture, brutality and similar outrageous conduct'.[155]

However, the entire area was reconsidered by the United States Supreme Court in the case of *United States v Alvarez Machain*,[156] where the facts were as follows. A Mexican citizen had been abducted to the United States by agents of the United States Drug Enforcement Agency to face charges of murder. The United States Supreme Court ruled that the assumption of jurisdiction was not unconstitutional and would only become so if the abduction was expressly prohibited in any extradition treaty between the two states. The argument of the majority was that if abduction was not expressly prohibited then the assumption of jurisdiction did not constitute a flouting of the treaty. However, it is open to argument that even if there is no express prohibition such conduct does undermine the object and purpose of the extradition treaty. This unusual interpretation of the 1978 United States-Mexico Extradition Treaty showed a peculiar regard for international law[157] and attracted a protest by the government of Mexico.[158] However, such a decision is at variance with the general movement of authority in municipal courts which tends to the view as in Bennett that irregular or unlawful conduct either vitiates jurisdiction or constitutes a discretionary ground for the court to refuse jurisdiction on the basis of abuse of process.[159]

---

152 *R v Staines Magistrates Court ex p Westfallen* [1998] 4 All ER 2101; *R v Mullen* [1999] 3 All ER 777.

153 *Ker v Illinois* (1886) 119 US 436; *Frisbie v Collins* (1952) 342 US 519 (sometimes referred to as the Ker-Frisbie doctrine).

154 *United States v Toscanino* (1974) 500 F 2d 267; 61 ILR 190.

155 *United States ex rel Lujan v Gengler* (1975) 510 F 2d 62; 61 ILR 206.

156 *United States v Alvarez Machain* (1992) 95 ILR 355; see R Rayfuse, 'International abduction and the United States Supreme Court: the law of the jungle reigns' (1993) 42 ICLQ 882; M Halberstam, 'In defense of the Supreme Court decision in *Alvarez Machain*' (1992) 86 AJIL 736; M J Glennon, 'State sponsored abduction: a comment on *United States v Alvarez Machain*' (1992) 86 AJIL 746.

157 Particularly when the court appeared to consider that any breaches of international law were a matter for the executive branch.

158 Such cases concerning abduction proceed on the basis that the court has jurisdiction. In this case the allegations concerned the torture and murder in Mexico of an American citizen; the links with the United States were very limited and jurisdiction could only have been asserted on the basis of the passive personality principle or possibly the universal principle (because it concerned torture). There is clearly a distinction between those cases where state A abducts an individual to face trial in state A in respect of offences committed in state A and situations such as *Alvarez Machain* where abduction takes place in order to try an individual in respect of a matter over which the courts of state A can only justify jurisdiction by reference to the passive personality principle.

159 On the assumption that the executive branch had full knowledge of the irregular conduct as appears to have been the case in *Alvarez Machain*. At a later date the case against the defendant was dismissed by a federal trial court judge.

7 EXTRA-TERRITORIAL JURISDICTION

In the last quarter of a century particular difficulties have arisen in the context of competition law. Most advanced capitalist states have some form of competition law designed to curtail restrictive practices, abuses of monopoly power and the various forms of cartel. The United States has had such legislation since the end of the 19th century.[160] While there can be no objection when jurisdiction is founded on territory or nationality difficulties have arisen where jurisdiction is exercised under the terms of the 'effects doctrine'.

It will be recalled that under the objective territorial principle some of the constituent elements of the offence are committed within the jurisdiction and the causal chain is normally direct and immediate. However, in anti-trust matters there has been a consistent attempt to invoke either the protective principle or the 'effects' doctrine. As indicated above the protective principle allows the state to claim jurisdiction over acts committed by an alien abroad which are deemed prejudicial to the security of the state. So that in *Joyce v DPP*[161] the acts were directed towards the military defeat and conquest of the United Kingdom while in *Attorney General of Israel v Eichmann*[162] the acts were directed to the systematic destruction of the Jewish people. In such cases the acts have been directed against the organs of Government or the entire people of a state; thus, the protective principle is invoked to protect a clearly identified national or public interest. Normally there is a general acceptance that a state is entitled to indict those who seek to destroy it.

The difficulty arises with the 'effects doctrine' whereby a state may seek to claim jurisdiction on the grounds that the conduct of a party is producing 'effects' within its territory. In the context of competition law the problem is complicated by the relationship in company law between a holding company and its subsidiary companies. The United States has sought to proceed against United States holding companies in respect of acts of their subsidiaries abroad or has proceeded against foreign companies with subsidiaries in the United States even if the offending acts have taken place abroad. The combination of the 'effects doctrine' and a reluctance to respect the separate legal personality of the subsidiary company has resulted in wide claims of jurisdiction in anti-trust matters.

Thus, the 'effects doctrine' operates on a wider basis in that the consequences taking place within the second jurisdiction need not be constituent elements of the offence. In the normal situation company A and company B make an agreement in state X which has an effect in state Y such as to give the courts of state Y jurisdiction. Alternatively a United Kingdom company trading lawfully in the United Kingdom might become subject to United States anti-trust laws because of its interest in a subsidiary trading in the United States.

---

160 Political pressure against railroad abuses and cartels caused the United States to develop a body of law earlier than the United Kingdom. The main legislation pertaining to restraint of trade and monopoly is the Sherman Act 1890; the Clayton Act 1914 and the Federal Trade Commission Act 1914.

161 *Joyce v DPP* [1946] AC 347. (In that case the treasonable adhering to an enemy of the Crown took place abroad but the actual conduct was intended to have an actual effect in England by breaking the resistance of the civilian population.)

162 *Attorney General of Israel v Eichmann* (1961) 36 ILR 5; (1962) 36 ILR 277. (One difficulty in applying the protective principle was that at the time of the conduct the state of Israel did not exist.)

A number of points need to be made. First, the effects doctrine is not widely accepted as a principle of international law. Secondly, while in many cases there will be an overlap with the objective territorial principle, a head of jurisdiction founded on consequences rather than the constituent elements of the offence is potentially much wider. Thirdly, some of the United States cases can be explained on the basis of nationality in that the United States court is asserting jurisdiction over the wholly owned foreign subsidiary of a United States corporation.[163] Fourthly, it is arguable that the effects doctrine is much wider than the protective principle because the legislation extends beyond cardinal matters of public or security interest.

The modern case law is said to originate with the well known statement in the case of *United States v Aluminium Company of America*.[164] In that case which concerned the question whether a Canadian company could be liable under the United States anti-trust legislation the court observed:

> ... it is settled law ... that any state may impose liabilities, even upon persons not within its allegiance, for conduct outside its borders that has consequences within its borders which the state reprehends.[165]

The increasingly expressed concerns of other states has lead the United States courts to place limits on the doctrine. It is possible to note three requirements: (i) that the acts of the aliens abroad must have an actual or intended effect within the United States; (ii) that the effects should be quantifiable and substantial; (iii) that the effects on the United States economy should in the balancing exercise outweigh the concerns of other states as to the exercise of extra-territorial jurisdiction. This approach is to be detected in the case of *Timberlane Lumber Co v Bank of America*[166] and in the subsequent case of *Mannington Mills v Congoleum Corporation*.[167]

However, there are indications in some of the later case law that the court should decline any balancing act with regard to the effect on other states; but simply ask whether on the evidence the acts have had a substantial effect within the jurisdiction. Considerations of comity and foreign relations, it is argued, are matters for the executive branch of government to resolve through normal channels.[168] The modern tendency to simply assess effect is indicated by the United States Supreme Court judgment in *Hartford Fire Insurance Co v California*[169] where the defendants (a group of United Kingdom insurers) did not dispute that their activities had some effect in the United States but

---

163 Sometimes described as 'the enterprise entity doctrine', the American courts are prepared to 'lift the veil' and exercise jurisdiction over a foreign corporation which is closely linked by shareholding or contractual obligations to an American corporation.

164 *United States v Aluminium Company of America* (1945) 148 F 2d 216; for a similar approach in subsequent cases, see *United States v Timken Roller Bearing Co* (1949) 83 F Supp 284; (1951) 341 US 593; *United States v General Electric Company* (1949) 82 F Supp 753; (1953) 115 F Supp 835; *United States v Watchmakers of Switzerland Information Centre Inc* (1955) 133 F Supp 40; (1955) 134 F Supp 710.

165 *United States v Aluminium Co of America* (1945) 148 F 2d 416, p 443, *per* Judge Learned Hand.

166 (1976) 549 F 2d 597; 66 ILR 270.

167 (1979) 595 F 2d 1287; 66 ILR 487.

168 *Laker Airways v Sabena Airways* (1984) 731 F 2d 909.

169 *Hartford Fire Insurance Co v California* (1993) 113 S Ct 2891. For discussion of the case, see A Lowenfeld (1995) 89 AJIL 42; P Trimble (1995) 89 AJIL 53; L Kramer (1995) 89 AJIL 750.

argued that the United States Courts should decline jurisdiction because such acts were lawful in the United Kingdom and that any balancing act between domestic effect and international comity would tend in favour of declining jurisdiction. By a majority of 5:4 the United States Supreme Court held: (i) the Sherman Act extended to situations where some substantial effect was produced in the United States; (ii) that the conduct in question was not required under United Kingdom legislation; (iii) that in the circumstances no form of balancing act was required. However, the minority took the view that the exercise of jurisdiction in such circumstances was subject to an overall requirement of reasonableness.

The conduct of the United States in anti-trust matters has resulted in differences of opinion with the European Union although a memorandum of understanding has been reached on the question;[170] the case of the European Union is weakened by its own endorsement of the 'effects doctrine' in respect of competition matters arising under the Treaty of Rome.[171]

Other states have viewed with increasing misgivings the wide claims made by United States anti-trust authorities to jurisdiction; they have argued that such conduct represents an infringement of their territorial sovereignty. Concern was expressed in the United Kingdom as early as the 1960s and legislation enacted[172] to limit the effects of extra-territorial jurisdiction. It seems to be agreed by all parties that there must be some limit to extra-territorial jurisdiction but no agreement as to how such a consensus is to be reached. In the context of the United Kingdom the response was the enactment of the Protection of Trading Interests Act 1980.[173] This legislation[174] permits the Secretary of State for Trade and Industry to make orders prohibiting legal persons of United Kingdom nationality from complying with certain orders made by a foreign court; such orders may include a prohibition on the supplying of evidence. Failure to comply will be a criminal offence.[175]

The legislation contains restrictions on the enforcement in England and Wales of certain overseas judgments in particular those for multiple damages.[176]

---

170 US/EU Agreement on the Application of Competition Laws (1995 OJ 95/45).

171 *Wood Pulp* case; *A Ahlstrom Oy v Commission* [1988] 4 CMLR 901.

172 See Shipping Contracts and Commercial Documents Act 1964. For case law see *British Nylon Spinners Ltd v Imperial Chemical Industries Ltd* [1953] 1 Ch 19; *Rio Tinto Zinc Corporation v Westinghouse Electric Corporation* [1978] AC 547. The 1964 Act has now been repealed but paved the way for the 1980 Act; the 1964 legislation had been enacted in response to the discovery demands of the Federal Maritime Commission.

173 In many respects a most unusual piece of legislation (particularly s 6) to have been passed, given the otherwise traditionally friendly relations between the two states. Indeed, the relevant Minister introducing the legislation (Mr John Nott) indicted his regret over 'a problem which we have failed to deal with at diplomatic level over many years'.

174 Legislation to like effect has been enacted in Australia (Foreign Anti-Trust Judgments (Restriction of Enforcement) Act 1979) and in Canada (Foreign Extraterritorial Measures Act 1984). For comment on the controversy, see Jones [1981] CLJ 41; AV Lowe (1981) 75 AJIL 257; Huntley (1981) 30 ICLQ 213; Blythe (1983) 31 AJCL 99; Collins (1986) JBL 372. The problem of. enforcing competition law and yet avoiding giving offence to other states is not restricted to the United States; similar problems have been experienced by the European Community when seeking to enforce the then Arts 85 and 86 of the Treaty of Rome (1957). See Case 48/69, *ICI v Commission* [1972] ECR 619; CMLR 557; 48 ILR 106; Case 89/85, *A Ahlstrom v Commission* [1988] 4 CMLR 901; FA Mann (1989) 38 ICLQ 375.

175 Protection of Trading Interests Act 1980, s 3.

176 *Ibid*, s 5.

The most controversial element of the legislation is probably s 6 which enables a United Kingdom national or resident to sue in the United Kingdom to recover sums paid in multiple damages by order of a foreign court. The creation of such a cause of action is designed to discourage private plaintiffs from seeking multiple damages in the United States and acts in effect as a 'claw back provision'. Since the prospective defendant (who will have been the plaintiff in the foreign proceedings) is unlikely to be present within the jurisdiction s 6(5) of the legislation provides for the amendment of RSC Order 11 to permit enable a claim form to be served out of the jurisdiction without the leave of the court.[177]

While the willingness of the American courts to make wide claims of jurisdiction in anti-trust matters has given rise to problems these concerns have been heightened in respect of actions by the United States Congress. In the last decade the United States has sought to bring trade pressure through sanctions against regimes considered to have violated international law. The first step was taken in the Cuban Democracy Act 1992 which prohibited the granting of licences in respect of certain transactions with Cuba; the scope of the legislation extended to United States companies owned or controlled in the United Kingdom. This original legislation was amended by the Cuban Liberty and Democratic Solidarity Act 1996 (LIBERTAD or the Helms Burton legislation).[178] In essence the legislation provided for the imposition of penalties on individuals or companies investing in Cuba regardless of their nationality; further the legislation provided for legal proceedings in the United States courts against foreign persons or companies deemed to be 'trafficking' in property expropriated by Cuba from American nationals. The legislation also provided for the United States to deny entry into the country of those executives whose companies were considered to be engaged in such 'trafficking'. The purpose of such legislation was to promote the foreign policy objectives of the United States not to protect domestic markets. In the same year Congress enacted the Iran-Libya Sanctions Act 1996 (D'Amato Act) which imposed sanctions on individuals or companies investing in these two countries regardless of their nationality. These two pieces of legislation resulted in protests by the European Union and an indication by the United States Government that it would suspend some aspects of the Helms-Burton Act. The legislation also resulted in criticism from the Inter-American Juridical Committee of the Organisation of American states. The substance of the European objection was that the United States was seeking to regulate the conduct of European subsidiaries of United States companies and to exercise control over goods and technology of United States origin situate beyond its territory.[179]

Experience indicates that there is a potential conflict between the traditional territorial principle and attempts to extend the protective principle and the 'effects doctrine' The traditional United Kingdom view is that a state 'acts in excess of its own jurisdiction when its measures purport to regulate acts which are done outside its territorial jurisdiction by persons who are not its own nationals and which have no, or no

---

177 See RSC Ord 11 r 1(2)(b).

178 See generally, AF Lowenfeld, 'Congress and Cuba: the Helms Burton Act' (1996) 90 AJIL 419.

179 In the context of Cuba, the United States General Assembly had called on the United States to end the embargo against Cuba in GA Res 50/10 (1995).

substantial, effect within that jurisdiction'.[180] So where acts are unlawful in state A but lawful in state B then it is argued that in respect of acts undertaken in state B then the authorities of state A should claim jurisdiction only against their own nationals. However, while the international community tends to understand that a state might need to act to protect its own domestic interests less tolerance is likely to be exhibited when the state is using extra-territorial legislation to accomplish foreign policy objectives particularly where those foreign policy objectives can be obtained by diplomacy or through the agency of the United Nations.

---

180 Sir John Hobson (Attorney General) July 1964; for an earlier problem, see Shipping Contracts and Commercial Documents Act 1964.

CHAPTER 9

SOVEREIGN IMMUNITY[1]

1 INTRODUCTION

In considering the topic of jurisdiction it was posited that state A would *prima facie* enjoy jurisdiction within its own territory in criminal and civil matters by virtue of its sovereignty. Such jurisdiction would in principle embrace its entire territory. It was noted elsewhere that in customary international law each state was in principle equal and none superior to another. Thus, simply at the theoretical level it was difficult to contemplate a situation in which the courts of state A could sit in judgment over a ruler of state B in respect of sovereign acts committed within his own territory. The concept of immunity from jurisdiction has from the outset been closely linked with the related concept of the sovereign equality of states. Aside from the principle that *par in parem non habet imperium* a number of justifications were advanced. Some argued that the immunity was linked to questions of comity while others argued that if a ruler of state B entered the territory of state A then the immunity arose by implied grant. Neither of these explanations was completely satisfactory but it was recognised in the 18th century that in some circumstances a foreign head of state, a diplomatic representative or a public ship might enjoy a certain immunity from jurisdiction. Such an immunity might take the form of immunity from the process of the court or it might concern the property belonging to a foreign state.[2]

The role of immunity is to act as a barrier to the jurisdiction of the state which would exist but for the operation of the doctrine of immunity. It is normally said that the immunity can be waived by the state entitled to assert it. The concept of state immunity is a doctrine of public international law and has to be distinguished from the related doctrines of non-justiciability and act of state. The concept of non-justiciability is a doctrine of private international law and holds that in certain circumstances the courts of state A will refrain from adjudicating on the domestic or foreign acts of a sovereign government.[3] Related to this is the doctrine of act of state much favoured by courts in the United States which holds that in certain circumstances the courts cannot review the

---

1   See generally, RY Jennings and AD Watts, *Oppenheim's International Law*, 9th edn, 1992, p 341; I Brownlie, *Principles of Public International Law*, 5th edn, 1998, pp 325–48; H Lauterpacht, 'The problem of the jurisdictional immunities of foreign states' (1951) 28 BYIL 220; S Sucharitkul, 'Immunities of foreign states before national authorities' (1976) 149 HR 87; I Sinclair, 'The law of sovereign immunity: recent developments' (1980) 167 HR 113; J Crawford, 'International law of foreign sovereigns: distinguishing immune transactions' (1983) 54 BYIL 75; P Trooboff, 'Foreign state immunity: emerging consensus on principles' (1986) 200 HR 235; C Whomersley, 'Some reflections on immunity of individuals for official acts' (1992) 41 ICLQ 848; H Fox, 'Jurisdiction and immunities', in AV Lowe and M Fitzmaurice (eds), *Fifty Years of the International Court of Justice*, 1996, pp 210–36.

2   *Compania Naviera Vascongado v SS Cristina* [1938] AC 385.

3   *Duke of Brunswick v Hanover* (1848) 1 HLC 1; *Buttes Gas and Oil Co v Hammer (No 3)* [1982] AC 888.

executive acts of a foreign government committed within its own territory.[4] This matter will be returned to later in the chapter.

The doctrine of sovereign immunity came to be accepted in the 18th century when the state was but the individual ruler and the immunity might only concern himself a limited number of diplomatic officials and a some naval vessels. That the doctrine followed from the principles of equality and territorial sovereignty was recognised by Marshall CJ in *The Schooner Exchange v McFaddon*[5] where the judge observed:

> One sovereign being in no respect amenable to another, and being bound by obligations of the highest character not to degrade the dignity of his nation, by placing himself or its sovereign rights within the jurisdiction of another, can be supposed to enter a foreign territory only under an express license or in the confidence that the immunities belonging to his independent sovereign station, though not expressly stipulated, are reserved by implication, and will be extended to him.

> This perfect equality and absolute independence of sovereigns, and this common interest compelling them to mutual intercourse, and an interchange of good offices with each other, have given rise to a class of cases in which every sovereign is understood to waive the exercise of a part of that complete exclusive territorial jurisdiction which has been stated to be the attribute of every nation.

In the early 19th century the actual role of government was very limited so that the grant of immunity extended to the ruler and diplomats in respect of all forms of activity. Such an unqualified concept of immunity was referred to as the doctrine of absolute immunity and it held that subject to limited exceptions a foreign state or sovereign was immune from the jurisdiction of the courts.[6] Although some early cases[7] in England are rather ambiguous, the judiciary had adopted the doctrine of absolute immunity by the last quarter of the 19th century. In the *Parlement Belge* the Court of Appeal[8] ruled that a sovereign state[9] could not be impleaded either by being served *in personam* or indirectly

---

4   This has to be kept separate from the doctrine in English constitutional law of act of state whereby an English court may refrain from adjudicating upon executive acts. See *Buron v Denman* (1848) 2 Ex 167; 145 ER 450 *Walker v Baird* [1892] AC 491; *Johnstone v Pedlar* [1921] AC 262; *Nissan v Attorney General* [1970] AC 179. Sometimes writers draw a distinction between act of state and act of foreign state.

5   (1812) 7 Cranch 116.

6   The exceptions to the general rule of absolute immunity were: (a) where the dispute concerned title to land in England; (b) where the dispute concerned trust funds situated in England or monies for payment of creditors (*Lariviere v Morgan* (1872) 7 Ch App 550); (c) debts incurred in respect of services to its property here (see Lord Denning MR in *Thai Europa Tapioco Service Ltd v Government of Pakistan* (1975)); (d) cases where a foreign government enters into a contract in England in respect of property situate here, although in such cases there might be some form of arbitration clause that constituted a voluntary submission to arbitration (see *President of India v Metcalfe Shipping Co Ltd* [1970] 1 QB 289).

7   *The Prins Frederick* (1820) 2 Dod 451; *Duke of Brunswick v King of Hanover* (1848) 2 HLC 1; *De Haber v Queen of Portugal* (1851) 17 Cl B 171.

8   (1880) 5 PD 197 reversing the ruling at first instance on this point of Phillimore J (1879) 4 PD 129. Phillimore J had adopted a much more cautious approach in the earlier case of *The Charkieh* (1873) LR 8 QB 197.

9   The immunity of the foreign ruler also embraced acts conducted in his private life, see *Mighell v The Sultan of Johore* [1894] 1 QB 149 (where the Court of Appeal applied the principle in *Parlement Belge* (1880) LR 5 PD 197 to an action for breach of promise to marry). Noted by M Nash (1999) 149 NLJ 182.

by proceedings against its property. The general outlook of the English courts was set out by Brett LJ in the Court of Appeal in the *Parlement Belge* where he observed:

> The principle to be deduced from all these cases[10] is that, as a consequence of the absolute independence of every sovereign authority, and of the international comity which induces every sovereign state to respect the independence and dignity of every other sovereign state, each and every one declines to exercise by means of its Courts any of its territorial jurisdiction over the person of any sovereign or ambassador of any other state, or over the public property of any state which is destined to public use, or over the property of any ambassador, though such sovereign, ambassador or property be within its territory, and therefore, but for common agreement subject to its jurisdiction.

The actual decision in the *Parlement Belge*[11] turned on a public vessel being used to transport mail and was in many ways indicative of the problems that began to arise at the end of the 19th century when states began to engage in a wide variety of commercial activities. At the time the Court of Appeal judgment appeared to indicate that a foreign state owned ship was entitled to immunity even though engaged in commercial activities or undertaking acts beyond those of public service.

The alternative to the doctrine of absolute immunity was the doctrine of restrictive immunity; in broad terms this doctrine drew a distinction between the acts of a state in its sovereign capacity (*acta jure imperii*) and acts of a state of a commercial or private law nature (*acta jure gestionis*). In principle under this doctrine immunity would be granted to the former but not to the latter. The problem began to emerge around the time of the First World War when governments began to undertake acts and direct economies to a much greater extent than their *laissez-faire* predecessors would have contemplated.[12] At this point, certain civil law countries began to move towards the restrictive approach while common law countries remained with the absolute immunity doctrine. Thus, a number of judgments can be cited in Italy[13] and Belgium[14] where the court had refused immunity to a foreign state in respect of *acta jure gestionis*.

2 THE EVOLUTION OF THE LAW ON IMMUNITY IN ENGLAND

Although the absolute immunity doctrine remained the orthodox position in England until after 1945 an examination of the case law indicates increasing judicial misgiving.

---

10   In a detailed reserved judgment, Brett LJ considered *The Schooner Exchange* (1812) 7 Cranch 116; *The Prins Frederick* (1820) 2 Dod 451; *The Santissima Trinidad* (1822) 7 Wheat 283; *Duke of Brunswick v King of Hanover* (1848) 6 Beav 1; *De Haber v The Queen of Portugal* (1851) 17 QB 171; *Vavasseur v Krupp* (1878) 9 Ch D 351.

11   The case of *Parlement Belge* (1879) 4 PD 129; (1880) 5 PD 197 concerned an unarmed packet belonging to the King of the Belgians which was engaged in the carrying of mails, as well as passengers and merchandise. The action was one *in rem* arising out of a collision. At first instance, Phillimore J had held that the *Parlement Belge* was not a public vessel. This determination was reversed by the Court of Appeal (Brett, James, Baggallay LJJ).

12   The change in state conduct is referred to by Scrutton LJ in *The Porto Alexandre* [1920] P 30 and Lord Maugham in *The Cristina* [1938] AC 485.

13   *Storelli v French Republic* (1924) 2 ILR 66; *Perrucchetti v Puig y Castro* (1928) 4 ILR 247.

14   *Soc Monnoyer et Bernard v France* (1928) 4 ILR 112; *Brasseur v Republic of Greece* (1932) 6 ILR 85. See H Lauterpacht, 'The problem of jurisdictional immunities of foreign states' (1951) 28 BYIL 220.

The confirmation of the absolute immunity doctrine in *The Parlement Belge*[15] was followed for over 50 years but with increasing reservations. The matter came before the Court of Appeal in *The Porto Alexandre*[16] which concerned a writ issued against a Portuguese requisitioned vessel for non-payment of salvage charges. A strong Court of Appeal[17] upheld the ruling of Hill J that immunity could be claimed simply on evidence that the vessel was the property of a sovereign state notwithstanding the fact that it was engaged in private trading operations. It was therefore important to determine whether an entity was or was not a state so as to attract immunity. In *Duff Development Company v Kelanton*[18] the House of Lords accepted that the statement in the executive certificate as to whether the entity was a state was conclusive. An unrecognised entity would not be able to claim immunity.[19]

Further evidence of judicial dissatisfaction with the rule of absolute immunity was displayed in the case of *The Cristina*.[20] In that case the Spanish Republican government made an order requisitioning all vessels in Bilbao but at the time of the issue of the decree the Cristina was on the high seas. When the vessel docked at Cardiff the Republican authorities took possession of the vessel and the owners sued for possession. The proceedings turned on the question as to whether the Republican government was entitled to have the case dismissed by virtue of sovereign immunity. However, in the course of giving judgment Lord Thankerton and Lord Macmillan questioned the correctness of the *Porto Alexandre*[21] while Lord Maugham openly indicated that the immunity extended to public ships engaged in commercial undertakings was inappropriate having regard to the growth in state owned commercial fleets after 1919. However, notwithstanding the criticism of the state of the law there was little doubt that the doctrine of absolute immunity extended to the ruler and state property and this continued to represent the law into the post-war period.

A further problem arose as to what exactly constituted a department of state. In *Krajina v The Tass Agency* the Court of Appeal[22] was prepared to accept the evidence of the Soviet Ambassador that the Tass Agency was a department of state and entitled to immunity in respect of libel proceedings. However, Singleton LJ used his judgment to indicate how unsatisfactory such a conclusion was. Further problems could arise if the entity had separate legal personality. In *Baccus SRL v Servicio Nacional del Trigo*[23] the defendants were able to claim immunity as a department of state of the Spanish government notwithstanding that they enjoyed corporate status and separate legal

---

15 *Parlement Belge* (1880) 5 PD 197.

16 [1920] P 30.

17 *The Porto Alexandre* [1920] P 30 (Hill J, Scrutton, Bankes and Warrington LJJ). It is not without interest that even in 1920 the judges expressed concern at such a degree of immunity. Scrutton LJ in particular thought the position was in need of reform.

18 [1924] AC 797; (1924) 2 ILR 124.

19 *The Gagara* [1919] P 95; *The Annette and The Dora* [1919] P 105; *The Jupiter* [1927] P 122.

20 *Compania Naviera Vascongado v SS Cristina* [1938] AC 485.

21 *The Porto Alexandre* [1920] P 30.

22 *Krajina v The Tass Agency* [1949] 2 All ER 274; 16 ILR 129 (Birkett J; Tucker, Cohen, Singleton LJJ).

23 *Baccus SRL v Servcio Nacional del Trigo* [1957] 1 QB 438 (Pearce J; Parker, Jenkins, Singleton LJJ dissenting).

personality. It seemed that whether a body was a department of state or not was to be determined under the relevant law constituting the body.[24] Although the rule of absolute immunity remained firmly in place signs could be detected of a more sceptical judicial attitude.[25] In *Rahimtoola v Nizam of Hyderabad*,[26] Lord Denning called for the adoption of the restrictive theory by the English courts and addressed the problem thus:

> ... sovereign immunity should not depend on whether a foreign government is impleaded, directly or indirectly, but rather on the nature of the dispute ... Is it properly cognisable by our courts or not? If the dispute brings into question, for instance, the legislative or international transactions of a foreign government, or the policy of its executive, the court should grant immunity if asked to do so ... but if the dispute concerns, for instance, the commercial transactions of a foreign government (whether carried on by its own departments or agencies or by the setting up separate legal entities) and it arises properly within the territorial jurisdiction of our own courts, there is no ground for immunity.[27]

3 THE MOVEMENT TOWARDS THE DOCTRINE OF RESTRICTIVE IMMUNITY

The end of the Second World War had left the Soviet Army in a position to dominate Eastern Europe and within a couple of years single party governments operating a command economy became the norm. This had the consequence that may more state agencies might seek to claim immunity in the courts of Western Europe. Not surprisingly the trend of Western European opinion began to move in favour of the restrictive doctrine of immunity.

By the late 1950s, a number of states had either adopted the approach of restrictive immunity or they had limited the circumstances in which absolute immunity arose. Thus, in the United States the Supreme Court considered that the doctrine of absolute immunity was inappropriate in the modern age[28] and it was settled that a state owned vessel was not entitled to claim immunity when it had been chartered to a private company.[29] Part of the concern in the United States was the unfair advantage that might be available to state concerns in Eastern Europe if the law did not evolve. This concern was shared elsewhere and in *Drelle v Republic of Czechoslovakia* the Supreme Court of Austria questioned whether the rule of absolute immunity remained a rule of international law.[30]

---

24 So that in the *Tass Agency* case it would be a matter of Soviet law while the status of Servicio del Trigo was to be determined under Spanish law.

25 *United States and France v Dollfus Mieg et Compagnie* [1952] AC 582; 19 ILR 163; *Juan Ysmael v Republic of Indonesia* [1955] AC 72; 21 ILR 95.

26 *Rahimtoola v Nizam of Hyderabad* [1958] AC 379.

27 *Ibid*, p 422.

28 *Larson v Domestic and Foreign Corporation* (1949) 337 US 682, p 703: '... the principle of sovereign immunity is an archaic hangover not consonant with modern morality and that it should be limited whenever possible.'

29 *The Navemar* (1938) 303 US 68; 9 ILR 176; *Republic of Mexico v Hoffman* (1945) 324 US 30; 12 ILR 143.

30 *Drelle v Republic of Czechoslovakia* (1950) 17 ILR 155; see Abell (1951) 45 AJIL 354. See also the speeches of Lord Evershed MR in the *Dollfus Mieg* case [1950] 1 Ch 333 and Lord Simon in the Privy Council in *Sultan of Johore v Abubakar* [1952] AC 318.

An important step was taken in 1952 when the United States Department of State in the form of the 'Tate Letter' expressly adopted the restrictive doctrine of immunity.[31] This statement of executive policy was followed in the courts both in the Court of Appeals in *Victory Transport Inc v Comisaria General de Abastecimentos y Transportes*[32] and later in the Supreme Court in *Alfred Dunhill of London Inc v Republic of Cuba*.[33] This movement in the United States was mirrored in Europe. In Germany in 1963 the *Bundesverfassunsgericht* came down in favour of the restrictive approach in *The Claim against the Empire of Iran*[34] while judgments to like effect were delivered in Switzerland[35] and The Netherlands.[36]

So that, by the late 1960s, the restrictive doctrine was being applied in most European states and in the United States. However, the United Kingdom became one of the last to renounce the absolute doctrine. Thus, in *Mellenger v New Brunswick Development Corporation*[37] the Court of Appeal was prepared to accept that a claim of sovereign immunity could be made in respect of a corporate body established by the Province of New Brunswick to promote industrial development. In the subsequent case of *Thai Europe Ltd v Pakistan Government*[38] the Court of Appeal recognised that while there might be exceptions to the principle of sovereign immunity they would only be relevant where there was some connection with the jurisdiction. In that case, German shipowners sued the government of Pakistan as successors in title under bills of lading to recover sums as demurrage in respect of the carriage of goods from Poland to Pakistan when such a contract had been disrupted by the 1971 India-Pakistan war. Lord Denning MR in upholding the setting aside the writ was influenced by the fact that not only was the claim *in personam* but that the entire transaction took place outside the United Kingdom and was outside any then recognised exception to sovereign immunity.

The movement towards the restrictive theory in England took place in stages. The first breach was made in *The Philippine Admiral*[39] which was a Privy Council appeal from Hong Kong in an action *in rem*. The claim itself was made by two Hong Kong shipping corporations against a vessel owned by the Philippine government. In giving judgment for the Privy Council, Lord Cross held that sovereign immunity could not be claimed in an action *in rem* in respect of a state owned vehicle engaged in commerce. The learned judge ruled that *The Porto Alexandre*[40] had been wrongly decided and the criticisms made in *The Cristina* were valid. Secondly, that the majority of the trading world was moving

---

31 The letter written by JB Tate, Acting Legal Adviser to the Department of State, indicated the future policy of the Department in respect of questions of immunity. Although, of course, the courts would be free to follow their own course in those cases where the advice of the Department was not required.

32 *Victory Transport Inc v Comisaria General de Abastecimientos y Transportes* (1964) 35 ILR 110.

33 (1976) 15 ILM 735; (1976) 66 ILR 212.

34 *Claim against the Empire of Iran* (1963) 45 ILR 57 (which concerned payment for the cost of repairs to the heating at the Iranian Embassy).

35 *Arab Republic of Egypt v Cinetelevision International Registered Trust* (1965) 65 ILR 425.

36 *Krol v Bank Indonesia* (1958) 26 ILR 180.

37 *Mellenger v New Brunswick Development Corporation* [1971] 1 WLR 601 (Kilner Brown J; Lord Denning MR, Salmon, Phillimore LJJ). Although there was no question of commercial dealing in this case.

38 [1975] 1 WLR 1485; 64 ILR 81.

39 *The Philippine Admiral* [1977] AC 373; see (1976) 92 LQR 166.

40 *The Porto Alexandre* [1920] P 30.

towards the restrictive theory and even more relevantly that if a state could be sued on trading contracts in its own courts it was anomalous that it could claim a general immunity in the courts of other states. Had such a judgment stood for long then the rules would have been different for actions *in rem* and actions *in personam*. However, such a division did not last long because the Court of Appeal was required to consider a claim for immunity when an action was brought *in personam*. In *Trendtex Corporation v Central Bank of Nigeria*[41] the plaintiffs sued the defendants for refusing to honour a letter of credit in respect of a contract for the supply of concrete. In allowing an appeal from Donaldson J and refusing immunity the majority of the Court of Appeal held not only that customary international law now favoured the restrictive approach but also that the court was not bound by the doctrine of *stare decisis* to apply the rule of absolute immunity.[42] So by the late 1970s, the English courts[43] had moved in favour of the restrictive approach.[44] Any uncertainty as to the state of the common law was clarified by the judgment of Lloyd J in *Planmount Ltd v Republic of Zaire*[45] where the learned judge after reviewing a number of conflicting authorities concluded that 'prior to the passing of the State Immunity Act 1978, a foreign state had no absolute immunity in the English courts whether the action be *in rem* or *in personam*'.[46]

In the wider world, civil law countries already accepted the restrictive approach but they were now joined by common law countries who passed legislation to give effect to the qualified or restrictive approach. Amongst the more significant pieces of legislation were the United States Foreign Sovereign Immunities Act (1976),[47] the Canadian State Immunity Act 1982 and the Australian Foreign States Immunities Act (1985).[48] On the international stage the European Convention on State Immunity (1972) and the Montreal Draft Convention on State Immunity prepared by the International Law Association in 1982 both proceeded on the basis of qualified or restrictive immunity.[49] In these circumstances it was inevitable that the United Kingdom would come into line and the enactment of the State Immunity Act 1978 provided for the adoption of the restrictive approach by stipulating in s 3 that foreign states would not be able to claim immunity in respect of commercial contracts.

---

41 *Trendtex Trading Corporation Ltd v Central Bank of Nigeria* [1977] QB 529.

42 *Ibid* (at least this was the view of the majority, Lord Denning MR and Shaw LJ. The third judge Stephenson LJ accepted that customary law had changed to recognise a rule of restrictive immunity but felt bound by the doctrine of precedent to follow the rule of absolute immunity). See B Markesinis (1977) 36 CLJ 211; White (1977) 26 ICLQ 674; see also (1977) 93 LQR 330.

43 Some reference to the general history in England is made in *Holland v Lampen-Wolfe* [2000] 1 WLR 1573.

44 See *Uganda Co (Holdings) Ltd v Government of Uganda* [1979] 1 Lloyd's Rep 481; *Hispano Americana Mercantil SA v Central Bank of Nigeria* [1979] 2 Lloyd's Rep 277.

45 *Planmount Ltd v Republic of Zaire* [1981] 2 All ER 1064; 64 ILR 309. (Although decided in 1980, the case concerned a contract concluded prior to the coming into effect of the State Immunity Act 1978 and was thus governed by common law.)

46 [1981] 2 All ER 1064, p 1068, *per* Lloyd J.

47 See (1976) 70 AJIL 298.

48 Other examples being State Immunity Act 1979 (Singapore); State Immunity Ordinance 1981 (Pakistan); Foreign States Immunities Act 1981 (South Africa).

49 As indeed so do the ILC Draft Articles on Jurisdictional Immunities of States and their Property (1991).

4 THE DISTINCTION BETWEEN SOVEREIGN AND NON-SOVEREIGN ACTS

With the adoption of the restrictive theory it becomes important to distinguish between those acts for which immunity can be claimed and those where it cannot. In most countries it will be a question of statutory interpretation and there is some authority for the view in the United Kingdom that the State Immunity Act 1978 represents a complete code beyond which no recourse is necessary.[50] The tendency in modern legislation[51] has been to set out the general principle of immunity and then to stipulate a number of exceptional cases where the immunity does not arise. In these circumstances as a matter of statutory construction it will be for the party alleging that the case is within one of the exceptions to bear the *onus probandi*. This drafting approach is taken by the International Law Commission in their Draft Article on the Jurisdictional Immunities of States and Their Property. Article 5 reads:

> A state enjoys immunity in respect of itself and its property, from the jurisdiction of the courts of another state subject to the provisions of the present articles.

Adopting the restrictive theory means drawing a distinction between sovereign acts (*acta jure imperii*) and non-sovereign acts (*acta jure gestionis*). In some cases this is obvious, such as the decision to order military operations. However, in many cases drawing a distinction is not so straightforward. One approach is to look at the nature of the act in issue (that is, the objective approach); a second approach is to look at the purpose of the act (that is, the subjective approach). Suppose we take the case of state A purchasing 10,000 pairs of boots for its army. According to the objective approach that is a commercial contract and a non-sovereign act; however it is strongly arguable that by the subjective approach it would be a sovereign act. The modern tendency has been to follow the objective or nature test and this approach has found favour in a number of jurisdictions.[52] Indeed it is arguable that the purpose test is unsatisfactory because all of the *intra vires* acts of the state have some form of public purpose;[53] the state is always acting on behalf of the community as a whole. Thus, there have been a number of authorities that hold that the purpose is irrelevant to the determination.[54]

A third possible approach alluded to by the United States Court of Appeals in the *Victory Transport* case[55] was to examine the different type of state acts and classify them in advance as to whether they were *acta jure imperii* or *acta jure gestionis*. In principle such classification would be done by municipal legislature so that legislative acts regarding the armed forces might be categorised as *jure imperii*. The difficulty with such an approach is that acts are rarely so clear cut and such a system lacks the flexibility that individual cases

---

50 *Al Adsani v Government of Kuwait* [1996] 1 Lloyd's Rep 104.

51 This is the approach adopted in State Immunity Act 1978, s 1. See, also, s 1604 United States Foreign Sovereign Immunities Act 1976; s 9 Australian Foreign State Immunities Act 1985.

52 *Claim Against the Empire of Iran* (1963) 45 ILR 57; *I Congresso del Partido* [1983] 1 AC 244.

53 *Victory Transport Inc v Comisaria General De Abastecimientos y Transpertos* (1963) 35 ILR 110.

54 *Trendtex Trading Corporation v Central Bank of Nigeria* [1977] QB 529; *I Congresso del Partido* [1983] 1 AC 244; *Kuwait Airways Corporation v Iraqi Airways Company* [1995] 1 WLR 1147.

55 (1963) 35 ILR 110.

may require. When many of the individual cases turn on judgments of fact and degree there seems little value in such an approach.

It is sometimes argued that a fourth approach can be detected in the judgment of the House of Lords in the case of *I Congresso del Partido*.[56] Although the case reached the highest tribunal after the State Immunity Act 1978 had come into effect the facts arose prior to that date and were governed by customary international law. The case concerned two ships (*The Playa Larga* and *The Marble Islands*) which had been transporting sugar to Chile when they were ordered by the Cuban government to abort the voyage and to discharge the cargo elsewhere. The conduct of the Cuban government was dictated by news a change of government in Chile.[57] At a later date, the Chilean owners of the cargo brought an action *in rem* against *I Congresso*, another ship owned by the Cuban government. The Cuban government claimed sovereign immunity.

The approach of the House of Lords was to insist that the entire context had to be surveyed and in particular both the initial relationship between the parties and the act giving rise to the dispute. Once a state had entered the trading arena in order to claim immunity it would be necessary to demonstrate some act was clearly done *jure imperii*. In the context of the *Playa Larga* the original contract was a trading contract and the decision to order the vessel to cease unloading at Valpariso was a decision that any owner could have taken and thus there was no room for a plea of immunity. In the context of the other vessel the *Marble Islands* the minority took the view that the decision of the Cuban government to order the disposal of the cargo was an act done in its governmental capacity while the majority held that the acquisition of title to the vessel had made the Cuban government bailee of the sugar and the subsequent decision to hand it over to unauthorised third parties was a private law act giving rise to liability in conversion.

The case itself indicates the importance of a two stage test namely that examination of the initial relationship should be followed by an examination of the act that gave rise to the dispute and that a plea of immunity could only be maintained if a state could point to an act that was *jure imperii*.

The matter was succinctly stated by Lord Wilberforce when he observed:[58]

> Under the 'restrictive theory' the court has first to characterise the activity into which the defendant state has entered. Having done this, and (assumedly) found it to be of a commercial, or private law, character it may take the view that commercial breaches, or torts, *prima facie* fall within the same sphere of activity. It should then be for the defendant state to make out a case that the act complained of is outside that sphere, and within that of sovereign action.

So as the learned judge indicated the task of the court is to:

> ... consider the whole context in which the claim against the state is made, with a view to deciding whether the relevant act(s) upon which the claim is based, should, in that context,

---

56 *I Congresso del Partido* [1983] 1 AC 244. For earlier proceedings, see (1980) ILR (Waller LJ, Lord Denning MR); [1978] QB 500 (Robert Goff J). For a general discussion, see H Fox, 'State immunity: the House of Lords' decision in *I Congresso del Partido*' (1982) 98 LQR 94.

57 The military coup against President Allende in September 1973 and the assumption of power by General Pinochet.

58 *I Congresso Del Partido* [1983] 1 AC 244.

be considered as fairly within an area of activity, trading or commercial, or otherwise of a private law character, in which the state has chosen to engage, or whether the relevant act(s) should be considered as having been done outside that area, and within the sphere of governmental or sovereign activity.[59]

However, while the test can be easily stated its application may be difficult as the differing opinions in the case indicate.[60] Notwithstanding such difficulties, the two stage test was applied by Browne WIlkinson J in *Sengupta v Republic of India*[61] and by Hoffmann LJ in *Littrell v United States of America (No 2)*[62] both being cases which fell to be decided outside the State Immunity Act 1978. Further, in *Holland v Lampen-Wolfe*[63] which also fell to be decided at common law the House of Lords approved the approach in *I Congresso* and held that whether an act is to be categorised as *jure imperii* or *jure gestionis* 'must be judged against the background of the whole context in which the claim is made'.[64]

In other jurisdictions there has been a willingness to look at the entire background and in assessing the nature of the transaction it has been held proper to look at the context or location in which the dispute arose. Thus, in *United States v The Public Service Alliance of Canada*,[65] the Canadian Supreme Court was prepared to look at both the nature of the act (an employment contract) and the location or context in which it arose (the military base of a foreign state) before concluding that immunity could be claimed under that Canadian State Immunity Act 1985. This flexible two stage approach lead the court to conclude that the United States was able to claim immunity.

In some jurisdictions a desire for flexibility has lead the court to stress the importance of determining the nature of an act by considering evidence as to its purpose[66] while some courts have stressed the difficulty of completely disentangling the act from its purpose.[67]

---

59 *I Congresso Del Partido* [1983] 1 AC 244.

60 The case revealed a division of opinion between the majority (Lord Diplock, Lord Bridge and Lord Keith) and the minority (Lord Wilberforce and Lord Edmund Davies) as to the application of the test.

61 *Sengupta v Republic of India* (1983) ICR 221. In that case, the claim arising from an employment dispute was excluded from the State Immunity Act 1978 by s 4(2)(a). Of interest is the passage in ruling of the Employment Appeal Tribunal given by Browne-Wilkinson J where he observed: 'Mrs Higgins further submitted that the question of immunity has to be decided by reference solely to the terms of the contract without regard to the breach of it by the state ... We reject this submission ... the decision of the House of Lords in *I Congresso del Partido* shows that the question does not fall to be decided solely by reference to the nature of the underlying contract and without reference to the nature of the breach.'

62 *Littrell v United States of America (No 2)* [1995] 1 WLR 82 (a case of personal injuries brought in respect of alleged conduct at a United States military hospital in the United Kingdom and thus outside the State Immunity Act 1978 by virtue of s 16(2)). The same approach was followed by a differently constituted Court of Appeal (Nourse and Hutchison LJJ, Sir John Balcombe) in *Holland v Lampen Wolfe* [1998] 1 WLR 188 where sovereign immunity was raised in the context of a libel claim arising from conduct within a military establishment.

63 *Holland v Lampen-Wolfe* [2000] 1 WLR 1573 (the substance of the dispute was excluded from the State Immunity Act 1978 by s 16(2)).

64 *Holland v Lampen-Wolfe* [2000] 1 WLR 1573, p 1585, *per* Lord Millett.

65 *United States v The Public Service Alliance of Canada* (1993) 32 ILM 1.

66 *De Sanchez v Banco Central de Nicaragua and others* (1985) 770 F 2d 1385; 88 ILR 75.

67 *Reid v Republic of Nauru* (1993) 1 VR 251; 101 ILR 193.

In the United Kingdom the doctrine of precedent has meant that in subsequent cases the guidelines in *I Congresso del Partido* have been applied,[68] although there has been a willingness to express the matter in terms of context in particular where the problem arises under domestic legislation. As Mummery J noted in *Arab Republic of Egypt v Gamal Eldin*,[69] 'the proper approach to the question whether an activity is commercial or in the exercise of sovereign authority involves looking at all the circumstances in relation to the activities and their context and then consider all the factors together. No one factor is in itself determinative in characterising the activity as sovereign or non-sovereign. It is relevant to look at the nature of the activity, the identity of those who deal with it, and the place where it takes place in order to resolve this question'.

In the context of immunity two other questions arise that deserve consideration. First, can an act that is classified as *jure imperii* cease to be so by subsequent conduct? Secondly, are there any circumstances in which immunity cannot be claimed because the act in question is at variance with general rules of public international law? It is proposed to deal with the second question later in the Chapter 10.

In respect of the first question it is clear that in some circumstances the classification of an act may change by virtue of subsequent event. This was illustrated by the House of Lords judgment in *Kuwait Airways Corporation v Iraqi Airways Co*.[70] In essence the facts were that following the invasion of Kuwait by Iraq in August 1990 the Iraqi Airways Corporation were ordered by Iraqi government to seize a number of aircraft belonging to the plaintiffs and to fly them to Iraq. In September 1990, an Iraqi legislative enactment purported to dissolve the plaintiff company and vest title to the aircraft in the Iraqi Aircraft Company. In 1991, the plaintiffs bought proceedings in London seeking a return of the aircraft and damages and the defendants raised a defence of state immunity. A majority of the House of Lords held that while immunity could be claimed in respect of the seizure of the planes as they were acts directly ordered by government once the planes had been vested in the defendant company then the subsequent retention of the aircraft was not done under sovereign authority and represented a continuing act of conversion for which an action could be maintained in private law. The case itself turned on whether at any time the Iraqi Aircraft Company was acting independently of the Republic of Iraq. Having regard to the factual situation it was perhaps not surprising that two Law Lords concluded that it was unrealistic to separate the time periods and they were prepared to conclude that at all times the defendants were acting under sovereign orders.

---

68 *Kuwait Airways Corporation v Iraqi Airways Company* [1995] 1 WLR 1147.

69 *Arab Republic of Egypt v Gamal Eldin and Another* [1996] 2 All ER 237, p 247.

70 *Kuwait Aircraft Corporation v Iraqi AIrways Co* [1995] 1 WLR 1147 (Lord Goff, Lord Jauncey and Lord Nicholls forming the majority; Lord Slynn and Lord Mustill constituting the minority). The matter was remitted for trial in the commercial court before Mance J who on 12 May 1998 rejected arguments drawn from private international law that the English court should recognise the legislative acts of the Iraqi government.

5 THE OPERATION OF THE STATE IMMUNITY ACT 1978[71]

(a) The general principles

As indicated above the State Immunity Act 1978 was enacted to provide a code as to the circumstances in which immunity might be granted. It came into effect on 22 November 1978 and is not retrospective; it therefore follows that cases will come before the courts where the legislation does not pertain either because the events took place before the operative date[72] or because the facts come within one of the exceptional situations where the legislation does not apply.[73] The express purpose of the legislation was to enable the United Kingdom to ratify both the 1926 Brussels Convention on the Unification of Certain Rules relating State Owned Vessels and the 1972 European Convention on State Immunity.[74] It is arguable that the legislation would be sufficient to meet the United Kingdom's obligations under the draft of the International Law Commission should that document one day enter into force. Another important objective was to ensure that the United Kingdom as a centre of trade was not damaged by rules that were thought to be unfavourable to trading interests.[75]

The legislation begins with the general principle[76] that a state will be immune from the jurisdiction of the courts of the United Kingdom save in respect of exceptional situations listed in ss 2–11. Section 2 of the legislation provides that a state shall not have immunity if it submits to the jurisdiction after the dispute giving rise to the proceedings has arisen or where there is a prior written agreement.[77] The effect of this provision is to set aside the old common law rule that a state could not agree to submit to the jurisdiction in advance.[78] Thus, Saville J was able to rule in *A Company Ltd v Republic of X*[79] that a written submission in advance could on its construction extend to both process and to pre-judgment attachment. However, a choice of law clause in favour of the law of the United Kingdom does not constitute submission.[80] Section 2(3)(a) provides that a state is

---

71 See D Bowett [1978] CLJ 193; R White (1979) 42 MLR 72; FA Mann (1979) 50 BYIL 43; G Delaume (1979) 73 AJIL 185.

72 *Hispano Americana Mercantile SA v Central Bank of Nigeria* [1979] 2 Lloyd's Rep 277; *I Congresso del Partido* [1983] 1 AC 244.

73 *Littrell v United States of America (No 2)* [1994] 2 All ER 203. (The case concerned medical provision within a military establishment). Section 16(2) of the State Immunity Act 1978 disapplies Part I of the Act where proceedings relate 'to anything done by or in relation to the armed forces of a state while present in the United Kingdom'. The provision is traceable to a like provision in Art 31 of the European Convention on State Immunity (1972).

74 The European Convention on State Immunity was signed in Basle by seven countries including the United Kingdom on 16 May 1972 and came into force on 11 June 1976.

75 See, also, Arbitration Act 1979. This concern was mentioned several times during the Parliamentary debates and was precipitated by fears that the United States Foreign Sovereign Immunities Act 1976 could lead to financial transactions being lost by the city of London.

76 State Immunity Act 1978, s 1; see also Art 15 of the European Convention on State Immunity (1972).

77 See, also, Art 1 and 2 of the European Convention on State Immunity (1972).

78 *Kahan v Pakistan Federation* [1951] 2 KB 1003; *Baccus SRL v Servicio Nacional del Trigo* [1957] 1 QB 438.

79 *A Company Ltd v Republic of X* [1990] 2 Lloyd's Rep 520 (although by operation of s 16 of the Act property subject to the Diplomatic Privileges Act 1964 will be immune).

80 State Immunity Act 1978, s 2(2).

deemed to have submitted if it has instituted the proceedings and normally submission will arise if the state has intervened in or taken any steps in the proceedings.[81] However, there will be no submission if the purpose of intervening is to assert immunity[82] or to claim an interest in property in circumstances where the state would have been able to claim immunity had the proceedings been brought directly against it.[83] For there to be waiver then there must be clear evidence of an intention to waive so that a written letter to an employee indicating that she might have certain right under United Kingdom employment could not be construed as being capable of creating a prior written agreement under s 2.[84] Similarly as a matter of construction a letter sent by a medical officer to an industrial tribunal did not constitute submission to the jurisdiction.[85] Any submission will be deemed to extend to any appeal arising out of the action but not to any counterclaim unless it arises out of the same legal relationship or facts as the claim.[86] Any submission to the jurisdiction must be by a person having the capacity to act such as the head of diplomatic mission or by an authorised agent.[87] Any question of possible immunity should in principle be decided at the outset of the hearing before the court at first instance examines the merits of the case.[88] It would seem that if a tribunal at first instance fails to consider the question of immunity because of the absence of relevant evidence then the appellate body is under a duty to consider the matter and is not precluded by rules restricting the submission of new evidence on appeal.[89]

(b) Commercial transactions[90]

It is arguable that the most important provision of the legislation is s 3, which provides that a state will not be immune in respect of 'a commercial transaction' or:

> ... an obligation of the State which by virtue of a contract (whether a commercial transaction or not) falls to be performed wholly or partly in the United Kingdom. In these circumstances the definition of a 'commercial transaction' is central and this is provided by s 3(3) which defines a commercial transaction as:
>
> (a) any contract for the supply of goods and services;
>
> (b) any loan or other transaction for the provision of finance and any guarantee or indemnity in respect of any such transaction or of any other financial obligation; and

---

81 State Immunity Act 1978, s 2(3)(b); *High Commissioner for India v Ghosh* (1960) 1 QB 134, 28 ILR 150.

82 *Ibid*, s 2(4)(a).

83 *Ibid*, s 2(4)(b). This would in principle cover the situation in *Compania Naviera Vascongada v Steamship Cristina* (1938) AC 485.

84 *Ahmed v Government of Saudi Arabia* [1996] 2 All ER 248.

85 *Arab Republic of Egypt v Gamal-Eldin* [1996] 2 All ER 237.

86 State Immunity Act 1978, s 2(6); reflecting to some extend the position at common law, see *Sultan of Johore v Abubaker Tunka Aris Bendahar* [1952] AC 318; *High Commissioner for India v Ghosh* [1960] 1 QB 134; 28 ILR 150 (CA).

87 State Immunity Act 1978, s 2(7).

88 *Maclaine Watson v Department of Trade* [1988] 3 All ER 257, p 317.

89 *United Arab Emirates v Abselghafar* (1995) ICR 65; *Arab Republic of Egypt v Gamal-Eldin* [1996] 2 All ER 237.

90 See European Convention on State Immunity (1972), Art 4.

(c) any other transaction or activity (whether of a commercial, industrial, financial professional or other similar character) into which a state enters or in which it engages otherwise than in the exercise of sovereign authority.

It is clear that the draftsman has chosen to avoid the distinction between acts *jure imperii* and acts *jure gestionis*. It is evident that matters falling within s 3(3)(a) or s 3(3)(b) are automatically commercial transactions while for the purposes of s 3(3)(c) they must be 'otherwise than in the exercise of sovereign authority' In respect of this latter expression Evans J in *Australia and New Zealand Banking Group v Commonwealth of Australia*[91] held that in interpreting s 3(3)(c) it was important to pay regard to the overall context and that a claim for negligent misstatement arising out of a loan transaction might be caught by both s 3(3)(b) and s 3(3)(c). Secondly, in respect of s 3(1)(b) it would seem that in contrast to s 3(1) (a) the contract need not have been entered into by the state itself and the formulation is wide enough to include contracts of indemnity and guarantee.[92] One of the difficulties in this context will be whether an analysis of conduct is to be subject to minute dissection or is one entitled to take a broad view of what constitutes 'sovereign activity'. Although the case did not concern commercial dealings this division of opinion is to be found in the speeches in *Kuwait Airways Corporation v Iraqi Airways Company;*[93] this latter case indicates that conduct has to be analysed in detail over time so that subsequent conduct with third parties may deprive the transaction of the protection of 'sovereign activity'.

While it is clear that a United Kingdom judge will simply follow the words of the State Immunity Act 1978 some guidance can be obtained by observing practice in the United States where the restrictive approach was adopted much earlier. The relevant United States legislation defines a 'commercial activity' as 'a regular course of commercial conduct or a particular commercial transaction or act'. The approach of the United States courts has been to focus upon the nature rather than the purpose of the act and they have not been slow to find that an activity is in substance commercial. Thus, attempts to engage in price fixing by states[94] or the operation of an insurance monopoly[95] will constitute commercial activities as will the issuing of commercial bonds.[96] In like terms the conduct of a state airline[97] or the purchase of cement[98] will be regarded as commercial activities as indeed will the issuing of foreign treasury notes.[99]

Particular difficulty has been encountered in the United States in respect of the activities of state controlled or state owned banks. In such cases a distinction has emerged between those case where the state bank acts as an internal regulator in which the act of state doctrine may preclude jurisdiction[100] and those instances where the state bank is

91 *Australia and New Zealand Banking Group v Commonwealth of Australia* (1989) (see transcript).

92 *Maclaine Watson & Co Ltd v Department of Trade and Industry* [1989] Ch 72.

93 [1995] 1 WLR 1147.

94 *International Association of Machinists and Aerospace Workers v OPEC* (1979) 477 F Supp 533; (1982) 76 AJIL 160.

95 *American International Group Inc v Islamic Republic of Iran* (1981) 75 AJIL 371.

96 *Carl Marks & Co v Union of Soviet Socialist Republics* (1988) 82 AJIL 129.

97 *Argentine Airlines v Ross* (1974) 63 ILR 195.

98 *National American Corporation v Federal Republic of Nigeria* (1977) 16 ILM 505; (1978) 17 ILM 1407.

99 *Schmidt v Polish People's Republic* (1984) 742 F 2d 67.

100 *Callejo v Bancomer SA* (1985) 24 ILM 1050.

engaged in normal operations within capital markets; in the latter instance the activity will be regarded as commercial and not subject to immunity.[101]

Although the United States has followed the restrictive doctrine since 1952 the relevant law is now set out in s 1605(a)(2) of the Foreign Sovereign Immunities Act 1976 which provides that the foreign state will not be immune in any situation 'in which the action is based upon a commercial activity carried on in the United States by the foreign state; or upon an act performed in the United States in connection with a commercial activity of the foreign state elsewhere: or upon an act outside the territory of the United States in connection with a commercial activity of the foreign state elsewhere and that act causes a direct effect in the United States'.

The sub-section embraces three elements. In respect of the first element it is clear that the commercial activity taking place in the United States must be substantial and not *de minimis*.[102] Where the act performed in the United States is in connection with a commercial activity of a foreign state elsewhere then the act within the United States must be sufficient to constitute the foundation of a legal claim.[103] In respect of the third element namely that of direct effect something of legal significance must take place within the United States.[104]

(c) Contracts of employment[105]

Section 4 of the State Immunity Act 1978 makes specific provision in respect of contracts of employment which were specifically excluded from s 3.[106] Section 4 provides that there will be no immunity in respect of contracts of employment where the contract is made in the United Kingdom or the work was to be wholly or partly performed there.[107] However, the section excludes those cases where when the proceedings are brought the individual is a national of the state concerned[108] or where the individual was neither a national of the United Kingdom nor habitually resident[109] there or where the parties have

---

101 *Alfred Dunhill of London Inc v Republic of Cuba* (1976) 425 US 682; 66 ILR 212; *Republic of Argentina v Weltover Inc* (1992) 100 ILR 509.

102 *Zedan v Kingdom of Saudi Arabia* (1988) 82 AJIL 828; 849 F 2d 1511 (US Court of Appeals).

103 *Zedan v Kingdom of Saudi Arabia* (1988) 849 F 2d 1511; *Saudi Arabia v Nelson* (1993) 100 ILR 545.

104 *Transamerican Steamship Corporation v Somali Democratic Republic* (1986) 76 AJIL 357; 767 F 2d 998; *Texas Trading & Milling Corporation v Federal Republic of Nigeria* (1981) 20 ILM 620; 647 F 2d 300; 63 ILR 552; *Zedan v Kingdom of Saudi Arabia* (1988) 849 F 2d 1511; but see also *Republic of Argentina v Weltover Inc* (1992) 100 ILR 509.

105 See Art 5, European Convention on State Immunity (1972); see H Fox, 'Employment contracts as an exception to state immunity: is all public service immune?' (1995) 66 BYIL 97; R Garnett, 'State immunity in employment matters' (1997) 46 ICLQ 81.

106 State Immunity Act 1978, s 3(3)(c).

107 *Ibid*, s 4(1).

108 As was the case in *Arab Republic of Egypt v Gamal Eldin* [1996] 2 All ER 237. This would have been the case in *Sengupta v Republic of India* (1983) ICR 221 had it not been outside the legislation because the employee had been appointed prior to the commencement date. See State Immunity Act 1978, s 4(2)(a).

109 State Immunity Act 1978, s 4(2)(b). For recent consideration of the expression 'habitually resident', see *Nessa v Chief Adjudication Officer* [1998] 2 All ER 728 (CA); [1999] 1 WLR 1937 (HL). For a review of the concept, see P Rogerson, 'Habitual residence: the new domicile' (2000) 49 ICLQ 86.

reached an agreement in writing to the contrary.[110] However, the exclusions in respect of contracts of employment have to be read with s 16(1) which disapplies the provisions in respect of members of a diplomatic mission or consular staff.[111]

(d) Other exclusions

The State Immunity Act 1978 contains a number of specific exclusions from immunity in ss 5–11. Section 5 provides that the state is not immune in respect of death or personal injury or damage to or loss of tangible property caused by an act or omission in the United Kingdom.[112] While s 6 removes immunity in respect of interests in immovable property,[113] save in respect of disputes concerning title or the right to possession of the diplomatic mission.[114] The provision also governs indirect impleading and provides that there shall be no immunity in such circumstances unless the state would have enjoyed immunity if it had been sued directly.[115] So that where Mr X sues Mr Y in respect of property and state Z also has a proprietary claim then state Z will only enjoy immunity if it would have had in a direct action. In *Re Rafidain Bank*[116] Browne Wilkinson J ruled that s 6(3) gave the court jurisdiction to hear a winding up petition in respect of a bank[117] notwithstanding that the Republic of Iraq was a substantial creditor.

Section 7 of the State Immunity Act 1978 provides that the state will not enjoy immunity in respect of proceedings relating to patents, trade marks and copyright;[118] the wording of the section is wide enough to include both disputes as to the existence of intellectual property rights and also disputes as to the exercise of such rights.[119] The provisions of s 8 prohibit immunity being claimed in respect of disputes as to the constitution of bodies corporate, unincorporated bodies or partnerships which are controlled from or have their principal place of business in the United Kingdom.

In some circumstances a state may agree in writing to submit a dispute to arbitration; s 9 of the State Immunity Act 1978 provides that in the absence of agreement to the

---

110 State Immunity Act 1978, s 4(1)(c).

111 See *Ahmed v Government of the Kingdom of Saudi Arabia* [1996] 2 All ER 248.

112 See also Art 11 of the European Convention on State Immunity (1972); Art 12, ILC Draft Articles 1991; Singapore State Immunity Act 1979, s 7; South African Foreign Sovereign Immunity Act 1981, s 6; Canadian State Immunity Act 1982, s 6. See also the somewhat wider provision in s 1605(a)(5) of the United States Foreign Sovereign Immunities Act 1976.

113 See Art 9, European Convention on State Immunity (1972).

114 State Immunity Act 1978, s 16(1)(b).

115 *Ibid*, s 6(4). For consideration of past case law on indirect impleading in the United Kingdom, see *Parlement Belge* (1880) 5 PD 197; *The Broadmayne* [1916] P 64; *Compania Naviera Vasconggad v SS Cristina* [1938] AC 485; *United States of America and Republic of France v Dollfus Mieg et Cie SA and Bank of England* [1952] AC 582; *Juan Ismael & Co Inc v Indonesian Government* [1955] AC 72; *Rahimtoola v Nizam of Hyderabad* [1958] AC 379.

116 *Re Rafidain Bank* (1992) BCLC 301.

117 Although the judge observed that different considerations arose in respect of the position of a state as owner of a company (see (1992) BCLC 301, p 304).

118 See Art 8, European Convention on State Immunity (1972); *A Ltd v B Bank and Bank of X* [1997] FSR 165.

119 For the difficulties that can arise see *Tyburn Productions Ltd v Conan Doyle* [1991] Ch 75; *Pearce v Ove Arup Partnership* [1997] Ch 293. In principle, the appropriate jurisdiction being that in which the intellectual property right arises or is granted.

contrary a state will not enjoy immunity in respect of court proceedings that relate to the arbitration.[120] Much of the litigation giving rise to problems of state immunity had concerned state owned ships used for commercial purposes. Thus, s 10 of the State Immunity Act 1978 is an important provision[121] because it provides that state owned ships used for commercial purposes should not enjoy immunity; the provisions of the enactment are broad enough to embrace not only ships owned by states but also ships in which a state has an interest. The section is widely enough drawn to include both actions *in rem*, actions *in personam* and claims in respect of cargoes. The final operative exclusion is contained in s 11 which provides that a state shall not be immune in respect of value added tax, customs duties agricultural levies and commercial rates.

6 THE STATUS OF THE ENTITY

One of the most difficult problems in the law of state immunity is who has the status to claim immunity. The question therefore arises as to when is an entity a 'state' for the purposes of the State Immunity Act 1978. Before the legislation was enacted the court would proceed on the basis of the evidence disclosed in the certificate from the Secretary of State for Foreign and Commonwealth Affairs.[122] This general approach is continued under the State Immunity Act 1978 where a certificate of the Secretary of State will be conclusive evidence as to whether any country is a state for the purpose of Part I of the legislation or whether any territory is a constituent part of a federal state.

Under s 14 of the State Immunity Act 1978 immunity is accorded to a 'state'; thus the question arises as to the status of the component parts of a federal state. In summary such a province will not have immunity and to that extent one may detect a departure from the prior law.[123] However, under the terms of s 14(5) an Order in Council may be made by the Secretary of State extending immunity to the constituent parts of a federal state.[124]

The second difficulty arises as to where the executive branch of government ends; this was a problem under the prior law as states began to engage a wide range of activities. In most cases, the argument had turned on whether the entity in question was a department of state.[125] The case law indicated that the constitution of the body in question had to be determined by reference to the *lex domicilii* but the decision as to whether the entity had the status of a department of state was to be determined according to English law.[126] The fact that an entity had corporate status or separate legal personality did not necessarily imply that it was not a department of state;[127] it was necessary to look beyond the issue

---

120 See Art 12, The European Convention on State Immunity (1972).
121 Which enabled the United Kingdom to ratify the International Convention for the Unification of Certain Rules relating to the Immunity of State owned Vessels (1926) as well as the Protocol to it (Cmnd 5763).
122 *Duff Development Corporation v Kelanaton* [1924] AC 797.
123 *Mellenger v New Brunswick Development Corporation* [1971] 1 WLR 604.
124 See SI 1993/2809 in respect of Germany. This treatment of the constituent part of the federal state is consistent with Art 28 of the European Convention on State Immunity (1972).
125 *Krajina v Tass Agency* [1949] 2 All ER 274.
126 *Ibid*; *Baccus SRL v Servicio National del Trigo* [1957] QB 438; *Trendtex Trading Corporation v Central Bank of Nigeria* [1977] QB 529.
127 *Baccus SRL v Servicio Nacional del Trigo* [1957] 1 QB 438.

of personality to examine the reason for formation and the precise nature of the functions performed. Thus, in *Baccus SRL v Servicio Nacional del Trigo*,[128] a majority of the Court of Appeal were prepared to allow immunity to a separate corporate entity engaged in the export and import of grain on behalf of the Spanish Government. The same readiness to look at the constitution is to be observed in *Trendtex Trading Corporation v Central Bank of Nigeria*[129] where the court in determining whether immunity arose were prepared to look at three elements namely the constitutional structure under Nigerian law as well as the actual functions performed together with the extent of effective control by the executive branch. As Shaw LJ expressed the matter:

> I cannot find in the constitution of the bank or in the functions it performs or in the activities it pursues or in all those matters looked at together any compelling or indeed satisfactory basis for the conclusion that it is so related to the Government of Nigeria as to form part of it.[130]

Shortly after the House of Lords in *Czarnikow Ltd v Rolimpex*[131] were prepared to accepted that a body while established by the Polish government might have such a degree of ordinary commercial freedom as to preclude immunity. So running through the case law prior to the State Immunity Act 1978 was a concern: (i) to examine the constitution of the entity in question; (ii) to inquire whether it was a department of state; (iii) to examine whether it enjoyed separate legal personality; (iv) to inquire into the degree of control by the executive branch; and (v) to examine the actual functions performed.

The question of the limits of the state are expressly dealt with in s 14 of the State Immunity Act 1978. The operative provisions read as follows:

14 States entitled to immunities and privileges:

  (1) The immunities and privileges conferred by this Part of this Act apply to any foreign or commonwealth State other than the United Kingdom; and references to a State include references to–

    (a) the sovereign or other head of that State in his public capacity;

    (b) the government of that State; and

    (c) any department of that government,

    but not to any entity (hereinafter referred to as a 'separate entity') which is distinct from the executive organs of the government of the State and capable of suing or being sued.

  (2) A separate entity is immune from the jurisdiction of the courts of the United Kingdom, if, and only if–

    (a) the proceedings relate to anything done by it in the exercise of sovereign authority; and

    (b) the circumstances are such that a State (or, in the case of proceedings to which section 10 above applies, a State which is not a party to the Brussels Convention) would have been immune.

---

128 *Baccus SRL v Servicio Nacional del Trigo* [1957] 1 QB 438; (1957) 23 ILR 160.
129 *Trendtex Trading Corporation v Central Bank of Nigeria* [1977] 1 QB 529.
130 *Ibid.*
131 *C Czarnikow Ltd v Centrala Handlu Zagranicznego Rolimpex* [1979] AC 351.

Thus, where an entity has separate legal personality and is distinct from the executive organs of government it will not be part of the state and *prima facie* not entitled to claim immunity by virtue of s 14(1)(c). However, if such a separate entity can demonstrate that it meets the two limbs of s 14(2) then a claim for immunity can be made. The problem arises as to how s 14(2) is to be approached; in a complex factual situation is it sufficient to take a broad overall view as to whether the terms of s 14(2) have been met or is it sensible to analyse individual elements of a particular transaction? This was in essence the problem facing the House of Lords in the case of *Kuwait Airways Corporation v Iraqi Airways Co*[132] where the salient facts were as follows.

In August 1990 Iraq invaded Kuwait. Pursuant to ministerial orders 10 civil aircraft belonging to the Plaintiffs were taken to Iraq by the Iraqi Aircraft Company (IAC). Iraqi Resolution 369 on 17 September 1990 purported to dissolve the plaintiff company and vest the ownership of the aircraft in the IAC. Thereafter the IAC had treated the aircraft as its own. Four were subsequently destroyed in allied action while six were sent to Iran. In January 1991 the plaintiffs issued a writ in London seeking delivery up of the aircraft and damages. After summary judgment had been entered the Republic of Iraq and the IAC moved to set aside the judgment. Evans J and the Court of Appeal held: (i) that service of proceedings on Iraq was ineffective; (ii) that the IAC was entitled to claim immunity under the State Immunity Act 1978. On appeal to the House of Lords the majority ruled: (i) that service on Iraq had been ineffective; and (ii) the IAC was only entitled to partial immunity under s 14(2) of the State Immunity Act 1978.

In respect of the question as to whether the IAC was entitled to claim immunity under State Immunity Act 1978, s 14(2), there was a division of opinion.[133] The majority[134] held that while the initial seizure was a sovereign act the subsequent use and retention of the aircraft although done at the behest of a sovereign power did not possess the character of a governmental act within the terms of ss 14(2)(a) and s 14(2)(b) when read with s 3 of the State Immunity Act 1978. The minority preferred to take a broader view asserting that it was important to view the entire transaction in its overall context (that is, seizure, retention and use of the aircraft) and they deprecated any attempt to introduce a subtle dissection of events. They argued that it was unreal and impermissible to seek to separate out IAC's eventual use of the disputed aircraft pursuant to the State's Decree from the circumstances of their initial acquisition. Moreover, they took the view that the IAC had acted throughout in harness with the Republic of Iraq. Further they reasoned that even if s 14(2) had to be read with s 3 that section was directed to removing the immunity of the trading state and had no applicability in the present case where the IAC was simply participating in the seizing the spoils of war; it was not possible they argued to view the transaction as commercial act simply because there was a future intention to operate the

---

132 [1995] 1 WLR 1147. (It is not without interest that in February 2001 an application was made to the House of Lords to aside part of the judgment on grounds that new evidence had come to light. Not surprisingly, the House of Lords refused to do so and instead directed that any new factual matters should be determined before a judge of the Commercial Court.)

133 It is worth remembering that this was not the only issue in the case. The four issues were: (i) whether the writ was effectively served on IAC; (ii) whether the writ was effectively served on Iraq; (iii) whether IAC as a separate entity was entitled to immunity under s 14(2).

134 [1995] 1 WLR 1147. (The majority comprised Lord Goff, Lord Jauncey and Lord Nicholls; the minority comprised Lord Mustill and Lord Slynn.)

aircraft as part of the civil airfleet. Thus, the division between the majority and the minority turned partly on whether the acts could be subject to separate analysis and partly on the question of statutory construction.

It has to be admitted that there is a considerable volume of case law that tends to the approach of the minority namely that one should look at the entire act in its overall context. Support for this view may be found in *I Congreso*,[135] *Littrell*,[136] *Republic of Egypt v Gamal Eldin*[137] and in the most recent case of *Holland v Lampen Wolfe*.[138]

An example of the willingness to examine the entire context is afforded by the case of *Re Rafidain Bank*,[139] where two companies – the Iraqi Reinsurance Company and Iraqi Airways Ltd claimed to be organs of the state of Iraq. At first instance, Browne Wilkinson J noted that both had separate legal personality and neither had governmental duties but were engaged in commercial activities; he therefore concluded that both were separate commercial entities and were precluded by s 3(1)(a) from claiming immunity.[140]

One of the more unusual claims to immunity was advanced in *Maclaine Watson v Department of Trade and Industry*.[141] It was argued that the EEC was entitled to immunity not under the terms of the State Immunity Act 1978,[142] but at common law. The submission was rejected by Kerr LJ in the Court of Appeal in which he was supported by the other judges. In giving judgment the court noted the distinction between the existence of legal personality on the international plane and a claim to immunity before a municipal court. The fact that the EEC possessed the former did not necessarily entail the latter;[143] further Kerr LJ held that claims to immunity representing a departure from normal rules on jurisdiction had to be established by the clearest evidence.

The claims by distinct entities have given rise to problems in other jurisdictions. In the United States, s 1603 of the Foreign Sovereign Immunities Act 1976 permits claims for immunity to be made by an entity which has a separate legal personality but which is yet an organ of a foreign state. Thus, in *First National City Bank v Banco Para el Comercio Exterior de Cuba (Bancec)*[144] the United States Supreme Court indicated that a distinct legal personality would give rise to a presumption of separateness; such a presumption might be rebutted by evidence of some form of agency relationship with the executive branch of the state. Although a separate legal entity the degree of governmental control may be such that it should be regarded as an organ of the state.

---

135 *I Congresso del Partido* [1983] 1 AC 244.

136 *Littrell v United States of America (No 2)* [1995] 1 WLR 82.

137 *Republic of Egypt v Gamal-Eldin* [1996] 2 All ER 237.

138 *Holland v Lampen Wolfe* [2000] 1 WLR 1573.

139 *Re Rafidain Bank* (1992) BCLC 301.

140 In essence the case concerned an application by the Republic of Iraq, the Iraqi Reinsurance Company and Iraqi Airways seeking an order that preferential payments be made by the liquidators of the Bank, T.

141 *Maclaine Watson v Department of Trade and Industry* [1988] 3 WLR 1033; 80 ILR 49 (CA) (Kerr, Ralph Gibson and Nourse LJJ).

142 Because it was not itself a state.

143 Article 210 of the Treaty of Rome (1957) provided: 'The Community shall have legal personality.'

144 (1983) 462 US 611; 80 ILR 581.

7 WAIVER OF IMMUNITY

As indicated above it has always been the case that a state might waive any claim to immunity; such a waiver might be express or implied. However, a distinction has to be maintained between waiver of immunity from jurisdiction and waiver of immunity from execution. Prior to the enactment of the State Immunity Act 1978 the court required convincing and unambiguous evidence of waiver. It was not enough for a Head of State to reside in England and participate in English life,[145] while a submission to arbitration proceedings was insufficient.[146] A clause in a contract was normally ineffective[147] and even where a state had litigated it could still raise a plea of immunity in respect of an unrelated counter claim.[148] Only a clear waiver of immunity at the time of commencement of legal proceedings would be judged adequate.[149]

Under the terms of s 2 of the State Immunity Act 1978 it is provided that a state may submit to the jurisdiction after a dispute has arisen or by a prior written agreement. Whether such a waiver will extend to forms of interlocutory relief is a matter of construction.[150] The principle of waiver is recognised in both the European Convention on State Immunity[151] and in the International Law Commission Draft Articles on Jurisdictional Immunities.[152] In principle a waiver of immunity will extend to any appeal.[153] Any waiver of immunity will oblige the state to submit to the normal obligations arising under codes of civil procedure.[154] It will be a matter for the domestic legislation of each state as to when waiver may be said to have arisen. In the United Kingdom waiver will be deemed to have been made if the state has instituted proceedings,[155] or has intervened or taken any step in proceedings.[156] However, it will not constitute waiver when the purpose of the intervention was to claim immunity[157] or to assert an interest in property in circumstances where the state would have been entitled to claim immunity had proceedings been brought against it.[158]

---

145 *Mighell v Sultan of Johore* [1894] 1 QB 149.

146 *Duff Development Co v Kelanton Government* [1924] AC 797.

147 *Kahan v Pakistan Federation* [1951] 2 KB 1003.

148 *High Commissioner for India v Ghosh* [1960] 1 QB 134 (CA); *South African Republic v La Compagnie Franco Belge du Chemin de Fer du Nord* [1898] 1 Ch 190.

149 *Kahan v Pakistan Federation* [1951] 2 KB 1003.

150 *A Company v The Republic of X* [1990] 2 Lloyd's Rep 520; 87 ILR 412.

151 Article 12.

152 Article 17.

153 *Sultan of Johore v Abubakar Tunku Aris Bendahar* [1952] AC 318.

154 *Prioleau v United States of America* (1866) LR 2 Eq 659; *Republic of Peru v Weguelin* (1875) LR 20 Eq 140; *Republic of Costa Rica v Erlanger* (1876) 3 Ch D 62; *Queen of Holland v Drukker* [1928] Ch 877.

155 State Immunity Act 1978, s 2(3)(a).

156 *Ibid*, s 2(3)(b).

157 *Ibid*, s 2(4)(a).

158 *Ibid*, s 2(4)(b).

8 THE HEAD OF STATE[159]

The position of the head of state acting in his public capacity[160] is governed by s 14 of the State Immunity Act 1978 which provides for immunity in similar terms to that of the state itself. Whether an individual is a head of state or a head of government will in cases of dispute be resolved by reference to the certificate of the Secretary of State under the terms of s 21 of the legislation. Such provisions reflect the well established position in customary international law that the serving head of state is entitled to immunity from civil and criminal jurisdiction in respect of official acts.

One of the most difficult problems in the last two decades has been when proceedings have been brought against a former head of state or government in respect of acts committed during his period in office Because such cases also rise problems of diplomatic status they are dealt with below.[161]

In respect of the head of state and his family who are present in the United Kingdom s 20 of the State Immunity Act 1978 provides that members of the family forming part of the household and private servants shall enjoy the immunity conferred on the head of a diplomatic mission and his family as set out in the Diplomatic Privileges Act 1964.

9 STATE IMMUNITY AND VIOLATIONS OF INTERNATIONAL LAW

A problem that has arisen in recent years is the question as to whether a state may make a claim for immunity before a municipal court in respect of acts that are themselves generally considered to be contrary to international law (for example, genocide, torture etc). There is some evidence that municipal courts are prepared to deny immunity in such circumstances.[162] The problem is complicated however by the fact that some of the cases have concerned claims for immunity by former rulers where there is the difficulty as to whether the immunity is that of the former rule or the state.

The problem but without this complication was illustrated by the case of *Al-Adsani v The Government of Kuwait,* where the plaintiff alleged that he had been tortured by officials of the Government at the instigation of a member of the royal family. In the course of preliminary proceedings[163] to determine whether leave should be granted to serve a foreign state out of the jurisdiction under RSC Order 11, Evans LJ ruled that as public international law was considered to be part of the law of England it was certainly arguable that no claim of immunity could be made for such conduct under the terms of the State Immunity Act 1978. At a later date, the Government of Kuwait applied to set

---

159 See generally, A Watts, 'The legal position in international law of heads of states, heads of governments and foreign ministers' (1994) 247 HR 9.

160 See *BCCI v Price Waterhouse* [1997] 4 All ER 108; J Hopkins (1998) 57 CLJ 4.

161 *Republic of the Philippines v Marcos (No 1)* (1986) 806 F 2d 344; 81 ILR 581. *In Re Grand Jury Proceedings* Doe No 770 (1987) 817 F 2d 1108; 81 ILR 599; *United States v Noriega* (1990) 746 F Supp 1506; 99 ILR 143; *Hilao v The Estate of Marcos* (1994) 25 F 3d 547.

162 *Filartiga v Pena-Irala* (1980) 630 F 2d 876; 77 ILR 169.

163 *Al Adsani v Government of Kuwait* (1995) 100 ILR 465 (Pain J, Evans, Rose and Butler Sloss LJJ). The appeal to the Court of Appeal simply being concerned with whether leave should be granted to serve the Government of Kuwait out of the jurisdiction.

aside the writ on the ground that they were entitled to immunity under the State Immunity Act 1978. This was granted by Mantell J[164] and a subsequent appeal to the Court of Appeal was dismissed.[165] In giving judgment in Court of Appeal, Stuart Smith LJ held that the State Immunity Act 1978 was a comprehensive code and that a claim for immunity could be made unless it was expressly prohibited by the legislation and it would be wrong to infer that torture while contrary to international law could not be the subject of immunity. The learned judge was influenced by the approach in the United States where both the Supreme Court[166] and the Court of Appeals[167] had indicated that conduct arguably in breach of international law could still be the subject of immunity unless it was expressly exempted under the Foreign State Immunities Act 1976. The rationale for this approach was that torture was unlawful as a matter of customary international law but any such rule of customary international law must yield to the clear provisions of an Act of Congress.

However, a different approach was taken by the majority of the House of Lords in *R v Bow Street Metropolitan Magistrate ex p Pinochet Ugarte (No 1)*.[168] In that case, the court was considering the claim of General Pinochet[169] to immunity from extradition proceedings. In giving judgment for the majority both Lord Nicholls and Lord Steyn argued that in principle immunity would only extend to official governmental acts and that what was an official governmental act was not a matter of constitutional law but of customary international law. So as customary international law regarded torture and hostage taking as unlawful acts these could not be the subject of a claim to immunity.[170]

In the second full hearing of the matter in *R v Bow Street Metropolitan Stipendiary Magistrate ex p Pinochet Ugarte (No 3)*[171] although much of the substance of the case

---

164 *Al Adsani v Government of Kuwait* 103 ILR 420 (Mantell J).

165 *Al Adsani v Government of Kuwait* [1996] 1 Lloyd's Rep 104; 107 ILR 536.

166 *Argentine Republic v Amerada Hess Shipping Corporation* (1989) 488 US 428; 81 ILR 658. (The case itself concerned an attack on an oil tanker by Argentine aircraft during the Falklands War (1982).)

167 *Siderman de Blake v Republic of Argentina* (1992) 965 F 2d 699. (A claim of torture by Argentine military officials.)

168 *R v Bow Street Metropolitan Magistrate ex p Pinochet Ugarte (No 1)* [2000] 1 AC 61. (The majority comprising Lord Steyn, Lord Nicholls and Lord Hoffmann. It is of note that impressive dissenting judgments were given by Lord Slynn and Lord Lloyd.) The minority argued that: (a) there was no evidence that the Convention Against Torture (1984) or the State Immunity Act 1978 expressly removed the traditional immunity of the Head of State; (b) that in any event the matters in question were non-justiciable within the act of state doctrine. See H Fox (1999) 48 ICLQ 207.

169 Ruler of Chile from September 1973 until March 1990, having lead a military coup against the government of President Allende.

170 The judgment was set aside in *R v Bow Street Metropolitan Stipendiary Magistrate ex p Pinochet Ugarte (No 2)* [2000] 1 AC 119 on the basis that the earlier tribunal had not been properly constituted.

171 *R v Bow Street Metropolitan Stipendiary Magistrate ex p Pinochet Ugarte (No 3)* [2000] 1 AC 147. The reasoning of the majority involved holding: (i) Extradition Act 1989, s 2, required the alleged conduct the subject of the extradition request to be a crime in the United Kingdom at the time when the offence was committed; (ii) extra-territorial torture did not become an offence under United Kingdom law until s 134 of the Criminal Justice Act 1988 came into effect on 29 September 1988; it followed that all allegations of torture prior to that date which did not take place in Spain were not extraditable offences; (iii) that in principle a head of state had immunity from jurisdiction in the United Kingdom for acts done in his official capacity (see s 20 State Immunity Act 1978 when read with Art 39(2) of Sched 1 of the Diplomatic Privileges Act 1964); [contd]

turned on the workings of the double criminality rule in the law of extradition,[172] the majority accepted that immunity could not be claimed in the United Kingdom in respect of acts which the United Kingdom had agreed by international convention to punish and which had been enacted into domestic law as criminal offences. It would therefore seem that immunity will not be able to be claimed under the State Immunity Act 1978 in respect of conduct which the United Kingdom has agreed on the international plane to punish and which has been made a criminal offence in domestic law. To this extent the assertion in *Al Adsani v Government of Kuwait* that the State Immunity Act 1978 was a comprehensive and self-contained code must now be viewed with a degree of caution.

10 INTERLOCUTORY ORDERS

A particular difficulty arises in the case of some forms of interlocutory relief. In the last two decades the courts in the United Kingdom have expanded the range of injunctive relief to enable the plaintiff to seek pre-trial orders designed to ensure that the defendant does not remove assets from the jurisdiction. In the United Kingdom the best known forms are the Mareva injunction[173] and the Anton Pillar order;[174] such orders are designed to prevent the plaintiff's rights at trial being frustrated by the pre trial conduct of the defendant. In the vast majority of circumstances the plaintiff will apply for the order *ex parte* on affidavit and will be subject to the general duty to disclose any material fact. However, under s 13(2) and 13(3) of the State Immunity Act 1978 no relief shall be given against a state by way of injunction or order of specific performance without the consent in writing of the state. It is therefore possible that an application for an injunction might be made and the defendant state would be in a position of seeking to set aside the order at a subsequent *inter partes* hearing. The procedure was examined by Saville J in *A Co Ltd v Republic of X*[175] where the learned judge ruled that in such circumstances on an inter partes hearing the judge must determine whether immunity exists because if it does the injunction must be discharged. Such an approach he felt followed logically from the observations of the Court of Appeal in *Maclaine Watson & Co Ltd v Department of Trade and*

---

171 [contd] (iv) however, torture was an international crime and since the coming into effect of the Torture Convention (1984) in 1987, it was a crime of universal jurisdiction; (v) since the Torture Convention (1984) had been ratified by Spain, Chile and the United Kingdom by 8 December 1988 there could be no immunity for offences of torture committed after that date. It is sensible to consider the dissenting speech of Lord Goff who argued: (i) that the immunity of the head of state after leaving office was *ratione materiae*; (ii) that it arose under international law in the Vienna Convention on Diplomatic Relations (1961); (iii) that it had been incorporated into English Law in legislation in 1964 and 1978; (iv) that the immunity attached to the state; (v) that it could be expressly waived but not impliedly waived; (vi) that the negotiating history of the Torture Convention (1984) did not reveal an intention to interfere with existing rules on immunity. For a review, see H Fox (1999) 48 ICLQ 687.

172 The request by Spain was based in part on allegations of torture of its citizens in Chile; such acts of extra-territorial torture did not become a criminal offence in England until s 134 of the Criminal Justice Act 1988 came into effect on 29 September 1988.

173 *Mareva Compania Naviera SA of Panama v International Bulk Carriers SA* [1975] 2 Lloyd's Rep 509.

174 *Anton Piller KG v Manufacturing Processes Ltd* [1976] Ch 55.

175 *A Co Ltd v Republic of X* [1990] 2 Lloyd's Rep 520.

Industry[176] where it was said that questions of immunity should in general be determined at the outset. The learned judge refrained form expressing an opinion as to the status of an *ex parte* order set aside for want of jurisdiction.

A not dissimilar regime operates in the United States under the terms of s 1610(d) of the Foreign Sovereign Immunities Act 1976 which prohibits the attachment of the property of a foreign state prior to judgment unless the state has expressly waived its immunity from attachment prior to judgment. A problem that has arisen before courts in the United States is as to whether treaty provisions that imply a waiver from pre-judgment attachment of property are sufficient to meet the statutory requirement that the waiver is 'express'.[177]

11 EXECUTION OF JUDGMENTS[178]

The case law establishes a distinction between immunity from jurisdiction, immunity from pre-judgment orders and immunity from the execution of judgments. The enforcement of a court judgment is the most sensitive of these matters and is so regarded by the various international instruments. Article 18 of the ILC Draft Articles on Jurisdictional Immunities stipulates that no measure of execution may be taken against the property of a state unless that state has expressly consented. Similarly, Art 23 of the European Convention on State Immunity 1972 prohibits any measures of execution against the property of a contracting state in the absence of written consent. Although some states have permitted execution against state property[179] the general trend has been to include restrictions in domestic legislation prohibiting execution against the property of a foreign state without its express consent.

Section 13(2)(b) of the United Kingdom State Immunity Act 1978 provides that 'the property of a state shall not be subject to any process for the enforcement of a judgment or arbitration award or, in an action *in rem*, for its arrest, detention or sale'. It is further provided in s 13(3) that such immunity may be waived by the written consent of the state concerned but mere submission to the jurisdiction of the courts will not constitute such consent. Similar provisions are to be found in other municipal legislation on the subject.[180]

The distinction between immunity from jurisdiction and immunity from execution was raised in the House of Lords case of *Alcom Ltd v Republic of Columbia*.[181] In that case a

---

176 *Maclaine Watson v Department of Trade and Industry* [1988] 3 WLR 1033, p 1103–04, 1157–58.

177 *Reading & Bates Corporation v National Iranian Oil Co* (1979) 478 F Supp 724; 63 ILR 305; 18 ILM 1398; *Chicago Bridge & Iron Co v Islamic Republic of Iran* (1980) 19 ILM 1436; *New England Merchants National Bank v Iran Power Generation and Transmission Co* (1980) 19 ILM 1298; 63 ILR 408.

178 See generally, J Crawford, 'Execution of judgments and foreign sovereign immunity' (1981) 75 AJIL 820.

179 *Société Commerciale de Belgique v L'Etat Hellenique* (1952) 79 Clunet 244 (Belgium); *Société Européenne d'Etudes et d'Enterprises v Yugoslavia* (1973) 14 ILM 71.

180 Singapore State Immunity Act 1979, s 15; Pakistan State Immunity Ordinance 1981, s 14; South African Foreign Sovereign Immunity Act 1981, s 14; Australian Foreign States Immunities Act 1985, s 31.

181 *Alcom Ltd v Republic of Columbia* [1984] AC 580.

default judgment had been obtained against the Republic of Columbia and a garnishee order had been made by the High Court in respect of the Embassy bank account held in London. At first instance Hobhouse J agreed to set aside the garnishee order but it was reinstated in the Court of Appeal.[182] In allowing the subsequent appeal, Lord Diplock indicated that a bank account held for an embassy will normally be immune from execution under s 13(4) of the State Immunity Act 1978 unless there is unambiguous evidence that it is used solely for commercial purposes and in normal circumstances the certificate filed by the head of mission will be conclusive. In the course of giving judgment Lord Diplock indicated his approval of the judgment of the *Bundesverfassungsgericht* in the *Philippine Republic* case(1977)[183] where the court had indicated that immunity from legal process of execution was required by public international law to be accorded to the bank account of a diplomatic mission when it was used for defraying the expenses of the mission.

Broadly the same approach was followed by the Italian Supreme Court in *Benmar v Embassy of the Democratic and Popular Republic of Algeria*[184] and it would seem that in most states an account used exclusively for diplomatic purposes will be immune as probably will a mixed account.[185]

12 OUTSTANDING QUESTIONS UNDER THE STATE IMMUNITY ACT 1978

Section 1 of the State Immunity Act 1978 provides that the state is immune from the jurisdiction of the courts of the United Kingdom save as provided by the Act. Section 1(2) provides that the courts shall give effect to this immunity even though the state does not appear. It is therefore clear that those who argue that immunity does not apply bear the onus probandi of demonstrating that the matter comes within a relevant exception.[186] As the exceptions relate to civil matters then the relevant standard will be that of the balance of probabilities.[187] As a claim to immunity is a matter pertaining to jurisdiction then the proper course for the court to adopt is to consider the matter as a preliminary issue.[188]

---

182 Interesting submissions advanced to the House of Lords by the then Simon Brown and Rosalyn Higgins who argued that the Court of Appeal had failed to preserve the distinction in the State Immunity Act 1978 between immunity from judgment and immunity from execution. The Court of Appeal judgment had been given under pressure of time; the judgment of Sir John Donaldson MR indicates that he wished to reserve judgment but circumstances required otherwise.

183 *Philippine Republic* case (1977) 46 B Verf GE 342; 65 ILR 146.

184 (1990) 87 ILR 56; 84 AJIL 573. Although the Italian Constitutional Court approached the matter differently in *Condor and Filvem v Minister of Justice* (1992) 101 ILR 394.

185 *Alcom Ltd v Republic of Columbia* (1984) 1 AC 580 reversing the Court of Appeal judgment [1984] 1 All ER 1; see PA Ghandi (1984) 47 MLR 597.

186 *Al Adsani v Government of Kuwait* [1996] 1 Lloyd's Rep 104; 107 ILR 536; *Rayner v Department of Trade and Industry* (1987) BCLC 667.

187 In accordance with the normal rule in England following the judgment in *Hornal v Neuberger Products Ltd* [1957] 1 QB 247.

188 *Maclaine Watson v Department of Trade and Industry* [1988] 3 WLR 1103; 80 ILR 49 approved by Saville J in *A Company Ltd v Republic of X* [1990] 2 Lloyd's Rep 520.

The case law in the United Kingdom since 1978 has raised a number of points concerning the interpretation of the legislation. Two particular matters call for consideration. A first problem of application has arisen in the context of the service of proceedings upon a foreign state.[189] An example is afforded by the case of *Westminster City Council v Islamic Republic of Iran*.[190] In that case the Iranian embassy in London had been stormed by security forces in May 1980 so that hostages might be rescued. The subsequent damage to the building was such that the local authority were required to exercise their statutory powers under the London Building Acts (Amendment) Act 1939 to repair the building. In seeking to recover the cost, the local authority then registered charges under the Local Land Charges Act 1975 and sought to register as chargees under the Land Registration Act 1925. Under the terms of s 12 of the State Immunity Act 1978 proceedings were required to be served on the Iranian Ministry of Foreign Affairs; at the time diplomatic relations had been severed. In the Chancery Division of the High Court, Peter Gibson J was forced to accept that the summons seeking registration could not be heard because of a failure to comply with the method of service stipulated in State Immunity Act 1978, s 12(1).

A problem of a similar nature arose in the case of *Kuwait Airways Corporation v Iraqi Airways Company*.[191] As indicated above the case arose out of the seizure of civil aircraft during the invasion of Kuwait. When proceedings were begun in London, the plaintiffs sought to serve both the Republic of Iraq and the Iraqi Airways Corporation. In the case of Iraq, the difficulty arose because of the absence of British diplomatic representation in Baghdad. The writ was passed by the Foreign And Commonwealth Office in London to the Iraqi Embassy in London with a request that it be passed to the Iraqi Ministry of Foreign Affairs in Baghdad. At first instance, Evans J[192] rejected a submission that service on a diplomatic mission was service on the foreign ministry and this refusal was upheld by the House of Lords. Thus, the failure to transmit the writ to Baghdad prevented the proceedings from having been properly served on the Republic of Iraq.[193]

A second source of litigation has arisen under the provisions of s 16(2) of the State Immunity Act 1978 which has the effect of disapplying Part I of the legislation in respect of 'proceedings concerning anything done by or in relation to the armed forces of a state

---

189 The relevant section being the State Immunity Act 1978, s 12.

190 *Westminster City Council v The Government of Iran* [1986] 1 WLR 979 (Peter Gibson J). The purpose of the application being to give the council the powers of legal mortgagees under the Land Registration Act 1925. In the circumstances, the learned judge was correct to reject any suggestion that the matter could be dealt with on an *ex parte* basis. Interestingly the case also indicates that the protection of Art 22 of the Vienna Convention on Diplomatic Relations 1961 will only be available when the premises are being used by a mission. At the time of the hearing in January 1986 the premises had been unused since May 1980.

191 [1995] 1 WLR 1147.

192 For consideration of the first instance judgment of Evans J, see H Fox (1994) 43 ICLQ 193; for the subsequent trial proceedings on wrongful interference, see (1999) CLC 31.

193 The House of Lords concluded that proceedings had been properly served on the Iraqi Aircraft Corporation under RSC Ord 65 r 3 (repeating the prior RSC Ord 9 r 8, as discussed in *Dunlop Pneumatic Tyre Co Ltd v Actien Gesellschaft fur Motor und Motorfahrzeugbau vorm Cudell & Co* [1902] 1 KB 342). It was not necessary to come to a conclusion as to whether IAC was an 'oversea company' within Companies Act 1985, s 744.

while present in the United Kingdom'.[194] The disapplying of Part I includes s 1 so that cases under s 16(2) fall to be decided at common law. In *Littrell v United States of America (No 2)*,[195] an operation on a United States military base fell within s 16(2) and was thus governed by common law. The Court of Appeal considered that at common law, having regard to the particular context and circumstances, the provision of medical services within a military base was a sovereign act entitled to immunity. This approach was accepted by the House of Lords in *Holland v Lampen Wolfe*[196] who considered that educational services provided to visiting forces fell within s 16(2) so that any claim to immunity would also have to be made at common law. Their Lordships held further that the provision of educational services within a military establishment attracted immunity at common law. One interesting argument raised on the appeal to the House of Lords was whether allowing immunity to the defendant would violate the plaintiff's right to a fair trial under Art 6 of the European Convention on Human Rights and Fundamental Freedoms (1950); it seems that Lord Millett in giving the leading judgment was correct in rejecting this superficially attractive[197] contention.

13 THE EUROPEAN CONVENTION ON STATE IMMUNITY[198]

One of the objects of enacting the State Immunity Act 1978 was to enable the United Kingdom to ratify the European Convention on State Immunity (1972) Work on the Convention had begun under the auspices of the Council of Europe in 1963 and the final text was signed in 1972; the instrument came into force in 1976. The Convention reflects the spirit of its times and so broadly favours the restrictive approach. However, it achieves this objective by outlining the principle of absolute immunity and then providing for a number of exceptions where the rule will not apply. The same technique was later used by the draftsman of the State Immunity Act 1978 to slightly different effect.[199]

In respect of substantive differences it is to be noted that the State Immunity Act 1978 provides for a broader class of exceptions than the European Convention and the provisions of Part I of the 1978 Act will apply to all states before the United Kingdom courts regardless of whether they are parties to the European Convention. Secondly, it is

---

194 See the analysis by Lord Millett in *Holland v Lampen Wolfe* [2000] 1 WLR 1573, p 1584, where learned judge compares the provision to Art 31 of the 1972 European Convention and speculates on the drafting technique employed to exclude the entire Part I of the Act so that s 1 is disapplied and the matter is governed by common law.

195 *Littrell v United States of America (No 2)* [1995] 1 WLR 82; [1994] 4 All ER 203.

196 *Holland v Lampen Wolfe* [2000] 1 WLR 1573, affirming [1998] 1 WLR 188 (CA).

197 The arguments against the contention are: (i) the purpose of Art 6 is to provide for a fair adjudicative powers not to extend those powers; (ii) those powers are subject to well established rules of customary international law; (iii) normally a treaty provision will only prevail over such a rule if it is express and specific; (iv) the United States was not a party to the European Convention (1950); (v) there is no express reference in the 1950 Convention to the curtailment of traditional immunity; (vi) the degree of immunity claimed was consistent with customary international law and no wider than international law allowed.

198 I Sinclair (1973) 22 ICLQ 254; FA Mann (1973) 36 MLR 18.

199 See *Holland v Lampen Wolfe* [2000] 1 WLR 1573, p 1584–85, where Lord Millett contrasts the drafting techniques employed in the 1972 Convention and the State Immunity Act 1978.

to be noted that the European Convention is concerned not only with matters of jurisdictional immunity but also with questions pertaining to the recognition and enforcement of judgments given against a foreign state.

The European Convention proceeds on the basis of the general immunity of the state in Arts 1–3 and then stipulates a number of activities in which immunity cannot be claimed. Article 4 provides no claim for immunity can be made in respect of contractual disputes and Art 5 excludes contracts of employment; succeeding articles prevent claims for immunity being made in respect of matters concerning internal company law,[200] intellectual property,[201] immovable property[202] and disputes concerning succession.[203]

The Convention preserves the distinction between immunity from jurisdiction and immunity from execution. Thus, Art 23 prohibits execution of a judgment against the property of a state but it combines it with provisions in Arts 20–22 whereby each contracting state accepts an obligation in international law to give effect to judgments pronounced against it by the courts of another contracting state in those cases where the rule of non-immunity prevails. These provisions are given effect to in Part II of the State Immunity Act 1978 (ss 18 and 19). By the terms of s 18 a final judgment given against the United Kingdom in a court of another contracting state which is a party to the Convention, not being a matter in which the United Kingdom had immunity, is to be recognised and enforced by the courts of the United Kingdom save in respect of a limited number of grounds[204] set out in s 19 of the Act.

It has to be admitted that, while the European Convention has been given effect to in the State Immunity Act 1978 and is sometimes alluded to in the United Kingdom courts,[205] it has suffered because it has only attracted a limited number of ratifications.[206] It is arguable that it has had most effect in the United Kingdom because, when that country signed in May 1972, it was still an exponent of the school of absolute immunity. Signing the Convention was a clear indication that legislation would be forthcoming.

---

200 European Convention on State Immunity (1972), Art 6.

201 *Ibid*, Art 7.

202 *Ibid*, Art 9.

203 *Ibid*, Art 10.

204 Some of these are traditional grounds in private international law such as: (i) recognition would be contrary to public policy; (ii) that there was not an adequate opportunity to present a case; (iii) that procedural requirements of the Convention have not been met; (iv) that there are prior similar proceedings before a United Kingdom court; (v) that in a matter under State Immunity Act 1978, s 6(2), the foreign court has assumed jurisdiction on a wider basis than accepted in the United Kingdom.

205 *Holland v Lampen Wolfe* [1999] 1 WLR 188.

206 Although the Convention entered into force in 1976, by 1996 it had only attracted eight parties. It should be noted that there is an additional Protocol which established a European Tribunal for the determination of certain disputes under the Convention.

14 THE ILC DRAFT ARTICLES ON THE JURISDICTIONAL IMMUNITIES OF STATES AND THEIR PROPERTY[207]

The International Law Commission has been working for some time on the subject of state immunity and has produced a series of Draft Articles. The Draft Articles have been subject to consideration by the Sixth (Legal) Committee of the General Assembly and have not passed without comment. The wide differences in practice even by those states that adopt the restrictive view has made it desirable to seek codification on the basis of an international convention. In broad terms, the Draft Articles favour the restrictive approach; however, Art 2 allows the purpose of the transaction to be taken into account in determining the nature of the transaction.[208] It may be that the difference of opinion between the 'nature' and 'purpose' of a transaction is less important than it was thought to be and the two tests are inter related.[209] Article 5 of the Draft Articles set out the general rule of immunity subject to exceptions:

> A state enjoys immunity in respect of itself and its property, from the jurisdiction of the courts of another state subject to the provisions of the present articles.

In considering the meaning of the expression 'state' Draft Article 2(1)(b) provides that the expression extends not only to the normal executive branch but to sub divisions and entities exercising sovereign authority.

Much of the Draft Articles are accepted by many states already. Draft Article 10 provides that a state will not be immune in respect of a commercial transactions[210] while other articles remove immunity in respect of employment contracts (Draft Article 11) and cases of personal injury and tangible property (Draft Article 12). In respect of immunity from execution Draft Articles 18 and 19 provide a broad immunity from execution.

The Draft Articles that emerged in 1991 were subject to some criticisms from major trading nations and were relayed to the Sixth (Legal) Committee of the General Assembly. This resulted in a Working Group of the ILC being established to consider those criticisms. In 1999 the Working Group of the ILC produced a Report for the Sixth Committee so the possibility remains that a multilateral convention might yet emerge.

In considering the compatibility with the existing State Immunity Act 1978 the Draft Articles give a greater role to 'purpose' and provide a different definition of a commercial transaction; they favour a more liberal approach both to the immunity of agencies and a more restrictive approach to questions of execution. Although the United Kingdom was

---

207 D Greig, 'Forum state jurisdiction and sovereign immunity under the ILC Draft Articles' (1989) 38 ICLQ 243; D Greig, 'Specific exceptions to immunity under the ILC Draft Articles' (1989) 38 ICLQ 560; M Byers, 'State immunity: Art 18 of the International Law Commission's Draft' (1995) 44 ICLQ 882.

208 This was felt to be more equitable in the case of developing countries operating economies subject to a greater degree of centralised control.

209 *United States v The Public Service Alliance of Canada* (1993) 32 ILM 1.

210 Under Art 2(1)(c) a commercial transaction is defined as: (i) any commercial contract or transaction for the sale or purchase of goods or the supply of services; (ii) any contract for a loan or other transaction of a financial nature, including any obligation of guarantee in respect of any such loan or of indemnity in respect of any such loan or transaction; (iii) any other contract or transaction, whether commercial whether of a commercial, industrial, trading or professional nature, but not including a contract of employment of persons.

one of the stoutest defenders of the absolute approach the emphasis on market based solutions in the last two decades has meant that the United Kingdom tends now to be sceptical of any modification of the restrictive approach. In the event of any multilateral treaty emerging, it should be noted that s 15 of the State Immunity Act 1978 empowers the making of delegated legislation to extend immunities and privileges to such extent as appears to be appropriate.

15 THE ACT OF STATE DOCTRINE[211]

As indicated above some of the cases coming before the courts raising problems of immunity also give rise to the doctrine of non-justiciability or the principle of act of state as it is sometimes described In a case of immunity it is asserted that the national court would have jurisdiction but for the claim of the defendant to immunity; such a claim depends on the status of the foreign state and is made *ratione personae*. In contrast there is a stream of case law in the common law world that holds that in certain circumstances a national court may decline jurisdiction by reason of the nature of the matter. The doctrine of act of state or non-justiciability can be traced back to the judgment in *Duke of Brunswick v King of Hanover*[212] but received its modern exposition in *Butes Gas and Oil Co v Hammer (No 3)*[213] where Lord Wilberforce indicated that:

> ... there exists in English law a general principle that the courts will not adjudicate upon the transactions of foreign sovereign states ... it seems desirable to consider this principle ... not as a variety of 'act of state' but one for judicial restraint or abstention.

A number of points need to be made. First, such a doctrine refers to the conduct of foreign sovereign states and is distinguishable from those cases in constitutional law where a foreigner begins an action (normally in tort) against the United Kingdom government.[214] Secondly, the doctrine is based on the principle of judicial restraint and is normally viewed as a part of private international law.[215] Thirdly, because of the different circumstances in which the phrase 'act of state' is employed it is probably sensible to refer to the doctrine as the principle of non-justiciability.

At varying times the doctrine has been applied in both the United States[216] and the United Kingdom[217] to justify a degree of judicial restraint in cases that would involve

---

211 FA Mann, 'The sacrosanctity of the foreign act of state' (1943) 59 LQR 42; M Zander, 'The act of state doctrine' (1959) 53 AJIL 826; M Singer, 'The act of state doctrine of the United Kingdom' (1981) 75 AJIL 283.

212 *Duke of Brunswick v King of Hanover* (1848) 1 HLC 1.

213 [1982] AC 888.

214 *Buron v Denman* (1848) 2 Ex 167; *Walker v Baird* [1892] AC 491; *Salaman v Secretary of State for India* [1906] 1 KB 613; *Johnstone v Pedlar* [1921] 2 AC 262; *Nissan v Attorney General* [1970] AC 179.

215 Referred to as such in *R v Bow Street Metropolitan Stipendiary Magistrate ex p Pinochet Ugarte (No 1)* [2000] 1 AC 61 by Lord Lloyd and Lord Slynn.

216 *Underhill v Hernandez* (1897) 168 US 250; *Oetjen v Central Leather Co* (1918) 246 US 297; *Banco Nacional de Cuba v Sabbatino* (1964) 376 US 398. See J Charney, 'Judicial deference in foreign relations' (1989) 83 AJIL 805.

217 *Duke of Brunswick v King of Hanover* (1848) 2 HLC 1; *Buck v Attorney General* [1965] Ch 765; *Buttes Gas and Oil Co v Hammer* [1982] AC 888; *R v Bow Street Magistrate ex p Pinochet Ugarte (No 1)* [1998] 3 WLR 1456 (where the minority would have applied the principle).

adjudicating on the conduct of a government of a foreign state. However, as the doctrine is one of private international law, public policy requires that it is not applied where breaches of public international law are in issue.[218] The normal circumstance in which the doctrine is applied is when an individual appears before the courts of state A in respect of acts undertaken while the agent or servant of state B. However, the doctrine has been applied in the United States in cases where property has been expropriated in state A and sold to a purchaser who is then sued by the true owner in courts of state B. The doctrine is not applied in this respect in civil law countries or in the United Kingdom where in such situations the case is resolved on the basis of the normal conflict of law rules.[219] While in the United Kingdom the doctrine is viewed as an aspect of private international law, in the United States the courts tend to stress that the constitutional principle of the separation of powers demands that the courts do not embarrass the executive in the conduct of foreign affairs. However, not every case concerning foreign affairs demands the operation of the doctrine;[220] the question is one of fact and degree and much will depend on whether a particular cause of action can be isolated.[221]

16 CONCLUSIONS[222]

The doctrine of sovereign immunity constitutes one of the older doctrines of public international law. The doctrine itself is said to arise as a consequence of the fundamental principles of equality and territorial sovereignty of states. Most of the relevant cases tend to arise before municipal courts and thus much will depend on the particular wording of the relevant municipal legislation.

A review of the subject leads to the following general conclusions. First, the majority of states tend to favour the restrictive approach; such an approach is consistent with the market based economies of Western Europe and is harmonious with the efforts at privatisation of state industries in Eastern Europe. Secondly, in most states whether sovereign immunity can be claimed will depend on domestic legislation; most of this legislation has been passed in the last quarter of a century. Thirdly, it is now clear that there is a growing willingness in municipal courts to refuse immunity where the allegations concern abuses of human rights; this may be asserted directly[223] or indirectly as a matter of statutory construction.[224] Fourthly, as the doctrine of absolute immunity recedes there is a willingness in some common law jurisdictions to explore further the

---

218 *Kuwait Airways Corporation v Iraqi Airways Corporation* (1999) CLC 31. (The judgment of Mance J noted with approval in *R v Bow Street Magistrate ex p Pinochet Ugarte (No 1)* [1998] 3 WLR 1456.)

219 English law traditionally favouring the *lex situs*, see *Luther v Sagor* [1921] 3 KB 532 (a case that turned on the extent of recognition of the Soviet Union); *Winkworth v Christie Manson and Woods Ltd* [1980] Ch 496; *Williams and Humbert Ltd v W and H Trade Marks (Jersey) Ltd* [1986] AC 368.

220 *Baker v Carr* (1962) 369 US 168.

221 *Linder v Portocarrero* (1992) 963 F 2d 332; 99 ILR 54.

222 The related question of the immunity of an international organisation and its staff is considered in Chapter 10.

223 For a direct attack on the use of immunity to shield abuses of human rights see the speech of Lord Steyn in *R v Bow Street Magistrate ex p Pinochet Ugarte (No 1)* [2000] 1 AC 61, p 1502.

224 *Letelier v Republic of Chile* (1980) 488 F Supp 665; 63 ILR 378.

doctrine of non-justiciability. Fifthly, many cases concerning sovereign immunity also raise problems of diplomatic immunity not least because the domestic legislation is often linked. It is to the subject of diplomatic immunity that one must now turn.

CHAPTER 10

DIPLOMATIC AND CONSULAR RELATIONS[1]

1 INTRODUCTION

The custom by which one state might send an individual to represent its interests in another state is one of the oldest practices in international society. In an age devoid of telegraph or telephone communications, a representative was the most practical option for the ruler who wished to communicate with a ruler of another state. It is not a matter of coincidence that some of the earliest writers on international law had served in some form of diplomatic capacity. Indeed, after the study of international law passed from the theologians in the 16th century many of the writers on international law had some direct experience of diplomatic service. In the broadest terms a diplomat is a person who represents his state in another state and is concerned with political relations between the two states. The powers and immunities of such persons grew up steadily as a result of state practice in the 17th and 18th centuries and were well understood by the time of the Congress of Vienna in 1815. The first permanent legations date from the 13th century and by 1500 England, France, Spain and Germany kept permanent representatives at each other's courts. The role of the permanent legation increased under Cardinal Richelieu not least because of the opportunities it provided for the gathering of information. Originally, the language of diplomacy was Latin but by the time of Louis XIV diplomatic affairs were regularly conducted in French. By 1919 English was employed on an equal footing with French; the emphasis on language is of some consequence because treaties tended to be drafted in the language used by the diplomats.

Diplomatic relations have tended to be conducted by Ambassadors who represent the sending state in the receiving state and act as the Head of Mission. At the Congress of Vienna in 1815 three classes of representative were identified: (a) ambassadors; (b) ministers plenipotentiary; and (c) *chargés d'affaires*. Under the terms of Art 14 of the Vienna Convention on Diplomatic Relations 1961 heads of a diplomatic mission are divided into three classes: (a) ambassadors; (b) envoys; and (c) *chargés d'affaires*. It will be for the individual states to determine the precise title. Normally the Ambassador will be assisted by other junior staff and will operate from an embassy building in the capital of the receiving state. In the 19th century, such Ambassadors tended to be persons of aristocratic background with an interest in foreign affairs; today the ambassador is more likely to be a career diplomat who has served in more junior posts before becoming an ambassador.

---

1   RY Jennings and AD Watts, *Oppenheim's International Law*, 9th edn, 1992, pp 1053–153; Lord Gore Booth, *Satow's Guide to Diplomatic Practice*, 5th edn, 1979; E Denza, *Diplomatic Law: Commentary on the Vienna Convention on Diplomatic Relations*, 2nd edn, 1998; C Lewis, *State and Diplomatic Immunity*, 3rd edn, 1990; RE Vaughan Williams, 'Les méthodes de travail de la diplomatie' (1924) HR 225; G Stuart, 'Le droit et la pratique diplomatiques et consulaires' (1934) 48 HR 459; R Higgins, 'United Kingdom Foreign Affairs Committee Report on the Abuse of Diplomatic Immunities and Privileges: government response and report' (1986) 80 AJIL 135; J Brown, 'Diplomatic immunity: state practice under the Vienna Convention on diplomatic relations' (1988) 37 ICLQ 53; S Nahlik, 'Development of diplomatic law, selected problems' (1990) 222 HR 187; A James, 'Diplomatic relations and contacts' (1991) 62 BYIL 347.

The law concerning diplomatic relations has a reputation of being well observed; the reason for this is not surprising. All states send diplomats and all states receive diplomats; each state has a vested interest in respecting the rules. The rules are seen as neutral and of benefit to all states both large and small and do not give rise to the problems of cultural and economic difference encountered in areas such as state responsibility and the law of human rights. The rules themselves have grown up over a long period of time. As early as 1708, when the Russian Ambassador was arrested for debt in London, the Russian Czar Peter the Great considered such conduct to be a criminal offence and when the Court of Queen's Bench[2] was uncertain about the position the Diplomatic Privileges Act 1708,[3] provided that no proceedings should be brought against a diplomat or their servant. Indeed, some of the earliest cases on international law coming before the English courts concerned aspects of diplomatic privilege.[4]

In England prior to the Diplomatic Privileges Act 1964 the law was contained in a number of statutes[5] and decided cases.[6] A person accepted as a member of the diplomatic staff was immune from civil and criminal jurisdiction. Such an immunity was immunity from the jurisdiction and did not constitute exemption from legal liability.[7] This immunity would cover claims to local rates,[8] as well as contributions sought by a liquidator in a company liquidation.[9] Any writ issued against a serving ambassador was void,[10] but a diplomat could with the knowledge and consent of his superior waive any immunity from jurisdiction.[11] Although the case law in England turned on the interpretation of the Diplomatic Privileges Act 1708, it was assumed to be declaratory of the common law of which the Law of Nations was deemed part.[12] English law prior to

---

2   *Mattueof's Case* (1709) 10 Mod Rep 4.

3   It is of interest that the preamble to the 1708 Act describes its purpose as 'preserving the privileges of Ambassadors'; under s 3, any proceedings were to be regarded as void and under s 4 anyone issuing such proceedings would be guilty of a criminal offence. It has to be borne in mind that the diplomatic community in London was at that time not large. As late as 1822 only six states had Ambassadors in London. By 1990 that figure (including High Commissioners) had reached 149; see *Oppenheim*, p 1060.

4   *Buvot v Barbuit* (1737) Cases Talbot 281; *Triquet v Bath* (1764) 3 Burr 1478.

5   Diplomatic Privileges Act 1708; Diplomatic Immunities (Commonwealth Countries and Republic of Ireland) Act 1952; Diplomatic Immunities Restriction Act 1952; Diplomatic Immunities (Conferences with Commonwealth Countries and Republic of Ireland) Act 1961.

6   See generally, *Triquet v Bath* (1764) 3 Burr 1478; *Viveash v Becker* (1814) 3 M & S 284; *Taylor v Best* (1854) 14 CB 487; *Magdalena Steam Navigation Co v Martin* (1859) 2 E & E 94; *Baron Penedo v Johnson* (1873) 29 LT 452; *Parkinson v Potter* (1885) 16 QBD 152; *Macartney v Garbutt* (1890) 24 QBD 368; *In re LW Cloete* (1891) 7 TLR 565; *Musurus Bey v Gadban* [1894] 2 QB 352; *In re Republic of Bolivia Exploration Syndicate* [1914] 1 Ch 139; *Re Suarez* [1917] 2 Ch 131; [1918] 1 Ch 176; *Fenton Textile Association Limited v Krassin* (1922) 38 TLR 259; *Assurantie Compagnie Excelsior v Smith* (1923) 40 TLR 105; *Engelke v Musmann* [1928] AC 433; *Dickinson v Del Solar* [1930] 1 KB 376; *R v Kent* [1941] 1 KB 454; *Parker v Boggan* [1947] KB 346; All ER 46; *Price v Griffin* (1948) 2 ILQ 266; *In re C (An Infant)* [1959] 1 Ch 363; *High Commissioner for India v Ghosh* [1960] 1 QB 134; *R v Madan* [1961] 2 QB 1; *Empson v Smith* [1966] 1 QB 426.

7   *Dickinson v Del Solar* [1930] 1 KB 376; 45 TLR 637.

8   *Parkinson v Potter* (1885) 16 QBD 152.

9   *In re Republic of Bolivia Exploration Syndicate Limited* [1914] 1 Ch 139 (Astbury J).

10 *Magdalena Steam Navigation Co v Martin* (1859) 2 E & E 94.

11 *Taylor v Best* (1854) 14 CB 487; *Re Suarez* [1918] 1 Ch 176 (CA).

12 *Triquet v Bath* (1764) 3 Burr 1478; *Viveash v Becker* (1814) 3 M & S 284; *Taylor v Best* (1854) 14 CB 487; *Magdalena Steam Navigation Co v Martin* (1859) 2 E & E 94.

the enactment of the Diplomatic Privileges Act 1964 was regarded as more generous in according a wider degree of immunity than was the case in some other countries. In cases of doubt, the question as to who was a diplomat was to be settled by a statement by the Foreign Office.[13]

The years after 1945 witnessed the process of decolonisation and a steady increase in the number of independent states. Many such states developed their diplomatic staff to include specialists in military. cultural and economic matters; at the same time, the consular role expanded reflecting the increase in foreign travel in the developed world. The importance of diplomatic law meant that it received the early attention of the International Law Commission which produced final draft articles in 1958 and organised a conference on the subject in 1961. The Vienna Convention on Diplomatic Relations of 1961 has attracted near universal support and was given effect to in the United Kingdom by the Diplomatic Privileges Act 1964.[14] It was implemented in the United States by the Diplomatic Relations Act 1978. In the United Kingdom, the Diplomatic Privileges Act 1964 applies many of the provisions of the Convention to all states regardless of whether they are parties to the Convention.

Although in general the rules work reasonably well the last three decades have witnessed problems arising either from misconduct within a diplomatic mission[15] or by attacks on diplomatic staff and premises by terrorist groups.

The most serious breakdown in the operation of the normal rules came in the *Case Concerning United States Diplomatic and Consular Staff in Tehran*[16] which arose out of the occupation by militants of the United States embassy in Tehran and the consulates in Tabriz and Shiraz. The International Court of Justice took the opportunity to stress the importance of stable diplomatic relations. In the Case Concerning United States Diplomatic and Consular Staff in Tehran (Provisional Measures) the ICJ stressed that:

> ... there is no more fundamental prerequisite for the conduct of relations between States than the inviolability of diplomatic envoys and embassies so that throughout history nations of all creeds and cultures have observed reciprocal obligations for that purpose.[17]

The Court returned to the theme at the merits hearing[18] where it observed:

> The rules of diplomatic law, in short, constitute a self-contained regime which, on the one hand, lays down the receiving State's obligations regarding the facilities, privileges and immunities to be accorded to diplomatic missions and, on the other, foresees their possible abuse by members of the mission and specifies the means at the disposal of the receiving State to counter any such abuse.[19]

---

13 *Engelke v Musmann* [1928] AC 433.

14 See Samuels (1964) 27 MLR 689; Buckley (1966) 41 BYIL 321; J Brown (1988) 37 ICLQ 53.

15 In the years of the Cold War particular problems arose in respect of diplomats engaged in espionage activities (eg, the expulsion by the United Kingdom of over 100 Soviet staff in 1971). In 1984 the Libyan People's Bureau in London was closed following the shooting of a Police Officer. In 1986 the United Kingdom severed diplomatic relations with Syria following evidence of very serious misconduct by staff at the Embassy in London.

16 (1979) ICJ 19; (1980) ICJ 3.

17 (1979) ICJ 19 (Order 15, December 1979).

18 (1980) ICJ 3.

19 *Case concerning United States Diplomatic and Consular Staff in Tehran* (1980) ICJ 3, p 40; 61 ILR 504, p 556.

2 THE VIENNA CONVENTION ON DIPLOMATIC RELATIONS (1961)[20]

The Vienna Convention on Diplomatic Relations (1961) began life as a series of Draft Articles prepared by the International Law Commission. The final draft articles were tabled at the United Nations Conference on Diplomatic Intercourse and Immunities in 1961 and the Convention is a result of that conference. It is generally recognised that the Convention is one of the most successful efforts undertaken to promote codification. Article 51 of the Vienna Convention provided that 22 ratifications were required to bring the Convention into force; these were speedily obtained and the Convention entered into force on 24 April 1964. It is also clear that the widespread pattern of acceptance of the Convention means that most of the provisions form part of customary international law. There has been a steady increase in the number of state parties. In January 1990 the figure stood at 152 and by January 1996 it had reached 174. The fundamental nature of the Convention and its important role in facilitating peaceful intercourse between states was stressed in the *Iran* case[21] and it is clear that a considerable part of the Convention represents customary international law. The large number of state parties and the scope of the Convention means that most questions can be resolved by reference to its contents.

The purpose of the Convention can be gleaned from the preamble which recalls that the Charter of the United Nations (1945) is designed to promote friendly relations among nations and that diplomatic intercourse promotes this objective. The preamble notes that the purpose of the privileges and immunities 'is not to benefit individuals but to secure the efficient performance of the functions of diplomatic missions as representing states'. It is to be noted that it is also stated that rules of customary international law will continue to govern matters not expressly provided for in the Convention.

In customary international law where each state was deemed sovereign there was no entitlement to diplomatic relations with another state. This principle is continued in Art 2 of the Convention which provides that diplomatic relations between states take place by mutual consent. This principle is reinforced in Art 4 which provides that the sending state must seek the consent (agreement) of the receiving state in respect of the person it intends to send as head of the mission. No reasons need be given for the refusal of such consent. This provision must be read with Art 9 which allows a receiving state at any time to declare a particular individual is *persona non grata*; in such circumstances the person must be recalled or cease to function within the mission. The receiving state is under no obligation to give reasons and so Art 9 is often invoked when states engage in tit for tat expulsions.

(a) The diplomatic mission

Article 3 of the Vienna Convention sets out the functions of the diplomatic mission. In broad terms these include representing the sending state and conducting negotiations on its behalf. The diplomatic mission may obtain information by lawful means and it may promote friendly relations and represent the interests of its own nationals. In the absence

---

20   For text, see (1961) 10 ICLQ 597; 55 AJIL 1064; see Kerley (1962) 56 AJIL 88.
21   *Case concerning United States Diplomatic and Consular Staff in Tehran* (1979) ICJ 19; (1980) ICJ 3; 61 ILR 504.

of specific agreement the receiving state may require that the size of a mission be kept within limits.[22] The head of the mission will be considered as having taken up his duties when he has presented his credentials to the Ministry of Foreign Affairs. Under the terms of Article 14 the Head of Mission must fall within one of three classes.[23]

The most important provision in the Convention in relation to the mission is contained in Art 22 which provides that:

(1) The premises of the mission[24] shall be inviolable. The agents of the receiving State may not enter them, except with the consent of the head of mission.

(2) The receiving State is under a special duty to take all appropriate steps to protect the premises of the mission against any intrusion or damage and to prevent any disturbance of the peace of the mission or impairment of its dignity.

(3) The premises of the mission. their furnishings and other property thereon and the means of transport of the mission shall be immune from search, requisition, attachment or execution.

Difficulties can arise when there is a suspicion of misconduct on the premises[25] or entry might be desired for some *bona fide* purpose such as to fight fire. In this context it is important to note Art 41(3) which states that: 'The premises of the mission must not be used in any manner incompatible with the functions of the mission as laid down in the present Convention.' In cases where an entry has been sought this provision has been raised as a justification.

The clearest example of a breach of the rule of inviolability arose in the *Iran*[26] case where the International Court of Justice took the opportunity to stress the importance of this principle and the duties that it imposed on the receiving state in particular the special duty arising under Art 22(2) 'to take all appropriate steps to protect the premises of the mission'. The clear tone of the Court's judgment was to stress the obligatory nature of the duty placed on the receiving state in Arts 22, 24, 25, 26, 27 and 29 to ensure proper functioning of diplomatic premises. It might be argued that the Iran case was a very particular dispute arising from the partial collapse of government in the course of the Iranian revolution but the content of the judgment makes it clear that even though the occupation may have been commenced by outsiders a receiving state and its government

---

22 In reality, much will depend on the level of social and economic contact between the sending and receiving state. If the two states have close links and many of their nationals travel to the other state then a larger mission will be appropriate.

23 Article 14 provides for: (a) ambassadors or nuncios accredited to Head of State and other heads of mission of equivalent rank; (b) envoys, ministers and internuncios accredited to Heads of State; (c) *chargés d'affaires* accredited to Ministers of Foreign Affairs.

24 The phrase is defined in Art 1(i) as 'the buildings ... and the land ... ancillary thereto ... used for the purposes of the mission'; thus premises that have ceased to be used will be outside Art 22 and may be made safe by a local authority acting under statutory powers. See *Westminster City Council v Government of Islamic of Iran* [1986] 1 WLR 979 .

25 Such as in the Sun Yat Sen incident in 1896 when Wright J declined to make an order of habeas corpus in respect of a person who appeared to be detained in the Chinese Embassy in London; the case was later settled through diplomatic means. See A McNair, *International Law Opinions*, 1956, Vol 1, p 85. Sun Yat Sen (1867–1925) survived the incident to participate in the overthrow of the Manchu Dynasty in 1911 and to become President of China in 1912.

26 *US Diplomatic and Consular Staff in Tehran* case (1979) ICJ 7; (1980) ICJ 3.

is under an immediate duty to act to restrain such conduct. Under Art 22(2) a receiving state will be liable in cases of inaction.

A second relevant incident concerns the events in London in April 1984.[27] In 1979 the Libyan Embassies had been renamed Libyan People's Bureaux and were considered to be under the control of local 'revolutionary committees'. On 17 April 1984 a peaceful demonstration was taking place outside the Embassy Building when shots were fired that resulted in the death of a policewoman. Although it is clear that consideration was given to the question of storming the embassy as the situation developed it became clear that a negotiated solution would be possible.[28] Several days later diplomatic relations with Libya were severed and a negotiated end to the siege was effected. At the conclusion of the siege, those leaving were questioned and electronically searched; diplomatic bags that left the Bureau were not searched or scanned. On 30 April 1984, after the personnel had left, British officials together with a representative of the Saudi Arabian Embassy searched the building and weapons and forensic evidence were found. The incident itself raised a number of questions of which the most important were, first, in what circumstances could force be used?[29] A second issue was power to search after the event; a third question was the duty that a receiving state owes to protect an Embassy from demonstrators under Art 22. This is of some importance in the United Kingdom because of the common law tradition that respects the right of peaceful assembly.[30]

(b) Immunities relating to the person

Article 1 of the Vienna Convention on Diplomatic Relations (1961) draws a distinction in respect of personnel. In broad terms there are four distinct categories: (a) the Head of Mission; (b) the members of the diplomatic staff; (c) administrative and technical staff; (d) service staff (for example, butler, valets, cleaners, kitchen staff). In general, different levels of immunity will be accorded to each category. In the United Kingdom any question as to whether a person is within such a category is to be regarded as concluded by any certificate given by the Secretary of State for Foreign and Commonwealth Affairs under the Diplomatic Privileges Act 1964, s 4.

---

27 See S Sutton, 'Diplomatic immunity and the siege of the Libyan people's Bureau' [1985] PL 193.

28 The conduct of the siege was considered by the House of Commons Select Committee on Foreign Affairs which published a report on 'The Abuse of diplomatic immunities and privileges' in December 1984. In giving evidence Sir John Freedland (then Legal Adviser at the Foreign Office) indicated that an actual assault on the embassy would only be justified on the same criteria as operate for the exercise of force in lawful self defence. See R Higgins (1985) 79 AJIL 641; I Cameron (1985) 34 ICLQ 610; R Higgins (1986) 80 AJIL 135.

29 One consideration, of course, being the number of United Kingdom citizens working in Libya; a second factor being the policy adopted in respect of hijacked aeroplanes namely to use every effort to seek a peaceful solution within the general legal framework.

30 The right of citizens in the United Kingdom to assemble and demonstrate raises questions now under the Public Order Act 1986 and the Human Rights Act 1998. At the time of the incident, the House of Commons noted the practice of the Commissioner of the Metropolitan Police of allowing peaceful demonstrations on the opposite side of the road to an Embassy premises. The then Permanent Under Secretary at the Foreign Office (Sir Anthony Acland) in giving evidence to the House of Commons Committee stressed the need for an adequate level of policing of such demonstrations to meet the duties placed upon the United Kingdom under Art 22.

The operative provisions of the Vienna Convention begin with Art 29 which proclaims the person of diplomatic agent to be inviolable and he may not be detained or arrested. The article provides that he shall be treated with dignity and respect In conjunction with this Art 30 provides that the private residence of the diplomat is to be inviolable[31] and his papers, correspondence and property[32] are subject to the same protection. In respect of criminal jurisdiction, the diplomatic agent will enjoy complete immunity in the receiving state. In the case of serious offences,[33] it will be appropriate for the receiving state to have the individual declared *persona non grata* under Art 9.

Article 31 provides that the diplomatic agent will enjoy immunity in respect of civil jurisdiction[34] save in respect of three specific areas. First, in cases concerning private immovable property situated in the receiving state.[35] This exception respects the rule in private international law that the proper court to determine title to property is that of the *lex situs*. Secondly, in cases concerning succession where the diplomat is involved as a private person and is not acting on behalf of the sending state.[36] Thirdly, the diplomat will not be exempt in respect of professional or commercial activity undertaken outside his official functions.[37] It should be noted that Art 32(2) provides that the diplomat will not be a compellable witness in judicial proceedings. Moreover, Art 32(3) stipulates that no execution of judgment shall be made in respect of a diplomat save in respect of the exceptional cases listed in Art 31(1). The privileges of the diplomat listed in Art 31 may be enjoyed by the members of the family of the diplomat forming part of his household provided they are not nationals of the receiving state. In broad terms, the diplomat will be immune from social security contributions and personal taxes levied by the receiving state.[38]

The Vienna Convention on Diplomatic Relations (1961) makes separate provision in respect of administrative and technical staff. Under the terms of Art 37 and Art 31, such staff will enjoy immunity from criminal jurisdiction but in respect of civil and administrative jurisdiction this is restricted to their official acts.[39] As with the diplomat such privileges may be enjoyed by members of their family forming part of the household. Under the terms of Art 37(3) members of the service staff of the mission who are not nationals of the receiving state enjoy immunity in respect of acts performed in the course of their duties including exemption form taxes on emoluments. The justification

---

31 This means that the premises will be defended against intruders; it does not mean that a state and the executive branch are entitled to evict a person who may be in lawful occupation without a court order. See *Agbor v Metropolitan Police Commissioner* [1969] 1 WLR 703; 52 ILR 382, where the Court of Appeal (Lord Denning MR, Salmon and Winn LJJ dissenting) set aside an exercise in self help by the executive branch which had proceeded on the basis of an error of fact as to whether it was the private residence of a diplomat.

32 Save in respect of exceptions listed below.

33 For the response of the United States and the United Kingdom in respect of the troublesome question of unpaid parking fines see (1994) 88 AJIL 312; (1992) 63 BYIL 700.

34 For an example of a case where proceedings were begun before immunity applied, see *Ghosh v D'Rozario* [1963] 1 QB 106; 33 ILR 361 (where the Court of Appeal held that immunity precluded the continuance of pre-existing proceedings).

35 Vienna Convention on Diplomatic Relations (1961), Art 31(1)(a).

36 *Ibid*, Art 31(1)(b).

37 *Ibid*, Art 31(1)(c).

38 *Ibid*, Arts 33 and 34.

39 *Ibid*, Art 37(2).

for separate treatment is that the duties of the junior staff are less sensitive and that there is thus less justification for interfering with the private law rights of those in the receiving state.

Difficulties have arisen as to the point at which immunity arises. Under the terms of Art 39(1) immunity arises when the person enters the receiving state to take up his post. In respect of termination Art 37(2) provides that immunities will continue until the individual has left the territory or after the expiry of a reasonable time in which to do so.[40] However, in respect of acts performed in the conduct of his official duties immunity shall continue to subsist.

A number of difficulties have arisen in respect of the question as to when immunity may be said to have arisen. In the United Kingdom prior to 1964 the rule was that the diplomatic agent must have been subject to reception by the receiving state. The matter was reconsidered in *R v Governor of Pentonville Prison ex p Teja*[41] which concerned an attempt by an individual to resist rendition to India under the Fugitive Offenders Act 1967. In rejecting the assertion that the individual had diplomatic status, Lord Parker LCJ[42] noted that Arts 2 and 4 of the Vienna Convention were predicated upon the assumption that the diplomat was present with the consent of the receiving state. In *R v Lambeth Justices ex p Yusufu*[43] Watkins LJ indicated agreement with *Teja* and expressed the view that Art 39 of the Vienna was only procedural in content. This view was followed in *Re Osman*[44] but was doubted in *R v Secretary of State for the Home Department ex p Bagga*[45] where Parker LJ in analysing the Vienna Convention in the context of a case on immigration control expressed the view that Art 39 operated from the time of entry into the territory and that, in the case of appointment of a person within the territory, Art 39 simply required notification. It therefore cannot be regarded as a settled question as to whether the sending state is or is not under a duty to notify in respect of permanent appointments within a reasonable period.

In respect of personal immunity, the operative date will be when the proceedings come before the court for determination. So a legal action in which a diplomat could have entered a plea of immunity will be allowed to continue if circumstances change and the

---

40 *Magdalena Steam Navigation Co v Martin* (1859) 2 El & El 94; *Musurus Bey v Gadban* [1894] 2 QB 352; *Re Suarez* [1918] 1 Ch 176.

41 *R v Governor of Pentonville Prison ex p Teja* [1971] 2 QB 274 (Lord Parker LCJ, Cairns LJ and Melford Stevenson J). In this case, the individual was claiming diplomatic immunity to resist proceedings under the Fugitive Offenders Act 1967.

42 The learned judge placed emphasis on Arts 2 and 4 to which it is arguable Art 39 is subject as Art 39(1) begins 'Every person entitled', ie, entitlement is a precondition of the application of the Article.

43 *R v Lambeth Justices ex p Yusufu* [1985] Crim LR 510 (Divisional Court) (Watkins LJ and Nolan J) This was an application for *certiorari* to quash a committal for trial arising out of the kidnapping of Mr Dikko in London in July 1984. The defendant argued unsuccessfully that he had diplomatic status from the time of entry under Art 39 notwithstanding no effort had been made to inform the Foreign Office.

44 *R v Governor of Pentonville Prison ex p Osman* (1988) *The Times*, 24 December (a case concerning an individual seeking to resist rendition under the then Fugitive Offenders Act 1967). See 59 BYIL 478.

45 *R v Secretary of State for the Home Department ex p Bagga* [1990] 3 WLR 1013; 1 All ER 777 (Parker, Glidewell and Leggatt LJJ).

immunity is withdrawn;[46] in like terms a divorce petition issued will remain valid if not struck out and can be determined[47] if at the time of the hearing any prior diplomatic immunity has ceased under Art 39(2). Difficulties have arisen in cases where diplomats and their wives in the course of divorce proceedings seek to restrain the removal of children from the jurisdiction; in normal circumstances immunity can be claimed by a departing husband and children.[48] In a case where departure has taken place a claim for state immunity may be upheld if the diplomat was acting under the orders of the state notwithstanding that the diplomat might not be able to claim immunity under Art 39(2).[49]

(c) Immunities in respect of property

As indicated above one of the cardinal provisions of the Vienna Convention is the inviolability of the mission.[50] Such inviolability extends to any property thereon and the means of transport of the mission. Thus, Art 22(3) provides that means of transport shall be 'immune from search, requisition, attachment or execution'. The mission itself will be immune in respect of local property taxation. Further, it is provided by Art 24 that the archives and documents of the mission shall be inviolable at any time and wherever they may be.[51] The protection accorded by Art 24 is an important consideration where libel proceedings are brought founded in an internal embassy document; the normal approach is either to regard the document as subject to absolute privilege or to rule that the entire dispute is non-justiciable for reasons of international comity.[52]

It is quite clear from Art 1(i) that the mission must be used for diplomatic purposes; it follows that premises that have ceased to be used for diplomatic purposes may be subject to civil claims. So that in *Westminster City Council v Government of Iran*,[53] it was possible to

---

46 *Empson v Smith* [1966] 1 QB 426 (where the defendant had immunity when the action was issued but failed to act and by the time of the substantive hearing the Diplomatic Privileges Act 1964 had come into effect his immunity had been restricted under Arts 31 and 37 in respect of acts outside his official duties) (Diplock, Sellers and Dankwerts LJJ).

47 *Shaw v Shaw* [1979] 3 All ER 1. (Husband had returned to the United States at the time of the hearing but at the time of the issue of the petition was a serving diplomat.) (Balcombe J following *Empson v Smith* [1966] 1 QB 426 allowed the petition to proceed. The English court having jurisdiction because the parties were habitually resident in England for one year prior to the presentation of the petition.)

48 *Re P (No 1)* (1998) 114 ILR 479 (Stuart White J rejecting the submission that the principle of the welfare of the child and the Children Act 1989 should prevail. The husband not having yet departed from the jurisdiction); 1 FLR 625.

49 *Re P (No 2)* (1998) 114 ILR 485; 1 FLR 1027 (Stephen Brown P; Lord Woolf MR, Butler Sloss and Simon Brown LJJ).

50 Vienna Convention on Diplomatic Relations (1961), Art 22.

51 In *Shearson Lehman v Maclaine Watson (No 2)* [1988] 1 WLR 16. (In the course of the case Lord Bridge indicated that he thought the expression 'archives and documents of the mission' in Art 24 should be read as meaning the archives or documents 'belonging to or held by the mission'.)

52 *Fayed v Al Tajir* [1988] 1 QB 712 (libel action arising from document circulating within London Embassy of the United Arab Emirates. Case concerns detailed review of competing considerations by Mustill LJ). See, also, *M Isaacs and Sons Ltd v Cook* [1925] 2 KB 391; *Szalatnay-Stacho v Fink* [1947] KB 1.

53 *Westminster City Council v Islamic Republic of Iran* [1986] 1 WLR 979.

conclude that the Iranian Embassy in London had ceased to be used for diplomatic purposes in May 1980. In similar terms, the departure of personnel from the Libyan People's Bureau in April 1984 marked the end of the use of that building for diplomatic purposes. One of the problems that has arisen in the last two decades is the problem of the abandonment of diplomatic premises. In the United Kingdom this resulted in separate legislation in the Diplomatic and Consular Premises Act 1987 and this is considered below.

In respect of bank accounts it would seem that such are immune from execution in customary international law and under the State Immunity Act 1978 unless they can be shown to be used solely for commercial purposes. This principle is reflected in Art 25 of the Vienna Convention which provides the receiving state shall accord full facilities for the performance of the functions of the mission.

Article 30 of the Vienna Convention on Diplomatic Relations (1961) provides that the private residence of the diplomatic agent shall enjoy the same inviolability[54] as the premises of the mission; the papers and correspondence shall likewise enjoy inviolability. In this context problems can arise where the state also claims an interest. In *Intpro Properties (UK) Ltd v Sauvel*,[55] an action was begun against a diplomat alleging breaches of covenant; the lease was granted to the French government who used the premises to house a diplomat and sometimes to hold social events. At a later date, the Republic of France attempted to argue that immunity arose under the State Immunity Act 1978, s 16(1)(b). The Court of Appeal in reversing Bristow J rejected this assertion and held that a premises do not become part of a diplomatic mission simply because they may occasionally be used for embassy social functions.

(d) Freedom of communication

The broad principle is that the diplomat should not be subject to excessive restrictions by the receiving state. Thus, by the terms of Art 26 the receiving state is required to ensure freedom of movement for all members of the mission save in respect of 'zones entry into which is prohibited or regulated for reasons of national security'.

Article 27 of the Vienna Convention on Diplomatic Relations (1961) contains a number of important provisions concerning communication. Article 27(1)–(4) read as follows:

(1) The receiving State shall permit and protect free communication on the part of the mission for all official purposes. In communicating with the government and the other missions and consulates of the sending State. wherever situated. the mission may employ all appropriate means. including diplomatic couriers and messages in code or cipher. However. the mission may install and use a wireless transmitter only with the consent of the receiving State.

(2) The official correspondence of the mission shall be inviolable. Official correspondence means all correspondence relating to the mission and its functions.

---

54 See *Agbor v Metropolitan Police Commissioner* [1969] 1 WLR 703 for consideration by Lord Denning MR as to when a diplomat may be said to have left his private residence.

55 *Intpro Properties (UK) Ltd v Sauvel* [1983] 1 QB 1019; 64 ILR 384 (CA) (Watkins and May LJJ).

(3) The diplomatic bag shall not be opened or detained.

(4) The packages constituting the diplomatic bag must bear visible external marks of their character and may contain only diplomatic documents or articles intended for official use.

There is no doubt that in recent years these provisions have given rise to public debate. A balance has to be sought between freedom of communication and the equally important need to guard against abuse. Allegations have circulated about the diplomatic bag being used to smuggle drugs, weapons, art treasures and sometimes individuals.[56] The 'bag' itself may vary in size from a small packet to a large crate. The issue has acquired a degree of prominence because of suspicions of diplomatic bags being used to facilitate terrorist conduct.[57] In such circumstances a state may feel in the presence of *prima facie* evidence that it has a duty to ascertain the full facts. In this context the question of screening of diplomatic bags is of some moment. The United Kingdom view is that the screening of such bags is not unlawful under Art 27(3).

When the siege of the Libyan Embassy concluded in April 1984 the United Kingdom took the decision not to search or screen any diplomatic bags leaving the premises. This was of particular interest because Libya had entered a reservation to Art 27(3) permitting it to request the opening of a diplomatic bag in the presence of an official representative of the state concerned. However, the subsequent House of Commons Select Committee was informed that the decision not to seek to open such bags was made on political rather than legal grounds.[58]

In July 1984 a former Nigerian Minister was found in a crate at Stanstead Airport ready to be flown to Nigeria.[59] In that particular case, the crate did not contain external markings and was not strictly a diplomatic bag. However, the subsequent statements issued by the Foreign and Commonwealth Office made it clear that where the preservation of human life was in issue then consideration would inevitably have to be given as to whether a diplomatic bag should be opened.

Disquiet about possible abuses of the diplomatic bag has lead to examination of the problem by the International Law Commission (ILC). The ILC has now produced Draft

---

56 In recent incidents: (a) in 1964 Italy expelled two Egyptians after an Israeli was found drugged in a crate described as 'diplomatic mail' in an airport in Rome; (b) in 1980 a crate destined for the Moroccan Embassy in London was found to contain drugs; (c) the crate containing Mr Dikko was opened at Stanstead in July 1984 before he could be flown to Nigeria; (d) when the siege of the Libyan Embassy in London in ended in April 1984, no attempt was made to search the diplomatic bags taken from the building.

57 The fear of Western states being that the diplomatic bag might be used to smuggle guns for use in terrorist activity or to employ against dissident exiles. Such conduct is, of course, a clear breach of Arts 3 and 41 of the Vienna Convention and the accepted rules of customary international law. It poses problems because of the duty of the executive branch of government to maintain law and order within its own territory. In these circumstances, some argue that such conduct constitutes such a fundamental breach as to warrant forfeiture of the protection of the Convention. For a review, see R Higgins (1985) 79 AJIL 641.

58 In the form of evidence from Sir John Freeland then Legal Adviser to the Foreign Office; for the subsequent House of Commons Foreign Affairs Select Committee Report; see R Higgins (1985) 79 AJIL 641; (1986) 80 AJIL 135. See also I Cameron (1985) 34 ICLQ 610.

59 For the incident of July 1984 concerning Mr Dikko, see A Akinsanya, 'The Dikko affair and Anglo-Nigerian relations' (1985) 34 ICLQ 602; see also (1985) 55 BYIL 493.

Articles on the Diplomatic Courier and the Diplomatic Bag;[60] the most relevant provision is Art 28 which concerns protection of the diplomatic bag. In the debates within the ILC there were two possible choices; either to continue with the absolute inviolability rule or to move to the 'request or return' approach.[61] In the event, Draft Article 28 adopts the traditional position by providing that the 'diplomatic bag shall be inviolable wherever it may be; it shall not be opened or detained and shall be exempt from examination directly or through electronic or other technical devices'. It is to be noted that Draft Article 28(2) continues the 'request or return' rule for the consular bag as it is presently set out in Art 35(3) of the Vienna Convention on Consular Relations (1963).

It has to be conceded that the Draft Articles do little to meet legitimate concerns about abuses of the diplomatic bag and it must be open to doubt as to whether any multilateral treaty founded on these provisions would be capable of attracting sufficient ratifications.

(e) Waiver of immunity

Under the terms of Article 32 of the Vienna Convention the sending state may waive the immunity from jurisdiction of the diplomatic agent and persons enjoying immunity under Art 37.[62] However, such a waiver must always be made expressly.[63] Where a diplomatic agent initiates litigation then he cannot claim immunity in respect of any counter claim that directly relates to that cause of action although immunity can be claimed in respect of an unrelated cause of action.[64] It is well established that waiver must be by the sending state and not by the individual himself. So that in *R v Madan*[65] a waiver by the individual was ineffective. In the context of normal litigation, the waiver may be by the state itself or by its chief diplomatic representative.[66] For the purpose of Art 32 in the United Kingdom it is provided in s 2(3) of the Diplomatic Privileges Act 1964 that a waiver by the head of the mission by any state shall be deemed to be a waiver by that state. In respect of execution of judgments, Art 32(4) provides that any waiver of immunity from jurisdiction will not imply a waiver from execution, for which a separate waiver will be necessary. In cases where a waiver has been granted by the Ambassador,

---

60 In 1989 the ILC adopted a set of 32 Articles and two draft Protocols under the title of Draft Articles on the Diplomatic Courier and the Diplomatic Bag.
61 Where a state requests permission to open the bag in the presence of an official of the mission and then refuses entry, if the request is not complied with, this would seem to violate Art 27.
62 Vienna Convention on Diplomatic Relations (1961), Art 32(1).
63 *Ibid*, Art 32(2).
64 See *High Commissioner for India v Ghosh* [1960] 1 QB 134 (action for debt counterclaim for defamation; claim for immunity allowed). See, also, *Duke of Brunswick v King of Hanover* (1844) 6 Beav 1; *South African Republic v La Compagnie Franco Belge du Chemin de Fer du Nord* [1898] 1 Ch 190; 14 TLR 65.
65 *R v Madan* [1961] 2 QB 1 (where Lord Parker LCJ left open the question as to whether a waiver could ever be retrospective).
66 *In re Republic of Bolivia Exploration Syndicate Ltd* [1914] 1 Ch 139; 30 TLR 78; *Dickinson v Del Solar* [1930] 1 KB 376; 45 TLR 637. In *A Company v The Republic of X* [1990] 2 Lloyd's Rep 520, Saville J indicated that any waiver in respect of Arts 22 and 30 would have to be given directly to the court and could not be founded upon *inter partes* agreement.

then it will not be possible for the individual to claim immunity in subsequent proceedings.[67]

Much will depend on the nature of the act in issue. While there has been concern in some capital cities as to the level of parking tickets issued the evidence does indicate a measure of co-operation where serious offences are in issue. In the United Kingdom the matter will be passed to the Foreign Office who will contact the diplomatic mission and request a waiver of immunity under Art 32; if a waiver is not offered then the person will be declared *persona non grata* under Art 9. United Kingdom policy has remained unchanged since 1952.[68] In the United States the same policy is adopted although there is perhaps a greater level of concern because of the presence of so many staff from international organisations based in Washington or New York.[69]

(f) The employment of diplomats[70]

In recent years there have been a number of cases where diplomats or other members of a mission have appeared as plaintiffs before the courts of a receiving state. One reason for this is that many states now include some form of employment protection legislation as part of their municipal law.[71] It is also clear that the ending of restrictive immunity and the willingness of states to employ foreign nationals in order to promote economic growth has lead to a number of employment disputes coming before municipal courts. In these circumstances the courts of the receiving state are faced with balancing the desire to protect its own labour force[72] with the need to preserve good relations with a foreign state by abstaining from exercising jurisdiction over matters internal to a diplomatic mission.

Although much will depend on precise municipal legislation, a common scenario is for a claim to be made against the sending state by a dismissed employee, and the court will be forced to consider both the law relating to diplomatic immunity but also any argument raised concerning state immunity. In *Sengupta v Republic of India*,[73] the

---

67 *R v AB* [1941] 1 KB 454 (Lord Caldecote LCJ citing Lord Ellenborough in *Marshall v Critico* (1808) 9 East 447 where he observed: 'This is not a privilege of a person, but of the state which he represents'). See also *Re Suarez* [1918] 1 Ch 176.

68 See Interdepartmental Committee on State Immunities, *Report on Diplomatic Immunity*, Cmnd 8460.

69 See Department of State, *Guidance for Law Enforcement Officers with Regard to Personal Rights and Immunities of Foreign Diplomatic and Consular Personnel* (1988) 27 ILM 1617.

70 H Fox, 'Employment contracts as an exception to state immunity' (1995) 66 BYIL 97; R Garnett, 'State immunity in employment matters' (1997) 46 ICLQ 81.

71 In the United Kingdom, the right to bring an action for unfair dismissal was placed on the statute book in 1971 in the Industrial Relations Act of that year; the provisions were later consolidated into Employment Protection (Consolidation) Act 1978. See now Employment Rights Act 1996.

72 In *Ahmed v Government of Saudi Arabia* [1996] 2 All ER 248, Peter Gibson LJ remarked 'I have considerable sympathy with the argument that a locally employed person of British nationality should be able to enjoy the rights and protection afforded by the Employment Protection(Consolidation) Act 1978', p 252.

73 *Sengupta v Republic of India* (1983) ICR 221; 64 ILR 352. (The case itself was governed by common law rather than the State Immunity Act 1978 because the contract of employment had been entered into in 1975.)

Employment Appeal Tribunal considered that at common law the tribunal lacked jurisdiction because any attempt to probe the performance of the employee's duties would trespass upon the claim of India to sovereign immunity in respect of the internal workings of its embassy. In dismissing the application Browne-Wilkinson J observed that 'the fairness of any dismissal from such employment is very likely to involve an investigation by the industrial tribunal into the internal management of the diplomatic representation in the United Kingdom of the Republic of India. an investigation wholly inconsistent with the dignity of the foreign state and an interference with its sovereign functions'.

Such cases will inevitably depend on the precise terms of the municipal law. In the United Kingdom while certain contracts of employment may not attract a claim of state immunity[74] this will not normally be the case with members of the diplomatic mission.[75] So that in *Arab Republic of Egypt v Gamal Eldin*[76] the Employment Appeal Tribunal allowed a claim for immunity by the state of Egypt in respect of two drivers at the embassy while, in *Ahmed v Government of Saudi Arabia*,[77] the defendants were able to raise a claim of state immunity in respect of an application by an embassy secretary. In those states where there is no specific legislation then the matter will be regarded as governed by common law and the *jure imperii/ jure gestionis* distinction will be applied. Thus, in Ireland a state has claimed immunity in respect of the employment claim of a chauffeur[78] while in New Zealand the Court of Appeals[79] upheld a claim for immunity in respect of an action by a secretary. The position in civil law countries is not markedly different so that in Germany the United Kingdom was able to plead immunity in respect of a claim by a secretary.[80] The attitude to such claims was well put in the Irish Supreme Court where one of the judges observed: 'I think once one approaches the embassy gates one must do so on an amber light. *Prima facie* anything to do with the embassy is within the public domain of the government in question.'[81] However, there are a number of examples in civil law courts where the emphasis has been placed on the status of the employee and a low level employee has been permitted to sue and claims for immunity have been rejected.[82]

---

74 State Immunity Act 1978, s 4.

75 By State Immunity Act 1978, s 16(1)(a), the terms of s 4 of the Act do not apply to the members of the mission under Diplomatic Privileges Act.

76 [1996] 2 All ER 237 (EAT).

77 [1996] 2 All ER 248 (CA) (Peter Gibson, Stuart Smith, Hutchinson LJJ).

78 *Canada v The Employment Appeals Tribunal and Burke* (1992) IR 484 (Supreme Court of Ireland).

79 *Governor of Pitcairn v Sutton* (1995) 1 NZLR 426.

80 *Conrades v United Kingdom* (1981) 65 ILR 205 (Hanover *Arbeitsgericht*).

81 *Canada v The Employment Appeals Tribunal and Burke* (1992) IR 484, p 500, *per* O'Flaherty J.

82 *British Embassy Drivers* case (1978) 65 ILR 20 (Superior Provincial Court of Vienna); *S v Republic of India* (1984) 82 ILR (Swiss Federal Tribunal); *MK v Turkey* (1985) 94 ILR 350 (Sub-District Court of the Hague); *Van Hulst v United States of America* (1990) NYIL (Supreme Court of The Netherlands). It is of course the case that Austria, Switzerland and The Netherlands have all signed the European Convention on State Immunity ('the Basle Convention').

(g) Abuses of the system

Although there have been a number of complaints in recent years about abuses of diplomatic privileges the basic structure of the Vienna Convention on Diplomatic Relations (1961) remains in place. The duties imposed on diplomats are set out in Art 41 of the Vienna Convention which reads:

(1) Without prejudice to their privileges and immunities, it is the duty of all persons enjoying such privileges and immunities to respect the laws and regulations of the receiving State. They also have a duty not to interfere in the internal affairs of that State.

(2) All official business with the receiving State entrusted to the mission by the sending Sate shall be conducted with or through the Ministry for Foreign Affairs of the receiving State or such other ministry as may be agreed.

(3) The premises of the mission must not be used in any manner incompatible with the functions of the mission as laid down in the present convention or by other rules of general international law or by any special agreements in force between the sending State and the receiving State.

It is clear that the privileges of diplomats are linked by Art 41(3) to the legitimate functions of the mission. It is equally clear that the diplomat is obliged not only to respect the laws of the receiving state but not to interfere in the affairs of that state.[83] The wording of the Article indicates that the duty of diplomats to obey internal laws is 'without prejudice to their privileges and immunities'. Thus, on the conventional interpretation abuse by a diplomat does not entail the loss of privilege. The reason for this is to protect the diplomat from any attempt by an unscrupulous receiving state to fabricate evidence and promote a case with the object of securing some form of advantage. The interpretation is of limited relevance because if cogent evidence exists of abuse by a diplomat most states will not hesitate to declare the individual *persona non grata* under Art 9.

There is little doubt that individual abuses by certain diplomats have resulted in a demand for restrictions and modification of the Vienna Convention on Diplomatic Relations (1961). Such a project is unlikely in the immediate future because of the need to secure such a wide range of agreement. However, in the cases of the grossest abuses the receiving state can expel particular individuals[84] or choose to break off diplomatic relations completely.

---

83 This has not always proved possible to resist, so that in 1584 Mendoza the Spanish Ambassador to England was ordered to leave the country after plotting to depose Queen Elizabeth I. In 1654 the French Ambassador to England was required to leave after conspiring against Oliver Cromwell. In recent times, expulsions have normally been concerned with allegations of spying or improper attempts to influence political parties. In 1980 New Zealand expelled the Ambassador of the Soviet Union for passing money to a political party. In 1985, when the United States Ambassador to France commented on the presence of communists in the government, France protested to the United States about interference in its internal affairs.

84 Examples would be: (a) the events at the Libyan People's Bureau in London in 1984 resulted in the termination of diplomatic relations between the United Kingdom and Libya; (b) the abduction of the former Nigerian minister in July 1984 resulted in two members of the Nigerian High Commission being expelled; (c) in 1986 evidence arising from a criminal prosecution at the Central Criminal Court of a non-diplomat lead to the breaking of diplomatic relations with Syria.

3 THE VIENNA CONVENTION ON CONSULAR RELATIONS (1963)[85]

As indicated above, the consular role[86] has increased considerably in the last 50 years. Consuls act on behalf of the sending state in the discharge of administrative functions; they are not confined to the capital and are to be found in substantial provincial cities. Their privileges and immunities are less extensive than the diplomat and this is a reflection of their different role. However, this is complicated by the modern tendency of some states to merge their diplomatic and consular functions. Consuls traditionally have an administrative role in respect of the nationals of the sending state in the receiving state such as keeping a register of nationals, recording births, witnessing documents, performing marriages[87] and providing for the taking of evidence. The importance of the consular role in the modern world was indicated by the International Court of Justice in the *Hostages* case[88] where it observed that:

> ... the unimpeded conduct of consular relations, which have also been established between peoples since ancient times. is no less important in the context of present day international law, in promoting the development of friendly relations among nations, and ensuring protection and assistance for aliens resident in the territories of other states; and ... therefore the privileges and immunities of consular officers and consular employees, and the inviolability of consular premises and archives are similarly principles deep rooted in international law.[89]

The normal distinction between a consul and a diplomat is that the latter is concerned with political relations with the receiving state. The consul may have dealings with local government institutions but is subordinate to the local diplomatic envoy. Although it has been accepted since the 18th century[90] that the privileges of the consul should be inferior to those of the diplomat the position has been complicated in the last quarter of a century by the tendency of some states to merge their diplomatic and consular functions. In principle the individual who acts simultaneously as diplomat and consul is entitled to the privileges of the former.

In the 18th and 19th centuries the role and status of the consul was governed by the rules of customary international law. The role of the consul began to increase in the 19th

---

85 See generally, Baron Alphonse Heyking, *'La théorie et la pratique des services consulaires'* (1930) 34 HR 811; G Stuart; *'Le droit et la pratique diplomatiques et consulaires'* (1934) 48 HR 459; J Zourek, *'Le statute et les fonctions des consuls'* (1962) 106 HR 357; A Maresca, *'Les rélations consulaires et les fonctions du consul en matière de droit privé'* (1971) 134 HR 105.

86 Although certain English novelists have portrayed the consular official as a broken sad case worthy of sympathy, see Malcolm Lowry, *Under the Volcano*, 1947; Graham Greene, *The Honorary Consul*, 1976.

87 The Foreign Marriage Act 1892 as amended by Foreign Marriage Act 1947 and the Foreign Marriage (Amendment) Act 1988 provides subject to certain conditions that any marriage conducted before a marriage officer in a foreign country will be valid in England provided one party is a United Kingdom national. The consular official may act as a marriage officer, see *Hay v Northcote* [1900] 2 Ch 262; *Ramsay Fairfax v Ramsay Fairfax* (1956) P 115; *Collett v Collett* (1968) P 482.

88 *Case concerning United States Diplomatic and Consular Staff in Tehran (Provisional Measures)* (1979) ICJ 7, pp 19–20.

89 (1979) ICJ 7, pp 19–20.

90 *Barbuitt's* case (1737) Cases Talbot 281; *Viveash v Becker* (1814) 3 M & S 284; *United States v Ravara* (1794) 2 Dall 299; *Re Biaz* (1890) 135 US 403.

century with the expansion of international commerce and shipping. In 1963 the United Nations organised a conference at Vienna which resulted in the signing of the Vienna Convention on Consular Relations (1963).[91] The Convention which entered into force in 1967 is partly a document of codification and partly an attempt at progressive development. Any questions outside the Convention will continue to be governed by the rules of customary international law.

Before an individual can be considered as a consul he must have a commission from the sending state and a permission (*exequatur*) from the receiving state. In general, a consul will operate within a particular consular district; such consular districts will be agreed between the sending state and the receiving state.[92] The Vienna Convention distinguishes between the paid career consul and the honorary consul who may be a local business man. Most states appoint both forms of consul; the Vienna Convention on Consular Relations (1963) recognises four classes of consular officer.[93] The extensive list of consular functions are set out in Art 5 of the Vienna Convention.[94] In principle, the consul will be responsible to his local embassy; in many capital cities the embassy will establish its own consular section.

In respect of premises the Vienna Convention provides for the inviolability of consular premises,[95] exemption from taxation[96] and inviolability of consular archives. A particularly important provision is Art 36 which gives the consul the right to communicate with a national of the sending state who is in prison in the receiving state and further provides that a national in prison shall be able to communicate with a consul and shall be informed of his right under the article. This particular provision gave rise to legal action before the International Court of Justice when both Paraguay and Germany brought a case alleging breaches[97] of Art 36 in respect of two of their nationals awaiting execution in the United States. Both applications alleged breaches of Art 36 and in both cases the Court was prepared to order Provisional Measures designed to restrain the executions. In the event the executions took place; although the Secretary of State did subsequently write to all Governors within the United States stressing the importance of observance of the Convention.

To an extent the Vienna Convention assimilates the status of diplomats and consuls. Of particular relevance is Art 41 which provides that a consul shall not be arrested save in connexion with a grave crime while Art 43 stipulates that the consul will enjoy immunity in respect of acts undertaken in the course of his official duties. Under the terms of Art 44 the consul enjoys a limited privilege preventing him being compelled to give evidence as

---

91   Text (1963) 57 AJIL 995.

92   Vienna Convention on Consular Relations (1963), Art 4.

93   Under Art 9, Consuls General, Consuls, Vice Consul or Consular Agent.

94   Such functions include protecting the nationals of the sending state in the receiving state, furthering commercial activity issuing passports, extending assistance to vessels and aircraft.

95   Vienna Convention on Consular Relations (1963), Art 31.

96   *Ibid*, Art 32.

97   *Vienna Convention on Consular Relations (Paraguay v United States of America)* (1998) ICJ 248, but subsequently discontinued; see (1998) ICJ 426. *Vienna Convention on Consular Relations (Germany v United States)* (1999) ICJ 9. For a discussion on the two cases see M Addo (1999) 48 ICLQ 673.

to the discharge of his official duties. In general the Convention draws a distinction between the career consul and the honorary consul with the former acquiring wider privileges and immunities.[98]

4 THE PARTICULAR PROBLEM OF ASYLUM

One of the most debated questions in diplomatic and consular law is as to whether international law recognises a right of asylum; such a form of asylum is sometimes described as 'diplomatic asylum'. In brief the question is whether a diplomatic mission in a receiving state is entitled to offer refuge to an individual fleeing from police or military forces.[99] Such questions may become acute during periods of civil disorder or revolution where there may be grounds for questioning whether an individual will be accorded a fair trial. There is little doubt that the practice is long standing and is frequently invoked but it a matter of considerable doubt as to whether it is part of an established rule of public international law.

There is no doubt that a right to grant asylum may arise pursuant to treaty[100] and in Latin America local custom[101] and treaty obligations often specify for such a right. Similarly there is little doubt that some states take the view that the granting of refuge or asylum is to be considered in situations where law and order has broken down and the concern[102] is to protect human life. In some instances refuge is granted pending negotiations to permit safe conduct out of the territory. While a state may be minded to grant refuge if it is sympathetic to a particular cause, there is some evidence to indicate that a state will be more likely to offer refuge if basic human rights cannot be guaranteed to the refugee in the receiving state. Although the Vienna Convention in Art 41(3) requires that the premises of the mission should not be used 'in any manner incompatible with the functions of the mission' most states do grant refuge in extreme circumstances. Writing in 1913, Sir Edward Grey[103] asserted a decision to grant refuge could only be 'from motives

---

98 Articles 40–57 (career consuls); Arts 58–67 (honorary consuls).

99 This is the usual situation although there may be other reasons such as where individuals are seeking to emigrate. Such was the case in some German Embassies in Eastern Europe prior to the fall of the Berlin Wall in 1989.

100 *Asylum* case (*Columbia v Peru*) (1950) ICJ 266; see HW Briggs (1951) 45 AJIL 728; GG Fitzmaurice (1950) 27 BYIL 31; F Morgenstern (1948) 25 BYIL 241; (1951) 647 LQR 362; van Essen (1952) 1 ICLQ 533.

101 Many of the cases arising out of unsuccessful coups where those fleeing had grounds to believe that justice might be summary and severe.

102 Examples would be: (a) the granting of asylum to Cardinal Mindzenty in the United States Embassy in Hungary in 1956. The Cardinal remained until 1971 when in old age he was allowed to leave for Rome; (b) the decision by Sweden and some other states in Santiago to offer sanctuary to those fleeing after the military coup that overthrew President Allende in September 1973; (c) the decision of the United States Embassy in Peking to offer refuge to Professor Fang Lizhi following the action of the Chinese authorities in Tianemen Square in June 1989. In all three instances, the state granting refuge was broadly in favour of causes adopted by the refugee and in all three cases had reason to doubt that normal standards of civil liberty would be respected. Another example is afforded by the French Embassy in Phnom Penh affording refuge in 1975. In three of the four incidents cited not only were civil liberties at risk but the legitimacy of the government itself was in issue.

103 Sir Edward Grey (1862–1933) (Foreign Secretary 1905–16). Grey was writing to HM Minister in Haiti on 30 May 1913: 7 BDIL 922. The United Kingdom policy remains as indicated by Grey.

of humanity in cases of instant or imminent personal peril'; while in 1981 the United States asserted that its policy was 'to grant temporary refuge for humanitarian reasons in extreme or exceptional circumstances when the life or safety of a person is put in immediate danger'.[104]

Thus, practice depends on the discretion exercised by individual states; when a decision is made to grant refuge the state of the territory will have the option of negotiating or using force against the mission. The latter course will normally be regarded as unacceptable.[105]

5 SPECIAL MISSIONS

In some instances a state may send a special mission[106] to another state in order to deal with a particular problem or to attend a conference. In normal circumstances, such staff will not be part of the permanent diplomatic staff. The fact that in certain instances immunity may be needed to be extended to non-diplomats was recognised by the United Kingdom during the Second World War when the presence of a number of governments in exile precipitated the need for domestic legislation.[107] Although the ILC had considered the question of special missions when preparing the draft articles for the 1961 Convention, the position of the *ad hoc* mission was considered again after 1961 at the request of the General Assembly. In 1967 the ILC produced a series of draft articles which were adopted by the General Assembly in December 1969 in the form of the Convention on Special Missions; the Convention entered into force on 21 June 1985. It was acknowledged by the ILC that the draft articles represented both a codification and a development of customary international law. Many of the provisions in the 1969 Convention on Special Missions mirror earlier provisions in the 1961 Convention on Diplomatic Relations and the 1963 Convention on Consular Relations.

Under Art 2 of the 1969 Convention the mission must have the consent of the receiving state and while a mission may be sent in the absence of diplomatic or consular relations,[108] the sending state must provide information as to the size of the mission.[109] While the agreement of the receiving state is necessary in respect of the site of the mission,[110] it is provided that the premises of the mission are inviolable[111] as is the private accommodation of members of the staff.[112] Members of the mission are to be

---

104 (1989) 75 AJIL 142.

105 During the Liberian Revolution of 1980, Liberian soldiers entered the French Embassy in Monrovia to arrest the son of a former President. France made a strong diplomatic protest.

106 In *R v Governor of Pentonville Prison ex p Teja* [1971] 2 QB 274, Lord Parker CJ appears to have considered that Mr Teja might be said to have been on a special mission. It is arguable that was the situation in *Fenton Textile Association Ltd v Krassin* (1921) 38 TLR 259.

107 Diplomatic Privileges (Extension) Act 1941; Diplomatic Privileges (Extension) Act 1944.

108 Convention on Special Missions (1969), Art 7.

109 *Ibid*, Art 8.

110 *Ibid*, Art 17.

111 *Ibid*, Art 25.

112 *Ibid*, Arts 30, 36, 39.

granted such freedom of movement as is necessary for the function of the mission;[113] they will enjoy immunity from criminal jurisdiction.[114] In respect of civil and administrative matters, they are placed in the same position as the diplomatic agent save that there is no immunity in respect of an action for damages arising from an accident caused by a vehicle used outside official functions.[115]

The 1969 Convention does not apply to those attending international conferences; in customary international law such persons are entitled to immunity from civil and criminal jurisdiction. It is sensible to conclude that a state that has consented to the conference being held on its territory is under a duty to accord freedom of movement and to regard official papers and documents as inviolable. Such persons are entitled to the protection accorded by the Convention on the Prevention and Punishment of Crimes against Internationally Protected Persons 1973.

6 THE IMMUNITIES OF INTERNATIONAL ORGANISATIONS[116]

The extent to which the staff of an international organisation enjoyed immunity was a matter of some debate in customary international law; indeed the entire question of legal personality was subject to some uncertainty.[117] Since 1945, the problem has become more acute with a proliferation in the number of international organisations; sometimes the matter may be dealt with in the form of a detailed treaty between the organisation and the state in which the headquarters are situated. The normal concern of such organisations is that staff should be immune in respect of acts undertaken in their official capacity. In a number of cases there is some reference to the question in the constitution of the organisation. Thus, Art 105 of the United Nations Charter (1945) provides that 'the Organisation shall enjoy in the territory of each of its members such privileges and immunities as are necessary for the fulfilment of its purposes' and further that 'representatives of the members of the United Nations and its officials shall similarly enjoy such privileges and immunities as are necessary for the independent exercise of their functions in connexion with the Organisation'.[118] However, such general references need to be supplemented by more detailed texts. In the case of the United Nations there are two detailed Conventions,[119] together with a Headquarters Agreement[120] concluded

---

113 *Ibid*, Art 27.

114 *Ibid*, Art 31.

115 *Ibid*, Art 31.

116 See generally, CW Jenks, 'Some constitutional problems of international organisations' (1945) 22 BYIL 11; J Kunz, 'Privileges and immunities of international organisations '(1947) 41 AJIL 828; C Eagleton, 'International organisation and the law of responsibility' (1950) HR 323; RJ Dupuy, '*Le Droit des rélations entre les organisations internationales*'(1960) HR 457–587; JES Fawcett, 'The place of law in an international organisation' (1960) 36 BYIL 321.

117 See CW Jenks, 'The legal personality of international organisations' (1945) 22 BYIL 267–75.

118 Article 105-2 United Nations Charter (1945).

119 General Convention on the Privileges and Immunities of the United Nations (approved by the General Assembly 13 February 1946); Convention on Privileges and Immunities of the Specialised Agencies (approved by the General Assembly on 21 November 1947).

120 See M Brandon, 'The legal status of the premises of the United Nations' (1951) 28 BYIL 100.

between the United Nations and the United States in 1947.[121] The normal practice is for states to provide for immunity in the form of municipal legislation; in the United Kingdom,[122] the operative legislation is now the International Organisations Act 1968 and the International Organisations Act 1981.

In the case of the United Nations the immunities are extensive. The General Convention of 1946 provides the United Nations shall enjoy immunity from legal process[123] and its premises, assets, archives and documents are inviolable.[124] Such provisions are necessary to prevent the functions of the organisation being frustrated by individual litigants. Members of the organisation enjoy immunity from income tax on their salary.[125] The Secretary General of the United Nations enjoys diplomatic immunity while other staff members enjoy immunity in respect of official acts.[126] It is provided in s 29 that the United Nations must make appropriate provision for resolving claims against it. The desire only to claim immunities necessary to operational efficiency is illustrated by s 20 which provides that the Secretary General must waive staff immunity if it can be done without damage to the interests of the United Nations.

An attempt to deal with immunities on a wider scale has been attempted in the Vienna Convention on the Representation of States in their Relations with International Organisations of a Universal Character which was adopted in 1975. The Convention applies to state representatives in any international organisation of a universal character and it also applies to delegations sent to conferences convened by the organisation. The purpose of the Convention is to approximate to the position under the Vienna Convention on Diplomatic Relations. So the Convention provides for the inviolability of the premises and the immunity of diplomatic staff. The Convention has had little direct effect because it was objected to by a number of governments on the basis that the analogy with a diplomatic mission was inappropriate and that the granting of immunities took insufficient account of the interests of the host state.[127]

---

121 See *PLO Observer Mission* case (1988) ICJ 12.

122 In the United Kingdom, the legislation permits Orders in Council to be made conferring legal personality or immunity as is appropriate. The legislation originated in the Diplomatic Privileges (Extension) Act 1941; the Diplomatic Privileges (Extension) Act 1944 and continued in the Diplomatic Privileges (Extension) Act 1946; Diplomatic Privileges (Extension) Act 1950. The legislation was consolidated in the International Organisations Act 1950 which was itself replaced by the International Organisations Act 1968. The International Organisations Act 1981 has the effect of extending the 1968 Act to commonwealth organisations. The history of the matter in the United Kingdom is discussed in the impressive judgment of Lord Oliver in *JH Rayner (Mincing Lane) Ltd v Department of Trade and Industry* [1990] 2 AC 418.

123 General Convention 1946, s 2.

124 *Ibid*, s 3.

125 *Ibid*, s 18 (otherwise state contributions would be indirectly paid to the states in which the main offices were located, ie, Switzerland and the United States, if those states levied tax).

126 General Convention 1946, ss 18 and 19.

127 See JG Fennessy, 'The 1975 Vienna Convention on the Representation of States in their Relations with International Organisations of a Universal Character' (1976) 70 AJIL 62. It is of note that France, the United States, Switzerland, Austria, Canada and the United Kingdom did not vote for the Convention. The Convention requires 35 ratifications or accessions before it comes into force.

7 THE INTERNATIONALLY PROTECTED PERSON

The diplomat serving in a foreign state[128] represents the sending state and has thus often been vulnerable to attacks by those in dispute with the sending state. The increase in terrorist attacks in the 1960s and early 1970s prompted the General Assembly to adopt the Convention on the Prevention and Punishment of Crimes Against Internationally Protected Persons including Diplomatic Agents.[129] In broad terms, the Convention provides that in respect of the 'murder. kidnapping or other attack upon the person or liberty of an internationally protected person',[130] a state party shall either prosecute[131] or extradite; Art 3 of the Convention provides that state parties shall establish jurisdiction over such offences. Such offences shall be included in any future extradition treaty between state parties.[132] The Convention further provides that state parties shall co-operate in the supply of evidence[133] and an arbitration procedure exists in the event of dispute.[134] In the absence of an extradition treaty the Convention may act as a legal basis to extradite.[135] The Convention was given effect to in the United Kingdom in the Internationally Protected Persons Act 1978 which creates a criminal offence in respect of attacks or threats of attack on a protected person;[136] further it makes such acts extraditable offences for the purpose of extradition law.[137]

8 THE UNITED KINGDOM

A few remarks are appropriate in respect of the position in the United Kingdom. The protection of the diplomat in customary international law was given effect to in the Diplomatic Privileges Act 1708 and this enactment afforded protection to the diplomat from civil and criminal process; the legislation was thought to reflect the position at common law of which customary international law was part. In the years after 1708, a

---

128 For the duty of 'special vigilance' towards such a person, see *United States v Mexico* (1927) 4 RIAA 173; (1924) 18 AJIL 543.

129 Annexed to Resolution 3166 (XXVIII) of 14 December 1973. The Convention came into force on 20 February 1977, given effect to in the United Kingdom in the Internationally Protected Persons Act 1978. See Rozakis (1974) 23 ICLQ 32; Wood (1974) 23 ICLQ 791.

130 The Convention on the Prevention and Punishment of Crimes Against Internationally Protected Persons, Including Diplomatic Agents (1973), Arts 2, 3 (jurisdiction), 6, (prosecute) 7 (extradite).

131 *Ibid,* Art 6.

132 *Ibid,* Art 8.

133 *Ibid,* Art 10.

134 *Ibid,* Art 13.

135 *Ibid,* Art 8.2.

136 Internationally Protected Persons Act 1978, s 1.

137 *Ibid,* s 3.

steady stream of case law developed on the subject;[138] it was generally assumed that the United Kingdom adopted a liberal approach to questions of diplomatic immunity. In respect of Commonwealth countries the legislation was supplemented by the Diplomatic Immunities (Commonwealth Countries and Republic of Ireland) Act 1952. At the time of the passing of the 1708 Act there were less than 10 diplomatic missions in London but by 1964 there were 83 with nearly 6,000 persons enjoying full diplomatic immunity.

The Vienna Convention on Diplomatic Relations of 1961 acquired the necessary twenty two ratifications and came into force on 24 April 1964. On 31 July 1964 the Diplomatic Privileges Act 1964 acquired the Royal Assent; after that date the United Kingdom ratified the Convention. The legislation came into effect on 1 October 1964.

By the terms of s 1 of the 1964 Act the prior law was displaced by the new legislative provisions; under the terms of s 2 of the legislation the articles of the Vienna Convention set out in Schedule 1 to the Act[139] were to be given the force of law in the United Kingdom. The case law prior to 1964 is therefore of only of relevance where it is directed to a question of general principle. The same technique was followed in respect of consular relations; the Vienna Convention on Consular Relations of 1963 was given effect to by the Consular Relations Act 1968. Section 1 of that legislation gave effect to those articles of the Vienna Convention on Consular Relations (1963) as set out in Sched 1 to the Act.

Although the legislation was modified in respect of taxation in 1971[140] and more substantively in the State Immunity Act 1978 the 1964 and 1968 Acts provide the basic statutory code today In 1985 the House of Commons Foreign Affairs select committee received evidence that there were 45,000 diplomatic agents in London of whom 15,000 enjoyed full immunity. Although there has been a considerable increase in the number of persons affected the universal nature of the Vienna Convention on Diplomatic Relations of 1961 has meant that comparatively few legal cases[141] have come before the English courts in the years since 1964.

---

138 See generally, *Triquet v Bath* (1764) 3 Burr 1478; *Viveash v Becker* (1814) 3 M & S 784; *Taylor v Best* (1854) 14 CB 487; *Magdalena Steam Navigation Company v Martin* (1859)2 E & E 94; *Baron Paredo v Johnson* (1873) 29 LT 452; *Parkinson v Potter* (1885) 16 QBD 152; *Macartney v Garbutt* (1890) 24 QBD 368; *In re L W Cloete* (1891) 7 TLR 565; *MusurusBey v Gadban* [1894] 2 QB 352; *In re Republic of Bolivia Exploration Syndicate* [1914] 1 Ch 139; *Re Suarez* [1917] 2 Ch 131; [1918] 1 Ch 176; *Fenton Textile Association Ltd v Krassin* (1922) 38 TLR 259; *Assurantie Compagnie Excelsior v Smith* (1923) 40 TLR 105; *Engelke v Musmann* [1928] AC 433; *Dickinson v Del Solar* [1930] 1 KB 376; *R v Kent* [1941] 1 KB 454; *Parker v Boggan* [1947] All ER 46; *Price v Griffin* (1948) 2 ILQ 266; *In re C (An Infant)* [1959] 1 Ch 363; *High Commissioner for India v Ghosh* [1960] 1 QB 134; *R v Madan* [1961] 2 QB 1; *Empson v Smith* [1966] 1 QB 426.

139 The relevant articles in Sched 1 being Arts 1, 22–24, 27–40. It is to be noted that Art 45 became part of English law under Diplomatic and Consular Premises Act 1987, s 6 and Sched 2.

140 Diplomatic and Other Privileges Act 1971.

141 Eg *Empson v Smith* [1966] 1 QB 426; *Agbor v Metropolitan Police Commissioner* [1969] 1 WLR 703; *R v Governor of Pentonville Prison ex p Teja* [1971] 2 QB 274; *Shaw v Shaw* [1979] Fam 62; *Intro Properties (UK) Ltd v Sauvel* [1983] QB 1019; *Alcom Ltd v Republic of Columbia* [1984] AC 580; *R v Lambeth Justices ex p Yusufu* [1985] Crim LR 510; *Westminster City Council v Government of Islamic Republic of Iran* [1986] 1 WLR 979; *Fayed v Al Tajir* [1988] 1 QB 712; *R v Secretary of State for Foreign Affairs ex p Samuel* (1989) 83 ILR 232; *Westminster City Council v Tomlin* [1990] 1 All ER 920; *R v Secretary of State for the Home Department ex p Bagga* [1991] 1 QB 485; *Re P (No 1) (Children Act: Diplomatic Immunity)* (1998) 1 FLR 624; *Re P (No 2) (Diplomatic Immunity: Jurisdiction)* (1998) 1 FLR 1026.

One area that has given rise to particular difficulty in London is the question of responsibility for unoccupied diplomatic premises particularly where the condition of the premises poses a threat to public safety or to adjoining occupiers. To this end the United Kingdom enacted the Diplomatic and Consular Premises Act 1987 to confer greater powers on the Secretary of State. Under the terms of s 1(1) where land is to be used as diplomatic or consular premises after the coming into effect of the legislation then the consent of the Secretary of State is required. Such a consent is not required in respect of land used for diplomatic and consular services prior to the coming into effect of the legislation.[142] Such consent may be withdrawn after which case the land ceases to be diplomatic or consular premises.[143] Where land has ceased to be used as diplomatic or consular premises then the Secretary of State may under s 2 if acting in accordance with international law[144] make a statutory instrument and deed poll vesting title to the premises in himself.[145] When such an order has been made then s 3 requires the Secretary of State to sell the premises[146] and to hold the proceeds of sale after certain deductions for the person divested of the estate or interest.[147]

Although problems had been experienced with other states the most acute case was that of the Cambodian Embassy in London where in 1975 after the arrival in power of the Pol Pot regime the staff at the London Embassy withdrew and handed over the keys to the Foreign Office. In 1979 the Heng Samrin government assumed power backed by Vietnamese forces. The United Kingdom withdrew recognition from the Pol Pot regime but did not recognise the new regime because of its dependence on foreign forces; thus there was no recognised government although diplomatic relations were not formally severed. By mid August 1976 squatters had occupied the premises but no attempt was made to remove them until 1988; at that stage there was a risk that the squatters might acquire title by adverse possession under the Limitation Act 1980. The Secretary of State took the view that to permit that to happen would be a breach of duty owed to Cambodia in international law to protect its embassy premises;[148] thus, a statutory instrument[149] and vesting order was made under the terms of s 2 of the Diplomatic and Consular Premises Act 1987.

---

142 Diplomatic and Consular Premises Act 1987, s 1(2).

143 Under the terms of s 1(3) although any withdrawal of consent must by s 1(4) be consistent with international law.

144 As provided under Diplomatic and Consular Premises Act 1987, s 2(2).

145 Under the terms of s 2, the Secretary of State makes a statutory instrument which is laid before Parliament providing that s 2 shall apply to the land (see s 2(1), 2(4)). If such an order is not annulled it will be followed by the deed poll which operates as the vesting document (see s 2(5)).

146 Diplomatic and Consular Premises Act 1987, s 3(1).

147 *Ibid*, s 3(2).

148 The duty arising under Art 45 of the Vienna Convention 1961 and made part of English Law by s 6 and Sched 1 to the 1987 Act.

149 Diplomatic and Consular Premises (Cambodia) Order 1988, SI 1988/30.

At a later date one of the squatters sought judicial review of the decision of the Secretary of State to make the order; at first instance that application was dismissed by Henry J.[150] The subsequent appeal was dismissed by a unanimous Court of Appeal.[151]

An earlier example of such difficulties was illustrated by the case of *Westminster City Council v The Islamic Republic of Iran*[152] which had arisen following the abandonment of the Iranian Embassy in London in 1980. It would seem from the tenor of the judgment of Peter Gibson J that failure to use or to manifest any interest in premises for a period of four years will be sufficient evidence that the building can no longer be considered diplomatic premises for the purpose of Art 22 and Art 1(i) of the Vienna Convention on Diplomatic Relations (1961).

Under the terms of s 3 of the Diplomatic Privileges Act 1964 the United Kingdom may restrict any privileges granted by it. if it appears that they are greater than those granted to a United Kingdom mission in another state. Any such withdrawal is to be effected by Order in Council. Under the terms of s 4 any certificate issued as to whether a person has been notified as a diplomat will be conclusive as to matters of fact.[153] In like terms, s 7 provides that where an special or bilateral agreements have been entered into by the United Kingdom providing for the extension of immunity that agreement shall have the force of law for as long as it remains in force.

9 THE PARTICULAR POSITION OF THE HEAD OF STATE

A difficulty that arises under the United Kingdom legislation concerns the position of the Head of State. Part of the difficulty is caused by the decision to draft the State Immunity Act 1978 by reference to the Diplomatic Immunity Act 1964. It is arguable that this causes undue difficulty because the immunities of the 1964 Act are enjoyed *ratione personae* while those of the latter legislation operate *ratione materiae*. The recent litigation in the United Kingdom indicates that one must be careful to distinguish a number of questions of which three are presently relevant: (a) is the claim for immunity made by a serving or a former head of state?; (b) is the claim made in respect of an official governmental act or is

---

150 *R v Secretary of State for Foreign and Commonwealth Affairs ex p Samuel* (1988) *The Times*, 10 September (Henry J). The argument advanced on behalf of the squatters (who described themselves as the Guild of Transcultural Students) was: (a) that the Secretary of State was not entitled to act to frustrate the acquisition of rights under the Limitation Act 1980; and (b) that the Secretary of State was under a duty to protect the embassy premises and could not be so acting when the course he had adopted would lead to sale of the premises under s 3. The two propositions are of course contradictory.

151 *R v Secretary for Foreign Affairs ex p Samuel* (1989) 83 ILR 232 (Fox, Croom Johnson and Mann LJJ). For parallel proceedings concerning the liability of squatters in the Embassy to pay rates, see *Westminster City Council v Tomlin* [1990] 1 All ER 920 (Henry J, Fox and Croom Johnson LJJ).

152 *Westminster City Council v The Islamic Republic of Iran* [1986] 1 WLR 979. The building had been stormed in May 1980 at the request of the Iranian government to enable those held hostage to be released. The damage done to the building posed a threat to public safety; consideration of public safety is one of the matters that the Secretary of State is required to have regard to under the terms of ss 2(3) and 1(5) of the Diplomatic and Consular Premises Act 1987.

153 The powers under s 4 of the 1964 Act exist also in s 11 of the Consular Relations Act 1968 and s 8 of the International Organisations Act 1968. See E Wilmhurst, 'Executive certificates in foreign affairs: the United Kingdom' (1986) 35 ICLQ 157. In principle, the request for a certificate should come from the court and not an individual party.

it made in respect of a private act?; (c) is the making of the claim consistent with international law?

It would seem following the different opinions expressed in recent case law that the following propositions can be stated with only a modest degree of confidence:

(i)   That the serving head of state will be entitled to claim immunity in England in respect of acts done in his official capacity as head of state (State Immunity Act 1978, s 1(14)).

(ii) Whether a particular person is at a specific time a serving head of state can be determined from the constitution of that state but an English court is obliged to act on the certificate of the Secretary of State (State Immunity Act 1978, s 21(a)).[154]

(iii) If a serving head of state is acting in his private capacity then he will enjoy the immunity of the head of a diplomatic mission (State Immunity Act 1978, s 20, Diplomatic Privileges Act 1964, s 2, Sched 1).

(iv) In respect of a former head of state then, he will enjoy immunity in respect of acts undertaken as part of his official duties as head of state (State Immunity Act 1978, s 20; Diplomatic Privileges Act 1964, s 2, Sched 1).

(v)   It would seem that there can be no claim to immunity in respect of private acts undertaken by a former head of state.[155]

(vi) Where a claim for immunity has been made by a former head of state then it will be rejected if: (a) the acts in question cannot in international law form part of the duties of a head of state;[156] or (b) the acts in question are prohibited in international law;[157] or (c) if the state in question has impliedly waived such an immunity by ratifying or acceding to an international convention that provides for the punishment of such acts.[158]

The position of the former Head of State was considered at length in England in the Pinochet litigation[159] which arose out of the request by Spain to extradite Augusto Pinochet, the military ruler of Chile from 1973 until 1990. The case itself indicated the potential conflict between traditional conceptions of immunity and the increasing emphasis placed on the observance of human rights. In the background was the question whether it would be more appropriate for a former ruler to be tried before an international forum rather than before a municipal court.

---

154 For earlier authorities, see *Taylor v Barclay* (1828) 2 Sim 213; *Duff Development Co Ltd v Government of Kelantan* [1924] AC 797; *The Fagernes* (1927) P 311; *Engelke v Musmann* [1928] AC 433; *R v Bottrill ex p Kuechenmeister* [1947] KB 41; [1947] 2 All ER 434.

155 *R v Bow Street Metropolitan Stipendiary Magistrate ex p Pinochet Ugarte (No 1)* [1998] 3 WLR 1456, p 1484; [2000] 1 AC 61.

156 *Ibid.*

157 *Ibid.*

158 *R v Bow Street Metropolitan Stipendiary Magistrate ex p Pinochet (No 3)* [2000] 1 AC 147; [1999] 2 WLR 827.

159 *R v Bow Street Metropolitan Stipendiary Magistrate ex p Pinochet (No 1)* [1998] 3 WLR 1456 (Lords Steyn, Nicholls and Hoffmann formed the majority; Lords Slynn and Lloyd formed the minority); *R v Bow Street Metropolitan Stipendiary Magistrate ex p Pinochet Ugarte (No 2)* [1999] 2 WLR 272; *R v Bow Street Metropolitan Stipendiary Magistrate ex p Pinochet Ugarte (No 3)*]1999) 2 WLR 827 (Lords Browne-Wilkinson, Hope, Hutton, Saville Phillips and Millett, with Lord Goff dissenting in part).

The litigation attracted considerable publicity and was not without its bizarre aspects.[160] However, in *Pinochet (No 1)*[161] a majority in the House of Lords was prepared to accept that no claim for immunity could be made at common law in respects of acts such as torture which are contrary to customary international law. However, the force of this conclusion was somewhat weakened by two powerful dissenting judgments which held that such immunity did arise and that in any event conduct during a *coup d'état* was essentially non-justiciable. The failure to comply with the rules of natural justice persuaded the House of Lords in *Re Pinochet (No 2)*[162] to rule that the earlier order be set aside and a fresh hearing take place

The hearing in *Pinochet (No 3)*[163] was conducted under less pressure of time and resulted in a wider range of arguments being presented. Although not fully discussed in *Pinochet (No 1)*, a considerable number of allegations were discharged by the majority because, as extra-territorial torture was not a crime in England until 1988, they failed to meet the double criminality rule that lies at the foundation of extradition law. Secondly, in respect of immunity the majority drew a distinction between immunity *ratione personae* and immunity *ratione materiae*. The majority held that the immunity of a serving Head of State is immunity *ratione personae* so that had General Pinochet been still in office he would have immunity in respect both his public and private acts. In respect of a former Head of State it was considered that immunity was *ratione materiae* and so General Pinochet could only be immune in respect acts coming within his functions as Head of State. Thirdly, the majority held that no immunity could be claimed by an individual or the state where the state had signed and ratified an international convention outlawing such acts; thus no claim for immunity could be made by Chile in respect of torture after its signature and ratification of the 1984 Torture Convention because such conduct constituted an implied waiver. In the context of immunity the force of the majority opinions was weakened by a dissenting judgment by Lord Goff in which he rejected the concept of any implied waiver holding that any waiver of immunity had to be express and that such a waiver could not arise from a state signing an international agreement that itself contains no mention of immunity.

A number of general points can be noted in the *Pinochet* litigation. First, the case indicates the general emphasis on pursuing those alleged to have violated human rights. Secondly, as many judges indicated it is probably preferable for the former rule of state A to be tried either by the courts of state A or by an international tribunal but not by the courts of state B. Thirdly, in the context of the United Kingdom the case raised difficult problems of reconciling the drafting in the Diplomatic Privileges Act 1964 with the

---

160 One of the more unusual aspects was that case began in October 1998 with an attempt to seek judicial review of warrants issued ;this had the consequence that the Divisional Court and the House of Lords were forced to consider the matter before a normal hearing before a magistrate at Bow Street, at which normally some of the evidential and factual matters might have been clarified.

161 *R v Bow Street Metropolitan Stipendiary Magistrate ex p Pinochet (No 1)* [1998] 3 WLR 1456 (the argument being that the common law included the relevant rule of customary international law).

162 *R v Bow Street Metropolitan Magistrate ex p Pinochet Ugarte (No 2)* [1999] 2 WLR 272 (the judgment of Lord Browne-Wilkinson contains a strong endorsement of the rule in *R v Sussex Justices ex p McCarthy* [1924] 1 KB 256).

163 *R v Bow Street Metropolitan Stipendiary Magistrate ex p Pinochet (No 3)* [1999] 2 WLR 827.

language adopted in the State Immunity Act 1978. Fourthly, the case has left unresolved difficult questions as to which acts of a Head of State are official acts and which are acts of personal conduct.

Fifthly, although in both substantive cases the majority came down against immunity important dissenting judgments were given and it does seem difficult to comprehend how a state can waive its immunity by signing an international agreement that contains no express reference to immunity.

CHAPTER 11

THE LAW RELATING TO TREATIES

1 THE NATURE AND FUNCTION OF TREATIES[1]

In municipal law, legal rights and duties may be created by a wide variety of legal mechanisms. Legislation may create rights and legally enforceable agreements may have the same effect; in certain circumstances rights may arise by operation of judicial precedent. The wide category of rights in an advanced economy are reflected in the volume of of legislation on the statute book. In the area of contract there may be a general law of contract, but there will also be particular provisions regulating commercial contracts, consumer contracts, employment contracts and property agreements. So detailed is the picture that question is raised as to whether there remains any general law of contract.

In contrast, international law is a less developed system. Legal rules may arise when acknowledged as part of customary international law; however, customary rules are limited in scope and normally require a considerable time to evolve. The reality is that in the 20th century the instrument of the treaty has to perform a wide variety of tasks that are performed in a municipal system by different concepts. A treaty may establish a legal code between different parties; it may serve to conclude hostilities or it may operate to transfer territory or to provide a measure of protection for the environment.

In short, the treaty is a concept that exists to perform a wide variety of tasks in international society; it is a true all purpose vehicle. In considering the general rules pertaining to treaties, it is important to bear in mind the varied nature of transactions that are founded upon treaty law.

Although agreements between rulers can be traced back before the Roman Republic, most writers consider the first modern instrument to be the Treaty of Westphalia (1648) which served to terminate the Thirty Years' War in Europe. From that date, a number of rules grew up in customary international law as to formation and interpretation of treaties. To an extent, these have been codified in the Vienna Convention on the Law of Treaties (1969), which came into effect in 1980.[2] Having regard to the wide variety of tasks that the treaty had to perform, the International Law Commission considered that that the subject would benefit from a degree of clarity and certainty.

The subject of the law of treaties is bedevilled by two difficulties. First, there is the need to find an agreed definition of the concept of a 'treaty'. Lord McNair in his standard work[3] defined a treaty as 'a written agreement by which two or more states or

---

1 See on the subject, A McNair, *The Law of Treaties*, 1961; I Detter, *Essays on the Law of Treaties*, 1967, Oxford: I Sinclair, *The Vienna Convention and the Law of Treaties*, 1st edn, 1973; 2nd edn, 1984; C Parry, 'The Law of Treaties', in M Sorensen (ed), *Manual of Public International Law*, 1968,London, TO Élias, *The Modern Law of Treaties*, 1974; J Klabbers, *The Concept of the Treaty in International Law*, 1996.

2 The Convention applies to only those treaties which are concluded by states after the date the convention enters into force for those states (see Art 4, Vienna Convention). See P McDade, 'The effect of Art 4 of the Vienna Convention on the Law of Treaties (1969)' (1986) 35 ICLQ 499.

3 A McNair, *The Law of Treaties*, 1961.

international organisations create or intend to create a relation between themselves operating within the sphere of international law'. This was propounded as a general definition and it is sensible to contrast this with the general definition set out in Art 2(1)(a), which reads:

For the purpose of the present Convention:

(a) 'Treaty' means an international agreement concluded between States in written form and governed by international law,[4] whether embodied in a single instrument or in two or more related instruments and whatever its particular designation.

It will be noted that the definition in the 1969 Vienna Convention is narrower and designed only to apply for the purpose of the Convention itself. Although the definition has acquired a wide degree of acceptance, a number of points can be made.[5] First, the definition indicates that the precise designation is not material; this reflects the fact that a wide variety of terminology may be employed. Secondly, the precise number of instruments comprising the agreement does not affect the substance of the matter. Thirdly, the definition refers only to agreement between states; this was of course because of the intention to proceed to a separate convention in respect of international organisations.[6] Fourthly, the definition requires the agreement to be in written form. This was designed to provide for ease of registration as was first required under Art 18 of the Covenant of the League of Nations (1919) and as now stipulated under Art 102 of the United Nations Charter. In this context, it should be noted that Art 3 preserves the legal force of an oral agreement. Fifthly, the definition refers to the agreement being 'governed by international law'. The *travaux preparatoires* indicate that this was intended to cover difficulties as to whether there had been 'an intention to create legal relations'.[7] It should be noted that there is no requirement for any element of reciprocity as stipulated under the English law doctrine of consideration. Sixthly, as indicated the definition includes the phrase 'governed by international law'; according to the International Law Commission Commentary this phrase indicates the intention to create obligations under international law. If there is no such intention then the document will not be a treaty. Thus one must be cautious about documents headed 'Memorandum of Understanding' (MOUs). Whether such a document is a treaty will depend on its terms;[8] sometimes an MOU is preferred on grounds of confidentiality. There has been a growing trend since 1945 to use such documents rather than a treaty.[9]

---

4   This has the effect of excluding 'gentlemen's agreements', 'non-binding agreements', *'de facto* agreements' sometimes referred to as MOUs.

5   *Qatar v Bahrain* (1994) ICJ 112.

6   Vienna Convention on the Law of Treaties between States and International Organisations or between International Organisations (1986).

7   In practice, this is reflected in the distinction between a treaty and a memorandum of understanding, however, confusion can arise because sometimes a treaty may be described as a 'memorandum of understanding' (MOU). Whether a document creates one or the other is a matter not of nomenclature but intention; where a treaty is intended the language will include terminology such as 'shall', 'agree', 'undertake', 'rights', 'obligations' and 'enter into force'; the document may include an express statement as to status. For a discussion of the distinction, see A Aust, *Modern Treaty Law and Practice*, 2000, Chapters 2 and 3.

8   See, eg, 'Inter-Organisation Programme for the Sound Management of Chemicals' (1995) ILM 1315.

9   See A Aust, 'The theory and practice of informal international instruments' (1986) 35 ICLQ 787.

Although not arising directly under the 1969 Convention there is authority for the view that a mandate agreement[10] will be regarded in customary international law as a treaty but such a status might not be accorded to an agreement between a state and a private company.[11] Thus while every treaty is founded upon agreement, not every agreement will be classified as a treaty.

The process therefore is to determine whether state conduct is to have legal effect and if so whether it is capable of creating a treaty. The first difficulty arises as to whether the parties have intended that legal relations should arise. This is a difficulty that arose particularly in the 19th century and early 20th century when Foreign Ministers such as Lord Salisbury and Sir Edward Grey were in the habit of entering into gentleman's agreements that were regarded as binding only the parties to them.[12] At the same time, others have argued that the Atlantic Charter of 1941 and the Helsinki Final Act of 1975 were not strictly treaties because of an absence of an intention to be legally bound. As in municipal law, whether legal relations are intended is a question of inference to be drawn from conduct. There is some argument in the case law as to whether the status of a treaty is to be determined by whether it has been registered under Art 102[13] of the United Nations Charter (1945). This argument seems misconceived; the provisions of Art 102 serve to determine enforceability vis à vis the United Nations, they are not designed to determine the status of a particular instrument.[14] After some hesitation, it would appear that declarations lodged under Art 36(2) of the Statute of the International Court of Justice will be regarded as having legal effect and being similar to treaty provisions.[15]

A question that commonly arises is as to whether acts or conduct by a state not intended to create an agreement may yet be said to have legal effect. In short the answer depends on the circumstances although much should depend on whether the declaration is unilateral or made as part of a reciprocal understanding. In the *Eastern Greenland* case[16] the Permanent Court of International Justice took the view that a declaration could have legal effect. In that case, Denmark had indicated through its Ambassador in Norway that it would raise no objection to the Norwegian claim to Spitzbergen. The intention was to secure Norwegian assurances in respect of the Danish claim to Greenland. In conversation with the Danish Ambassador, the Norwegian Foreign Minister indicated

---

10 *Re South West Africa* case (1962) ICJ 319.

11 *Anglo Iranian Oil Company* case (1952) ICJ 93.

12 Which is perhaps just as well because there seems to be some evidence that the Anglo French negotiations conducted by Theophile Delcasse (French Foreign Minister 1898–1905) and the London Ambassador, Paul Cambon, were not fully disclosed to members of the French Government; in the years 1898–1905 there were six French governments. It is quite clear that Lord Salisbury and Lord Landsdowne regarded the understandings as not binding on a subsequent French Government. For the oral discussions leading to *entente*, see Robert K Massie, *Dreadnought: Britain Germany and the Coming of the Great War*, 1991.

13 *Case concerning the Territorial Dispute (Libya v Chad)* (1994) ICJ 6 (see Judge *ad hoc* Sette-Camara).

14 If an MOU is intended rather a treaty this will be determined by: (a) intention; (b) not by contents alone; (c) by reference to any express provision as to status. Registration under Art 102 cannot confer on a document the status of a treaty if it does not already possess it. In marginal cases registration may be evidence that the parties regard the document as a treaty.

15 *Anglo Iranian Oil Co (Jurisdiction)* case (1952) ICJ 93 (doubtful); the *Fisheries Jurisdiction* cases (1973) ICJ 3 (probably yes); *Nicaragua v United States* (1984) ICJ 392 (declarations regarded as subject to the general obligation to act in good faith that arises in the law of treaties).

16 *Eastern Greenland* case (1933) PCIJ, Ser A/B, No 53.

that Norway would cause no difficulties in respect of Greenland. At a later date when the matter came before the PCIJ the majority of the court held that Norway was bound by such a declaration as it was made within the express authority of a Foreign Minister. However, it is clear from the facts that the declaration was founded on an element of reciprocity. So that it might be argued that the case was one of oral agreement rather than one of unilateral declaration.

In the subsequent *Nuclear Tests* case,[17] the majority appear to have taken the view that a unilateral declaration could have legal consequences. In that case, Australia and New Zealand had brought an action against France in respect of that country's atmospheric nuclear testing in the South Pacific. Before the court could determine the merits the President of France and the Prime Minister had indicated that the round of atmospheric nuclear testing would cease. The court was therefore obliged to consider whether the proceedings had any further object. The majority held that such a unilateral statement was binding upon France because the statements were made publicly and that the court could infer an intention to be legally bound. However there is much force in the dissenting judgment of *ad hoc* Judge Barwick who pointed out that, in principle, statements limiting a state's freedom of action should receive a restrictive interpretation and that there was nothing in the language or circumstances that indicated that those making the statement were intending to enter into a binding legal obligation. In the event the majority view prevailed and it was held that a dispute between the parties no longer existed. It has to be admitted that this is not a very satisfactory case and a lawyer naturally hesitates to affix binding consequences to statements made at a press conference.[18]

A more conservative approach was followed by a Chamber of the Court in the *Frontier Dispute* case,[19] where the court accepted that a unilateral statement could have legal consequences, but this would only arise where there was clear evidence that there was an intention to be legally bound and the statement was made to the international community as a whole. In the instant case a statement made in bilateral negotiations was not of that character.

2 QUESTIONS OF FORM AND LANGUAGE[20]

It is accepted by most writers that the law of treaties is bedevilled by a variety of forms and little uniformity of language. First, a treaty may be concluded between Heads of State, although this is unusual and is reserved for the most important forms of treaty. Secondly, for technical and political matters the treaty may be made between

---

17 *Nuclear Tests (Australia v France; New Zealand v France)* case (1974) ICJ 253. (In that case, one statement had been made to the legislature, one had been made at a press conference and another before the General Assembly.)

18 The Court does not seem to have been influenced by the fact that 1974 had seen the death in office of one French President (Georges Pompidou (1911–74)) and the election of a successor in the form of Valéry Giscard d'Estaing who, while technically from a different political party (Union pour la Democratie Francaise), had served as Finance Minister under President Pompidou (1969–74). There was, however, reason to believe that a new Administration was re-examining some of the foreign policy commitments of its predecessor.

19 *Frontier Dispute* case *(Burkina Faso v Mali)* (1986) ICJ 554.

20 A McNair, 'The functions and differing legal character of treaties' (1930) 11 BYIL 100.

governments. Thirdly, having regard to the nature of the treaty, it may be appropriate for the treaty to define the parties as 'states' for example, as in the North Atlantic Security Treaty (1949). Fourthly, treaties may be signed between political leaders, foreign ministers and departmental heads. An interesting combination of techniques is afforded by the Treaty of Rome (1957) where the instrument is made between Heads of State through the acts of their plenipotentiaries. A more straightforward example is provided by the Joint Declaration of 19 December 1984 made between the British Prime Minister and the Prime Minister of China as to the future of Hong Kong.

In addition to questions of form, there are also problems of nomenclature and language. A treaty may simply be described as a 'treaty' but a wide variety of other names are used and it is sensible to say a little about some of them.

(a) Convention

This term was used indiscriminately prior to 1945 to apply to treaties of a bilateral or multilateral nature. Since 1945, the expression is confined to treaties of a multilateral nature and is usually employed in respect of multilateral law making treaties (for example, Genocide Convention (1948) Law of the Sea Convention (1982); Convention against Torture and Other Cruel, Inhuman or Degrading Treatment or Punishment (1984)).

(b) Protocol

In general the expression 'protocol' indicates an instrument less formal than a Convention. However, the terms is used in a variety of senses and may be employed to mean: (i) as a document contemporaneous with the Convention and drawn up by the same negotiators to govern questions of interpretation. In these circumstances, ratification of the Convention will normally entail ratification of the Protocol; (ii) it may indicate a supplementary treaty concluded at a later date and requiring separate ratification; (iii) it may indicate a contemporaneous document ancillary to a Convention but requiring independent ratification; (iv) it may simply be a form of *procès verbal* not itself requiring ratification.

(c) *Procès verbal*

This is normally a document that simply summarises the proceedings and indicates any conclusions reached. It is not normally subject to ratification.

(d) Agreement

This is less formal than a Convention or treaty; it normally concerns technical or administrative matters but it may be employed in respect of political issues of considerable moment, for example, the Dayton Peace Agreement (1995). If it is of a provisional nature it may be known as an 'Arrangement'.

(e) Statute

This will be a document that sets out the detailed rules regulating the function of an institution that may itself have been established by treaty. Examples are afforded by the Statute of the International Court of Justice (1946), the statute of the European Central Bank or the Statute of the International Criminal Court (1998).

(f) *Modus vivendi*

A *modus vivendi* is a document recording an agreement of a temporary nature. It is usually informal and does not require ratification.

(g) Covenant

In municipal law the term denoted a solemn promise under seal and had been invoked in the constitutional and religious quarrels of 17th century Scotland. The phrase was taken up and employed to indicate the serious nature of the obligations assumed in the Covenant of the League of Nations (1919).[21] The term has been revived more recently in the United Nations Covenant on Civil and Political Rights (1966) and the Covenant on Economic, Social and Cultural Rights (1966). At the same time, the solemn nature of obligations was sometimes referred to as a 'Pact' as in the Kellogg Briand Pact of 1928 which was better known as the General Treaty for the Renunciation of War (1928).

(h) Declaration

The expression 'declaration' may or may not indicate a treaty relationship. The term is employed to indicate: (i) an intention to accept compulsory jurisdiction under Art 36(2) of the Statute of the International Court of Justice; (ii) it may be part of a General Assembly Resolution, for example, the Declaration on the Granting of Independence to Colonial Peoples (1960); (iii) it may indicate a treaty as in the 1984 Joint Declaration relating to the future of Hong Kong; (iv) it may simply be a statement of general principles issued after a summit meeting or other diplomatic exchange.

(i) Final Act

This expression is usually reserved for the document that concludes a major diplomatic conference. It will indicate the history and objects of the conference, the delegates who have attended and any other resolutions and decisions that were not incorporated into the final convention. Such a document does not require ratification and is to be be distinguished from the expression 'General Act' which may be a treaty.

---

21 Woodrow Wilson (1856–1924) learned in both History and Law was of Scottish descent. Wilson was probably the most scholarly and high minded United States President of the 20th century and such a title indicated to him both the ethical and the legal nature of the obligations contained within the document. For Wilson, see AS Link, *Wilson the Diplomatist*, 1957.

As will be seen from the above the expression 'treaty' is a generic term and in each case much will depend not on the terminology used but the nature and purpose of the transaction.

3 THE PARTIES TO A TREATY

As a general rule a treaty may not impose obligations or confer rights on a third party without its consent.[22] In customary international law, this was often expressed in terms of the Latin maxim '*pacta tertiis nec nocent nec prosunt*'; the general principle is now stated in Art 34 of the Vienna Convention on the Law of Treaties (1969) which reads: 'A treaty does not create either obligations or rights for a third state without its consent.' In the modern world, one can detect a number of exceptions to this general rule:

(a) The United Nations Charter (1945) contains a number of provisions that apply to non-member states. In particular, Art 2(6) imposes obligations on non-Members while Arts 32, 35(2) and 50 confer rights. It is open to argument that the United Nations Charter (1945) is a particular form of global constitution whose fundamental objective of securing peace would be frustrated if the reach of the treaty did not extend to non-members.

(b) A multilateral treaty declaratory of existing customary international law will have effect upon non-parties; however in this instance the non-party is bound not by the treaty but by the customary rule.

(c) A multilateral treaty may have the effect of creating a new rule of customary international law but it is clear from the judgments in the North Sea Continental case[23] and *Nicaragua v United States (The Merits)*[24] that a heavy *onus probandi* lies on the party so asserting. Once again the non-party state will be governed not by the treaty but by the customary rule so established.

(d) In respect of third party rights arising under a treaty, it has been accepted that such rights might arise although questions did occur as to whether the third party could claim directly or merely through a contracting party and whether the parties to the treaty could abolish the stipulation without the consent of the third party. The matter of rights '*in favorem tertii*' was considered by the PCIJ in the case of the *Free Zones of Upper Saxony and the District of Gex*,[25] where the court ruled that for a benefit to arise in favour of a third party: (i) the treaty must be examined to determine whether a right has been created; (ii) it must then be ascertained whether the right has been accepted by the third party; and (iii) in certain circumstances the right must not be terminated without the consent of the third party. The general tenor of the judgment is reflected in Art 36(1) of the Vienna Convention which reads:

> A right arises for a third State from a provision of a treaty if the parties to a treaty intend the provision to accord that right either to the third State, or to a group of States to

---

22   E Jimenez de Arechaga (1956) 50 AJIL 338.
23   (1969) ICJ 3.
24   (1986) ICJ 14.
25   (1932) PCIJ, Ser A/B, No 46; (1932) 6 ILR 362.

which it belongs, or to all States and the third State assents thereto. Its assent shall be presumed so long as the contrary is not indicated, unless the treaty otherwise provides. 'This provision is to be read with article 37(2) which provides that a third party right may not be revoked or modified by the parties' if it is established that the right was intended not to be revocable or subject to modification without the consent of the third State.

(e) However customary international law was hostile to the concept of a treaty imposing obligations on a non-party. This reluctance is now reflected in Art 35 of the Vienna Convention which reads:

> An obligation arises for a third State from a provision of a treaty if the parties to a treaty intend the provision to be the means of establishing the obligation and the third State expressly accepts that obligation in writing.

(f) Some jurists have argued that there is a distinct exception to the general rule in the form of a category of dispositive treaties that create an objective legal regime binding upon third parties. The principal examples are those treaties applying to international waterways that purport to create a legal regime. Thus, Art 1 of the Constantinople Convention of 1888 provides that 'the Suez Maritime Canal shall always be free and open in time of war as in time of peace, to every vessel of commerce or of war without distinction of flag'. Similarly, the judgment of the Permanent Court of International Justice in the *Wimbledon* case[26] was to the effect that Art 380 of the Treaty of Versailles 1919 concerning the Kiel Canal was to benefit all nations.

4 THE FORMATION OF TREATIES[27]

As indicated above, parties may use a wide variety of methods to conclude a treaty and different language may be employed to describe the final outcome. However it is normally claimed that a number of common criteria can be discerned: (i) the agreement must be in writing;[28] (ii) the parties must possess legal personality on the international plane; (iii) the document must be governed by international law; and (iv) it must be intended to create a legal obligation.

Who actually negotiates the treaty in practice will be a question for the constitutional law of each state. In the United Kingdom, matters concerning the negotiation, signature and ratification of treaties fall within the royal prerogative of foreign affairs. In the United States, Art II, s 2 of the Constitution provides that the President 'shall have power by and with the advice and consent of the Senate to make treaties, provided two-thirds of the Senators present concur'.

There must be some question as to whether it can be said that writing is an actual requirement. Such a requirement is stipulated in the definition contained in the Vienna Convention[29] but there must be some hesitation following those cases where it has been

---

26 *Wimbledon* case (1923) PCIJ, Ser A, No 1, p 24; 2 ILR 99.

27 See C Parry (1950) 36 TGS 149; K Widdows, 'What is an international agreement in international law?' (1979) 50 BYIL 117.

28 See Vienna Convention on the Law of Treaties (1969), Art 2(1)(a).

29 See *ibid*, Art 2(1)(a), but note also the *Eastern Greenland* case (1933) PCIJ, Ser A/B, No 53 as to the effect of oral declarations.

held that oral declarations may have some legal effect. However, Art 102 of the United Nations Charter (1945) provides for the registration and publication of treaties; it is difficult to imagine how an oral agreement could meet these procedures and failure to comply will mean that such a 'treaty' cannot be relied upon before the International Court of Justice.

The second element is that a treaty must be made between parties that possess international legal personality. This concept normally causes no difficulty in the context of states, but may give rise to problems where colonies or federal entities are in issue. In the case of a colony, everything will depend on the precise circumstances while, in respect of a federal entity, the matter will depend on the constitutional structure. Thus, Art 33(3) of the German Constitution (1949) permits individual *Länder* to conclude treaties subject to the approval of the Federal Government. In respect of international organisations, the power to enter into a treaty may arise expressly or impliedly from the constitutional document establishing the organisation. In the case of corporations, it is often argued that the agreement will be subject to municipal law, expressly or impliedly chosen, unless the contract can be said to have been internationalised. Such an approach stems from the judgment in the *Anglo Iranian Oil Co* case[30] and the arbitration in *Texaco v Libya*;[31] however, in the latter case it is clear that the parties had entered into a choice of law clause that expressly referred to international law. Thirdly, for a treaty to arise it is necessary that the agreement be subject to international law; this will therefore exclude those situations where a state or international organisation chooses to enter into a contract governed by municipal law. Fourthly, as stated above it is important that there should be an intention to create legal relations; this was expressly stated in the first draft of the International Law Commission in 1953 but, in the final definition in Art 2 of the Vienna Convention, it was felt by the Special Rapporteur[32] that this element was covered by the use of the words 'governed by international law'.

The process by which a treaty is concluded can be reduced to a number of steps; these can be summarised as: (i) the identification and accrediting of negotiators; (ii) negotiation and adoption; (iii) authentication and signature; (iv) ratification; (v) accession and adhesion; (vi) entry into force; and (vii) registration and publication.

While states have the capacity to make treaties it is important that those acting as the human agents should establish their credentials. Such a process is known as the production of full powers. Article 7(1) of the Vienna Convention indicates that full powers should be produced, save in those situations where full powers are presumed by virtue of office, as in the case of Heads of State, Heads of Government and Ministers of Foreign Affairs. It is normal for the text of a treaty to record that evidence of full powers have been produced. Article 8 of the Vienna Convention provides that any act performed by a person not possessing full powers as required under Art 7 shall be of no legal effect unless confirmed by the state. In an international conference, one of the tasks will be to establish the authority of the delegates attending and the extent of their powers.

---

30 *Anglo Iranian Oil Co* case (1952) ICJ 93; 19 ILR 507.
31 *Texaco v Libya* (1977) 53 ILR 389; (1978) 17 ILM 1.
32 In actual fact, the fourth Special Rapporteur Sir Humphrey Waldock (1960–69) who had followed JL Brierly (1949–52); H Lauterpacht (1953–54) and G Fitzmaurice (1955–60).

The second stage will be for the process of negotiation to take place, leading to the adoption of a draft text. Negotiation may take place in formal sessions or in committee or informally, but such negotiations will be directed to producing a draft treaty.

The normal process will be for those participating to produce a draft treaty. Article 9(1) of the Vienna Convention (1969) provides that the text will be adopted by the consent of all states participating. However, this general rule gives way to a particular provision in respect of international conferences. Article 9(2) of the Vienna Convention (1969) provides that the text will be adopted if there is a vote in favour by two-thirds of the states present, unless there is a decision to apply a different rule. In some international conferences, a decision is taken not to proceed unless there is unanimity. Where the conference is being held under the auspices of an international organisation, then the voting procedure will be governed by the constitution of that body. Article 10 of the Vienna Convention provides that the text may be authenticated[33] in whatever manner the parties so determine.

The basis of the law of treaties is the consent of the individual state; thus, Art 11 of the Vienna Convention on the Law of Treaties (1969) provides that consent may be expressed:

... by signature, exchange of instruments constituting a treaty, ratification, acceptance, approval or accession or any other means if so agreed.

Signature may be evidence of authentication of the text or it may indicate consent if it comes within the terms of Art 12 of the Vienna Convention. This provides that signature will have that effect if the treaty so provides or where it is otherwise agreed or where it appears from the full powers of the representative or was so expressed during the negotiation.

While consent by ratification is the norm, many treaties provide that signature shall indicate consent. Where ratification is required, then a state that has so signed is obliged in the interim to refrain from any action that might defeat the object and purpose of a treaty.[34] In cases where ratification is required, then a party that signs but does not ratify will not be contractually bound by the provisions.[35] It is not unusual for a final treaty draft to be left open for a period of time to allow for signature; the object is to obtain as many signatures for the convention as possible. When such a time has elapsed any state that wishes to consent must accede or adhere.

Some treaties may provide that the instrument shall be binding upon signature and where a treaty is subject to ratification there may be a clause indicating that the treaty will be provisionally binding pending ratification. If the treaty is not subject to ratification or approval or is silent, then in the absence of a contrary intention, it would seem that the document is binding upon signature. Article 12 of the Vienna Convention on the Law of Treaties (1969) preserves the rights of states to agree that they may be bound by signature alone. In cases where a treaty is to be effected by exchange of instruments, then Art 13 of the Vienna Convention (1969) stipulates that the parties will be so bound if: (i) the

---

33 Authentication is the process of certification that the document contains the definitive and authentic text.

34 Article 18.

35 *North Sea Continental Shelf* case (1969) ICJ 3 (where the Federal Republic of Germany had signed but did not ratify the Geneva Convention on the Continental Shelf (1958)).

instruments provide that the exchange shall have this effect; or (ii) it can be otherwise established that the states were agreed that the exchange of instruments should have this effect.

The 19th century view[36] was that a treaty could not be effective unless it had been ratified. Today, many treaties do not require ratification. By 'ratification' is meant 'the international act ... whereby a state establishes on the international plane its consent to be bound by a treaty'. The modern view is that whether ratification is required depends on the intention of the parties. This view is reflected in Art 14 of the Vienna Convention which provides for the consent of a state to be expressed by ratification when: (i) the treaty expressly so provides;[37] (ii) the negotiating states agree that ratification should be required;[38] (iii) the treaty has been signed subject to ratification;[39] and (iv) an intention to sign subject to ratification appears from the full powers or was expressed during negotiations.[40]

The principle of ratification is founded on the following considerations. First, a state may wish to consider carefully the precise obligations that its delegates have chosen to assume. Secondly, in a federal state legislation may be required by the constituent parts and time is needed to permit consultation. Thirdly, treaty negotiations are normally conducted by the executive branch of government; if there are to be changes in municipal law then the democratic principle requires that these are implemented by the legislative branch.

In the United Kingdom, the negotiation and ratification of treaties are conducted under the terms of the royal prerogative although some treaties will require Parliamentary approval either because of their subject matter or because there is a prior statute placing limits on ratification.[41]

Because treaty obligations are founded on the consent of states it must follow that there cannot be a legal duty to ratify a treaty. However reluctance to ratify can give rise to problems and lengthy delays in the coming into force of international conventions. A particular example is afforded by the Law of the Sea Convention (1982) which only secured the necessary number of ratifications in 1993.[42] Sometimes, if a treaty is drafted too quickly, defects may justify a state refusing to ratify. Moreover, where domestic legislation is required pressure on parliamentary time may cause delay. Under the Treaty of Rome (1957) if a member state failed to implement a directive into national law then

---

36 See *The Eliza Ann* (1813) 1 Dods 244; *Ambatielos* case (Jurisdiction) (1952) ICJ 43; *Mavrommatis Palestine Concessions (Jurisdiction)* case (1924) PCIJ Ser A No 2, p 57.

37 Vienna Convention on the Law of Treaties (1969), Art 14.1(a).

38 *Ibid*, Art 14.1(b).

39 *Ibid*, Art 14.1(c).

40 *Ibid*, Art 14.1(d).

41 European Parliamentary Elections Act 1978, s 6(1) (no treaty increasing the powers of the European Parliament to be ratified unless approved by legislation); *R v Foreign Secretary ex p Rees Mogg* [1994] QB 552. See for comment, G Marshall [1993] PL 402; R Rawlings [1994] PL 254, p 367.

42 Under the terms of Art 308, the Convention came into force in 1994, 12 months after the date of the deposit of the 60th instrument of ratification.

action could be taken by the European Commission before the European Court of Justice under Art 169.[43] That option does not exist within the wider international community.

In a situation where a state seeks to become a party to a treaty it has not signed, then the normal method is that of accession (sometimes known as adhesion or adherence). The terms of Art 15 of the Vienna Convention (1969) provide that accession is possible, if the terms of the treaty so provide or that the the negotiating states agree to permit such a method; such an agreement may be at the time of negotiations or subsequently. The difference between accession and signature and ratification is that in the former case the state seeking to accede will not have taken part in the negotiations that produced the treaty.[44] It is normal to provide that an important multilateral convention will remain open for signature. Thus, Art 83 of the Vienna Convention itself permits the Convention to remain open for accession by the states indicated in Art 81. Accession has the same effect as signature or ratification; thus, Art 84 of the Vienna Convention provides that the Convention will come into force 30 days after the receipt of the 35th instrument of ratification or accession. It is normal for a multilateral convention to include distinct articles regulating signature, ratification, entry into force and accession.[45]

5 RESERVATIONS TO TREATIES[46]

In negotiations for a bilateral treaty, it is possible for the states to have various disagreements; if such differences are fundamental then there will be no treaty, just as in municipal law: if prospective parties cannot agree then no contract will result. However, in multilateral negotiations it is most unlikely that all states will agree on every point in the final text. This is particularly the case where states contain governments with different economic and social philosophies. Thus, international law permits a state to become a party to a treaty while not agreeing with all its terms.

In general terms, a reservation might be defined as an assertion made by a state which is made with the object of amending or excluding obligations which would otherwise arise under a treaty. Such an assertion may be made when a state is broadly content with a treaty but that there are a number of provisions that it cannot accept. The procedure enables a state to become a party to the treaty when otherwise it might be obliged to reject it. Article 2(1)(d) of the Vienna Convention on the Law of Treaties defines a reservation as:

---

43 Now Art 226 of the EC Treaty revised following the Treaty on European Union (TEU; Treaty of Amsterdam 1997). Generally speaking, the European Court of Justice did not accept pressure on parliamentary time as an excuse for failing to implement a directive.

44 A relevant example being the United Kingdom, signing an Act of Accession in 1972 to permit entry into the European Community in 1973.

45 See Law of the Sea Convention (1982), Art 305 (signature), Art 306 (ratification), Art 307 (accession), Art 308 (entry into force).

46 G Fitzmaurice, 'Reservations to multilateral conventions' (1953) 2 ICLQ 1; JM Ruda, 'Reservations to treaties' (1975) 146 HR 95; D McRae, 'The legal effect of interpretative declarations' (1978) 49 BYIL 155; DW Bowett, 'Reservations to non-restricted multilateral treaties' (1976–77) 48 BYIL 67; JK Gamble, 'Reservations to multilateral treaties: a macroscopic view of state practice' (1980) 74 AJIL 372; C Redgwell, 'Universality of integrity? Some reflections on reservations to multilateral treaties' (1993) 64 BYIL 245; PH Imbert, 'Reservations to the European Convention on Human Rights' (1984) 33 ICLQ 558; S Marks, 'Reservations unhinged: the *Belilos* case before the ECHR' (1990) 39 ICLQ 300.

... a unilateral statement, however phrased or named, made by a State, when signing, ratifying, accepting, approving or acceding to a treaty, whereby it purports to exclude or to modify the legal effect of certain provisions in the treaty, in their application to that State.

A distinction has to be drawn between a reservation and 'political statements, "declarations" "understandings" or "statements on interpretation" or "interpretative declarations"'.[47]

It is clear from the *Anglo French Continental Shelf* case[48] that in the event of dispute it will be for the international tribunal to determine whether the statement is in substance a reservation or merely some form of political declaration. However, even if such a statement is categorised as a reservation it will necessary to consider whether such a reservation is consistent with the treaty in question. Thus, in *Belilos v Switzerland*, the European Court of Human Rights held that a statement described as an 'interpretative declaration' might be categorised as a reservation and thus subject to the rule prohibiting general reservations in Art 64 of the Treaty.[49] If one accepts that the test is one of substance not form or nomenclature, then for a statement to constitute a reservation it must be one that unambiguously seeks to exclude or modify the legal effect of a particular provision of the treaty and that anything less will not be sufficient.

If a reservation has been made then the next question is one of effect. The rule in customary international law was that for a reservation to be accepted in respect of a multilateral treaty all other parties would be obliged to consent; if not then that state was not to be considered as a party to the treaty even in respect of those states that had accepted the reservation. The object of such a regime was to protect the integrity and coherence of international treaties and to some extent reflected the theory that the law of treaties was analogous to the law of contract where a counter offer did not constitute a valid acceptance. However, to this approach there were two objections. First, a state might be excluded from participation in the treaty even though its objections were marginal. Secondly, such an approach would make it difficult to codify international law in the form of multilateral conventions. In the event, the conventional view of unanimity was accepted by the League of Nations,[50] even though by 1932 the Pan American Union was prepared to adopt a more liberal approach to the question of reservations.

The traditional view of unanimity remained the dominant principle into the post-war period. In 1948, the Convention on the Prevention and Punishment of Genocide was opened for signature and a number of states indicated that they wished to enter reservations. Other states objected, so the General Assembly requested an Advisory Opinion from the International Court of Justice. In the *Reservations to the Convention on Genocide* case[51] the Court ruled that:

---

47   D McCrae, 'The legal effect of interpretative declarations' (1978) 49 BYIL 155.

48   *Anglo French Continental Shelf* case (1979) 54 ILR 6 (concerning a French reservation to Art 6 of the Geneva Convention on the Continental Shelf (1958)).

49   *Belilos v Switzerland* (1988) ECHR Ser A Vol 132. For discussion see S Marks, 'Reservations unhinged: the *Belilos* case before the European Court of Human Rights ' (1990) 39 ICLQ 300.

50   Report of the Committee of Experts for the Progressive Codification of International Law (1927).

51   (1951) ICJ 15.

... a State which has made and maintained a reservation which has been objected to by one or more of the parties to the Convention but not by others, can be regarded as being a party to the Convention if the reservation is compatible with the object and purpose of the Convention; otherwise, that State cannot be regarded as being a party to the Convention.

However, the Court also ruled: (i) that if a party to the Convention objects to a reservation which it considers to be incompatible with the object and purpose of the Convention, it can in fact consider that the reserving state is not a party to the Convention; and (ii) that if, on the other hand, a party accepts the reservation as being compatible with the object and purpose of the Convention it can in fact consider that the reserving state is a party to the Convention.

In the particular case of the Genocide Convention (1948), which did not have a reservation clause, the Court ruled that the universal nature of the obligation, the fact that the Convention had been the product of majority votes, and the fact that the objective of the treaty was humanitarian, were all considerations that justified a flexible approach. Thus, the Court favoured the Pan American approach and leaned towards flexibility at the expense of uniformity. The relevant provisions in the Vienna Convention on the Law of Treaties (1969) follow the flexible approach of the court. The International Law Commission had pointed out in the interim that the increase in the number of states and the fact that reservations tended to be on one or two matters were considerations which justified a flexible approach.

The provisions relating to reservations are contained in Arts 19–25 of the Vienna Convention. Under Art 19 a state may formulate a reservation unless: (a) the reservation is prohibited by the treaty; or (b) the attempted reservation is prohibited by the treaty; or (c) where the reservation is incompatible with the object and purpose of the treaty.

The Vienna Convention (1969) then proceeds to make particular provision in respect of a number of specific situations:

(i) Under the terms of Art 20(1) a reservation expressly authorised by a treaty does not require the consent of another state. The state making the reservation will be a party to the treaty and the reservation will serve to modify its obligations in respect of the other parties.

(ii) Under the terms of Art 20(2) when it appears from the limited number of negotiating States and the object and purpose of a treaty that the application of the treaty in its entirety between all the parties is an essential condition of the consent of each one to be bound by the treaty, a reservation requires acceptance by all parties. Thus a state whose reservation is accepted by the other parties will be a party to the treaty but a state whose reservation is objected to will not be a party to the treaty. It will be necessary to examine the history of the treaty and its actual text to determine whether it comes within this particular class. It is most unlikely that a multilateral treaty would come within this category.

(iii) Under the terms of Art 20 (3) when a treaty is a constituent instrument of an international organisation and unless it otherwise provides, a reservation requires the acceptance of the competent organ of that organisation.

(iv) In cases not dealt with above Art 20(4) of the Vienna Convention (1969) provides:

(a) acceptance by another contracting state of a reservation constitutes the reserving state a party to the treaty in relation to that other state if or when the treaty is in force for those states;

(b) an objection by another contracting state to a reservation does not preclude the entry into force of the treaty as between the objecting and reserving states unless a contrary intention is definitely expressed by the objecting state;

(c) an act expressing a state's consent to be bound by the treaty and containing a reservation is effective as soon as at least one other contracting state has accepted the reservation.

Thus, in relation to the above, if state A makes a reservation to the Z Convention and it is accepted by state B then both state A and state B are parties to the Convention in their relations with each other (Arts 20(4)(a) and 21(1)(a) and (b)). However, if state A makes a reservation to the Z Convention which is objected to by state B then the Z Convention will still be in force between state A and state B unless the latter has expressly declared otherwise(Arts 20(4)(b) and 21(3)). This is designed to ensure that as far as possible multilateral conventions can be made to operate and thus goes beyond the judgment in the *Genocide* case.

If the objecting state declares that it does not regard the reserving state as a party to the treaty then the treaty will not govern their relations. The treaty will not be in force between them but it will not affect the position of other parties to the treaty (Art 20(2)). However, if the objecting state does not oppose the entry into force of the treaty with the reserving state then 'the provisions to which the reservation relates do not apply as between the two states to the extent of the reservation' (Art 21(3)).

The interrelation of the provisions may be illustrated by an example. Suppose state A and state B are parties to the Z Multilateral Convention. If state B seeks to make a reservation such as 'it does not accept Art 4' then the process of reasoning would be along the following lines:

(i) The first question would be whether the purported reservation was in law a reservation; this will be a matter for the tribunal. On the assumption that it is, one proceeds.

(ii) It will then be necessary to determine whether the reservation is prohibited by the treaty (see Art 19(a)).

(iii) It will then be important to determine whether the reservation has been expressly authorised (Art 20(1)).

(iv) It will then be necessary to determine whether the reservation comes within the particular classes specified in Art 20(2) or Art 20(3)).

(v) If none of the above pertains then if the reservation is accepted by state A then the Z Convention comes into force between state A and state B as modified, that is, Art 4 does not apply (see Art 20 (4)(a)).

(vi) If the reservation is objected to by state A and that state declares that it does not regard state B as a party to the treaty then the Z Convention will not be in force between the two states (Art 20(4)(b)) but this will not affect other parties (Art 21(2)).

(vii)If the reservation is objected to by state A but that state allows the treaty to enter into force then the Z Convention comes into force between state A and state B save that 'the provisions to which the reservation relates do not apply ... to the extent of the reservation'. Thus, the Z Convention will apply between the two states but Article 4 will not (Art 21(3)).

The scheme of the Vienna Convention is to provide for differential treatment in respect of reservations. The provisions though sometimes convoluted are designed to ensure that a reserving state cannot impede the movement towards codification through the vehicle of the multilateral convention. The uniformity approach may have had the virtue of clarity but had it remained in place it is unlikely that progress would have been made other than at the speed of the most reluctant member. The present position does mean that in each case one has to consider carefully the nature of any reservations made by an individual state and that a multilateral convention gives rise to a number of distinct bi lateral relationships.

6 THE ENTRY INTO FORCE OF TREATIES

Broadly, a treaty will enter into force when the parties so intend. This rule is reflected in Art 24(1) of the Vienna Convention; however in the absence of express provision Art 24(2) provides that the treaty will enter into force when consent to be bound by the treaty has been established for all negotiating states.

As with municipal legislation, it is usual to make express provision as to when a treaty is to come into force. In the case of multilateral conventions, the normal procedure is to stipulate that the treaty will come into force when a certain number of ratifications have been received; in a world of over 150 states it is unrealistic to expect every state to ratify. In these circumstances, a particular number of ratifications or accessions is specified. Thus, the Geneva Convention on the Territorial Sea and the Contiguous Zone (1958) came into effect 30 days after 22 ratifications or accessions had been lodged with the Secretary General.[52] In contrast, the Vienna Convention on the Law of Treaties (1969) came into effect 30 days after 35 instruments of ratification or accession had been received.[53] More recently, the Law of the Sea Convention (1982) provided in Art 308 that the treaty would come into force 12 months after the date of the reception of the 60th instrument of ratification or accession.

When the requisite number of ratifications have been received then the treaty will come into force but only between those states that have ratified; those who have simply signed will not be bound by the treaty unless in the particular circumstances signature is to be regarded as sufficient evidence of consent to be bound.

Article 102 of the United Nations Charter (1945) and Art 80 of the Vienna Convention on the Law of Treaties (1969) provide that after a treaty enters into force the treaty should be submitted to United Nations Headquarters for registration and publication. These provisions reflect the original objective of Woodrow Wilson to secure an end to those

---

52   As stipulated in Art 29.
53   As stipulated in Art 84.

secret treaties which were thought to have contributed to the outbreak of the First World War (1914–18). These provisions also enable the United Nations Treaty Series to be as complete as possible.[54]

7 THE APPLICATION OF TREATIES

When a treaty has entered into force, problems may arise as to its scope or application. In principle, a treaty is not retrospective unless it is expressly stated to be so. Under Art 29 of the Vienna Convention on the Law of Treaties (1969), a treaty is binding upon each state party in respect of its entire territory unless the contrary was stated. In the past, it was not unusual for European powers to stipulate whether the treaty provisions would apply in respect of colonial territory.

In recent years, the increase in both the number of states and the volume of treaties has lead to problems in respect of successive treaties that relate to the same subject matter. In order to regulate the relationship, Art 30 of the Vienna Convention makes detailed provisions which are as follows:

(1) Subject to Art 103 of the Charter of the United Nations, the rights and obligations of states parties to successive treaties relating to the same subject matter shall be determined in accordance with the following paragraphs.[55]

(2) When a treaty specifies that it is subject to, or that it is not to be considered as incompatible with, an earlier or later treaty, the provisions of that other treaty shall prevail.

(3) When all the parties to the earlier treaty are parties also to the later treaty but the earlier treaty is not terminated or suspended in operation under Art 59, the earlier treaty applies only to the extent that its provisions are compatible with those of the later treaty.[56]

(4) When the parties to the later treaty do not include all the parties to the earlier one –

   (a) as between states parties to both treaties the same rule applies as in para 3;

   (b) as between a state party to both treaties and a state party to only one of the treaties, the treaty to which both states are parties governs their mutual rights and obligations.

(5) Paragraph 4 is without prejudice to Art 41[57] or to any question of the termination or suspension of the operation of a treaty under Art 60[58] or to any question of responsibility which may arise for a state from the conclusion or application of a treaty,

---

54 The provisions replace like requirements stipulated in Art 18 of the Covenant of the League of Nations. However, there is a distinction between the process of diplomacy being conducted in private and the eventual treaty being in public. See Harold Nicholson, *Diplomacy*, 1939.

55 Article 103 stipulates that obligations under the United Nations Charter take precedence over any other treaty obligations; see the *Lockerbie* case (19992) ICJ 3; (1992) 94 ILR 478.

56 Article 59 is concerned with the termination or suspension of a treaty by a later treaty.

57 Article 41 is concerned with agreements to modify multilateral treaties between certain of the parties only.

58 Article 60 is concerned with material breach of a treaty and is discussed below.

the provisions of which are incompatible with its obligations towards another state under another treaty.

The object of Art 30 is to provide a general set of provisions but in most instances the parties will make express provision to govern any potential conflict.

8 INVALID TREATIES

To prevent states seeking to evade treaty obligations, Art 42(1) of the Vienna Convention provides that 'the validity of a treaty or of the consent of a state to be bound by a treaty may be impeached only through the application of the present Convention'. The purpose of the provision is to prevent states undermining the integrity of the treaty system by absurd claims. As in municipal law, the circumstances in which agreements freely entered into can be set aside must always be limited in scope. In pursuance thereof, Art 44(1) stipulates that a state may only withdraw or suspend the operation of a treaty as a whole and not particular parts unless the treaty so provides or the provisions of Art 44(3) pertain, namely:

(a) the said clauses are separable from the remainder of the treaty with regard to their application;

(b) it appears from the treaty or is otherwise established that acceptance of those clauses was not an essential basis of the consent of the other party or parties to be bound by the treaty as a whole; and

(c) continued performance of the remainder of the treaty would not be unjust.

It will be evident that the Convention takes a conservative approach on the question of severability of treaty obligations. Further, in certain circumstances the right to invalidate a treaty may be lost. Article 45 provides that a ground for invalidity may be forfeited where a state becomes aware of the relevant facts and then agrees that the treaty is valid or consents to its operation or by reason of its subsequent conduct is deemed to have acquiesced. Such a provision is in line with the doctrine of estoppel in municipal law.

A common problem that arises in the context of validity is the relationship with constitutional law. The written constitutions of some countries may provide that the executive branch should not undertake certain treaty obligations without the consent of the legislature. The question arises as to the effect in international law of the non-compliance by a state of its own constitutional requirements. Historically, there have been a number of answers to this question. One opinion holds that the treaty is automatically void or at least will be when the constitutional provision is well known. The argument being that the executive branch of government draws its authority from the constitution and has no authority independent of that document. The other school of thought holds that the treaty is valid but may not be so if the other party knew that the state in question was acting contrary to its own constitutional requirements. This second approach is supported by Art 46 of the Vienna Convention which reads as follows:

(1) A State may not invoke the fact that its consent to be bound by a treaty has been expressed in violation of a provision of its internal law regarding competence to

conclude treaties as invalidating its consent unless that violation was manifest and concerned a rule of its internal law of fundamental importance.

(2) A violation is manifest if it would be objectively evident to any State conducting itself in the matter in accordance with normal practice and in good faith.

These are demanding requirements – the provision must be: (a) manifest; (b) objectively evident; and (c) be of fundamental importance. Article 46 is directed to the situation where a negotiating government (that is, the executive branch) exceeds its constitutional powers.

A problem of a different nature arises if an individual seeks to exceed his negotiating powers; to an extent this matter is regulated by the provisions as to powers contained in Arts 7 and 8 which have been alluded to above. However, there may be situations where an individual is given negotiating powers subject to a specific restriction and then he exceeds that limitation. In this context, Art 47 provides the state will normally be bound unless the other party had notice. The text of the Art 47 reads:

If the authority of a representative to express the consent of a State to be bound by a particular treaty has been made subject to a specific restriction, his omission to observe that restriction may not be invoked as invalidating the consent expressed by him unless the restriction was notified to other negotiating States prior to his expressing such consent.

The basis of the law of treaties is the free and open consent of independent sovereign states. Therefore, Art 49 of the Vienna Convention provides that a treaty may be invalidated by the fraudulent conduct of the other state. In cases where one negotiating state has sought directly or indirectly to corrupt the negotiations of the other then Art 50 provides that this may be invoked as a ground for invalidating the treaty. Thus, if state A and state B conclude a treaty but the representatives of state B were bribed by state C on the instructions of state A then this would be a ground of such invalidity. Having regard to the fact that treaties are negotiated by career civil servants such instances will in practice be very rare indeed.

The emphasis on free consent is fortified by the provisions of Art 51 which provide that a treaty shall be of no legal effect if an attempt is made to coerce the representatives of a negotiating state.[59] A different problem arises in respect of attempts to coerce the state itself by threats to use force. Prior to the First World War, threats to use force were sometimes employed to secure favourable treaty terms; the subsequent treaty was not thought to be unlawful. However, under the Covenant of the League of Nations (1919) and the Kellogg Briand Pact of 1928 the threat to use force against another state is *prima facie* unlawful and is a breach of Art 2(4) of the United Nations Charter (1945). Thus Art 52 of the Vienna Convention provides that: 'A treaty is void if its conclusion has been procured by the threat or use of force in violation of the principles of international law embodied in the Charter of the United Nations.'[60] At the time of drawing up the Convention there was some debate as to whether the concept should extend to the

---

59 Arguable that this took place in 1939, when Germany coerced the representatives of Czechoslovakia to secure a treaty granting a protectorate over Bohemia and Moravia; more obviously, coercion was used in 1968 by the USSR to secure agreement to station troops in Czechoslovakia to curtail the effects of the 'Prague Spring'.

60 The evidence would have to be compelling; see the *Fisheries Jurisdiction* case (1973) ICJ 14.

employment of economic pressure, but the International Law Commission did not show much enthusiasm for such an extension. This concern was met by the issuing of a contemporaneous Declaration on the Prohibition of Military, Political or Economic Coercion in the Conclusion of Treaties. The terms of Art 52 refer to conduct at variance with the United Nations Charter (1945); this would therefore not apply where members of the United Nations pursuant to Security Council Resolutions seek to persuade a sovereign state to sign an agreement.[61]

A more common cause of dispute is where one party alleges that the treaty does not properly reflect the agreement reached. Having regard to the manner in which treaty negotiations are conducted, this is unlikely to occur very often. The general approach of Art 48 of the Vienna Convention is to restrict claims based on mistake or error; the text of the article makes this clear by providing:

(1) A State may invoke an error in a treaty as invalidating its consent to be bound by the treaty if the error relates to a fact or situation which was assumed by that State to exist at the time when the treaty was concluded and formed an essential basis of its consent to be bound.

(2) Paragraph 1 shall not apply if the State in question contributed by its own conduct to the error or if the circumstances were such as to put that State on notice of a possible error.

The text of Art 48 follows upon the prior case law and, in particular, the *Temple of Preah Vihear* case,[62] where the International Court of Justice indicated that a plea of error could not be entertained where the state advancing it contributed by its own conduct to the error. Where the state has contributed to the error or having been put on notice failed to act, then such a plea will be not succeed.

The Vienna Convention on the Law of Treaties (1969) provides that a treaty will be void if it conflicts with certain fundamental norms of international law (*jus cogens*). This is expressly stated in Art 53 which reads:

A treaty is void if, at the time of its conclusion, it conflicts with a peremptory norm of general international law. For the purposes of the present Convention, a peremptory norm of general international law is a norm accepted and recognised by the international community of States as a whole as a norm from which no derogation is permitted and which can be modified only by a subsequent norm of general international law having the same character.

The difficulty with this provision is that there is no agreement as to which rules are of such a fundamental character. It is clear that any such rule must be established by a wide cross section of states. Moreover, the provision has to be read with Art 64 which provides that: 'If a new peremptory norm of general international law emerges, any existing treaty which is in conflict with that norm becomes void and terminates.'

The Convention contains a number of provisions regulating invalidity; it would seem that the precise consequences differ according to the form of invalidity. In situations within Art 8 and Arts 51–53 then the treaty will be void and have no legal force. In

---

61 As was the case in February–March 1999 where the Republic of Yugoslavia was requested to sign an agreement in Paris regulating its future conduct in the province of Kosovo.

62 *Temple of Preah Vihear* case (1962) ICJ 6.

contrast, under Arts 46–50 it is at least arguable that the treaty will be *prima facie* valid unless and until the other state establishes a vitiating factor and in certain circumstances as under Art 45 acquiesence may prevent the establishment of such an impediment. In these circumstances this is more likely to be viewed as voidable than void.

In any event, both category of defects are subject to the requirement to give the other state notice and, in both situations, there is an obligation to invoke the methods of peaceful settlement stipulated in Art 33 of the United Nations Charter (1945); in cases where no solution has been reached after 12 months then the matter should be referred to the special conciliation commission established under the Annex to the Convention.[63] Where acts have been performed in reliance upon an invalid treaty then Arts 69 and 71 provide for an equitable restoration of the *status quo ante*.

9 THE INTERPRETATION OF TREATIES[64]

One of the most common problems in the law of treaties is that of interpretation. Clearly, where a problem arises the evidence will have to be analysed and the facts determined and the relevant treaty provisions examined. At this stage, a difficulty may arise as to the precise meaning and scope of expressions used in the treaty; as with statutes in municipal law, problems of interpretation and construction will arise. To avoid difficulty, some treaties contain extensive definition sections outlining the meaning to be attached to common terms.[65]

As with statutory construction in municipal law, there are a number of schools of thought that seek to determine how treaty interpretation should be undertaken; examples can be found in the decided cases of each of these schools of thought. It is sensible to say a little about each, before considering how they may have been affected by the terms of the Vienna Convention on the Law of Treaties (1969):

(a) The literal, textual or grammatical approach – according to this school the treaty is to be interpreted by seeking to ascertain the ordinary, natural meaning of the words employed in the treaty. The object is to determine the intention of the parties at the time of agreement by reference to the actual words used. Sometimes, however, it is difficult to determine the natural or plain meaning of a word used. This approach draws upon the Anglo American tradition of statutory interpretation, whereby the role of the judge or tribunal is strictly limited and where there is a reluctance to engage in any form of legislative conduct. This approach, which is founded on a

---

63 Vienna Convention (1969), Art 66(b).

64 H Lauterpacht, 'Restrictive interpretation and the principle of effectiveness in the interpretation of treaties' (1949) 26 BYIL 48; G Fitzmaurice, 'The law and procedure of the International Court of Justice: treaty interpretation and certain other treaty points' (1951) 28 BYIL 1; G Fitzmaurice, 'The law and practice of the International Court of Justice (1951–1954): treaty interpretation and other treaty points' (1957) 33 BYIL 203; E Gordon, 'The World Court and the interpretation of constitutive treaties' (1965) 59 AJIL 794; M McDougal, 'The ILC, "Draft Articles upon Interpretation"' (1967) 61 AJIL 992; MK Yasseen, 'L'Interprétation des traites d'après la Convention de Viènne sur le droit des traités' (1976) 151 HR 1-114.

65 As indeed in Art 2 of the Vienna Convention on the Law of Treaties (1969).

precise analysis of the words used, has been followed in a number of cases, both before international tribunals but also before municipal courts.[66]

(b) The actual intention of the parties – this approach seeks to interpret the treaty by reference to the actual intention of the parties at the time of its conclusion. The difficulty with such an approach is one of evidence; on close examination the intentions of the parties may have been different.

(c) The object or purpose of the treaty. Sometimes described as the teleological approach, this school of thought argues that the terms of the treaty should be interpreted so as to give effect to the object and purpose that the parties are deemed to have intended.[67] To a considerable extent, this has been the approach of the European Court of Justice in respect of the Treaty of Rome (1957); such an approach is facilitated if the treaty sets out certain broad principles in advance of its detailed provisions. The latter provisions can then be interpreted by reference to the broad principles that the parties have accepted.[68] In principle, the 'object and purpose' is that of the parties not that of the court or tribunal.

(d) Linked to the above is the effectiveness principle.[69] This principle holds that the treaty should be interpreted so as to ensure the effective implementation of the object and purpose of the treaty. This is clearly linked to the teleological principle but imports a greater element of objective policy determination. It is arguable that the *Reparations* case[70] is an example of the principle in operation. However, to rely upon effectiveness as a principle presupposes that the tribunal has determined the overall object of the treaty. Clearly, the principle cannot be invoked to undermine the clear letter and spirit of the parties intentions.[71] This approach is defensible where the tribunal is considering the express or implied powers contained within the constitution of an international organisation.[72] However, such an approach may be open to question where the issue is simply a question of reciprocal obligations between states and where reservations on sovereignty should not be lightly presumed.

(e) Consistency. It is sometimes argued that there is a principle in treaty interpretation that a consistent meaning should be given to different parts of the treaty instrument. To some extent consistency may be achieved by including an extensive definition section within the text of the treaty itself.

---

66   *Advisory Opinion on the Constitution of the Maritime Safety Committee of the Inter-Governmental Maritime Consultative Organisation* (1960) ICJ 150; *Polish Postal Service* case (1925) PCIJ, Ser B, No 11. For such an approach in municipal courts, see *United States v Alvarez Machin* (1992) 31 ILM 902 (United States Supreme Court).

67   The teleological approach was discussed by Lord Denning MR in the Court of Appeal hearing in *James Buchanan & Co Ltd v Babco Forwarding and Shipping* [1978] AC 141; see R Munday (1978) 27 ICLQ 450. See also *The Ambatielos* case (1952) ICJ 28.

68   As indeed is often the practice of the European Court of Justice which often seeks to refer to the general principles set out in Arts 1–7 of the Treaty of Rome (1957).

69   Sometimes expressed in the maxim *ut res magis valeat quam pereat* – it is better that the thing to have effect than be rendered a nullity.

70   *Reparations for Injuries* case (1949) ICJ 179.

71   *Interpretation of Peace Treaties* case (1950) ICJ 221; 19 ILR 416.

72   *Reparations for Injuries* case (1949) ICJ 174; 16 ILR 318; *Competence of the General Assembly for the Admission of a State* case (1950) ICJ 4; 17 ILR 326; *Certain Expenses of the United Nations* case (1962) ICJ 151.

(f) Human Rights treaties. It is sometimes argued that different considerations apply to the interpretation of human rights treaties. First, it is argued that the intention is to create a new legal order based on the objective determination of minimum standards of conduct. Secondly, in such cases the tribunal will be more than usually aware that its interpretation will be relied upon as setting down standards of conduct within other signatory states. Thus, it is argued that the emphasis should be upon the objects and purpose of the Convention as establishing an autonomous legal order capable of creating individual rights and whose validity is not to be judged against external criteria.[73]

(g) Extrinsic evidence. In normal circumstances, a tribunal will be restricted to the terms of the treaty itself, but in appropriate cases the court may consider: (i) the past history; (ii) the *travaux preparatoires*;[74] (iii) subsequent agreements between the parties regarding the interpretation of the treaty or the application of its provisions;[75] (iv) subsequent practice in the application of the treaty, establishing agreement regarding its implementation;[76] (v) interpretative protocols.

As in municipal law, while principles of interpretation are sometimes alluded to, much depends on the character of the text; the International Court of Justice may feel that a liberal approach is justified where the constitution of an international organisation is in issue but that a more conservative approach is called for when the treaty concerns the reciprocal obligations of states.

Part III, s 3, of the Vienna Convention on the Law of Treaties (1969) is devoted to the subject of interpretation and the relevant provisions are set out in Arts 31–33. The cardinal principle is set out in Art 31 (1) which reads:

> A treaty shall be interpreted in good faith in accordance with the ordinary meaning to be given to the terms of the treaty in their context and in the light of their object and purpose.

This is expanded upon in Art 31(2) which reads:

> The context for the purpose of the interpretation of a treaty shall comprise, in addition to the text, including its preamble and annexes:
>
> (a) any agreement relating to the treaty which was made between all the parties in connexion with the conclusion of the treaty;
>
> (b) any instrument which was made by one or more parties in connexion with the conclusion of the treaty and accepted by the other parties as an instrument related to the treaty.

Article 31(1) sets out the fundamental rule and is consistent with the prior case law;[77] since 1969, the International Court of Justice has indicated that the principle represents

---

73 *Tyrer v United Kingdom* (1978) 2 EHRR 1; *Soering v United Kingdom* (1989) 11 EHRR 439.
74 Vienna Convention on the Law of Treaties (1969), Art 32.
75 *Ibid*, Art 31(3).
76 *Ibid*.
77 *Competence of the General Assembly for the Admission of a State to the United Nations* case (1950) ICJ 4; (1950) 17 ILR 326.

the state of customary law[78] and the same approach has been followed by the European Court of Human Rights.[79] The concept of 'context' is amplified in Art 31(2) and includes any preamble, annex or subsequent agreement made by the parties at the conclusion of the treaty. The intention that the broad picture should be reviewed is confirmed by Art 31(3) which reads:

> There shall be taken into account together with the context:
>
> (a) any subsequent agreement between the parties regarding the interpretation of the treaty or the application of its provisions;
>
> (b) any subsequent practice[80] in the application of the treaty which establishes the agreement of the parties regarding its interpretation;
>
> (c) any relevant rules of international law applicable in the relations between the parties.

The intention is that Art 31 should set out the primary rules of interpretation, with emphasis being given in Art 31(1) to the object and purpose of the treaty. However, there may be circumstances in which the interpretation under Art 31 is unclear or is susceptible of corroboration. The International Court of Justice has confirmed that Art 31 represents the customary law of treaty interpretation;[81] it can therefore be invoked even in respect of those states not a party to the Convention. [82]

Article 32 provides for a supplementary means of interpretation. The text of Art 32 reads:

> Recourse may be had to supplementary means of interpretation, including the preparatory work of the treaty and the circumstances of its conclusion in order to confirm the meaning resulting from the application of Art 31, or to determine the meaning when the interpretation according to Art 31:
>
> (a) leaves the meaning ambiguous or obscure; or
>
> (b) leads to a result which is manifestly absurd or unreasonable.

Thus, Art 32 permits *travaux preparatoires* to be consulted. However, a number of points can be made. First, Art 32 refers to 'recourse may be had'; this raises the question as to whether it is necessary to proceed to Art 32 if the meaning is clear under Art 31. Secondly, there is some authority that indicates that if the text is clear, then recourse to Art 32 is not required.[83] Thus, in the *Maritime and Territorial Dispute* case,[84] the International Court of Justice considered that the treaty text was sufficiently clear cut and that there was thus no need to have recourse to *travaux preparatoires*. Thirdly, the structure of Art 31 not only sets

---

78 *Territorial Dispute* case (*Libya v Chad*) (1994) ICJ 6; 100 ILR 1; *Qatar v Bahrain* case (1995) ICJ 6; 102 ILR 47.

79 *Golder v United Kingdom* (1975) 1 EHRR 524; *James v United Kingdom* (1986) 8 EHRR 123; *Lithgow v United Kingdom* (1986) 8 EHRR 329.

80 See *Land, Island and Maritime Frontier Dispute* (*El Salvador v Honduras, Nicaragua Intervening*) (1992) ICJ 351; *Jan Mayen* (*Denmark v Norway*) case (1993) ICJ 37; (1993) 99 ILR 395.

81 *Territorial Dispute* (*Libya v Chad*) case (1994) ICJ Rep 6; *Kasikili/Sedudu Island* (*Botswana v Namibia*) case, ICJ, 13 December 1999.

82 *Asian Agricultural Products Ltd* (*AAPL*) *v Republic of Sri Lanka* (1992) 30 ILM 577.

83 *Territorial Dispute* case (*Libya v Chad*) (1994) ICJ 6; *Maritime and Territorial Dispute* (*Qatar v Bahrain*) case (1995) ICJ 5.

84 *Maritime and Territorial Dispute* (*Qatar v Bahrain*) case (1995) ICJ 5.

out the central principle in Art 31(1) but the Article is headed 'General rule of interpretation'. Fourthly, a tribunal may be reluctant to consult Art 32 if the state in question did not participate in the preparatory work.[85]

Fifthly, in the recent *Kasikili/Sedudu Island* case,[86] the International Court of Justice proceeded to interpret the treaty by reference to its language before reviewing that finding by examining the treaty's object and purpose.

In some cases it will be necessary to pay regard to Art 31(4) which provides that 'a special meaning shall be given to a term if it is established that the parties so intended'. However, it is clear that if one party alleges a particular meaning then the *onus probandi* lies upon that party.[87] Article 32 of the Vienna Convention refers to supplementary means of interpretation, however, in the *Maritime and Territorial Dispute* case,[88] the majority of the ICJ considered that as the principal treaty text had a clear meaning it was not necessary to refer to the *travaux preparatoires* to confirm that interpretation.

In cases where the treaty has been drawn up in more than one language,[89] and each is to be considered authentic or official, then Art 33(4) provides that in the absence of agreement as to the prevailing text then 'when a comparison of the authentic texts discloses a difference of meaning which the application of Arts 31 and 32 does not remove, the meaning which best reconciles the texts, having regard to the object and purpose of the treaty shall be adopted'.[90]

10 AMENDMENT AND MODIFICATION OF TREATIES

Although the expressions 'amendment' and 'modification' share a common theme in that they both pertain to the revision of treaties, the terms do in fact have different meanings. Amendment indicates a formal alteration of treaty provisions affecting all parties while the process of modification concerns the revision of treaty provisions in respect of a limited number of states.

Article 39 of the Vienna Convention provides: 'A treaty may be amended by agreement between the parties. The rules laid down in Part II apply to such an agreement except in so far as the treaty may otherwise so provide.' The effect of this provision is that any agreement to amend must be subject to the same formalities as operate in the making of the treaty unless the treaty itself so provides. The motivation for amending a treaty will vary but, in the modern world, circumstances and conditions change rapidly and the

---

85   *River Oder* case (1929) PCIJ, Ser A, No 23.

86   *Kasikili/Sedudu Island* (*Botswana v Namibia*) case, ICJ, 13 December 1999.

87   *Eastern Greenland* case (1933) PCIJ, Ser A/B, No 53; 6 ILR 95.

88   *Maritime Delimitation and Territorial Questions* (*Qatar v Bahrain*) case (1994) ICJ 112.

89   Clearly, there is less likely to be difficulty if all parties co-operate on drawing up the different texts rather than relying on one party to simply translate. An account of the drawing up of the Russian version of the United Nations Charter (equally authentic under Art 111) is provided by Michael Ignatieff in *Isaiah Berlin; A Life*, 1998, who relates that the philosopher oversaw the Russian translation of the Charter.

90   In the *Mavrommatis Palestine Concessions* case (1926) PCIJ, Ser A, No 2, the court advanced the view that where there was inconsistency between two official texts then the tribunal should adopt the more limited of the two definitions; the court was also influenced by which draft had drawn up first.

average treaty may have a life span longer than a commercial contract in municipal law. Thus, many treaties contain express provisions to deal with amendment. Perhaps the best known provision is that contained in Art 108 of the United Nations Charter, which provides that the Charter can be amended by a vote of two thirds of the members of the General Assembly together with votes by each of the permanent members of the Security Council.

While many multilateral treaties contain express provision for amendment those that do not will be governed by the provisions of Art 40 of the Vienna Convention.[91] This article provides that the proposed amendment shall be circulated to all state parties.[92] Each state is entitled to have the right to participate in the decision making process,[93] and the process for the negotiation and conclusion of any agreement to amend the treaty.[94] Every state which is entitled to become a party to the treaty may become a party to the treaty as amended.[95] However, the amended agreement does not bind any state which is a party but declines to become a party to the amending agreement.[96] Article 40(5) governs the position where a state has become a party to the treaty after the amending agreement has come into effect. Such a state will be a party to the amended treaty[97] save as regards those regards those states that are not a party to the amending agreement. In such circumstances the acceding state will be a party to the unamended treaty in respect of those states.[98]

In contrast, modification arises where two or more parties decide to change the treaty between themselves alone. This procedure is known as modification and is acceptable either where it is expressly provided for in the treaty[99] or where it does not affect the rights and obligations of other states, and the provision is not one 'derogation from which is incompatible with the effective execution of the object and purpose of the treaty as a whole'.[100]

11 THE TERMINATION OF TREATIES[101]

As in the municipal law of contract there are a number of methods by which a treaty may come to an end. It is important to say a little about each.

---

91 Vienna Convention on the Law of Treaties (1969), Art 40(1).

92 *Ibid*, Art 40(2).

93 *Ibid*, Art 40(2)(a).

94 *Ibid*, Art 40(3)(b).

95 *Ibid*, Art 40(3).

96 *Ibid*, Art 40(4).

97 *Ibid*, Art 40(5)(a).

98 *Ibid*, Art 40(5)(b).

99 *Ibid*, Art 41(1)(a).

100 *Ibid*, Art 41(1)(b)(i) and (1)(b)(ii).

101 A Vamvoukis, *Termination of Treaties in International Law*, 1985; R Plender, 'The role of consent in the termination of treaties' (1986) 57 BYIL 133.

(a) Termination in accordance with the treaty or by agreement

The commonest method is for a treaty to come to an end is as provided by the treaty itself. Examples would be where the treaty is for a particular period,[102] or where there is a specific minimum period before the option to withdraw arises or where there is a right to withdraw at any time or where the treaty is to endure until a particular project has been accomplished. This practice has been recognised by the Vienna Convention (1969) which provides in Art 54(1)(a) that a state party may withdraw 'in conformity with the provisions of the treaty'. However, a treaty may also come to an end by agreement and Art 54(1)(b) provides that it may do so 'at any time by consent of all the parties after consultation with the other contracting states'.

In the event that the treaty makes no express provision for denunciation or withdrawal such a right might arise impliedly under the terms of Art 56.[103] The text reads:

(1) A treaty which contains no provision regarding its termination and which does not provide for denunciation or withdrawal is not subject to denunciation or withdrawal unless –

    (a) it is established that the parties intended to admit the possibility of denunciation or withdrawal; or

    (b) a right of denunciation or withdrawal may be implied by the nature of the treaty.

(2) A party shall give not less than twelve months notice of its intention to denounce or withdraw from the treaty under paragraph 1.

Although not strictly a form of limitation Art 58 of the Vienna Convention provides that two or more parties to a multilateral treaty may agree to the suspension of the multilateral treaty as between themselves if such suspension is provided for in the treaty or the suspension does not affect the rights and duties of other parties and is not incompatible with the object and purpose of the treaty.

Where all the parties to a treaty later conclude a treaty on the same subject matter then Art 59 provides that the earlier treaty may be regarded as impliedly terminated if it appears from the later treaty that the parties intended that the matter should be governed by that treaty or the provisions of the earlier treaty are so incompatible with the earlier one as not to be capable of being applied at the same time.

(b) Material breach[104]

As with the municipal law of contract, difficulties will arise when a state breaches a particular term of a treaty. It may be that the other state will wish to terminate the treaty or claim some form of compensation. As in domestic law, there is the same problem as to

---

102 *Rainbow Warrior Arbitration* (*New Zealand v France*) case (1990) 82 ILR 499.

103 Held to be an accurate statement of customary international law in *Nicaragua v United States* (*Jurisdiction*) (1984) ICJ 392, p 420.

104 See S Rosenne, *Breach of Treaty*, 1985; DN Hutchinson, 'Solidarity and breaches of multilateral treaties' (1988) 59 BYIL 151.

distinguishing between a serious breach and a trivial one. In respect of bilateral treaties the general rule is set out in Art 60(1) which reads:[105]

> A material breach of a bilateral treaty by one of the parties entitles the other to invoke the breach as a ground for terminating the treaty or suspending its operation in whole or in part.

However, the position is more complicated where there is a multilateral treaty. It is objectionable that a breach by state A should entitle state B to regard the treaty as terminated because this would be unfair on States C, D and E. For this reason separate provision is made in Art 60(2) of the Vienna Convention which reads:

> A material breach of a multilateral treaty by one of the parties entitles:
>
> (a) the other parties by unanimous agreement to suspend the operation of the treaty in whole or in part or to terminate it either;
>
>   (i) in the relations between themselves and the defaulting State, or
>
>   (ii) as between all the parties;
>
> (b) a party specially affected by the breach to invoke it as a ground for suspending the operation of the treaty in whole or in part in the relations between itself and the defaulting State;
>
> (c) any party other than the defaulting State to invoke the breach as a ground for suspending the operation of the treaty in whole or in part with respect to itself if the treaty is of such a character that a material breach of its provisions by one party radically changes the position of every party with respect to the further performance of its obligations under the treaty.

However, before a breach can give rise to an entitlement to terminate it must be capable of being described as 'material'. The International Law Commission had chosen this expression in preference to 'fundamental' because the latter indicated that the breach must be directed to the object of the treaty. The purpose is to distinguish the material breach from a breach that might be regarded as trivial; this distinction was recognised in customary international law.[106] Thus, Art 60(3) provides that a breach will be material if it is either a repudiation of the treaty not sanctioned by the convention or it represents a violation of a provision essential to the accomplishment of the object and purpose of the treaty.[107] There is every reason to believe that a tribunal will be slow to find that a breach is material. In the *Danube Dam* case,[108] the International Court of Justice held that Hungary was not entitled to regard a breach by Czechoslovakia as material when that breach had been precipitated by the prior conduct of Hungary.

---

105 Article 60 was held to represent a rule of customary law in the *Gabcikovo-Nagmaros Project* case (ie, the *Danube Dam* case), ICJ, 27 September 1997; (1997) ICJ 7; (1998) 37 ILM 162.

106 See *Tacna-Arica Arbitration* case (1925) 2 RIAA 921, p 943 (where there was a border dispute between Chile and Peru, the Arbitrator being President Coolidge); see also the *Namibia* case (1971) ICJ 16, p 47; 49 ILR 2, p 37 (where the failure by South Africa as the Mandatory Power to co-operate with the United Nations was regarded as fundamental).

107 See the *Rainbow Warrior Arbitration* case (*New Zealand v France*) (1990) 82 ILR 499 (where the conduct of France was found to be a material breach of the 1986 New Zealand-France Agreement).

108 *Case concerning the Gabcikovo-Nagymaros Project* (*Hungary v Slovakia*) (1997) ICJ 7; 38 ILM 162.

On the assumption that the breach can be categorised as material, its effect is not to terminate the treaty but to confer upon the innocent state an option to terminate or suspend the treaty. However, such a right may be modified or excluded by the treaty itself or lost by acquiescence.[109]

It is important to note that Art 60(5) provides that the principles set out in Art 60(2) and 60(3) do not apply in respect of treaties of a humanitarian nature where the purpose is to establish an objective legal regime.

(c) Supervening impossibility of performance

Article 61 of the Convention is directed to a situation where a treaty becomes impossible of performance because of 'the permanent disappearance or destruction of an object indispensable for the execution of the treaty'. In including this provision the International Law Commission had in mind situations such as the submergence of an island or the disappearance of a river where the performance of the treaty has been rendered impossible. As the wording of the article indicates the disappearance must be permanent and not temporary; in the latter case it would seem there is merely a right to suspend treaty obligations. This particular head has some affinity with the doctrine in common law countries of frustration of a contract by reason of destruction of subject matter.[110] At the Vienna Conference a proposal by Mexico to broaden the text of Art 61 to include reference to *force majeure* was rejected. Recent case law indicates that Art 61 represents the position in customary international law;[111] in the *Danube Dam* case,[112] the ICJ indicated that the article required the destruction of something 'indispensable' for the performance of the treaty. The Court did not exclude the possibility that environmental concerns might come within Art 61 but sensibly reasoned that they could not arise in cases where the treaty provided for consultation on such issues. In principle, where a treaty has made specific provision for a particular event, then that event cannot normally constitute the basis of discharge by supervening impossibility.

(d) Fundamental change of circumstances (*rebus sic stantibus*)[113]

International law recognises a principle that one party may be entitled to withdraw from treaty obligations where there has been a fundamental change of circumstances arising since the making of the treaty. Whereas the concept of impossibility is directed to the proper object of the treaty, Art 62 allows for termination if the circumstances prevailing at the time when the treaty was concluded have fundamentally changed.

---

109 See Vienna Convention on the Law of Treaties (1969), Art 45.

110 The prior common law doctrine of absolute obligation in *Paradine v Jane* (1647) Aleyn 26 giving way to the modern doctrine of frustration set out by Blackburn J in *Taylor v Caldwell* (1863) 3 B & S 826. For a modern discussion of the evolution of the common law, see *National Carriers Ltd v Panalpina (Northern) Ltd* [1981] AC 675.

111 *Rainbow Warrior Arbitration (New Zealand v France)* (1987) 82 ILR 499; the *Danube Dam* case (1998) 37 ILM 162.

112 For comment on this case concerning treaty obligations in the context of environmental concerns, see P Okowa (1998) 47 ICLQ 688; D Reichert-Facilides (1998) 47 ICLQ 837.

113 J Brierly (1925) 11 Grotius Society, p 11; S Schwebel (1959) 8 ICLQ 320.

Sometimes, this doctrine is referred to as the principle of *rebus sic stantibus*. A number of points should be made. First, this doctrine has some overlap with the doctrine of impossibility of performance set out in Art 61 of the Vienna Convention on the Law of Treaties (1969). Secondly, the doctrine is a recognition that treaties may be intended to endure for many years, but international society is never static and circumstances can change in a manner which the parties could not have foreseen. Thirdly, such a doctrine is recognised in municipal systems in common law countries where the doctrine of frustration embraces both destruction of subject matter and fundamental change of circumstances. Fourthly, some writers have urged caution under his head fearful that such a doctrine might be employed as a vehicle by states anxious to avoid international obligations.[114]

The precise text of Art 62 of the Vienna Convention is as follows:

(1) A fundamental change of circumstances which has occurred with regard to those existing at the time of the conclusion of a treaty, and which was not foreseen by the parties, may not be invoked as a ground for terminating or withdrawing from the treaty unless:

   (a) the existence of those circumstances constituted an essential basis of the consent of the parties to be bound by the treaty; and

   (b) the effect of the change is radically to transform the extent of obligations still to be performed under the treaty.

(2) A fundamental change of circumstances may not be invoked as a ground for terminating or withdrawing from a treaty:

   (a) if the treaty establishes a boundary; or

   (b) if the fundamental change is the result of a breach by the party invoking it either of an obligation under the treaty or of any other international obligation owed to any other party to the treaty.

(3) If, under the foregoing paragraphs, a party may invoke a fundamental change of circumstances as a ground for terminating or withdrawing from a treaty it may also invoke the change as a ground for suspending the operation of the treaty.

It should be noted that the article is drafted in such a manner as to make a claim difficult to sustain. The object was to recognise the existence of the doctrine but to establish demanding criteria and a clear *onus probandi* on those who seek to assert. It is generally accepted that the article states the position in customary international law[115] and this approach was followed in the *Fisheries Jurisdiction* case,[116] where the court observed that the doctrine could only be invoked where subsequent changes have rendered the performance 'something essentially different from that originally undertaken'.[117] It is clear that the change of circumstances must operate as regards the future so that the facts must have changed so fundamentally that the parties cannot be taken to have consented to performance in such changed circumstances. This provision was raised by Hungary in the *Danube Dam* case.[118] Not surprisingly, it was rejected by International Court of Justice

---

114 See J Garner, 'The doctrine of *rebus sic stantibus* and the termination of treaties'(1927) 21 AJIL 409.

115 For discussion see *Free Zones of Upper Saxony and the District of Gex* case (1932) PCIJ, Ser A/B, No 46.

116 *Fisheries Jurisdiction* case (1973) ICJ 3.

117 See (1974) ICJ 3, para 43.

118 *Case concerning the Gabcikovo-Nagymaros Project* (*Danube Dam* case) (1997) ICJ 7; (1998) 37 ILM 162.

on the basis that changes in environmental knowledge since 1977[119] would not necessarily affect the parties obligations and in any event to an extent had been forseen by the treaty. The Court proceeded to observe that the stability and integrity of treaty law required that Art 62 could only be invoked in exceptional cases.

(e) Other grounds for questioning a treaty obligation

Until relatively recently it had been thought that a state could only justify breach of a treaty obligation by reference to the three specific grounds set out in the Vienna Convention (1969), namely, material breach (Art 60), supervening impossibility (Art 61) and fundamental change of circumstances (Art 62). However, in the *Rainbow Warrior Arbitration*,[120] France successfully argued that a state could avail itself of the 'circumstances precluding wrongfulness' set out in the International Law Commission draft on *State Responsibility*, In the subsequent *Danube Dam* case,[121] it was accepted by the ICJ that Hungary could raise a defence based on the ILC Draft Articles on State Responsibility even though the particular defence of 'necessity' could not be sustained on the facts of the case. The ICJ went on to examine the interrelationship of these two pleas. It ruled that the validity of a suspension or termination of a treaty had to be examined by reference to the requirements of the Vienna Convention; such a plea was a plea that there had been no treaty violation. In contrast, the consequences of an illegal termination, in particular, whether it gave rise to responsibility on the part of the state had to be examined with reference to the law of state responsibility. Thus, in this second situation the plea accepted that there had been a treaty violation but precluded 'wrongfulness' if one of the 'defences' under the law of state responsibility applied.

(f) Consequences of termination or suspension

In respect of termination, Art 70 provides that unless the treaty otherwise provides termination releases a party from future obligations to further perform the treaty but it does not operate retrospectively so it does not affect obligations that have arisen prior to the date of termination. In respect of suspension, Art 72 provides that unless the treaty otherwise provides the effect of suspension is to release the parties from the duty to perform obligations for the period of the suspension. When a state party wishes to withdraw from a treaty it will normally do so by notice of termination or by act of denunciation. The expression 'denunciation' indicates the notification by a state to another state that it intends to withdraw from a treaty. Because of the practical difficulties that can arise in the context of multilateral treaties, it is usual to stipulate a time period before an act of denunciation can take effect.

---

119 The case of Hungary was cumulative in that it preyed in aid: (i) political changes since 1977; (ii) problems of economic viability; (iii) progress in environmental knowledge; (iv) new norms of environmental law.

120 *Rainbow Warrior Arbitration (New Zealand v France)* (1987) 26 ILM 1346; 82 ILR 499.

121 *Gabcikovo (Hungary v Slovakia)* (1997) ICJ 7; (1998) 37 ILM 162.

12 THE RESOLUTION OF DISPUTES

The Vienna Convention on the Law of Treaties (1969) places considerable emphasis on the peaceful resolution of disputes. Article 65(3) provides for the peaceful settlement of disputes under the terms of Art 33 of the United Nations Charter (1945). In addition, Art 66 of the Vienna Convention provides that if any dispute arises under Art 53 or 64 then any one of the parties may submit the matter to the International Court of Justice, unless the matter is, by common consent, referred to arbitration. If the dispute concerns other matters arising under the Vienna Convention (1969), then Art 66(b) provides that any one of the parties may request the Secretary General of the United Nations to put in place the conciliation arrangements set out in the Annex to the Convention. It is now standard practice to insert a disputes clause into a multilateral convention providing a number of methods for the peaceful settlement of a dispute. As the United Nations Law of the Sea Convention (1982) indicates, the nature of the dispute will determine which method is appropriate; proceedings that require detailed examination of evidence are different to those where a question of treaty interpretation is in issue.

13 REGISTRATION OF TREATIES[122]

Article 80 of the Vienna Convention provides that treaties shall after entry into force be transmitted to the Secretariat of the United Nations for registration or filing and recording, as the case may be, and for publication. Under the terms of Art 102, only treaties that have been registered may be relied upon before the International Court of Justice.[123] However, an unregistered treaty will be binding between the parties *inter se*.[124] As indicated above, the provisions of Art 102 replaced those of Art 18 of the Covenant of the League of Nations (1919). The object was to ensure publicity and to minimise international tension caused by the practice of secret treaties: in 1919 it had been felt that secret treaties had played a role in clouding the diplomatic environment in the years immediately preceding the First World War.[125] In any event, the treaties registered are published in the United Nations Treaty Series. It is to be noted that the terms of Art 102 refer to 'every treaty and every international agreement'; such a formulation is wide enough to include unilateral statements and declarations made on membership of the United Nations or in respect of the Optional Clause. However, registration under Art 102 does not confer on an instrument the status of a treaty if it does not already possess it.

Sometimes, a treaty may required to be registered under more than one regime. Article 83 of the Chicago Convention on International Civil Aviation (1944) requires the registering of 'arrangements' with the ICAO Council.

---

122 M Brandon, 'The validity of non-registered treaties' (1952) 29 BYIL 186; R Lillich, 'The obligation to register treaties and international agreements with the United Nations' (1971) 65 AJIL 771; M Tabory, 'Recent developments in United Nations treaty registration and publication practices' (1982) 76 AJIL 350; D Hutchinson, 'The significance of the registration or non-registration of an international agreement in determining whether or not it is a treaty' (1993) 46 CLP 257.

123 By 1998, nearly 40,000 had been registered. About 1,200 are registered each year. See A Aust, *Modern Treaty Law and Practice*, 2000, Chapter 19.

124 *Maritime and Territorial Questions (Qatar v Bahrain)* case (1994) ICJ 112, p 122.

125 For the diplomatic background, see P Kennedy, *The Rise of Anglo-German Antagonism 1860–1914*, 1980 and J Charney, *Splendid Isolation: Britain and the Balance of Power (1874–1914)*, 1984.

The United Kingdom is a party to over 12,400 treaties; since 1892 every treaty that has entered into force for the United Kingdom has been published in the United Kingdom Treaty Series. As explained elsewhere, publication in the United Kingdom Treaty Series is of no constitutional effect.[126]

14 VIENNA CONVENTION ON THE SUCCESSION OF STATES IN RESPECT OF TREATIES (1978)[127]

The question of the succession of states is considered in detail in Chapter 18. However, a number of points can usefully be made in respect of the law of treaties. State succession takes place where one state replaces another as an international legal person and becomes responsible for a particular area of territory. State succession can occur when a colonial power gives way to an independent state or when a federal structure dissolves into a number of constituent parts each asserting their independent statehood as was the case in the Soviet Union and the former Socialist Federal Republic of Yugoslavia. In these circumstances, the question arises as to whether the new state will be a party to the treaty obligations of its predecessor. In respect of the cases of Yugoslavia and the Soviet Union, a number of points can be made. First, both situations indicate that the international community tends to approach such problems on a case by case basis rather than in accordance with any general rule. Secondly, pressure will normally be brought on the newly independent state to honour the main treaty obligations of its predecessor state.[128] Thirdly, recent events in these two cases indicate that recognition by the international community will be contingent on the new state agreeing to honour treaty obligations. Fourthly, in the case of the Soviet Union where treaty obligations related to nuclear weapons of mass destruction experience indicates that the matter is best resolved by individual negotiation particularly when the newly independent state is seeking financial support from the wider international community. In essence, a general rule that a newly independent state should start from scratch with a clean slate may be attractive in positivist theory but will not be acceptable to the wider international community.

This approach is to be contrasted with the provisions of the Vienna Convention on the Succession of States in Respect of Treaties (1978);[129] this Convention, which was drawn up before the recent events in Eastern Europe, is now in force having received the requisite 15 ratifications.[130] However, some states have questioned the relevance of the Convention and much of the preliminary work was done during the period of decolonisation which was itself at an end by 1978. Under the terms of Art 7, the Convention does not apply to any succession of states that occurs prior to the date of its entry into force. The Convention is an example of the progressive development of international law rather than an exercise in codification; it is not therefore a statement of the rules of customary law on treaty succession.

---

126 For the constitutional position in the United Kingdom, see Chapter 4.

127 For further consideration of the topic, see Chapter 18 on state succession.

128 A state that indicates its willingness to honour existing obligations is more likely to be favourably treated if and when it seeks economic help from an international organisation.

129 The Convention had acquired eight ratifications by 1990 and had only obtained 15 by 1996.

130 Under the terms of Art 49, the Vienna Convention on the Succession of States in Respect of Treaties (1978) came into effect in 1996 (VCSST 1978).

The Convention is concerned with the question as to whether the new state will be bound by the treaty obligations of its predecessor. In broad terms, the Convention provides in Art 16 (VCSST) that the newly independent state is not so bound and starts with a blank sheet or clean slate; these provisions contrast with those in Art 15 which govern the situation when territory is transferred from one state to another. In such circumstances, the treaty obligations of the predecessor state cease when the territory passes to the successor.[131] While the provisions of Art 15 are understandable, the text of Art 16 would seem to be a source of difficulty; the wording reads:

> A newly independent State is not bound to maintain in force, or to become a party to, any treaty by reason only of the fact that at the date of the succession of States the treaty was in force in respect of the territory to which the succession of States relates.

Such a broad principle is not workable in the modern world and the Convention itself provides that it does not apply in respect of boundary regimes[132] or other territorial regimes in respect of territory.[133] It is clear that such a broad principle as in Art 16 has to be modified in those very difficult cases where a federal state disintegrates and succession to treaty rights has to be part of a wider equitable settlement.[134]

The practical reality in the modern world is that it is unlikely that an newly independent state will come into existence without a need for financial and other support from the wider international community; in these circumstances, as events in the former Soviet Union and Yugoslavia have demonstrated, the *quid pro quo* for such support will normally be a readiness to accept some treaty obligations of the predecessor state at least in the areas of human rights and arms limitation.

15 VIENNA CONVENTION ON THE LAW OF TREATIES BETWEEN INTERNATIONAL ORGANISATIONS OR BETWEEN STATES AND INTERNATIONAL ORGANISATIONS (1986)[135]

This treaty is designed to regulate relations between international organisations and between international organisations and states. The original determination of the International Law Commission had been to try and deal with these matters in the Convention of 1969, but they came to the conclusion that treaties drafted by international organisations had a number of special characteristics and the need to avoid delay and undue complexity indicated that the 1969 Convention should be limited in scope.[136] In these circumstances, the 1969 Vienna Convention applied simply to treaties between states and its effect has been either to codify rules of customary international law or to

---

131 Article 15 would apply to situations such as Alsace Lorraine which was subject to French rule until 1871 and German rule from 1871–1919 and French rule again after 1919.

132 Article 11.

133 Article 12.

134 See *Arbitration Commission of EC Conference on Yugoslavia Opinion No 1*, 29 November 1991; (1991) 92 ILR 162.

135 See G Gaja, 'A "new" Vienna Convention on Treaties between States and International Organisations or between International Organisations: a critical commentary' (1987) 58 BYIL 253; PK Menon, *The Law of Treaties between States and International Organisations*, 1992.

136 See (1966) YBILC (II), p 187.

permit the orderly development of such rules. The International Law Commission prepared draft articles in respect of international organisations in 1982 and these were adopted in 1986.

The Vienna Convention on the Law of Treaties between States and International Organisations (1986) has much in common with the 1969 Vienna Convention in terms of both structure and provisions; this tends to fortify the view that the 1969 provisions mirror the rules of customary international law. The Convention will come into force when 35 ratifications have been obtained. Article 73 of the 1986 Convention provides for possible problems of overlap by indicating that 'as between states parties parties to the Vienna Convention on the Law of Treaties of 1969, the relations of those states under a treaty between two or more states and one or more international organisation shall be governed by that Convention'. This provides that in these cases the 1969 Convention will prevail.

One of the more difficult problems was that of the liability of states for treaties concluded by international organisations where those states were not themselves parties to the treaty. An example arises in respect of the external treaty making power of the European Community. After some hesitation, it was decided that the Convention would not apply and Art 74(3) expressly excludes such difficulties. In such cases, the liability of the state would depend on the internal constitution of the international organisation. Another area of modification was in respect of the resolution of disputes; as an international organisation cannot be a party to contentious proceedings before the International Court of Justice a modification was introduced in respect of the seeking of an advisory opinion in the event of dispute.[137]

---

137 See Art 96, United Nations Charter; Art 66(2), Vienna Convention (1986).

CHAPTER 12

THE LAW OF STATE RESPONSIBILITY[1]

1 INTRODUCTION

In any legal system the violation of a legally binding obligation will normally entail a measure of responsibility. The topic of state responsibility is concerned with the circumstances in which a state may be adjudged to have violated an international obligation and the consequences that may result therefrom. Sometimes, the subject is alluded to as that of 'state liability'; this is acceptable because the subject is concerned with liability for wrongful acts. The broad philosophy that influences the subject was set out by Judge Huber in the *Spanish Zone of Morocco* case where he stated:[2]

> ... responsibility is the necessary corollary of a right. All rights of an international character involve international responsibility. Responsibility results in the duty to make reparation if the obligation in question is not met.[3]

The principles of the law of state responsibility were developed in customary international law and involve both procedural and substantive aspects. The subject is concerned with questions such as: (i) in what circumstances may state A make a claim against state B?; (ii) for what acts will state B be liable?; (iii) upon what principles should liability be assessed?

The topic of state responsibility has been under consideration by the International Law Commission for a considerable period of time. In the period 1956–61, the Special Rapporteur[4] produced a number of reports on the limited question of state responsibility for damage to the property or persons of aliens but this was not proceeded with as the International Law Commission decided to examine the matter against a broader canvas.

In 1975, the Commission decided on a three part structure. Part I would concern the fundamentals of state responsibility. Part II would comprise the content and degrees of state responsibility while Part III would be devoted to questions of implementation and the settlement of disputes. In the period 1969 until 1980, the Special Rapporteur had produced eight reports and the International Law Commission had provisionally approved 35 draft articles. After 1980, work commenced on Part II and later on Part III; by 1996 60 draft articles had been produced. In 1996, the International Law Commission

---

1   RY Jennings and AD Watts, *Oppenheim's International Law* 9th edn, 1992, p 499; FV Garcia-Amador, 'State responsibility. Some new problems' (1958) 94 HR 365; H Accioly, *'Principes generaux de la responsibilité internationale d'après la doctrine et la jurisprudence'* (1959) 96 HR 349; M Sorensen, *'Principes de droit international public'* (1960) 101 HR 1, pp 217–33; P Reuter, *'Principes de droit international public'* (1961) 103 HR 425, pp 583–619; E Jimenez de Arechaga, 'International law in the past third of a century' (1978) 159 HR 1, pp 267–313.

2   *Spanish Zone of Morocco Claims* (1923) 2 RIAA 615; 2 ILR 157.

3   *Ibid.*

4   On 7 December 1953, the General Assembly had adopted Resolution 799 (VIII) requesting the International Law Commission to take up the matter. Mr FV Garcia-Amador served as Special Rapporteur from 1956 until 1961. Professor Roberto Ago served as Special Rapporteur from 1963; although elected a member of the International Court of Justice in 1979, he completed his work in 1980. In the period 1963 until 1980 he submitted eight reports.

provisionally adopted its Draft Articles[5] but these were to be reconsidered when governments had a opportunity to comment on them. Since that date a considerable number of comments have been made; in August 2000, the International Law Commission gave a second reading to revised draft articles on state responsibility.[6] The general view was that these draft articles would not be the basis for a convention but they might, in the future, be commended by states in the form of a General Assembly Resolution. In any event much of Part I of the Draft Articles restates accepted principles of customary international law.[7]

The law on state responsibility contains a number of principles well established in customary international law. The sources of the law on state responsibility are to be found not only in the customary rules. Many inter-state problems have been resolved by arbitral commissions so there is a considerable volume of past case law on which to draw.[8] Many of the past cases have been determined by Mixed Claims Commissions; in recent years the Iran-United States Claims Tribunal has made a considerable contribution to the jurisprudence in this area.

Since the state cannot itself commit acts of commission or omission, responsibility arises by reason of the acts of individuals; those individuals may be acting as part of a branch of government or in their private capacity.[9] In consequence, many of the actual cases are concerned with the capacity in which an individual happens to be acting. The subject itself is concerned with the nature of acts or omissions that give rise to responsibility and the persons by whom such acts must be committed if the state is to be held responsible. It is proposed to consider first the nature of state responsibility before dealing with attribution, nationality of claims and the requirement to exhaust local remedies. The particular question of expropriation will be considered in the Chapter 19 on international economic law.

---

5   ILC's 1996 Report, GAOR 51st Session, Supp 10, p 125. The Draft comprised 60 Articles in three parts and are concerned with general principles. The draft articles do not deal with the specific question of conduct towards aliens. The 60 Articles divide into Part I (on the nature of state responsibility), Part II (the rights of the 'innocent or injured' state against the 'wrongdoer state'), Part III (the consequences and the resolution of disputes). Many of the draft articles (particularly in Part I) re state or codify existing rules in customary law. Those customary rules are themselves supported by a wide variety of case law in the form of arbitral awards; state responsibility is a subject with a considerable volume of case law not least as regards the duty of the state towards aliens.

6   The revised Draft Articles of August 2000 involve considerable renumbering and are divided into Part One – The Internationally Wrongful Act of a State (Arts 1–27); Part Two – Content of International Responsibility of a State (Arts 28–42) Part Two bis (Arts 43–59).

7   But not Draft Article 19 of the 1996 Articles, see Nicaragua v United States (The Merits) (1986) ICJ 14.

8   One of the most of cited sources on this topic are the reports of the Mexico/United States Claims Commission. This itself being a reflection of the emphasis of the United States from the end of the 19th century to promote arbitration as a method of the peaceful settlement of disputes.

9   In which case, the individual may be personally liable in municipal law but state responsibility will normally not arise; see below for the question of attribution.

2 THE NATURE OF STATE RESPONSIBILITY

The ongoing work of the International Law Commission in the area of state responsibility has built upon earlier efforts in this field.[10] The general principles are set out in the International Law Commission's Draft Articles 1[11] and 2[12] which read as follows:

(1) Every intentionally wrongful act of a State entails the international responsibility of that State.

(2) There is an internationally wrongful act of a State when conduct consisting of an act or omission:

    (a) is attributable to the State under international law; and

    (b) constitutes a breach of an international obligation of the State.

International law does not draw distinctions between tortious and contractual liability as pertain in municipal law. However, a distinction is drawn between international delicts and international crimes. This distinction was indicated in Draft Article 19(2) of the 1996 Draft Articles which read as follows:

(2) An internationally wrongful act which results from the breach by a State of an international obligation so essential for the protection of fundamental interests of the international community that its breach is recognised as a crime by that community as a whole constitutes an international crime.

Draft Article 19(3) then proceeded to indicate acts that might be regarded as international crimes such as aggression, slavery, massive pollution, genocide and the forcible maintenance of colonial domination.[13] However, while it may be helpful to distinguish such acts from ordinary delicts, they are all acts already variously prohibited in customary international law and clearly contrary to the United Nations Charter (1945). In any event, such provisions do not appear in the Draft Articles of 2000 where the matter is addressed in more general terms in Draft Art 12[14] which reads:

There is breach of an international obligation by a State when an act of that State is not in conformity with what is required of it by that obligation, regardless of its origins and character.

Whether an act gives rise to responsibility is a matter to be judged by international law. Thus, Art 3 of the Draft Articles[15] indicates:

---

10 In the 1929 Harvard Draft on the Responsibility of States for Damage Done in their Territory to the Person or Property of Foreigners, and the Hague Conference of 1930 where the topic was discussed under the same title. See also Harvard Draft Convention on the International Responsibility of States for Injuries to Aliens (1961).

11 Article 1 remained the same in both the 1996 and 2000 drafts of the ILC; all subsequent references will be to the second reading of 2000 although the 1996 provision will be noted.

12 Draft Article 2 in the Second Reading of 2000 represents a redraft of Art 3 in the 1996 Draft Articles.

13 It should be noted that Draft Article 19 was not well received in 1996 and in the second reading by the ILC in 2000 Draft Articles 41 and 42 represent an attempt to find a compromise acceptable both to those who supported and those who opposed the concept of international crimes as set out in the draft articles adopted on a first reading.

14 Which draws upon Arts 16, 17 and 18 of the 1996 Draft Articles.

15 Which repeats Art 4 of the 1996 ILC Draft Articles.

> The characterisation of an act of a State as internationally wrongful is governed by international law. Such characterisation is not affected by the characterisation of the same act as lawful by internal law.

Thus any act or omission is to be determined by rules of international law regardless of how the matter may be categorised or classified in a municipal system. Thus Draft Article 2 of the ILC Draft[16] refers to 'conduct consisting of an action or omission'[17] which is 'attributable to the State under international law' and 'constitutes a breach of an international obligation of the State'. Further the obligation must exist at a particular point in time so that Draft Art 13 of the ILC Draft stipulates that: 'An act of state shall not be considered a breach of an international obligation unless the state is bound by the obligation in question at the time the act occurs.'

A difficulty that arises is as to whether the law of state responsibility overlaps with any other area of international law although the modern tendency is to view it as a distinct topic.[18] The entire matter was canvassed in the *Rainbow Warrior Arbitration* case.[19] The facts in the case were as follows.

In 1985 two French agents participated in the attack and destruction of the *Rainbow Warrior* vessel which was moored at harbour in New Zealand. New Zealand protested and the Secretary General gave a ruling[20] as mediator which was followed by an agreement between the two states. In brief the agreement provided for the imprisonment of the two agents at a French base in the Pacific for a period of three years.[21] However, both agents were allowed to return to France before the expiration of the three year period. New Zealand invoked the arbitration clause under the Agreement and argued that there had been a breach of treaty. France asserted that the law of treaties was not relevant and under the law of state responsibility it had a defence under either force majeure or distress.[22] In giving their ruling and holding that France had established a *prima facie* defence the tribunal was prepared to accept that a State might not be liable if it could show that it had a defence under the general law of state responsibility.[23]

The holding of the arbitrators was to the effect that as international law did not differentiate between contractual and tortious obligations it followed that any breach *prima facie* gives rise to a question of state responsibility and that in principle a state could raise a defence under the law of state responsibility that was not available under the Vienna Convention on the Law of Treaties. That the origin of an international obligation is irrelevant for purposes of state responsibility is confirmed by Draft Article 12 of the ILC Articles.[24]

---

16 Which repeats Art 3 of the 1996 ILC Draft Articles.

17 See *James Claim (United States v Mexico)* (1926) 4 RIAA 82; *Corfu Channel (The Merits)* (1949) ICJ 4.

18 See *EC Arbitration Commission on Yugoslavia* Opinion No 13 (1993) 96 ILR 726.

19 (1990) 82 ILR 499.

20 For the ruling of the Secretary General, see (1987) 81 AJIL 325; 74 ILR 256.

21 For the agreement between France and New Zealand of July 1986, see (1987) 74 ILR 274.

22 Articles 24 and 25 of the ILC Draft Articles (2000) repeating Draft Articles 31 and 32 of the 1996 Draft.

23 For consideration of the same point see *Gabcikovo-Nagymaros Project (Hungary v Slovakia)* (1996) ICJ 7.

24 Repeating the substance of Draft Article 17 of the 1996 Draft.

On the assumption that state may be liable for acts of omission the question arises as to whether this liability should be described as absolute,[25] strict or dependent on the production of evidence of intention or negligence. Before outlining the theories it is important to note that the cases themselves depend on the acts of individuals and much will depend on the inferences that the tribunal chooses to draw from the facts. With that covenant in mind, the first school of thought holds that liability is absolute or strict. Thus if an act is committed by an agent of the state and causes damage then liability arises independent of any question of negligence or intention. This approach is sometimes referred to by writers as the 'objective' approach.[26] This school of thought is to be contrasted with the subjective approach which holds that there must be evidence of fault be it intention (*dolus*) or negligence (*culpa*) before a state can be liable.

The precedents can be preyed in aid to support both schools of thought and it is probably the case that one cannot find a single principle that reconciles harmoniously all the authorities. An example of the objective approach is said to arise in the *Neer Claim*[27] where the facts were as follows.

An American citizen was shot dead by a group of men while working in Mexico. The efforts of the local police were dilatory and were subject of criticism by the Governor and the Attorney General. The United States brought a claim on behalf of the widow and daughter based on the failure to pursue the matter. The claim was rejected by the General Commission who appeared to apply the objective formula.[28]

Although the case is open to a number of interpretations, support for the objective formula may be found in the *James* claim,[29] where the facts were not dissimilar. A more open endorsement of the objective approach is to be found in the Caire claim,[30] where the facts were as follows.

A French citizen was killed in Mexico by Mexican soldiers who had demanded money from him. A claim was brought on behalf of his dependants by France.

The Commission determined that Mexico was liable under the accepted principles which were to be interpreted 'in accordance with the doctrine of the objective responsibility of the state, that is, the responsibility for the acts of the officials or organs of a state, which may devolve upon it even in the absence of any "fault" of its own'. Whether the case is actually is an authority for the objective approach is a matter that will be explored below.[31]

---

25 It is probably sensible to differentiate 'absolute' liability, where the state is liable on the basis of injury caused by conduct, from 'strict' liability, where the state is liable subject to a limited number of defences. As both turn on the fact of injury caused by conduct, it is usual to refer to them both as forms of 'objective' responsibility.

26 See *Neer Claim (United States v Mexico)* (1926) 4 RIAA 60; 3 ILR 213; *Caire Claim (France v Mexico)* (1929) 5 RIAA 516; 5 ILR 146. See also *The Jessie* (1921) 6 RIAA 57; *The Wanderer* (1921) 6 RIAA 68.

27 *Neer Claim (United States v Mexico)* (1926) 4 RIAA 60; 3 ILR 213.

28 Some parts of the ruling are ambiguous; reference is also made to an international minimum standard, on which see below.

29 *James Claim* (1926) 4 RIAA 82.

30 *Caire Claim* (1929) 5 RIAA 516; 5 ILR 146.

31 See under the question of imputability; it is arguable that the *Caire* case was concerned with questions of attribution rather than abstract theories as to state responsibility.

Those who favour the subjective approach and insist upon evidence of negligence point to the *Home Missionary Society Claim*,[32] where the facts were as follows.

The British administration of the protectorate of Sierra Leone imposed a tax on the native population. This lead to rioting, during which missionaries were killed and Society property destroyed. The United States brought a claim against Great Britain.

In rejecting the claim, the tribunal appeared to favour the subjective approach, noting that: 'It is a well established principle of international law that no Government can be held responsible for the act of rebellious bodies of men committed in violation of its authority, where it is itself guilty of no breach of good faith, or of no negligence in suppressing insurrection.' There are a number of statements indicating the need for knowledge and fault in the *Corfu Channel* case,[33] where some of the judges held that a state could not be liable for mines within its territorial waters unless knowledge and fault could be demonstrated. There are similar statement in the *Lighthouses Arbitration* case.[34]

However, these statements concerning the objective and subjective principle must be regarded with a considerable degree of caution. In the *Home Missionary* case,[35] the result can be explained by the fact that the damage was caused not by state organs or agents but by an insurrection which the state put down as efficiently as possible. In the *Corfu Channel* case,[36] the central issue was whether Albania had known about or had participated in the laying of mines; this was a question of evidence which was itself linked to the *onus probandi*.

Where a claim is made on the international plane, then the issues are normally quite complex and cannot be resolved by the simple application of labels such as 'objective' or 'subjective' responsibility. Let us consider an example. Suppose X, a citizen of state A, visits state B, where he is murdered by private individuals. State B then makes no proper effort to bring the wrongdoers before the courts. In such a case, it is possible that state A might bring a claim on behalf of his dependants. However, the issues in the case can be divided into: (a) who caused the death of X?; and (b) to what extent is state B liable in international law?

In respect of the first question, clearly the private individuals caused the death of X and, in principle, they should be brought before the criminal courts of state B. This is not a case such as the *Caire* case,[37] where soldiers caused the death. In respect of the second aspect, the allegation against state B is one of omission: that its officials failed to act properly to bring the wrongdoers to justice. This raises difficult questions as to the minimum standard of law enforcement: whether there was as was said in the *Neer* case[38] to be 'an insufficiency of governmental action as far short of international standards that every reasonable and impartial man would recognise its insufficiency'.

---

32   *Home Missionary Society Claim* (1920) 6 RIAA 42; 1 ILR 173.
33   *Corfu Channel (The Merits)* (1949) ICJ 4; 16 ILR 155.
34   *Lighthouses Arbitration (France v Greece)* (1956) 12 RIAA 217; *In re Rizzo* (1955) 22 ILR 317.
35   *Home Missionary Society Claim* (1920) 6 RIAA 42; 1 ILR 173.
36   *Corfu Channel (The Merits)* (1949) ICJ 4; 16 ILR 155.
37   *Caire Claim* (1929) 5 RIAA 516; 5 ILR 146.
38   *Neer Claim (United States v Mexico)* (1926) 4 RIAA 60; 3 ILR 213.

Since all cases on state responsibility begin with the acts of individuals it is sensible to be cautious about labels and to consider the precise manner in which responsibility is imputed. It is to that question one must now turn.

3 THE QUESTION OF ATTRIBUTION OR IMPUTABILITY

Since unlawful acts or omissions can only be committed by individuals the question arises as to which acts or omissions can be attributed or imputed to the state. Only if such acts can be imputed will the state be responsible in international law.

The modern state operates through its governmental organs; since the time of Montesquieu,[39] it has been usual to distinguish between the acts of: (a) the legislature; (b) the executive; and (c) the judiciary. In the law of state responsibility, armed forces will be regarded as part of the executive, although in most states subject to the direction of civilian politicians. In addition, there may be complications where the state is federal and problems arise as to the activities of component parts. In normal cases, the act complained of will be that of the officials. It is therefore important to distinguish a case such as *Caire*,[40] where there was an act of commission by soldiers, from a case such as the *Home Missionary Society* case,[41] where the allegation was one of omission. In principle, it does. not matter that the official was junior in the hierarchy; the precise status will be irrelevant Thus in the *Massey* claim,[42] the United States was successful in recovering damages where a United States citizen was murdered in Mexico. An individual, Saenz, was arrested but allowed to escape by the assistant gaol keeper. The tribunal rejected an assertion by Mexico that it was not liable because of the lowly status of the official. In any event, the liability of the state was compounded by the subsequent failure of the authorities to re-arrest Saenz. The position was clearly expressed by Commissioner Nielsen where he stated:

> I believe that it is undoubtedly a sound general principle, that whenever misconduct on the part of (persons in the service of the state), whatever may be their particular status or rank under domestic law, results in the failure of a nation to perform its obligations under international law, the nation must bear the responsibility for the wrongful acts of its servants.[43]

The same approach was followed in the *Quintanilla* case,[44] where the United States was held liable for the acts of a deputy sheriff when a Mexican citizen died in custody. Similarly, in the *Maal* case,[45] the Venezuelan Government were held liable for an improper public search conducted by subordinate officials.[46]

---

39   Charles Louis Baron Montesquieu (1689–1755) in *De L'Esprit des Lois*, 1748.

40   *Caire Claim* (1929) 5 RIAA 516; 5 ILR 146.

41   *Home Missionary Society Claim* (1920) 6 RIAA 42; 1 ILR 173.

42   *Massey Claim* (1927) 4 RIAA 155; the claim was brought by the United States on behalf of the widow and two dependant children.

43   *Ibid*.

44   *Quintanilla Claim (Mexico v United States)* (1926) 4 RIAA 101.

45   *Maal Claim (Netherlands v Venezuela)* (1903) 10 RIAA 730.

46   *Ibid*.

While the category of official may be varied so, indeed, can be the acts subject to complaint. Acts that attract claims and liability may range from mine laying[47] and the shooting down of civilian aeroplanes[48] to the destruction of maritime vessels.[49] What is important in each case, is the precise duty breached and the link between the relevant official and the state. In principle, if a clear duty has been breached by a public official then a state will find it difficult to defend a claim. However, there are a number of aspects that require to be considered separately.

(a) Acts of a public official outside his authority (the *ultra vires* problem)

The relevant case law indicates that a state may still be liable if an official acts *ultra vires*. The approach of the case law shows some similarity with concepts of agency and course of duty that arise in the municipal law of torts, company law and constitutional law. In respect of an official, his authority might be actual authority which could be express or implied. Alternatively, in respect of third parties, the authority might be extended further and the act might be described as being within his apparent or ostensible authority. Thus, it is possible to imagine an act of an official beyond his actual authority, express or implied, which might be described as *ultra vires* but is, in fact, regarded as being within his apparent or ostensible authority as perceived by a third party. In such circumstances, states have been held liable for the *ultra vires* acts of officials. Thus, in the *Union Bridge Company* case,[50] where a British official of the Cape Government mistakenly appropriated neutral property during the Boer War, the tribunal found in favour of the United States who brought the action on behalf of one of its citizens. Even though the tribunal found the mistake to have been made in good faith, this did not affect liability.

Such an approach was followed in *Youman's* case,[51] where Mexican militia ordered to protect American citizens instead joined in rioting in which American citizens were killed. Such actions were clearly outside their actual authority, but Mexico was held liable. Likewise, in the *Caire* case,[52] Mexico was held liable when Mexican soldiers demanded money and then murdered a French national. In both *Youman's* case[53] and *Caire's* case,[54] emphasis was laid upon the fact that the soldiers were acting under the order of an officer who was on duty. Traditionally, tribunals tend to regard the state as liable for the actions of the military if the forces are on official duty and acting under the direction of an officer. It is arguable in such cases that the fault imputed to the state is the failure of the officer to exercise proper control over the soldiers under command.

There has been a considerable reliance on the principle of apparent authority in order to hold the state liable; thus, it can be said that the state will be liable for the *ultra vires* acts

---

47 *Corfu Channel (The Merits)* (1949) ICJ 4; 16 ILR 155; *Nicaragua v United States (The Merits)* (1986) ICJ 14; 76 ILR 349.

48 The *Aerial Incident* case (1959) ICJ 127; 27 ILR 557; a recent example being the incident of 1 September 1983 when Soviet jets shot down Korean Airlines Flight 007; see (1983) 22 ILM 1148, pp 1190, 1419; (1984) 23 ILM 864; F Hassan (1984) 33 ICLQ 712; M Leich (1984) 78 AJIL 244.

49 For the *Rainbow Warrior Incident* see (1987) 81 AJIL 325; 74 ILR 241.

50 *Union Bridge Company* case (1924) 6 RIAA 138; 2 ILR 170.

51 *Youman's* case (1926) 4 RIAA 110; 3 ILR 223.

52 *Caire Claim* (1929) 5 RIAA 516; 5 ILR 146.

53 *Youman's* case (1926) 4 RIAA 110; 3 ILR 223.

54 *Caire Claim* (1929) 5 RIAA 516; 5 ILR 146.

of officials if those acts can be said to have been within the apparent authority of the official. Thus, in the *Jessie*[55] and the *Wanderer*,[56] an unauthorised search gave rise to liability, as did a failure to control looting seamen in the *Zafiro Claim*,[57] while in the *Mosse* case,[58] the principle of apparent authority was expressly endorsed. Difficulties can arise with private acts but if a public servant uses his official position to pursue a private vendetta then the state will be liable.[59] However, if an officer has resigned or withdrawn from employment, then the state will not normally be liable.[60]

Article 4 of the ILC Draft Articles[61] provides that the act of a state organ shall be regarded as an act of state provided it was acting in that capacity in the case in question. However, the draft article does not indicate how it is to be determined whether an organ is 'acting in that capacity'. Article 4 is supplemented by Draft Article 5 which attributes to the state the conduct of entities exercising elements of the governmental authority.

The thrust of the past case law is reflected in Art 10 of the ILC Draft which provides:

> ... that the conduct of an organ of state entitled to exercise governmental authority shall be considered an act of State even if it exceeded its competence or contravened instructions concerning its activity.

(b) The acts of private individuals

The general principle is stated in Arts 6 and 7 of the Draft Articles,[62] which read as follows:

> (6) The conduct of a person or group of persons shall be considered an act of the State under international law if the person or group of persons was in fact acting on the instructions of, or under the direction or control of, that State in carrying out the conduct.
>
> (7) The conduct of a person or group of persons shall be considered an act of State under international law if the person or group of persons was in fact exercising elements of the governmental authority in the absence or default of the official authorities and in circumstances such as to call for the exercise of those elements of authority.

In all such cases it will be a question of evidence. Thus, if an Englishman visits Germany and is murdered by a German citizen in a fight, no liability will attach to the German state. The duty of the German government will be to investigate the incident and bring the wrongdoers before an appropriate criminal court.[63] However, cases may not be this simple; an action that appears to start as a private initiative may be adopted by the state.

---

55 *The Jessie* (1921) 6 RIAA 57.
56 *The Wanderer* (1921) 6 RIAA 68.
57 *Zafiro (Great Britain v The United States)* case (1925) 6 RIAA 160.
58 *Mosse* case (1953) 13 RIAA 494; 20 ILR 217.
59 *Mallen Claim* (1927) 4 RIAA 173.
60 *Cibich Claim (United States v Mexico)* (1927) 4 RIAA 57.
61 Articles 4 and 5 of the 2000 Draft draw upon Arts 5 and 7 in the 1996 Draft.
62 Which draw upon Art 8 of the 1996 ILC Draft Articles.
63 *Neer Claim (United States v Mexico)* (1926) 4 RIAA 60; 3 ILR 213.

The classic examination of this is to be found in the circumstances of the *Hostages* case[64] arising out of the turbulent events of the Iranian Revolution (1978–80). In that case it appears to have been accepted that initial attack on the United States Embassy by militants could not be attributed to the state. The fact that certain leaders issued statements of approval would not make such conduct an act of state, but the situation changed when the conduct was subsequently adopted by the government of Ayatollah Khomeini. Manifestly, it is difficult sometimes to know whether an act is an act of state where private individuals may have been incited to act for example by government controlled newspapers.[65] It is clear that a court must proceed cautiously in this area so that, in the *Nicaragua* case,[66] the International Court of Justice, when confronted with the question of the responsibility of the United States for actions by *Contras* forces in Nicaragua, held that there would be no state responsibility in the absence of evidence of actual effective control of military operations, whereas manifestly the United States would be answerable for the actions of its own armed forces and covert operatives.[67]

(c) Acts of mob violence and insurrection

The starting point for discussion under this head is the general principle that normally a state will not be held responsible for damage done by mob violence or by insurrectionaries.[68] Article 10 of the ILC Draft Articles reads:

(1) The conduct of an insurrectional movement, which becomes the new government of a State shall be considered an act of that State under international law.

(2) The conduct of a movement, insurrectional or other, which succeeds in establishing a new State in part of the territory of a pre-existing State or in a territory under its administration shall be considered an act of the new State under international law.

However, to this general principle of non-responsibility a number of caveats require to be entered. Mob violence incited by a state can lead to responsibility and the state will also be liable in circumstances where the state has failed to show due diligence in restoring law and order.[69] What constitutes due diligence will be a question of fact and degree to be weighed against the relevant circumstances.

As indicated above, the state will not normally be responsible for the acts of insurrectionaries. Thus, in the *Sambaggio* case,[70] an Italian national had made a claim for damage done by revolutionaries in Venezuela. In rejecting his claim, Umpire Ralston advanced three justifications. First, that revolutionaries are not the agents of Government. Secondly, their acts are committed to destroying the Government and no one should be

---

64 *US Diplomatic and Consular Staff in Tehran* case (1980) ICJ 3; 61 ILR 550.

65 Eg the attacks on the United States Embassy in Beijing during the Kosovo conflict in 1999 following the deaths of three Chinese citizens in the Chinese Embassy in Belgrade. In the event, the United States apologised for the bombing of the Embassy and agreed to pay compensation.

66 *Nicaragua v United States* (1986) ICJ 14; 76 ILR 349.

67 *Ibid.*

68 *Home Missionary Society Claim* (1920) 4 RIAA 42; *Pinson Claim* (1928) 5 RIAA 327.

69 Judge Huber in *Spanish Zones of Morocco Claims* (1925) 2 ILR 157; 2 RIAA 617; cited with approval in *Asian Agricultural Products Ltd v Sri Lanka* (1991) 30 ILM 577.

70 *Sambaggio (Italy v Venezuela)* case (1903) 10 RIAA 499.

held responsible for the acts of an enemy attempting his life. Thirdly, revolutionaries are in principle beyond government control, and the Government cannot be held responsible for those who have escaped its restraint. However, while non-responsibility will be the normal principle, this will not be the case where the state has shown a lack of due diligence in protecting installations. Thus in *AAPL v Sri Lanka*, Sri Lanka[71] was held responsible for not exercising due diligence to protect an installation from the Tamil Tigers. It is arguable that in the modern world a state should be able to produce evidence that it has used appropriate technology to exercise surveillance in respect of those who have shown a willingness to act violently or unlawfully.

Where an insurrectionary movement succeeded in establishing itself as the government of the state, then the rule was that it would become responsible for its acts prior to its installation in power.[72] This approach is followed in Art 10(1) of the ILC Draft Articles which reads: 'The conduct of an insurrectionist movement which becomes the new government of a state shall be considered an act of that State under international law.'[73]

The position of the liability of the state in respect of acts prior to entry into power has fallen to be considered in a number of cases arising from the confused circumstances of the Iranian Revolution. The issue before the Iran-United States Claims Tribunal was invariably whether a particular individual had been forced to leave Iran because of the action of public officials or because of the general instability arising from the revolutionary situation. In *Rankin v The Islamic Republic of Iran*,[74] the claimant was unable to demonstrate that his departure from Iran was after the assumption of power by the new regime and he was unable to show that his leaving was a result of the action of public officials or the Revolutionary Guard, as distinct from being precipitated by the generally difficult atmosphere that prevailed. In *Short v The Islamic Republic of Iran*,[75] the claimant was actually withdrawn from Iran by his employers prior to the new regime taking power. The Iran-US Claims Tribunal followed the reasoning of the International Court of Justice in the *Hostages* case[76] and held that: 'The acts of supporters of a revolution (as distinct from its agents) cannot be attributed to the government following the success of the revolution just as the acts of supporters of an existing government are not attributable to the government.' The claim was therefore rejected on the basis that the withdrawal was not attributable to the conduct of agents of the revolution. In contrast, in the case of *Yeager v The Islamic Republic of Iran*,[77] compensation was awarded because the individual was expelled by the Revolutionary Guard after the installation of the new regime. While the Guard might not be a constituted public body they were acting with the approval and knowledge of the new regime.

---

71 *Asian Agricultural Products Ltd v Sri Lanka* (1991) 30 ILM 577.

72 *Bolivar Railway* case (*Great Britain v Venezuela*) (1903) 9 RIAA 445.

73 The same principle but with slightly different wording appeared in Draft Article 15(1) of the 1996 Articles.

74 *Rankin v The Islamic Republic of Iran* (1987) 17 Iran-US CTR 135; (1988) 82 ILR 204; 82 AJIL 353.

75 *Short v Islamic Republic of Iran* (1987) 16 Iran-US CTR 76; (1988) 82 ILR 148; 82 AJIL 140.

76 *United States v Iran* (1980) ICJ 3.

77 *Yeager v The Islamic Republic of Iran* (1987) 17 Iran-US CTR 92; (1988) 82 ILR 178; 82 AJIL 353.

4 THE NATIONALITY OF CLAIMS

The subject of state responsibility is founded upon one state having the capacity to make a claim against another state in respect of acts or omissions that are attributable to that other state. In principle, state A will only take up the claims of its own nationals or those of companies registered within its own territory. Each state will have its own internal rules as to the cases in which it will offer full diplomatic and consular protection. Thus, in the United Kingdom the Rules relating to International Claims issued by the Foreign and Commonwealth Office in 1985 indicate in Rule 1 that: 'Her Majesty's Government will not take up the claim unless the claimant is a United Kingdom national and was so at the date of the injury.'[78] It was accepted in customary international law that a state was under a general duty to protect its own nationals and such a state had a discretion whether to take up their claims. Thus the United Kingdom will not normally take up a claim after a person ceases to be a United Kingdom[79] national or where there has been undue delay,[80] but may continue to act on behalf of a personal representative when the claimant has died.[81] Although each state may, in principle, draft its own rules, such rules must be in accordance with the broad principles of international law in order for the claim to be admissible.

When a state takes up the case of an individual, it is asserting its own rights in international law. Partly, this is a legacy of the 19th century view that the individual was not a subject of international law. As the Permanent Court of International Justice expressed the matter in the *Mavrommatis Palestine Concessions* case,[82] 'a state is in reality asserting its own rights, its rights to ensure, in the person of its subjects, respect for the rules of international law'. As was noted elsewhere, the theoretical basis can be traced back to Vattel, in that the injury to the national became an injury to the nation and thus should be espoused internationally by the nation injured.[83] The requirement of continuing citizenship has been criticised by some writers, on the basis that if the wrong done to the individual is also done to the state then it must vest at the time of injury and should not be affected by any subsequent change of citizenship.

In normal circumstances, a state will not take up a claim unless it is satisfied that the individual is a citizen; however, problems can arise in respect of recently acquired citizenship and where an individual is the national of more than one state. The entire area was traversed in the *Nottebohm* case,[84] the salient facts of the dispute being as follows.

Friedrich Nottebohm was born in Hamburg in 1881. Between 1905 and 1943, he lived in Guatemala where he developed business interests. He was in the habit of taking

---

78 The rules having been issued in 1971 and revised in 1983 and 1985. The requirement that a claim is attached to a national is followed by the United States; see (1982) 76 AJIL 836; for the 1985 Rules, see (1988) 37 ICLQ 1006. For a review, see Ian Sinclair, 'Nationality of claims, British practice' (1950) 27 BYIL 125. Under the 1985 Rules, the expression 'United Kingdom National' includes a company incorporated under the law of the United Kingdom or of any territory for which the United Kingdom is internationally responsible.

79 1985 Rules, r 2.

80 1985 Rules, r 9.

81 1985 Rules, r 11.

82 (1924) PCIJ, Ser A, No 2, p 12.

83 Administrative Decision No 5 (*United States v Germany*) (1924) 7 RIAA 119; 2 ILR 349.

84 *Nottebohm* case (*Second Phase*) (1955) ICJ 4; see Jones (1956) 5 ICLQ 230.

holidays in Germany and Liechtenstein (where his brother lived). In October 1939, he obtained Liechtenstein nationality in the course of a short visit. In 1943, he was deported from Guatemala to the United States, where he was interned as an alien until his release in January 1946. In the interim, his business interests in Guatemala had been confiscated. In January 1946, he was refused permission to reenter Guatemala. At a later date, Liechtenstein brought a claim against Guatemala; the latter then asserted that Liechtenstein had no *locus standi* to present a claim.

In agreeing with Guatemala, the International Court of Justice ruled:[85] (i) that a grant of nationality normally carried with it the right to diplomatic protection; (ii) that while each state was entitled to its own citizenship laws, a grant of nationality might, in certain circumstances, not operate on the international plane where there was the absence of a genuine connection between the individual and the state; (iii) that a review of the history in the present case led to the inference that such a connection was little more than tenuous. Since that ruling, the case has been cited as authority for the proposition that there must be a genuine connection between the individual and the claimant state. It may be, however, that such a proposition is too broad; much will depend on the relationship of claimant and respondent:

(i) First, where an individual is stateless then 'no state is empowered to intervene or complain on his behalf either before or after the injury'.[86]

(ii) A second situation is where the individual in question is both a national of the claimant and the respondent state. This difficulty was faced in the *Canevaro* case,[87] where Italy brought a claim on behalf of one Raphael Canevaro; not only did Canevaro hold Peruvian citizenship but he had participated in public life in Peru and had also represented that country abroad. Not surprisingly, the Permanent Court of Arbitration ruled that his dominant and effective nationality was Peruvian and that the Government of Peru had every right to consider him as a Peruvian citizen and to reject his status as an Italian claimant. The test of dominant and effective nationality was followed in the *Merge* claim,[88] where the United States had brought a claim under the 1947 Italian Peace Treaty on behalf of an individual who had both United States and Italian nationality. The tribunal applied the test of dominant and effective nationality to determine whether a claim could be brought. The emphasis on dominant and effective nationality has been applied in dual nationality cases by the Iran-United States Claims Tribunal.[89] While the test of dominant and effective nationality has often been invoked, an alternative test is to be found in Art 4 of the Hague Convention on the Conflict of Nationality Laws (1930) which reads: 'A State may not afford diplomatic protection to one of its nationals against a State whose nationality such a person also possesses.'[90]

---

85 *Nottebohm* case (*Second Phase*) (1955) ICJ 4; see J L Kunz (1960) 54 AJIL 558.

86 *United States of America v Mexico* (1931) 4 RIAA 669.

87 *Canevaro (Italy v Peru)* case (1912) 11 RIAA 397; 6 AJIL 746.

88 The *Merge Claim* (1955) 22 ILR 443.

89 *Esphahanian v Bank Tejerat* (1983) 2 Iran-US CTR 157; 72 ILR 478; *Islamic Republic of Iran v USA*, Case No A / 18 (1984) 5 Iran-US CTR 251; 75 ILR 176.

90 In the United Kingdom such a formulation appears in the 1985 Rules, r 3 to the effect that a claim will not be taken up if the respondent state is the state of his second nationality.

(iii) The third factual situation is where the individual has the nationality of the claimant state but has a long standing and close nexus with the respondent state. In these circumstances, the *Nottebohm* case[91] would indicate that a claim can will only be admissible if there is evidence of a genuine connection between the individual and the claimant state. In such a case the court will look at the precise circumstances in which citizenship of the claimant state was acquired; it will also be important to weigh the nature, duration and character of connections with the respondent state.

(iv) A fourth possibility is where an individual is the national of the claimant state but also the national of a third state. It would seem that, in such a situation, the respondent state is not able to set up the possible nationality of the third state to defeat the standing of the claimant state. Thus, in the *Salem* case[92] the tribunal held that Egypt was not able to set up possible Persian nationality to defeat a claim brought by the United States on behalf of one of its citizens. The tribunal noted 'the rule of international law being that in a case of dual nationality a third power is not entitled to contest the claim of one of the two powers whose nationality is interested in the case by referring to the nationality of the other power'.[93]

Thus, although the *Nottebohm* case attracted a degree of criticism, it was probably correctly decided on its particular facts; in the course of giving judgment, the Court had made it plain that it was not intended to be taken beyond the limited question as whether the nationality of Nottebohm could be relied upon against Guatemala. This narrow *ratio* was endorsed shortly after in the *Flegenheimer Claim*.[94] The facts of this case concerned a claim brought by the United States under the terms of the 1947 Peace Treaty between the Allied Powers and Italy. On the facts, the Tribunal concluded that the applicant was not a United States citizen. However, in the course of the hearing, Italy submitted[95] that a link with a third state might negate a nationality held with the claimant state; the tribunal rejected this submission holding that the *Nottebohm* case was limited to its particular facts and in any event was not intended to introduce a general principle of opposability based on a link with a third state.[96]

Although most claims concern individuals there will be occasions when a state might seek to make a claim on behalf of a company;[97] this raises the question of the separate legal personality of the company and the position of both the company and its

---

91 The *Nottebohm (Second Phase)* case (1955) ICJ 4.

92 The *Salem (Egypt v USA)* case (1932) 2 RIAA 1161; but see also *Mackenzie v Germany* (1926) 7 RIAA 288; 20 AJIL 595.

93 The *Salem (Egypt v USA)* case (1932) 2 RIAA 1161, p 1188.

94 *Flegenheimer Claim* (1958) 25 ILR 91.

95 In the *Flegenheimer Claim* (1958) 25 ILR 91, the Tribunal declared the claim inadmissible on grounds that the individual was not a United States citizen; the individual had links with Germany but lost his nationality under a 1940 enactment. The limited scope of the *Nottebohm* judgment was recognised when the tribunal noted that the ICJ had indicated in that case that 'the Court does not propose to go beyond the limited scope of the question which it has to decide, namely, whether the nationality conferred on Nottebohm can be relied upon as against Guatemala in justification of proceedings instituted before the Court' (1955) ICJ 17 cited in *Flegenheimer's Claim* (1958) 25 ILR 91.

96 Which, as the Tribunal noted in *Flegenheimer* (1958) 25 ILR 91, had been rejected in the *Salem* case (1932) 2 RIAA 1161.

97 WE Beckett (1931) 17 Trans Grot Soc 175; JW Jones (1949) 26 BYIL 225; Harris (1969) 18 ICLQ 275.

shareholders. The matter was considered in some detail by the International Court of Justice in the *Barcelona Traction* case.[98] The salient facts of the case were as follows.

The Barcelona Traction, Light and Power Company was established in 1911 and was concerned with the supply of electricity in Spain; the majority of the shares was held by Belgian nationals. After 1945, the Spanish Government took a number of measures which brought the company to the point of bankruptcy. Canada made a number of representations to the Spanish Government but then withdrew. Belgium brought an action on behalf of the shareholders. Spain objected claiming that as the damage had been done to the company not the shareholders Belgium lacked *locus standi*. The Court agreed in 1964 to add this preliminary objection to the hearing of the merits.

In rejecting the claim of Belgium and finding for Spain, the International Court of Justice[99] advanced a number of reasons. First, that in most cases international law would recognise well established principles of municipal law. Secondly, that it was a well established principle of municipal law that the company was a legal person distinct from its members. This principle had been accepted for many years in a large number of different jurisdictions. Thirdly, it was a well established rule of international law that *prima facie* it was the national state of the company that was entitled to exercise diplomatic protection. Fourthly, different considerations might arise if the acts had been directed not at the company but at the shareholders *per se*. Fifthly, that the normal right of the national state to represent the company might be displaced: (i) if the company had ceased to exist legally by reason of liquidation; or (ii) that the state in question was incapable of acting. Sixthly, that the company continued to exist in Canada[100] and that state had the diplomatic resources to act. Seventhly, the court rejected that Belgian contention that on equitable grounds there should be an independent secondary right of action on behalf of shareholders. Such a right, it was thought, could not accommodate the rapidly changing ownership of shares and might lead to such a proliferation of diplomatic claims as to cause confusion and insecurity in international society. Thus, several states amended their rules on international claims following the *Barcelona Traction* case; thus, the United Kingdom rules provide that a case may be taken upon behalf of a national shareholder where the company has ceased to exist;[101] or where the wrong was directed against the shareholders by reason of their nationality;[102] or where the national state of the company lacked the capacity to make the claim.[103] It is of note that the principle of the separate legal personality of the company as it pertains to claims on the international plane was recently confirmed by Judge Oda in his Separate Opinion in the *Elettronica Sicula SpA (ELSI)* case.[104]

---

98 *Barcelona Traction (Second Phase)* case (1970) ICJ 3; see also *Barcelona Traction (Preliminary Objections)* case (1964) ICJ 6. For comment, see Briggs (1971) 65 AJIL 327; Lillich (1971) 65 AJIL 522.

99 *Barcelona Traction* case (*Second Phase*) (1970) ICJ 3; see HW Briggs (1971) 65 AJIL 327; Lillich (1971) 65 AJIL 522.

100 The company was in receivership, not in liquidation.

101 1985 Rules, r 5.

102 1985 Rules, r 3.

103 1985 Rules, r 6.

104 *Elettronica Sicula SpA (United States v Italy)* case (1989) ICJ 15. This was in fact heard by a Chamber of the International Court of Justice. See Adler (1990) 39 ICLQ 641; M Dixon (1992) 41 ICLQ 119; FA Mann (1992) 86 AJIL 92.

In respect of the national state of the company, this is normally determined by the place of incorporation of the company, but it can also be determined by where real control is held or where the centre of management exists. The rules as to nationality of claims are reflected in ILC Draft Article 45,[105] which provides that:

> The responsibility of a State may not be invoked if:
>
> (a) The claim is not brought in accordance with any applicable rule relating to the nationality of claims...

In some cases, a tribunal may itself be operating under a treaty that expressly deals with *locus standi*. Thus, in the United States-Iran Claims Settlement Declaration (1981),[106] the agreement provided that a state wishing to bring a claim on behalf of a company would have to show that it was incorporated in the state and that 50% or more of its ownership was held by nationals of that state.

5 THE EXHAUSTION OF LOCAL REMEDIES

There is a well recognised rule of customary international law that holds that before a state may bring a claim on the international plane on behalf of one of its citizens then that individual must be shown to have exhausted all internal remedies in the respondent state. Thus, if state A wishes to bring a claim against state B on behalf of its citizen X then it must first satisfy itself that X has exhausted all remedies made available by the legal system of state B. A number of reasons for this rule are advanced. First, as a matter of courtesy and comity it enables state B to correct any injustice before being subject to an international claim. Secondly, as the matter arose within the sovereign territory of state B then that state enjoys sovereignty and has jurisdiction to correct the wrong. Thirdly, the rule itself has a practical value in preventing international relations being disrupted by a proliferation of trivial claims. Fourthly, it does mean that, by the time an international claim has been presented, the facts have normally been clearly established. Fifthly, such a rule is not unique to international law; in many aspects of constitutional law a citizen has to exhaust his internal remedies before seeking to raise a matter before the superior courts. Sixthly, the individual or company has impliedly agreed to accept the legal system of the country when they visit that state or choose to transact business there. Seventhly, in many cases where the facts are in dispute, the witnesses will be in the respondent state and are easily able to give evidence before the local courts. The rule itself is of long standing and is reflected in Draft Article 45[107] of the International Law Commission's Draft Articles on State Responsibility which provides that the responsibility of a state may not be invoked if: '... (b) The claim is one to which the rule of exhaustion of local remedies applies, and any available and effective remedy has not been exhausted.'

Questions will arise as to the meaning of the expression 'failure to exhaust local remedies'; this has been taken to mean that the remedy must by available and effective. Thus, a claim may be dismissed if the other party can point to steps not taken which

---

105 See Draft Article 22 in the 1996 ILC Draft.
106 Providing for the establishment of the Iran-US Claims Tribunal.
107 See, also, Draft Article 22 in the 1996 ILC Draft.

would have been available and effective in respect of the claim. The matter was considered in the *Finnish Shipowners Arbitration*,[108] where the facts were as follows.

Finnish shipowners brought a claim against the United Kingdom Government in respect of the use of 13 of their ships in the First World War. After negotiations failed, the matter was determined by the Admiralty Transport Arbitration Board who, after hearing the relevant evidence, found as a fact that the ships had been requisitioned by Russia not the United Kingdom; they therefore rejected the claim for compensation. There was a possible appeal to the Court of Appeal, but that was limited to questions of law. An appeal based on such findings of fact would have been doomed to failure.[109] The shipowners chose not to appeal but took the matter to arbitration. The United Kingdom raised the question of non-exhaustion of internal remedies. The Arbitrator rejected the assertion that failure to appeal by itself represented a non-exhaustion of internal remedies because the available appeal was so limited in scope as not to be an effective remedy.

The operation of the rule was illustrated by the *Ambatielos* arbitration[110] where the facts were as follows.

In 1919, Ambatielos, a Greek national, entered into a contract to purchase certain ships from the United Kingdom. The relevant British negotiator was a Major Laing. In 1922 Ambatielos began proceedings in the Probate Divorce and Admiralty Division of the High Court before Mr Justice Hill, but failed to call vital evidence including that of Major Laing. He appealed to the Court of Appeal but abandoned his appeal when that Court refused leave to call evidence that could have been called before the trial court.[111] At a later date, Greece took up his case and was met by claim of non-exhaustion of remedies. The tribunal accepted this contention holding either that there had been a failure to appeal to the Court of Appeal and House of Lords and, even if such appeals would have been futile, they were rendered futile by the claimant's conduct before the court of first instance in failing to call available and admissible evidence.[112]

The result in this case was probably dictated by the fact that Ambatielos had broken a rule common to many municipal law systems that relevant evidence, if available, must be called before the trial court.

While there is an obligation to exhaust available and effective internal remedies, this will not be the case if there is evidence of constitutional impropriety that indicates there is no justice to exhaust.[113] Similarly, there will be no obligation to proceed to the local courts if it would be 'obviously futile'[114] and there will be no obligation to appeal against a

---

108 *Finnish Ships Arbitration (Finland v United Kingdom)* (1934) 3 RIAA 1479.

109 Having regard to the fact that any error was within the jurisdiction of the tribunal, an appeal would have had little prospect of success while English law followed the principles in *R v Nat Bell Liquors* [1922] AC 128; the position would not change until *Anisminic Ltd v Foreign Compensation Commission* [1969] 2 AC 147.

110 The *Ambatielos Arbitration* case (1956) 12 RIAA 83; 23 ILR 306.

111 This is, of course, the normal common law rule that evidence is not normally admissible on appeal if that evidence was available and could have been called before the trial court and there is no good reason for the failure to call the evidence.

112 The tribunal being influenced by the fact that the claimant had advanced no convincing reason for his failure to call evidence at the appropriate time.

113 The case of *Robert E Brown (United States v Great Britain)* (1923) 6 RIAA 120.

114 *Norwegian Loans* case (1957) ICJ 9 (see Judge Read).

decision at first instance if it is inevitable that it would be 'a repetition of a decision already given',[115] unless that repetition was brought about by a failure to follow reasonable rules of civil procedure in municipal law.[116]

The fact that local remedies may be slow is not a defence to the charge of failing to exhaust them. This would appear to be the inference that is to be drawn from the *Interhandel* case;[117] the facts of the case were as follows.

In 1942, the United States Government acting under the Trading with the Enemy Act 1942 seized the assets of a company, the General Aniline and Film Co (GAF) which had been incorporated in the United States. The majority of the shares in the company were owned by a Swiss company, Interhandel. At that time, the United States Government considered Interhandel to be under the direction and control of IG Farben, a German company.[118] The Swiss Government took the view that Interhandel had severed all connection with IG Farben in 1940 and that, at the operative date, GAF was controlled by an independent Swiss company. In 1946, the Washington Accord was signed between the Allied Powers and Switzerland. This provided for the unblocking of Swiss assets. However, the United States continued to regard GAF as subject to German ownership and did not lift the order of seizure. In the years 1948 until 1957, the Swiss Government and Interhandel brought proceedings in the courts of the United States. In 1957, the Swiss Government brought proceedings before the International Court of Justice under the Optional Clause. However, after the application had been launched the Supreme Court of the United States ruled that Interhandel could continue legal proceedings. The United States thus argued that there had been a failure to exhaust internal remedies.

The International Court of Justice accepted the argument of the United States and rejected the Swiss case. Switzerland argued that the obligation to exhaust local remedies did not apply to the conduct of central government or in respect of treaty obligations. The Court rejected this limitation, holding: (i) that the local remedies rule applied to the conduct of central government where there was an independent judiciary; (ii) that Interhandel had *locus standi* to continue with legal proceedings in the United States and therefore it could not be said that local remedies had been exhausted. The Court was therefore acknowledging that where the wrong is alleged to have been committed by the executive or legislative branch if there is an independent judiciary operating a system of judicial review of administrative acts then such an avenue must be exhausted before bringing a claim on the international plane.

There may be a limited number of cases where local remedies may not need to be exhausted. Examples would be: (i) where the municipal court is compelled by law to reject the claim or where the jurisdiction of the municipal court has been ousted by legislation; (ii) where the municipal courts are corrupt; (iii) where the municipal courts discriminate against foreign claims or are subservient to the executive branch; (iv) where

---

115 *Panevezys-Saldutiskis Railway* case (1939) PCIJ, Ser A/B, No 76, p 18.

116 *Ambatielos Arbitration* case (1956) 12 RIAA 83; (1956) 23 ILR 306.

117 *Interhandel (Switzerland v United States)* case (1959) ICJ 6; 27 ILR 475.

118 Not just any German company, IG Farben had been the object of suspicion in the First World War in respect of the use of poison gas on the Western Front; it would be reconstituted in1925, bringing together BASF, Hoechst and Bayer. By 1941, the company was under suspicion in respect of the employment of Jewish concentration camp prisoners. Several IG Farben executives would stand trial for war crimes in one of the United States trials of leading industrialists at Nuremberg in 1948. In 1951, the company was broken up into several parts.

an appeal from a lower court would be manifestly futile because of the limited scope of the appellate function; (v) where the claim concerns a diplomatic agent; (vi) where the claim itself is brought pursuant to a treaty provision and that treaty expressly excludes the local remedies rule. Such exceptions will be limited indeed and it would seem that a party who asserts that the local remedies rule does not operate will bear the *onus probandi* in displacing a well established rule of international law.[119]

The question of the local remedies rule arose again for consideration in the *Elettronica Sicula (ELSI) SpA* case. The facts of the case were as follows.

This was a case brought by the United States against Italy in respect of damage to a company (ELSI) which was wholly owned by two United States corporations. The claim was brought under the 1948 Treaty of Friendship, Commerce and Navigation which provided for the jurisdiction of the International Court of Justice but made no reference to the local remedies rule.

The United States[120] argued that the local remedies rule did not apply because the treaty was silent on the matter. This argument was rejected by the Court, who held that such a well established rule of customary international law could only be displaced by express words in a treaty. The Chamber of the Court rejected the Italian argument that the remedies had not in fact been exhausted; in respect of the application of the rule, the Chamber held that the party alleging non-compliance with the rule bears the *onus probandi*. It was held further that a party will comply with the rule if he can show that he has in substance exhausted the available remedies. It was also held that as exhaustion is a matter of inference it is to be determined by looking at all the circumstances of the case including the obligation of states to act in good faith.[121]

Thus, it would seem that a party alleging that the local remedies rules does not apply will bear the *onus probandi*. On the assumption that it does apply, then the party alleging non-compliance with the rule will bear the onus.

6 IS THERE A MINIMUM STANDARD?

One of the problems that often arises in respect of international claims is as to whether there are objective international standards. Manifestly, administrative and judicial proceedings differ from state to state; to take an obvious example, some states adopt an adversarial system of proceedings while others adopt a more inquisitorial system.[122] Western nations have tended to place emphasis on minimum international standards

---

119 See United States-Mexico General Claims Convention (1923), Art V; Convention on International Liability for Damage Caused by Objects Launched into Outer Space (1972), Art 11; for discussion see, T Meron (1959) 25 BYIL 95; see also FCO International Claims Rules (1985), rr 7 and 8.

120 A United States argument that the rule did not apply in respect of declaratory actions between states was also rejected.

121 FA Mann (1992) 86 AJIL 92; M Dixon (1992) 41 ICLQ 119; M Adler (1990) 39 ICLQ 641.

122 There are, of course, considerable differences over matters of procedure and evidence; some states permit the general admissibility of documentary evidence and have liberal provisions as regards the admissibility of hearsay evidence. Other states stress the importance of oral testimony and the opportunity for cross examination; often this is accompanied by limits on the admissibility of hearsay evidence. In matters of procedure, some states have criminal trials before a panel of judges followed by a written judgment; other states employ the jury system.

beyond which no state should be allowed to fall. To some extent, this objective has been achieved in the period since 1945 by the development of an international law of human rights which protects persons regardless of whether they are nationals or aliens. Thus, Art 1 of the European Convention on Human Rights and Fundamental Freedoms (1950) requires parties to 'secure for everyone within their jurisdiction the rights and freedoms defined in Section 1 of the Convention'. This emphasis is also to be found in the Universal Declaration of Human Rights (1948), where many of the articles commence with the word 'everyone'. In contrast, some states have argued that minimum standards do not apply or are 'culturally relative' or that the attempt to assert such common standards represents an unjustified interference in domestic affairs. In the years since 1945, such arguments are unlikely to prevail as more and more states have become party to one or other regional human rights instrument.

However, the case law on state responsibility does indicate that even, before 1945, tribunals were reluctant to accept the argument that an individual state had done its inadequate best or had accorded the same level of treatment to an alien as it did to its own national. To some extent, this was a reflection of the natural law background of international law. Thus, in the *Neer Claim*[123] which concerned the killing of an United States citizen in Mexico, the United States-Mexican Claims Commission could refer to 'governmental action so far short of international standards that every reasonable and impartial man would readily recognise its insufficiency'.[124] In the *Janes*[125] claim, the tribunal felt justified in awarding compensation when no attempt was made to bring an identified murderer to justice. One explanation for such cases is drawn from constitutional law and political theory; this explanation is that there are certain minimum acts that all governments must undertake and, if they are unable to do so, then no government can be said to exist. The most basic of such non-delegable duties would be the protection of human life and property within the territory; such a view is consistent with the approach in international law which held that recognition of a government should be contingent on control. It is also consistent with state practice, in that Foreign Ministries will counsel their citizens not to travel to those states where a minimum system of law and order is not in operation. The case law contains a number of examples of references to international standards in respect of human life[126] and the concept of common standards has also be raised in cases of criminal procedure. Thus, in the *Roberts* case,[127] where a United States citizen shared a room of 35 feet by 20 feet with 30 or 40 others and without sanitation, it was no defence to argue that he had received the same treatment as Mexican nationals. Much will depend on the case in question, but tribunals have been vigorous in asserting minimum standards where human life is in issue. Thus, in the *Swinney* claim,[128] where an American was killed by Mexican forces, the tribunal noted that: 'Human life in these parts, on both sides, seems not to be appraised so highly as international standards prescribe.'[129]

---

123 *Neer Claim* (1926) 4 RIAA 77; 3 ILR 213.
124 *Ibid.*
125 *Janes Claim* (1926) 4 RIAA 82; 3 ILR 218.
126 *Garcia* case (1926) 4 RIAA 119.
127 *Roberts Claim* (1926) 4 RIAA 77; 3 ILR 227.
128 *Swinney Claim* (1926) 4 RIAA 98.
129 *Ibid.*

In the years since 1945, it is likely that the state in question will have become a signatory to one or other regional human rights convention.[130] However, simply as a matter of state responsibility, four points deserve comment. First, the respondent state will be expected to show a minimum level of competence and good faith; evidence of bad faith or collusion will be fatal to its case. Secondly, in cases turning on matters of criminal procedure then the state will be expected through its organs to have investigated the crime, collected relevant evidence and brought the matter before an impartial tribunal within a reasonable period of time. Thirdly, in matters of civil procedure, the requirement will be that the dispute has been brought before an impartial tribunal. In civil and criminal cases, there will be an obligation to respect the normal rules of natural justice.[131]

A fourth area of difficulty concerns the expulsion of aliens. Recent years have witnessed increasing attempts by those fleeing persecution or pursuing a better standard of living to seek residence in other states. In most states, there will be detailed rules of immigration control and most will provide that those who are not lawfully entitled to stay may be deported. However, a distinction must be drawn between such cases and the alien who has a lawful entitlement to reside but is then expelled. In such circumstances, question will arise as to whether the expulsion is collective or individual. Collective expulsion is in principle discriminatory and contrary to the European Convention on Human Rights.[132] In cases where the expulsion concerns a single individual, then most municipal legal systems provide that the executive branch may deport an alien on grounds of national security or where the presence is not conducive to the public good.[133] In the United Kingdom, aliens are subject to the normal law and have access to the courts;[134] an alien who is a European citizen will be able to rely on the protection of European Community law.[135]

7 DEFENCES

Sometimes, in municipal law, the breach of a legal obligation may not give rise to responsibility because the matter may be subject to a particular defence. International law has broadly accepted that a state may raise particular defences to allegations of unlawful conduct. In the terminology of the ILC Draft Articles, there are a number of 'circumstances precluding wrongfulness' and these are set out in Chapter V (Arts

---

130 Matters pertaining to human rights obligations will be considered in Chapters 14 and 15.

131 The rules of natural justice tend to be stressed in common law jurisdictions and play a significant role in constitutional law; the two principal rules *audiatur est et altera pars* (the court should hear both sides) and *nemo judex in causa sua* (no one should be judge in his own cause) have acquired widespread acceptance. For case law in the United Kingdom, see *R v Sussex Justices ex p McCarthy* [1924] 1 KB 256; *Ridge v Baldwin* [1964] AC 40; *R v Gough* [1993] AC 646; *R v Bow Street Metropolitan Stipendiary Magistrate ex p Pinochet Ugarte (No 2)* [1999] 2 WLR 272; *Locabail (UK) Ltd v Bayfield Properties Ltd* [2000] QB 451.

132 Fourth Protocol (1963), Art 4.

133 *R v Home Secretary ex p Hosenball* [1977] 3 All ER 452 (the role of judicial review being strictly limited as the Home Secretary is answerable to Parliament).

134 See *Netz v Chuter Ede* [1946] Ch 244; *R v Bottrill ex p Keuchenmeister* [1947] KB 41; *Keuchenmeister v Home Office* [1958] 1 QB 496; *R v Home Secretary ex p Cheblak* [1991] 2 All ER 319; see I Leigh [1991] PL 331; F Hampson [1991] PL 507.

135 Case 131/79, *R v Home Secretary ex p Santillo* [1981] QB 778.

20–27).[136] The terminology itself is not without interest because it appears to indicate that responsibility has not arisen as distinct from providing a defence when responsibility has been established.

The circumstances include consent by the potential victim state (Art 20) or where the act is required in the circumstances by a peremptory norm of international law (Art 21). Further responsibility is precluded where the act is a lawful one of self-defence (Art 22) or where the act complained of was a legitimate countermeasure to an internationally wrongful act of the complaining state (Art 23). In situations of *force majeure* or an unforeseen event making it materially impossible to perform the international obligation which is violated then wrongfulness is precluded (Art 24). Instances where the individual was in a situation of extreme distress where there was no other means available of saving the author's life or the lives of other persons in the author's care (Art 25) also constitutes a 'defence'. A narrow ground of state necessity is also available (Art 26).

Recent jurisprudence has given additional impetus to defences arising in the law of state responsibility. In the *Rainbow Warrior* case,[137] the arbitral tribunal ruled that even where compliance with a treaty was in issue it was open to a state not only to raise 'defences' under the law of treaties but also to advance any 'defences' arising under the law of state responsibility. This general approach was confirmed in *Danube Dam* case,[138] where the International Court of Justice held that, while the validity of a suspension or termination of a treaty had to be determined under the law of treaties, the consequences of an illegal termination and, in particular, whether it gave rise to state responsibility had to be determined under the general law of state responsibility. While this distinction may have a theoretical appeal, much is likely to depend on how a tribunal categorises and determines a specific obligation and the particular facts arising in each case.

8 THE TAKING OF FOREIGN OWNED PROPERTY[139]

One of the commonest problems in the law of state responsibility concerns the taking of the property of foreign investors.[140] This matter is considered further in Chapter 19, but at this stage a number of points may usefully be made. In the modern world, it is often the case that a company registered in state A may seek to invest in state B. It is normally a matter for each state as to whether it wishes to accept foreign investment, but if it decides to do so then public international law sets out a number of rules as to how it treats the foreign investor. In general terms, the foreign investor is expected to abide by the laws of the host state; however, problems may arise as to the conduct of such a foreign investor.

---

136 In the 1996 Draft Articles the relevant articles were Arts 29–34.

137 *Rainbow Warrior (France v New Zealand)* case (1987) 82 ILR 499.

138 *Gabcikovo-Nagymaros (Hungary v Slovakia)* case (1997) ICJ 7.

139 See generally I Christie, 'What constitutes taking of property under international law'(1962) 33 BYIL 307; O Schachter, 'Compensation for expropriation' (1984) 78 AJIL 121; P Norton, 'A law of the future or a law of the past? Modern tribunals and the international law of expropriation' (1991) 85 AJIL 474; GH Aldrich, 'What constitutes a compensable taking: the decisions of the Iran-United States Claims Tribunal' (1994) 88 AJIL 585.

140 As Professor Schachter has observed: 'Apart from the use of force, no subject of international law seems to have aroused as much debate – and often strong feelings – as the question of the standard for payment of compensation when foreign property is appropriated' (1984) 78 AJIL 121.

Sometimes, such difficulties can be avoided by setting out minimum standards in a bilateral investment agreement. In this area of international law, there has traditionally been a problem of differences of opinion between capital exporting countries and capital importing countries.

The law of state responsibility often becomes relevant when a host state decides to expropriate the assets of a foreign investor. In such circumstances, the private investor in state B may request that its own state (state A) takes up its case and seeks some form of recompense. As a preliminary matter, one must be careful about the meaning of the term 'expropriate'; the expression 'expropriation' may embrace nationalisation, levying of punitive taxation, requisition, compulsory acquisition or many other forms[141] of conduct. Past case law indicates that four questions commonly arise: (a) has there been expropriation?; (b) is the expropriation consistent with the requirements of international law?; (c) if the expropriation is unlawful how should compensation be assessed?; (d) how should compensation be assessed in cases of lawful expropriation? Past experience indicates that disputes in this area are best resolved either by arbitration or by a tribunal hearing.

On the assumption that some form of expropriation is in issue, the question arises as to the approach of public international law. International law has traditionally drawn a distinction between lawful expropriation and unlawful expropriation. As a matter of general principle, for expropriation to be lawful the expropriating act[142] must be: (a) not arbitrary; (b) for a public purpose;[143] (c) without discrimination; and (d) subject to payment of appropriate compensation. It therefore follows that there is a distinction between those expropriatory acts that are unlawful from the outset and those that may be rendered unlawful by a refusal to pay compensation. Conventional textbook opinion has held that expropriation will be lawful if there is compliance with the United Nations General Assembly Resolution on Permanent Sovereignty over Natural Resources (1962),[144] which requires that expropriation 'shall be based on grounds or reasons of public utility, security, or the national interest which are recognised as overriding purely individual or private interests, both domestic and foreign. In such cases the owner shall be paid appropriate compensation in accordance with the rules in force in the state taking such measures in the exercise of its sovereignty and in accordance with international law'.[145]

---

141 According to M Sornarajah (1994), the expression 'expropriation' may embrace: (a) forced sales of property; (b) forced sale of shares; (c) transfer from foreign interests to local interests; (d) application of management control; (e) a physical takeover of the property; (f) failure to provide protection when there is interference with the foreign investment; (g) licensing decisions; (h) exorbitant taxation; (i) expulsion of the foreign investor contrary to international law; (j) acts of harassment such as freezing of a bank account.

142 For consideration of the concept of expropriation, see *Agip SpA v The Government of the Popular Republic of the Congo* (1979) 67 ILR 319; *Benvenuti and Bonfant v The Government of the Popular Republic of the Congo* (1980) 67 OLR 345; *Harza Engineering Co v The Islamic Republic of Iran* (1982) 1 Iran-US CTR 96; 70 ILR 118; *Starrett Housing Corporation v Government of the Islamic Republic of Iran* (1984) 4 Iran-US CTR 122; *Kalamazoo Spice Extraction Company v The Provisional Military Government of Socialist Ethiopia* (1984) 86 ILR 4590; 78 AJIL 902.

143 See *Lithgow v United Kingdom* (1986) 75 ILR 439; *James v United Kingdom* (1986) 75 ILR 397.

144 GA Res 1803 (XVII).

145 But see also United Nations Declaration on the Establishment of a New International Economic Order (1974 GA Res 3201) and United Nations Charter of Economic Rights and Duties of States (1974 GA 3281).

The requirement of public utility imports the principle that the act must be for public benefit[146] and this will not be the case where the motivation is retaliatory;[147] while the requirement of public benefit has not been stressed in all cases,[148] the weight of opinion favours it.[149] Evidence of discriminatory conduct renders any expropriation unlawful.[150]

In principle, 'property' includes not only real property but also contractual rights[151] and intellectual property rights.

The requirements for lawful expropriation have been thrown into some doubt in the last quarter of a century because of action by the United Nations General Assembly. In 1974, the General Assembly adopted a Declaration on the Establishment of a New International Economic Order[152] and a Charter of Economic Rights and Duties of States.[153] Both these documents assert the legality of expropriation but fail to stipulate any requirement as to 'public purpose' or 'non-discrimination'.

While there may be differences of opinion about the requirements for a lawful expropriation the real difference between developed and developing nations tends to focus on the question of compensation. In developed countries the state is normally not entitled to take the property of the citizen without making payment in compensation; the individual who has his property taken for a public purpose is compensated by the general body of taxpayers.[154] In developing countries, the matter is viewed differently as emphasis is placed on the sovereignty over natural resources and the desire to avoid the remittance of profits abroad. These concerns may be heightened if the developing state seeks to develop a command economy or there has been a history of exploitation by the foreign investor.

The precise rule in customary international law as to compensation is by no means easy to determine. The *Norwegian Shipowners Claims*[155] arbitration of 1922 referred to 'just compensation' to be ascertained by 'fair actual value at the time and the place' 'in view of all surrounding circumstances'. Shortly after, in the *Spanish Zone of Morocco* case,[156] reference was made to full compensation. In 1928, in the *Chorzow* case[157] the Permanent Court of International Justice required only 'payment of fair compensation'. However, in 1938 Secretary of State Cordell Hull, when writing to the Mexican Government on the subject of the expropriation of agrarian lands owned by United States nationals,

---

146 *Certain German Interests in Polish Upper Silesia* (1926) PCIJ, Ser A, No 7, p 22.

147 *BP v Libya* (1974) 53 ILR 329.

148 *Liamco* case (1981) 20 ILM 1; 62 ILR 141.

149 *Amoco Finance v Iran* (1987) 15 Iran-US 189.

150 *Aramco* case (1963).

151 *Amoco Finance v Iran* (1987) 15 Iran-US CTR 189.

152 GA Res 3201.

153 GA Res 3281.

154 The issue of principle in placing the burden on the general body of taxpayers to compensate the citizen whose property has been taken, emerges in the House of Lords judgment in *Attorney General v De Keyser's Royal Hotel* [1920] AC 508; the rationale for taking the property of the citizen for social purposes is discussed by the European Court of Human Rights in *Lithgow v United Kingdom* (1986) 8 EHRR 329. See also *Earl of Lonsdale v Attorney General* [1982] 1 WLR 887; United States Constitution 5th Amendment (1791).

155 *Norwegian Shipowners' Claims* (1922) 1 RIAA 307.

156 *Spanish Zone of Morocco* case (1925) 2 RIAA 615.

157 *Case concerning the Factory at Chorzow (Merits)* (1928) PCIJ, Ser A, No 17.

demanded 'prompt, adequate and effective compensation'; since that date, this particular phrase has been invoked by the United States and others ,but it is open to question as to whether the 'Hull formula' ever constituted a rule of customary international law. The formulation, however, has found favour with capital exporting countries and it is often employed in bilateral investment agreements. It was also assumed that what was 'prompt, adequate or effective' was to be tested by reference to the requirements of international law not municipal law. However, many treaties use other formulations and there is little evidence of full compensation being paid in recent years.[158]

Moreover, since 1938, there has been not been a uniform use of language. The General Assembly Resolution of 1962 on the Permanent Sovereignty over Natural Resources,[155] referred to 'appropriate' compensation and support for this approach is to be found in both the *Texaco* case[160] and the *Aminoil* case.[161] In the *Aminoil* case,[162] 'appropriate' was seen as desirable because it reflected the desire to investigate all the relevant facts in a particular case and also to weigh all material considerations with a degree of flexibility. A review of the arbitral decisions[163] in the years from 1945 to the early 1970s tended to show that full compensation was required and that arbitrators tended to be guided by past awards.

However, by the early 1970s, the position was becoming less clear. Decolonisation in the 1960s had resulted in a large number of newly independent states who had a different view of compensation.[164] According to many, compensation was not to be determined by what was 'appropriate' according to international law; instead, the foreign investor was entitled to be compensated by the 'national standard'. This entitlement was no more than would have been paid to a national and such a level was to be considered appropriate.

Support for this view was to be found in both the Declaration on the Establishment of a New International Economic Order[165] and the Charter of Economic Rights and Duties of States;[166] developed countries did not accept this approach.

In the circumstances, such differences of opinion have not proved so damaging and subsequent arbitral awards have tended to focus on a middle way as arbitrators have tended to look at past awards. The reasons for this are not hard to seek. A state that expropriated without paying compensation might obtain a short term benefit but it would attract little private investment in the future. Secondly, the collapse of communist states tended to weaken the ideological objection to the payment of compensation.

---

158 See M Sornarajah (1994).

159 GA Res 1803 (XVII).

160 *Texaco v Libya* (1978) 53 ILR 389; 17 ILM 1.

161 *Aminoil v Kuwait* (1982) 21 ILM 976; 66 ILR 518.

162 *Ibid.*

163 See generally *Petroleum Development Ltd v Sheik of Abu Ahabi* (1951) 18 ILR 144; *Ruler of Qatar v International Marine Oil Co* (1953) 20 ILR 534; *The Lighthouses Arbitration* (1956) 23 ILR 299; *Saudi Arabia v Arabian American Oil Co* (1958) 27 ILR 117; *Saphire International Petroleum Ltd v National Iranian Oil Co* (1963) 35 ILR 136.

164 In some cases, this was linked to some form of Marxist approach as many developing countries in the 1960s and 1970s tended to be sympathetic to the Soviet Union and the traditional communist view that the state was entitled to control the means of production, distribution and exchange.

165 GA Res 3201.

166 GA Res 3281.

Thirdly, many developing states anxious to attract foreign investment were prepared to sign bilateral investment agreements. Fourthly, the tendency of arbitrators was to be guided by past practice In *BP v Libya*,[167] the emphasis was on full compensation while in *Texaco v Libya*[168] the arbitrator held that the principle of *restitutio in integrum* enunciated in the *Chorzow* case[169] remained valid, while in the *Liamco* case.[170] the arbitrator favoured 'equitable compensation'. The tendency has been to avoid ideological differences and to emphasise that compensation should be appropriate,[171] just[172] or fair.[173]

On the assumption that a general principle to govern compensation can be arrived at the question arises as to the actual method of assessment. The following general points arise from past arbitral awards:

(1) Claims for damage which is adjudged too remote will be rejected.[174]

(2) Arbitral awards tend to distinguish between *damnum emergens* (loss suffered) and *lucrum cessans* (expected profits).[175]

(3) Arbitral awards and tribunals tend to distinguish between expropriation unlawful at the outset and expropriation unlawful by reason of failure to offer compensation. In such a situation compensation might be regarded as damages.[176]

(4) In cases of expropriation unlawful from the outset full compensation for real property may be awarded.[177]

(5) In respect of concessionary contracts one approach is to assess the revenue to be earned during the period of the concession and then discount the revenues actually earned prior to the date of the expropriation. The difficulty with such a discounted cash flow approach (DCF) is that it requires evidence of past conduct and the keeping of accurate records.

(6) In respect of fixed assets one approach has been to proceed on the basis of net book value that is, the value of the assets minus depreciation and making no allowance for goodwill. Such a method is not likely to be popular with foreign investors but is often taken as a starting point for negotiations.

(7) In cases of unlawful expropriation and in many cases of lawful expropriation the claimant has sought compensation on the basis of the business as a going concern.[178]

---

167 *BP v Libyan Arab Republic* (1973) 53 ILR 297.
168 *Texaco v Libya* (1977) 53 ILR 389.
169 *Factory at Corzow (Germany v Poland)* (1928) PCIJ, Ser A, No 17.
170 *Libyan American Oil Co v Libyan Arab Republic* (1981) 20 ILM 10.
171 *Animoil* case (1982) 21 ILM 976.
172 *Amoco International Finance Corporation v The Islamic Republic of Iran* (1987) 15 Iran-US CTR 189; 83 ILR 500.
173 *Southern Pacific Properties (Middle East) Ltd v Arab Republic of Egypt* (1993) 32 ILM 933.
174 *AMCO v Indonesia* (1985) 24 ILM 1022; 89 ILR 405.
175 *Ibid*.
176 *Amoco International Finance Corporation v The Islamic Republic of Iran* (1987) 15 Iran-US CTR 189; 83 ILR 500.
177 *Texaco v Libya* (1977) 53 ILR 389.
178 *AIG v The Islamic Republic of Iran* (1983) 4 Iran-US CTR 96; *Amco International Finance Corporation v The Islamic Republic of Iran* (1987) 15 Iran-US CTR 189; *Phillips Petroleum Co Iran v The Government of the Islamic Republic of Iran* (1989) 21 Iran-US CTR 79; *Starrett Housing Corporation v The Islamic Republic of Iran* (1989) 21 Iran-US CTR 112.

This involves determining how much a notional purchaser would pay in respect of the assets, goodwill and some measure of future profits. but disregarding the actual fact of expropriation.

The uncertainty of the rules of customary international law and the desire of some states to attract foreign investment has lead to a proliferation of bilateral investment agreements. The object of such agreements is to create a framework that balances the interest of the capital importing state and the capital foreign investor. It is common to include terms that provide for the equitable treatment of the foreign investor and prohibit discriminatory treatment; in respect of expropriation, it is normal to include a term that both limits the circumstances in which such action is allowed and provides for the payment of compensation. The majority of such agreements include provision for the resolution of disputes. A very high proportion of such agreements have been concluded in the 1990s, as the collapse of communism has lead to more emphasis on international investment; many such agreements provide for international arbitration through the auspices of the ICSID.[179]

In respect of the actual payment of compensation, a state may pay either by lump sum or by a series of sums to be paid over a number of years; in cases where there are many individual claimants, the state may pay a lump sum to the claimant state who will then set up some administrative machinery to meet the claims on a *pro rata* basis. In the United Kingdom, that task is performed by the Foreign Compensation Commission.[180]

A matter that has given rise to considerable comment in recent years is the action that an individual foreign investor might take in respect of a concessionary contract with a state. The following points can be made:

(1) Such an agreement is generally viewed as a contract and not a treaty;[181] it is not an international agreement. According to its particular terms, there may well be remedies in the relevant municipal law but the best view is that a breach of contract of itself does not give rise to responsibility on the international plane.[182] It would seem that such responsibility can only arise if the state seeks to extinguish all contractual rights in a manner similar to expropriation.

(2) To guard against such conduct, one course of action has been to insert a choice of law clause that seeks to internationalise the contract; this is done by making some reference to the rules of public international law.[183] The object is to ensure that conduct under the contract is considered by reference to international law. The effectiveness of such arrangements is open to doubt. It is normally thought that to be effective the contract must also include a stabilisation clause. Such a clause is an undertaking by a state not to take legislative or executive action in the future to

---

179 The International Centre for Settlement of Investment Disputes (ICSID) was established under the Washington Convention on the Settlement of Investment Disputes between States and Nationals of Other States in 1965. By 1997, it was said that of the 1,100 bilateral investment treaties in existence over 900 chose the ICSID as the form of dispute resolution.

180 See Foreign Compensation Act 1950; Foreign Compensation Act 1969; Foreign Compensation (Amendment) Act 1993. For consideration of the general role of the Commission, see *Anisminic Ltd v Foreign Compensation Commission* [1969] 2 AC 147.

181 *Anglo Iranian Oil Co* case (1952) ICJ 93.

182 See I Brownlie, *Principles of Public International Law*, 5th edn, 1998, p 550.

183 On this see *Texaco v Libya* (1977) 53 ILR 389.

negate the contract. A stabilisation clause is also the subject of some controversy because a sovereign government cannot fetter its freedom of action indefinitely; it is therefore thought that such clauses can only be valid for a limited period of time. The basis of such a clause is to indicate that any subsequent termination of contractual rights should be viewed as an act of expropriation; in certain cases this might increase the level of compensation awarded.[184]

(3) It should be noted that some writers[185] have taken a different view and assert that a breach of contract by a state does entail international responsibility as part of an international law of contract. Such writers support this position by reference to the doctrine of acquired rights, the principle of *pacta sunt servanda* and *dicta* in a number of arbitral and tribunal decisions.[186]

9 INDIVIDUAL CONDUCT

In this chapter, attention has been devoted to the subject of state responsibility for acts contrary to international law. However, an important theme since 1945 has been the attempt to place responsibility upon individuals for acts contrary to international law. One legacy of the Nuremberg trials, and one product of human rights law, is the conviction that criminal prosecutions may have a role to play in ensuring respect for international law. Such individuals may be prosecuted before a national court or before a specially constituted international tribunal (for example, the Yugoslav War Crimes Tribunal) or in future before the International Criminal Court. The jurisdiction of such bodies is considered further in Chapter 24.

10 CALVO CLAUSES

A matter worthy of attention is the Calvo clause.[187] Such a clause[188] may be included in a contract between a foreign national and a state whereby the foreign national agrees to renounce any right to diplomatic protection and to bring any dispute before the local courts. Such clauses were commonly included by Central and Latin American states in respect of foreign investors. The clauses stemmed from a desire to restrict interference in domestic affairs.

If the clause is merely a requirement to exhaust local remedies then it is valid[189] and such was the conclusion of the United States-Mexico General Claims Commission in the

---

184 *Animoil* case (1963) 27 ILR 117.

185 RY Jennings, 'State contracts in international law' (1961) 37 BYIL 156; JN Hyde, 'Economic development agreements' (1962) 105 HR 267.

186 *Delagoa Bay Railway Company* case (1900) Moore Int Arbitrations 1865; *El Trunfo Claim* (1901) 15 RIAA 46; *Landreau Claim* (1921) 1 RIAA 347; *Shufeldt Claim* (1930) 2 RIAA 1079; *Saudi Arabia v Arabian American Oil Co* (1958) 27 ILR 117; *Texaco v Libyan Government* (1978) 53 ILR 389.

187 Named after the Argentinian jurist Carlos Calvo.

188 The precise wording of the clause may differ.

189 And in many cases redundant. It was not redundant in the *North American Dredging Company* case (1926) since the relevant Convention under which the Commission had been established included a term excluding the local remedies rule.

North American Dredging Company case.[190] It is strongly arguable that the other form of the Calvo clause, where the foreign investor agrees to waive the right of diplomatic representation, is probably ineffective.[191] First, a state enjoys the sovereign right to protect its citizens. Secondly, the right of making representations on the international plane is accorded by international law to the state and thus cannot be disclaimed by an individual.

---

190 *North American Dredging Company (United States v Mexico)* case (1926) 4 RIAA 26.
191 *Mexican Union Railways (Ltd)* (1929) AD No 129; *El Oro Mining and Railway Co Ltd* (1931) AD No 100.

CHAPTER 13

THE LAW OF THE SEA[1]

1 INTRODUCTION

The subject of the law of the sea has been a central concern of international lawyers since at least the time when European adventurers set out to discover and conquer the New World if not before. In an age devoid of aviation[2] and naval power, the domination of the high seas represented the best guarantee of both regular trade and secure defence. For those states, such as Great Britain, dependent on the import of food and raw materials control of maritime routes could not be a matter of indifference. By the end of the 20th century a considerable part of international law pertaining to the law of the sea was contained in the United Nations Convention on the Law of the Sea (1982). However, to understand the nature of this multilateral law making treaty it is necessary to say something of the history.

By 1400, if not before, rulers had come to recognise that certain distinctions could be made. Common sense dictated a distinction between internal waters (ports, harbours, roadsteads and closed in bays) and all other waters. At the end of the 15th century European states began to assert rights over the oceans. Prior to that date the high seas had been regarded as free for all to sail and fish.[3] Pope Alexander VI[4] in a series of papal bulls attempted to apportion territory and the oceans between Portugal and Spain. In the papal bull *Inter Caetera* (1492) he drew an imaginary boundary line from north to south 100 miles west of the Azores and the Cape Verde Islands and ruled that the oceans and territory beyond were subject to Spanish sovereignty. This was not acceptable to Portugal who began direct negotiations with Spain that resulted in the Treaty of Tordesillas (1493) under which the Portuguese claimed the route to India as well as part of the South Atlantic while Spain asserted rights over the Pacific and the Gulf of Mexico. The extent to

---

1   RY Jennings and AD Watts, *Oppenheim's International Law*, 9th edn, 1992, pp 719–826; CJ Colombus, *The International Law of the Sea*, 6th edn, 1967; ED Brown, *International Law of the Sea*, 1994, Vols 1 and 2; R Churchill and AV Lowe, *The Law of the Sea*, 3rd edn, 1999; D Bowett, *Law of the Sea*, 1967; DP O'Connell, *The International Law of the Sea*, 1982 and 1984 (I Shearer (ed)), Oxford: OUP; P Allott, 'Mare nostrum: a new international law of the sea' (1992) 86 AJIL 764; T Treves, 'Codification du droit international et pratique des Etats dans le droit de la mer' (1990) 223 HR 9.

2   Aviation was not of critical importance in international law until just before the outbreak of the First World War. Part of the reason for the tension between England and Germany in the years prior to 1914 was caused by the efforts of Admiral von Tirpitz (1849–1930) as Secretary for the Navy (1897–1916) to establish a strong German naval force. For the background, see RK Massie, *Dreadnought*, 1991.

3   The traditional Roman law position was that the sea was open to all men and it was incapable by nature of becoming the object of private property. See P Fenn, 'Origins of the theory of territorial waters' (1926) 20 AJIL 465.

4   Alexander VI (1431–1503) (Pope 1492–1503) (Rodrigo Borgia) was of Spanish origin and was disposed to favour Spanish claims, not least because he wished for Spanish help to support the territorial ambitions of his son Cesare in Italy. The two principal papal bulls *Inter Caetera* and *Dudum Siquidem* place Portugal at a disadvantage and lead to direct negotiations.

which the rules were uncertain is illustrated by the fact that the Portuguese were obliged to ask later popes[5] to confirm the territorial arrangement made in the Treaty.

Assertions of sovereignty over the high seas were challenged by the Protestant trading interests of Northern Europe. Hugo Grotius produced his *Mare Liberum* (1609), partly at the behest of his employers in the Dutch East India Company who sought to challenge the influence of the Portuguese in the Indian ocean.[6] Such a publication asserted the principle of the freedom of the high seas and did not go unchallenged. Both Welwood in his *Abridgement of all Sea Laws* (1613) and Selden in the somewhat later *Mare Clausum* (1635)[7] sought to advance the claims of Great Britain to control navigation in the North Sea. However, the principle propounded by Grotius began to hold sway partly because it was of mutual benefit and facilitated trade and partly because a single state could not effectively assert sovereignty over the high seas unless it was prepared to commit considerable naval forces to policing disputed areas.

At the same time it was recognised that a state might claim a maritime belt adjacent to its coast for purposes of defence[8] and over which it had rights akin to sovereignty. The precise origin of this concept is a matter of dispute but, by the end of the 18th century, a distance of three nautical miles was claimed by Great Britain and some other states. However, a number of Scandinavian countries claimed different widths. Some writers link the emergence of the concept to the publication in 1702 of Bynkershoek's[9] *De Dominio Maris Dissertatio* in which he endorsed the canon shot rule that held that the littoral state had rights over the coastal waters within the range of a cannon shot fired from its shores. But some writers have questioned whether the rule did emerge from this source.[10] Indeed, Great Britain introduced, in the 18th century, the concept of a maritime belt beyond territorial waters known as the contiguous zone over which certain policing functions might be exercised.[11]

So that, in the early 19th century, any international law of the sea was based on customary rules and those rules recognised the concept of the high seas over which no state could claim jurisdiction, and also a maritime belt of territorial waters whose breadth was sometimes said to be three nautical miles. That position would remain unchanged into the 20th century.[12] One of the reasons was that colonisation meant that much of the

---

5   Pope Julius II (1443–1513) (Pope 1503–13) confirmed the Treaty division in his papal bull *Ea Quae* (1506). Portuguese claims were also supported by Leo X (1475–1521) (Pope 1513–21) who sanctioned Portuguese claims to the Indian ocean in his papal bull *Praecelsae devotionis* (1514).

6   For an evaluation of Hugo Grotius (1583–1645), see H Lauterpacht, 'The Grotian Tradition in International Law' (1946) 23 BYIL 1; RW Lee, 'Hugo Grotius' (1946) 62 LQR 53.

7   W Welwood, *The Abridgement of all the Sea Laws*, 1613; J Selden, *Mare Clausum*, 1635.

8   The assertion of a distinct maritime belt can be found in the works of Bartolus of Sassoferrato (1314–57) and later in the work of Jean Bodin, *Les Six Livres de la République*, 1576, Paris. See P Fenn, 'Justinian and the freedom of the sea' (1925) 19 AJIL 716; 'Origins of the theory of territorial waters' (1926) 20 AJIL 465.

9   Cornelis van Bynkershoek (1673–1743); *De Dominio Maris Dissertatio* (Essay on Sovereignty over the Sea) expressed the principle *Terrae potestas ubi finitur armorum vis* (territorial sovereignty extends as far as the power of arms carries).

10 WW Walker, 'Territorial waters, the Canon Shot rule' (1945) 22 BYIL 210; HS Kent, 'The historical origins of the three mile limit' (1954) 48 AJIL 537.

11 See Hovering Acts 1736–1876.

12 *R v Keyn* (1876) 2 Ex D 63 contains an interesting if inconclusive discussion of the state of the law of the sea as it appeared to the English judiciary in the late 19th century.

world's oceans were indirectly subject to colonial powers. In the 20th century, decolonisation would increase the number of independent coastal states who would seek to achieve a greater measure of control over adjacent waters.

It was recognised after the First World War that it was not sensible to found the law of the sea on customary law alone. In 1924, the League of Nations requested its Committee of Experts to draw up a list of subjects suitable for codification. Included among the list was the topic of 'territorial waters'. The Committee began consultations with interested governments and sufficient porgies was made to warrant holding a conference at the Hague in 1930. However, this conference was only a limited success as no international convention emerged; nevertheless, a series of draft articles on the subject of territorial waters were produced. Although no further substantive progress was to be made in that decade, interest in the subject of the law of the sea grew as individuals speculated on the possibility of sustained deep sea drilling and exploration.

The establishment of the United Nations in 1945 lead to the creation of the International Law Commission in 1947 and this body has, since that date, been active in seeking codification of the law of the sea. However, the main impetus for action derived from action taken by the United States in the form of the Truman Declaration issued in September 1945. In that statement, President Truman asserted:

> ... having concern for the urgency of conserving and prudently utilising its natural resources, the Government of the United States regards the natural resources of the subsoil and sea bed of the continental shelf beneath the high seas but contiguous to the coasts of the United States as appertaining to the United States, subject to its jurisdiction and control.

In essence, the Truman Proclamation comprised two statements, one in respect of the natural resources of the subsoil and seabed of the continental shelf and the other with respect to coastal fisheries in certain areas of the high seas. The danger of such unilateral law making was not only that it broke with the traditional maritime zones recognised by customary international law but that it prompted others to act. In the years between 1945 and 1955, many Latin American states unilaterally declared maritime zones of varying breadths. The Latin American states unilaterally declared maritime zones in respect of coastal waters and subsoil to a distance of 200 nautical miles.[13] In the same period, the *Anglo Norwegian Fisheries* case[14] indicated that there were considerable differences of opinion about the meaning of even long established customary rules in particular in respect of the drawing of baselines.

The developments prompted by the Truman Declaration if left unchecked would have meant that there was no uniform law of the sea. Thus, the International Law Commission began work on the subject in the early 1950s and by 1956 had consulted sufficient states and produced a detailed enough report to warrant the calling of an international conference. The first United Nations Conference on the Law of the Sea (UNCLOS I)[15] was attended by 86 states, nearly double the number participating in the 1930 Conference. The conference produced four conventions: the Convention on the

---

13 See generally LDM Nelson, 'The patrimonial sea' (1973) 22 ICLQ 668.

14 (1951) ICJ 116 (where the court rejected the United Kingdom contention that straight baselines could only be drawn across bays).

15 Meeting in Geneva from 24 February 1958 to 27 April 1958.

Territorial Sea and the Contiguous Zone; the Convention on the High Seas; the Convention on the Continental Shelf; the Convention on Fishing and Conservation of the Living Resources of the High Seas. The first three of these conventions were based on existing rules of customary international law as analysed in the documentation of the International Law Commission. Not surprisingly these three conventions attracted a high number of ratifications. The fourth convention went somewhat beyond the existing customary law and attracted only a limited number of ratifications.

However, the one problem that defeated the conference was the question of the precise breadth of the territorial sea; this was partly because different state traditions applied in this area. It was decided to call a second conference to discuss this question and the related but increasing problem of fishery limits. The second United Nations Conference on the Law of the Sea (UNCLOS II) took place in the months of March and April 1960; a compromise proposal of a six mile territorial sea together with a six mile fishery zone failed to win acceptance by a single vote. The conference had failed to agree partly because of an element of distrust about off shore submarine surveillance activities and partly because there was doubt as to whether states would be able to discharge the increased responsibilities that went with a broader territorial sea.

So, after 1960, a number of problems remained unresolved. These were: (i) the precise width of the territorial sea; (ii) questions pertaining to the right of passage for warships through straits; (iii) problems of conservation in the area beyond the territorial sea; (iv) the rights of passage that might be enjoyed in respect of the waters close to an archipelago.

The fact that agreement could not be reached in 1960 did not mean that there were not a number of reasons why the task should not be attempted again. First, technical improvements in fishing methods made agreement on this question important. Secondly, newly independent states that had not participated in the 1958 conference were anxious to ensure recognition of their control over coastal waters. Thirdly, the 1958 Convention had made no provision for deep sea mineral mining; in 1967 the General Assembly had voted to establish a committee to study the problem. Fourthly, it was becoming increasingly clear that a number of problems in relation to the law of the sea were inter-related and interlocking and that it was difficult to make progress in one area without considering the impact on other questions. Fifthly, it was considered undesirable that no agreement could be reached on the breadth of the territorial sea. Sixthly, one of the most serious problems after 1960 was the problem caused when large oil tankers encountered difficulties and the spillage of oil would damage the marine environment. The situation was well illustrated in March 1967 when the Torrey Canyon ran aground off the southern coast of the United Kingdom; such an incident served to indicate the need for a more comprehensive legal framework in respect of the law of the sea, The specific problem of marine pollution was dealt with in two international conventions adopted in 1969; the first was the International Convention relating to Intervention on the High Seas in cases of Oil Pollution Casualties (sometimes described as the Intervention Convention)[16] and the second was entitled the International Convention on Civil Liability for Oil Pollution

---

16 To be read with the Protocol relating to Intervention on the High Seas in cases of Marine Pollution by Substances other than Oil, adopted in London in 1973.

Damage (sometimes described as the Liability Convention).[17] However, both conventions were restricted in terms; the first was designed to enable defensive measures to be taken and the second was concerned to limit liability and provide for insurance.

However, these conventions were only limited in scope and pressure had grown within the General Assembly for a more comprehensive approach. In 1967, Mr Arvid Pardo of Malta urged the United Nations to take action in respect of possible deep sea mining beyond the continental shelf. This was followed between 1967 and 1969, by a number of General Assembly Resolutions,[18] declaring that the exploration of the seabed and the ocean 'beyond the limits of national jurisdiction' should be undertaken for the benefit of mankind.

With these considerations in mind the General Assembly in December 1970 adopted two resolutions which provided first for a Declaration of Principles Governing the Seabed and Ocean Floor and the Subsoil Thereof beyond the Limits of National Jurisdiction;[19] the second resolution provided for the calling of a third United Nations Conference on the Law of the Sea (UNCLOS III).[20]

The Law of the Sea Conference that met from 1974 until 1982 was faced with a number of pressing questions. First, many newly independent states wished to establish a clear entitlement to exclusive fishing rights in an area of 200 nautical miles. Secondly, many developing states wished to see detailed rules established in respect of deep sea ocean mining and to limit the activities of western based exploration companies. Thirdly, it was clear that the different groupings – developing states, western states and communist states – each had their own priorities. Fourthly, the diversity of interests meant that the conference did not start by working from an agreed draft by the International Law Commission.

From 1975, it was decided to proceed not by formal vote but by seeking to find a consensus; such a procedure was necessary not only to prevent maritime nations from being outvoted but also to ensure that the final text would be both comprehensive and yet capable of attracting the widest possible number of ratifications. That the objective would require delicate political compromises was illustrated by the fact that negotiations fell within the ambit of the United Nations General Assembly's First (Political and Security) Committee rather than in the Sixth (Legal) Committee.

With over 150 states attending it was clear that compromises were inevitable; thus, Western states were prepared to accept a wider territorial sea in exchange for clear provisions relating to passage in international straits. However, such was the level of agreement that in the period 1975 until 1982 some of the provisions were translated into municipal law before the treaty itself was concluded.

---

17 To be read with the Convention for the Establishment of a Fund for Compensation for Oil Pollution Damage (1971) which makes provision for additional compensation to that available under the Liability Convention.
18 GA Res 2340 (XXII) of 18 December 1967; 2467 (XXIII) of 21 December 1968; and 2574 (XXIV) of 15 December 1969.
19 GA Res (1970) 2749 (17 December 1970).
20 GA Res (1970) 2750 (17 December 1970).

The text of the Law of the Sea Convention (1982) was adopted on 30 April 1982 by 130 votes to four with 17 abstentions.[21] The Convention was open for signature for a period of two years; at the end of that period it had been signed by 159 states. Article 308 provided that the Convention would come into effect 12 months after the receipt of the sixtieth ratification. On 16 November 1993, Guyana deposited the sixtieth ratification so that the Convention would come into force on 16 November 1994. In the period from 1982 until 1994, it was clear that a considerable number of Western states including the United States might refrain from ratifying if changes were not made in respect of Part XI of the Convention dealing with the subject of the International Seabed Area. To enable the Convention to enter into force an Agreement relating to the Implementation of Part XI of the Convention was adopted on 29 July 1994. This enabled the Law of the Sea Convention 1982 to enter into force on 16 November 1994. According to Art 311(1) of the Convention, in respect of those state parties to it, the Convention will prevail over the four 1958 Conventions.

Thus, the state of the law of the sea can be summarised as follows. All states are governed by the relevant rules of customary international law which in many cases have been repeated in the provisions of the Law of the Sea Convention (1982). Secondly, the Law of the Sea Convention has had the effect of creating new rules of customary international law. Thirdly, those states that have ratified the Law of the Sea Convention (1982) are bound by its terms. However, as some states have not adhered to the 1982 Convention such states may be bound by the terms of the 1958 Conventions. One of the objectives of the Law of the Sea Convention (1982) was that it should be comprehensive and universal and the position can be contrasted with the law on human rights where there has been tendency for the law to develop on a regional basis.

2 INTERNAL WATERS[22]

Internal waters are those waters not part of any maritime zone nor part of the high seas. More specifically they are defined in Art 5(1) of the 1958 Convention on the Territorial Sea and the Contiguous Zone where it is stated that 'waters on the landward side of the baseline of the territorial sea form part of the internal waters of the State'. This definition is for the most part repeated in Art 8(1) of the 1982 Convention on the Law of the Sea. The waters form part of the territory of the coastal state and are distinguishable from the territorial sea because of the absence of any right of innocent passage. The sovereignty of the coastal state over internal waters is expressly stated in both international conventions.[23]

---

21   Israel, Turkey, the United States and Venezuela voted against; the Federal Republic of Germany and the United Kingdom.

22   See generally, AH Charteris, 'The legal position of merchantmen in foreign ports and national waters' (1920) 1 BYIL 45-96; R Laun, 'Le régime international des ports' (1926) 15 HR 1; P Jessup, The Law of Territorial Waters and Maritime Jurisdiction, 1927; L Caflisch, 'Règles générales du droit des cours d'eau internationaux' (1989) 219 HR 9–226.

23   Articles 1 and 2 of 1958 Convention; Art 2 of the UN Convention on the Law of the Sea (1982) (LOSC).

Thus, it is accepted that a state may exercise jurisdiction over acts taking place on vessels within its internal waters[24] even though the Flag state of the vessel may exercise a concurrent jurisdiction. In general the coastal state will not interfere with the exercise of disciplinary powers by a captain over his crew.

This concurrent jurisdiction is illustrated by *R v Anderson*,[25] where the Court of Crown Cases Reserved ruled that English courts had jurisdiction to try an American citizen in respect of manslaughter committed on a British vessel in French internal waters even though jurisdiction could also have been claimed by France or the United States. Similarly, in the case of *United States v Wildenhus*,[26] the United States Supreme Court upheld the right of a United States court to try a Belgian citizen for the murder of a fellow Belgian crew member on a Belgian merchant vessel when it was docked at the port of Jersey City, New Jersey. In giving judgment, Waite CJ alluded to the practice that disorders that affect only the ship may be dealt with by the Flag state but disorders that affect the public peace may be dealt with by the coastal state. The fact that agreements may be made to share responsibilities does not affect the reality of concurrent jurisdiction.

In cases of foreign warships the position is different; the warship is regarded as an extension of the sovereign Flag state.[27] The theory is that by allowing the foreign warship to enter its port, the coastal state impliedly indicates not to exercise that jurisdiction in relation to matters which occur on that vessel.[28] Members of the crew of a foreign warships may be tried by the courts of the Flag state for crimes committed on the warship while the warship was in the territorial sea. It would seem that members of the crew of a foreign warship are immune from prosecution by the coastal state for crimes committed on board the ship and for crimes committed on shore if they were in uniform and on official business. However, the Flag state may waive its immunity. In such circumstances, the permission of the captain or the sovereign state will be required; such permission is normally accorded by the formal waiver of immunity.[29] So that in *Chung Chi Cheung v The King*,[30] the Privy Council upheld the jurisdiction of the Supreme Court of Hong Kong to try a British subject for a murder committed on a Chinese customs carrier in the territorial waters of Hong Kong; in this particular case, there was no express waiver by the Flag state but it was held that such a waiver could be implied by participation in the proceedings.

---

24 AH Charteris, 'The legal position of merchantmen in foreign ports and national waters' (1920) 1 BYIL 45.

25 *R v Anderson* (1868) 1 Cox CC 198 (Bovill CJ, Byles and Lush JJ, Channel B) (the defendant had been found guilty at the Central Criminal Court in respect of an offence committed on the River Garonne in France while the vessel was on its way to Bordeaux).

26 *United States v Wildenhus* (1887) 120 US 1.

27 *Schooner Exchange v McFaddon* (1812) 7 Cranch 116 (*per* Marshall CJ).

28 *Ibid*.

29 *Chung Chi Cheung v The King* [1939] AC 160.

30 *Ibid*.

3 BASELINES[31]

The concept of the baseline is of supreme importance in the law of the sea because it constitutes the point from which the breadth of any particular maritime zone is calculated. At customary international law the baseline was formed by the low water mark around the coast of a state. This principle was reflected in Art 3 of the Geneva Convention on the Territorial Sea and Contiguous Zone (1958) which reads: 'Except where otherwise provided ... the normal baseline for measuring the breadth of the territorial sea is the low water line along the coast as marked on largescale charts officially recognised by the coastal state.' This wording is repeated in Art 5 of the Law of the Sea Convention (1982) and the text of the article appears under the heading 'Normal Baseline'.

In many cases such an approach will be acceptable however some coasts are not straight and are subject to indentation. It is therefore necessary to formulate rules that can provide for different geographical conditions; such rules need to be precise to prevent states engaging in generous interpretation. Where the baseline is drawn will determine the extent of internal waters and states may be tempted to increase the breadth of such waters for defence purposes.

The method of drawing baselines in abnormal geographical circumstances was considered in detail in the *Anglo Norwegian Fisheries* case.[32] In that case a Norwegian enactment of 1935 had set a baseline along almost a thousand miles of coastline. The decree had been foreshadowed in earlier decrees of 1869 and 1889. The Norwegian coast comprises fjords rocks, reefs and islands some of which run parallel to actual coast and this part is known as the *skjaergaard* (a Norwegian word meaning a rock rampart). Rather than drawing the line by reference to the appropriate low water mark of each island and rock the Norwegians had, since the 19th century, drawn a straight baseline linking the outermost points of the *skjaergaard*. Such a method had the effect of widening the area covered within internal waters and the territorial sea thus reducing the area that would otherwise be high seas. However, such a method, unlike the conventional method, did allow the Norwegian territorial sea to be determined with reasonable precision. From the late 1930s, disputes arose with Great Britain as to fishing rights in these waters. In 1949, the United Kingdom brought a case before the International Court of Justice arguing that Norwegian method of drawing baselines was contrary to international law.

In a judgment which has had a considerable influence on the evolution of the law of the sea, the Court ruled that the method of drawing baselines must take proper account of geographical realities. Secondly, it was ruled that the *skjaergaard* was an extension of the mainland thus it was the outer limit of the *skjaergaard* that constituted the dividing line with the sea and as such should be used as the place for drawing the baseline. Thirdly, that the normal method for drawing baselines (*tracé parallèle*) was not appropriate having

---

31 See generally, CHM Waldock, 'The *Anglo Norwegian Fisheries* case' (1951) 28 BYIL 114; J Evenson, 'The *Anglo Norwegian Fisheries* case and its legal consequences' (1953) 47 AJIL 609; DH Johnson, 'The *Anglo Norwegian Fisheries* case (1952) 1 ICLQ 145; G Marston, 'Low tide elevations and straight baselines' (1972–1973) 46 BYIL 405.

32 *Anglo Norwegian Fisheries* case (1951) ICJ 116. See CHM Waldock, 'The *Anglo Norwegian Fisheries* case' (1951) 28 BYIL 114; J Evenson, 'The *Anglo Norwegian Fisheries* case and its legal consequences' (1952) 46 AJIL 609; G Marston, 'Low tide elevations and straight baselines' (1972) 46 BYIL 405.

regard to the indentations of the coast. Fourthly, that the straight baseline method founded upon geometric conceptions was appropriate in the circumstances. Fifthly, that on the facts of the case the straight baseline method had been adopted by Norway over many years and had been acquiesced in by other states.

The effect of the judgment in the *Anglo Norwegian Fisheries* case was to endorse the straight baseline system as a valid method of drawing baselines. However, to ensure a degree of uniformity of state conduct the court set out a number of principles. First, it was asserted that the drawing of baselines was not a matter for the discretion of the individual state. Secondly, that such baselines must 'not depart to any appreciable extent from the general direction of the coast'.[33] Thirdly, the baselines must be drawn so that any waters lying within them are sufficiently connected to the land to be subject to a regime of internal waters. Fourthly, in the actual drawing of the lines it may be appropriate to consider 'certain economic interests peculiar to a region, the reality and importance of which are clearly evidenced by a long usage'.[34]

The judgment in the *Anglo Norwegian Fisheries* case was viewed at the time as an instance of judicial law making but the general principles were soon adopted as part of international law. Thus, Art 4 of the Geneva Convention on the Territorial Sea (1958) recognised and adopted the principles set out by the International Court of Justice and went further by stressing that the straight baseline method was a distinct method rather than a permissible departure from the low watermark system.[35] Article 4 of the Geneva Convention provides:

(1) In localities where the coastline is deeply indented and cut into, or if there is a fringe of islands along the coast in its immediate vicinity, the method of straight baselines joining appropriate points may be employed in drawing the baseline from which the breadth of the territorial sea is measured.

(2) The drawing of such baselines must not depart to any appreciable extent from the general direction of the coast.

(3) Baselines shall not be drawn to and from low tide elevations, unless lighthouses or similar installations which are permanently above sea level have been built on them.

(4) Where the method of straight baselines is applicable under the provisions of paragraph 1, account may be taken, in determining particular baselines, of economic interests peculiar to the region concerned, the reality and the importance of which are clearly evidenced by long usage.

The same approach is taken in Art 7 of the Law of the Sea Convention which reads as follows:

(1) In localities where the coastline is deeply indented and cut into, or if there is a fringe of islands along the coast in its immediate vicinity, the method of drawing straight baselines joining appropriate points may be employed in drawing the baseline from which the breadth of the territorial sea is measured.

---

33 (1951) ICJ 116, p 133; (1951) 18 ILR 86, p 95.

34 *Ibid*, p 133; p 95.

35 So much so that the United Kingdom (which had finished on the losing side in the *Fisheries* case) has employed the straight baselines system off the west coast of Scotland.

(2) Where because of the presence of a delta and other natural conditions the coastline is highly unstable, the appropriate points may be selected along the furthest seaward extent of the low water line and, notwithstanding subsequent regression of the low water line, the straight baselines shall remain effective until changed by the coastal State in accordance with the Convention.

(3) The drawing of straight baselines must not depart to any appreciable extent from the general direction of the coast, and the sea areas lying within the lines must be sufficiently closely linked to the land domain to be subject to the regime of internal waters.

(4) Straight baselines shall not be drawn to and from low tide elevations, unless lighthouses or similar installations which are permanently above sea level have been built on them or except in instances where the drawing of baselines to and from such elevations has received general international recognition.

(5) Where the method of straight baselines is applicable under paragraph 1, account may be taken, in determining particular baselines, of economic interests peculiar to the region concerned, the reality and the importance of which are clearly evidenced by long usage.

(6) The system of straight baselines may not be applied by a State in such a manner as to cut off the territorial sea of another State from the high seas or an exclusive economic zone.

Where the result of adopting the straight baseline system is to enclose as internal waters areas which had not previously considered as such a right of innocent passage shall be deemed to exist under the terms of Art 5(2) of the 1958 Convention and Art 8(2) of the 1982 Convention.

4 ISLANDS[36]

In respect of islands the normal principles set out above apply. An island is defined by Art 121(1) of the 1982 Convention as 'a naturally formed area of land, surrounded by water, which is above water at high tide',[37] and such an island will have a maritime belt.[38] The definition makes it clear that where land is above the sea at low tide but below at high tide then it will not be an island but it may be employed as basepoint under the straight baselines system if lighthouses or similar installations have been built.[39]

In this context it should be noted that Art 121(3) of the 1982 Convention provides that rocks which cannot sustain human habitation or economic life of shall have no exclusive economic zone or continental shelf of their own. The precise wording here stresses capacity to sustain human habitation rather than actual habitation. Cases of uninhabitable

---

36 CR Symmons, *The Maritime Zones of Islands in International Law*, 1979.
37 Convention on the Territorial Sea (1958), Art 10(1); LOSC (1982), Art 121(1).
38 See *ibid*, Art 10(2); LOSC (1982), Art 121(2).
39 See Art 7(4) of the 1982 Convention. Though this requirement may not always be observed in practice.

rocks have given rise to difficulty and there is reason to believe that Art 121(3) does not restate a rule of customary international law.[40]

5 ARCHIPELAGIC STATES[41]

One of the problems that had been left open in the 1958 Geneva Conventions had been the question of the drawing baselines around archipelagos. There is a natural tendency for an archipelagic state to draw straight baselines around the entire island territory thus enclosing the whole territory. Concern however had arisen prior to 1958 when Indonesia and the Philippines had indicated in 1955 and 1957 respectively that they would enclose their entire territory within straight baselines. Domestic legislation had followed in 1960 and 1961 respectively. After 1958 many archipelagic states in the Indian and Pacific Ocean had become independent so there was a need to produce an agreed scheme. Prior to 1973 many maritime states had opposed any special regime for archipelagic states fearing that such a regime would lead to the expansion of the territorial sea and limitations on rights of shipping. However, archipelagic states[42] advanced their case with considerable force during UNCLOS III and special provision was made in the 1982 Convention.

For the provisions to apply there must be an archipelagic state and this is defined in Art 46 as follows:

(a) 'archipelagic state' means a State constituted wholly by one or more archipelagos and may include other islands;

(b) 'archipelago' means a group of islands, including parts of islands, interconnecting waters and other natural features which are so closely inter-related that such islands, waters and other natural features form an intrinsic geographical, economic and political entity, or which historically has been regarded as such.

The effect of Art 46 is to exclude the mainland state which includes a non-coastal archipelago[43] and it is only the state which comes within Art 46 that will be able to draw baselines under the terms of Art 47. That provision permits the archipelagic state to draw straight archipelagic baselines joining the outermost points of the outermost islands but this privilege is subject to a number of limitations. Such requirements can be best appreciated by the text of Art 47 which reads:

(1) An archipelagic state may draw straight archipelagic baselines joining the outermost points of the outermost islands and drying reefs of the archipelago provided that within

---

40 The United Kingdom had proclaimed a 200 nautical mile fishing zone around Rockall in the Fishery Limits Act 1976, but renounced such a claim in summer 1997 when the new administration acceded to the LOSC (1982). For background, see CR Symmons, 'The Rockall dispute deepens: an analysis of recent Danish and Icelandic actions' (1986) 35 ICLQ 344. See, also, R O'Keefe, 'Palm-fringed benefits, island dependencies in the New Law of the Sea' (1996) 45 ICLQ 408; see *Jan Mayen* (*Denmark v Norway*) case (1993) ICJ 37. For a general review, see C Symmons, *The Maritime Zone of Islands in International Law*, 1979.

41 E Brown, *The International Law of the Sea*, 1994, Chapter 8; R Churchill and V Lowe, *The Law of the Sea*, 3rd edn, 1999, Chapter 6; DP O'Connell, 'Mid-ocean archipelagos in international law' (1971) 45 BYIL 1; CF Amersinghe, 'The problem of archipelagos in the international law of the sea' (1974) 23 ICLQ 539.

42 Such states would now include Antigua, Bahamas, Barbuda, Comoros, Fiji, Phillipines, Indonesia.

43 Ecuador (The Galapagos Islands), Portugal (The Azores).

such baselines are included the main islands and an area in which the ratio of the area of the water to the area of the land, including atolls, is between 1 to 1 and 9 to 1.

(2) The length of such baselines shall not exceed 100 nautical miles, except that up to 3 per cent of the total number of baselines enclosing any archipelago may exceed that length, up to a maximum length of 125 nautical miles.

(3) The drawing of such baselines shall not depart to any appreciable extent from the general configuration of the archipelago.

(4) Such baselines shall not be drawn to and from low tide elevations, unless the lighthouses or similar installations which are permanently above sea level have been built on them or where a low tide elevation is situated wholly or partly at a distance not exceeding the breadth of the territorial sea from the nearest island.

(5) The system of such baselines shall not be applied by an archipelagic state in such a manner as to cut off from the high seas or the exclusive economic zone the territorial sea of another state.

(6) If a part of the archipelagic waters of an archipelagic state lies between two parts of an immediately adjacent neighbouring state, existing rights and all other legitimate interests which the latter state has traditionally exercised in such waters and all rights stipulated by agreement between those states shall continue and be respected.

(7) For the purpose of computing the ratio of water to land under paragraph 1, land areas may include waters lying within the fringing reefs of islands and atolls, including that part of a steep-sided oceanic plateau which is enclosed or nearly enclosed by a chain of limestone islands and drying reefs lying on the perimeter of the plateau.

(8) The baselines drawn in accordance with this article shall be shown on charts of a scale or scales adequate for ascertaining their position. Alternatively, lists of geographic co-ordinates of points, specifying the geodetic datum, may be substituted.

(9) The archipelagic states shall give due publicity to such charts or lists of geographical co-ordinates and shall deposit a copy of each such chart or list with the Secretary General of the United Nations.

The waters within such baselines are archipelagic waters and the state will have sovereignty;[44] closing lines may be drawn within such waters for the purpose of determining internal waters.[45] The baselines drawn for the purpose of determining archipelagic waters are also employed for measuring the territorial sea, contiguous zone and exclusive economic zone.[46] Within archipelagic waters the state is required to respect existing rights, fishing rights and existing submarine cables.[47] It is further provided that ships of all states shall enjoy a right of innocent passage through archipelagic waters;[48]

---

44 LOSC (1982), Art 49; the sovereignty extends to airspace Art 49(2). The point being that archipelagic waters form all the waters within the archipelagic baselines. However, within archipelagic waters a state may draw closing lines to delimit internal waters; the normal rules as to drawing such baselines will apply.

45 *Ibid*, Art 50.

46 *Ibid*, Art 48.

47 *Ibid*, Art 51.

48 *Ibid*, Art 52.

the state may designate sea lanes and air routes suitable for continuous and expeditious passage.[49]

6 BAYS[50]

The bay gave rise to two particular problems in customary international law. The first difficulty was whether an indentation on the coast was wide enough to constitute a bay; the second difficulty was whether a straight baseline could be drawn across the mouth of the bay. In respect of the first point, the Permanent Court of Arbitration admitted in the *North Atlantic Coast Fisheries* case[51] that there was no agreed position as to the legal criteria for the existence of a bay. In respect of the second question, the position in customary international law was far from clear[52] for while it was accepted that a straight baseline might be drawn across the mouth of the bay there was no agreement as whether this was prohibited beyond a certain point. It was argued in the *Anglo Norwegian Fisheries* case that a straight baseline could be drawn up to a width of 10 nautical miles but such a contention was not accepted by the court. [53]

These two questions were clarified by Art 7 of the 1958 Geneva Convention on the Territorial Sea and Contiguous Zone. Article 7(2) defines the 'bay' in the following terms:

> For the purpose of these Articles, a bay is a well-marked indentation whose penetration is in such proportion to the width of its mouth as to contain landlocked waters and constitute more than a mere curvature of the coast. An indentation shall not, however be regarded as a bay unless its area is as large as, or larger than, that of the semicircle whose diameter is a line drawn across the mouth of that indentation.

This definition is repeated in Art 10(2) of the 1982 Law of the Sea Convention. In respect of the second question, namely, the drawing of a straight baseline across the mouth of the bay, Art 7(4) of the 1958 Convention provides as follows:

> If the distance between the low water marks of the natural entrance points of a bay exceeds twenty four miles, a closing line may be drawn between these two low water marks, and the waters enclosed thereby shall be considered as internal waters.

This provision is repeated in Art 10(2) of the 1982 Law of the Sea Convention and provides a workable method of distinguishing a bay from a mere indentation.

However, the provisions of Art 7 of the 1958 Convention and Art 10 of the 1982 Convention do not apply to historic bays and these deserve separate consideration.[54]

Neither the 1958 Convention nor the 1982 Convention contain any specific reference to historic bays so the position has to be determined under customary international law.[55]

---

49   *Ibid*, Art 53.
50   See G Westerman, *The Juridical Bay*, 1987.
51   *North Atlantic Fisheries* case (1910) 11 RIAA 167.
52   See *North Atlantic Coast Fisheries* case (1910) 11 RIAA 167; *Anglo Norwegian Fisheries* case (1951) ICJ 116.
53   See (1951) ICJ 116, p 131.
54   See exclusions in Art 7(6) and Art 10(6).
55   See *Tunisia/Libya Continental Shelf* case (1982) ICJ 18; *Land, Island and Maritime Frontier* case (1992) ICJ 351; 97 ILR 266.

A historic bay is a bay whose waters are regarded as internal by the coastal state on the basis of a historic entitlement that has been accepted or acquiesced in by other states. Most such historic bays will be wider than the bays covered under Art 7 of the 1958 Convention or Art 10 of the 1982 Convention because otherwise a state will simply claim the rights arising under those provisions. A number of historic bays exist, of which the Hudson Bay in Canada is probably the best known, although in some cases the status as a historic bay may be a matter of dispute.[56]

The criteria for the existence of an historic bay have been examined on a number of occasions by the United States Supreme Court and it would seem that the criteria are: (i) the actual exercise of sovereignty over the bay for a considerable period of time; (ii) that such an exercise of sovereignty must have been open, effective and continuous; (iii) during the period the exercise of sovereignty must have been acquiesced in by other states; (iv) there should be evidence of the exclusion of foreign vessels and control of rights of navigation.[57] These requirements were impliedly accepted by the International Court of Justice in the *Land, Island and Maritime Frontier* case.[58]

In recent years, one of the most controversial episodes has been the claim by Libya that the Gulf of Sidra (Sirte) should enjoy the status of an historic bay. This claim was articulated in 1973 and a closing line drawn across the 296 miles; such conduct resulted in international protests and the United States sent naval forces into the Gulf. In the last two decades, there have been a number of incidents and the evidence in favour of Libya's claim has not been exposed to independent scrutiny.[59] The claim must be regarded as very doubtful.

A further difficulty in the context of bays is the position of the bay bordered by more than one state (sometimes referred to as the pluri-state bay). Such bays are not expressly provided for under the terms of the Geneva Convention on the Territorial Sea (1958) or the 1982 Law of the Sea Convention.[60] However, the position has been subject to judicial consideration in the case of the Gulf of Fonseca bordered by Honduras, Nicaragua and El Salvador. In 1917, the then Central American Court of Justice[61] considered that the Gulf was an historic bay and thus constituted internal waters; the Court ruled that save in respect of the three miles of territorial waters the bay was subject to the common ownership of the riparian states. In 1992, in the *Land, Island and Maritime Frontier* case[62] the International Court of Justice reached broadly the same conclusion save that it

---

56 Russia claims the Peter the Great Bay; Vietnam claims part of the Gulf of Thailand and the the Gulf of Tonkin; Thailand claims part of the Gulf of Thailand. Not all these claims to historic bays have been accepted.

57 For case law in the United States Supreme Court, see *United States v California* (1965) 381 US 139; *United States v Louisiana (Louisiana Boundary)* case (1969) 394 US 11; *United States v Alaska* (1975) 422 US 184; *United States v Louisiana* (1985) 470 US 93; *United States v Maine* (1985) 471 US 375.

58 (1992) ICJ 351.

59 See F Francioni, 'The Gulf of Sidra incident and international law' (1980) 5 Italian Yearbook of International Law 85.

60 Eg, Passamaquoddy Bay (Canada-United States).

61 *El Salvador v Nicaragua* (1917) 11 AJIL 674.

62 (1992) ICJ 351; 97 ILR 266 (of interest is the dissenting opinion of Judge Oda who argued that a multistate bay could not be a historic bay). There is little doubt that the International Court of Justice was influenced by the prior judicial decision of 1917. See MN Shaw, '*Case concerning the Land, Island and Maritime Frontier Dispute*' (1993) 42 ICLQ 929; A Gioia, 'The law of multinational bays and the case of the *Gulf of Fonseca*' (1993) NYIL 81.

expressly stated that there was a right of innocent passage for each state for purposes of access.

7 THE TERRITORIAL SEA[63]

As indicated above, it has been accepted for over 300 years that a state was entitled to claim a maritime belt adjacent to its coast. There is little doubt that this entitlement was linked to questions of defence. It would seem that the distinction between the coastal belt and the high seas was accepted by the time Bynkershoek published his *De Dominio Maris Dissertatio* in 1702. In this work, the author indicated the distinction between the freedom of the high seas and the rights that a coastal state might enjoy over the waters adjacent to its coast. However, while it was clear that a coastal belt might be claimed there was little agreement as to the width of such a belt. Great Britain and, later, the United States claimed three nautical miles[64] but greater claims were made by others and it could not be said, in the 18th and 19th century, that there was any uniformity as to the width. The United States adopted the three mile principle when Thomas Jefferson declared a three mile zone of neutrality adjacent to the United States coast at the outbreak of war between Great Britain and France in 1793.

Secondly, there was no agreement as to the precise rights enjoyed over the coastal belt; a division of opinion existed as to whether such rights should be described as 'sovereignty' 'jurisdiction' or some other form of policing right. In the United Kingdom, the matter was considered extensively in the *Franconia* case[65] in the later part of the 19th century. In that case the facts were as follows.

A German Keyn was the captain of a vessel the *Franconia* which was in collision with a British vessel the *Strathclyde* two and a half nautical miles from Dover. The collision resulted in considerable loss of life and Keyn was prosecuted and convicted at the Central Criminal Court. He sought to set aside the conviction on the basis of absence of jurisdiction. By 7:6 the Court of Crown Cases Reserved agreed to set aside the conviction.

Although the judgments contained a number of different opinions, a common theme was that while Great Britain might be able to claim a territorial sea of three nautical miles it could not exercise criminal jurisdiction unless the right to do so had been expressly asserted in legislation. The judgment itself came as something of a surprise and the

---

63 PT Fenn, 'Origins of the theory of territorial waters' (1926) 465; DP O'Connell, 'The juridical status of the territorial sea' (1971) 45 BYIL 303; HS Kent, 'Historical origins of the three mile limit' (1954) 48 AJIL 537.

64 Eg, Lord Stowell in *The Anna* (1805) 5 Ch Rob 573; 165 ER 809. There was a tendency in the 18th century for Scandinavian counties to claim a breadth of four nautical miles. The background is discussed in HS Kent, 'The historical origins of the three mile limit' (1954) 48 AJIL 537.

65 *R v Keyn (The Franconia)* (1876) 2 Ex D 63.

passing of the Territorial Waters Jurisdiction Act 1878[66] served to restore English law to the position that had been thought to pertain prior to the *Franconia* case. In the period before 1914, a number of states were prepared to accept the principle of the three mile limit.[67]

After the First World War, a wide variety of state practice could be seen to exist. In 1930 no agreement was possible on the breadth of the territorial sea at the Hague Conference and the only measure of accord was the recognition that there was no general rule as to a three mile limit. The making of the Truman Declaration in 1945, and the emerging concept of the continental shelf, had the consequence that many states were prompted to make wider claims to a territorial sea.[68] In these circumstances, it was not surprising that no agreement on the width of the territorial sea could be reached at the 1958 Geneva Conference. Two years later at UNCLOS II (1960), a proposal to fix the territorial sea at six miles and to stipulate a fishery zone of a further six miles failed to win sufficient support. The general trend since 1945 had been for coastal states to seek wider maritime zones and as part of the compromise package at UNCLOS III (1974–82) the width of the territorial sea was fixed at 12 nautical miles; this rule being expressly stated in Art 3 of the Law of the Sea Convention (1982). Many states had been moving in that direction already including the traditional maritime nations such as the United States and the United Kingdom. In the case of the United Kingdom, a territorial sea of 12 nautical miles was adopted in the Territorial Sea Act 1987 and the United States followed shortly after.[69]

Although a number of theories had been advanced as to the juridical nature of rights over the territorial sea the matter was clarified by Arts 1 and 2 of the 1958 Geneva Convention which read:

Article 1

(1) The sovereignty of a State extends, beyond its land territory and its internal waters, to a belt of sea adjacent to its coast, described as the territorial sea.

(2) This sovereignty is exercised subject to the provisions of these Articles and to other rules of international law.

Article 2

The sovereignty of a coastal State extends to the air space over the territorial sea as well as to its bed and subsoil.

Since the juridical nature is that of sovereignty, the coastal state is entitled to take measures to control fishing, provide for defence and enforce customs regulations.

---

66 It is interesting to note the terms of the preamble of the Territorial Waters Jurisdiction Act 1878. The draftsman begins with the phrase: 'Whereas the rightful jurisdiction of Her Majesty, her heirs and successors, extends and has always extended over the open seas adjacent to the coasts of the United Kingdom and of all other parts of Her Majesty's dominions to such a distance as is necessary for the defence and security of such dominions ...' That no fundamental change was intended is indicated by the purpose of the legislation which is stated as being: 'An Act to regulate the Law relating to the Trial of Offences committed on the Sea within a certain distance as is necessary for the defence and security of such dominions.'

67 Argentina (1871); Brazil (1859); Chile (1855); Japan (1870); Mexico (1902); Netherlands (1889).

68 On this see LDM Nelson, 'The patrimonial sea' (1973) 22 ICLQ 668.

69 Presidential Proclamation No 5928 (President Reagan), December 1988.

However, the extent to which this is done will depend partly on the municipal legislation of the coastal state and its resources to enforce such regulations.

In customary international law, it was accepted that foreign merchant ships had a right of innocent passage through the territorial sea. This, of course, raised the difficult question as to when passage is 'innocent'. This concept is expanded in Art 14 of the Geneva Convention on the Territorial Sea (1958). Article 14(1) restates the entitlement to a right of innocent passage and this is then amplified in Art 14(2), 14(3) and 14(4) which read as follows:

> (2) Passage means navigation through the territorial sea for the purpose either of traversing that sea without entering internal waters, or of proceeding to internal waters, or of making for the high seas from internal waters.

> (3) Passage includes stopping and anchoring but only in so far as the same are incidental to ordinary navigation or are rendered necessary by force majeure or by distress.

> (4) Passage is innocent so long as it is not prejudicial to the peace, good order or security of the coastal State. Such passage shall take place in conformity with these Articles and with other rules of international law.

If the right of innocent passage is not being exercised, then the coastal state may take appropriate steps to intervene; the coastal state is not required to regard passage as innocent if there is an attempt to flout municipal rules applying to fishing.[70] In the case of submarines, vessels are required to navigate on the surface and show their flag.[71] The concept of innocent passage was developed in the 1982 Convention. Article 19 seeks to define the concept further by listing a number of prohibited acts. The wording of Art 19(2) indicates that certain Acts are *prima facie* not innocent. The detailed provision reads:

> Passage of a foreign ship shall be considered to be prejudicial to the peace, good order or security of the coastal State if in the territorial sea it engages in any of the following activities:

> (a) any threat or use of force against the sovereignty, territorial integrity or political independence of the coastal State, or in any other manner in violation of the principles of international law embodied in the Charter of the United Nations;

> (b) any exercise or practice with weapons of any kind;

> (c) any act aimed at collecting information to the prejudice of the defence or security of the coastal State;

> (d) any act of propaganda aimed at affecting the defence or security of the coastal State;

> (e) the launching, landing or taking on board of any aircraft;

> (f) the launching, landing or taking on board of any military device;

> (g) the loading or unloading of any commodity, currency or person contrary to the customs, fiscal, immigration or sanitary laws and regulations of the coastal State;

> (h) any act of wilful and serious pollution contrary to this Convention;

> (i) any fishing activities;

---

70   Convention on the Territorial Sea (1958), Art 14(5).
71   *Ibid*, Art 14(6).

(j)   the carrying out of research or survey activities;

(k)   any act aimed at interfering with any systems of communication or any other facilities or installations of the coastal State;

(l)   any other activity not having a direct bearing on passage.

Alongside these list of prohibited acts the 1982 Convention provides that the coastal state shall not hamper the exercise of innocent passage by the imposition of discriminatory conditions.[72]

One of the most difficult problems today is to ensure that naval passage close to a coast is subject to supervision to reduce the risk of collision. Thus Art 17 of the Geneva Convention (1958) requires those exercising the right to comply with the regulations of the coastal state. This is built on in Art 21(1) of the 1982 Convention which stipulates that those exercising the right of innocent passage should respect the rules of the coastal state concerning:

(a)   the safety of navigation and the regulation of maritime traffic;

(b)   the protection of navigational aids and facilities and other facilities or installations;

(c)   the protection of cables and pipelines;

(d)   the conservation of the living resources of the sea;

(e)   the prevention of infringement of the fisheries laws and regulations of the coastal State;

(f)   the preservation of the environment of the coastal State and the prevention, reduction and control of pollution thereof;

(g)   marine scientific research and hydrographic surveys;

(h)   the prevention of infringement of the customs, fiscal, immigration or sanitary laws and regulations of the coastal State.

This provision has to be read with Art 22 which permits a coastal state to establish designated sea lanes and traffic separation schemes and particular types of vessel may be required to stay within the designated lanes.[73]

It is accepted that a coastal state may take measures to deny or suspend the right of innocent passage.[74] However, a more difficult question is whether the right of innocent passage extends to foreign warships. It has to be admitted that there has been movement on this question in the 20th century and this is not unconnected with the emergence of the United States as a major naval power after 1919. In the *North Atlantic Coast Fisheries Arbitration* case,[75] Elihu Root appearing for the United States appeared to think that the right did not extend to foreign warships. By the Hague Conference of 1930 the view

---

72   LOSC (1982), Art 24.

73   *Ibid*, Art 22(2).

74   Territorial Sea Convention (1958), Art 16(1); LOSC (1982), Art 25(1).

75   *North Atlantic Coast Fisheries Arbitration* case (1910) 11 RIAA 167; the views of Elihu Root (1845–1937) were of some interest not only because he was regarded as one of the most distinguished lawyers of his time but because he had served as Secretary of State (1904–09). He would go on to play a role in drafting the Statute of the Permanent Court of International Justice in 1919.

appeared to be that the right was contingent on prior notification and authorisation. It is arguable that the *Corfu Channel* case[76] being concerned with passage through straits did not progress the matter much further. Thus in 1958 the division of opinion continued to exist. The preparatory materials to the 1958 Convention reflect this division of opinion and the final text is headed 'Section 3: Right of Innocent Passage; Rules applicable to all ships'. It is arguable that Art 14 extends the right of innocent passage to warships if only because Art 14(6) makes specific provision in respect of submarines.[77] The same considerations apply to Arts 17 and 20 of the 1982 Law of the Sea Convention (1982) which as a matter of interpretation appear to extend the right of innocent passage to foreign warships.

This has not been accepted by all coastal states and some have formally demanded prior authorisation, The position has been clarified because in the period of rapprochement between the United States and the Soviet Union an agreement has been reached on this question. In September 1989, the Soviet Union and the United States indicated that they had reached a bilateral understanding on the Uniform Interpretation of Norms of International Law Governing Innocent Passage. This document begins by asserting that the relevant rules are set out in the 1982 Law of the Sea Convention and then declares that:

> All ships, including warships regardless of cargo, armament or means of propulsion, enjoy the right of innocent passage through the territorial sea in accordance with international law, for which neither prior notification nor authorisation is required.[78]

This understanding was of some significance because the United States and the Soviet Union were at that time the two major naval powers in the world. Second in the period of the Cold War there had been much concern particularly in Scandinavian countries in respect of submarines entering territorial waters below the surface.

A reading of the relevant provisions in the 1982 Convention indicates that passage will be innocent provided it does not fall within the matters set out under Art 19(2). Such passage is also conditional upon the vessel complying with the regulations of the coastal state as to safety as provided for in Arts 21, 22, 23 and 25.

A further problem that arises is as to the enforcement jurisdiction of the coastal state. Can the coastal state exercise criminal jurisdiction in respect of a vessel passing through the territorial sea? At the 1930 Hague Conference, draft articles had been prepared to the effect that the coastal state should not exercise criminal jurisdiction in respect of vessels passing through save where the peace of the coastal state was threatened or where the Flag state had requested the intervention of the coastal state. The spirit of this principle formed the basis of Art 19(1) of the 1958 Territorial Sea Convention and these provisions have now been re-stated in Art 27 of the 1982 Law of the Sea Convention (1982). The provision stipulates that criminal jurisdiction is not to be exercised in respect of a foreign vessel passing through save:

(a) if the consequences of the crime extend to the coastal State;

---

76 *Corfu Channel (The Merits)* (1949) ICJ 4.
77 At the time of drafting and indeed today all submarines are warships so that Art 14(6) only makes sense if Art 14(1) extends to warships.
78 (1989) 24 ILM 1444.

(b) if the crime is of a kind likely to disturb the peace of the country or the good order of the territorial sea;

(c) if the assistance of the local authorities has been requested by the master of the ship or by a diplomatic agent or consular officer of the Flag State; or

(d) if such measures are necessary for the suppression of illicit traffic in narcotic drugs or psychotropic substances.

These limitations on criminal jurisdiction do not apply in respect of a vessel passing through the territorial sea after it has left internal waters.[79] Officials of the coastal state cannot act if the offence was committed prior to entering the territorial sea provided that the vessel does not enter or has not entered internal waters.[80]

Article 28 of the Law of the Sea Convention (1982) provides that the coastal state should not stop or divert a ship entering territorial waters for the purposes of the enforcement of civil jurisdiction.[81] This limitation does not apply in respect of those vessels lying in the territorial waters or passing through the territorial waters after being in internal waters.[82]

However, warships and Government ships operated for non-commercial purposes are not subject to the enforcement jurisdiction of the coastal state because they are entitled to immunity in customary international law. This was provided for in Art 22(2) of the Territorial Seas Convention (1958) and the provisions have been amplified in Arts 29–32 of the Law of the Sea Convention (1982). However, the claim is to immunity from jurisdiction so the vessel is *prima facie* subject to the legislative provisions of the coastal state and failure to comply may result in a request to leave the territorial sea.[83]

8 INTERNATIONAL STRAITS[84]

Although the term 'strait' is not defined anywhere in the United Nations Law of the Sea Convention (1982) the general concept is well known. A strait is a narrow natural passage of water connecting two larger passages of water.[85] The importance of international straits has been recognised since the 18th century; it was Vattel who pointed out that the freedom of the high seas could be rendered meaningless if a coastal state could close an international strait without good reason. Prior to 1958, the matter was governed by customary international law and everything depended on the nature of the strait. If the waters were part of the high seas then foreign ships in passing through the straits were simply exercising the general freedom of the high seas; if however the straits comprised

79   LOSC (1982), Art 27(2).

80   *Ibid*, Art 27(5).

81   *Ibid*, Art 28(1).

82   *Ibid*, Art 28(3).

83   Territorial Seas Convention (1958), Art 23; *ibid*, Art 30.

84   H Caminos, 'The legal regime of Straits in the 1982 United Nations Convention on the Law of the Sea' (1987) 205 HR 9-246.

85   R Churchill and AV Lowe, *The Law of the Sea*, 3rd edn, 1999, Chapter 5.

territorial waters then the foreign vessel was simply exercising the right of innocent passage.

The nature of international straits was considered in the *Corfu Channel* case[86] arising between the United Kingdom and Albania. In that case, British warships passing through the Corfu Channel were fired on by Albanian guns. Some months later a force of cruisers and destroyers sailed through the strait and a number of vessels were damaged after coming into contact with mines. Three weeks later British naval forces swept the entire channel of mines When the matter came before the International Court of Justice[87] the Court emphasised the particular nature of straits, observing:

> ... that states in time of peace have a right to send their warships through straits used for international navigation between two parts of the high seas without the previous authorisation of a coastal state, provided the passage is innocent.[88]

In giving judgment the court accepted that the nature of a strait was to be inferred from the geographical characteristics of the waterway and not from the actual volume of traffic or the availability of alternative routes. The principle that derived from the majority judgment in the Corfu Channel case was that under customary international law foreign warships had a right of passage through international straits which could not be suspended by the coastal state.

The position in customary international law was reinforced by Art 16(4) of the 1958 Geneva Convention on the Territorial Sea which reads:

> ... there shall be no suspension of the innocent passage of foreign ships through straits which are used for international navigation between one part of the high sea and another part of the high seas or the territorial sea of a foreign state.

In the years after 1958 there had been a tendency for coastal states to claim a wider territorial sea; this had the consequence that many straits would now comprise territorial seas rather than high seas. At the same time, some of the major maritime nations were concerned about the extensive claims of coastal states and were not prepared to concede such claims unless new provisions were introduced clarifying the position in respect of international straits. Thus, the Law of the Sea Convention (1982) introduced a new regime in respect of straits and this is contained in Arts 34–45. Article 34 provides that any right of passage through an international strait shall not affect the legal status of the waters. Article 37 identifies and singles out for special treatment those straits which link one part of the high seas or part of an exclusive economic zone to another part of the high seas or exclusive economic zone, so that there will be a number of straits not caught by the definition.[89] By Art 38 it is provided that there shall be a right of transit passage in respect of ships and aircraft; transit passage means the exercise of freedom of navigation and overflight for the purpose of continuous and expeditious transit of the strait. However, it

---

86 *Corfu Channel (Merits)* (1949) ICJ 4.

87 *Ibid.*

88 (1949) ICJ 4, p 28; 16 ILR 155, p 161

89 In broad terms, those excluded would be: (i) where there is a high seas route (Art 36); or (ii) where the strait is formed by the island of a state bordering the strait and its mainland and there exists seaward of the island a high seas route (Art 38(1)) (eg, the straits of Messina); and (iii) the straits connect an area of the high seas or exclusive economic zone to the territorial sea of another state (LOSC, Art 45).

is further stipulated that ships and aircraft exercising the right of transit passage shall observe all relevant international regulations. It is further provided that states bordering the strait should not hamper the right of transit.[90] By Art 45 it is stipulated that there shall be a right of innocent passage in respect of those straits excluded from the right of transit passage by Art 38(1) or by Art 45(1)(b).

However, some international straits have because of their importance been subject to detailed international regulation. Thus, Art 35(c) provides that such legal regimes are not to be affected by the right of transit created under the Law of the Sea Convention. Thus, the Treaty of Lausanne (1923) acknowledges the 'principle of freedom of transit and navigation' in the Dardanelles and the Bosphorous and this principle is restated in the 1936 Montreux Convention. In like terms, the 1979 Treaty of Peace between Israel and Egypt provides for 'unimpeded and non-suspendable freedom of navigation and overflight' through the Strait of Tiran and the Gulf of Aqaba.[91]

A question of some difficulty is whether there is a right of transit passage arising under customary international law. The difficulty is that many states were not prepared to concede a right of non-suspendable innocent passage and in the period prior to 1958,[92] when claims as to territorial sea were much narrower there would normally be a high seas corridor down the middle of the international strait. With the broadening of the maritime zones the circumstances prevailing in 1958 were very different and the relevant question is whether practice since 1982 is some evidence of a subsequently created rule of international law in favour of transit passage.

One approach has simply been to make new declarations. In 1987, when the United Kingdom extended the territorial sea to 12 nautical miles, this had the effect of removing the high seas corridor in the Straits of Dover. In November 1988, the United Kingdom and France issued a joint declaration by which both governments indicated their intention to:

> ... recognise the rights of unimpeded transit passage for merchant vessels, State vessels and, in particular warships following their normal mode of navigation, as well as the right of overflight for aircraft, in the Straits of Dover. It is understood that, in accordance with the principles governing this regime under the rules of international law, such passage will be exercised in a continuous and expeditious manner.[93]

---

90 LOSC (1982), Art 44.

91 On this particular peace treaty, see M Elbareidi, 'The Egyptian-Israeli Peace Treaty and access to the Gulf of Aqaba: a new legal regime' (1982) 76 AJIL 532; R Lapidoth, 'The Strait of Tiran, the Gulf of Aqaba and the 1979 Treaty of Peace between Egypt and Israel' (1983) 77 AJIL 84.

92 Article 16(4) of the 1958 Convention provides for a non-suspendable right of innocent passage.

93 Declaration of the United Kingdom and France issued 2 November 1988, reproduced in E Brown, *The International Law of the Sea*, 1994, Vol II, p 94.

9 THE CONTIGUOUS ZONE[94]

The contiguous zone may be defined as a 'zone of sea contiguous to and seaward of the territorial sea'[95] in which the coastal state may seek to enforce immigration, customs sanitary and fiscal laws. The concept appears to have originated in the 18th century when, after 1736, Great Britain passed a series of Hovering Acts which provided that customs control might be exercised beyond the three mile territorial sea; the principal object was to ensure some control over smugglers who remained outside the three mile territorial limit. The concept is in essence a compromise between the need of the coastal state to exercise control beyond the narrow belt of the territorial sea while at the same time respecting the traditional doctrine of the freedom of the high seas. Early in the 19th century, such legislation had been defended as a matter of convenience,[96] but difficulties began to arise as the legislation was enforced against foreign vessels well beyond the territorial sea. Thus, in 1850 a French smuggler, the *Petit Jules*, was seized by the Revenue 23 miles off the Isle of Wight. The difficulty for the United Kingdom was that it traditionally supported a narrow territorial sea of three nautical miles and in the 19th century was anxious to discourage other states from making more extensive claims. Thus when customs legislation was consolidated in the Customs Consolidation Act 1876 and the original provisions were retained there was less enthusiasm for enforcement against foreign vessels beyond the territorial sea.[97]

At the end of the 19th century Law Officers advised the Foreign Secretary in 1893 that where a British vessel had been seized beyond the three mile limit while seeking to breach the Revenue Laws of another country it had not been the practice to issue a diplomatic protest.[98] However, by the end of the 19th century the United Kingdom adhered to the three mile limit of the territorial sea[99] and was reluctant to go beyond that limit save for questions of defence; it also protested where others sought to go beyond that limit.[100] When states protested that provisions in the Customs Consolidation Act 1876 went beyond the three mile limit the then Foreign Secretary Sir Edward Grey prepared legislation to ensure that the limit of three miles was adhered to.[101] Thus, by

---

94 See R Churchill and AV Lowe, *The Law of the Sea*, 1999, 3rd edn; G Gidel, '*La mer territoriale et la zone contigue*' (1934) 48 HR 241; P Jessup, *The Law of Territorial Waters and Maritime Jurisdiction*, 1927; AV Lowe, 'The development of the concept of the contiguous zone' (1981) 52 BYIL 109; S Oda, 'The concept of the contiguous zone' (1962) 11 ICLQ 131.

95 R Churchill and AV Lowe, *The Law of the Sea*, 1999, 3rd edn.

96 Le Louis (1817) 2 Dods 210; 165 ER 1464 (Lord Stowell).

97 The provisions were re-enacted in ss 53 and 179 of the Customs Consolidation Act 1876. These provisions were repealed by the Customs and Excise Act 1952. However, the essence of s 53 was re-enacted in s 26 of the 1952 Act and then s 35(7) of the Customs and Excise Management Act 1979. However, the provisions re-enacting s 179 indicated an intention not to enforce against foreign vessels beyond the three mile limit, see ss 75 and 76 of the 1952 Act and ss 88 and 89 of the 1979 Act.

98 See Law Officers (Russell, Rigby) to the Earl of Roseberry, 18 March 1893.

99 So that the Foreign Office paid compensation after the judgment in *Mortensen v Peters* 1906 14 SLT 226.

100 Thus, Sir Edward Grey (Foreign Secretary 1905–16) protested in 1911 about Russian legislation before the Duma that sought to claim jurisdiction over four nautical miles.

101 *Ibid*.

1918 the United Kingdom remained a loyal supporter of the three mile limit and no longer enforced statutory provisions at variance with this basic principle.

In the 1920s, difficulties arose when the United States Tariff Act 1922 subjected foreign ships within 12 miles of the coast to United States liquor laws as set out in the Volstead Act 1919; at the same time, other states particularly in Latin America began to make claims that went beyond the narrow three mile limit. So, in *El Salvador v Nicaragua*,[102] the Central American Court of Justice was able to make reference to a zone beyond the territorial sea in which a state might 'exercise the right of imperium for defensive and fiscal purposes'. A wide variety of opinions on the question surfaced at the Hague Conference of 1930 but no agreement could be reached on the recognition of a supervisory zone beyond the limit of the territorial seas. The distinguished French jurist Professor Gidel advanced the theory of the contiguous zone at the conference as a means of reconciling the conflicting practice of states. However, the United Kingdom viewed the notion of a contiguous zone as but a device to extend the territorial sea.[103]

The United Kingdom continued to protest about the exercise of wider claims by other states[104] until the early 1950s but by then it became clear that the various assertions by other states necessitated a reconsideration of opposition to the concept of a contiguous zone.

At the Geneva Conference in 1958 agreement was reached on the concept of the contiguous zone and this was stipulated in Art 24 of the Territorial Sea Convention which provided as follows:

In a zone of the high seas contiguous to its territorial sea, the coastal state may exercise the control necessary to:

(a) prevent infringement of its customs, fiscal, immigration or sanitary regulations within its territory or territorial sea;

(b) prevent infringement of the above regulations committed within its territory or territorial sea.

This provision was reproduced in almost identical form as Art 33(1) of the 1982 Law of the Sea Convention which reads:

In a zone contiguous to its territorial sea, described as the contiguous zone, the coastal State may exercise the control necessary to:

(a) prevent infringement of its customs, fiscal, immigration or sanitary laws and regulations within its territory or territorial sea;

(b) punish infringement of the above laws and regulations committed within its territory or territorial sea.

---

102 *El Salvador v Nicaragua* (1917) 11 AJIL 674; see PC Jessup, *The Law of Territorial Waters and Maritime Jurisdiction*, 1927.

103 Professor Gidel played an important role at the 1930 conference and his views were set out shortly after in '*La mer territoriale et la zone contigue*' (1934) 48 HR 241.

104 For developments in the courts, see *Croft v Dunphy* [1933] AC 156 (where Canadian legislation operating beyond territorial waters was upheld by the Privy Council on the basis that it was analogous to 18th century English legislation); see, also, *Attorney General v Hunter* [1949] 1 All ER 1006 (Morris J) for the operation of the Customs Consolidation Act 1876 beyond territorial waters. See also AV Lowe (1978) 94 LQR 255.

Although the Geneva Conference had not been able to reach agreement on the breadth of the territorial sea, it was stipulated in Art 24(2) of the Territorial Sea Convention (1958) that the contiguous zone should not extend 'beyond 12 miles from the baselines from which the breadth of the territorial sea is measured'. So in the years that followed, it was open to a state to claim a three mile territorial sea and a nine mile contiguous zone or a six mile territorial sea and a six mile contiguous zone. The effect of Art 24(2) was to place an outer limit on both maritime zones. In the period after 1958, the tendency had been to make wider claims in respect of the territorial sea so that at UNCLOS III when the breadth of the territorial sea was fixed at 12 nautical miles (Law of the Sea Convention (1982), Art 3) it was consistent with broadening of the maritime belts to permit a further contiguous zone of 12 nautical miles. Thus Art 33(2) of the Law of the Sea Convention (1982) provides that 'the contiguous zone may not extend beyond twenty four nautical miles'.

It is clear from the wording of Art 24 of the Territorial Sea Convention (1958) and Art 33 of the Law of the Sea Convention (1982) that the jurisdiction of the coastal state is to prevent infringements within its territory or territorial sea; the jurisdiction is not legislative but one of enforcement. Moreover, under the 1958 Convention the contiguous zone was part of the high seas, but under the 1982 Convention the contiguous zone will be part of the exclusive economic zone.[105]

10 THE EXCLUSIVE ECONOMIC ZONE[106]

The exclusive economic zone is a product of a number of factors arising in the past half century. First, there has been a movement to larger maritime belts after the Truman Declaration of 1945. Some states went so far as to claim a territorial sea of up to 200 nautical miles.[107] Secondly, there had been a greater emphasis on larger fishing zones after 1945. Thirdly, the state of the present law owes much to pressure from newly independent states in the period of the negotiations culminating in the Law of the Sea Convention (1982). The tendency in Latin America had been for coastal states to make sovereignty claims up to a distance of 200 miles. Thus, the state of the present law is to some extent a compromise between those seeking full sovereignty up to a distance of 200 nautical miles and those anxious to limit the power of the coastal state. The concept is also linked to developments in the law of the continental shelf.

One of the major problems in the law of the sea has been the increasing emphasis on fishing zones; the *Anglo Norwegian Fisheries* case[108] was an early post-war example of a case prompted by differences of opinion as to fishery zones. In 1958, the United Kingdom formally objected to a claim by Iceland to a 12 mile fishery zone (EFZ). In the same year,

---

105 Article 55 of the LOSC (1982) reads: 'The exclusive economic zone is an area beyond and adjacent to the territorial sea.'

106 D Attard, *The Exclusive Economic Zone in International Law*, 1987; R Churchill and AV Lowe, *The Law of the Sea*, 3rd edn, 1999, Chapter 9.

107 See Chile (1947); Peru (1947); Costa Rica (1948). The distance of 200 miles had been selected as the outer limit of the Humboldt Current. See LD Nelson, 'The patrimonial sea' (1974) 22 ICLQ 668.

108 *Anglo Norwegian Fisheries* case (1951) ICJ 116; (1951) 18 ILR 86.

the Geneva Conference on the law of the sea was unable to reach agreement on fishery zones and the provisions on the contiguous zone contained in Art 24 of the Geneva Convention on the Territorial Sea (1958) did not create any exclusive fishing right in favour of the coastal state. So, while the United Nations conferences of 1958 and 1960 failed to reach agreement on fishery zones, technical improvements in fishing methods and increased activity by developing countries made a solution to the problem more urgent.

The European Fisheries Convention of 1964 permitted a coastal state to claim exclusive fishing rights in a belt of six nautical miles while access to a belt between six and 12 nautical miles was restricted to those state parties who had habitually fished in the past decade. Such harmony was disrupted in 1971 when Iceland made a unilateral claim to an exclusive fishing zone of 50 nautical miles. This claim was resisted both by the United Kingdom and West Germany. Iceland argued that such a declaration was necessary in view of the heavy dependence of the economy on fishing and the increasing scientific evidence of depletion of stocks. The United Kingdom attempted to resist such a declaration both by naval protection vessels and also by legal action before the International Court of Justice.[109] In the *Fisheries Jurisdiction* case,[110] the International Court of Justice accepted the legality of a 12 mile limit in customary international law but rejected the claim to a 50 mile limit on the basis that no such entitlement existed within customary international law and also that any such claim had been continuously opposed by West Germany and the United Kingdom. However, in the wider world a large number of claims were being made to 200 mile fishing zones so much so that, in 1977, the United Kingdom which had opposed the more modest claim of Iceland introduced a fishery zone of 200 nautical miles.[111] Indeed, in the *Fisheries Jurisdiction* case itself the Court had alluded to the preferential rights of a coastal state in circumstances of 'special dependence on coastal fisheries'. Had such an approach been pursued it might have lead to particular rules in respect of coastal states such as Iceland who were particularly dependent on fishing.

However, the demands of newly independent coastal states resulted in a complete code being established under the Law of the Sea Convention (1982). The operative provisions are contained in Part V (Arts 55–75) of the Convention. Article 55 provides that the exclusive economic zone is 'an area beyond and adjacent to the territorial sea' and subject to the relevant provisions of the Convention. Article 56 attempts to state the general position by providing:

(1) In the exclusive economic zone, the coastal State has:

   (a) sovereign rights for the purpose of exploring and exploiting, conserving and managing the natural resources, whether living or non-living, of the waters superjacent to the sea-bed and of the sea-bed and its subsoil, and with regard to other activities for the economic exploitation and exploration of the zone, such as the production of energy from the water, currents and winds;

---

109 *Fisheries Jurisdiction* case (1973) ICJ 3; The *Fisheries Jurisdiction* (*The Merits*) case (1974) ICJ 3.

110 *Fisheries Jurisdiction* (*The Merits*) case (1974) ICJ 3.

111 The Fishery Limits Act 1976 permits states to fish within a 200 mile limit. By this time, the United Kingdom was a member of the European Community and thus subject also to the Common Fisheries Policy (CFP) arising under Art 38 of the Treaty of Rome (1957).

(b) jurisdiction as provided for in the relevant provisions of this Convention with regard to:

    (i) the establishment and use of artificial islands, installations and structures;

    (ii) marine scientific research (iii) the protection and preservation of the marine environment.

(2) In exercising its rights and performing its duties under this Convention in the exclusive economic zone, the coastal State shall have due regard to the rights and duties of other States and shall act in a manner compatible with the provisions of this Convention.

Article 57 provides that 'the exclusive economic zone shall not extend beyond 200 nautical miles from the baselines from which the breadth of the territorial sea is measured'. The purpose of Art 58 is to stipulate the rights and duties of other states in the exclusive economic zone; in broad terms these are the freedom of navigation, the right of overflight and the right of laying submarine cables and pipelines. It is further provided in Art 58(3) that in exercising their rights and performing their duties such states shall have due regard to the rights, duties, laws and regulations of the coastal state. Article 59 further provides that in the event of conflict as to rights and duties within the zone then such a matter is to be resolved 'on the basis of equity and in the light of all relevant circumstances, taking into account the respective importance of the interests involved to the parties as well as to the international community as a whole'. To some extent, the word 'exclusive' is less than accurate because Art 62 and Arts 69–71 of the 1982 Convention provide that a coastal state which is unable to avail itself of the fish or living resources of its exclusive economic zone is obliged to allow other states upon payment,[112] access to its surplus. The coastal state has power to restrain pollution and control scientific research.[113]

In the event of disputes as to delimitation of the exclusive economic zone, Art 74 provides that 'the delimitation of the exclusive economic zone between states with opposite or adjacent coasts shall be effected by agreement on the basis of international law as referred to in Art 38 of the Statute of the International Court of Justice in order to achieve an equitable solution'. It is to be noted that this provision is in like terms to Art 83 of the Convention which regulates the delimitation of the continental shelf and both provisions have arisen in disputes where states have sought to establish a single maritime zone applicable both to the continental shelf and the exclusive economic zone.

The problem of delimitation has arisen in a number of cases where states have sought to determine a single maritime boundary applicable in respect of the continental shelf and the exclusive economic zone. In the *Gulf of Maine* case,[114] a Chamber of the International Court of Justice was required to draw a single maritime boundary line in respect of both the continental shelf and the exclusive economic zone (in this instance a fisheries zone). Although both states were parties to the Geneva Convention on the Continental Shelf (1958), Art 6 of that Convention was rejected as a basis since it related only to the seabed. In respect of a single maritime boundary where one state was opposite or adjacent to another the Court indicated: (i) that no such delimitation should be unilateral; (ii) that any

---

112 LOSC 1982, Art 62(4)(a).
113 *Ibid*, Arts 211(5), 211(6), 220 and 246–55.
114 *Gulf of Maine (Canada v United States)* case (1984) ICJ 246.

delimitation should be based upon agreement; (iii) that such an agreement should be founded upon equitable principles but should also pay regard to the geographical features of the area; (iv) in the absence of express agreement states should require a competent third party to make the determination.

The principles set out in the *Gulf of Maine* case were followed in the *Guinea/Guinea Bissau Maritime Delimitation* case.[115] In the latter case, the tribunal was required to produce a single maritime boundary line in respect of the territorial sea, exclusive economic zone and continental shelf. In applying the earlier principles set out in the *Gulf of Maine* case, the tribunal was minded to pay regard to the configuration of the West African coast, the prior conduct of colonial powers and the security interests of each state. In the *Gulf of Maine* case the Court had rejected any attempt to consider matters such as oil exploration rights so in the *Guinea/Guinea Bissau* case[116] economic factors were rejected as being too transient to constitute relevant criteria.

A similar example involving the delimitation of a single maritime boundary arose in the *St Pierre and Miquelon (Canada/France)* case,[117] where the arbitration tribunal was required to determine the relevant maritime belt of islands lying off the Newfoundland coast. The tribunal followed the *Gulf of Maine* case[118] in: (i) rejecting Art 6 of the Geneva Convention on the Territorial Sea (1958) as the basis for determination; (ii) accepting that where conflicts arose between adjoining states then it was appropriate to take geographical considerations into account; (iii) accepting that any solution would have to be based on equitable principles; (iv) accepting that any delimitation would have to avoid encroaching on the maritime belts of adjacent states. It has been argued that the application of equitable principles in this area together with concepts such as proportionality may make the exercise rather arbitrary.[119] Such a case however is an illustration of the problems that can arise because an island can generate its own maritime zones.

A later instance of the problems that can develop is afforded by the *Jan Mayen Maritime Delimitation (Denmark/Norway)* case[120] where the International Court of Justice operating under Art 36(2) was required to stipulate a common maritime boundary[121] between Jan Mayen Island and Eastern Greenland. In that case, the Court emphasised that while questions of delimitation of the continental shelf might be governed by the equidistance principle contained in Art 6 of the 1958 Convention questions of the delimitation of the exclusive economic (or fisheries) zone being governed by customary

---

115 *Guinea/Guinea Bissau Maritime Delimitation* case (1985) 25 ILM 251; 77 ILR 635.

116 *Ibid.*

117 (1992) 31 ILM 1149.

118 *Gulf of Maine* case (*Canada v United States*) (1984) ICJ 246.

119 A view expressed in the dissenting opinion of Professor Weil (1992) 31 ILM 1149, p 1197. For discussion of the case see K Highet, 'Delimitation of the maritime areas between Canada and France' (1993) 87 AJIL 452; MD Evans 'Less than an ocean apart: the St Pierre and Miquelon and Jan Mayen Islands and the delimitation of maritime zones' (1994) 43 ICLQ 678.

120 (1993) ICJ 37; 99 ILR 395. See MD Evans, '*Case concerning Maritime Delimitation in the Area Between Greenland and Jan Mayen (Denmark v Norway)*' (1994) 43 ICLQ 697: MD Evans, 'Delimitation and the common maritime boundary' (1994) 64 BYIL 283.

121 The expression itself having no precise legal significance but often being used when a court or tribunal is required to fix a boundary for both the exclusive economic zone or fishery zone and the continental shelf.

international law were required to produce an equitable result. Thus, it may be possible to start with a presumption in favour of the equidistance principle in cases involving adjacent or opposite states but it will still be necessary to consider all relevant or special circumstances and the weight given to each factor will be a matter for the tribunal. In particular, it will be necessary to consider the general geography, the configuration of the coast and the length of the coastline, the past conduct of the parties and any relevant security considerations. However, while much of the relevant case law has concerned delimitation of the continental shelf[122] and the principles of such delimitation are indicated below there remains an impression that boundary delimitation represents a judgment *ex aequo et bono*.

Some of the cases principally concerning the continental shelf have elucidated the status of the exclusive economic zone. In 1982, the International Court of Justice observed that 'the concept of the exclusive economic zone ... may be regarded as part of modern international law'[123] and, in 1985, the same tribunal was prepared[124] to accept that it could extend to 200 miles as a matter of customary international law. By 1998, 93 states claimed an EEZ of 200 miles while nine claimed an EFZ of 200 miles.[125] It is to be noted that Art 73 of the Law of the Sea Convention (1982) authorises the coastal state to enforce its laws by 'boarding, inspection and judicial proceedings'. In respect of those states that are members of the European Union the principle of sharing of exclusive fishing zones is part of the Common Fisheries Policy deriving from the Treaty of Rome (1957).[126]

11 THE LAND LOCKED STATE[127]

It has been calculated that of the nearly 190 states in the world, 42 have no sea coast at all. An additional number suffer from other disadvantages such as a small coastline or a limited EEZ or continental shelf because of the presence of adjacent states. In some instances the maritime belt is poor in natural resources.

In the 17th and 18th century it had been recognised that the desire of a landlocked or geographically disadvantaged state to acquire a port could be a cause of international instability.[128] Before 1914, it was subject to debate as to whether the vessels of a landlocked state had the right to sail on the high seas and fly the flag of that state. The

---

122 The principles emerging in cases mainly concerned with delimiting the continental shelf; see *North Sea Continental Shelf* case (1969) ICJ 3; *Anglo-French Continental Shelf* case (1977) 18 ILM 397; *Dubai/Sharjah Border Arbitration* (1981) 91 ILR 543; *Continental Shelf (Tunisia/Libya)* case (1982) ICJ 18; *Continental Shelf (Libya/Malta)* case (1985) ICJ 3; *Case concerning Maritime Delimitation in the Area between Greenland and Jan Mayen Island* (1993) ICJ 38.

123 *Continental Shelf (Tunisia v Libya)* (1982) ICJ 18, p 74.

124 *Continental Shelf (Libya v Malta)* (1985) ICJ 13, p 33.

125 Including the United States, Japan and the United Kingdom.

126 See EC Regulation 170/83. For the dangers of unilateral legislative action, see *R v Transport Secretary ex p Factortame Ltd (No 1)* [1990] 2 CMLR 353 (CA); 2 AC 85 (HL); Case 213/89 *R v Transport Secretary ex p Factortame Limited (No 2)* [1991] AC 603 (ECJ and HL).

127 E Lauterpacht, 'Freedom of transit in international law' (1958) 44 TGS 313; L Caflisch, 'Landlocked states and their access to and from the sea' (1978) 49 BYIL 71.

128 Manifested in concern at Russian attempts to secure ports with access to the Mediterranean and the traditional concern of the United Kingdom in respect of access to the Channel ports by any power other than France.

traditional maritime powers had argued that, in the absence of an identified port, control could not be exercised. This was modified by Art 273 of the Treaty of Versailles (1919) which permitted recognition of the flag of the landlocked state. Parity between the landlocked state and the coastal state derives from the 1921 League of Nations Conference on Communications and Transit which issued a Declaration on the subject.[129]

The principle of equality of treatment was stated in the Geneva Conventions of 1958. Article 2 of the High Seas Convention (1958) provides that freedom of the high seas shall be enjoyed by coastal and non-coastal states. Article 3 of the High Seas Convention further provides that 'States having no sea coast should have free access to the sea'. Article 14(1) of the Territorial Seas Convention stipulated that the right of innocent passage was to be enjoyed by coastal and non-coastal states. The Law of the Sea Convention (1982) provides in favour of the landlocked states a right of innocent passage in territorial waters,[130] a right of transit passage through straits[131] and right of innocent passage through archipelagic waters.[132]

These provisions as to equality of treatment were carried over into the Law of the Sea Convention (1982); the cardinal provision is that contained in Art 125 which reads:

(1) Landlocked States shall have the right of access to and from the sea for the purpose of exercising the rights provided for in this Convention including those relating to the freedom of the high seas and the common heritage of mankind. To this end, landlocked States shall enjoy freedom of transit through the territory of transit States by all means of transport.

(2) The terms and modalities for exercising freedom of transport shall be agreed between landlocked States and transit States concerned through bilateral, sub-regional or regional agreements.

(3) Transit States, in the exercise of their full sovereignty over their territory shall have the right to take all measures necessary to ensure that the rights and facilities provided for in this Part for landlocked States shall in no way infringe their legitimate interests.

It can be seen that Art 125 does not confer an unqualified right but such a right is contingent on the need of the landlocked state to reach agreement with the transit state. The general principle that agreement should be reached between the two states is carried further in Arts 127–30 of the 1982 Convention which provide for co-operation on matters of customs and transport. Of particular importance is Art 131 which stipulates that 'ships flying the flag of landlocked states shall enjoy treatment accorded to other foreign ships in maritime ports'.

In respect of the Exclusive Economic Zone, the Law of the Sea Convention (1982) provides that the land locked state 'shall have the right to participate, on an equitable basis, in the exploitation of an appropriate part of the surplus of the living resources of the exclusive economic zones of coastal states of the same sub-region or region'.[133] The

---

129 Declaration Recognising the Right to a Flag of States Having No Sea Coast 7 LNTS 73; in force from 20 April 1921.
130 LOSC (1982), Art 17.
131 *Ibid*, Art 38(1).
132 *Ibid*, Art 52(1).
133 *Ibid*, Art 69(1).

terms and modalities of such participation shall be established by the states concerned by the appropriate form of agreement.[134] Article 70 of the Law of the Sea Convention (1982) provides for the same rights in favour of the geographically disadvantaged state.

In respect of the international seabed area the Law of the Sea Convention (1982) provides for the effective participation of land locked and geographically disadvantaged states.[135]

12 THE HIGH SEAS[136]

(a) Introduction

The papal bulls of Pope Alexander VI (1492–1503) and Pope Julius II (1503–13) in 1493 and 1503 respectively had endeavoured to divide the high seas between the demands of Spain and those of Portugal. Such claims were at variance with the interests of the Protestant trading states of Northern Europe and were subject to challenge.[137] From the time of Grotius, such states began to advance the doctrine of the open seas. Such a doctrine formulated in *Mare Liberum* (1609)[138] was consistent not only with trading interests but also with practical realities; it was not sensible for a state to claim sovereignty over large stretches of ocean that it was unable to police. Hugo Grotius argued that the seas could not be state property because they could not be taken into possession and in the absence of effective possession could not be subject to state sovereignty. The views of Grotius did not prevail immediately and a different approach advanced in Selden's *Mare Clausum* (1635) was endorsed by Charles I who paid for the work to be printed. By the latter half of the 17th century, however, the principle of freedom of navigation was coming to be accepted.

In time, the doctrine of the open seas came to prevail. In the early 18th century writers began to draw a distinction between the maritime belt adjacent to the coastal state over which sovereignty might be claimed and the open seas over which sovereignty could not be asserted and which was free for all states to navigate upon. These views can be detected in Bynkershoek's *De Dominio Maris Dissertatio* which appeared in 1702 and Vattel's *Le droit des gens* (1758).

---

134 *Ibid*, Art 69(2).

135 *Ibid*, Arts 148, 152, 160 and 161.

136 See generally ED Brown, *The International Law of the Sea*, 1994, Chapter 14; R Churchill and AV Lowe, *The Law of the Sea*, 2nd edn, 1988; 3rd edn, 1999. A van Swanenberg, 'Interference with ships on the high seas' (1961) 10 ICLQ 785; J Siddle, 'Anglo American co-operation in the suppression of drug smuggling' (1982) 31 ICLQ 726; IA Shearer, 'Problems of jurisdiction and law enforcement against delinquent vessels' (1986) 35 ICLQ 320.

137 The most obvious being the rejection by Elizabeth I (1558–1603) of Spanish protests at the activities of Francis Drake (1545–96) who had acted as a pirate against Spanish interests in the Caribbean (1567–72) and in December 1577 received royal sponsorship for his voyage round the world (1577–80). The demand by the Spanish Ambassador that he should be punished resulted in him being knighted on the *Golden Hind*. Elizabeth rejected the assertion of the Ambassador that Spanish permission was required to navigate the Pacific.

138 The full title being *Mare Liberum sive de jure quod Batavis competit ad Indicana commercia dissertatio*, a chapter of the work *De Jure Praedae*.

The doctrine of the freedom of the high seas holds that no state may acquire sovereignty over parts of the high seas. This broad proposition is stated in Art 2 of the Geneva Convention on the High Seas (1958) and is repeated in Art 87 of the Law of the Sea Convention (1982). Article 2 of the 1958 Convention reads:

> The high seas being open to all nations, no State may validly purport to subject any part of them to its sovereignty. Freedom of the high seas is exercised under the conditions laid down by these articles and by the other rules of international law. It comprises, *inter alia,* both for coastal and non-coastal States:
>
> (1) freedom of navigation;
>
> (2) freedom of fishing;
>
> (3) freedom to lay submarine cables and pipelines;
>
> (4) freedom to fly over the high seas.

These freedoms, and others which are recognised by the general principles of international law, shall be exercised by all states with reasonable regard to the interests of other states in their exercise of the freedom of the high seas.

This article was thought of as being consistent with past case law[139] and as generally declaratory of international law. The difficulty is that the development of other maritime zones since 1945 has meant that the definition of the 'high seas' has required to be modified. Article 1 of the Geneva Convention on the High Seas (1958) defines the high seas as 'all parts of the sea that are not included in the territorial waters or internal waters of the state'. Thus under the Convention the contiguous zone was part of the high seas.[140] In the Law of the Sea Convention (1982), Art 86 modifies the definition by providing that the high seas are 'all parts of the sea that are not included in the exclusive economic zone, in the territorial sea or in the internal waters of a state, or in the archipelagic waters of an archipelagic state'. Article 87 builds upon Art 2 of the 1958 Convention by providing that there shall be freedom of the high seas and that this shall be exercised subject to the provisions of the Convention and the general rules of international law. The same article repeats the freedom stipulated in Art 2 of the 1958 Convention but adds two new freedoms in Art 87(1)(d) and 87(1)(e), namely:

> (d) freedom to construct artificial islands and other installations permitted under international law, subject to Part VI;[141]
>
> (e) freedom of scientific research, subject to Parts VI and XIII.[142]

By the terms of Art 87(2) these freedoms are to be exercised with due regard for the interests of other states and also in accordance with rights under the Convention in respect of activities in the international seabed area.[143] Article 88 requires that 'the high

---

139 See the *Behring Sea Fisheries Arbitration* (1893); Moore, *International Arbitrations,* 1878, New York, Vol 1, p 935; *Behring Sea Fisheries Arbitration* (1902) 9 RIAA 51.

140 See Geneva Convention on the Territorial Sea (1958), Art 24.

141 Which concerns the continental shelf. On this, see below.

142 Which concerns marine scientific research.

143 LOSC (1982), Art 87(2).

seas shall be reserved for peaceful purposes'[144] and Art 89 stipulates that 'no State may validly purport to subject any part of the high seas to its sovereignty'.

The freedom of fishing is seen as a traditional aspect of freedom of the high seas and is referred to as such in Art 2 of the 1958 Convention and Article 87(1)(e) of the 1982 Convention. Such a freedom was alluded to in the *Anglo Norwegian Fisheries* case[145] and was used as a justification for declaring invalid the unilateral extension of fishing zones by Iceland in the *Fisheries Jurisdiction* case.[146]

A second aspect of freedom of the high seas is the traditional freedom of navigation;[147] this aspect can be traced back to Grotius. This freedom has been traditionally defended by the major trading states. Particular concern was expressed during the Iran-Iraq war (1980–88) when both parties were involved on attacks on civilian shipping.

(b) Jurisdiction and the maintenance of order on the high seas

The absence of state sovereignty over the high seas has meant that in principle jurisdiction has been linked to the nationality of the vessel; in customary international law a Flag state would have jurisdiction over the ship. Such a state will enforce its own rules of municipal law and any relevant rules of international law. A vessel that is stateless and does not fly a flag may be boarded and seized on the high seas.[148]

Each state is required to fix rules under its own municipal law for the registration of vessels. However, after 1945 concern grew at the practice of registration of vessels in states with low taxation and minimum requirements on employment conditions. In broad terms, Art 5 of the Geneva Convention on the High Seas (1958) required a genuine link between the vessel and the state. The terms of the article read as follows:

(1) Each State shall fix the conditions for the grant of its nationality to ships, for the registration of ships in its territory, and for the right to fly its flag. Ships have the nationality of the State whose flag they are entitled to fly. There must exist a genuine link between the State and the ship; in particular, the State must effectively exercise its jurisdiction and control in administrative, technical and social matters over ships flying its flag.

(2) Each State shall issue to ships to which it has granted the right to fly its flag documents to that effect.

This provision was reproduced Art 91 of the Law of the Sea Convention (1982) save in respect of that part of para 1 that referred to the exercise of actual control. There is little doubt that the draftsmen in 1958 were influenced by the recently decided *Nottebohm* case.[149] Although the Convention was said to be declaratory of customary international

---

144 One of the submissions by Australia and New Zealand in the *Nuclear Tests* case (1974) ICJ 253, p 457; (1974) 57 ILR 350, p 650 was to the effect that nuclear testing by France in the Pacific was at variance with the freedom of the high seas. However, the court did not rule on this point.

145 *Anglo Norwegian Fisheries* case (1951) ICJ 116; 18 ILR 86.

146 The *Fisheries Jurisdiction* case (*The Merits*) (1974) ICJ 4.

147 The *Corfu Channel* case (1949) ICJ 4; *Nicaragua v The United States* (1986) ICJ 14.

148 *Naim Molvan v Attorney General for Palestine* [1948] AC 351.

149 The *Nottebohm* case (*The Merits*) (1955) ICJ 4.

law it must be doubtful if this is so.[150] In any event the 1958 provisions did little to curb the growth of flags of convenience and the last 40 years have witnessed a steady growth in the number of vessels registered in states such as Panama, Liberia, Cyprus and the Bahamas. By the early 1980s, nearly one-third of the world's shipping was registered in such states.[151] Such registrations may be advantageous in terms of cost and taxation but it has been questioned as to whether there are sufficient provisions to regulate safety and personnel. One of the most obvious causes of concern is the fact that much of the recent law of the sea on matters such as pollution and safety standards is contained in treaty law; the effect of such law could be negated if registrations are made in states that are not party to these conventions or do not employ the personnel necessary to ensure compliance.

Little attempt was made to clarify the concept of a genuine link; in 1960 the International Court of Justice declined to do so in the *Constitution of the Maritime Safety Committee of IMCO* case.[152] Although little progress was made on defining a genuine link, the requirement was reproduced in Art 91 of the Law of the Sea Convention (1982).

The possible abuses of flags of convenience lead to action by UNCTAD (United Nations Conference on Trade and Development). In the late 1970s, a number of reports were commissioned and a conference was later summoned which met from 1984 until 1986 and resulted in the adoption of the United Nations Convention on Conditions for Registration of Ships (1986). The purpose of the Convention is to establish a close link between the vessel and the Flag state; to this end, the Convention provides that municipal laws shall not only establish control over vessels but shall provide detailed provisions for the identification of ownership so that proprietorship may not be concealed behind a number of interlocking corporations. Another practice designed to curb flags of convenience has been the action by some European states such as Germany and Denmark to set up additional 'international registers' alongside the national register. In some cases, this has resulted in an increase in registrations in the last decade as owners sought to register under the parallel register.

The question of a genuine link between the vessel and the state arose during the latter stages of the Iran-Iraq war (1980–88). During the hostilities, there had been a pattern of attacks on Kuwaiti vessels. The government of Kuwait requested the United States and the United Kingdom to reflag certain Kuwaiti vessels; the two governments agreed to do so, asserting that the requirements as to a genuine link had in fact been met.

In respect of jurisdiction for acts committed on the the high seas the ordinary principles of criminal jurisdiction as recognised by public international law will apply. Thus, if an Italian on a Swedish ship fires a shot and kills a person on a Danish vessel then he could, in principle, be tried by the Italian courts (nationality principle), the Swedish courts (the subjective territorial principle) and the Danish courts (objective territorial principle). Thus, for these purposes the vessel is treated as if it were the territory of the Flag state.

---

150 See the *Muscat Dhows* case (1905) (1908) 2 AJIL 921.
151 *Monterosso Shipping Company Ltd v International Transport Workers Federation* [1982] 3 All ER 841.
152 (1960) ICJ 150; 30 ILR 426.

However, the position was not so clear cut as regards collisions at sea. This matter was considered in the rather confused case of *The Lotus*.[153] In that case, the *Lotus,* a French vessel, collided with a Turkish vessel the *Boz Kourt.* In the collision eight Turkish nationals were killed. When the *Lotus* reached Constantinople the officer of the watch, one Lieutenant Demons, was prosecuted for manslaughter before the Turkish court. The municipal court rejected a plea of no jurisdiction and following conviction France and Turkey agreed to submit the question of jurisdiction to the Permanent Court of International Justice. The court decided by the casting vote of its President that Turkey had jurisdiction; such a conclusion was grounded on either the objective territorial principle or the passive personality principle. However, the decision was contrary to expectations and caused alarm amongst seamen who had assumed that criminal jurisdiction would reside in the Flag state alone. Following representations, the actual result in the *Lotus* case[154] was reversed in respect of collisions or 'other incidents of navigation'. This was effected by Art 11(1) of the Geneva Convention on the High Seas (1958) which reads as follows:

> In the event of a collision or of any other incident of navigation concerning a ship on the high seas, involving the penal or disciplinary responsibility of the master or of any other person in the service of the ship, no penal or disciplinary proceedings may be instituted against such persons except before the judicial or administrative authorities either of the Flag State of the State of which such a person is a national.

This provision is reproduced in Art 97(1) of the Law of the Sea Convention (1982) and so the *ratio* of the *Lotus* case must be taken as reversed in so far as it pertains to collisions or other incidents of navigation. However, the wider discussion of the principles of jurisdiction is unaffected save that the divisions within the court and the split nature of the vote tend to weaken the authority of the case. Such a judgment has now to be read with Arts 95 and 96 of the Law of the Sea Convention (1982). The former provision stipulates that warships on the high seas have complete immunity from the jurisdiction of any state other than the Flag state while the latter extends this immunity to ships used on non-commercial service.

(c) Qualifications to the principle of freedom of the high seas

There are a number of distinct exceptions to the general principle of the freedom of the high seas and the other broad principle of the presumption in favour of Flag state jurisdiction. It is convenient to note a number of exceptions under this heading.

Piracy[155]

It was well established in customary international law that piracy was an offence of universal jurisdiction. In this context one means piracy by the law of nations because municipal law may give an extended definition to the concept. The special treatment of

---

153 The *Lotus* case (1927) PCIJ, Ser A, No 10; for comment see JL Brierly (1928) 44 LQR 154.
154 *Ibid.*
155 See an interesting discussion of the history of the concept by the Privy Council in *In re Piracy Jure Gentium* [1934] AC 586.

piracy was noted by Judge Moore in his dissenting speech in the *Lotus* case[156] where the learned jurist observed:

> Piracy by the law of nations, in its jurisdictional aspects, is sui generis. Though statutes may provide for its punishment, it is an offence against the law of nations; and as the scene of the pirates operations is the high seas, which it is not the right or duty of any nation to police, he is denied the protection of the flag which he may carry, and is treated as an outlaw, as an enemy of all mankind – *hostis humani generis* – whom any nation may in the interest of all capture and punish.

The definition of piracy was not without its difficulties not least because of the approach of the municipal courts. It is generally accepted that Art 15 of the Convention on the High Seas states the position in customary international law and this is reproduced in almost identical terms in Art 101 of the Law of the Sea Convention (1982) which provides:

> Piracy consists of any of the following acts:
>
> (1) any illegal acts of violence or detention, or any act of depredation, committed for private ends by the crew or the passengers of a private ship or a private aircraft, and directed:
>
> > (a) on the high seas, against another ship or aircraft, or against persons or property on board such ship or aircraft;
> >
> > (b) against a ship, aircraft, persons, or property in a place outside the jurisdiction of any State;
>
> (2) any act of voluntary participation in the operation of a ship or an aircraft with knowledge of the facts making it a pirate ship or aircraft;
>
> (3) any act of inciting or of intentionally facilitating an act described in sub paragraph 1 or sub paragraph 2 of this article.

The essential element of piracy is the acting for private ends; for this reason the hijacking motivated by political ends will not be piracy. Where a warship has reasonable grounds for suspecting that a merchant vessel is engaged in piracy then it may board it on the high seas for the purpose of investigation.[157] If evidence is obtained then the vessel may be seized and the persons on board may be arrested and tried.[158] Seizures on account of piracy may only be carried out by warships or authorised vessels.[159] Confusion in this area may have arisen because of the tendency of municipal law to employ a wider definition of piracy. For example some municipal laws categorise mutiny as a species of piracy,[160] but it does not meet the definition in international law.[161] It would seem that a vessel under the control of mutineers may only be arrested by the Flag state and not by others.

---

156 The *Lotus* case (1927) PCIJ, Ser A, No 10.

157 High Seas Convention (1958), Art 22; LOSC (1982), Art 110.

158 *Ibid*, Art 19; LOSC (1982), Art 105.

159 *Ibid*, Art 21; LOSC (1982), Art 107.

160 For the approach in municipal law, *The Magellan Pirates* (1853) 1 Sp Ecc & Ad 81; *The Ambrose Light* (1885) 25 Fed 408; *Republic of Bolivia v Indemnity Mutual Marine Assurance Co* [1909]) 1 KB 785; *Athens Maritime Enterprises Corporation v Hellenic Mutual War Risks Association (Bermuda) Ltd* [1983] QB 647; *Castle John and Nederlandse Stichting Sirius v NV Mabeco and NV Parfin* (1986) 77 ILR 537.

161 Under Art 15(1)(a) it must be 'directed against another ship'; see also LOSC (1982), Art 101.

Stateless ships

Since it is argued that the high seas are open to the vessels of all nations, it is sometimes asserted that a state is entitled to seize a stateless ship on the high seas. Reasoning to this effect was accepted by the Privy Council in the case of *Naim Molvan v Attorney General for Palestine*[162] which concerned the seizure by the British Navy of a stateless ship attempting to transfer immigrants to Palestine.

The rights of belligerents

It is generally accepted that in time of war a warship of a belligerent state may seize an enemy merchant ship. It is also accepted that a belligerent warship is entitled to stop and search a neutral merchant ship (but not in neutral territorial waters[163]) to determine whether it is carrying contraband or seeking to avoid a blockade. If the search produces evidence that justifies the suspicion then the vessel will be taken into port and an order sought that it be adjudged a 'lawful prize' by a Prize court[164] set up by the belligerent/ captor state.[165]

Self-defence/necessity

Although not accepted by all, some states have asserted a right to intervene on the high seas in situations falling short of war; such action has been defended on the basis of being proportionate self-defence designed to restrain the spread of civil conflict. Such an argument was advanced by France in the late 1950s, when the French navy was authorised to stop and search foreign merchant vessels suspected of carrying weapons to rebel factions in Algeria.

A related argument is that of necessity, which was advanced by the United Kingdom administration of Mr Harold Wilson in 1967 when a Liberian tanker, the *Torrey Canyon*, ran aground off Lands End spilling large quantities of oil into the sea and causing pollution to both the French and English coasts. In a desperate effort to restrain the spread of pollution, aircraft were ordered to bomb the tanker and set it alight. At the time, the treaty regime on intervention had not been developed and the action was justified on the grounds of necessity. It is noteworthy that no complaint was received from the Liberian government.

Right of approach

As the merchant vessel on the high seas is subject to the jurisdiction of the Flag state, it may be necessary for a warship to determine the nationality of a vessel or to determine whether it is engaged in unlawful conduct (for example, piracy, trading in slaves). In the

---

162 [1948] AC 351.

163 This explains the decision of the United States to adopt the three mile limit in 1793 at the outbreak of war in Europe, the breadth being claimed by Secretary of State Jefferson and remaining the position of the United States until after 1945.

164 *The Zamora* [1916] 2 AC 77.

165 The role of the Prize Court in developing rules of Public International Law should not be underestimated. This was particularly the case during the Napoleonic Wars, when the Prize Court in England was presided over by the Admiralty judge Sir William Scott (Lord Stowell) (1745–1836) (Judge in Admiralty 1798–1827); see, eg, *The Anna* (1805) 5 Ch Rob 373.

absence of hostilities or specific treaty provision, Art 22 of the High Seas Convention (1958) permits a warship to approach and to board for the purpose of checking documents. However, a degree of restraint has to be shown because Art 22(3) provides that if the suspicions prove unfounded, then compensation may be payable for any damage caused. In strict terms, three elements arise: namely, the right of approach; the right to board; and the right to search. Article 22 proceeds on the basis that such rights depend on reasonable suspicion. [166]

The provisions of Art 22 have been extended in Art 110 of the Law of the Sea Convention (1982) so that reasonable suspicion of unauthorised broadcasting may also be invoked. The article itself brings the three elements together by describing the right as a 'right of visit'.

The slave trade[167]

One of the most important concerns of international law in the 19th century was to restrict the activities of the slave trade. This emphasis has continued into modern treaty law. Article 13 of the 1958 High Seas Convention requires states to prevent their flag being used for such operations on the High Seas. This provision is repeated in Art 99 of the Law of the Sea Convention (1982) while, under Art 110 of the same Convention, it is provided that reasonable suspicion of slave trading is a justification for a warship to board a merchant vessel.

The doctrine of hot pursuit[168]

The right of hot pursuit is a doctrine that developed in customary international law to ensure that a vessel that had violated the laws of the coastal state could not escape liability by fleeing to the high seas. The right was recognised in the *I'm Alone* case,[169] where a British schooner was pursued by United States vessels from a point 10 miles from the United States coast to a point beyond 200 miles. The right itself was set out in detail in Art 23 of the High Seas Convention (1958) and developed in Art 111 of the Law of the Sea Convention (1982).

For the right to arise, the competent authorities of the coastal state must have good reason to believe that the vessel has violated the laws and regulations of that state.[170] The pursuit must commence when the foreign ship or one of its boats is within the internal waters, territorial sea or contiguous zone of the pursuing state. However, if the pursuit commences when the vessel is within the contiguous zone it may only be undertaken if there has been a violation of the rights for the protection of which the zone was established.[171] The right of hot pursuit ceases as soon as the ship pursued enters the

---

166 A concept used in many systems of municipal law to enable law enforcement officers to stop, search and arrest; see, eg, in the United Kingdom the use of the concept in the Police and Criminal Evidence Act 1984.

167 See Hugh Thomas, *The Slave Trade*.

168 P Poulantzas, *The Right of Hot Pursuit in International Law,* 1969; Fitzmaurice (1936) 17 BYIL 82; Williams (1939) 20 BYIL 83; WC Gilmore (1995) 44 ICLQ 949.

169 *I'm Alone* case (1935) 3 RIAA 1609; 7 ILR 203.

170 LOSC (1982), Art 111(1).

171 *Ibid.*

territorial sea of its own country or of a third state. The right of hot pursuit applies *mutatis mutandis* to violations in the exclusive economic zone or on the continental shelf, in respect of the relevant regulations pertaining to such areas.[172] The Article further provides that the right may only be exercised after a visual or an auditory signal to stop has been given at a distance which enables it to be seen or heard by the foreign ship.[173] The right of hot pursuit may be exercised only by warships or military aircraft or aircraft clearly marked and identifiable as being on government service.[174]

The award in the *I'm Alone* case indicates that the right to engage in hot pursuit does not extend to a right to sink the vessel although different considerations may apply where the sinking is caused accidentally in the course of the pursuit.[175]

Unauthorised broadcasting

Under the terms of Art 109 of the Law of the Sea Convention (1982), all states have agreed to co-operate in the suppression of unauthorised broadcasting from the high seas. By Art 109(2), this is defined as meaning 'the transmission of sound radio or television broadcasts from a ship or installation on the high seas intended for reception by the general public contrary to international regulations, but excluding the transmission of distress calls'. Under the terms of Art 109(3), it is provided that any person engaged in unauthorised broadcasting may be prosecuted before the court of the Flag state of the ship, the state of registry of the installation, the state of which the person is a national, any state where the transmission can be received or any state where authorised radio communication is suffering interference. It is further provided in Art 109(4) that any of the states specified in Art 109(3) may arrest any person or ship engaged in unauthorised broadcasting on the high seas and seize the broadcasting apparatus.[176]

Treaties

Since the Flag state in principle enjoys jurisdiction over a vessel on the high seas, it is possible for that state to enter into a treaty with another state enabling that state to enjoy powers of visit and search over its vessels. Such agreements became popular in the 19th century whereby European powers agreed[177] to the searching of vessels suspected of being engaged in the slave trade.[178] Thus, the Convention for the Protection of Submarine Cables (1884) allowed the right to approach but not to board suspected offenders in order to determine nationality, while the 1967 Convention on the Conduct of Fishing Operations in the North Atlantic conferred the right to visit and search. In the last

---

172 *Ibid*, Art 111(2).

173 *Ibid*, Art 111(4).

174 *Ibid*, Art 111(5).

175 *I'm Alone* case (1935) 3 RIAA 1609; 7 ILR 203.

176 For a discussion of the difficulties in the municipal sphere, see *Post Office v Estuary Radio Ltd* [1968] 2 QB 740 (CA).

177 General Act for the Suppression of the Slave Trade 1890.

178 A slightly different example being the 1924 Convention between the United States and the United Kingdom, whereby the latter agreed to 'raise no objection to the boarding of private vessels under the British flag outside the limits of territorial waters by the authorities of the United States' in order to restrict the smuggling of liquor. The Convention itself is discussed in the *I'm Alone* case (1935) 3 RIAA 1609.

two decades, such treaties have been adopted as part of the struggle against drug trafficking, terrorism and other unlawful acts.[179] Thus, the 1981 United States-United Kingdom Agreement on Vessels Trafficking in Drugs permitted the visit search and seizure of such vessels on the high seas. This objective was carried further in the 1988 Vienna Convention Against Illicit Traffic in Narcotic Drugs and Psychotropic Substances; under Art 17 of the Convention which entered into force in 1990, a state party which suspects that a vessel is engaged in unlawful conduct may request permission from the Flag state to take appropriate measures in respect of the vessel. The terms of Art 17 have been followed in the 1995 Council of Europe Agreement on Illicit Traffic by Sea.

Collisions

As noted above in respect of collisions at sea, the rule propounded in the *Lotus* case[180] has been modified by international convention. Thus, Art 11 of the Geneva Convention on the High Seas (1958) provides that, in the event of a collision or of any other incident of navigation concerning a ship on the high seas, involving the penal or disciplinary responsibility of the master, or of any other person in the service of the ship, no penal or disciplinary proceedings may be instituted against such persons except before the judicial or administrative authorities either of the Flag state or of the state of which such a person is a national. Article 11(3) further provides that no arrest or detention of the ship, even as a measure of investigation, shall be ordered by any authorities other than those of the flag state. These provisions are repeated in identical form in Art 97(1) and 97(3) of the Law of the Sea Convention (1982).

(d) The problem of pollution on the high seas[181]

The problem of pollution of the high seas has assumed an increasing importance in the years since 1945. In particular, the problem has become a central concern in the years since the late 1950s. To some extent, this is an extension of a general interest in environmental questions and partly it is a consequence of a number of high profile disasters that having been broadcast have raised public awareness; in part such disasters have had more far reaching effects because of technological changes such as the increasing use of large tanker fleets. In addition, developments in marine science have lead to a greater awareness of the environmental consequences of such incidents.[182] The general concern was expressed in Art 24 of the Geneva Convention on the High Seas

---

179 See the 1988 Rome Convention for the Suppression of Unlawful Acts Against the Safety of Maritime Navigation; see, also, 1988 Rome Protocol for the Suppression of Unlawful Acts Against the Safety of Fixed Platforms Located on the Continental Shelf. For discussion, see G Plant, 'The Convention for the Suppression of Unlawful Acts Against the Safety of Maritime Navigation' (1990) 39 ICLQ 27.

180 The *Lotus* case (1927) PCIJ, Ser A, No 10; (1927) 4 ILR 153.

181 Churchill and Lowe, *Law of the Sea*, Chap 15, pp 328–400; E Brown, *International Law of the Sea*, Chap 15, pp 336–98.

182 One of the reasons undoubtedly must be developments in television news reporting which have raised public awareness of such incidents. The list begins with *Torrey Canyon* (1967), and includes *Amoco Cadiz* (1978), *Exxon Valdez* (1989), *Aegean Sea* (1992), *Braer* (1993), *Sea Empress* (1996). For discussion, see G Plan, 'Safer ships, cleaner seas'; Lord Donaldson's Inquiry, *The UK Government's Response and International Law* (1995) 44 ICLQ 939.

(1958), which required that: 'Every State shall draw up regulations to prevent pollution of the seas by the discharge of oil from ships or pipelines or resulting from the exploitation and exploration of the seabed and its subsoil, taking account of existing treaty provisions on the subject.'

Following the highly publicised incident involving the *Torrey Canyon* in 1967,[183] international action manifested itself in the signing in 1969 of the International Convention relating to Intervention on the High Seas in Cases of Oil Pollution Casualties which entered into force in 1975. The Convention pledged state parties to take action to prevent damage to coastlines which might be caused by oil pollution. To ensure that compensation was paid, the International Convention on Civil Liability for Oil Pollution Damage, signed in 1969, provided as a general principle that those causing oil pollution should pay compensation.[184] To provide for circumstances not covered by this convention, an international fund was established under the terms of the 1971 Convention on the Establishment of an International Fund for Compensation for Oil Pollution Damage.[185] Indeed, these were not the first international instruments seeking control over oil pollution; most would view the 1954 Convention for the Preservation of the Seas by Oil as the first significant international agreement in this sphere.

Thus, by the time the Law of the Sea Conference began to meet in 1973, a framework of international agreements was already been put in place to deal with specific aspects of pollution. Among the more significant instruments regulating specific matters are:

(i) The International Convention for the Prevention of Pollution from Ships (1973) (sometimes referred to as the MARPOL Convention).[186]

(ii) The International Convention for the Safety of Life at Sea (1974) (sometimes referred to as the SOLAS Convention).[187]

(iii) The Convention for the Prevention of Marine Pollution by Dumping Wastes and Other Matters (1972) (sometimes referred to as the London Convention).[188]

(iv) The Convention for the Prevention of Marine Pollution by Dumping from Ships and Aircraft (1972) (sometimes referred to as the Oslo Convention).[189]

(v) The Convention for the Prevention of Marine Pollution from Land Based Sources (1974)(sometimes referred to as the Paris Convention).[190]

---

183 In 1967, a Liberian tanker ran aground off Lands End and large quantities of oil spilled from the vessel causing damage to both the French and English coasts. The incident was widely reported and culminated in aircraft bombing the tanker in order to set it alight and thus prevent further spillage.

184 The Convention came into force in 1975 but was subject to amendment by Protocols in 1976, 1984 and 1992.

185 The Convention was subject to amendment by Protocol in 1976, 1984 and 1992.

186 In force October 1983.

187 In force May 1980.

188 Entered into force August 1975; see (1972) 11 ILM 1294.

189 This convention, which applied to the North East Atlantic and North Sea, was drafted at the same as the London Convention and came into force in 1974.

190 In force May 1978. It should be noted that the Paris Convention and the Oslo Convention were both replaced by the 1992 Convention for the Protection of the Marine Environment of the North East Atlantic (also known as the Paris Convention) when it came into force in 1998.

Thus, there had been a considerable number of international and regional instruments drawn up prior to the Law of the Sea Convention (1982). The task for the conference in 1973 was not to set out detailed standards in particular areas but to lay down a framework of general principle. The participants at the law of the sea conference were anxious to provide clearer guidelines to define the regulatory powers of the coastal state, to ensure that those powers were employed with a degree of uniformity and to clarify questions of jurisdiction. To this end, over 40 articles of the Law of the Sea Convention (1982) are devoted to the marine environment and its protection. The basic provisions are set out in Part XII (Arts 192–238) of the Convention, although other provisions are stated elsewhere. Article 192 provides that 'States have the obligation to protect and preserve the marine environment'. The duty to take appropriate measures is set out in Article 194 which reads as follows:

(1) States shall take, individually or jointly as appropriate, all measures consistent with this Convention that are necessary to prevent, reduce and control pollution of the marine environment from any source, using for this purpose the best practicable means at their disposal and in accordance with their capabilities, and they shall endeavour to harmonise their policies in this connection.

(2) States shall take all measures necessary to ensure that activities under their jurisdiction or control are so conducted as not to cause damage by pollution to other States and their environment, and that pollution arising from incidents or activities under their jurisdiction or control does not spread beyond the areas where they exercise sovereign rights in accordance with this Convention.

(3) The measures taken pursuant to this Part shall deal with all sources of pollution of the marine environment. These measures shall include, *inter alia*, those designed to minimise to the fullest possible extent:

(a) the release of toxic, harmful, or noxious substances, especially those which are persistent, from land based sources, from or through the atmosphere or by dumping;

(b) pollution from vessels, in particular measures for preventing accidents and dealing with emergencies, ensuring the safety of operations at sea, preventing intentional and unintentional discharges, and regulating the design, construction, equipment, operation and manning of vessels;

(c) pollution from installations and devices used in exploitation of the natural resources of the seabed and subsoil, in particular measures for preventing accidents and dealing with emergencies, ensuring the safety of operations at sea, and regulating the design, construction, equipment, operation and manning of such installations or devices;

(d) pollution from other installations and devices operating in the marine environment, in particular for preventing accidents and dealing with emergencies, ensuring the safety of operations at sea, and regulating the design, construction, equipment, operation and manning of such installations or devices.

(4) In taking measures to prevent, reduce or control pollution of the marine environment, states shall refrain from unjustifiable interference with activities carried out by other states in the exercise of their rights and in pursuance of their duties under this Convention.

In addition to these general provisions, the Convention stipulates that states are under a duty to co-operate with each other to preserve the marine environment[191] and to provide

---

191 LOSC (1982), Art 197.

assistance to developing states to facilitate this objective.[192] State parties are required to adopt laws to restrain not only land based pollution,[193] but also pollution by vessels[194] and pollution by dumping.[195] The Convention further provides that such laws shall be enforced by the coastal state or the Flag state as appropriate.[196]

(e) The regulation of straddling stocks[197]

Although the freedom to fish on the high seas is regarded as one of the important aspects of freedom of the high seas it is a freedom that is not absolute.[198] Such a principle has had to be further modified in the light of the development of the concept of the exclusive economic zone; such zones now extend into what was formerly the high seas and are themselves subject to much closer regulation. Article 56(1) of the 1982 Convention provides that coastal states shall have sovereign rights in the Exclusive Economic Zone for the purpose of exploring, exploiting, conserving or managing natural resources. Under Art 61, the coastal state is under a duty both to promote conservation of living resources[199] and Art 62 requires such a state subject to this prior duty to promote the objective of the optimum utilisation of living resources. In cases where the same stock passes between the exclusive economic zones of two different coastal states, then the Convention provides for mutual co-operation.[200]

However, fish tend to be found in those areas where there is most zoo plankton and on which many species feed; amongst these areas will be the shallow continental shelf waters adjacent to a coast. Although generalisations have to be treated cautiously, it is widely accepted that much of the commercial fishing in the world takes place within 200 miles of land as these waters hold the greatest volume of fish stocks.[201] Thirdly, the bare text of the Law of the Sea Convention (1982), at first blush,[202] gives the impression that fish are confined to various zones; however, many stocks are migratory and will therefore pass from the Exclusive Economic Zone to the high seas or to some other Exclusive Economic Zone. Such stocks are sometimes referred to as 'straddling stocks or shared stocks'. Clearly, if such stocks were not subject to some form of regulation unrestricted

---

192 LOSC (1982), Arts 202 and 203.

193 *Ibid*, Art 207.

194 *Ibid*, Art 211.

195 *Ibid*, Art 210.

196 *Ibid*, Arts 213–222.

197 See Churchill and Lowe, *The Law of the Sea*, 3rd edn, 1999, Chap 14.

198 See Art 2 of the Geneva Convention on the High Seas (1958), which refers to the 'reasonable regard to the interests of other states'; see, also, Arts 1 and 6 of the Geneva Convention on Fishing and Conservation of the Living Resources of the High Seas (1958).

199 Article 61(1).

200 Article 63(1).

201 See Churchill and Lowe, *The Law of the Sea*, 2nd edn, 1988, p 235; 3rd edn, 1999, p 296.

202 Although, of course, the Convention contains a number of specific provisions in respect of particular species. Article 64 provides for co-operation in respect of highly migratory species such as marlins and tuna. Article 65 provides for co-operation in respect of conservation of marine mammals, such as whales. Article 66 provides for co-operation and conservation of anadromous stocks. Article 67 makes specific provision in respect of catadromous stock. By the combined effect of Art 68 and Art 77(4), sedentary species are treated under the Convention as part of the natural resources of the continental shelf of the coastal state.

fishing on the high seas could deplete the fish stock within the exclusive economic zone and completely undermine the conservation measures of a coastal state. This problem is recognised by Art 63(2) of the 1982 Convention which requires the coastal state and those states fishing on the high seas to reach agreement, either directly or indirectly, in respect of the conservation measures appropriate to such stocks. Those states fishing on the high seas are obliged to co-operate in such joint efforts at conservation, having regard to the provisions of Arts 116–20 of the Law of the Sea Convention (1982).

However, it has to be acknowledged that the provisions of the Convention stipulate that agreement shall be reached but require others to establish the machinery so to do. In a number of parts of the world where there are straddling stocks bordering an exclusive economic zone, there have been problems of overfishing and a temptation arises for coastal states to seek to legislate beyond the 200 mile limit.[203] To ensure respect for the general spirit of the provisions within the Law of the Sea Convention (1982), the United Nations General Assembly[204] supported a call for a conference on the subject of straddling stocks and this met from 1993–95 and resulted in an Agreement for the Implementation of the Provisions of the United Nations Convention on the Law of the Sea relating to the Conservation and Management of Straddling Fish Stocks and Highly Migratory Fish Stocks (usually referred to as the Straddling Stocks Agreement).[205]

The Straddling Stocks Agreement 1995,[206] which requires the ratification of 30 states seeks to build upon the general provisions of the Law of the Sea Convention. It provides that states should co-operate to ensure the conservation of migratory stocks and further stipulates that such conservation should be founded on the precautionary principle.[207] Such co-operation might be accomplished directly or through existing or newly established regional organisations.[208]

In respect of compliance with the conservation and management rules of international and regional organisations, the agreement provides that Flag states shall ensure compliance by its own vessels irrespective of where violations occur. Article 21 is concerned with co-operation between regional organisations and provides that a state which is a party to such an organisation may board and inspect fishing vessels flying the flag of another state that is party to the Agreement. Where a boarding or inspection reveals breaches of the relevant regulations, then the inspecting state must inform the Flag state which must take enforcement action itself or allow the inspecting state to act. Whether the Agreement will have the desired effect will depend on whether it can attract a sufficient number of ratifications from those states with interests in high seas fishing.

---

203 In particular, the North West Atlantic, the Bering Sea, the Sea of Okhotsk, the Barents Sea; and off the coast of Argentina; in consequence some states have sought to regulate beyond the 200 mile limit, such as Canada, Chile and Argentina.

204 Resolution 47/192 (1992).

205 See DH Anderson, 'The Straddling Stocks Agreement of 1995 – an initial assessment' (1996) 45 ICLQ 463.

206 PG Davies and C Redgwell, 'The international legal regulation of straddling fish stocks' (1996) 67 BYIL 199.

207 Articles 5 and 6 of the Straddling Stocks Agreement 1995.

208 Article 8, Straddling Stocks Agreement 1995.

One of the best known regional organisations charged with managing the problem of straddling stocks is the Northwest Atlantic Fisheries Organisation (NAFO),[209] which was established under the Northwest Atlantic Fisheries Convention (1978). The organisation operates through a Fishery Commission, which is charged with managing straddling stocks in the area of the Grand Banks off Newfoundland; this area extends beyond Canada's 200 nautical mile EFZ (now EEZ). The European Community is a party to the 1978 Convention. After 1986, Spain and Portugal became members of the European Community and persuaded the European Community to object to quotas set by NAFO. Spain having objected to the quotas established its own quotas. Because of this, and after evidence had come to light of vessels employing flags of convenience in respect of states not members of NAFO, the Canadian legislature passed the Coastal Fisheries Protection Act 1994, amending earlier legislation, and which enabled Canadian authorities to take action against vessels fishing on the high seas for straddling stocks contrary to NAFO regulations. A serious incident arose in March 1995, when the Canadian authorities arrested a Spanish vessel[210] on the high seas; on 28 March 1995 Spain instituted proceedings against Canada before the International Court of Justice, claiming jurisdiction on the basis of the optional clause declarations of both parties. Following intensive diplomatic negotiations, a compromise was agreed between the EC and Canada in April 1995, whereby the quotas for Greenland halibut were adjusted and Canada agreed to adjourn domestic proceedings against the vessel.[211] The Spanish case questioning the validity of the Canadian domestic legislation continued before the International Court of Justice; however, Canada had entered a reservation to its optional clause declaration. On 4 December 1998, the International Court of Justice delivered its judgment in the *Fisheries Jurisdiction* case (*Preliminary Objections*) (*Spain v Canada*)[212] ruling that the relevant Canadian reservation to the declaration of acceptance precluded its jurisdiction to adjudicate.

---

209 Of the regional fishery commissions one can note the North West Atlantic Fisheries Organisation (NAFO), established under the 1978 Convention on Future Multilateral Co-operation in the North West Atlantic Fisheries; the Northeast Atlantic Fisheries Commission established under the 1980 Convention on Future Multilateral Co-operation in the North East Atlantic Fisheries; the General Fisheries Council for the Mediterranean established by the 1949 Agreement for the Establishment of the General Fisheries Council for the Mediterranean; the Commission for the Conservation of Antarctic Marine Living Resources (CCAMLR) established by the 1980 Convention on the Conservation of Antarctic Marine Living Resources.

210 The Spanish trawler in question was named the Estai and was fishing for turbot (sometimes described as Greenland halibut); the relevant Canadian regulations had imposed a 60 day moratorium.The vessel was released after a week on the posting of a bond.

211 For the factual background, see PG Davies, 'The EC/Canadian fisheries dispute in the Northwest Atlantic' (1995) 44 ICLQ 927

212 *Fisheries Jurisdiction Case (Preliminary Objections) (Spain v Canada)* (1998) ICJ. For an assessment, see Louise de la Fayette (1999) 48 ICLQ 664.

13 THE CONTINENTAL SHELF[213]

The expression the 'continental shelf' is used both by geographers and lawyers and it is important to be clear as to exactly what is being referred to. It is therefore sensible to consider first the use made of the expression by physical geographers. If one considers the seabed adjacent to a coast then, in many instances, it can be observed that there are three distinct sections before the bed of the ocean is reached. Immediately adjacent to the coast, the seabed will gradually slope down from the low water mark to a point of about 130 metres in depth: this is the continental shelf in the sense used by a physical geographer. At or about that point, the angle of declination is observed to increase (that is, the slope becomes much steeper) and this will continue to a point between 1,200 and 3,500 metres in depth; this second section, having the steeper slope, is known as the continental slope. Thirdly, in many instances there will be a part beyond the slope where the angle of decline is more gradual until the actual bed of the ocean is reached; this third section is known as the continental rise and may descend to a depth of between 3,500 or 5,500 metres before the actual ocean bed is reached. Geographers then describe all three sections[214] as comprising the continental margin. It has been estimated that about one-fifth of the seabed comes within the scope of the continental margin.

It has been accepted for over 50 years that the area of the continental margin – and in particular the continental shelf strictly so called – might be rich in oil and gas deposits, as well as constituting rich sources of fish, particularly the sedentary species. Indeed, at the Hague Conference in 1930 it was recognised that a coastal state might enjoy certain rights over the subsoil within the territorial sea. Prior to 1930, this might be of marginal significance, such as the assertion by the United Kingdom as to the rights in respect of pearl fisheries off the coast of Ceylon. However, it also became clear during the 1930s that it would not be long before mining technology had so developed to enable extensive and profitable offshore drilling for oil and gas beyond the traditional three mile limit.[215] As with so many areas of activity in the municipal sphere, changing technology presented opportunities to profit and it became clear that some form of regulatory regime would be required; in short, it was necessary for a legal regime to be put in place that could regulate such developments. However, that did not happen immediately, because the first instinct of states was simply to begin to make extensive claims in respect of the waters adjacent to their coasts. The United Kingdom had made a treaty with Venezuela as early as 1942, but

---

213 See generally, CJ Hurst, 'Whose is the bed of the sea?' (1923–24) 4 BYIL 34; H Lauterpacht, 'Sovereignty over submarine areas' (1950) 27 BYIL 376; L Goldie, 'Sedentary fisheries and Article 2(4) of the Continental Shelf Convention' (1969) 63 AJIL 86; R Young, 'The legal status of submarine areas beneath the high seas' (1951) 45 AJIL 225; D Hutchinson, 'The seaward limit to the continental shelf jurisdiction in customary international law' (1985) 56 BYIL 133.

214 Ie, the three sections (the continental shelf, the continental slope and the continental rise) comprise the continental margin.

215 For an early discussion, see C Hurst, 'Whose is the bed of the sea? Sedentary fisheries outside the three mile limit' (1924) 3 BYIL 34. (The article is of interest because the author who was the Legal Adviser to the Foreign Office advanced the view that the submarine area beyond the belt of the territorial sea was *res nullius*; this remained the official position in the United Kingdom until 1945.)

the real scramble began after the Truman Proclamation of September 1945.[216] In that statement, the United States indicated that it regarded:

> ... the natural resources of the subsoil and seabed of the continental shelf beneath the high seas but contiguous to the coasts of the United States as appertaining to the United States, subject to its jurisdiction and control.

Although the general nature of the proclamation was clear, what remained uncertain was the precise seaward limit of the continental shelf. An accompanying memorandum issued by the State Department indicated that: 'The continental shelf is usually defined as that part of the undersea land mass adjacent to the coast, over which the sea is not more than 100 fathoms (600 feet) in depth.' The proclamation had been prompted by the knowledge that extensive off shore drilling was technically possible but the danger was that the unilateral act of the United States would elicit a response. In the years immediately following the Truman Proclamation,[217] many coastal states began to make extensive maritime claims so that, between 1945 and 1958, there was little consensus on the subject.[218] Thus, the absence of clear customary law[219] on the subject and the need to respond to technical change had lead to unilateral action.

The Truman Proclamation did not affect the legal status of the waters above the shelf; for the most part these would remain part of the high seas.[220] However, many states in Latin America issued proclamations claiming sovereignty in respect of distances of up to 200 nautical miles from the coast. In some instances, the Latin American countries had no continental shelf in the geographical sense and the tenor of such announcements was to call into question the traditional distinction between the territorial sea and the high seas. Therefore, much work was required in the years prior to the 1958 Conference on the Law of the Sea to produce agreement on the areas of difficulty such as the legal definition of

---

216 An interesting reaction was that of the United Kingdom. First, the attitude of the United Kingdom had been to warn of the dangers of unilateral proclamations, fearing a scramble would be set off. Secondly, the area beyond the territorial sea had been regarded as *res nullius*. However, soon the United Kingdom followed the spirit of the Proclamation, making statutory instruments in respect of various colonies. By 1951, the United Kingdom (in the form of the legal adviser WE Beckett) was moving away form the *res nullius* view towards the concept of an inchoate right. For the evolution, see G Marston, 'The incorporation of continental shelf rights into United Kingdom law' (1996) 45 ICLQ 12.

217 Although technically referred to as the Truman Proclamation, the statement of 28 September 1945 did, in fact, contain two proclamations, one concerning the natural resources of the subsoil and the seabed of the continental shelf, and the other concerning right in respect of coastal fisheries in areas the high seas. To an extent the entire development of the post 1945 law of the sea can be traced to this statement.

218 For the scramble after 1945, see L Nelson, 'The patrimonial sea' (1973) 22 ICLQ 668; for contemporary comment, see H Lauterpacht, 'Sovereignty over submarine areas' (1950) 27 BYIL 395; MacGibbon, 'Some observations on the part of protest in international law' (1953) BYIL 119. The important date was 18 August 1952, when Chile, Ecuador and Peru issued the Declaration of Santiago, which made claim to sovereignty in respect of 200 nautical miles. Argentina had asserted a claim to its continental shelf in 1946 and like claims were made by Costa Rica in 1948 and El Salvador in 1950.

219 As late as 1951, Lord Asquith was able to indicate that he saw no clear customary law on the subject of the continental shelf of coastal states; see *Re Arbitration between Petroleum Development and the Sheikh of Abu Dhabi* (1953) 47 AJIL 156; 18 ILR 144; (1952) 1 ICLQ 247.

220 That is if, in 1945, one treated differently that part of the shelf under the then three mile territorial sea since, by the Hague Conference of 1930 if not earlier, it had been accepted that possession of a territorial sea gave the coastal state rights over the bed and subsoil of that sea.

the continental shelf, the precise breadth and the legal rights of the coastal state. In the interests of clarity, it is proposed to examine these questions in turn.

(a) The definition of the continental shelf

Article 1 of the 1958 Geneva Convention on the Continental Shelf (1958) defined the continental shelf in the following terms:

> For the purpose of these Articles the term 'continental shelf' is used as referring:
>
> (a) to the seabed and the subsoil of the submarine areas adjacent to the coast but outside the area of the territorial sea, to a depth of 200 metres or, beyond that limit, to where the depth of the superadjacent waters admits of the exploitation of the natural resources of the said areas;
>
> (b) to the seabed and subsoil of similar submarine areas adjacent to the coasts of islands.

This definition was far from satisfactory. First, it did not link the legal concept of the continental shelf with accepted geomorphic concepts. Secondly, it was dangerously vague because it defined the continental shelf in terms of exploitability. However, drilling technology was developing rapidly and it was uncertain as to where the boundary of exploitability would be; moreover, on this definition, the legal breadth of the continental shelf depended on exploitability but the question arose as to whether this was the ability to fish or to engage in oil exploration. The test of exploitability not only raised questions as to what form of exploitation was in issue, but the matter was complicated by the problem as to whether the capacity to exploit was to be that of the coastal state or of some other state.

However, be that as it may, the definition was accepted by the International Court of Justice in the *North Sea Continental Shelf* cases[221] as stating customary international law, although the court did emphasise that title over the shelf arose by virtue of it being the natural prolongation of the land territory, rather than by virtue of concepts arising in other areas, such as the doctrines of occupation or effective control. The lack of precision caused difficulties in the years after 1958; it was clear that technological change would enable much deeper exploitation. If the 1958 definition were allowed to stand, then more advanced states might justify a breadth of continental shelf that covered much of the ocean floor. Such a development would have been unsatisfactory in itself, but would also clash with demands for common entitlement to the deep seabed which were increasingly made after 1967.[222] The task therefore for the Third Law of the Sea Conference was to produce a definition which would import some maximum breadth to the legal concept of the continental shelf. During the conference, it became clear that the claims of coastal states to an EEZ of 200 nautical miles were likely to be accepted so that Art 76(1) of the Law of the Sea defined the continental shelf as follows:

> The continental shelf of a coastal State comprises the seabed and subsoil of the submarine areas that extend beyond its territorial sea throughout the natural prolongation of its land territory to the outer edge of the continental margin, or to a distance of 200 nautical miles

---

221 *North Sea Continental Shelf* cases (1969) ICJ 3; 41 ILR 29.
222 The matter being raised by Dr Arvid Pardo of Malta before the General Assembly in 1967.

from the baselines from which the breadth of the territorial sea is measured where the outer edge of the continental margin does not extend up to that distance.

The wording posits a link between the legal definition and the geological realities. Article 76(1) has to be read with Art 76(2) which provides the continental shelf shall not extend beyond 200 nautical miles save as expressly authorised in Art 76(4)–76(6). Where the continental margin[223] does not extend up to 200 nautical miles, then areas of the seabed will be included up to a distance of 200 nautical miles. The effect is to deem that each coastal state will be entitled to a legal continental shelf of 200 nautical miles regardless of the actual geomorphic realities.[224] Where the actual continental margin extends beyond 200 nautical miles, then the legal continental shelf will be determined in accordance with a formula stipulated in Arts 76(4) and 76(5), but in no circumstances must the shelf extend beyond 350 nautical miles from the baselines from which the breadth of the territorial sea is measured.[225] To avoid disputes about the precise limits of the shelf between 200 and 350 nautical miles, Art 76(8) provides for the coastal state to make submissions to a Commission on the Limits of the Continental Shelf where there is an intention to claim a continental shelf of more than 200 nautical miles; however, the wording of the sub Article leaves some doubt as to whether the recommendations are final. The experience since 1994 has been that state claims have tended to be made in accordance with Art 76 and some national legislation has focused on the formula of '200 nautical miles or the outer edge of the continental margin'.[226] The controversy over the precise breadth of the continental shelf is not a matter of mere academic interest; in many areas of the world, the ocean floor is likely to be covered with manganese nodules which contain not only manganese but also cobalt, copper and nickel. It is such considerations that have heightened the interest of states in the precise breadth of the continental shelf.

(b) Rights and duties in respect of the continental shelf

Article 77 of the Law of the Sea Convention (1982) provides that the coastal state exercises over the continental shelf sovereign rights for the purpose of exploring and exploiting its natural resources.[227] It is further provided that such rights are exclusive and no other state may exercise such rights without the consent of the coastal state.[228] The original Truman Proclamation had referred only to mineral resources, but Art 2(4) of the 1958 Continental Shelf Convention provided that sovereign rights extended beyond mineral rights to living organisms of the sedentary species. This description of sovereign rights is continued in Art 77(4) of the Law of the Sea Convention but it will not extend to non-natural rights such as wrecks, for which particular provision is made elsewhere.[229]

---

223 As defined in Art 76(3) to included the continental shelf, continental slope and continental rise.
224 *Tunisia/Libya Continental Shelf* case (1982) ICJ 18; *Gulf of Maine* case (1984) ICJ 246; *Libya/Malta Continental Shelf* case (1985) ICJ 13.
225 LOSC (1982), Art 76(6).
226 Federal Law on the Continental Shelf of Russian Federation (1995).
227 LOSC (1982), Art 76(1); see 1958 Continental Shelf Convention, Art 2(1).
228 LOSC (1982), Art 76(2); see 1958 Continental Shelf Convention. Art 2(2).
229 See LOSC (1982), Art 303.

It is provided that rights over the continental shelf do not affect the legal status of superadjacent waters[230] and the coastal state may may not impede the laying or maintenance of submarine cables or pipelines on the shelf.[231] However, the coastal state may authorise artificial islands and installations on the shelf[232] and has the exclusive right to authorise and regulate drilling.[233]

In those cases where the continental shelf extends beyond 200 nautical miles,[234] special provision is made because the superadjacent waters are high seas and not part of the coastal state's EEZ. First, in relation to fishing, the distinction between sedentary and non-sedentary species will be important because the latter will be subject to the high seas regime of freedom of fishing.[235] Secondly, Art 82 makes express provision in respect of the exploitation of non-living resources beyond the 200 mile limit; the article provides that the coastal state shall, after five years, make a percentage contribution based on the volume of production to the International Seabed Authority. Under the terms of Art 82(2), the percentage will rise from 1% in the sixth year to 7% in the twelfth and succeeding years.[236] Under the terms of Art 82(4), the payments will be distributed by the Authority to state parties 'on the basis of equitable sharing criteria taking into account the interests and needs of developing states'.

(c) The delimitation of the continental shelf

The growing importance of the continental shelf has lead to a number of disputes and considerable literature on the principles that are to be applied where a court or tribunal has to resolve a dispute between opposite or adjacent states. One can exclude the cases where there has been an application to fix a single maritime boundary.[237] In those cases where the continental shelf alone is in issue, then the general principle is that delimitation should be determined by agreement founded on equitable principles.

Article 6 of the Geneva Convention on the Continental Shelf (1958) had stipulated that such delimitation should be by agreement but, in the absence of special circumstances, the boundary would be 'the median line, every point of which is equidistant from the nearest point of the baselines from which the the breadth of the territorial seas is measured'. In the *North Sea Continental Shelf* case (1969), a dispute arose between the then Federal Republic of West Germany and Denmark and Holland. If the equidistance principle had been applied, then Germany with its concave northern coastline would only have been allocated a small part of the North Sea Continental Shelf between Holland

---

230 LOSC (1982), Art 78.

231 *Ibid,* Art 79.

232 Article 80 to be read with Art 60 of the Convention.

233 LOSC (1982), Art 81.

234 For consideration of the status of the continental shelf in the context of a European Community Directive (92/43), see *R v Secretary of State for Trade and Industry ex p Greenpeace Ltd* (2000) unreported, 19 January, QBD.

235 In 1994, a dispute arose between Canada and the United States as to the status of scallops which US fishermen were catching outside Canada's 200 mile fishing zone. See (1995) 10 I JMCL 221.

236 It is important to pay regard to Art 82(3), which stipulates that a developing state which is a net importer of a particular mineral resource shall be exempt from such payments.

237 The *Gulf of Maine* case (1984) ICJ 246; *Case concerning Maritime Delimitation in the Area between Greenland and Jan Mayen (Denmark v Norway)* (1993) ICJ 37.

and Denmark. One of the questions in the case was whether the equidistance principle could be binding on Germany which had not ratified the 1958 Convention not as a matter of treaty law but because the provisions of Art 6 constituted a rule of customary international law. The Court ruled that the equidistance principle was not a rule of customary international law and thus was not binding on Germany. However, in considering the relevant rule of customary international law, the court ruled that:

> ... delimitation is to be effected by agreement in accordance with equitable principles, and taking account of all the relevant circumstances, in such a way as to leave as much as possible to each Party all those parts of the continental shelf that constitute a natural prolongation of its land territory into and under the sea, without encroachment on the natural prolongation of the land territory of the other.

The Court's judgment gave rise to a number of consequences. First, the right of a coastal state to a continental shelf was linked to the 'natural prolongation of its land territory'. Secondly, the principle of delimitation was so general and required the consideration of all relevant circumstances that the difficulty would arise when applying it in different geographical circumstances. Thirdly, in the case in question, the parties subsequently reached agreement on the boundary by reference to the principles enunciated by the court. Fourthly, although the case appeared to indicate a different rule in customary international law from that provided under Art 6, it was open to debate as to whether the equidistance plus special circumstances test was much different in practice from the test of equitable principles plus all relevant circumstances; the latter is, in principle, broader because a circumstance may be relevant without being special.

In the *Anglo French Continental Shelf* case,[238] the arbitral tribunal was charged with fixing a delimitation of the Western Approaches. Both states were parties to the Geneva Convention on the Continental Shelf (1958) so that Art 6 applied. In giving the award, the arbitral tribunal viewed both rules as expressions of a single principle which, in effect, 'gives particular expression to a general norm that, failing agreement, the boundary between states abutting the same continental shelf is to be determined on equitable principles'.[239] On the facts of the case, the tribunal made allowance for the position of both the Channel Islands and the Scilly Isles.

The fact that the two tests would normally lead to the same result was expressly acknowledged by the International Court of Justice in the *Jan Mayen (Denmark v Norway)* case,[240] where it was noted that 'it must be difficult to find any material difference – at any rate in regard to delimitation between opposite coasts – between the effect of Art 6 and the effect of the customary rule which also requires a delimitation based on equitable principles'.[241]

The Law of the Sea Convention (1982) makes reference to the process of delimitation in Art 83 which provides that:

---

238 *Anglo French Continental Shelf* case (1977) 54 ILR 6.

239 (1979) 54 ILR 6, p 57; 18 ILM 398, p 421; see, also, DW Bowett, 'The arbitration between the United Kingdom and France concerning the continental shelf boundary in the English Channel' (1978) 49 BYIL 1.

240 (1993) ICJ 38.

241 *Ibid*, p 58.

The delimitation of the continental shelf between States with opposite or adjacent coasts shall be effected by agreement on the basis of international law, as referred to in Article 38 of the Statute of the International Court of Justice, in order to achieve an equitable solution.

Thus, it is reasonable to infer that delimitation in respect of opposite or adjacent coasts is to be determined on the basis of equitable principles, taking into account all relevant factors in order to achieve an equitable result. Although no list can be comprehensive, past judicial and arbitral decisions have given some indication as to the factors that will be considered by a tribunal:

(i) In the first instance the parties should seek to reach an agreement founded on equitable principles.[242]

(ii) In no circumstances is unilateral determination acceptable.[243]

(iii) In each particular case careful attention must be given to the overall geographical context.[244]

(iv) In respect of competing states it is proper to consider both the length of the coastline and its configuration.[245]

(v) Where there are areas of overlap in the continental shelf between competing states then there is a presumption that an equal division of such areas will constitute an equitable solution.[246]

(vi) It will be proper to take into account the past conduct of the parties in relation to the disputed area.[247]

(vii) It will be proper to take into account not only the existence of natural resources in a disputed area but also access to those resources.[248]

(viii) While a tribunal should strive for proportionality between coastline and continental shelf it is more important to avoid a result that is disproportionate.[249] Proportionality is not itself a principle but may act as a test to determine whether the decision reached is in fact equitable.[250]

(ix) It would seem that within a distance of 200 nautical miles geological factors will not weigh heavily and that natural prolongation is a factor that will not be itself decisive as to what represents and equitable solution.[251]

---

242 *North Sea Continental Shelf* case (1969) ICJ Rep 3, pp 46–47; LOSC (1982), Art 83(1).

243 The *Gulf of Maine* case (1984) ICJ 246; (1984) 71 ILR 74.

244 *Anglo French Continental Shelf* case (1977) 54 ILR 6; *Libya/Malta Continental Shelf* case (1985) ICJ 13; (1985) 81 ILR 239; *Guinea-Guinea (Bissau)* case (1985) 77 ILR 635.

245 *North Sea Continental Shelf* case (1969) ICJ 3, pp 17–18; *Gulf of Maine* case (1984) ICJ 246, pp 298–99, 312–13, 323; *Guinea-Guinea (Bissau)* (1985) 77 ILR 635, p 681; *Jan Mayen* case (1993) ICJ 37, pp 65–70.

246 *North Sea Continental Shelf* case (1969) ICJ 3; *Libya/Malta Continental Shelf* case (1985) ICJ 13; (1985) 81 ILR 239.

247 *Tunisia/Libya Continental Shelf* case (1982) ICJ 18.

248 *North Sea Continental Shelf* case (1969) ICJ 3; *Jan Mayen (Denmark v Norway)* case (1993) ICJ 37.

249 *Anglo French Continental Shelf* case (1977) 54 ILR 6.

250 *Libya/Malta Continental Shelf* case (1985) ICJ 13; (1985) 81 ILR 239.

251 *Tunisia/Libya Continental Shelf* case (1982) ICJ 18, p 46; (1982) 67 ILR 4; *Libya/Malta Continental Shelf* case (1985) ICJ 13, pp 32–37; (1985) 81 ILR 239.

(x) A distinction has to be drawn between those cases where delimitation is between opposite states where there may be a presumption in favour equidistance in contrast to those cases between adjacent states where no such presumption arises and an equitable solution will require consideration of a wide number of factors.[252]

(xi) The relative economic position of the two competing states will not normally be legally relevant.[253]

(xii) The degree of relevance and weight to be given to each factor will vary in each particular case.[254]

It might be thought from the above that the rules are so open ended that prediction is difficult and a tribunal would have considerable freedom to reach a decision. However, it is clear that a distinction has to be drawn between those cases where a single maritime boundary is in issue and those cases where only the limit of the continental shelf falls to be determined. Secondly, it is also evident that, in the latter situation, a distinction has to be drawn between claims made by opposite states where equidistance may at least be a starting point for discussion and those cases arising between adjacent states where a wider number of considerations will have to be drawn upon in order to reach an equitable result.

In the last two decades, questions of maritime delimitation[255] have occupied the International Court of Justice for a considerable period of time and much academic comment has been generated; however, there has been a remarkable consistency of approach. The decided cases have revealed a consistent willingness not only to consider each case as geographically distinct, but to ensure that relevant criteria lead to an equitable result and to deprecate any attempt to overconceptualise the subject.[256] In the *North Sea Continental Shelf* cases, the ICJ observed 'that there is no limit to the considerations which states may take into account for the purpose of making sure that they apply equitable procedures'.[257] In the *Anglo French Continental Shelf* case,[258] the tribunal observed that Art 6 of the 1958 Convention existed to give effect to 'a general norm that, failing agreement, the boundary abutting on the same continental shelf is to be determined by equitable principles'.

In the *Tunisia/Libya Continental Shelf* case,[259] the Court was obliged to proceed on the basis of customary international law as neither state was a party to the 1958 Convention. Although the Court rejected purely economic factors, it was prepared to accept that an

---

252 *North Sea Continental Shelf* case (1969) ICJ 3, pp 36–37.

253 *Libya/Malta Continental Shelf* case (1985) ICJ 13, pp 40–41; (1985) 81 ILR 239, p 283.

254 *North Sea Continental Shelf* case (1969) ICJ 3, pp 50–51.

255 In actual fact, somewhat longer. The relevant cases being the *North Sea Continental Shelf* case (1969) ICJ 3, (1969) 41 ILR 29; *Tunisia/Lybia Continental Shelf* case (1982) ICJ 18; (1982) 67 ILR 4; *Gulf of Maine* case (1984) ICJ 246, (1984) 71 ILR 74; *Libya Malta Continental Shelf* case (1985) ICJ 13, (1985) 81 ILR 239; *Jan Mayen (Denmark v Norway)* case (1993) ICJ 38. There have also been some important decisions by arbitral tribunals, of which the most important have been *Anglo French Continental Shelf* case (1977) 54 ILR 6; *Guinea/Guinea Bissau Maritime Boundary* case (1986) 25 ILM 251; (1986) 77 ILR 636; *St Pierre and Miquelon* case (1992) 31 ILM 1145.

256 *Tunisia/Libya Continental Shelf* case (1982) ICJ 18, p 92; (1982) 67 ILR 4, p 85.

257 *North Sea Continental Shelf* cases (1969) ICJ 3, p 50.

258 *Anglo-French Continental Shelf* case (1978) 54 ILR 6.

259 *Tunisia/Libya Continental Shelf* case (1982) ICJ 18.

equitable solution required it to consider a wide range of relevant circumstances.[260] Indeed, the judgment has attracted some criticism because the Court seemed to regard the object of an equitable result as more important then limiting the relevant factors that determined the result. Some expressed concern that such an approach can lead to the facts giving rise to an equitable solution for which particular circumstances are then preyed in aid to justify the original determination.[261] In any event, the judgment does support the view that maritime boundaries are to be determined in accordance with equitable principles, taking account of all the relevant circumstances in order to achieve an equitable result.

Although the *Gulf of Maine* case[262] concerned only a Chamber of the Court and was concerned with a single maritime boundary between Canada and the United States, both parties in their pleadings urged the Chamber to consider geographical, geological and environmental circumstances, as well as the prior conduct of the parties. In giving judgment, the Chamber stressed the importance of geographical factors and regarded socio economic factors as being of little direct relevance.[263] The Chamber also indicated that what might be relevant in determining the EEZ might not be so in the case of the continental shelf. The case indicates a slightly less liberal approach, with the main emphasis being placed on geographical considerations and a reluctance to consider environmental factors.

In the *Libya/Malta Continental Shelf* case[264] Libya was not a party to the Geneva Convention on the Continental Shelf (1958) so the case was determined under the rules of customary international law. The parties in their pleadings advanced a wide range of criteria that might be considered material and the judgment of the Court recognised that security considerations and political status might have some relevance. The case itself indicates not only a more liberal approach than the *Gulf of Maine* case,[265] but also a willingness to consider the existence of the exclusive economic zone as an important factor. The Court ruled that while the EEZ and the continental shelf are subject to separate regimes, they should be developed so that they can operate in an harmonious unity. Thus, it accepted that since customary international law allowed the state to claim an EEZ of 200 nautical miles, greater emphasis had to be placed on the consideration of distance from the coast. Some of the wider submissions of the parties were not accepted. The Court rejected arguments based on landmass or on narrowly economic considerations. However, the Court accepted that criteria relating to the configuration and length of the coast were important as indeed was the need to avoid excessive disproportion between the length of the coast and the continental shelf.

In the *Guinea/Guinea Bissau* case,[266] an arbitral tribunal was required to consider the maritime boundary between the two states. Once again, it was stated that the object was

---

260 Amongst which were: (i) the coastal direction; (i) the presence of islands and islets; (iii) the configuration of the seabed; (iv) potential claims by third states; (v) the past conduct of the parties.

261 See the dissenting speech by Judge Gross (1982) ICJ 18, p 153; (1982) 67 ILR 4, p 146.

262 (1984) ICJ 246.

263 *Gulf of Maine* case (1984) ICJ 246.

264 (1985) ICJ 13; (1985) 81 ILR 239.

265 (1984) ICJ 246.

266 (1988) 25 ILM 251.

to find an equitable solution having regard to all the relevant circumstances but, in so doing, the tribunal considered that in the instant case arguments based on proportionality, prolongation or economic strength carried little weight. The emphasis on finding an equitable solution in the precise geographical circumstances was stressed by the tribunal in the *St Pierre and Miquelon (Canada/France)* case,[267] which concerned islands lying off the southern coast of Newfoundland. In this particular case, which concerned settling a common maritime boundary to the west and south of the islands, the tribunal stressed that any solution should not only be equitable in the circumstances but should avoid encroaching on the maritime zone of Canada. Thus, in considering the western aspect, and mindful that it would encroach on Canada's maritime zone, the tribunal decided to award a 12 mile exclusive economic zone beyond the 12 mile territorial sea. However, in respect of the southern aspect, the islands were permitted a zone of 200 nautical miles but limited in breadth so as to avoid encroaching upon adjacent maritime zones. Having reached such a conclusion, the tribunal asked itself whether the proposed solution was proportionate and not 'radically inequitable'.

In the *Jan Mayen (Denmark v Norway)* case,[268] the International Court of Justice was charged with delimiting the continental shelf and fishing zone between the islands of Greenland and Jan Mayen. Being concerned with opposite states, and being subject to Art 6 of the Geneva Convention on the Continental Shelf (1958), the court began by drawing a median line and then moving it eastwards towards Jan Mayen island to reflect the greater length of the Greenland coast and the importance of fishing to the Greenland economy. It was not considered appropriate to consider security interests or the limited population on Jan Mayen island. In essence, the court considered that, in the situation of opposite states, the disproportion in coastal length and the principle of equitable access to fishing resources could modify the median line.

14 THE INTERNATIONAL SEABED AREA

It has been known since the 19th century that the seabed beyond the continental shelf was rich in metallic nodules; such nodules which might comprise a variety of metallic substances have come to be referred to as 'manganese nodules'. Particularly rich stocks are to be found on the bed of the Indian Ocean and in parts of the Pacific Ocean. In the last half century it has become evident that such deposits were in excess of the land based resources. The presence of such nodules posed three questions. At what point in time would it become possible to exploit such resources? Secondly, was it not likely that the consortia seeking to develop such resources would be drawn from the capital rich economies of the developed world? Thirdly, what would be the effect of such developments on those developing states whose economies were dependent on the export of particular minerals?

Increasingly in the 1960s, it came to be accepted that the answer to these questions would involve some form of regulatory regime in respect of the international seabed.

---

267 (1992) 31 ILM 1145; (1992) 95 ILR 645; see M Evans (1994) 43 ICLQ 678.
268 (1993) ICJ 38; see M Evans (1994) 43 ICLQ 697.

Developing countries were particularly anxious that if the matter remained unregulated there was the risk of a scramble by companies based in developed states.

When these questions first came to the fore in the 1960s, one difficulty was that if the continental shelf remained subject to the 'exploitability' criterion in the 1958 Convention, then companies might be able to justify expanding further and further from the coast into ever deeper waters. For this reason, it was necessary to produce a much more precise definition of the continental shelf. A second difficulty was that some developed nations took the view that deep sea exploration was justified even in the middle of an ocean as an aspect of the traditional freedom of the high seas. However, this was not a view accepted by developing nations who increasingly sought the introduction of a regulatory regime.

In November 1967, Dr Arvid Pardo the Maltese Ambassador to the United Nations proposed that a declaration should be drawn up regulating the use of the international seabed in the interests of mankind.[269] Such a proposal was well received by many developing states and, in 1968, a committee was established under the title of 'the Committee on the Peaceful Uses of the Sea Bed and Ocean Floor beyond the Limits of National Jurisdiction'. From the outset, it was clear that developing states wished to move rapidly to introduce a regulatory regime. In 1969, the General Assembly adopted Resolution 2574 (described as the 'Moratorium Resolution') which provided that, in broad terms, there should be a moratorium of all activities on the seabed and ocean floor pending the introduction of an international regulatory regime.[270] In 1970, the General Assembly built upon this by adopting Resolution 2749 which comprised a 'Declaration of Principles Governing the Seabed and Ocean Floor and the Subsoil Thereof, beyond the Limits of National Jurisdiction' ('the Area'). The resolution was widely drawn and susceptible of a variety of interpretations, but it declared that that the Area and its resources were the 'common heritage of mankind' and could not be appropriated by any single state and that no rights could the acquired over the Area save under the international regulatory regime that was to be established.

Thus, when the conference on the law of the sea opened in 1973 there was a clear difference of view. Developing states were anxious to establish an international seabed authority as a regulatory body with comprehensive powers, while some of the developed nations viewed this as excessively bureaucratic and would have been content with a limited form of registration of claims. However, the movement of opinion was generally towards developing nations and the detailed provisions were set out in Part XI of the Law of the Sea Convention (1982) (Arts 133–91).

Article 136 provides that the Area[271] and its resources are to be the common heritage of mankind and Art 137 stipulates that no state should claim or exercise sovereignty over any part of the Area; however, minerals recovered may be alienable in accordance with Part XI. In general, all rights in the resources of the Area are vested in mankind as a

---

269 The full title of the proposed declaration was 'A Declaration and Treaty Concerning the Reservation Exclusively for Peaceful Purposes of the Sea Bed and Ocean Floor Underlying the Seas beyond the Limits of National Jurisdiction and the Use of their Resources in the Interests of Mankind'.

270 General Assembly Resolution 2574(XXIV) passed by 62 votes to 28 with 28 abstentions. Western nations abstained or voted against.

271 The Area being defined in Art 1(1) as 'the sea bed and ocean floor and subsoil thereof, beyond the limits of national jurisdiction'.

whole, on whose behalf the International Seabed Authority is to act[272] and all activities shall be carried out for the benefit of mankind as a whole.[273] Article 140(2) further provides that the Authority shall provide for the equitable sharing of financial and other economic benefits derived from activities in the Area.

Under the terms of the Convention, the Authority was itself to engage in operations in the Area, through its mining arm the Enterprise. Article 153 provided that exploration and exploitation was to be conducted by the Enterprise, by state parties and by other natural and juridical persons. Annex III of the Convention provided that qualified applicants were to submit formal written proposals; such proposals would specify two particular sites for exploration. In respect of one site, permission would be granted to explore while the second site would be 'banked' by the Authority so as to permit future exploitation. The logic of such arrangements was to promote a system of parallel development of the Area both by mining companies and by the Enterprise and developing states. However, by the time that the final text of the Law of the Sea Convention (1982) was drawn up, it was clear that such arrangements were not acceptable to the United States and certain other Western states so that, in early 1982, attempts were made to find a compromise acceptable to all parties. To this end two resolutions were passed.

Resolution 1 provided for the establishment of a Preparatory Commission (referred to as Prep Com) comprised of representatives from those states who had signed the Convention. One of the tasks of this body was to prepare for the constitution of the International Seabed Authority. At the same time, it was recognised that a number of companies had expended considerable sums on research and development in seabed mining. In consequence, Resolution 2 made special provision for eight pioneer investors[274] drawn from a number of states. Each investor was required to produce evidence of having invested a sum of $30 million in seabed mining. These pioneer investors were to be permitted to undertake exploration activities prior to the coming into force of the Convention and would have priority as regards other applicants in the distribution of exploration contracts.

It had been hoped that the concessions made in Resolution 2 would have been sufficient to secure the consent of a number of Western European states, but circumstances played a part. By 1982, conservative regimes in London, Washington and later Bonn objected not only to the bureaucratic structure and regulatory regime but also to provisions on the compulsory transfer of intellectual property rights. The content of Part XI was given as the reason why neither the United States nor the United Kingdom were prepared to sign the Convention in 1982.

The failure to produce an acceptable scheme within the Convention on deep sea mining precipitated a move towards national legislation on the subject. The United States began with the Deep Seabed Hard Materials Resources Act 1980 and the United Kingdom followed with the Deep Sea Mining (Temporary Provisions) Act 1981. Legislation to

---

272 Article 137(2).
273 Article 140.
274 Four were to come from France, Japan, India and the then USSR while the other four comprised multinational consortia.

similar effect was passed in Japan,[275] West Germany,[276] France, Italy and the USSR. In broad terms such legislation provided for the granting of licences for exploration and exploitation and for the mutual recognition of licences granted by other states.

In the case of the United Kingdom, s 1 of the 1981 Act prohibited unlicensed deep sea mining while s 2 provided for the granting of licences. As with other national legislation, s 3 provided for the recognition of licences granted by other reciprocating countries. The legislation provided that the granting of licences should take account of the need to protect the marine environment[277] and the licensee[278] was obliged to respect the freedom of the high seas. Section 9 of the 1981 Act provided for the imposition of a Deep Sea Mining Levy to be paid by the holder of a licence into a Deep Sea Mining Fund. Under the terms of s 10 such a fund would be paid over to the relevant international organisation if the Law of the Sea Convention (1982) should enter into force for the United Kingdom.

The co-operative effort by a number of states outside the scope of the Law of the Sea Convention (1982) was alluded to as the 'mini treaty' regime. It came to be underwritten by agreements made in 1982[279] and 1984[280] designed to improve the level of co-operation. The rationale for this co-operation was that it constituted the regulation by states of the activities of their own nationals upon the high seas. However, developing states did not accept this analysis asserting that the reciprocating states regime was at variance with earlier General Assembly Resolutions and likely to undermine the objective of universal participation in the 1982 Convention. This viewpoint was endorsed by Prep Com which indicated in 1985 that the scheme was inconsistent with the Convention in general and with Art 137 in particular as being an unlawful disposition of part of the Area. More controversially, Prep Com declared the entire scheme contrary to customary international law. At one stage, it was proposed that the entire question be subject to an advisory opinion by the International Court; however, it is doubtful what practical value there would have been when the situation remained highly fluid. One reason was that the decline in world metal prices in the 1980s made deep sea mining less attractive as an immediate commercial proposition. Secondly, the increasing influence of market based solutions in the 1980s and the decline of centrally planned economies in Eastern Europe tended to strengthen western objections to Part XI of the Convention. Thirdly, it remained clear that if an agreement could be reached on Part XI, most states would be prepared to accede to the Convention. Fourthly, the task of establishing the International Seabed Authority would be financially burdensome unless major western nations were prepared

---

275 Japan (1983) 22 ILM 102.

276 West Germany (1981) 20 ILM 393; France (1982) 21 ILM 808; Italy (1985) 24 ILM 983; USSR (1982) 21 ILM 551.

277 Deep Sea Mining (Temporary Provisions) Act 1981, s 5.

278 *Ibid*, s 7.

279 The 1982 Agreement concerning Interim Arrangements relating to Polymetallic Nodules of the Deep Sea Bed (France, West Germany, United States, United Kingdom). In effect, provided for consultation to prevent overlapping claims (1982) 21 ILM 850.

280 Provisional Understanding Regarding Deep Sea Bed Matters (1984) (Belgium, France, Federal Republic of Germany, Italy, Japan, Netherlands, United Kingdom, United States) (the title of the document testifies to its interim nature) (1984) 23 ILM 1354. The agreement contained further provisions to prevent overlapping claims. Thus, no state was to issue a licence in respect of an area included in a claim filed elsewhere.

to participate. These factors tended to the view that it was less important to ascertain the legality of the reciprocating states regime; what was important was to resume negotiations to see whether a *modus vivendi* could be reached.

After 1990, this task was undertaken by the United Nations Secretary General. Negotiations made such progress[281] that by summer 1993 there were grounds for optimism. On 28 July 1994, the Agreement Relating to the Implementation of Part XI of the United Nations Convention on the Law of the Sea was accepted by the General Assembly by 121 votes to none with seven abstentions. In effect, Part XI was modified to meet the concern of western states. Article 1 of the 1994 Agreement required state parties to implement Part XI in accordance with the agreement and Art 2 provided that Part XI and the agreement were to be interpreted as a single document. Under the terms of Art 4, a state could not consent to the agreement without becoming a party to the Convention. At the time, the agreement was concluded it was known that the Law of the Sea Convention would come into effect on 16 November 1994, so that Art 7 of the 1994 Agreement provided for its provisional application from that date if the consent of 40 states had been obtained under Art 6.

The actual modifications to the Law of the Sea Convention are contained in the Annex to the 1994 Agreement. Section 1 stipulates that organs and institutions established under the Convention on a cost effective basis. Section 2 of the Annex provides that the work of the Enterprise shall, in the first instance, be carried out by the Secretariat of the Authority and the Enterprise shall conduct its initial deep seabed operations through joint ventures. In respect of decision making within the Authority, s 3 provides that decision making in the organs of the Authority should be by consensus and that the Assembly may at any time conduct a review of any of the matters stipulated in Art 155, notwithstanding the specific provisions of the article. In respect of the transfer of technology, Art 5 provides that the Enterprise and developing states shall seek to obtain such technology on fair and reasonable commercial terms and conditions on the open market.

The agreement reached in July 1994 had the consequence that when the Law of the Sea Convention came into effect in November 1994, there was a realistic prospect of universal participation. On 25 July 1997, the United Kingdom deposited an instrument of accession[282] and an instrument of ratification of the Implementation Agreement which both took effect 30 days later on 24 August 1997. The United Kingdom was the 119th State to indicate its consent to be bound by the Convention and the 82nd party to the Agreement of July 1994. By July 1998, 127 states had ratified or acceded to the Law of the Sea Convention (1982) so that the objective of 'a constitution for the Oceans' has broadly been achieved. Having regard to the large number of states and the diverse interests involved, this has been a considerable achievement.

---

281 See BH Oxman, 'The 1994 Agreement and the Convention' (1994) 88 AJIL 687; LB Sohn, 'International law implications of the 1994 Agreement' (1994) 88 AJIL 696; JI Charney, 'US provisional application of the 1994 Deep Seabed Agreement' (1994) 88 AJIL 705; DH Anderson, 'Efforts to ensure universal participation in the United Nations Convention on the Law of the Sea' (1993) 42 ICLQ 654; DH Anderson, 'Further efforts to ensure universal participation in the United Nations Convention on the Law of the Sea' (1994) 43 ICLQ 886.
282 DH Anderson, 'British accession to the UN Convention on the Law of the Sea' (1997) 46 ICLQ 761.

15 THE RESOLUTION OF DISPUTES[283]

The Law of the Sea Convention (1982) contains a considerable number of articles designed to promote the peaceful settlement of disputes; the relevant provisions are contained in Part XV (Arts 279–299). Article 279 commits all state parties to the principle of the peaceful settlement of disputes while Art 280 permits such parties to reach agreement as to a particular method of peaceful resolution. It will be open to parties in dispute to seek conciliation.[284]

In the absence of such resolution then other avenues will arise. Under the terms of Art 287, when a state ratifies or accedes to the Convention it may choose one of the following methods of dispute resolution: (i) the International Tribunal for the Law of the Sea;[285] (ii) the International Court of Justice; (iii) an arbitral tribunal established under Annex VII; or (iv) a special arbitral tribunal established under Annex VIII. In addition, Art 187 provides that the Sea Bed Disputes Chamber of the Tribunal shall have jurisdiction in respect of disputes concerning the deep seabed and the International Sea Bed Authority. In most situations, much will depend on the precise nature of the dispute and the appropriate forum will depend not only on whether the dispute is of a factual or legal nature but also whether a decision is required quickly.[286]

Since states may resolve their disputes outside the Convention, examples arise of cases coming before other judicial bodies; of particular relevance is the role of the European Court of Justice in dealing with disputes both between member states and between member states and the European Commission. In the past century there are numerous examples of disputes being resolved by inquiry,[287] conciliation,[288] arbitration[289] or by a hearing before the International Court of Justice.[290]

---

283 JG Merrills, *International Dispute Settlement*, 3rd edn, 1998; JG Collier and AV Lowe, *The Settlement of Disputes in International Law*, 1999, Chapter 5; R Churchill and AV Lowe, *The Law of the Sea*, 3rd edn, 1999, Chapter 19. See, also, AO Adede (1975) 69 AJIL 798; (1978) 72 AJIL 84; S Oda, 'Dispute settlement prospects in the law of the sea' (1995) 44 ICLQ 863.

284 LOSC (1984), Art 284.

285 For the first case, see *The M/V Saiga* (1998) 110 ILR 736; 37 ILM 360. For comment, see AV Lowe, 'The *M/V Saiga* case: the first case in the International Tribunal for the Law of the Sea' (1999) 48 ICLQ 187.

286 *In the M/V Saiga (No 1)* (1997). The International Tribunal for the Law of the Sea gave a decision on 4 December 1997 in respect of an application made on 13 November 1997. The decision itself was concerned with an order for prompt release of the vessel. The substantive hearing took place in March 1999 and concerned the attempt by Guinea to enforce customs rules in its EEZ and to employ force. In a judgment given on 1 July 1999, the International Tribunal for the Law of the Sea found that Guinea had been acting unlawfully in seeking to impose a customs zone beyond that permitted in Art 33 of the LOSC and further emphasised that rights within the EEZ were restricted to those set out in Arts 56 and 58. Rather unusually, much of the hearing was devoted to the hearing of oral evidence; the tribunal made an award in favour of St Vincent and the Grenadines of a sum of US $2,123,357. For an evaluation of proceedings, see Louise de la Fayette 'The *M/V Saiga (No 2)* case (*St Vincent and the Grenadines v Guinea)*' (2000) 49 ICLQ 467.

287 The Dogger Bank Inquiry (1905) in JB Scott (ed), *The Hague Court Reports* (1916), pp 403–13; The Red Crusader Inquiry (1962) (1967) 35 ILR 485.

288 *Jan Mayen Island Continental Shelf Dispute (Iceland v Norway)* (1981) 20 ILM 797; (1981) 62 ILR 108; see, also, EL Richardson, '*Jan Mayen* in perspective' (1988) 82 AJIL 443.

289 *Anglo French Continental Shelf* case (1977) 54 ILR 6; *Guinea/Guinea Bissau Maritime Boundary* case (1986) 25 ILM 251.

290 *Anglo Norwegian Fisheries* case (1951) ICJ 116; *North Sea Continental Shelf* case (1969) ICJ 3; *Tunisia/Libya Continental Shelf* case (1982) ICJ 18, (1982) 67 ILR 4; *Gulf of Maine* case (1984) ICJ 246; *Libya/Malta Continental Shelf* case (1985) ICJ 13; (1985) 81 ILR 239.

CHAPTER 14

AIR LAW AND SPACE LAW

1 AIR LAW[1]

(a) Introduction

The law in respect of airspace began to be discussed towards the end of the 19th century.[2] A number of approaches were possible. First, some sought to argue that air space was free and open to all. Secondly, some asserted that all superjacent airspace was subject to the exclusive sovereignty of the state by analogy with the principle in municipal law of *cujus est solum, ejus est usque ad coelum et ad infernos*;[3] a principle which had been subject of comment in those cases concerning trespass to airspace.[4] A third possible approach was to argue that in line with the law of the sea, the state was entitled to a 'belt of airspace' and that beyond that point airspace was like the high seas open to all. A fourth possibility was to accept the second approach, namely sovereignty of the individual state but to assert that it was subject to a right of innocent passage. These debates were being conducted in a Europe which was subject to increasing tension, particularly after 1890, between Germany and its neighbours. In these circumstances, state practice tended to be concerned with problems of national security and the fear of surprise attack. While most accepted that the airspace above the high seas was open to all, there were divisions of opinion prior to 1914; the United Kingdom tended to the view of state sovereignty over airspace but this was not a view shared by all European states. The United Kingdom legislated on the matter in the Aerial Navigation Act 1911[5] which enabled the Secretary of State to make delegated legislation prohibiting the navigation of aircraft within certain

---

1 Shawcross and Beaumont, *Air Law*, 4th edn, 1977 (2 Vols subject to regular supplements); B Cheng, *The Law of International Air Transport*, 1962; R Jennings and AW Watts, *Oppenheim's International Law*, 9th edn, 1992, p 650; RY Jennings, 'Some aspects of the international law of the air' (1949) 75 HR 509; D Goedhuatts, 'Questions of public international air law' (1952) 81 HR 201; DW Greig, *International Law*, 2nd edn, 1976, London: Butterworths; A McNair, *The Law of the Air* (ME Kerr and AH Evans (eds)), 3rd edn, 1964; E Pepin, '*Le droit aerien*' (1947) 71 HR 477; P De Geouffre de La Pradelle, '*Les frontières de l'air*' (1954) 86 HR 117.

2 By the time problems of air law began to emerge at the turn of the century, the principles of territory and jurisdiction were already well established.

3 The expression appear to have been first coined by Accursius in the 13th century. Accursius through his commentaries on Roman Law is seen as one of the earliest writers on private international law. In essence, the phrase means that the owner of the land is presumed to own everything 'up to the sky and down to the centre of the earth'. For a discussion in the municipal law context, see *Corbett v Hill* (1870) LR 9 Eq 671; *Pountney v Clayton* (1883) 11 QBD 820, p 838, *per* Bowen LJ; *Wandsworth Board of Works v United Telephone Company* (1884) 13 QBD 904; *Commissioner for Railways v Valuer General* [1974] AC 328, p 351, *per* Lord Wilberforce; *Bernstein of Leigh (Baron) v Skyviews & General Ltd* [1978] QB 479.

4 See Co Litt 4a; *Blackstone Commentaries*, Vol II, Chapter 2, p 18. For early discussion of the principle, see *Baten's* case (1610) 9 Rep 53b; *Pickering v Rudd* (1815) 4 Camp 219.

5 This was followed by the Aerial Navigation Act 1913 which was followed by the Aerial Navigation Act 1919; this legislation being replaced by the Air Navigation Act 1920. The 1920 Act was amended by the subsequent Air Navigation Act 1936. Many of the provisions finding their way into the consolidating Civil Aviation Act 1949.

areas.[6] However, most writers accept that the rules of customary international law remained unsettled at the time of the outbreak of the European War in 1914.

The experience of the war of 1914–18 profoundly changed European society and the subsequent conduct of international relations. In the early months of the war, aeroplanes were used for scouting and then fighter planes were sent to intercept them. Zeppelin raids on England began in 1915 and bombing by aeroplane followed. By 1918, Britain was preparing an independent bomber force. Although only 1,100 people died in air raids in England during the conflict, the effect on public opinion was considerable; aircraft could bring home to a civilian population the effects of a far away conflict. Military strategists realised that control of the air would be of crucial importance in any future conflict.

In these circumstances it was not surprising that statesmen[7] came to the view that sovereignty in airspace was essential and that military success in the future would be determined to a considerable extent by control of airspace.

International Law was quick to respond to these new developments. Article 1 of the Paris Convention for the Regulation of Aerial Navigation 1919 adopted the common law principle of sovereignty of the individual state for an unlimited distance into airspace; the sovereignty was to be enjoyed by each state not merely each contracting state. Under Art 2, each party undertook to allow in time of peace innocent passage to private aircraft so long as they complied with rules made by or under the authority of the Convention.[8] Although the Convention established an International Commission for Air Navigation, and while the Convention was signed by 26 states, the number of ratifications proved a disappointment. However, the principle that aviation would have to be subject to international regulation and the principle that a state enjoyed sovereignty in its own airspace had been established within the first two decades of the 20th century. The establishment of state sovereignty in airspace had the consequence that any unauthorised intrusion would in principle be a trespass; not surprisingly the action that a state should take in such circumstances has been the subject of some debate.

Some states which did not ratify the Paris Convention participated in the Havana Convention on Commercial Aviation (1928) which, although restricted to commercial aviation, contained similar provisions. The growth in aviation in the 1920s and 1930s and the desire by states for a broader and more detailed set of rules lead to the summoning of the International Civil Aviation Conference which convened in Chicago in November 1944. The United States acted as host of the conference and, as the most significant state, was anxious to secure agreement on a number of principles which became known as the

---

6   Interestingly, the principal object of the legislation as stated in the preamble was the protection of the public.

7   An important event was the publication of the Smuts Report in October 1917 for the War Cabinet of David Lloyd George, which raised the question that provided sufficient aeroplanes could be constructed military victory might be achieved without mass casualties in land combat. The publication of the report prompted an independent air ministry in England and the establishment of the Royal Air Force. The report raised the question as to whether attacks could be directed on a civilian population. For the effect in the First World War, see AJP Taylor, *The First World War*, 1965; AJP Taylor, *English History (1914–1945)*, 1965. For a discussion as to the debate on bombing of civilian areas in World War II, see Jonathan Glover, *Humanity: A Moral History of the Twentieth Century*, 1999, Chapter 6.

8   The right of passage was excluded for international aircraft so that scheduled services were dependent on the consent of the individual state concerned (see Art 15).

Five Freedoms; these were (a) the right of the airlines of each state to fly across foreign territory without landing; (b) the right of the airlines of each state to land for non-traffic purposes; (c) the right of the airlines of each state to disembark in a foreign country traffic originating in the state of origin of the aircraft; (d) the right of the airlines of each state to pick up in a foreign country traffic destined for the state of origin of the aircraft; (e) the right of the airlines of each state to carry traffic between two foreign countries. The first two rights are transit rights; the first 'freedom' enables the state granted to fly and carry traffic non-stop over the territory of the grantor state. The second 'freedom' is the right to fly and carry traffic but also to stop for non-traffic purposes (that is, refuelling and repair). The third and fourth rights are transit rights. The third 'freedom' enables traffic to be carried from the Flag state (that is, the grantee state) to the territory of the grantor state while the fourth 'freedom' is the right to carry traffic from the territory of the grantor state to the territory of the Flag state. The fifth 'freedom' is the most extensive and the least granted. It involves the right to carry traffic between the grantor state and a third state. Clearly, such rights are required in the conduct of long haul flights. The fifth right proceeds by tracing the route from the flag state to the grantor state.

Thus, in the case of a right granted by the United States (grantor state) to the United Kingdom (Flag state or grantee), the fifth 'freedom' may embrace the rights respect of traffic that originates or is destined for (i) a place anterior to the United Kingdom (for example, Norway) (that is, anterior point fifth freedom); (ii) a place intermediate between flag state and grantor state (for example, France) (that is, intermediate point fifth freedom); (iii) a place beyond the grantor state (for example, Canada) (that is, beyond point fifth freedom).

The existing five 'freedoms' are supplemented by a number of other so called 'freedoms'. Thus, where state A has third and fourth rights in respect of state B and state C, it can create an effective fifth freedom in respect of state C by the organisation of its services from state B to state A and then to state C; such a situation is sometimes alluded to as the 'Sixth Freedom'. Sometimes, reference is made to a 'Seventh Freedom', namely where an airline based in state A seeks to conduct operations outside its territory between states B and C. Finally, where routes are between points in the grantor state, this is sometimes referred to as an ' Eighth Freedom' or, more usually, it is described as cabotage.

The principal product of the 1944 conference was the Chicago Convention on International Civil Aviation which was concluded in December 1944 and entered into force in April 1947.[9] The conference itself indicated that there was a difference of opinion between the United States preference for a liberal regulatory framework and the European desire for some form of 'predetermination', whereby routes and capacity were predetermined by contracting parties.

As events unfurled it became clear that it would not be possible, beyond the level of general principle, to regulate every question arising by multilateral convention.[10]

---

9   Now ratified or acceded to by over 150 states. The Convention has of course been amended on a number of occasions since 1944. The original text was in English but authentic texts were subsequently produced in Spanish, French and Russian. Legislation to give effect to the Convention was contained in Air Navigation Act 1947.

10 Unlike the law of the sea where this has proved possible aviation law more closely resembles human rights law where international conventions have been supplemented by action at the regional level.

(b) The modern law

Article 1 of the Chicago Convention asserted the principle that 'every state has complete and exclusive sovereignty over the airspace above its territory' and by the terms of Art 2 such territory will include both 'the land areas and the territorial waters adjacent thereto'. The scope of the Convention is restricted by Art 3 to civil aircraft and so does not extend to state aircraft such as military, customs and police aircraft. The emphasis on state sovereignty is reinforced in Art 6, which provides that no scheduled international air service may be operated over or into a contracting state, except with the special permission or authorisation of that state. However, this provision has to be read with Art 5 which stipulates that:

> Each contracting State agrees that all aircraft of the other contracting States, being aircraft not engaged in scheduled international air services shall have the right, subject to the observance of the terms of this Convention, to make flights into or in transit non-stop across its territory and to make stops for non traffic purposes without the necessity of obtaining prior permission, and subject to the right of the State flown over to require landing.

The exclusion of scheduled air services from Art 5[11] has meant that individual agreements have had to be created to provide the basic structure in which international scheduled flights can operate.[12] The interpretation of Arts 5 and 6 has depended on the definition to be accorded to the phrase 'scheduled international air service'. Although in 1952 the ICAO Council placed a narrow meaning on the expression which would have made Art 5 the governing rule and Art 6 the exception, this has not been accepted by state parties many of whom control national airlines. The practice has been to make Art 6 the general rule and Art 5 the exception restricted to private flight; so that permission is required for charter flights even though, on the plain wording, they may be considered outside the terms of Art 6. After 1944, the number of states increased considerably and many newly independent states spent large sums sustaining the operations of a national airline; in such circumstances they were not anxious to expose designated national carrier to further competition.

In respect of the nationality of aircraft, Art 17 provides that aircraft shall have the nationality of the state in which they are registered and although an aircraft cannot be registered in two states such registration may be changed from one state to another. The Convention provides that national law shall govern matters affecting registration.

One of the most enduring legacies of the Convention was the establishment, under Art 43, of the International Civil Aviation Authority which in 1947 became a specialised agency of the United Nations; the intention being that the organisation would administer the Convention[13] and co-ordinate co-operation in legal and technical matters. To facilitate harmonisation, Art 37 provides that the ICAO would be able to formulate International Standards and Recommended Practices. The organisation operates through an Assembly

---

11 The distinction between Scheduled International Air Services that required the permission of states and non-scheduled flights that had restricted rights of overflight and landing was carried over from the earlier Paris Convention.

12 For consideration of the Chicago Convention see *Italy-United States Air Arbitration* (1964) 16 RIAA 96; 45 ILR 393.

13 At least after the provisional body, the PICAO, ceased to operate in 1947.

and a Council[14] and such other bodies as may be necessary.[15] The organisation is charged with developing a safe and orderly growth of international civil aviation and is obliged to insure the avoidance of wasteful competition, the promotion of safety and the development of airports and aircraft design.[16] It has to be admitted that in the half century since it became operational it has some impressive achievements to its credit not least the promotion of safe and affordable civil aviation.[17]

An important provision was contained in Art 68, which stipulated that each state was entitled to prescribe the particular air route and airport that an international air service might use. This article provided the basis for post-1945 co-operation on matters of air traffic control. It is clear that much of the Chicago Convention followed upon the earlier Paris Convention; the general approach to sovereignty (Arts 1–2) and to questions of nationality and registration (Arts 17–21) draw upon the earlier instrument.[18] The Convention also included important provisions about harmonising safety standards, the investigation of accidents[19] and the reduction of customs and immigration controls[20] as well as documentation.[21]

The Chicago Convention on International Civil Aviation set out the general principles and provided the basis for the orderly development of civil aviation in the period after 1945. However, the statement of general principle did not go as far as some desired and an attempt was made to carry matters further in two other agreements drawn up at the conference. The most ambitious attempt was contained in the Chicago International Air Transport Agreement (sometimes described as the Five Freedoms Agreement). This agreement was intended to lead to promote the objective of freedom of international navigation and embraced the five freedoms indicated above. However, this policy which was promoted by the United States was at variance with the cautious instincts of many other states; thus, few states signed the agreement and only a limited number of ratifications were obtained.[22] However, the states also drew up a less ambitious agreement known as the Chicago International Air Services Transit Agreement (sometimes known as the Two Freedoms Agreement) which provided for two of the five freedoms, namely flying without landing and landing rights for non-traffic purposes (that is, refuelling and repair) in foreign territories. This agreement was in the nature of a compromise, but was signed in February 1945 and by 1989 had over 100 state parties. Such an agreement is important even in a world of bilateral agreement, suppose states X and Z agree in a bilateral agreement to accord the four freedoms in respect of a particular

---

14 For consideration of the role of the ICAO Council, see *The Appeal Relating to the Jurisdiction of the ICAO Council (India v Pakistan)* (1972) ICJ 46.

15 Article 43.

16 Article 44.

17 The 1948 Geneva Convention on the International Recognition of Rights in Aircraft; the Rome Convention of 1952 on Damage caused by Foreign Aircraft to Third Parties on the Surface.

18 The 1944 Convention retained in Art 7 the approach of the Paris Convention to air cabotage, ie, the right to carry traffic within the state itself.

19 Article 26.

20 Articles 23 and 24.

21 Article 29.

22 Only 11 states accepted the agreement. The United Kingdom did not accept it and the United States withdrew in 1946.

number of flights. However, such an agreement will be facilitated if there is no need to fly around state Y because it is a party to the Two Freedoms Agreement.

It has, however, to be admitted that the original objective of the Chicago Conference, of producing a series of multilateral conventions that would govern all major questions pertaining to international civil aviation, had not been achieved so that much would depend on either bilateral or regional agreements. Such agreements tended to be of a specialised and technical nature. Perhaps the most important was the Bermuda Agreement of 11 February 1946[23] made between the United Kingdom and the United States if only because it provided a model that others followed with some variations. The Bermuda Agreement proceeded on the principle that international air services should made available and should reflect the level of public demand and that there should be a fair and equal opportunity for the air carriers of both nations to compete in the provision of services. The Agreement proceeds on the basis of reciprocity, non-discrimination and regular consultation in respect of traffic requirements. The administrative and technical clauses have been followed in subsequent agreements. In July 1946 the United States withdrew from the Air Transport (or Five Freedoms) Agreement, acknowledging that the international regulation of air traffic by multilateral convention was unlikely to proceed further. A dispute between the United Kingdom and United States about landing rights for Concorde resulted in the United Kingdom denouncing the Bermuda Agreement in June 1976. New negotiations took place and a second agreement (usually known as Bermuda II) emerged. Bermuda II[24] reaffirmed the principles of Bermuda I, but also included provisions on infrastructure charges[25] and points of access.

However, while bilateral agreements have played a significant part since 1945 there are some important agreements of a regional nature. In respect of charter flights between some European Countries, reference should be made to the Multilateral Agreement on Commercial Rights of Non-Scheduled Air Services, which was signed in Paris in 1956 following work by the International Civil Aviation Organisation and to which the United Kingdom acceded in 1960. Secondly, an example is afforded by the Brussels Convention for the safety of Air Navigation of 1960 (known as the Eurocontrol Convention) which provides for the international traffic control of high flying aircraft.[26]

In considering the international organisation of aviation, it is important to note the role of the International Air Transport Association which is not a governmental organisation but comprises members of the airline industry who meet on a regular basis to discuss matters of common interest such as the level of fares, access to routes, safety and the appropriate action to be taken in respect of unlawful acts such as hijacking.

---

23 See R Jennings, 'International civil aviation and the law' (1945) 23 BYIL 191; 'Some aspects of the international law of the air' (1949) 75 HR 509.

24 For consideration of the status of Bermuda II in the English courts, see *British Airways Board v Laker Airways Ltd* [1985] AC 58; Collier [1984] CLJ 253; Carter (1984) 44 BYBIL 358.

25 See the *Heathrow Airport User Charges Arbitration* (1993) 102 ILR 215; S Witten, '*The United States- United Kingdom Arbitration concerning Heathrow Airport User Charges*' (1995) 89 AJIL 174.

26 The Civil Aviation (Eurocontrol) Act 1962 provided for the status and immunities of the body within the United Kingdom.

(c) The Warsaw Convention system

In the early years of civil aviation, there were concerns that the development of the infant industry might be damaged by large damages awards in municipal courts made in respect of accidents.[27] An attempt to reach agreement on claims in private law was made in the Warsaw Convention for the Unification of Certain Rules relating to International Carriage by Air (1929).[28] The object of the Convention was first to produce a degree of uniformity in respect of documentation, tickets and liability rules. The second objective was to limit the potential liability of carriers in respect of personal injury or death in exchange for restricting the carrier's defences. Under the Convention, the carrier was entitled to restrict his liability while the passenger or cargo owner did not have to prove negligence. Fault on the part of the carrier was presumed in the event of damage; the broad principle of the convention is both to establish liability but also to limit liability. The establishment of such a position in the municipal law of tort made it easier for infant carriers to obtain the necessary level of insurance cover. The Convention was amended by the Hague Protocol of 1955.[29] A Convention supplementary to the Warsaw Convention was signed at Guadalajara in 1961; it concerns the situation where the 'contracting carrier' contracts all or part of the contract of carriage to an 'actual carrier'.[30] However, the United States expressed dissatisfaction with the position following the Hague Protocol and, in 1966, the Montreal Agreement was negotiated, whereby a number of United States and foreign carriers agreed to higher limits and effective absolute liability. In 1971, the Hague Convention was further amended following a conference in Guatemala City organised by ICAO in 1971.[31]

In 1975, an international conference at Montreal accepted three additional Protocols[32] modifying the three earlier versions of the Warsaw Convention, with the object of specifying the liability of the carrier in terms of Special Drawing Rights rather than gold francs under the original Warsaw Convention. In addition, Montreal Protocol No 4 applied to international carriers of cargo and postal items a form of strict liability similar to that as applied to passengers under the Guatemala Protocol.

---

27 For litigation in municipal courts, see *Aslan v Imperial Airways Ltd* (1933) 149 LT 276; 45 LlL Rep 316; 49 TLR 415 (Mackinnon J); *Westminster Bank v Imperial Airways Ltd* [1936] 2 All ER 890 (Lewis J); *Grein v Imperial Airways Ltd* [1937] 1 KB 50; 8 ILR 453; *Phillipson v Imperial Airways Ltd* [1939] AC 332; *Harabin v BOAC* [1952] 2 All ER 1016 (Barry J); *Rotterdamsche Bank NV v BOAC* [1953] 1 WLR 493; *American Smelting & Refining Co v Philippine Airlines Inc* (1954) 21 ILR 286; *Chisholm v BEA* [1963] 1 Lloyd's Rep 626 (Fenton Atkinson J); *Seth v BOAC* [1964] 1 Lloyd's Rep 268 (US Court of Appeals); *Lisi v Alitalia Linee Aeree Italienne SpA* [1967] 1 Lloyd's Rep 140; [1968] 1 Lloyd's Rep 505; *Corocraft Ltd v Pan American Airways Inc* [1969] 1 QB 616; *Restenberg Platinum Mines Ltd v South African Airways* [1977] 1 Lloyd's Rep 564; *Fothergill v Monarch Airlines* [1981] AC 251; (1980) 74 ILR 627; *Sidhu v British Airways plc* [1997] AC 430.

28 Given effect to in the United Kingdom in the Carriage by Air Act 1932.

29 Given effect to in the United Kingdom by the Carriage by Air Act 1961, which came into force on 1 June 1967; see SI 1967/479. See generally, RM Forrest, 'Carriage by air: the Hague Convention' (1961) 10 ICLQ 726.

30 Given effect to in the United Kingdom by the Carriage by Air (Supplementary Provisions) Act 1962. In both the 1961 Act and the 1962 Act, if there is a conflict between the French text and the English text, then the former prevails (1961 Act, s 1(2); 1962 Act, s 1(2)).

31 The Guatemala Protocol (1971) was designed to replace the Montreal Agreement of 1966 and raise the relevant limits; it was signed by the United Kingdom but required 30 states (embracing 40% of scheduled air traffic in 1970) for it to come into effect.

32 Legislation to enable the United Kingdom to give effect to Protocol, s 3 (the Guatemala version) and Protocol 4 was enacted in the form of the Carriage by Air and Road Act 1979.

In respect of the Warsaw Convention itself, the central provision is Art 17 which renders the carrier liable for damage sustained in the event of death or any other bodily injury suffered by a passenger, if the accident which caused the damage[33] so sustained took place on board the aircraft or in the course of any operations of embarking or disembarking. In such circumstances, Art 20 applies and provides that the carrier is not liable if he proves that he and his agents have taken all necessary measure to avoid the damage or that it was impossible for him or them to take such measures. In respect of limits on liability, Art 22 provides for limits in terms of gold francs or Poincare francs; however, such limits on liability may be displaced under Art 25 if the damage is caused by wilful misconduct by the carrier or one of his agents.

In the last quarter of a century, the low limits under the Warsaw Convention have prompted plaintiffs to seek to sue other persons, often the manufacturer, in the hope of securing higher damages. Sometimes, such cases involve difficult questions[34] as to which is the appropriate jurisdiction and, in cases outside the Brussels Convention (1968),[35] questions may arise either as to the doctrine of *forum non conveniens* or whether an anti-suit injunction should be granted. The desire to select a particular forum will be influenced by different rules on both liability and the assessment of damages, but also as to whether a plaintiff wishes to finance the litigation through some method of contingency fee system.[36] In the particular context of aviation litigation, the motivating feature may be a desire to sue the manufacturer rather than the carrier; in many cases this will require issuing proceedings in the particular jurisdiction in which the manufacturing company has its headquarters.[37]

---

33 Of course, in some jurisdictions it may be possible to argue that there was no accident and that damages should be assessed at common law. Thus, in *Krys v Lufthansa* (1999), the United States Supreme Court rejected a petition where an Appeals Court had upheld an award of $3 m where aircrew had failed properly to detect cardiac arrest. The argument of Lufthansa that the matter was an accident within the Warsaw Convention was rejected.

34 For a recent case turning on whether an anti suit injunction should be granted, see *Airbus Industrie GIE v Patel* [1999] 1 AC 119; [1998] 2 WLR 686. For an earlier example, see *Société Nationale Industrielle Aerospatiale v Lee Kui Jak* [1987] AC 871.

35 The Brussels Convention on Jurisdiction and Enforcement of Judgments in Civil and Commercial Matters (1968) provides a mandatory allocation of jurisdiction in respect of those states within the European Union. It was given effect to in the United Kingdom by the Civil Jurisdiction and Judgments Act 1982 (operative 1987). In those cases outside the Convention, scheme excessive claims to jurisdiction may be restrained by the doctrine of *forum non conveniens* and, where that did not operate, by the anti suit injunction. Since the early 1970s, the English courts have recognised the desire of plaintiffs to forum shop; see *Castanho v Brown and Root (UK) Ltd* [1981] AC 557.

36 In a case turning on competing jurisdictions, the method of financing the legal action and the cost of preparing evidence will be a relevant consideration in any balancing exercise, see *Connelly v RTZ Corporation plc* [1998] AC 854.

37 Given the nature of aircraft manufacture, this will often be in either California or Texas. There is no doubt that a perception that higher levels may be awarded by a jury in the United States has prompted actions against manufacturers in certain states. The practice of 'forum shopping' began to emerge in the early 1970s prompted by (i) advertising by foreign lawyers; (ii) an awareness of larger awards abroad; (iii) the possibility of employing a form of contingency fee system abroad; (iv) a desire to avoid the limits of the Warsaw Convention in respect of carriers. If there is an important incident that drew attention to this trend, it may have been the Paris air crash of 2 March 1974 when the crash of a Turkish Airlines American built plane near Paris resulted in the death of over 300 people. Some of the deceased were prominent professional persons and some chose to proceed against the manufacturer rather than Turkish Airlines. See *In Re Paris Air Crash of March 2 1974* (1975) 399 F Supp 732.

(d) Unlawful acts directed against aircraft

As has been discussed elsewhere, one of the most disturbing aspects in the history of modern aviation has been an increase in the incidence of unlawful attacks directed against aircraft; such acts may take the form of seizure, hijacking or merely acts directed against passengers and crew. The last four decades have witnessed an attempt by the international community to secure agreement on the suppression of such acts. The vehicle of the multilateral law making convention has been employed to extend the bases of jurisdiction, to ensure that certain acts are considered criminal offences by all state parties; further, the general scheme of the conventions has been to provide for the principle of prosecute or extradite. To this end, the Tokyo Convention on Offences and Certain Other Acts Committed on Board Aircraft (1963) is concerned with jurisdiction over acts committed on board an aircraft which threaten safety.[38]

An increase in terrorist activity in the late 1960s, led to the Hague Convention for the Suppression of Unlawful Seizure of Aircraft (1970) which provides that state parties will claim jurisdiction and impose severe penalties in respect of those involved in the unlawful seizure of an aircraft. The Convention adopts the principle of *punire aut dedere*. A further step was taken in the Montreal Convention for the Suppression of Unlawful Acts against the Safety of Civil Aviation (1971),[39] which adopts a similar approach in respect of both jurisdiction and extradition to the Hague Convention but is directed not to hijacking but to outlawing acts of sabotage against civil aircraft, either in flight or on the ground. The Montreal Convention has been supplemented by a Protocol of 1988, which is concerned with those acts directed at damage or injury in respect of airport premises. The Conventions broadly provide for: (i) the claiming of jurisdiction; (ii) the obligation to punish or to extradite; (iii) the imposition of severe penalties. At the same time, terrorist attacks have given rise to interesting litigation in municipal courts as to the civil liability of the carrier under the Warsaw Convention.[40]

It should be noted that in respect of damage caused to persons or property on the surface by an aircraft in flight the matter is regulated by the Rome Convention on Damage Caused by Foreign Aircraft to Third Parties on the Surface (1952)[41] and the Montreal Protocol 1988. The Convention proceeds on a basis of strict liability following the establishment of a causal connection between the act and the damage. Liability is placed on the aircraft operator who is presumed to be the registered owner. The limiting of compensation in such situations has acted as an obstacle to a high level of ratifications.

---

38 Noted elsewhere.

39 It was obligations arising under the Montreal Convention that formed the basis of the *Case concerning Questions of Interpretation and Application of the 1971 Montreal Convention Arising From the Aerial Incident at Lockerbie* (1992) ICJ 3.

40 *Krystal v BOAC* (1975) 403 F Supp 1322; *Day v TWA Inc* (1975) 528 F 2d 31 cert denied; (1976) 428 US 890.

41 The Convention replaced the Rome Convention on Damage Caused by Foreign Aircraft to Third Parties on the Surface (1933); see note by RO Wilberforce (1953) 2 ICLQ 90.

(e) Unauthorised intrusion and the interception of aircraft

A matter that has given rise to considerable discussion in the period since 1945 has been that of unauthorised aerial intrusion. If one starts from the assumption of state sovereignty in airspace, then it follows that an unauthorised intrusion is *prima facie* a trespass; in principle, such an intrusion would justify an interception and a request to land. However, it is clear from state practice that a distinction has to be drawn between cases concerning civilian aircraft and those pertaining to military flights.

In the years of the Cold War a number of incidents arose in which complaint was made that certain states had been over ready to forcibly intercept intruding planes. A number of cases[42] were brought before the International Court of Justice but they did not proceed to judgment because of lack of jurisdiction. Perhaps the best known arose out of an incident on 27 July 1955 when a civilian airliner owned by El Al was shot down by Bulgarian airplanes over Bulgarian airspace. Both Israel and the United States initiated proceedings before the International Court Justice but the proceedings were not proceeded with because of lack of jurisdiction.[43] However, the consistent theme of the pleadings in such cases was that, in respect of civilian airliners, a state should make the intruder aware of the fact of intrusion and in appropriate cases send a protest by diplomatic channels but that in no circumstances should force be used against a civilian airliner, the rationale being that the obligation to respect innocent human life must take priority over the technical fact of trespass to airspace.

During the years of the Cold War, some states[44] asserted their entitlement to shoot down any military plane that had intruded into their airspace and such conduct was justified on the basis of legitimate self-defence.[45] However, in cases where a civilian airliner had been shot down, then the normal practice came to be for the matter to be referred to the Council of the ICAO and any adverse finding would result in an obligation to make recompense.[46] Although a flexible approach was suggested in an important

---

42 *Treatment in Hungary of Aircraft and Crew of the United States* (1954) ICJ 99; *Case concerning the Aerial Incident of 7 October 1952 (United States v USSR)* (1956) ICJ 9; *Aerial Incident of 4 September 1954 (United States v USSR)* (1958) ICJ 158; *Case concerning the Aerial Incident of 7 November 1954 (United States v USSR)* (1959) ICJ 26.

43 *Case concerning Aerial Incident of 27 July 1955* (1959) ICJ 127; 27 ILR 557; (1960) ICJ 146.

44 The most celebrated incident concerned the American pilot, FG Powers, who was shot down on a military mission above the Soviet Union in May 1960. At the trial before the USSR Supreme Court Military Collegium, the court justified such conduct by reference to: (a) the principle of sovereignty in airspace dating from the 1919 Paris Convention; (b) the text of the judgment indicates that the court felt that in the nuclear age a sudden military attack might have been anticipated. The court sentenced Powers under the relevant espionage law. Powers himself was eventually released in 1962 in exchange for Rudolph Abel, a Soviet spy; he later published his account of events under the title *Operation Overflight* in 1970. For a contemporary analysis of the legal issues see Quincy Wright, 'Legal aspects of the U2 incident' (1960) 54 AJIL 836.

45 For a comprehensive survey of the incidents in the period 1945–53, see O Lissitzyn, 'The treatment of aerial intruders in recent practice and international law' (1953) 47 AJIL 554.

46 In 1973, Israeli planes shot down a Libyan airliner that had intruded into Israeli occupied Sinai. There was a conflict of evidence as to whether a warning had been given and defied. In any event, the Council of the ICAO condemned the action and Israel paid compensation. See (1973) 12 ILM 1180.

article by Lissitzyn in 1953,[47] most states have tended increasingly to the view that there is an absolute rule against using force against a civilian airliner regardless of the circumstances of any trespass.

This was illustrated by the most serious incident in recent years, which arose on 1 September 1983 when a Soviet fighter shot down a Korean Air Lines flight (KA 007) resulting in the deaths of all 269 persons on board. The response of the international community was immediate and unequivocal.[48] Although a draft Security Council resolution was vetoed by the Soviet Union, the Council of the ICAO investigated the matter and recommended the strengthening of the provisions of the 1944 Chicago Convention. The original provision in Art 3(d) had read:

> The contracting States undertake, when issuing regulations for their State aircraft, that they will have due regard for the safety of navigation of civil aircraft.

Following upon the report of the Council of the ICAO a new Art 3 *bis* provided that:

> (a) The contracting states recognise that every state must refrain from resorting to the use of weapons against the civil aircraft in flight, and that in case of interception, the lives of persons on board and the safety of aircraft must not be endangered. This provision shall not be interpreted as modifying in any way the rights and obligations of states set forth in the Charter of the United Nations.

The Article further provides in 3 *bis* (b) that where the aircraft is flying above territory without permission or where there are reasonable grounds for believing that it may be acting contrary to the Convention then any contracting state may require the aircraft to land at a designated airport.

The Article raises a number of points. First, the prohibition relates to the use of 'weapons' rather than force so that the form of interception may involve force falling short of the firing of weapons. Secondly, as a general proposition the intruding aircraft must obey all reasonable orders of the territorial sovereign. Thirdly, the territorial sovereign in its efforts to control the movement of the intruding aircraft must not expose the aircraft or its occupants to unnecessary danger. Fourthly, it is important to note that each contracting state under Art 25 undertakes to provide measure of assistance to aircraft in distress.

In many of the incidents where a trespassing civil aircraft has been shot down there has either been a failure of communications or human error;[49] however, circumstances can arise in which a right of self-defence might be claimed.

---

47 O Lissitzyn, 'The treatment of aerial intruders in recent practice and international law' (1953) 47 AJIL 554. It has to be acknowledged that Lissitzyn was writing in the early and rather tense period of the Cold War when there was a greater degree of fear about a surprise attack. For an appreciation of the writer, see (1995) 89 AJIL 88.

48 F Hassan, 'The shooting down of Korean Airlines Flight 007 by the USSR and the furtherance of air safety for passengers' (1984) 33 ICLQ 712; MN Leich, 'Destruction of Korean Airliner: action by international organisations' (1984) 78 AJIL 244.

49 The enquiry after the Korean Airlines incident in 1983 concluded that the USSR believed it was dealing with an American plane engaged on espionage tasks see (1984) 23 ILM 937; (1994) 33 ILM 310. For compensation claims arising out of the incident, see (1985) 56 BYIL 511. The incident took place during the period of President Andropov 18 months before the arrival in power of President Gorbachev and thus before the western world was fully aware of the level of incompetence and inefficiency that permeated some aspect of Soviet administration.

Such an issue was raised in July 1988, when the USS Vincennes, a US naval vessel protecting neutral shipping in the Persian Gulf during the Iran-Iraq War, shot down an Iranian civil airliner in the mistaken belief that it was an Iranian military aircraft; 290 lives were lost. The incident was, of course, not strictly one of aerial intrusion and it has to be acknowledged that the vessel was operating in a *de facto* war zone. Subsequent reports placed the blame on the warship[50] and although Iran began proceedings before the International Court of Justice the legal action was terminated pending agreement upon compensation.[51]

It is clear now that in respect of civilian aircraft in flight Art 3 *bis* states a rule of customary international law and represents an absolute prohibition[52] against the use of force save in circumstances consistent with the United Nations Charter.[53] In the case of military aircraft, it would seem that force can only be used as a last resort in proportionate self-defence[54] and only then after all reasonable steps have been taken to establish whether the intrusion is accidental or intentional;[55] in such circumstances, there is a duty to warn and discourage. As state practice has emerged since 1945, it is certainly the case that any use of force in peacetime against even a military aircraft will have to be justified and one starts from a presumption that a territorial sovereign should have been able to deal with intrusion by methods short of the use of weapons.

---

50 Agora, 'The downing of Iran Flight 655' (1989) 83 AJIL 318; H Maier, '*Ex gratia* payments and the Iranian Airline tragedy' (1989) 83 AJIL 325.

51 *Aerial Incident of July 3 1988 Case (Iran v United States)* (1989) ICJ 132; (1996) ICJ 9. The United States agreed to pay $300,000 for each wage earner and $150,000 for each non-wage earner see (1996) 90 AJIL 278; 35 ILM 493.

52 This was the view stressed by the President of the UN Security Council in respect of the conduct of Cuban military aircraft in February 1996 in shooting down two civilian aircraft registered in the United States. In March 1996, President Clinton approved sanctions against Cuba under the Cuban Liberty and Democratic Solidarity (Libertad) Act 1996.

53 A circumstance in which shooting down might be justified was in the tragic and bizarre case in the United States in autumn 1999 when a civilian executive jet taking off from Florida continued to fly on after all personnel were either dead or unconscious. United States fighter planes were alerted and flew alongside to establish the basic facts. At that point, the President of the United States was informed as Commander in Chief. In the event, the jet did not land in a populated area. Subsequent statements by US government sources indicated that an order to shoot the plane down might have had to be given had the plane been about to land in a populated area. In such circumstances, if the aircraft is not subject to control then it has ceased to be 'in flight' in the accepted sense. The incident attracted widespread attention because one of the passengers was the popular United States Golf Champion, Mr Payne Stewart.

54 Cases concerning aerial incidents are often a symptom of tense relations and mistrust between two states as indicated by the *Aerial Incident of 10 August 1999* where Pakistan instituted proceedings before the ICJ against India in respect of the destruction of a Pakistani aircraft.

55 An example of recent controversy is afforded by the China/United States spying incident in April 2001 where the United States plane appeared to be operating in international airspace when it was subject to challenge by Chinese aircraft objecting to the gathering of intelligence. The fact that the United States plane was operating in international airspace was influential in the refusal of the United States to issue an apology; in contrast, in April 1999, the United States had apologised for the attack on the Chinese Embassy in Belgrade.

2 SPACE LAW[56]

(a) Introduction

The law relating to airspace has proceeded on the basis of state sovereignty since the Paris Convention of 1919. This principle has been modified by the multilateral and bilateral treaties that permitted normal civil aviation activities to proceed. However, in the last 50 years the *usque ad coelum* principle has had to be modified to accommodate activities in outer space. The decision by the USSR to launch the first satellite to circle the earth in 1957 was followed within a few years by manned space flight which increased in ambition until a landing on the moon was accomplished in July 1969. In these circumstances, the international law in relation to outer space has had to develop rapidly, although only a small number of states initially had any direct interest in the subject matter.

The development in this area owes much to the establishment in 1958 of the United Nations Committee on the Peaceful Uses of Outer Space (UNCOPUOS) which operates through two sub-committees, the Scientific and Technical Subcommittee and the Legal Subcommittee. The executive branch of UNCOPUOS is the United Nations Office for Outer Space Affairs which is based in Vienna. However, not all matters concerning Outer Space will come within the remit of UNCOPUOS; questions of telecommunications are within the remit of the International Telecommunication Union (ITU) while military matters remain within the jurisdiction of the various arms control bodies.

In the years after 1957, agreement was straightforward because only the United States and the USSR had a significant interest in the process. The first matter of consequence was to define 'outer space'. In the late 1950s, it seemed as a matter of principle that there must come a point at which airspace met outer space; such a point would be above the highest point of conventional aviation, but below the lowest point at which a satellite could orbit the earth. Some writers argued that this point was between 50 and 100 miles above the surface of the earth.[57] As other states began to take an interest in outer space, a difference of opinion arose as to whether it was possible or desirable to draw a clear distinction between airspace and outer space.

(b) The evolution of the law on outer space[58]

The launch of the Russian satellite in 1957 prompted a serious attempt to clarify the law on outer space. An early Resolution of the General Assembly in December 1959 (GA Res

---

56 See generally, CW Jenks, *Space Law*, 1965; JES Fawcett, *International Law and the Uses of Outer Space*, 1968; *Outer Space: New Challenges to Law and Policy*, 1984; M Lachs, *The Law of Outer Space*, 1972, Leiden; C Christol, *The Modern Law of Outer Space*, 1982; C Christol, *Space Law: Past, Present and Future*, 1991; M Lachs, 'The international law of outer space' (1964) 113 HR 1-116; D Goedhuis, 'Conflicts of law and divergencies in the legal regimes of air space and outer space' (1963) 109 HR 257–346; D Goedhuis, 'The problems of the frontiers of outer space and air space' (1982) 174 HR 367; JF McMahon, 'Legal aspects of outer space' (1962) 38 BYIL 339.

57 D Goedhuis, 'The problems of the frontiers of outer space and air space' (1982) 174 HR 367.

58 For the historical development of this area of law, see B Cheng, 'The United Nations and outer space' (1961) 14 CLP 247; B Cheng, 'The extraterrestrial application of international law' (1965) 18 CLP 132; B Cheng, 'United Nations Resolutions on Outer Space: "instant" international customary law?' (1965) 5 Indian JIL 23.

1472(XIV)) urged international co-operation in the peaceful uses of outer space.[59] This was followed by General Assembly Resolution 1721 of December 1961 which attempted to provide for the orderly development of international law in the context of outer space. Two years later[60] in December 1963, Resolution 1962(XVIII) was adopted[61] under the title of the Declaration of Legal Principles Governing the Activities of States in the Exploration and Use of Outer Space. This resolution provided that outer space should be subject to international law, that the right of exploration should be open to all states and that outer space should not be subject to appropriation by any individual state. During this period, it was argued by at least one writer that the effect of the adoption of unanimous General Assembly Resolutions on outer space might be to create a form of 'instant' customary international law where the binding force of stated principles arises not from the Resolution itself but from the general acceptance by member states as part of international law.[62]

However, there was a desire for a treaty based framework and these general resolutions were followed in the next two decades by five multilateral law making treaties which were as follows:

(1) The 1967 Treaty on Principles Governing the Activities of States in the Exploration and Use of Outer Space including the Moon and other Celestial Bodies (sometimes referred to as the Outer Space Treaty).

(2) The 1968 Agreement on the Rescue of Astronauts, the Return of Astronauts and the Return of Objects Launched into Outer Space (sometimes referred to as the Rescue Agreement).[63]

(3) The 1972 Convention on Liability for Damage Caused by Objects Launched into Outer Space (sometimes referred to as the Liability Convention).[64]

(4) The 1975 Convention on Registration of Objects Launched into Outer Space (Registration Convention).

(5) The 1979 Agreement Governing the Activities of States on the Moon and other Celestial Bodies (the Moon Treaty).[65]

It is necessary to say a little about each of these international instruments; it is proposed to deal with the first two before considering later the remaining three treaties.

The legal regime of outer space was clarified by the 1967 Treaty on Principles Governing the Activities of States in the Exploration and Use of Outer Space (the Outer

---

59 Which itself followed upon the Resolution on the Question of the Peaceful Use of Outer Space, UN GA Res 1348 (XIII) of December 1958.

60 The intervening period had witnessed Resolution 1884 (XVIII) of 17 October 1963, which had called upon states to refrain form placing in orbit around the Earth any objects carrying nuclear weapons or any other kinds of weapons of mass destruction; this was adopted unanimously on 17 October 1963.

61 GA Res 1962 (XVIII) of 13 December 1963.

62 A view advanced by Bin Cheng in an influential article 'United Nations Resolutions on Outer Space: "instant" international customary law?' (1965) 5 Indian JIL 23. The writer was particularly concerned with the example of resolutions on outer space passed in the early 1960s.

63 For text see (1969) 63 AJIL 382.

64 (1971) 10 ILM 965.

65 (1979) 18 ILM 1434.

Space Treaty). The document itself is modelled on the Antarctica Treaty of 1959. As the preamble indicates, the treaty builds upon the earlier General Assembly Resolutions; the treaty provides that outer space is to be free for the exploration and use by all states (Art 1) and cannot be subject to appropriation by any single state (Art 2). It is further provided that exploration and use of outer space must be carried out in accordance with international law and for the benefit of mankind (Arts 1 and 3). A provision that has attract comment is that contained in Art 4 which reads in part:

> State parties to the Treaty undertake not to place in orbit around the Earth any object carrying nuclear weapons or any other kind of weapons of mass destruction, install such weapons on celestial bodies, or station such weapons in outer space in any other manner.

This provision is designed to ensure the demilitarisation of outer space and has attracted some comment.[66] Further, the treaty provides that activities in outer space shall not cause damage to the environment (Art 9) and that, in the conduct of such activities, states shall be prepared to display the greatest possible openness in providing information (Arts 10, 11 and 12).

As a general rule international law does not hold the state liable for the acts of the autonomous individual; however Art 6 of the Outer Space Treaty provides that a state will be liable not only for national activities in outer space but also for the activities of non-governmental organisations. Further, thereto Art 7 stipulates that where any object is launched into outer space and causes damage to another state then liability will fall upon the state that has launched or procured the launching of the object. The treaty further provides that property rights are not affected by the launching of an object into outer space (Art 8); so that where an object is found it is to be returned to the state enjoying title. It is to be noted that the provisions of Arts 5, 7 and 8 have been extended by the 1968 Rescue Agreement, the 1972 Liability Convention and the 1974 Registration Convention.

In considering the Outer Space Treaty it is worthy of note that the draftsmen did not consider it necessary to provide a precise definition as to where air space and state sovereignty ended and outer space and the rule of *res communis* began. At about the time of the Treaty Fawcett[67] argued that the dividing line should be drawn at the lowest point at which a satellite can safely orbit the earth. This would seem to be correct in principle and has been endorsed by other writers.

The movement towards holding states liable for conduct in outer space was extended by the 1972 Convention on International Liability for Damage Caused by Space Objects (the Liability Convention). Article 2 of the Liability Convention provides that a 'launching state shall be absolutely liable to pay compensation for damage caused by its space object on the surface of the earth or to the aircraft in flight'. In cases where two states participate in launching a space object then liability will be joint and several (Art 5). The Convention

---

66 The question arose in 1983/1984, when President Reagan announced the United States Strategic Defence Initiative which centred around the principle of anti missile systems based in space. However, the reception accorded to the idea and the reduction in tension between East and West served to postpone any consideration as to whether the objective violated Art 4. The subsequent administrations of President Bush (1989–93) and President Clinton (1993–2001) have shown markedly less enthusiasm for the project.

67 JES Fawcett, *International Law and the Uses of Outer Space*, 1968, pp 23–24. See also D Goedhuis, (1982) 174 HR 367–408; I Brownlie, 'Principles of public international law', 5th edn, 1998, pp 262–67.

provides for the presentation of claims by the state which suffers damage (Art 8); such a claim is to be made through diplomatic channels (Art 9) and should normally made within one year of the date of the occurrence of the damage (Art 10). If no agreement is reached within one year of the submission of the claim,[68] then provision is made for the establishment of a Claims Commission;[69] this procedure has something in common with an international arbitration save that the decision is to be final and binding only if the parties have so agreed.[70] Article 22 accords *locus standi* to the international organisation active in space if such an organisation has made a declaration of its acceptance of rights and duties under the Convention. In such circumstances the organisation will bear primary responsibility for any damage[71] and it is only if the organisation has not responded to a claim within six months that a claimant state may 'lift the veil' and invoke the joint and several liability of the state members of that organisation.[72] A number of international organisations have made declarations under Art 22. It has not been necessary as yet to apply the full settlement procedures of the 1972 Liability Convention. In the 1978 case of *Cosmos 954* which concerned the disintegration of a Soviet nuclear powered satellite and the contamination of Canadian territory the entire matter was resolved by diplomatic negotiation. [73]

Space law is a rapidly changing aspect of international law and it is therefore not surprising that most questions are subject to treaty provision and thus customary international law has only a limited relevance. It is arguable that some of the provisions of the 1967 Outer Space Treaty have acquired the status of a rule of customary law in the absence of any evidence of persistent objection.

The development of space law in the decade 1960–70 was stimulated by the attention paid to manned space flight.[74] Part of this interest lead to signing in April 1968 of the Agreement on the Rescue of Astronauts, the Return of Astronauts and the Return of Objects Launched into Outer Space.[75] The Agreement provided that a contracting state would inform the launching state in respect of any spacecraft which might have made an emergency landing within its territory[76] and would do everything appropriate to provide

---

68 Liability Convention (1972), Art 14.

69 *Ibid*, Art 14.

70 *Ibid*, Art 29.

71 *Ibid*, Art 22.

72 *Ibid*, Art 22(3).

73 The claim by Canada in January 1979 was formulated on the basis of the 1972 Liability Convention and was for the sum of $6,041,174.70; the matter was later resolved through diplomatic channels. See C Christol, 'International liability for damage caused by space objects' (1980) 74 AJIL 346; AF Cohen, 'Cosmos 954 and the international law of satellite accidents' (1984) 10 YJIL 78.

74 The first manned space flight was undertaken by Yuri Gagarin (1934–68) who on 12 April 1961 completed one orbit of the earth in 108 minutes in the spacecraft Vostok 1. The first manned spaceflight by a United States citizen was undertaken by Alan Shepherd on 5 May 1961. However, the more ambitious effort of Colonel John Glenn followed shortly after on 20 February 1962 when he orbited the earth three times in Mercury spacecraft Friendship 7. In 1974, Glenn was elected Senator for Ohio and in 1984 unsuccessfully sought the Democratic Presidential nomination. On 20 July 1969, the United States astronaut Neil Armstrong became the first person to set foot on the Moon. During the decade 1960–70, it was necessary to develop space law by treaty to reflect the rapid progress in manned flight. In this context, it is noteworthy that on 26 April 1962 the first United Kingdom satellite, Ariel, was launched by the United States.

75 The Agreement entered into force in December 1968 under the terms of Art 7 upon receipt of the requisite ratifications.

76 Rescue Agreement (1968), Art 1.

emergency assistance;[77] in principle a contracting party could claim from the launching state expenses incurred in undertaking rescue duties.[78] The Convention provides for the safe and speedy return of astronauts landing within the territory of another state.[79]

The Conventions of 1967, 1968 and 1972 evidenced an increasing need to regulate activities in outer space; the next step was achieved by the 1975 Convention on Registration of Objects Launched into Outer Space which came into force in 1976. Under the terms of the Art 2 of the Convention, each launch state shall maintain a registry of objects launched into outer space and shall inform the Secretary General of the United Nations of the existence of such a registry.

The pace of multilateral law making activity was certainly considerable and what was noteworthy was the readiness of the international community to accept the principle of regulation by international agreement. By 1985, there were 85 states who had ratified the 1967 Outer Space Treaty[80] and the figures in respect of the other conventions[81] were equally impressive.

Further, progress in constructing an international law of outer space was effected in 1979 when the Agreement Governing the Activities of States on the Moon and other Celestial bodies was adopted. Pursuant to Art 19 the Agreement came into force on 11 July 1984 on receipt of the fifth instrument of ratification. The treaty itself applies to both the moon and other celestial bodies[82] and provides that all activities undertaken shall be consistent with international law[83] and the need for peace and security between states Consistent with that principle, Art 3 provides that the moon shall only be used for peaceful purposes and the establishment of military installations is prohibited.[84] Further, Art 4 provides that any exploration shall be the province of all mankind and shall be carried out for the benefit of all. State parties are obliged to keep the Secretary General informed as to exploratory activities on the moon[85] and in their activities guard against damage to the environment.[86] Of particular relevance is Art 11 which provides that the moon and its natural resources are the common heritage of mankind[87] and is not to be

---

77 Rescue Agreement (1968), Art 2.

78 *Ibid*, Art 5.

79 *Ibid*, Art 4.

80 By 1998, there were 94 parties.

81 By 1985, there were 78 parties to the 1968 Rescue Agreement; 69 bound by the 1972 Liability Convention and 34 bound by the 1975 Registration Convention. See C Christol (1985) 79 AJIL 163. By 1998, there were 86 parties to the 1968 Rescue Agreement; 76 parties to the 1972 Liability Convention and 39 parties to the 1975 Registration Agreement.

82 Moon Treaty (1979), Art 1.

83 *Ibid*, Art 2.

84 *Ibid*, Art 3(4).

85 *Ibid*, Art 5.

86 *Ibid*, Art 7.

87 The concept 'the common heritage of mankind' had, of course, been raised in the context of the law of the sea by Ambassador Arvid Pardo on 17 August 1967. Thus, the 1979 Moon Treaty rather than the 1982 Law of the Sea Convention was the first to adopt this principle. Thus, we can distinguish: (a) national territory; (b) *res nullius*, ie, areas which may be acquired as national territory; (c) *res extra commercium*, ie, areas which by law are not susceptible of national appropriation; (d) the common heritage of mankind, ie, an area not only beyond national appropriation but the resources of which are considered to be the property of mankind at large. See B Cheng, 'The Moon Treaty' (1980) 33 CLP 213.

subject to national appropriation by any claim of sovereignty. Article 11(4) provides that states shall explore on the basis of equality and shall keep the Secretary General informed about their activities. Article 11(5) provides that when exploitation of the natural resources becomes feasible then an international regulatory regime will be established to ensure:

(a) the orderly and safe development of the natural resources of the moon;

(b) the rational management of those resources;

(c) the expansion of opportunities in the use of those resources;

(d) an equitable sharing by all states parties in the benefits derived from those resources whereby the interests and needs of the developing countries, as well as the efforts of those countries which contributed either directly or indirectly to the exploration of the moon, shall be given special consideration.

It has to be conceded that progress in respect of the Moon Treaty has been less impressive.[88] The Treaty came into effect on 11 July 1984, following receipt of the fifth ratification but of the limited number of signatory states only France has extensive space interests. To an extent, the treaty was designed to introduce a regulatory regime in the future and thus one should withhold judgment. Another point of interest is whether the common heritage principle in Art 11 of the Moon Treaty is consistent Art 1 which provides for the free exploitation of the space environment.[89]

The developing international law on outer space has required the introduction of municipal legislation. In the United Kingdom this has taken the form of the Outer Space Act 1986.[90] The legislation provides that the launching of space objects or the operation of such objects or any activity in outer space will when performed by a United Kingdom national be unlawful save where a licence has been granted by the Secretary of State. As with normal licensing legislation the enactment enables the Secretary of State to impose conditions. To fulfil the international obligations of the United Kingdom, s 7 provides that a register is to be kept of space objects. Of particular relevance is s 10 which provides that in the event of a space activity resulting in an international law claim against the United Kingdom then the government may claim an indemnity from the individual or company so responsible.

As with aviation law earlier in the century international has evolved remarkably quickly alongside unprecedented technical advances. It may be that much of the progress in the initial decades was due to fact that only the United States and the USSR considered the matter of any real consequence however the increasing use of satellites for telecommunications purposes has caused may states to modify this original view and to take an active part in the regulatory regime appropriate to outer space.

---

88 By 1998, there were nine parties but none of the permanent members of the Security Council are parties. See (1979) 18 ILM 899.

89 C Christol, 'The Moon Treaty enters into force' (1985) 79 AJIL 163.

90 The legislation acquired the royal assent on 18 July 1986. The object of the legislation is stated in the preamble to be to 'confer licensing and other powers on the Secretary of State to secure compliance with the international obligations of the United Kingdom with respect to the launching and operation of space objects and the carrying on of other activities in outer space by persons connected with this country'.

CHAPTER 15

THE INTERNATIONAL LAW OF HUMAN RIGHTS[1]

1 INTRODUCTION

Few would dispute that the evolution of a distinct law on human rights has been one of the most significant developments in public international law in the years since 1945. It is fashionable to date this development from either the United Nations Charter (1945) or the United Nations Declaration on Human Rights (1948); however, the impetus for the establishment and maintenance of minimum standards can, in fact, be traced back much further. However, it is possible to observe a marked increase in human rights law on the international plane while at the same time noting significant developments at the regional level. It is proposed in this chapter to deal with the former aspect while in the following chapter to consider the development of regional systems.

Although the history of human rights law can be traced back a considerable way few dispute that the experience of the Second World War and the disclosure of fundamental abuses in Germany has served as an impetus to develop this aspect of international law in the years since 1945. The abuses perpetrated by the Nazi regime have stimulated three distinct trends. First, the enshrining of certain basic guarantees in the written constitutions of individual states in the years since 1945. Secondly, the development of an international law of human rights that stems from the United Nations Charter. Thirdly, the development of various regional systems.

Any discussion of the subject of human rights involves difficult questions of definition in particular about the nature of a 'right'. Indeed even if one can reach agreement on a definition about the concept of a right a distinction has to be drawn between ethical or moral rights and legal rights. In normal circumstances a legal right will be one that will be recognised and enforced through the judicial process. In modern society there may be many moral rights that it is simply not possible fully to give effect to through the municipal legal system.[2] In essence, a question will arise as to those values that a society considers so important that they require them to be given effect to through the municipal legal system. However, the expression 'right' is used very loosely and on closer examination one may need to distinguish between a claim, a duty, a power or

---

1 H Lauterpacht, *International Law and Human Rights*, 1950; L Sohn and T Buergenthal, *International Protection of Human Rights*, 1973; M McDougall, H Laswell and I Chen, *Human Rights and World Public Order*, 1980; P Sieghart, *The Law of Human Rights*, 1983; RY Jennings and AD Watts, *Oppenheim's International Law*, 9th edn, 1992, Chapter 8; S Davidson, *Human Rights*, 1993, Buckingham: Open University Press; A Robertson and J Merrills, *Human Rights in the World*, 4th edn, 1996; H Steiner and P Alston, *International Human Rights in Context*, 1996; R Wallace, *International Human Rights*, 1997.

2 In municipal law, see *Day v Brownrigg* (1878) 10 Ch D 294; *Thorne v British Broadcasting Corporation* [1967] 1 WLR 1104: 'It is a fundamental rule that the court will only grant an injunction at the suit of a private individual to support a legal right', *per* Lord Denning MR, p 1109; *Paton v Trustees of the British Pregnancy Advisory Service* [1979] QB 276; 95 LQR 332; 30 CLP 217.

immunity and it has only been in the last century[3] with the increasing emphasis on linguistic analysis that these distinctions have come to the fore. Moreover, even if one can reach agreement on the meaning of the expression 'right' then questions arise as to what the word 'human' adds to the expression. Many would accept that the concept is best explained historically and this matter is examined below, but a working provisional definition would be that the concept of human rights is employed to indicate that all individuals simply by being human have moral rights which no state or society should deny. Sometimes, these rights are described as 'fundamental' or 'basic' to a civilised society. When such rights are being discussed in the municipal law context, then such an area of law is referred to as the law of civil liberties; in most modern states certain basic civil liberties will be set out either in a bill of rights or within the constitution. Finally, in any discussion of the topic it will be necessary to consider in what circumstances state authorities may modify or restrict a particular human right or civil liberty in pursuit of some higher goal. It can therefore be seen that the law of human rights is closely related to questions of morality, political philosophy and constitutional law.

The development of human rights law on the international plane must be set in its historical context and it is to that matter that one must now turn.

2 THE NATURE AND EVOLUTION OF HUMAN RIGHTS LAW[4]

As noted elsewhere the earliest writers on international law were theologians who thus approached the subject from a natural law perspective. They were concerned to stipulate that there might be higher moral laws binding on the secular ruler. In its most elementary aspect this took the form of a concern as to the duties that a ruler owed to his subjects, the circumstances in which war might be engaged in and the circumstances in which a subject might disobey.

However, such reflections were of little direct relevance until in the ferment of the Reformation Europe began to break into distinct nation states and philosophers began to consider the nature of government. In broad terms such thinkers began to articulate the view that political power came from the people and not from the individual ruler. Although the principle of the social contract can be traced back to Plato it was in the 17th century that it began to emerge as a distinct concept. Grotius (1583–1645) employed the concept to explain the internal stability of the state but it is in later political philosophers that beginnings of a concern for human rights can be detected.

---

3   Much of the discussion being prompted by W Hohfeld in *Fundamental Legal Conceptions as Applied in Judicial Reasoning* (published posthumously and edited by WW Cook in 1923). The same attempt to elucidate the concept of a 'right' is to be found in Salmond's *Jurisprudence*, 7th edn, 1902.

4   The general nature of a legal right and the distinction between legal and moral rights has generated a considerable volume of literature. The most prominent contributors are HL Hart, *The Concept of Law*, 1961; J Rawls, *A Theory of Justice*, 1973; R Dworkin, *Taking Rights Seriously*, 1977; R Dworkin, *A Matter of Principle*, 1986; R Dworkin, *Law's Empire*, 1986. The background to natural law thinking is set out clearly in J Finnis, *Natural Law and Natural Rights*, 1980. The relationship between human rights law and civil liberties in the United Kingdom is considered in D Feldman, *Civil Liberties and Human Rights in England and Wales*, 1993. General surveys are provided in M Cranston, *What Are Human Rights?* 1973; J Waldron (ed), *Theories of Rights*, 1984; NE Simmonds, *Central Issues in Jurisprudence*, 1986.

Thomas Hobbes (1588–1679),[5] writing at the time of the English Civil War, argued that natural law was not an objective order but comprised at best certain limited natural rights which men transferred to a ruler who would govern exercising absolute power. Individual self-interest caused men to vest power in such a ruler so that order might be maintained and the natural desire of self-preservation be ensured.

The social contract of Hobbes was at best an artificial construct arising less by express action and more as a matter of inference. It is for this reason that many writers on human rights see John Locke as the central figure. Locke argued[6] that individuals enjoyed certain rights in the state of nature before they entered civil society. Among these rights were the right to life, liberty and property; when men entered into civil society they did not surrender these rights. According to Locke, men surrendered to the state the power of enforcement they did not surrender the rights themselves. Under Locke, the exercise of governmental power depended on respecting the terms of a contract between the rulers and the ruled. Locke did not face the problem of the circumstances in which the majority might override individual rights and it was for others to apply his thought. Although the Bill of Rights (1689) in England was concerned with restricting the power of the Crown at the expense of Parliament, it was important in recognising the need for the executive branch of government to be subject to legislative control.

Later writers expanded on these general themes. Montesquieu[7] in his *De L'Esprit des Lois* identified the need for balance in the exercise of governmental power and argued that sociological factors influenced the content of positive laws. Although some would not describe him as a philosopher, Voltaire[8] was influential in stressing the case for social and religious tolerance and emphasising the need of individuals to confront the problem of evil conduct in the real world. Of more direct relevance was the writing of Jean Jacques Rousseau[9] who in in his *Du Contrat Social* (1762) asserted that individual freedom and citizenship could only be secured by a social contract with the entire community.

The 18th century thinkers of the enlightenment exhibited a number of common features and the law of human rights can be linked to their writings. A constant theme is the recognition that government is a necessary evil, that the role of government is to

---

5   Thomas Hobbes (1588–1679). In *De Cive* (1642) and *Leviathan* (1651), the revised Latin version being published in 1668), Hobbes argued that cities or states were founded on the need for self-preservation and that the law making power of government derives form the consent of those governed.

6   John Locke (1632–1704). In his *Essay concerning Human Understanding* (1689), Locke argued for an empirical view of knowledge. In his *Second Treatise of Civil Government* (1689), Locke put the case for a contractual theory of government. It is of note that Locke's lesser known work the *Letters concerning Toleration* (1689, 1690, 1692) argued for toleration in matters of religion, at least in respect of all those not claiming allegiance to a foreign ruler. Locke has some claims to be regarded as the founder of the modern law of evidence; the classic proponent of the liberal theory of the state the most influential 17th century writer on questions of civil liberty. On John Locke, see M Cranston, *John Locke: A Biography*, 1957; John W Yolton, *Locke: An Introduction*, 1985.

7   Charles Louis, Baron de Montesquieu (1689–1755). Montesquieu argued in *L'Esprit des Lois* (1749) that the ideal form of government was a constitutional government with a clear separation of legislative, executive and judicial roles.

8   Voltaire, pen name of François Marie Arouet (1694–1778). His concern with the problem of evil conduct permeates *Zadig* (1747) and *Candide* (1759).

9   Jean Jacques Rousseau (1712–78). One aspect of Rousseau's social contract between ruler and people is the writer's emphasis upon reciprocal rights and obligations.

protect certain natural rights such as life, liberty and property and that the power of government should be limited to prevent oppression. At the end of the 18th century, political ferment provided the opportunity to implement some of these ideas.

The leaders of the American Revolution were men well versed in 18th century political philosophy. Thomas Jefferson was familiar with the work of Locke and Montesquieu and he attempted in the Declaration of Independence of 4 July 1776 to give practical effect to the theories of limited government and natural rights. The second paragraph of the declaration reads:

> We hold these truths to be self evident, that all men are created equal, that they are endowed by their Creator with certain unalienable Rights, that among these are Life, Liberty and the Pursuit of Happiness.

In similar terms, the leaders of the French Revolution drew up a Declaration of the Rights of Man and the Citizen on 26 August 1789 which noted that 'the aim of every political association is the preservation of the natural and imprescriptible rights of man' and it proceeds to identify these rights as 'Liberty, Property, Safety and Resistance to Oppression'. Practical effect was given to these sentiments in the Bill of Rights of 1791 which, when annexed to the United States Constitution (1787), provided for freedom of belief, freedom of the press and freedom of assembly; the two documents when read together give effect to the theories of Montesquieu on limited government and the opinions of Locke on natural rights. At the same time, in Europe the works of Immanuel Kant[10] contained within them statements of principle sympathetic to the development of a distinct law of human rights. Kant's assertion that one should 'act in such a way that you always treat humanity, whether in your own person or in the person of any other, never simply as a means but always at the same time as an end'.

It should not be thought that natural rights thinking went unchallenged; Burke questioned whether civil rights could be deduced from natural law, while both Hume and Bentham denied the existence of natural rights. Later, John Stuart Mill would argue that rights are founded on utility. The revival of historical studies in England and Germany caused Henry Maine and Friedrich Karl von Savigny to argue that rights are determined by the particular cultural, environmental and social factors in a community while the Benthamite jurist John Austin stressed the need for a clear separation between ethical concepts and legal rules. In short, the 19th century was not a fertile ground for natural law thinking, but a number of other developments were taking place that would have enduring consequences.

With the benefit of hindsight, the movement against slavery which gathered pace in the 18th century was an early attempt on the international plane to promote human rights. The efforts to outlaw the slave trade grew with the prohibition within the British Empire in 1807 and action against the slave trade was provided for in the Treaty of Paris in 1814 and the Congress of Vienna in 1815. However, the trade itself proved resistant to

---

10 Immanuel Kant (1724–1804), *Critique of Pure Reason*, 1781; *Groundwork of the Metaphysic of Morals*, 1785; *Critique of Practical Reason*, 1788; *Critique of the Power of Judgment*, 1790. Although, of course, considered today as the greatest of modern philosophers, Kant spent much time thinking about problems of international comity and in *Perpetual Peace* (1795) he examined the need for a Federation of Nations to preserve international law.

treaty provisions and the matter was returned to at the Congress of Berlin in 1885 and the Brussels Conference of 1890.[11]

The industrialisation of the 19th century led to more effective armaments. In 1859, Henri Dunant shocked by the level of suffering at the Battle of Solferino was motivated to establish the *Comite International et Permanent de Sécours aux Blessés Militaires*. The adoption of the first Geneva Convention in 1864 marked the beginning of international humanitarian law. In short, in certain circumstances the treatment of the sick and wounded would become a matter of concern to international society. Thus, Art 25 of the Covenant of the League noted that:

> The Members of the League agree to encourage and promote the establishment and co-operation of duly authorised voluntary national Red Cross organisations having as purposes the improvement of health, the prevention of disease and the mitigation of suffering throughout the world.

A third strand in the history of human rights law concerns the treatment of minorities within Europe. At the Treaty of Berlin (1878), Bulgaria, Montenegro, Serbia, Rumania and Turkey all agreed to allow religious freedom to those within their boundaries. Matters were taken further in 1919, when it became clear that there were limits to the principle of self-determination and that, in many circumstances, minorities would be included within state boundaries following the dissolution of the Austro Hungarian Empire. Treaties were made for the protection of minorities with newly created states such as Poland (Versailles 1919), with Czechoslovakia and Yugoslavia (St Germain en Laye 1919), with Romania (Trianon 1920), and with Greece (Sevres 1920); and in respect of the ex enemy states provision was made in the relevant peace treaties, as with Austria (St Germain en Laye 1919), with Bulgaria (Neuilly), with Hungary (Trianon 1919), and finally with Turkey (Lausanne 1923). A further development was that new members of the League made declarations on admission in respect of minorities ,as in the case of Finland (1921), Albania (1921), Lithuania (1922), Latvia (1923), Estonia (1923) and Iraq (1932).

At or about 1900, one can therefore detect three main strands in the development of modern human rights law: namely the Western tradition of natural rights; the emphasis upon humanitarian law; and the increasing efforts to protect minorities on the dissolution of the Ottomann Empire. The significance of these changes was not always apparent at the time, so that LH Oppenheim, in the first edition of his *International Law* published in 1905, could confidently assert that the rights of man were not part of International Law.

In the inter-war years, the guarantees given to minorities in Eastern Europe led to a steady stream of case law. Where an allegation of breach of a state's obligations was in issue, then the Council of the League might refer the matter to an *ad hoc* Minorities Committee. In appropriate cases, the Council could refer the matter to the Permanent Court of International Justice; thus, in the *Minority Schools in Albania*[12] case the Court emphasised the need to preserve equality of treatment in educational provision. A particular vehicle for the case law arose from the German Polish Convention on Upper Silesia of 1922 which was designed to ensure equality of treatment for German and Polish

---

11   The matter was returned to in the Universal Declaration of Human Rights (1948), in which Art 4 reads: 'No one shall be held in slavery or servitude;slavery and the slave trade shall be prohibited in all their forms.'

12   *Minority Schools in Albania* case (1935) PCIJ, Ser A/B, No 64, p 17.

minorities on either side of the German Polish frontier. The Convention provided for a Mixed Commission and an Arbitral Tribunal; the former body was concerned with conciliation and the latter body was judicial in nature and its decisions were binding on the courts of both states. In cases of dispute, a matter might be referred to the Permanent Court of International Justice, as indeed was the case in the *Rights of Minorities in Upper Silesia* case,[13] so that gradually the general idea began to emerge of an international court passing judgment on the conduct of individual state authorities. To that extent these embryonic efforts were to be built on later.

In addition to specific regional systems designed to resolve problems arising because of boundaries, another important step was taken in 1919. Article 22 of the Covenant of the League provided for the establishment of a mandate system to guide the future of certain territories formerly held by enemy powers. It was declared in Art 22 that the 'well being and development of such peoples form a sacred trust of civilisation'. Pursuant to this objective, Art 23 set out a demanding list of obligations of which one was 'to secure just treatment of the native inhabitants of territories under their control'.

It is relevant to add that the Treaty of Versailles provided for the establishment of the International Labour Organisation in 1919 whose objective was to improve the working conditions of peoples and to promote the principle of freedom of association. The climate of 1919 was therefore conducive to the development of a law on human rights; governments were expected to take a closer interest in the welfare of their peoples and efforts were to be made to redress the balance between the interests of capital and labour.

The breakdown in diplomatic order in Europe after 1933, led to widespread abuses of human rights and finally to all out conflict. As the hostilities unfolded, it became clear that the rulers of Germany were abusing state power to a degree previously not encountered. Moreover, from the outset of the conflict, many urged[14] that one of the objects of victory should be to ensure a world order based on a form of basic rights and this was taken up by President Roosevelt in 1941, when he demanded action to secure the 'four essential freedoms – freedom of speech and worship, and freedom from want and fear'. Thus, in 1945 when the United Nations Charter[15] was being drawn up, a number of references to human rights were included within the document. The Preamble asserts a determination 'to reaffirm faith in fundamental human rights, in the dignity and worth of the human person', while Art 1(2) refers to the 'principle of equal rights and self-determination of peoples'. Article 13 indicates that the topic is one that shall be studied by the General Assembly while Art 55(c) provides that the United Nations 'shall promote universal respect for, and observance of, human rights'. To re-emphasise the point, Art 56 provides that: 'All Members pledge themselves to take joint and separate action in co-operation with the Organisation for the achievement of the purposes set forth in Art 55.'

---

13 *Rights of Minorities in Upper Silesia* case (1928) PCIJ, Ser A, No 15, p 46.

14 The desire to state clear war aims based on a bill of rights was taken up as early as October 1939 by HG Wells in a letter to the *Times* and amplified in a paperback book that sold widely, entitled *HG Wells on the Rights of Man*. In essence, HG Wells argued for a New World Order of international human rights founded on the rule of law and democracy rather than diplomacy. There is some evidence that the case put by HG Wells influenced Franklin Roosevelt.

15 On the historical background, see J Burgers, 'The road to San Francisco' (1992) 14 HRQ 4471; J Morsink, 'World War Two and the Universal Declaration' (1993) 15 HRQ 357; S Marks, 'The roots of the Universal Declaration of Human Rights in the French Revolution' (1998) 20 HRQ 483.

Further, in respect of the trusteeship system which replaced the mandate system, Art 73 provided for 'just treatment and protection against abuses', while Art 76(c) required 'respect for human rights'.

Although the references might only be in the most general terms, it was clear that the promotion of human rights would be an important task of the United Nations.[16] The reasons for this are not hard to seek; the experience of the Second World War had lead to a revival of natural law thinking. The danger of philosophies that extolled state power were all too visible and the point of view began to emerge that states that abused human rights tended to be aggressive towards their neighbours.[17] It could therefore be argued that by promoting human rights one was likely to produce a more stable world; a functioning democratic state with a free press is less likely to threaten its neighbours.[18] However, any developing law of human rights has to operate within certain accepted principles of public international law and it is sensible to say a little about these.

3 FUNDAMENTAL PRINCIPLES

Any emerging law of human rights would have to accommodate itself to accepted principles of public international law. In the 19th century, it was accepted that a state was sovereign within its own territory and this view was supported by Westlake and Oppenheim. The primacy of domestic jurisdiction was acknowledged in Art 15(8) of the Covenant of the League of Nations and this approach was continued in Art 2(7) of the United Nations Charter (1945) which reads:

> Nothing in the present Charter shall authorise the United Nations to intervene in matters which are essentially within the domestic jurisdiction of any state or shall require Members to submit such matters to settlement under the present Charter; but this principle shall not prejudice the application of enforcement measures under Chapter VII.

It is common for a state to raise Art 2(7) when its domestic conduct has been the subject of some criticism but such arguments do not normally prevail.[19] First, it has been accepted

---

16 A matter analysed by Professor H Lauterpacht in his *International Law and Human Rights* which was published in 1950.

17 An argument advanced by President Truman in closing the San Francisco conference in June 1945. The argument was advanced at the conference by the American delegate, Mr Dulles, who referred to the future role of the United Nations as being to deal with 'the underlying causes of war as well as to deal with crises leading to war', cited by DJ Harris in *Cases and Materials on International Law*, 5th edn, 1998, p 973. As Secretary of State between 1953–59, John Foster Dulles (1888–1959) played an important role in the early years of the United Nations.

18 A theme that became very influential in United States foreign policy in the years after 1945. See Warren Christopher, *In the Stream of History*, 1998, p 61.

19 Obviously, every state raises Art 2(7) when it wishes to deter others from investigating its conduct. A recent example would be its employment by Russia in the face of demands that there be some form of investigation as to conduct in Chechnya. The question therefore arises as to the correct interpretation and application of Art 2(7) which must be a matter for the United Nations to interpret and apply as it is contained within the Charter. An attempt to interpret the provision in three propositions was made by the United States Ambassador to the United Nations (Henry Cabot Lodge) in March 1960 where he stressed that Art 2(7) involved three assertions: (i) the right of a state to regulate its internal affairs; (ii) the right and obligation of the United Nations to investigate national policies that affect the world community; (iii) that this right arose to a greater degree where obligations arising under the Charter were in issue.

since 1945 that the provision is not to be interpreted liberally. Secondly, it is a matter for the United Nations not the individual state to determine whether a matter is 'essentially domestic'. Thirdly, the provisions of the sub clause are clearly subordinate to the enforcement powers of the Security Council arising under the Charter. Fourthly, it is evident as a matter of interpretation that the principles in Art 2 are subordinate to the purposes of the United Nations as stated in Art 1 and in other parts of the Charter. Fifthly, it is perverse for a state that has voluntarily entered into human rights treaties to prey in aid its domestic jurisdiction when faced with an individual petition or a hostile report form a human rights body. Sixthly, it is well accepted that international action can be taken if the abuses of domestic jurisdiction cause regional insecurity.[20] Thus, in respect of human rights violations a state will not normally be able to prey in aid the provisions of its domestic law, however the status of the state and the nature of the violations may determine the response of the international community.

Since in public international law each state is territorially sovereign, it follows that if there has been an abuse within the state then it is for the institutions of that state to remedy the matter. This is a basic rule of the law of state responsibility[21] and most human rights treaties require the exhaustion of domestic remedies provided that such a remedy is available and practical. This limitation is justified on grounds of comity but also on grounds of convenience; the state where the abuse has arisen is also the state in which the evidence is more likely to be available.

A third feature that will be noted is that the law of human rights tends to operate by means of regional instruments. Although these draw upon the Universal Declaration of Human Rights (1948), they vary in content but some general points can be made. First, some rights will be absolute in the sense that such conduct is always unlawful whatever the justification. Thus, Art 3 of the European Convention on Human Rights reads simply: 'No one shall be subjected to torture or to inhuman or degrading treatment or punishment.' However, some of the provisions the right is stated but then it is stated that a state may restrict the right in the interests of some other social good. Thus, Art 10(1) of the European Convention on Human Rights states the general principle of freedom of expression but in Art 10(2) provides for its limitation or restriction in a number of defined circumstances.

Secondly, while a state will be bound to respect all rights while it remains a signatory circumstances may arise in which observance is not possible. Thus, Art 15 of the European Convention provides that a state may avail itself of a right of derogation in certain limited circumstances in times of emergency.[22] Thirdly, it may be that when signing a human rights treaty a state may feel that it cannot abide by a particular provision because of the provisions of its domestic law. It may be that the human rights treaty will permit such a signatory to make a limited reservation.[23]

---

20   See *Iraqi Safe Havens* case, Security Council Resolution 668 (April 1991).

21   *The Finnish Ships Arbitration* (1934) 3 RIAA 1479; *The Ambatielos Arbitration* (1956) 12 RIAA 83; 23 ILR 306; (1957) 24 ILR 291.

22   *Brogan v United Kingdom* (1989) 11 EHHR 117; *Brannigan and McBride v United Kingdom* (1993) 17 EHRR 539.

23   See generally, *Belilos v Switzerland* (1988) 10 EHRR 466; S Marks (1990) 39 ICLQ 300 in respect of Art 64 of the European Convention on Human Rights (1950).

Fourthly, while most precise human rights are governed by treaty a question may arise as to whether a particular abuse is to be regarded as contrary to customary international law; in this context would fall genocide,[24] torture,[25] slavery[26] in view of the large number of states adhering to basic treaties on these subjects.

A difficult question that should be noted at this point is the problem as to whether human rights should be regarded as universal. In principle, this is a philosophical or ethical question rather than a legal one. If a state signs a human rights treaty and submits itself to external surveillance then, legally, it is not open to it challenge the obligations that it has voluntarily assumed. Broadly, the approach is to recognise that human rights are universal in scope but that, in appropriate cases, allowance must be made for historical, cultural and religious factors. The position was clearly stated in Chapter 1, para 5, of the 'Vienna Declaration and Programme of Action' issued following the Second United Nations Conference on Human Rights held in Vienna in June 1993. The relevant paragraph reads:

> All human rights are universal, indivisible and interdependent and interrelated. The international community must treat human beings globally in a fair and equal manner, on the same footing, and with the same emphasis. While the significance of national and regional peculiarities and various historical, cultural and religious backgrounds must be borne in mind, it is the duty of States, regardless of their political, economic and cultural systems, to promote and protect all human rights and fundamental freedoms.

While some writers question the validity of universal human rights,[27] the prevailing trend has been to stress the 'human' nature of human rights and to point to the fact that such rights are vested in individuals not states and exist independent of the conduct of particular states. Such writers point to the law of human rights being founded on the universal principle of human dignity[28] and the empirically established fact that some human wants are universal.[29]

4 THE INTERNATIONAL LAW OF HUMAN RIGHTS

As indicated above, the United Nations Charter (1945) contains a number of references to human rights. The most significant references are contained in Art 55 which provides that the United Nations shall promote 'universal respect for, and observance of, human rights and fundamental freedoms for all without distinction as to race, sex, language or religion'. This is then followed by Art 56 which stipulates that:

---

24 Convention on the Prevention and Punishment of the Crime of Genocide (1948).

25 Convention against Torture and other Cruel, Inhuman or Degrading Treatment or Punishment (1984). For a discussion of the position in customary international law, see *R v Bow Street Metropolitan Stipendiary Magistrate ex p Pinochet Ugarte* [1998] 3 WLR 1456.

26 The Slavery Convention (1926); Protocol Amending the Slavery Convention (1953).

27 J Donnelly, *Universal Human Rights in Theory and Practice*, 1989; Y Ghai, 'Human rights and governance' (1994) 15 AYIL 5.

28 O Schachter, 'Human dignity as a normative concept' (1983) 77 AJIL 848.

29 See Rosalyn Higgins, *Problems and Process: International Law and How We Use It*, 1994.

All Members pledge themselves to take joint and separate action in co-operation with the organisation for the achievement of the purposes set forth in Article 55.

It has been suggested that Art 55 places the obligation on the United Nations as a collective entity, while Art 56 imposes an obligation upon the Members to take joint and separate action in co-operation with the organisation to achieve particular objectives. In any event, much debate took place as to whether the relevant articles in the United Nations Charter were merely aspirational because of the absence of any method of enforcement[30] or whether they were to be interpreted as creating legal obligations.[31]

However, theoretical disputes amongst scholars in the late 1940s are of less significance than the actual conduct of the United Nations. From the birth of the organisation, states have been condemned for conduct seen as violating the human rights principles of the Charter.[32]

Although the Charter did contain limitations in respect of domestic jurisdiction, these have been interpreted narrowly and the steady emphasis since 1945 has been on the increasing legal protection of human rights on the international plane. In autumn 1945, the Preparatory Commission recommended that the Economic and Social Council should establish a Commission on Human Rights charged with preparing an international Bill of Rights. The Commission and its drafting committee[33] prepared both a Declaration and a Convention which included provisions for legal enforcement. However, the Third Session of the General Assembly held in the autumn of 1948 decided to proceed only on the Declaration and this was accepted by the General Assembly on 10 December 1948, with 48 votes in favour, none against and eight abstentions.[34] The Declaration was not intended as an immediately enforceable legal text; instead, as Mrs Roosevelt informed the General Assembly, it was intended as 'a declaration of the basic principles to serve as a common standard for all nations'.

Although the original document may not have been intended to have legal consequences, the declaration has had a very considerable impact both directly and indirectly on the general law of human rights. In 1967, the Secretary General considered that its provisions had been adopted in the written constitutions of 43 states. The document has been referred to in subsequent documents on international human rights[35]

---

30 M Hudson, 'Integrity of international instruments' (1948) 42 AJIL 105; H Kelsen, *The Law of the United Nations*, 1950.

31 P Jessup, *A Modern Law of Nations*, 1948; H Lauterpacht, *International Law and Human Rights*, 1950. For other contributions to the debate, see, J Kunz (1949) 43 AJIL 43; Q Wright (1945) 45 AJIL 62; Preuss (1952) 46 AJIL 289.

32 GA Res 285(III) of 1949 (Treatment of Married Women with Foreign Spouses in USSR); General Assembly Res 1353(XIV) of 1959; 4723(XVI) of 1961 and 2079(XX) of 1965 (in relation to civil liberties within Tibet).

33 The Commission and the drafting committee were chaired by Eleanor Roosevelt (1884–1962) widow of the 32nd President. There is little doubt that Mrs Roosevelt saw the purpose of the document was to stand alongside the references to the rights of man in the 1776 Declaration of Independence and the 1789 Declaration of the Rights of Man.

34 The abstentions were Czechoslovakia, Poland, USSR, Bylorrussia SSR, Ukraine SSR, Yugoslavia and Saudi Arabia. Of these abstentions, seven were directly or indirectly influenced by Marxist Leninist governments.

35 The Convention on the Status of Refugees (1951).

and in important regional human rights instruments.[36] The instrument has been referred to in subsequent important General Assembly resolutions[37] and by virtue of its wide acceptance many of its principles may be regarded as rules of customary international law.

The Declaration itself comprises 30 articles and broadly concentrates on civil and political liberties. The document begins by asserting that man is born free and equal in dignity and rights (Art 1) and that everyone has the right to life liberty and the security of the person (Art 3). The Declaration prohibits slavery (Art 4) or the subjection of torture or cruel, inhuman or degrading treatment (Art 5); it requires equality before the law (Art 7), effective remedies (Art 8) and due process of law (Arts 10 and 11). The draftsmen stipulated for the right of privacy (Art 12) and the right to freedom of movement (Art 13) together with the right to seek asylum (Art 14) and the right to a nationality (Art 15). Traditional civil liberties are included so that the declaration provides for the right to marry (Art 16), the right to own property (Art 17) and the right to freedom of thought (Art 18) and expression (Art 19).

It is further provided that there shall be a right of peaceful assembly (Art 20) and a right to participate in the government of one own country (Art 21). In the context of social rights, it is noteworthy that the Declaration provides for the right to work (Art 23), the right to social security (Art 25) and the right to education (Art 26).

The Declaration itself draws on the Western liberal tradition of the state which is traceable back to Locke and Jefferson but in its reference to social provisions it draws on social democratic thinking that had developed as a reaction to the slump of the 1930s and is to be found in the New Deal activism of Franklin Roosevelt. Although the document was not intended to be legally binding its widespread acceptance both in state constitutions and regional human rights treaties has given it a status *sui generis*. The Declaration has been referred to in numerous cases,[38] both before municipal and international tribunals. The special nature of the United Nations Declaration was referred to in 1968. In that year, a United Nations Conference was held in Tehran to review the progress made in the 20 years since that date. The Conference concluded with a Proclamation and 29 resolutions. The Proclamation noted the special status of the Declaration and the need for continued progress while Resolution 22 referred to the principles set out in the Declaration as representing 'ethics common to all members of the international community'.

The nature of the General Assembly as a body renders it unsuitable for detailed consideration of human rights problems; its role has normally been to consider questions of broad principle. Article 68 of the United Nations Charter provided that the Economic and Social Council should establish a commission for the promotion of human rights. The United Nations Commission on Human Rights has since 1946 played an important role in

---

36 See the Preamble to the European Convention on Human Rights (1950); the Preamble to the American Convention on Human Rights (1969); the Preamble to the African Charter on Human and People's Rights (1981).

37 Res 1514(XV), the Declaration on Colonialism.

38 *Re Flesche* (1949) 16 ILR 266; *The State (Duggan) v Tapley* (1951) 18 ILR 336; *Robinson v Secretary General of the United Nations* (1952) 19 ILR 49; *Camacho v Rogers* (1961) 32 ILR 368; *The Basic Right to Marry Case* (1971) 72 ILR 295; *Namibia (Legal Consequences)* case (1971) ICJ 6, p 46.

the preparation of international conventions but it was soon accepted that it did not have power to entertain individual applications.[39] However, the Commission has played an active role in the conventions relating to Racial Discrimination,[40] Civil and Political Rights,[41] and Economic and Social Rights.[42] These matters will be considered below.

The United Nations Commission on Human Rights was created in 1946 with a membership of nine. In the period since that date, the membership was increased to the 53 that it now contains.[43] In the first 20 years dominated by the Cold War and decolonisation, there was little demand for an investigatory role and its inability to investigate particular complaints was confirmed in 1947.[44] However, in 1966 the General Assembly urged the Economic and Social Council to consider how the United Nations capacity might be increased to counter human rights violations. In May 1970, in ECOSOC Resolution 1503, the Council introduced procedures whereby the Sub Commission on the Prevention of Discrimination and Protection of Minorities could consider communications involving serious allegations of human rights violations and refer them to the Commission on Human Rights. The Commission can then decide whether to pass the matter on to the Council at which point the matter ceases to be confidential. However, the Commission might establish an *ad hoc* conciliation committee or appoint an independent expert or special rapporteur. However, the Commission has no enforcement powers and will not be able to question witnesses in the territory in question.

It has been argued that the procedure is slow and is designed to accomplish its goals by discreet pressure. It has been the practice since 1978 for the Chairman of the Commission to announce those countries that are the subject of consideration.[45] A country may be removed from the list when an abusive government gives way to a democratic regime operating within the rule of law. In defence of the system, it provides a vehicle for raising the matter in an international forum and it provides a mechanism for putting discreet pressure on an infringing government.

In June 1967, the Economic and Social Council adopted Resolution 1235[46] in which it approved the decision of the Commission to give annual consideration to a matter entitled 'Questions of the violation of human rights and fundamental freedom, including policies of racial discrimination and segregation and of apartheid in all countries, with particular reference to colonial and other dependent countries and territories'. The procedure under Resolution 1235 which involves the investigation of a particular country is public and may be initiated by a member state or a group of states or the Sub

---

39 ECOSOC Res 75(V) (1947) reaffirmed in ECOSOC Res 728 F (XXVIII) (1959).
40 International Convention on the Elimination of All Forms of Racial Discrimination (1966).
41 International Covenant on Civil and Political Rights (1966).
42 International Covenant on Economic, Social and Cultural Rights (1966).
43 By a variety of resolutions (ECOSOC 1946, 6 (I), 9 (II); 1961/845 1966/1147; 1979/36 and 1990/48) the membership was increased to 21, in 1966 to 32, in 1980 to 43 and in 1990 to 53.
44 ECOSOC Res 75(V).
45 Between 1978 and 1985, 29 countries were subject to consideration under the process. See M Bossuyt (1985) 6 HRLJ 179. An interesting example is Uruguay which went on the list in 1980 following widespread reports. In 1985, there was a change of regime and the country was removed from the list and the new administration complimented by the Human Rights Committee for its co-operative attitude.
46 Which followed on from GA Res 2144 (XXI).

Commission on the Prevention of Discrimination and the Protection of Minorities. Thereupon the Commission may decide to investigate the matter through a working group or through a special rapporteur. In any event the Commission will report through the Council to the General Assembly. While a large number of countries have been subject to consideration by the Commission there seems to be a reluctance to mount a full investigation in the absence of actual conflict so that in the 1980s human rights abuses in Latin America were subject to special investigation,[47] but there was a reluctance to move against other powerful states whose co-operation might be needed in other fora.

Further institutional change resulted from the United Nations World Conference on Human Rights held at Vienna in June 1993. The conference produced a detailed document entitled the Vienna Declaration and Programme of Action. Chapter 1, para 8, noted that: 'Democracy, development and respect for human rights and fundamental freedoms are interdependent and mutually reinforcing.' Chapter II, paras 13–16, called for the strengthening of the United Nations Centre for Human Rights,[48] while paras 17 and 18 called for the establishment of a United Nations High Commissioner for Human Rights charged with the promotion and protection of all human rights. In December 1993, the General Assembly agreed[49] on the appointment of a United Nations Commissioner who would be the principal officer with responsibility for co-ordinating the efforts of United Nations agencies. Since that time, the United Nations High Commissioner has been active in visits to member states and sources of international concern.

5 CLASSIFICATION

The western tradition from the middle of the 18th century was to emphasise role of the individual and his entitlement to rights; manifestly many rights are individual such as the right to life or the right not to be subject to inhuman treatment. However, certain individual rights will be exercised and enjoyed collectively such as the right to assemble or to worship. In the present century, human rights law has witnessed the emergence of the collective right where the object is to protect the rights of a group or a class. Examples of such rights would be the right not to be discriminated against on grounds of colour or sex or the right as a minority to enjoy cultural or linguistic freedom; in such a context one might also include the right to protection against acts of genocide. Clearly, where a

---

47 See P Alston, *The Commission on Human Rights in the United Nations and Human Rights: A Critical Appraisal*, 1992, Oxford: Clarendon. The learned author notes that Eastern Europe was only subject to two special procedure investigations (ie, Special Rapporteurs, Rapporteurs, Special Representatives, Working Groups).

48 At the time, the United Nations Human Rights Centre in Geneva only had a limited number of staff and absorbed less than 1% of the total United Nations budget.

49 GA Res 48/141 (20 December 1993). The first holder of the post was Ayala Lasso from Ecuador who took office in April 1994 as High Commissioner and with the status as Under Secretary General of the United Nations. The difficulties of the task are indicated by Art 3 of the relevant General Assembly Resolution whereby the holder of the post is expected to balance promotion of human rights with the principle of state sovereignty. See A Clapham, 'Creating the High Commissioner for Human Rights: the outside story' (1994) 5 EJIL 556. The second holder of the post, Mrs Mary Robinson (former President of the Irish Republic), has drawn attention to abuses in Kosovo and called for Russia to investigate the conduct of its forces in Chechnya arising from the military offensive of 1999/2000.

collective right is in issue then it must be exercised in a manner consistent with the interests of others within the state. Thus, one can classify such rights as either exclusively individual or partly individual and partly collective and lastly as entirely collective.

A second classification has been alluded to above. Political and civil rights are sometimes referred to as first generation human rights and are consistent with the general western liberal tradition. Economic and social rights are sometimes described as second generation rights although such rights are not without their critics and some governments are distinctly ambivalent. It is sensible to reflect on the difference between first generation and second generation rights.[50] While the first generation right may not involve a great sum of public expenditure, second generation rights involve complex questions of macro economic management, as well as considerable expenditure of public money. Moreover, it is argued that second generation rights have a variable quality according to the level of economic development of the state.

In classifying rights, it is important to bear in mind the so called 'third generation' rights which tend to be of a collective nature and often reflect the impact of 'third world' countries in the years after 1945. Amongst these might be said to be the right to self-determination, the right to development, the right to a clean environment and the right to enjoy natural resources. In particular some of these rights now arise within the scope of international economic law or international environmental law. These 'rights' raise difficult questions about the balance that has to be struck between promoting economic growth and higher standards of living and the equally important consideration of safeguarding the environment. These matters will be returned to below.[51]

While first generation rights may be regarded as strictly 'legal' and can be secured by appropriate constitutional guarantees there is no doubt that second and third generation rights give rise to difficult economic questions; many of these rights can only be secured by an efficient state raising revenue in taxation and redistributing such revenue.

However, before considering United Nations action in particular areas it is necessary to examine the two major instruments that provide the present day basis of international human rights law.

6 THE INTERNATIONAL COVENANT ON CIVIL AND POLITICAL RIGHTS[52]

In the years after 1948, it was recognised that work would need to be undertaken to ensure that the content of the United Nations Declaration on Human Rights (1948) might assume the form of a legal obligation. By 1950, the General Assembly recognised that

---

50 See E Vierdag, 'The legal nature of the rights granted by the International Covenant on Economic, Social and Cultural Rights (1978) 9 NYIL 69; M Bossuyt, 'La distinction entre les droits civils et politiques et les droits economiques, sociaux et culturels' (1975) 8 HRJ 783.

51 See Chapter 17, International Environmental Law, and Chapter 19, International Economic Law.

52 See T Opsahl, 'The Human Rights Committee', in P Alston (ed), The United Nations and Human Rights (1992); D McGoldrick, The Human Rights Committee, 1991 (rev edn 1994); E Schwelb (1968) 62 AJIL 827; D Fischer (1982) 76 AJIL 142; F Jhabvala (1984) 6 HRQ 81; F Jhabvala (1985) 15 Israel Yearbook on Human Rights 184; A Robertson (1969) 43 BYIL 21; PR Ghandi, 'The Human Rights Committee and the right of individual communication' (1986) 57 BYIL 201.

there were two broad categories of rights that needed to be considered namely civil and political rights and economic and social rights. A wide variety of ideas were advanced by interested states; some were happy to establish wide ranging investigative bodies but others such as the USSR pointed to the provisions of Art 2(7) of the Charter. By 1952, the General Assembly accepted that the two categories of rights would need to be set out in two different documents. By 1954, the Commission on Human Rights had prepared the text of two covenants and submitted the texts to ECOSOC and the General Assembly. However, 12 years were to pass before agreement could be reached on substantive rights and methods of enforcement. The Covenants as approved by the Third Committee were accepted unanimously by General Assembly in December 1966 and required 35 ratifications to enter into force and these were obtained by 1976. In addition, an Optional Protocol to the Covenant on Civil and Political Rights was approved by a majority and entered into force at the time of the two covenants.

One of the commonest complaints made of the covenants is that the enforcement systems are rather weak. Before turning to the substantive content, it is first important to remember that the covenants were being drawn up at the time of the Cold War when some states resented any criticism of governmental conduct. Secondly, it is sensible to bear in mind the possible methods of enforcement; in broad terms, these might be:

(a) the possibility of an individual complaint on the international plane;

(b) the possibility of inter-state complaint;

(c) the possibility of a reporting obligation placed on a state;

(d) the establishment of an external body with powers of investigation.

The International Covenant on Civil and Political Rights commences with an affirmation of the right of self-determination (Art 1) and then proceeds to require each state to accord to persons within their territory the rights afforded by the Convention (Art 2). The substantive rights protected by the Covenant are:

Art 6:   The right to life;

Art 7:   Freedom from torture and inhuman treatment;

Art 8:   Freedom from slavery and forced labour;

Art 9:   The right to liberty and security;

Art 10:   The right of detained persons to be treated with humanity;

Art 11:   Freedom from imprisonment for debt;

Art 12:   Freedom of movement and of choice of residence;

Art 13:   Freedom of aliens from arbitrary expulsion;

Art 14:   The right to a fair trial;

Art 15:   Prohibition of conviction under retroactive criminal laws;

Art 16:   The right to recognition as a person before the law;

Art 17:   The right to privacy;

Art 18:   The right to freedom of thought, conscience and religion;

Art 19:   The right to freedom of opinion and expression;

Art 20:   The prohibition of propaganda for war and of incitement to national, racial or religious hatred;

Art 21:   The right of assembly;

Art 22:   The right to freedom of association;

Art 23:   The right to marry and found a family;

Art 24:   The rights of a child;

Art 25:   The right to participate in political life;

Art 26:   The right to equality before the law;

Art 27:   The protection of the rights of minorities.

This is a longer list expressed in more detailed terms than appears in the Universal Declaration of Human Rights; several rights appear which had not been included in the 1948 Declaration. Some of the rights are spelt out in considerable detail and are intended to operate progressively. For example, Art 6 while stating the inherent right to life refers to 'countries which have not abolished the death penalty' implying that such a development was likely in the future. The rights themselves fall within the classic civil and political rights of western tradition and clearly favour open democratic government (Art 25) and proper respect for the language and culture of minorities (Art 27). To the common lawyer some of the rights might seem dangerously vague but the draftsmen had to secure sufficient agreement and much could be left to subsequent interpretation. It was felt that precise definitions were of less importance than enforcement and general observance.

The principal institution for the enforcement of the Covenant is the Human Rights Committee[53] which was established under the terms of Art 28 and would comprise eighteen elected persons of high moral character.[54] The elections were to be held by secret ballot[55] and each state could nominate two persons. The term of office is four[56] and the elections are designed to ensure representation of the different forms of civilisation and of the principal legal systems.[57] The Committee meets three times a year in either New York or Geneva. Members serve in a personal capacity[58] and are expected to make a declaration as to impartiality.[59] The Committee has power to make its own rules of procedure save that there must be a quorum of 12 and that decisions are to be made by a majority.[60]

Under the terms of Art 40 the Covenant is implemented by a reporting system which envisages a report after one year and then reports submitted every five years.[61] Members of the Committee may receive information from other sources and some states have been

---

53 See D McGoldrick, *The Human Rights Committee*, 1991 (rev edn 1994).

54 ICCPR (1966), Art 28.

55 *Ibid*, Art 29.

56 *Ibid*, Art 32.

57 *Ibid*, Art 31.

58 *Ibid*, Art 28(3).

59 *Ibid*, Art 38.

60 *Ibid*, Art 39.

61 See *Ibid*, Art 40(1)(a) and (b).

criticised for the limited content of their reports.[62] The Committee is entitled to comment on the content of state reports and under the terms of Art 40(5) the state party is entitled to make observations on those comments. The rationale of such a system is that human rights are likely to be improved by a constructive dialogue between the Committee and the state party. The Committee itself has issued a number of general comments on matters of topical and widespread concern and its specific comments in respect of state reports tend to divide into 'positive aspects' 'suggestions and recommendations' and 'causes of concern'.[63] Following guidelines issued in 1977 and revised in 1981, state reports should be structured so as to set out first the constitutional protection afforded to human rights and the remedies available and then the report should detail individual areas of substantive law. Actual meetings tend to be poorly attended and members of the Human Rights Committee are part time; the form will normally be for individual members to question the state representative as to the content of his report. Since 1992, it has been the practice for the Committee to make a collective comment on on the state report.

Under the terms of Art 41 of the Covenant a state party may at any time recognise by declaration[64] the competence of the Committee to receive and consider a complaint by another state party. However, the jurisdiction to hear such complaints only arises if both parties have made such a declaration. If such a complaint is made, then the Committee is bound, under Art 41, to use its good offices to achieve a resolution and, if this is not possible, it is obliged to collect relevant information and to produce a report. If the matter is not resolved to the satisfaction of the parties under Art 41, then Art 42 allows the Committee with the consent of the parties to appoint an *ad hoc* Conciliation Commission.

One specialist has described the procedure in Art 41 and Art 42 as 'complex, delicate and long winded'[65] although it is also true that the procedure, to some extent, reflects the Cold War origins of the 1966 Covenant.

The powers of the Human Rights Committee were extended by the First Optional Protocol of 1966[66] which, by Art 1, 'recognises the competence of the Committee to receive and consider communications from individuals subject to its jurisdiction who claim to be victims of a violation by that state party of any of the rights set forth in the Covenant'. Under the terms of the Protocol, it is necessary to be a victim of a violation of rights arising under the Covenant and to have exhausted all available domestic remedies; an application cannot be made if the matter is subject to investigation by some other international body. In broad terms, the procedure before the Committee involves a two stage process: first, to determine admissibility and, secondly, to examine the merits. Under the terms of Art 5(4), the Committee shall produce a report to be forwarded to the

---

62   M Nowak (1981) 2 HRLJ 168; (1984) 5 HRLJ 199.

63   In dealing with the third periodic report of Iraq under Art 40 (UN Doc A/46/40 (1991) Supp No 40 at 150 and UN Doc A/47/40 (1994) supp No 40 at 41), the Committee relied upon external sources from NGOs to pose questions as to extra judicial executions and torture and expressed regret that many of their questions had not received satisfactory replies.

64   As of July 1997, 40 states had made declarations, including the United Kingdom. See Leckie (1988) 10 HRQ 249.

65   PR Ghandi, 'The Human Rights Committee and the right of individual petition' (1986) 57 BYIL 201.

66   The First Protocol came into effect in 1976; by 1998, 89 parties to the ICCPR were also party to the 1966 First Protocol.

state party and the individual. Secondly, under Art 6 activities under the Protocol are to be included in the annual report made under Art 45 of the Covenant. Thus, it is not correct to view the Committee as having the power of final judgment and extensive methods of enforcement.

In the early years, the Committee considered on average 20 cases a year but, from 1985, the number of state parties increased and the volume of work began to grow. It is clear that an individual must meet a minimum requirement as to *locus standi*; there is no form of *actio popularis* and thus some interest in the matter must be established.[67] An application before a regional human rights tribunal cannot be determined[68] but where the state has injured a number of victims then a complaint by one can be considered even if another has chosen to proceed in another forum.[69]

In respect of substantive rights, the Committee has upheld the right to participate in political life in Uruguay[70] and the residential rights of minorities in Canada.[71] Some of the case law has arisen from political turmoil in Central and South America and the Committee has been vigorous in condemning the practice of declaring citizens 'disappeared' in Uruguay,[72] and has found breaches of Art 6 of the Covenant by police and military forces in Columbia.[73] Similarly, there have been a number of cases in which the practice of torture and other abusive conduct has been condemned.[74] The Committee has upheld the right of privacy in sexual matters[75] and has favoured equality before the law[76] and freedom of expression save in those cases where restriction was necessary.[77]

One area that has caused difficulty is the approach to be adopted in death penalty cases. As can be seen, the death penalty is not prohibited in Art 6; indeed, there are many states that have reintroduced the death penalty after a period of suspension. This has led to a developing case law. In some cases, problems have arisen as to whether a state will be

---

67 *Aumeeruddy-Cziffra v Mauritius* (the *Mauritian Women* case) (1981) 1 Selected Decisions HRC 67 (unmarried women not victims in respect of deportation policy pertaining to husbands although married women were); *Hertzberg v Finland* (1982) 1 Selected Decisions HRC 124.

68 *Millan v Uruguay* (1980) 1 Selected Decisions HRC 52; *DF v Sweden* (1985) 2 Selected Decisions HRC 55.

69 *Fanalli v Italy* (1983) 2 Selected Decisions HRC 99.

70 *Silva v Uruguay* (1981) 1 Selected Decisions HRC 65.

71 *Lovelace v Canada* (1981) 2 Selected Decisions HRC 28.

72 *Bleier v Uruguay* (1982) 1 Selected Decisions HRC 109. In fairness to Uruguay, it should be noted the elected government which took office in 1985 has been complimented for its co-operation. The cases concern the regime operating between the revolution of 1970 and that of 1984. See *Conteris v Uruguay* (1985) 2 Selected Documents HRC 168; see, also, *Bautista de Arellana v Columbia* (1996) 3 IHRR 315; *Celis Laureano v Peru* (1997) 4 IHRR 54.

73 See *Guerrero v Columbia* (1982) 1 Selected Decisions HRC 112; *Herrara Rubio v Columbia* (1985) 2 Selected Documents HRC 192.

74 *Estrella v Uruguay* (1983) 2 Selected Decisions HRC 93; *Carabell v Uruguay* (1981) 1 Selected Decisions HRC 63.

75 *Toonen v Australia* (1994) 1-3 IHRR 97 (private homosexual conduct in Tasmania).

76 *Broeks v Netherlands* (1987) 2 Selected Documents HRC 196 (social security laws in The Netherlands).

77 *Mukong v Cameroon* (1995) 2 IHRR 131 (arrested for criticising the President of the Cameroons and the Government on the BBC). *Faurrison v France* (1996) 4 IHRR 444. A conviction was upheld where the prosecution had been brought under the Gayssot Act 1990, which makes it a criminal offence to challenge the factual conclusions and verdict of the Nuremberg Military Tribunal (1946).

in breach of the covenant by agreeing to extradite without seeking assurances that the death penalty or a particular method of death penalty should not be sought.[78] Problems have arisen as to whether a delay on death row constitutes a breach of Art 7 and the answer appears to be it does not unless accompanied by special factors.[79] Failure to accord an opportunity for legal representation on a capital charge will be a breach of Art 14.[80] The Committee has shown itself ready to request that a sentence not be carried out pending a hearing,[81] but such requests have not always been respected.[82]

In the particular context of the death penalty, a Second Optional Protocol to the International Covenant on Civil and Political Rights Aiming at the Abolition of the Death Penalty was opened for signature in 1989 and acquired the necessary 10 ratifications to enter into force in 1991.[83] By Art 1 of this Second Optional Protocol no one within the jurisdiction of a state party is to be executed.

7 THE INTERNATIONAL COVENANT ON ECONOMIC, SOCIAL AND CULTURAL RIGHTS[84]

The International Covenant on Economic, Social and Cultural Rights was adopted in 1966 and secured the requisite number of ratifications to enter into force in 1976.[85] The Covenant is closely linked to the ICCPR and, prior to 1954, there had been an intention to include both rights in a single document. There are, however, differences of language; where the ICCPR uses terms such as 'everyone has the right to', the International Covenant on Economic, Social and Cultural Rights uses such neutral expressions as 'State Parties ... recognise the right of everyone to ...'. Thus, it is argued that the Covenant is of an aspirational or promotional nature rather than an instrument that requires immediate implementation. It will be recalled that the Universal Declaration of Human Rights listed only six rights in 1948 but by 1966 these had expanded, partly under the influence of social democratic thinking in western nations. The economic, social and cultural rights protected by the Covenant are listed in Part III and are as follows:

---

78 *Kindler v Canada* (1994) 1-2 IHRR 98; *Ng v Canada* (1994) 1-2 IHRR 161; *Cox v Canada* (1995) 2 IHRR 307.

79 For consideration of the so called 'death row phenomenon' before various tribunals, see *Soering v United Kingdom* (1989) 11 EHRR 439; *Pratt v Attorney General* (1994) 2 AC 1; *Johnson v Jamaica* (1997) 4 IHRR 21.

80 *Robinson v Jamaica*, HRC Report GAOR 44th Session (1989), p 241.

81 *Pratt and Morgan v Jamaica*, HRC Report GAOR 44th Session Supp 40 (1989), p 222.

82 *Ashley v Trinidad*, HRC Report GAOR 49th Session Supp 40, Vol 1, (1994), p 70.

83 The Protocol was annexed to GA Res 44/128. It entered into force in 1991, three months after the tenth ratification was obtained. On 1 April 1999 it had attracted 36 state parties. On that same date, the First Protocol had obtained 95 state parties and the Covenant itself had obtained 144 state parties.

84 See generally, M Craven, *The International Covenant on Economic, Social and Cultural Rights*, 1995; P Alston, 'The Committee on Economic, Social and Cultural Rights', in *The United Nations and Human Rights: A Critical Appraisal*, 1992. See also P Alston (1987) 9 HRQ 332; P Alston and G Quinn (1987) 9 HRQ 156; P Alston (1990) 84 AJIL 365; S Leckie (1991) 13 HRQ 545.

85 See E Schwelb (1976) 70 AJIL 511; Hevener and Mosher (1978) 27 ICLQ 596.

Art 6:   The right to work;

Art 7:   The right to just and favourable conditions of work, including fair wages, equal pay for equal work and holidays with pay;

Art 8:   The right to form and join a trade union including the right to strike;

Art 9:   The right to social security;

Art 10:   Protection of the family, including assistance for mothers and children;

Art 11:   The right to an adequate standard of living, including adequate food, clothing and housing;

Art 12:   The right to the highest attainable standard of physical and mental health;

Art 13:   The right to education. Primary education is to be compulsory and free to all. Secondary and higher education is to be generally accessible (Art 14 permits the progressive implementation of this right);

Art 15:   The right to participate in cultural life and enjoy the benefits of scientific progress.

The language of the provisions has not escaped criticism. First, some argue that the emphasis on progressive implementation makes it difficult to measure whether a state has honoured its obligations. Secondly, some of the obligations are so onerous that no state could possibly be in full compliance. Thirdly, the rationale of the Covenant depends on a degree of redistribution of wealth that may not be acceptable to many electorates and may be difficult for developing countries. A fully functioning social security system may be possible in a complex western economy, where there is a high level of employment, but it is simply impossible in countries such as India or Pakistan, where there are insufficient immediate resources. Some argue that the rights can only be secured by effective state action and this depends on a state apparatus of sufficient size and competence to deliver such rights. Moreover, questions arise as to whether such rights are sufficiently precise as to be capable of legal analysis; this problem of justiciability is also raised in the context of whether lawyers and judges should determine such questions or whether the skills of the welfare economist are required. The Vienna World Conference on Human Rights expressed concern in 1993 at the seeming lack of progress in the area of economic and social rights. Some writers have argued that the only sensible approach is to examine how a state spends its GDP, so that a democratic state spending a high proportion on health, education, housing and social security should be encouraged by the developed world, but a government that spends only a small proportion on such matters and devotes large resources to military expenditures projects of 'state prestige' should be subject to censure. It may be that such statistics are difficult to collate but if a state spends more on arms imports than it does on public health then this might be some evidence of non-compliance with the International Covenant on Economic, Social and Cultural Rights.

The Covenant operates on the basis of state reporting. The reporting obligations are set out in Art 16 and Art 17. The reports submitted under Art 16(2) are to be considered by the Economic and Social Council. In 1978, a Special Working Group comprising 15 members elected by ECOSOC performed this function but it did not operate very well so, in 1985, it was decided to modify the institutions. In 1987, a new Committee on Economic, Social and Cultural Rights with 18 independent experts met for its first meeting in March

1987.[86] Under Art 18 reports may be obtained from the Specialised Agencies and under Art 19 may transmit state reports to the Commission on Human Rights for their comments. Although the state reports are examined by independent expert it is arguable that an annual session of three weeks is not adequate to discharge this task.

A number of difficulties arise in implementing the Covenant. First, the terms of the text are vague and to some extent aspirational. Secondly, there is a problem of obtaining relevant information from sources other than states. This is because many of the reputable NGOs operate in the field of civil and political rights rather than that of economic and social rights. Thirdly, although the Committee draws upon statistical information supplied by the Secretariat there has been a problem of states that report late or inadequately. In broad terms, a state party is expected to supply an initial report in two years and subsequent reports are required every five years. Fourthly, although the reports are now investigated by a committee of independent experts, the time available is very limited. Fifthly, the committee is not an autonomous body like the Human Rights Committee but a subordinate organ set up by ECOSOC which can only in turn report to the General Assembly. Sixthly, the Committee has no jurisdiction to hear individual complaints and it has no competence to hear inter-state complaints.

Having considered the two main general instruments promoted by the United Nations in the field of human rights, it is now necessary to examine those specific areas where international action has been directed to a particular topic.

8 GENOCIDE

The unequivocal testimony presented to the Nuremberg Tribunal and the evidence of contemporary accounts created strong pressure for international action to restrain and punish systematic murder conducted by state officials. The United Nations was set up at a time when it was becoming clear that the National Socialist regime in Germany had murdered at least six million of its fellow citizens. The Convention on the Prevention and Punishment of Genocide was adopted by the General Assembly on 9 December 1948.[87] By the terms of Art 1, the contracting parties 'confirm that genocide, whether undertaken in time of peace or in time of war, is a crime under international law which they undertake to prevent and punish'. The definition of genocide is contained in Art 2 which reads:

> In the present Convention, genocide means any of the following acts committed with intent to destroy, in whole or in part, a national, ethical, racial or religious group, as such:
>
> (a) killing members of the group;
>
> (b) causing serious bodily or mental harm to members of the group;

---

86 See P Alston and B Simma, 'The First Session of the UN Committee on Economic, Social and Cultural Rights' (1987) 81 AJIL 747; 'Second Session of the UN Committee on Economic Social and Cultural Rights' (1988) 82 AJIL 603.

87 By 1998 there were 122 state parties. The Convention was given the force of law in the United Kingdom in the Genocide Act 1969. See Lemkin (1947) 41 AJIL 145; Kunz (1949) 43 AJIL 738.

(c) deliberately inflicting on the group conditions of life calculated to bring about its physical destruction in whole or in part;

(d) imposing measures intended to prevent births within the group;

(e) forcibly transferring children of the group to another group.

It is further provided under Art 4 that there shall be no immunity for state officials[88] and contracting parties agree to implement legislation to ensure that genocide is tried either where it has been committed or before an international tribunal. The crime of genocide has long been regarded as constituting the most serious example of an international crime that broke the necessary compact between the government and the governed. In 1951, in the Advisory Opinion on Reservations to the Convention on the Prevention and Punishment of the Crime of Genocide, the International Court of Justice affirmed that genocide was 'contrary to moral law and to the spirit and aims of the United Nations' and that 'the principles underlying the Convention are provisions which are recognised by civilised nations as binding on states even without any conventional obligation'.[89]

In 1945, it had been hoped that genocide was a matter that was not likely to be of concern in the future, however sadly the subject has acquired a renewed degree of prominence in recent years in respect of the events arising out of the dissolution of Yugoslavia and the Civil War in Rwanda. In respect of Yugoslavia, the Statute of the International Tribunal includes in Art 4 express jurisdiction to try persons for genocide;[90] in similar terms, the Statute of the International Tribunal for Rwanda[91] established under Security Council Resolution 955 of 1994 includes jurisdiction in Art 2 to try crimes of genocide. The emphasis of both tribunals is on prosecution and affixing individual criminal responsibility. This policy is continued in the Rome Statute of the International Criminal Court which in Arts 5 and 6 confers jurisdiction on the court to hear allegations of genocide.[92]

An example of the issue of genocide being considered in inter-state litigation arose in the *Case concerning Application of the Convention on the Prevention and Punishment of the Crime of Genocide (Bosnia-Herzegovina v Yugoslavia (Serbia and Montenegro))*, where Bosnia alleged breaches of the Convention against Yugoslavia. In its Order of 8 April 1993 on a Request for indication of Provisional Measures, the Court held that Art IX of the Convention provided a basis for jurisdiction.[93] The Court broadly affirmed the approach of the court in the *Reservations to the Genocide Convention* case in stressing the particularly offensive nature of genocide as an international crime.[94] The Court ordered the parties

---

88 In *R v Bow Street Metropolitan Stipendiary Magistrate ex p Pinochet Ugarte (No 1)* [1998] 3 WLR 1456, it was noted by the House of Lords that Art 4 of the Genocide Convention had not been given the force of law in England in the Genocide Act 1969.

89 Reservations to the Convention on the Prevention and Punishment of the Crime of Genocide (1951) ICJ 15, p 22.

90 See Security Council Resolutions 1991/713; 1993/808; 1993/827.

91 L Sunga, 'The Commission of Experts on Rwanda and the Creation of the International Tribunal for Rwanda' (1995) 16 HRLJ 121.

92 Adopted in Rome on 17 July 1998. Under the terms of Art 126, the statute will enter into force one month after the 60th day following the deposit of the sixtieth instrument of ratification.

93 (1993) ICJ 3; 95 ILR 1.

94 Reservations to the Genocide Convention (1951) ICJ 15; 18 ILR 364.

not to extend the scope of the dispute pending a full hearing and this was repeated in the Order of Provisional Measures of 13 September 1993.[95] On 11 July 1996, the International Court of Justice rejected Preliminary Objections raised by Yugoslavia and stressed that a state could be held directly liable for genocide even though the events were directed by particular individuals.[96]

Although international instruments today use the expression 'genocide', such acts were treated within the category of 'crimes against humanity'[97] for the purpose of Art 6(c) of the Charter of the International Military Tribunal of 8 August 1945.

9 DISCRIMINATION ON GROUNDS OF RACE

The principle of equality before the law precludes discrimination on grounds race sex or religion. This principle of non-discrimination was noted by the Permanent Court of International Justice in the *Minority Schools in Albania* case.[98] Although France and the United Kingdom with colonial empires had expressed some concern, the final text of the United Nations Charter is premised on the principle of non-discrimination. In particular, the preamble refers to 'the equal rights of men and women' and this is amplified by the provisions of Arts 55 and 56; the principle of non-discrimination is expressly stated in Arts 2 and 7 of the Universal Declaration of Human Rights (1948).

The first moves on the international plane to assert the principle were associated with the condemnation of apartheid in South Africa which had been implemented in that country after 1948. From the early 1950s, concerns were expressed within the General Assembly[99] and later in the Security Council as the threat to regional harmony became apparent.[100]

The first concrete statement on the international plane was the United Nations Declaration on the Elimination of All Forms of Racial Discrimination (1963) which was adopted by the General Assembly. Article 1 of the Declaration read:

> Discrimination between human beings on grounds of race, colour or ethnic origin is an offence to human dignity and shall be condemned as a denial of the principles of the Charter of the United Nations, as a violation of the human rights and fundamental freedoms proclaimed in the Universal Declaration of Human RIghts as an obstacle to

---

95 (1993) ICJ 325; 95 ILR 125. Of particular interest is the opinion of Judge Lauterpacht (*ad hoc*) who considers in some detail the question as to whether the ICJ can review resolutions of the security council on grounds either of *ultra vires* or because they might unintentionally violate a rule of *jus cogens*.

96 (1996) ICJ 565. The objections of Yugoslavia in broad terms were: (i) that, at the relevant time, Bosnia was not a party to the Convention; (ii) that, at the relevant time, the Genocide Convention was not in force between parties; (iii) that the claim was outside Art IX in that the conflict was a civil war and that, at the relevant time, Yugoslavia did not exercise control over the relevant territory. All these objections were rejected. For an earlier dispute before the ICJ, see *Trial of Pakistani Prisoners of War* (1973) ICJ 328.

97 See generally, *Public Prosecutor v Menten* (1981) 75 ILR 331; *Fédération Nationale des Déportes et Internes Resistants et Patriotes v Barbie* (1985) 78 ILR 125.

98 (1935) PCIJ, Ser A/B, No 64; 8 ILR 386.

99 GA Res 616/1952; 1761/1962; 3151/1973.

100 Security Council Resolution 282/1973.

friendly and peaceful relations among nations and as a fact capable of disturbing peace and security among peoples.

The remainder of the Declaration called on states to take steps to prevent racial discrimination in the main areas of civil liberties, and various articles in the Declaration stressed the link between the principle of non-discrimination and the terms of both the United Nations Charter and the Universal Declaration of Human Rights. The emphasis on the principle of non-discrimination was echoed by action at the municipal level.[101]

Within two years, the United Nations had adopted the International Convention on the Elimination of All Forms of Racial Discrimination which was opened for signature on 7 March 1966.[102] The Convention defines 'racial discrimination' as meaning 'any distinction, exclusion, restriction or preference based on race, colour, descent or national or ethnic origin which has the effect of nullifying or impairing the recognition, enjoyment or exercise, on an equal footing, of human rights and other fundamental freedoms in the political, economic, social, cultural or any other field of public life' (Art 1). The parties to the Convention condemn racial discrimination and undertake certain obligations to counter such practices (Art 2). Further, they agree to prohibit racial discrimination and not only to allow equality before the law (Art 5) but to take measures particularly in the educational to combat the prejudices which lead to racial discrimination (Art 7).

To ensure observance of the Convention, Art 8 provides for the establishment of a Committee on the Elimination of Racial Discrimination which comprises 18 persons serving in a personal capacity who hold office for four years, state parties are to submit reports and the Committee is to report annually on its activities. If a state party considers that another state party is not implementing the Convention, then it may bring the matter to the attention of the Committee;[103] if the matter is not settled by agreement then the Committee may appoint a Conciliation Commission[104] and it may report back to the Committee with recommendations for resolving the dispute.[105] In addition to the provisions for state reports and inter-state complaints, Art 14 introduces a procedure whereby a state may consent to the Committee considering individual applications. Under the terms of Art 14.9 the procedure was implemented from 1 January 1983, when the tenth state declaration was received. The Committee meets twice a year and, although there have been some difficulties on funding, the system of state reports has found widespread acceptance. The Committee on the Elimination of Racial Discrimination is

---

101 In the United States, President Johnson signed the Civil Rights Act 1964; the case law had been moving in favour of the principle of non-discrimination from *Brown v Board of Education* (1954) 347 US 483, which had overruled *Plessy v Ferguson* (1896) 163 US 537, the prior leading case on the 13th and 14 amendments. For discussion of the background, see C Lofgren, *The Plessy Case*, 1987, Oxford: OUP; JR Pole, *The Pursuit of Equality in American Life*, 1978. In the United Kingdom, the principle of freedom of contract could lead to discrimination (see *Constantine v Imperial Hotels* [1944] KB 693). However, Parliament legislated in the form of the Race Relations Act 1965; Race Relations Act 1968 and the Race Relations Act 1976.

102 Res 2106(XX). The Convention entered into force on 4 January 1969 following the deposit of 27 instruments of accession. See E Schwelb (1966) 15 ICLQ 1048. By 1998 there were 148 state parties.

103 International Convention on the Elimination of All Forms of Racial Discrimination (1966), Art 11.

104 *Ibid*, Art 12.

105 *Ibid*, Art 13.

generally adjudged to have been a success; it demands specific information in state reports and pursues those states who have failed to submit reports on time. state representatives are invited to attend meetings of the Committee and an attempt has been made to establish a dialogue.

In addition, to the Convention itself note should also be taken of the Declaration on the Elimination of All Forms of Intolerance and Discrimination based on Religion or Belief adopted by consensus by the United Nations General Assembly on 25 November 1981.[106] A matter that deserves consideration is whether there is a rule of customary international law favouring the principle of non-discrimination; having regard to the number of judicial utterances[107] and the widespread acceptance of the Convention it would be reasonable to conclude that the principle is supported in customary international law

10 DISCRIMINATION AGAINST WOMEN[108]

One of the most significant social changes in many western societies since 1945 has been in the status and role of women. In 1945, ECOSOC established a Commission on the Status of Women. The principle of non-discrimination between the sexes has been stressed from the earliest years of the United Nations. Support for the principle is to be found in Art 2 of the Universal Declaration on Human Rights and Art 3 of both the ICCPR and ICESCR. In the years after 1950, economic affluence in many western societies and progressive legislation has enabled women to enjoy improvements in health education and general welfare; large numbers of women are employed in a full time capacity and in many western countries an increasing number of women participate in national legislatures.[109] In these circumstances, writers began to draw attention to the disproportionate effect on women of poverty, illiteracy and malnutrition; the same writers[110] pointed to the discriminatory and insecure conditions of employment that many women were subject to in developing countries. Many of these writers might be

---

106 GA Res 36/55; see D Sullivan (1988) 82 AJIL 487.

107 See in particular, the dissenting opinion of Judge Tanaka in the South West Africa case (1966) ICJ 3; (1966) 37 ILR 243; Legal Consequences for States of the Continued Presence of South Africa in Namibia (1971) ICJ 16.

108 See generally, R Cook (ed), *Human Rights of Women; National and International Perspectives*, 1994; A Byrnes (1989) 14 YJIL 1; C Bunch (1990) 12 HRQ 486; R Cook (1993) 15 HRQ 230; M Galey (1984) 6 HRQ 463; M McDougall, H Laswell and I Chen (1975) 69 AJIL 497.

109 It is worth remembering how recent these changes were. Prior to the 19th century property legislation (Married Women's Property Act 1870; Married Women's Property Act 1882), the property rights of a woman in England were subject to restriction; it was only in 1918 that women acquired the right to vote and not until 1928 did they acquire the vote on the same basis as men.

110 H Charlesworth, C Chinkin and S Wright (1991) 85 AJIL 613.

grouped within the general school of 'feminist legal theory'[111] and, while individual approaches differ, they tend to concentrate on evidence of the suppression and subordination of women and they analyse law and international conventions by reference to the actual or potential contribution to alleviating or removing such oppression.

In the early years after the founding of the United Nations, the General Assembly adopted a number of conventions most of which had been promoted by the United Nations Commission on the Status of Women. Among these were the Convention for the Suppression of the Traffic in Persons and of the Exploitation of the Prostitution of Others,[112] the Convention on the Political Rights of Women,[113] the Convention on the Nationality of Married Women[114] and the Convention on the Consent to Marriage, Minimum Age for Marriage and Registration of Marriages.[115]

However, in a comprehensive manner international action has taken the form of the adoption in December 1979 of the Convention on the Elimination of All Forms of Discrimination against Women.[116] The expression 'discrimination against women' was defined in Art 1 as meaning 'any distinction, exclusion or restriction made on the basis of sex which has the effect or purpose of impairing or nullifying the recognition, enjoyment or exercise by women, irrespective of their marital status, on a basis of equality of men and women, of human rights and fundamental freedoms in the political, economic, social, cultural, civil or any other field'. By Art 2 state parties condemn discrimination against women and agree to take all appropriate steps to promote equality (Art 3). The Convention commits state parties to ensuring that women can play a full part in the political life of the state[117] and to ensure that equality is achieved in areas of education,[118] employment,[119] healthcare[120] and legal status.[121] It has been noted that, in some societies, the status and role of women may be influenced by cultural or religious considerations. This raises a delicate problem as to whether establishing fundamental rights for women may impinge on cultural and religious freedoms which are themselves a legitimate concern of human rights law.[122]

The Convention provides in Art 17 for the establishment of a Committee on the Elimination of Discrimination against Women. The Committee is made up of 23

---

111 See generally, N Lacey (1987) 14 JLS 411; R West (1988) 55 U Chi Law Rev 1; N Duclos (1990) 38 Buff Law Rev; K Bartlett (1990) 103 Harv L Rev 829.
112 1950.
113 1953.
114 1957.
115 1962.
116 See N Burrows (1985) 32 Netherlands Int L Rev 419.
117 Convention on the Elimination of All Forms of Discrimination against Women (1979), Arts 7 and 8.
118 *Ibid*, Art 10.
119 *Ibid*, Art 11.
120 *Ibid*, Art 12.
121 *Ibid*, Art 15.
122 Donna Sullivan (1992) 24 NYU J Int Law & Politics 795.

independent experts who sit in their personal capacity and not as representatives of state parties. The duties of the Committee are set out in Arts 18–21 and the scheme has some similarity with that of the Committee on the Elimination of Racial Discrimination. Under Art 18, state reports are to be submitted in the first instance after a year and thereafter at four yearly intervals. By Art 20, the Committee is to meet for two weeks annually but it is open to question whether this is sufficient time. It is provided that the Committee may make suggestions on the basis of state documentation and it reports annually through ECOSOC to the General Assembly. The Committee issues General Recommendations as to be matters included in reports. One of the most detailed being General Recommendation No 14, designed to eradicate the different forms of female circumcision.

A matter that should not pass without comment is that of reservations to the Convention.[123] Although 150 states have become parties to the Convention, over 80 reservations have been lodged.[124] This indicates that states with different cultural traditions do not easily agree as to what conduct constitutes discrimination against women. Although there have been a number of requests by the Committee on the Elimination of Discrimination Against Women few states have withdrawn or modified their reservations.[125]

In the context of discrimination against women it should be borne in mind that a number of cases have come before the Human Rights Committee under the Optional Protocol which raise the same issues. Among these are *Lovelace v Canada*, *Aumeeruddy-Cziffra v Mauritius* and *Ato del Avetellanal v Peru* thus indicating that there is some overlap with the International Covenant on Civil and Political Rights.

There is some evidence that the subject of discrimination against women has acquired a greater prominence in the last two decades. In the last quarter of a century there have been four United Nations world conferences on women. The first held in International Women's Year in Mexico City in 1975 resulted in a Plan of Action and led to the 1979 Convention. A second conference in Copenhagen, Denmark in 1980 highlighted concerns in respect of education, employment and health. The third conference in Nairobi, Kenya in 1985 resulted in the issue of *A Strategy for the Advancement of Women to the year 2000*. From the mid-1980s, the emphasis came to be placed on both countering threats to violence against women and responding to the health threat posed by HIV/AIDS. In March 1995, the Secretary General announced a Strategic Plan of Action designed to improve the level of representation of women at the United Nations. In September 1995, 180 governments were represented at the fourth United Nations Conference held in Beijing, China which resulted in the Beijing Declaration which reviewed progress and set out goals to be achieved in the areas of poverty, education and health.

---

123 See R Cook (1990) 30 Va JIL 643; for a more general consideration, see C Joyner, *The United Nations and International Law*, 1997, p 181.
124 This contrasts with the International Convention on the Elimination of All Forms of Racial Discrimination where of 146 parties only two have lodged substantive reservations.
125 CEDAW General Recommendation 4 (on Reservations), Report of the Committee on the Elimination of Discrimination against Women (Sixth Session) A/42/38 (1987).

11 THE OUTLAWING OF TORTURE

Although torture was employed in common law countries in the 17th century, it gradually came to be accepted that state authorities should collect evidence themselves and that, in the detention and interviewing of suspects, certain minimum basic standards should be observed; as the rationalist tradition in the law of evidence emerged so torture died out.[126] However, the practice continued to be employed in political dictatorships to silence opponents and was resorted to by a number of regimes in the 1930s.[127] Thus, Art 5 of the Universal Declaration of Human Rights (1948) reads: 'No one shall be subject to torture or to cruel or degrading treatment or punishment.' This basic prohibition is re-stated in Art 7 of the International Covenant on Civil and Political Rights (1966).[128] In many states, the absorption of the principles of the Universal Declaration of Human Rights (1948) into the written constitution has served to act as a firm deterrent to such conduct. However, since 1945 there has been considerable evidence that in some states the practice of torture has been used normally with the object of controlling political opponents. There is considerable evidence assembled by NGOs that the practice of torture is still widely used to crush domestic political opposition.[129] To restrict this development a number of international and regional treaties have been adopted. The most important international document[130] was the Declaration on the Protection of All Persons from Being Subjected to Torture and Other Cruel, Inhuman or Degrading Treatment or punishment which was adopted by the General Assembly in 1975.[131]

The Convention against Torture and Other Cruel and Inhuman or Degrading Treatment or Punishment was adopted on 10 December 1984 and entered into force in 1987 after receipt of the 20th document of ratification.[132] The expression 'torture' is defined in Article 1 as meaning:

---

126 For the development of the law of evidence as the only foundation upon which to establish facts in the judicial context, see W Twining, *Theories of Evidence, Bentham and Wigmore*, 1985.

127 Historical research indicates that torture was employed in Germany in the period 1933–45 and also in the Soviet Union under Josef Stalin (1924–53).

128 The prohibition is also contained in Art 3 of the European Convention on Human Rights; Art 5 of the American Convention on Human Rights (1969), and Art 5 of the African Charter of Human and People's Rights (1981).

129 See *Torture in the Eighties*, 1984, Amnesty International. See, for example, the questioning of the Iraqi representative on the question of torture by the Human Rights Committee at the time of the Third Periodic Report under Art 40 of the ICCPR (UN Doc A/46/40 (1991) Supp No 40, p 150; UN Doc A/47/40 (1994) Supp No 40, p 41).

130 But one should also note the Inter American Convention on Torture (1985) 24 ILM 519; the European Convention for the Prevention of Torture and Inhuman or Degrading Treatment (1987) 27 ILM 1152. See A Cassesse (1989) 83 AJIL 128. Note also UN Standard Minimum rules for the Treatment of Prisoners (1957) as amended in 1977 (see ECOSOC Res 2076 (LXII)) and detailed in N Rodley, *The Treatment of Prisoners in International Law*, 1987.

131 While it is arguable that the provisions in the UDHR (1948) were a reaction to state conduct in Germany and the Soviet Union in the 1930s, the renewed interest by the international community in the 1970s was linked to reports by NGOs concerning torture and political repression in states such as Chile (after 1973), Argentina (after 1976) and Uruguay. Attention was also directed to conduct in South Africa, particularly after the death in custody of the political activist Steve Biko (1946–77) in September 1977.

132 By January 1999, 110 states had ratified or acceded to the Convention. See *R v Bow Street Stipendiary Magistrate ex p Pinochet Ugarte (No 3)* [2000] 1 AC 147; [1999] 2 WLR 147.

... any act by which severe pain or suffering, whether physical or mental, is intentionally inflicted on a person for such purposes as obtaining from him or a third person information or a confession, punishing him for an act he or a third person has committed or is suspected of having committed, or intimidating or coercing him or a third person, or for any reason based on discrimination of any kind, when such pain or suffering is inflicted by or at the instigation of or with the consent or acquiesence of a public official or other person acting in an official capacity. It does not include pain or suffering arising only from, inherent in or incidental to lawful sanctions.

Under Part I of the Convention state parties are obliged to ensure that torture does not take place on their territory (Art 2) and they are required to refuse to expel or extradite a person to a country where there is a risk that he may be tortured (Art 3). Further state parties are required to make torture a criminal offence[133] and to take steps to exercise jurisdiction.[134] In broad terms, a state is obliged to prosecute or extradite those alleged to have committed who are found within its territory.[135] By the terms of Art 10, positive duties are placed on states to ensure that state officials are educated and trained to be aware of the unlawfulness of torture.[136]

It is provided in Art 17 that a Committee Against Torture was to be established. The Committee comprises 10 independent experts of high moral standing. Interestingly Art 17(2) requires state parties to have regard to the claims of those who have served on the Human Rights Committee operating under the International Covenant on Civil and Political Rights; this is justified in the interests of consistency. The Committee receives state reports[137] and in the event of a state making a declaration then it may hear inter-state complaints.[138] Further if a state party makes a declaration under Art 22 then the Committee acquires a competence to hear individual claims. Under the terms of Art 20 if the Committee receives reliable evidence of torture being practised in the territory of a state party it may invite that state party to co-operate in examining the evidence[139] or it may choose to send one of its members to make a confidential enquiry.[140] The state party will be expected to co-operate in allowing such a visit[141] and will receive the findings of the rapporteur together with any recommendations of the Committee. Until this stage, the proceedings remain confidential but in the last analysis the Committee[142] has the right to include the matter in its annual report. It must be doubtful whether this is a severe sanction particularly as state parties have the right to enter a reservation against the entire procedure under Art 28.

---

133 Convention against Torture and Other Cruel and Inhuman or Degrading Treatment or Punishment (1984), Art 4.

134 *Ibid*, Art 5.

135 The Convention was implemented in the United Kingdom in the Criminal Justice Act 1988, ss 134–38. Under the terms of s 134, torture committed anywhere in the world may be prosecuted in the United Kingdom but only under s 135 with the consent of the Attorney General. The provisions themselves came into effect on 29 September 1988.

136 See Torture Convention (1984), Arts 10 and 11.

137 *Ibid*, Art 19.

138 *Ibid*, Art 21.

139 *Ibid*, Art 20(1).

140 *Ibid*, Art 20(2).

141 *Ibid*, Art 20(3).

142 For consideration of the working of the Committee, see E Zoller (1989) 7 NQHR 250; A Dormenval, 'United Nations Committee Against Torture: practice and perspectives' (1990) 8 NQHR 26.

The emphasis on state reports and constructive dialogue draws upon the experience of both the United Nations Human Rights Committee and the evolving practice under the Convention for the Elimination of All Forms of Discrimination Against Women. A state that indulges in torture is likely to be in breach of both the IICCPR 1966 and the 1984 Torture Convention.; some of the most serious offenders have not ratified the Convention or choose not to co-operate with the Committee.

In 1985 the United Nations Commission on Human Rights appointed a Special Rapporteur on Torture who is charged with collecting information on torture and he is charged with increasing individual country visits and co-operating with the Committee on Torture. That torture remains widespread is attested to by reports of the Human Rights Committee and evidence from NGOs and is corroborated by the establishment of a Voluntary Fund for the Victims of Torture established by the General Assembly. Although the practice is far from eliminated the Convention provides a mechanism for bringing those responsible to justice; as will be seen below it is well established in municipal case law that torture is also contrary to customary international law.[143]

12 THE PROTECTION OF CHILDREN[144]

It is a matter of common experience that political instability, war and famine tend to have a disproportionate effect on children and the vulnerable. Just as municipal legal systems make special provision to protect children international law has has been active since 1945 in finding methods of extending protection to children. This process may be said to have originated with the establishment of UNICEF in 1946.[145] In 1948, the Universal Declaration recognised in Art 25[146] that children are entitled to care, assistance and protection as well as impliedly acknowledging the rights and dignity of children.[147]

The broad principles were set out in the United Nations Declaration of the Rights of the Child (1959) which drawing upon the Universal Declaration noted that that 'the child by reason of his physical and mental immaturity, needs special safeguards and care

---

143 *Attorney General of Israel v Eichmann* (1962) 36 ILR 18,p 277; *Re The Extradition of Demajanjuk* (1985) 776 F 2d 571; *R v Bow Street Metropolitan Stipendiary Magistrate ex p Pinochet Ugarte (No 3)* [2000] 1 AC 147; [1999] 2 WLR 827.

144 See generally, G Van Bueren, *The International Law on the Right of the Child*, 1995; D McGoldrick (1991) 5 International Journal of Law and the Family 132; T Hammarberg, 'The UN Convention on the Right of the Child and how to make it work' (1990) 12 HRQ 26.

145 The United Nations International Children's Emergency Fund (UNICEF) was established under GA Res 57(1) (1946). See also Res 417(V) (1950) and Res 802 (1953).

146 In demanding equal treatment for children whether or not born within wedlock, Art 25 was ahead of its time. In the United Kingdom, an illegitimate child was regarded as *filius nullius* and subject to considerable legal disability until well after 1945. Legislative change was effected by the Family Law Reform Act 1969, the Inheritance (Provision for Family and Dependents) Act 1975 and the Fatal Accidents Act 1976, but the disadvantages were not fully removed until the Family Law Reform Act 1987.

147 UDHR (1948), Art 1.

including appropriate legal protection, before as well as after birth'.[148] The Declaration sets out a number of principles designed to ensure a healthy and happy childhood. Particularly noteworthy is the obligation upon state authorities offer parental care in appropriate cases[149] and to make available education[150] and health care.[151] These concerns were taken further in 1966 when Arts 23[152] and 24 of the International Covenant on Civil and Political Rights made express reference to the rights of children. In similar terms, Art 10 of the International Covenant on Economic, Social and Cultural Rights provides for protection and assistance of children without regard to conditions of parentage.

These early measures resulted in the adoption by the General Assembly on 20 November 1989 of the Convention on the Rights of the Child[153] which under Art 49 came into effect on 2 September 1990 following the receipt of the 20th instrument of ratification. For the purpose of the Convention, a 'child' is a human being under the age of 18 unless under the law applicable to the child majority is acquired prior to that age.[154] As a guiding principle, the Convention requires that in decisions affecting a child the best interests of the child should be the primary consideration.[155] The Convention applies in both peace and war and concerns both civil rights and economic and social rights; the instrument embraces 41 substantive obligations.[156]

The Convention stipulates for a number of basic rights such as the right to life,[157] to a name,[158] and to a nationality.[159] It is further provided that the child shall not be unlawfully removed abroad[160] and shall enjoy the right of freedom of expression,[161] thought and conscience.[162] State parties agree to protect the child from forms of mental or

---

148 The document also drew upon the 1924 Geneva Declaration on the Rights of the Child. This document set out seven basic principles but was not intended to create legal obligations. The principles were drawn from the work of Eglantyne Jebb, the founder of the Save the Children Union.

149 Declaration of the Rights of the Child (1959), Principle 6.

150 *Ibid*, Principles 5 and 7.

151 *Ibid*, Principles 2 and 4.

152 Article 23 refers to the right to marry freely and found a family. This was of some concern in the 1960s and 1970s. In the Soviet Union and some other Eastern European countries barriers were placed on those citizens who sought to marry foreigners. In South Africa, mixed race marriages might be subject to non-recognition, criminal prosecution and other legal disability.

153 GA Res 44/25; (1989) 28 ILM 1448.

154 Convention on the Rights of the Child (1989), Art 1.

155 *Ibid*, Art 3.

156 By 1997 the Convention had been accepted by 187 state parties.

157 Convention on the Rights of the Child (1989), Art 6.

158 *Ibid*, Art 7.

159 *Ibid*, Art 8.

160 *Ibid*, Art 11. Or more correctly that states shall co-operate to combat illicit transfers. There is, of course, a detailed legal framework in place under the terms of the Hague Convention on the Civil Aspects of International Child Abduction (1980). A possible problem has arisen as to the relationship between Art 12 of the 1989 Convention and Art 13(2) of the Hague Convention which has been considered in municipal courts; see *Re S (A Minor) (Abduction: Custody Rights)* [1993] Fam 242; *Re M (A Minor) (Child Abduction)* (1994) 1 FLR 390.

161 Convention on the Rights of the Child (1989), Art 13.

162 *Ibid*, Art 14.

physical violence[163] and from economic[164] or sexual exploitation,[165] as well as the illicit use of drugs.[166] Article 37 requires state parties to refrain from torture and other cruel and inhuman punishment; state parties agree further to refrain from the employment of children under the age of 15 in armed conflict.[167]

The structures for implementing the Convention are contained in Part II of the instrument. Under the terms of Art 43 a Committee on the Rights of the Child has been constituted; originally elected in 1991, it comprised 10 independent experts and under Art 44 had competence to receive state reports. An initial report was to be submitted after two years and thereafter every five years. The Committee is to report to the General Assembly every two years through the agency of ECOSOC. In respect of state reports the emphasis as elsewhere is on constructive dialogue and state representatives are encouraged to attend. The Committee may issue observations in respect of individual state reports and it has shown itself willing to discuss specific topics.[168]

The near universal acceptance of the Convention has given it within a short period of time a special status and municipal courts[169] are beginning to take it into account.

13 ACTION IN RESPECT OF MIGRANT WORKERS[170]

One of the most vulnerable groups in modern international society is that of the migrant worker. Such a person will be a national of state A who travels to state B to engage in paid employment. This will include specialist personnel, offshore workers but not refugees or stateless persons. To ensure protection of this vulnerable category, the General Assembly adopted in December 1990 the International Convention on the Protection of the Rights of All Migrant Workers and Members of their Families.[171] Although the ILO had been active

---

163 *Ibid*, Art 19.

164 *Ibid*, Art 32.

165 *Ibid*, Art 34.

166 *Ibid*, Art 33.

167 This arose from the publicity given to young children engaged in military conflicts in Africa and also to reports arising from the Iran-Iraq war (1980–88).

168 At the second session in 1992, it discussed the question of the use of children in armed conflicts; see generally, G Van Bueren (1994) 43 ICLQ 809.

169 By 1 April 1999, the Convention had acquired 191 state parties; for an example of it being relied upon in a municipal court, see *Minister of State for Immigration v Teoh* [1995] 128 ALR 353 (case in which the Australian High Court was prepared to accept that an unincorporated treaty might give rise to a legitimate expectation that the executive branch would act in accordance with the treaty). See R Piotrowicz [1996] PL 190.

170 See generally, S Hune and J Niessen (1991) 9 NQHR 133; for a detailed discussion of the Convention, see articles in (1991) 25 International Migration Review (special issue on the Migrant Labour Convention); S Hune and J Niessen (1994) 12 NQHR 393.

171 GA Res 45/158 (18 December 1990).

in the area of migrant workers,[172] concern grew in the 1970s because of the numbers of workers entering Western Europe and the United States; some of these entered unlawfully and many were left without basic rights.[173] At first, it was proposed that the ILO might take action but it was considered that a broader consensus might be achieved if action was taken through the General Assembly. The drafting of the Convention took place over an eleven year period from 1990.[174]

Under the terms of Art 2, the Convention defines a 'migrant worker' as a person who is to be engaged, is engaged or has been engaged in a remunerated activity in a state of which he or she is not a national. The article further provides that the term will include the frontier worker, the seasonal worker or the worker on an offshore installation. However, by the terms of Art 3 the category will not include students, refugees or staff working with international organisations. It has to be admitted that some of the provisions reproduce matters included in previous human rights treaties.[175] In addition to basic civil liberties, the Convention provides that migrant workers are entitled to equality of treatment before courts and tribunals[176] and shall not be subject to collective expulsion;[177] further they are entitled to participate in trade unions[178] and have access to social security[179] and medical treatment.[180] The Convention provides that cultural identity is to be respected[181] and the child of the migrant worker should have the right of access to education.[182]

Under the terms of Part VII (Arts 72–78) provision is made for the establishment of a Committee of 14 independent experts. The Committee will be charged with receiving state reports[183] and in the event of appropriate declarations being made inter-state complaints may be determined.[184] Further in cases of a declaration by state parties individual complaints may be entertained under Art 77.

---

172 The efforts of the ILO had not always been fruitful. The first convention (No 66) was adopted in 1939 and did not receive a single ratification; the second (No 97) adopted in 1949 had only acquired 40 ratifications by 1995; the third (No 143) adopted in 1975 had only acquired 17 ratifications by 1995. For detailed consideration, see Virginia Leary in *The United Nations and International Law*, 1997 (Christopher Joyner (ed)), p 208.

173 It is interesting that migrant workers have also given rise to problems in private international law in respect of the tort committed abroad, where problems can arise as to jurisdiction and choice of law: see *Sayers v International Drilling Co NV* [1971] 1 WLR 1176; *Castanho v Brown and Root (UK) Ltd* [1981] AC 557; *Coupland v Arabian Gulf Oil* [1983] 1 WLR 1136; *Johnson v Coventry Churchill International Ltd* [1992] 3 All ER 14. Such case law in the United Kingdom has now to be read in the light of the Private International Law (Miscellaneous Provisions) Act 1995.

174 Under the terms of Art 87, 20 ratifications are necessary to bring the Convention into force; by 1995, three ratifications had been achieved and by January 1997 that figure had risen to 7.

175 Convention on Migrant Workers (1990), Art 9 (the right to life); Art 10 (no migrant worker to be subjected to torture, or to cruel, inhuman or degrading treatment).

176 *Ibid*, Art 18.

177 *Ibid*, Art 22.

178 *Ibid*, Art 26.

179 *Ibid*, Art 27.

180 *Ibid*, Art 28.

181 *Ibid*, Art 31

182 *Ibid*, Art 30.

183 *Ibid*, Art 73.

184 *Ibid*, Art 76.

14 DOES THE PRINCIPLE OF SELF-DETERMINATION CONSTITUTE A HUMAN RIGHT?

As has been noted elsewhere the principle of self-determination was introduced[185] into international society by Woodrow Wilson at Versailles in 1919.[186] In the most general terms, it refers to the right of persons living in a particular territory to determine the political and legal status of that territory. As has often been noted the principle is fraught with dangers[187] and is potentially at conflict with the other principle of international law, namely respect for the territorial integrity of states. If such a principle constitutes a human right then it is a human right exercised collectively.

It is quite clear that the principle was accepted after 1945 in the colonial context, that is, that the persons of a territory under the control of a colonial power had the right to move towards self-government. It is referred to in that sense in Art 1(2) and Art 55 of the United Nations Charter (1945) and it is not surprising that it was included in both the 1966 Covenants which were drawn up during the time of decolonisation and included an identical Art 1 which read:

> All peoples have the right of self determination. By virtue of that right they freely determine their political status and freely pursue their economic social and cultural development.

The limitations to the principle can be noted in the 1970 Declaration on Principles of International Law where after stating the principle the Declaration notes that:

> Nothing ... shall be construed as authorising or encouraging any action which would dismember or impair, totally or in part, the territorial integrity or political unity of sovereign and independent States conducting themselves in compliance with the principle of equal rights and self-determination of peoples and thus possessed of a government representing the whole people belonging to the territory without distinction as to race, creed or colour.

The clear import of the statement was that the principle would have to be balanced by other considerations where colonial rule was not in issue. In practical terms the principle raises at least two questions, namely: (a) who are the people?; and (b) what is the relevant territorial unit in which they should exercise self-determination? The difficulties with the principle were succinctly expressed by Sir Ivor Jennings, when he noted:

> On the surface, it (the principle of self-determination) seemed reasonable; let the people decide. It was in fact ridiculous because the people cannot decide until somebody decides who the people are.

---

185 See generally, A Cobban, *Nation State and National Self Determination*, 1969, London: Penguin; M Pomerance (1976) 70 AJIL 1; P Thornberry (1989) 38 ICLQ 867; A Whelan (1994) 43 ICLQ 99; M Koskenniemi (1994) 43 ICLQ 241; R McCorquodale (1994) 43 ICLQ 857; H Quane (1998) 47 ICLQ 537.

186 The idea itself can be traced back to both the American Declaration of Independence (1776) and the French Revolution of 1789; it was endorsed by Giuseppe Mazzini in the push for Italian unification in the mid-19th century. The doctrine was advanced by VI Lenin in both *On Imperialism*, 1916, and in his *Theses on the Socialist Revolution and the Right of Nations to Self Determination*, 1916. For an outline of the historical background, see A Cassesse, *Self Determination of Peoples: A Legal Reappraisal*, 1995.

187 This was realised even at Versailles and was subject to criticism by JM Keynes in *The Economic Consequences of the Peace*, 1919, London.

This difficulty was avoided in the years after 1919 because, at the Paris Peace conference of 1919, ethnic groups that had developed national aspirations were simply extracted from the wreck of the German, Russian, Austro Hungarian and Ottomann Empires and new states were created on simply ethnic lines.[188] After 1945, the principle was extended to permit independence from colonial rule for multi ethnic communities. However, while the principle was used as a justification for decolonisation only limited thought was given to who was to exercise the right because decolonisation was executed on the basis of the principle of *uti possidetis* and this principle was confirmed in General Assembly resolutions[189] and subsequent rulings of the International Court of Justice.[190] Secondly, if one examines actual conduct between 1947 and 1991, secession was actively discouraged[191] by the Security Council; established borders were regarded as permanent and not to be changed save by agreement.

Since 1991, the problem of self-determination has become more acute as multinational states have disintegrated[192] in accordance with ethnic patterns; however, the general view of international law was set out by the Arbitration Commission on Yugoslavia in Opinion No 2, where they asserted that the principle of *uti possidetis* would normally prevail over any principle of self-determination. They observed that 'it is well established that, whatever the circumstances, the right to self-determination must not involve changes to existing frontiers at the time of independence (*uti possidetis juris*) except where the states concerned agree otherwise'.

An assessment of the historical record induces a degree of scepticism about any general principle of self-determination and a clear willingness by international organisations to examine problems on a case by case basis. Secondly, even if a principle of self-determination can be asserted, it is evident that in many situations it will have to yield to the principle of *uti possidetis*.

As an aspect of human rights law a certain degree of caution is justified, when considering the principle of self-determination. Many states drawing up the 1966 Covenants understood the common Art 1 to mean no more than that despotic non-constitutional government should be avoided. It was argued by some western nations that self-determination was a political principle and not a justiciable right.[193] Secondly, it

---

188 For consideration of the concept of an ethnic group in the context of Race Relations legislation, see *Mandla v Dowell Lee* [1983] 2 AC 548.

189 See GA Res 1514(XV) Declaration on the Granting of Independence to Colonial Countries and Peoples (1960), where the text attempts to balance the two principles. See, also, GA Res 1541 (XV) (1960); in the regional context see Organisation of African Unity Resolution 16 (I), 1964.

190 In the *Burkina Faso v Mali* case (1986) ICJ 554, the Court stressed the importance of the principle of *uti possidetis* and emphasised that the critical date would normally be the date of independence but might be different depending on the conduct of the parties. The court, 20 years after decolonisation, was anxious to avoid increasing boundary disputes in post-colonial Africa; see Naldi (1987) 36 ICLQ 893.

191 The one actual instance being Bangladesh in 1971; for a review of the political considerations arising in respect of secession, see Margaret Moore (ed), *National Self-Determination and Secession*, 1998.

192 Ie, Soviet Union, Yugoslavia, Czechoslovakia, Ethiopia. For examples of secessionist problems in the modern world, see Quebec, Flanders, Sudan, Sri Lanka, Kashmir, Punjab, Iraq (Kurdish regions), Turkey (Kurdish regions).

193 See, for example, the United Kingdom in its statement of 2 July 1955 UN Doc a/2910/Add 1 Xth Session Annexes 5. Other states raised other objection such as: (i) as a collective right it should not be included in the Covenants; (ii) that Art 1(2) of the Charter rendered it redundant; (iii) that it might serve to stimulate secession.

is strongly arguable that the presence of Art 27 in the International Covenant on Civil and Political Rights indicates that Art 1 should be given a narrow and limited meaning because of the clear recognition that many states will contain ethnic minorities. In this context, it is sensible to examine the approach of the Human Rights Committee. The rulings of the Committee have tended to place limits on the meaning of Art 1 and the principle of self-determination. First, the Committee has pointed out the general duty of states to observe the United Nations Charter and respect the territorial integrity of other states.[194] Secondly, the efforts of the Committee seem to be directed to securing political pluralism within a state under the rule of law rather than asserting any right of self-determination.[195] Thirdly, the Committee has consistently taken the view that, under the Optional Protocol, only the individual has *locus standi qua* individual to bring a complaint and that he cannot do so as an agent for a group or in some form of *actio popularis*. Since the complaint must be in respect of an individual right,[196] the Committee has ruled that this cannot apply in respect of collective rights.

It is quite clear, therefore, that one must draw a distinction between the anti-colonial self-determination which is well established and is sometimes referred to as external self-determination and the modern concept employed in the post-colonial world of internal self-determination based on a democratic pluralist constitutional structure.

15 THE RIGHTS OF MINORITIES[197]

When the boundaries of Europe were redrawn in 1878[198] and 1919,[199] new independent sovereign states were created. To ensure that conflict did not resume the major powers tried to extract guarantees that minorities within the new states would receive minimum standards of treatment. After 1919, this took the form of drawing up peace treaties with

---

194 See *Report of the Human Rights Committee to the General Assembly* UN Doc A/39/40 1984, p 143, para 6. See D McGoldrick, *The Human Rights Committee*, 1991, pp 247–68; A Cassesse, *Self Determination of Peoples: A Legal Reappraisal*, 1995, pp 37–67.

195 In the early years, the Committee seemed content to accept single party government (see the debate Romania in 1979 as set out in the *Report of the Human Rights Committee to the General Assembly* 1980 UN Doc A/36/40, para 178; however, in recent years, there has been more emphasis on the need for political pluralism (see the assessment of the position in Zaire (CCPR/C/SR 995) paras 43, 49, 54, 60; see also *Report of the UN Human Rights Committee to the General Assembly* 1990 UN Doc A/45/40, paras 542–46, 576–77). This has become slightly easier in the last decade with the end of single party government in large parts of Eastern Europe.

196 The Committee has declared inadmissible complaints by tribes in Canada.

197 See generally, CA Macartney, *National States and National Minorities*, 1934; I Claude, *National Minorities, An International Problem*, 1955; P Thornberry (1980) 15 Texas International Law Journal 421; H Hannum, *Autonomy, Sovereignty and Self Determination*, 1990; T Franck, *The Power of Legitimacy Among Workers*, 1990; P Thornberry, *International Law and Minorities*, 1991; RY Jennings and AD Watts, *Oppenheim's International Law*, 9th edn, 1992, pp 972 *et seq*; F Ermacora (1983) 182 HR 251; N Rodley (1995) 17 HRQ 48.

198 At the Congress of Berlin (1878), Bulgaria, Montenegro, Serbia, Romania and Turkey all accepted the duty to grant religious freedom to their nationals.

199 The end of the First World War resulted in a large number of treaties, most of which provided guarantees of civil liberties for the relevant minorities. The treaties were with Poland (Versailles 1919), Czechoslovakia (St Germain en Laye 1919), Yugoslavia (St Germain en Laye 1919), Romania (Trianon 1919), Greece (Sevres 1920).

the newly independent states incorporating the principle that minorities were to receive the same civil liberties as the majority group and that discrimination would be outlawed. The individual treaties provided for the right of petition to the League of Nations and the 1922 German-Polish Convention on Upper Silesia went further in allowing an action in the last analysis to be brought before the Permanent Court of International Justice.[200] It has to be admitted that the system did not work very well; newly independent states tend to be resentful of any external monitoring and often regard it as a a qualification of their sovereign rights. Secondly, after 1933 the National Socialist regime in Germany deliberately inflated minority concerns in neighbouring states as part of an attempt to undermine the basis of the Versailles settlement.

After 1945, the emphasis was on the establishment of individual human rights but in 1947 the Sub Commission on the Prevention of Discrimination and Protection of Minorities was established by the United Nations High Commission on Human Rights and later the Sub Commission itself established Working Groups on both Slavery[201] and the Rights of Indigenous Populations.[202] At the same time efforts were made by treaty[203] to ensure proper treatment of minorities.

As indicated above the most important source is contained in Art 27 of the International Covenant on Civil and Political Rights (1966) which reads:

> In those States in which ethnic, religious or linguistic minorities exist, persons belonging to such minorities shall not be denied the right, in community with other members of their group, to enjoy their own culture, to profess and practise their own religion, or to use their own language.

The Human Rights Committee in considering cases of minority rights either in the context of state reports or in ruling on individual applications have been anxious to steer a middle course between preserving civil liberties and the principle of non-discrimination but also seeking to avoid any pronouncement that could promote secessionist claims; it is arguable that this concern has increased since the dissolution of Yugoslavia in 1991–92. It is noteworthy in examining the language of Art 27 that it is directed to protecting 'persons belonging to such minorities' rather than the minority group as such.

---

200 See *Certain German Interests in Polish Upper Silesia* case (1926) PCIJ, Ser A, No 7; *Rights of Minorities in Polish Upper Silesia* case (1928) PCIJ, Ser A, No 15; *Chorzow Factory (Indemnity) (Merits)* case (1928) PCIJ, Ser A, No 17; *Minority Schools in Albania* case (1935) (1935) PCIJ, Ser A/B, No 64, p 17.

201 Established in 1974 as the Working Group on Slavery; the name was changed in 1988 to the Working Group on Contemporary Forms of Slavery. For a general review, see K Zoglin (1986) 8 HRQ 306.

202 In 1982, the Working Group on Indigenous Populations (WGIP) was established charged with considering the position of indigenous peoples across the world. The 1983 definition propounded by the United Nations Sub Committee on the Prevention of Discrimination and Protection of Minorities begins 'indigenous communities, peoples and nations are those which, having a historical continuity with pre-invasion and pre colonial societies that developed on their territory, consider themselves distinct from the sectors of the societies now prevailing in those territories or parts of them'.

203 See Treaty of Peace with Italy (Art IV) (1947); India-Pakistan Peace Treaty (1950).

In these circumstances, it is not surprising that the case law has tended towards a responsible and cautious approach. In *Lovelace v Canada*[204] the question was whether a female applicant should forfeit the right to live on an Indian reservation following the dissolution of her marriage to a non-Indian when a male in the same position would not be so disadvantaged. The Committee found that there had been a breach of Art 27. In giving reasons, the Committee held that a particular enactment affecting a member of a minority must meet a two fold test. It must be objectively and reasonably justified on the facts and, secondly, the provision must be necessary for the continued viability and welfare of the minority as a whole. This approach was followed in *Kitok v Sweden*[205] where the Committee in applying the same test found that the Reindeer Husbandry Act designed to protect the economic interests of the Sami people in Sweden did not infringe Art 27 when it operated to the disadvantage of a particular individual. However, in *Ominyak and Lubicon Lake Band v Canada*[206] the Committee found that there had been a breach of Art 27 when the provincial government of Alberta had consented to the expropriation of the applicants' territory at the behest of private corporate interests.[207]

In the interests of further protection of minority rights the United Nations General Assembly adopted a Declaration on the Rights of Persons Belonging to National or Ethnic, Religious and Linguistic Minorities in December 1992. The document builds upon Art 27 of the ICCPR and is premised on the principle that 'the promotion and protection of the rights of persons belonging to national, ethnic religious and linguistic minorities contribute to the political and social stability of the states in which they live'. Article 1 of the instrument provides that 'states shall protect the existence and the national or ethnic, cultural, religious and linguistic identity of minorities within their respective territories and shall encourage conditions for the promotion of that identity'.

Under the terms of Art 2 it is provided that persons belonging to minorities have the right to enjoy their own culture, profess and practise their own religion and use their own language without interference or discrimination. The Declaration further provides that states shall ensure that members of minorities are enabled to enjoy the rights stipulated in the Declaration. However, the Declaration does not refer to the right of self-determination or any right of secession; indeed Art 8(4) reads:

> Nothing in the present Declaration may be construed as permitting any activity contrary to the purposes and principles of the United Nations, including sovereign equality, territorial integrity and political independence of States.

---

204 *Lovelace v Canada* (1981) 2 Selected Decisions HRC 28 (1981) 68 ILR 17. (In actual fact the Committee considered that the provision violated Art 27 by preventing the applicant returning to live with her parents on the Tobique Indian Reserve after divorce so that it was not necessary to consider the sex discrimination aspect.)

205 *Kitok v Sweden* (1989) HRC Report GAOR 44th Session Supp 40, p 271; (1989) 96 ILR 637.

206 *Ominyak and Lubicon Lake Band v Canada* HRC Report GAOR 45th Session Supp 40, Vol II, p 1; (1990) 96 ILR 667; See, also, *Lansmann v Finland* (1995) 2 IHRR 287.

207 Where the cultural objects of a minority group are in issue then the matter will normally be determined by the relevant rules of private international law pertaining to the passing of property see *AG of New Zealand v Ortiz* [1984] AC 1.

The question of the rights of minorities has acquired an added importance in the last decade with the dissolution of the Soviet Union and Yugoslavia; manifestly, there cannot be self-determination for every minority[208] but there has been an attempt to recognise that the stability of a state often depends on ensuring that a particular minority has been accorded a minimum degree of civil liberty. To this end, the Council of Europe has produced a Framework Convention for the Protection of National Minorities which was adopted by the Committee of Ministers in November 1994 and opened for signature on 1 February 1995. In broad terms contracting parties agree to allow minorities equality with the majority and the guarantee that the culture of a 'national minority' is respected.

In recent years particular attention has been devoted to the problem of indigenous peoples.[209] Although accurate figures are difficult to obtain, it is probably the case that nearly 300 million people in over 35 states come within the conventional definition. The best known are the Maori (New Zealand), the Indians (Native Americans), the Aborigines (Australia) and the Sami (Lapps) in Scandinavia and Russia. Although there may be some problems as to the overlap between a 'minority' and an 'indigenous people', a workable definition has been in place since 1983[210] and interest in the problems has been steadily growing since the 1960s. Within the United Nations, the Sub Commission on Prevention of Discrimination and Protection of Minorities decided in 1982 to establish a Working Group on Indigenous Populations and this resulted in a Draft Declaration on the Rights of Indigenous Peoples which was submitted to the UN Commission on Human Rights in August 1994. The draft declaration[211] includes a rather ambiguous Art 3 which reads :

> Indigenous peoples have the right of self determination. By virtue of that right they freely determine their political status and freely pursue their economic, social and cultural development.

Indigenous people have the right to participate in the life of the state[212] and to live in freedom and security[213] and to practise their cultural and spiritual traditions.[214]

---

208 Because this would simply lead to an accumulation of small states, many of which would lack economic or political viability, it would also frustrate the work of regional and international organisations.

209 See generally, R Barsh (1986) 80 AJIL 369; H J Heintze (1990) 50 Zao RV 39; Douglas Sanders (1991) 13 HRQ 368; R Barsh (1994) 7 Harv Hum Rts J 33; E Stamatopoulou (1994) 16 HRQ 58; WM Reismann (1995) 89 AJIL 350; SJ Anaya, *Indigenous Peoples in International Law*, 1996, Oxford.

210 The definition accepted by the Working Group on Indigenous Populations reads in part: 'Indigenous communities, peoples and nations are those which, having a historical continuity with pre-invasion and pre-colonial societies that developed on their territories, consider themselves distinct form other sectors of the societies now prevailing in those territories or parts of them.' Clearly, in most cases the 'indigenous population' will be a minority within the state but on this broad definition not all minorities will be an indigenous population.

211 The Draft Declaration was accepted by the Working Group which then submitted it to the UN Sub Commission which accepted the draft and passed it in August 1994 to the UN High Commission of Human Rights which on 3 March 1995 in Res 1995/32 decided to establish a working group of the Commission to facilitate further consideration. This was validated by ECOSOC on 25 July 1995. See RT Coulter (1995) 13 NQHR.

212 Draft Declaration 1994, Art 4.

213 *Ibid*, Art 6.

214 *Ibid*, Arts 12 and 13.

16 THE RIGHT TO DEVELOPMENT[215]

At the time of the Universal Declaration of Human Rights (1948) the international community comprised 56 states; today there has been nearly a fourfold increase. However, alongside this increase there has been a growing disparity between rich and poor. Many new states suffer from debt, low incomes, illiteracy, low investment, low economic growth and political instability. In contrast, many of the richer states have experienced steady increases in levels of income, health care, education and capital investment. In these circumstances, there has been a growing demand by poorer states that richer states are under an obligation to assist. Indeed, some poorer states argue that the right of development is derived from the principle of self-determination. The argument is advanced that individual human rights cannot prosper in conditions of economic backwardness and instability. To this, a number of points require to be made. First, a considerable number of international institutions do exist and have been functioning since 1945 with the object of redressing economic disparities; these are examined in the chapter entitled International Economic Law. Secondly, it is a separate question as to whether the poorer states are entitled to claim a distinct right to development. This is disputed by Western states on the grounds that for the most part the western tradition of human rights is directed to individual rather than collective rights. Thirdly, it is argued that matters of such an economic nature are not susceptible of being reduced to the legal language of rights and obligations. Fourthly, it is not without relevance that the right began to be asserted in the early 1970s after western states having decolonised were reluctant to enter into continuing obligations towards former colonies. The right in question was first acknowledged by the UN Commission on Human Rights in 1977 and it received its most tangible manifestation in the UN Declaration on the Right to Development in 1986, but it is the subject of controversy and criticism; some argue that it is inconsistent with General Assembly guidelines as to the creation of new human rights.[216]

Be that as it may, Art 1 of the 1986 UN Declaration defines the right in terms that 'the right to development is an inalienable human right by virtue of which every human person and all peoples are entitled to participate in, contribute to, and enjoy economic, social, cultural and political development, in which all human rights and fundamental freedoms can be fully realised'. In Art 2 it is declared that 'the human person is the central subject of development and should be the active participant and beneficiary of the right of development'; this is then followed by Arts 3, 4 and 5 which place the obligations on

---

215 On the subject generally, see O Schachter (1976) 15 Columbia Journal of Transnational Law p 1; R Rich (1983) 23 Va JIL 287; C Weeramantry (1985) 25 Indian Journal of International Law 482; J Donnelly (1985) 15 Calif WILJ 473; R Barsh (1991) 13 HRQ 322; P Alston (1991) 18 Melb UL Rev 216.

216 In 1986, the General Assembly indicated that states should consider the following before creating new human rights instruments: (a) whether the right was consistent with the existing body of human rights law; (b) was the right of a fundamental character and derived from the inherent dignity and worth of the human person?; (c) was the right sufficiently precise to give rise to identifiable and practicable rights and obligations?; (d) did the right provide where appropriate realistic and effective implementation machinery including reporting systems?; (e) was the right capable of attracting broad international support? See GA Res 41/121.

states to act at the national and international level to facilitate the right of development. Of particular note is Art 3 which reads in part: '... states have the primary responsibility for the creation of national and international conditions favourable to the realisation of the right to development.' This is in line with the general position in human rights law that the primary responsibility falls on the individual state. Thus, is is arguable that the individual state is under a duty both to follow macro economic policies designed to promote the right to development and also to co-operate with the relevant international institutions to secure that end.

The declaration has been the subject of criticism in that the elements of the right are unclear and the tone of the document is aspirational. An example is afforded by the concluding sentence in Art 8 which reads: 'Appropriate economic and social reforms should be carried out with a view to eradicating all social injustices.'

In 1992, the Rio Declaration on Environment and Development noted in Principle 3 that 'the right to development must be fulfiled so as to equitably meet development and environmental needs of present and future generations'. One year later, the United Nations re-emphasised the right to development in the UN Vienna Declaration and Programme of Action in 1993 and referred to it as 'a universal and inalienable right and an integral part of human rights'. While it is accepted that states have a duty to co-operate within international organisations to ameliorate conditions in poorer states,[217] it must be questionable whether progress will be made using the language of rights. However, beyond this it is doubtful whether any such right can be asserted.

17 HUMAN RIGHTS LAW AND CUSTOMARY INTERNATIONAL LAW

Although human rights law is a subject that has developed in the last half century in the form of treaty obligations, there may be cases in which it is necessary to assert that the action in question is contrary to established rules of customary international law. Although there is not complete agreement, judgments in municipal courts together with the level of ratifications would appear to indicate that it can be safely concluded that genocide, slavery, the murder of individuals, torture, prolonged arbitrary detention and sustained racial discrimination are all acts contrary to customary international law.

Such matters have tended to arise where a claim is brought before the municipal courts of state A alleging breaches of customary international law by the government of state B; such cases may be complicated by claims to immunity. A number of cases have been brought before courts in the United States alleging misconduct by government officials in South America. In *Filartiga v Pena Irala*,[218] two Paraguayaun citizens brought a civil action before a United States district court against the defendant a former police chief in Paraguay claiming damages for the torture and death of a family member.[219] The

---

217 This emerges from General Comment No 3 (1991) of the Committee on Economic, Social and Cultural Rights and is broadly in line with the duties arising from the UN Charter.

218 *Filartiga v Pena-Irala* (1980) 630 F 2d 876; ILM 966 (United States Circuit Court of Appeals, 2nd Circuit).

219 Paraguay being ruled from 1954 until 1989 by Alfredo Stroessner who lead a military regime that was subject to criticism on account of its repressive nature. The regime was overthrown in 1989 and Stroessner sought asylum in Brazil.

United States Court of Appeals was obliged principally to consider whether the court had jurisdiction under the Judiciary Act 1789 and the Alien Tort Act 1790;[220] the court held not only that it possessed jurisdiction but that torture was a crime contrary to customary international law. The argument that torture was a crime contrary to customary international law was advanced in *Al Adsani v Government of Kuwait*,[221] but had to yield to the requirements of the doctrine of state immunity. However, this is now questionable following the House of Lords judgment in *Re Pinochet (No 1)*[222] where the majority of the House of Lords were prepared to accept that certain acts were clearly contrary to international law. As Lord Steyn asserted, 'the development of international law since the Second World War justifies the conclusion that by the time of the 1973 *coup d'état*, and certainly ever since, international law condemned genocide, torture, hostage taking and crimes against humanity ... as international crimes deserving of punishment'. This approach was followed in *Re Pinochet (No 3)*[223] where Lord Browne-Wilkinson stressed[224] that the concept of acts contrary to international law stated in the Judgment of the Nuremberg International Military Tribunal had been subsequently endorsed by the General Assembly on 11 November 1946.[225] In these circumstances, there can be little doubt that a number of serious abuses of human rights[226] will be held to be breaches of customary international law.

18 INTERNATIONAL INSTITUTIONS

The development of human rights law on the international plane has been the task of a number of international institutions of which the International Labour Organisation[227] and the United Nations Educational, Scientific and Cultural Organisation[228] have played a prominent role role. These institutions are considered together with other international institutions in Chapter 23.

---

220 Necessary because the tort in question took place outside the United States; in cases where tort was committed in the United States then the court will have jurisdiction under traditional principles, see *Letellier v Republic of Chile* (1980) 488 F Supp 665, 63 ILR 378 (claim made in tort in respect of death caused by car bomb in Washington DC); *Paul v Avril* (1993) 812 F Supp 207 (acts of torture in Haiti).

221 *Al Adsani v Government of Kuwait* (1996) 107 ILR 536 CA; see S Marks (1997) 57 CLJ 8.

222 *R v Bow Street Metropolitan Stipendiary Magistrate ex p Pinochet Ugarte* [1998] 3 WLR 1456.

223 *R v Bow Street Metropolitan Stipendiary Magistrate ex p Pinochet Ugarte (No 3)* [2000] 1 AC 147; [1999] 2 WLR 827.

224 [1999] 2 WLR 827, p 840.

225 GA Res 95 1st Sess 1144; UN Doc A/236 (1946). See, also, the collection of papers on the subject of human rights in customary international law in (1995–96) 25 Ga JICL 1.

226 See *Third Restatement of United States Foreign Relations Law*, Vol 2 (1987), p 165.

227 The Organisation was established under Part XIII of the Treaty of Versailles and became an agency of the United Nations under Art 63 following GA Res 50(1).

228 The United Nations Educational Scientific and Cultural Organisation was established in 1945 and its relationship with the United Nations was fixed in December 1946; see GA Res 50(1).

19 CONCLUSIONS

It is sensible to review the state of human rights law on the international plane. First, there is no doubt that a state that violates human rights will not be able to hide behind assertions of territorial sovereignty or the provisions of Art 2(7) of the United Nations Charter (1945). Secondly, there are a wide range of treaty provisions in force that broadly provide for a threefold method of enforcement,[229] namely, state reporting, inter-state complaints and individual applications. Thirdly, it is now widely accepted that the grossest abuses of human rights constitute breaches of customary international law. Fourthly, many of the international instruments have established Committees charged with handling specific cases but also with issuing general guidance as to how the principles are to be observed. Fifthly, there has been some concern as to whether the bodies established under treaty have sufficient funds to discharge their tasks and this concern manifested itself in the Vienna Declaration and Programme of Action in 1993. Sixthly, there are increasing numbers of NGOs and sympathetic governments ready to draw the attention of the world community to cases of abuse. Seventhly, the system of human rights enforcement has developed considerably on the regional plane and the recent decision to proceed with an International Criminal Court has increased the likelihood of prosecutions in the most serious cases. Eighthly, there are increasing signs that in criminal and civil actions brought before municipal courts such courts are not prepared to accept that a plea of immunity from the jurisdiction can be entered in respect of serious allegations of human rights abuse.

While each of the methods of international enforcement have something to commend them,[230] there can be little doubt that the surest method of observance is for each state to operate within a constitutional framework that protects basic human rights and provides for their enforcement in municipal courts. It may be that the role of international law in the future will be to set out general principles and to provide for individual accountability in cases of gross abuse. This is not to detract from the important promotional work undertaken by the United Nations but as indicated above the enforcement mechanism under the International Covenants is not rigorous and much will depend on how human rights law develops at the regional level.

It might be argued that human rights law develops chronologically. It was observed by the sociologist TH Marshall[231] that the 18th century was the century of civil rights, the 19th the century of political rights and the 20th century that of social rights. While one must be cautious about such generalisations, there is some evidence that human rights law is now grappling with the problem that, unless there is a certain level of economic prosperity, then human rights are unlikely to take root. In this context, there is now increasing emphasis being placed not only on economic and social rights but also on the workings of international economic law.

---

229 There is, however, no room for complacency; the complaints frequently made against the Human Rights committee include: (i) insufficient time; (ii) absence of oral hearings and exclusive reliance on documentary evidence; (iii) no independent fact finding capacity. For robust criticism of the sate of international human rights law see Geoffrey Robertson, *Crimes Against Humanity*, 1999.

230 Ie, state reporting, inter-state complaints, individual applications.

231 TH Marshall, *Citizenship and Social Class*, 1950.

It is now necessary to outline how human rights law has developed on the regional plane.

CHAPTER 16

HUMAN RIGHTS: THE REGIONAL FRAMEWORK

1 INTRODUCTION

As indicated in the previous chapter, the development of an international law of human rights has proceeded apace since 1945. However, these developments on the international plane have coincided with movement on the regional plane. As a broad generalisation, one can note the development of a distinct regional law in Western Europe which then spreads to other parts of the world following decolonisation and the collapse of Marxist Leninist systems in Eastern Europe. It is also important to note that, as the number of states expanded after 1945 and as many written constitutions were withdrawn and redrafted, it became common to include within the basic constitutional documents certain fundamental human rights or civil liberties which were entrenched against interference by the legislative or executive branch of government. In the early years after the Second World War the emphasis was initially upon civil or political rights with the scope widening in subsequent decades.

In Western Europe there is no doubt that the development of a regional law on human rights was linked to the revelations of the abuses of state power practised since 1933. First, the nature and scope of the policies of the National Socialist regime in Germany prompted demands for guarantees of basic rights at both the national level and the regional level. Secondly, associated with the movement towards a regional law of human rights was the gathering attempts to foster forms of European integration which culminated initially in the Treaty of Rome of 1957. The new Europe was to be based on open markets and accountable and limited constitutional government. Thirdly, many Western European states were anxious to demonstrate the contrast with those regimes in Eastern Europe which operated a single party form of government, a centralised economy and limited emphasis on individual rights. Thus, the growth of human rights law in Western Europe after 1945 was in part a reaction against past abuses and also a step on the road to closer European integration; it was also an attempt to draw a clear contrast between liberal democracy of Western Europe and single party forms of government in Eastern Europe.

In this chapter, it is proposed to examine the position in Europe before considering the regional systems operating in other parts of the world.

2 EUROPE

(a) Introduction[1]

The first reference to a Charter of Human Rights in Europe was made in May 1948, at the Congress of Europe held at the Hague, which linked the production of a Charter with progress on European integration. In 1949, the Council of Europe was established to secure inter-governmental and inter-parliamentary co-operation. The objects of the organisation were set out in the Statute. Article 1 provided that the Council should seek to achieve a 'greater unity between its Members for the purposes of safeguarding and realising the ideals and principles which are their common heritage and facilitating their economic and social progress'. Article 3 of the Statute provided that respect for human rights and the rule of law was to be a condition of membership. The Council of Europe operated with two principal organs namely a Committee of Ministers and a Consultative Assembly. In September 1949, the Legal and Administrative Committee of the Assembly proposed that certain rights drawn from the Universal Declaration of Human Rights (1948) should be set out in a detailed document which should be respected by member states of the Council of Europe. The matter was then passed to the Committee of Ministers who, working through two committees in the early months of 1950, produced a draft Convention. This Convention, known as the European Convention on Human Rights and Fundamental Freedoms, was signed by Foreign Ministers in Rome on 4 November 1950 and entered into force following 10 ratifications on 3 September 1953. Since that date, there has been a steady increase in the number of state parties.[2] The general objective of the Convention was to provide for the enforcement at the regional level of rights set out in the Universal Declaration of Human Rights. This is made clear when one looks at the Preamble to the European Convention which records states parties as 'being resolved, as governments of European countries which are likeminded and have a common heritage of political traditions, ideals, freedom and the rule of law to take the first steps for the collective enforcement of certain of the rights stated in the Universal Declaration'.

---

1   See generally P Van Dijk and GHJ Van Hoof, *Theory and Practice of the European Convention on Human Rights*, 2nd edn, 1990; R Beddard, *Human Rights in Europe*, 3rd edn, 1993; J Fawcett, *The Application of the European Convention on Human Rights*, 2nd edn, 1987; DJ Harris, M O'Boyle and C Warbrick, *Law of the European Convention on Human Rights*, 1st edn, 1995; M Janis, R Kay and A Bradley, *European Human Rights Law: Text and Materials*, 1st edn, 1995; AH Robertson and J Merrills, *Human Rights in the World*, 4th edn, 1996; AH Robertson and J Merrills, *Human Rights in Europe*, 3rd edn, 1993; F Jacobs and R White, *The European Convention on Human Rights*, 2nd edn, 1996; S Davidson, *Human Rights*, 1st edn, 1992, Buckingham: Open University Press; C Gearty, 'The European Court of Human Rights and the Protection of Civil Liberties' (1993) 52 CLJ 90.

2   By the year 2000 the number had reached 41.

(b) The European Convention on Human Rights[3]

The philosophy underlying the European Convention is alluded to in the Preamble; the draftsmen reaffirm 'their profound belief in those fundamental freedoms which are the foundation of justice and peace in the world and are best maintained, on the one hand, by an effective political democracy and, on the other, by a common understanding and observance of the human rights upon which they depend'. The Convention[4] sets out a number of civil and political rights and requires state parties to secure such rights to everyone within their jurisdiction. The rights reflect the basic civil and political rights, such as the right to life (Art 2)[5] and the prohibition of torture or inhuman or degrading treatment or punishment (Art 3).[6] The Convention outlaws slavery (Art 4) and provides for the right to liberty and security of the person (Art 5),[7] as well as the right to a fair and public hearing within a reasonable time by an independent and impartial tribunal established by law (Art 6).[8] The Convention further provides for the prohibition of retrospective criminal legislation (Art 7),[9] while stipulating for the respect for privacy and family life, (Art 8)[10] as well as for freedom

---

3   For case law on the status of the European Convention in the United Kingdom prior to the coming into force of the Human Rights Act 1998, see *Birdi v Secretary of State for Home Affairs* (1974) 119 SJ 322; *R v Chief Immigration Officer, Heathrow Airport ex p Salamat Bibi* [1976] 1 WLR 979; *Ahmad v Inner London Education Authority* [1978] QB 36; *Malone v Commission of Police of the Metropolis* [1979] Ch 344 *R v Lemon and Gay News Ltd* [1979] AC 617; *Associated Newspaper Group v Wade* [1979] 1 WLR 697; *Attorney General v BBC* [1981] AC 303; *Schering Chemicals Ltd v Falkman Ltd* [1982] QB 1; *Trawnik v Lennox* [1985] 1 WLR 532; *Attorney General v Guardian Newspapers Ltd* [1987] 1 WLR 1248; *Attorney General v Guardian Newspapers Ltd* [1990] 1 AC 109; *Secretary of State for the Home Department v Brind* [1991] AC 696; *R v Chief Metropolitan Magistrate ex p Choudhury* [1991] 1 QB 429. For comment on the position in the United Kingdom, see A Lester [1984] PL 46; S Greer (1999) 24 ELR 3; D Feldman (1999) LS 165.

4   It should be noted at the outset that the Convention was amended after 1950 by Protocols 3, 5 and 8 which entered into force on 21 September 1970, 20 December 1971 and 1 January 1990. However, the more significant change is the coming into effect of Protocol XI on 1 November 1998; this has resulted in a renumbering of the articles from Art 19 but those articles set out in Section 1 (Arts 1–18) remain unaffected by the insertion of Protocol XI.

5   *Paton v United Kingdom* (1980) 3 EHRR 408; *Stewart v United Kingdom* (1985) 7 EHRR 453; *McCann v United Kingdom* (1996) 21 EHRR 97.

6   *Tyrer v United Kingdom* (1978) 2 EHRR 1; *Republic of Ireland v United Kingdom* (1978) 2 EHRR 25; *Soering v United Kingdom* (1989) 11 EHRR 439; *Vilvarajah v United Kingdom* (1992) 14 EHRR 248; *Costello Roberts v United Kingdom* (1995) 19 EHRR 112.

7   *Lawless v Ireland* (1961) 1 EHRR 15; *X v United Kingdom* (1981) 4 EHRR 188; *Brogan v United Kingdom* (1989) 11 EHRR 117; *Fox, Campbell and Hartley v United Kingdom* (1990) 13 EHRR 157; *Thynne, Wilson and Gunnell v United Kingdom* (1990) 13 EHRR 666; *Brannigan v United Kingdom* (1994) 17 EHRR 539.

8   *Kostovski v Netherlands* (1989) 12 EHRR 434; *Windtisch v Austria* (1990) 13 EHRR 281; *Saunders v United Kingdom* (1990) 13 EHRR 313; *McMichael v United Kingdom* (1995) 20 EHRR 205; *Murray v United Kingdom* (1996) 22 EHRR 29; *Benham v United Kingdom* (1996) 22 EHRR 293.

9   *SW and CR v United Kingdom* (1996) 21 EHRR 363.

10 *Klass v Federal Republic of Germany* (1979) 2 EHRR 214; *Dudgeon v United Kingdom* (1981) 4 EHRR 149; *Silver v United Kingdom* (1983) 5 EHRR 347; *Malone v United Kingdom* (1984) 7 EHRR 14; *Leander v Sweden* (1987) 9 EHRR 443; *Rees v United Kingdom* (1989) 9 EHRR 56; *Gaskin v United Kingdom* (1990) 12 EHRR 36; *Norris v Republic of Ireland* (1991) 13 EHRR 186; *Cossey v United Kingdom* (1991) 13 EHRR 622; *Ludi v Switzerland* (1992) 15 EHRR 173; *Campbell v United Kingdom* (1993) 15 EHRR 137; *Buckley v United Kingdom* (1997) 23 EHRR 101; *Stubbings v United Kingdom* (1997) 23 EHRR 213.

of thought and religion (Art 9).[11] The draftsmen also stipulated for the right to freedom of expression (Art 10),[12] the right to peaceful assembly and freedom of association (Art 11),[13] the right to marry and found a family (Art 12),[14] the right to an effective remedy before a national authority in the event of violation of a right stipulated under the Convention (Art 13)[15] and the right to non-discrimination in the enjoyment of such rights (Art 14).[16]

Since 1950, the Convention has been subject to amendment by various protocols[17] which have added to the substantive rights protected. In March 1952, the First Protocol created additional rights in respect of property[18] and education as well as in area of free elections.[19] The Second Protocol of May 1963 granted the Court a competence to give advisory opinions,[20] while the Third Protocol of the same date introduced procedural reforms in respect of the Commission. The Fourth Protocol[21] created additional rights in respect of freedom of movement while the Fifth Protocol[22] is directed to the subject of elections to the court and the Commission. The Sixth Protocol, which was concluded in April 1983 and entered into force in March 1985, provides for the abolition of the death penalty. The Seventh Protocol of November, which came into effect in November 1988, is concerned with procedural and substantive safeguards in criminal matters, while the Eighth, Ninth and Tenth Protocols concern matters of a procedural nature.

---

11 *X v Austria* (1965) Yearbook VIII 174; *Huber v Austria* (1971) Yearbook VIII 174; *Choudhury v United Kingdom* (1991) 12 HRLJ 172; *Hoffman v Austria* (1994) 17 EHRR 293; *Kokkinakis v Greece* (1994) 17 EHRR 397; *Otto Preminger Institute v Austria* (1994) 19 EHRR 34; *Holy Monastries v Greece* (1995) 20 EHRR 1.

12 *Handyside v United Kingdom* (1976) 1 EHRR 737; *Arrowsmith v United Kingdom* (1978) 3 EHRR 218; *Sunday Times Ltd v United Kingdom* (1979) 2 EHRR 245; *Gay News Ltd v United Kingdom* (1982) 5 EHRR 123; *Glasenapp v Federal Republic of Germany* (1986) 9 EHRR 25; *Kosiek v Federal Republic of Germany* (1987) 9 EHRR 25; *Muller v Switzerland* (1991) 13 EHRR 212; *Observer, Guardian and Sunday Times Ltd v United Kingdom* (1991) 14 EHRR 153, p 229; *Thorgeir Thorgeirson v Iceland* (1992) 14 EHRR 843; *Open Door Counselling and DWW v Ireland* (1992) 15 EHRR 244; *Informationsverein Lentia v Austria* (1994) 17 EHRR 93; *Cascado Coca v Spain* (1994) 18 EHRR 1; *Jersild v Denmark* (1995) 19 EHRR 1; *Jacubowski v Germany* (1995) 19 EHRR 64; *Oberschlick v Austria* (1995) 19 EHRR 389; *Piermont v France* (1995) 20 EHRR 301; *Tolstoy Miloslavsky v United Kingdom* (1995) 20 EHRR 442; *Prager v Austria* (1996) 21 EHRR 1; *Vogt v Germany* (1996) 21 EHRR 205; *Goodwin v United Kingdom* (1996) 22 EHRR 442.

13 *Young, James and Webster v United Kingdom* (1981) 4 EHRR 38; *Platform 'Artze für das Leben' v Austria* (1988) 13 EHRR 204; *Sibson v United Kingdom* (1994) 17 EHRR 204; *Holy Monastries v Greece* (1995) 20 EHRR 1; *Vogt v Germany* (1996) 21 EHRR 205.

14 *Rees v United Kingdom* (1989) 9 EHRR 56; *Cossey v United Kingdom* (1990) 13 EHRR 622.

15 *Leander v Sweden* (1987) 9 EHRR 443; *Vilvarajah v United Kingdom* (1992) 14 EHRR 248.

16 *Abdulaziz and Others v United Kingdom* (1984) 6 EHRR 28.

17 The broad division is that the First Protocol (property), the Fourth Protocol (movement), the Sixth Protocol (the death penalty) and the Seventh Protocol (criminal matters) contain substantive guarantees and remain binding on those states that have ratified them. However, the Second, Third, Fifth, Eighth, Ninth and Tenth Protocols are of a procedural nature and are replaced after the coming into effect of Protocol X1.

18 *James and Others v United Kingdom* (1986) 8 EHRR 123; *Lithgow v United Kingdom* (1986) 8 EHRR 329.

19 The First Protocol was adopted in March 1952 and entered into force on 18 May 1954.

20 See now Art 47 of the amended Convention.

21 The Fourth Protocol of 1963 achieved the five ratifications needed and entered into force in May 1968. The Protocol is widely drawn and embraces: (i) prohibition on imprisonment for contractual obligations; (ii) freedom of movement within a state; (iii) restrictions on the expulsion of aliens and a prohibition on the expulsion of nationals.

22 The Fifth Protocol came into force in 1974.

Of specific relevance is the Eleventh Protocol, which was adopted on 11 May 1994 and entered into force on 1 November 1998, which is of particular importance in that it replaces the Court and the Commission with a single court and is dealt with further below.[23] It is, however, necessary to make reference to the system which existed prior to the coming into effect of Protocol XI.

A number of general points about the Convention can usefully be made. First, its provisions have gained wide acceptance and have been incorporated into the domestic law of most member states.[24] Secondly, while the Convention applies within a particular territory, it serves to protect individuals within that territory even though, by so doing, it may restrict the rights of a non-contracting state.[25] Thirdly, the rules of interpretation followed by the European Court of Human Rights adopt the teleological or purposive approach with the emphasis being on a form of interpretation consistent with contemporary conditions.[26] Fourthly, ratification of the Convention enables the Commission to receive only inter-state applications; individual applications require a declaration under Art 25[27] in respect of competence and an additional declaration conferring jurisdiction on the Court under Art 46.[28] Fifthly, there has been a steady increase in the number of member states resulting in a higher volume of judicial activity.[29] Sixthly, member states may derogate from many[30] but not all of their obligations in time of war or public emergency but they must inform the Secretary General of the Council of Europe of the reasons for such conduct.[31]

The Commission

Under the original scheme of the Convention,[32] the structure provided for both a European Commission of Human Rights and a European Court of Human Rights.[33] The

---

23 It operates by inserting new Arts 19–51 into the text of the Convention.

24 The United Kingdom doing so in the Human Rights Act 1998.

25 *Soering v The United Kingdom* (1989) 11 EHRR 439 (a case concerning extradition from the United Kingdom of an individual facing a capital charge in the United States).

26 The distinction between European and English methods of interpretation is discussed by Lord Denning MR in the Court of Appeal in *James Buchanan and Co Ltd v Babco Forwarding and Shipping (UK) Ltd* [1978] AC 141 CA.

27 Under the terms of the original Art 25 an individual application could only be made if the relevant state against which the complaint had been made had declared that it recognised the competence of the Commission to receive such petitions. In contrast, the successor provision in Art 34 inserted by Protocol XI allows the Court to receive individual applications. There is no requirement of a separate declaration.

28 No such provision is included in the Convention as amended by Protocol XI.

29 When Russia was admitted as a member of the Council of Europe and signed the Convention in February 1996 it was the thirty ninth member state of the Council of Europe. Russia did not however sign the Sixth Protocol concerning the abolition of the death penalty.

30 Under the ECHR only four rights are non-derogable: Art 2 (right to life); Art 3 (freedom from torture or other ill treatment); Art 4 (prohibition of slavery and forced labour); and Art 7 (prohibition on the retrospective application of the criminal law).

31 See European Convention on Human Rights (1950), Art 15, see *Lawless v United Kingdom* (1961) 1 EHRR 15; *Brannigan and McBride v United Kingdom* (1993) 17 EHRR 539.

32 A general expression meaning prior to the coming into effect of Protocol XI on 1 November 1998.

33 European Convention on Human Rights (1950), Art 19, see now Art 19 of the Amended Convention which provides that the Court takes over the work of the present Commission.

Commission consisted of a number of members equal to that of the High Contracting Parties;[34] the members of the Commission were elected by the Committee of Ministers.[35] They were to serve for a period of six years and were eligible for re-election. Candidates for the Commission were to be of high moral standing[36] and were to serve on the Commission in their individual capacity.[37] In effect, the role of the Commission was to act as a recipient of petitions and to function as a preliminary filter.[38] In accordance with traditional principles of international law, the Commission was not to deal with a matter unless and until all domestic remedies had been exhausted.[39] Article 25 of the original Convention provided that in the event of a declaration by a state party then an individual might have the right of individual petition although the declaration might be subject to a time limit and therefore need to be renewed thereafter; reservations other than temporal are probably unacceptable.[40]

In respect of the obligation to exhaust internal remedies if the applicant demonstrates a *prima facie* case then the onus will be upon the state to demonstrate that procedures exist which afford an effective remedy. The Convention required that the petition be lodged within six months of the final municipal decision.[41] The normal procedure was for a petition to be examined by a Rapporteur. Under the terms of Art 27(3), the Commission was entitled to declare a petition inadmissible if it was incompatible with the Convention, manifestly ill founded or an abuse of the right of petition.[42] The rules of procedure permitted the Commission to give priority to urgent applications; since the mid 1970s, there has been a steady increase in the number of applications[43] so that, by the early 1990s, the volume of work was making it very difficult for the Commission staff to cope. even though a high proportion of applications are subsequently not proceeded with[44] or declared inadmissible.

---

34   *Ibid*, Art 20.
35   *Ibid*, Art 21.
36   *Ibid*, Art 21(3).
37   *Ibid*, Art 23.
38   *Ibid*, Arts 25 and 28. See now Art 34 of the Amended convention.
39   *Ibid*, Art 26. See now Art 35 of the Amended Convention.
40   The Amended Convention proceeds on the basis of the automatic competence of the Court in respect of individual petitions so that provisions similar to Arts 25 and 46 are not required. See now, Art 34 of the Amended Convention. .
41   European Convention on Human Rights (1950), Art 26. See now Art 35 of the Amended Convention,
42   See now Art 35 of the Amended Convention which allows the Court to reject a petition on similar grounds.
43   Broadly, there was a fourfold increase in the number of applications between 1976 and 1993.
44   See HG Schermers, 'The Eleventh Protocol to the European Convention on Human Rights' (1994) 17 ELR 367, where the learned author draws upon official figures to demonstrate: (a) the increase in the number applications; and (b) the heavy workload caused by applications that require preliminary examination but are not finally proceeded with. The statistics produced by the Commission draw a distinction between provisional files and registered applications. In 1993, the last full year before the adoption of Protocol XI, there were 9,323 provisional files and 2,037 registered applications.

In the event of the Commission declaring the application admissible then there was a second stage at which the facts were ascertained[45] and the Commission might seek to facilitate a friendly settlement consistent with the objectives of the Convention.[46] If a friendly settlement was obtained, then a written report would be passed to the Committee of Ministers. If a friendly settlement is not reached, then the Commission would state its opinion as to whether the facts disclosed a breach of the Convention and a report will be made to the Committee. At the same time, the Commission would meet to decide whether to refer the case to the Court under the terms of Art 48(a).[47]

The Court

The European Court of Human Rights which is based in Strasbourg dates from 1959. Under the original terms of the Convention the role of the Court was set out in Section IV of the text (Arts 38–56).[48] It was provided that members of the Court should be elected by the Consultative Assembly[49] and that membership should correspond to the member states of the Council of Europe.[50] It was provided that candidates were required to be of high moral character[51] and were elected for a period of nine years.[52] Members of the Court were to sit in their individual capacity and were not to hold any incompatible position while serving as judges of the Court.[53] The Court was to operate under a President and a Vice President;[54] in normal circumstances cases would be heard by a Chamber of nine judges.[55] Only a state party or the Commission could bring a case before the Court as of right[56] and the jurisdiction of the Court extended to all matters of interpretation or application arising under the Convention.[57] For a case to be brought against a state, it was necessary that the requisite declaration had been made under Art 46; in normal circumstances, the Court would only deal with a case if prior efforts at a friendly settlement had failed.[58] In the event of a dispute as to admissibility or

---

45 European Convention on Human Rights (1950), Art 28.

46 *Ibid*, Art 28(1)(b).

47 With the abolition of the Commission, these provisions have no precise equivalent under Protocol XI although Arts 38 and 39 contain provisions designed to facilitate a friendly settlement.

48 See now Arts 19–51 of the Amended Convention.

49 European Convention on Human Rights (1950), Art 39. See now Art 22 of the Amended Convention.

50 *Ibid*, Art 39.

51 *Ibid*, Art 39(3). See Art 21 of the Amended Convention.

52 *Ibid*, Art 40. Article 23 of the Amended Convention provides for a period of six years.

53 *Ibid*, Art 40(7). See Art 21 of the Amended Convention.

54 *Ibid*, Art 41; under Art 26 of the Amended Convention the Court is to elect a President and Vice President.

55 *Ibid*, Art 43.

56 *Ibid*, Art 44.

57 *Ibid*, Art 45. See Art 32 of the Amended Convention.

58 *Ibid*, Art 47.

jurisdiction, then such a question was to be determined by the Court.[59] Any judgment of the Court was to include reasons[60] and was to be final.[61] The parties to the Convention expressly agreed to abide by decisions of the Court in any case in which they were parties.[62] Under the terms of Protocol IX, which came into effect on 1 October 1994, the terms of Art 48 were broadened to enable the following to bring cases before the Court. The operative provision read:

(1) The following may bring a case to the Court, provided that the High Contracting Party concerned, if there is only one, or the High Contracting Parties, concerned, if there is more than one, are subject to the compulsory jurisdiction of the Court or, failing that, with the consent of the High Contracting Party concerned, if there is only one, or of the High Contracting Parties concerned if there is more than one:

(a) the Commission;

(b) a High Contracting Party whose national is alleged to be a victim;

(c) a High Contracting Party which referred the case to the Commission;

(d) a High Contracting Party against which the complaint has been lodged;

(e) the person, non governmental organisation or group of individuals having lodged the complaint with the Commission.[63]

Although the Court was entitled to sit in Chambers with only nine judges it might defer to the Grand Chamber of 17 judges. The vast majority of cases since 1960 have been brought by the Commission, but there have been examples of inter-state applications[64] and cases where a state has brought an action on behalf of one of its own nationals.[65] The rules of procedure permit the Court to adopt interim measures. In respect of remedies, Art 50 of the Convention obliged the Court to review the relevant remedies in municipal law and then to ensure 'just satisfaction to the injured party'.[66]

There has been a steady increase in the volume of case law. In 1960, the court decided one case on its merits; by 1976 the annual figure had risen to six cases. As recently as 1984, the number of cases in a year remained in single figures. However, thereafter the number of cases began to rise so that, by 1989, 25 cases a year were being disposed of. In the subsequent decade, the figure nearly doubled increasing the emphasis on procedural reform. As one judge of the court noted, it took 30 years for the court to dispose of its first 200 cases but it dealt with its next 200 in three years.[67]

Although the actual volume of case law developed slowly the jurisprudence of the Court has grown impressively; there is hardly an article of the Convention that has not

---

59 *Ibid*, Art 49.

60 *Ibid*, Art 51. See Art 45 which provides for reasons for a judgment and Art 49 which requires reasons for an advisory opinion.

61 *Ibid*, Art 52.

62 *Ibid*, Art 53. See Art 46 of the Amended Convention.

63 The rules on jurisdiction under the Amended Convention are contained in Arts 32, 33, 34 and 47.

64 *Republic of Ireland v United Kingdom* (1978) 2 EHRR 25.

65 *Soering v United Kingdom* (1989) 11 EHRR 439.

66 Now to be found in Art 41 following the implementation of Protocol XI.

67 Judge Ryssdal (Norway).

been subject to detailed judicial consideration. The Court has been obliged to rule on sensitive matters such as action taken to interrogate prisoners[68] and administrative measures to monitor the contacts of detainees.[69] The Court has considered the issue of corporal punishment,[70] the application of capital punishment[71] and the limits to pre-trial reporting;[72] in the sphere of private life judgments have been given in respect of homosexual relations[73] and changes of gender.[74] The Court has been obliged to consider the circumstances in which the property of the citizen might be taken[75] and the action that the state might take to restrain possible attack.[76] In the sphere of employment, the Court has shown itself ready to assert the rights of the individual[77] and in the sphere of public health it has been anxious to safeguard the rights of those compulsorily detained.[78] In general, the evidence is that states accept the judgment of the court and in many instances a court judgment has lead to legislative change in a particular state;[79] the Convention gives a residual authority to the Committee of Ministers to supervise the execution of the judgment and in cases of absolute defiance a threat of expulsion[80] from the Council of Europe might arise. The broad philosophy of the Convention as with most human rights treaties is that of balance. As the Court observed in *Soering v UK*,[81] 'inherent in the whole Convention is a search for a fair balance between the demands of the general interest of the community and the requirements of the protection of the individual's fundamental rights'.

The Committee of Ministers

The third institution operating under the Convention is the Committee of Ministers. This is a political rather than a judicial body being drawn from the Foreign Ministers of the member states of the Council of Europe.[82] Under the statute of the Council of Europe it

---

68 *Republic of Ireland v United Kingdom* (1978) 2 EHRR 25.

69 *Golder v United Kingdom* (1975) 1 EHRR 524; *Silver v United Kingdom* (1983) 5 EHRR 347.

70 *Tyrer v United Kingdom* (1978) 2 EHRR 1.

71 *Soering v United Kingdom* (1989) 11 EHRR 439.

72 *Sunday Times Ltd v United Kingdom* (1979) 2 EHRR 245.

73 *Dudgeon v United Kingdom* (1981) 4 EHRR 149.

74 *Rees v United Kingdom* (1989) 9 EHRR 56; *Cossey v United Kingdom* (1990) 13 EHRR 622.

75 *James v United Kingdom* (1986) 8 EHRR 123; *Lithgow v United Kingdom* (1986) 8 EHRR 329.

76 *McCann v United Kingdom* (1995) 21 EHRR 97.

77 *Young, James and Webster v United Kingdom* (1981) 4 EHRR 38.

78 *X v United Kingdom* (1981) 4 EHRR 188.

79 An example is afforded by the United Kingdom which, in the 1950s and 1960s, had taken the view of AV Dicey that civil liberties were properly protected by the development of the common law. In the 1970s and 1980, as the United Kingdom began to be challenged in the European Court, it would introduce legislative changes to give effect to the judgment. Eg, *Sunday Times Ltd v United Kingdom* (1979) 2 EHRR 245, given effect to in the Contempt of Court Act 1981; *X v United Kingdom* (1981) 4 EHRR 188, given effect to by the Mental Health (Amendment) Act 1982, now consolidated in the Mental Health Act 1983; *Malone v United Kingdom* (1985) 7 EHRR 14 given effect to in the Interception of Communications Act 1985.

80 Greece was forced to withdraw from the Council of Europe under threat of expulsion in 1969, following the assumption of power by the military regime. On the restoration of democratic government in 1974, Greece was readmitted to the Council of Europe.

81 *Soering v United Kingdom* (1989) A 161, para 89; (1989) 11 EHRR 439.

82 In most cases the work being delegated to junior ministers.

has certain supervisory powers. In respect of its duties concerning human rights arising under the European Convention, it has a number of supervisory and facilitating functions. Pursuant to Art 21 of the Convention, it was concerned with the election of members of the Commission while, under Art 32, when a case was not taken to the Court by the Commission, the Committee of Ministers might determine whether there had been a violation of the Convention. On a more mundane level, the Committee was charged under Art 42 with determining rate of compensation for judges sitting in the court. In most cases, the Committee of Ministers would follow the recommendations of the Commission, but there might be situations arising under Art 32, where it was not possible to obtain the necessary two thirds majority to act or it may be expedient to find a political resolution of the problem.

Under Art 54,[83] the Committee of Ministers has an enforcement role. Once the court has delivered judgment then, in principle, a state is expected to give effect to that judgment under Art 53.[84] However, when the terms of the judgment are submitted to the Committee of Ministers, it will be for that body to determine whether the defaulting state has acted with sufficient resolve to give effect to the judgment. In practice, the Committee tends to note action taken by the individual states rather than subject the matter to detailed analysis. Some have expressed the view that it is unsatisfactory that a non-judicial body should be charged with determining whether municipal law has been modified to give effect to the Convention.

The implementation of Protocol XI

The steady increase in the number of state parties and the inexorable growth in the number of petitions provided cause for reflection as to how procedures might be simplified and cases expedited. In 1985, the Committee of Ministers requested a Committee of Experts to study the question of possible reforms of procedure. Procedural reforms were introduced under the Eighth Protocol which entered into force on 1 January 1990 and which permitted the Commission to operate by Chambers and in committee, but this modest reform could not prevent a fourfold increase in registered applications between 1983 and 1993. To ensure further progress on procedural reform, the Eleventh Protocol was opened for signature on May 11 1994 and, after acquiring the necessary ratifications, came into effect on 1 November 1998. In essence, Protocol XI introduces far reaching structural reform by replacing the two prior agencies of commission and court with a single court. In drafting terms, the original Arts 1–18 remain while new articles are inserted in the form of Arts 19–51 and under the terms of Protocol XI, Art 2, certain further changes are made to Section V of the Convention[85] which becomes Section III of the amended Convention.

The Court is now required to do the work of the two prior agencies (that is, the Court and the Commission) and will function on a permanent basis.[86] Judges are subject to the

---

83 See Art 46 of the Amended Convention.

84 See *ibid*.

85 In essence, the original Art 57 becomes Art 52, while the original Arts 58 and 59 are deleted. Articles 60 to 66 of the original Convention become Arts 53 to 59 of the modified Convention.

86 Article 19 of the Amended Convention.

same requirements as to qualification[87] but will sit for only six years.[88] The Court is entitled to sit in committee with three judges, in Chambers with seven judges, or in Grand Chamber with 17 judges.[89] Under the terms of Art 29, a committee of the court may determine admissibility of individual cases while a Chamber of the court will perform the same function in respect of inter-state applications.[90] The amended Convention continues the established rule in international law that domestic remedies must be exhausted first.[91] If the Court determines that the application is admissible, then efforts will be made to seek a friendly settlement.[92] The normal rule will be that substantive cases are heard before judges in Chambers, save in serious questions of interpretation where jurisdiction may be relinquished to the Grand Chamber.[93] In normal circumstances, the judgment of the Chamber will be effective after three months,[94] save in those exceptional cases where there is an appeal to the Grand Chamber.[95]

The Grand Chamber has jurisdiction to give advisory opinions[96] requested by the Committee of Ministers. Under Art 34,[97] an individual application does not require a prior state declaration. Article 35 continues the previous rule that all relevant domestic remedies must be exhausted,[98] while applications that are anonymous,[99] or not original,[100] will be rejected; the Court will not deal with applications that, at the time, are before other international fora.[101] It is further provided that the application must be made within a period of six months from the date on which the final decision was taken.[102]

As before, the Court has power to strike out applications that are incompatible with the provisions of the Convention,[103] or where the petition is abusive,[104] or manifestly ill founded.[105] In considering a case, the Court may explore the possibility of a friendly settlement;[106] in such a situation, the case will be struck from the list.[107] In principle,

---

87 *Ibid*, Art 21.
88 *Ibid*, Art 23.
89 *Ibid*, Art 27.
90 *Ibid*, Art 29(3).
91 *Ibid*, Art 35.
92 *Ibid*, Arts 38 and 39.
93 *Ibid*, Art 30.
94 *Ibid*, Art 43.
95 *Ibid*, Art 43.
96 *Ibid*, Art 31(b).
97 *Ibid*, Art 34.
98 *Ibid*, Art 35.1.
99 *Ibid*, Art 35.2(a). (Ie, the complaint must not be a matter that has been investigated and ruled upon previously.)
100 *Ibid*, Art 35.2(b).
101 *Ibid*, Art 35.2(b).
102 *Ibid*, Art 35.1.
103 *Ibid*, Art 35.3.
104 *Ibid*. (It is abusive where the complaint is brought for an improper motive.)
105 *Ibid*, Art 35.3. These provisions are similar to the prior Art 27 which conferred a similar jurisdiction on the Commission. By ill founded is meant that there must be *prima facie* evidence to sustain the complaint.
106 *Ibid*, Arts 38 and 39.
107 *Ibid*, Art 39.

hearings are in public[108] and any judgment of a Chamber of the Court must be accompanied by reasons.[109] In exceptional cases, a party may apply to refer the matter to the Grand Chamber.[110] The Court may award just satisfaction to the injured party if it finds a violation of the Convention;[111] the Committee of Ministers will supervise the execution of the judgment.[112] The objective of the changes is to produce a more streamlined system that will process cases more quickly; it also has the advantage that the complainant could bring his case directly before a judicial body. Under the prior system, whether a case reached the Court depended on the conduct of the Commission or a state party;[113] under the new system, it is the judicial branch which will decide which cases proceed to a full hearing. Protocol XI entered into force in November 1998, being one year after ratification by all state parties to the Convention.[114] Under the transitional arrangements set out in Art 5,[115] members of the Commission remained in office for one year until October 1999 for the purpose of dealing with cases declared admissible.

(c) The European Social Charter

In the early 1950s, the principal concern of the Council of Europe, and thus the European Convention on Human Rights (1950), had been with civil and political rights. This was understandable in the aftermath of the Second World War; however, it was not long before attention began to turn to the subject of economic and social rights. In the broadest sense, such rights are designed to ensure a reasonable standard of living for all citizens. However, such a standard depends on the level of economic performance and cannot simply be imposed in a legal instrument. Moreover, there were clearly differences between the industrialised economies of Northern Europe and the agricultural economies of Southern Europe. In particular, there were many in post-war Europe who saw the priority as trying to raise living standards generally through economic growth; the economic needs of each state after 1945 differed greatly and much depended on how economic life had been affected in the Second World War. Further, there was much room for debate as to which sectors of economic activity should be owned and operated by the state.

In these circumstances, it is perhaps not surprising that although the Council of Europe turned its attention to economic and social rights in 1954, it was not until 1961 that agreement was finally reached. Because of differing economic and social conditions,

---

108 *Ibid*, Art 40.
109 *Ibid*, Art 49.
110 *Ibid*, Art 43 .
111 *Ibid*, Art 41.
112 *Ibid*, Art 46.
113 See Arts 32 and 48 of the original Convention. These provisions were unsatisfactory in that in many cases the action if it did not proceed to the court would terminate with the Committee of Ministers.
114 Articles 3 and 4 of Protocol XI.
115 Article 5 of Protocol XI.

the European Social Charter (1961)[116] was drafted not in terms of immediately enforceable legal rights but was premised on general principles and objectives to be attained. The document itself is divided into five parts. Part I (Arts 1–19) sets out certain general rights. However, this part of the Charter is not drafted in terms of immediate binding legal obligation as it is prefaced that: 'The Contracting Parties accept as the aim of their policy, to be pursued by all appropriate means, both national and international in character, the attainment of conditions in which the following rights and principles may be effectively realised.' Part II contains a number of specific obligations which are set out in Arts 1–19.

To accommodate the fact that there is such diversity in economic conditions Part III (Art 20) requires signatories to indicate which five of seven specific articles set out in Part III they are prepared to accept. In addition, such acceptance of Part III must extend to 10 articles or 45 numbered paragraphs.[117] Part IV is concerned with implementation while Part V is concerned with derogations. The Charter was signed on behalf of the 13 members of the Council of Europe on 18 October 1961 and it came into force on 26 February 1965 following the deposit of the fifth instrument of ratification.

Methods of implementation are provided for in Part IV of the Charter. A Committee of Experts reviews every two years the reports of contracting parties[118] as to how they are discharging their responsibilities under the Charter.[119] Copies of the report are sent to relevant national organisations who are entitled to make comments.[120] These materials, together with the comments of the Committee of Experts,[121] are then considered by a Governmental Committee on the Social Charter.[122] The comments of the Committee of Experts are also passed to the Consultative Assembly of the Council of Europe which then refers the matter to the Committee of Ministers.[123] These methods of enforcement may be more convoluted than simply factual findings by a court, but they do ensure that state parties are under pressure to conduct themselves in a manner consistent with the spirit of the Charter.

An attempt to clarify and strengthen enforcement mechanisms has been made in the Protocol amending the Social Charter (the Turin Protocol) which was adopted at Turin in October 1991, thus coinciding with the 30th anniversary of the Charter. One of the reasons for renewed emphasis on enforcement was that the Charter has a new role as a guarantor of minimum standards as the free market system is extended to states in Eastern Europe. It was felt that the existing enforcement mechanisms embodied an overlap between the Committee of Independent Experts and the Governmental Committee. Under the Turin

---

116 In general, the Charter is designed to protect the following; the right to work, to just conditions of work, to safe and healthy working conditions, to fair remuneration, to reorganise, to bargain collectively, to protection for children and young persons in employment, to vocational guidance and training, to social security, to social and welfare services, to assistance for the disabled.

117 European Social Charter (1961), Art 20(1)(c).

118 *Ibid*, Art 21.

119 *Ibid*, Art 25.

120 *Ibid*, Art 23.

121 *Ibid*, Art 24.

122 *Ibid*, Art 27.

123 *Ibid*, Art 28.

Protocol, the Committee of Independent Experts is strengthened by being increased in size and being given the exclusive authority to interpret the Charter. The role of the Governmental Committee will be to advise the Committee of Ministers on appropriate policies to facilitate Charter obligations. The decision to strengthen the Committee of Independent Experts was necessitated by an increasing workload;[124] to improve enforcement the Committee was given additional power to request information or to hold oral hearings either at its own initiative or upon request.

(d) The European Convention for the Prevention of Torture[125]

The European Convention for the Prevention of Torture and Inhuman and Degrading Treatment or Punishment was adopted in 1987 and entered into force on 1 February 1989. The Convention derives from the Legal Affairs Committee of the Council of Europe and to some extent represents a regional extension of the 1984 International Convention against Torture and other Cruel, Inhuman or Degrading Treatment or Punishment. Both instruments were precipitated by the information coming to light in the 1970s of the wide use of torture by repressive non-democratic regimes. As the preamble to the Convention indicates, the intention is to build upon the safeguards provided by Art 3 of the European Convention on Human Rights (1950). It had been asserted by some that there was an overlap with the European Convention on Human Rights (1950) in that under Art 28(1)(a)[126] a fact finding exercise could be undertaken but this was only in respect of a specific application while the Torture Convention is wider in providing for general visits. Moreover it is made clear in Art 17(2) of the Torture Convention (1987) that information yielded might later be used for an individual application under the European Convention. It is also relevant to observe that the 1987 Convention is directed to the 'prevention' of torture whereas Arts 3 and 25[127] of the European Convention on Human Rights (1950) are clearly directed to individual actions being brought in respect of past violations.

Under the terms of Art 1 of the European Convention for the Prevention of Torture a European Committee for the Prevention of Torture and Inhuman or Degrading Treatment or Punishment (hereinafter referred to as 'the Committee') is established and it is stipulated that the Committee shall monitor allegations of torture by visits and fact finding missions. There is thus a preventative element that supplements the individual remedies under the European Convention on Human Rights (1950). By the terms of Art 2,

---

124 The Additional Protocol of 1988 had the effect of adding four more economic and social rights, namely: (i) non-discrimination in employment on grounds of sex; (ii) consultation of workers within an undertaking; (iii) participation in the improvement of working conditions; (iv) protection of elderly persons. The Protocol entered into force on 4 September 1992.

125 See generally, A Cassesse (1989) 83 AJIL 128; M Evans and R Morgan (1991) 41 ICLQ 590; J Murdoch (1994) 5 EJIL 220; M Evans and R Morgan (1994) 5 EJIL 249; M Evans and R Morgan (1997) 46 ICLQ 663.

126 Article 28(1)(a) of the original Convention; a slightly more restricted formulation appears in Art 38(1)(a) inserted under Protocol XI.

127 Now Art 34 as inserted by Protocol XI.

state parties are obliged to permit such visits and are under a duty to co-operate. Members of the Committee are to be persons of 'high moral character, known for their competence in the field of human rights'[128] and are to be elected by the Committee of Ministers of the Council of Europe.[129] The Committee for the Prevention of Torture is to meet *in camera* and decisions are to be taken by a majority.[130] The Committee will organise periodic visits which will normally be carried out by two members who may if necessary be assisted by experts and interpreters.[131] A state party will be notified of the intention to visit and is required to grant entry to its territory,[132] to provide information,[133] and to grant access to any place where persons are deprived of their liberty. In limited circumstances a state party may object to a visit on grounds of national defence or public safety.[134] Following a visit the Committee will produce a report and the state party is expected implement the report in good faith.[135] If a state party refuses to co-operate then the Committee may choose to make a public statement.[136] Information gathered is confidential and the report itself will only be published when requested by a state party.[137] Each year the Committee will produce a general report which will be submitted to the Committee of Ministers who will transmit such a report to the Consultative Assembly.

(e) The European Community[138]

The Treaty of Rome (1957) did not itself contain express provisions in respect of human rights. However, the preamble to the treaty did pledge state parties to 'ensure economic and social progress' and affirmed that the essential objective of their efforts was 'the constant improvement of the living and working conditions of their peoples'. It might, however, be argued that human rights were expressly recognised from the very outset because the preamble went on to confirm that European solidarity was to be constructed 'in accordance with the principles of the Charter of the United Nations'. Moreover, the Treaty stipulated that Community institutions were to operate within the rule of law subject to final determination by the European Court of Justice.[139] The Treaty from the

---

128 European Convention for the Prevention of Torture (1987), Art 4.

129 *Ibid*, Art 5.

130 *Ibid*, Art 6.

131 *Ibid*, Art 8.

132 *Ibid*, Art 8(2)(a).

133 *Ibid*, Art 8(2)(b).

134 *Ibid*, Art 9.

135 *Ibid*, Art 10(1).

136 *Ibid*, Art 10(2).

137 *Ibid*, Art 11.

138 See generally, M Akehurst (1981) 52 BYIL 29; M Mendelson (1981) 1 YEL 126; H Schermers, 'The scales in balance: *National Constitutional Court v Court of Justice*' [1990] 27 CMLR 97; H Schermers, 'The European Community bound by fundamental human rights' [1990] 27 CMLR 249; R Dallen, 'An overview of EEC protection of human rights' [1990] 27 CMLR 761; G De Burca (1993) 13 OJLS 283.

139 Treaty of Rome (1957), Art 164.

outset embraced a distinct philosophy that economic prosperity was to secured by free markets operating within the rule of law.

As Community law developed certain basic principles began to be asserted in the case law of which perhaps the most important was the principle of the supremacy of community law over national law.[140] However, this raised difficult problems as to whether a provision of community law could prevail over a provision in the written constitution of a state. More particularly, this touched upon rather sensitive issues, not least because some of the written constitutions contained guarantees of basic rights and had been specifically drawn up following prior abuses.[141] Further, difficult questions of constitutional law[142] might arise when it was asserted that a government operated under a constitution and was therefore unable to cede rights entrenched within a written constitution particularly when those entrenched rights had been drafted as a response to prior abuses of state power.[143]

In these circumstances, there are a number of avenues by which the European Community has been able to promote the maintenance of human rights at the regional level. First, membership of the European Community has depended on the maintenance of a democratic government operating within the rule of law.[144] Secondly, the European Court of Justice has been most anxious not to antagonise the constitutional courts of member states[145] and has thus noted the existence of certain fundamental human rights that are part of both community law and national law; the technique has been to identify certain common principles shared by states on the international plane and given effect to

---

140 In general terms, one can note four basic legal principles: (i) that Community law is an independent legal order; (ii) that Community law is common to all member states; (iii) that Community law prevails over any national law that is incompatible with it; (iv) that Community law can confer rights and impose obligations directly on private persons in the member states. The principle of the supremacy of Community law was established shortly after the establishment of the community; see Case 26/62 *Van Gend en Loos v Nederlandse Administratie der Belastingen* [1963] ECR 1; CMLR 29; Case 6/64 *Costa v Ente Nationale per l'Energia Elettrica (ENEL)* [1964] ECR 585; CMLR 425.

141 The obvious example being Germany, where the *Grundgesetz* of 1949 sets out a number of fundamental rights, of which perhaps the most relevant is Art 1(2) which reads: 'The German people therefore acknowledge inviolable and inalienable human rights as the basis of every community, of peace and justice in the world.' The intent of this provision is reinforced by Art 1(3) which provides: 'The following basic rights shall bind the legislature, the executive and the judiciary as directly enforceable law.' Also relevant is Art 19(2) which reads 'in no case may the essential content of a basic right be encroached upon'.

142 By those who took the traditional position in constitutional law that a government derives its power from and under the constitution. As Thomas Paine had expressed it in *The Rights of Man*, 1791: 'A constitution is a thing antecedent to government, and a government is only the creature of a constitution.' See AJ Ayer, *Thomas Paine*, 1989.

143 The written constitution may not only set out basic rights and provide they shall not be derogated from, but it may also expressly declare that the rights are binding on all three branches of government.

144 Thus, Greece (with a prior military regime) did not sign an act of accession until 1979, and Spain (post-General Franco) and Portugal (post-Dr Salazar) did not sign acts of accession until 1986.

145 For obvious reasons of history, this is a very sensitive issue in Germany where the *Bundesverfassungsgericht* has been vigilant in ensuring that the written constitution is respected; see *Internationale Handelsgesellschaft mbH* [1974] 2 CMLR 540; *Steinike und Weinleg* [1980] 2 CMLR 531; *Application of Wünsche Handelsgesellschaft* [1987] 3 CMLR 225; *Brunner v European Union Treaty* [1994] 1 CMLR 57.

in national constitutions.[146] In essence, the European Court of Justice has absorbed these principles into community law so as to avoid a conflict with the constitutional traditions of member states.

The third technique that has been employed has been to develop European community law as founded on certain basic principles that are themselves consistent with a developed regional case law of human rights. Thus, in European community law there is evidence of the doctrine of proportionality,[147] legal certainty,[148] legitimate expectation,[149] the right to a fair hearing[150] and the principle of equality of treatment. A fourth approach has been to make express reference to human rights in subsequent treaty documents. The preamble to the Single European Act (1986) made reference to fundamental human rights and this approach was taken further in the Treaty on European Union (the Maastricht Treaty) (1992). Article F(2) of Title I reads:

> The Union shall respect fundamental rights, as guaranteed by the European Convention for the Protection of Human Rights and Fundamental Freedom signed in Rome on 4 November 1950 and as they result from the constitutional traditions common to the Member States, as general principles of Community law.

Of equal relevance is Title V, which pledges the parties to a Common Foreign and Security Policy and under the terms of Art J1 one of the objectives of that policy is 'to preserve peace and strengthen international security, in accordance with the principles of the United Nations Charter as well as the principles of the Helsinki Final Act and the objectives of the Paris Charter'. Further, in Title VI provision is made for co-operation in the fields of Justice and Home Affairs, but this co-operation is to be conducted 'in compliance with the European Convention for the Protection of Human Rights and Fundamental Freedoms of 4 November 1950'.[151] So that the Treaty on European Union (1992) provides for the recognition and enforcement of human rights both internally as part of the community legal order but also externally[152] in the conduct of foreign affairs.

The movement for the recognition of human rights within EC law has proceeded steadily. Part of the reason for this undoubtedly is the effect on Western European opinion

---

146 Case 29/69 *Stauder v City of Ulm* [1969] ECR 41; [1970] CMLR 112; Case 11/70 *Internationale Handelsgesellschaft mbH* [1970] ECR 1125; [1972] CMLR 255; Case 4/73 *Nold v Commission* [1974] ECR 491; 2 CMLR 338; Case 44/79 *Haur v Land Rheinland Pfalz* [1979] ECR 3727; [1980] 3 CMLR 42; Case 85/87 *Dow Benelux* [1989] ECR 3137.

147 Case 11/70 *Internationale Handelsgesellschaft mbH* [1970] ECR 1125; Case 118/75 *Watson and Belmann* [1976] ECR 1185; 2 CMLR 482.

148 Case 43/75 *Defrenne v Sabena (No 2)* [1976] ECR 455; [1976] 2 CMLR 98; Case 169/80 *Gondrand Frères* [1981] ECR 1931.

149 Case 120/86 *Mulder* [1988] ECR 2321; [1989] 2 CMLR 1. For a review of the case law on the topic, see E Sharpston (1990) 15 ELR 103.

150 Case 17/74 *Transocean Marine Paint Association v Commission* [1974] ECR 1063; 2 CMLR 459.

151 See Treaty on European Union (1992), Title VI (Art K2).

152 This, of course, is inevitable as two of the members of the European Community are also permanent members of the Security Council. Since 1990, European Community Foreign Ministers have had cause to stress the human rights aspect of foreign policy when negotiating with Iraq, Iran, Nigeria, Sierra Leone, as well as in diplomatic interventions in Rwanda, the former Yugoslavia and during the Kosovo conflict in the spring of 1999. While there may be differences between European states on matters of tactics the broad principles of foreign policy now have to be acceptable to the European Parliament.

of the events in the former Yugoslavia. Although there has been a long standing desire to expand the community, many have wished to see a firmer framework of human rights guarantees before such expansion proceeds further. This is of particular concern when the Community expands to embrace former communist states which have only limited experience of multiparty democracy. This momentum has been continued by consolidating the prior provisions relating to human rights in the consolidated version of the treaties following upon the Treaty of Amsterdam (1997).[153] Thus, Art 11 of the Treaty of Amsterdam (1997) repeats the Union's 'attachment to the principles of liberty democracy and respect for human rights and fundamental freedoms and the rule of law'.[154]

However, it is clear that in the wider European landscape the European Court of Justice will have an important influence on the development of human rights law so that some thought it sensible for the European Community to formally accede to the European Convention on Human Rights (1950). However, it has been held that the European Community lacks competence to accede to the European Convention on Human Rights (1950)[155] so that any future act of accession would require an amendment of existing treaties. In these circumstances, it has been decided[156] to seek to establish a European Union Charter of Fundamental Rights; the intention is to produce a visible document declaratory in nature which does not compete with the European Convention on Human Rights but serves as a guide to European institutions and a benchmark against which future membership applications are to be judged.

(f) The Organisation for Security and Co-operation in Europe (OSCE)

The movement for *rapprochement* and *detente* in Europe which can, at the latest, be dated from the arrival in power in Germany of Chancellor Brandt[157] which led to initiatives for a final settlement of post-1945 disputes. The practical response was the establishment of the Conference on Security and Co-operation in Europe (CSCE) which opened in Helsinki, Finland on 3 July 1973 and concluded there on 1 August 1975. The Helsinki Final Act 1975 was a declaratory statement of a political nature and was designed to represent a *modus vivendi* between Eastern and Western Europe. The document set out a number of general principles[158] which were designed to regulate relations between

---

153 Thus, the original preamble to the Treaty of Rome (1957) appears in the consolidated version of the Treaty of Rome established by the Treaty of Amsterdam (1997). Article F(2) of the Treaty on European Union (1992) is now contained in Art 6 of the TEU as amended by the Treaty of Amsterdam (1997) while Art J.1 now appears as Art 11 in the consolidated version.

154 Treaty of Amsterdam (TEU) (1997), Art 11 (previously TEU 1992, Art J.1).

155 Opinion 2/94 *Re Accession of the Community to the European Human Rights Convention* [1996] 2 CMLR 265.

156 At the meeting of the Heads of Government (Cologne June 1999).

157 The policy of reconciliation followed by Willy Brandt as Foreign Minister (1966–69) and then as Federal Chancellor (1969–74) was sometimes described as Ostpolitik; the policy did much to reduce tension within Europe and earned Brandt the Nobel Peace Prize in 1971.

158 The relevant principles were: (i) sovereign equality between states; (ii) refraining from the use of force; (iii) inviolability of frontiers; (iv) territorial integrity of states; (v) peaceful settlement of disputes; (vi) non-intervention in internal affairs; (vii) respect for human rights; (viii) self-determination of peoples; (ix) co-operation among states; (x) fulfilment in good faith of obligations under international law.

states; of the 10 general principles para 7 is of particular relevance in calling for 'respect for human rights and fundamental freedoms, including the freedom of thought, conscience, religion or belief'. Much of the document was concerned with problems of security and confidence building measures designed to reduce tension between NATO and Warsaw Pact forces; part of the text was devoted to the promotion of co-operation in areas such as science and technology. One of the objectives of the Final Act had been to resist any implementation of the so called 'Brezhnev Doctrine'[159] and some of the human rights provisions were consistent with demands made by intellectuals[160] in the Soviet Union.

The intention after Helsinki was that 'follow up' meetings should be held to explore possible future areas of co-operation; pursuant to this intention, subsequent meetings were held in Belgrade in 1977 and Madrid in 1983. However, when the third follow up meeting was summoned to Vienna on 4 November 1986, the general landscape had shifted. The Vienna Conference met from 4 November 1986 until 19 January 1989 at a time when there was a gradual movement of liberalisation in Eastern Europe in response to the arrival in power of Mikhail Gorbachev.[161] The Vienna Conference culminated in a Concluding Document (1989); the document set out certain basic principles relevant to Security in Europe. Paragraph 12 of the statement of principles contained a 'determination to guarantee the effective exercise of human rights and fundamental freedoms'; paras 13–27 contained more specific undertakings. The document welcomed further co-operation in the sphere of science, technology and the environment while recording that artificial barriers to family reunions should cease and that in matters of the travel of minors the welfare of the child should be of paramount concern. Of particular, relevance in the Concluding Document was a section entitled 'The Human Dimension of the CSCE' which resulted in subsequent meetings in Paris in 1989 and Copenhagen in July 1990. The Copenhagen Conference was devoted to the 'Human Dimension of the CSCE' and concluded with a 'Document of the Conference on the Human Dimension of the CSCE'; in the changed atmosphere in Europe the document stressed the need for democracy, the rule of law and the freedom of each state to choose its own political, economic and cultural system. Of particular significance was the fact that the document expressly linked the law of human rights to democratic government within the rule of

---

159 Named after Leonid Brezhnev (1906–82), General Secretary of the Communist Party of the Soviet Union 1964–82. The doctrine was propounded at the time of the invasion of Czechoslovakia (1968) and held that the Soviet Union was entitled to intervene by force if necessary in any state within its sphere of influence and in which 'socialism was threatened'. Such an imperialist approach was at variance with the United Nations Charter, but was invoked again at the time of the invasion of Afghanistan.

160 The Helsinki Final Act (1975) was drawn up at a time when human rights groups in the Soviet were beginning to demand a greater measure of civil liberties. The campaign was associated with the physicist Andrei Sakharov (1921–89), who was awarded the Nobel Peace Prize in 1975, and Alexander Solzhenitsyn (1918–) who, in novels such as *One Day in the life of Ivan Denisovitch* (1962), was critical of the state of civil liberties under Josef Stalin. He was awarded the Nobel Prize for Literature in 1970. As an example of the efforts of the author to secure publication of his works outside the Soviet Union, see *Bodley Head Ltd v Flegon* [1971] 1 WLR 680 (Brightman J).

161 Mikhail Gorbachev (b 1931) followed Konstantin Chernenko (1911–85) as General Secretary of the Soviet Communist Party in 1985 (CPSU). Gorbachev was the first Soviet leader since VI Lenin (1870–1924) to have had a legal training. The three strands of Gorbachev's policies would directly impact on human rights in Eastern Europe: (i) *perestroika* or restructuring; (ii) *glasnost* or openness; and (iii) the movement towards *detente* and arms control.

law. The signatories called for 'free elections that will be held at regular intervals by secret ballot'. Thus, para 5.7 demanded that 'human rights and fundamental freedoms will be guaranteed by law and in accordance with ... obligations under international law', while para 7 noted that 'the will of the people serves as the basis of the authority of government'. The document itself drew upon the Locke-Jefferson tradition of constitutional law.

The changes in Eastern Europe were of such a nature that Heads of Government met in Paris in November 1990 to agree upon a Charter for a New Europe. In broad terms, the document was intended to chart a course for Europe in the post-Cold War period. The preamble of the document required a 'steadfast commitment to democracy based on human rights and fundamental freedoms'. The document endorsed the 10 principles of the Helsinki Final Act and proclaimed that the New Europe was to be constructed on the basis of the pillars of human rights, democracy and the rule of law. It is of particular note that the document endorsed 'economic co-operation based on a market economy' but such economic liberty was to be 'exercised in democracy and protected by the rule of law'.

The subsequent meeting of the Human Dimension of the CSCE took place in Moscow in October 1991 which resulted in a Concluding Document. The Concluding Document of the Moscow Conference reaffirmed the content of the Helsinki Final Act and introduced a scheme for experts to assist participating states in resolving 'questions in its territory relating to the human dimension of the CSCE'. Following this initiative, a number of missions were sent to assist newly independent states.

The CSCE follow up meeting took place in Helsinki in 1992 and resulted in a document entitled 'The Helsinki Summit Declaration'. The document welcomed the development of democratic government, the rule of law and the initial steps to a market economy that were being taken in Eastern Europe; it further noted the abuses being perpetrated against minorities and provided for the establishment of the office of High Commissioner on National Minorities. The entire tone of the document was directed at establishing structures that could manage the economic and social changes set in train by the collapse of communist regimes. Since the Charter of Paris (1990), much of the day to day co-operation has been in the hands of a Committee of Senior Officials working through an Office of Democratic Institutions and Human Rights.

In the years since the Helsinki Conference of 1973–75, the work of the Conference on Security and Co-operation in Europe had increased considerably as attempts have been made to assist in the reconstruction of Eastern Europe; a number of *ad hoc* and semi permanent institutions had been set up to facilitate this process so that, in these circumstances, it was understandable that at Budapest in 1994 the CSCE should change its name to OSCE (the Organisation for Security and Co-operation in Europe). It would seem sensible to regard the OSCE as a political structure designed to promote reconstruction based on democracy, human rights and the rule of law. To this extent its objectives are long term and political in contrast to the European Convention on Human rights where the emphasis is upon the application of existing law to proven or admitted facts.

3 THE INTER AMERICAN SYSTEM[162]

The American continent contains a large number of states of varying size and at different stages of economic and social development. First, the economic power of the United States stands in contrast to the relative poverty of some Central and Latin American states. Secondly, the long tradition of democratic government in the United States under the terms of a written constitution contrasts with the military regimes that, at various times, this century have held power in states such as Argentina, Chile, Uruguay and Paraguay. Thus, this is both the continent which produced the Declaration of Independence of 1776 and so set out in clearest terms the case for limited government under the rule of law; however, it is also the continent in which in some countries of Latin America there is irrefutable evidence of the most serious abuses of human rights including unlawful detentions, state torture and arbitrary executions. In some states, the normal constitutional principle that civilian authority should prevail over military force has been openly flouted; such problems have been accentuated by difficulties arising from grossly unequal distributions of wealth and an immature political culture in which extremism and violence constitute the normal methods of discourse. Insecure democratic structures, wide differences of income, problems of acute poverty and illiteracy have posed serious problems in some states in Latin and South America. So that the American continent has played a large part in the birth of human rights law but it has also been the location of some of the most serious abuses.

The inter-American system is traceable back to the establishment in 1948 of the Organisation of American States[163] which operates as a regional agency for the purposes of Art 48 of the United Nations Charter (1948). The Organisation of American States has a structure broadly in line with that of the United Nations in comprising a Permanent Council and a General Assembly. The legal basis of the Organisation of American States is founded on the 1947 Inter American Treaty of Reciprocal Assistance (the Rio Treaty) and the 1948 Pact of Bogota which constitutes the original Charter. The Charter was amended by the Protocol of Buenos Aires in 1967.[164] The original Charter itself contains a number of general references requiring states to respect individual rights; however, the absence of

---

162 See generally, S Davidson (1992); LR Scheman (1965) 59 AJIL 335; T Buergenthal (1975) 69 AJIL 828; T Buergenthal (1982) 76 AJIL 231; T Buergenethal (1985) 79 AJIL 1; C Crena (1992) 63 BYIL 135; S Davidson (1995) 44 ICLQ 405.

163 This was not the first step at co-operation. Reference should be made to the International Union of American Republics established in 1890; this was assisted by a Commercial Union and both were referred to as the 'Pan American Union'; after 1910, it had its headquarters in Washington in a building sometimes referred to as the 'House of the Americas'. Schemes of co-operation had been floated from the time of Simon Bolivar (1783–1830), but the United States had tended to claim a dominant influence in Latin America, while the Monroe Doctrine (1823) held sway. After the Montevideo Conference of 1933 and that of Buenos Aires in 1936, the United States indicated its willingness to conduct its relations on the principles of 'good neighbourliness' and non-intervention in domestic affairs.

164 The 1948 Charter entered into force in December 1951 and was subsequently amended by the Protocol of Buenos Aires of 1967, the Protocol of Cartagena de Indias, the Protocol of Washington of 1992 and the Protocol of Managua of 1993.

detailed provisions was cured by the adoption of a resolution entitled the American Declaration of the Rights and Duties of Man. This was not, however, incorporated into the Charter system.

The next step chronologically was the establishment of the Inter American Commission on Human Rights. This was established by the Permanent Council of the Organisation of American States in 1960 and by Art 2 of its statute human rights were to be 'the rights set forth in the American Declaration of the Rights and Duties of Man'. In its early years, the function of the Commission was simply advisory but following a Special Inter American Conference in Brazil in 1965, a new Art 9 *bis* was added to the statute to enable the Commission to receive individual petitions. In 1967, the Protocol of Buenos Aires amended the OAS Charter with the purpose of establishing the Commission as an organ of the OAS.[165] Under the provisions of Art 112, the Commission was to preserve and maintain the state of human rights observation until an American Convention on Human Rights could enter into force.

After some preparatory work a Specialised Conference on Human Rights was held in San Jose, Costa Rica and in November 1969 the text of the American Convention on Human Rights (1969) was adopted; the instrument entered into force on 18 July 1978, upon receipt of the eleventh instrument of ratification.[166] The American Convention sets out 26 rights and freedoms of which 21[167] appear in the United Nations Covenant on Civil and Political Rights.[168] When the American Convention came into effect, a new statute entered into force for the Inter American Commission stipulating that there would be a single Commission with distinct powers under both the Charter and the Convention. Under the terms of Art 1(2) of the statute, the Commission would be charged with preserving human rights established under the Convention and in respect of non-party states it would enforce those human rights standards stipulated by the American Declaration of the Rights and Duties of Man. Thus, the Inter American Commission on Human Rights had a dual mandate; its duties under the Convention ran from 1978 and in

---

165 See T Buergenthal (1975) 69 AJIL 828.

166 As stipulated by Art 74, American Convention on Human Rights (1969).

167 The relevant 21 being: (i) the right to life; (ii) freedom from torture and inhuman treatment; (iii) freedom from slavery and servitude; (iv)the right to liberty and security; (v) the right to a fair trial; (vi) prohibition on retroactive criminal laws; (vii) privacy and family life; (viii) conscience and religion; (ix) freedom of thought and expression; (x) freedom of assembly; (xi) freedom of association; (xii) freedom to marry and establish a family; (xiii) freedom of movement; (xiv) the right to free elections; (xv) the right to a proper remedy when rights are violated; (xvi) the right to legal personality; (xvii) the right to compensation in the event of miscarriages of justice; (xviii) the right to a name; (xix) the rights of a child; (xx) the right to a nationality; (xxi) the right to equality before the law. The five rights appearing in the American Convention which do not appear in the United Nations Covenant are: (i) the right of property; (ii) freedom form exile; (iii) restriction on the collective expulsion of aliens; (iv) the right of reply; (v) the right of asylum.

168 ACHR rights which are not protected under the ICCPR are: (i) the right to compensation (Art 10); (ii) freedom of aliens from arbitrary expulsion (Art 13); (iii) right of reply (Art 14); (iv) equal rights of children born out of wedlock and those born in wedlock as a right of the family (Art 17(5)); (v) right to a name (Art 18); (vi) right to a nationality (Art 20); (vii) right to property (Art 21); (viii) right to equal protection (Art 24); (ix) right to judicial protection (Art 25).

respect only of state parties and its other duties ran from 1960 and arose under the Charter as modified in 1965[169] and 1967.

In the early years of the Commission, it devoted its energies to fact finding investigations in particular states. Since the early 1960s, it has considered the state of human rights in Cuba, Haiti, Dominican Republic, Argentina, Nicaragua, Guatemala and El Salvador. After the amendment of the governing statute in 1965 at Rio de Janeiro, it became entitled to receive individual petitions. In accordance with traditional principles of international law, no application could be considered until external remedies had been exhausted. If the application was considered admissible, then the Commission would seek to establish the basic facts; this would include giving the state in question the opportunity to comment. At that stage, the Commission will make a determination which involves a finding of facts, conclusions and recommendations for a settlement. Under the Charter system, the only sanction is that of publicity since there is no binding judicial determination and the system does not provide for a mediated settlement or monetary compensation.

As indicated above the American Convention on Human Rights (1969)[170] protects the traditional civil and political rights: as with the European Convention the rights arising are subject to appropriate limitations.[171] To ensure implementation and supervision, the Convention provides for the continuance of the Inter American Commission on Human Rights and the establishment of a court to be known as the Inter American Court of Human Rights.[172] Article 34 provides that the Commission shall be composed of seven members; the extensive jurisdiction of the Commission is set out in Art 41 and it is noteworthy that these roles are educational, investigative, advisory and supervisory.

Chapter VIII of the Convention (Arts 52–69) provides for the establishment of the Inter American Court of Human Rights;[173] the Convention contains safeguards for the election of judges[174] and stipulates that the Court shall normally sit in a quorum of five.

In respect of the jurisdiction of the Commission, Art 44 provides that any person, or non-governmental organisation may lodge a petition with the Commission alleging a violation of the Convention.[175] Under the terms of Art 45 an inter-state complaint may be

---

169 At a Second Special Inter American Conference in Rio de Janeiro in Brazil in 1965, the statute was amended to include Art 9 *bis* to permit individual petitions;this provision became Art 20 of the new statute in 1979.

170 See T Buergenthal (1971) 21 Buffalo Law Review 121.

171 See for example, Arts 12 and 13 of the American Convention on Human Rights (1969).

172 *Ibid*, Art 33. See T Buergenthal (1982) 76 AJIL 231.

173 American Convention on Human Rights (1969), Art 52.

174 *Ibid*, Art 53.

175 In recent years, the Inter American system has had an effect in the United Kingdom where appeals heard by the Privy Council from Caribbean countries have sometimes raised questions as to whether an individual should be allowed time to exhaust his rights under the Inter American system; such appeals also raise a related human rights point because the post-independence written constitutions of some Caribbean states contain provisions modelled on the European Convention on Human Rights (1950). For the developing case law in this area, see *Pratt v Attorney General for Jamaica* [1994] 2 AC 1; *Bradshaw v Attorney General of Barbados* [1995] 1 WLR 936; *Henfield v Attorney General of Bahamas* [1997] AC 413; *Fisher v Minister of Public Safety and Immigration* [1998] AC 649; *Fisher v Minister of Public Safety and Immigration (No 2)* [1999] 2 WLR 349; *Thomas v Baptiste* [1999] 3 WLR 249 (PC).

submitted if a prior declaration of competence has been made by the state parties. In general terms, the complaint must be brought within a period of six months[176] and all relevant internal remedies must have been exhausted;[177] the substance of the petition must not have been raised with any other international organisation.[178] The first duty of the Commission is to determine the admissibility of the petition under the Convention;[179] if it does so decide, then it will seek to establish all the basic facts and in doing so is entitled to demand the co-operation of state parties.[180] In appropriate cases, the Commission may assist in promoting a friendly settlement.[181] In cases where a friendly settlement is reached, then a report will be sent to the Secretary General of the Organisation of American States.[182] If a friendly settlement is not reached, then a formal report will be produced and if the report has not been implemented within a period of three months then it will be for the Commission to determine by a majority what further action to take.[183] It is noteworthy that the acceptance of this competence is obligatory,[184] while in respect of inter-state complaints a state declaration is required.[185]

In respect of the Court, only state parties or the Commission have the right to initiate proceedings;[186] the Convention did not confer a right on the individual to proceed directly to the court. In 1969, there had been some debate as to the desirability of a judicial organ so that under Art 62 the jurisdiction of the Court will be affected by declarations filed by state parties.[187] In the event of jurisdiction arising under Art 62, the Court has competence to rule on violations of the Convention.[188] Further, the Court has considerable power to give advisory opinions.[189] Such an advisory jurisdiction extends not simply to the American Convention but to other human rights treaties entered into by state parties.[190] It is stipulated that the Court shall give reasons for its judgment and dissenting opinions may be attached to the judgment.[191] The judgment of the Court is final and not subject to appeal.[192] The Convention stipulates that state parties shall comply with the judgment of the Court.[193] Where a judgment includes a monetary

---

176 American Convention on Human Rights (1969), Art 46(1)(b).

177 *Ibid*, Art 46(1)(a).

178 *Ibid*, Art 46(1)(c).

179 *Ibid*, Art 47.

180 *Ibid*, Art 48.

181 *Ibid*, Art 48(1)(f).

182 *Ibid*, Art 49.

183 *Ibid*, Arts 50 and 51.

184 *Ibid*, Art 44.

185 *Ibid*, Art 45.

186 *Ibid*, Art 61.

187 Under the terms of Art 62, parties may declare that they accept the jurisdiction of the court unconditionally or on condition of reciprocity and for a limited or indefinite time.

188 *Ibid*, Art 63.

189 *Ibid*, Art 64.

190 See *Definition of Other Treaties Subject to the Interpretation of the Inter-American Court* (1983) 22 ILM 51; 67 ILR 594; (1982) 3 HRLJ 140. See T Buergenthal (1985) 79 AJIL 1.

191 American Convention on Human Rights (1969), Art 66.

192 *Ibid*, Art 67.

193 *Ibid*, Art 68.

award, then such an award is to be enforced in that state by the normal methods appropriate for the enforcement of judgments.[194]

In respect of conduct, it is noteworthy that the Commission has extensive powers under the terms of Art 41[195] and this competence has been employed to give advice and to prepare reports both on individual countries and also in respect of specific topics. The Court has acknowledged the competence of the Commission to give rulings as to whether a particular piece of domestic legislation is contrary to the Convention. It might be argued that the procedure of the Commission in individual petitions is slow and convoluted but one justification for this is that the objective is not to filter cases for the Court but to guide and influence the parties towards a friendly settlement.

It has to be admitted that it is the advisory jurisdiction of the Court[196] that has been the most prominent. In the *Definition of Other Treaties Subject to the Interpretation of the Inter American Court* case,[197] the Court was prepared to give a wide interpretation to Art 64 of the Convention in holding that any human rights treaty which concerned a state party might be the subject of an advisory opinion. In the *Effect of Reservations* case,[198] the Court ruled that reservations under Art 75 do not have to be accepted by other parities. In the *Restrictions to the Death Penalty* case,[199] the Court ruled that it had jurisdiction to give an opinion on the validity of a reservation submitted by Guatemala under Art 4(4). Shortly after, in the *Proposed Amendments* case,[200] the Court was called upon to rule on the compatibility with the Convention of certain amendments proposed to the constitution of Costa Rica. In the subsequent *Licensing of Journalists* case,[201] the Court was required to consider whether the licensing of journalists was compatible with Art 13 and in coming to a view the court was influenced by case law arising under the European Convention on Human Rights. There have been a number of cases when the Court has been required to consider possible limitations. In the *Interpretation of 'Laws'* case,[202] such a question arose under Art 30 following a request by Uruguay, while in the *Right of Reply* case,[203] Costa Rica raised a question as to the interpretation of Art 14; later in the *Habeas Corpus* case,[204] the question at issue was the possible suspension of rights in emergency situations under Art 27.

In contrast, in contentious cases the record of the Court is more limited; as noted above, under the terms of Art 62 contentious proceedings can only be initiated if the state

---

194 *Ibid*, Art 68.

195 In essence, Arts 41–43 provide for the continuance of the old supervisory system of the Commission, while Arts 44–47 provide for the new supervisory system alluded to above.

196 See *ibid*, Art 64.

197 *Definition of Other Treaties Subject to the Interpretation of the Inter American Court* (1983) 22 ILM 51; 67 ILM 594; (1982) 3 HRLJ 140.

198 *Effect of Reservations* case (1983) 22 ILM 33; 67 ILR 559; (1982) 3 HRLJ 182.

199 *Restrictions to the Death Penalty* case (1983) 4 HRLJ 339.

200 *Proposed Amendments to the Naturalisation Provisions of the Constitution of Costa Rica* (1984) 5 HRLJ 161.

201 *Compulsory Membership in an Association prescribed by Law for the Practice of Journalism* (1986) 7 HRLJ 74; 75 ILR 31. The court referred to case law arising under the European Convention on Human Rights such as *Sunday Times v United Kingdom* (1979) 2 EHRR 245.

202 *The Word 'Laws' in Art 30 of the American Convention on Human Rights* (1986) 7 HRLJ 231.

203 *Character and scope of the right of reply or correction recognised in the American Convention* (1986) 7 HRLJ 238.

204 *Habeas Corpus in Emergency Situations* case (1988) 9 HRLJ 94.

party or state parties have accepted the jurisdiction of the Court. The importance of precise compliance with procedural compliance is indicated by the ruling of the Court in the *Viviana Gallardo* case.[205] The application was made by Costa Rica in the context of the murder of a suspected terrorist. Costa Rica attempted to bring the matter directly before the Court without approaching the Commission; the attempt was rejected. The Court indicated that the conciliatory functions of the Commission were not to be short circuited and that the jurisdiction of the Court on the merits was contingent on prior procedural compliance.

However, the evidence is clear that, in appropriate cases, the Court will employ the full range of its powers under the Convention. Thus, in the *Valasquez Rodriguez* case the Court was prepared to make an interim order under Art 63(2) to prevent interference with witnesses.[206] At a subsequent hearing, the Court ordered compensation for violations of Arts 4, 5 and 7.[207] Indeed, at a subsequent hearing, the Court was prepared to accept that damages might go beyond pecuniary loss and extend to moral and emotional damage.[208] It seems right in principle that, where state organs have been guilty of serious abuses, then there should not be technical or artificial limits on claims for damages.

In respect of other initiatives, the Organisation of American States has not been inactive. In 1985, the Inter American Convention to Prevent and Punish Torture was adopted; Art 2 of the same stipulated that state parties would prevent and punish torture, while Art 12 provided that states should legislate to ensure jurisdiction over torture as a criminal act; to complement these provisions, Art 13 required that torture should be included as an extradition crime between states. In a related matter, a Protocol on the Abolition of the Death Penalty was adopted in June 1990,[209] whereby state parties agreed not to apply the death penalty although a limited reservation was permissible in respect of serious conduct in time of war.

One of the most significant abuses of the 1970s had been the forced disappearance of individuals in certain Latin American states. This concern has been given effect to in the Inter American Convention on the Forced Disappearance of Persons (1994) in which such conduct is described in the preamble as a crime against humanity. Such a practice is outlawed by Art 1 and, under the terms of Art 3, such conduct is to be made criminal by all state parties; under the terms of Arts 13 and 14, state parties agree that where a complaint is made to the Inter American Commission on Human Rights such a matter is to be investigated as quickly as possible and that any such government should respond as quickly as possible to requests for information.

In the sphere of economic and social rights further steps have been taken. In 1988, an Additional Protocol on Economic and Social Rights was adopted.[210] The Protocol

---

205 *The Application of Costa Rica concerning the case of Viviana Gallardo* (1981) 20 ILM 1424; 67 ILR 578; 2 HRLJ 328.

206 *Valasquez Rodriquez* case (Judgment of 29 July 1988) (1988) 9 HRLJ 212.

207 *Valasquez Rodriguez* case (Judgment of 21 July 1989) (1989) 11 HRLJ 127.

208 *Valasquez Rodriguez – Interpretation of Compensatory Damages ond the Judgment of 21 July 1989* (1991) 12 HRLJ 14.

209 Technically it was the Protocol to the American Convention on Human Rights to Abolish the Death Penalty (1990).

210 Known as the Protocol of San Salvador of 14 November 1988 (1989) 14 ILM 156. The full tile is 'The Additional Protocol to the American Convention on Human rights in the Area of Economic, Social and Cultural Rights (The Protocol of San Salvador) (1988)'.

provides for just conditions of work,[211] social security[212] and the right to trade union membership[213] as well as the right to health[214] and education.[215] Under the terms of Art 19 of the Protocol periodic reports are to be submitted to the Secretary General of the Organisation of American States which will then be sent to a number of bodies, including the Inter American Commission on Human Rights. In cases where rights of trade union membership or education are being flouted then an application may be made under the enforcement procedures of the American Convention on Human Rights.[216]

4 AFRICA[217]

There are now 50 African states that are members of the United Nations. The political landscape of the continent has been transformed since the late 1950s, when decolonisation began to gather pace. As has been noted by political scientists the newly established states have faced problems of poverty, illiteracy and health provision; ethnic difficulties and boundary disputes are present in a number of areas. These burdens are compounded by limited capital investment, problems of corruption and, in some areas, the absence of representative democratic government. In these circumstances, with the absence of political homogeneity there are bound to be considerable problems in establishing and promoting a regional framework of human rights.

Decolonisation in the early 1960s stimulated interest in efforts at regional co-operation. The tangible result was the drafting of the Charter of the Organisation of African Unity in 1963. Article II of the Charter includes among the aims of the organisation the desire 'to promote the unity and solidarity of African states' and 'to eradicate all forms of colonialism from Africa' as well as 'to promote international co-operation, having due regard to the Charter of the United Nations and the Universal Declaration of Human Rights'. The Organisation of African Unity (OAU) is based in Addis Ababa and operates through an Assembly of Heads of State and Government and a Council of Foreign Ministers. After 1963, much discussion took place as to the desirability of a regional human rights treaty and conferences on the subject were held in 1969, 1971 and 1973;[218] in 1979, the Assembly of Heads of State of the Organisation of

---

211 Protocol of San Salvador, Art 7.

212 *Ibid*, Art 9.

213 *Ibid*, Art 8.

214 *Ibid*, Art 10.

215 *Ibid*, Art 13.

216 *Ibid*, Art 19(6).

217 See generally, TO Elias (1964) 40 BYIL 336; TO Elias (1965) 59 AJIL 243; R Gittleman (1982) 22 Va JIL 667; U Umzorike (1983) 77 AJIL 902; S Neff (1984) 33 ICLQ 331; R Kikwanuka (1988) 82 AJIL 80; T Muluwa (1989) 38 ICLQ 299.

218 In Cairo, Addis Ababa and Dar-es-Salaam respectively. All three being held under the auspices of the United Nations.

African Unity requested the Secretary General to prepare a draft instrument. The preliminary version of the African Charter of Human and People's Rights was drafted in Banjul (Gambia) in 1980 and formally adopted at the 18th Assembly Meeting of the Heads of State and Government of the Organisation of African Unity at Nairobi, Kenya in June 1981; the instrument entered into force on 21 October 1986.[219]

A number of general points can usefully be made about the African Charter. First, the Charter is concerned to protect not only civil and political rights but also economic and social rights. The preamble contains the observation that 'it is henceforth essential to pay particular attention to the right to development and that civil and political rights cannot be dissociated from economic, social and cultural rights in their conception as well as universality and that the satisfaction of economic, social and cultural rights is a guarantee for the enjoyment of civil and political rights'. Secondly, the Charter is concerned to protect not simply 'individuals' but also 'peoples'; the latter are protected in respect of collective rights sometimes described as third generation rights.[220] Thirdly, the African Charter emphasises that the individual while the beneficiary of rights also owes duties to the family, society and the state,[221] thus reflecting the African view of the obligations that the individual owes to the wider community.

In respect of the structure of the Charter, Art 1 commits all member states to respect the rights and duties arising under the Charter while Art 2 stipulates that all rights and duties are to be enjoyed without discrimination. Thereafter, Arts 3–16 are concerned to set out traditional civil and political liberties[222] and draw upon the contents of other human rights instruments. One interesting feature is the seeming freedom allowed for national law. Thus, Art 10(1) reads: 'Every individual shall have the right to free association provided that he abides by the law.' Articles 17 and 18 set out the economic, social and cultural rights which have some affinity with those set out in the International Covenant on Economic, Social and Cultural Rights (1966).

The rights in respect of peoples are set out in Arts 19–24. Articles 19 and 20 set out the right of equality and the right of self-determination; these two concepts draw upon the United Nations Covenants of 1966. These two documents also inspired Art 21 which asserts rights in respect of wealth and natural resources. The history of Africa has been such that it is not surprising that Art 22 recognises the right of people's to economic, social and cultural development. Article 23 stipulates a right to peace and security while Art 24 provides that 'all people's shall have the right to a generally satisfactory environment'. Clearly, the nature of such rights is designed to have implications both for the conduct of domestic and foreign policy. The implications of such rights for the

---

219 At March 2000, 53 African states were parties.

220 References to 'people' appear in Art 19 (equality), Art 20 (existence and self-determination), Art 21 (natural resources), Art 22 (economic development), Art 23 (peace), Art 24 (the environment).

221 See Arts 27, 28, 29 of the Charter.

222 These being: (i) the right to equality before the law; (ii) the right to respect for life and integrity of the person; (iii) freedom from exploitation and degradation; (iv) the right to liberty and security of the person; (v) the right to a fair trial; (vi) freedom from retrospective laws; (vii) freedom of conscience; (viii) the right to receive information and express opinions; (ix) freedom of association; (x) freedom of assembly; (xi) freedom of movement; (xii) prohibition of mass expulsion; (xiii) the right to participate in government; (xiv) the right of access to public service; (xv) the right of access to public property; (xvi) the right to property.

conduct of government has been taken into account by stipulating a number of duties[223] that are owed by the individual to his family and the state. This is perhaps not so unusual when one considers that the purpose of Art 29 is to qualify rights stated earlier. It has to be borne in mind that the European Convention on Human Rights contains qualifications in a number of individual articles; in the case of the African Charter Art 29 acts as an general article of limitation.

The implementation of the Charter is the responsibility of the African Commission on Human and People's Rights.[224] The Commission comprises 11 members of the highest moral standing;[225] the commissioners serve in their personal capacity[226] and no state may at any one time contribute more than one commissioner.[227] Elections are supervised by the Secretary General of the Organisation of African Unity;[228] commissioners serve for a six year period[229] and are obliged to discharge their duties impartially and faithfully.[230] The Commission functions through a Chairman and a Vice Chairman.[231] The role of the Commission is both to promote Human and People's Rights as well as to ensure their protection.[232]

If one state party has reason to believe that another state party is responsible for violating the Charter, then it may draw the matter to the attention of that other party[233] and, if no satisfactory explanation is received within a period of three months, then it may submit the matter to the Commission.[234] The Commission may only deal with the matter if all obvious local remedies have been invoked.[235] In the event of an investigation, the Commission has freedom as to the manner in which it investigates, but it is entitled to serve notice on a state to provide it with all relevant information.[236] Having obtained all relevant information, the Commission will seek to reach an amicable solution,[237] but if that is not possible it will submit a report together with recommendations to the Assembly of Heads of State and Government.[238] In respect of complaints from individuals or non-governmental organisations,[239] while there is freedom to complain no communication can be examined unless it can overcome the rather demanding criteria of

---

223 Article 29 stipulates eight duties: (i) the duty to the family; (ii) the duty to use one's abilities for the service of the state; (iii) the duty to avoid damaging the security of the state; (iv) the duty to strengthen social solidarity; (v) the duty to preserve national independence; (vi) the duty to work and pay taxes; (vii) the duty to preserve African cultural values; (viiii) the duty to do one's best to promote African unity.
224 African Charter on Human and Peoples' Rights (1981), Art 30.
225 *Ibid*, Art 31.
226 *Ibid*, Art 31(2).
227 *Ibid*, Art 32.
228 *Ibid*, Art 35.
229 *Ibid*, Art 36.
230 *Ibid*, Art 38.
231 *Ibid*, Art 42.
232 *Ibid*, Art 45.
233 *Ibid*, Art 47.
234 *Ibid*, Art 48.
235 *Ibid*, Art 50.
236 *Ibid*, Arts 46 and 51.
237 *Ibid*, Art 52.
238 *Ibid*, Arts 52 and 53.
239 *Ibid*, Art 55.

Art 56. In particular, no communication can be considered if it is 'based exclusively on news disseminated through the mass media'. Moreover, prior to any substantive consideration the matter must be brought to the attention of the state concerned.[240] In cases of a pattern of individual complaints that disclose evidence of serious violations, then the Commission may draw the matter to the attention of the Assembly of Heads of State and Government.[241]

It has to be admitted that the original Charter lacking a judicial body, with rather vague provisions and operating with limited resources was likely to encounter difficulties.[242] First, there is a well established historical link between democratic government and the observance of human rights; in 1981, few of the states launching the African Charter could be described as fully functioning democracies. Secondly, there have been complaints since 1986 that the non-binding findings of the Commission have had limited effect. Thirdly, while the Charter requires reports to be submitted every two years,[243] compliance has been limited and the constructive dialogue envisaged does not seem to have taken place.[244]

Thus, by the mid 1990s, a view began to emerge that the system needed to be strengthened by the addition of a judicial branch. This change of heart was precipitated by atrocities in a number of states[245] and a greater level of interest by the outside world. In these circumstances, in June 1994 the Assembly of Heads of State and Government requested the Secretary General of the Organisation of African Unity to convene the appropriate meeting of experts. Following three such meetings,[246] in June 1998 the Protocol to the African Charter on Human and People's Rights on the Establishment of an African Court on Human and People's Rights (AHRC) was adopted by the Organisation of African Unity. The broad intention is that the AHRC should complement and strengthen the efforts of the Commission.

---

240 *Ibid*, Art 57.

241 *Ibid*, Art 58.

242 It has been pointed out by commentators that: (i) only a limited number of the states in question were functioning democracies; (ii) the absence of a judicial branch was a serious flaw; although (iii) some argued that the Charter was simply a starting point and largely promotional. For a review, see Makau Mutua (1999) 21 HRQ 342.

243 African Charter on Human and Peoples' Rights (1981), Art 62.

244 See Felice D Gaer (1992) 10 NQHR 29 for a consideration of state reporting under the African Charter. It has been pointed out that the Charter: (i) does not specify the reports to be submitted; (ii) does not stipulate criteria for judgment; (iii) does not indicate what action should be taken in event of non-compliance. See also O Okere (1984) 6 HRQ 141; J Cobbah (1987) 9 HRQ 309.

245 The tragic events in Rwanda and violations in Nigeria, Liberia, Somalia, Ethiopia, Sudan and Sierra Leone, Burundi, the Republic of the Congo and the Democratic Republic of the Congo. Several were of such a serious nature as to lead to a breakdown of law and order and a need for outside help (eg, Sierra Leone). For litigation arising from such events see *Republic of Somalia v Woodhouse, Drake & Carey (Suisse) SA* [1993] QB 54 (Hobhouse J); *Sierra Leone Telecommunications Co Ltd v Barclays Bank plc* [1998] 2 All ER 821 (Cresswell J).

246 The preliminary meetings taking place in South Africa (September 1995), Mauritania (April 1997) and Addis Ababa, Ethiopia (December 1997).

The Protocol provides for the establishment within the Organisation of African Unity of an African Court on Human and People's Rights.[247] The purpose of the Court is to complement the jurisdiction of the Commission;[248] the Court will have jurisdiction to deliver advisory opinions.[249] Access to the court will be enjoyed by the Commission and by state parties that have complained, together with those state parties against whom a complaint has been made or whose citizen is the victim of a human rights violation.[250] The Court is instructed to apply the provisions of the Charter[251] and, while conducting hearings in public,[252] may try to effect an amicable settlement between the parties.[253] The Court itself is to be composed of 11 judges[254] who will be elected by the Assembly of the Organisation of African Unity;[255] the term of office will be six years[256] and individual judges are to discharge their duties with independence and impartiality.[257] A judge may only be removed by a unanimous vote of the Court;[258] the tribunal will operate with a quorum of seven judges. The court is entitled to receive written, oral and expert testimony;[259] in appropriate cases, it may make a finding of a violation of a human or peoples' rights and order compensation or reparation.[260] The state parties undertake to comply with the judgment of the Court in those cases to which they are party.[261] Under the terms of Art 34 the Protocol[262] requires 15 ratifications to come into effect.

5 THE ARAB WORLD[263]

The dissolution of the Ottoman Empire after 1919 gave way to the mandate system established by the League of Nations. It was, however, only after 1945 that a significant number of Arab states began to emerge so as to make regional co-operation a viable option. In March 1945, the League of Arab States was established when seven countries (Egypt, Iraq, Jordan, Lebanon, Saudi Arabia, Syria and Yemen) signed the Pact of the League of Arab States. The general objectives of the League were set out in the Pact and

---

247 Protocol on the Establishment of an African Court on Human and Peoples' Rights (1998), Art 1.
248 *Ibid*, Art 2.
249 *Ibid*, Art 4.
250 *Ibid*, Art 5.
251 *Ibid*, Art 7.
252 *Ibid*, Art 10.
253 *Ibid*, Art 9.
254 *Ibid*, Art 11.
255 *Ibid*, Art 14.
256 *Ibid*, Art 15.
257 *Ibid*, Arts 16 and 17.
258 *Ibid*, Art 19.
259 *Ibid*, Art 26.
260 *Ibid*, Art 27.
261 *Ibid*, Art 30.
262 Article 34.2 provides that the Protocol will come into effect 30 days after the receipt of the 15th ratification. By mid 2000, 11 instruments of ratifications had been obtained.
263 For general background, see B Boutros Ghali, 'The Arab League (1945–70)' (1969) 25 *Revue Egyptiènne de Droit International* 67.

included 'the strengthening of the relations between the member states; the co-ordination of their policies in order to achieve their independence and sovereignty; and a general concern with the affairs and interests of the Arab countries'. In 1950, a Treaty for Joint Defence and Co-operation was signed by Egypt, Lebanon, Syria, Saudi Arabia, and Yemen; it was acceded to by Iraq in 1951 and Jordan in 1952. The remaining Arab countries joined in 1964. The Joint Defence Treaty describes the Arab League as a regional organisation for the purposes of the United Nations Charter. In the 1950s, Arab states had different political structures; some were hereditary monarchies while others were presidential republics. At the outset, the regional arrangements were based on military security and diplomatic co-operation.

In 1966, the Arab League was asked to participate in the International Conference on Human Rights to be held in Tehran in 1968. In 1967, the Arab League decided in principle to establish a Commission on Human Rights. In December 1968, the Council of the League held a regional Conference on Human Rights in Beirut; at the conference it was announced that a Permanent Arab Commission on Human Rights was to be established. The subject had acquired a greater degree of prominence because of concern arising form the occupation of territory following the Arab-Israeli conflict of June 1967.

The Commission which includes representatives of all Arab states is charged with preparing proposals for the Council. In principle, it is concerned with the promotion of human rights; to this end, it has urged the establishment of human rights commissions in Arab states and it has made representations on behalf of those living in territory occupied since 1967. From the 1970s, a number of schemes had been put forward for codifying human rights in a single document which would reflect the Islamic basis of such rights. However, little progress was made during the years of the Iran-Iraq[264] war and it was not until after the Gulf War[265] that, in 1994, an Arab Charter on Human Rights was adopted by the League of Arab States. The document stresses both the Islamic tradition of equality and brotherhood but also the legacy of the Universal Declaration of Human Rights (1948). Articles 5–39 set out a wide range of civil, political and economic rights; of particular notice are the requirements as to proper criminal procedure and restrictions on the use of the death penalty which, by Art 10, is to be confined to the most serious crimes and is not to be inflicted on a person under 18 years of age. Interestingly, Art 19 asserts that 'the people are the source of political authority' while Arts 27 and 37 provide for freedom of religious observance. The Charter is to be enforced by a reporting system. Article 40 provides for the establishment of a Committee of Experts on Human Rights which is to be elected by secret ballot. Article 41 requires state parties to make an initial report and thereafter to make reports every three years. Under the terms of Art 42 the Charter will come into effect on the receipt of the seventh instrument of ratification.

---

264 1980–88.
265 1990–91.

6 CONCLUSIONS

In some areas of public international law the emphasis has been to produce a single codifying treaty which although founded on certain compromises is valid upon ratification throughout the entire world. Examples of such documents would be the Vienna Convention on Diplomatic Relations (1961) or the United Nations Law of the Sea Convention (1982). In the case of human rights law, the subject operates at both the international level and the regional level. Given differences in economic and social conditions and the need to provide measures of enforcement, regional supervision has much to commend it, not least on grounds of proximity and practicality.

Manifestly, improved education, publicity and modes of transport have contributed to a better understanding of human rights violations. New techniques of journalism and news gathering have enabled one part of the world to learn almost simultaneously of violations committed many thousands of miles away. In consequence, a wider range of institutions now exist to promote, protect and restrain abuses of human rights. While generalisations should normally be qualified, the evidence does seem to indicate that human rights (at least civil and political rights) are best protected by those states possessed of an openly elected democratic government operating under a written constitution and within the rule of law.

In contrast, the least respect for human rights appears to be found in regimes of a totalitarian nature where there is a reluctance to allow freedom of discussion and participation in civic life. Thus, some of the grossest abuses are to be found existing under military juntas, individual dictatorships or hardline communist regimes. To the extent that Marxist Leninist regimes have largely been swept away, the general prospects have improved for observance of human rights.

Related to the question of human rights are considerations of economic prosperity and peace. Those states that respect human rights tend to be stable societies that attract capital investment and do not threaten their neighbours; those states that abuse human rights often threaten their neighbours and, save in the case of military equipment, are often unable to attract foreign investment. Respect for human rights provides the contented and stable society that encourages investment and thus economic growth. A failure to respect basic civil liberties discourages investment and acts as an obstacle to economic growth.

While there may be legitimate concerns about methods of enforcement the present procedures are grounded in experience; methods of state reporting, inter-state complaint and individual application complement each other very well. Allied to this is the growing conviction that individuals charged with gross abuses should stand trial before criminal courts. The recent attention devoted to restricting claims of immunity[266] and the efforts being made to establish an International Criminal Court are steps in the same direction.

Although it is certainly true that international and regional protection has a proper role in raising standards it is sensible to bear in mind the domestic element. The most reliable method of ensuring respect for human rights is to ensure that democratically

---

266 *R v Bow Street Metropolitan Stipendiary Magistrate ex p Pinochet Ugarte (No 1)* [2000] 1 AC 61; *R v Bow Street Metropolitan Stipendiary Magistrate ex p Pinochet Ugarte (No 3)* [2000] 1 AC 147.

elected governments operate under a written constitution that enshrines the principles if not the text of the Universal Declaration on Human Rights (1948); the acts of such a government should be subject to review by an independent judiciary. It is thus no coincidence that the rise in human rights law since 1945 has been matched by increasing emphasis on the importance of constitutional law, particularly in the sphere of judicial review of administrative action.

In reviewing progress much is a matter of individual opinion. Many will accept that the United Nations has been active in promotional work and the Universal Declaration of Human Rights (1948) has proved to be a model for many written constitutional documents. However, the enforcement provisions under the 1966 Covenants are limited indeed and in many situations the United Nations has seemed unable to restrain gross abuses.[267] It is clear that proper account has to be taken of economic, cultural and social factors and a tension exists between those who argue that human rights ought to be universal and those who assert that human rights are universal. Some human rights are now so sophisticated that it is absurd not to pay regard to the economic background. To take an obvious example the entitlement to proper health care involves complex questions as to how revenue is raised through taxation; in many states there will be a variety of opinions as to how this is to be achieved. If a state has no proper system of tax collection or a corrupt structure of government, then some collective human rights will prove impossible to establish.

In these circumstances, many look to progress being made at the regional level. This has proved possible in Europe where many states share a common social background and where levels of economic prosperity do not vary significantly. However, in other regional systems this degree of homogeneity is not present and thus less progress has been made.

In the circumstances, while much remains to be done, most would agree that human rights law, which barely existed in 1945, now occupies a central position within the overall corpus of public international law. To some extent differences of opinion centre on methods rather than objectives.

---

267 The most obvious being the events in Rwanda in 1994.

CHAPTER 17

INTERNATIONAL ENVIRONMENTAL LAW[1]

1 INTRODUCTION

In the last 30 years the topic of international environmental law has assumed an increasing prominence. However, it would be wrong to think of the topic as a distinct subject with its own terminology;[2] traditional concepts such as the principle of territorial sovereignty and the doctrine of state responsibility have a continuing role to play. Nevertheless, there has been a steady increase in the number of institutional structures and the volume of treaty law. The area of international environmental law is indeed extensive and embraces the problems posed by transboundary air pollution, the use of nuclear power and the carriage of hazardous waste while also attempting to mitigate the damage posed by acid rain, ozone depletion, climate change and loss of biodiversity. The agenda is broad and ever increasing.

At first blush, such problems arise from the interdependence of the world environment and are difficult to resolve because they raise fundamental questions about the balance to be struck between the pace of economic growth and the need for limitations on personal or corporate conduct. Moreover, in a world of over 180 states there will always be difficulties as to where this balance is to be struck; in some situations, scientific evidence may provide a clear pointer but, in other situations, scientific opinion may be equivocal and there may be strong economic arguments to consider. In many instances, the opinion of the developed state may differ from that of the developing state.

The increase in interest in environmental matters has been part of the general landscape since 1945. In some states this is a matter of history and, in others, it may be the result of a particular political viewpoint but, be that as it may, there is little doubt that concern for the environment is in most states a matter that engages the attention of senior politicians and administrators. The reasons for this are not difficult to discern. First, scientific advances have made man aware of the damage that his activities can do to the planet. Secondly, in some instances the evidence has indicated that the damage may be irreversible. Thirdly, in some situations a link has been made between environmental conditions and individual health so that questions have arisen as to the relationship between human rights law and a clean environment. Fourthly, in many wealthier states

---

1   See generally, A Kiss and D Shelton, *International Environmental Law*, 1991; P Birnie and A Boyle, *International Law and the Environment*, 1992; P Sands, *Principles of International Environmental Law*, 1995; I Brownlie, *Principles of Public International Law*, 5th edn, 1998, Chapter 13; HL Dickstein (1974) 23 ICLQ 426; A Springer (1977) 26 ICLQ 531; M Lachs (1990) 39 ICLQ 663; P Sands (1994) 65 BYIL 303; D McGoldrick (1996) 45 ICLQ 796; PN Okowa (1996) 67 BYIL 275; D French (2000) 49 ICLQ 35.

2   It is probably better to adopt the approach of Professor Brownlie who, in the fifth edition of his *Principles of Public International Law* (1998), adopts the title of 'Legal Aspects of the Protection of the Environment' rather than 'International Environmental Law'. As the learned author notes, 'the legal underpinnings of the protection of the environment continue to be the institutions of general international law'.

improvements in technology have enabled a choice to be made in favour of production methods that do less damage to the environment. A fifth important element is the steady rise in the influence of NGOs[3] in this area; such organisations have steadily increased in both membership and resources.[4]

Concern for the environment is at least as old as the process of industrialisation. The industrial revolution beginning in England and extending to Europe and the United States was based in its early phase on heavy industries such as coal, iron and steel all of which posed a threat to the immediate environment. In England, the response at first was to rely on the law of nuisance;[5] later, the law of restrictive covenants[6] introduced a degree of private control and then hazardous activities began to be subject to the rule in *Rylands v Fletcher*.[7] In short, municipal law had to develop to protect the environment from particular activities. However, these forms of legal action were based on private law so that it soon became necessary for governments to introduce some form of planning legislation[8] specifying which activities could be conducted in particular areas. As the Bhopal incident in India[9] indicated, there are obvious dangers if certain industrial processes are conducted adjacent to residential areas. Many developed states will have detailed systems of planning law that require permission before certain activities can be conducted. To put the matter another way there is a clear distinction in many systems of municipal law between the ownership of property and the use that can be made of that property.

It is possible to discern the same evolution in the sphere of international law; in the 19th century states in Europe began to co-operate on matters of common interest[10] and certain rather vague rules of customary law began to emerge as to the duties that one

---

3   For an account of one such organisation, see Robert Lamb, *Promising the Earth*, 1996.

4   A noteworthy feature in the United Kingdom has been the willingness of the courts to liberalise the rules on *locus standi* to enable pressure groups to bring environmentally related claims. See *R v Poole BC ex p Beebee* (1991) JPL 643; *R v Her Majesty's Inspectorate of Pollution ex p Greenpeace (No 2)* [1994] 4 All ER 329; *R v Secretary of State for Foreign and Commonwealth Affairs ex p World Development Movement* [1995] 1 All ER 611.

5   See *St Helens Smelting Co v Tipping* (1865) 11 HLC 642 (for subsequent injunction, see (1865) LR 1 Ch 66); *Gaunt v Fynney* (1872) 8 Ch App 8; *Salvin v North Brancepeth Coal Co* (1874) 9 Ch App 706n, affd (1874) 9 Ch App 706.

6   Following the judgment in *Tulk v Moxhay* (1848) 2 Ph 774, the landowner in England who sold off land was entitled to impose restrictive conditions on the use by the future purchaser (ie, covenantor) of that land and to enforce that covenant by injunction against any future assignee of the purchase who had actual or constructive notice of the covenant.

7   *Rylands v Fletcher* (1866) LR 1 Ex 265; affd (1868) LR 3 HL 330.

8   In England, such a system was introduced as late as 1909 in the Housing, Town Planning etc Act 1909, which was followed by the Town and Country Planning Act 1932 and later considerably extended in the Town and Country Planning Act 1947. Since that date planning law in England has been subject to consolidation in 1962, 1971 and 1990. The basic law being contained in the Town and Country Planning Act 1990.

9   At Bhopal, In India in December 1984 an incident at a plant owned by Union Carbide India Ltd resulted in the escape of methyl isocyanate (MIC – a chemical precursor used in the manufacture of the pesticide Sevin) causing the deaths of around 3,000 people and injured very many more. The incident prompted discussion as to the need for planning systems to ensure that potentially dangerous industrial processes are kept away from residential areas.

10 The Congress of Vienna (1815) resulted in the establishment of the Rhine Commission which had legislative and judicial powers and in which littoral states participated. It was followed by the European Commission on the Danube (1856); at the same time commissions for the Elbe (1821), Douro (1835) and the Po (1849) were established with more limited powers.

state might owe another. Gradually, it came to be recognised that more than vague rules would be required. However, any the scope for development was constrained by certain basic factors. First, international law traditionally proceeded on the basis of the territorial sovereignty of the state and its freedom to act within its own territory. By 'territory' is meant the land within the relevant boundaries, the internal waters,[11] territorial sea and airspace.[12] Secondly, international law traditionally proceeded on the basis that one state would not interfere in the affairs of another or act so as to do damage to it. These assumptions have, however, had to be modified since 1945. First, the environmental problems caused by state A may affect state B (for example, transboundary pollution) or indeed the more remote state C (for example, where pollution in state A causes acid rain in state C); alternatively, negligent conduct in state A may affect the entire region (for example, a nuclear accident). Although the general movement has been towards greater protection of the environment, the emphasis has changed according to circumstances. In the 1930s, much attention was devoted to problems of transboundary pollution. However, by the 1950s, the growth in the size of oil tankers shifted the emphasis to problems of marine pollution and international action was taken. By the 1970s, attention was focused on problems of chemical dumping and damage to flora and fauna. During that same decade, scientific research was being undertaken that lead in the 1980s to concerns about ozone layer depletion, climate change and lack of biodiversity. In short, there is a steady movement from the local problem in the 19th century to the transboundary problem and then to the regional and global problem. It is also relevant to note that improvements in televised news reporting enabled the full consequences of environmental damage to be brought home to the general public in western Europe and North America.

At this stage it is sensible to say a little about definitions. The word 'environment' is one of those widely used expressions whose meaning varies according to the context in which it is employed. It has been defined as 'surrounding; surrounding objects, region or circumstances'.[13] Thus, the expression is broader than 'nature'. A second widely used expression is 'ecology', which has been defined as a 'branch of biology dealing with living organisms'[14] habits, modes of life, and relations to their surroundings'. More recently, the word 'ecosystem' has been employed and this has been defined as 'a unit of ecology, which includes the plants and animals occurring together, plus that part of their environment over which they have an influence'.[15] However, the meaning of such expressions will have to be displaced where a specific treaty gives a particular meaning to an expression. Thus, a distinction has in this area has to be drawn between precise scientific definitions, the use in general political discourse and the employment of terms in international treaties. Secondly, as noted above, it is clear that the scope of environmental law is wide and getting wider embracing the atmosphere the land, the seas and outer space. Scientific discoveries often lead to demands for national or international regulation thus creating a specialist area of law.

---

11 UNCLOS (1982), Art 8.
12 *Ibid*, Art 2.
13 The *Concise Oxford Dictionary*, 5th edn, 1964; see the French verb *envirroner* – to surround.
14 The *Concise Oxford Dictionary*, 5th edn, 1964, see Greek *oikos* meaning 'house'.
15 The *Compact Oxford English Dictionary*, 2nd edn, 1991.

At this point it is necessary to make a few general remarks about the broad evolution of the subject.

2 THE EVOLUTION OF INTERNATIONAL ENVIRONMENTAL LAW

As a distinct subject international environmental law is less than two decades old but it draws upon earlier developments. A number of writers have identified four historical periods, namely: (i) the period from the development of industrialisation until the establishment of the United Nations; (ii) the period from 1945 until the United Nations Conference on the Human Environment held in Stockholm in June 1972; (iii) the period from 1972 until the United Nations Conference on Environment and Development held in June 1992 in Rio de Janeiro, Brazil; (iv) the period from 1992. It is sensible to say a little about each period.

(a) The first period: from industrialisation to 1945

Interest in the natural environment can be traced at least to the period of the Enlightenment when scientists sought to understand the nature and history of the physical universe and to reconcile the facts found with traditional thought. The emphasis on empirical evidence and human reason prompted this development. Thus, Buffon[16] having outlined natural history had considered the cooling of the earth by 1778 while Montesquieu[17] wrote about both the history of the planet and the nature of plant life. At the same time Diderot[18] viewed the world as but matter and motion and assumed in 1769 in *Rêve de d'Alembert* that all life was relative to its material environment. However, the writers of the Enlightenment were, in the pre-industrial age, less concerned with protection of the environment than with understanding the history of the universe and how it might be reconciled with the works of scripture and the authority of the classics.

The process of industrialisation[19] stimulated concern for environmental conditions; observers noted the damage caused by early industrialisation and such misgivings[20]

---

16 Jean Louis Comte de Buffon (1707–88). The first volume of *L'Histoire Naturelle* appeared in 1749; in 1778 in *Epoques de la Nature* he examined the history of the earth and the length of time required for the planet to cool.

17 Charles Baron de Montesquieu (1689–1755). In 1721, in *Lettres Persanes* Montesquieu discussed whether a date for the creation of the earth could be arrived at. In the years 1719–21, he delivered papers at the Academy of Bordeaux on the nature and structure of plant life. He is, of course, better known today for *De l'Esprit des Lois* (1748) which, amongst other insights, held that the laws of any society tended to reflect the social, political and geographical forces within that society.

18 Denis Diderot (1713–84). In *Rêve de d'Alembert* (1769), he linked the condition of human life and human values with the material environment.

19 For 19th century attempts in England to invoke the law of nuisance, see *Attorney General v Birmingham* (1858) 4 K & J 528; *St Helens Smelting Co v Tipping* (1865) 11 HLC 642; *Sturges v Bridgman* (1879) 11 Ch D 852.

20 In Chapter 5 of his *The Condition of the Working Class in England* (first published Leipzig 1845) Frederick Engels describes the dirt and semi permanent clouds of coal smoke that hung over some industrial towns in England in 1844. That the situation persisted is indicated by the Royal Commission on Noxious Vapours which, in 1878, referred to those 'whose houses are rendered almost uninhabitable by the stench of sulphurretted hydrogen'.

resulted in pressure for public health[21] and housing legislation[22] in England. As the century progressed, a local government structure[23] was put in place and the scope of such legislation was extended. On the international plane progress was limited; treaties were adopted to prevent overfishing[24] and to protect migratory birds.[25] The year 1900 witnessed the first treaty designed to protect wildlife[26] and this was extended in 1933;[27] two years earlier, the first international agreement on whaling was concluded.[28] However, taken in the round the law making effort was rather sporadic and devoted to particular issues; in the circumstances this is probably not surprising given the increasing tension in Europe after 1933. Elsewhere, Canada and the United States had concluded the Water Boundaries Treaty in 1909 which constituted the first international instrument which imposed burdens on parties to avoid pollution.

Of perhaps more enduring significance was the fact that the general movement in favour of arbitration had resulted in two instances of international awards developing the customary law in this area. The awards in the *Pacific Fur Seal Arbitration*[29] and the later *Trail Smelter* case[30] were to have a considerable effect on the development of customary international law and are therefore considered below. However, by 1939 the efforts at international co-operation were limited and indeed many Western European economies were dependent on traditional heavy industry (coal, steel, iron, textiles, engineering, mining) while others adhered to accepted principles of territorial sovereignty.

(b) The second period: 1945–72

The second period begins with the signing of the United Nations Charter in 1945. The charter itself did not contain any express reference to the environment although Art 1(3) is certainly wide enough to include the topic if only by implication. Two other events in 1945 prompted discussion as to environmental damage. First, the decision to employ nuclear weapons in armed conflict in August 1945 prompted discussion as to the environmental consequences of such weapons and raised in the starkest terms the related question as to the ethical limits on certain forms of human conduct. Secondly, one of the

---

21 Public Health Act 1848; Public Health Act 1875.

22 Housing of the Working Classes Act 1885 and 1890.

23 Municipal Corporations Act 1835; Local Government Act 1888 and 1894.

24 North Seas Fisheries (Overfishing Convention) 1882.

25 Convention between United States and Great Britain for the Protection of Migratory Birds in the United States and Canada (1916).

26 Convention Destinée a Assurer la Conservation des Diverses Espèces Animales Vivant à l'Etat Sauvage en Afrique qui sont Utiles a l'Homme, London, 19 May 1900.

27 Convention on the Preservation of Fauna and Flora in their Natural State, London, 8 November 1933.

28 Convention for the Regulation of Whaling, Geneva, 24 September 1931.

29 (1893) 1 Moore's International Arbitration Awards 755.

30 *Trail Smelter Arbitration (US v Canada)* (1941) 3 RIAA 1905.

justifications for the Truman Declaration on the Continental Shelf in September 1945 was to ensure 'conservation and prudent utilisation'.[31]

The specialised agencies set up after 1945 did not include a body specifically devoted to the environment but the constitutional documents of both the Food and Agriculture Organisation (FAO) and the United Nations Educational, Scientific and Cultural Organisation (UNESCO) include matters that pertain to the environment and conservation. However, in 1947 ECOSOC resolved[32] to call a conference devoted to environmental concerns. The resolution while acknowledging the importance of conservation provided for the calling of a United Nations Conference on the Conservation and Utilisation of Resources (UNCCUR). The Conference met in New York from 17 August 1949 until 6 September 1949 and many of the topics discussed centred upon the relationship between conservation and development. It is arguable that the significance of the conference lay less in policy announcements but in generally broadening the terms of the agenda.

On a wider canvass the General Assembly were beginning to discuss problems such as oil pollution and atmospheric nuclear testing which would in the course of the next decade lead to the 1963 Test Ban Treaty.[33] In respect of the marine environment the efforts of the International Maritime Organisation resulted in 1954 in the adoption of the International Convention for the Prevention of Pollution of the Sea by Oil[34] and this instrument was to be followed by others in the next two decades as the threats of spillage to the marine environment became ever more apparent. At the same time, the International Law Commission began preparatory work on the codification of the law of the sea. The 1958 Geneva Convention on the High Seas (1958) contained specific article dealing with pollution and the matter was taken further in the Geneva Convention on Fishing and Conservation of the Living Resources of the High Seas (1958). At about the same time, the Antarctic Treaty (1959) contained provisions designed to prevent environmental damage through the disposal of radioactive waste. While on the regional level the European Commission began to take a close interest in environmental protection notwithstanding the absence of specific provisions in the Treaty of Rome in 1957 and, in Africa, the African Nature Convention of 1968 was wider in scope than anything previously attempted for that region.

During the same period there were a number of cases that sought to clarify obligations in customary international law.[35] The principles of state responsibility in this

---

31 It is not without relevance that when CAR Crosland published *The Future of Socialism* in 1956, the author drew particular attention to regional and environmental concerns; the author returned to the topic in *Socialism Now*, 1974.

32 ECOSOC Resolution 32(IV) (1947).

33 The 1963 Treaty Banning Nuclear Weapons Testing in the Atmosphere, Outer Space and Under Water. This was followed by the Treaty on the Prohibition of the Emplacement of Nuclear Weapons of Mass Destruction on the Sea Bed (1971). At the same time, regional initiatives resulted in the signing of the Treaty for the Prohibition of Nuclear Weapons in Latin America (1967) and the South Pacific Nuclear Free Zone Treaty (1985).

34 Came into force on 26 July 1958.

35 The nature of customary international law is considered below.

context were examined by the International Court of Justice in the *Corfu Channel* case[36] and later by the arbitration tribunal in the *Lac Lenoux Arbitration*.[37] However, by the late 1960s there was growing concern about the relationship between development and growth and comment on the absence of a single body charged with the issue.[38] These concerns were ventilated further at the International Conference of Experts on the Scientific Basis for Rational Use and Conservation of the Resources of the Biosphere which was convened by UNESCO in 1968. The conference contrasted the growth of interest in environmental questions with the failure to make progress at the international level. In July 1968, ECOSOC passed a resolution in favour of an international conference[39] and in December 1968 this was endorsed by the General Assembly which called for a conference on the Human Environment.[40] This conference met in Stockholm in June 1972. It is also relevant to add that the years 1945–72 had been the years of decolonisation so that the number of states had risen to over 100 by 1972

(c) The third period: 1972–92

The United Nations Conference on the Human Environment was held in Stockholm, Sweden between 5 June 1972 and 16 June 1972. The Conference resulted in three non-binding documents: (i) an instrument on institutional and financial arrangements; (ii) a Declaration that set out 26 principles; and (iii) an Action Plan which comprised 109 recommendations. Of the most significance for the development of international law was the document setting out certain basic principles. The document was a compromise between those states who saw it simply as a declaratory document and those who viewed it as the basis for intergovernmental action in the future. Of the 26 principles those of most legal relevance are 21, 22, 23, 24. The relevant principles are as follows:

Principle 21

States have in accordance with the Charter of the United Nations and the principles of international law, the sovereign right to exploit their own resources pursuant to their own environmental policies, and the responsibility to ensure that activities within their jurisdiction or control do not cause damage to the environment of the other States or of areas beyond the limits of natural jurisdiction.

Principle 22

States shall co-operate to develop further the international law regarding liability and compensation for the victims of pollution and other environmental damage caused by activities within the jurisdiction or control of such States to areas beyond their jurisdiction.

---

36 The *Corfu Channel* case (*The Merits*) (1949) ICJ 4.
37 *Lac Lanoux Arbitration* (1957) 24 ILR 101.
38 It was probably inevitable that this should arise at the end of the 1960s. In the years after 1945, the emphasis had been on reconstruction and economic growth. By the end of the decade, the growth in social science research in disciplines such as economics, sociology was beginning to question the cost of economic growth. Such concerns ventilated in Germany and France and became caught up in agitation against the Vietnam war; at the same time environmental concerns were also raised by various groupings seeking nuclear disarmament.
39 ECOSOC Res 1346 (XLV) (1968).
40 GA Res 2398(XXIII) (1968).

Principle 23

Without prejudice to such criteria as may be agreed upon by the international community, or to standards which will have to be determined nationally, it will be essential in all cases to consider the systems of values prevailing in each country, and the extent of the applicability of standards which are valid for the most advanced countries but which may be inappropriate and of unwarranted social cost for the developing countries.

Principle 24

International matters concerning the protection and improvement of the environment should be handled in a co-operative spirit by all countries, big or small, on an equal footing. Co-operation through multilateral or bilateral arrangements or other appropriate means is essential to effectively control, prevent, reduce and eliminate adverse environmental effects resulting from activities conducted in all spheres in such a way that due account is taken of the sovereignty and interests of all States.

Some have argued that the Stockholm Principles have had an effect similar to the Universal Declaration of Human Rights in that, while it was not intended to impose immediate binding legal duties, the document has changed the nature of the discourse and provided a benchmark against which any subsequent proposals are to be judged. Of the other relevant principles, Principle 1 linked the quality of the environment with the requirements of human rights law[41] while some of the other Principles are directed to similar objectives. Principles 2, 3 and 5 emphasise the need to protect natural resources while Principles 4, 6 and 7 are directed to particular environmental threats. In respect of developing countries. Principles 8–15 concern the relationship between development and environmental protection; related to this, Principles 16–20 lay down principles in relation to demographic policies and in particular the question of population growth.

The Stockholm Conference had an immediate effect; its general conclusions were endorsed by the General Assembly[42] and the establishment of the United Nations Environment Programme[43] lead to a determined effort to promote standards by both regional action and global multilateral law making treaties. During this period the Geneva Convention on Long Range Transboundary Air Pollution was followed by the 1985 Vienna Convention on the Protection of the Ozone Layer and later by the Montreal Protocol on Substances that Deplete the Ozone Layer.

After the Stockholm Conference pressure to consider environmental questions began to be felt across the entire spectrum. First, international organisations began to take a greater interest; in 1971 the GATT established a Group on Environmental Measures and International Trade. Secondly, on the regional plane the amendments to the Treaty of Rome 1957 contained in the Single European Act 1986[44] included express legislative

---

41 A number of state constitutions include such a reference; it is also included in Art 24 of the African Charter on Human and People's Rights (1981) and Art 24 of the Convention on the Rights of the Child (1989).

42 See GA Res 2994(XXVII); GA Res 2995(XXVII); GA Res 2996(XXVII) GA Res 2997–GA Res 3004(XXVIII).

43 The United Nations Environment Programme was established after the Stockholm Conference and based in Kenya; it comprises a Governing Council elected by the General Assembly.

44 A new Title VII on the Environment, comprising Arts 130r to 130t was added to Part Three of the then EEC Treaty by Art 25 of the Single European Act.

powers in environmental matters. Thirdly, the UNEP produced in 1978 a draft 'Principles of Conduct in the Field of the Environment for the Guidance of States in the Conservation and Harmonious Utilisation of Natural Resources Shared by Two or More States'. Fourthly, in 1981 at Montevideo an intergovernmental conference held by the UNEP decided to formulate priorities for action in environmental matters. Fifthly, in 1980 the efforts of UNESCO, the FAO and the WWF resulted in a World Conservation Strategy that attempted to link the needs of conservation and development by adopting the principle of 'sustainable development'. Sixthly, in 1982 the United Nations General Assembly[45] adopted a World Charter of Nature which was designed to outline 'principles of conservation by which all human conduct affecting nature is to be guided and judged'.

However, perhaps the most significant development was the establishment in 1983 of a World Commission on Environment and Development (WCED) whose report (the Brundtland Report)[46] was published in 1987. First of all, the report emphasised the need to deal with environmental problems generally rather than in specific traditional categories. Secondly, it stressed the need for education of the general public in environmental dangers. Thirdly, it recognised that international law had not developed adequately to deal with the threat posed and it called for legislative initiatives at the municipal and international level. Fourthly, the report endorsed the principle of sustainable development as a general guide in this evolving area of law.

In December 1987, the General Assembly took note of the Brundtland Report[47] and in December 1989 in a further resolution[48] the same body called for a UN Conference on Environment and Development which met in June 1992 in Rio de Janeiro, Brazil. The purpose of the Conference was 'to elaborate strategies and measures to halt and reverse the effects of environmental degradation in the context of strengthened national and international efforts to promote sustainable and environmentally sound development in all countries'.

(d) The fourth period: 1992 to the present

The United Nations Conference on the Environment and Development (UNCED) was held in Rio de Janeiro from 3–14 June 1992. At its conclusion UNCED adopted three non-binding instruments, as follows: (i) the Rio Declaration on Environment and Development (the Rio Declaration); (ii) a non-legally binding Statement of Principles for a Global Consensus on the Management, Conservation and Sustainable Development of All Types of Forest (the UNCED Forest Principles); and (iii) Agenda 21. At the same time, two treaties were opened for signature: (i) the Convention on Biological Diversity;[49] and

---

45   UNGA Res 37/7 28 October 1982. The Charter received 111 votes in favour, 18 abstentions and one vote against (United States); see (1983) 23 ILM 455.

46   Gro Harlem Brundtland (b 1939) had served as Norwegian Prime Minister at various times after 1981, but more relevantly had been environment minister in the years 1974–76.

47   GA Res 42/187 (1987).

48   GA Res 44/228 (1989).

49   Article 36 of the Convention on Biological Diversity (1992) required 30 ratifications for the Treaty to enter into force. The Treaty entered into force on 29 December 1993.

(ii) the United Nations Framework Convention on Climate Change.[50] These two treaties will be considered below.

Although the Rio Declaration was not intended to be formally binding, its adoption at the end of a long negotiating process and following an international conference makes it an important source of 'soft law'. Principle 1 reaffirms that human beings are 'entitled to a healthy and productive life in harmony with nature'; Principle 2 reaffirms in amended form Art 21 of the Stockholm Declaration and reads:

> States have, in accordance with the Charter of the United Nations and the principles of international law, the sovereign right to exploit their own resources pursuant to their own environmental and developmental policies, and the responsibility to ensure that activities within their jurisdiction or control do not cause damage to the environment of other states or of areas beyond the limits of national jurisdiction.

It must be doubtful as to how much has been changed by the modification in the wording of Principle 21 of the Stockholm Declaration. Indeed, it is arguable that the new wording places a twofold responsibility on states. The essence of the declaration is contained in Principles 3 and 4 which read as follows:

> Principle 3
>
> The right to development must be fulfiled so as to equitably meet developmental and environmental needs of present and future generations.
>
> Principle 4
>
> In order to achieve sustainable development, environmental protection shall constitute an integral part of the development process and cannot be considered in isolation from it.

The Rio Declaration is more specific than the prior Stockholm Declaration and endorses the principles both of co-operation and sustainable development; further it commits all states to effective environmental legislation. Principle 15 adopts the precautionary approach while Principle 16 stipulates that the polluter should pay.

In addition UNCED produced a document known as Agenda 21 which was an action plan to move forward environmental and development concerns. Following UNCED the General Assembly passed a number resolutions[51] calling for further work on particular issues raised.

3 CUSTOMARY INTERNATIONAL LAW

Although international environmental law is of comparatively recent origin and thus comprises a number of multilateral law making treaties it is important also to consider the role of customary international law.[52] In the *Trail Smelter Arbitration*[53] between

---

50 Article 23 of the United Nations Convention on Climate Change (1992) required 50 ratifications for the treaty to come into effect. The treaty entered into force on 21 March 1994.

51 GA Res 47/188 (1992); 47/189 (1992); 47/190 (1992); 47/191 (1992); 47/192 (1992).

52 For earlier *dicta*, see the *Trail Smelter Arbitration* (1928) 2 RIAA 829; The International Commission on the River Order (1929) PCIJ, Ser A, No 23; 5 ILR 830.

53 The *Trail Smelter Arbitration* (1941) 35 AJIL 686.

Canada and the United States the facts were that a smelter in British Columbia emitted sulphur dioxide and caused physical damage to property within the state of Washington. In awarding damages the arbitral award is generally thought to have established the proposition that no state may allow its territory to be used in such a manner as to cause physical damage to the territory of another. The principle was accepted later in the *Lac Lanoux* case[54] where the arbitral tribunal was concerned with whether France had complied with its obligations under treaty and customary law before diverting a water course that it shared with Spain. Emerging from the case was the related principle that in cases of potential transboundary hazards there is a duty upon states to co-operate and negotiate to resolve potential problems.

There are a number of cases where the International Court of Justice have held that a state must act responsibly so as not to injure the interests or territory of another. In the *Corfu Channel* case[55] the court held that each state was under a duty 'not to allow knowingly its territory to be used for acts contrary to the rights of other states'. Although the court was not obliged to come to a conclusion, Australia's argument in the *Nuclear Tests* case[56] was founded on the assertion that environmental damage constitutes an infringement of state sovereignty. Twenty years later in the *Request for an Examination of the Situation in Accordance with Paragraph 63 of the Nuclear Tests* case 1974[57] the dissenting opinion of Judge Weeramantry observed that there is 'a fundamental principle of environmental law' which must here be noted. It is well entrenched in international law and goes back as far as the *Trail Smelter* case, and perhaps beyond.

The basic principle is that 'no nation is entitled by its own activities to cause damage to the environment of any other nation'.

A little later in the *Advisory Opinion on the legality of the Threat or Use of Nuclear Weapons*, the Court noted in the clearest terms 'the existence of the general obligation of states to ensure that activities within their jurisdiction and control respect the environment of other states or of areas beyond national control is now part of the corpus of international law relating to the environment'.

Related to the general rule of customary law not to do harm to other states, it is sometimes asserted that there are a number of emerging principles that may be in the process of acquiring the status of rules of customary international law:

(1) Principle 21 of the Stockholm Declaration and Principle 2 of the Rio Declaration re-state the customary law rule that states should not cause damage to the environment of other states.

(2) It is sometimes argued that there is now a principle of environmental law known as the 'precautionary principle'. This often arises where a state argues that it will not agree to sign a treaty or to restrict a practice because it has not been established to a standard of full scientific certainty that the practice causes environmental harm. The 'precautionary principle' holds that a state is under a duty to take preventive action if

---

54 The *Lac Lanoux Arbitration* (1957) 24 ILR 119; see, also, the *Gut Dam Arbitration (United States-Canada)* (1968) 8 ILM 118.

55 The *Corfu Channel* case (1949) ICJ 4, p 22; (1949) 16 ILR 155, p 158.

56 *Nuclear Tests* case (1974) ICJ 253.

57 (1995) ICJ 288.

the evidence is such as to show that it is probable or reasonably foreseeable that serious environmental damage will result. This principle is endorsed in Principle 15 of the Rio Declaration and essentially turns on the inferences to be drawn from equivocal evidence and raises the question at what point the prudent state should take preventive action. To some extent, it is a question of the standard of proof and probability which may vary according to the nature of the harm involved. Principle 15 of the Rio Declaration reads that: 'In order to protect the environment, the precautionary approach shall be widely applied by states according to their capacities. Where there are threats of serious or irreversible damage, lack of full scientific certainty shall not be used as a reason for postponing cost-effective measures to prevent environmental degradation.' The precautionary principle has been referred to in a number of international law making conventions[58] and has been cited with approval in the International Court of Justice.[59]

(3) Given that many environmental problems are of a transboundary nature it is often asserted there is a general duty on states to co-operate at least in matters of a transboundary nature. This principle is said to derive from the *Lac Lanoux Arbitration* case but it is equally arguable that it arises under Art 1(3) of the United Nations Charter (1945). This principle is stated in Principle 24 of the Stockholm Declaration (1972) and Principles 7 and 19 of the Rio Declaration(1992).

(4) A further principle that deserves consideration is that of 'sustainable development'.[60] Some view this as a principle while others argue that it is an emerging rule of customary international law. The general consensus is that it is too vague to constitute a rule but useful as a guiding principle. The principle itself emerged in the early 1970s in the *Icelandic Fisheries* case[61] when it was argued that there was an obligation in customary international law for states to co-operate in the conservation and sustainable development of the common property resources of the high seas.[62] A number of points can usefully be made. First, the principle is sometimes invoked to demonstrate that environmental law is founded in rights of nature; this contrasts with those environmental lawyers who view the subject from an anthropocentric perspective and thus see it as linked to human rights law or as an extension of it. Secondly, sometimes the expression 'sustainable development' is used to indicate forms of economic activity which are environmentally friendly or ecoefficient. A third sense in which the expression is used is in indicating the general balance that has to

---

58 The principle appears in the preamble to the Vienna Convention for the Protection of the Ozone Layer (1985); it also appears in the Montreal Protocol to the Vienna Convention (1987). The principle arises by implication in the preamble to the United Nations Convention on Biological Diversity (1992). It is expressly stated in both the Convention on the Protection and Use of Transboundary Watercourses and Lakes (1992) in Art 2(5) and in the Framework Convention on Climate Change (1992) in Art 3(3).

59 The serious view taken of environmental damage was set out by Judge Weeramantry in his dissenting opinion in the *Request for an Examination of the Situation in Accordance with Paragraph 63 of the Court's Judgment in the 1974 Nuclear Tests Case* (1995) ICJ 288. The same learned judge placed the general forefront of his approach in his separate opinion in the later *Danube Dam* case (*Hungary v Slovakia*) (1997) ICJ Rep 1.

60 P Sands (1994) 65 BYIL 303; For a general discussion of the concept, see D McGoldrick (1996) 45 ICLQ 796.

61 *Fisheries Jurisdiction* cases (1974) ICJ 3.

62 See PW Birnie and A Boyle, *International Law and the Environment*, 1992, p 122.

be struck between economic development and environmental protection. This dilemma has been recognised by the International Court of Justice and was well expressed by Judge Weeramantry who observed in the *Danube Dam* case[63] (*Hungary v Slovakia*):

> The protection of the environment is ... a vital part of contemporary human rights doctrine, for it is a *sine qua non* for numerous human rights such as the right to health and the right to life itself. It is scarcely necessary to elaborate on this, as damage to the environment can impair and undermine all the human rights spoken of in the Universal Declaration and other human rights instruments ...

> While therefore, all peoples have the right to initiate development projects and enjoy their benefits, there is likewise a duty to ensure that those projects do not significantly damage the environment.

The sensible conclusion must be that the principle of sustainable development[64] is one that is too vague to constitute a rule of customary international law. This indicates one of the difficulties with this recent and rapidly expanding subject namely that while some is founded on clear treaty provisions the distinction between rules of customary international law and general principles that may serve as a guide is not always clear. Thus, while it may be said that the duties on states to co-operate represents a rule of customary international law the concept of sustainable development probably only represents a general principle. The present state of the evidence indicates that the concept of sustainable development, the precautionary principle, the duty to carry out an environmental impact assessment, and the obligation to enter into consultation with an affected state have not advanced beyond the stage of general principles.[65]

4 STATE RESPONSIBILITY

As international environmental law is a relatively new subject within public international law there has been a tendency to place it within the traditional area of state responsibility. It is sensible therefore to examine a number of general aspects arising from that law.

(a) Damage

In respect of obligations arising under treaty environmental law has tended to go beyond the requirement of evidence of actual physical damage. Thus, Art 1(a) of the Convention on Long Range Transboundary Air Pollution (1979)[66] defines 'air pollution' as 'the introduction by man, directly or indirectly of substances or energy into the air resulting in deleterious effects of such a nature as to endanger human health'. The emphasis in each treaty will be to identify on scientific grounds the harmful damage and then to draft the

---

63 *Danube Dam* case (*Hungary v Slovakia*) (*Case concerning The Gabcikovo-Nagymaros Project*) (1997) ICJ 1. (The case itself turned on obligations arising under a treaty.)

64 See I Brownlie (1998), p 287.

65 See PN Okowa (1996) 67 BYIL 275.

66 Entered into force 16 March 1983.

treaty so as to cast the net sufficiently wide to prohibit all acts that may reasonably be thought to cause the harm in question. Thus, in Art 1(4) of the Law of the Sea Convention (1982) the definition of marine pollution refers to acts which 'result or is likely to result in such deleterious effects as harm to living resources and marine life'.

The tendency has been to identify the damage in the widest possible terms; thus Art 1(4) of the Law of the Sea Convention (1982) in defining marine pollution refers to 'impairment of quality for use of sea water' while Art 1(2) of the Vienna Convention on the Ozone Layer (1985)[67] is drafted to protect the ozone layer from 'changes in the physical environment ... which have significant deleterious effects'.

(b) Liability

In accordance with traditional principles of state responsibility, the state will be liable for the acts of its officials and state enterprises which cause damage to other states. However, questions will arise where the activity arises from a private enterprise located within the territory of that state. In such cases, an injured party may have an action in the municipal law of tort. It is to be noted, however, that the principle in the *Trail Smelter Arbitration*[68] is to the effect that 'no state has the right to use or permit the use of territory in such a manner as to cause injury ...'. This is clearly indicates that a state is liable for activities taking place on its territory that cause harm and it will be liable if fails to restrain such conduct.

The liability of the state in international law will further depend on the precise obligation accepted under any treaty. In many environmental treaties, the state assumes the responsibility to legislate[69] to prohibit certain acts and to enforce that legislation[70] and, in many instances, to take immediate action in the cases of non-observance or upon notice of harm being caused. In some instances, the treaty may provide expressly for state liability in respect of non-state enterprises; an example is afforded by the Outer Space Treaty (1967)[71] which imposes liability in respect of national activities in outer space 'whether such activities are carried out by governmental agencies or non-governmental agencies'.

(c) The nature of liability

A problem that sometimes arises is whether liability is strict. Is the state under an absolute and unqualified obligation to prevent environmental damage so that it will be liable in the absence of fault? The answers in customary international law are equivocal. In the *Trail Smelter* case,[72] the liability of Canada was not in issue while the *Corfu Channel* case

---

67 Entered into force on 22 September 1988.
68 The *Trail Smelter Arbitration* (1941) 35 AJIL 716; (1941) 9 ILR 317.
69 See, eg, The Convention on Nuclear Safety (1994), Art 7.
70 See, eg, Convention for the Protection of the Ozone Layer (1985), Art 2.
71 Adopted on 19 December 1966, opened for signature 27 January 1967, entered into force 10 October 1967.
72 The *Trail Smelter* case (1939) 33 AJIL 182; (1941) 35 AJIL 681; 9 ILR 315.

does not support the strict liability approach.[73] In the *Nuclear Tests* case,[74] the matter did not fall to be decided but in any event as the acts in question were the intentional acts of the French Government it is difficult to imagine how questions of fault could be in dispute. It is clear that the *Gut Dam* case,[75] is no basis to assert any rule of strict liability because of the presence of an express guarantee of indemnity and the absence of any discussion of the point.

In treaty law there are some examples of strict liability[76] but everything depends on the precise language of the treaty and the general approach has been to require that a state exercise a proper standard of diligence and take appropriate measures having regard to the relevant facts and scientific and technical criteria.[77] In respect of liability, it would seem, following the *Danube Dam* case,[78] that when the conduct of a state is called into question then it will be able to produce evidence of any of the circumstances precluding wrongfulness as set out in the general law of state responsibility.[79] In that particular case, it was accepted that Hungary was able to raise a 'defence' of necessity in respect of a breach of a treaty even though on the evidence no such defence could be sustained.

(d) Limitations

The law of state responsibility is to a large extent concerned with bilateral relations and the duties that one state might owe to another. It provides a sensible framework to resolve disputes when a citizen of state A has been ill treated or denied justice in state B. Indeed many of the cases concern tortious acts committed by state officials where the facts can be easily ascertained.[80]

However, with environmental problems a number of difficulties arise. First, in many cases the scientific evidence is equivocal and action may have to be taken on the basis of probability and incomplete information. Secondly, in many cases it is the conduct of a number of states that is contributing to the problem rather than the unlawful act of a single state. Thirdly, in many cases action may have to be taken before irreversible damage is done and at a time when not all states are prepared to accept that a problem exists. Fourthly, the action needed to be taken may involve considerable economic sacrifice or lifestyle changes in particular states that impinge on sovereignty whereas in the conventional case of state responsibility a single payment will be sought as financial compensation. It is for this reason that many argue that the law of state responsibility has only a limited role to play and that as many environmental questions are global in nature there is an emerging principle that each state is under an international duty to co-operate.

---

73 *Corfu Channel* case (1949) ICJ 4; 16 ILR 155.
74 *Nuclear Tests* case (1974) ICJ 253; 57 ILR 350.
75 The *Gut Dam Arbitration (United States v Canada)* (1969) 8 ILM 118.
76 The Convention on International Liability for Damage Caused by Objects Launched into Outer Space (1972), Art 2.
77 See, eg, Art 2, Geneva Convention on Long Range Transboundary Air Pollution (1979); Art 2, Vienna Convention for the Protection of the Ozone Layer (1985).
78 *Case concerning the Gabcikovo-Nagymaros Project (Hungary v Slovakia)* (1997) ICJ 7.
79 See ILC Draft Articles on State Responsibility Provisionally Adopted on Second Reading, August 2000, Chapter V, Arts 20–27.
80 See, eg, the *Caire Claim* (1929) 5 RIAA 516; 5 ILR 146.

5 THE INTERNATIONAL DUTY TO CO-OPERATE

The early and rather tentative case law under customary international law had concentrated upon the duty of one state not to knowingly allow activities upon its territory to damage the territory or interests of another state.[81] However, from this general proposition can be deduced a duty to notify other states of environmental harm. Thus, Principle 18 of the Rio Declaration (1992) provides that 'States shall immediately inform other States of any natural disasters or other emergencies that are likely to produce sudden harmful effects on the environment'.[82] This is supplemented by Principle 19, which provides that 'States shall provide prior and timely notification and relevant information to potentially affected States on activities that may have a significant adverse transboundary effect and shall consult with those States at an early stage and in good faith'.

It is one thing for a state to notify in cases of emergency it is quite another for a state to be under a general and continuing duty to co-operate in environmental matters. There is a growing school of thought that there is such a duty and this duty extends both to other states and to international organisations. This can be traced back to the *Lac Lanoux Arbitration*[83] where the arbitral tribunal emphasised the need to negotiate on transboundary problems. Thus, Principle 24 of the Stockholm Declaration reads in part: 'International matters concerning the protection and improvement of the environment should be handled in a co-operative spirit by all countries, big or small on an equal footing.' A duty towards international institutions might also be inferred from Principle 25 of the Stockholm Declaration. Moreover, as has been noted elsewhere a general duty to co-operate can be inferred from Art 1(3) of the United Nations Charter. An aspect of the duty to co-operate is the obligation to inform other states through the publication of environmental impact assessments;[84] this has been followed by regional organisations[85] and endorsed by the International Court of Justice.[86]

Although one can infer a general duty to co-operate the scope and level of that duty will vary from one state to another. Indeed co-operation should be such that the interests of future generations are considered. This matter is dealt with in the Rio Declaration (1992) in Principles 3 and 7. Principle 3 reads: 'The right to development must be fulfiled so as to equitably meet developmental and environmental needs of present and future

---

81 The *Trail Smelter Arbitration* (1939) 33 AJIL 182, (1941) 35 AJIL 684, 9 ILR 315; the *Corfu Channel* case (*Merits*) (1949) ICJ 4.

82 For a duty to inform, see also International Convention for the Prevention of Pollution from Ships (1973), Art 8; Law of the Sea Convention (1982), Art 192; Basel Convention on the Control of Transboundary Movements of Hazardous Wastes and their Disposal (1989), Art 13.

83 *Lac Lanoux Arbitration* (1957) 24 ILR 101. The principle that states should negotiate and co-operate in a constructive manner has been extended to those cases that turn on the delimitation of the continental shelf. See the *North Sea Continental Shelf* case (1969) ICJ 3.

84 An example is afforded by the Law of the Sea Convention (1982), Part XII, (Arts 204–06). Article 204 provides for the monitoring of the risks or effects of pollution while Art 205 and Art 206 provide for the publication of reports to international organisations and other states in respect of such risks or in respect of planned activities that may have an effect on the environment.

85 EC Directive 85/337.

86 Discussed by Judge Weeramantry in his opinion in the *Request for an Examination of the Situation in Accordance with Paragraph 63 of the Court's Judgment in the 1974 Nuclear Tests case* (1995) ICJ 288.

generations.' The need to secure differential treatment between states is provided by Principle 7 which reads in part: 'States shall co-operate in a spirit of global partnership to conserve, protect and restore the health of the Earth's ecosystem. In view of the different contributions to global environmental degradation, States have common but differentiated responsibilities. Thus co-operation should be based on a recognition of the different pressures on states as well as a need to provide for the interests of future generations.'

Taking a broad view of the matter and drawing together the requirements of customary international law, treaty obligations and emerging principles one can posit at least eight general duties that a state is subject to under international environmental law. Those duties can be summarised as:

(i)   a general duty not to damage the environment or to allow others on one's territory so to do;[87]

(ii) a general duty to co-operate with other states and international organisations in furthering environmental protection;[88]

(iii) a general duty to monitor risks to the environment in one's own territory and to inform international organisations and other states in appropriate circumstances;[89]

(iv) a general duty to give effect to the precautionary principle;[90]

(v)   a general duty to ensure in appropriate cases by municipal legislation that those responsible for pollution pay for the ensuing damage;[91]

(vi) a particular duty to co-operate on transboundary matters;[92]

(vii) a general duty to respect the principle of sustainable development particularly in matters of conservation;[93]

(viii) a general duty to recognise that the environmental obligations of each individual state may differ;[94]

(ix) a general duty to bear in mind the need to protect the interests of future generations;[95]

(x)   a general duty to be guided in environmental questions by the weight of scientific and technical opinion rather than by ideological considerations;

(xi) a general duty to help develop international law in the area of environmental protection;[96]

---

87   *Trail Smelter Arbitration* (1939) 33 AJIL 182; (1941) 35 AJIL 684; *Danube Dam* case (1997) ICJ 1.
88   Rio Declaration (1992), Principles 2, 7, 18, 19.
89   *Ibid*, Principles 17 and 18.
90   *Ibid*, Principle 15.
91   *Ibid*, Principle 16.
92   *Lac Lanoux Arbitration* (1957) 24 ILR 101.
93   Rio Declaration (1992), Principle 4.
94   *Ibid*, Principle 6.
95   *Ibid*, Principle 3.
96   *Ibid*, Principle 27.

(xii) a general duty to be guided in all environmental matters by the principles of co-operation between states enshrined in the United Nations Charter.[97]

Because international environmental law is a relatively new but rapidly expanding discipline it is difficult to draw the normal clear distinctions between customary rules and emerging principles. In any event the subject is likely to be governed in specific areas by multilateral law making treaties and it is to these matters one must now turn.

6 THE ATMOSPHERE

The industrial revolution caused the first significant concern about air pollution as observers noted the semi permanent clouds of smoke[98] that hung over industrial cities following the burning of coal in factories and other enterprises. In most states the process of industrialisation has had to be followed by legislation designed to protect the environment from certain forms of production. Today the main source of air pollution is caused by sulphur dioxide and nitrogen oxide produced by the use of fossil fuels for power generation and industrial processes together with the exhaust emissions from petrol and diesel vehicles. This last source is of considerable importance because the affluence of the post-1945 world has produced a very considerable ownership of such vehicles not only in developed states but also in developing countries.

Modern scientific research has demonstrated that sulphur dioxide and nitrogen oxides react with water vapour in the atmosphere to form into acid compounds and they are then dispersed by wind and weather over many miles; the evidence indicates that the dispersal may extend to thousands of miles. Such acid compounds may fall as rain or snow and as such increase acidity in soil lakes and forests; in many cases this can contribute to reduced crop growth or threaten wildlife and fish. The simple point is that state A is not only threatened by industrial processes on its own territory but also by the activities of those within its immediate region or beyond.

One of the difficulties in this area is the uncertain legal status of the atmosphere. It is well established that the airspace above a state is part of its territory but this does not extend to the atmosphere. As noted elsewhere the *Trail Smelter Arbitration*[99] had indicated that one state would be answerable for air pollution above the territory of another state. However, it was not until the early 1960s that concentrated attention began to focus upon the effect of human activity on the environment.[100] However, from that date the focus of

---

97   United Nations Charter (1945), Art 1; Rio Declaration (1992), Principle 2.

98   However, the presence of smoke was not always viewed in the same light as in the 20th century. In 1887, when the then Prince of Wales opened a new Town Hall in Middlesborough, he was told by the local Mayor that the presence of smoke was an indication of prosperity and work. See Asa Briggs, *Victorian Cities*, 1968, p 263. As Professor Briggs indicates industrialisation lead to the formation of urban communities. In 1837, England and Wales had only five provincial cities with populations over 100,000 by 1891 there were 23 and they contained one-third of the population.

99   *Trail Smelter Arbitration* (1939) 33 AJIL 182; (1941) 35 AJIL 681.

100 This was perhaps only to be expected with the years 1945–60 devoted to post-war reconstruction in Europe. Some writers see the publication in 1962 of Rachel Carson's *Silent Spring* as an important event in raising public awareness.

attention has narrowed. Following the Stockholm Conference in 1972 and the Helsinki Conference on Security and Co-operation in Europe the United Nations Economic Commission for Europe was instrumental in the drafting of the Geneva Convention on Long Range Transboundary Air Pollution[101] which was opened for signature in November 1979 and came into force on 16 March 1983. For the purposes of the Convention, 'air pollution' is defined as 'the introduction by man, directly or indirectly, of substances or energy into the air resulting in deleterious effects of such a nature as to endanger human health, harm living resources and ecosystems and material property and impair or interfere with amenities and other legitimate uses of the environment'. It has to be acknowledged that the obligations assumed under the Convention are limited indeed. Under Art 2, state parties agree 'to limit and, as far as possible, gradually reduce and prevent air pollution including long range transboundary air pollution'. This is to be achieved by exchanges of information[102] and a review of policies[103] which is to be facilitated by consultation[104] and the employment of 'the best available technology which is economically feasible and low and non-waste technology'.[105] In addition to co-operation on research[106] and information,[107] the parties agreed to the establishment of a co-operative programme for the monitoring and evaluation of the long range transmission of air pollutants in Europe (EMEP).[108]

The Convention has been supplemented by a number of Protocols which have progressively strengthened the regulatory regime. In 1984, a Protocol was adopted on financial matters[109] and this was followed in 1985[110] by a Protocol which required substantial reductions in sulphur emissions and subjected states to an obligation to report to the Executive Body established under the Convention.[111] Matters were taken further in 1988 with the adoption of the Sofia Protocol[112] which provided for the control of nitrogen oxide emissions. In 1991, the Geneva Protocol[113] introduced control over the emissions of

---

101 The Convention was less important for its specific content but more significant for establishing a legal and institutional basis for future co-operation on questions of acid rain and transboundary air pollution. See A Rosencranz (1981) 75 AJIL 975; J Fraenkel, 'The Convention on Long Range Transboundary Air Pollution' (1989) 30 Harv ILJ 447.

102 Article 3.

103 Article 4.

104 Article 5 .

105 Article 6.

106 Article 7.

107 Article 8.

108 Article 9.

109 Protocol on Long Term Financing of a Cooperative Programme for Monitoring and Evaluation of the Long Range Transmission of Air Pollutants in Europe, Geneva, 28 September 1984. In force 28 January 1988. See (1988) 27 ILM 701.

110 Protocol on the Reduction of Sulphur Emissions or their Transboundary Fluxes, Helsinki, 8 July 1985. In force 2 September 1987. See (1988) 27 ILM 707.

111 See 1979 Convention on Long Range Transboundary Air Pollution, Art 10.

112 Protocol Concerning the Control of Emission of Nitrogen Oxides or Their Transboundary Fluxes, Sofia, 31 October 1988. In force 14 February 1991. See (1989) 28 ILM 212.

113 Protocol Concerning the Control of Emissions of Volatile Organic Compounds, Geneva, 18 November 1991; (1992) 31 ILM 573.

volatile organic compounds and in 1994 the Oslo Protocol[114] introduced further controls on sulphur emissions and stipulating targets for the years 2000, 2005 and 2010.

7 THE OZONE LAYER AND CLIMATE CHANGE

It has been accepted for over a quarter of a century that certain human activities could do damage, possibly irreparable damage, to the ozone layer.[115] This layer located in the stratosphere is important in acting as a filter for sunlight and protecting the earth from ultra violet radiation. From the mid 1960s there came to be a vigorous scientific debate about which human activities affected the ozone layer and how they did so.[116] Further, there was much discussion as to the possible consequences of damage to the ozone layer. Broadly it came to be accepted that damage to the ozone layer howsoever caused might result in serious effects on agriculture, fisheries and human health. The task facing the international community was to try and promote a degree of co-operation when a scientific consensus was only just emerging.[117]

The first effort at international co-operation was contained in the Vienna Convention for the Protection of the Ozone Layer (1985) which entered into force on 1 January 1989. The convention is general in terms but represents a move towards preventive action and is consistent with the precautionary principle set out subsequently in the Rio Declaration (1992). For the purpose of the convention the 'ozone layer' is defined as 'the layer of atmospheric ozone above the planetary boundary layer'[118] and 'adverse effects' are defined as 'changes in the physical environment or biota, including changes in climate, which have significant deleterious effects on human health or on the composition, resilience and productivity of natural and managed ecosystems, or on materials useful to mankind'.[119]

In broad terms the Convention is a framework document envisaging future protocols under which more specific action will be taken.[120] The Convention obliges state parties to

---

114 Protocol on Further Reductions of Sulphur Emissions, Oslo, 14 June 1994 (1994) 33 ILM 1542.

115 The word ozone derives from the Greek *ozein*, to smell. In the early 1960s, the emphasis was on activities above the earth; it was thought that hydrogen and nitrogen compounds released by supersonic air transport might damage the ozone layer. It was also thought that the testing of nuclear weapons in the atmosphere would also damage the ozone layer. In 1974 scientists at the University of California published a paper asserting that chlorine found in chlorofluorocarbons (CFCs) had the potential to rise and damage stratospheric ozone. This changed the terms of the scientific debate because it raised new questions about common activities at ground level.

116 See generally, I Rowlands (1995).

117 The years 1975–85 witnessed considerable scientific research and disagreement as to the precise cause of ozone layer depletion. The CFC chemical cause was not the only explanation advanced. The differing scientific views made it more difficult to obtain a legal consensus so that the initial 1985 Vienna Convention was drafted in the terms of a framework convention. For the state of the scientific debate at the time, see John Gribben (1988).

118 Article 1, Vienna Convention for the Protection of the Ozone Layer (1985).

119 *Ibid.*

120 Article 8.

co-operate and to take appropriate measures to safeguard the ozone layer.[121] Further, the convention provides for co-operation in research,[122] and legal and scientific matters[123] as well as in the sharing of information. As a basis for future action the Convention provides for the establishment of a Conference[124] and a Secretariat[125] which will be concerned with the adoption of future protocols and the settlement of disputes.

The Convention was built upon in the Montreal Protocol of 1987.[126] The scheme of the Montreal Protocol was to list a number of substances which were thought to deplete the ozone layer[127] and then to seek to regulate both production and consumption. In the original Protocol, the intention had been to freeze production and consumption at 1986 levels and then to move towards a progressive reduction. However, other scientific evidence emerged that caused those meeting in Helsinki in May 1989 to determine revised targets to phase out halons and those CFCs subject to the Protocol as well as to secure further reductions in other substances thought to contribute to the depletion of the ozone layer.

Amendments to the Protocol were adopted in London in 1990[128] and in Copenhagen in 1992.[129] The most significant points being changes to phasing out times in respect of particular substances. However, special rights were stipulated for the interests of developing countries and provision was made in respect of the transfer of alternative technologies.

The amendments further refined the procedures in respect of settlement of disputes that had been stipulated under Art 11 of the Ozone Convention.

Related to the question of the protection of the ozone layer has been the wider question of climate change which has also been of increasing significance in the last quarter of a century. The concern of the General Assembly was indicated by Resolution 45/53,[130] which declared in para 1 that climate change was to be regarded as 'a common concern of mankind, since climate is an essential condition which sustains life on earth'.

Following the urging of the UNEP and action in other fora the United Nations Framework Convention on Climate Change was opened for signature at the United Nations Conference on Environment and Development held at Rio in 1992 and entered into force on 21 March 1994. The broad objective of the Convention is set out in Art 2 which stipulates that:

---

121 Article 2.

122 Article 3.

123 Article 4.

124 Article 6.

125 Article 7.

126 Montreal Protocol on Substances that Deplete the Ozone Layer (1987). See (1987) 26 ILM 1541.

127 As listed in the Montreal Protocol (1987), Annex A.

128 (1991) 30 ILM 537.

129 (1993) 32 ILM 874. (The Copenhagen meeting being the fourth meeting under the Montreal Protocol; the tightening standards were precipitated by further scientific evidence of ozone.)

130 United Nations General Assembly Resolution 45/53, but see also prior resolutions 42/182 (1987) 42/184 (1987); 42/186 (1987); 42/187 (1987) and also 44/207.

The ultimate objective of this Convention and any related legal instruments that the Conference of the Parties may adopt is to achieve, in accordance with the relevant provisions of the Convention, stabilisation of greenhouse gas concentrations in the atmosphere at a level that would prevent dangerous anthropogenic interference with the climate system. Such a level should be achieved within a time frame sufficient to allow ecosystems to adapt naturally to climate change, to ensure that food production is not threatened and to enable economic development to proceed in a sustainable manner.

In general terms the document is a framework Convention in which the state parties have agreed to protect the climate system[131] and to co-operate with other state parties on research education and training.[132] The main thrust of the Convention is contained in Art 4 which commits state parties to provide information on greenhouse gas emissions not controlled by the Montreal Protocol. In broad terms information on such emissions must be supplied within six months of the Convention coming into effect[133] and must be accompanied by information as to measures taken to reduce such emissions.[134] The Convention operates on the questionable basis of dividing the world into Annex I developed countries who are to cut the level of their carbon emissions and the rest.

Further, states included in Annex II are obliged to assist developing countries by allowing appropriate transfers of technology so as to permit reductions in pollution. The objective is to ensure the returning of such emissions to the 1990 level.[135] One feature of the Convention of note is that it commits developed countries to assisting in the transfer of technology to those states with particular environmental problems. The difficulty with the general scheme is that it does little to restrict emission levels in developing nations.

The Convention establishes both a Conference of the Parties[136] and a Secretariat;[137] the purpose of the former is to meet regularly to receive and review reports by state parties and to act as a medium for the exchange of information. The Conference is to be assisted by a Secretariat and a subsidiary body charged with providing scientific and technological advice.[138] It has to be conceded that while the Convention is described as a framework document it is remarkably detailed and some of the obligations assumed by developed states appear open ended.

The Convention entered into force on 21 March 1994 and the first meeting of the Conference took place in Berlin in 1995. At that meeting dissatisfaction was expressed with the obligations assumed under Art 4(2)(a) and 4(2)(b) of the Convention. So that when the Conference met again in Geneva it was decided to draw up a legally binding protocol to clarify and strengthen the obligations assumed under Art 4. At the third meeting of the Conference at Kyoto in December 1997 the Protocol[139] adopted stipulated

---

131 United Nations Framework Convention on Climate Change (1992), Art 3.
132 *Ibid*, Arts 5 and 6.
133 Article 4(2)(b).
134 Article 4(2)(b) and Art 12 .
135 Article 4(2)(b).
136 Article 7.
137 Article 8.
138 Article 9.
139 By November 1999 the Protocol had acquired 84 signatures.

particular targets on emissions for various blocs[140] such as the European Community, the United States, Japan and those countries making the transition to a market economy in Eastern Europe. The Kyoto Protocol enables a practice of emission trading to be instituted whereby a developed country may earn credit other than by domestic reductions such as by investing in projects in developing countries.

The Kyoto Protocol to the United Nations Framework Convention was adopted on 11 December 1997; the Protocol follows the original Convention in drawing a distinction between industrialised Annex 1 countries who agreed to curb the emissions of greenhouse gases and other countries who were not subject to restriction on grounds that it would restrict their prospects of economic growth. Whether it was sensible to disregard the pollution growth in developing countries has been a matter increasingly in contention since 1997. The Kyoto Protocol will come into force when 55 countries that account for 55% of carbon dioxide choose to ratify.[141] Under the terms of the Protocol developed countries are to reduce their emissions of greenhouse gases[142] – essentially carbon dioxide (CO_2) produced by burning fossil fuels – by a figure of 5% of the 1990 level and this target is to be reached between 2008 and 2012. Amongst such developed countries the precise reduction required would vary;[143] in contrast some developed countries might be able to increase their emissions. Developing countries are exempt from the restrictions on emissions. The justification for this uneven treatment was that some developed countries produce more pollution than others although since 1997 the precise terms of the Kyoto Protocol have been subject to criticism as not doing sufficient to restrain pollution in those developing countries where a premium is being placed on economic growth.

8 INTERNATIONAL WATERCOURSES[144]

The expression 'international watercourse' is but a convenient expression to describe those rivers or lakes that may be shared by two or more states. The rivers may straddle a boundary or they may flow through more than one state. Clearly such waterways raise questions as to how the riparian states should co-operate and the rights of upstream and downstream states. Moreover, a geographical problem arises of defining the extent of the watercourse. Is it to be restricted to the part which crosses a boundary or does it embrace the whole including the basin and any associated tributaries. A narrow definition may make management difficult; a broad definition may unduly intrude on the internal waters of a state.

---

140 The Protocol divides the parties into Annex 1 parties (developed states) and non Annex 1 parties (developing states or states in a transition to a market economy).

141 By March 2001, 84 states had signed; 33 states had ratified but this included only one industrialised state.

142 The Protocol embraces carbon dioxides, methane and other industrial products such as hydroflurocarbons.

143 In general, Europe was to achieve a reduction of 8% while the United States was to attain a reduction of 7%; reductions of 6% were to be achieved by Canada, Russia and Japan.

144 See generally, P Birnie and A Boyle, *International Law and the Environment*, 1992, Chapter 6.

One of the earliest forms of co-operation between states in Europe was in respect of international waterways and this question absorbed some of the time of the delegates at the Congress of Vienna in 1815.[145] A significant question is that of allocation. In principle there are three possible views. The first view sometimes described as that of territorial sovereignty would allow the upstream state to take any action such as diversion or abstraction regardless of how it might affect the rights of the downstream state.[146] The second view that of territorial integrity would allow the lower riparian state a right to a full flow of water. Both the first and the second views have only attained limited support. However, the widest support is accorded to the third view which holds that international watercourses are shared resources and should be subject to the principle of equitable utilisation by riparian states. This principle is grounded in common sense, practicality and fairness and has received a certain degree of support in the case law;[147] it is also the principle least likely to lead to resentment and dispute and pays some regard to the need for comity and fair dealing between sovereign states.

The third school of thought was endorsed by the International Law Association in 1966 when in drafting its Helsinki Rules[148] it identified the principle of 'reasonable and equitable share' in the beneficial use of watercourses as 'the key principle of international law in this area'. Further, the Helsinki Rules required states to prevent damage by pollution 'consistent with the principle of equitable utilisation'.

On the international plane the most significant advance was the adoption in 1992 of the Convention on the Protection and Use of Transboundary Watercourses and Lakes. For the purpose of the Convention 'transboundary waters' means 'any surface or ground waters which mark, cross or are located on boundaries between two or more States; wherever transboundary waters flow directly into the sea, these transboundary waters end at a straight line across their respective mouths between points on the low water line of their banks'.[149] The purpose of the Convention is to prevent adverse effects on the environment including 'effects on human health safety, flora, fauna, soil, air, water climate landscape'.[150] State parties are required to take action to prevent, control and reduce pollution of water[151] and in doing so are to be guided by both the precautionary principle and by the associated principle that the polluter should pay.[152] The Convention requires state parties to take appropriate action to prevent pollution and this will include

---

145 The Congress of Vienna (1815) had resulted in the establishment of the Rhine Commission being the first attempt at inter state co-operation in respect of a waterway.

146 This view is sometimes described as the 'Harmon Doctrine' as it was invoked by United States Attorney General Harmon in 1895, who asserted the right of the United Sates to divert the Rio Grande. The theory did not enjoy much support in Europe which since the Congress of Vienna in 1815 had tended to favour the principle of equitable utilisation.

147 Some support is to be found in *Territorial Jurisdiction of the International Commission of the River Oder* case (1929) PCIJ, Ser A, No 23; *Diversion of Water from the Meuse* case (1937) PCIJ, Ser A/B, No 70; *Lac Lanoux Arbitration* (1957) 24 ILR 101.

148 The ILA Helsinki Rules Report of the 52nd Conference (1966).

149 Convention on the Protection and Use of Transboundary Watercourses and Lakes (1992), Art 1(1).

150 *Ibid*, Art 1(2).

151 *Ibid*, Art 3 .

152 *Ibid*, Art 2(5).

monitoring,[153] research[154] and the exchange of information.[155] It is stipulated that where bilateral and multilateral agreements do not exist then they should be entered into by riparian states.[156] It is further stipulated that in such agreements Riparian states shall provide for mutual assistance[157] and the exchange of information.[158]

For some years the International Law Commission has been working on draft articles to govern those international waterways that may or may not constitute boundaries. The draft articles on the Non-Navigational Uses of International Watercourses were adopted by the International Law Commission at its 46th session in 1994. In May 1997, the General Assembly[159] adopted the Convention on the Law of Non-navigational. Uses of International Watercourses. The general principle is set out in Art 5 which reads:

> Watercourse States shall in their respective territories utilise an international watercourse in an equitable and reasonable manner. In particular, an international watercourse shall be used and developed by watercourse States with a view to attaining optimal and sustainable utilisation thereof and benefits therefrom, taking into account the interests of the watercourse States concerned, consistent with adequate protection of the watercourse.

This principle is supplemented by an express obligation not to cause significant harm. Thus Art 7 reads in part: 'Watercourse States shall, in utilising an international watercourse in their territories, take all appropriate steps to prevent the causing of significant harm to other watercourse States.' This is followed by a requirement under Art 8 to co-operate in good faith. The Convention provides that there should be a regular exchange of information between watercourse states[160] and requires timely notification of measures that might have an adverse effect on other watercourse states.[161] In such circumstances other states should have a period of six months to evaluate the proposal;[162] in the absence of a reply then the watercourse state may go ahead and implement the measure.[163] If a reply or objection is given under Art 15 then the state parties are required to consult and negotiate.[164] Where one watercourse state believes that another is planning measures that may have an adverse effect then it may itself initiate the notification and consultation procedure.[165]

In respect of ecosystems Art 20 provides that watercourse states shall act both individually and jointly to protect such ecosystems. It is further stipulated that watercourse states shall act to reduce and control pollution and take all measures to

---

153 *Ibid*, Art 4.
154 *Ibid*, Art 5.
155 *Ibid*, Art 6.
156 *Ibid*, Art 7.
157 *Ibid*, Art 15.
158 *Ibid*, Art 13.
159 General Assembly Resolution 49/52 .
160 Convention on the Law of the Non-navigational Uses of International Watercourses (1997), Art 11.
161 *Ibid*, Art 12.
162 *Ibid*, Art 13.
163 *Ibid*, Art 16.
164 *Ibid*, Art 17.
165 *Ibid*, Art 18.

protect and preserve the marine environment. Consistent with other such instruments Art 33 of the Convention provides detailed provisions in respect of the peaceful settlement of disputes.

9 WILDLIFE[166]

Wildlife have from the outset given rise to transboundary problems. It is thus not surprising that wildlife law constitutes one of the oldest forms of environmental law. International wildlife law is concerned in part to protect valuable animals which are at risk of being exploited irresponsibly for commercial gain. In this context one can note five principal treaties that are designed to protect particular species from commercial exploitation; the relevant instruments are the International Convention for the Regulation of Whaling (1946)[167] (known as the 'Whaling Convention');[168] the International Convention for the Protection of Birds (1950);[169] the Interim Convention on the Conservation of North Pacific Fur Seals (1957);[170] the Convention for the Conservation of the Vicuna (1969); the Agreement on the Conservation of Polar Bears (1973).[171] These five treaties share the common objective of restricting exploitation by introducing limits to avoid depletion of the species. In general such treaties are not concerned with matters such as pollution and habitat loss that may also pose a threat to the species.

In addition, one should note those international conventions designed to protect wildlife in particular geographical areas. In chronological order the most important are the Convention on Nature Protection and Wildlife Preservation in the Western Hemisphere (the 'Western Hemisphere Convention') (1940);[172] the African Convention on the Conservation of Nature and Natural Resources (1968); the Convention on the Conservation of European Wildlife and Natural Habitats (sometimes known as the 'Berne Convention') (1979); the Convention on the Conservation of Antarctic Marine Living Resources ('CCAMLR' (1980)). These treaties of a distinct geographical nature have been supplemented by four treaties which are not confined to a distinct species or a particular area; they are the Convention on Wetlands of International Importance Especially as Waterfowl Habitat (sometimes known as 'RAMSAR') (1971),[173] the Convention

---

166 See generally, S Lyster, *International Wildlife Law*, 1985.

167 Replacing the earlier Convention for the Regulation of Whaling (1931) and two subsequent protocols, namely The International Agreement for the Regulation of Whaling (1937) and the Protocol Amending the International Agreement of 8 June 1937 for the Regulation of Whaling (1938).

168 Article 3(1) of the Convention establishes the International Whaling Commission which has power to adopt regulations on quotas.

169 Replacing the Convention for the Protection of Birds useful to Agriculture (1902). In 1916, the United States and Great Britain (on behalf of Canada) agreed the Convention for the Protection of Migratory Birds (1916). See *Missouri v Holland* (1920) 252 US 415 where the United States Supreme Court upheld a federal statute enacted to give effect to the treaty.

170 Replacing the Treaty for the Preservation and Protection of Fur Seals ('the 1911 Treaty').

171 Signed in Oslo, 15 November 1973, entered into force pursuant to Art 10(4) on 26 May 1976.

172 The Convention was drawn up by Members of the Pan American Union (now the Organisation of American States) and entered into force on 30 April 1942.

173 Known as RAMSAR as the Convention was drawn up and signed on 2nd February 1971, in the Iranian town of that name. Under the terms of Art 10(1) the Convention came into effect on 21 December 1975.

Concerning the Protection of the World Cultural and Natural Heritage (the 'World Heritage Convention') (1972),[174] the Convention on International Trade in Endangered Species of Wild Fauna and Flora ('CITES') (1973),[175] the Convention on the Conservation of Migratory Species of Wild Animals (the 'Bonn Convention') (1979).[176] These latter four treaties are limited in scope; RAMSAR is confined to wetlands while the World Heritage Convention is restricted to 'natural sites or precisely delineated areas of outstanding universal value from the point of view of science, conservation or natural beauty'. The scope of CITES is limited to the regulation of international trade while the 'Bonn Convention' is confined to migratory species.

Thus, wildlife law has a longer history than some other aspects of environmental law but it has seen increased activity in the last quarter of a century. The earlier treaties were designed to prevent depletion by killing or commercial exploitation; in contrast the modern emphasis is to prevent disturbance of the habitat. A modern treaty regime such as the Convention on International Trade in Endangered Species of Wild Fauna and Flora (1973) (CITES) has provided for state parties to establish bodies to administer the permit system instituted by the treaty[177] and it stipulates for regular reports by state parties[178] to a central body; further in appropriate circumstances it allows qualified non-governmental organisations to be represented.[179]

10 ULTRA HAZARDOUS ACTIVITIES

In many municipal law systems certain activities are regarded as ultra hazardous and liability in the law of tort is likely to be imposed strictly[180] on proof of the act causing damage irrespective of whether negligence or failure of due diligence has been demonstrated by the plaintiff. There is no reason why such a principle should not apply on the international plane particularly in the context of transboundary disputes however this requires agreement to be reached on what activities are to be categorised as 'ultra

---

174 The Convention was drawn up under the auspices of UNESCO on 16 November 1972 and under the terms of Art 33 came into force on 17 December 1975.

175 The Convention was concluded in Washington on 6 March 1973 and under Art 22(1) entered into force on 1 July 1975.

176 At the United Nations Conference on the Human Environment held in Stockholm in 1972, it was noted in recommendation 32 of the Action Plan that governments should consider treaties to protect species which were to be found in international waters or were prone to migrate from one territory to another; the Convention followed the initiative of the Federal Republic of Germany and was concluded on 23 June 1979 in Bonn but did not enter into force until 1 November 1983 under the terms of Art 18(1).

177 See Art 3, Convention on International Trade in Endangered Species of Wild Fauna and Flora (1973).

178 *Ibid*, Art 8(7).

179 *Ibid*, Art 11(7).

180 For the 19th century approach, see *Rylands v Fletcher* (1865) LR 1 Ex 265; (1868) LR 3 HL 330; for later qualification, see *Rickards v Lothian* (1913) AC 263 PC; *Rainham Chemical Works Ltd v Belvedere Fish Guano Co* [1921] 2 AC 465; *Read v J Lyons & Co* [1947] AC 156. For a review of the position at common law, see W Stallybrass [1929] 3 CLJ 376 .

hazardous'. It is widely accepted that nuclear activities (of a civil or military nature) fall within that category but beyond this there is little agreement. The examples of strict liability being asserted are limited but an example is afforded by Art 2 of the Convention on International Liability for Damage caused by Space Objects (1972) which reads: ' A launching State shall be absolutely liable to pay compensation for damage caused by its space object on the surface of the earth or to aircraft in flight.' However, the most obvious area for the application of the principle concerns nuclear activity and this is a matter to which one must now turn.

11 NUCLEAR ACTIVITY[181]

The development of nuclear technology and its deployment to such effect in the late summer of 1945 concentrated the minds of statesmen and international lawyers. Nuclear weapons could not be disinvented and thus effort would be required both to promote the peaceful settlement of disputes and to ensure non-proliferation of such weapons. On the other hand nuclear energy devoted to civil purposes seemed to offer a system in which the benefits of cheap energy outweighed any risk factors. From the outset the international community had three problems to confront. First, how to prevent the proliferation of nuclear technology for weapons purposes. Secondly, how to ensure that the testing of nuclear weapons did not do serious harm to the environment. Thirdly, how to ensure that the operation of civil nuclear power installations did not pose a threat to immediate neighbours. Given that the state of scientific knowledge was only gradually developing the framework of international law has had to adjust to the developing scientific consensus in a new field of activity. Moreover, as with space exploration in the early years nuclear technology was the concern of only a limited number of states.

In the context of nuclear weapons it was soon established after 1945 that one of the objectives must be to prevent the spread of nuclear weapons technology beyond the five permanent members of the Security Council. The tension of the Cold War was perhaps not the most encouraging backdrop but, in 1968, the principle of non-proliferation was endorsed in the Nuclear Non Proliferation Treaty of that year. Such a treaty was designed to prevent acquisition by new states but it did nothing to reduce the stockpiles of existing nuclear states. The essence of the treaty is contained in Arts I and II. Article I requires nuclear weapon states not to transfer to a non-nuclear weapons state any form of nuclear weapons or related technology and not to permit or in any manner encourage a non-nuclear weapons state to become a nuclear power. Article II requires those state parties that are non-nuclear weapons states to refrain form accepting the transfer of nuclear weapons or related devices. Further, Art IV permits all state parties to employ nuclear energy for peaceful purposes.

Since the early 1950s it had been the pattern of nuclear states to engage in various forms of weapons testing;[182] gradually it came to be recognised that such testing in the atmosphere or under water might itself have serious environmental consequences. These

---

181 See generally, A Boyle (1989) 60 BYIL 257 .
182 See *Pearce v Secretary of State for Defence* [1988] AC 755.

reservations lead to the 1963 Test Ban Treaty[183] which was accepted by three of the then five nuclear states. The treaty effectively banned all testing in the atmosphere, outer space or under water. but was not signed by France or China who were both intent on continuing further testing. The nuclear testing undertaken by the French government resulted in Australia and New Zealand seeking a declaration that atmospheric testing in the South Pacific was contrary to international law[184] and an infringement of sovereign rights; in the event the Court[185] found that it was unable to determine the issue as the French government had issued a statement indicating its intention to cease atmospheric nuclear testing.[186] At a later date when a new French administration[187] announced its intention in 1995 to resume underground nuclear testing New Zealand sought to reopen the 1974 judgment on the basis that radioactive material would be introduced into the environment such as to infringe sovereignty and that in any event such testing was contrary to international law in the absence of an environmental impact assessment. The Court rejected an attempt[188] to reopen the 1974 judgment under para 63 on the basis that the earlier judgment was concerned with atmospheric testing and could not be preyed in aid in respect of the resumption of underground testing. Although the decision of the majority disposed of the case much attention has focused on the scholarly dissenting opinions of Judges Weeramantry and Komora who were prepared to give considerable emphasis to the environmental duties that one state bore towards another.

The most recent consideration of the deployment of nuclear weapons came in the case of the Legality of the Use by a State of Nuclear Weapons in Armed Conflict[189] where the International Court of Justice declined to give an Advisory Opinion requested by the WHO Assembly. However, it did give an Advisory Opinion requested by the United Nations General Assembly reasoning that subject to one possible exception the threat or use of nuclear weapons 'would generally be contrary to the rules of international law applicable in armed conflict'.

On the civil side the 1950s had witnessed an increasing interest in the development of nuclear power for energy generation. It was clear that the economic growth of the post-war period could only be sustained by cheap and plentiful energy sources; nuclear power seemed to offer an energy source cheap in cost, containable and safe. As early as 1956, the

---

183 Treaty Banning Nuclear Weapons Tests in the Atmosphere, in Outer Space and Under Water.

184 In 1973, the Court had concluded that there was a *prima facie* case for jurisdiction and ordered interim measures see Nuclear Tests (Interim Protection) (1973) ICJ 99.

185 *Nuclear Tests* cases (*Australia v France; New Zealand v France*) (1974) ICJ 253; see T Franck (1975) 69 AJIL 612 The decision of the Court was reached by nine votes to six on the basis that a declaration by the French government rendered the entire issue academic; interestingly the minority judges included Sir Humphrey Waldock and *ad hoc* judge Sir Garfield Barwick.

186 The statement was issued by President Giscard d'Estaing (1974–81) who had been elected following the death of President Pompidou (1969–74) in April 1974. The Court took the view that New Zealand and Australia were principally objecting to atmospheric nuclear testing.

187 President Chirac having been elected in 1995 following the conclusion of the second term of François Mitterand (1981–95).

188 *Request for an Examination of the Situation in Accordance with Paragraph 63 of the Court's Judgment of 1974 in the Nuclear Tests case* (1995) ICJ 228; see R Volterra [1996] CLJ 3.

189 *Legality of the Use by a State of Nuclear Weapons in Armed Conflict* (1996) ICJ 66. For a detailed analysis, see P Sands and L Boisson de Chazournes (eds), *International Law, the International Court of Justice and Nuclear Weapons*, 1997; MJ Matheson (1997) 91 AJIL 419.

International Atomic Energy Agency had been established to facilitate the growth of nuclear power. However, by the early 1970s, questions of energy were at the forefront of debate; concerns were expressed about the disposal of nuclear waste,[190] controversy arose as to the safety of different forms of nuclear reactor[191] and a number of high profile incidents changed the terms of the debate.[192] In a number of countries, environmental groups began to campaign against the building of new nuclear power facilities.[193] These however were purely domestic concerns normally to be determined through the relevant planning law process.

Although concern about the safety of nuclear power had been a subject of discussion in a number of states the international aspect did not become fully apparent until after the accident at Chernobyl in the then Soviet Union. On 26 April 1986, an accident occurred during the testing of a turbo generator unit in the fourth unit of the Chernobyl Nuclear Power Plant. The following day increased levels of radiation were noticed in Sweden, Denmark and Poland. It was only on 28 April 1986, 72 hours after the original incident that the Soviet Government informed the International Atomic Energy Agency. In the interim the outside world had relied on information gleaned from spy satellites. The experience of Chernobyl gave rise to a number of relevant legal questions; the salient problems were as follows:

(a) Does a state owe a legal duty to prevent the escape of radioactive material?

(b) What is the nature of its duty in respect of any consequent damage?

(c) Is such a state obliged to inform neighbouring states of such an escape?

(d) What legal arrangements exist to provide for mutual assistance?

The failure of the Soviet Union to respond quickly resulted in the adoption, under the auspices of the IAEA, of the Vienna Convention on Early Notification of a Nuclear Accident (1986).[194] Under the terms of Art 2 of the Convention, a state party is obliged to 'forthwith, notify, directly or through the International Atomic Energy Agency ... those states which are or may be physically affected ... of the nuclear accident, its nature, the time of its occurrence and its exact location where appropriate ...'. The Convention further provides that full, detailed and precise information is provided[195] so that neighbouring states may minimise the radiological consequences.[196] The Convention confers a co-

---

190 Partially banned under the London Dumping Convention (1972).

191 By the early 1970s, debates arose in the United States and the United Kingdom as to the relative safety records of the British made gas cooled nuclear reactor and the American Pressurised Water Reactor.

192 Although the first civil nuclear accident was at Windscale in 1957, it did not attract much publicity. Of more consequence was the accident in a PWR at Three Mile Island near Harrisburg, Pennsylvania in 1979, which attracted considerable press interest and coincided with the release of the mainstream film, *The China Syndrome* (1979) which took as its theme the issues of nuclear safety and transparency.

193 In the United Kingdom, those campaigning against an expansion of nuclear facilities were able to submit evidence to the Windscale Enquiry (1976–77) chaired by Mr Justice Parker.

194 Convention on Early Notification of a Nuclear Accident (1986) 25 ILM 1370. In force 27 October 1986.

195 Convention on the Early Notification of a Nuclear Accident (1986), Art 5.

196 *Ibid*, Art 2.

ordinating role on the IAEA[197] and further provides for consultation[198] and the mandatory settlement of disputes.[199]

The Notification Convention was the first multilateral convention on the topic and, while it may reflect some of the prior learning on transboundary obligations,[200] it is limited in that it only applies in respect of non-military accidents. It should also be noted that, by the terms of Art 1(1), the notification obligations only arise if the release or escape 'could be of radiological safety significance for another state'. The Notification Convention of 1986 has been followed by a number of bilateral agreements on the same topic.[201]

The second instrument to emerge was the Vienna Convention on Assistance in Cases of Nuclear Emergency (1986), although this document had been anticipated in the 1963 Nordic Mutual Emergency Assistance Agreement in Connection with Radiation Accidents.[202] In general, there is no obligation in international law for one state to assist another in respect of a major disaster although many do so on the basis of shared humanitarian concern. However, it is desirable that questions of control of assistance, finance and liability should be clearly established in advance. The 1963 Nordic Mutual Assistance Agreement sets out the terms for mutual assistance[203] and provides a co-ordinating role for the IAEA;[204] in general the requesting state is to bear all risks and claims resulting from assistance rendered on its territory and covered by the Agreement.[205]

The policy of mutual assistance between states in respect of major disasters was endorsed by the General Assembly in 1971 and this initiative resulted in the establishment of a United Nations Disaster Relief Office with a Disaster Relief Co-ordinator.[206] Even before Chernobyl, it was recognised that a speedy response was essential in any nuclear accident. The heightened concern after Chernobyl resulted in the adoption of the Vienna Convention on Assistance in the Case of a Nuclear Accident or Radiological Emergency.

The Convention provides that state parties acting between themselves and through the IAEA shall co-operate in the event of a nuclear accident.[207] A state may seek

---

197 *Ibid,* Art 4.

198 *Ibid,* Art 6.

199 *Ibid,* Art 11.

200 At least by analogy with the *Trail Smelter* case (1941) 3 RIAA 1907; *Corfu Channel* case (*United Kingdom v Albania*) (1949) ICJ 4; *Lac Lanoux Arbitration* (1957) 24 ILR 101.

201 See eg, 1987 Agreement between Belgium and the Netherlands on Co-operation in Nuclear Safety (1988) 41 NLB 42; 1987 Norway-Sweden Agreement on Exchange of Information and Early Notification Relating to Nuclear Facilities (1987) 17 EPL 41; 1987 United Kingdom-Norway Agreement on Early Notification Cmnd 371.

202 Adopted in Vienna on 17th October 1963 and subsequently ratified by Denmark, Finland, Norway and Sweden.

203 Nordic Mutual Emergency Assistance Agreement (1963), Art 1.

204 *Ibid,* Art 2.

205 *Ibid,* Arts 3 and 4.

206 GA Res 2816 (XXVI) had provided for the establishment of a Disaster Relief Co-ordinator. The resolution was adopted on 14 December 1971 by 86 votes in favour and none against.

207 Vienna Convention on Assistance (1986), Art 1; see (1986) 25 ILM 1377.

assistance whether or not the emergency originates within its own territory.[208] The IAEA must respond to detailed requests for assistance[209] by making available appropriate resources and transmitting promptly the request to other states and international organisations.[210] It is provided that the requesting state shall have overall control of the assistance unless otherwise agreed.[211] The Convention indicates the duties placed upon the IAEA including the obligation to provide experts, equipment and materials.[212] Assisting states may provide assistance without cost or subject to reimbursement.[213] The Convention makes provision for immunities and rights of transit;[214] in the case of death or injury to the personnel of an assisting state the obligation to compensate shall fall upon the requesting state.[215] Thus, the overall principle of the Convention is to balance the need for immediate, co-ordinated expert assistance with the principle of respect for the sovereign authority of the requesting state.

A second area of concern arises under the subject of prevention. One of the principal concerns in the last two decades has been that damage might be caused by reason of the obsolescence or faulty operation of a civil nuclear installation. As a matter of customary international law the principal responsibility for the safety of a nuclear installation falls upon the state in which the facility is situated. This has been a particular concern following the break up of the Soviet Union where the western world perceived that a number of installations were old and subject to an immature safety culture. Following discussions initiated in 1991, the IAEA adopted in 1994 the Vienna Convention on Nuclear Safety which is broadly intended to establish a policing and review system in this sensitive area. The Convention proceeds on the basis that responsibility for nuclear safety rests with the state having jurisdiction over a nuclear installation.[216] Each contracting state is obliged to take legislative, administrative and regulatory action to ensure nuclear safety.[217] Under the terms of Art 7 it is provided that municipal legislation should include a licensing scheme for the operation of nuclear installations with safeguards permitting suspension, modification and revocation in appropriate cases. The Convention sets out a number of general principles relevant to siting,[218] design and construction,[219] operation[220] and emergency preparedness of nuclear installations.[221] The Convention envisages a system of state reporting to a review committee.[222] Under the terms of Art 31,

---

208 *Ibid,* Art 2(1).
209 *Ibid,* Art 2(2).
210 *Ibid,* Art 2(6).
211 *Ibid,* Art 3.
212 *Ibid,* Art 5.
213 *Ibid,* Art 7.
214 *Ibid,* Arts 8 and 9.
215 *Ibid,* Art 10.
216 See Preamble (iii) Vienna Convention on Nuclear Safety (1994).
217 *Ibid,* Art 4.
218 *Ibid,* Art 17.
219 *Ibid,* Art 18.
220 *Ibid,* Art 19.
221 *Ibid,* Art 16.
222 *Ibid,* Arts 5 and 20.

the Convention is to come into force on receipt of 22 ratifications of which 17 must be by states having at least one nuclear installation.

A related matter that deserves consideration is the question of liability in civil law for dangerous escapes or discharges. In principle any escape or damaging discharge of radiation is prima facie tortious and so one possible solution is to engraft suitable rules of private international law so that those damaged in state B by a discharge originating in state A should be allowed to bring actions directly before the courts of state A where the damage originated or in the courts of state B where the harmful effects arose.[223]

However, it has long been recognised that transboundary discharges are best dealt with by specific international agreement. The first specific attempt was made in the OEEC[224] Paris Convention on Third Party Liability in the Field of Nuclear Energy (1960) which was then supplemented by the Brussels Supplementary Convention on Third Party Liability in the Field of Nuclear Energy (1963).[225] Article 3 of the 1960 Convention provides that the operator of the nuclear installation shall be liable for damage to or loss of life of any person and damage to or loss of any property.[226] The Paris Convention provides a financial ceiling on liability which was then modified in 1963. The Paris Convention was opened for signature on 29 July 1960 and entered into force on 1 April 1968 by which time there had been acts of ratification or accession by 14 European states.

Related to the Paris Convention (1960) is the Brussels Convention on the Liability of Operators of Nuclear Ships (1962) which stipulates in Art 2 that the operator of the nuclear ship shall be strictly liable for any damage on proof of causation. In this context it is sensible to compare the Paris Convention (1960) with the Brussels Convention (1962). Both conventions impose strict liability upon the operator[227] and both instruments stipulate that the operator shall be obliged to possess liability insurance.[228] The two conventions together with the Vienna Convention (1963) are concerned to impose financial limits on the extent of liability.[229] The provision of absolute liability subject to financial limits has been thought appropriate in the past. Both the Paris Convention and the Vienna Convention deal expressly with competence by providing that the courts of the contracting party in whose territory the incident occurred shall have jurisdiction;[230] it is further provided that judgments given by a competent court shall be recognised[231] in the territory of other contracting parties.

---

223 As an example, see Brussels Convention on Jurisdiction and the Enforcement of Judgments in Civil and Commercial Matters (1968), Art 5(3); see Case 21/76 *Bier BV v Mines de Potasse D'Alsace SA* [1978] QB 708; [1976] ECR 1735; *Shevill v Presse Alliance SA* [1995] 2 AC 18; [1996] AC 959; C Forsyth [1995] CLJ 515; A Briggs (1996) 67 BYIL 586.

224 Now OECD.

225 Given effect to in the United Kingdom in the Nuclear Installations Act 1965 as amended by Nuclear Installations Act 1969, as extended by Congenital Disabilities (Civil Liability) Act 1976.

226 Save to the extent excluded under Art 3(a)(1) and (2) Paris Convention (1960).

227 Paris Convention (1960), Art 3; Brussels Convention (1962), Art 2.

228 Paris Convention (1960), Art 10; Brussels Convention (1962), Art 3.

229 See Paris Convention (1960), Art 7; Brussels Convention (1963), Art 3; Vienna Convention (1963), Art V.

230 See Paris Convention (1960), Art 13; Vienna Convention (1963), Art XI.

231 See Paris Convention (1960), Art 13(d); Vienna Convention (1963), Arts XI and XII. (It is of note that Art XII provided that recognition may be refused on the traditional grounds of fraud, abuse of natural justice or violation of public policy.)

It has to be admitted that the conventions have had only limited effect. An accident such as Chernobyl would not be within the scope of the Conventions because the USSR was not a party at the operative date. Secondly, it is far from clear whether the citizens of non-parties can invoke the conventions. Thirdly, while a significant number of Western European states are parties to the Paris Convention only a limited number of states have chosen to become parties to the three relevant global conventions.[232] In cases where the conventions do not operate then litigation will be subject to the normal principles of state responsibility and transboundary civil proceedings.

12 HAZARDOUS WASTE[233]

The problem of the disposal of toxic, chemical dangerous and hazardous waste has grown noticeably in the last quarter of a century. Partly this is because of increased scientific knowledge about the risks posed to human health by certain practices and partly because certain NGOs have sought to focus greater attention on the issue. There has been a desire to introduce a regulatory system to control dumping at sea and disposal in underdeveloped countries; the latter being at particular risk because of the presence of strict planning controls in most developed states.

The dumping of waste was subject to few restraints prior to the 1970s. However, regional co-operation in the North East Atlantic area was advanced by the Convention for the Prevention of Marine Pollution by Dumping from Ships and Aircraft (1972) (the 'Oslo Convention'), which introduced a ban on the dumping of certain substances while subjecting others to regulatory control. On a global basis, the Convention on the Prevention of Marine Pollution by Dumping of Wastes and Other Matter (1972)[234] (the 'London Convention') subjects dumping[235] outside internal waters to prohibition save where expressly permitted.

In addition to restraints on dumping attempts have been made to curtail transboundary traffic in hazardous waste; under the auspices of the United Nations Environment Programme (UNEP) the Basel Convention[236] on the Control of Transboundary Movements of Hazardous Wastes and their Disposal (the 'Basel Convention') was adopted in 1989 and entered into force on 5 May 1992. The Convention itself owed much to the determined approach of the Council of Ministers of the

---

232 Ie, Brussels Convention on Nuclear Ships (1962); Vienna Convention on Civil Liability for Nuclear Damage (1963); Convention on Maritime Carriage of Nuclear Material (1972).

233 See K Kummer (1992) 41 ICLQ 530; K Kummer, 1st edn, 1995; 2nd edn, 2000.

234 (1972) 11 ILM 1294; in force from 30 August 1975.

235 Dumping was defined in Art 19 of the Oslo Convention as 'any deliberate disposal of of substances and materials into the sea'. The London Convention defines dumping as the deliberate disposal of waste from ships and aircraft.

236 Drawn up at the Basel Conference in the Control of Transboundary Movements of Hazardous Wastes which met in March 1989; it required 20 ratifications to enter into force and these were secured by 5 February 1992.

Organisation of African Unity[237] who had sought a strong Convention with detailed safeguards against waste traffic from developed to developing countries.

The Basel Convention rejects the concept of a complete ban on transboundary movements; it applies to those wastes stipulated in the relevant Annexes[238] to the instrument. The Convention takes as a basic principle the need to ensure that the generation of hazardous wastes should be reduced to a minimum and where such generation cannot be avoided then the waste should be disposed as closely as possible to the source of generation. The Convention further requires state parties to co-operate 'in order to improve and achieve environmentally sound management of hazardous wastes and other wastes'.[239] Under the terms of Art 4 it is provided that state parties shall prohibit the export of hazardous wastes to those states that have prohibited such imports. Where such imports are not prohibited then exports shall only be permitted where a state issues a consent in writing to a specific import.

In cases where transboundary movement of hazardous waste is not prohibited it must be carried out in accordance with the prior informed procedure stipulated in Arts 6 and 7. Transboundary movements that are not in accordance with the Convention are categorised as unlawful; the Convention requires its parties to adopt and enforce municipal legislation to prevent and punish unlawful traffic.[240] Transit states can prohibit transit passage and the exporting state must not permit transboundary movement to commence until it has the written consent of the transit state.[241]

The Basel Convention does not apply to the movement of radioactive waste but this omission has been filled by the Code of Practice adopted in 1990 by IAEA on the International Transboundary Movement of Radioactive Waste which seeks to ensure that such movement should not take place without the prior consent of the sending, receiving and transit states as stipulated by the terms of their municipal law.

13 MARINE POLLUTION

The problem of marine pollution has attracted a considerable degree of prominence in the last quarter of a century. Marine pollution may arise from the operations of shipping, dumping at sea, conduct on the sea bed and the effects of land based activities. In the last two decades an attempt has been made to obtain a degree of international co-operation in respect of the four main sources of marine pollution namely the operation of ships, dumping, sea bed activities and land based activities.

---

237 In the OAU Council of Ministers Resolution on Dumping of Nuclear and Industrial Wastes in Africa CM/Re 1153(XLVIII), it was declared that the import of such waste into Africa was a crime against the African people. African states took an active part in the negotiations prior to the adoption of the Basel Convention. On 29 June 1991, the OAU adopted the Bamako Convention on the Ban on the Import of all Forms of Hazardous Wastes into Africa and the Control of Transboundary Movements of Such Wastes Generated in Africa. In broad terms, the Convention prohibits the importation of wastes into Africa by non-parties.

238 See Basel Convention (1989), Art 1 and Annexes I to III. Broadly such wastes comprise a core list together with those prohibited by individual state legislation.

239 Basel Convention (1989), Art 10.

240 Articles 4(4), 9(5).

241 Article 6(4).

In respect of pollution from ships a problem arises because some pollution is caused by normal shipping operations. In particular, when a tanker washed its empty tanks prior to taking on a new cargo some pollution would be caused by the normal discharge. The first attempt to introduce a degree of control was effected by the International Convention for the Prevention of Pollution of the Sea by Oil (1954)[242] which had the effect of prohibiting discharges within a certain distance of land. However, this instrument was superseded by the International Convention for the Prevention of Pollution from Ships (1973)[243] (usually referred to as the MARPOL Convention) which was adopted under the auspices of the IMO.[244] The MARPOL Convention is intended to deal with all forms of intentional pollution from ships other than dumping and it contains detailed regulations set out in a number of Annexes which deal with oil, noxious substances, harmful substances, sewage and garbage. The scope of the Convention is such that it applies to all vessels of a state party other than warships and those engaged in non-commercial purposes.

The desire to increase the power of states over vessels flying their flag was evidenced by UNCLOS, Art 211(2) which reads:

> States shall adopt laws and regulations for the prevention, reduction and control of pollution of the marine environment from vessels flying their flag or of their registry. Such laws and regulations shall at least have the same effect as that of generally accepted international rules and standards established through the competent international organisation or general diplomatic conference.

In principle, the coastal state may legislate to prevent pollution within the territorial sea[245] or the EEZ. In respect of enforcement, UNCLOS, Art 217 provides that Flag states must enforce violations of pollution laws wheresoever committed; while the coastal state may exercise enforcement powers under UNCLOS, Art 220. In cases where a vessel within territorial waters has committed offences, then the coastal state has powers of inspection and detention.

One of the commonest causes of marine pollution is the accidental not the intentional act and the danger of such accidental pollution became apparent after the *Torrey Canyon* incident (1967); thereafter questions arose as to the precise powers of the coastal state to act. The immediate response was the Convention relating to Intervention on the High Seas in cases of *Oil Pollution Casualties* (1969) (sometimes known as the Intervention Convention).[246] In broad terms, Art 1 provides for the freedom of the coastal state and reads:

---

242 International Convention for the Prevention of Pollution of the Sea by Oil (1954). In force from 26 July 1958. Amendments to the Convention were adopted in 1962 and 1969.

243 International Convention for the Prevention of Pollution from Ships (1973) as amended by Protocol London 1 June 1978. In force 2 October 1983.

244 The International Maritime Organisation was established in 1958 under the terms of a treaty adopted in 1948. Until 1982 it was known as the Intergovernmental Maritime Consultative Organisation (IMCO). The IMO operates through a Council and an Assembly but most of the work in formulating international conventions is done in the various technical committees.

245 UNCLOS (1982), Art 21.

246 International Convention relating to Intervention on the High Seas in Cases of Oil Pollution Casualties (1969). In force 6 May 1975.

State parties may take such measures on the high seas as may be necessary to prevent, mitigate or eliminate grave and imminent danger to their coastline or related interests from pollution or threat of pollution of the sea by oil, following upon a maritime casualty or acts related to such casualty, which may reasonably be expected to result in major harmful consequences.

To ensure that states are prepared to take active measures in case of accidents concerning oil certain minimum obligations are stipulated under the International Convention on Oil Pollution Preparedness, Response and Co-operation (1990).[247] The Convention provides for the establishment of effective national systems to respond to such incidents; it further provides for the provision of information and the obtaining of assistance from other states and the financing of such assistance. The worth of the Convention was demonstrated in January 1991 when the IMO acted as if the Convention were in force in respect of the discharge of oil into the Gulf from oil terminals in Kuwait.

In respect of liability compensation is governed by the International Convention on Civil Liability for Oil Pollution Damage (sometimes referred to as the Civil Liability Convention) (1969).[248] In broad terms the Convention imposes strict liability on the shipowner for the escape of oil subject to certain financial limits which operate unless the shipowner is at fault. The Convention provides for the maintenance of insurance and sets out rules for the bringing of civil claims. The Civil Liability Convention is supplemented by the International Convention on the Establishment of an International Fund for Compensation for Oil Pollution Damage (1971) (sometimes referred to as the Fund Convention). The Convention provides for compensation[249] where the shipowner is not liable or where he is liable but is unable to meet his obligations. The 1969 Civil Liability Convention and the 1971 Fund Convention have been modified by two Protocols which were adopted in 1992 and came into force in 1996.[250] The Protocols change the relevant financial limits and provide for two new conventions: the 1992 Civil Liability and Fund Conventions.

In respect of dumping at sea the practice had grown steadily in the 1950s as land based dumping became subject to increasing legislative control. Article 25 of the 1958 High Seas Convention had required states to take measures against marine pollution caused by radioactive waste. The demand for global regulation lead to the adoption of the Convention on the Prevention of Marine Pollution by Dumping of Wastes and Other Matter (1972)[251] (usually referred to as the London Convention). The London Convention sets out a detailed scheme to control dumping of waste and state parties are then required

---

247 The International Convention on Oil Pollution Preparedness, Response and Co-Operation (1990). In force 13 May 1995.
248 As modified by Protocols in 1976, 1984, 1992.
249 From the International Oil Pollution Compensation Fund established under the Convention.
250 The International Convention on Civil Liability for Oil Pollution Damage (1969) subject to amendment by the London Protocol of 27 November 1992 and in force on 30 May 1996. This has the effect of renaming the 1969 Convention as the International Convention on Civil Liability for Oil Pollution Damage (1992). The International Convention on the Establishment of an International Fund for Compensation for Oil Pollution damage (1971), as amended by the London Protocol of 27 November 1992. in force 30 May 1996. This has the effect of renaming the 1971 Convention as the International Convention on the Establishment of an International Fund for Oil Pollution Damage 1992.
251 Convention on the Prevention of Marine Pollution by Dumping of Wastes and Other Matter London, 29 December 1972. In force 30 August 1975.

to take legislative action to impose the controls on vessels or aircraft registered in its territory or flying its flag. as well as those loading within its territory or otherwise under its jurisdiction.

The problem of pollution from deep sea mining on the high seas is provided for in UNCLOS, Art 145 which requires the International Seabed Authority to make rules to prevent pollution from deep sea mining. In respect of land based sources of marine pollution there has been a hesitation in acting because of the implications for state sovereignty. Articles 207 and 213 of UNCLOS require state parties to make and enforce laws designed to restrict 'pollution of the marine environment from land based sources'. Attempts have been made to secure regional co-operation of which the best known effort is the Convention for the Prevention of Marine Pollution from Land based Sources (usually referred to as the Paris Convention) (1972) which was replaced by the 1992 Convention for the Protection of the Marine Environment of the North East Atlantic.

14 OUTER SPACE[252]

It is provided in Art 1 of the Outer Space Treaty (1967)[253] that 'the exploration and use of outer space, including the moon and other celestial bodies, shall be carried out for the benefit of all countries ... and shall be the province of all mankind'. It is further provided in Art 4 that nuclear weapons and other weapons of mass destruction shall not be placed in orbit around the earth. Liability of state parties for objects launched into outer space is provided for by Art 7 of the same. The broad thrust of treaty law in respect of outer space is not simply to restrain causes of conflict but also to ensure that undue damage is not inflicted on the general environment. Thus, Art 7 of the Agreement Governing the Activities of States on the Moon and other Celestial Bodies (1979)[254] provides that:

> In exploring and using the moon, States Parties shall take measures to prevent the disruption of the existing balance of its environment, whether by introducing adverse changes in that environment, by its harmful contamination through the introduction of extra-environmental matter or otherwise.

A particular contemporary problem is that of space debris arising from space objects. A 'space object' is the generic term used to describe all objects that human beings have launched or attempted to be launch into outer space; this designation will include spacecraft, satellites and launch vehicles. Such a designation is recognised in the Outer Space Treaty (1967),[255] the Convention on International Liability for Damage Caused by Space Objects (the Liability Convention) (1972)[256] and the Agreement Governing the

---

252 See generally, B Cheng (1997).
253 Adopted on 19 December 1966, opened for signature 27 January 1967, entered into force 10 October 1967.
254 Adopted on 5 December 1979, opened for signature on 18 December 1979, entered into force on 11 July 1984. See CQ Christol (1985) 79 AJIL 163.
255 See Art 7, Outer Space Treaty (1967).
256 Adopted on 29 November 1971; entered into force 1 September 1972. See Arts 2 and 3 of the Liability Convention (1972).

Activities of States on the Moon and other Celestial Bodies (1979).[257] As a broad principle the state is liable for damage caused by its space objects to other states and their nationals.

It would seem that the ownership of such objects is a matter of municipal law and such objects or debris are not to be treated as *res derelicta* simply because there may be no *animus domini*.[258] Liability may arise under the 1967 Outer Space Treaty,[259] the 1972 Liability Convention[260] or the 1979 Moon Treaty[261] and there is authority for the view that a state should be strictly liable for damage resulting from space debris generated by a space object.[262]

15 SUMMARY

It therefore follows from the above that international environmental law for the most part comprises those multilateral law making instruments concluded in the last quarter of a century of which the most significant can be summarised as follows:

(1) Convention on Long Range Transboundary Air Pollution, Geneva, 13 November 1979;[263]

(2) Convention for the Protection of the Ozone Layer, Vienna, 22 March 1985;[264]

(3) Convention on Early Notification of a Nuclear Accident, Vienna, 26 September 1986;[265]

(4) Protocol on Substances that Deplete the Ozone Layer, Montreal, 16 September 1987;[266]

(5) Convention on the Control of Transboundary Movements of Hazardous Wastes and their Disposal, Basel, 22 March 1989;[267]

(6) Convention on the Protection and Use of Transboundary Watercourses and Lakes, Helsinki 17 March 1992;

(7) Framework Convention on Climate Change, New York, 9 May 1992;[268]

(8) Protocol on the Further Reduction of Sulphur Emissions, Oslo, 14 June 1994;

(9) Convention on the Law of the Non Navigational Uses of International Watercourses, New York, 8 July 1997.

---

257 Agreement Governing the Activities of States on the Moon and Other Celestial Bodies (1979) entered into force 11 July 1984; see Art 14(2).

258 See B Cheng (1997), p 416.

259 Outer Space Treaty (1967), Arts 7 and 8.

260 Liability Convention (1972), Arts 2 and 3.

261 Moon Treaty (1979), Art 14(2).

262 See the International Instrument on the Protection of the Environment from Damage Caused by Space Debris adopted by the International Law Association at its Sixty Sixth Conference in 1994.

263 Entered into force 16 March 1983.

264 Entered into force 22 September 1985.

265 Entered into force 27 October 1986.

266 Entered into force 1 January 1989.

267 Entered into force 5 May 1992.

268 Entered into force 21 March 1994.

It is to be noted that the need for specific and detailed provision has lead to the growth of treaty law. It would seem that the pattern of future development is likely to be on the basis of specific treaties. The pattern of drafting a Framework Convention and then proceeding to detailed protocols[269] has proved to be a sensible *modus operandi*.

16 CONCLUSIONS

As indicated above the scope of international environmental law has grown rapidly in the last quarter of a century. The limited nature of customary rules and the upsurge in activity since 1972 has meant that much of the relevant law is contained in multilateral law making treaties. A number of points can usefully be made. First, although environmental concerns will be of direct relevance in international disputes they will have to be accommodated within the traditional principles of international law of which the law of state responsibility is of continuing relevance. Secondly, it is clear that the success of multilateral law making treaties will depend not only on methods of enforcement but also on the extent to which a scientific consensus can be established. Thirdly, while the International Court of Justice has established a special Chamber[270] to consider cases raising problems of environmental law it is open to question as to whether the International Court is the appropriate forum where the disputes turns on the inferences to be drawn from conflicting scientific evidence. rather than on pure questions of law.[271]

---

269 See, for example, the Framework Convention on Climate Change (1992) followed by the Kyoto Protocol (10 December 1997) (1998) 37 ILM 22.

270 A matter that had been been under consideration for some years. See the statement made by Sir Robert Jennings (then President of the ICJ) to the Rio Conference in 1992 entitled 'The role of the ICJ in the development of international environmental protection law'. Jurisdiction to establish such a Chamber arises under Art 26(1) of the Statute. On the question of the Chambers system, see S Schwebel (1987) 81 AJIL 831; S Oda (1988) 82 AJIL 556; R Ostrihansky (1988) 37 ICLQ 30.

271 See PN Okowa, 'Environmental dispute settlement, some reflections on recent developments', in MD Evans (ed), *Remedies in International Law, The Institutional Dilemma*, 1998, London: Hart.

CHAPTER 18

STATE SUCCESSION[1]

1 INTRODUCTION

The purpose of this chapter is to outline the principles pertaining to the area of 'state succession' which as a subject should be distinguished from the related topic of 'succession of governments'. It has been said on more than one occasion that the area of state succession is one of the less clearly defined areas of public international law. Thus, the Badinter Commission established by the Conference on Yugoslavia could assert that 'there are few well established principles of international law that apply to state succession. Application of these principles is largely to be determined case by case, though the 1978 and 1983 Vienna Conventions do offer some guidance'. Similar sentiments have been expressed by municipal courts. One of the problems in this area is that the expression 'state succession' is used to describe a wide number of different factual situation and it is misleading to embark on analogies with private law where on death or personal and corporate insolvency legislation provides for the assets of the prior legal person to vest or fall under the control of another legal person. In most municipal systems such rules will be established by legislation and are routinely applied each year in large numbers of cases.

One definition of state succession might be that state succession arises when there is 'a definitive replacement of one state by another in respect of sovereignty over a given territory' Another approach would be to follow the definition contained in Art 2 of the Vienna Convention on the Succession of States in respect of Treaties (1978) in which the expression 'succession of states' was defined to mean 'the replacement of one state by another in the responsibility for the international relations of territory'. In reality, it is sensible to regard the expression 'state succession' as an omnibus expression designed to cover a wide number of factual situations. Secondly, when in municipal law an individual dies or a company becomes insolvent the event will affect a number of immediate individuals but the general legal system will apply its rules to the determination of property rights. In contrast, in some situations of state succession the entire existence of the state may be in issue, political passions may be heightened and an atmosphere of conflict may prevail;[2] in these circumstances, there may a reluctance to apply general principles and an insistence that all questions of dispute should be regulated by specific treaty.

---

1   See generally, DP O'Connell (1967), 2 Vols; K Zemanek (1965) 116 HR 181; DP O'Connell (1970) 130 HR 95; I Brownlie (1998), Chap 28; *Oppenheim's International Law*, 9th edn, (RY Jennings and AD Watts (eds)), Vol 1, pp 208–45; FA Mann (1972) 88 LQR 57; R Lavalle (1979) 73 AJIL 407; R Mullerson (1993) 42 ICLQ 473.

2   The obvious example being the violent events surrounding the dissolution of the former Socialist Federal Republic of Yugoslavia in 1991.

In practice, sovereignty in respect of territory may change in a variety of ways; for example:

(1) Part of the territory of state A may become incorporated in state B or it may be divided between states X, Y, and Z.

(2) Part of the territory of state A is taken to form a second state (ie, one state becomes two). This would be the case where there has been secession such as the creation of Bangladesh in 1971. To an extent this would also be the case where territory subject to a colonial power becomes a separate sovereign state.

(3) The whole of the territory of state X becomes part of state Y (ie, two states become one state).

(4) The whole of the territory of state A is divided between states X, Y and Z (ie, four states become three).

(5) The whole of the territory of state X forms the basis of several new sovereign states (eg, where there has been the dissolution of a federal state).[3]

These are simply a number of possible changes of sovereignty; moreover the method may vary and may involve cession, secession or agreement. A merger between state A and state B to form state C is clearly different from the absorption of state A by state B. If state A cedes part of its territory to state B this is different from the secession of part of state X to form state Y This situation has to be distinguished from the dissolution of state Z to form several distinct states or the granting of independence by state A to its former colony which is now to become state B.

There are thus a variety of possible situations so that many have doubted whether general rules can be any more than the starting point for discussion In each case it is important to establish the facts clearly before deciding whether general principles may be applicable. Be that as it may, it would seem that the fundamental distinction is whether the process is being achieved peacefully by consent or whether the change in sovereignty is being effected against a background of disagreement or violence.

The situation is complicated by the fact that the concept of succession may itself be disputed. It may be argued that although there have been changes the emerging entity may assert that it is simply the continuation of a prior entity. Thus, in 1991 the Russian Federation took the position that for many purposes it was simply a continuation of the USSR but within different borders. In contrast the complex and violent dissolution of the Socialist Federal Republic of Yugoslavia lead the Arbitration Commission of the EC Conference on Yugoslavia to conclude that the prior state no longer existed.

The difficulties that may arise when there is a change of sovereignty has lead many states to deal with such problems by specific treaty. Thus, in 1919 the Treaty of St Germain regulated the obligations concerning public debt that would fall upon the successor states of the Austro Hungarian Monarchy. In many cases of decolonisation a detailed agreement has been drawn up to regulate outstanding questions. Such agreements may have the virtue of certainty but there may be questions of equality of bargaining power at the time of independence.

---

3   Eg, as in 1991–92 where it was clear that the former Socialist Federal Republic of Yugoslavia was dissolving to form the states of Croatia, Slovenia, Macedonia and Bosnia-Herzegovina.

The unsatisfactory nature of the law and the problems posed by decolonisation caused the International Law Commission to embark on a study of the subject in the 1970s; a report was produced in 1977 and two codifying treaties were drawn up. The first was the 1978 Vienna Convention on State Succession in Respect of Treaties[4] and the second the 1983 Vienna Convention on State Succession in Respect of State Property, Archives and Debts.[5] It is accepted by most that this effort at codification has had only had a very limited impact. First, it is arguable that the text of the conventions is only appropriate in respect of the position of the newly independent state. Secondly, state practice has tended to diverge from the provisions of the convention. Thirdly, the very limited number of ratifications and accessions has done little to modify the view of some states that problems of state succession are best resolved on a case by case basis. However, the actual question of state succession has acquired a degree of prominence in the last decade in view of the dissolution of the Soviet Union, Yugoslavia and Czechoslovakia, the unification of Yemen and Germany together with the secession of Eritrea from Ethiopia. In the particular instance of Yugoslavia it is clear that where there is an atmosphere of mistrust and violence then problems of succession can probably only be clarified by specific treaty provision.

In many cases, the question arises as to whether a new sovereign entity is to be liable for the obligations incurred by the prior entity; these may be private rights such as concessions, contracts or property rights. Some writers have sought to argue that the governing principle is that of vested or acquired rights; this appears to mean that the change of sovereignty should not affect the rights of foreign nationals. This is not very helpful, first because the doctrine of vested right derives from private international law where it is traceable to Huber and has been espoused in this context by jurists such as AV Dicey and OW Holmes Jr. However, in the context of changes in sovereignty it begs the question; the new entity will in principle be sovereign and being endowed with legislative and judicial organs the prior rights will or will not be enforced. It must be doubtful whether any light is shed on the matter by asserting a right established under a prior sovereign and presuming it must be enforced by a subsequent sovereign. Secondly, as will be seen below it is difficult to find any clear support for the principle in the case law.

A matter that deserves noting at this stage is that in many cases of state succession a new entity may desire recognition by the wider international community or admission to an international organisation; such favours are more likely to be granted if there is a willingness to accept certain previously established obligations. It therefore follows that in this area more than many others there is a divergence between the abstract rules and actual conduct.

---

4   (1978) 17 ILM 1488. In force 1996, 15 parties.
5   (1983) 12 ILM 306. Not in force, 15 parties required.

2 STATE SUCCESSION AND THE LAW OF TREATIES

(a) Preliminary observations

One of the most important aspects of state succession in the effect of changes in sovereignty upon treaty obligations. In the modern world many technical matters are governed by treaty and any change of sovereignty is a matter of concern. In general there has been an attempt to differentiate between those treaties that concern rights over territory and other treaty obligations. The latter class would include multilateral law making treaties, bilateral treaties, and human rights treaties together with a wide category of political agreements.

In respect of succession the general rules are those of customary international law which have in part been codified by the 1978 Vienna Convention on Succession of States in respect of Treaties. However save in cases of special agreement the Convention will only apply in respect of succession taking place after the coming into force of the Convention. It is arguable that the confusion in the subject stems from an attempt in some instances to strike a balance between the Roman law tradition where all obligations devolved upon the heir and the position advanced by the United States after 1783 of the so called 'clean slate' to the effect that former colonies were not bound by treaties to which Great Britain was a party.

(b) Treaties concerned with rights over property

The general rule is that where a treaty is concerned with rights over property then there will be a succession to rights and obligations. A treaty of this category (sometimes known as a 'dispositive treaty') may relate to boundaries or to servitudes. Thus, if a boundary treaty is made between state A and state B and then the territory of state A falls under state C then that state will bound by the terms of the boundary treaty. The rule of succession in this instance is based on the need for order and stability in international relations.

This principle of territorial integrity may be traced back to the dissolution of the Spanish Empire in South America early in the 19th century; in that instance the newly independent states were obliged to follow the prior administrative of the Spanish authorities. Since that date the general principle has been that where a state succeeds to territory then in principle it succeeds to the boundaries of that territory. This has been justified on the general equitable principle that 'he who takes the benefit must also bear the burden'.

This principle also applies in the case of servitudes so that if the servient land passes to a new state then *prima facie* that new state will be bound to observe the terms of the obligation. Thus, in the *Free Zones of Upper Saxony and the District of Gex* case[6] the Permanent Court of International Justice held that France was obliged to honour a promise by Sardinia to maintain a customs free zone in respect of territory that had subsequently been acquired by France.

---

6   *Free Zones of Upper Saxony and the District of Gex* case (1932) Ser A / B, No 46.

The principle of respect for territorial boundaries is justified in the interests of maintaining stability but it can cause problems as it has in Africa where the prior colonial boundaries paid little regard to the ethnic and economic interests.[7] However, in the absence of agreement between newly independent states, the Organisation of African Unity[8] has been forced to insist upon respect for existing administrative boundaries and has generally deplored attempts at secession in the former Belgian Congo or Nigeria. The principle of respect for territorial boundaries was stressed by the International Court of Justice in the *Burkina Faso v Mali* case[9] where it noted that: 'There is no doubt that the obligation to respect pre-existing international frontiers in the event of a State succession derives form a general rule of international law whether or not the rule is expressed in the formula of *uti possidetis*.' Similarly in the confused and violent circumstances that surrounded the break up of Yugoslavia the Badinter Arbitration Commission established by the Conference on Yugoslavia observed that:[10]

> Except where otherwise agreed, the former boundaries become frontiers protected by international law. This conclusion follows from the principle of respect for the territorial status quo and, in particular from the principle of uti possidetis. *Uti possidetis* though initially applied in settling decolonisation issues in America and Africa is today recognised as a general principle, as stated by the International Court of Justice.

As the Commission indicated this principle is stated in Art 11 of the 1978 Vienna Convention in the clearest terms that:

> A succession of States does not as such affect:
>
> (a) a boundary established by a treaty; or
>
> (b) obligations and rights established by a treaty and relating to the regime of a boundary.

The emphasis on the permanence of boundaries was reiterated in the *Libya/Chad* case[11] where the Court stressed that 'once agreed, the boundary stands, for any other approach would vitiate the fundamental principle of the stability of boundaries, the importance of which has been repeatedly emphasised by the court'. The special nature of boundary arrangements is also recognised in Art 62(2) of the Vienna Convention on the Law of Treaties which stipulates that the principle of fundamental change of circumstances cannot be invoked if the treaty establishes a boundary.

It is sometimes the case that a treaty that establishes a boundary makes other territorial stipulations, for example, as to a demilitarised zone or to some other servitudes. Although this was not without controversy, Art 12 of the 1978 Vienna Convention on Succession of States in respect of Treaties provides that a succession of states does not affect such a treaty. However although boundaries are in general to be regarded as fixed a sovereign state may choose as an attribute of sovereignty to modify its own borders. Thus, in Africa, Eritrea[12] was permitted to establish itself as a distinct state when a new regime in Ethiopia agreed to allow it to do following a referendum.

---

7   See MN Shaw (1986).

8   Organisation of African Unity (1964) AHG Res / 16(1).

9   *Burkina Faso v Republic of Mali* (1986) ICJ 5554, p 566; 80 ILR 459.

10   See Opinion No 3 of 11 January 1992; (1992) 31 ILM 1499.

11   *Libya/Chad* case (1994) ICJ 6, p 37; 100 ILR, pp 1, 36.

12   Eritrea was admitted as a member of the United Nations on 28 May 1993.

(c) Political treaties

It seems to be generally accepted that where the agreement is no more than a treaty of friendship or alliance, or neutrality and where the agreement is with a particular regime then such a treaty will not bind a subsequent government or a succeeding state.

(d) Where the treaty states rules of customary international law

In cases where the multilateral treaty simply declares rules of customary international law as with parts of the United Nations Convention on the Law of the Sea (1982) then the successor state will be bound on the same principles as any other state.

(e) Objective regimes

It is argued by some writers that there is a class of treaty sometimes described as 'dispositive' treaties which regulates a particular region or location. In practice, the topic overlaps with that of servitudes but there is some support for the view amongst writers and in the wording of Art 12 that state succession does not affect such obligations and they are thus, transmissible. There is little consensus on such treaties but they certainly comprise those that regulate international waterways such as the Kiel or Suez canal.[13] In *Case concerning the Gabcikovo-Nagymaros Project (Hungary/Slovakia)*,[14] the International Court of Justice was prepared to assume not only that a treaty in respect of the Danube created an objective regime but that Art 12 of the Vienna Convention had the effect of providing for the transmissibility of objective regimes; further the Court held that Art 12 represented a rule of customary international law.

(f) Absorption and merger

Where State A is absorbed by State B and no new state is created then the former ceases to exist and the latter continues in a somewhat larger form. Such was the situation in 1990 where the Länder that comprised East Germany acceded to the Federal Republic. In this situation, the general principle is that the treaties of state B will apply to the enlarged territory but the treaties of state A of a political nature will perish with the state. This will not be the case with treaties of a territorial nature. Thus, the treaties of the predecessor state will cease to apply while the treaties of the successor state will apply unless there has been an agreement to the contrary.[15] This phenomenon is sometimes described as that of 'moving treaty boundaries'.

---

13   Eg, Permanent Neutrality and Operation of the Panama Canal Treaty (1978) (in relation to the Panama Canal); Art 1 of the Constantinople Convention (1888) (relating to passage through the Suez canal); Art 380 of the Treaty of Versailles (1919) (concerning the Kiel canal); see the *Wimbledon* case (1923) PCIJ, Ser A, No 1; 2 ILR 99.

14   *Case concerning the Gabcikovo-Nagymaros Project (Hungary/Slovakia)* (the *Danube Dam* case) (1997) ICJ 7.

15   The Unification of Germany was a special case and is noted below; however, it is relevant to observe that Annex I of the Unification Treaty excluded from the new Lander certain obligations arising from the Federal Republic's NATO obligations.

Where two or more states unite to form one successor state then the position is as set out in Art 31 of the 1978 Vienna Convention on Succession to Treaties. It is provided that 'any treaty in force at the date of the succession of States in respect of any of them continues in force in respect of the successor State'[16] unless the successor state and the other state parties otherwise agree or it appears from the treaty or is otherwise established that the application would be incompatible with the object of the treaty or would radically change the conditions for its operation.[17] By the terms of Art 31(2), it is stipulated that such a treaty will only continue in force in respect of that part of the territory that it was in force at the date of the unless it is a multilateral treaty which the successor state gives notification that it is to apply in respect of the entire territory[18] or if the multilateral treaty in issue which under its terms or by virtue of the limited number of participants and its object and purpose, the participation of any other state must be considered as requiring the consent of all the parties,[19] the successor state and the other state parties agree.

As a matter of interpretation Art 31 of the Vienna Convention on Succession to Treaties is directed to the situation where two states combine to form a third state; the provisions are not directed to the situation where one state absorbs another state and that latter entity ceases to exist. The former situation is illustrated by the merger of Egypt and Syria to form the United Arab Republic in 1958 and the coming together of Tanganyika and Zanzibar to form Tanzania in 1964; in both instances, the prior treaties continued to apply subsequent to the merger in their relevant areas. The latter situation is exemplified by the unification of Germany which is discussed below.

(g) Where territory is ceded from one state to another

Where territory formerly part of state A becomes part of state B then the general rule in customary international law is that the treaties of state A shall cease to apply while the treaties of state B will extend to the newly acquired territory. This example of the 'moving frontiers rule' is evidenced by Art 15 of the Vienna Convention on the Succession of States to Treaties which provides for the application of the treaties of the successor state save where 'it appears from the treaty or is otherwise established that the application of the treaty to the territory would be incompatible with the object and purpose of the treaty or would radically change the conditions for its operation'. Thus, when France recovered the provinces of Alsace Lorraine in 1919 it was accepted that German treaties would cease to apply and French treaties would extend to the recovered provinces. To this extent, it would seem that Art 15 codifies the practice[20] in customary law.

---

16 Vienna Convention on Succession to Treaties (1978), Art 31(1).

17 *Ibid*, Art 31(1)(a) and 31(1)(b).

18 *Ibid*, Art 31(2)(a). Unless, under the terms of Art 31(3), it appears from the treaty or is otherwise established that the application of the treaty in respect of the entire territory of the successor State would be incompatible with the object and purpose of the treaty or would radically change the conditions for its operation.

19 Vienna Convention on Succession to Treaties (1978), Art 17(3).

20 The same being the case when the United States annexed Hawaii in 1898; see DP O'Connell, *State Succession in Municipal Law and International Law*, Vol II, p 377.

(h) Where there is secession from one state to form a new state or states

The circumstances in which there can be separation are considerable. Historical examples would be the secession of Belgium in 1830 and the secession of Cuba from Spain in 1898 or the secession of Finland after 1919. However, it may be that a previously established entity has split into its component parts as with the 1961 dissolution of the United Arab Republic.[21]

It has to be acknowledged that secession has never been encouraged by the international community and, after 1945, the examples are limited.[22] It seems to be accepted[23] that the new state does not succeed to the treaties of the former state of which it was previously a part, even though the evidence of actual practice is conflicting; the principle does seem to be one of a clean slate and there are a number of examples[24] that support this view. From a positivist perspective, it is argued that the new state should not be bound by a treaty that it has not signed and is, thus, entitled to take free of the obligations of the predecessor state. However, while this approach may have had a logical simplicity[25] 100 years ago when treaty obligations were limited it is hardly realistic in the modern interdependent world.

In these circumstances, it is relevant to consider the provisions of Art 34 of the 1978 Vienna Convention on the Succession of States to Treaties which provides that 'any treaty in force at the date of the succession of States in respect of the entire territory of the predecessor State continues in force in respect of each successor State so formed'. This provision will not apply if the states concerned otherwise agree or it appears that the application of the treaty in respect of the successor State would be incompatible with the object and purpose of the treaty. In *Case concerning the Gabcikovo-Nagymaros Project (Hungary/Slovakia)*[26] the International Court of Justice reserved its position as to whether Art 34 represented a rule of customary international law. In respect of the predecessor state, Art 35 provides that existing treaties remain in force unless the states concerned otherwise agree or it is established that the treaty related only to the territory that had separated or the application of the treaty to the predecessor state would be incompatible with the object and purpose of the treaty or would radically change the conditions for its operation.

It is likely, however, that any state that secedes will be anxious to secure recognition, financial assistance and membership of the relevant international organisations. In these circumstances, the international community is in a position to exert some pressure.

---

21 See, eg, the dissolution of the Federation of Mali upon the secession of Senegal; for a general discussion, see Cohen (1960) 36 BYIL 375.

22 The most significant example being Bangladesh which seceded from Pakistan in 1971 and was admitted to the United Nations in 1974; however, the outcome was different in the case of the Congo (1960) and Biafra (1967).

23 See *Oppenheim's International Law*, p 222; O'Connell, *State Succession*, Vol II, p 88.

24 Belgium from the Netherlands (1830); Cuba from Spain (1898); Finland from Russia (1919).

25 An interesting example is afforded by the United States. The Third Restatement of US Foreign Relations Law comes down in favour of the clean slate principle which had found favour with the United States after 1783. However, in the case of the dissolution of the Soviet Union the administration took the view that Russia and the non-Baltic Republics should assume the treaty obligations of the USSR.

26 *Case concerning the Gabcikovo-Nagymaros Project (Hungary/Slovakia)* (1997) ICJ 7.

(i) Decolonised and newly independent states

One of the reasons for the International Law Commission considering the question of succession to treaties had been concerns arising from the process of decolonisation and this fact is stressed in the preamble to the 1978 Vienna Convention on the Succession of States to Treaties. The document recognises a particular category of state defined in Art 2(1)(f) as the 'newly independent state' As a general proposition, the clean slate principle[27] is recognised in Art 16 which provides that the 'newly independent State is not bound to maintain in force, or to become a party to, any treaty by reason only of the fact that at the date of the succession of states the treaty was in force in respect of the territory to which the succession of state relates'.

In addition to this general rule the Vienna Convention makes two specific further provisions. First, in respect of bilateral treaties Art 24 provided that a new state succeeds to a bilateral treaty which the predecessor state made with another state, only if that other state and the new state agree. However, in the absence of express assertion such an agreement may be inferred from conduct. Secondly, in respect of multilateral treaties the 1978 Vienna Convention provides an expedited procedure. Thus, Art 17 provides that a new state may become a party to a multilateral treaty, to which the predecessor state was a party simply by notification of the depository that it regards itself a succeeding to the treaty.[28] As an exception it is provided that a state will not succeed if succession would be regarded as incompatible with the nature and purpose of the treaty. The reason for the liberal approach in Art 17 is that multilateral conventions are more effective with a greater number of participants.

It is clear that the 1978 Vienna Convention preserves the clean slate principle in that it is expressly stated in Art 16 and no state need succeed under Arts 17 or 24 if it does not wish to do so. In the years of decolonisation, there was some uncertainty as to the clean slate principle because some newly independent states found it convenient to adopt a degree of automatic succession and often this was done in co-operation with the former colonial power. This often took the form of a devolution agreement between parent state and independent state[29] and while there might be doubt about the legal effect on third states such a procedure did contribute to clarity.

(j) Dissolution of states

When a state ceases to exist as a legal person and is replaced by other states then it is generally accepted that political or personal treaties will terminate but that treaties of pertaining to territory will continue to have effect. History affords many examples of the dismemberment of prior unions such as Norway/Sweden in 1905, the United Arab Republic in 1960 the Federation of Mali in 1960, the Federation of Rhodesia and Nyasaland in 1963 and more recently the Czech Republic and the Slovak Republic in 1992.

---

27 See generally, DP O'Connell (1949) 26 BYIL 454; (1962) 38 BYIL 84 (1964) 13 ICLQ 1450; see, also, *Lensing v HZA Berlin-Packhof* (1973) 53 ILR 153; *State v Oosthuizen* (1976) 68 ILR 3; *M v Federal Department of Justice and Police* (1979) 75 ILR 107; *Re Bottali* (1980) 78 ILR 105.

28 Article 17(1), 1978 Vienna Convention.

29 See E Lauterpacht (1958) 7 ICLQ 524; Francis (1965) 14 ICLQ 612.

Dissolution in such circumstances is likely to be a significant political event and detailed provision is likely to be made by treaty. Where there is a degree of consent then specific agreements can be made but difficulties can arise where the fact of dissolution is disputed.

Thus, in the case of Yugoslavia there was a dispute as to whether the Socialist Federal Republic of Yugoslavia continued in a different form following secession by others[30] or whether the number of withdrawals was such as to bring the original state to an end. On the assumption that it is a case of dissolution, then Art 34 of the 1978 Vienna Convention on the Succession of States to Treaties provides for the continuance of treaties of the predecessor state unless the states concerned otherwise agree or where 'the application of the treaty would be incompatible with the object and purpose of the treaty or would radically change the conditions for its operation'.

(k) International human rights treaties

A question that often arises is whether the rules on state succession affect obligations arising under international human rights documents. It is sometimes argued that human rights treaties are different in that their purpose is not to regulate the relations of states but to secure minimum standards of treatment for the people of a territory Just as a successor state may be subject to boundary treaties and should in principle extend citizenship to those in the territory so it is argued a successor state should be bound by the human rights regime that protects the persons of a territory. First, it is argued that international law has already recognised those treaty documents whose purpose is to preserve minimum standards as being different in character from normal treaties.[31] Secondly, it is argued that the effect of the human rights treaty is to vest those rights in the population so that they become acquired rights vis à vis the successor state. Thirdly, since the rights under an international human rights treaty are normally traceable back to the Universal Declaration of 1948 the successor state is not being asked to observe any more than is stipulated in the United Nations Charter. Fourthly, it is argued that the effect of an international human rights treaty is to fix an objective legal regime for the people of the territory which should in principle be binding on a successor. Fifthly, it is contended that the successor state having acquired the benefit of the territory and its people is in principle bound by any 'burden'. Sixthly, human rights treaties are viewed as imposing fundamental norms whereas the law of state succession is viewed rather like changes of corporate personality in municipal law as a technical matter that must be subordinated to more important considerations,[32] such as respect for the international human rights regime. Thus, in 1992 during the dissolution of the Socialist Federal Republic of Yugoslavia the Human Rights Committee had no hesitation in asserting that 'all peoples within the territory of the former Yugoslavia are entitled to the guarantees of the Covenant'[33] and this was reinforced by a resolution of the Commission on Human

---

30 For Yugoslavia, see below.

31 *Reservations to the Genocide Convention* case (1951) ICJ 15; the *Barcelona Traction* case (1970) ICJ 4.

32 As in municipal law, where the principle of separate legal personality is overridden and the corporate veil lifted where considerations of public policy demand.

33 CCPR/C/79 Add 14–16, 28 December 1992.

Rights.[34] There was no inconsistency in this position because the successor states of the former Yugoslavia were seeking admission as members of the United Nations and would thus be bound by the human rights obligations of the United Nations Charter.

This policy has also found favour with the International Court of Justice; in *Case concerning the Application of the Genocide Convention (Bosnia-Herzegovina v Yugoslavia) (Preliminary Objections)*[35] two of the judges were prepared to consider that there might be automatic state succession to human rights treaties as a principle of customary international law so as to avoid any gap in human rights protection between the dissolution of the predecessor state and the acceptance of obligations by a successor state.

3 STATE SUCCESSION AND NATIONALITY[36]

It is a matter of trite law that it is for each state to determine its rules of nationality.[37] Thus, much will depend on the precise terms of the municipal law of the predecessor and the successor states. It has however to be admitted that on the question of nationality there is much that remains unclear.

Some writers commence with the presumption that nationality will change when sovereignty changes. Professor Brownlie indicates that 'the evidence is overwhelmingly in support of the view that the population follows the change of sovereignty in matters of nationality'.[38] Broadly, supporting evidence is to be found in the post-1919 treaties of Versailles, St Germain, Trianon and Paris which required newly established states in Europe to extend nationality to those born in the territory or habitually resident there unless they sought to disclaim such a right within a particular period of time. This was consistent with British and United States practice in the 19th century as being to extend rights of citizenship to the nationals of the predecessor state resident in the territory.

However, in many cases the predecessor state may make arrangements by treaty or municipal law for citizens in the former territory to retain their citizenship. Although this will only be relevant if the predecessor or parent state continues in existence. Similarly, the successor state may be prepared to grant citizenship[39] although this may be on the basis of birth, residence or domicile. In some instances, when there has been a change of sovereignty, the state parties may allow inhabitants an option to select citizenship of either within a limited period of time. In matters of such detail, it is clearly wise to resolve such problems not by reference to general propositions but by municipal law or specific treaty provision. In cases where there has been no express agreement, then there is a

---

34 Commission on Human Rights Resolution 1994/16, 25 February 1994.

35 (1996) ICJ 565 (see Separate Opinions of Judge Weeramantry and Judge Shahabuddeen).

36 See P Weiss, *Nationality and Statelessness in International Law*, 2nd edn, 1979; DP O'Connell, *State Succession*, Vol 1, Chaps 20 and 21.

37 See *The Acquisition of Polish Nationality* case (1923) PCIJ, Ser B, No 7 p 16; *Nationality Decrees in Tunis and Morocco* case (1923) PCIJ, Ser B, No 4, p 24; 2 ILR 349; the *Nottebohm* case (1955) ICJ 23; 22 ILR 349.

38 I Brownlie, *Principles of Public International Law*, 5th edn, 1998, p 657.

39 See generally, *Slouzak Minority in Teschen (Nationality)* case (1940) AD 11 (1919–41) No 93; *In Re Andries* (1950) 17 ILR No 26; *Ministry of Home Affairs v Kemali* (1962) 40 ILR 191; *North Transylvania Nationality* case (1965) 43 ILR 191.

degree agreement that the annexing state takes both the territory and the population and is obliged to grant its nationality to the inhabitants of the territory who were citizens of the ceding state.

In cases where the succession is by way of independence then there has been a tendency for matters to be settled by express agreement between the parties.[40] Interesting questions can arise when there has been secession[41] and a loss of nationality and then a restoration of the *status quo ante*.

Thus, actual practice is varied but it is germane to observe that the Universal Declaration of Human Rights (1948) asserts that 'everyone has the right to a nationality' and the 1961 Convention on the Reduction of Statelessness provides that states involved in the cession of territory should ensure that no one becomes stateless as a result of a change in sovereignty. However, the uncertainty of the general position caused the International Law Commission to put the matter of nationality in cases of state succession on the agenda for detailed study. The working group that reported in 1995 held that statelessness was the most serious consequence of state succession and all states engaged in transfers of territory were under a duty to prevent it arising.

4 STATE SUCCESSION AND INTERNATIONAL ORGANISATIONS

When a state ceases to exist and is replaced by another sovereign power, then the membership of the former will cease and the latter will have to make an application for full membership of the relevant international organisation. In principle, questions of applications for membership, of status and cessation are matters that fall to be determined by the terms of the constitution of the international organisation in question. In some cases, it will be a case of determining which is the continuing state and which is the new state, as was the case when India was subject to partition in 1947 and Pakistan became a member of the United Nations in its own right. When Egypt and Syria merged to form the United Arab Republic in 1958, the latter entity was considered as a member of the United Nations; three years later, on dissolution of the union, Syria was allowed to resume its former membership. In 1990, when there was a merger between North and South Yemen the new state replaced the two predecessor entities. In the case of the Socialist Federal Republic of Yugoslavia the emerging of Bosnia-Herzegovina, Croatia, Slovenia and Macedonia were admitted as new members of the United Nations as was the case with the Czech Republic and Slovakia in 1993. In that same year, the secession of Eritrea was followed by its admission as a member of the United Nations.

A number of points emerge from the past history. First, international organisations operate best when states are participating members so there is a natural reluctance to create unnecessary difficulties. Secondly, if state A loses part of its territory that is in principle no obstacle to state A remaining as a member of an international organisation.

---

40 The United Kingdom tended to deal with such matters in the legislation conferring independence; see Belize Act 1981, ss 4 and 5; see, also, negotiations between France and Algeria in 1962 (1963) 57 AJIL 716.

41 As indicated by the experience of Austria after annexation by Germany in the years 1938–45 and its resumption of independence in 1945; see *Austrian Nationality* case (1953) 20 ILR 250; *Nationality (Secession of Austria)* case (1954) 21 ILR 175; *Austrian Nationality* case (1955) 22 ILR 430.

Thirdly, any entity that has acquired recognition as a state must in principle apply for membership of an international organisation in accordance with the constitutional procedures of the organisation. Fourthly, given the many different problems that can arise in respect of state succession the general view is that each case should be determined on its own specific facts.

5 STATE SUCCESSION AND PUBLIC PROPERTY RIGHTS

The principles of state succession in respect of property are those developed in customary international law. The 1983 Vienna Convention on the Succession of States in Respect of Property, Archives and Debts is not in force and is unlikely to be so in the immediate future. Having regard to the complex property issues that can arise, the basic principle is that the predecessor state and the successor state should endeavour to reach agreement on property questions. Thus, in the context of Yugoslavia[42] Opinion No 14 of the Arbitration Commission stressed that 'the first principle applicable to state succession is that the successor states should consult with each other and agree a settlement of all questions relating to the relating to the succession'.

The broad principle is that public property of the predecessor state will pass to the successor state.[43] This raises questions as to the meaning of public property because the extent of state involvement in an economy may vary. In general, such property will be that under the ownership directly or indirectly of the executive, legislative or judicial branch of government. To determine this question, the relevant law will be the internal law of the predecessor state; such law will determine whether the property is within public ownership. This principle of customary law is adopted in Art 8 of the 1983 Vienna Convention which stipulates that state property shall be 'property, rights and interests which, at the date of the succession of states, were, according to the internal law of the predecessor state owned by that state'. In principle, the operative date will be the date of succession[44] and this will normally be the date of independence although in a case of multiple succession there may be more than one operative date. In cases of a federal state where property has under a constitution been transferred to constituent parts then that property cannot be regarded as property of the federal state.[45]

However, while the property must be state property to pass a distinction has to be drawn between immovable property and movable property. If the immovable property[46] is situated in the territory to which the succession relates, then the property passes to the

---

42 Where it is arguable that there was no predecessor state but a number of successor states.

43 *Peter Pazmany University* case (1933) PCIJ, Ser A/B, No 61; in *Haille Selassie v Cable and Wireless Ltd* [1938] 2 Ch 182 (the Court of Appeal holding that the grant of *de jure* recognition operating retrospectively prevented the plaintiff the former Emperor of Ethiopia form suing to recover a public debt which must be deemed to pass to the successor sovereign. At first instance, Bennett J had held that a *de facto* grant of recognition did not displace the title to sue of the *de jure* sovereign).

44 The principle adopted in Art 10 of the 1983 Vienna Convention on the Succession of States.

45 As was to some extent the case in respect of Yugoslavia, see Arbitration Commission Opinion No 14; 96 ILR 732; (1993) 32 ILM 1589 *et seq*.

46 Whether the property is to be categorised as movable or immovable property is a matter for the *lex situs*.

successor state. This is supported not only by the 1983 Vienna Convention,[47] state practice[48] and also by the traditional preference for the *lex situs*. If the immovable property is located outside the territory, then in customary international law this would remain with the predecessor state if it existed although such a rule can be modified by agreement; if the predecessor state no longer exists then the property should be divided between the successor states.

The 1983 Vienna Convention makes special provision for the newly independent state and provides in Art 15(b) that immovable property 'having belonged to the territory to which the succession of States relates, situated outside it and having become State property during the period of dependence, shall pass to the successor state' and other immovable state property situated outside the territory 'shall pass to the successor State in proportion to the contribution of the dependent territory'. These rules had no equivalent in customary international law and reflected the perceived unequal relationship when negotiations for decolonisation were taking place.

In respect of movable property, if it was employed for local use the rule in customary international law was that it was to pass to the successor state. This is confirmed by Art 17(1)(b) of the 1983 Vienna Convention which reads 'movable State property of the predecessor State connected with the activity of the predecessor State in respect of the territory to which the succession of States relates shall pass to the successor State'.

In respect of movable property not employed within the territory, the position is less clear Art 17(1)(c) of the Vienna Convention 1983 provides that such property 'shall pass to the successor State in an equitable proportion', although there must be some doubt as to whether that reflects the position in customary international law. By Art 18(1)(d) the same rules is adopted in the case of the dissolution of the predecessor state although in this instance the rule appears more logical.

Although general rules do exist recent state practice indicates that such matters will be dealt with expressly by treaty provision. In the case of Yugoslavia the Arbitration Commission[49] contented itself with observing that in the case of the state property, debts and archives of the SFRY (other than immovable property within each successor state) the general principle should be one of equitable division.

A particular type of property that gives rise to difficulty is that of archives. Archive material represents the history and cultural heritage of a particular community and may also be of considerable economic value. The archive may comprise prints, films coins documents exhibits and many may be particularly attached to buildings or personalities within a particular territory. In these circumstances, UNESCO has taken a close interest in disputes about archives and tends to the view that such material should be located in the state of origin or creation. It is normal when dealing with cession of territory to include a specific provision about archive material. Two practical considerations arise; first, where the archive is of interest to both the predecessor state and the successor state there may be

---

47 Vienna Convention (1983), Art 14 (where there is a transfer of part of the territory to another state); Art 1 (i)(a) (immovable property passes to the newly independent state); Art 16 (where there is a uniting of states); Art 17 (where there is a separation of part of the territory of a state to form a successor state); Art 18 (where there is a dissolution of a state).

48 See Arbitration Commission on Yugoslavia Opinion No 14; 96 ILR 731(1993) 32 ILM 1589.

49 *Ibid.*

two claimants; secondly, difficulties can be circumvented if parts of the archive can be reproduced. There is no doubt that disputes about archives do generate considerable differences between states[50] partly because the legitimacy of a state is to some extent linked with its history and the culture of its people; the archive often provides the best evidence of this continuity.

The matter is dealt with under the terms of the 1983 Vienna Convention; Art 20 provides a definition of a 'state archive' and Arts 21 and 22 stipulate that the archive of the predecessor state shall pass on the date of succession; it is further provided that in the absence of agreement the archive shall pass without compensation.[51] In cases where there has been a transfer of part of territory then that part of the archive which relates 'exclusively or principally to the territory to which the succession of States relates, shall pass to the successor State'. Article 28 contains specific provisions in respect of newly independent states designed to ensure that archives that originate in the territory in question but have been absorbed within the archive of the predecessor state shall pass to the newly independent state;[52] the article further imposes a duty on the predecessor state to help recover material of a pre colonial nature.[53] It is not unknown for restitution of archive material to be included within a treaty. Under the terms of the Treaty of Peace with Italy in 1947, the Republic of Italy was obliged to return all archival and historical material removed from Ethiopia after October 1935. Under the terms of Art 28(2), archive material of interest to the successor state (other than that provided for in Art 28(1)) shall be reproduced 'in such a manner that each of those States can benefit as widely and equitably as possible form those parts of the State archive of the predecessor State'. Further, Art 28(3) provides that the predecessor state shall provide the newly independent state with the best available evidence from state archives which bears upon the title or the boundaries of the independent territory.

In cases of merger, Art 29 of the 1983 Vienna Convention provides that the archives of the former states shall pass to the successor state. Further, in cases of secession Art 30(1) provides for the passing to the successor state of the archive material that relates to that territory. In cases of dissolution Art 31 stipulates that the archive relating to normal administration will pass to the successor[54] but all other archive material shall pass to the various successor states in an equitable manner having regard to all relevant circumstances.

An area of particular sensitivity in matters of state succession to property is that of public debt. First, the sums involved tend to be large and the debt is in essence monies owed by the predecessor state to third parties. Often such parties are reluctant to see a transfer of the debt; thus, it is normally necessary for the successor state to assume full liability.[55] This is easier if the prospective successor enjoys a high degree of credit

---

50 France and Algeria having been in dispute for nearly thirty years on the question of archive material.

51 Vienna Convention on the Succession of States in respect of State Property (1983), Art 23.

52 *Ibid*, Art 28(1)(a).

53 *Ibid*, Art 28(4).

54 *Ibid*, Art 31(1)(a).

55 In essence, this took place on German unification when the Federal Republic (a wealthy state with a reputation for financial rectitude) simply assumed responsibility for the debts of the German Democratic Republic.

worthiness. The 1983 Vienna Convention defines 'state debt' as 'the financial obligation of a predecessor state arising in conformity with international law'[56] and Art 36 provides that 'a succession of States does not as such affect the rights and obligations of creditors'. It is usual to divide public debt into the national debt itself being the monies owed by central government and local debts which may have been incurred by subordinate government bodies. In respect of the former. it is normal to make specific provision although. in customary international law. in the absence of such provision. if the predecessor state continues to exist after succession then it is probable that the predecessor state remains liable.[57] Some writers hold that, in some circumstances, the successor state should bear liability either on the basis that having acquired the territory it should also bear the burden or in those cases where the loan has been employed in permanent improvements on the territory.[58] It would seem that localised debts being connected to the specific territory probably pass to the successor state. The principles are somewhat uncertain in this area partly because of a paucity of actual case law and partly because in matters of public debt it is usual to make specific provision.

The matter is dealt with in the 1983 Vienna Convention in Arts 36–41.[59] As indicated above, Art 36 provides that a succession of states does not as such affect the rights of creditors; so that, in principle, an agreement between a predecessor state and a successor state cannot be preyed in aid in respect of a claim by a creditor third state or by a creditor international institution. When there is a transfer of part of the territory of a state to another state it is provided by Art 37 that an equitable proportion of the public debt shall pass to the successor state. In the case of a newly independent state, Art 38 provides that no debt of the predecessor state shall pass save by agreement and any such agreement shall not infringe the principle of the permanent sovereignty of the newly independent state. In cases of merger, then 'the State debt of the predecessor States shall pass to the successor State'. In cases where part of the territory of a state forms a new state or where there is dissolution and the formation of a number of successor states, then Arts 40 and 41 provide that the successor states shall bear an 'equitable' proportion of the predecessor's state debts.

In matters of public debt, it is certainly not possible to harmoniously reconcile all the precedents. After the secession of Texas from Mexico in 1840, an *ex gratia* payment was made. However, in 1871 Germany refused to accept any liability after the taking of Alsace Lorraine while, in 1898, the United States rejected any obligation to take over Cuban debts arguing that the debts had been incurred for the benefit of Spain. Shortly after, Panama accepted no obligations when it separated from Columbia in 1903. However, in contrast, after the Treaty of Berlin in 1878, Serbia, Montenegro and Bulgaria accepted obligations in respect of Ottoman debts and this practice was broadly followed in the

---

56 The definition on its face excluding debts to private creditors.

57 *Ottoman Public Debts Arbitration* (1925) 1 RIAA 529. If only because the contractual arrangements are with that legal person and so the rights of the creditors cannot be affected by the dealings with a third party unless they are party to the new arrangements. In some cases, if the successor state is financially more reliable then they may be happy to consent to an arrangement whereby the successor assumes the responsibilities of the predecessor state.

58 Hyde, *International Law*, 2nd edn, 1947, Vol 1, pp 409–10.

59 Articles 36-41, Vienna Convention on the Succession of States in Respect of State Property, Archives and Debts (1983).

peace treaties of 1919 with the successors to the Austro Hungarian monarchy while Turkey assumed responsibility for a proportion of the Ottoman debt. Shortly after, when the Anglo Irish Treaty of 1921 provided for the establishment of Eire, it was agreed that public debt was to be apportioned on an equitable basis.

Thus, the sensible conclusion must be that while practice is far from uniform it is reasonable to assume that a successor state will succeed to a proportion of the public debt[60] if contracted for and on behalf of the former territory

6 STATE SUCCESSION AND CONTRACTUAL RIGHTS AND OBLIGATIONS

The question arise as to whether contractual rights arising in respect of state A may be enforced against state B as the successor state. In this context a distinction is drawn between contractual claims that simply give rise to a claim for unliquidated damages and contractual rights that may be said to liquidated in the sense that they have become vested or acquired by recognition by a court or acknowledgement by the predecessor state. It has to be admitted that terminology in this area is not uniform but a distinction can be made between matters that are the subject of claim and matters where it would be unjust or unconscionable for a successor state not to acknowledge or give effect to the right.

There is little doubt that the case law has undergone a degree of change. In the 19th century, municipal courts influenced by the principle of privity of contract found it difficult to accept that a contract with state A could be binding on a state in the absence of acceptance by the latter. Thus, in *Cook v Sprigg*[61] the appellants failed to persuade the Privy Council that a concession granted by a former ruler should be honoured when Cape Colony annexed the territory of East Pondoland. The approach that the grantee did not assume the liabilities of the grantor was followed in the *West Rand Central Gold Mining Co v The King*[62] where the Divisional Court of King's Bench rejected the argument that there was a rule of customary international law that the conquering state became liable for the financial and legal obligations of its predecessor.

However, this approach has been departed from in subsequent case law and in some instances an attempt has been made to prey in aid the doctrine of 'acquired rights'. The meaning of this expression is the subject of some debate and at its lowest it may mean that private rights should be affected as little as possible by changes of sovereignty. A number of cases came before the Permanent Court of International Justice in the inter-war years arising from events in Poland. The newly independent Poland had been created out

---

60 See generally, K Zemanek, 'State succession after decolonisation' (1965) 116 HR 181, pp 255–70; *Poldermans v State of The Netherlands* (1956) 24 ILR 69; *Re Marchi* (1965) 47 ILR 83; *Demol v Etat Belge, Ministre des Finances* (1964) 47 ILR 75.

61 *Cook v Sprigg* [1899] AC 572; (the Privy Council rejected the appeal from the Supreme Court of the Colony of Good Hope mainly on the basis that annexation was an act of state and thus not a matter which a municipal court could entertain).

62 *West Rand Central Gold Mining Co v The King* [1905] 2 KB 391; (the applicant in the case was a British company and the seizure of its assets by the South African Republic may have been unlawful under the local law).

of former German, Russian and Hapsburg land and problems arose when the Polish administration sought to act against persons who had acquired rights under German rule. In the *German Settlers'* case the Polish authorities attempted to evict certain German settlers arguing that they did not have full legal title; the German settlers successfully resisted this demonstrating that they had acquired title under a method recognised by German law and that in any event they were protected under the Minorities Treaty of 1919. However, of more importance was the broader proposition expressed by the court where it stated:

> ... private rights acquired under existing law do not cease on a change of sovereignty ... even those who contest the existence in international law of a general principle of state succession do not go so far as to maintain that private rights including those acquired from the state as the owner of the property are invalid as against a successor in sovereignty.

The principle that the successor state was obliged in international law to respect existing rights was restated in the *Case concerning Certain German Interests in Polish Upper Silesia*[63] and it therefore follows that it should pay compensation if it revokes a concession[64] or otherwise interferes with existing property rights,[65] These inter-war cases shifted the presumption in favour of respecting existing property rights, although it is clear that the right must be one clearly established and not a mere claim or the subject of dispute. In respect of concession contracts, it cannot be said that state practice is uniform; at the risk of oversimplification, the position probably is that the successor state is not bound to continue the concession but, if it decides to terminate it, then it must pay compensation at the appropriate standard or consent to such compensation being fixed by an independent third party. As regards the right itself, it would seem that the right must be one existing and enforceable under the law of the predecessor state and not so inchoate as to be a mere claim. If it is categorised as a mere claim, then it will not bind a successor state; in principle, categorisation or classification must be determined under the law of the predecessor state.

7 STATE SUCCESSION AND CLAIMS IN TORT

It seems to be established that the successor state is not bound by an unliquidated claim for damages in tort. This proposition is said to arise from the case of *Robert E Brown*.[66] Brown was a United States citizen and mining engineer who had claims to certain prospecting rights in the South African Republic; in 1895, however, his claim was frustrated by conflict between the executive and judicial branches. When Great Britain acquired the territory during the Boer War, he persuaded the United States to take up his claim. The Arbitral Tribunal in 1923 rejected his assertion that Great Britain as the successor state was liable to right the wrongs done by the former state. This was followed in the *Hawaiian claims* case,[67] where a number of British subjects brought an action in

---

63 *Certain German Interests in Polish Upper Silesia* (1926) PCIJ, Ser A, No 7; 3 ILR 429.
64 *Mavrommatis Palestine Concessions* case (1924) PCIJ, Ser A, No 5.
65 *Chorzow Factory* case *(Indemnity) (Merits)* (1928) PCIJ, Ser A, No 17; 4 ILR 268.
66 *Robert E Brown's* case (1923) 2 ILR 66; 6 RIAA 120.
67 The *Hawaiian Claims* case (1925) 3 ILR 80; 6 RIAA 157.

respect of false imprisonment by the authorities of the Hawaiian Republic and the Arbitral Tribunal rejected the claim asserting that there was no principle of succession to liability for torts. Although in principle the successor state will not be liable for unliquidated claims in tort there will be liability in cases where the successor state recognises, adopts and continues a wrong perpetrated by its predecessor.[68] In such an example, it is less a question of succession and more a matter of a separate cause of action arising.

8 STATE PRACTICE

Although the era of decolonisation produced examples of state succession and indeed stimulated the initiatives of the International Law Commission the problems tended to be those associated with the withdrawal of the prior colonial power. However the disintegration of the communist system in Eastern Europe has given the subject an unusual degree of prominence. It is sensible to note the salient points.

(a) Yemen

An example of unification as a form of state succession is provided by the case of the Yemen. By virtue of an agreement dated 22 April 1990,[69] the Yemen Arab Republic and the People's Democratic Republic of the Yemen came together as two states to form a single state, to be known as the Republic of Yemen. This is an example of two states merging to create a new third entity. The agreement provided that the new state was to be considered a party to all the treaties concluded by the two prior entities with effect from the first date on which either had become a party.

(b) Czechoslovakia

In the case of the former Czech and Slovak Federal Republic, it was agreed that the single state would be extinguished and would be replaced by the two states of the Czech Republic and Slovakia. It was further agreed that state assets would be split in a proportion of two to one (broadly in line with the proportion of the respective populations). The two new states[70] came into existence on 1 January 1993 and indicated that they were prepared to assume the international obligations of the former state. The succession of Slovakia to a treaty which was held to establish an objective territorial regime was considered in the *Gabcikovo-Nagymaros Project case (Hungary v Slovakia)*[71] as falling within Art 12 of the Vienna Convention on Succession of States (1978).

---

68 The *Lighthouses Arbitration (France v Greece)* (1956) 12 RIAA 155; 23 ILR 659.
69 For the text of the Agreement on the Establishment of the Republic of the Yemen, see (1991) 30 ILM 820. The substance of the merger is set out in Art 1, which reads in part 'there shall be established between the State of the Yemen Arab Republic and the State of the People's Democratic Republic of Yemen ... a full and complete union, based on a merger, in which the international personality of each of them shall be integrated in a single international legal person called 'the Republic of Yemen'.
70 M Hoskova, '*Die Selbstuflosung der CSFR-Ausgewahlte rechtliche Aspeckte*' (1993) 53 Zo RV 697.
71 *Gabcikovo-Nagymaros Project* case (*Hungary v Slovakia*) (1997) ICJ 7.

(c) The Baltic states

The Baltic states (Estonia, Latvia, Lithuania) were absorbed into the Soviet Union in 1940 by forcible annexation. In consequence, many states viewed this as a breach of the Stimson Doctrine and refused to accord full recognition.[72] In 1990, as the Soviet Union began to disintegrate, the three declared their independence and were recognised as such by a number of states. On 6 September 1991, the Soviet Union granted recognition and on 17 September 1991 all three states became members of the United Nations. Having regard to the history it is doubtful whether the three states should be regarded as 'newly independent' for the purpose of Art 2(e) of the 1978 Vienna Convention. The Baltic states do not regard themselves as successors to the Soviet Union and have broadly asserted their adherence to the 'clean slate' principle as far as the prior treaties of the Soviet Union are concerned.

(d) Hong Kong

A recent but unusual example of state succession is afforded by the case of Hong Kong. Under the Treaty of Nanking (1842), the island of Hong Kong had been ceded by China in perpetuity; this was followed by the Convention of Peking (1860) under which the southern part of the Kowloon peninsula with Stonecutters island was ceded on the same terms. Finally, in 1898 by Convention the New Territories (being the land opposite the island of Hong Kong and comprising 92% of the territory) were leased to Great Britain for a period of 99 years to expire on 30 June 1997.

Conscious that the territories subject to the lease would revert to China, the United Kingdom began negotiations with China to secure a comprehensive settlement of the future of Hong Kong. The United Kingdom and China concluded an Agreement of 26 September 1984 together with three Annexes (described as the Joint Declaration and Three Annexes) whereby the entire Hong Kong territory would revert to China on 1 July 1997. It was agreed that, thereafter, Hong Kong would become the Hong Kong Special Administrative Region[73] and this region would enjoy a considerable degree of autonomy, save in matters of foreign affairs and defence. It was further provided that the government should be drawn from the local population[74] and the economic, social and legal system should remain in place, as would the framework of civil liberties.[75] The detail of the Joint Declaration is expanded upon in Annex I, which provides for the continuance in office of public servants and by Art XIII of Annex 1 the provisions of the International Covenant on Civil and Political Rights (1966) are to remain in force for the territory. By Art 3(12) of the Joint Declaration, it was provided that the principles set out in the Declaration and the Annexes should be formulated by the National People's

---

72 The United Kingdom had regarded the three states as *de facto* part of the Soviet Union. The United States did not recognise the incorporation. For consideration in the municipal courts, see for municipal case law, *Latvian State Cargo and Passenger Line v Clark* (1948) 15 ILR No 16; *Latvian State Cargo and Passenger Line v McGrath* (1951) 18 ILR No 27; *Pulenciks v Augustovskis* (1951) 18 ILR No 20; *Re Kovas' Estate* (1958) 26 ILR 76; *Re Mitzkel's Estate* (1962) 33 ILR 43.

73 Article 3(1) of the Joint Declaration provides for the establishment of a Special Administrative Region in accordance with the provisions of Art 31 of the Chinese Constitution.

74 Joint Declaration 1984, Art 3(4).

75 *Ibid*, Art 3(5).

Congress of the Republic of China in a Basic Law of the Hong Kong Special Administrative Region.[76]

Such detailed provisions as to the future governance of a territory are unusual but reflect the need to enable the culture of free enterprise Hong Kong to coexist alongside the state socialist system operated by China since 1949. In pursuance of these arrangements the entire Hong Kong territory passed to China on 1 July 1997.

(e) The Soviet Union

The arrival in power of Mikhail Gorbachev in February 1985 set in train a period of reform which lead to the failed *coup d'état* of August 1991 and the dissolution of the Soviet Union. Although this process took place over many months, constitutionally the Soviet Union may be said to have come to an end on 21 December 1991 when the Alma Ata Declaration lead to the establishment of the Commonwealth of Independent States (CIS)[77] and an assertion by the former Soviet Republics not only that they would honour prior international agreements binding the USSR, but also that the Russian Federation was entitled to assume the membership position of the USSR at the United Nations. This proposal did not encounter opposition and in January 1992 the Russian Foreign Ministry indicated that the Russian Federation would carry out the treaty obligations of the USSR as they related to its territory. While there has been some debate as to the claim of the Russian Federation to continuity with the USSR, the important consideration has been to ensure the continued observance of treaty obligations relating to nuclear weapons. In this context, the willingness of Russia to give such guarantees and the decision of Ukraine, Belarus and Kazakstan to seek non-nuclear status has lead to a willingness to adopt a pragmatic approach.

(f) Germany[78]

At the conclusion of the Second World War, Germany had been divided into four zones of allied occupation (US, UK, France and the Soviet Union[79]) with specific arrangements for Berlin[80] which did not form part of any zone. The territory subject to western

---

76   For the Basic Law of the Hong Kong Special Administrative Region in force from 1 July 1997, see (1990) 29 ILM 1511. See generally, White (1987) 36 ICLQ 483; G Ress, 'The legal status of Hong Kong after 1997' (1986) 46 Zao RV 647; DR Fung, 'The basic law of the Hong Kong Special Administrative Region of the People's Republic of China' (1988) 37 ICLQ 701.

77   See (1992) 31 ILM 138; 31 ILM 147. See, also, Y Blum, 'Russia takes over the Soviet Union's seat at the United Nations' (1992) 3 EJIL 354; SA Voitovich, 'The Commonwealth of Independent States: an emerging institutional model' (1992) 3 EJIL 403; R Mullerson, 'The continuity and succession of states by reference to the former USSR and Yugoslavia' (1993) 42 ICCQ 473.

78   See generally, JA Frowein, 'Germany reunited' (1991) 51 Zao RV 331; S Oeter, 'German unification and state succession' (1991) 51 Zao RV 349; JP Jacque, 'German unification and the European Community' (1991) 2 EJIL 1; K Heilbronner, 'Legal aspects of the unification of the two German states' (1991) 2 EJIL 18; JA Frowein, 'The reunification of Germany' (1992) 86 AJIL 152.

79   Not all of the Soviet Zone came under Soviet occupation, as the Russians had ceded to Poland territory within the zone east of the Oder/Neisse line. At the Potsdam conference in 1945, there was some division of opinion as to the precise boundary of Germany. After some disagreement, the starting point for discussion was the 1937 boundary. (See WS Churchill, *The Second World War*, Vol VI, p 563).

80   See I Hendry and M Wood, *The Legal Status of Berlin*, 1987.

administration formed the basis of the Federal Republic of West Germany, which came into existence in 1949 under the terms of a written constitution. By the Convention on Relations between the Three Powers and the Federal Republic of Germany which came into operation in 1955, the occupation was ended but the Allied Powers retained certain residual powers in respect of Berlin and also in the event of reunification with the territory of East Germany which had been constituted in the former Soviet Zone. The actual status of the Federal Republic and its claim to be a continuation of pre-1933 Germany attracted a considerable degree of academic debate[81] not least because reunification might at some point become a practical political issue as relations improved during the period in office of Chancellor Brandt (1969–74).[82]

Although the years after 1974 had witnessed an improvement in relations between the Federal Republic and East Germany, it was changes within the Soviet Union which stimulated the upsurge against communist rule and the collapse of the East German state.

On 18 May 1990, a treaty between the two German states provided for Economic, Monetary and Social Union.[83] In essence, the Deutsche Mark became the currency for East Germany and the Bundesbank became the relevant monetary authority.

On 31 August 1990, a second treaty was signed which provided for the accession of the of East Germany under the terms of Art 23 of the Federal Constitution to take effect on 3 October 1990. On 12 September 1990, the Treaty on the Final Settlement with Respect to Germany[84] was signed by the four allied powers and the two German states; it confirmed the boundary of the new German state as the Oder-Neisse frontier with Poland. This boundary was confirmed in a treaty made between Germany and Poland signed in November 1990 and ratified in January 1992.

The Treaty between the Federal Republic of Germany and the German Democratic Republic of 31 August 1990 made it clear that the latter was being absorbed into the former. Thus, Art 1 provides 'upon the accession of the German Democratic Republic to the Federal Republic in accordance with Art 23 of the Basic Law taking effect on 3 October 1990, the Länder of Brandenburg, Mecklenburg, Western Pomerania, Saxony, Saxony Anhalt and Thuringia shall become Länder of the Federal Republic of Germany'. Thus, the constitution of the Federal Republic is simply being extended to the former provinces of East Germany. In like terms, Arts 7 and 8 provided for the application of the economic and monetary system to the new territory. In respect of treaties, Art 11 provided that the treaties of the Federal Republic would extend to the new territory, while Art 12 provided that territories made by the German Democratic Republic would be subject to individual negotiation. Thus, the legal documentation made clear that the German Democratic republic would be extinguished.

---

81   R Jennings (1946) 23 BYIL 112; FA Mann (1947) 33 TGS 119; Q Wright (1952) 46 AJIL 299; J Simpson (1957) 6 ICLQ 83; Lush (1965) 14 ICLQ 742; FA Mann (1967) 16 ICLQ 760; See generally, *Netz v Chuter Ede* [1946] Ch 224; *R v Bottrill ex p Kuechenmeister* [1947] KB 41; *Carl Zeiss Stiftung v Rayner & Keeler* [1967] AC 853; *Re Treaty on the Basis of Relations between the Federal Republic of Germany and the German Democratic Republic* (1972) 78 ILR 150; *Trawnik v Lenox* [1985] 2 All ER 368.

82   As Foreign Minister from 1966 and Federal Chancellor from 1969–74, Willy Brandt followed a policy towards East Germany of *Wandel durch Annaherung* (Change through Convergence) which came to be known as *Ostpolitik* and resulted in the signing with East Germany of the Basic Treaty in 1972. Brandt was awarded the Nobel Peace Prize in 1971.

83   See (1990) 29 ILM 1108; the treaty entered into force on 30 June 1990.

84   See (1990) 29 ILM 1186.

(g) Yugoslavia[85]

The Socialist Federal Republic of Yugoslavia as established by Josef Tito in 1945 had adopted a federal solution towards the problem of ethnic tension. However difficulties increased after his death in 1980 and the collective leadership was driven by rivalry, ethnic division and mutual suspicion. On 25 June 1991 Slovenia and Croatia declared their independence and were able to secure recognition by the European Union and a number of other states by January 1992. In April 1992 Bosnia-Herzegovina declared its independence and acquired recognition. In that same month Serbia and Montenegro established the Federal Republic of Yugoslavia claiming to be the continuing state of the Socialist Federal Republic of Yugoslavia. In May 1992 the European Union indicated its willingness to recognise Macedonia as a sovereign state. At or about the same time these newly independent states[86] were admitted as members of the United Nations although the Security Council rejected the claim of the Federal Republic of Yugoslavia to assume the seat of the Socialist Federal Republic of Yugoslavia[87] on the grounds that it was not the successor state.

However these legal changes were accompanied by fighting on the ground as the Serb controlled Yugoslav Army tried to prevent dissolution in 1991 and then as Bosnian Serbs resisted the declaration of independence by Bosnia-Herzegovina. In the period between 1991 and the Dayton Peace Agreement of 21 November 1995 a number of Security Council resolutions[88] were passed seeking to restrain the various contending parties on the ground. Yugoslavia has not been an example of orderly state succession but a tragic illustration of the dissolution of a federal state being effected against a background civil war and ethnic conflict.

9 CONCLUSION

As the Badinter Committee on Yugoslavia indicated,[89] the rules on state succession in international law suffer from being rather vague and in any event require to be applied

---

85 See generally, M Glenny, *The Fall of Yugoslavia: The Third Balkan War*, 1992; M Weller, 'The international response to the dissolution of the Socialist Federal Republic of Yugoslavia' (1992) 86 AJIL 569; Y Blum, 'UN membership of the "new" Yugoslavia: continuity or break?' (1992) 86 AJIL 830; A D'Amato, 'Peace v accountability in Bosnia' (1994) 88 AJIL 500; M Weller, 'Peacekeeping and peace enforcement in the Republic of Bosnia-Herzegovina' (1996) 56 Zao RV 70.

86 Bosnia-Herzegovina (22 May 1992); Croatia (22nd May 1992); Macedonia (8 April 1993); Slovenia (22nd May 1992).

87 Yugoslavia had been a member since 24 October 1945. General Assembly ruled that the new entity must apply for membership itself (GA Res 41/1 (1992)). At 1 January 2000 no application had been received.

88 The more significant being SC Res 713 (25 September 1991 indicating territorial gains made by force would not be acceptable and imposing an arms embargo); SC Res 752 (15 May 1992) (calling for an end to conflict in Bosnia-Herzegovina); SC Res 757 (30 May 1992) (imposing economic sanctions); SC Res 764 (13 July 1992) (indicating personal liability under international humanitarian law); SC Res 769 (7 August 1992) (calling for an end to abusive conduct); SC Res 770 and 771 (13 August 1992) (condemnation of ethnic cleansing); SC Res 787 (16 November 1992) (sanctions against Serbia and Montenegro); SC Res 816 (31 March 1993) (all necessary measures to control airspace over Bosnia); SC Res 819 (16 April 1993) (declaration of safe areas including Srebrenica); SC Res 824 (6 May 1993) (declaration of further safe areas).

89 See *Arbitration Commission of the EC Conference on Yugoslavia Opinion No 1*, 29 November 1991; 92 ILR 162.

with caution. Unlike municipal law, problems of succession may arise in a variety of forms and what is appropriate in one context may not be in another. A review of recent state practice indicates a clear division between those cases where the problem of succession has been dealt with peacefully in an atmosphere of trust and good will[90] and those cases where there has been mistrust and the use of force.[91] In the former situation, agreement on specific problems is normally recorded in a treaty while in the latter situation terms often have to be imposed on contending parties by an external body. If there is a lesson to be drawn from the tragic events in the former Yugoslavia, it must be that dissolution or secession should be on the basis of agreement conducted in a peaceful manner and with reference to equitable principles and proper respect for the human rights of each community.

90   As with Germany and Czechoslovakia.
91   As in the former Yugoslavia.

CHAPTER 19

INTERNATIONAL ECONOMIC LAW[1]

1 INTRODUCTION

In many textbooks on international law published in the United Kingdom only limited reference to international economic law is made. Indeed, some dispute the existence of the topic as a distinct subject of study.[2] One reason for this is, of course, that the subject is of comparatively recent origin; a second reason has been that the subject has been dominated by economists and lawyers have had less direct influence than they have had in developing subjects such as the law of the sea. Thirdly, in the United Kingdom there has tended to be a rather distant relationship[3] between economics and law so that it cannot be said that there was a distinct corpus of competition law prior to 1948.[4] At the end of the 19th century, the law of contract had developed some restrictions on contracts adjudged to be in restraint of trade[5] and there was some legislation on customs and import controls but, unlike in Europe and the United States, there was no emerging competition law.

The United Kingdom view in the 19th century had been been broadly to favour free trade, although questions of protection and tariff controls had demonstrated a singular ability to destabilise administrations particularly those of a conservative colour.[6] In the decade prior to 1914, the United Kingdom had been governed by a liberal administration which favoured free trade and this coincided with the general view of the United States that there should not be internal or external barriers to the movement of goods. Although the age of domestic *laissez faire* was coming to an end and the claims of organised labour

---

1   See G Schwarzenberger, 'The principles and standards of international economic law' (1966) 117 HR 1-98; I Seidl-Hohenveldern, *International Economic Law*, 2nd edn, 1992; DM McRae, 'The contribution of international trade law to the development of international law' (1996) 260 HR 99.

2   This, of course, is now a minority viewpoint but is grounded in the opinion that the subject simply comprises the application of traditional sources to the economic field. However, it is now clear that economic law and environmental law have the capacity to generate their own distinct concepts. See P Sands, 'International law in the field of sustainable development' (1994) BYIL 303.

3   This, of course, contrasts with the position in the United States; the relationship between lawyers economists in establishing international economic institutions was alluded to by JM Keynes in his closing speech at the Bretton Woods Conference in 1944; see D Moggridge, *Maynard Keynes: An Economist's Biography*, 1992, p 746; R Skidelsky, *John Maynard Keynes: Fighting for Britain, 1937–46*, Chapter 10.

4   In the United Kingdom, the subject dating from the Monopolies and Restrictive Practices (Inquiry and Control) Act 1948 in contrast to countries such as the United States which had enacted anti trust legislation in the form of the Sherman Act 1890 and the Clayton Act 1814.

5   In fact, the earliest case being *Dyer's Case* (1414) YB II Hen 5 fo 5. The recent law being traceable from *Nordenfelt v Maxim Nordenfelt Guns and Ammunition Company* [1894] AC 535; *Mason v Provident and Clothing and Supply Co Ltd* [1913] AC 724. See, also, *Morris v Saxelby* [1916] AC 688; *Esso Petroleum Co Ltd v Harper's Garage (Stourport) Ltd* [1968] AC 269. On the general attitude of the common law, see Simpson, 'How far does the Law of England forbid monopoly?' 41 LQR 393; P Atiyah, *The Rise and Fall of Freedom of Contract*, 1979.

6   The decision to repeal the Corn Laws in 1845 having brought to an end the administration of Robert Peel (1841–46). Later the decision in 1903 of Joseph Chamberlain to raise the question of tariff reform and protection paralysed the administration of AJ Balfour (1902–05).

were beginning to be heard in many European states, free trade was consistent with the foundations of Gladstonian liberalism and was viewed in the United Kingdom as consistent with the national interest provided that it could be secured by adequate naval strength.

The turning point can be identified as the accession to power of the Bolsheviks in Russia under VI Lenin[7] in October 1917. Drawing upon the writings of Karl Marx and Friedrich Engels, the new Soviet Government asserted the ethical superiority of state owned enterprises and claimed the right to take over foreign businesses without compensation in the interests of their own citizens. This practice was immediately condemned by other European states and difficult questions began to arise as to whether the confiscatory decrees of the Soviet Government should be acknowledged in the municipal laws of other states.[8]

While the changes in the Soviet Union were attributable to the adoption of a distinct philosophy developments took place in Europe that would prompt the emergence of international economic law. First, after 1918 most European states were governed on the basis of open democratic elections and electorates tended to be influenced by the level of economic prosperity. Secondly, mass unemployment and political instability in some European States prompted much thought as to the role of government in macro economic management.[9] Thirdly, it was clear to many that a single state could not act alone and it became evident that there was a proper role for international co-operation which would be designed to stimulate economic growth through a measure of exchange rate stability in contrast to the extreme fluctuations that characterised the inter war years. Fourthly, many of these ideas were associated with developments in the subject of economics as writers began to analyse the role of government in securing sufficient level of demand in a modern economy.

In addition, to these general factors it was evident to all in 1944 and 1945 that a major task of reconstruction needed to be performed in Western Europe and that such reconstruction was urgent if a barrier was to be built to resist the threat of Soviet Expansion. Action on exchange rate stability and free trade required international co-operation; such objectives could not be attained by any one state acting alone. In these circumstances, the attitude of the United States was crucial and the experience of the domestic New Deal had tended to show that there was a proper role for government in promoting those economic conditions in which private enterprise could flourish. The effort of securing victory in 1945 had lead many to believe economic and social problems were susceptible of rational analysis and that governments could act and plan to avoid future problems. The international economic institutions established after 1945 were

---

7   VI Lenin (1870–1924).

8   *AM Luther v James Sagor & Co* [1921] 1 KB 453 (Roche J) reversed by Court of Appeal [1921] 3 KB 532; *Princess Olga Paley v Weisz* [1929] 1 KB 718; *Re Russian Bank for Foreign Trade* [1933] Ch 745; see, also, in a different context, *Oppenheimer v Cattermole* [1976] AC 249. See generally, A McNair (1946) 31 Grotius Society 30.

9   This re-evaluation of the role of government and the nature of macroeconomic management was particularly associated with the writings of JM Keynes (1883–1946) whose General Theory of Employment, Interest and Money was published in February 1936. Keynes was more knowledgeable than most about the limits of international co-operation having attended the Versailles Conference and he went on to play a significant role at the Bretton Woods Conference in 1944.

therefore grounded in the belief that co-operation and planning might achieve more than leaving matters to the free operation of markets.

Even before the conclusion of conflict in 1945, the causal link between economic instability and political extremism in inter-war Germany was evident to all. In these circumstances, the Bretton Woods Conference in 1944[10] was designed to establish a post-war economic structure and facilitate progress on tariff reform. Pursuant to the conference, the International Monetary Fund (IMF) was established and an International Bank for Reconstruction and Development (known as 'the World Bank') was also created to accomplish longer term economic objectives. Within a further three years, the General Agreement on Tariffs and Trade (1947) had come into existence and, in due course, these three institutions[11] formed the basis of the post-war economic structure. In time, the role of the World Bank was extended by the creation of a number of related institutions. The International Finance Corporation was established in 1956 and was followed shortly thereafter in 1960 by the establishment of the International Development Agency (IDA). At a later date, the International Centre for the Settlement of Investment Disputes (ICSID) became effective and the Multilateral Investment Agency (MIGA) was established in 1988. Collectively these institutions are referred to as 'the Word Bank Group'.

These international institutions were complemented by regional institutions of which one of the most important was the Organisation for European Economic Co-operation (OEEC); in 1960, when the immediate task of post-war economic reconstruction was complete this body was reconstituted as the Organisation for Economic Co-operation and Development (OECD). The immediate post-war world witnessed a number of economic pacts designed to promote economic growth by creating larger markets free of internal tariff restrictions and often operating a common external tariff. Examples are afforded by the Benelux Union,[12] the European Economic Community (EEC),[13] the European Free Trade Association (EFTA)[14] and the Canada-United States Free Trade Agreement (FTA)[15] which in turn was expanded to become the North Atlantic Free Trade Association (NAFTA).[16] The general trend towards regionalisation and larger trading blocks is not restricted to the developed world. In Africa the Economic Community of West African States (ECOWAS)[17] was established in 1975 and was followed by the African Economic Community in 1991[18] and the Common Market for Eastern and Southern Africa in 1993. Although the precise motivation differed in each case, the general objective was founded on a belief that a larger market was likely to generate economic growth.

---

10 UN Monetary and Financial Conference, Bretton Woods, New Hampshire USA, 1–22 July 1944. The United Kingdom delegation included the economists JM Keynes, Lionel Robbins and Dennis Robertson with WE Beckett as the Legal Adviser; the United States team included Henry White, Fred Vinson (later Chief Justice of the United States) and Henry Morgenthau.

11 It is not strictly speaking the case that the GATT is an institution; for its precise identity see below.

12 Between Belgium, Netherlands and Luxembourg and in effect from 1 January 1948.

13 Under Treaty of Rome (1957); effective from 1 January 1958.

14 Effective from 1959 and including the United Kingdom, Austria, Demark, Portugal, Sweden, Switzerland and Norway.

15 1988, see (1988) 27 ILM 281.

16 Ie, Canada, United States, Mexico (1992); for text see (1993) 32 ILM 289, p 605.

17 For text see (1975) 14 ILM 1200 for amended version see (1996) 35 ILM 660.

18 (1991) 30 ILM 1241; M Ndulo, 'Harmonisation of trade laws in the African Economic Community' (1993) 42 ICLQ 101.

So, in a comparatively short period after the Second World War, a number of international and regional institutions came into existence with the broad objective of promoting economic growth. At the centre stands the International Monetary Fund whose membership now comprises 180 states. The broad objectives of the International Monetary Fund are set out in the Articles of Agreement of 1945[19] which were amended in 1969, 1978 and 1992. Article 1 of the Articles of Agreement sets the objective as being to secure the expansion and balanced growth of international trade which is to be secured by stable exchange rates, international liquidity and the exercise of financial discipline to avoid balance of payments disequilibriums.

The nature of international economic law is closely linked with the jurisdiction of the relevant institutions. Thus, the work of the International Monetary Fund is usually described as comprising the topic International Monetary Law. The work of the General Agreement on Tariffs and Trade (1947) and related institutions is normally described as being part of International Trade Law while the activities of the World Bank group are often described as falling within International Development Law. These three elements are said to comprise International Economic Law. However, before turning to substantive matters it is necessary to refer to matters of theory.

2 THE NATURE OF INTERNATIONAL ECONOMIC LAW[20]

As to the juridical nature of international economic law there are a number of schools of thought. The first school views it as comprising the public international law rules for inter-state relations;[21] this is an acceptable but limited definition. Other writers such as Petersmann[22] take the view that the subject embraces both private law and the national and international regulation of the world economy; this second school of thought views the subject as focused upon the law relating to international trade in goods, financial services and monetary affairs together with the relevant rules of public international law on foreign investment. A third school of thought links the topic to the United Nations Charter (1945) and places stress upon the right to development in respect of third world countries.[23]

As well as disputes about basis and content, there is also room for debate about as to its subjects; clearly, the subject concerns the activities of states and international organisations, but it also embraces the activities of multinational organisations. One approach is simply to accept that the subject concerns activities within the world

---

19 Drawn up at the Bretton Woods Conference (July 1944).

20 See I Seidl Hohenveldern, *International Economic Law*, 2nd edn, 1992.

21 Thus, G Schwarzenberger saw IEL as being concerned with '(1) the ownership and exploitation of natural resources; (2) the production and distribution of goods; (3) invisible international transactions of an economic or financial character; (4) currency and finance; (5) related services; (6) the status and organisation of those engaged in such activity'; see G Schwarzenberger, *The Principles and Standards*.

22 EU Petersmann, 'International economic theory and international economic law', in R St J Macdonald and DM Johnstone (eds), *The Structure and Process of International Law, Essays in Legal Philosophy, Doctrine and Theory*, 1983.

23 SR Chowdry (ed), *The Right to Development in International Law*, 1992; A Carty (ed), *Law and Development*, 1992.

economy that may be subject to rules arising in national law, public international law and sometimes under the rubric of private international law. To take a simple example, an agreement between state A and state B is clearly susceptible of analysis within the scope of public international law however an agreement between state A and a multinational company may give rise to questions of choice of law and the relevant law may be domestic law or public international law.[24] Further, an agreement between two multi national companies both domiciled in different states may also give rise to problems of jurisdiction.

Another characteristic of the subject is its aspirational nature;[25] it is a matter of fact that some states are poor and under developed so that some of the materials of the subject draw on soft law sources which seek to set frameworks for improvement in the living standards of those in the poorest states. In this context, should be noted documents such as the United Nations General Assembly Resolution on Permanent Sovereignty over Natural Resources[26] and the 1974 Declaration on the Establishment of a New International Economic Order[27] and the Charter of Economic Rights and Duties of States.[28] There is some ground for scepticism about the subject in view of its lack of certainty, imprecision and impermanence so that it is sensible to review the actual evidence of the working of its most prominent institutions.

3 INTERNATIONAL MONETARY LAW[29]

In general terms international monetary law is derived from treaty law and the role of custom is a best marginal. Although international monetary regulation may be effected at both the international and regional level there is little doubt that the dominant institution is the International Monetary Fund (IMF). Established in 1945 under the terms of the Articles of Agreement the organisation now comprises 182 states.[30] Although there is an important role for lawyers, the system works on the basis of co-operation, consensus, diplomacy and soft law.[31]

The jurisdiction of the International Monetary Fund is based on the Articles of Agreement of 1945 which were themselves amended in 1969,[32] 1978 and 1992. The principal purpose of the IMF is 'to facilitate the expansion and balanced growth of international trade and to contribute thereby to the promotion and maintenance of high

---

24 *Serbian Loans* case (1929) PCIJ, Ser A, Nos 20–21.
25 See Hazel Fox, 'The definition and sources of international economic law', in Hazel Fox (ed), *International Economic Law and Developing*.
26 UN GA Res 1803 (XVII).
27 UN GA Res 3201 (1 May 1974).
28 UN GA Res 3281 (XXIX) (12 December 1974).
29 H James, *International Monetary Co-operation Since Bretton Woods*, 1996; J Gold, *Legal Effect of Fluctuating Exchange Rates*, 1990.
30 As at December 1998.
31 See generally, H James, *International Monetary Co-operation Since Bretton Woods*, 1996; J Gold, *Interpretation, The IMF and International Law*, 1996.
32 In 1969, in respect of special drawing rights; in 1978, in respect of the introduction of discretionary exchange rate arrangements.

levels of employment'[33] and this is to be secured by stable exchange rates, financial discipline and the avoidance of balance of payments disequilibriums. The regulatory power of the IMF is exercised through regular surveillance[34] and through measures recommended when any member state seeks the help of the Fund.

The formal legal sources of the International Monetary Fund comprise: (i) the Articles of Agreement; (ii) relevant by laws;[35] (iii) resolutions of the Board of Governors; (iv) decisions of the Executive Board; and (v) directives of the Managing Director. Provision is made for the amendment of the Articles of Agreement although the articles themselves provide for certain enabling powers and some degree of flexibility.[36] Member states are under a duty to co-operate with the Fund[37] which itself has international legal personality.[38]

In respect of its internal constitution the IMF operates through a Board of Governors,[39] an Interim Committee, an Executive Board and a Managing Director. In addition, there is a Development Committee which advises the IMF and the Governors of the World Bank on matters concerning developing countries.

Although decision making is often by consensus in a system of weighted voting operates with the weight of voting power allocated according to economic strength. However, the requisite majority depends on the nature of the decision to be taken.[40] The system of decision making within the IMF has not escaped criticism by developing countries and various proposals for reform have been advanced;[41] such criticisms centre upon the system of weighted voting and lack of transparency. It is trite law that any decision of any organ of the IMF has to be *intra vires* the Articles of Agreement.

In matters of dispute settlement there has been a remarkable lack of litigation. Decisions of the Executive Board can in principle be referred to the Board of Governors.[42] The Fund has the authority to seek an advisory opinion from the International Court of Justice on any relevant legal question pertaining to its jurisdiction however none has been requested so far.[43] The Articles contain a number of sanctions against the member states in breach;[44] voting rights can be suspended[45] and member states may be refused access to the Fund.[46] The IMF traditionally co-operates closely with the World Bank Group and

---

33 See Article 1(ii) of the Articles of Agreement (1945).
34 See Article IV of the Articles of Agreement (1945 as amended).
35 Article XII, s 2(g) of the Articles of Agreement of the IMF (1945).
36 Article IV, s 2(c); Article V s 7(c) of the Articles of Agreement of the IMF (1945).
37 Article IV, s 1 of the Articles of Agreement (1945).
38 Article IX of the Articles of Agreement (1945).
39 Article XII, s 2 of the Articles of Agreement of the IMF.
40 For very important matters, an 85% vote is required; see Article 111, s 2(c); Article XIII, s 1; for less important decisions, a vote of 70% will suffice while for many other matters a simple majority will be sufficient.
41 See E Osieke, 'Majority voting systems in the International Labour Organisation and the International Monetary Fund' (1984) 33 ICLQ 381; AH Quereshi (1988) 28 Indian Journal of International Law 481.
42 Article XXIX of the Articles of Agreement of the IMF.
43 Article VIII of the Agreement between the United Nations and the IMF (1947).
44 Article XII, ss 7 and 8 (communication of views).
45 Article XXVI, s 2(6) of the Articles of Agreement of the IMF.
46 Article V, s 5 of the Articles of Agreement of IMF.

now seeks to work with the World Trade Organisation;[47] its relationship with the United Nations is governed by a formal agreement.[48]

One of the principal concerns of the international community has been in respect of the movement of exchange rates. It is arguable that in customary law a state had the entitlement to determine the value of its currency.[49] However, as international trade developed in the 20th century, it became clear that currency changes affected other countries. At the turn of the century, the principal currencies were linked to the gold standard but, after 1918, the deflationary policies this often entailed made such a nexus increasingly difficult to sustain;[50] in the 1930s, most states left the gold standard and operated some form of floating exchange rates. In 1945, the newly established IMF instituted a system of fixed exchange rates whereby member states agreed to keep their currency at a certain par value both in relation to the United States dollar and indirectly in relation to gold. After 1945, the United States agreed to link the dollar to gold and this connection remained until it was ended by President Nixon in 1971.[51] From 1971 until the amendment of the articles in 1978, currencies floated in an extra legal regime.

The 1978 Amendment of the Articles followed upon the shock to the international monetary system occasioned by the energy crisis of 1973/1974; this in turn had produced differing rates of domestic inflation and thus exchange rate instability. A number of committees met from 1974 to examine the problem. The 1978 Amendment allowed states a discretion as to the method of fixing their exchange rate. It will be recalled that Art 1(iii) had provided that one of the purposes of the IMF was 'to promote exchange stability, to maintain orderly exchange arrangements among members, and to avoid competitive exchange depreciation'. Pursuant to this objective, the amended Art IV allows a state a choice of method in relation to the exchange rate (eg, fixed, floating or pegged to a particular currency); however, states remained under a duty to co-operate with the Fund and to consult in the event of any proposed change. Under the terms of Art IV, s 1, the member state is expected 'to direct its economic and financial policies toward the objective of fostering orderly economic growth with reasonable price stability'. Secondly, the 1978 Amendment entailed a diminution in the role of gold in that gold was no longer to be employed as the 'common denominator' of the par value system.

The objective of the IMF was not restricted to securing exchange rate stability; the principal purpose was to 'facilitate the expansion and balanced growth of international trade' and this could only be done by minimising the incidence of exchange control

---

47 There are a number of memoranda regulating formal agreement.

48 The relationship between the IMF and the United Nations is governed by an Agreement between the United Nations and the IMF (1947).

49 *Case concerning the Payment of Various Serbian Loans Issued in France* (1927) PCIJ, Ser A, No 10, p 44; quoted in FA Mann, *The Legal Aspect of Money*, 1982, p 465.

50 The United Kingdom had returned to the gold standard in 1925 but withdrew in September 1931; the United States withdrew in April 1933.

51 In the years after 1968, the par value system had come under pressure by reason of differing levels of productivity and inflation. In November 1967, the United Kingdom had devalued; in August 1971, the United States decided to end the conversion into gold of foreign held dollars. In June 1972, the United Kingdom allowed the pound to float. The par value system had been characterised by crises after 1968 because of differing economic performance. The War of 1973 and the consequent oil price rise caused such inflationary pressure as make the par value system unworkable. The exchange rate had to 'take the strain' of differing economic performance.

regulations. Pursuant to this objective, Art 1(iv) had stipulated that a purpose of the Fund was 'to assist in the establishment of a multilateral system of payments in respect of current transactions between members and in the elimination of foreign exchange restrictions which hamper the growth of world. Exchange control restrictions may take many forms,[52] but they all have the same effect, namely undermining the objective of a freely convertible currency. Thus to ensure the multilateral system of payments the Articles of Agreement stipulate certain rules under Art VIII and for those states not able to comply with the full rigor of that provision an interim arrangement is made available under Art XIV.

The majority of members of the IMF have accepted the restrictions under Art VIII. In broad terms, a member state agrees not to impose, without the approval of the Fund any restrictions on the making of payments and transfers for current international transactions. Thus, the Fund has found it necessary to give rulings on whether particular forms of exchange regulations violate Art VIII. In principle, the article will prohibit governmental measures restrictive of market operations or causing undue delay or being discriminatory in nature; some practices, however, escape on the ground that the obligation arises by way of surrender rather than on the 'making of payment'.

There are a number of states, particularly developing states, who are unable or unwilling to submit to the full rigours of Art VIII. In these circumstances they may elect to be covered by the interim provisions available under Art XIV. However, the objective of this transitional regime is to enable the member state to move towards a full multilateral systems of payments as soon as the position of its balance of payments permits. If a state is adjudged ready to accept the full regime, then the IMF may indicate that it should do so and if a state declines then it may be deprived of the right of access to the Fund. Once a member state elects to submit to Art VIII that decision is irrevocable.

Once a member state is subject to Art VIII there may be circumstances where it wishes to act in order to protect its own currency. In principle, the member must seek the permission of the Fund and such permission is unlikely to be granted unless the application is made for balance of payments reasons and the proposed measures are necessary, limited in duration and without damaging effect on other members. The IMF has a number of methods for implementing the multilateral payments system. As with other international organisations, a member state in breach may be deprived of its voting rights or prohibited from access to the Fund; in some instances, it may impose conditions on access to the Fund. Member states are subject to surveillance and conditions may be imposed. Further, Art VIII(2)(b) of the Articles of Agreement provides that where an exchange contract is in breach of the regulations of another state that are *intra vires* the Articles of Agreement then such a contract shall be unenforcable in the other state. This creates an exception to the rule in Anglo American private international law that stipulates that one state does not normally acknowledge the revenue or penal laws of another state. The approach of the English courts in considering compatibility with

---

52 Such as: (i) prohibition on sums held by non citizens; (ii) non-availability of currency; (iii) licensing requirements; (iv) limits on sums capable of being dealt with; (v) deposit requirements; (vi) quotas for importers; (vii) delay in availability of foreign exchange.

Art VIII s 2(b)[53] has been to consider the matter not as one of interpretation of the contract but as one requiring the determination of the substance of the transaction.[54]

In addition to its duties in relation to monitoring exchange rates and its role in promoting currency convertibility, the IMF is also charged with providing international liquidity. A system of floating currencies depends on the extent of a state's reserves and any system of international liquidity. An absence of liquidity might be covered by the imposition of import controls but such measures would not be acceptable internationally. At Bretton Woods in 1944, JM Keynes had suggested a new form of international reserve to underpin the world economy and the idea was taken forward in the 1969 amendment of the Articles of Agreement. The 1969 Amendment provided for the creation of Special Drawing Rights (SDRs) to promote international liquidity and thus to assist member states confronted with balance of payments problems. There is some dispute as to the precise proprietary right represented by the SDR, some argue that it is a form of international money while others contend that it is simply a credit recorded by the IMF. In principle, the SDR is a right assigned to members of the Fund as a reserve asset to support the value of their currency.

4 INTERNATIONAL TRADE LAW[55]

International Trade Law is one of the most developed forms of international economic law. In essence, it is concerned with the flow of goods and services across frontiers. The subject itself divides into the public law and private law sphere. In the private sphere the lawyer is concerned with contractual questions, standard form agreements, questions of jurisdiction and problems arising from choice of law clauses and methods of dispute resolution. In its public international law aspect, it is concerned with the circumstances in which a state may impose quantitative restrictions or tariffs and the extent to which it can discriminate in favour of particular states. Related to this is the political argument that open, free and non-discriminatory trade promotes good relations between states and is itself conducive to peace: such an argument draws upon the economic principle of comparative advantage traceable to David Ricardo which holds that international trade is itself an engine of economic growth. One of the lessons learned from the economic depression of the 1920s and 1930s was that the post-war world would benefit from steps taken to promote international trade.

After Bretton Woods and the establishment of the United Nations (1945) a charter to create an International Trade Organisation was drafted in Havana, Cuba. However, the agreement was not accepted by the United States Congress and so the charter never entered into force and so the institution was never set up. The International Trade

---

53 Given effect to in England in the Bretton Woods Agreement Order in Council 1946 made under the Bretton Woods Act 1946.

54 *United City Merchants (Investments) Ltd v Royal Bank of Canada* [1983] 1 AC 168; see, also, *Wilson Smithett & Cope Ltd v Teruzzi* [1976] QB 683; *Batra v Ebrahim* [1982] 2 LR 11; *Mansouri v Singh* [1986] 1 WLR 1393; *Overseas Union Insurance v AA Mutual International Insurance* [1988] 2 LR 63.

55 RE Hudec, *The GATT Legal System and World Trade Diplomacy*, 1975; JH Jackson, *World Trade and the Law of GATT*, 1969l; JH Jackson, *The Jurisprudence of GATT and the WTO*, 2000.

Organisation had been intended to operate alongside a General Agreement on Tariffs and Trade (1947); when it became clear that the International Trade Organisation would not come into existence 23 states signed a Protocol of Provisional Application stipulating for the operation of the GATT. In the following four decades nearly 150 states joined the system so that the GATT operated as a quasi institution. The abbreviation GATT was used in two senses namely to indicate the treaty itself and to specify the Geneva based institution that administered the treaty. However, the GATT itself was not an international institution although it was certainly arguable that it had developed into something approaching an international institution notwithstanding the absence of a proper constitutional structure.

As a treaty the objective was to establish a common code in respect of international trade by providing mechanisms both for consultation and for reducing and stabilising tariffs. In essence the annual negotiating sessions[56] would reach agreement on tariffs and such an agreement would become binding when adopted by the Council of the Contracting Parties. The obligations thus acquired contractual force between the contracting parties; by virtue of the Most Favoured Nation Clause, tariff concessions in favour of one party become available to all parties. The GATT agreement itself sets out a number of fundamental principles, of which the most important are: (i) the principle of the most favoured nation state;[57] (ii) the reduction of tariff barriers; (iii) non-discrimination between imported and domestic goods;[58] (iv) elimination of import or export quotas;[59] (v) restriction on export subsidies; (vi) a prohibition on dumping. Special provisions are made in respect of developing countries and those states experiencing balance of payments problems,[60] and in circumstances of serious damage to domestic producers.

The objective of the GATT was thus to set out certain general principles designed to liberalise international trade. Subsequent agreements have lead to its amendment or extension as instanced by the Cotton Textiles Agreement of 1962 which was itself replaced by the Multi Fibre Textiles Agreement of 1973. The initial objective was to extend the GATT provisions to the trade in a wide number of products. However, the liberal objectives of the 1950s and 1960s in regard to tariffs were placed at risk by efforts at regional co-operation in the 1970s and the introduction of non-tariff restrictions to trade.

To meet these concerns the Uruguay Round was launched in 1986 with the purpose of ending non-tariff restrictions and also with the object of extending the GATT to new areas such as trade related intellectual property rights (TRIPS) and trade related investment measures (TRIMS). In essence, the objective of the Uruguay Round was to improve entry into traditional GATT areas, to extend the GATT provisions into new areas and to

---

56 The Multilateral Trade Negotiations which take place under the framework of GATT are normally described as 'rounds' and are as follows: Geneva (1947); Annecy, France (1949); Torquay, England (1950); Geneva (1956); the fifth round in Geneva in 1960 was named the Dillon Round; the sixth round was known as the Kennedy round and took place in Geneva in 1964; the seventh round was known as the Tokyo round and took place in Geneva in 1973; the eighth round known as the Uruguay round was launched in 1986 and concluded in December 1993.

57 GATT, Art 1.

58 *Ibid*, Art 3.

59 *Ibid*, Art IX.

60 *Ibid*, Art XIV.

promote institutional change. The Uruguay Round of GATT took seven and a half years and concluded on 15 April 1994 with the signing of the Marakesh agreement establishing the World Trade Organisation. The Uruguay Round itself was a considerable success in that GATT rules were extended to new areas of activity such as agriculture, film, broadcasting and intellectual property rights and the decision was taken to extend the operation of the Multifibre Agreement (MFA). Perhaps the most significant step was the decision of the 117 states to establish a proper institutional structure in the form of the World Trade Organisation.

The World Trade Organisation[61] came into existence on 1 January 1995 and is designed to provide the common institutional framework for the conduct of trade relations:[62] it is further charged with administering and implementing the multilateral trade agreements[63] and with providing a forum for negotiations. The structure of the World Trade Organisation comprises the Ministerial Conference which meets every two years,[64] while day to day business is in the hands of a General Council[65] which also convenes a Dispute Settlement Body[66] and a Trade Policy Review Body;[67] there are three other specialist delegated bodies namely the Council for Trade in Goods; the Council for Trade in Services and the Council for Trade related Aspects of Intellectual Property Rights.

The objectives of the WTO are twofold namely to ensure a reduction in tariffs and to eliminate discriminatory treatment in trade relations.[68] However, these principles have to take account of the need to promote sustainable development and the requirement to safeguard the interests of developing nations. Membership of the WTO is open to any state or separate customs territory which enjoys autonomy over external commercial relations.[69] While the WTO is not a specialised United Nations agency it is required to co-operate with both the IMF and the World Bank Group; the object of such co-operation is to achieve greater coherence in global economic policy making.[70] The WTO is endowed with separate legal personality.[71]

The regime of open trade involves a prohibition on quantitative restrictions on imports and exports;[72] the respect for tariff reductions already agreed upon;[73] the prohibition of discrimination against member countries;[74] the prohibition on treatment at

---

61 Established under Art 1 of the Marrakesh Agreement of 15 April 1994.
62 Marrakesh Agreement (1994), Art II(1).
63 *Ibid*, Art III(1).
64 *Ibid*, Art IV(1).
65 *Ibid*, Art IV(2).
66 *Ibid*, Art IV(3).
67 *Ibid*, Art IV(4).
68 See *ibid*, preamble.
69 *Ibid*, Arts XI and XII.
70 *Ibid*, Art III(5).
71 *Ibid*, Art VIII.
72 GATT (1994), Art XI.
73 *Ibid*, Art II.
74 *Ibid*, Art I.

variance with the national standard;[75] the obligation of transparency namely the obligation to disclose all trade related measures.[76]

The WTO operates through a code which extends to its three particular activities namely goods, services and trade related aspects of intellectual property rights – that is, GATT 1994[77] and the Multilateral Agreements on Trade, GATS,[78] and TRIPS.[79] GATT 1994 is supplemented by a number of agreements specific to particular sectors;[80] these agreements together with GATT 1994 are referred to as the Multilateral Agreements on Trade in Goods. The Multilateral Agreements on Trade in Goods, GATS, TRIPS, the Understanding on Rules and Procedures Governing the Settlement of Disputes and the Trade Policy Review Mechanism form a corpus of legal obligations subsumed within the Marrakesh Agreement of 1994;[81] all parties to the Marrakesh agreement are bound by these agreements.[82]

One of the most significant features of the new WTO structure is the attention given to matters of enforcement.[83] In broad terms, this task falls to the WTO Dispute Settlement Mechanism and the WTO Trade Policy Review Mechanism (TPRM). In respect of dispute settlement, it has to be acknowledged that the prior GATT dispute machinery was subject to justified criticism for undue delay and the absence of an identifiable appellate structure. The WTO dispute settlement structure[84] is outlined in the Understanding on the Rules and Procedures Governing the Settlement of Disputes (normally referred to as 'the Understanding').[85] A Dispute Settlement Body (DSB) has been established to administer the rules and procedures in respect of the Understanding.[86] Access to the dispute settlement machinery is available only to members of the WTO; the obligations under the WTO pertain only to states and there does not appear to be any obligation to exhaust internal remedies. Since the obligations arising under the GATT/WTO system are inter-state matters the admissibility of complaints is not contingent on the prior exhaustion of local remedies.[87] Normally, private parties will be obliged to request their

---

75   *Ibid*, Art III.

76   *Ibid*, Art X.

77   The contents of GATT 1947 and subsequent amendments having been re-enacted in GATT 1994.

78   The Agreement on Trade in Services (GATS).

79   Agreement on Trade Related Aspects of Intellectual Property Rights (TRIPS).

80   Which will normally prevail in the event of a conflict with GATT 1994; see Annex 1A to the Marrakesh Agreement (1994). These agreements include the Agreement on Trade Related Aspects of Investment Measures (TRIMS).

81   Marrakesh Agreement 1994, Arts II(I) and II(2).

82   *Ibid*, Art II(2).

83   See J Collier and AV Lowe, *The Settlement of Disputes in International Law*, 1999, pp 99–104; EU Petersmann (ed), *International Trade Law and the GATT/WTO Dispute Settlement System*, 1997; TJ Schoenbaum, 'WTO dispute settlement, praise and suggestions for reform' (1998) 47 ICLQ 647; AW Sharpe, 'The first three years of WTO dispute settlement: observation and comment' (1998) 1 Journal of International Economic Law 277.

84   See Arts XXII and XXIII of GATT 1994 and the Understanding.

85   The 1994 Understanding on Rules and Procedures Governing the Settlement of Disputes is set out in (1994) 33 ILM 1226.

86   Article 2 of the Understanding.

87   For a general discussion of this point, see EU Petersmann, 'The dispute system of the World Trade Organisation and the evolution of the GATT dispute settlement system since 1948' [1994] 31 CMLR 1157.

government to invoke the dispute machinery the Understanding proceeds on the basis of both consultation and adjudication; further the Understanding permits disputes to be sent to arbitration if the parties so decide.[88] States which are in dispute are expected to engage first in direct consultations.[89] Such consultations are subject to time limits to prevent unfair advantage being obtained by protracted and inconclusive negotiations.[90] If efforts at the consultation stage fail then the dispute is adjudicated upon by a panel;[91] such a panel comprises members serving in their individual capacity[92] who are charged with reviewing the evidence in an objective manner, finding the facts and applying the relevant regulations.[93] The panel is normally required to report within a period of six months.[94] A right of appeal exists in respect of a panel report but only on a point of law;[95] the manner in which a panel weighs evidence and determines facts is regarded as a point of law.[96] The Appellate Body is comprised of lawyers with a specialist knowledge of international trade law.[97] The Appellate Body may uphold or reverse a finding of the panel[98] and its determination will normally be accepted by the Dispute Settlement Body (DSB).[99]

In principle remedies will normally involve the withdrawal of the offending measure. The report of the panel or the Appellate Body is to be implemented without undue delay;[100] in the event of failure to agree the time period then this matter may be resolved by arbitration.[101] Implementation of panel and appellate reports is subject to surveillance by the Dispute Settlement Body (DSB). A third party state may participate at the consultation stage[102] or the panel stage and may make written submissions to the appellate body. It does not however have an independent right of appeal. The Understanding contains a number of provisions designed to protect the interests of developing countries and further directs that where relevant the position of developing countries is to be considered in any panel report.[103]

---

88 Article 25 of the Understanding.
89 Article XXII of GATT 1994; Art 4 of the Understanding.
90 Article 4(3) of the Understanding.
91 *Ibid*, Art 6.
92 Under the terms of Art 8 they will be well qualified persons (though not always lawyers) who have a background in international trade – this background may have been acquired in practical experience within the WTO system or may be grounded in teaching or writing on international trade.
93 Article 11 of the Understanding.
94 Article 12 of the Understanding.
95 Article 17(6) of the Understanding.
96 See Art 11 of the Understanding; see also European Communities Measures Concerning Meat and Meat Products (Hormones) (Report of the Appellate Body 1998).
97 The Appellate Body comprises seven lawyers who serve for a four year period.
98 Article 17(3) of the Understanding.
99 Under the prior GATT system, a report would not be adopted unless there was a consensus for adoption; under the terms of the Understanding the report is adopted unless there is a consensus against adoption. See Art 17(14).
100 Article 26(1) of the Understanding.
101 *Ibid*, Art 21.
102 *Ibid*, Art 4(11).
103 *Ibid*, Art 12(11).

A second method of enforcement within the WTO is provided by the Trade Policy Review Mechanism[104] as operated by the Trade Policy Review Body (TPRB);[105] this process[106] is designed not to consider individual cases[107] but to review the foreign trade regime of a member state to ensure compliance with the WTO code and the principle of transparency. Member states are expected to submit reports at the time of review by the TPRB. The interval between reviews depends on the influence that a state has on overall world trade; the more influential the state the more frequent the reviews. The review process is designed to consider the trade practices of a state against the obligations in the WTO code; such a practice bears some affinity with the reporting regimes operating under human rights treaties.

5 INTERNATIONAL DEVELOPMENT LAW

It is sometimes argued that International Development Law represents the third aspect of International Economic Law. A number of international organisations are engaged in work that might loosely be described as pertaining to International Development Law. In this context it is important to remember that the preamble to the Charter of the United Nations stipulates that one of the objectives of the organisation is 'to employ international machinery for the promotion of the economic and social advancement of all peoples'.[108] To facilitate this objective, it is sensible to regard international development law as embracing the laws that promote foreign investment and the laws that provide for co-operation and participation in international institutions. While, in general, customary international law it was strongly arguable that there was no duty placed on one state to aid another such a broad proposition requires qualification after 1945. In respect of terminology, there is a widespread acceptance that states can be classified into developed countries, developing countries and less developed or under developed. The increase in the number of states and the economic and technological advances made in the developed world have served to widen the differences in living standards between developed countries and the remainder of states.

The general obligation towards the less developed countries was set out in Art 55 of the Charter of the United Nations which reads in part:

> With a view to the creation of conditions of stability and well being which are necessary for peaceful and friendly relations among nations based on respect for the principle of equal rights and self determination of peoples, the United Nations shall promote:
>
> (a) higher standards of living, full employment, and conditions of economic and social progress and development;

---

104 See Annex 3 of the Marrakesh Agreement (1994).
105 PC Mavroidis, 'Surveillance schemes: the GATT's new trade policy review mechanism' (1992) 13 Michigan Journal of International Law 374.
106 See Art III (4) and IV of the Marrakesh Agreement (1994).
107 Although evidence disclosed under the TPRM might be the subject of action through the WTO dispute settlement procedures.
108 Preamble to Charter of the United Nations (1945).

(b) solutions of international economic, social, health, and related problems; and international cultural and educational co-operation ...

Thus, from 1945 at the latest, there has been an emphasis on promoting economic growth or development in the poorer nations of the world. The term 'development' was defined in Art 1 of the Declaration on the Right to Development (1986) as being 'the process which facilitates for every human person and all peoples the enjoyment of economic, social, cultural and political development'. However, while development might in 1945 have been equated with economic growth there has been since that date an increasing emphasis on environmental protection; thus, the need to ensure development and the obligation to ensure environmental protection has manifested itself in the principle of 'sustainable development'.

It has been questioned by one leading authority as to whether the concept of 'sustainable development' is any more than an emerging principle of customary international law.[109] Be that as it may, those who espouse the principle[110] have isolated four elements, namely: (i) the principle of inter generational equity; (ii) the sustainable use of natural resources; (iii) the equitable use of natural resources – that is, so that the needs of other states are taken into account; (iv) the principle of integration – namely the integration of environmental and development objectives.[111] The principle of sustainable development suffers the problem of being vague and open ended but it has attracted attention in recent international judgments and it certainly serves at present to indicate the need to find a balance between the requirement of economic growth and the no less pressing need to ensure environmental protection.[112] Alongside the principle of sustainable development, there are a number of relevant principles some of which find support in customary international law; examples would be the duty of states to co-operate and to act as a good neighbour,[113] the precautionary principle and the principle that the polluter should pay.

As indicated above it is the emergence of international institutions in the years since 1945 that have promoted the cause of development. This is particularly associated with the efforts of the World Bank Group which comprises the International Bank for Reconstruction and Development (1946)[114] and its associated bodies namely the International Finance Corporation (IFC 1956), the International Development Association (IDA 1960); the International Centre for the Settlement of Investment Disputes (ICSID 1966) and the Multilateral Investment Guarantee Agency (MIGA 1988). In broad terms, the relevant legal sources are: (i) the relevant Articles of Agreement and Bye-Laws; (ii)

---

109 See I Brownlie, *Principles of Public International Law*, 5th edn, 1998, p 287; on the concept, see P Birnie and A Boyle, *International Law and the Environment*, 1992, p 122; P Sands, 'International law in the field of sustainable development' (1994) 65 BYIL 303; W Lang (ed), *Sustainable Development in International Law*, 1995.

110 See P Sands, 'International law in the field of sustainable development', in W Lang (ed), *Sustainable Development in International Law*, 1995, p 58.

111 See separate opinion of Vice President Weeramantry in *Case concerning Gabcikovo-Nagymaras Project* (1997) ICJ 4 (Hungary/Slovakia).

112 *Ibid*.

113 As in the general law of state responsibility see *Trail Smelter Arbitration* (1938/1941) 3 RIAA 1905.

114 Better known as the World Bank and deriving from the United Nations Monetary and Financial Conference held in Bretton Woods, New Hampshire.

agreements with other international organisations; (iii) relevant loan and credit agreements.

Thus Art 1 of the Articles of Agreement of the IBRD notes that its purposes are: 'To assist in the reconstruction and development of territories of members, including the restoration of economies destroyed or disrupted by war, the reconversion of productive facilities to peacetime needs and the encouragement of the development of productive facilities and resources in less developed countries'.[115] These objectives are to be achieved by the facilitation of the investment of capital, the promotion of private investment and the supplementing of private investment by the Bank.[116] To a large extent, these objectives are reiterated in the statute of the IDA,[117] while the constitutional documents of the IFC, MIGA and ICSID are more concerned with private sector solutions. The work of the various institutions within the World Bank Group is designed to be complementary and the constitutional documents provide that decisions are not to be made on political grounds.[118]

Membership of the World Bank Group is restricted to States.[119] As regards constitutional structure each organ[120] operates through a Board of Governors, Executive Board, and a President,[121] save in the case of the ICSID which operates through an Administrative Council and a Chairman; the organisations operate by means of weighted voting.[122] In general, each organ will interpret its own constitutional document and there are provisions for amendment. All the organs within the World Bank Group enjoy international legal personality. States are expected to make some contribution to the funds and, in the case of the ICSID, they are expected to contribute towards expenses. In respect of operations, the work of the IBRD[123] and the IDA concentrates upon the provision of loans to those states which have a limited per capita GNP; in general such loans must be for productive, reconstructive or development purposes.[124] Such criteria will normally exclude loans for military purposes; loans granted are subject to periodic review.[125] In contrast, the role of the IFC is to facilitate loans to private enterprises;[126] the investment may be made by direct loan or by subscribing to a share of the equity. Such investment is designed to stimulate the local economy but must be consistent with good environmental practice.[127] This work is supplemented by the efforts of of MIGA,[128] which provides

---

115 Articles of Agreement of IBRD (1945), Art 1.
116 *Ibid*, Art 1.
117 See Art 1 of IDA (1960).
118 See IBRD, Art 10; IDA Art V s 6; IFC Art III s 9; MIGA Art 34.
119 By linking such membership to that of the IM or IBRD; see IBRD, Art II; IDA, Art II IFC, Art II; ICSID Art 67.
120 See IBRD, Art V; IFC, Art IV; IDA, Art VI; MIGA, Art 30.
121 There are some provisions for interlocking membership.
122 See IBRD, Art V; IDA, Art VI, s 3; IFC, Art IV, s 3; MIGA, Art 39; save in the case of ICSID which operates on the basis of one member one vote.
123 See IBRD, Art 1 and III, s 4.
124 See IBRD, Art 1 and IDA, Art V.
125 See IBRD, Art III, s 4(v).
126 See Articles of Agreement of the IFC, Art 1.
127 IFC, Art 1.
128 The Multilateral Investment Guarantee Agency (MIGA) established in 1988.

guarantees[129] against non-commercial risks[130] and in respect of certain investments. In contrast, the role of the ICSID is to provide a mechanism for the peaceful resolution of investment disputes. Stimulated by an initiative of the World Bank and grounded in the Washington Convention of 1965, the role of the ICSID is to provided a method of dispute resolution between Contracting States and the nationals of other Contracting States. Under the terms of Art 25, the jurisdiction only extends to investment disputes; the Convention provides two methods namely conciliation and arbitration. Jurisdiction is contingent on the submission of the parties although today there are a large number of bilateral investment treaties which provide for submission to the ICSID. In the case of a valid submission to arbitration, contracting states are required to desist from taking the matter up as a diplomatic claim. An arbitral award is binding and not subject to appeal. However, in certain circumstances a party may move for the annulment of an award under Art 52 on grounds of procedural irregularity, irregular constitution or improper exercise of power.[131] In recent years some criticism has arisen as a result of an increase in the number of annulment requests.[132] However, many cases submitted to ICSID are settled before a full hearing. In respect of enforcement such awards are to be recognised and enforced as if a judgment of that state's own courts. Although as the Convention does not require individual states to set aside their own rules on sovereign immunity there may be difficulties in actual enforcement.[133]

Although international development law is concerned with the promotion of development and the activities of the relevant international organisations to achieve this goal an equally important aspect is that of foreign investment not least because it may be a fertile ground for legal disputes. In the world after 1945, many writers are tempted to divide the international community into capital exporting states and capital importing states. More precisely, problems can arise when a private corporation registered and with a place of business in state A chooses to invest in the territory of state B; sometimes the foreign investor may object to action subsequently taken by the government of state B. It is broadly accepted that in customary international law it is a matter for each state to determine whether it wishes to accept foreign investment;[134] however if it decides to accept foreign investment then public international law sets out a number of rules as to

---

129 For the United Kingdom, see the Multilateral Investment Guarantee Agency Act 1988, which provides for United Kingdom participation.

130 For contribution by the United Kingdom, see Multilateral Investment Guarantee Agency Act 1988 s 2. For a general discussion, see SK Chatterjee, 'The Convention Establishing the Multilateral Investment Guarantee Agency' (1987) 36 ICLQ 76. Examples of non commercial risk would be: (i) civil war; (ii) expropriation; (iii) currency restrictions by the host state. See Art 11, Convention Establishing the Multilateral Investment Guarantee Agency (1985).

131 *Amco Asia Corporation, Pan American Development Ltd and PT Amco Indonesia v Republic of Indonesia Ad Hoc Committee acting under Article 52* (1986) 1 ICSID Reports 509; 25 ILM 1439; in this case, there had been a jurisdictional hearing in 1983, a decision on merits in 1984, an annulment in 1986 and new decisions on merits and jurisdiction in 1988 and 1991.

132 *Maritime International Nominees Establishment v Government of the Republic of Guinea ad hoc Committee acting under Article 52* (1989) 4 ICSID Reports 79.

133 Article 55 of the Washington Convention on the Settlement of Investment Disputes between States and Nationals of Other States (the 'ICSID Convention').

134 This is the view taken in the World Bank, *Guidelines on the Treatment of Foreign Direct Investment*, 1992, Guideline II.

how the state should behave towards the foreign investor.[135] In many instances minimum standards are set out in bilateral investment agreements with a stipulation for arbitration under the auspices of the ICSID.[136]

The most urgent concern of the foreign investor is that its assets might be subject to expropriation[137] by the host state. The expression 'expropriation' covers a wide number of situations. According to one writer[138] it may embrace at least 10 different actions so that some care must be taken in respect of the precise action[139] adopted by the host state; indeed, it would seem that the expression 'expropriation' is a general term[140] that embraces distinct concepts such as requisition, nationalisation, compulsory acquisition and confiscation. Expropriatory decrees give rise to problems in private international law as to whether they should be recognised and enforced in the courts of other states and they also have to be considered against the background of the accepted rules of public international law.

International law has traditionally drawn a distinction between lawful expropriation[141] and unlawful expropriation.[142] Lawful expropriation embraces acts undertaken for a public purpose and which are non-discriminatory in nature; there is room for doubt as to the precise meaning of public purpose, however it is arguable this should be given a wide interpretation having regard to the traditional freedom international law allows to states to select their own social and economic system.[143] In principle an act of lawful expropriation gives rise to an entitlement to compensation although there is wide scope for argument as to how that compensation is to be assessed. In contrast an act of expropriation which does not meet the criteria of legality will be

---

135 As indicated in the World Bank, *Guidelines on the Treatment of Foreign Direct Investment*, 1992, Guideline III, which refers to transparency, accountability and the principle of equitable treatment.

136 The treatment of the foreign investor is considered in Chapter 12 on State Responsibility.

137 See generally, W Friedmann, *Expropriation in International Law*, 1953; RL Bindschelder 'La protection de la propriété privée en droit international public' (1956) 90 HR 173; B Wortley, *Expropriation in Public International Law*, 1959; G White, *Nationalisation of Foreign Property*, 1961; R Higgins, 'The taking of property by the state: recent developments in international law' (1982) 176 HR 259; M Sornarajah, *The International Law on Foreign Investment*, 1994.

138 According to M Sornarajah, *The International Law on Foreign Investment*, 1994, the expression 'expropriation' may embrace: (a) forced sales of property; (b) forced sale of shares; (c) transfer from foreign interests to local interests; (d) application of management control; (e) a physical takeover of the property; (f) failure to provide protection when there is an interference with the foreign investment; (g) licensing decisions; (h) exorbitant taxation; (i) expulsion of the foreign investor contrary to international law; (j) acts of harassment such as freezing of a bank account.

139 *Starrett Housing Corporation v Government of the Islamic Republic of Iran* (1983) 4 Iran-US CTR 122; 85 ILR 349.

140 For a general discussion, see *Williams and Humbert Ltd v W and H Trade Marks (Jersey) Ltd* [1986] AC 368, in particular the discussion by Nourse J at first instance on the classification of foreign expropriatory decrees. For the approach of the English courts, see *Luther v Sagor* [1921] 3 KB 532; *Princess Olga Paley v Weisz* [1929] 1 KB 718; *Re Helbert Wagg & Co Ltd* [1956] Ch 323; *Oppenheimer v Cattermole* [1976] AC 249; *Buttes Gas and Oil Co v Hammer (No 3)* [1982] AC 888; *Williams and Humbert Ltd v W and H Trade Marks (Jersey) Ltd* [1986] AC 368.

141 The World Bank *Guidelines on the Treatment of Foreign Direct Investment*, 1992, 31 ILM 1363 stipulate that expropriation must be: (i) for a public purpose; (ii) without discrimination; and subject to (iii) payment of appropriate compensation.

142 *Amoco International Finance Corporation v The Islamic Republic of Iran* (1987) 15 Iran-US Claims Tribunal 189; 83 ILR 500.

143 *Nicaragua v The United States* (1986) ICJ 14.

categorised as an act of unlawful expropriation; such acts are said to give rise to an obligation to pay damages.

In respect of lawful expropriation, the emphasis has been on the obligation to make 'prompt, adequate and effective compensation'; this principle[144] derives from a letter sent by Cordell Hull[145] to the Mexican Government on 22 August 1938 and is sometimes alluded to as the 'Hull formula'. This formulation has found favour with capital exporting states[146] and international tribunals; it is often employed in bilateral investment agreements. However, in the last two decades the emphasis has been on the awarding of 'appropriate compensation',[147] which enables a tribunal to consider all relevant evidence and there has been a greater willingness to examine the overall context.[148] While valuation of physical assets may be subject to negotiation, difficulties can arise as to the extent to which claims can be made for loss of future profits.[149] In respect of physical assets, the emphasis does appear to be on compensation at the level of fair market value[150] but in respect of loss of future profits there may be difficulties of evidence and any such sum may be discounted on grounds of remoteness. In the case of an unlawful taking then full restitution[151] represents the starting point of assessment.

In practice many claims are settled by the diplomatic negotiations under the terms of a bilateral investment agreement and the payment of a lump sum by state A to state B. It will then be the duty of state B to distribute such sums to those citizens with a legitimate claim. In the United Kingdom this task is accomplished by the Foreign Compensation Commission although this has proved to be not without some difficulty.[152]

Uniformity of practice is achieved by bilateral investment agreements between capital exporting states and capital importing states. In general, such agreements after

---

144 But it was not used in the early case law; see *Norwegian Shipowners' Claims* case (1922) 1 RIAA 307; *Chorzow Factory* case (1928) PCIJ, Ser A, No 17, p 46; see J Fischer Williams (1928) 9 BYIL 1. For an interesting discussion as to whether the 'Hull formula' ever acquired the status of a general rule of law applicable in all circumstances, see O Schachter, 'Compensation for expropriation' (1984) 78 AJIL 121.

145 Cordell Hull (1871–1955) (Secretary of State 1933–44) (Winner of the Nobel Peace Prize 1945): his preparatory work on the United Nations Charter gained him the unofficial title of 'Father of the United Nations'.

146 Adopted by the United States in respect of agrarian reform in Mexico in the 1930s; raised by the United Kingdom in respect of Iranian oil nationalisation in 1951 and by both states at the time of the nationalisation of the Suez Canal in 1956. The principle has been invoked by the United States in respect of Cuba and Ceylon; see (1962) 56 AJIL 166; (1964) 58 AJIL 168.

147 See United Nations Declaration on Permanent Sovereignty over Natural Resources (1962) GA Res 1803 (XVII); *Texaco v The Government of Libya* (1978) 17 ILM 3; 53 ILR 389; *Aminoil v Kuwait* (1982) 21 ILM 976; 66 ILR 518; see FA Mann (1983) 54 BYIL 213.

148 *INA Corporation v The Islamic Republic of Iran* (1985) 8 Iran-US CTR 373; 75 ILR 595.

149 *AMCO v Indonesia* (1985) 24 ILM 1022; 89 ILR 405 (where a distinction was expressly drawn between *damnum emergens* (loss incurred) and *lucrum cessans* (anticipated profits)).

150 *INA Corporation v The Islamic Republic of Iran* (1985) 8 Iran-US CTR 373, 75 ILR 595.

151 *Ibid*; *Amco International Finance Corporation v The Islamic Republic of Iran* (1987) I5 Iran-US CTR 189; (1986) 82 AJIL 358.

152 The Foreign Compensation Act 1950 had provided that the decisions of the Commission 'shall not be called in question in any court of law'; this lead to *Anisminic Ltd v Foreign Compensation Commission* [1969] 2 AC 147, which revolutionised the law of judicial review in the United Kingdom. See HW Wade (1969) 85 LQR 198; B Gould [1970] PL 358. For the response of the United Kingdom Parliament, see Foreign Compensation Act 1969.

establishing their particular scope will be concerned to deal *inter alia* with the admission of investment, the standard of treatment and methods of dispute resolution. Such agreements may deal with the issue of subsequent legislation by the host state. One of the main causes of concern for the potential foreign investor is that subsequent legislation by the host state may operate to its detriment. To this end, some foreign investors may seek to enter into agreements with the host state that combine a stabilisation clause with some form of choice of law clause in favour of international law,[153] or a reference to international arbitration.[154] The object of a stabilisation clause is to provide that subsequent legislation by the host state shall not adversely affect the foreign investor.[155] It has to be admitted that such arrangements are not without their difficulties. First, an agreement between a private organisation and a state is not normally considered an international agreement.[156] Secondly, a stabilisation clause in seeking to freeze the state of the law of the host state is contrary to the principle of the legislative sovereignty of a state and may indeed be unconstitutional within the domestic sphere. Thirdly, a stabilisation clause is at variance with the principle of the permanent sovereignty over natural resources. While many contracts between a state and an alien entity may be governed by municipal law there has been a growing attempt to seek to 'internationalise' the contract by including stabilisation clauses, choice of law clauses and references to international arbitration.[157] It is then argued that such conduct 'internationalises' the contract so as to enshrine the principle of *pacta sunt servanda* and thus prevent the unilateral variation of the contract by the host state. While it is accepted that stabilisation clauses are legitimate[158] some theoretical difficulties arise and in the event of breach the presence of the clause may simply be another ground for compensation rather than the basis for specific performance.

6 CONCLUSION

It can therefore be seen that the efforts of United Nations agencies since 1945 to raise the standard of living of poorer countries has lead to the emergence of a distinct corpus of international economic law. The subject now embraces those international rules normally treaty based which are designed to secure monetary co-operation, to liberalise trade and

---

153 This, of course, is quite different from the so called 'Calvo clauses' which were often inserted in contracts between South American states and persons to whom concessions had been granted. Such clauses involved the foreign investor agreeing not to make diplomatic representations through his own government and also undertaking to submit to the courts of the host state. The legality of such clauses is a matter of debate: see *North American Dredging Company* claim (1926) 20 AJIL 800; (1926) 4 RIAA 26; 3 ILR, p 4.

154 *BP Exploration Co v Libya* (1974) 53 ILR 297; *Texaco v Libya* (1974) 53 ILR 389; *Aminoil v Kuwait* (1982) 66 ILR 518.

155 *LIAMCO v Libya* (1981) 62 ILR 140; AZ El Chiati, 'Protection of investment in the context of petroleum agreements' (1987) 204 HR 9.

156 *Anglo Iranian Oil* case (1952) ICJ 93.

157 A Fatouros, 'International law and the internationalised contract' (1980) 74 AJIL 134; C Greenwood, 'State contracts in international law – the Libyan Oil Arbitrations ' (1982) 53 BYIL 27; DW Bowett, 'State contracts with aliens: contemporary developments on compensation for termination or breach' (1988) 59 BYIL 49.

158 The *Aminoil* case, *Kuwait v American Independent Oil Co* (1982) 21 ILM 976 (see in particular the Separate Opinion of Sir Gerald Fitzmaurice).

to promote development. In all three areas, there has been an evolution of institutions designed to facilitate the peaceful settlement of disputes. As indicated above, the corpus of international economic law has been growing steadily since 1945 and has expanded further with the collapse of communist central planning in 1989; the difficulty that now arises is that the desire to promote economic growth in poorer states has to take account of environmental concerns. To this extent, the future of international economic law is likely to be inextricably linked with the requirements of international environmental law; the need for a balance between these two branches of international law is already evident in the emerging concept of 'sustainable development'.

CHAPTER 20

THE PEACEFUL SETTLEMENT OF DISPUTES BETWEEN STATES

1 INTRODUCTION[1]

From the earliest times and certainly from 16th century it was recognised that a breach of international order leading to conflict could set in train undesirable consequences. Thus, from the outset writers on international law have given much thought to the topic of how international disputes could be resolved short of conflict; such reflections were also motivated by the ethical consideration that unrestrained conflict would entail considerable loss of human life. Thus, from the 16th century as international law began to develop, much thought was given as to the question of how international society could be managed so as to avoid conflict and a descent into widespread war. As the capacity of armaments increased in the 19th century, so a number of methods began to emerge designed to resolve international problems short of conflict. In general terms methods of peaceful resolution of disputes can be divided into: (i) diplomatic methods of dispute settlement; (ii) legal or judicial methods of dispute resolution; (iii) methods arising under the particular rules of an international organisation.

Before turning to specific methods of dispute resolution it is necessary to say a word about terminology. A 'dispute' is founded on the fact of disagreement; one authority[2] defines a dispute as 'a specific disagreement concerning a matter of fact, law or policy in which a claim or assertion of one party is met with refusal, counter claim or denial by another'. Thus, an international dispute may be said to arise when the disagreement concerns the government of a sovereign state, an international organisation or some other legal person. For the most part however the dispute will be those between sovereign states. It is sensible to distinguish the 'dispute' from the 'conflict'. A 'conflict' has been defined as signifying 'a general state of hostility between the parties'. Certainly, a dispute if unresolved may give rise to a conflict; the methods of peaceful resolution are designed to ensure that this does not happen. In contrast, a distinction should be drawn between peaceful methods of dispute resolution and vehicles of conflict resolution that may be employed, say, to end a civil war, that is, methods that are employed when the conflict has been in existence for some considerable time.

It should not be thought that the existence of international disputes testifies to the weakness of international order. Disputes sometimes arise within families and may indeed lead to divorce. Likewise, in civil society there may be disputes about the terms of a contract, the powers of the police or the rights to a piece of land; some of these disputes may indeed be emotionally charged but a lawyer would argue that they are capable of legal analysis. Evidence can be taken, facts found and rules applied or an appropriate discretion exercised by an independent and impartial tribunal. It may be that the decision

---

1   See generally, J Merrills, *International Dispute Settlement*, 2nd edn, 1991; J Merrills, *International Dispute Settlement*, 3rd edn, 1998; J Collier and AV Lowe, *The Settlement of Disputes in International Law*, 1st edn, 1999.

2   See J Merrills, *International Dispute Settlement*, 2nd edn, 1991, p 1.

will not satisfy the parties; the divorced spouse may seek a greater share of the family assets or the company may be unhappy that it was not able to rely on an exclusion clause. However, in any mature society there will be well established methods of dispute resolution. It may be that a citizen may not agree with the outcome so for example pressure might be brought on the legislature to increase the damages available in respect of tortious claims. However, what is clear is that in mature post-industrial societies the citizen agrees to pursue his disputes by exclusively peaceful means. Generally speaking the criminal law prohibits the use of force and even the recovery of property must normally be effected by a court order. Thus, an examination of municipal law demonstrates that disputes inevitably arise that the nature of disputes change with variations in economic activity and that the use of force is best avoided by the provision of a variety of methods of peaceful resolution.

So in international society with over 180 states with conflicting aims and ambitions it is perhaps natural that disputes should arise. In municipal law the fact that more persons travel in the 20th century has increased the number of accident related claims so too in international law; the ability to explore outer space or the deep sea bed has generated new areas of potential dispute. It should therefore be accepted that disputes between states are the natural reflection of the dynamic nature of international society. The basic question is how such inevitable disputes should be resolved.

It is clear beyond doubt that one of the fundamental objectives of the United Nations Charter is the promotion of the peaceful resolution of disputes. This is referred to in Art 1(1) and is more explicitly stated in Art 2(3) which reads:

> All Members shall settle their international disputes by peaceful means in such a manner that international peace and security, and justice, are not endangered.

This principle is built upon in Art 33(1) of the Charter which reads:

> The parties to any dispute, the continuance of which is likely to endanger the maintenance of international peace and security, shall, first of all, seek a solution by negotiation, enquiry, mediation, conciliation, arbitration, judicial settlement, resort to regional agencies or arrangements, or other peaceful means of their own choice.

It is to be further to be noted that Art 33(2) entitles the Security Council to call upon both parties to adopt one or other method of peaceful resolution. In 1970, in the Declaration on Principles of International Law, the General Assembly after referring to Art 2(3) noted:

> States shall accordingly seek early and just settlement of their international disputes by negotiation, inquiry, mediation, conciliation arbitration, judicial settlement, resort to regional agencies or arrangements or other peaceful methods of their choice.

It is proposed to examine each of these methods in turn. However, it should be noted that the methods do depend on the free consent of states and in any particular situation more than one method may be appropriate. Secondly, such methods may not be sufficient in those limited cases where a government considers vital national issues to be at stake; in such circumstances a government may submit any negotiated or agreed terms to its people in a referendum. Thirdly, in some international instruments the parties are allowed a degree of choice as to the particular method to be adopted.

2 NEGOTIATION AND CONSULTATION

It is sometimes argued that a state is under a duty in customary international law to consult another state if a decision that it is about to take will affect that state.[3] However, the concept of 'consultation' should be distinguished between cases of 'prior notification' and those cases of 'prior consent'. In the former instance the affected state is given an opportunity to comment and such a process may properly be called consultation. However, in the latter instance state A is seeking to obtain the consent of state B before it takes a decision. Having regard to the basic principle of the sovereignty of states international law will be slow to assume that an obligation of prior consent arises[4] although it may in cases of joint sovereignty over territory or where there is a provision for joint decision taking arising under a treaty. It may be that an agreement provides for a measure of consultation and examples are afforded by the Antarctic Treaty 1959 or by the 1990 Interim Reciprocal Information and Consultation System established to defuse tension and to regulate the movement of British and Argentine forces in the South Western Atlantic. It is doubtful whether there is a general duty to negotiate (which includes consultation) arising in customary international law, but it is common to find such duties arising by treaty.

If a duty to consult has arisen then in principle it must be meaningful. So that consultation must be at a time when the proposals are at a formative stage; the proposing state must give sufficient information and time to permit intelligent response and the product of the consultation must be conscientiously taken into account. If a duty to negotiate has arisen, then international tribunals have required that such negotiations should be undertaken in good faith[5] and this involves giving serious consideration to relevant proposals advanced by the other side. The duty to negotiate in good faith does not imply a duty in all circumstances to reach agreement[6] although much will depend on the phraseology of the treaty imposing the duty and possibly also on the gravity of the subject matter. It is clear that the duty to negotiate involves a duty to pursue the negotiations[7] so that abruptly terminating discussions would be a breach. It is clear that negotiation involves discussions between the parties in the appropriate manner and form; a dispute between parties at an international assembly does not constitute negotiation and is likely to be characterised as disputation.[8] There is no general rule of international law that negotiations should be concluded before a party may invoke another method of

---

3   Although the actual authority for the proposition seems limited; it arises by implication from the undoubted proposition that state A is obliged to respect the sovereignty of state B.

4   This would seem to follow from the reasoning in the *Lac Lanoux Arbitration (France v Spain)* (1957) 24 ILR 101.

5   *North Sea Continental Shelf* cases (1969) ICJ 3; *Fisheries Jurisdiction* cases (1974) ICJ 3.

6   The *German External Debts Arbitration* (1980) 19 ILM 1357; 47 ILR 418.

7   *Railway Traffic between Lithuania and Poland* (1931) PCIJ, Ser A/B, No 42, p 108; 6 ILR 403.

8   *South West Africa (Preliminary Objections)* case (1962) ICJ 319; *Northern Cameroons* case (1963) ICJ 15.

dispute settlement.[9] Where a party refuses to engage in negotiations at all then an international tribunal is likely to regard itself as having jurisdiction.[10]

One practical question that sometimes arises is that if the negotiations break down and it is resolved to proceed to judicial determination the parties may decide to exclude the evidence of the negotiations from the tribunal. Thus, in the *Gulf of Maine* case[11] the parties agreed that proposals and matters arising in negotiations would be inadmissible in evidence at the subsequent hearing before the chamber of the International Court of Justice. This is not dissimilar to the principle of 'without prejudice' negotiations in municipal law, but it may be more important before an international tribunal where there is less emphasis on the application of clear rules and more attention paid to a settlement based on questions of reasonableness and equity.

3 GOOD OFFICES AND MEDIATION

In some disputes the relationship between the parties is so fraught and the animosity so great that direct negotiations are unlikely to be initiated. In these circumstances, the intervention of a third party may be beneficial. If the third party simply encourages the two parties and acts as a vehicle for communication then that third party is said to be discharging his good offices. However, if the third party participates in the discussion of the substance of the dispute then he is said to be acting as a mediator. Clearly the distinction between good offices and mediation is a fine one and the processes do overlap.

For good offices or mediation to arise there has to be a third party capable of so acting; in practice this may be an individual, an international organisation or a state. In many instances the individual or state has a tradition of friendship or history that makes acting as a mediator acceptable to both parties. An early example is afforded by President Theodore Roosevelt using his good offices in 1905–06 to secure the ending of the Russo Japanese War.[12] In slightly different fashion the United Kingdom used its good offices to effect a ceasefire in 1965 in the Rann of Kutch dispute[13] between India and Pakistan while those same states were content to accept the USSR as a mediator in respect of a dispute in

---

9   *Aegean Sea Continental Shelf* case (1978) ICJ 3; *Nicaragua v United States* (1984) ICJ 392; *Case concerning Land and Maritime Boundary between Cameroon and Nigeria* (1998) ICJ 275.

10 *United States Diplomatic and Consular Staff in Tehran* (1980) ICJ 3 (where the ICJ indicated that Iran's refusal to negotiate with the United States as required by the Vienna Convention on Diplomatic Relations (1961) could not constitute a bar to legal action).

11 *Delimitation of the Maritime boundary in the Gulf of Maine Area* (1984) ICJ 246.

12 Theodore Roosevelt (1858–1919) (President 1901–09) Roosevelt won the Nobel Peace Prize for his efforts. Roosevelt began a trend taken up by subsequent US Presidents; the most obvious examples being President Carter (1977–81) and President Clinton (1993–2001) acting as third parties to resolve issues in the Middle East.

13 An account of such negotiations appears in Harold Wilson, *The Labour Government 1964–1970: A Personal Record*, 1971, pp 112–13. The efforts of the United Kingdom were made possible by the presence of the Indian Prime Minister and President of Pakistan in England for a Commonwealth meeting.

the Kashmir the same year.[14] In 1978 when Chile and Argentina were in dispute about the Beagle Channel award, the Pope offered the services of Cardinal Antonio Samore to act as arbitrator; an offer that was accepted by both states.[15] In the period 1980–81, Algeria acted as a mediator between the United States and Iran in securing the peaceful release of the American consular and diplomatic staff; in this particular instance mediation was tried after judicial proceedings had proved fruitless and an attempt to use force had failed. In the early phase of the Falkland Islands dispute in 1982, Mr Alexander Haig[16] attempted to act as mediator between the United Kingdom and Argentina while at a later date the Secretary General[17] offered his good offices to both parties in an attempt to secure a peaceful resolution.

Mediation cannot be effected without the consent of both parties; a mediated settlement is likely to include elements of compromise so that there may be cases where mediation is not appropriate.[18] If one party feels that a compromise is not acceptable, then mediation is unlikely to be fruitful; mediation stands a reasonable prospect of success when both parties are exhausted by conflict.[19] However, recent examples indicate that where one state has clearly breached international law[20] and has been condemned by the Security Council then a mediated settlement can only normally be on the basis of the *status quo ante*.

---

14   The Soviet Union having an interest in both avoiding instability near its southern border but also in preventing any attempt by China at increasing its influence. The Soviet Union was acceptable as a mediator because although it had friendly relations with India it had not condemned the actions of Pakistan.

15   The *Beagle Channel Arbitration Award* (1977) 52 ILR 93; (1978) 17 ILM 634 (the initial arbitral award in favour of Chile was not acceptable to Argentina). However, by 1984 the mediation of the Pope served to resolve the dispute (1985) 24 ILM 7. The decision to call upon the Pope reflected the long history of Roman Catholic interest in the affairs of Latin and South America.

16   Mr Alexander Haig (b 1924) (Secretary of State 1981–82); in this instance, the United States had every interest in offering to mediate between a fellow member of the Security Council and a member of the Organisation of American States. Mediation was of course more difficult because conduct of Argentina had been ruled by the Security Council to have been a breach of the United Nations Charter.

17   At the time Javier Perez de Cuellar (1982–91).

18   So that the Soviet Union rejected efforts of mediation by the Secretary General in respect of Hungary in 1956 and Nigeria declined mediation in respect of the secession of Biafra in 1967.

19   An example is afforded by the conduct of the Secretary General in seeking an end to the Iran-Iraq War in 1988.

20   In essence, this was a problem in the Falkland Islands dispute in 1982 where there was a risk that a mediated settlement allow Argentina to have retained some of the gains that had been secured by force and in breach of the United Nations Charter. This problem arose again prior to the Gulf War when France and the Soviet Union offered to mediate; such attempts failed because the Security Council had ordered a withdrawal from the territory of Kuwait. Both examples illustrate that where there has been an unlawful use of force contrary to the United Nations Charter it is likely that there will be resistance to any mediated settlement that leaves the aggressor with some benefit from his unlawful conduct particularly where there is a Security Council resolution demanding a return to the *status quo ante*.

4 INQUIRY[21]

Where a dispute arises between two states which turns on a disagreement as to basic facts, then it may be appropriate to set up an international body which is capable of hearing all relevant evidence and producing clear factual findings upon which remedies may be determined. Such a method became popular at the end of the 19th century, when in the Maine incident of 1898 a Spanish and an American Board of Enquiry reached different conclusions in respect of the same incident.[22] The unsatisfactory nature of national enquiries prompted the 1899 Hague Peace Conference[23] to suggest international commissions charged with an impartial investigation of the facts. These proposals were included in six articles of the Hague Convention for the Peaceful Settlement of Disputes (1899).[24] The value of such a system was demonstrated in the Dogger Bank incident of October 1904 when Russian naval forces attacked a number of Hull fishing trawlers in the mistaken belief that they were Japanese vessels. Prompted by France an international board of enquiry was set up in November 1904 and delivered its report in February 1905. The report was accept by Russia who paid a sum in compensation.[25] The experience was seen as successful so that the Hague Convention of 1907[26] expanded the procedural rules to permit and expedite further enquiries.

In subsequent years, a number of Commissions of Enquiry were established in Europe and they adopted the procedure stipulated in the Hague Convention of 1907; in the early years, the commissions tended to comprise naval officers seeking to determine the facts of a disputed naval incident.[27] In addition to developments in Europe influential changes were being introduced by the United States. After 1911 the United States began the practice of entering into treaties with other states which contained a clause that any future dispute with the United States would be submitted to arbitration or to a Commission of Enquiry. This was a practical manifestation of the American position that international affairs could be subjected to the rule of law; this would be carried further by Woodrow Wilson at Versailles. Such treaties were sometimes known as 'Taft'[28] or 'Bryan'[29] treaties of arbitration.

---

21 See generally, J Merrills, *International Dispute Settlement*, 3rd edn, 1998, Chap 3; J Collier and AV Lowe, *The Settlement of Disputes in International Law*, 1999, p 24.

22 On 15 February 1898, the *USS Maine* exploded in a harbour in Havana with a loss of 259 lives. The mistrust caused by two different enquiries was one of the events leading to the Spanish-American War.

23 The proposal was made by Russia as part of a number of initiatives to reduce international tension.

24 Hague Convention for the Pacific Settlement of Disputes (1899), Arts 9–14.

25 For the Report, see JB Scott, *The Hague Court Reports First Series*, 1916, p 404. Russia paid a sum of £65,000 in compensation. The idea of a commission of enquiry had been proposed by France whose Foreign Minister Theophile Delcasse was anxious to promote good Anglo Russian relations as part of his scheme of building on the Franco-Russian *entente*.

26 Hague Convention for the Pacific Settlement of Disputes (1907), Arts 9–35.

27 As in The Tavignano Commission (1912); The Tiger Commission (1917); The Tabantia Commission (1921–22). For the reports, see JB Scott, *The Hague Court Reports First Series*, 1916, p 413 and *Second Series*, 1932, p 135.

28 William Howard Taft (1857–1930) served as Secretary of War (1904–08) under President Roosevelt before becoming President (1909–13). Taft later went on to serve as Chief Justice of the United States (1921–30) and during that period gave the important arbitral award on recognition in the *Tinoco Arbitration* (1923) 1 RIAA 369.

29 William Jennings Bryan (1860–1925) served as Secretary of State under President Wilson (1913–15).

One advantage of the enquiry is that it permits an impartial investigation of the evidence and it allows passions aroused by the incident to cool. The cooling of passions aroused in public opinion makes it easier to negotiate a compromise solution. By the time of the Red Crusader enquiry in 1962,[30] it was accepted that the tribunal should include legally qualified personnel and that both oral and written evidence should be received. A more recent use of the procedure arose in the Letelier and Moffitt cases where an international commission of enquiry was set up under the Bryan-Suarez Mujica Treaty of 1914 to determine compensation after inconclusive litigation before the United States courts.[31]

It is sensible to ask why the flexible machinery under the Hague Convention is not employed more often. First, in many incidents the establishment of the facts often leads to the payment of compensation by the state in the wrong; in many cases it is simpler to pay compensation than to risk damaging a long term relationship.[32] Secondly, enquiries are often carried out by officials of international organisations without being formally constituted under the Hague Convention;[33] evidence is received, facts are established and liability under international law is determined. Third, in past years there was sometimes a reluctance by communist states to submit to international enquiries but this may be passing away with the changes in Eastern Europe since 1989.

5 CONCILIATION

Conciliation is a method of resolving disputes which combines the characteristics of inquiry and mediation. An independent third party investigates the evidence, finds the facts and puts forward proposals for a settlement which are not themselves binding on the parties. Conciliation became popular at the end of the 19th century to resolve difficulties in labour relations and in some countries legislation was passed to make provision for the process.[33a] It is generally accepted that the method acquired prominence on the international plane after 1919 as statesmen sought to increase the range of methods available to facilitate the peaceful settlement of disputes.

The first treaty to include express provision as to conciliation was the treaty concluded between Sweden and Chile in 1920. In 1922, the League of Nations adopted a resolution encouraging states to resolve disputes through conciliation commissions. However, the most influential reference to the subject was contained in a treaty between

---

30　See 35 ILR 485.

31　The case itself arose out of a tort committed in the United States, namely the murder of Mr Orlando Letelier (a former Foreign Minister of Chile) and an American citizen Mrs Moffitt. A plea of sovereign immunity was rejected and damages awarded against Chile (63 ILR 378) but attempts to enforce the judgment against the national airline failed (79 ILR 561). For the Commission of Enquiry see 88 ILR 727; (1992) 31 ILM 1.

32　A good example being the decision of the United States to pay a sum to China in 1999 as compensation for the physical damage and loss of life caused when the Chinese Embassy in Belgrade was hit during the Kosovo campaign in the spring of 1999.

33　An example being the decision of the ICAO to require its Secretary General to conduct an enquiry in September 1983 following the shooting down of Korean Air Lines Boeing 747 above Soviet territory. The incident involved a very considerable life and the enquiry did not receive full co-operation from the Soviet authorities.

33a　As an example, see United Kingdom Conciliation Act 1896.

France and Switzerland in 1925 which provided for a Permanent Conciliation Commission and this was echoed in the Locarno treaties signed by Germany in the same year; in these treaties made with Belgium, France, Czechoslovakia and Poland it was provided that disputes were to be subject to conciliation save where judicial determination or arbitration was selected.

Conciliation acquired a degree popularity in the inter-war years; the process of conciliation was embodied in the General Act for the Pacific Settlement of International Disputes (1928) which was itself revised in 1949. These development were, however, not confined to Europe; in 1923 the United States entered into the Treaty of Washington with five Central American state which provided for the employment of conciliation commissions. The impetus provided by the Bryan treaties was evidenced in 1923 when 16 American states concluded the Gondra Treaty which made provision for the use of commissions of enquiry. However, in 1929 the Inter American General Convention of Conciliation amended the Gondra Treaty to provide for commissions of conciliation. The inter war years were the golden age of conciliation with nearly 200 treaties concluded between 1920 and 1940 that included some form of conciliation provision.

Situations in which conciliation is employed tend to involve matters of both politics and law. Since 1919 conciliation has been adopted in a wide variety of factual circumstances.

In 1931, a German Lithuanian Commission met to consider the expulsion of German citizens from Memel. Two years previously, the Charco Commission had met to consider a border dispute between Paraguay and Bolivia;[34] a similar type of territorial dispute gave rise to the Franco Siamese Conciliation Commission in 1947. A conciliation commission may be practical where it is necessary to consider complex factual and legal issues; thus the method was used in the Belgium Danish Commission of 1952 and the Franco Swiss Commission of 1955 to consider issues arising from the confused events of 1940.[35] A Conciliation Commission normally involves a number of persons with a legally qualified chairman but in 1977 Kenya, Uganda and Tanzania asked a single individual to make provision for the distribution of the assets of the former East African Community.[36]

While conciliation is often employed in technical property matters an example in the maritime context arose in 1980 when Iceland and Norway established a commission to determine the dividing line of the continental shelf between Iceland and Jan Mayen Island.[37]

There is no reason why a conciliation commission should not be used for a variety of forms of dispute. The broad distinction is between disputes of a factual nature and those where questions of law are involved. In both however there is a need to receive evidence, weigh such evidence, make the appropriate findings of fact and consider and evaluate the submissions of the parties before coming forward with practical proposals for a settlement.

34　See L Woolsey, 'Commission of inquiry and conciliation, Bolivia and Paraguay' (1929) 23 AJIL 110; (1930) 24 AJIL 122, p 573.

35　Ie, disputes arising from the German invasion of Belgium and France in 1940.

36　Ie, Dr Victor Umbricht; for discussion, see V Umbricht.

37　For the report, see (1981) 20 ILM 797; 62 ILR 108. For acceptance of the report, see (1982) 21 ILM 1222. For the reflexions by the chairman EL Richardson see (1988) 82 AJIL 443.

While many of the conciliation commissions are today *ad hoc* arrangements, a large number of regional treaties support the principle of conciliation. References to the same are to be found in the American Treaty of Pacific Settlement (1948) (the Pact of Bogota); the European Convention for the Peaceful Settlement of Disputes (1957); the Charter of the Organisation of African Unity (1963)[38] and the Treaty Establishing the Organisation of Eastern Caribbean States (1981). In addition, references to the principle are to be found in general treaties such as the Vienna Convention on the Law of Treaties (1969); the Law of the Sea Convention (1982); and the Vienna Convention on the Protection of the Ozone Layer (1985).

6 ARBITRATION

The methods examined above, namely negotiation, mediation, inquiry and conciliation, are sometimes termed diplomatic means of resolution because the parties retain control of the dispute; they retain the right to accept or reject the terms of any proposed settlement. In contrast, arbitration and judicial settlement are normally chosen when a binding decision is required; normally the parties will require facts to be found and international law to be applied. Since 1922, there has been a functioning international court but this grew out of the earlier process of international arbitration and it is to this that we must now turn.

International arbitration has grown steadily as a method of dispute resolution since the 18th century. Arbitration involves the determination of a dispute between states (or between a state and some other entity) through the legal determination by one or more arbitrators or by a tribunal other than the International Court of Justice. In many instances the arbitration is concerned with a particular dispute. The modern form of international arbitration is traceable back to the 1794 Treaty of Amity, Commerce and Navigation (the 'Jay Treaty'[39]) between the United States and Great Britain which set up national commissions[40] comprising equal numbers appointed by each state to determine disputes concerning the citizens of each state. The commissions set up under the Jay Treaty determined each case and made their awards by applying legal principles. The system

---

38 See the 1964 Protocol on the Commission of Mediation, Conciliation and Arbitration to the Charter of the Organisation of African Unity.

39 Named after John Jay (1745–1829). Jay had helped negotiate the Treaty of Paris (1783); he was a co-author of the Federalist Papers (1788) and was appointed Chief Justice of the United States in 1789 and while in office served as envoy to Great Britain in 1794 and negotiated the Treaty that bears his name. In 1795 he resigned his judicial office to serve as Governor of New York. It is worthy of note how the independence of the United States prompted the development of international law not only as the first significant non European power but also because so many of its significant early figures (eg Madison, Jefferson, Jay) tended to view international affairs from a legal perspective and had a knowledge of both the law and practice of diplomacy together with an interest in writers such as Vattel. It is, of course, a short step from applying the principle of government under the rule of law (enshrined in the Declaration of Independence of 1776 and the United States Constitution of 1787) not only in the domestic sphere but also on the international plane.

40 The phrase mixed commission or mixed tribunal indicating that the composition of the tribunal is drawn from the nationals of more than one state. This is to be contrasted with the expression 'mixed arbitration' which normally indicates that the arbitration is between a state and a non-state entity.

was extended under the Treaty of Ghent (1814) whereby the United States and Great Britain agreed that in the event of disagreement the ruling of a third party could be obtained. However, in the early part of the 19th century such commissions tended to be viewed as extensions of diplomacy and it was not yet accepted that an award should be accompanied by detailed reasons. But as the century moved towards its close awards by mixed commissions tended to become more frequent. and the giving of reasons was not unusual.[41]

Another form of arbitration employed in the 19th century was that of sovereign arbitration where the dispute was referred to the judgment of a foreign ruler; this had its origins in the medieval practice of referring disputes to the Pope. However, for much of the 19th century it was not the practice to give a reasoned ruling and it was not until the award by the King of Italy in the *Clipperton Island Arbitration*[42] that the giving of detailed reasons founded on international law could be said to be the norm.

It is generally agreed that an important development took place with the *Alabama Arbitration* (1872).[43] By the Treaty of Washington 1871, Great Britain and the United States agreed that an arbitral tribunal should determine the United States claim for naval losses incurred when the Alabama was supplied to the Confederate forces during the Civil War in breach of Great Britain's duty of neutrality. The success of the *Alabama Arbitration* resulted in a discernible move towards arbitration as a method of resolving international disputes as illustrated by the *Bering Sea Fur Arbitration* (1893)[44] and the *British Guiana-Venezuela Boundary Arbitration*(1899).[45] This example was adopted by the delegates to the Hague Conference of 1899 who, anxious to expand arbitration as a method of peaceful settlement, decided to establish the Permanent Court of Arbitration (PCA). The PCA is governed by Hague Convention 1 for the Pacific Settlement of International Disputes (the 1899 Convention), as amended by Convention 1 of 1907 (the 1907 Hague Convention). It has often been observed that the PCA is not permanent, is not a court and does not arbitrate. Instead being based at the Hague, it provides list of arbitrators and rules for such arbitrations if the Parties wish to adopt them. The PCA was quite active in the period until 1922[46] when the establishment of a permanent international court of justice served to divert away potential cases. However, no inter-state case has been referred to the PCA for over half a century.

In respect of the selection of arbitrators, it will normally be for the parties to make the choice; in some instances, such as the *Rann of Kutch Arbitration*, the arbitrators were

---

41 See *Bolivar Railway Company Claim (Great Britain v Venezuela)* (1903) 9 RIAA 445.

42 *Clipperton Islands* case *(France v Mexico)* (1932) 26 AJIL 390 (King Victor Emmanuel III of Italy) (acquisition of territory *res nullius* by occupation).

43 See JB Moore, *History and Digest of the International Arbitrations to which the United States has been a Party*, 1898, London, Vol 1, p 653.

44 *Bering Sea Arbitration (United States v Great Britain)* (1893) (1898) 1 Moore Int Arbitrations 935.

45 *British Guiana v Venezuela Boundary Arbitration* (1899–1900) 92 BFSP 160.

46 Examples being *Pious Funds of the California* case (1902) 9 RIAA 1; *Venezuela Preferential Claims* case (1904) 6 RIAA 99; *Japanese House Tax* case (1905) 11 RIAA 51; *Muscat Dhows* case (1905) 11 RIAA 83; *North Atlantic Coast Fisheries* case (1910) 11 RIAA 167; *Canevaro* case (1912) 11 RIAA 397; *Russian Indemnity* case (1912) 11 RIAA 421.

chosen by an appropriate third party.[47] To avoid procrastination, some international agreements stipulate that in the absence of choice by the parties then, after a period of time, the arbitrators may be chosen by an appropriate third party.[48] Although the Hague Conventions of 1899 and 1907 stipulate procedural rules, it will be for the parties to resolve such questions; they may choose to adopt the procedural rules of an international organisation.[49]

It will be for the parties to settle upon the issues for determination by the arbitrators; this is an important matter because, if the issues are not properly delineated, the tribunal may consider that it lacks jurisdiction to determine a particular matter.[50] A further consideration of relevance is the criteria that the arbitrators are to adopt; this may be set out in the agreement or compromise that provided for the arbitration. In many instances the parties are content to instruct the arbitrators 'to decide in accordance with the principles of international law'; in other cases, the parties may stipulate that certain propositions are to constitute the *lex specialis*.[51] In some situations, the tribunal may be entitled to consider both municipal and international law particularly where the latter is uncertain.[52] Sometimes, an arbitrator may be expressly requested to take account of equitable considerations[53] and, in some instances, a tribunal may be asked to go beyond a specific case and set out general guidelines for the future.[54] After the award has been made, the parties may still seek guidance on interpretation; in certain circumstances, a challenge might be brought on the ground that the arbitrator has exceeded his jurisdiction or that he failed to exercise his jurisdiction properly.[55]

It has to be admitted that the figures for inter state arbitrations since 1945 outside the auspices of the PCA have been disappointing. In the years 1900 to 1945, some 178 cases have been recorded but, in the years from 1945–90, the figure had fallen to 43 even though the number of states has increased nearly fourfold.[56] It is arguable that this phenomenon can be explained by the fact that a state will not submit politically sensitive matters to arbitration while politically unimportant matters are not submitted because they can be resolved by negotiation.

---

47   See the *Indo-Pakistan Western Boundary (Rann of Kutch) case (India v Pakistan)* (1968) 50 ILR 2; see generally, JG Wetter, 'The Rann of Kutch Arbitration' (1971) 65 AJIL 346. On the same point, in the *Lac Lanoux Arbitration (France v Spain)* (1957) 24 ILR 101, both France and Spain asked the King of Sweden to nominate a president of the tribunal.

48   Pact of Bogota (1945), Art 45; European Convention for the Peaceful Settlement of Disputes (1957), Art 21.

49   In the *United States-Untied Kingdom Arbitration concerning Heathrow Airport User Charges* (1993) 102 ILR 216.

50   See *Haji-Bagherpour v United States* (1983) 71 ILR 600; *Grimm v Iran* (1983) 71 ILR 650.

51   To an extent, this was done in the *Alabama* case (1872) where Art 6 of the Treaty of Washington (1871) set out certain propositions on the duty of neutrals in time of war that may not have reflected the state of customary international law.

52   As was the case in the *Trail Smelter Arbitration (US v Canada)* (1941) 3 RIAA 1905. (At that time, the state of international environmental law could only be described as vague.)

53   So that in 1907, in a treaty on boundary disputes between Columbia and Ecuador the arbitral tribunal was instructed that it may 'leaving to one side strict law, adopt an equitable line in accordance with the necessities and convenience of the two countries'.

54   *North Atlantic Coast Fisheries Arbitration (Great Britain v United States)* (1910) 11 RIAA 173.

55   *Arbitral Award of 31 July 1989* (1991) ICJ 53; noted (1992) 41 ICLQ 891; 86 AJIL 553.

56   MW Janis, *An Introduction to International Law*, 2nd edn, 1993.

It is important to distinguish those conventional arbitrations between states and those arbitrations that involve private parties. In principle, an arbitration may raise questions as to: (i) the law governing the arbitration agreement; (ii) the law governing the arbitration proceedings; (iii) the law according to which the arbitration is to be determined; (iv) the arrangements for enforcement. In respect of arbitrations between states then: (i) will be governed by the rules of public international law; while (ii) and (iii) will be determined by the choice of the parties; this may be public international law but it may involve municipal law. Where the international arbitration is conducted between private entities then matters (i)–(iv) will be governed by the relevant rules of private international law. In recent years there has been an increase in so called 'mixed arbitrations', that is, between a state and a private party; in many cases such arbitrations will concern investment disputes. In such circumstances it is usual for the parties to accept the rules set out by the International Centre for the Settlement of Investment Disputes (ICSID).[57]

State parties to the treaty agree to recognise awards made by arbitral tribunals operating under the ICSID.[58] It is often the case that bilateral investment treaties often provide that in the event of dispute the matter may be arbitrated under the ICSID; the precise terms of submission will vary from treaty to treaty and in some instances the instrument may require arbitration to be preceded by conciliation. A very high proportion of investment agreements make some reference to ICSID involvement. Under the terms of the ICSID access to the municipal courts is barred but a problem has arisen in recent years of parties that fail in the arbitration seeking to annul the award by challenging it before an *ad hoc* committee of the ICSID. This has lengthened the process and introduced an unintended appellate element into the system.[59]

An arbitral body that has proved remarkably influential in the last two decades is the Iran-United States Claims Tribunal;[60] this body was established under the settlement mediated by Algiers[61] as a resolution of the Hostages crisis[62] and was concluded on 19

---

57 The ICSID is in effect a structure in which arbitration can take place. It derives from the Washington Convention on the Settlement of Investment Disputes between States and Nationals of Other States (1965). The ICSID was instigated by the World Bank (the International Bank for Reconstruction and Development) and is based at the World Bank headquarters in Washington DC.

58 Article 54 of the Washington treaty requires state parties to provide for methods of enforcement similar to those of judgments in their own courts. For the United Kingdom, the relevant legislation is the Arbitration (International Investment Disputes) Act 1996.

59 See M Reisman, 'The breakdown of the control mechanism in ICSID arbitration' (1989) 4 Duke Law Journal 739.

60 W Mapp, *The Iran-United States Claims Tribunal: The First Ten Years 1981–1991*, 1993; GH Aldrich, *The Jurisprudence of the Iran United States Claims Tribunal*, 1996; G Wegen, 'Discontinuance of international proceedings: the *Hostages* case (1982) 76 AJIL 717; SH Amin, 'Iran-United States claims settlement' (1983) 32 ICLQ 750; D Lloyd Jones, 'The Iran-United States Claims Tribunal: private rights and state responsibility' (1984) 24 Va JIL 259; TL Stein, 'Jurisprudence and jurists' prudence: the Iranian forum clause decisions of the Iran-US Claims Tribunal' (1984) 78 AJIL 1; DD Caron, 'The nature of the Iran-US Claims Tribunal and the evolving structure of international law' (1990) 84 AJIL 104.

61 Sometimes referred to as the Algiers Declarations embracing the General Declarations and the Claims Settlement Declaration which provided for the establishment of the Iran-United States Claims tribunal. For text see (1981) 20 ILM 224.

62 *United States Consular and Diplomatic Staff in Tehran* (1980) ICJ 1.

January 1981.[63] In broad terms, the tribunal was charged with dealing with a wide number of outstanding disputes when the principal issues had been settled between the two states.[64] The experience of the tribunal is remarkable considering that relations between the two states continued to be very tense; by the end of 1998, nearly 4,000 cases had been considered in whole or in part. In general terms the jurisdiction of the tribunal embraces four areas, namely: (i) claims by United States nationals against Iran and claims by Iranian nationals against the United States; (ii) claims *ex contractu* arising between Iran and the United States; (iii) property disputes arising in respect of the former Shah, Reza Pahlevi; (iv) disputes concerning the interpretation or application of the Algiers Declaration. The Tribunal Rules are a modified form of the UNCITRAL Arbitration Rules which the United Nations had prepared in 1976 as a model for conducting international commercial arbitrations. In respect of the applicable law the tribunal is instructed to apply the rules of public international law or private law where appropriate. In order to ensure that United States nationals might be paid, one of the terms of the Algiers Accords was that Iran would provide for the establishment of a Security Account in a sum of $1 billion and would ensure that such a fund did not fall below the level of $500 million. A second feature of the arrangements is that the actual events which precipitated the crisis are excluded from the jurisdiction of the tribunal. Thirdly, the tribunal does not have jurisdiction in respect of those contracts where there is a clear choice of jurisdiction in favour of the Iranian courts. Fourthly, the tribunal follows traditional international law in requiring claims for less than $250,000 to be made by the government on behalf of its citizens but claims in excess of that sum may be made and compromised by private entities. Fifthly, the general approach of municipal courts has been to respect the decisions of the Iran-US Claims tribunal even in those cases where there may be have been technical non-compliance with the other international conventions on the recognition and enforcement of arbitral awards.[65]

The advantages of arbitration in municipal law are often said to be speed, informality and flexibility. This remains the case on the international plane, where an arbitral board of three is normal but as the *Tinoco Arbitration*[66] or the *Island of Palmas* case[67] indicates, in certain circumstances, a significant contribution can be made by a single individual. In the period since 1945, many states have found arbitration to be a sensible method of resolving disputes; in many treaties arbitration is indicated as an optional method of dispute resolution. There may sometimes be difficulties in the enforcement of awards but these

---

63 The crisis had started with the seizure of the hostages in November 1979 and an application to the ICJ (see *United States Consular and Diplomatic Staff in Tehran* (1980) ICJ 1) which was followed in April 1980 by an unsuccessful attempt to rescue the hostages. In November 1980, President Carter (1977–81) failed to secure re-election and so 19 January 1981 was his last day in office.

64 Ie, the return of the hostages and the unblocking of the Iranian assets that had been frozen in many western states in November 1979.

65 See *Ministry of Defence of Iran v Gould Inc* (1988) 82 AJIL 591; 969 Fed 2d 764 (9th Cir 1992); *Dallal v Bank Mellat* [1986] QB 441 (claim bought by US citizen and rejected by the claims tribunal would be struck out as an abuse of process when subsequently litigated in England even though there may not have been strict compliance with the 1958 New York Convention).

66 *Tinoco Arbitration (Great Britain v Costa Rica)* (1923) 1 RIAA 369 (William H Taft, then Chief Justice of the United States Supreme Court) (the case itself being important in the area of recognition of governments).

67 *Island of Palmas* case *(Netherlands v United States)* (1928) 2 RIAA 829 (Max Huber: at the time Judge of the Permanent Court of International Justice).

can be avoided by establishing the appropriate structure or fund prior to the commencement of the arbitration.

7 JUDICIAL SETTLEMENT – THE INTERNATIONAL COURT OF JUSTICE

(a) Introduction

Of the limited number of permanent international courts[68] and tribunals the most important is the International Court of Justice (ICJ) and it is necessary to say a little about its role. Sometimes, the Court is described as the 'World Court', particularly by politicians anxious to stress its supranational quality. As has been indicated above the period from 1800–1900 witnessed a steady increase in the emphasis on the peaceful resolution of disputes and this came to the fore with the development of arbitration in the final quarter of the century; these initiatives had already been extended with the establishment of the Permanent Court of Arbitration after the Hague Conference of 1899.[69] After 1918, there was a feeling that the conflict had been caused not by the intentional act of any one state but by a breakdown in international forms and procedures so that measures taken to strengthen such structures were justified. Secondly, the unprecedented loss of life resulted in a willingness to examine how international relations might be conducted on a more orderly basis. Thirdly, 1919 witnessed the arrival of the United States at Versailles as a major world power and many, such as President Wilson, were of the view that peace was more likely to be maintained by the acceptance of the principle of the rule of law in international relations rather than any undue reliance on the balance of power. Fourthly, in many European countries there had been opposition to the war and the rise in social democratic thinking had led to demands for a more structured international environment.[70]

---

68 One can note also the European Court of Justice, the European Court of Human Rights, the Inter American Court of Human Rights, the Central American Court of Justice, the Law of the Sea Tribunal.

69 It is worth bearing in mind the success of arbitration prior to 1914. Between 1902 and 1914, the Court of Arbitration at the Hague dealt successfully with 15 cases in which 17 states were a party. The territorial sweep of the disputes involved Europe, Asia, Africa and the Americas.

70 It is worth also recalling that many Universities in Europe and the United States had established chairs in International Law so that the subject was being more widely studied. Secondly, both the State Department in Washington and the Foreign Office in London employed legal advisers. This is confirmed by a study of membership of the Commission of Jurists who, in 1920, prepared the scheme for the Permanent Court. The chairman, Baron Descamps, was an authority on international arbitration; there were several professors of international law on the committee. Elihu Root who served on the committee had considerable experience of international arbitrations having appeared amongst others in the *North Atlantic Fisheries Arbitration* (1910) 11 RIAA 167. A number of the members had experience as legal advisers to foreign ministries.

In these circumstances, when the proposal was made at Versailles to consider an international court[71] it received a favourable reception and Art 14 of the Covenant of the League provided that the Council of the League would adopt plans for the establishment of a Permanent Court of International Justice. The Committee of Jurists who produced a statute for the Permanent Court intended that it should build on the groundwork done in the field of international arbitration in the pre-war years and that the Court should take its place alongside other peaceful methods of settling disputes. The general desire in 1920 was to get the Court established and to allow practical difficulties to be settled as and when they arose; there is some evidence that members of the Commission of Jurists had been impressed by the work of the United States Supreme Court[72] in ironing out disputes within a federal system and hoped the Court might achieve the same on the international plane. The report of the Committee of Jurists drew upon earlier efforts[73] and the draft statute did include provisions for compulsory jurisdiction but these did not survive the scrutiny of the Council and the Assembly of the League of Nations. The Statute as amended came into force in 1921 and remains with minor changes the basis of the ICJ today.

The Permanent Court of International Justice operated from 1922 to 1940 and became an accepted actor on the international stage. In the period of its active life, it dealt with 33 contentious cases and 28 requests for advisory opinions. States tended to nominate individuals of considerable distinction so that the rulings of the court have been influential in the development of international law.

On the German invasion of Holland in 1940 the officials of the Court moved to Geneva. During the conflict a number of allied committees began to plan for a judicial body after the War.[74] The results of these deliberations were submitted to the San Francisco Conference in 1945. The new judicial body was to be named the International Court of Justice; it would have a new statute, and a more formal legal relationship with the United Nations. However, in substance if not in law the new Court was the successor of the former; the statute is almost identical to its predecessor. The element of continuance is evidenced by Art 36(5) and Art 37 which provide for a transfer of jurisdiction. The two

---

71 It seems that the credit for persuading the Conference to opt for a permanent international court belongs to Cecil Hurst (1870–1963) who attended the Conference as Legal Adviser to the Foreign Office. Hurst was building upon the experience of the 1907 Hague Conference which he had attended and the various pre-1914 arbitrations in which he had been engaged. Hurst became a judge of the court in 1929 serving until 1946. The spirit of co-operation that Hurst managed to engender amongst other delegations did much to contribute to the success of the conference. (For a detailed assessment of this influential international lawyer, see the note in the *Dictionary of National Biography* by M Lauterpacht).

72 See Lord Phillimore (1920) 6 TGS 89. However such an analogy is of limited value; the United States Supreme Court rules on the duties of individual states under the written constitution. The role of the PCIJ was to deal with disputes between sovereign states who might or might not consent to its jurisdiction. It is interesting that the view of the distinguished jurist Sir Frederick Pollock (1845–1937) in 1919 was that the important matter was to establish the court and then to deal with practical problems as and when they arose. (See his contribution to the debate in Phillimore (1920) 6 TGS 89.)

73 In particular, the Draft Convention Relative to the Creation of a permanent Court of Arbitral Justice at the Second Hague Peace Conference of 1907 which was not adopted.

74 A detailed history of the administrative plans is given by G Marston in 'The London Committee and the International Court of Justice', in A Lowe and M Fitzmaurice, *Fifty Years of the International Court of Justice*, 1996.

reasons for the change as evidenced in the debates at San Francisco were the desire to break any link with institutions associated with the League of Nations and the drafting difficulties that would have arisen if the statute of the Permanent Court on International Justice had continued in being. The new court has a more formal link with the United Nations.

Article 92 of the United Nations Charter (1945) stipulates that the court is 'the principal judicial organ of the United Nations'. By the terms of Art 93(1), 'All members of the United Nations are *ipso facto* parties to the Statute of the International Court of Justice'.

(b) Composition

The Court comprises fifteen judges[75] and such individuals serve for a term of nine years; five are elected every three years so that such limited triennial elections provide a degree of continuity. The system of election is drawn from the previous practice under the Permanent Court of International Justice. This is a sensitive issue because an international court must command confidence and while not all 180 states can have a representative on the court it is desirable that the major legal and cultural systems of the world are acknowledged. To meet this problem, in 1920 Elihu Root had suggested that as in municipal law the political branch of government (that is, the executive and legislature) should play a role while others on the 1920 Committee of Jurists wished to provide for a link with the Court of Arbitration.[76] The compromise scheme balancing these two considerations continues today in the Statute of International Court of Justice (1945). Article 2 requires that such individuals be 'persons of high moral character, who possess the qualifications required in their respective countries for appointment to the highest judicial offices, or are jurisconsults of recognised competence in international law'. Persons are nominated by the national groups in the Permanent Court of Arbitration;[77] before making such nominations national groups should consult the appropriate legal institutions within their own country.[78] In accordance with the principle of Elihu Root, persons appearing on the list of those nominated are then eligible for election by the General Assembly and the Security Council;[79] both such organs should operate independently. Article 9 of the Statute provides that electors should bear in mind that in the Court as a whole 'the representation of the main forms of civilisation and of the principal legal systems of the world should be assured'. To be elected a candidate must secure a majority in both the Security Council and the General Assembly.[80] In recent years, the geographical split within the Court has been that one judge is drawn from the United States, four from Western Europe, six from Africa and Asia, two from South America and two from Eastern Europe. The tendency has been for those elected to have acquired their specialist knowledge of international law either within a foreign ministry

---

75 See Statute of the International Court of Justice (1945), Art 3.

76 See Lord Phillimore, 'Scheme for the Permanent Court of International Justice' (1920) 6 TGS 89.

77 Statute of the International Court of Justice (1945), Art 4.

78 *Ibid*, Art 6.

79 *Ibid*, Art 4.

80 For comment on past elections, see (1952) 46 AJIL 38; (1961) 37 BYIL 527; (1965) 59 AJIL 908; (1993) 86 AJIL 173; (1994) 88 AJIL 178.

or as a University teacher of the subject;[81] in many cases this past record has also included some experience of private practice.

The need to ensure that the Court is viable and commands confidence lead the draftsmen to provide in Art 31 of the statute that a party to a case before the court may nominate an *ad hoc* judge if the bench does not contain a national of that party.[82] It therefore follows that, in appropriate cases, the court may comprise 17 judges. Such a concession is based not on logic[83] but on a desire to build confidence in the court. The practice follows on the tradition in international arbitration in appointing one member from each of the parties.

As is to be expected the highest standards are required of judges so that no serving judge may act in a political or administrative capacity[84] or appear as an advocate.[85] Any judge enjoys a degree of independence and may only be dismissed by a unanimous vote of the Court.[86] Members engaged on official business enjoy the appropriate diplomatic privileges and immunity.[87] Salaries are fixed by the General Assembly; they are free of taxation and may not be decreased during the term of office.[88]

(c) Jurisdiction and legal disputes

In broad terms, the jurisdiction of the International Court of Justice is divided between jurisdiction in contentious cases and the jurisdiction to give an advisory opinion. Each will be considered in turn but before doing so a number of general points can usefully be made.

Since its inception in 1922, the Court has been charged with deciding admissible cases on the basis of the application of international law at the relevant date.[89] The role of the Court is to declare the law and where appropriate develop the existing law,[90] but it is a judicial body and thus is not charged with formal law making. This is not to say that particular cases may not have political overtones; indeed, in certain circumstances related matters may be the subject of discussion in other organs of the United Nations.[91] However, the Court is charged with determining those cases over which it has

---

81 This is certainly true of the United Kingdom, where the judges nominated have tended to have had a record of teaching and publishing works on the subject, ie, Arnold McNair (1946–55); Hersch Lauterpacht (1955–60); Gerald Fitzmaurice (1960–73) (former Legal Adviser at Foreign Office 1953–60 and member of the Committee of Jurists in 1945 that helped draw up the plans for the ICJ); Humphrey Waldock (1973–82); RY Jennings (1982–95); Rosalyn Higgins (1995–).

82 An example being the *Nuclear Tests* case (*Australia v France*) (1974) ICJ 253 where the distinguished Australian judge Sir Garfield Barwick sat as an *ad hoc* judge.

83 Because Art 20 requires all judges to act impartially.

84 Statute of the International Court of Justice (1945), Art 16.

85 *Ibid*, Art 17.

86 *Ibid*, Art 18, para 1.

87 *Ibid*, Art 19.

88 *Ibid*, Art 32.

89 The *Northern Cameroons* case (1963) ICJ 15; 35 ILR 353.

90 An example being the *Anglo Norwegian Fisheries* case (1951) ICJ 116.

91 The *Nicaragua* case (1984) ICJ 392; 76 ILR 104; the *Lockerbie* case (1992) ICJ 3 (see esp Judge Lachs and Judge Weeramantry).

jurisdiction in accordance with recognised sources of law. There will however be cases where it might be appropriate to decline jurisdiction because to exercise it would involve ruling on the rights of third states or for reasons of judicial restraint.[92] It should be noted at the outset that one of the problems for an international court is that of jurisdiction; in a world of sovereign states, as a general principle it will be necessary for the state to consent to the jurisdiction of the court. This problem was recognised both in 1920 and 1945 when some of the smaller states raised the issue of compulsory jurisdiction but this was regarded as premature by the larger states.

It is generally accepted the jurisdiction of the Court extends only to legal disputes. In the *Mavrommatis Palestine Concessions (Jurisdiction)* case,[93] the court considered that a dispute might be defined as 'a disagreement over a point of law or fact, a conflict of legal views or of the interests between two persons'. For the dispute to be 'legal' or 'justiciable' it must be one capable of legal analysis.[94] For a dispute to arise there must be evidence of a disagreement; a disagreement will arise where an assertion by state A of fact, law or opinion is either not accepted or rejected by state B.[95] Whether such a situation exists is capable of objective determination[96] and could be demonstrated by evidence of conflicting conduct.[97] Thus, in the *Interpretation of Peace Treaties* case[98] a dispute could be said to arise where two states held differing views on performance of treaty obligations, while in the *Application of the Obligation to Arbitrate under s 21 of the United Nations Headquarters Agreement* case,[99] the Court found evidence of a dispute in a pattern of conflicting conduct. In a number of cases, the Court has found a dispute where an assertion by state A is not accepted by state B. Thus, in the *East Timor* case[100] the Court was prepared to accept the existence of a dispute because the assertions by Portugal had not been accepted by Australia, while in the case of *Bosnia-Herzegovina v Yugoslavia*[101] the Court was prepared to infer the existence of a dispute from the rejection by Yugoslavia of complaints by Bosnia-Herzegovina.

The existence of a dispute is a pre condition of jurisdiction. On the assumption that a dispute exists the Court will have to inform itself of the ambit of the dispute and this is achieved in a two stage process.[102] The first stage is achieved by the submission of written pleadings which will then be followed by an oral hearing. Although the official languages of the Court are English and French,[103] it may at the request of a party

---

92 See below.

93 *Mavrommatis Palestine Concessions (Jurisdiction)* case (1924) PCIJ, Ser A, No 2, p 11.

94 *Case concerning Border and Transborder Armed Actions (Nicaragua v Honduras)* (1988) ICJ 69.

95 *Interpretation of Peace Treaties* case (1950) ICJ 65; 17 ILR 331.

96 *Interpretation of Peace Treaties* case (1950) ICJ 65; 17 ILR 331.

97 *Applicability of the Obligation to Arbitrate under Section 21 of the United Nations Headquarters Agreement* (1988) ICJ 12; 82 ILR 225.

98 (1950) ICJ 65; 17 ILR 331.

99 (1988) ICJ 12; 82 ILR 225.

100 In the *East Timor* case (1995) ICJ 90 while the Court was prepared to accept the existence of a dispute it declined to rule on the merits and invoked the *Monetary Gold* principle (1954) ICJ 54; on this see below. See AV Lowe (1995) ICJ 484.

101 *Case concerning the Application of the Geneva Convention (Bosnia-Herzegovina v Yugoslavia) (Request for Provisional Measures)* (1993) ICJ 3; (*Further Request for Provisional Measures*) (1993) ICJ 325.

102 Statute of the International Court of Justice (1945), Art 43.

103 *Ibid*, Art 39, para 1.

authorise a language other than the two official languages.[104] The Court is given power to make its own rules of procedure for the disposal of cases subject to the procedural stipulations of the statute itself.[105] Following the oral hearing the Court will deliberate in private but it will deliver its judgment in public; dissenting opinions are permitted and are not unusual.[106] It is clear that the dispute must exist at the time of the hearing; if circumstances have changed even by unilateral act so that there is no longer in reality a dispute then the matter cannot proceed; it is not the role of the court to settle academic controversies[107] or to speculate on matters of political motivation.[108]

Although generalisations should be taken cautiously the record since 1946 indicates that cases before the International Court of Justice may take three distinct stages. An aggrieved state may seek interim relief or preliminary measures from the Court;[109] the Court will be required to rule on this application. Secondly, the opposing state may well seek at a second hearing to persuade the Court that it does not have jurisdiction to hear the full case on its merits.[110] Thirdly, somewhat later the Court may be required to hear the full case on its merits.[111]

Questions have come to the fore in recent years as to the relationship between the powers of the Security Council and the jurisdiction of the ICJ. In particular, it has been suggested that in some circumstances a power of judicial review might arise. The traditional view has been that each organ under the United Nations Charter is the arbiter of its own competence. Thus, the International Court of Justice was quite entitled to determine an application even though the matter was subject to consideration by the Security Council[112] or was the subject of diplomatic activity by the Secretary General[113] or subject to negotiation between the parties.[114] So that it is possible for a case to be heard before the ICJ when at the same time the Secretary General is organising a fact finding mission.[115]

The relationship between the powers of the Security Council under Chapter VII and the jurisdiction of the ICJ was raised in the *Lockerbie (Provisional Measures)* case;[116] it

---

104 Statute of the International Court of Justice (1945), Art 39, para 3.

105 See the Statute of the International Court of Justice (1945), Art 30, para 1; Rules of Procedure were made in 1946 and redrafted in 1978.

106 During the years of the PCIJ, there seems to have been a concern that indiscriminate dissenting opinions would damage the standing of the infant court. This seems to have been the view of Judge Hurst who served as President 1934–36 (see appreciation by Professor Lauterpacht in *Dictionary of National Biography* cited above).

107 *Nuclear Tests* case (1974) ICJ 253; 57 ILR 398.

108 *Case concerning Border and Transborder Armed Actions* (1988) ICJ 69; *Advisory Opinion on the Legality of the Use by a State of Nuclear Weapons in Armed Conflict* (1996) ICJ 66.

109 See *Case concerning the Application of the Genocide Convention (Bosnia-Herzegovina v Yugoslavia (Serbia and Montenegro) (Provisional Measures)* (1993) ICJ 3.

110 See eg, *Fisheries Jurisdiction* case *(United Kingdom v Iceland) (Jurisdiction)* (1973) ICJ 3.

111 *Corfu Channel* case *(United Kingdom v Albania) (The Merits)* (1949) ICJ 4.

112 The *Nicaragua* case *(Jurisdiction)* (1984) ICJ 392, p 431; 76 ILR 104.

113 *United States Diplomatic and Consular Staff in Tehran* (1980) ICJ 7; 61 ILR 530.

114 *Aegean Continental Shelf* case (1976) ICJ 3; 60 ILR 562.

115 *Case concerning the Land and Maritime Boundary between Cameroon and Nigeria (Cameroon v Nigeria)* (1996) ICJ 13.

116 *Lockerbie (Provisional Measures)* case (1992) ICJ 1; in the subsequent proceedings, *Lockerbie (Jurisdiction and Admissibility)* case (1998) 37 ILM 587; (1998) ICJ 3, the Court did not feel it necessary at the preliminary stage to rule on whether the terms of a Security Council Resolution were such as to render a hearing on the merits redundant.

would seem that a Security Council resolution must be presumed to be valid and will normally prevent an order of provisional measures where there is a clear Security Council resolution to the contrary.[117]

(d) Jurisdiction in contentious cases

As indicated above the jurisdiction of the court divides into the contentious and the advisory. In this part it is proposed to discuss the contentious jurisdiction; the advisory jurisdiction will be considered below. The fundamental provision is contained in Art 34 para 1 of the statute[118] which reads: 'Only states may be parties in cases before the Court.' This has the consequence that neither individuals nor international organisations can bring contentious proceedings. In 1920, the Committee of Jurists considered the case for an individual to bring an action against his own state but rejected it;[119] the view was that as many inter state complaints arise from the wrongs done by a state to individuals[120] it was sensible to restrict jurisdiction to complaints between states.

Under the terms of Art 93 of the United Nations Charter, 'All members of the United Nations are *ipso facto* parties to the Statute of the International Court of Justice'. In the case of states which are not members of the United Nations, they may become parties to the Statute on conditions to be specified by the General Assembly.[121] Any decision to allow a non-member of the United Nations to participate in proceedings must respect the principle of the equality of parties before the Court.[122] The Security Council has determined that access to the Court is to be permitted to those non-member states who lodge a declaration with the Registrar of the Court and an acknowledgment that they will respect the decisions of the Court.[123]

The operative provision in respect of jurisdiction is contained in Art 36, para 1, which reads: 'The jurisdiction of the Court comprises all cases which the parties refer to it and all matters specially provided for in the Charter of the United Nations or in treaties or conventions in force.' It is clear from the wording that it is the 'parties' that must consent

---

117 No problem arises if the provisional measures sought are likely to be consistent with a relevant Security Council resolution as was arguably the case in the action brought by Bosnia-Herzegovina which raised the question of the legality of the arms embargo. See *Case concerning the Application of the Genocide Convention (Bosnia-Herzegovina v Yugoslavia) (Provisional Measures)* (1993) ICJ 3, 325. See generally, TM Franck, 'The "powers of appreciation": who is the ultimate guardian of UN legality?' (1992) 86 AJIL 519; V Gowlland Debbas, 'The relationship between the International Court of Justice and the Security Council in the light of the *Lockerbie* case' (1994) 88 AJIL 643; JE Alverez, 'Judging the Security Council' (1996) 90 AJIL 1. For a recent example where provisional measures were granted in terms very similar to a Security Council resolution, see the *Congo* case (*Democratic Republic of the Congo v Burundi, Rwanada, Uganda*) 1 July 2000, ICJ (see SC Res 1304, 16 June 2000).

118 Statute of the International Court of Justice (1945), Art 34, para 1.

119 Lord Phillimore (1920) 6 TGS 89.

120 A classic example being fishing disputes where the actual dispute concerns individual commercial interests; see *Anglo Norwegian Fisheries* case (*United Kingdom v Norway*) (1951) ICJ 116.

121 In general, the conditions are an agreement to accept the judgment of the Court and a willingness to pay a proportion in expenses. Since 1945, this has at various times been a problem for Liechtenstein, San Marino, Japan (before becoming a member of the United Nations in 1956) and Nauru.

122 Statute of the International Court of Justice (1945), Art 35, para 2.

123 See eg, Albania in the *Corfu Channel* case (1949) ICJ 4; 16 ILR 155; SC Res 9 (1946).

to the jurisdiction of the Court. A distinction is sometimes drawn between situations where the parties have agreed to jurisdiction prior to the dispute arising and those situations where consent of both parties is said to arise after the commencement of the dispute. In broad terms there will be four methods by which the Court can acquire jurisdiction in contentious proceedings. These are: (i) consent may be given in advance on the basis of a compromissory clause in a treaty;[124] (ii) consent may be given in advance by reason of a declaration under the optional clause of Art 36, para 2, of the Statute of the International Court of Justice;[125] (iii) consent may be given by an express agreement between the states subsequent to the dispute arising;[126] (iv) consent may be said to exist where one party has initiated proceedings and the agreement of the other may arise by subsequent express act or by an inference drawn from its conduct.[127]

Where it is argued that a subsequent agreement confers jurisdiction then it will be for the court to examine the documentary materials and determine the nature and scope of the agreement.[128]

As indicated above, one of the commonest sources of jurisdiction is where the parties have entered into a treaty which stipulates that the Court should have jurisdiction in particular categories of dispute. Such clauses are sometimes referred to as 'compromissory clauses' and appear in many multilateral and bilateral treaties. The existence of such clauses as a distinct head of jurisdiction is recognised in Art 36(1) of the Statute of the International Court of Justice and has formed the basis for a number of cases of which the *United States Diplomatic and Consular Staff*[129] and the *Nicaragua (Jurisdiction Phase)* case[130] are but two recent examples.[131]

---

124 *United States Diplomatic and Consular Staff in Tehran* (1980) ICJ 3.

125 See *Norwegian Loans* case (*France v Norway*) (1957) ICJ 9; *Interhandel (Switzerland v United States)* case (1959) ICJ 6; *Nicaragua (Jurisdiction and Admissibility)* case (*Nicaragua v United States*) (1984) ICJ 392.

126 *Minquiers and Ecrehos* case (*France v United Kingdom*) (1953) ICJ 47; *Frontier Land* case (1959) ICJ 209; *Libya/Chad* case (1974) ICJ 6; *Tunisia/Libya Continental Shelf* case (1982) ICJ 18.

127 This is sometimes described as a situation of *forum prorogatum* but it would seem to embrace two responses, namely that of express consent and that of consent inferred from conduct. See *Corfu Channel* case (*United Kingdom v Albania*) (*Preliminary Objection*) (1948) ICJ 15. See generally, CHM Waldock, '*Forum prorogatum* or acceptance of a unilateral summons to appear before the International Court' (1948) 2 ILQ 377.

128 *Qatar v Bahrain* (1994) ICJ 112; (1995) ICJ 6; see M Evans, '*Case concerning Maritime Delimitation and Territorial Questions Between Qatar and Bahrain (Jurisdiction and Admissibility)*' (1995) 44 ICLQ 691.

129 *United States Diplomatic and Consular Staff in Tehran* case (1980) ICJ 3, where jurisdiction was founded on Art 1 of the Optional Protocol Concerning the Compulsory Settlement of Disputes which follows both the Vienna Convention on Diplomatic Relations 1961 and the Vienna Convention on Consular Relations 1963.

130 *Nicaragua (Jurisdiction Phase)* case (1984) ICJ 329 (where the majority found jurisdiction to arise under the Treaty of Friendship, Commerce and Navigation (1956) between Nicaragua and the United States).

131 Other examples would be *Case concerning Application on the Prevention and Punishment of the Crime of Genocide (Bosnia-Herzegovina v Yugoslavia) (Provisional Measures)* (1993) ICJ 3, 325 (where jurisdiction was founded on Art IX of the Genocide Convention (1948); *Case concerning Border and Transborder Armed Actions (Nicaragua v Honduras) (Jurisdiction and Admissibility)* (1988) ICJ 69 (where the court founded jurisdiction under Art 31 of the Pact of Bogota (1948)). See also, *Territorial Dispute* case (*Libya v Chad*) (1994) ICJ 6 (where jurisdiction arose under a bilateral treaty); *Application of the* [cont]

It is important to distinguish between arguments that are advanced as to jurisdiction and arguments that are advanced as to admissibility. In principle, jurisdiction relates to the competence of the court and admissibility concerns the nature of the claim. Logically arguments about admissibility should only be taken when it is accepted that jurisdiction arises.[132] The case law indicates that the International Court of Justice prefers to consider arguments of jurisdiction and admissibility prior to any hearing on the merits;[133] there has been a tendency to hear disputes on jurisdiction and admissibility together. Arguments founded on admissibility may concern the absence of prior diplomatic negotiations,[134] or the absence of a legal interest by a petitioner[135] or the failure to establish a genuine link between the state and an individual;[136] objection to admissibility may also be grounded in a failure to exhaust local remedies[137] or an attempt to assert *locus standi* in a manner inconsistent with basic principles of municipal law[138] or an assertion of a waiver by one party.[139]

In respect of the principle of *forum prorogatum* much depends on the *ratio* to be drawn from the judgments in the *Corfu Channel (Preliminary Objections)* case.[140] In that case, the United Kingdom was in dispute with Albania over mine laying in the Corfu Channel between October 1944 and November 1946. In January 1947, Albania had indicated that it was prepared to accept recommendations of the Security Council. In April 1947, the Security Council recommended that both parties submit the dispute to the International Court of Justice.[141] In May 1947, the United Kingdom began an action before the ICJ; in July 1947, Albania indicated its acceptance of the jurisdiction of the Court. At a later date,

---

131 [cont] *Convention on the Prevention and Punishment of the Crime of Genocide (Bosnia Herzegovina v Yugoslavia) (Preliminary Objections)* (1996) ICJ 595; *Oil Platforms (Islamic Republic of Iran v United States of America) (Preliminary Objections)* (1996) ICJ 803 (where jurisdiction arose under Art XX(2) of the Treaty of Amity, Economic Relations and Consular Relations (1955) between Iran and the United States).

132 It therefore follows that the three stages posited above are in fact four, namely: (i) provisional measures; (ii) jurisdiction; (iii) admissibility of the claim; (iv) merits. There has been a tendency to take (ii) and (iii) together. It might be argued by analogy with private international law that the stages could be increased to five, namely: (i) should the court consider provisional measures? (ii) does the court possess jurisdiction?; (iii) should the court decline jurisdiction for some reason of judicial propriety?; (iv) are there objections to the admissibility of the claim?; (v) the merits stage. In practice the tendency is for three stages.

133 The matter is governed by Art 79 of the 1978 Rules of Court which allows the Court to dispose of matters of a preliminary nature at a preliminary stage. Difficulties have arisen when the court has taken the view that the matter cannot be disentangled from the merits (see *South West Africa* case (1966) ICJ 3; *Barcelona Traction* case (1970) ICJ 3). The 1978 Rules replace those of 1946 which were amended in in 1972 and were based on those of 1946. For a recent instance of the difficulty between jurisdiction, admissibility and preliminary matters, see *Cases concerning Questions of Interpretation and Application of the 1971 Montreal Convention arising from the Aerial Incident at Lockerbie (Jurisdiction and Admissibility)* (1998) ICJ 3.

134 *Right of Passage (Preliminary Objections)* (1957) ICJ 125.

135 *Northern Cameroons* case (1963) ICJ 15.

136 *Nottebohm* case *(Liechtenstein v Guatemala)* (1955) ICJ 4.

137 *Norwegian Loans* case (1957) ICJ 9 (esp Judge Lauterpacht); *Barcelona Traction* case *(Second Phase)* (1970) ICJ 3.

138 *Barcelona Traction* case *(Second Phase)* (1970) ICJ 3.

139 *Certain Phosphate Lands in Nauru* case *(Preliminary Objections)* (1992) ICJ 240.

140 *Corfu Channel (Preliminary Objection)* case (1948) ICJ 15.

141 As they were entitled to do under Art 36, paras 1 and 3, of the United Nations Charter.

Albania challenged the jurisdiction of the Court. In resisting this challenge the United Kingdom advanced three arguments: (i) that the Court had jurisdiction by reason of Art 36(1) of the Statute of the International Court of Justice when read with Art 36(1) and 36(3) of the Statute of the United Nations; (ii) that Albania had expressly consented to jurisdiction subsequent to the application to court; (iii) that Albania had impliedly consented to jurisdiction subsequent to the application to court. The majority of the Court held that there had been an express acceptance of jurisdiction;[142] however, seven members of the Court went on to rule against submission (i) that jurisdiction might arise by virtue of a Security Council recommendation. Although it is not easy to reconcile the wording of Art 36(1) of the Statute of the Court (that is, 'matters specially provided for in the Charter of the United Nations') with that of Art 36 of the UN Charter, it is generally accepted that the Statute of the Court was drawn up at a time when it was thought that the San Francisco conference might accept some measure of compulsory jurisdiction. One effect of the judgment is that the recommendation of the Security Council under Art 36(1) and Art 36(3) does not establish a distinct head of compulsory jurisdiction.

A further head of jurisdiction is provided by the provisions of Art 36(5) and Art 37 of the statute of the International Court of Justice; the former is concerned with prior declarations under the optional clause and is considered below.[143] Article 37 provides that where a state was a party to a treaty providing for reference to a tribunal instituted by the League of Nations or to the Permanent Court of International Justice then that reference shall be taken as a reference to the International Court of Justice However, such a provision will only operate if the treaty remains in force and the parties to the dispute are also parties to the new statute. This 'deemed transfer' of a compromissory clause has constituted the basis of jurisdiction in a number of cases.[144]

As indicated above jurisdiction in contentious cases depends on the consent of states.[145] It therefore follows that difficulties may arise where a case between state A and state B would involve giving a decision on the legal rights of state C; according to the principle in the *Monetary Gold* case,[146] the court will decline to decide between states A and B if to do so would necessitate giving a ruling on the legal rights of state C. However, there are limits to this principle. In the *Nicaragua* case,[147] the Court rejected an argument by the United States that jurisdiction should be declined under the *Monetary Gold* principle simply because the position of third parties might have to be considered. The Court held that the *Monetary Gold* principle applies only in those situations where the

---

142 Therefore, strictly speaking, it was not necessary to rule on (i) or (iii).

143 For consideration of the optional clause, see below.

144 The *Ambatielos* case (*Preliminary Objection*) (1952) ICJ 28; *South West Africa* cases (*Preliminary Objections*) (1962) ICJ 319; *Barcelona Traction* case (*Preliminary Objections*) (1964) ICJ 6.

145 The position was well put by Judge Oda when he observed: 'When considering the jurisdiction of the International Court of Justice in contentious cases, I take as my point of departure the conviction that the Court's jurisdiction must rest upon the free will of sovereign States, clearly and categorically expressed, to grant the Court the competence to settle the dispute in question.' (Judge Oda: *Nicaragua v Honduras (Jurisdiction and Admissibility)* (1988) ICJ 69, p 109).

146 *Monetary Gold Removed from Rome* case (*Preliminary Question*) (1954) ICJ 19 (where a majority of states consented to jurisdiction but Albania, whose property was the subject of dispute, did not).

147 *Military and Paramilitary Activities in and against Nicaragua (Jurisdiction and Admissibility)* (1984) ICR 392.

position of the third party 'would not only be affected by a decision, but would form the very subject matter of the decision'. It is also germane to observe that any non-party is protected by the terms of Art 59 of the Statute as well as the provisions relating to intervention of third parties contained in Arts 62 and 63. Thus, the mere fact that the position of a non-party might be subject to consideration is no barrier to jurisdiction and this approach was followed by a Chamber of the Court in the *Frontier Dispute* case (*Burkina Faso v Mali*).[148] It would seem that the Court will endeavour to hear the case unless the interest of the non-party can be described as inextricably linked and absolutely central to the main dispute; it is therefore necessary to be clear as to the substance of the dispute between the main parties. So in the *Nauru* case (*Nauru v Australia*)[149] the Court declined to dismiss the action of Nauru against Australia even though New Zealand and the United Kingdom were also members of the Administering Authority of Nauru; the Court preyed in aid the provisions of Art 59 and characterised the dispute as pertaining to the particular responsibilities of Australia. Just as characterisation (or classification) can be used to determine the choice of law in private international law, so it can be used in this sphere to determine whether or not to accept jurisdiction. The *Monetary Gold* principle was applied with full rigor in the *East Timor* case (*Portugal v Australia*)[150] where Portugal brought an action against Australia in respect of its treaty dealings with Indonesia as *de facto* occupier of East Timor. The Australian case was that the real dispute was between Portugal and Indonesia and arose from the unlawful entry of Indonesia into East Timor. Secondly, it was argued by Australia and accepted by the Court that the legality of Australia's treaty dealings could not be determined without first reaching a conclusion on Indonesia's occupation of East Timor. If one is seeking a distinction between the *Nauru* case and the *East Timor* case it could be argued that in the former the claim of Nauru against Australia could be determined without any determination of the conduct of third parties but in the *East Timor* case a prior determination of the role of Indonesia was an essential pre condition to determining the claim against Australia. The difficulty with the Monetary Gold principles lies not in description but in application; it does seem from the case law that it will be applied in those cases where findings against the non-party are a precondition to any adjudication against the defendant state.

A question that does arise is as to whether the court is more disposed than in the past to find jurisdiction if at all possible; there is some case law that would justify that interpretation.[151] There may be certain cases of such a degree of gravity that international order would be damaged if jurisdiction were to be refused on a narrow technical ground.[152] Much will depend on whether, at the preliminary stage, the 'plaintiff state' has

---

148 *Frontier Dispute* case (*Burkina Faso v Mali*) (1985) ICJ 6; (1986) ICJ 554.

149 *Certain Phosphate Lands in Nauru (Nauru v Australia) (Preliminary Objections)* (1992) ICJ 240.

150 *East Timor* case (*Portugal v Australia*) (1995) ICJ 90; See C Chinkin (1995) 45 ICLQ 712; P Bekker (1996) 90 AJIL 94.

151 *Nicaragua* case (1984) ICJ 169.

152 *Application of the Convention on the Prevention and Punishment of Genocide (Bosnia-Herzegovina v Yugoslavia) (Preliminary Objections)* (1996) ICJ 595; see C Gray (1997) 46 ICLQ 688.

to show a definite case of jurisdiction[153] or whether a plausible case is sufficient.[154] It seems that a plausible case is sufficient at the preliminary stage.

(e) Jurisdiction under Art 36(2) – the optional clause

Although the statute does not provide for compulsory jurisdiction; a provision was included allowing states to declare in advance that they would accept the jurisdiction of the court. That provision is now contained in Art 36(2) and reads as follows:

> 36.2 The States Parties to the present statute may at any time declare that they recognise as compulsory *ipso facto* and without special agreement, in relation to any other state accepting the same obligation, the jurisdiction of the Court in all legal disputes concerning:
>
> (a) the interpretation of a treaty;
>
> (b) any question of international law;
>
> (c) the existence of any fact which, if established, would constitute a breach of an international obligation;
>
> (d) the nature or extent of the reparation to be made for the breach of an international obligation.

The provisions of Art 36(2) require to be read with Art 36(3) and 36(6) which read as follows:

> 36.3 The declaration referred to above may be made unconditionally or on condition of reciprocity on the part of several or certain States, or for a certain time.
>
> 36.6 In the event of a dispute as to whether the Court has jurisdiction, the matter shall be settled by a decision of the Court.

The Article is itself a compromise between those who in 1920 and 1945 wanted a compulsory system of jurisdiction and those who were not prepared to accept such a power. The intention was that the jurisdiction of the Court would expand as the number of declarations increased; such optimism has not proved to be well founded. A number of points can usefully be made. First, the article itself applies to legal disputes in the sense described above so that a matter solely within the domestic jurisdiction of the respondent state will not will come within its terms.[155] Secondly, the declarations filed by a state may be made conditionally and will be subject to the principle of reciprocity;[156] the vast majority of declarations fall within this category. Thus, in the recent *Fisheries Jurisdiction (Spain v Canada)* case,[157] the International Court of Justice rules that a reservation in

---

153 An approach that flows from *Mavrommatis Palestinian Concessions* case (1926) PCIJ, Ser A, No 2.

154 See *Ambatielos* case (1953) ICJ 10; *Nicaragua* case (1984) ICJ 169; *Nauru v Australia (Preliminary Objection)* (1992) ICJ 240; the *Genocide* case (1996) ICJ 595; *Oil Platforms (Islamic Republic of Iran v United States)* (1996) ICJ 803; the *Lockerbie* case *(Jurisdiction and Admissibility)* (1998) ICJ 3.

155 *Rights of Passage over Indian Territory (Preliminary Objections)* (1957) ICJ 125.

156 It is arguable that the principle of reciprocity arises under Art 36(2) 'in relation to any other state accepting the same obligation' rather than 36(3) which is directed to conditions that a state may or may not choose to add.

157 *Fisheries Jurisdiction* case *(Spain v Canada)* (1998) ICJ; on questions of jurisdiction see *Aegean Sea Continental Shelf* case (1978) ICJ 3; *Case concerning East Timor (Portugal v Australia)* (1995) ICJ 90.

Canada's declaration precluded its jurisdiction to adjudicate upon the dispute. Thirdly, the declaration is effected by deposit of the instrument with the Secretary General of the United Nations.[158] Fourthly, the number of declarations has been disappointing. No communist state ever signed the optional clause so that the number of declarations in 1955 totalled only 32; the numbers have steadily increased reaching 59 in 1996, but this is a modest percentage when balanced against the 180 states that now constitute the international community. Some have attributed this reluctance to a lack of confidence in international adjudication, others have alluded to the reaction to particular judgments,[159] while others have pointed to the lukewarm attitude displayed by permanent members of the Security Council.[160]

The emphasis on the imposition of conditions and the principle of reciprocity means that the jurisdiction of the Court will be based on the common will of the parties or the lowest common denominator.[161] Thus, where state A makes a declaration excluding subject X then a declaration filed by state B on the principle of reciprocity will enable state B to argue that no jurisdiction exists in subject X; that is, one party may rely on the condition or reservation expressed in the declaration of another. So in the *Norwegian Loans* case,[162] Norway was entitled to take advantage of a reservation in the French declaration; since France had excluded cases relating to its domestic jurisdiction then Norway was entitled to exercise the same right. The principle of reciprocity enables the state which has made the wider acceptance of the jurisdiction of the Court to rely upon the reservations to the acceptance laid down by the other party; so the state making the wider declaration can rely upon terms included in the narrower. declaration. However, the principle cannot be extended to enable the state making the narrower declaration to rely on terms which the other state has not chosen to include within its own declaration. So in the *Interhandel* case,[163] the United States was unable to rely on a restriction which the other Party. Switzerland had not included within its own declaration of acceptance. The principle of reciprocity will not be enforced in respect of time limits. In the *Nicaragua* case[164] the United States was held to the six month period of notice within its own declaration even though Nicaragua could have terminated its own declaration without notice.

A declaration made for the purpose of an application to court is not an abuse of process[165] while if a matter is properly before the Court then jurisdiction is not defeated by any subsequent termination of the declaration.[166]

Two matters have given rise to particular jurisdictional problems under Art 36(2). The first concerns the so called 'automatic' or 'self-judging' reservation. An example would be

---

158 Statute of the International Court of Justice (1945), Art 38(4).

159 In particular, the reaction to the *South West Africa* case (*Second Phase*) (1966) ICJ 3.

160 After 1984 only the United Kingdom had a valid declaration in force.

161 *Norwegian Loans* case (1957) ICJ 9; 24 ILR 782.

162 *Ibid.*

163 The *Interhandel* case (1959) ICJ 6.

164 *Nicaragua* case (*Jurisdiction and Admissibility*) (1984) ICJ 392.

165 *Right of Passage over Indian Territory* case (*Preliminary Objections*) (1957) ICJ 125; *Case concerning Certain Phosphate Lands (Nauru v Australia)* (1992) ICJ 240.

166 *Right of Passage over Indian Territory* case (1957) ICJ 125; *Nicaragua* case (1984) ICJ 392.

that set out in proviso (b) of the United States Declaration of 14 August 1946, which reserves 'disputes with regard to matters essentially within the domestic jurisdiction of the United States of America as determined by the United States of America'. Such reservations[167] have been the subject of controversy; it has been argued that such a reservation is invalid either because it does not constitute a valid declaration of acceptance under Art 36 or because it is contrary to the clear words of Art 36(6) which require that in cases of dispute it is for the court to determine whether or not it possesses jurisdiction. As a matter of logic and construction it is difficult to imagine how a declaration can be validly made under article when seemingly in conflict with Art 36(6).

A second matter that has given rise to problems are the provisions contained in Art 36(5) which provide for a transfer of jurisdiction from the PCIJ to the ICJ. In the *Case concerning the Aerial Incident of July 27 1955 (Preliminary Objections)*,[168] the ICJ ruled that such prior declarations were only transferable in respect of those states attending the San Francisco conference and signing the Statute of the Court; all other prior declarations were deemed to have lapsed with the dissolution of the PCIJ. However, in the *Preah Vihear Temple* case *(Preliminary Objections)*[169] it was ruled that a declaration made after 1946 purporting to renew an earlier declaration was valid under the present Statute in that such a subsequent declaration could only be referable to the present court.

The problem of the survival of a prior declaration arose again in the *Nicaragua* case[170] where Nicaragua had made a declaration in 1929 that it would accept the compulsory jurisdiction of the PCIJ but it had not ratified it. The United States therefore argued that Nicaragua had not become a party to the Statute of the PCIJ and therefore could not avail itself of Art 36(5). The Court however ruled that the interpretation of the words 'in force' in Art 36(5) were wide enough to encompass an unconditional declaration of potential effect and that such a declaration was rendered valid and effective by Nicaragua's ratification of the Statute of the ICJ in 1945.

(f) Interim measures

Under the terms of Art 41 of its Statute, the International Court of Justice has power to grant appropriate provisional measures. The terms of this power are to be exercised if the court 'considers the circumstances so require' and the purpose of the measures is to 'preserve the respective rights of either party'.[171] Such a discretionary power has its equivalent in interlocutory proceedings in municipal law; the purpose being to ensure that the situation is not radically changed to the disadvantage of one party before a

---

167 In the context of the United States such a reservation is known as the 'Connally Reservation' following the amendment introduced by Senator Connally in the Senate debate in 1946. Although some did include similar reservations the number has gradually diminished. See R Jennings (1958) 7 ICLQ 349; K Simmonds (1961) 10 ICLQ 522; J Crawford (1979) 50 BYIL 87. There are indications in the *Norwegian Loans* case (1957) ICJ 9 and the *Interhandel* case (1959) ICJ 6 that a number of judges consider such reservations invalid. See also, L Henkin, 'The Connally reservation'.

168 (1959) ICJ 127.

169 (1961) ICJ 17.

170 The *Nicaragua* case (1984) ICJ 169.

171 See *Aegean Sea Continental Shelf* case (1976) ICJ 3 (to protect those rights that are the subject of dispute in judicial proceedings).

hearing on the merits can take place. Under the terms of Rule 73, any party may seek such interim measures at any time in the course of proceedings and, under Rule 75, such provisional measures may be ordered by the Court of its own motion. Preliminary measures may be mandatory or prohibitory in nature[172] and may fall on only one party to the proceedings.

A party seeking provisional measures probably has to show that there is a plausible case of jurisdiction on the merits;[173] manifestly, difficulties could arise if interim measures were ordered in respect of a matter which the Court did not possess jurisdiction. So, provisional measures will not be ordered where there are doubts as to jurisdiction or where the application may not have been made in good faith.[174] There is a willingness to grant provisional measures if the matter appears urgent[175] or there seems to be a clear breach of international law.[176] Provisional measures are unlikely to be granted where they would frustrate action taken by other United Nations organs.[177] In only one case have provisional measures been granted and jurisdiction been found not to arise;[178] in no case has a successful applicant for provisional measures failed in a fully contested hearing on the merits. In broad terms, the purpose of provisional measures is either to preserve rights which may be the subject of the case[179] or to prevent action being taken that would aggravate or extend the dispute.[180] Relief will be refused where the measures seek to go beyond the merits of the present case[181] or where no element of urgency can be shown.[182] In cases of grave breaches of international law, provisional measures will be ordered.[183] Provisional measures may be indicated by the court independent of the submissions of the parties.[184]

At present it is unclear whether a state which obtained a grant of provisional measures but lost the proceedings[185] or where the application was subsequently

---

172 *United States Diplomatic and Consular Staff in Tehran (Provisional Measures)* (1979) ICJ 7.

173 See *Anglo Iranian Oil Co* case (1951) ICJ 89 (where provisional measures were granted and subsequently jurisdiction was not established); *Nuclear Tests* case (1973) ICJ 99; *Nicaragua v The United States* (1984) ICJ 169; *Burkina Faso v Republic of Mali* (1986) ICJ 554.

174 *Legality of the Use of Force (Yugoslavia v Belgium and Others)* (1999) ICJ. (In this case, the court in considering the military action in Kosovo rejected claims to jurisdiction based on: (i) Art IX of the Genocide Convention; or (ii) the Optional Clause. It is noteworthy that many of the respondents argued in their written case that in any event provisional measures should be refused on grounds of (a) the bad faith of the applicants; (b) abuse of process.)

175 *Cameroons v Nigeria* (1996) ICJ 13.

176 The *Hostages in Iran* case (1979) ICJ 7; *Nicaragua v The United States* (1984) ICJ 169.

177 The *Lockerbie* case *(Provisional Measures)* (1992) ICJ 1.

178 *Anglo Iranian Oil Co (Interim Measures)* case (1951) ICJ 89; *Anglo Iranian Oil Co (Jurisdiction)* case (1952) ICJ 93.

179 The *Interhandel* case *(Provisional Measures)* (1957) ICJ 105 (rejected because of lack of urgency); the *Aegean Sea Continental Shelf* case (1976) ICJ 3 (no risk of irreparable prejudice).

180 *Fisheries Jurisdiction* cases (1972) ICJ 12; *Nuclear Tests* cases (1973) ICJ 99; *United States Diplomatic and Consular Staff* case (1979) ICJ 7; *Application of the Genocide Convention* case (1993) ICJ 3.

181 *Arbitral Award of 31 July 1989 (Guinea-Bissau v Senegal)* (1990) ICJ 64.

182 *Passage through the Great Belt (Finland v Denmark)* (1991) ICJ 12.

183 *Application of the Genocide Convention* (1993) ICJ 3.

184 *Cameroons v Nigeria* (1996) ICJ 13.

185 Of which there are at present no examples.

dismissed[186] should be answerable for any intermediate loss. In cases of a highly charged political nature the grant of provisional measures has normally had limited effect. In the *Fisheries Jurisdiction* cases,[187] the matter was resolved by the emergence of the 200 mile fisheries zone while the *Nuclear Tests* cases[188] was resolved by a change of policy by France. In the case of the *Tehran Hostages*[189] the overall problem was resolved by negotiation and conciliation.

(g) The position of third parties

The Statute of the Court contains a number of provisions relating to the third party state. Article 59 of the Statute of the Court provides that a decision of the Court has no binding force 'except between the parties and in respect of that particular case'; this provision has frequently been invoked by the Court when it has sought to avoid the strict application of the *Monetary Gold* principle. There is no right to appear as a third party before the International Court of Justice. However, this broad principle is qualified by the terms of Art 62 which provides that a state which considers that it has an interest of a legal nature may submit a request to the Court to be permitted to intervene. The article provides that it shall be 'for the Court to decide upon this request'. The provisions of Art 62 require to be read with those of Art 63 which stipulates that where the Court is concerned with the construction of a convention to which states other than those concerned in the case are parties then the Registrar shall notify all such states forthwith. Further it is provided that every state so notified has the right to intervene in the proceedings but if it chooses to do so then the construction given by the judgment shall be equally binding upon it.

In approaching Art 62,[190] the Court has tended towards a cautious approach. In the *Haya de la Torre* case,[191] the Court stressed that there must be proceedings in existence so that in the *Nuclear Tests* case[192] once it was decided that there was no legal dispute between Australia and New Zealand and France then there was no legal basis for the intervention of Fiji. While the Court has no authority to reject an application to intervene on policy grounds the basis of the application must be clear and there must be an interest in the present case rather than a general interest arising from being a state within the region.[193] In considering whether to allow intervention, it is legitimate to ensure that undue delay to the original parties is avoided. While clearly the purpose of intervention is to enable states to protect against the impairment of vital rights, intervention will not be allowed if it will introduce an extraneous dispute.[194]

---

186 As in the *Anglo Iranian Oil Co* case (1952) ICJ 93.

187 *Fisheries Jurisdiction* cases *(Provisional Measures)* (1972) ICJ 12; *Fisheries Jurisdiction* cases *(Jurisdiction)* (1973) ICJ 3; *Fisheries Jurisdiction* cases *(Merits)* (1974) ICJ 3.

188 *Nuclear Tests* cases *(Interim Protection)* (1973) ICJ 99.

189 *United States Diplomatic and Consular Staff in Tehran* case (1979) ICJ 7.

190 To be read with Art 81 of the Rules of Court.

191 *Haya de la Torre* case (1951) ICJ 71.

192 *Nuclear Tests* case (1974) ICJ 253.

193 *Case concerning the Continental Shelf (Libya/Tunisia)* (1982) ICJ 18; *Application of Malta to Intervene* (1981) ICJ 3.

194 *Case concerning the Continental Shelf (Libya/Malta)* (1985) ICJ 13; *Application of Italy to Intervene* (1984) ICJ 3.

More recently, a Chamber of the Court permitted Nicaragua to intervene under the terms of Art 62 in the *Case concerning the Land, Island and Maritime and Frontier Dispute* case (*El Salvador/Honduras*)[195] but stipulated that the state seeking to intervene bore the *onus probandi* of demonstrating a legal interest which might be affected by part of the judgment of the court on the merits of the case. It is clear that the Court will consider the nature of the case made by the intervenor rather than any objections by the parties. The intervening state does not itself need to demonstrate jurisdiction because the jurisdiction of the Court has already been established by the contending parties. In giving judgment on the merits of the case the Chamber of the Court noted that the terms of intervention may be specifically limited and the intervenor does not become a party to the case.[196] The intervenor acquires the right to be heard but is not bound by the decision itself.

In considering third party intervention reference should also be made to Art 63, which permits third party intervention where the issue arises of 'the construction of a convention to which states other than those concerned in the case are parties'. If a state seeks to intervene under Art 63, then it must satisfy the Court that the proposed intervention relates to the subject matter of the dispute between the parties or that the convention that it invokes is in issue in the case.[197]

(h) Interpretation and revision

Article 60 of the Statute of the International Court of Justice provides that a judgment is final and without appeal. However, it further provides that in the event of a dispute as to the meaning or scope of the judgment the court shall construe it upon the request of any party. For the provisions of the article to be operative it is necessary that there should be a *bona fide* dispute as to the interpretation or scope of the judgment.[198]

A related matter concerns the powers of the court under Art 61 to revise a judgment. This power is strictly limited to prevent obvious abuse. Any application under Art 61 must be based on the discovery of a fact of such a decisive nature which at the time the judgment was given was unknown to the Court or the party claiming revision. Any application must be made within six months of the discovery of the new fact. No application may be made after the lapse of 10 years from the date of the judgment. The fact must be of a decisive nature and must not be one that at the time of the original action could have been discovered by a party through the exercise of reasonable diligence.[199] It is not possible for an applicant to rely on his own negligence in failing to ascertain a matter reasonably discoverable at the time of the original hearing.

---

195 *Land, Island and Maritime Frontier Dispute* case (*Intervention*) (1990) ICJ 3.

196 *Case concerning the Land, Island and Maritime Frontier Dispute (El Salvador v Honduras, Nicaragua intervening)* (1992) ICJ 351.

197 *SS Wimbledon* (1923) PCIJ, Ser A, No 1 (the Court allowed intervention on the basis of Art 63); *Haya de la Torre* case (1951) ICJ 76; *Case concerning Military and Paramilitary Activities in and against Nicaragua* (1984) ICJ 215.

198 *Request for the Interpretation of the Judgment of 20 November 1950 in the Asylum case* (1950) ICJ 402.

199 *Application for Revision and Interpretation of the Judgment of 24 February 1982 in the Case concerning the Continental Shelf (Tunisia v Libya)* (1985) ICJ 191.

A variation on this theme is where the original court judgment makes provision for liberty to apply in certain circumstances. In para 63 of the Court's judgment in the *Nuclear Tests* case[200] it was provided that the matter might be re-examined if there were to be a resumption of atmospheric nuclear testing by France. Thus, when France resumed underground nuclear testing at Mururoa Atoll in the South Pacific in 1995, New Zealand applied to the Court seeking a re-examination of the earlier decision.

In the *Request for an Examination of the Situation in Accordance with Paragraph 63 of the Court's Judgment of 20 December 1974*,[201] the Court dismissed the request on the basis that as the earlier judgment had concerned solely with atmospheric testing, the case could not be re-examined because of the resumption of underground testing. However, in the course of giving judgment the Court accepted that the concept of the re-examination of a judgment was different in character to an application under Art 60 or Art 61; the object of re-examination was not to change the original judgment but to re-establish its character in the face of subsequent conduct by one or other party.

(i) The question of non-appearance[202]

As with municipal systems that provide for default judgments the same problem has to be faced on the international plane, namely the attitude that the court should adopt in respect of the state that fails to appear or otherwise defend the case. Express provision is made by Art 53 of the Statute of the Court which stipulates that where one of the parties does not appear before the court or fails to defend its case then the other party may call upon the Court to decide in favour of its claim. However, before doing so the court must satisfy itself that it has jurisdiction in the matter and that the claim is well founded in fact and law. The subject of non-appearance gained greater prominence in the 1970s in cases such as the *Fisheries Jurisdiction* case,[203] the *Nuclear Tests* case,[204] the *Aegean Continental Shelf* case,[205] and most pointedly in the *Hostages* case.[206] Sometimes a state appears in part of the proceedings; in the *Nicaragua* case,[207] the United States unsuccessfully contested the jurisdiction of the court and then declined to appear at the merits stage. In some cases, the reason for non-appearance is that the conduct of the state is so clearly in breach of international law as to leave little room for legal argument.[208] In other cases, the state in question has decided that the matter is too politically sensitive to continue to submit to judicial adjudication.[209]

---

200 *Nuclear Tests Cases (Australia v France and New Zealand v France)* (1974) ICJ 253.

201 *Nuclear Tests Case (New Zealand v France)* (1995) ICJ 288.

202 G Fitzmaurice, 'The problem of the "non-appearing" defendant government' (1980) 51 BYIL 89; I Sinclair, 'Some procedural aspects of recent international litigation' (1981) 30 ICLQ 338.

203 *Fisheries Jurisdiction* case (1974) ICJ 3.

204 *Nuclear Tests* cases (1974) ICJ 253.

205 *Aegean Continental Shelf* case (1976) ICJ 3; (1978) ICJ 3.

206 *Case concerning United States Diplomatic and Consular Staff in Tehran* (1980) ICJ 3.

207 *Military and Paramilitary Activities* case (*Request for Interim Measures*)(1984) ICJ 169; (*Jurisdiction and Admissibility*) 392; (*Merits*) (1986) ICJ 14.

208 *Case concerning United States Diplomatic and Consular Staff in Tehran* (1980) ICJ 3.

209 *Nuclear Tests* case (1974) ICJ 253.

(j) *Ad hoc* chambers

Under the new Rules of Court introduced in 1978 there has been an increasing willingness to take advantage of the provisions of Art 26(2) of the Statute and permit the operation of *ad hoc* chambers to dispose of particular cases. Under Art 26(3), a chamber may be established if the parties so request. When the Court sits in full there will be fifteen judges (or possibly 16 or 17 judges if *ad hoc* judges are appointed). Under the terms of Art 26(2), the parties may influence the number of judges appointed to the chamber. Such a process may lead to a smaller bench and speedier resolution; however, some have suggested that it can lead to the parties having undue influence on the composition of the court. In the *Gulf of Maine* case[210] the rules provided for the parties to be consulted and for a secret ballot of the court to take place to settle composition. However, Canada and the United States indicated that unless their wishes on composition were met they would submit the case instead to arbitration. In the face of this insistence the Court elected the chamber that the parties had requested although only after protests by two judges. Although there is no minimum number specified the tendency following the *Gulf of Maine* case[211] has been to appoint a chamber of five judges. There has been some concern that this might lead to a narrower bench of judges drawn from particular legal cultures but this fear does not appear to be substantiated by the evidence.

At first it was thought that the procedure would only be used in cases of a technical legal nature and an example of this was provided by the *Gulf of Maine* case[212] which concerned a case of continental shelf delimitation. However, since that date the procedure has been more varied. In the *Frontier Dispute* case[213] and the *ELSI* case[214] there was a heavy volume of evidence while in the *Land, Island and Maritime Frontier* case,[215] difficult issues on the acquisition of territory fell to be addressed. Judgments given under the chambers system have been subsequently referred to with approval by the full court.[216]

It is worthy of note that there has been, since 1993, a chamber for environmental disputes which comprises seven judges having a particular interest in the field. However, this has not prevented subsequent case on the subject being heard by the full court.[217]

(k) The enforcement of judgments

A judgment given will be final and without a right of appeal. In principle the decision binds only the parties to the dispute but the reasoning contained therein may be influential in the development of international law. The International Court of Justice is not concerned with problems of enforcement.

---

210 *Delimitation of the Maritime Boundary in the Gulf of Maine Area. Constitution of the Chamber Order of 20 January 1982* (1982) ICJ 3.
211 The *Gulf of Maine* case (1984) ICJ 246.
212 *Ibid.*
213 *Frontier Dispute* case *(Burkina Faso v Mali)* (1986) ICJ 554.
214 *Case concerning Elettronica Sicula SpA (ELSI)* (1989) ICJ 15.
215 *Land, Island and Maritime Frontier Dispute (El Salvador/Honduras: Nicaragua Intervening)* (1992) ICJ 351.
216 *Continental Shelf (Libya/Malta)* case (1985) ICJ 13.
217 *Gabcikovo-Nagymaros Project (Hungary/Slovakia)* (1997) ICJ 7.

Under the terms of Art 94, of the United Nations Charter each member of the United Nations undertakes to comply with the decision of the International Court of Justice in any case to which it is a party. In cases of non-compliance, the other party may have recourse to the Security Council which may make recommendations or decide upon measures to be taken to give effect to the judgment. Such action would require to be taken under Chapter VI of the Charter. Enforcement through the Security Council is liable to be difficult. In the case of *Nicaragua v The United States*, the attempt by Nicaragua to secure enforcement through the Security Council was frustrated by the decision of the United States to employ the veto.

Past experience has indicated that there has not been a difficulty with enforcement *per se*. The difficulty has been in persuading states to accept the jurisdiction of the court; if they are prepared to do so then they are normally prepared to give effect to the judgment rendered. There have, however, been a number of cases where there has been an initial refusal to enforce the judgment. Instances of non-compliance are afforded by the conduct of Albania in the *Corfu Channel* case,[218] the refusal of Iceland in the *Fisheries Jurisdiction* case[219] and the initial non-compliance by Iran in the *Hostages* case.[220]

(l)   The advisory jurisdiction of the Court[221]

In addition to the jurisdiction of the Court to determine disputes between states (that is, contentious proceedings) the Court also has jurisdiction to render advisory opinions (that is, the advisory jurisdiction). Article 96 of the Charter of the United Nations provides:

(1) The General Assembly or the Security Council may request the International Court of Justice to give an advisory opinion on any legal question.

(2) Other organs of the United Nations and specialised agencies, which may at any time be so authorised by the General Assembly, may also request advisory opinions of the Court on legal questions arising within the scope of their activities.

These provisions require to be read with Art 65 of the Statute of the Court which stipulates that:

(1) The Court may give an advisory opinion on any legal question at the request of whatever body may be authorised by or in accordance with the Charter of the United Nations to make such a request.

The advisory procedure provided is not open to states but only to international organisations. At the time of writing, this comprises six organs of the United Nations

---

218 *Corfu Channel* case (*The Merits*) (1949) ICJ 4.
219 *Fisheries Jurisdiction* case (1974) ICJ 3.
220 *United States Diplomatic Staff in Tehran* case (1980) ICJ 3.
221 See generally, E Hambro, 'The authority of the advisory opinions of the International Court of Justice' (1954) 3 ICLQ 2; D Greig, 'The advisory jurisdiction of the International Court and the settlement of disputes between states' (1966) 15 ICLQ 325; R Ago, 'Binding advisory opinions of the International Court of Justice' (1971) 85 AJIL 439; S Schwebel, 'Authorising the Secretary General of the United Nations to request advisory opinions of the International Court of Justice' (1984) 78 AJIL 869; S Schwebel, 'Was the capacity to request an advisory opinion wider in the Permanent Court of International Justice than it is in the International Court of Justice?' (1991) 62 BYIL 77.

together with 16 specialised agencies. In the case of the specialised agency, the question posed must be one that is *intra vires* the constitutional document. So that, in 1996, the International Court of Justice declined to provide an opinion requested by the General Assembly of WHO on the legality of the use of nuclear weapons by a state reasoning that the constitution of the World Health Organisation confined it *inter alia* to the effects on health of the use of nuclear weapons. On the same day the Court gave an advisory opinion to the General Assembly of the United Nations on the legality of the threat or use of nuclear weapons.[222]

The purpose of the advisory opinion is to offer legal advice which is not binding on the requesting bodies and unlike the contentious jurisdiction the object is not to settle a particular inter state dispute. The question itself will be phrased in abstract terms. The principle propounded in the *Status of Eastern Carelia* case[223] is that the court will not permit its advisory jurisdiction to extend to a dispute between parties where one of the parties refuses consent to the jurisdiction of the court. It has to be recognised, however, that the jurisdiction of the PCIJ extended to 'disputes' while that of the ICJ under Art 65 extends to 'any legal question'. In these circumstances, it is perhaps not surprising that the *Eastern Carelia* case was distinguished in the *Interpretation of Peace Treaties* case[224] where the position of the ICJ as an organ of the United Nations was stressed and a distinction was drawn between pronouncing on the merits of a dispute[225] and advising on dispute settlement machinery. In the *Namibia* case[226] and the *Western Sahara* case[227] the *Eastern Carelia* case was distinguished on the basis that the situation did not constitute a dispute and the request by a political organ for an opinion was referable to its duties under the United Nations Charter.

While an advisory opinion is not designed to settle a particular dispute, such opinions have made a significant contribution to the development of international law in the period since 1946. Influential opinions have been delivered on the admission to United Nations membership[228] and the reparation for injuries suffered in the service of the United Nations[229] which clarified issues of legal personality on the international plane. In the sphere of territorial disputes, advisory opinions have been given in the *Namibia* case[230] and the *Western Sahara* case;[231] in both instances, the *Eastern Carelia* approach was distinguished and the emphasis placed on permitting the General Assembly to carry out its obligations in respect of decolonisation. A particularly important advisory opinion was delivered in the *Reservations to the Genocide Convention* case[232] which not only lead to change in the substantive law of treaties but was important in that the Court stressed that

---

222 *Legality of the Threat or Use of Nuclear Weapons* (1996) ICJ 66, p 226; see AV Lowe (1996) 55 CLJ 45.
223 *Status of Eastern Carelia* case (1923) PCIJ, Ser B, No 5.
224 *Interpretation of Peace Treaties* case (1950) ICJ 65.
225 As would have been the situation in the *Eastern Carelia* case (1923) PCIJ, Ser B, No 5.
226 The *Namibia* case (1971) ICJ 16.
227 The *Western Sahara* case (1975) ICJ 12.
228 *Conditions of Membership of the United Nations* case (1948) ICJ 57.
229 *Reparation for Injuries Suffered in the Service of the United Nations* (1949) ICJ 174.
230 The *Namibia* case (1971) ICJ 16.
231 The *Western Sahara* case (1975) ICJ 12.
232 *Reservations to the Genocide Convention* case (1951) ICJ 15.

an important role of the advisory opinion was 'to guide the United Nations in respect of its own action'.

It is clear, however, that the tendency has been for advisory opinions to have been most readily sought in the early years of the United Nations when there was some degree of uncertainty concerning the relationship between the various organs of the United Nations and the member states. The advisory opinion has been particularly useful in respect of technical institutional matters such as judgments rendered by administrative tribunals,[233] the expenses of United Nations operations[234] and the applicability of the United Nations Headquarters Agreement.[235]

It has to be admitted that the role of the advisory opinion is very limited. In the years 1948–75, only 16 were delivered. While there has been an increase in the number of contentious cases since 1980, there has been no such rise in the number of advisory opinions; in the period 1980–89 only five were delivered; one of the reasons for this undoubtedly is that those organisations entitled to seek advisory opinions all employ large numbers of well qualified legal advisers so there is perhaps less role for the ICJ as 'an in house counsel of last resort'.

(m) Reflections on the role of the Court

Judging an institution by the number of cases that it processes is an imperfect yardstick. In the years 1946–90 the International Court of Justice dealt with 52 contentious cases and delivered 21 advisory opinions. In the years 1981–91, judgments in 12 contentious cases were delivered. However one expresses it the workload has not been heavy. In respect of advisory opinions, it is arguable that those organisations that might seek them already possess well qualified legal staff. Secondly, there seems little doubt that the unfortunate judgments in the *South West Africa* cases[236] caused many newly independent states not to sign the optional clause. At the time, there was an under representation of Afro-Asian states on the bench and many newly independent states preferred to resolve problems through diplomatic channels being rather sceptical of some of the principles of classic customary international law. One of the legacies of the *South West Africa* case was that the Court began to manifest a willingness to accommodate the needs of potential litigants and stressed its role as an organ of the United Nations, in contrast to its earlier image as an extension of a 19th century arbitral tribunal. In pursuance of this, one can note the use of *ad hoc* chambers, a more liberal attitude to third party intervention[237] and a readiness to resort to equitable principles *intra legem*. In respect of access, one impediment to poorer countries was the legal cost involved so that in 1989 there was established a UN Trust Fund to Assist States in the Settlement of Disputes through the International Court of Justice.

---

233 *Effect of Awards of Compensation Made by the United Nations Administrative Tribunal* (1954) ICJ 47.

234 *Advisory Opinion on Certain Expenses of the United Nations* (1962) ICJ 151.

235 *Applicability of the Obligation to Arbitrate under Section 21 of the UN Headquarters Agreement* (1988) ICJ 12.

236 *South West Africa* case (*Preliminary Objections*) (1962) ICJ 319; *South West Africa* case (*Second Phase*) (1966) ICJ 6.

237 *Land, Island and Maritime Frontier Dispute (El Salvador v Honduras)* (1990) ICJ 92.

Until 1989, Marxist regimes were reluctant to use the court at all but since that date there has been a steady increase in the number of contentious cases. In some instances, the initiating of proceedings has served to clarify the issues and make a negotiated settlement possible. As one distinguished former President of the Court has noted, 'the Court procedure is beginning to be seen as a resort to be employed in close relationship with normal diplomatic negotiations'.[238]

It has also to be noted that, unlike in 1946, the International Court of Justice is not the only court administering justice on the international plane. It operates alongside the European Court of Justice, the European Court of Human Rights, the Inter American Court of Human Rights and the International Tribunal on the Law of the Sea. In the future, it will need to develop a relationship with the International Criminal Court as it has with the two tribunals established to investigate war crimes in Bosnia and Rwanda. Some writers have argued that the International Court of Justice would have a higher degree of relevance if it had the capacity to give preliminary rulings on international law, in the same manner as the European Court of Justice has operated under Art 177 of the Treaty of Rome (1957).[239] However, this suggestion seems misplaced. The European Court of Justice exists to safeguard a regional system of a limited number of states working together but accepting the principle of the supremacy of European Community Law. In contrast, the International Court of Justice serves an international community of over 200 states of different cultural traditions who tend to guard their sovereignty jealously and, in many cases, have little in common save membership of the United Nations. A related concern lies in the relationship between the court and the Security Council. This raises two issues, namely whether there are any legal limits to the powers of the Security Council and, secondly, whether there is a procedure of judicial review of the exercise of such powers. It was never intended in 1945 that the Court should exercise a power of judicial review over the Security Council,[240] but this issue has arisen indirectly without having to be resolved in two cases in the last decade;[241] it is, of course, the case that the scope of judicial review in most systems of municipal law has increased greatly since 1945 so such arguments on the international plane are perhaps inevitable.

It is certainly true that the role of the International Court of Justice could be more prominent but in the 1990s it has been kept busy with a flow of contentious cases from developing countries. The newly available chambers procedure has been employed on a number of occasions. It is, however, disappointing that only a limited number of states accept jurisdiction under the optional clause Art 36(2) and it is that only one of the five permanent members of the Security Council has a valid declaration in force. However,

---

238 Sir Robert Jennings (President 1991–94) in an address to the United Nations General Assembly, 8 November 1993 (UN Doc A/48/PV 31).

239 See now Art 234 of the Treaty of Amsterdam (1997).

240 The *Namibia* case (1971) ICJ 6.

241 *Lockerbie (Provisional Measures)* case (1992) ICJ 1. See also *Case concerning Application of the Convention on the Prevention and Punishment of the Crime of Genocide* (1993) ICJ 325, in particular the separate opinion of Judge *ad hoc* Lauterpacht who, while not accepting any unlimited power of the Court to review the Council, went on to add 'that the Court has some power of this kind can hardly be doubted'. Since he continued 'the Court, as the principle judicial organ of the United Nations, is entitled, indeed bound, to ensure the rule of law within the United Nations system and, in cases properly brought before it, to assist on adherence by all United Nations organs to the rules governing their operation ...'.

time is probably on the side of the Court. The virtual disappearance of Marxist regimes in Eastern Europe has lead to an increasing emphasis on the rule of law in international affairs. The greater emphasis on co-operation through the vehicle of multilateral treaties will extend the jurisdiction of the Court. The fundamental principle of the United Nations Charter is the peaceful settlement of disputes and this is now almost universally accepted within the international community; although some states may decide that particular disputes are more suitable for arbitration there seems no reason why the Court should not also benefit from an increasing readiness to submit to adjudication. Finally as the number of democratic states increases it is likely that public opinion will induce governments to favour peaceful settlement; although some disputes may be properly described as 'political' there seems no good reason why even the most politically charged dispute between states should not be capable of legal analysis.[242]

8 INSTITUTIONS AND DISPUTE SETTLEMENT

In addition to the methods outlined above, the United Nations Charter broadly supports the principle of regional co-operation to settle disputes. Article 52.1 reads: 'Nothing in the present Charter precludes the existence of regional arrangements or agencies for dealing with such matters relating to the maintenance of international peace and security as are appropriate for regional action, provided that such arrangements or agencies and their activities are consistent with the Purposes and Principles of the United Nations.' Article 52.2 provides that where a state enters into such an arrangement then it should make every effort to settle local disputes peacefully through such regional agencies before referring them to the Security Council. However, the role of the Security Council is expressly preserved by Art 52.4.

Under the terms of Art 53.1, the Security Council may utilise such a regional organisation for enforcement action but so that the agency acts under its authority. However, the article further states that no regional enforcement action shall be taken without the authorisation of the Security Council. However, any such regional action is clearly subordinate to the powers and duties of the Security Council and General Assembly as indicated by Arts 103, 24, 35 and 36 of the United Nations Charter. Thus, while a regional organisation may have an appropriate role to play it is subordinate to and does not detract from the prime responsibilities of the Security Council and General Assembly under the United Nations Charter. In appropriate cases, where there is not an immediate threat to international peace and security, the Security Council may be content to allow the regional organisation to explore means of resolution.

Of the relevant regional organisations the least advanced is probably the Arab League. It provides for co-operation between Arab States, regular meetings and informal ministerial contacts. The Arab League played a role in organising an Inter Arab Force to diffuse tension between Iraq and Kuwait in 1961 and, in 1990, Ministers of the Arab

---

242 The example cited by the Secretary General Javier Perez de Cuellar in his last annual report in 1991 was that of the Iraq-Kuwait border (before the invasion of August 1990) which was capable of legal analysis and determination. It is arguable that the influence of the Court is less likely to be pronounced in the civil war situations that now pose greatest threats to peace and security.

League undertook consultations to try to produce an agreed solution after the Iraqi invasion of Kuwait. The League itself operates through a Council where each member has one vote. Members of the League have agreed to renounce the use of force and to accept the decisions of the Council as binding.

A longer tradition of regional co-operation exists in respect of the American states. Drawing upon earlier initiatives, the Organisation of American States founded in 1948 provides the vehicle for regional co-operation. This co-operation is based on a framework of three treaties. The Inter American Treaty of Reciprocal Assistance (or the Rio Treaty (1947) establishes a defensive alliance and provides for the consultation and the collective exercise of self-defence. The Charter of Bogota (1948) provides for the establishment of the Organisation of American States and, in Art 23, it is stipulated that international disputes shall be submitted to the Organisation for peaceful settlement. The third treaty is the American Treaty on Pacific Settlement (or Pact of Bogota) (1948), which contains provision for mediation, inquiry and judicial settlement. This latter treaty has not been particularly successful so that the OAS has employed the Inter American Peace Committee which was established in 1940; this body was reconstituted in 1970 as the Inter American Committee on Peaceful Settlement, operating as a subsidiary body of the Council of the OAS. In practice, the actual task of dispute resolution falls to the Permanent Council of the OAS operating at ambassadorial level and the Consultation Meetings of the Ministers of Foreign Affairs deriving from the Rio Treaty. Associated with this is the role of the Secretary General of the OAS who, under the amended terms of Art 116, may bring to the attention of the Organisation matters 'threatening the peace and security of the hemisphere'.

A more recent but less complex structure applies in relation to Africa.[243] The Organisation of African Unity was established in 1963 with the object of promoting co-ordination amongst African states. The Organisation embraces four institutions, namely an Assembly of Heads of State, a Council of Ministers, a General Secretariat and a Commission of Mediation, Conciliation and Arbitration. Article XIX of the Charter of the OAU refers to the principle of the peaceful settlement of disputes and the Commission of Mediation and Conciliation and Arbitration was established under a Protocol of 21 July 1964 to facilitate this objective. However, the African tradition has been to avoid quasi judicial methods in favour of informal diplomatic contacts through the auspices of the OAU. The tendency of the OAU in the most intractable problems has been to set up *ad hoc* fact finding commissions; this has been adopted in respect of the disputes between Somalia and Ethiopia, Morocco and Algeria as well as in respect of the competing claims to the Western Sahara and the civil war in Chad.

As is to be expected, Europe has a number of regional instruments designed to promote the peaceful settlement of disputes. In respect of those states that are members of the European Community, any disputes arising under the constituent treaties of the Community will be determined in the final analysis by the European Court of Justice whose judgments are binding on member states. Since 1992, in certain circumstances failure to observe a judgment may result in a financial penalty. Secondly, in the area of

---

243 See TO Elias, 'The Commission of Mediation, Conciliation and Arbitration of the Organisation of African Unity' (1964) 40 BYIL 336; T Muluwa, 'The peaceful settlement of disputes among African states 1963–1983; some conceptual issues and practical trends' (1989) 38 ICLQ 299.

human rights the European Convention on Human Rights has included limited scope for inter state complaints. Thirdly, if the matter turns on defence or security then those states that are signatories to the North Atlantic Treaty Organisation (1949) are obliged to avail themselves of the methods of conciliation mediation and arbitration which may involve the good offices of the Secretary General of the Organisation.

Work on the peaceful resolution of disputes had proceeded after the Helsinki Final Act 1975 under the auspices of the Conference on Security and Co-operation in Europe. One initiative was the Convention on Conciliation and Arbitration which was signed in 1992 and came into force in 1994. This provided for the establishment of the Geneva Court of Conciliation and Arbitration. In the same year, the Conference on Security and Co-operation in Europe was re named the Organisation for Security and Co-operation in Europe (OSCE) with permanent arrangements for dispute resolution. With a membership of over 50 states, it will receive reports from the Geneva Court of Conciliation in the event that the parties have rejected settlement proposals. In the years since 1994, the OSCE has sent various missions to states to find facts and contribute to conflict resolution.

As is to be expected, the record of regional action is mixed. In 1957, the OAS had some success in mediating between Honduras and Nicaragua in respect of an arbitral award.[244] In 1961 and 1973, the good offices of NATO were employed to persuade Iceland and the United Kingdom to terminate their fishing dispute. In 1963, the Organisation of African Unity[245] had some success in resolving a border dispute between Algeria and Morocco. In 1948 and 1955, the OAS provided personnel to monitor the border between Costa Rica and Nicaragua. However, the success of regional initiatives should not be overstated. Some disputes are inter regional, in other instances the regional organisation may be unwilling to commit resources and in some cases a state may simply use a regional organisation to bolster support.[246]

---

244 See CG Fenwick, 'The *Honduras-Nicaragua boundary dispute*' (1957) 51 AJIL 761; *Arbitral Award Made by the King of Spain on 23 December 1906* (1960) ICJ 192.

245 See G Naldi, 'Peace-keeping attempts by the Organisation of African Unity' (1985) 34 ICLQ 593.

246 Examples being the attitude of Argentina to the OAS during the Falklands War in 1982 and threats by Iceland to leave NATO in 1973.

CHAPTER 21

INTERNATIONAL LAW AND THE USE OF FORCE BY STATES[1]

1 INTRODUCTION

One of the earliest concerns of international law has been to determine the circumstances in which the use of force might be justified. This aspect of the subject is generally referred to as 'the laws of war' although this expression requires qualification. The expression governs both the rules that determine when resort to force may be justified (*jus ad bellum*) and the rules that determine the actual conduct of armed conflict (*jus in bello*). It is intended in this chapter to deal with the former category of *jus ad bellum*.

The circumstances in which a ruler might resort to force concerned the earliest writers of international law and the topic remains at the heart of the subject as set out in the provisions of the United Nations Charter. In the municipal law of most states, the general position has been to prohibit the citizen using force save in cases of self-defence and the entitlement to employ force under the authority of the law resides in the relevant police force or armed forces. The citizen has given up the right to employ force subject to the guarantees that the agencies of the state will protect his person and his property. The general objective of international law in the last century was to move in the same direction namely to outlaw the use of force save in very exceptional circumstances. However this took some time to be the case and it is necessary to examine how restrictions on the use of force came to be accepted.

2 FROM THE DOCTRINE OF THE 'JUST WAR' TO THE LEAGUE OF NATIONS[2]

From earliest time philosophers have considered the circumstances in which force might be adopted. Aristotle[3] in *Politics* deplored the ready recourse of Sparta to force and attempted to set out the possible justifications of a morally just war of which one was to prevent enslavement. Aristotle considered that the objective of any war must be to establish a durable peace and this was taken further by Cicero[4] in *De Republica* where he argued that war would only be lawful if the purpose was to drive out an invader or to

---

1   See generally, D Bowett, *Self Defence in International Law*, 1958; I Brownlie, *International Law and the Use of Force by States*, 1963; Y Dinstein, *War, Aggression and Self Defence*, 2nd edn, 1994; G Best, *War and Law since 1945*, 1994. See also CHM Waldock, 'The regulation of the use of force by individual states in international law' (1952) 81 HR 451; C Greenwood, 'The concept of war in modern international law' (1987) 36 ICLQ 283.

2   J von Elbe, 'The evolution of the concept of the Just War in international law' (1939) 33 AJIL 665.

3   Aristotle (384–322BC). For a review of his political thought, see GER LLoyd, *Aristotle, the Growth and Structure of his Thought*, 1968; RG Mulgan, *Aristotle's Political Theory: An Introduction for Students of Political Theory*, 1977; J Barnes, *Aristotle*, 1982. For the complete works, see the two volumes edited by J Barnes, 1984.

4   Marcus Tullius Cicero (106–43 BC). In his early works – *On the Orator, On the Republic*, and *On the Laws* – Cicero was concerned not only to demonstrate that Rome's laws and institutions embodied the best in Greek philosophy but also to show that the wise statesman would seek to guide political affairs through persuasion rather than violence. For both Aristotle and Cicero, there was a connection between the conduct of domestic affairs and the conduct of external relations.

redress an injury. So that there is evidence in the classical period of reflection on the limitations as to force.

Serious thought about the role of force in political affairs coincided with the adoption of Christianity as one of the religions of the Roman Empire.[5] The association of church and state meant that Christian writers would have to consider in what circumstances the use of force might be justified. The earlier Christian writers had been pacifists[6] but as Christians began to hold office under the Roman Empire these concerns required to be modified.

Traditional Christian thought favoured an orderly society, so that war could only be justified if it was consistent with the divine purpose; in these circumstances the doctrine of the 'just war' began to be developed. According to St Augustine[7] (AD 354–430), war might be justified to punish a wrong where the wrongdoer has refused to restore the *status quo ante*. However, the means used must be proportionate to the wrong inflicted. It was also thought that wars against unbelievers or heretics might in certain circumstances be regarded as divinely sanctioned. The doctrine that resort to war by a ruler had to meet certain requirements constituted the doctrine of 'the just war' and remained so for over 1,000 years.

The doctrine was further developed by St Thomas Aquinas[8] who, in the *Summa Theologiae*, stipulated three conditions for a just war, namely: (a) a proper authority; (b) a just cause; and (c) the possession of the right intention. The first requirement meant that war should only be initiated by a properly constituted ruler. The second requirement imported the notion that those attacked were deserving of such treatment. The third requirement stipulated that war was not to be motivated by hatred or revenge. The doctrine of the just war attracted widespread comment and was alluded both in Bracton[9] and also by the Italian post-glossator Bartolus (1314–57).[10]

The doctrine of the just war acquired support in the schools of theology and it was from these schools of theology that the earliest writers on international law were to emerge. The writers Francisco Vitoria (1480–1546)[11] and Francisco Suarez (1548–1617)

---

5   In the form of the *Edict of Milan*, AD 313, issued by the Emperor Constantine (AD 274–337) who became sole Emperor in 324 and summoned and presided over the first general council of the Church at Nicea in 325.

6   Such as Tertullian (160–240) and Origen (185–254) who argued that with the return of Christ imminent the believer should ignore the conflicts of the world. This attitude became harder to endorse when, after Constantine, Christians began to hold positions of authority in the Empire.

7   Augustine's (354–430) views on the conduct of external relations were set out in his *The City of God* written between 413 to 427, the writing of which was partly prompted by the sacking of Rome by Alaric and the Goths in 412 which caused many refugees to flee to North Africa. For Augustine, see H Deane, *The Political and Social Ideas of St Augustine*, 1957; H Chadwick, *Augustine*, 1986.

8   St Thomas Aquinas (1224–74); the *Summa Theologiae* was written between 1266–73. For Aquinas, see JA Weisheipl, *Friar Thomas D'Aquino, his Life, Thought and Works*, 1874; A Kenny, *Aquinas*, 1979; J Marenbon, *Later Medieval Philosophy*, 1987.

9   Bracton's *De Legibus* having been written by 1265.

10 C Woolf, *Bartolus of Sassoferrato, His Position in the History of Medieval Political Thought*, 1913.

11 Francisco Vitoria (his name being variously spelt as Francisci de Victoria, Francisco de Victoria, Francisco de Vitoria and Franciscus de Vittoria) was a Dominican Frar and a Professor at Salamanca. In *De Indis et de Iure Belli Relectiones*, 1532, he raised questions about Spanish treatment of races in South America and argued that differences of religion, the expansion of empire or personal glory did not constitute good reasons for war.

contributed the concept of proportionality which remains important today. Suarez argued that not every cause would justify war and the injury to the state must be equivalent to the damage that would probably arise from conflict. In this period before the commencement of international law, writers tended to be concerned with the morality of war rather than its legality; during this period of natural law thinking if a conflict was immoral then it would naturally be regarded as unlawful.

As Europe began to break into distinct sovereign states in the 16th century and international law as a discipline began to emerge, much thought was given to the circumstances in which force was justified. In seeking to give the just war doctrine a more secular grounding, Hugo Grotius examined the concept in his work *De Jure Belli ac Pacis* (1625). Grotius agreed that war should only be initiated by a competent ruler. He then proceeded to examine the concept of the just cause; Grotius argued that force was justified in defence of persons or property and in cases of immediate danger a state might invoke the doctrine of anticipatory self-defence. Grotius discussed a number of 'unjust' causes of war such as the desire to acquire territory or to oppress a people in contrast to a desire to punish a state which had caused an injury. So, until 1700, some form of just war doctrine secular or religious dominated the subject. As developed since St Augustine, it comprised a number of elements, namely: (a) the need for a competent authority; (b) the need for a just cause; (c) the presence of the right intention; (d) the requirement of proportionality in taking action; (e) the requirement that conflict be the last resort after other methods such as diplomatic exchanges have been exhausted; (f) a reasonable prospect that the war will succeed.

The 18th and 19th centuries witnessed the decline of the just war doctrine as positivism became the dominant philosophy in international affairs. Drawing upon the political philosophy[12] of Jean Bodin (1529–96) and Thomas Hobbes (1588–1679) such a philosophy stressed that the state was bound only by those rules that it chose freely to accept. Such an intellectual climate rejected natural law and any higher law and stressed the sovereign rights of the state;[13] such a sovereign right might include the right to declare war. If states were sovereign and equal then it was argued that it was inconsistent for one state to judge the validity of another's conduct. After the Treaty of Westphalia (1648), Europe divided into states who assessed national interests in secular terms and alliances were built and war declared to promote or destroy the balance of power that was seen to exist in Europe. A distinction was drawn between ethical considerations and matters of legal regulation so that in the 18th century laws developed governing the status of neutrality or the conduct of a blockade, but it was not regarded as appropriate in the positivist environment to question the sovereign right of a state to declare war. This was perhaps inevitable in 18th century Europe, which had witnessed the invasion of Silesia in 1740 and Saxony in 1756 and three partitions of Poland, although even Frederick the Great did attempt to justify his invasion of Saxony in 1756 and protested against the invasion of Bavaria by Joseph II in 1777. At the same time, Emerich de Vattel (1714–67) in *Le Droit des Gens* (1758) argued that it was not the role of the Law of Nations to sit in

---

12 The questioning of the just war doctrine can be traced back at least to Machiavelli (1469–1527) who had observed in *Il Principe* (1513) 'that war is just which is necessary'.

13 Thus Richard Zouche (1589–1650) thought that neither belligerent could be acting unjustly if they were acting in good faith. Both Bynkershoek (1673–1743) and Christian Wolff (1679–1754) held that no nation could act as judge over combatants.

judgment on the justice of a conflict because of the sovereign independence and equality of states and the instability that would arise if a judgment had to be made between a just and an unjust conflict.

Some attempt might be made by treaty to provide guarantees against attack,[14] but beyond this it was not thought unlawful to commence war; although towards the end of the 19th century public opinion was beginning to make itself felt in the conduct of foreign affairs and this led to the increasing interest in methods of peaceful resolution. At the same time, the growing power of armaments and actual experience caused many to consider that the price of unrestricted freedom to wage war was too great. Thus, the second Hague Convention of 1907 drawn up at the initiative of Latin American states prohibited the use of force to recover debts, save where the debtor state had refused to consent to arbitration. In the third Hague Convention of 1907, it was provided that war should be preceded by a formal declaration of war. However, in the years before 1914 it was not disputed that a state might engage in war to advance its national interests. In so far as attempts were made to restrict the use of force, they comprised either proposals for naval and arms reduction or the formation of strategic and defensive alliances. The fact that there had not been an all out conflict in Europe since 1815 seemed to give grounds for optimism.

Such optimism and complacency was shattered by the experience of the First World War; the unprecedented loss of human life and the duration of the conflict resulted in a profound change in the attitude to conflict. Prior to 1914, conflict had been regarded as part of the natural order of things disagreeable but necessary as an aspect of state power. The pacifist opposition to the war in several European countries and the impact of the individual losses and suffering had an important effect on European public opinion. The scale of suffering was such that between 1914–18 more people were killed than in all the prior European conflicts of the the 19th century. Moreover, European nations had fought the war in part with conscripted forces so that the impact of the losses was widely felt throughout society. In the immediate aftermath, the main conclusion drawn was that the War had resulted from accident and miscalculation rather than from the intentional aggressive act of a single state. Those gathering in Paris in 1919 saw the need for an international organisation that would include a number of procedural checks to prevent the escalation of normal tensions; Woodrow Wilson and others saw the need for a greater role for law in international relations as well as the requirement for more open diplomatic exchanges in contrast to the secret diplomacy that had characterised the end of the 19th century.

3 THE LEAGUE OF NATIONS SYSTEM (1919–45)

The draftsmen of the Covenant of the League of Nations thought that the important matter was to provide procedural steps that would prevent the outbreak of war. The operative provision was contained in Art 12.1 of the Covenant which provided:

---

14 An example being the Treaty Protecting Belgium of 1839.

> The Members of the League agree that if there should arise between them any dispute likely to lead to a rupture, they will submit the matter either to arbitration or to inquiry by the Council, and they agree in no case to resort to war until three months after the award by the arbitrators or the report by the Council.

This provision reflected the movement towards peaceful settlement of disputes that had been growing in the years prior to 1914 and it was also drafted to include a compulsory 'cooling off' period; some in 1919 felt that conflict had arisen in 1914 because the mobilisation timetables of the European states had not allowed sufficient time for a diplomatic solution to be constructed. The provisions of Art 12 were supplemented by Art 13 which stipulated that members of the League should submit disputes to arbitration. If for any reason this was not done, then parties agreed under Art 15 to submit such disputes to the Council of the League and to await any report by the Council and to wait a period of three months before any recourse to war. In addition to these provisions, a broad restriction on the use of force was contained in Art 10 of the Covenant which read:

> The Members of the League undertake to respect and preserve as against external aggression the territorial integrity and existing political independence of all Members of the League. In case of any such aggression or in case of any threat or danger of such aggression the Council shall advise upon the means by which this obligation shall be fulfilled.

It has been suggested that there is some inconsistency in the provisions of Art 10 and Arts 12–15 of the Covenant but the general principle was that the Council of the League would act as the final arbiter. In the years after 1919 attempts were made to strengthen the provisions of the Covenant by introducing more express condemnation of the use of force. Thus, the Charter was followed by a Draft Treaty on Mutual Assistance (1923) and a Protocol for the Settlement of International Disputes (1924). Under the terms of the Protocol force was to be restricted to resistance to acts of aggression or where it had been sanctioned by the Council of the League. Although the Protocol did not receive sufficient ratifications to enter into force the basic idea was taken further in the Treaty for the Renunciation of War (sometimes known as the Kellogg-Briand Pact or the Pact of Paris). Article 1 of the treaty renounced war as an instrument of national policy while Art 2 pledged states to settle disputes by peaceful means. The Kellogg-Briand Pact was signed on August 27 1928 and entered into force on July 24 1929. Although the Pact did not deal with the use force short of war and while it did not prevent conflict it was ratified by a large number number of states and contributed to a clear distinction between the aggressive war and measures taken in self-defence and those situations where the use of force was authorised by the Legaue of Nations. In stressing the general prohibition of war followed by a number of strictly limited exceptions it represented the starting point of the modern law. Thus, the aggressive acts by Japan, Italy and Germany which culminated in the Second World War came to be condemned in legal terms as breaches of the Covenant of the League of Nations and the Kellogg-Briand Treaty of 1928. The readiness to condemn aggressive conduct was illustrated by the Stimson Doctrine of 1931 which was endorsed by the League of Nations in 1932 and held that acquisitions of territory by force were not to be recognised. Thus, many of the elements now found in the United Nations Charter (1945) had actually been put in place before 1939.

4 THE UNITED NATIONS CHARTER AND THE USE OF FORCE[15]

The draftsmen of the United Nations Charter intended to put in place an international organisation charged with maintaining international peace and security. To achieve this aim it was necessary to place restrictions on the use of force. Thus, Arts 2.3 and 2.4 set out the general position:

> 2.3 All Members shall settle their international disputes by peaceful means in such a manner that international peace and security, and justice are not endangered.

> 2.4 All Members shall refrain in their international relations from the threat or use of force against the territorial integrity or independence of any state, or in any other manner inconsistent with the Purposes of the United Nations.[16]

A number of points can usefully be made. First, Art 2.3 stresses the importance of the peaceful resolution of disputes. Secondly, Art 2.4 is widely drawn to refer not to 'war' but to 'the threat or use of force'. Thirdly, both articles must be read with Art 1.1 which sets the prime objective of the organisation being to 'maintain international peace and security'. Fourthly, it is relevant to add that Art 2.6 of the Charter specifies that non-members of the Organisation shall respect these principles so that international peace and security may be preserved.

The provisions themselves were expanded upon in the 1970 Declaration on Principles of International Law, in which it was stressed that force should not be used settle international issues. Secondly, that a war of aggression constituted an international crime and that boundary disputes should not be settled by the threat or use of force. Thirdly, that states must avoid armed reprisals and should not organise acts of civil strife in the territory of anther state.

The wording of Art 2.4 has not been without difficulty. One question that arises is whether the expression 'force' extends beyond armed force to economic pressure. The 1970 Declaration of Principles on International Law recalls the duty of states to refrain from economic coercion and Art 1 of the International Covenant on Civil and Political Rights (1966) guarantees to peoples the right to 'freely pursue their economic, social and cultural development'. There seems a reasonable case on the construction of Art 2.4 for holding the expression 'force' to include economic duress not least because any other interpretation would be inconsistent with the general duty to preserve friendly relations among nations. That the wording extends to threats of force was accepted by the International Court of Justice in the *Advisory Opinion on the Legality of the Threat or Use of Nuclear Weapons*[17] although the Court accepted that the mere possession of such weapons would not constitute a threat.

---

15 See generally, T Franck, 'Who killed Article 2(4)?' (1970) 64 AJIL 809; L Henkin, 'The reports of the death of Article 2(4) are greatly exaggerated' (1971) 65 AJIL 544; C Warbrick, 'The invasion of Kuwait by Iraq' (1991) 40 ICLQ 482, 965; C Gray, 'After the ceasefire, Iraq, the Security Council and the use of force' (1994) 65 BYIL 135.

16 It is worthy of note that the obligations are imperative: 'shall settle' and 'shall refrain' being the terms employed.

17 (1996) ICJ 66.

In those circumstance in which Art 2(4) has been alluded to by the International Court of Justice the tendency has been to give it a broad interpretation[18] and to regard it as setting out a general prohibition on the threat or use of force subject to a limited number of exceptions. Of these exceptions, there were originally four, although only two are of practical significance today. These are: (a) the right to use force in self-defence; (b) the right to use force when authorised by the United Nations Security Council; (c) force undertaken by the five major powers before the Security Council was functional; and (d) the use of force against 'enemy' states. The first two of these will be considered below and the second two are of now of only limited interest. Article 106 permitted the collective use of force before the Security Council was functional and Arts 53 and 107 permitted action against the enemy states of the Second World War.

In considering Art 2(4) it is important to remember that it was drafted at a time when statesmen were reflecting on the cost of all out conflict. It was not intended to restrict the power of a state within its own borders as is indicated by the prohibition of force 'against the territorial integrity or political independence of any State'. The intention was to create an international community in which change was not sought by force; in respect of cases of injustice it was hoped that these could be dealt with through the offices of the United Nations but that the maintenance of peace was to preferable to unilateral action. However, before exploring these matters further it is necessary to say a word about classification.

5 CLASSIFICATION

It is usual to classify the acts that a state might adopt and the three most important today are retorsion, reprisals and the exercise of the right of self-defence. It is necessary to say a little about each.

(a) Retorsion

Retorsion is a lawful act which is intended to injure a wrongdoing state normally as a method of retaliation against its conduct. The purpose of such a act is to demonstrate displeasure while preserving the forms of legality. For example, if state A were to expropriate the property of the citizens of state B then state B might reply by breaking off diplomatic relations or suspending foreign aid. Normally such conduct will be implemented under specific municipal legislation. The forms of retorsion may vary from the breaking off of diplomatic relations or the termination of foreign aid to the implementation of travel restrictions or the control of aliens; in some cases retorsion may take the form of fiscal measures.

The question arises as to the legitimacy of such measures under the United Nations Charter. Under the terms of Art 2.3, states are obliged to settle their disputes by peaceful means in such a manner that international peace and security and justice are not endangered. Clearly this places limits on the possible acts of retorsion.

---

18   *Corfu Channel (The Merits)* (1949) ICJ 4; *Nicaragua v United States (The Merits)* (1986) ICJ 14.

(b) Reprisals[19]

A reprisal is an act undertaken to redress an injury in time of peace. It is an act that would otherwise be a violation of international law, but is not so regarded if it is done in response to a prior unlawful act. A reprisal may be forcible or non-forcible.

The classic case on the law of reprisals is the *Naulilaa* case,[20] which arose out of a dispute between Germany and Portugal. In 1914, German forces raided the Portuguese colony of Angola destroying property following the mistaken killing of three German citizens who were lawfully in the territory. At a later date, Portugal brought a claim for compensation and Germany asserted that the action was a lawful reprisal. The tribunal rejected this assertion and held that there were three requirements to be met for a reprisal to be adjudged lawful. First, there had to be a previous violation of international law. Secondly, the reprisal had to be preceded by an unsuccessful attempt to claim redress and third, the reprisal must be proportionate to the injury suffered. On the facts the arbitral tribunal rejected the German defence.

It is now the case that while non-forcible reprisals may be undertaken within the Naulilaa framework forcible reprisals are subject to Art 2(4) of the United Nations Charter and will be unlawful unless they can be justified as an exercise of legitimate self-defence. It is often difficult to draw a distinction between self-defence and reprisals but the former is normally defensive action to repel while the latter is often retributive or punitive action.

Although there are documented examples of reprisals[21] the most controversial instance in recent years was on 15 April 1986 when the United States bombed various targets within Libya claiming this to be a legitimate reprisal following allegations that Libya had been behind indiscriminate violence against American citizens in Europe. It is quite clear that the United Nations Charter places limits on the forcible reprisal and this was emphasised in the Declaration on Principles of International Law Concerning Friendly Relations and Co-operation Among States in Accordance with the United Nations Charter adopted by the General Assembly on 24 October 1970, which states 'States have a duty to refrain from acts of reprisal involving the use of force'. In these circumstances, a state may seek to emphasise the element of lawful self-defence rather than that of reprisal. Although there is no strict usage in recent years 'reprisals' are often described as 'counter measures'.

(c) Pacific blockade

In time of war, it is usual to blockade the ports of a belligerent state to curtail trade and thus bring pressure on an adversary. However, the pacific blockade is a blockade

---

19 R Falk, 'The Beirut raid and the international law of retaliation' (1969) 63 AJIL 415; Y Blum, 'The Beirut raid and the international double standard' (1970) 64 AJIL 73; DW Bowett, 'Reprisals including recourse to armed force' (1972) 66 AJIL 1; RW Tucker, 'Reprisals and self defence: the customary law' (1972) 66 AJIL 581.

20 The *Naulilaa* case (1928) 2 RIAA 1011; 4 ILR 526.

21 The expulsion of Hungarians from Yugoslavia in 1935 and the shelling of the Spanish port of Almeira by German vessels in 1937.

employed in time of peace and it is sometimes classified as a form of reprisal. The practice of the pacific blockade developed in the 19th century when the stronger naval power wished to apply pressure against a weaker state. The pacific blockade is often thought of as a more flexible instrument than that of a declaration of war. It is generally agreed that in the case of a pacific blockade that the blockading state has no right to seize the maritime vessels of third states.

Although the pacific blockade is carried out in time of peace, it is as regards the blockaded state a hostile act and, being akin to a forcible reprisal, it must be very doubtful whether it can be described as consistent with the United Nations Charter, not least because it cannot be described as a peaceful method of dispute resolution under the terms of Art 33. Indeed, the enforcement nature of the pacific blockade is such that it is one of the methods that the Security Council may authorise under Art 42 to 'maintain or restore international peace or security'.

The best known example of the pacific blockade arose in October 1962[22] when the United States put in place such a blockade in respect of Cuba. This was a particularly unusual situation for a number of reasons. First, the main dispute was between the United States and the Soviet Union. Secondly, the main purpose was to intercept certain military equipment destined for Cuba. Thirdly, the vessels of third party states en route to Cuba might be subject to search. Fourthly, the United States purported to be acting following a resolution of the Organisation of American States and described the action as one of quarantine. Although many accepted[23] that such a blockade was contrary to Art 2(4), there was much comment that the action was justified either as a measure of regional enforcement or as an exercise in anticipatory self-defence.

A slightly different example was afforded by the announcement by the United Kingdom Government of a 200 mile Total Exclusion Zone (TEZ) around the Falkland Islands on 28 April 1982. The measure was part of the military operations designed to retake the Falkland Islands and was thus justified as a measure of self-defence under Art 51 of the United Nations Charter. As the purpose of the announcement was to make military operations possible this was not an example of a pacific blockade.

(d) The use of force in self-defence

A further relevant category is that of self-defence. It is very rare for force to be used today without one or other side claiming to act in self-defence. For this reason, it is important to examine this concept in some detail below.

---

22   See RF Kennedy, *Thirteen Days, A Memoir of the Cuban Missile Crisis*, 1968.
23   L Meeker, 'Defensive quarantine and the law' (1963) 57 AJIL 515; C Christol, 'Maritime quarantine: the naval interdiction of offensive weapons and associated material to Cuba' (1963) 57 AJIL 525; Q Wright, 'The Cuban quarantine' (1963) 57 AJIL 546; M McDougal, 'The Soviet-Cuban quarantine and self defence' (1963) 57 AJIL 597.

6 THE USE OF FORCE IN SELF-DEFENCE[24]

In customary international law it was well recognised that the state might employ force in self-defence. Provided a state acted within the formulation in the *Caroline* case,[25] there could be no objection. In that case, British citizens seized and destroyed a vessel in an American port. This action had taken place because it was believed that the *Caroline*[26] was supplying American nationals who had been mounting operations in Canadian territory. In subsequent correspondence with the United Kingdom Government, the Secretary of State Daniel Webster[27] argued that any action in self-defence must meet the test of necessity and proportionality. For the situation to be one of self-defence, there must be evidence of 'a necessity of self-defence, instant, overwhelming, leaving no choice of means and no moment for deliberation'. In respect of the response, Webster argued that it should be proportionate 'since the act, justified by the necessity of self-defence must be limited by that necessity and kept clearly within it'. The principle of self-defence had been acknowledged from the time of Aquinas, but the virtue of the *Caroline* test was that it set out certain criteria by which it could be determined whether there had been a legitimate exercise of the right; the test stressed that the action must be necessary and the means employed proportionate. The test was accepted by the United Kingdom and came to be accepted as part of customary international law. The test was referred to in the Nuremberg War Trials and in the Security Council debates on the Cuban Missile Crisis (1962), the Middle East War (1967) and the bombing of the Osarik Nuclear Reactor (1981).

When the United Nations Charter (1945) was being drawn up, it was therefore quite natural to include some reference to the principle of self-defence and this was included in Art 51 which reads in full:

Nothing in the present Charter shall impair the inherent right of individual or collective self-defence if an armed attack occurs against a Member of the United Nations, until the Security Council has taken measures necessary to maintain international peace and security. Measures taken by members in the exercise of this right of self-defence shall be immediately

---

24 See generally, DW Bowett, *Self Defence in International Law*, 1958; I Brownlie, *International Law and the Use of Force by States*, 1963; Y Dinstein, *War, Aggression and Self Defence*, 2nd edn, 1994. See also, D Grieg, 'Self defence and the Security Council: what does Article 51 require?' (1991) 40 ICLQ 366; J Hargrove, 'The *Nicaragua* judgment and the future of the law of force and self defence' (1987) 81 AJIL 135.

25 The *Caroline* case (1841) 29 British and Foreign State Papers 1137–38; 30 British and Foreign State Papers 195–96. Daniel Webster (1782–1852) served as Secretary of State 1841–43. In 1842, he helped negotiate the Ashburton Treaty which fixed the Maine-Canada border.

26 In actual fact, the *Caroline* was seized in the State of New York, set on fire and cast adrift so that it fell over the Niagara Falls; two United States citizens were killed in the incident. See RY Jennings, 'The *Caroline* and *McLeod* cases' (1938) 32 AJIL 82.

27 The actual incident took place on 29 December 1837 and resulted in a complaint by Secretary of State Forsyth in January 1838 to the British Government. The advice of the Law Officers had been that the case was one of self defence and the matter was not progressed until 1840, when a charge of murder was brought against one Alexander McLeod. In 1842, the British Government sent Lord Ashburton to Washington to negotiate a settlement of the boundary dispute between Canada and the United States and the formulation advanced by Secretary Webster was made in a letter to Ashburton in July 1842 (which repeated the contents of a letter of July 1841). McLeod, who had boasted of his participation in the incident, was released by a New York court in October 1841 on grounds of lack of evidence. See RY Jennings, 'The *Caroline* and *McLeod* cases' (1938) 32 AJIL 82. Webster and Lord Ashburton negotiated the Treaty of Washington (1842) which settled the boundary in Maine.

reported to the Security Council and shall not in any way affect the authority and responsibility of the Security Council under the present Charter to take at any time such action as it deems necessary in order to maintain or restore international peace and security.

Problems have arisen over the interpretation of Art 51 and the precise circumstances in which the right to self-defence may be exercised. First, the employment of the word 'inherent' may indicate that the framers did not intend to curtail rights arising in customary international law. Secondly, the use of the expression 'if an armed attack occurs against a Member' raised the question as to whether preventive or anticipatory self-defence is permissible. It has to be acknowledged that there are two schools of thought on the subject. One school argues that Art 51 is the only relevant law on self-defence and properly interpreted it prohibits anticipatory self-defence.[28] The other school of thought rejects this view and draws upon the failure of collective security in the post-1945 period.[29] Although the matter was raised in argument in the *Nicaragua* case,[30] it was not necessary for the International Court of Justice to rule on the question.

Those who place a narrow ambit on Art 51 argue that Art 2(4) places a total ban on the use of force and that Art 51 is an exception which must like all exceptions be interpreted strictly to prevent undermining the general principle. Secondly, they argue that the fact of an armed attack is easier to identify and provides a surer foundation to permit action. Thirdly, they argue that the wording of Art 53 would be redundant if Art 51 permitted anticipatory self-defence. In contrast, those who seek to establish a wider meaning for Art 51 argue that the reference to 'inherent' indicates that two rights exist, namely those arising under customary international law and those arising under Art 51 and there is some support for this view in the *Nicaragua* case. In practice, the question will be one of evidence; an attack on state A may be foreseeable or it may be imminent or it may be taking place. The Security Council debates in the period since 1945 indicate that states are nervous about introducing any concept of anticipatory self-defence because it undermines international order by leaving too much discretion to the individual state. Thus, the United States did not prey the concept in aid during the *Cuban Missile* crisis in 1962. Five years later, Israel argued in the context of the Middle East War (1967) that there was such a right if it could be shown that an attack was not merely foreseeable but imminent. In 1981, when the Security Council debated the bombing by Israel of the nuclear reactor near Baghdad even those states that were prepared to accept that force could be used in a pre-emptive fashion held that it must be demonstrated that the threat was imminent and all other means of addressing the threat had been exhausted. It was pointed out by more than one delegate that if Art 51 were to be interpreted to give a wide right to preventive action then this would undermine the role of the Security Council under Art 39.

It is arguable that more light is shed on the subject by sticking to first principles. In the modern world, the state that employs force has to justify it before the court of world opinion. If a state claims that it is acting in self-defence, then it will have to produce evidence that its actions are both necessary and proportionate;[31] this will depend on the

---

28 Included among such writers are I Brownlie, Y Dinstein, L Henkin, and P Jessup.
29 Included among such writers are J Stone, W O'Brien, D Bowett and M McDougal.
30 *Nicaragua v United States* (1986) ICJ 14.
31 *Ibid; Legality of the Threat or Use of Nuclear Weapons* (1996) ICJ 66.

circumstances, but it will also depend on whether there was sufficient time for alternative courses of action to be adopted bearing in mind the overall duty under Arts 2(3) and 33 of resolving disputes peacefully. As experience since 1945 indicates, when a state purports to act in self-defence the legitimacy of its action will have to be justified before the Security Council. It would seem from the debates on the subject in 1962, 1967 and 1981 that any state seeking to defend preventive action bears a heavy *onus probandi* and would have to demonstrate: (a) evidence of a serious threat; (b) evidence that all peaceful methods to resolve the problem have been exhausted; (c) evidence that the threat is imminent not merely foreseeable; (d) evidence that the action taken was proportionate and directed to relieving the imminent threat.

It follows from the above that the law of self-defence cannot be preyed in aid to justify the seizure of territory. Articles 2(3) and 33 require states to settle their disputes by peaceful means so that a state in possession of territory is entitled to to rely on the principle of self-defence even if the aggressor claims to hold a better title. Thus, in 1982 and 1990, the United Kingdom and Kuwait were entitled to rely on the principle of self-defence on the invasion of their sovereign territory.

A further matter that requires to be noted is that Art 51 refers to both individual and collective self-defence. The distinction between individual and collective self-defence has proved more troublesome than at first might seem apparent. In logical terms, there are four possibilities: (i) individual self-defence individually exercised, that is, state A attacks state B and state B exercises its individual right of self-defence; (ii) individual self-defence collectively exercised, that is, where state A attacks states B, C and D and these states each exercise their own rights of self-defence; (iii) collective self-defence individually exercised, that is, where state A attacks state B and state C although beyond the range of attack comes to the aid of state B; and (iv) collective self-defence collectively exercised, that is, where state A attacks state B and state C and state D join together to resist such an attack.

However, these technicalities have had little impact on state practice. After 1945, few states had the economic resources to defend themselves so that both NATO and the Warsaw Pact came into existence, relying on the right of collective self-defence set out in Art 51. Under the terms of Art 5 of the NATO Treaty (1949), an attack on one state is to be treated as an attack on all. It has been assumed since 1945 that a right of collective self-defence existed both in customary international law and under the Charter. However, there is a danger that 'the notion of collective self-defence is open to abuse and it is necessary to ensure that it is not employable as a mere cover for aggression disguised as protection'.[32] In the *Nicaragua* case,[33] the Court recognised that a right of collective self-defence existed at customary international law and also under the Charter. However, to ensure against abuse the Court stipulated a number of procedural safeguards. Thus, there must be evidence of an armed attack by state A against state B. Secondly, state B must form its own view that it has been subject to an armed attack. Thirdly, after making such an assessment state B must make a request for assistance by state C. Fourthly, state C must not exercise the right of collective self-defence simply on the basis of its own assessment of the situation. Clearly, such guidelines serve a useful purpose; collective self-defence may prevent the strong state abusing the weaker state but it is a practice that

---

32 Judge Jennings in the *Nicaragua* case.
33 *Nicaragua v United States* (1986) ICJ 14.

could be abused and it does carry with it the risk of spreading any conflict. It must also be open to question as to whether the whole matter is partly academic. If state A attacks state B then state B may exercise its own individual right of self-defence under Art 51 but it is obliged to report such measures to the Security Council who will then take cognisance of the issue and indicate how and in what manner force is to be used; so that if state C comes to the aid of state B it would normally do so following a Security Council resolution.

An example is afforded by the invasion of Kuwait in August 1990. The invasion was followed by a request from Kuwait for other states to help restore its sovereign territory. In the circumstances the request was made to the Security Council and the economic and military measures taken thereafter were undertaken under the authority of Security Council resolutions but the action was in essence collective and the collective right was referred to in Security Council resolutions.[34]

7 INTERVENTION TO PROTECT NATIONALS[35]

In the 19th century, it came to be accepted in customary international law that a state might have a right to intervene to protect the lives of its own nationals. This is, of course, distinct from humanitarian intervention where the purpose of action is to protect the lives of other nationals. The right has a certain logic; if a national of state A travels to state B he is entitled to expect that the government of that state will as a matter of constitutional law and the law of state responsibility protect his person and his property. Situations may arise where there is no functioning government in state B or the government is unwilling or unable to protect foreign citizens. In those circumstances, it is argued that state A as an aspect of the law of self-defence has the right to intervene to protect the lives of its own nationals. This right has to be distinguished from those situations where a state intervenes to protect its nationals with the consent of the other state.

While there is a danger that any such right might be abused and such a right tends to favour the powerful state with the military forces to execute a rescue mission, the fact remains that there have been a number of incidents since 1945 where this particular right has been invoked. In 1946, the United Kingdom moved troops to the Iran-Iraq border to protect its nationals in Iran. Between 1960 and 1964, Belgium and the United States used military force in the Belgium Congo to protect the lives of their nationals. In 1965, the United States intervened in the Dominican Republic and, in 1976, executed a rescue mission in Lebanon; in both instances, it argued that law and order had broken down and that it had the right to rescue its own nationals. In July 1976, Israeli airborne commandoes stormed a plane in Entebbe, Uganda to rescue 96 Israeli citizens taken hostage. In April 1980, the United States unsuccessfully employed force to rescue diplomats and consular officials held in Iran and justified the attempt as an exercise of the right to protect its own nationals. In 1983, one of the reasons given for the invasion of Grenada was the desire to protect foreign nationals following the instigation of a 'shoot on sight curfew'. In 1989,

34 See Security Council Resolution 1990/661.
35 M Akehurst, 'The use of force to protect nationals abroad' (1977) 5 International Relations 3.

Secretary of State James Baker explained that one of the reasons for intervention in Panama was a desire to save the lives of United States citizens. In 1990, when law and order had broken down in Liberia, the United States used force to rescue foreign nationals. In that case it was explained that the intervention was limited to saving human life and there was no intention to intervene in the domestic affairs of Liberia.

On most occasions, if nationals are rescued from a dangerous environment then other states will react sympathetically, particularly as is often the case the rescuing state has been prepared to rescue the nationals of other states. The evidence indicates that the intervening power will normally be a western state and the intervention will take place in a politically unstable part of the world. Although some scholars question whether the rescuing of foreign nationals is compatible with Art 2(4) and Art 51, a considerable number of writers take the opposite view.[36] They argue that the rescuing of foreign nationals is: (a) the survival of a pre-Charter practice; (b) consistent with Art 51; and (c) a use of force below the threshold of Art 2(4); (d) that the Security Council may be unable to act itself; (e) that the rescuing state is simply acting to protect human rights.

In respect of foreign nationals, the first distinction is whether the rescuing state has actually been invited by a functioning government. If it has not, then it will be legally safe in acting if the only purpose for its action is to rescue foreign nationals and any force used is proportionate and directed to preserving human life. It is likely that such interventions will continue; since 1945, developments in news reporting have enabled the live transmission of pictures of foreign conflicts. In such circumstances, a government is unable to take no action when there is a threat to the lives of significant numbers of its nationals. Another complexity is that, in some cases, the foreign nationals may be government employees so that the duty placed on the government is inescapable. It seems that this area of law can no longer be viewed in isolation but must be considered with reference to the law of state responsibility and the wider framework of human rights protection.

8 INTERVENTION ON HUMANITARIAN GROUNDS[37]

It is argued that distinct from rights in respect of foreign nationals there is a right to intervene on humanitarian grounds.[38] For an intervention to be justified on humanitarian

---

36 Professor Reisman, Professor Lillich and Professor McDougal.

37 See RB Lillich (ed), *Humanitarian Intervention and the United Nations*, 1973; T Franck and N Rodley, 'After Bangladesh: the law of humanitarian intervention by military force' (1973) 67 AJIL 287.

38 Since the end of the Cold War, one can point to three interventions of a humanitarian nature not expressly authorised by the Security Council: (i) the ECOWAS/ECOMOG intervention in Liberia in 1990/1991; (ii) the intervention to protect the Kurdish and Shi'a populations in Iraq in 1991/1992; (iii) the NATO intervention to protect the people of Kosovo. In the case of Kosovo, while there was not the express sanction of a Security Council Resolution it is germane to observe that SC Res 1199 (1998) had demanded that all parties to the conflict 'take immediate steps to improve the humanitarian situation and avert the impending humanitarian catastrophe'. In the case of Kosovo, there was a fear that any further Security Council Resolution might have been vetoed by China or Russia. A contrast is afforded by the intervention in East Timor in 1999, where the Australian government sought a Security Council Resolution before participating in the United Nations Mission in East Timor (UNAMET); this was provided by SC Res 1264 (1999). In all four situations (Liberia, Iraq, Kosovo, East Timor), there was reason to believe that the relevant government was unable or unwilling to restrain abuses of human rights and that a humanitarian crisis might ensue.

grounds, four aspects normally have to be considered. First, there must be within the state in question an immediate threat to human rights, particularly a threat of extensive loss of human life. Secondly, the intervention must be limited to protecting basic human rights. Thirdly, the action is one that has not been taken at the invitation of the government of the territory. Fourthly, the action is not one taken under the authority of a Security Council Resolution. The difficulty lies in identifying an example because, in many of the cases of humanitarian intervention, there may be other motives such as the desire to rescue foreign nationals or the wish to put in place a particular government. Some of the interventions, such as that of Belgium in the Congo in 1960, 1963 and 1964 or the United States in the Dominican Republic in 1965, had motives other than the simply humanitarian concern. Some writers point to the Indian invasion of East Pakistan in 1971 as an example, but this was not stressed by India in its contribution to subsequent Security Council debates; it cannot be said that the Indonesian invasion of East Timor in 1975 or the South African involvement in Angola meet the test of humanitarian intervention. It is arguable that the role of French force in the overthrow of the ruler of the Central African Republic came closest to the humanitarian objective. It was argued in 1983 that the invasion of Grenada constituted a humanitarian intervention but the invasion was also justified as a regional peacekeeping action and an operation designed to protect foreign nationals. So even if a right of humanitarian intervention is accepted, it is difficult to find clear cases in the post-war world.

Against this, there are those writers who deny any right of humanitarian intervention. They argue that the object of the United Nations Charter is to maintain international peace and that the United Nations has a monopoly right to use force save in cases of individual or collective self-defence and that to permit otherwise would be to countenance abuse. It is arguable that in the post-Cold War period one can point to three examples of humanitarian intervention not expressly authorised by the Security Council. These are the ECOWAS/ECMOG intervention in Liberia in 1990/1991; the intervention to protect the Kurdish and Shi'a populations in Iraq in 1991/1992; and the NATO intervention to protect the people of Kosovo in 1999.[39] What seems to be emerging is that if a state is unable or unwilling to protect human rights and regional instability and a humanitarian crisis ensues then intervention may be sought under this head.

The nature of any right of humanitarian intervention came to a head during the NATO military action in Kosovo in the form of Operation Allied Force (26 March 1999–10 June 1999). The military action was *prima facie* an intervention in a foreign state and contrary to Art 2(4) of the United Nations Charter; it was outside the ambit of Art 51 and had not been expressly authorised by Security Council.[40] The question arose as to whether any right of humanitarian intervention existed in customary international law or whether it was in the process of emerging; the following points are relevant:

---

39 The Kosovo situation had been the subject of a number of Security Council Resolutions which, even if they did not expressly authorise the use of force, made it abundantly clear that the Security Council viewed the humanitarian situation with concern; see SC Res 1160 (31 March 1998); SC Res 1199 (23 September 1998); SC Res 1203 (24 October 1998); SC Res 1207 (17 November 1998). For a review of the background, see D Kritsiotis, 'The Kosovo crisis and Nato's application of armed force against the Federal Republic of Yugoslavia' (2000) 49 ICLQ 330.

40 Of the relevant Security Council resolutions, Resolution 1160 (1988) stressed the need for 'peaceful resolution' of the crisis in Kosovo while Resolutions (1199) (1998) and 1203 (1998) and 1207 (1998) do not contain language justifying the use of force.

(i) The balance of textbook opinion in 1999 (that is, at the time of the action) doubted whether there was a right of humanitarian intervention in the absence of express Security Council Resolution.[41]

(ii) However, it had been asserted as early as November 1998 that 'a limited use of force was justifiable in support of purposes laid down by the Security Council but without the council's express authorisation when that was the only means to avert an immediate and overwhelming humanitarian catastrophe'.[42]

(iii) Recent years have seen growing emphasis on the protection of human rights and, in recent years, the Security Council has characterised the most serious violations of human rights where there has been widespread loss of life as threats to international peace and security.[43]

(iv) If the Security Council cannot authorise conduct to prevent threats to international peace and security because of the threat of a veto should not other states be able to act to restrain extreme abuses?

(v) While any right of international humanitarian intervention might be abused most legal rights in municipal or international law are capable of abuse; this is not a valid argument against the existence of such a right.[44]

(vi) If as seems arguable that a right of international humanitarian intervention may be emerging then the criteria would seem to be:[45]

   (a) prior determination by the Security Council of a grave crisis threatening international peace and security;

   (b) articulation by the Security Council of specific policies for the resolution of the crisis, the implementation of which can be secured or furthered by armed intervention;

   (c) objectively verified evidence of a grave humanitarian emergency;

   (d) that such an emergency can only be averted by the use of force;[46]

   (e) that intervention should be by a multilateral force;

   (f) that the objectives of such action are directed simply to averting the humanitarian catastrophe;

   (g) that throughout such action the force used is restricted to the limited objective.

Thus, it would seem following the Kosovo intervention that the best opinion is either that a last resort right of international humanitarian intervention exists or that it is in the

---

41   See I Brownlie (2000) 49 ICLQ 878 (being a memorandum prepared for the House of Commons Foreign Affairs Committee).
42   See Baroness Symons (Minister of State Foreign Office), HL Debs (1998–1999) WA 140, 16 Nov 1998.
43   C Greenwood, 'International law and the Nato intervention in Kosovo' (2000) 49 ICLQ 926.
44   Ibid.
45   See C Greenwood (2000) 49 ICLQ 926 (who takes the view that such a right of last resort exists) and V Lowe, 'International legal issues arising from the Kosovo crisis' (2000) 49 ICLQ 934 (who takes the view that such a right is emerging).
46   This must mean that efforts at a negotiated solution have been tried.

process of emerging but that it is is subject to very strict criteria. Manifestly it is preferable to secure the express authorisation of a Security Council Resolution.[47]

9 FORCE EXPRESSLY AUTHORISED BY THE UNITED NATIONS

While Art 2(4) of the United Nations Charter places a broad prohibition on the use of force, it is provided that under Chapter VII of the Charter the Security Council may authorise the use of force where there is a threat to international peace and security.[48] Because this aspect concerns the constitutional powers of the Security Council this exception is considered in the chapter concerning the United Nations. It should be noted at this point that there are some who take the view that all acts of force other than in self-defence are unlawful unless covered by an express Security Council resolution. The difficulty with this view is that it would mean that a state was powerless to act to restrain a humanitarian catastrophe in the absence of a Security Council resolution which cannot be obtained because of fear of a veto.

10 CIVIL WARS[49]

It is rare since 1945 for one state to seek to enlarge its territory by invading another. More common is the civil war which might be fought for control of a government or it may be borne out of a desire to secede. It may be that one group simply wishes the central government to grant a degree of regional autonomy. It may be that the civil war is founded on an ideological struggle with outside states backing one or other side. Technically, international law regards civil war as an internal matter and such conflicts tend only to involve the outside world when they contribute to regional instability, threaten established interests or result in allegations of abuses of human rights. Although the outside world may offer mediation or conciliation, there is a general reluctance on the part of the developed world to send expensive highly trained forces into complex conflicts often borne of ethnic or post-colonial tensions. It is certainly true that a civil war may develop into international problem, as might be said to be the case of the former Yugoslavia.

---

47 In this context, the history is of some relevance. Modern international law and the United Nations Charter (1945) grew out of the human rights abuses that characterised World War II. As Professor Greenwood has noted, 'an interpretation of international law which would forbid intervention to prevent something as terrible as the Holocaust, unless a permanent member could be persuaded to lift its veto, would be contrary to the principles on which modern international law is based ...'; see C Greenwood (2000) 49 ICLQ 926 at 930.

48 See United Nations Charter, Arts 39, 40, 42.

49 R Pinto, 'Les règles du droit international concernant la guerre civile' (1965) 114 HR 451; TJ Farer, 'The regulation of foreign intervention in civil armed conflict' (1974) 142 HR 291; *The International Regulation of Civil Wars* (E Luard (ed)), 1972; *Law and Civil War in the Modern World* (JN Moore (ed)), 1974.

Much practice concerning civil wars are matters of interpretation; each situation has to some extent to be judged on its merits. Even the language is far from uniform. One can speak of the established government or the democratically elected constitutional government; where there is such an entity then the presumption is that it is deserving of external support. One can also refer to rebels or revolutionaries who may exercise *de facto* control over some parts of the country. An interim classification of such groups is to describe them as insurgents while a more formal status is that of belligerents. According to customary international law, belligerent status might be conferred when there is evidence of an armed conflict, where there is *de facto* occupation of a substantial part of state territory, where a responsible body is conducting hostilities in accordance with the rules of war and where it is necessary for external powers to state their position. In practice, however, matters are not so clear cut so that there is little in common between the Spanish Civil War and the subsequent conflicts in Nigeria, Angola and Vietnam. What is clear is that during the years of the Cold War the number of civil wars increased, particularly in post-colonial states, and the resulting conflicts often involved external powers helping one or other faction. It is also clear that the broad prohibition on the use of force contained in Art 2(4) does not extend to civil wars.

It is argued by some states that it is always lawful to aid an established government. If that government has been democratically elected, and is supported by the relevant regional organisation, then it will probably be possible to secure a Security Council resolution regulating conduct. An example is the civil war in Sierra Leone from 1997,[50] when a Security Council resolution was passed designed to indicate support for the democratically elected government and condemning any attempt to give support to rebel forces. However, against this it has to be borne in mind that in some cases an outside power has fraudulently asserted that it is intervening at the behest of an established government as in Hungary (1956), Czechoslovakia (1968) and Afghanistan (1979). In such situations, where the established government is being used as an instrument of oppression the problem arises as to how much aid should be offered to opposition groups. Where the object is to assist a democratically elected government to stay in office, then it is likely that any action will have been co-ordinated not only through the Security Council but also through the relevant regional organisation.[51]

The general view of many states is that there should be no external intervention in a civil war and no attempt to supply weapons to either side. In some situations, such as in Sierra Leone in 1997, if the relevant regional organisation is in agreement, it may be possible to secure a Security Council resolution to this effect. If one reflects on past civil wars – Spain (1936–39), the Belgian Congo (1960), Angola (1975), Yugoslavia (1992) – the situation is often so complex that it is difficult to identify the legitimate government. Many states take the view that any aid to the established government may simply prolong the conflict by encouraging others to aid the insurgents. In some cases, a government may supply weapons but normally it will be reluctant to become further

---

50   See SC Res 1997/1132; 1998/1156; 1998/1162.

51   As has been the case with Sierra Leone since 1997, where the emphasis has been on support for the democratically elected government both through the Organisation of African Unity and through the Security Council. The state of the established government and its standing in the outside world will be relevant; see *Sierra Leone Telecommunications Co Ltd v Barclays Bank plc* [1998] 2 All ER 821 (where *locus standi* in a municipal court was held to depend in part on the nature and extent of recognition by regional organisations).

involved. The lesson to be derived from Yugoslavia (1992–2000) or Sierra Leone (1997–) is that if the civil war threatens regional stability then the problem will be passed to the Security Council who may seek to prevent the conflict spreading by imposing an arms embargo.

In respect of insurgents it seems to be accepted in state practice that it is unlawful for a state to aid insurgents seeking to overthrew the government of another state. As a matter of principle, it is an affront to the sovereignty of that state. The rule was accepted unanimously in GA Res (XX) 2131[52] which stated that 'no state shall organise, assist, foment, finance incite or tolerate subversive terrorist or armed activities directed towards the violent overthrow of the regime of another State, or interfere in civil strife in another state'.

The matter was considered in the *Nicaragua* case,[53] where a majority of the Court found that the United States had been in breach of international law in aiding the *contras* forces in their struggle against the Sandanista government of Nicaragua. In the course of the case, it was necessary for the court to consider the United States' argument that aid to insurgents in Nicaragua was justified as an exercise of the right of collective self-defence, because Nicaragua was allowing weapons to pass to anti-government forces in El Salvador. On the facts, the Court found there had been no armed attack against El Salvador so as to permit the exercise of the right of collective self-defence; it seems from the reasoning of the Court that if Nicaragua had sent troops to aid insurgents in El Salvador then that state and the United States might have been entitled to aid the insurgents in Nicaragua. Although there are a number of differing opinions in the case, it can be taken as authority for the general proposition that it will be unlawful to aid the insurgents against an established government.[54] It probably also follows from the case that if a state is threatened by insurgents who are being aided by foreign troops then it would be lawful for a third state to come to the assistance of the authorities.

A matter that requires comment is that there now seems to be a distinction between those civil wars that destabilise a region and result in Security Council action and those which are subject to the general rule that states should refrain from intervention.

11 FORCE AND SELF-DETERMINATION

As has been indicated elsewhere, the principle of self-determination indicates the right of a people of a particular territory to determine their political status. The principle emerged at the end of the 19th century and it must be distinguished from obligations placed upon states to protect minorities. Although no such right could arise in customary international law, it can be discerned in a number of treaty provisions arising after 1919, which

---

52 GA Res (XX) 2131; 21 December 1965.
53 *Nicaragua v United States* (1986) ICJ 14; see A D'Amato, 'Nicaragua and international law: the 'academic' and the real' (1985) 79 AJIL 657; K Highet, 'Evidence, the Court and the *Nicaragua* case (1987) 81 AJIL 1.
54 See also 1970 Declaration on Principles of International Law which provides that no state 'shall organise, assist, foment, finance, incite or tolerate subversive, terrorist or armed activities directed towards the violent overthrow of the regime of another state, or interfere in civil strife in another state'.

provided that the inhabitants of a particular territory might have the right to a plebiscite. After 1945, the principle was referred to in Arts 1(2), 55, 73 and 76 of the United Nations Charter, although these references are not specific and may be taken to mean either the right to independence or the entitlement to non-interference by others. The difficulty with the principle of self-determination lies in the application; it requires agreement on the 'people' and the 'territory' to which it relates.

Since 1945, the principle has been developed to permit decolonisation on a wide scale. This approach was endorsed in the General Assembly Declaration on the Granting of Independence to Colonial Peoples[55] and is to be found in Art 1 of both the International Covenant on Civil and Political Rights (1966) and the International Covenant on Economic, Social and Cultural Rights (1966). By 1970, the Declaration on the Principles of International Law[56] could declare that states were under a duty refrain from any act which would deprive peoples of their right to self-determination, although the same document went on to assert that nothing should be done to disrupt the territorial integrity of existing states. However, it is generally true that the international community has only been anxious to apply the principle of self-determination in the case of non-self-governing territories, mandated territories and trust territories. In principle, international law has stressed the importance of determining the wishes of the people of a territory.[57]

However, once the movement for decolonisation had run its course by the late 1970s, the international community lost any enthusiasm self-determination[58] and became very concerned about the problems posed by secession and ethnic conflict. Difficulties have arisen in respect of wars of liberation designed to achieve national self-determination. Western states have not been anxious to involve themselves and while there have been a number of General Assembly resolutions on the subject,[59] it has to be admitted that involvement normally comprises only the supply of weapons. There are many aspects about self-determination in the civil war context where the rules are vague or unclear and only become clear where one or other party brings the matter before the Security Council, which is then obliged to try and introduce ground rules to prevent the spread of the dispute and to facilitate a peaceful resolution of the conflict.[60]

12 FORCE IN THE TERRORIST CONTEXT

The use of terrorism has been a phenomenon since at least the time of the French Revolution, when the word came to accepted as describing the employment of violence for political purposes. Although political violence has had a long history, there is some evidence of an increase in terrorist activity at the end of the 19th century when anarchist

---

55   GA Res (1960)(XV) 1514 .

56   Set out in the Annex to Resolution 2625 (XXV) (1970).

57   The *Namibia* case (1971) ICJ 6; the *Western Sahara* case (1975) ICJ 12.

58   The experience the Belgian Congo (1960), Nigeria (1967), Angola (1976), Yugoslavia (1992), Rwanda (1994) having served as reminders of the dangers of secession and ethnic conflict.

59   G A Res 2105 (XX); 2160 (XX); 2465 (XXIII); 2649 (XXV); 2734 (XXV); 2787 (XXVI) 3070 (XXVIII), 3163 (XXVIII); 3421 (XXX).

60   As has been the case in Yugoslavia (1992), Rwanda (1994), Sierra Leone (1997).

and nationalist groups in Europe began more openly to employ violence for political objectives.[61] While there may be differences of definition, the general element of a terrorist offence embraces a violent act with a political objective designed to influence a particular audience. Manifestly, some states may regard a political group as terrorist while other states may regard the same individuals as freedom fighters; indeed, the terrorist leader of yesterday may be accepted as a legitimate constitutional ruler tomorrow. One of the difficulties faced by international law in this area is the division of opinion amongst different states.

The first question that arises is as to the nature of terrorist acts under international law. In normal circumstances, such acts will be subject to criminal jurisdiction under municipal law and attract punishment. On the international plane, it is strongly arguable such acts violate general rules of customary international law and are at variance with the general principles of law recognised by civilised nations.[62] In respect of treaty law, the 1937 Convention for the Prevention and Punishment of Terrorism did not receive sufficient ratifications to come into effect but, since 1945, there have been a considerable number of international instruments providing for the extradition and punishment of those concerned in terrorist acts. Examples are the Hague Convention for the Unlawful Seizure of Aircraft (1970); the Montreal Convention for the Suppression of Unlawful Acts against the Safety of Civil Aviation (1971); the International Convention against the Taking of Hostages (1979); the Convention on the Prevention and Punishment of Crimes against Internationally Protected Persons, Including Diplomatic Agents (1973). So, while it is not possible to point to a comprehensive general treaty, it is clear that on the international plane there are a wide number of instruments that outlaw specific terrorist acts.

It is generally assumed that state involvement in terrorist activity will be a breach of Art 2(4) of the United Nations Charter and this is a view that has been accepted by the Security Council.[63] In similar terms, the General Assembly have unanimously condemned state sponsored terrorist activity.[64]

The next two problems that arise in respect of terrorism are the questions: in what circumstances may a victim state respond to a terrorist incident and how should it do so? If the act is committed by individuals, then the correct course is to collect evidence and to seek the extradition or trial of those responsible. In the period since 1945, state practice has gone further and involved the abduction of suspected terrorists, the assassination of particular terrorists, military action against terrorist bases and military action against states allegedly involved. In cases where the terrorist activity is linked to a particular state, then it would seem that under the United Nations Charter a state should raise the matter first with the Security Council and demand appropriate action. The most debated incident of counter measures against terrorism arose with the United States military action against Libya on 15 April 1986, which later gave rise to eight meetings of the Security Council. The United States argument was that the counter measures against

---

61 See James Joll, *The Anarchists*. Historians have pointed to the number of Heads of State subject to assasination attempts in the period 1890–1914.

62 As stipulated in Art 38 of the Statute of the International Court of Justice.

63 SC Res 748 (1992) concerning the aftermath of the Lockerbie incident .

64 GA Res 40/61, 9 December 1985.

terrorism were justified as a discriminate and proportionate exercise of the right of self-defence. The argument, therefore, on the legality of force as a counter measure on terrorism depends on whether an armed attack has been made on that state, whether the response is timely, proportionate and discriminate. The question, therefore, depends on what form of action against a state constitutes an armed attack; in practice, it would seem that evidence of a pattern is looked for such as attacks on nationals, military personnel and strategic locations. It cannot be said that there is any agreed view on the legitimacy of counter measures against terrorism. However, any state that so acts will have to demonstrate its reasons for acting and this will entail producing evidence of hostile acts directed against it by state sponsored groups. While there are some who regard all reprisals as unlawful under the United Nations Charter, it is probably the case that no state should take it upon itself to adopt forcible counter measures unless and until it has reported the matter to the Security Council and given that body the chance to act.[65]

13 PEACEKEEPING

One of the circumstances in which force may require to be used is in the context of a United Nations peacekeeping operation. In essence, peacekeeping involves the interposition of a military force normally of a multinational character with the consent of the sovereign power and any other factions. The objectives of such a peacekeeping force may be to observe agreed positions or to supervise a negotiated peace accord. The number of such peacekeeping operations[66] has increased greatly since the conclusion of the Cold War but because the topic of peacekeeping raises questions of the constitutional structure of the United Nations it is proposed to consider the topic under that heading.

14 QUESTIONS OF DOCTRINE

There are a number of references in the literature to particular doctrines that are said to have some relevance to the employment of force. The three best known are the Monroe, Johnson and Brezhnev doctrines. None of these constitute rules of international law and simply represent the policy of a state at any particular point in time. The Monroe doctrine of 1823[67] held that the the United States would regard as a threat to its peace and security any further European colonial ambitions in the Western Hemisphere. In the post-colonial world, this is not a valid concern and the United States relations with its neighbours are now conducted under the terms of the Charter of the Organisation of American States (1948).

The second doctrine, the Johnson doctrine, was propounded in 1965 at the time of the sending of a force to the Dominican Republic. At the time, the intervention was explained

---

65 This certainly seems to follow from Arts 33, 34 and 35.1 of the United Nations Charter when read together.

66 The statistics are of some interest; from 1945–85, 13 peacekeeping operations were launched; however, from 1988 to 1994, 21 such operations were launched.

67 Named after James Monroe (1758–1831), Secretary of State 1811–17, 5th President of the United States 1817–25. The doctrine itself represented the response of the United States to the liberation of the Latin American republics by Simon Bolivar and others.

on the grounds of protecting lives of United States citizens and foreign nationals. In justifying the action President Johnson[68] indicated that the United States would not 'permit the establishment of another communist government in the Western hemisphere'. Since the collapse of such regimes after 1989, the statement, which was no more than a statement of United States foreign policy, has little direct relevance.

The third so called doctrine, the Brezhnev doctrine, was a clear affront to the norms of international law. Propounded by Leonid Brezhnev,[69] the doctrine held that the Soviet Union was entitled to regard certain states as within its sphere of influence and had the right to intervene where it adjudged the communist system was threatened. The doctrine was preyed in aid to justify the invasion of Czechoslovakia in 1968 and was raised in argument after the invasion of Afghanistan in 1979. The doctrine was an affront to the basic principle of the sovereign equality of states and did not survive the discrediting of its author. The doctrine was formally abandoned by the Soviet Union in 1989 and is now only of historical interest.

All three doctrines represent no more than statements of foreign policy. Decolonisation has rendered the Monroe doctrine redundant while the collapse of the Soviet Union has reduced the Brezhnev doctrine to being of only of historical interest. The Johnson doctrine[70] is, in its original terms, a dead letter but it has its modern day equivalent in the still strained relations that exist between Cuba and the United States.

15 CONCLUSIONS ON THE RULES PROHIBITING THE USE OF FORCE

It is agreed by most scholars that the threat of a widespread conventional war has diminished in the years since 1945. This fact is not due to international law itself but to changes in public attitude that can be dated to the beginning of the century. The experience of the First World War had a profound effect on society in Europe and the United States, producing a desire to avoid a repetition of the waste and carnage of that conflict. Any romantic notions about war borne out of the 19th century classical curriculum perished in the fields of Flanders. After 1919, statesmen were required to produce an international order in which disputes could be sensibly managed and peacefully resolved. Although the Legaue of Nations failed a general prohibition on the use of force rapidly gained public acceptance.

---

68 Lyndon Johnson (1908–73), 36th President of the United States 1963–69. The statement was influenced by the difficulties that the United States had experienced in dealing with Cuba during the Cuban Missile crisis of 1962. The United States was simply stating its long term foreign policy objective of discouraging any communist regime within the 'sphere of influence of the United States'. Although it is arguable that each state is entitled to choose its own social and economic system (see Art 1 ICESCR 1966), the concern of the United States at this point in the Cold War was that a communist regime might seek to install missiles within striking distance of the United States.

69 Leonid Brezhnev (1906–82), General Secretary of the Communist Party (1964–82). Under Brezhnev Soviet Foreign Policy was directed to expanding Soviet influence in Asia and Africa. Large defence spending served to coerce states of Eastern Europe. However a domestic policy that involved corruption and restraints on civil liberties was not flexible enough to adapt after 1985.

70 At the time of the invasion of Grenada in 1983 the question was raised as to whether this was an application of the Johnson doctrine see Dore, 'The US invasion of Grenada: resurrection of the "Johnson Doctrine?"' (1984) 20 Stan J Int Law 173. However, the three reasons given by President Reagan and Secretary of State Schultz were: (i) to protect US nationals; (ii) to forestall further chaos; (iii) to assist in the restoration of conditions of law and order. (See statement of 25 October 1983).

The experience of the Second World War indicated that the international order needed to be strengthened against potential aggressors and the Nuremberg Trials established the principle that there would be personal liability for those who waged aggressive wars. Secondly, the conflict illustrated that, in a modern war, there were unlikely to be any winners; the economic cost even to a victorious state was likely to be considerable. Thirdly, at the conclusion of the Second World War, the use of nuclear weapons indicated that the costs of any future conflict were likely to be incalculable. Fourthly, in the period from 1900–45, there had been a steady increase in democratic government in Europe so that any spending on defence had to compete with expenditure on other desirable social provision. As the Vietnam conflict (1965–75) was to indicate in the United States no democratic government could sustain a lengthy conflict and impose conscription without having the full support of its own public opinion. Therefore, the broad emphasis of the United Nations Charter in seeking both to outlaw the use of force and to promote the peaceful settlement of disputes, was in harmony with contemporary social developments. Where there have been aggressive acts between states since 1945 then, almost invariably, one of those states is not a functioning democracy; at the time of the invasion of the Falkland Islands in 1982, or of Kuwait in 1990, the invading state was not a functioning democracy operating with a free press under the rule of law. The experience since 1945 indicates that states that operate democratically and respect the civil liberties of their own citizens are most unlikely to threaten their neighbours with the use of armed force.

Since 1945, the two main problems have been the inability of the United Nations to function fully during the Cold War[71] and the increase in the number of civil wars and ethnic conflicts. In respect of the first matter, this is less likely now to be a problem with the collapse of Soviet power in Eastern Europe and a less ideological approach to Russian Foreign Policy. The second matter is more difficult, and the history of post-colonial Africa and post-communist Eastern Europe suggests that civil wars are most likely to pose the most difficult problems concerning the use of armed force. Given that such conflicts have such complex causes and, given the reluctance of major powers to become involved, these are likely to prove the intractable of problems. In some civil wars, the problems arise from an unequal and unjust distribution of wealth, in others there are problems of ethnic identity and demands for regional autonomy. In such conflicts, the rules of customary international law are dangerously vague and the habit of some states in freely selling weapons to the combatants only serves to exacerbate the problem. In the past, some states welcomed the vague nature of customary rules because it allowed them to intervene indirectly in such conflicts. With the ending of the Cold War, it is likely that the Security Council will seek to limit such conflicts by imposing restrictions on the sale of arms to the combatants.

The United Nations system prohibiting the use of force enjoys widespread support. It is worthy of note that those states that have flouted the rules since 1945 if they have not suffered outright military defeat have been subject to severe economic sanctions.[72]

---

71 Because of the ideological divisions of the Cold War and the threat of the use of the veto within the Security Council, at least until the arrival in power of Mikhail Gorbachev in 1985 and the more co-operative and pragmatic foreign policy of his foreign minister, Edvard Schevardnadze.

72 The obvious examples being Argentina (1982), Iraq (1991), Serbia (1999).

CHAPTER 22

THE UNITED NATIONS[1]

1 INTRODUCTION

Although the League of Nations had not been successful in preventing all out conflict in 1939, it was clear to the Allied statesmen during the Second World War that some form of international organisation would have to be established to manage tensions within the international community. The United States Department of State[2] had been working on plans for such an organisation since 1943 and in August 1944 representatives of China, Russia, Britain and the United States met to approve an American plan entitled 'Tentative United States Proposals for a General International Organisation' at Dumbarton Oaks, a country house near Washington DC. The proposal was approved and the terms made public in October 1944. In February 1945, an ailing President Roosevelt met with Winston Churchill and Joseph Stalin at Yalta to agree on post-war reconstruction. They decided that an international conference would meet to settle the new post-war structure at San Francisco in April 1945. By April 1945, France had rejoined the big five and invitations were sent to 46 nations to attend the conference at San Francisco; 45 nations agreed to attend. The San Francisco Conference was opened by President Truman on 25 April 1945 and concluded with the signing of the United Nations Charter on 26 June 1945. It is, therefore, relevant to observe that the Charter was drafted during the Second World War and, thus, proper emphasis was placed on the desire to avoid future conflict.

The United Nations Charter is a lengthy document of 19 Chapters containing 111 articles; however, the general objectives of the Organisation are set out in the Preamble to the Charter and may be summarised as both the maintenance of peace and the promotion of human welfare through social progress.[3] Fifty one states signed the Charter at the conclusion of the San Francisco Conference; under the terms of Art 110, the Charter was not to come into force until it had been ratified by the Big Five states together and a majority of the signatory states. This was obtained relatively quickly and the United Nations Charter came into force on 24 October 1945. The first meeting of the General Assembly took place in London on 10 January 1946. On 18 April 1946, the last session of

---

1   See generally, HG Nicholas, *The United Nations as a Political Institution*, 1959; DW Bowett, *The Law of International Institutions*, 4th edn, 1982; E Luard, *A History of the United Nations*, 1982, Vol 1; A Roberts and B Kingsbury (eds), *United Nations, Divided World*, 2nd edn, 1993; C Joyner (ed), *The United Nations and International Law*, 1997; FS Northedge, *The League of Nations*, 1986; R Righter, *Utopia Lost, The United Nations and World Order*, 1995.

2   The period of gestation was, in fact, much longer and can be traced through: (i) the meeting between FD Roosevelt and Winston Churchill in August 1941 in Newfoundland, Canada, which drew up the Atlantic Charter; (ii) The United Nations Declaration signed by 26 nations on 1 January 1942; (iii) The Moscow Declaration of October 1943 issued by the governments of the United States, the United Kingdom, Russia and China, which provided for a new general international organisation; (iv) the meeting at Dumbarton Oaks in August–October 1944, where final drafts were considered; (v) The San Francisco Conference of April 1945–June 1945.

3   It is of interest that the Preamble stresses the importance of respect for international law, the drafting of the Preamble owed much to the South African Prime Minister JC Smuts (1870–1950).

the League of Nations Assembly was held for the purpose of dissolving both the League and the Permanent Court of International Justice.

Chapter One of the United Nations Charter is devoted to setting out the purposes and principles of the Organisation. The relevant provisions are as follows:

Article 1

The Purposes of the United Nations are:

(1) to maintain international peace and security, and to that end: to take effective collective measures for the prevention and removal of threats to the peace, and for the suppression of acts of aggression or other breaches of the peace, and to bring about by peaceful means, and in conformity with the principles of international law, adjustment or settlement of international disputes or situations which might lead to a breach of the peace;

(2) to develop friendly relations among nations based on respect for the principle of equal rights and self determination of peoples, and to take other appropriate measures to strengthen universal peace;

(3) to achieve international co-operation in solving international problems of an economic, social, cultural, or humanitarian character, and in promoting and encouraging respect for human rights and for fundamental freedoms for all without discrimination as to race, sex, language or religion; and

(4) to be a centre for harmonising the actions of nations in the attainment of these common ends.

Article 2

The Organisation and its Members, in pursuit of the Purposes stated in Article 1, shall act in accordance with the following Principles:

(1) The Organisation is based on the principle of the sovereign equality of all its Members.

(2) All Members, in order to ensure to all of them the rights and benefits resulting from membership, shall fulfil in good faith the obligations assumed by them in accordance with the present Charter.

(3) All Members shall settle their international disputes by peaceful means in such a manner that international peace and security, and justice, are not endangered.

(4) All Members shall refrain in their international relations from the threat or use of force against the territorial integrity or political independence of any State, or in any other manner inconsistent with the purposes of the United Nations.

(5) All Members shall give the United Nations every assistance in any action it takes in accordance with the present Charter, and shall refrain from giving assistance to any State against which the United Nations is taking preventive or enforcement action.

(6) The Organisation shall ensure that States which are not Members of the United Nations act in accordance with these principles so far as may be necessary for the maintenance of international peace and security.

(7) Nothing contained in the present Charter shall authorise the United Nations to intervene in matters which are essentially within the domestic jurisdiction of any State or shall require the Members to submit such matters to settlement under the present

Charter; but this principle shall not prejudice the application of enforcement measures under Chapter VII.

A number of points can usefully be made. First, the objectives of the organisation are wide and are not restricted to the maintenance of international peace and security; equally important is the objective of promoting economic and social progress. Secondly, the Charter itself has been the subject of a number of disputes about interpretation. Under the terms of Art 111, there are five official or authentic texts in Chinese, French, Russian, English and Spanish. In actual fact, the San Francisco conference used English and French as the working languages and the other three texts were translations.[4] Thirdly, while a treaty may be interpreted by reference to the *travaux preparatoires*, this is a rather sensitive matter in the case of the United Nations Charter because the 51 original signatories have now grown to over 180 members.[5] Fourthly, the Charter is founded upon traditional principles of international law so that it provides for the sovereign equality of states and stipulates the need to observe treaty obligations. Fifthly, it should be borne in mind that, in 1945, France and the United Kingdom had large colonial empires so that Art 2(7)[6] was of some importance in preserving the principle that matters within the domestic jurisdiction of a state were excluded. This provision has given rise to much debate in the years after 1945, as the movement for decolonisation began to grow. Sixthly, the intention was that membership should be a permanent obligation so that, unlike the Covenant of the League,[7] no provision was made for withdrawal by a state. Seventhly, it should not be assumed that everything was the subject of agreement at San Francisco; there were spirited debates about the role and duties of the Security Council and the General Assembly. However, there was a widespread acceptance that compromises would have to be made to ensure that a viable international organisation was established. It is important to bear in mind the political background against which the Charter was drawn up; in the spring and summer of 1945, the world learned the full story of events in the concentration camps as Germany and occupied territories were liberated and, in August 1945, nuclear weapons were used for the first time in conflict. In these circumstances, it is understandable that many states took the view that the political imperative was to establish a new international organisation as quickly as possible and leave outstanding questions to be settled on the basis of future negotiations. Finally, in respect of future changes Art 108 provided for amendment of the Charter with the consent of two-thirds of the members of the General Assembly including all of the permanent members of the Security Council.

---

4   One of the most sensitive texts was the Russian version; this was prepared in May 1945 in the Veterans Building in San Francisco by a group that included Isaiah Berlin (1909–97); see Michael Ignatieff, *Isaiah Berlin, A Life*, 1998, pp 132–34.

5   By the end of 1997, the number had increased to 185. Much of the increase is due to decolonisation and later to the break up of the Soviet Union and Yugoslavia. Sometimes, merger can result in reduction, such as when Tanganyika (1961) and Zanzibar (1963) joined together to become Tanzania in 1964. In 1990, the Republic of Yemen became a single member, replacing Yemen (1947) and Democratic Yemen (1967).

6   To be compared with a similar but not identical provision in Art 15(8) of the Covenant of the League of Nations. Such a provision was, of course, desired by the Soviet Union whose system of one party rule was unlikely to survive external investigation.

7   See Art 1(4) of the Covenant of the League of Nations (1919).

2 MEMBERSHIP

A distinction is drawn between original members of the United Nations and states that are admitted to membership under the terms of Art 4 of the Charter. Under the terms of Art 3, an original Member is one that participated in the San Francisco Conference and signed and ratified the Charter, or one that signed the United Nations Declaration of 1 January 1942 and then signed and ratified the Charter. Fifty one states qualified as original members of the United Nations including the five permanent members of the Security Council. The draftsmen of the Charter envisaged that other states would wish to join and so Art 4 stipulates that membership is open 'to all other peace loving States which accept the obligations contained in the present Charter and, in the judgment of the Organisation, are able and willing to carry out these obligations'. It is further provided that admission is contingent on a decision of the General Assembly upon a recommendation of the Security Council.

In the early years after 1945, Cold War rivalry caused the Security Council to be reluctant to admit new states. In consequence, the General Assembly sought an Advisory Opinion from the International Court of Justice on: (a) the criteria for admission; and (b) the criteria that a state should have in mind when casting a vote for admission. In the Advisory Opinion on Conditions of Membership in the United Nations,[8] the International Court of Justice held by a majority that there were five conditions, namely that the applicant had to be: (i) a state; (ii) be peace loving; (iii) accept the obligations of the Charter; (iv) be able to carry out these obligations; (v) be willing to do so. Secondly, the Court ruled that when casting a vote for admission a state should have these criteria in mind and no others. However, such was the state of Cold War suspicion that the opinion did not result in an immediate change of policy. However, in a later Advisory Opinion, the Court[9] rejected an attempt by the General Assembly to admit states without a prior recommendation of the Security Council. Nevertheless, the situation became less tense on admissions after December 1955, when a 'package deal' was negotiated to enable 16 new states to become members.

As with any voluntary organisation, there are provisions in Art 5 for suspension from membership of the organisation and in Art 6 for expulsion. Expulsion can only be effected by a vote of the General Assembly on a recommendation by the Security Council, upon evidence of persistent violation of the Principles of the Charter. No state has been expelled, although Indonesia did withdraw for a year in 1965 and South Africa was barred from full participation in the work of the General Assembly in the years 1974 until 1993. One of the reasons for a reluctance to expel is the fact that the United Nations exists to protect peoples and it is felt that they should not be disadvantaged by the misconduct of their government.

The desire to secure the widest possible membership is also evident when considering the problem of micro states; the concern had been as to whether such entities were able to discharge the duties of membership. The description 'micro state' has tended to attach to those states with a population of less than 100,000 and an area of less than 500 square

---

8   The *Admissions* case (1948) ICJ 61.
9   The *Second Admissions to the United Nations* case (1950) ICJ 8.

miles. This has not proved to be an obstacle and Andorra,[10] Antigua and Barbuda, Grenada and the Federated States of Micronesia and Marshall Islands have all been admitted as have Liechtenstein, Monaco, San Marino and Palau.

In the context of membership, it is necessary to consider the provisions of Art 2(6) of the Charter. Some writers have argued that this provision seeks to impose obligations on non-members. This is going too far; the purpose of the sub-article is to stipulate the policy that the Organisation will follow in its relations with non-members.

One of the more debated questions of membership has concerned the position of China. As indicated above, China was an original member of the United Nations but, in 1949, the communists seized power in Peking.[11] However, from 1949 to 1971 China was represented at the United Nations by the nationalist government of Chiang Kai-shek which was based in Taiwan. The question, therefore, was which government should represent China; in principle, it should be the one that has effective control over the majority of the territory and enjoys recognition from other states. So in 1971, as part of 'opening the door to China', the General Assembly resolved 'to restore all its rights to the People's Republic of China and to recognise the representatives of its government as the only legitimate representatives of China in the United Nations, and to expel forthwith the representatives of Chiang Kai-shek from the place they unlawfully occupy at the United Nations, and in all the organisations related to it'.[12] A more recent case of difficulty has arisen in the context of the break up of the former Socialist Federal Republic of Yugoslavia; the new states that had seceded were allowed to become members[13] even though fighting was still continuing. The remaining territory of Serbia and Montenegro (now described as the Federal Republic of Yugoslavia) was refused permission to assume the seat of the Socialist Federal Republic of Yugoslavia because, it was argued, that the latter entity had ceased to exist; it was further resolved[14] that Serbia and Montenegro should themselves apply for membership as a new entity.

3 THE ORGANS OF THE UNITED NATIONS

There are six principal organs of the United Nations. The best known perhaps is the General Assembly which comprises all states; there are then three bodies which are of a specialist nature and comprise only a limited number of states, namely the Security Council, the Economic and Social Council and the Trusteeship Council. There are then two other bodies which are made up of individuals, the Secretariat and the International

---

10 Andorra (1993), Antigua and Barbuda (1981), Grenada (1974), Micronesia (1991), Liechtenstein (1990), Monaco (1993). San Merino (1992), Palau (1994).

11 For litigation arising therefrom, see *Civil Air Transport Inc v Central Air Transport Corporation* [1953] AC 70; [1952] 2 All ER 733; 2 LR 259.

12 United Nations General Assembly Resolution 2758 (XXVI) of 25 October 1971. The liberalisation was influenced by the foreign policy of President Nixon who had set out to improve relations with China and to persuade the government in Peking to play a more constructive role in international affairs.

13 Slovenia, Bosnia-Herzegovina and Croatia were admitted as members on 22 May 1992. See GA Resolutions 46/236, 46/236, 46/237.

14 GA Res 47/1 22 September 1992.

Court of Justice. It is arguable that the Security Council is the most important political and executive organ and it is proposed to consider that body first.

(a) The Security Council

Under the terms of Art 23 of the Charter the Security Council comprises 15 member states; of these, five are permanent members. Originally, these were the United States, the Soviet Union, the United Kingdom, China and France. In 1991, the Russian Federation acting with the support of the 11 members of the Commonwealth of Independent States indicated that it would assume the membership of the USSR in all relevant United Nations organs. Perhaps because of a desire to facilitate political change in the Soviet Union, there was no insistence by any other state that this change required any amendment of the Charter.[15] The allocation of permanent seats reflected the structure of political power in 1945 and the efforts of those states that had made a major contribution to securing military victory in the Second World War.

There are 10 other non-permanent members[16] of the Security Council who are elected by the General Assembly for a period of two years.[17] The broad jurisdiction of the Security Council is set out in Art 24.1 which reads:

In order to ensure prompt and effective action by the United Nations its Members confer on the Security Council primary responsibility for the maintenance of international peace and security, and agree that in carrying out its duties under this responsibility the Security Council acts on their behalf.

This provision has to be read with Art 25 which provides that members of the United Nations agree to accept and carry out decisions of the Security Council. The scheme, therefore, was to ensure that the Security Council would have the power to act effectively.

The important question was how the Security Council was to reach decisions. One of the problems in 1945 was the need to accommodate to the demands of the USSR. The USSR, conscious of the western bias on the Council and anxious to avoid limitations on its own conduct, pressed for a form of voting veto. Under the terms of Art 27, each member of the Security Council has one vote. If the matter is of a procedural nature then it requires nine affirmative votes to be carried.[18] If the matter is not of a procedural nature, then it requires nine votes including the concurring votes of the permanent members.[19] Hence, a negative vote by a permanent member would prevent action being taken. The important question, therefore, was whether a matter was procedural or not. A statement issued by the Four Sponsoring Powers at the time of the San Francisco Conference indicated that such a question was itself subject to the veto. Thus, the USSR might veto a matter being considered as procedural and then, when the matter was put to the substantive vote it would exercise a second veto. Such conduct did nothing for the

---

15 See Y Blum (1992) 3 EJIL 354.
16 The original number had been six but Art 23 was amended with effect from 1 January 1966 to reflect the increase in the membership of the General Assembly.
17 Under the terms of GA Res 1991(XVIII) elections are to provide: (a) five from African and Asian states; (b) one from Eastern European states; (c) two from Latin American states; (d) two from Western European states.
18 United Nations Charter (1945), Art 27(2).
19 *Ibid*, Art 27(3).

reputation of the Security Council, particularly if the matter was one on which the international community should act. However, while permanent members have not hesitated to use the veto, such conduct might[20] damage the institution itself, so that gradually the practice of abstention began to develop; this practice, which had not been envisaged under Art 27, was acknowledged by the International Court of Justice in the *Namibia* case as 'not constituting a bar to the adoption of resolutions'.[21] The practice today under the Rules of Procedure is for the President of the Council to propose a matter as procedural and if such a motion receives nine affirmative votes then it will be considered as such.

The essential problem is that the Security Council has a legislative, executive and quasi judicial role but the votes are cast by states who are influenced by their own particular national interests. This is not a problem if the foreign policy of that state is broadly to observe international law and to ensure that it allows full and open debate in its own domestic media. The problems arise in respect of states whose foreign policy is not subject to any form of domestic accountability.[22]

In broad terms, the Security Council has two important roles, namely the pacific settlement of international disputes likely to endanger international peace and the taking of enforcement action;[23] both these matters will be considered further below. In addition to these two basic duties, the Council has a role in trusteeship matters in the determination of strategic areas[24] and it plays a role in the admission, suspension and expulsion of states.[25] The decisions, but not the recommendations, of the Security Council are binding on fellow members.[26] In addition, the Security Council participates in the election of judges to the International Court of Justice.

It has to be candidly admitted that, in the years after 1945, the tensions and hostilities of the Cold War made it difficult for the Security Council to function effectively. Secondly, nothing could be more damaging for its reputation than evidence that permanent members were themselves engaged in conduct that violated the Charter.[27] The accession

---

20 See A Stavropoulos, 'The practice of voluntary abstentions by permanent members of the Security Council under Article 27(3) of the Charter' (1967) 61 AJIL 737.

21 *Legal Consequences for States of the Continued Presence of South Africa in Namibia* (1971) ICJ 16, p 22; 49 ILR 2, p 12.

22 This being, of course, the basic difference between the United States and the USSR in the 1950s and 1960s. Although the United States possessed considerable military power, any foreign policy act was subject to open debate in the Congress and in the media. As the Vietnam War was to indicate, there were limits to how far the Executive Branch could go if it lacked support in the legislature, the media and amongst public opinion.

23 For duties of the Security Council see Art 24 and Chaps VI, VII, VIII, and XII.

24 United Nations Charter (1945), Art 83 and 86.

25 *Ibid*, Arts 4, 5 and 6.

26 *Ibid*, Art 25.

27 It was very difficult to imagine how the conduct of the Soviet Union in respect of Czechoslovakia (1968) or Afghanistan (1979) could be considered consistent with the Charter; the repressive nature of Soviet society and its domineering attitude towards Eastern Europe damaged the reputation of the Security Council. While few of the members of the United Nations operate perfect democracies, the domestic and foreign conduct of the Soviet Union raised problems when it sought to sit in judgment on others. One of the problems for the Security Council is that it operates in a quasi judicial manner and is seeking to cast judgment on others. This raises problems if the conduct of a significant permanent member attracts criticism. Such criticism grew in the 1960s as western socialist parties became disillusioned with Soviet conduct and opposition began to accelerate after the award of the Nobel Prize to Alexander Solzhenitsyn in 1970.

to power of Mikhail Gorbachev in 1985 produced a change in approach and a desire to find common ground, and this was reflected in the conduct of his foreign minister, Edvard Shevardnadze, who replaced Andrei Gromyko[28] in the same year. Improved co-operation with the Soviet Union after 1985, and later with the Russian Federation, has enabled the Security Council to operate more effectively, as was instanced in August 1990 when the body was able to present a united front in response to the invasion of Kuwait. Since 1992, the economic weaknesses of the Russian Federation have made it more willing to co-operate and it is reasonable to assume that the suspicion and ideological conflict which nearly paralysed the Security Council in the 1950s is very much a thing of the past and the tendency amongst permanent members is now to examine each issue on its merits independent of ideological considerations.

(b) The General Assembly

Article 9(1) of the United Nations Charter provides that 'the General Assembly shall consist of all the Members of the United Nations'. The functions of that body are set out in Arts 10, 11 and 13 which read in part as follows:

> The General Assembly may discuss any questions or any matters within the scope of the present Charter or relating to the powers and functions of any organs provided for in the present Charter, and ... may make recommendations to the Members of the United Nations or to the Security Council or to both on any such questions or matters.[29]

The matter is amplified in Art 11(2) which reads:

> The General Assembly may discuss any questions relating to the maintenance of international peace and security brought before it by any Member of the United Nations, or by the Security Council, or by a state which is not a Member of the United Nations ... and ... may make recommendations with regard to any such question to the State or States concerned or to the Security Council or to both.

The broad role of the General Assembly is indicated in Arts 13 and 14 which read in part:

> The General Assembly shall initiate studies and make recommendations for the purpose of:
>
> (a) promoting international co-operation in the political field and encouraging the progressive development of international law and its codification;
>
> (b) promoting international co-operation in the economic, social, cultural, educational, and health fields, and assisting in the realisation of human rights and fundamental freedoms for all without discrimination as to race sex, language or religion.

The positive role of the General Assembly is stressed in Art 14 which reads in part:

> ... the General Assembly may recommend measures for the peaceful adjustment of any situation ... which it deems likely to impair the general welfare or friendly relations among nations.

---

28 Andrei Gromyko (1909–89). Although he had attended the Tehran, Yalta and Potsdam conferences Gromyko was associated with a negative attitude. As United Nations representative in the years 1946–49 he exercised the Soviet veto 26 times; he served as Soviet Foreign Minister from 1957 until 1985.

29 United Nations Charter (1945), Art 10.

To an extent the General Assembly is the institution that has changed most since 1945. In the early years with only 51 members it tended to reflect western preoccupations.

However, as the membership of the United Nations began to expand on decolonisation, it came to reflect the concerns of developing nations particularly as each member of the General Assembly has one vote.[30] Although such a vote may be lost if the state is in arrears with its financial contribution for a period of two years. [31]

The method of voting in the General Assembly is set out in Art 18 of the Charter which reads as follows:

(1) Each member of the General Assembly shall have one vote.

(2) Decisions of the General Assembly on important questions shall be made by a two thirds majority of the members present and voting. These questions shall include: recommendations with respect to the maintenance of international peace and security, the election of the non permanent members of the Security Council, the election of the members of the Trusteeship Council in accordance with paragraph 1(c) of Art 86, the admission of new Members to the United Nations, the suspension of the rights and privileges of membership, the expulsion of Members, questions relating to the operation of the trusteeship system, and budgetary questions.

(3) Decisions on other questions, including the determination of additional categories of questions to be decided by a two thirds majority, shall be made by a majority of the Members present and voting.

Save in respect of budgetary matters, a vote of the General Assembly does not have the force of a legislative chamber. It was not the intention of the founders that the General Assembly should resemble a legislative body.[32] The reasons for this are obvious; many states are small with populations of less than five million and it would be absurd for such states to be able to pass resolutions that bound states that comprised a majority of the world's population. However, a vote of the General Assembly is not without legal effect;[33] if it is unanimous it may be weighty evidence of the state of customary law or it may set in train such a degree of consistency of practice that a rule of customary law may be said to emerge. A resolution condemning state X for a breach of international law may persuade the Security Council to act and may influence other states in their assessment of the situation.

The draftsmen of the Charter were anxious to avoid any conflict with the Security Council so that it is provided in Art 12(1) that:

While the Security Council is exercising in respect of any dispute or situation the functions assigned to it in the present Charter, the General Assembly shall not make any

---

30   *Ibid*, Art 18(1).

31   *Ibid*, Art 19.

32   DH Johnson, 'The effect of resolutions of the General Assembly of the United Nations' (1956) 32 BYIL 97; R Falk, 'On the quasi legislative competence of the General Assembly' (1966) 60 AJIL 782; G Arangio-Ruiz, 'The normative role of the General Assembly of the United Nations and the Declaration of Principles of Friendly Relations' (1972) 137 HR 419.

33   Some resolutions have had an important effect on the development of international law, such as Resolution 1803 (XVII) (on natural resources), Resolution 2131 (XX) (on non-intervention) Resolution 2312 (XXII) (on territorial asylum).

recommendation with regard to that dispute or situation unless the Security Council so requests.

Under the terms of Art 20, the General Assembly meets in regular annual sessions but it may be summoned by the Secretary General to special sessions[34] at the request of the Security Council or a majority of the Members of the United Nations. The General Assembly operates under its own rules of procedure and elects a President for each session.

The role of the General Assembly has tended to fluctuate according to political constraints. In the years after 1945, Western nations tended to dominate the Assembly and were minded to stress its importance when contrasted with the Security Council which was handicapped by the veto. After 1960, the majority moved in favour of developing nations and communist regimes tried to ingratiate themselves with newly independent states by stressing the role of the General Assembly. Since 1985, the Security Council has tended to be less divided and this has lead to a more harmonious relationship with the General Assembly.

Under the terms of Art 22 of the Charter, the General Assembly is entitled to set up subsidiary organs as it deems necessary. Today, it operates through six principal committees which concern respectively; disarmament and international security; economic and financial matters; social, humanitarian and cultural matters; political and decolonisation matters; administrative and budgetary matters and legal matters. In addition to these specialist committees, there are two standing committees known as the General Committee and the Credentials Committee which are concerned with procedural matters. Also, there are two other committees which deal with budgetary matters and contributions.

Alongside the committee structure, the General Assembly has set up a number of specialist bodies whose composition will be outlined in the resolution which established the particular body.[35] Such bodies differ in function, membership, powers and duration. Some operate as distinct agencies with a specific secretariat and budget and the express power to negotiate with other governments. Although the establishment of such organisations has to be within the specific powers of the Assembly, such powers may be express or implied.[36]

In some quarters, it has been fashionable to deride the General Assembly as little more than a 'talking shop'; however, this judgment is unfair and takes no account of the evidence. The General Assembly played a positive role in both the Korean and Suez crises when unanimity was lacking in the Security Council; the Assembly has provided an opportunity for poorer states to raise their concerns on the international plane. In respect of Disarmament, the General Assembly has a positive record and has done much through agencies such as the United Nations Disarmament Commission to promote arms control

---

34   There have been special sessions on Palestine (1947), the Middle East (1956, 1958, 1967, 1980, 1982), South West Africa (Namibia) (1967, 1978, 1986) and on particular topics such as apartheid (1989), disarmament (1978, 1982, 1988).

35   Examples would be the United Nations Children's Fund (UNICEF), the Board of Auditors, the International Law Commission (ILC), the United Nations Commission on International Trade Law (UNCITRAL), the World Food Council (WFC), United Nations Environment Programme (UNEP).

36   *Effects of Awards of Compensation made by the UN Administrative Tribunal* (1954) ICJ 47.

agreements. It promotes economic and social co-operation through its supervision of the Economic and Social Council. In respect of international law, the sixth committee of the General Assembly has played a significant role in the preparation of the multilateral law making conventions that have served to clarify and codify particular topics. It was the General Assembly that resolved to call the Geneva Conference on the Law of the Sea in 1958 together with the Vienna Conferences of 1961, 1963 and 1968–69 on Diplomatic Relations, Consular Relations and the Law of Treaties. There are two other points that should be made. First, there is much to be said on the international plane for the exchange of views; the General Assembly provides a forum for the exchanging of views and thus prevents misunderstandings arising. Secondly, the draftsmen of 1945 realised that if a general international organisation was to endure, it needed an organ comprising a small number of states that could act quickly in an emergency, but it also needed to make each individual state feel they had a role to play in the organisation; this second and equally important role is performed by the General Assembly. Finally, it should be remembered that one of the roles of the General Assembly is to elect members of other organs such as the 10 non-permanent members of the Security Council, the members of the Economic and Social Council as well as participating with the Security Council International Court of Justice. While it is arguable that the Security Council has more immediate impact in the sense that it adjudicates on immediate threats to international peace and security, it is certainly arguable that the role of the General Assembly in developing international law through multilateral law making conventions is equally important and has not always received the credit it deserves.

(c) The Economic and Social Council

The experience of the League of Nations had been that the organisation was pressed, sometimes against its own will, to consider economic and social questions; the high level of unemployment in Europe and the general slump of 1929–31 increased this pressure. During the Second World War, there had been much economic and social co-operation as national rivalries were set aside in pursuit of the single goal of victory.

The draftsmen of the United Nations Charter were anxious to promote social and economic progress not only as desirable ends but also as likely guarantees of international peace and stability. To this end, Chapter X of the Charter provided for the establishment of an Economic and Social Council (ECOSOC). Under the terms of the amended Art 61, it comprises 54 Members of the United Nations who are elected for a period of three years but are subject to staggered elections. Under the terms of Art 62, ECOSOC may initiate studies, make recommendations to the General Assembly or specialised agencies and prepare draft conventions. It operates under the authority of the General Assembly.

The decisions of the Council are reached on the basis of a majority vote; the Council may assist the Security Council at the Security Council's request.[37]

One of the main tasks of ECOSOC arises under Art 63, which provides that it is to be responsible for co-ordination of the work of the specialised agencies; the agency comes into a relationship with ECOSOC by means of an agreement approved by the General

---

37   United Nations Charter (1945), Art 65.

Assembly.[38] At present, there are 16 such organisations,[39] including the ILO, FAO, UNESCO and WHO as well as the IMF and the IBRD. The powers and procedures of such organisations are governed by their constituent documents. Under the terms of Art 63(2), ECOSOC may co-ordinate the work of such specialised agencies through consultation and through recommendation to the General Assembly. The Council operates through a number of functional commissions[40] and five regional commissions.[41] In recent years, the Council has been responsible for organising the Drug Control Programme and playing a role in the administering of the Office of the UN High Commissioner for Refugees as well as UNEP and UNICEF.

(d) The Trusteeship Council[42]

The United Nations Charter continued the approach of the League of Nations mandate system in respect of those territories not ready for self-government. Chapter XII (Arts 75–85) and Chapter XIII (Arts 86–91) provided for the establishment of an International Trusteeship System and a Trusteeship Council. Under the terms of Art 77, the territories subject to the trusteeship system were territories held in 1945 under mandate, territories which were detached from enemy states as a result of the Second World War and territories voluntarily placed under the system by states responsible for their administration. The only former mandated territory which did not come within the new system was South West Africa (Namibia) and the status of that territory was before the International Court of Justice several times in the years 1950–70.[43] By 1955, there were 11 trust territories that fell under the administration of seven different states. However, over the course of time each reached self-governing status and the trusteeship agreement

---

38 *Ibid*, Art 63(1).

39 Examples would be the International Civil Aviation Organisation (ICAO); the United Nations Educational, Scientific and Cultural Organisation (UNESCO); World Health Organisation (WHO); the International Telecommunications Union (ITU); the International Maritime Organisation (IMO); the World Meteorological Organisation (WMO); the Food and Agriculture Organisation (FAO); International Fund for Agricultural Development (IFAD); International Union for the Protection of New Varieties of Plants (UPOV); Universal Postal Union (UPU); World Intellectual Property Organisation (WIPO); World Tourism Organisation (WTO).

40 Included within this category of bodies formally related to the UN Economic and Social Council would be the Commission for Sustainable Development (CSD); International Narcotics Control Board (INCB); United Nations Capital Development Fund (UNCDF); United Nations Children's Fund (UNICEF); United Nations Conference on Trade and Development (UNCTAD); United Nations Development Programme (UNDP); United Nations Environment Programme (UNEP); United Nations Fund for Drug Abuse Control (UNFDAC); United Nations Fund for Population Activities (UNFPA); United Nations High Commissioner for Refugees (UNHCR); United Nations Research Institute for Social Development (UNRISD); United Nations Special Fund (UNSF); World Food Council (WFC).

41 These include the Economic Commission for Europe (ECE); the Economic and Social Commission for Asia and the Pacific (ESCAP); the Economic Commission for Latin America (ECLA); the Economic Commission for Africa (ECA); and the Economic Commission for Western Asia (ECWA). The legal authority for setting up such commissions is contained in Art 68 of the United Nations Charter (1945).

42 See C Parry, 'The legal status of trusteeship agreements' (1950) 27 BYIL 164; JL Kunz, 'Chapter XI of the United Nations Charter in action' (1954) 48 AJIL 103.

43 For the lengthy saga, see *South West Africa* case Advisory Opinions (1950) ICJ 128; (1955) ICJ 67; (1956) ICJ 23; ICJ Judgments (1962) ICJ 319; (1966) ICJ 6; culminating in Advisory Opinion of 1971 (1971) ICJ 16.

was terminated. The last territory was that of Palau, which had formed part of the Trust Territory of the Pacific Islands administered by the United States and which chose, in a plebiscite, free association with that state. After some difficulties over the passage of nuclear powered submarines, agreement was reached and the Security Council terminated the trusteeship agreement.[44] Palau became independent on 1 October 1994 and the Trusteeship Council was in suspension therefrom although formal termination would require an amendment of the Charter.

(e) The Secretariat

Chapter XV of the United Nations Charter makes provision for a Secretariat which comprises about 14,000 staff working in New York or Geneva and a slightly higher figure who work for the secretariats of the subsidiary organs of the United Nations. Under the terms of Art 97 of the Charter the Secretariat is headed by the Secretary General[45] who is elected by the Security Council and the General Assembly and is designated as the chief administrative officer of the Organisation. As the veto operates any candidate for the post must possess the character and intellect that commands support in both the Security Council and the General Assembly. Under the terms of Art 98, the Secretary General is obliged to undertake tasks designated by the General Assembly, Security Council and Economic and Social Council as well as producing an annual report to the General Assembly on the work of the organisation. In accordance with Art 99, the Secretary General is entitled to bring to the attention of the Security Council 'any matter which in his opinion may threaten the maintenance of international peace and security'. One of the most important provisions in the Charter is that which guarantees the constitutional position of the Secretary General and that is set out in Art 100 which reads:

(1) In the performance of their duties the Secretary General and the staff shall not seek or receive instructions from any Government or from any other authority external to the Organisation. They shall refrain from any action which might reflect on their position as international officials responsible to the Organisation.

(2) Each Member of the United Nations undertakes to respect the exclusively international character of the responsibilities of the Secretary General and the staff and not seek to influence them in the discharge of their responsibilities.

The purpose of this provision is to protect the constitutional and quasi judicial role of the Secretary General.[46] It would be most undesirable if any state were to seek to put improper pressure on the Secretary General. In the early years, there is some evidence that the Soviet Union tried to do but this was resisted by other states;[47] in recent years, there has been some tension between one Secretary General and the United States, but this may owe more to the attitude of the United States Congress than to any particular

---

44   See SC Res 1994/956.

45   S Schwebel, *The Secretary General of the United Nations*, 1952.

46   References to the role and duty of the Secretary General are to be found not only in Arts 97, 98, 99, 100 and 101 but also in Arts 12(2), 20, 73(e), 101 and 110.

47   In the early years, the Soviet Union (possibly as a result of its own insecurity) seems to have found the concept of an independent Secretary General difficult to comprehend; the Soviet Union bore some responsibility for the resignation of Trygve Lie and sought (unsuccessfully) to put pressure on Dag Hammarskjold.

feeling by the executive branch.[48] As indicated above, much depends on the energy, character and intellect of the individual who holds the post; it has often been observed that the United Nations Charter requires a strong, independent Secretary General but the Member States would not find this palatable. Since 1946, the office has been held by a Norwegian (Trygve Lie, 1946–53);[49] a Swede (Dag Hammarskjold, 1953–61);[50] a Burmese (U Thant, 1961–71); an Austrian (Kurt Waldheim, 1972–81); a Peruvian (Javier Perez de Cuellar, 1982–91)[51] and an Egyptian (Boutros Boutros Ghali, 1992–97). The office has been held since 1 January 1997 by Kofi Annan of Ghana.

(f) The International Court of Justice

Under the terms of Art 92 of the Charter, the sixth organ of the United Nations is the International Court of Justice; having regard to its judicial and advisory role this organ is discussed in the context of the peaceful settlement of disputes.

(g) The specialised agencies

The term 'specialised agency' is a general expression designed to indicate those inter-governmental organisations funded on treaty that perform functions of an international character and have been brought into a relationship with the United Nations through agreements made under the terms of Arts 57 and 63. Basic questions, such as entitlement to membership, voting rights and organisational structure, will be dealt with in the founding constitutional document. In many instances, membership rights depend on the presence that a state has in a particular field of activity. Most of such organisations have some form of rule creating body capable of making recommendations and drafting treaties. It is possible for a state to withdraw from participation in one of the specialised agencies while remaining a full member of the United Nations. Some of the better known specialised agencies are as follows.

---

48 A matter discussed in some detail by Boutros Boutros Ghali in his memoirs *Unvanquished, A US-UN Saga*, 1999, in which the former Secretary General expresses some reservations about the conduct of the United States; however, there is some evidence that the administration itself was under pressure from the United States Congress.

49 See Trygve Lie, *The Cause of Peace*, 1959.

50 Dag Hammarskjold (1905–61). For an assessment of this most active of Secretary Generals, see Brian Urquhart, *Hammarskjold*, 1973. As Secretary General, Hammarskjold opposed France and Britain in respect of the Suez operation of 1956. He was voted wide powers to deal with the Congo crisis in 1960 (SC Res S/4387 (14 July 1960); SC Res S/4405 4405 (22 July 1960); SC Res S/4426 (9 August 1961)). The active role taken by Hammarskjold in the Congo crisis set the tone for the office; later Secretary Generals would take an active role at other times of crisis, eg, Cyprus (1964); Middle East War (1973); Falkland Islands Invasion (1982); Gulf Crisis (1990–91); and negotiations with Iraq concerning arms inspection (1997–2000). See also O Schachter, 'Dag Hammarskjold and the relation of law to politics' (1962) 56 AJIL 1.

51 For a warning on the difficulties of striking a balance, see J Perez de Cuellar, 'The role of the United Nations Secretary General', in A Roberts and B Kingsbury (eds), *United Nations, Divided World*, 1993, pp 125–42.

The International Labour Organisation (ILO)

The International Labour Organisation was set up in 1919 and linked to the League of Nations; indeed, its constitution was to be found in Part XIII of the Treaty of Versailles. In 1946, it was necessary to amend the constitution[52] to reflect the dissolution of the League. The broad purpose of the organisation is stated in its Preamble as being to improve the conditions of labour; this manifests itself in concern for the hours of work and the conditions under which such work is undertaken, together with support for the principles of freedom of association, equal pay and non-discrimination. The ILO had been the subject of a number of Advisory Opinions from the Permanent Court of International Justice[53] and was the first specialised agency to develop a nexus with the United Nations. The objectives of the organisation are effected by the drafting of international conventions, which are then ratified by individual states; if a state that is of the opinion that another is not meeting its obligations then it may complain to the International Labour Office. In the years since 1919, over 150 conventions have been produced in the field of employment relations and many of the principles propounded by the ILO are now to be found in many human rights documents. The ILO operates through a Council, a Secretariat and an International Labour Conference.

The Food and Agriculture Organisation (FAO)

The Food and Agriculture Organisation dates from 1943, although it draws upon the inspiration of the earlier International Institute for Agriculture which had been established in 1905 to act as a vehicle for information on matters of concern in the field of agriculture. In broad terms, the objects of the FAO are to promote information relating to food, nutrition and agriculture. The Organisation operates through a Conference, a Secretariat and a Director General. The increasing realisation, since 1945, of the problems posed by poverty and increasing population has tended to widen the activities of the FAO. Since 1963, the FAO has been responsible for the World Food Programme and related initiatives; the FAO Conference may approve conventions for submission to member states. Under the terms of its constitution, the FAO may offer help to individual governments and it has gained a considerable reputation for its field work.

The World Health Organisation (WHO)

It has been obvious for centuries that illness and disease are no respectors of national frontiers. As with matters of science, there is a long history of international co-operation as instanced by the establishment of the International Office of Public Health in Paris in 1903. The World Health Organisation dates from 1946 and it took over the functions of a number of bodies acting in this area. The objects of the organisation are 'the attainment by all peoples of the highest possible level of health'.[54] The organisation operates through a

---

52   The constitution was amended again in 1961, 1972 and 1986.
53   See PCIJ, Ser B, No 2; PCIJ, Ser B, No 3; PCIJ, Ser B, No 13; PCIJ, Ser A/B, No 50.
54   See Art 1 of the WHO Constitution. For consideration of the functions of WHO, see *Legality of the Threat or Use of Nuclear Weapons (WHO case)* (1996) ICJ 66. It is strongly arguable that the work of the organisation has become more important in the years since 1945. In general, post-war affluence has lead to increased health provision and increased life expectancy in the wealthier nations in contrast to the low levels of health expenditure and limited life expectancy in poorer states.

plenary body known as the World Health Assembly, which elects members to the Executive Board. In addition, there is a secretariat and a director general. The Assembly has a legal competence similar to that of the ILO and the FAO in that it may adopt by a two-thirds majority conventions or agreements 'which shall come into force for each Member when accepted by it in accordance with its constitutional processes'.

The United Nations Educational, Scientific and Cultural Organisation (UNESCO)

The UNESCO Constitution of 1945 states its objectives in general terms as being 'to contribute to peace and security by promoting collaboration among the nations through education, science and culture ...'. Although the history of UNESCO has not been without difficulty,[55] it has striven to reduce illiteracy by the promotion of teacher training programmes; in addition, it has sought to ensure that children in poorer states have access to educational material at reduced rates. In some areas, it has tried to promote a more balanced approach to the teaching of particular subjects; in particular, it has tried to ensure that the teaching of history gives a factually accurate picture and is not used as a vehicle for nationalist propaganda and indoctrination. Another part of its work is to protect cultural rights through the recognition of copyright as stipulated in the Universal Copyright Convention.

The organisation which is based in Paris operates through a General Conference which elects members of the Executive Board; in addition there is a secretariat and a director general.

The International Civil Aviation Organisation (ICAO)

The International Civil Aviation Organisation was established by the Chicago Convention of 1944 which was itself amended in 1947, 1954 and 1961. The objects of the ICAO are 'to develop the principles and techniques of international air navigation and to foster the planning and development of international air transport'.[56] In the period since 1945, the overriding objective has been to promote the safe and orderly growth of international air transport. The organisation operates through a Council which has power to set standards and make recommendations; in contrast to other international institutions, where the legislative power is in the Assembly, the ICAO structure is designed to ensure that those states that have a major interest in the subject have a greater say in the resolution of problems under the Convention.

Economic and financial organisations

The experience of the slump of the 1920s and 1930s, and the tension caused by high levels of unemployment, prompted much thought as to how international monetary co-operation could be improved so as to moderate the fluctuations of the business cycle. The basis for such co-operation seemed to lie in improving international monetary co-

---

55 Eg, the United States withdrew in 1984.
56 Article 44.

operation and by endorsing the macroeconomic views propounded by JM Keynes.[57] Pursuant to this, the United Nations Monetary and Economic Conference of 1944 (normally referred to as the Bretton Woods Conference), produced the Articles of Agreement of the International Monetary Fund which came into effect in December 1945. The broad objectives of the Fund are described in Art 1 as being the promotion of international monetary co-operation, the facilitation of the expansion and balanced growth of international trade and the promotion of exchange stability. The main organ of the IMF is a Board of Governors which comprises Finance Ministers and Central Bank Governors, but day to day control is exercised by an Executive Board. One of the tasks of the IMF is exchange rate co-ordination. The original Bretton Woods system had provided for a fixed gold parity with the United States dollar to which other currencies were linked; in the event, this system broke down in 1971 and, since 1976, the IMF has operated a system of flexible exchange rates

In addition to the Agreement providing for the IMF, the Bretton Woods Conference also resulted in an Agreement for the creation of an International Bank for Reconstruction and Development (usually known as 'the World Bank'). As set out in Art 1 of the Articles of Agreement, the purposes of the institution include assisting in the reconstruction and development of the territories of members by facilitating the investment of capital, promoting private foreign investment by means of guarantees or participation in loans and also the promotion of the long term balanced growth of international trade. The initial objective of the Bank had been to facilitate post-war reconstruction but in recent years the purpose of the Bank has been to assist with loans to developing countries for the purpose of infrastructure projects.

Although the Bank is a distinct legal entity from the IMF, there is a close relationship. To be a member of the Bank it is necessary to a member of the Fund. Neither institution acts in a legislative capacity. In essence, the Bank acts to raise money and then enters into agreements for the direct loan of that money or acts to guarantee the loan of money provided by another source.

The two immediate post-war institutions have been supplemented by other bodies. One difficulty with the World Bank was that it could only lend to governments or to private bodies able to offer a government guarantee. To widen the source of funds, the International Finance Corporation (IFC) was set up in 1956 to enable loans to be made to private enterprises. This institution is legally distinct from the Bank and has a separate agreement with the United Nations; however, Bank personnel serve on its Board of Governors. By 1960, it was felt that poorer countries might benefit from a more flexible loans system. To this end, the International Development Association (IDA) was established in 1960 to make concessionary loans (sometimes constituting grants) to those poorer states not able to raise finance through normal market operations. The World Bank and the IFC and the IDA are sometimes referred to collectively as the World Bank Group.

---

57 In his *General Theory of Employment, Interest and Money* published in February 1936, Keynes had attempted to show that: (i) consumption and investment demand can fall short of potential supply or capacity to produce resulting in mass unemployment; (ii) he argued that the level of demand or spending was the main determinant of economic activity; (iii) Keynes broadly favoured international co-operation in such matters having been present at the 1919 Peace Conference. For the man and his outlook, see R Skidelsky, *John Maynard Keynes Volume 1 (1883–1920)*, 1983; *Volume II (1920–37)*, 1992.

Associated with the World Bank Group is the International Centre for the Settlement of Investment Disputes (ICSID)[58] and the Multilateral Investment Guarantee Agency (MIGA).[59]

The Universal Postal Union (UPU)

The Universal Postal Union can be traced back to the Berne Convention of 1874, which established a General Postal Union which, in 1878 after the Congress in Paris, was named the Universal Postal Union. The Constitution was revised in 1964 and reflects its structure as a 'union' of postal administrations, and its objective is 'to secure the organisation and improvement of the postal services and to promote in this sphere the development of international collaboration'. The work of the organisation is principally concerned with expediting mail services.

The International Telecommunications Union (ITU)

An International Telegraphic Union was established in 1865 and this extended to radio after the Berlin Conference of 1906. However, following the Madrid Conference of 1932, the present title of the International Telecommunications Union was adopted. The constitutional structure was revised in 1947, 1952, 1961 and in 1965. The object of the organisation is to promote co-operation in all forms of telecommunications; to this end, the Union distributes the radio frequency spectrum and acts to avoid interference between radio operators in in different countries.

The World Meteorological Organisation (WMO)

An International Meteorological Organisation had been established as early as 1878 and its constitution was subject to revision in 1919, 1923, 1929 and 1935. The World Meteorological Organisation came into existence in 1950 and, the following year, the work assets and liabilities of the IMO were transferred to it. The simple objective of the organisation is to promote the rapid exchange of weather information and to further the application of meteorological information in the spheres of aviation, shipping and agriculture.

The International Maritime Organisation (IMO)

This organisation is of comparatively recent origin but of increasing importance in the light of the developments in the international law of the sea. In 1948, a United Nations Maritime Conference drafted the Intergovernmental Maritime Consultative Organisation Convention, but this instrument did not come into force until 1958, when the requisite ratifications were finally obtained. At that stage, the organisation was known as the Inter-

---

58 The ICSID as established by the World Bank in 1964. The legal basis is the Washington Convention on the Settlement of Investment Disputes between States and Nationals of Other States (the 'ICSID Convention') (1965) 4 ILM 532.

59 See SK Chaterjee, 'The Convention establishing the Multilateral Investment Guarantee Agency' (1986) 36 ICLQ 76; IF Shihata, 'The Multilateral Investment Guarantee Agency (MIGA) and the legal treatment of foreign investment' (1987) 203 HR 95.

governmental Maritime Consultative Organisation (IMCO), but in 1982 it changed its name to the International Maritime Organisation. The organisation operates through committees, a council and an Assembly; the Assembly comprises all member states which now number over 150. In broad terms, proposals originate in committee and if endorsed by the Council will be passed to the Assembly which may then proceed by recommendation or convention. The purpose of the organisation is to provide for inter-governmental co-operation in technical matters affecting shipping and also to encourage the adoption and observance of the highest possible standards in matters of maritime safety.[60]

The specialised agencies have been brought into a relationship with the United Nations by means of agreements negotiated by ECOSOC under the terms of Art 57 of the Charter. A number of points on this can usefully be made. First, all the agencies have in common a desire to promote a particular objective on the basis of international co-operation. Secondly, some of the agencies predate the United Nations and all have different constitutional structures. In some agencies, all states are regarded as equal; in others, an attempt has been made to accommodate to the fact that some states are more significant than others. Thirdly, the terms of the agreements vary so that those relating to the World Bank and the Fund stress the autonomy of these organisations. Fourthly, the agreements themselves differ in respect of financial matters and the sharing of information.

4 PACIFIC SETTLEMENT OF DISPUTES UNDER THE UNITED NATIONS CHARTER (CHAPTER VI)[61]

The idea of some form of collective security had been introduced in 1919, under the terms of the Covenant of the League of Nations. The basic obligation was contained in Art 12, which required Members of the League to submit any 'dispute likely to lead to a rupture' to arbitration, judicial settlement or inquiry by the Council. Further, they agreed not to go to war for a period of three months following any arbitral award or inquiry by the Council. Pursuant to this, under the terms of Art 15(2) member states agreed to submit to the Council all relevant facts about the dispute. After such an inquiry, and in the absence of a settlement, the Council was to publish a report and make such 'recommendations which are deemed just and proper in regard thereto'.[62] If the report was unanimous, then members agreed not to go to war with any state that honoured the terms of the report. If the report was not unanimous but simply founded on a majority, the Members of the League were said to reserve 'to themselves the right to take such action as they shall consider for the maintenance of right and justice'. It was arguable that the rather convoluted provisions did not actually outlaw war but simply imposed a 'cooling off'

---

60 The following other specialised agencies can be noted: the World Intellectual Property Organisation; the International Fund for Agricultural Development; the United Nations Industrial Development Organisation; the International Fund for Agricultural Development.

61 R Higgins, 'International law and the avoidance, containment and resolution of disputes' (1991) 230 HR 9; SR Ratner, 'Image and reality in the United Nations' peaceful settlement of disputes' (1995) 6 EJIL 426.

62 Covenant of the League of Nations (1919), Art 15(4).

period of three months, although the position was complicated by the prohibition against aggression contained in Art 10 of the Covenant. In any event, if a party resorted to war in disregard of the provisions contained in Arts 12–15, then sanctions might be sought under Art 16, although the power of the Council was restricted to making a recommendation which might or might not be accepted by the individual members. However, the record on sanctions was not encouraging; they were not pursued against Japan in 1932 and their application against Italy in 1935–36 lacked any serious intent.

The provisions of the Covenant may have lacked a degree of clarity but they did contain a condemnation of aggression;[63] the idea that disputes should be submitted to a central group of states would reappear in 1945. The provisions in respect of a 'cooling off' period were founded on the view that such a period would allow for further diplomatic exchanges and prevent the escalation by mobilisation that had characterised the days before the outbreak of the First World War. The fact that the League of Nations failed to prevent the Second World War is less important than the fact that it demonstrated that some form of collective security system was unavoidable in the modern world.

The United Nations Charter makes it clear that one of the purposes of the Organisation is to promote the peaceful settlement of disputes. Article 1(1) reads in part that the purposes of the organisation are:

... to bring about by peaceful means, and in conformity with the principles of justice and international law, adjustment or settlement of international disputes or situations which might lead to a breach of the peace.

Further, the obligation placed on member states is set out in Art 2(3) which reads:

All Members shall settle their international disputes by peaceful means in such a manner that international peace and security, and justice, are not endangered.

The United Nations Charter was drafted with the intention of conferring executive responsibility on the Security Council and confining the General Assembly to an advisory or parliamentary role. Because of tensions within the Security Council, matters have developed in a less straight forward manner. Additionally, the Secretary General by exercising his good office may play a significant role in the peaceful settlement of disputes.

The legal powers of the Security Council begin under Chapter V of the Charter and Art 24(1); this stipulates:

In order to ensure prompt and effective action by the United Nations, its Members confer on the Security Council the primary responsibility for the maintenance of international peace and security, and agree that in carrying out its duties under this responsibility the Security Council acts on its behalf.

This provision is to be read with Art 25 which reads:

All Members of the United Nations agree to accept and carry out the decisions of the Security Council in accordance with the present Charter.

In broad terms, the Security Council can act under Chapter VI (peaceful settlement) or Chapter VII) (enforcement action); it would seem doubtful that action under both is

---

63   As set out in Art 10 of the Covenant of the League of Nations (1919).

caught be the provisions of Art 25.[64] In practice, a case may be raised with the Security Council by a member state,[65] by a non-member state[66] or by the General Assembly[67] or Secretary General.[68] It will be for the Security Council to determine whether the matter is to be put on its agenda.

In respect of the powers arising in respect of the peaceful settlement of disputes, these are contained in Chapter VI (Arts 33–38). Under the terms of Art 33(1) members are under a duty to seek a peaceful resolution of their disputes; however, Art 34 allows the Security Council to investigate any dispute which is likely to endanger the maintenance of international peace and security. Further, under the terms of Art 35, any member of the United Nations may bring such a dispute to the attention of the Security Council. In such a case, while the Security Council may take into account any procedures adopted by the parties, it may itself, at any stage of the dispute, 'recommend appropriate procedures or methods of adjustment'. In making any such recommendation, the Security Council is to take into account the fact that, in principle, legal disputes should be submitted to the International Court of Justice in accordance with the provisions of the Statute of the Court. In addition, the General Assembly[69] or the Secretary General may draw matters to the attention of the Security Council.[70]

The Security Council was not intended to be a judicial body, although it must act within the provisions of the Charter and it has a basic duty to receive sufficient evidence so that it is in full possession of the facts of any dispute. The actions of the Council are a mixture of good offices, mediation and conciliation; states within the Security Council are not impartial and they have their own political and cultural motivations. Cases are taken before the Security Council for many different reasons. If state A has a strong case in a dispute with state B, then it may fortify its case further by raising the matter with the Security Council. However, the principle works in the opposite direction: if state A has a poor case in international law, but is under pressure from its own public opinion, then it may raise the matter before the Security Council simply to demonstrate that it has exhausted all possible avenues. In some cases, if the problem is susceptible of legal analysis, the Security Council may recommend that the matter is taken to the International Court of Justice.[71] Many disputes have a legal and a political aspect; as a general principle, the International Court will probably not award interim measures if the matter is subject to consideration by the Security Council.[72] It is clear that under Chapter VI the Security Council cannot impose a settlement on the parties, but it may seek in the form of a resolution to set out the general principles upon which a future

---

64 See the *Namibia* case (1971) ICJ 16, For consideration of the matter, see R Higgins, 'The Advisory Opinion on Namibia. Which United Nations Resolutions are Binding under Art 25 of the Charter?' (1972) 21 ICLQ 270.
65 United Nations Charter (1945), Art 35(1).
66 *Ibid*, Art 35(2).
67 *Ibid*, Arts 10, 11(2) and 11(3).
68 *Ibid*, Art 99.
69 *Ibid*, Arts 10 and 11.
70 *Ibid*, Art 99.
71 As was the case with the Corfu Channel incident.
72 The *Lockerbie* case (1992) ICJ 3.

settlement should be based;[73] this, then, has the effect of establishing negotiating parameters for the parties.

Although the principal role lies with the Security Council, the powers of the General Assembly should not be overlooked. The General Assembly has the power to discuss such matters under Art 10 and, under Art 11(1), it may make recommendations to the Security Council and, while it must refrain from acting when the Security Council is exercising its own powers,[74] it may nevertheless make recommendations under Art 14 of the Charter. Further, it should be noted in the context of pacific settlement that the Secretary General will have an important role which may involve the exercise of good offices or the negotiating with relevant regional organisations, although the role of the Secretary General will be limited in cases where there are clear Security Council Resolutions on the subject.[75]

5 THE COLLECTIVE SECURITY AND ENFORCEMENT SYSTEM (CHAPTER VII)[76]

While there may have been a variety of views as to the precise causes of the outbreak of the First World War, those statesmen charged with producing the United Nations Charter had little doubt that the Second World War had been caused in part by unrestrained aggression and the failure of states to respect the letter or spirit of the Covenant of the League of Nations. They were quite clear that more needed to be done to enforce respect for the rule of law on the international plane. The first manifestation of this view was the broad prohibition on the use of force set out in Art 2(4) of the Charter, which gave effect to the Stimson doctrine of non-recognition. The second step was to put in place a system of enforcement which would deter aggression, punish the wrongdoer and ensure that smaller states had confidence in the system of collective security.[77] These provisions are contained in Chapter VII of the Charter and it is worthy of note that this section of the Charter is designed to provide for 'Action with Respect to Threats to the Peace, Breaches of the Peace, and Acts of Aggression'.

The basic duty placed on the Security Council is set out in Art 39 which reads:

> The Security Council shall determine the existence of any threat to the peace, breach of the peace, or act of aggression and shall make recommendations, or decide what measures shall

---

73 The best known being SC Res 242 (1967), which sets out the general principles on which negotiations for a Middle East peace settlement should be based.

74 See United Nations Charter (1945), Art 12.

75 An example is afforded by the trip of the Secretary General Annan to Iraq in 1998, where it was made clear that the Secretary General was there to explain but not to negotiate in the light of the Security Council Resolutions on arms inspection.

76 See ND White, *Keeping the Peace, The United Nations and the Maintenance of International Peace and Security*, 1990; H McCoubrey and ND White, *International Law and Armed Conflict*, 1992; D Sarooshi, *The United Nations and the Development of Collective Security*, 1999.

77 The concept of 'collective security' has been defined as 'the proposition that aggressive and unlawful use of force by one nation against another will be met by the combined strength of all other nations' (see KP Sakensa, *The United Nations and Collective Security*, 1974).

be taken in accordance with Arts 41 and 42 to maintain or restore international peace and security.

This provision has to be read with the succeeding provisions, so that Art 40 permits the Security Council to order provisional measures while it considers what substantive action to take. In broad terms, enforcement action may take one of two forms as indicated in Arts 41 and 42. Thus Art 41 reads:

> The Security Council may decide what measures not involving the use of armed force are to be employed to give effect to its decisions, and it may call upon the Members of the United Nations to apply such measures. These may include complete or partial interruption of economic relations and of rail, sea, air, postal, telegraphic, radio, and other means of communication and the severance of diplomatic relations.

This provision is then followed by Art 42 which reads:

> Should the Security Council consider that measures provided for in Art 41 would be inadequate or have proved to be inadequate, it may take such action by air, sea or land forces as may be necessary to maintain or restore international peace and security. Such action may include demonstrations, blockade and other operations by air, sea or land forces of Members of the United Nations.

These provisions have to be read with Art 43, which envisaged the negotiation of special agreements for the provision of armed forces, with such agreements being executed by a Military Staff Committee established under Art 47. Since 1945, these arrangements have not been able to be executed so that the original scheme of Chapter VII has never become fully operational. Thus, the position is that, while the Security Council may require compliance with measures issued under Art 41, it cannot order a state to participate in measures authorised under Art 42.

Thus, under Chapter VII, the Security Council is given power not merely to make recommendations but to take decisions binding on other members. The key element is the expression 'any threat to peace, breach of the peace or act of aggression'; thus the Middle East War of 1948,[78] the Korean situation in 1950[79] or the Unilateral Declaration of Independence by Southern Rhodesia[80] have all come within the definition,[81] as did the invasion of the Falkland Islands in 1982.[82] The conclusion of the Cold War has led to a greater willingness to invoke Art 39, as evidenced by the resolutions passed in respect of Yugoslavia,[83] Somalia,[84] Liberia[85] and Rwanda.[86] However, at least three of these

---

78 SC Res 54 (1948).

79 See SC Res 83 (1950) and SC Res 84 (1950).

80 For Southern Rhodesia, see SC Res 217 (1965); SC Res 221 (1966); SC Res 232 (1966); SC Res 253 (1968); SC Res 277 (1970).

81 In recent years, the Security Council has been increasingly ready to accept that the provisions of Art 39 have been met; see SC Res 1199 (1998) (Kosovo) and SC Res 1264 (1999) (East Timor).

82 SC Res 502 (1982).

83 For resolutions passed during the Yugoslav crisis, see SC Res 713 (25 September 1991); SC Res 743 (21 February 1992); SC Res 752 (15 May 1992); SC Res 757 (30 May 1992); SC Res 764 (13 July 1992); SC Res 769 (7 August 1992); SC Res 770 (13 August 1992); SC Res 780 (6 October 1992); SC Res 787 (16 November 1992).

84 SC Res 733 (23 January 1992); SC Res 751 (28 April 1992); SC Res 794 (3 December 1992).

85 SC Res 788 (1992).

86 For Rwanda, see SC Res 912 (1994); SC Res 918 (1994); SC Res 929 (1994); SC Res 955 (1994).

situations were, in essence, complex internal civil wars so that, while there may have been a willingness to pass a resolution, there was some reluctance to contribute soldiers to enforce the resolution.

In most situations, it is not difficult to decide whether there has been any 'threat to the peace'. Such a threat might arise by a civil war causing regional tension, as in the cases of Yugoslavia[87] or Liberia[88] or by virtue of state conduct in the case of Libya[89] or by a failure to respect previously agreed democratic processes as in the case of Haiti.[90] The expression aggression was defined in a United Nations General Assembly Resolution of 1974.[91] Of particular interest is Art 3, which indicates that aggressive acts might include not only the use of weapons but also the blockade of ports and the sending of armed bands to carry out armed attack. However, such a resolution can only provide a general guide.[92] The Security Council is entitled to receive all relevant evidence and it will be for its Members to determine whether Art 39 has been triggered. Some of the past cases have left little room for doubt, such as the invasion of South Korea in 1950;[93] or the Falkland Islands in 1982;[94] or Kuwait in 1990.[95]

The exercise of powers under Chapter VII was not without difficulty in the Cold War because of the threat of the use of the veto power. Action had only been possible by the Security Council on Korea because of the absence of the Soviet Union. Western powers, conscious that the Security Council might be subject to the exercise of the veto power, sought to bolster the position of the General Assembly by the persuading that body to pass the Uniting for Peace Resolution on 3 November 1950.[96] In broad terms, the Uniting for Peace Resolution asserted that, in the event of the Security Council failing in its duty to maintain international peace and security, the General Assembly would meet with a view to making recommendations which might include the use of armed force. Such an approach was difficult to square with the division of responsibilities under the Charter, in particular Art 11(2) which provides that 'any such question on which action is necessary shall be referred to the Security Council by the General Assembly, either before or after discussion'. However, it is important to consider the background to the matter; the frivolous use of the Soviet veto ran the risk of paralysing the Security Council and there

---

87 See SC Res 713 (1991); SC Res 733 (1992).
88 SC Res 788 (1992).
89 SC Res 748 (1992).
90 SC Res 841 (1993) (imposition of arms and oil embargo; SC Res 873 (1993). The problem in Haiti arose from the ousting of a government which had been democratically elected in elections which had been monitored by the United Nations).
91 GA Res 3314 (XXIX).
92 See J Stone, 'Holes and loopholes in the 1974 definition of aggression' (1977) 71 AJIL 231.
93 See SC Res 83 (1950); SC Res 84 (1950).
94 See SC Res 502 (April 3 1982, which demanded a cessation of hostilities and withdrawal by Argentinian forces).
95 See SC Res 660 (August 2 1982, which demanded the immediate withdrawal of Iraqi forces from Kuwait).
96 GA Res 377(V) (3 November 1950).

was concern that the organisation might become as impotent as the League of Nations. Secondly, at the time the General Assembly[97] was a much smaller body than it has become and the subsequent use of the procedure has been limited.[98]

Once the Security Council has considered the evidence and found that the requirements of Art 39 have been met, it will then have to consider what measures are required. It may decide that provisional measures are appropriate under Art 40 to calm the situation and allow diplomatic exchanges to proceed; so in the past,[99] it has ordered a ceasefire in order that diplomatic exchanges can commence. Beyond this, it then has to consider whether to order, under Art 41, measures not involving the use of armed force or to act under Art 42 and authorise the use of force.

In respect of action under Art 41, examples of Security Council action are limited. The unilateral declaration of independence by the government of Mr Ian Smith in Southern Rhodesia in November 1965 resulted in Security Council action to limit trade in certain essential commodities.[100] At a later date, the United Kingdom government was given authority to search vessels[101] and, gradually, the sanctions regime was extended.[102] The granting of independence to Southern Rhodesia as Zimbabwe in 1979[103] resulted in the lifting of sanctions.[104] At the time, some argued that the action was unnecessary because Southern Rhodesia was not technically a state; however, the Security Council were acting to prevent a government holding office without the expressed consent of 90% of the population and were concerned that the tension within Southern Rhodesia would contribute to regional instability.[105] Similar action was taken in respect of South Africa, where an arms embargo had been imposed[106] under Art 41 against the apartheid regime, but such sanctions were lifted in 1994[107] with the introduction of a non-racial constitution.

Economic sanctions have been imposed under Chapter VII, at a time when other measures have been under active consideration. In the case of the Iraqi invasion of Kuwait, a number of economic sanctions were imposed after August 1990. Security Council Resolution 661[108] imposed economic sanctions on Iraq, while Resolution 666[109]

---

97 The Uniting for Peace Resolution was relied upon by the General Assembly in 1956 to authorise the United Nations Emergency Force in the Middle East.

98 Suez (1956); Hungary (1956); Lebanon (1958); Belgian Congo (1960); Middle East (1967); Pakistan (1971); Afghanistan (1980); Namibia (1981).

99 In the Middle East context, see SC Res 234 (1967); SC Res 338 (1973).

100 SC Res 217 (1965). See generally, JW Halderman, 'Some legal aspects of sanctions in the Rhodesian case' (1968) 17 ICLQ 672.

101 SC Res 221 (9 April 1966).

102 For subsequent resolutions drawing upon Art 39 and Art 41, see SC Res 232 (1966); SC Res 253 (1968); SC Res 277 (1970).

103 For legislation of the United Kingdom Parliament on the subject, see Southern Rhodesia Act 1965; Southern Rhodesia Act 1979; Zimbabwe Act 1979. For a discussion of the constitutional problems caused by the Unilateral Declaration of Independence, see the Privy Council judgment in *Madzimbamuto v Lardner Burke* [1969] 1 AC 645.

104 This was effected by SC Res 460 (1979).

105 The conduct of the regime was also a defiance of the general principle of self-determination.

106 See SC Res 418 (1977); this replaced the voluntary embargo that had been in place since 1963.

107 SC Res 919 (25 May 1994).

108 SC Res 661 (1990).

109 SC Res 666 (1990).

regulated the flow of foodstuffs, and the entire regime was tightened in Resolution 670,[110] when sanctions were extended to aviation links. Although the situation had to be resolved by the use of military force, Resolution 687 (1991) set out the terms of a long term peace settlement, and Resolution 692 provided for the establishment of the United Nations Compensation Commission. At a later date, Resolution 705[111] modified the terms of compensation, while Resolution 706[112] regulated the details of Iraq's petroleum exports. In short, the Iraq-Kuwait crisis resulted in a wide use of Chapter VII powers.

The tragic events of the civil war in Yugoslavia have resulted in a considerable number of resolutions under Chapter VII. On 25 September 1991, Resolution 713 imposed an arms embargo on all parties to the conflict. This was followed on 30 May 1992 by Resolution 757, which imposed economic sanctions on the Federal Republic of Yugoslavia; these sanctions were tightened in Resolution 787 of 16 November 1992. In the spring of 1993, the geographical scope of such sanctions was extended in Resolution 820, and this process was carried further in Resolution 942. The negotiations leading to the Dayton Peace Agreement of November 1995 were accompanied by a reduction of sanctions and a lifting of the arms embargo.[113]

It is arguable that the use of Art 41 sanctions in the case of Iraq and Yugoslavia was only of some effect because of the willingness and capacity to resort to forcible measures as well. Be that as it may, the Security Council has also employed Chapter VII to establish international tribunals[114] to prosecute those accused of criminal acts.

Alongside the jurisdiction to adopt non-forcible measures, the Security Council is entitled, if it considers such measures inadequate, to take 'such action by air, sea or land forces as may be necessary to maintain or restore international peace and security'. It was intended that these powers available under Art 42 should operate alongside the provision for military arrangements concluded under Art 43 and made effective under Art 45. In the event, these articles were not brought into effect so that action under Art 42 has depended on whether a consensus exists in the Security Council not only to pass a resolution but to provide the resources to implement it.

However, Art 42 has been relied on by the Security Council from the outset. The first serious use was in the Korean crisis of June 1950 which was precipitated by the invasion of South Korea by its neighbour North Korea. In the event, the Security Council met and, in a series of resolutions,[115] called for the withdrawal of North Korean troops beyond the 38th parallel and requested member states to place their armed forces under a Commander to be appointed by the United States.[116] These resolutions were only able to be passed because the Soviet Union had withdrawn from the Security Council; when the

---

110 SC Res 670 (1990).

111 SC Res 705 (1991).

112 SC Res 706 (1991).

113 The modification and reduction of sanctions can be traced in Security Council Resolutions 943 (1994); 988 (1995); 992 (1995); 1003 (1995); 1015 (1995); 1021 (1995); 1022 (1995); 1074 (1995).

114 See SC Res 808 (1992) and 827 (1992) in respect of the former Yugoslavia and Res 995 (1994) in respect of Rwanda.

115 See SC Res 82 (1950); Res 83 (1950); Res 84 (1950).

116 The first Commander being Douglas MacArthur (1880–1964), who was appointed by President Truman and relieved of command in April 1951.

Soviet Union returned the United States persuaded the General Assembly to pass the 'Uniting for Peace Resolution' to preserve the momentum behind the action.[117] The force dispatched was described as a United Nations force and contained personnel contributed by 16 member states.[118] This was a most unusual situation; the Soviet Union returned to the Security Council in August 1950[119] and some in the United States raised questions as to the procedures by which the force had been established. When the fighting ended and a peace conference took place at Geneva in 1954, those states that had sent troops were separately represented. Although the Uniting for Peace Resolution was relied upon again in 1956, because of the involvement of two members of the Security Council, enthusiasm for involving the General Assembly began to ebb.

In the years after Suez, the hostile relations between the two superpowers and the presence of the veto power placed limits on the possible action of the Security Council. This was particularly the case where there had been serious breaches of international law[120] involving the Soviet Union.[121] In some cases, the United States conducted matters outside the Security Council.[122] However, the tension between the superpowers ended with the arrival in power of Mikhail Gorbachev[123] and the retirement of Andrei Gromyko as Foreign Minister.[124] Thereafter, it became possible for the Security Council to co-operate without difficulties of ideology and the focus of United States' foreign policy began to move back towards[125] the Security Council.

---

117 The conduct of the Truman Administration raised questions in the United States. Senator Taft raised the question as to whether a vote without the Soviet Union was consistent with Art 27 of the Charter. Others argued that it was risky to build up the role of the General Assembly when the United States had only one vote in a body of 60; some pointed out that the General Assembly would come to be dominated by states not always minded to agree with the United States (see Congressional Record, 5 January 1951).

118 Australia, Belgium, Canada, Columbia, Ethiopia, France, Greece, Luxembourg, Netherlands, New Zealand, Philippines, Thailand, Turkey, South Africa, United Kingdom and United States.

119 The Soviet Union returned to the Security Council in August 1950 and in November 1950 it vetoed a resolution critical of the involvement of China. Thereafter, with the paralysis of the Security Council, effective conduct passed to a committee of the General Assembly; an armistice became effective in July 1953.

120 There has been a problem from the outset under the United Nations Charter. The Charter seeks the maintenance of international law and the Security Council is under a general duty to uphold the Charter.

121 It is difficult not to conclude that the conduct of the Soviet Union in Hungary (1956), Czechoslovakia (1968) and Afghanistan (1979), together with the Brezhnev Doctrine were not clear violations of the United Nations Charter. Allied to this was the policy of Soviet involvement in regional conflicts by the supplying of weapons and the sending of advisers. Further the considerable sums spent on military forces could only contribute to an atmosphere of mistrust in the Security Council.

122 To some extent, this is true of the Cuban missile crisis (1962), Vietnam (1961–75) and the Dominican Republic (1965).

123 Leader of the Soviet Union from the death of Konstantin Chernenko in 1985.

124 He had served as Foreign Minister from 1957 until 1985 and was personally associated with the policies of the Cold War years.

125 See R Higgins, 'Peace and security, achievements and failures' (1995) 6 EJIL 445. An important event was probably the election of George Bush as United States President in 1988. In his various previous posts, Bush had served as United States Ambassador to the United Nations (1971–73) as well as serving as special envoy to China for President Ford (1974–75). The general disposition to work through the United Nations was illustrated by the attempts of his Secretary of State, James Baker, to build a coalition of states against Iraq in the period 1990–91. Unlike some previous Presidents, George Bush had considerable experience of diplomatic and intelligence matters before holding the highest office. Some historians have indicated that one of the legacies of the Vietnam War (1963–75) in the United States is the need for foreign policy initiatives to have support both in Congress and with the general public. Acting with and through the institutions of the United Nations makes this more likely.

The post-Cold War climate was well illustrated by the response of the Security Council to the Iraqi invasion of Kuwait; it helped that the incident itself was a clear breach of the United Nations Charter. In the event, Security Council Resolution 660[126] condemned the invasion and demanded withdrawal and this was followed by nearly 30 Security Council resolutions on the same subject. Resolution 661[127] imposed a trade and arms embargo while Resolution 662[128] declared the purported Iraqi annexation of Kuwait to be null and void. The Security Council acting under Chapter VII passed resolutions to protect foreign nationals[129] and diplomatic personnel in Kuwait.[130] As these actions were being taken, a number of member states indicated their willingness to contribute forces, should that be necessary. On 29 November 1989, the Security Council adopted Resolution 678[131] which provided that, after 15 January 1990, 'all necessary measures' were authorised to ensure respect for Resolution 660. When a further round of diplomatic contacts failed, an air campaign began on 16 January 1991, followed by a land offensive which commenced on 24 February 1991. The land offensive succeeded in removing the Iraqi army from Kuwait and liberating the territory. Resolution 678 had included the phrase 'to restore international peace and security in the area' and, although coalition forces did enter southern Iraq, no attempt was made to remove the Iraqi government from office.[132] A temporary ceasefire was established in Resolution 686 of 2 March 1991, to be followed by the detailed terms of the ceasefire in Resolution 687 of 3 April 1991.

The action taken against Iraq gave rise to a number of points. First, the action involved the expulsion of the army of state A from the territory of state B; it was quite clear there had been a breach of the United Nations Charter and the considerable number of states who participated testified to this view.[133] The second issue was how, if at all, the Security Council could exercise any control over the actual conduct of military operations. A third issue that was raised at the time was whether more time should have been given

---

126 SC Res 660 (2 August 1990) referred to Arts 39 and 40 of the Charter.

127 SC Res 661 (6 August 1990) also made reference to the right of self defence.

128 SC Res 662 (9 August 1990).

129 SC Res 664 (18 August 1990) required that Iraq release foreign nationals held in Iraq or Kuwait. This was followed by SC Res 665 (25 August 1990) which authorised the searching of Iraqi vessels.

130 SC Res 667 (16 September 1990) condemned Iraq for its treatment of diplomatic personnel contrary to the Vienna Conventions of 1961 and 1963.

131 This was the last resolution prior to the ceasefire. Iraq objected on the grounds that there was a general reference to Chapter VII and not a specific reference to Arts 42 and 43.

132 One question at the time was legal, namely whether action against the regime was authorised under the Resolutions or whether military action should be restricted to expelling the Iraqi army from Kuwait. Another problem was that action against the regime might lead to the disintegration of the state itself and thus cause greater regional tension. A third argument was the need to preserve international goodwill for future co-operative ventures. In the event, a compromise was reached by imposing strict controls in the form of the cease fire and compensation Resolutions.

133 Between August 1990 and December 1990, 29 states came forward to assist the US lead coalition: Argentina, Australia, Bahrain, Bangladesh, Belgium, Canada, Czechoslovakia, Denmark, Egypt, France, Germany, Greece, Italy, Kuwait, Morocco, Netherlands, New Zealand, Niger, Norway, Oman, Pakistan, Qtar, Saudi Arabia, Senegal, Spain, Syria, United Arab Emirates, the United Kingdom and the United States.

for economic sanctions to work.[134] A fourth problem was whether those states affected by the operation of sanctions had any right to compensation under Art 50 of the Charter.[135]

The near degree of unanimity displayed by the Security Council in the Gulf War raised expectations that, in the post-Cold War period, the Security Council might be able to act more decisively under Chapter VII. However, it has to be said that, since that date, the Security Council has had to cope with intractable civil war situations stimulated by ethnic conflict and a collapse of normal political structures. As many observers have remarked, the problems posed by civil wars are much more difficult to resolve.[136]

During the Gulf War, a large number of Kurds fleeing from the Iraqi army had entered Turkey from Iran and Iraq; there was no dispute that widespread human suffering was being caused. In these circumstances, Security Council Resolution 688 was adopted on 5 April 1991 authorising the provision of humanitarian aid and pointing to the flow of refugees across international frontiers; some states had objected[137] to the resolution, questioning whether it was consistent with Art 2(7) of the Charter. As a matter of law, it can be defended either on grounds that the movement of refugees had caused regional instability or that Iraq subsequently consented to the resolution by agreeing to accept humanitarian aid; a third justification is that the resolution does not stand alone and has to be read with all other resolutions directed to the Iraqi government since August 1990.

In considering the nature of Security Council intervention, it is important to note also that it is becoming clear that actions by the Security Council may, in certain limited circumstances, be subject to a form of judicial review by the International Court of Justice. This was raised by several judges in the *Lockerbie* case[138] and also by Judge Lauterpacht in his separate opinion in the *Genocide* case.[139] However, this does not represent a fetter because, on the assumption that the Security Council has relevant evidence and power to act, it would be inconsistent with the nature of judicial review[140] for the International Court of Justice to substitute its discretion for that of the Security Council.

---

134 In between the final resolution of 28 November 1990 and the actual opening of the air campaign on 16 January 1991, the question of military action was debated in the United States Congress and the United Kingdom Parliament. A number of speakers recalled that one of the requirements for just war doctrine to apply was that all other avenues had been tried and exhausted. In point of fact, the invasion took place on 1 August 1990 and the air campaign did not begin until 16 January 1991.

135 For a detailed review of this see J Carver and J Hulsmann, 'The role of Article 50 of the United Nations Charter in the search for international peace and security' (2000) 49 ICLQ 528.

136 See A Parsons, *From Cold War to Hot Peace*, 1995.

137 The resolution raised the sensitive issue of internal sovereignty; in the Security Council, 10 states voted for, three voted against (Cuba, Yemen and Zimbabwe) and two abstained (China, India).

138 *Lockerbie* case (*Case concerning Questions of Interpretation and Application of the 1971 Montreal Convention arising from the Aerial Incident at Lockerbie*) (1992) ICJ 3.

139 *Case concerning Application of the Convention on the Prevention and Punishment of the Crime of Genocide (Bosnia-Herzegovina v Yugoslavia)* (1993) ICJ 325.

140 The essence of judicial review being to review the decision making process, not to act as a form of appeal.

While the Gulf War is the classic recent example of Security Council activism,[141] it is sensible to consider a number of other initiatives.

(a) Somalia

The collapse of the regime of President Siad Barre in 1991 had left the country[142] subject to effective civil war between rival warlords. Various international bodies had been engaged in humanitarian relief and on 23 January 1991 the Security Council imposed an arms embargo.[143] After a technical mission had considered the options,[144] the Security Council sent a limited force of military observers (UNSCOM);[145] however, the situation continued to deteriorate and the delivery of humanitarian aid was being blocked. By this stage, Somalia had no effective government to request help; however, the United States offered to lead a humanitarian mission and pursuant to this the Security Council adopted Resolution 794 on 3 December 1992.[146] The resolution made it clear that the ultimate responsibility for the country rested with the people of Somalia. In the period December 1992 to March 1993, about 37,000 personnel joined the relief mission. In March 1993, Resolution 814 renamed the force UNSCOM II and expanded its powers but divisions of opinion were already present as to how much military action should be taken against rival warlords. Although the mandate of the force was strengthened,[147] 25 Pakistani soldiers serving with UNSCOM II were killed in June 1993, followed by the death of 18 United States soldiers in October 1993; this prompted the United States to indicate that it would withdraw from Somalia in March 1994. The mission was effectively over by March 1995. Although the mission had had some effect in distributing aid, it raised concerns in the United States about the wisdom of such projects and it did nothing for the reputation of the United Nations.

(b) Rwanda

Rwanda had been independent since 1967 but, from 1989, it had been plagued by clashes between the Hutu[148] dominated forces of the French backed Government of Rwanda and

---

141 The degree of unity achieved in the Security Council and the broad support for the coalition owed much to the limited objective, namely a desire to enforce Art 2(4) of the Charter and require the Iraqi army to leave Kuwait. It also owed much to the vigour and diplomatic skill of the then Secretary of State James Baker (1989–92). In his published writing, Baker has expressed the fear that the United Nations might become 'a forum for lowest common denominator decision making unless America takes the lead in shaping the debate and forcing action'. One of the problems since 1989 has been the question: can the United Nations act effectively without a clear United States lead? This question has been raised in the published writings of both James Baker and Warren Christopher and surfaced again during the Kosovo campaign of 1999. There is clearly a difficult balance to be struck between 'shaping the debate' and dominating the organisation. The relationship between the United States and the United Nations is central to the memoirs of the most recent Secretary General. (See Boutros Boutros Ghali; *Unvanquished; A US-UN Saga*, 1999, New York.

142 Somalia having been a member of the United Nations since 1960.

143 SC Res 733 (1992).

144 SC Res 746 (1992).

145 SC Res 751 (1992).

146 The operation was known as Operation Restore Hope; the initiative was that of President Bush but it had been approved by President elect Clinton.

147 For other resolutions, see SC 865 (1993); 878 (1993); 885 (1993); 886 (1993).

148 The Hutus being the majority and the Tutsi the minority within the territory.

the Tutsi dominated Rwanda Patriotic Front (RPF) which operated from Uganda. On 22 June 1993, the Security Council agreed to set up the United Nations Observer Mission Uganda-Rwanda (UNOMUR), with the objective of policing the border area.[149] Following a peace accord reached in Arusha, Tanzania in August 1993, the United Nations set up a second force to implement the agreement and to secure the capital, Kigali, to be known as the United Nations Assistance Mission for Rwanda (UNAMIR);[150] it was intended to prepare for the election of a new government. Implementing the agreement proved difficult and, on 6 April 1994, the death of the President of Rwanda in an aircrash precipitated a civil war with genocidal acts perpetrated by various factions. Large numbers of refugees began to stream towards Uganda, Zaire Tanzania and Burundi. To avoid further loss of life, the size of UNAMIR was scaled down.[151] At the beginning of May 1994, the Security Council imposed an arms embargo;[152] serious discussions took place about a relief force but member states were unwilling to act. Eventually, in June 1994, France offered a force to rescue foreign nationals and to establish a safe area and this force was authorised under Resolution 929 on 22 June 1994.[153] The intensity of the civil war abated after the signing of a cease fire on 18 July 1994 and France combined with units from Ghana and Zimbabwe to provide a measure of security under the mandate of UNAMIR II which continued until March 1996. However, any action had been taken rather late; although estimates are difficult to verify, it is not seriously disputed that over half a million person died between March and September 1994 and an equal number became refugees. The extent of the slaughter and the seeming inability of the United Nations to take effective restraining action was the cause of much critical comment; once again, the episode raised the question of how the United Nations should act when there is a reluctance by member states to contribute armed forces.

(c) Yugoslavia

The Socialist Federal Republic of Yugoslavia had been subject to internal tension since the death of President Tito in 1980. However, disintegration began to accelerate when Croatia and Slovenia declared their independence in June 1991. After the European Community and the CSCE failed to make progress, the problem was passed to the Security Council which imposed an arms embargo in Resolution 713 in September 1991.[154] This was a controversial step because it appeared to leave the well equipped Yugoslav People's Army in a position to dictate terms. In February 1992, the Security Council resolved to set up a United Nations Protection Force (UNPROFOR), one of whose tasks was to assist the delivery of humanitarian aid.[155] However, throughout the conflict events moved faster on the ground and negotiated ceasefires were continually broken as the various parties sought to gain territorial advantage. As the fighting spread to Bosnia, the situation

---

149 See SC Res 846 (1993). For earlier action, see SC Res 812 (1993) and subsequently SC Res 891 (1993).
150 See SC Res 872 (5 October 1993); see also SC Res 893 (1994) and SC Res 909 (1994).
151 SC Res 912 (21 April 1994). The UNAMIR force was only lightly equipped and not organise to stop the violence.
152 SC Res 918 (1994).
153 SC Res 929 (1994).
154 SC Res 713 (1991).
155 SC Res 743 (February 1992).

deteriorated. Security Council Resolution 752 of 15 May 1992[156] was passed to restrain fighting in Bosnia Herzegovina but it was largely ignored and this resulted in economic sanctions being imposed in Resolution 757 of 30 May 1992.[157] From this time, reliable independent reports began to emerge of 'ethnic cleansing' and serious abuses of human rights. This conduct resulted in a succession of Security Council resolutions[158] endeavouring to regulate a situation that was now slipping out of control as the various factions engaged in all out military conflict.

At the London Conference of August 1992, a decision was taken to increase the personnel available to UNPROFOR[159] and this was followed by the imposition of a ban on military flights over Bosnia and Herzegovina.

By the autumn of 1992 there was irrefutable evidence of human rights abuses and the Security Council authorised an independent investigation;[160] however, by this stage the pattern of the conflict had been set, with fighting on the ground dictating the pace of events.[161] In spring 1993, the Security Council declared a number of safe areas,[162] but these were not respected as the parties sought to maximise their territorial gains in advance of the inevitable peace settlement. From 1994, air strikes were conducted by NATO to restrain the activities of the Bosnian Serb forces. By August 1995, the Bosnian Serb forces and Croatians had achieved the territorial gains that they sought and were responsive to proposals by the American envoy, Richard Holbrooke. In October 1995, the parties agreed to attend a peace conference at Dayton, Ohio, which resulted in a Framework Agreement being accepted there on 21 November 1995 and signed in Paris on 14 November 1995. Consequent upon the agreement, many of the earlier Security Council resolutions were lifted.[163]

The case of the disintegration of the former Socialist Federal Republic of Yugoslavia brought to an end any euphoria generated by the Gulf War. The civil war indicated the reluctance of member states to contribute. The United States tended to regard the matter as a European problem and the Europeans were unwilling to become involved and often unable to act collectively. In essence, the Security Council was unable to restrain the conduct of the parties in a brutally fought civil war when it lacked the military strength to enforce its will. Once again, the Yugoslav crisis brought into clear focus the distinction between the willingness to pass a resolution and the capacity to enforce it.

---

156 SC Res 752 (15 May 1992).

157 SC Res 757 (30 May 1992).

158 SC Res 764 (13 July 1992) (made reference to obligations under international humanitarian law and the Geneva Conventions); SC Res 769 (7 August 1992) (referred to the abuses perpetrated against the civilian population); SC Res 770 (13 August 1992); SC Res 771 (which condemned the practice of ethnic cleansing).

159 For the succession of resolutions relevant to UNPROFOR, see SC Res 727 (8 January 1992); SC Res 743 (21 February 1992); SC Res 749 (7 April 1992); SC Res 769 (7 August 1992); SC Res 776 (14 September 1992); SC Res 779 (6 October 1992).

160 SC Res 780 (6 October 1992).

161 SC Res 787 (16 November 1992) and SC Res 798 (17 December 1992) had both condemned ethnic cleansing; and SC Res 808 (22 February 1993) and SC Res 827 (25 May 1993) had provided for the establishment of the International Criminal Tribunal for the Former Yugoslavia.

162 See SC Res 819 (16 April 1993, Srebrenica) and SC Res 824 (6 May 1993, Sarajevo, Tuzla, Zepa, Gorazde, Bihac).

163 SC Res 1021 (1995) and SC Res 1022 lifting the arms embargo and suspending the economic sanctions against the Federal Republic of Yugoslavia.

6 PEACEKEEPING AND RELATED ACTIVITIES

In the years since the conclusion of the Cold War, there has been considerable United Nations activity in this area. However, it is important to be clear on terminology; in his document, *An Agenda for Peace*,[164] the Secretary General, Dr Boutros Ghali, attempted to set out some working definitions. First, he drew attention to the role of preventive diplomacy which might involve fact finding and good offices. Secondly, he identified 'peacemaking' which might be action taken under Chapter VI of the Charter. Thirdly, he defined peacekeeping as the deployment of United Nations personnel in an area with the consent of the parties. In contrast he went on to identify 'peace enforcement',[165] which involves peacekeeping undertaken without the consent of the parties and is normally authorised under the terms the provisions of Chapter VII. It has to be recognised that the basic distinction between 'peacekeeping' (with consent) and 'enforcement action' has become less clear with the emergence of forms of 'mixed keeping' which may involve elements of each. Secondly, the deployment of forces may be undertaken on a limited basis but circumstances may dictate a modification of the mandate once the force has arrived in theatre.[166]

It is clear that the modern law on peace keeping is a product of gradual evolution. The early actions of the United Nations were designed to supervise truces as was the case in the Balkans in 1947 or after the Middle East War in 1948. At the same time, it was clear that little progress was likely to be made on making forces available under Art 43 of the Charter. Secondly, while there is no express provision in the Charter dealing with peace keeping, there are a number of provisions that can be preyed in aid to legitimise the conduct of the Security Council,[167] the General Assembly[168] or the Secretary General[169] in this area. So the two relevant questions are 'What form of activity is in issue?' and 'What is the legal authority for the activity?'. However, given the complexities of civil war situations it has sometimes been difficult to prevent a blurring of these questions.

The evolution of the law is best considered historically. In the early years of the United Nations, it was clear that the provisions of Art 43 were unlikely to be implemented and it was also evident that, in many cases, the Security Council would be paralysed by the use of the veto. In these circumstances, the General Assembly sought to fill the vacuum. The first such peace keeping force was set up during the Suez crisis of 1956, when the Security Council was unable to act because of the involvement of two of its permanent members. The response of the General Assembly was to set up the United Nations Emergency Force in the Middle East (UNEF) in November 1956[170] to supervise the ceasefire; the force that was answerable to the General Assembly and the Secretary General remained in the area until 1967.

---

164 Accepted by the General Assembly in GA Res 47/120.
165 Confusion sometimes arises when the expression 'peace making' is used as synonymous for peace enforcement.
166 Sometimes referred to by the expression 'mission creep', which became common after the Somalia intervention in 1992.
167 See Arts 29, 34, 36, 37, 38, 39 and 42.
168 See Arts 11, 14; see also *Certain Expenses of the United Nations* case (1962) ICJ 151.
169 See Charter of the United Nations (1945), Art 98.
170 See GA Res 3276 (4 November 1956).

This initial precedent was followed in the more complicated Congo crisis of June 1960 where the Security Council authorised the Secretary General Hammarskjold to establish a peace keeping force.[171] Pursuant to this direction, the United Nations Force in the Congo (ONUC) was established and took its instructions from the Secretary General[172] because of division in the Security Council; as the situation in the Congo deteriorated the force was drawn into heavy military operations more akin to enforcement than peace keeping. The establishment of peace keeping forces in both the Middle East and the Congo was not without legal difficulty. The forces had been financed separately and not out of the general budget; some states objected to contributing on the grounds that the forces had not been lawfully established under the Charter. In these circumstances, the General Assembly sought an Advisory Opinion from the International Court of Justice as to whether there was an obligation to contribute arising under Art 17(2). In the *Expenses* case[173] the International Court of Justice held that the expenses of the forces fell within Art 17(2); in respect of the suggestion that the establishment of UNEF was unlawful, the Court noted the power of the General Assembly to Act under Art 11 or Art 14 while, in respect of ONUC, it was observed that Art 98 permitted a wide delegation of powers to the Secretary General.

In the Cyprus crisis of 1964, the force sent by the Security Council (UNFICYP) was subject to a detailed mandate as to how it was to conduct itself in dealing with the tension between the Greek and Turkish communities; however, the actual resolution[174] is not specific as to whether the force was set up under Chapter VI or Chapter VII. Although the wording of Chapter VI may have had to be stretched, it is strongly arguable if the General Assembly is authorised to act under Arts 11 and 14 then it seems logical that the Security Council should have the same implied power under Chapter VI.

In the years 1945–85, it is possible to identify at least 10 forces[175] that generally came within the ambit of United Nations peace keeping. Generally, such forces were only to act in self-defence and the usual objective was to ensure the observance of a ceasefire line. Thus, in the Middle East a second United Nations Emergency Force (UNEF II) policed the ceasefire between Egypt and Israel after the Yom Kippur war in November 1973, while in 1974 a disengagement observer force (UNDOF)[176] performed the same function between Syria and Israel; a more difficult task faced the United Nations Interim Force in Southern Lebanon (UNIFIL) which was sent in 1978[177] to restore the authority of the Lebanese Government in a situation verging on civil war. If there are any lessons from the first 40 years, they are probably that such forces operate best if they are sent with the approval of the entire international community, that they have limited and clearly defined tasks accepted by the various parties in the theatre and they have adequate resources to discharge those tasks. When the objectives are unclear, or the consent of the parties is lacking, or resources are inadequate then difficulties can easily arise.

---

171 For Security Council resolutions during the Congo crisis, see SC Res 4383 (14 July 1960); SC Res 4424 (9 August 1960); SC Res 4722 (21 February 1961).

172 See CC O'Brien, *To Katanga and Back*, 1962.

173 *Certain Expenses of the United Nations* case (1962) ICJ 151.

174 SC Res 186 (1964).

175 A list would include Middle East (UNEF 1 (1956); UNEF II (1973) UNDOF (1974) UNIFIL (1982)); Yemen (UNYOM 1963); New Guinea (UNSF 1962); India and Pakistan (UNMOGIP 1949; UNIPOM 1965); Dominican Republic (DOMREP 1965); Cyprus (UNFICYP 1964).

176 SC Res 350 (31 May 1974).

177 The crisis followed the Israeli invasion of Lebanon; see SC Res 425 and 426 (19 March 1978).

The conclusion of the Cold War resulted in the decline of the use of the veto in the Security Council and perhaps an undue degree of optimism as to what might be achieved by international peace keeping. A problem immediately arose because of a blurring of a distinction between peace making and peace enforcement and difficulties developed when forces were sent with fluctuating objectives into internal civil wars. After 1989, a considerable number of peace keeping operations[178] have been sanctioned, but it is a matter of record that such interventions (even though resolved upon for the highest humanitarian reasons) have had a very mixed track record and resulted in tension between the United Nations and certain important member states. Interventions in Yugoslavia, Somalia, Haiti and Rwanda may have been dictated by the noblest objectives, but difficulties have arisen when member states are reluctant to send large numbers of forces to undertake open ended commitments. Both Dr Boutros Ghali and Kofi Annan have drawn attention to the problems caused when member states pass resolutions for humanitarian or peace keeping action, but then are reluctant to provide the resources to effectively undertake those tasks.

In the years since 1989, there has been an increasing emphasis on the protection of human rights through the establishment of democratic government.[179] To this end, the United Nations has provided technical help in monitoring elections designed to usher in democratic government.[180]

However, the experience since 1989 has given cause for concern. First, there is a rather confused line between peace enforcement and peace keeping.[181] Secondly, some states are increasingly reluctant to commit forces to open ended commitments. Thirdly, there has been a developing call for the establishment of a special 'United Nations Rapid Reaction Force'[182] but it does seem that most states prefer to leave their options open and to contribute on a case by case basis. In some states, there will be constitutional difficulties in pledging forces in advance to unknown objectives. Fourthly, at the back of such concerns lies the realisation that substantial United Nations action over a long period of time requires the active participation of the United States;[183] those who argue for an

---

178 Since 1989 such missions have included Iran and Iraq (UNIMOG 1988); Iraq/Kuwait (UNIKOM 1991); Angola (UNAVEM 1989; UNAVEM II 1991); El Salvador (ONUSAL 1991); Namibia (UNTAG 1989); Somalia (UNOSOM 1992; UNOSOM II 1993); Mozambique (ONUMOZ 1992); Rwanda (UNOMUR 1993); Yugoslavia (UNPROFOR 1992); Liberia (UNOMIL 1993); Central America (ONUCA 1989).

179 For a general discussion, see S Marks, *The Riddle of all Constitutions*, 2000.

180 See Namibia (1989); Haiti and Nicaragua (1990); Angola (1992); Cambodia (1993); South Africa, Mozambique and El Salvador (1994).

181 Which can make for very difficult operating conditions for UN personnel on the ground, as was seen in Yugoslavia and to a lesser extent in Somalia.

182 See WM Reisman, 'Preparing to wage peace, toward the creation of an international peacemaking command and staff college' (1994) 88 AJIL 76.

183 After the military action in Kosovo in 1999, the published figures indicated the heavy reliance of NATO on United States aircraft. Without the support of the United States, it is unlikely that 'the Gulf War coalition' would have been formed to liberate Kuwait. A heavy proportion of the NATO air strikes during the conflict in Yugoslavia were undertaken by the United States Air Force. It is clearly desirable that the United Nations should be able to call on a wide range of states and not be overly dependent on the good will of the United States. Further, during the United States Presidential Election campaign of November 2000, one of the foreign policy issues concerned the circumstances in which the United States should contribute forces to open ended commitments abroad.

independent United Nations force see this as a solution to the problem of over-dependence on a single state.

Consideration of the state of United Nations peace keeping since 1989 indicates that the process has moved considerably from its Cold War origins. The distinction between peace keeping and peace enforcement has become very blurred and is now often hard to determine.[184] The United Nations has moved from policing ceasefire lines in Cyprus and Kashmir to the very hazardous task of intervening in civil wars. Such a move has taken place with only limited debate; there is no doubt that, since 1989, many resolutions have been passed and the number of personnel is over 35,000, but the cost is proving difficult to meet. Some states are reluctant to meet their budgetary contributions and others are unwilling to supply armed forces. While the desire to intervene is fuelled by an understandable and quite proper concern to protect human rights the problem is that democratically elected governments with small professional armies[185] are reluctant to expose their own soldiers to risk in far away lands in obscure and complex quarrels[186] that have no resonance with their own domestic electorate. Secondly, many such problems are now passed to the United Nations when earlier diplomatic efforts have failed and attitudes are entrenched.[187] Thirdly, the most serious difficulties have arisen for the United Nations when its forces are not operating with the consent of all parties; they can then be placed in the embarrassing position of not being able to help with humanitarian work or being insufficiently resourced to restrain serious abuses of human rights. It is a matter of record that hostile action was taken against United Nations peace keepers in Yugoslavia, Somalia and Rwanda although the problem has been less acute in Sierra Leone and East Timor.

The evidence indicates that many states are unlikely to favour open ended intervention and instead will insist on limited objectives to be conducted in a defined time scale and with the consent of the parties in the theatre. In most western states, the executive branch of government will be answerable to its legislature for the deployment of its armed forces. As the experience of Yugoslavia in 1994 and Kosovo in 1999 has indicated, if forcible measures are needed then the initial preference will be for the use of air power.

---

184 An interesting example is afforded by Haiti where, in September 1994, a multinational force lead by the United States intervened to assist in the restoration of democratic government. Although the action was taken under SC Res 940 (1994) and the objectives were noble, it is difficult to see how such action was consistent with Art 39 and the previous refusal to intervene against 'unwholesome' regimes. It is not without interest that China abstained on the Security Council vote. It might be argued that the circumstances were special in that the people of Haiti had suffered under the Duvalier regime (*père et fils*) and the United Nations had been specifically requested to oversee democratic elections; it was therefore logical to intervene when the democratically elected candidate was ousted. It is noteworthy that a large force was made available and such a force was likely to receive a generally friendly welcome. The emphasis on a democratically elected regime is also to be detected in the United Nations reaction to events in Sierra Leone in the period 1997–2000.

185 This is particularly the case in those states that have simply a volunteer army and do not rely on forms of national service or conscription.

186 Eg, in both Somalia and Rwanda foreign soldiers serving the United Nations were targeted and killed.

187 As illustrated by the initial efforts of the European Community to resolve the Yugoslav crisis in spring 1991.

The future of peace keeping was reviewed for the United Nations by Lakhdar Brahimi[188] in 1999 and a panel of experts and their conclusions were discussed at the United Nations Millennium Summit held in New York in September 2000. It was generally accepted that structural reform was needed, with some member states being asked to supply troops and others being required to make a more equitable contribution. However, before these practicalities are addressed there has to be some agreement as to whether intervention by the United Nations should be on a case by case basis or should be by reference to agreed criteria.

In looking at the broader picture, it is difficult not to conclude that United Nations peacekeeping has been the unintended victim of post-Cold War euphoria coming into contact with the development of the human rights movement; while the latter trend is certainly desirable, it is arguable that there has been an unwillingness to face up to the practical problems of sending limited United Nations forces into situations of unresolved conflict. In the 1990s, the United Nations has been defeated by warlords in Somalia, and embarrassed over 'safe areas' in Yugoslavia, while being humiliated over events in Rwanda. The two relevant questions are: 'In what circumstances should the United Nations intervene?' and 'How should any such intervention be managed?' There are some who argue that the United Nations should intervene whenever there is a serious risk of abuse of human rights; if that is to be the case the United Nations will need considerably greater resources.[189]

7 CONCLUSIONS

There is a tendency when evaluating the role of the United Nations taken as a whole either to claim too much or to err on the side of being overly critical.[190] However, a number of points can usefully be made. First, the fact that the organisation has attracted and retained such a high level of membership is some evidence of its value. Secondly, the prohibition on the use of force enshrined in the Charter has meant that it is now rare for one state to attempt to seize territory of another. Thirdly, there is no doubt that the organisation has found it difficult to make an effective contribution in cases of internal civil wars. Fourthly, on a practical level there is no doubt that, in some cases, the United Nations has found it difficult to persuade states to pay their contributions in full and on time. Fifthly, there is evidence that, since the conclusion of the Cold War, the Security Council has been more ready to pass resolutions under Chapter VII, but states have shown themselves reluctant to match such resolutions with military resources.[191] Since the conclusion of the Cold War, many states have sought to reduce defence spending as a

---

188 Very experienced United Nations envoy and former foreign minister of Algeria.

189 The point was put very clearly by President Clinton when addressing a special meeting of the Security Council in September 2000, when he observed 'We must do more to equip the United Nations to do what we ask it to do'.

190 As Rosemary Righter observed, 'for all the good will towards the Security Council, the United Nations entered the 1990s in the position George Kennan once described as the most dangerous for any institution, too many of its lovers were uncritical, and its critics were too often unloving' (see Rosemary Righter, *Utopia Lost; The United Nations and World Order*, 1995, p 19).

191 This was the point made by the Secretary General to the Security Council in September 2000 during the United Nations Millennium Summit.

proportion of GDP and are reluctant to make open ended peacekeeping commitments. In the years after 1989, the agenda has been dominated by the emphasis on the protection of human rights but a tension is clearly discernible between those who favour the establishment of a United Nations rapid reaction force[192] and those who remain sceptical about the wisdom of open ended commitments. Sixthly, it has to be recognised that there are some abuses that may well go unchecked unless the United States can be persuaded to lend practical help to any United Nations initiative. Seventhly, some of the achievements of the United Nations are real and substantial but they often do not receive the credit they deserve; among these are efforts at social and economic co-operation between states, decolonisation, and the development and codification of international law. Without the United Nations, it is highly unlikely that a treaty as ambitious as the Law of the Sea Convention (1982) would ever have been attempted and measures to codify international law would not have made the progress that they have.

There is a tendency by some to assert that not enough has been achieved. However, one of the difficulties is that, since 1945, in Europe, North America and many other states the years have been marked by steady economic growth, rising living standards within economies regulated by the rule of law. In contrast many newly independent states suffer from limited investment, intermittent conflict and a poor infrastructure; in some cases, these problems are compounded by high levels of illiteracy and political corruption. The difficulty is that, while there are many more states than in 1900, the differences in economic and social conditions have grown considerably. One way of addressing this problem is to try and ensure that a state has a democratically elected government operating within the rule of law; only then, it is argued, will there be sufficient capital investment to generate sustainable improvements in living standards. The challenge for the United Nations in the 21st century is to narrow the gap between rich and poor states.

---

192 See WM Reisman, 'Preparing to wage peace: toward the creation of an international peacemaking command and staff college (1994) 88 AJIL 76.

CHAPTER 23

INTERNATIONAL INSTITUTIONS

1 INTRODUCTION

As has been indicated elsewhere, a consistent theme in international society in the last 100 years has been the need for states to work together to achieve common objectives and, to a large extent, this need explains the proliferation of international and regional organisations. However, in the 19th century, the traditional view was that only states were legal persons in international law. Writing in 1912, in the second edition of his celebrated treatise, Lassa Oppenheim could note: 'Since the law of nations is based on the common consent of individual States, and not of individual human beings, States solely and exclusively are subjects of international law.'[1] In broad terms, states remain the principal legal persons on the international stage, but the presence of international and regional bodies has transformed the picture considerably. It should not be thought that this development stems directly from 1919; there is evidence of international co-operation in the 19th century in bodies such as the Commission for the Rhine (1815), the Elbe (1821), or the Po (1849) and, towards the end of that century, it had become clear that co-operation on technical matters was unavoidable as instanced by the establishment of bodies such as the Universal Postal Union (1874). Indeed, after the Congress of Vienna (1815), Metternich had tried to manage European affairs by regular diplomatic conferences and these continued after his fall, as instanced by the Paris Conference of 1856 on the Balkans and the Berlin Conferences of 1878 and 1884–85. Thus, prior to 1914, European peace depended on periodic conferences, diplomatic exchanges, defensive alliances and a broad adherence of the system of the balance of power. Indeed, the patchwork of defensive alliances that grew up before 1914 was testament to the fact that no European state felt a sufficient a degree of confidence to manage its own defence alone.

In respect of co-operative ventures in the 19th century, it is usual to point to the influence of those organisations of a non-governmental nature such as the International Committee of the Red Cross (1863), the International Law Association (1873) or the International Dental Federation (1900), which are sometimes described as private international unions. Indeed, so numerous were such bodies that a Union of International Associations was founded in 1910 to clarify and co-ordinate their activities. In contrast, it is usual to refer to 'public international unions' as being based on permanent co-operation between governments founded upon a multilateral treaty of which the Commission on the Rhine (1815) is often taken as the earliest example. However, as with all organisations it is necessary to pay regard to the contents of the constitutional document and to the law applicable to that document.

One of the reasons for the increase in public international unions in the second half of the 19th century was the pace of technical changes; improvements in transport, sanitation,

---

1   Lassa Oppenheim (1858–1919) in L Oppenheim, *International Law*, 2nd edn, 1912. At the relevant time, Oppenheim had held the Whewell chair since 1908; that he was not expressing a minority opinion is indicated by the fact that his predecessor in the chair, John Westlake (1828–1913) had asserted similar sentiments in his *International Law*, 1894.

medicine and communication stimulated the case for international co-operation on a permanent basis, so that a body such as the Universal Postal Union (founded in 1874) operated on the basis of a permanent bureau, regular conferences and with provision for decisions taken by a majority vote. At the end of the 19th century, although Europe was subject to increasing tension, naval rivalry and military tension, one can also detect the beginnings of the modern international organisation with the emphasis on the periodic legislative conferences, majority voting and a permanent bureau or secretariat.[2] It is also important to note that the gradual widening of the franchise in European states had brought to the fringes of power liberal or social democratic politicians who tended to favour forms of international co-operation, in contrast to the nationalism and imperialism favoured by others.

In considering the concept of the 'international organisation', one is normally concerned with an organisation established on the basis of an agreement between states. Such a body has to be distinguished today from a 'non-governmental organisation' (such as Amnesty International or Greenpeace), which is founded on an agreement between individuals. It may be that such a body may have the right to make representations on the international plane and, in the case of the International Committee for the Red Cross, such a body may be required by states to undertake certain tasks; however, there is a fundamental distinction between the NGO and the international organisation. Many NGOs started life concentrating on one particular area of activity and came into being because of a feeling that a particular activity was not receiving sufficient attention by established political structures.

There has been a considerable effort by historians and political scientists to analyse the nature and purpose of international and regional organisations. Whether this is of practical value is open to question, because of the different objectives of such organisations; however, such analysis is concerned in part to ask whether the 'state' remains the central unit in international society. The first school[3] is sometimes described as the traditional or legal school, which views international organisations as limited vehicles to promote co-operation between states and, in the case of the United Nations, to manage the inevitable conflicts between states. Some such writers[4] would go further and argue that the purpose of such bodies is to promote the rule of law in the conduct of international affairs. However, all would see the state as the cardinal unit and the international organisation as the vehicle through which states may co-operate. Thirdly, one can point to those lawyers who argue that the purpose of certain international organisations is to promote a form of world law.[5] Fourthly, and closely allied to this, are those who view such organisations as steps on the road to some form of international government.[6] This approach can be traced back to the turn of the century, when some liberal and socialist thinkers began to reflect on the waste, competition and aggression

---

2   See, for example, the International Telegraphic Union (1865) or the Radiotelegraphic Union (1906).

3   Writers within this school might include JL Brierly, CW Jenks, MO Hudson, H Schermers and DW Bowett.

4   One might include here H Lauterpacht and Lord Robert Cecil who wished to expand the role of law on the international plane. Lauterpacht argued that many if not all international disputes were in principle justiciable.

5   See G Clark and LB Sohn, *World Peace through World Law: Two Alternative Plans*, 3rd edn, 1966.

6   See C Eagleton, *International Government*, 1948.

engendered by the nation state.[7] A fifth stream of writers are those of the realist school who reflected on the failure of the League of Nations and the exercise of power in the conduct of international relations;[8] such writers tended to stress the role of national interest in international relations.[9] The most influential of these was Hans Morgenthau[10] who, in his *Politics among Nations*, advanced three propositions, namely that states are the central actors on the international stage; that there is a fundamental difference between domestic politics and international politics; and that the business of international relations is predominantly concerned with the struggle for power and peace. It is arguable that such an analysis concentrates too much on 'high politics' and places insufficient emphasis the role of law in matters of technical co-operation; while such writers wished to see a more rational conduct of international relations, they were influenced by the failure of the League of Nations and the paralysis of the Security Council. Sixthly, it is possible to identify a stream of writers, sometimes described as functionalists, who look beyond the nation state to functions being discharged at the regional level; however, much of this reflection arose from the Treaty of Paris (1950) and Treaty of Rome (1957) and may have some validity in that context, but it cannot be said to be of general application.[11] Seventhly, until recently there was a distinct strand of Soviet or Marxist thinking on international organisations which viewed them as facilitating peaceful co-existence between states and paid attention to the different levels of social and economic performance.[12] Eighthly, there are those writers of a 'globalist' persuasion, who see common problems demanding a greater legislative role for the United Nations.[13] Although there are a wide variety of views, the basic division is between those who accept that the state will remain the central unit in international society and those who believe that the regional or international organisation should assume some of its functions. Finally, it is perfectly possible to hold both views at the same time; many accept that defence matters should be organised through NATO while also expecting the United Nations to act on global warming but yet continue to argue that matters of asylum and immigration control should be the concern of the nation state. It is also important to draw a distinction between Europe, where integration has proceeded steadily since 1957, and other parts of the world, where such advances have been less marked.

7　To be associated with Fabian writers as well as liberals, see Leonard Woolf, *International Government*, 2nd edn, 1916. Other figures would be Philip Noel Baker and Gilbert Murray; Fabian thought had been associated with opposition to World War I and the search for a supranational authority that would prevent war.

8　Such writers were influenced by the failure of the legal mechanisms of the League of Nations and included EH Carr (better known today as the historian of the Soviet Union), George Schwarzenberger, whose *Power Politics*, 1941, had analysed the weaknesses of the League of Nations and raised question of ethical values in international relations, and Reinhold Niebuhr, who saw the role of the United Nations as being to create a sense of community. See R Niebuhr, 'The illusion of world government' (1948) 27 Foreign Affairs 379. Given the evidence disclosed at the Nuremberg Trials in 1945, this emphasis on ethics and values in the 1940s is understandable.

9　See EH Carr, *The Twenty Years Crisis 1919–39*, 2nd edn, 1946; Henry Kissinger, *Diplomacy*, 1994.

10　Hans Morgenthau was in fact a German born lawyer who published the first edition of *Politics among Nations* in 1948. The second edition was published in 1960 at the height of the Cold War.

11　See D Mitrany, *A Working Peace System*, 1966; *The Functional Theory of Politics*, 1975.

12　C Osakwe, *Participation of the Soviet Union in Universal International Organisations*, 1972.

13　RW Sterling, *Macropolitics: International Relations in a Global Society*, 1974.

As indicated above, in the final analysis the international organisation has to be analysed by reference to its basic constitutional document.[14] In broad terms, just as with a domestic constitution, one can discern legislative, executive and judicial functions; in the context of such organisations, it is also important to draw a distinction between promotional activities and operational duties. Normally, the basic document will set out the objects and functions of the organisation; it is a basic principle that the international organisation is not entitled to go beyond its stipulated functions.[15] In most documents, there will be some reference to the organisation having legal personality on the international plane, although whether it does so in municipal law will normally vary according to the status of treaties within domestic law;[16] further, the constitutional document will normally make reference to questions of privileges and immunity.[17] In respect of structure, the constitutional document will make some reference to the seat or headquarters of the organisation[18] and this will be followed by terms relating to conditions of membership and provisions for suspension or expulsion. In respect of operating bodies, the normal constitution draws a distinction between principal organs and subsidiary and regional organs.[19] In the case of principal organs, the normal arrangement is to have an 'Assembly' or 'Congress' with power delegated to a smaller executive body or council.[20] In the case of specialist organisations, it is usual to provide that the executive body or council should include representatives of the states most active in the field.[21] In respect of voting, the 20th century has witnessed a steady move away from the principle of unanimity towards a system of majority voting;[22] however, to ensure protection for the more substantial states, it is usual to include a form of weighted voting that bears some relation to financial contribution.[23]

As indicated above, it is possible to classify organisations into the international (or global) and the regional. It is also possible to distinguish between those organisations founded on a treaty between states and those resulting from a treaty between governments. It is probably also true that one can distinguish those organisations which claim to be supranational in the sense that they can legislate and have direct effect on the citizens in member states.[24] There is no agreement on classification so it proposed to examine international institutions before examining those operating on the regional plane.

---

14 See CW Jenks, 'Some constitutional problems of international reorganisations' (1945) 22 BYIL 18.

15 This matter will be considered further below.

16 This matter will be considered further below.

17 These matters are considered further below.

18 Although, of course, in the case of the United Nations no home was specified at the time the Charter was signed.

19 See generally, ZL Klepcki, *The Organs of International Organisations*, 1973.

20 To this extent, the United Nations Charter follows this model.

21 See, for example, the Council of the International Civil Aviation Organisation (ICAO). In some cases, the requirement is that the executive body should be representative of all geographical areas, as with the Executive Council of the Universal Postal Union.

22 The issue of which subjects require unanimity and which require a majority has been a live issue in the European Community since the original Treaty of Rome; the method of weighted voted can be traced back to the Central Commission for the Navigation of the Rhine (1815); see also Treaty of Rome (1957), Arts 138 and 148.

23 As is the case with the International Bank for Reconstruction and Development and the International Monetary Fund.

24 See DW Bowett, *The Law of International Institutions*, 4th edn, 1982.

2 INSTITUTIONS OPERATING ON A GLOBAL OR UNIVERSAL BASIS

(a) The League of Nations

The League of Nations was established in 1919 with the object of managing disputes between states. It represented an attempt by the then United States, President Woodrow Wilson, to replace the European concept of the balance of power with the American emphasis on collective security and the rule of law. The organisation was founded on the principles of respect for state sovereignty, the peaceful settlement of disputes and the desirability of disarmament; it sought to introduce a regime of collective security, with a system of sanctions in the event of aggression. It is of interest that the preamble to the covenant referred to 'the firm establishment of the understandings of international law as the actual rule of conduct among Governments'. Under the terms of Art 2 of the Covenant, the League operated through an Assembly, a Council and a Secretariat; by the terms of Art 4, the Council consisted of representatives of the principal allied powers together with a number of non-permanent members. Under the terms of Art 1, it was intended that the League should be a universal institution but in the event it remained predominantly European. The Council met when required while the Assembly met annually.

External aggression was outlawed by Art 10 of the Covenant and Arts 11–15 contained complicated and rather legalistic provisions as to the powers of the Council when there was a threat to peace. The effect of Art 16 was that it was a matter for individual member states as to whether they participated in economic sanctions or military action at the behest of the Council. Article 8 pledged members to disarmament but, from the early 1930, it was clear that these provisions were being ignored. The League itself did important work in promoting the peaceful settlement of disputes and there is evidence of its popularity amongst a general public exhausted by conflict.[25] However, the democracies supporting the League lacked the resources to resist aggression[26] from the non-democratic regimes in Italy, Germany and Japan. The organisation was fatally flawed by the non-involvement of the United States; the outbreak

---

25 The practical difficulty was that the economic crisis in Europe after 1931 had placed defence spending under pressure and, in cases such as the Japanese invasion of Manchuria, the American government was not prepared to support economic sanctions, still less military action. It is probably true that John Simon (Foreign Secretary 1931–35) would have been more suitable in another post, but the difficulties of supporting the League of resisting aggression and avoiding conflict while conducting foreign policy for a coalition government should not be underestimated. After the outbreak of hostilities in 1939, there was a tendency to place personal blame on John Simon for the foreign policy failures of the 1930s. However, there were those such as Leo Amery who felt that Simon had done his best to make the League system work. For a reasoned defence of this most controversial of foreign secretaries, see David Dutton, *Simon*, 1992.

26 The difficulties facing the League in the 1930s were well put in a memorandum prepared in the British Foreign Office which observed, 'The links in the chain fall together more or less in the following order. The monetary crisis leads inevitably back to the economic chaos in Europe. The economic chaos and all attempts to deal with it involve in their turn the political questions of reparations and war debts. These are linked by the United States with the question of disarmament, and the latter, in the eyes of the French Government, depends upon the problem of security. The problem of security in its turn raises the question of the territorial *status quo* in Europe ... which brings us to the maintenance or revision of the peace settlement'. (Memorandum by O Sargent and F Ashton-Gwatkin, 26 November 1931, cited in A Corzier, *Appeasement and Germany's Last Bid for Colonies*, 1988, p 28, and David Dutton, *Simon*, 1992, p 119).

of the Second World War sealed the fate of the League of Nations and the organisation was formally wound up in April 1946 following the coming into effect of the United Nations Charter in October 1945.

(b) The United Nations

The United Nations was established in 1945 as an attempt to provide an international organisation capable of managing the inevitable tensions between states. The draftsmen of the Charter of the United Nations attempted to learn the lessons of the failures of the League of Nations. The work of the United Nations Organisation is dealt with elsewhere.

(c) Monetary and economic organisations

One of the lessons drawn from the instability of the 1930s was that more needed to be done to provide for monetary co-operation to secure non-inflationary economic growth and thus avoid the high levels of unemployment that had lead to domestic instability and political extremism. To this end, a number of wartime conferences put in place a variety of international economic organisations that have operated since 1946–47. These are discussed elsewhere.[27]

3 REGIONAL ORGANISATIONS

One of the significant characteristics of the period since 1945 has been the growth in the number of regional organisations. There are a number of reasons for this. First, there are simply more states and many states wish to co-operate with those states that are geographically proximate or with which they have cultural ties. Secondly, there is the obvious economic motivation; it is widely recognised that the level of economic growth may be linked to the size of the market and there is a natural tendency for states to seek to work together to create larger trading areas for producers. Thirdly, in the modern world few states have the resources to provide entirely for their own defence and there is advantage in co-operating within a regional organisation that provides a degree of collective security. Fourthly, the United Nations Charter expressly recognises[28] the role of regional organisations and tries to work through them in resolving problems. Fifthly, some post-colonial states are so poor and so lacking in infrastructure that they require the support of other regional states to discharge the normal functions of government. Sixthly, in some cases, the emphasis towards regionalism was a reaction towards the superpower tensions of the Cold War.

In the case of Europe, the movement toward regionalism has gone much further than elsewhere founded on the European Economic Community established under the Treaty of Rome (1957). It is therefore sensible to say a little about significant regional organisations before considering the European Union.

---

27 See Chapter 19 on International Economic Law.
28 United Nations Charter (1945), Arts 52–54 .

(a) Africa[29]

The Organisation of African Unity is the principal regional organisation for Africa and was established in May 1963 under the terms of the Charter of the Organisation of African Unity. The supreme organ is the Assembly of Heads of State and Government which meets annually or in special session; preparatory work is effected by meetings of the Council of Ministers. Membership is open to all independent sovereign African states; it is a flexible and rather loose organisation designed to promote regional co-operation and is founded on the 'sovereign equality of all Member States'.[30] In its early years, the emphasis was on decolonisation and the struggle against apartheid however the actual objectives under the Charter are very broad, including co-operation in matters of economics, health, transport and defence.[31] The Organisation operates through a Secretary General and a secretariat and is based in Addis Ababa. There has been since 1964 a Protocol which established a Commission of Mediation, Conciliation and Arbitration. The basic tendency of the Organisation has been to seek to resolve inter-African disputes within Africa although it has to be candidly admitted that the record on the Western Sahara, Chad, Ethiopia, Rwanda and Sierra Leone has been disappointing.

Although the OAU is the principal regional organisation there are a number of regional economic organisations of which the best known is the West African Economic Community (ECOWAS) which dates from 1967 and provided for a free trade area in Dahomey, Ghana, Ivory Coast, Liberia, Mali, Mauritania, Benin, Nigeria, Senegal and Sierra Leone. The same year saw the establishment of the Economic Community of East Africa (ECEA) which performs a similar function in respect of East Africa.

(b) The Arab League[32]

The Arab League is the result of a pact signed in March 1944[33] and is an organisation providing for co-operation between sovereign states. Membership is open to independent Arab States. In practice, it is necessary to apply for membership and for that application to be accepted. The broad objective of the League is economic and financial co-operation,[34] although the League also provides for the peaceful settlement of disputes between states.[35] The headquarters of the League are in Tunis, having moved there from Egypt after President Sadat made an independent peace treaty with Israel in 1979. The central organ of the League is the Council which has acted as a forum for conciliation on a number of occasions such as during the Iraqi-Kuwait crisis of 1961; the League constitutes a regional organisation for the purpose of Chapter VII of the United Nations and it was in

---

29 TO Elias, 'The Commission of Mediation, Conciliation and Arbitration of the OAU' (1964) 40 BYIL 336; TO Elias, 'The Charter of the OAU' (1965) 59 AJIL 243.
30 Article III(I) of the 1963 Charter.
31 Article II(II) of the 1963 Charter.
32 Khadduri, 'The Arab League as a regional arrangement' (1946) 40 AJIL 756; B Boutros-Ghali, 'The Arab League (1945–1970)' (1969) 25 Revue Egyptiènne de Droit International, p 67. B Boutros Ghali, 'La Ligue des Etats arabes' (1972) 137 HR 1.
33 For text see (1945) 39 AJIL 266.
34 See Art III of the Pact.
35 See Art V of the Pact.

this capacity that it was consulted in the Gulf War crisis of 1990. The Council of the League operates with a number of committees who cover specialist areas such as economic or cultural affairs.

(c) Eastern Europe

Although all the relevant organisations dissolved with the collapse of the Soviet Union and many Eastern European countries are now seeking full membership of either the European Union or NATO, it is sensible to record the efforts at regional co-operation in Eastern Europe. The Council for Mutual Economic Aid (COMECON) had been established in 1949 and included Bulgaria, Cuba, Czechoslovakia, the German Democratic Republic, Hungary, Poland, Romania and the USSR; it is a matter of record that the organisation was not able to match the improvements in living standards that took place in Europe and was a casualty of the collapse of the Soviet Union. Alongside this was the Warsaw Treaty Organisation, established under a Treaty of Friendship, Co-operation and Mutual Assistance concluded in Warsaw in May 1955 (thereafter referred to as the Warsaw Pact); in its terms, the treaty provided for collective security and while in theory it was open to western countries it was in practice confined to Eastern European states. Both treaties proceeded on the basis that member states were free and independent but such language was difficult to square with the events in Hungary in October 1956 and in Czechoslovakia in August 1968. To a greater or lesser degree, member states operated repressive single party forms of government subservient to the armed forces of the Soviet Union; with the collapse of the Soviet Union neither organisation was viable. The influence of the Soviet Union over Eastern Europe was directly traceable to the conduct of Joseph Stalin in the closing months of the Second World War; the collapse of communist party rule in Eastern Europe lead the dissolution of the relevant regional organisations.

(d) Asia

The most significant economic and political organisation in the region is the Association of South East Asian Nations (ASEAN) which now comprises Thailand, Malaysia, Singapore, the Philippines, Brunei and Vietnam. It operates on the basis of an annual Ministerial meeting, together with a standing committee and a number of specialist committees. The organisation dates from 1967 and its work is co-ordinated by a Secretary General; in broad terms, the organisation has promoted a number of agreements to provide for the peaceful settlement of disputes and to further political and economic co-operation.[36]

---

36 The most significant being the Treaty of Amity and Co-operation (1976) (providing for the peaceful settlement of disputes); the Declaration of ASEAN Concord (1976) (which provided for increased political and economic co-operation); the Framework Agreement on Enhancing ASEAN Economic Co-operation (1992).

(e) The Americas[37]

The idea of regional co-operation in the American continent was first proposed by Simon Bolivar in 1822. However, the Monroe doctrine of the following year[38] created an obstacle to immediate co-operation. In 1890, a conference in Washington resulted in the establishment of the International Union of American Republics (sometimes known as the Pan American Union) which was not an organisation but a series of conferences. In 1910, the headquarters of the Pan American Union was established in Washington. After the First World War, conferences continued to be held but it was not until the Montevideo Conference of 1933 that the United States accepted the principle of non-interference in the affairs of other Latin American or Central American states. During the 1930s and 1940s, a steady improvement in relations lead to greater emphasis on co-operation.

The modern system of co-operation is based on two treaties. In 1947, the Inter American Treaty of Reciprocal Assistance (normally known as the Rio Treaty) provides for consultation and collective self-defence. At the ninth Inter American Conference at Bogota in 1948, the Pact of Bogota[39] was signed providing for the establishment. of the Organisation of American States (OAS). Article 1 of the Pact of Bogota records that the Organisation of American States is to be considered as a regional organisation for the purpose of the United Nations Charter and provision is made for the peaceful settlement of disputes and common action, both to resist aggression and to promote political and economic co-operation. The supreme body is the General Assembly which meets infrequently as much business is conducted through meetings of foreign ministers; in addition there is a general secretariat which is supervised by a permanent council which is a plenary body of ambassadorial rank. The best known product of the Organisation of American States is the American Convention on Human Rights (1969); the guiding principle of the organisation is co-operation between sovereign states. Clearly, the social and economic differences between such states are considerable; the organisation is founded on voluntary co-operation and has none of the supranational powers and ambitions of the European Community.

(f) The Council of Europe

At the conclusion of conflict in 1945, a number of political groupings sprang up each desiring to promote the cause of closer European co-operation. The practical effect of such campaigning was the signing of the Statute of the Council of Europe by 10 countries on 5 May 1949; to some extent, the document was a compromise between those who favoured progress towards a 'United States of Europe' based on some form of federation and those who simply wished for voluntary co-operation between independent sovereign states.

---

37 See DW Bowett, *The Law of International Institutions*, 4th edn, Chap 7.

38 The Monroe Doctrine issued by President Monroe in 1823 at the behest of his Secretary of State, John Quincy Adams, represented the reaction of the United States to the liberation movements in Latin America. It warned that the United States would not tolerate the establishment of colonial power in the western hemisphere; however, it was later invoked to justify the westward expansion of the United States (eg, by President Polk in 1845) and carried with it the implication that the United States had the right to intervene in the domestic affairs of its neighbours.

39 This has been amended by (i) the Buenos Aires Protocol of 1967; (ii) the Cartagena de Indias Protocol of 1985; (iii) the Washington Protocol of 1992; (iv) the Managua Protocol of 1993.

The principal aim of the Council, as set out in Art 1, was to promote common action in economic, social, cultural and related matters. In respect of membership a distinction is drawn between original members, full or admitted members and associate members. The institution has a Parliamentary Assembly made up of persons drawn from the legislative chambers of the member states and a Committee of Ministers drawn from those holding ministerial rank in the member states. The role of the Parliamentary Assembly is to deliberate and to recommend action to the Committee of Ministers.

The most significant work of the Council of Europe has been in the preparation of international conventions; the best known of these are the European Convention on Human Rights and Fundamental Freedoms (1950), but note should also be taken of the Convention on the Peaceful Settlement of Disputes (1957), the Convention on Extradition (1957) and the European Social Charter.

(g) The European Union[40]

There is no doubt that the European Union is the most sophisticated and advanced form of regional organisation in the world. Beginning life as the European Coal and Steel Community under the Treaty of Paris (1951), the concept of European integration was developed further by the creation of the European Economic Community (1957) under the Treaty of Rome and by establishment of the European Atomic Energy Community in the same year. The three communities have operated with a common set of institutions since the coming into effect of the Merger Treaty in 1967.[41] Starting with a core of six member states,[42] a number of treaties of accession have provided for enlargement. On 1 January 1973, the United Kingdom, Ireland and Denmark became members. Greece, having returned to democracy, joined with effect from 1 January 1981, and on 1 January 1986, Spain and Portugal, having thrown off dictatorship, gained admission. Austria, Finland and Sweden became members with effect from 1 January 1995. In 1991, an agreement made with the states of the European Free Trade Area provided for the creation of a European Economic Area but the first agreement[43] was held unlawful by the European Court of Justice and the second amended version[44] did not come into effect until January 1994.

The original objectives of the European Economic Community were set out in the Preamble to the Treaty of Rome and in Arts 1, 2, and 3 of the Treaty. On many occasions, the European Court of Justice when called upon to interpret a specific provision justifies its interpretation by reference to a particular principle contained in these initial articles. In essence, the Treaty of Rome (1957) provides for a single internal market[45] with a common

---

40 See generally, D Wyatt and A Dashwood, *European Community Law*, 3rd edn, 1993; *Lasok and Bridge's Law and Institutions of the European Community* (D Lasok and KP Lasok (eds), 6th edn, 1994; J Steiner and L Woods, *Textbook on EC Law*, 5th edn, 1998; S Weatherill and P Beaumont, *EC Law*, 1995, 2nd edn; T Tridmas, *The General Principles of EC Law*, 2000.

41 The Treaty Establishing a Single Council and a Single Commission of the European Communities (1965) (known as the Merger Treaty).

42 The original six being Belgium, Germany, France, Italy, Luxembourg and the Netherlands.

43 First EEA Case Opinion 1/91, (1991) ECR 1-6079.

44 Second EEA Case Opinion 1/92.

45 See Treaty of Rome (1957), Arts 30–36; see now Treaty of Amsterdam (TOA 1997), Arts 28, 29, 30, 31.

external tariff;[46] from the outset there have been detailed and specific provisions to outlaw internal tariffs,[47] to promote competition,[48] to restrict state aids[49] and to make possible the free movement of goods,[50] services,[51] capital[52] and labour.[53] Although drafted by lawyers, the Treaty of Rome adopts a distinct economic philosophy, namely that of promoting economic growth by legally enforced open competition within a large market operating a common external tariff. The Treaty of Rome (1957) provided for a Common Agricultural Policy[54] and for a series of association agreements with third world countries.[55] Alongside these economic objectives, the Treaty of Rome (1957) required progress towards 'an ever closer union among the peoples of Europe'. It would be foolish to ignore the fact that there has been tension since 1957 between those states who wish to progress towards some form of European federation and those states who do not view such an objective as a priority. After 1957, the Community operated through an Assembly,[56] a Council of Ministers[57] and a Commission.[58] Under the terms of Arts 164–188 of the Treaty of Rome, the final arbiter of legality was to be the European Court of Justice, which had the power to give preliminary rulings on references from municipal courts[59] and had power to adjudicate on disputes between the European Commission and member states. The increase in the number of member states and the wide scope of jurisdiction created such a volume of case law that it was necessary under the Single European Act (1986) to provide for a Court of First Instance to relieve the European Court of Justice of its burden. In principle, a member state and its court are

---

46 Treaty of Rome (1957), Arts 12, 28, 29; see now TOA 1997, Arts 25, 26, 27.

47 *Ibid*, Arts 30–36; see now TOA 1997, Arts 28, 29, 30, 31.

48 *Ibid*, Arts 85, 86, 87, 88; see now TOA 1997, Arts 81 ,82, 83, 84, 85, 86.

49 *Ibid*, Arts 92, 93, 94; see now TOA 1997, Arts 87, 88, 89.

50 *Ibid*, Arts 9, 10; see now TOA 1997, Arts 23, 24.

51 *Ibid*, Arts 59, 60, 61, 62, 63, 64, 65, 66; see now TOA 1997, Arts 49–55.

52 Treaty of Rome (1957 as amended), Arts 73b, 73c, 73d, 73f, 73g; see now TOA (1997), Arts 56–60.

53 Treaty of Rome (1957), Arts 48–51; see now TOA 1997, Arts 39, 40, 41, 42.

54 See *ibid*, Arts 38–47.

55 See *ibid*, Arts 131–36.

56 Under the Treaty of Rome (1957), Arts 137–44, the Assembly comprised delegates designated by the respective Parliaments. The Assembly adopted the title 'Parliament' in 1962 and it was formally re-named as such in the Single European Act 1986, Art 3(1). In 1976, the Council of Ministers acting under Art 138 decided upon direct elections. These took place first in 1979 and followed in 1984, 1989, 1994, 1999. The relevant legislation in the United Kingdom being the European Parliamentary Elections Acts 1978, 1993.

57 The Council of Ministers was established under Arts 145–54 of the Treaty of Rome (1957). Under the terms of the original Art 148, the Council of Ministers was to act by qualified majority voting save in those situations under the treaty where unanimity is required.

58 The Commission was established under Arts 155–63 of the Treaty of Rome (1957). As a body the Commission (i) has a legislative role in that it prepares legislation for the Council of Ministers; (ii) it has executive duties; (iii) in respect of areas such as competition policy and enforcement it has quasi judicial powers.

59 The jurisdiction to give preliminary rulings arose under Art 177 (see now Art 234) and was designed to promote the orderly development of European Community Law. The role of the European Court was to give guidance on interpretation; however, application was a matter for the national court. See Case 13/61 *De Geus en Uitdenbogerd v Robert Bosch GmbH* [1962] CMLR 39; Case 26/82 *Van Gend en Loos v Nederlandse Administratie der Belastingen* [1963] ECR 1; [1963] CMLR 105; Case 6/64 *Costa v ENEL* [1964] ECR 585; [1964] CMLR 425; Case 283/81 *CILFIT Srl v Ministro della Sanita* [1982] ECR 3415; [1983] 1 CMLR 472.

obliged to follow the rulings of the European Court of Justice and since 1993 such a state is at risk of a financial penalty in the event of non-observance.

The European Economic Community was never intended to be a static institution; the intention was to move forward on the basis of additional treaties. This was achieved in the 1970s by negotiations for the admission of new members and then attention focused on the development of the single internal market. The next significant step was taken in the Single European Act (1986)[60] which amended the Treaty of Rome to permit qualified majority voting on a wider range of matters and thus to facilitate the full operating of the internal market by 31 December 1992. However, the pace of integration quickened in the late 1980s[61] and following two inter-governmental conferences the Treaty on European Union (the Maastricht Treaty) was signed on 7 February 1992. The Treaty on European Union had the effect of establishing three pillars of the European Union; these were: (i) the European Community itself;[62] (ii) the common foreign and security policy;[63] and (iii) inter-governmental co-operation on home affairs and matters of justice.[64] The treaty itself was designed to advance the cause of European integration and it set out to achieve this by extending the scope of Community competence and strengthening the institutional structures, in particular by providing a greater role for the European Parliament in the legislative process. However, the most controversial provisions concerned the advance to economic and monetary union in 1999.[65] These provisions were not acceptable to Denmark or the United Kingdom, who both sought opt outs from these treaty provisions. The treaty itself was the subject of considerable debate and faced constitutional challenges in the courts in England,[66] Germany[67] and France;[68] there were signs in a number of European countries of concern at the steps taken towards integration. Work on the integrationist Maastricht Treaty had been under discussion since the early 1980s; however, the collapse of communist rule in Eastern Europe in 1989 opened up the possibility of further expansion of the Community. In these circumstances, a debate began to take place between those who favoured closer ties among existing members and those states that placed greater emphasis on increasing the membership of the Community. In these circumstances, it was not surprising that the Maastricht Treaty was followed by the much more modest Treaty of Amsterdam (1997), which was signed on 2 October 1997 and

---

60 Given effect to in the United Kingdom by the European Communities (Amendment) Act 1986.

61 The impetus for this coming from Jacques Delors (President of the Commission from 1985) and the high degree of agreement between the long serving President of France François Mitterand (1981–95) and the German Chancellor Helmut Kohl (1982–98).

62 As it was now to be called instead of the prior title of the European Economic Community.

63 See Title V(V) Treaty on European Union (1992).This was immediately subject to scrutiny when the European Community tried to formulate an agreed policy on Yugoslavia.

64 Title VI(VI) Treaty on European Union (1992).

65 The United Kingdom secured opt outs on economic and monetary union and on social policy, although the latter was then included in the Treaty of Amsterdam when the United Kingdom in 1997 decided to opt in.

66 The treaty was given effect to in English law in the European Communities (Amendment) Act 1993. The process of ratification was subject to challenge in *R v Foreign Secretary ex p Rees Mogg* [1994] QB 552. See R Rawlings 'Legal politics: the United Kingdom and the ratification of the TEU' [1994] PL 254; see also G Marshall [1993] PL 402.

67 For the *Bundesverfassungsgericht*, see [1994] 1 CMLR 57.

68 For France, see *Conseil Constitutionnel* (9 April 1992) [1993] 3 CMLR 345; see D Oliver, 'The French Constitution and the Treaty of Maastricht' (1994) 43 ICLQ 1.

effective from 1 May 1999. This treaty is much more limited in scope, but is noticeable for making a considerable number textual amendments and for consolidating and renumbering all the provisions in the EC Treaty of 1957 and the TEU (1992) the authority for which was given under Art 12 of the Treaty of Amsterdam.

One of the most significant characteristics of the European Community has been its law making and supranational character. At a risk of gross oversimplification, European Community Law can be expressed in a limited number of propositions. First, European Community Law is an independent legal order. Secondly, European Community Law is common to all member states. Thirdly, European Community Law prevails over any national law that is incompatible with it. Fourthly, European Community Law can confer rights and impose obligations directly on private persons in member states.[69] It can therefore be seen that the European Union is a unique form of regional organisation,[70] although the ultimate destination of the organisation is now a matter of active debate between those favouring closer integration and those believing that the process has already gone far enough.

(h) North Atlantic Treaty Organisation

The advance of the Soviet army in 1945 left a considerable part of Europe under the direct influence of the Soviet Union. In the part that remained free, there was concern that such states would unaided be unable to resist a Soviet land attack.[71] In such circumstances, the North Atlantic Treaty Organisation came into being designed to 'tie' the United States and Canada to the defence of Western Europe. The North Atlantic Treaty signed on 4 April 1949 was a response to the Berlin blockade and the Soviet coup in Czechoslovakia in 1948;

---

69 For the seminal cases on the nature of European Community law and its relationship with the municipal law of member states, see Case 26/62 *Van Gend en Loos v Nederlandse Administratie der Belastingen* [1963] ECR 63; CMLR 105; Case 6/64 *Costa v ENEL* [1964] ECR 585; CMLR 425; Case 11/70 *International Handelsgesellschaft mbH* [1970] ECR 1125; [1972] CMLR 255; Case 43/75 *Defrenne v Sabena (No 2)* [1976] ECR 455; 2 CMLR 98; Case 106/77 *Amministrazione delle Finanze dello Stato v Simmenthal SpA* [1978] ECR 629; 3 CMLR 263.

70 The matter being expressed very clearly in Case 6/64 *Costa v ENEL* where the Court observed 'By contrast with ordinary international treaties, the EEC Treaty has created its own legal system which, on the entry into force of the Treaty, became an integral part of the legal systems of the Member States and which their courts are bound to apply. By creating a Community of unlimited duration, having its own institutions, its own personality, its own legal capacity and capacity of representation on the international plane and, more particularly, real powers stemming from a limitation of sovereignty or a transfer of powers from States to the Community, the Member States have limited their sovereign rights, albeit within limited fields, and they have thus created a body of law which binds the nationals and themselves'.

71 NATO was an extension of the Brussels Treaty of 1948 (ie, the Treaty of Economic, Social and Cultural Collaboration and Collective Self Defence of 17 March 1948). From the late 1940s, one can detect two distinct trends in Western Europe: (i) the desire of states to co-operate on matters of self defence in the fact of the large military forces of the Soviet Union – this trend found expression in NATO and also in the 1952 European Defence Treaty of 1952 which was rejected by the French National Assembly in August 1952; (ii) the desire of smaller European states to come together in larger trading units to ensure a larger market and thus promote economic growth – this trend began with the Benelux Customs Union of 1948 made between Luxembourg, Belgium and the Netherlands and culminated in the Treaty of Rome (1957). Both developments were grounded in the view that the individual nation state was not large enough or populous enough to stand alone. This view was propounded by theorists such as Professor Laski in the 1948 edition of *Liberty in the Modern State*.

originally, the treaty was signed by 12 states but was open to others and membership reached 15 in 1955 when Konrad Adenauer secured the membership of West Germany.

By Art V of the Treaty, an attack on one state was to be viewed as an attack on all; the treaty provides for consultation on matters pertaining to territorial sovereignty.[72] The treaty came into being because the result of the Second World War was to leave Germany divided and France and the United Kingdom unable alone to defend themselves. The object was to create a regional defence alliance based on the consent of democratically elected governments. The treaty provides for a Council on which each member is represented in the form of officials. The Council functions through Defence and Military Committees; responsible to the Military Committee is the Supreme Allied Commander Europe (SACEUR),[73] who operates from headquarters in Belgium known as SHAPE. The geographical scope of the defensive alliance is set out in the treaty, although this has not prevented out of area action in 1999.[74] The administrative head of the organisation is the Secretary General.[75] In addition, there is a NATO Parliamentary Conference which first convened in 1955 and now meets annually.

In 1966, France withdrew from the military committee while remaining a member of the organisation thus preserving the integrity of the treaty itself. The collapse of the Warsaw Pact resulted in the establishment of a North Atlantic Co-operation Council which came into being in 1991 and included NATO states and former members of the Warsaw Pact. In 1994, NATO began participating in the Partnership for Peace Programme which involved defence and military co-operation with those European states who accept the principles of democratic government and international law. Since the collapse of communist rule in Eastern Europe, NATO has been the principal defence alliance[76] and it has co-operated in the enforcement of sanctions against Yugoslavia and acquired a greater degree of prominence during the Kosovo conflict of spring 1999.[77]

(i) Organisation for Economic Co-operation and Development[78]

In 1948 the Organisation for European Economic Co-operation (OEEC) had been established to administer the Marshall Aid programme[79] and to co-ordinate economic

---

72 See Art IV of the NATO treaty (1949).

73 Who, as a matter of convention, will be a serving United States officer; in recent years, the best known being Alexander Haig (1974–79) who later went on to serve as Secretary of State (1981–82).

74 As in the Kosovo campaign of spring 1999.

75 This post will be held by a European who will normally be a person who has served as a foreign or defence minister (eg, Joseph Luns, Lord Carrington, Manfred Worner, Javier Solano, and since 1999 Lord Robertson).

76 For the problems posed by proposed enlargement, see R Mullerson 'NATO Enlargement and Russia' (1998) 47 ICLQ 192.

77 For an analysis of the conflict see D Kritsiotis, 'The Kosovo crisis and Nato's application of armed force against the Federal Republic of Yugoslavia' (2000) 49 ICLQ 330.

78 See DW Bowett, *The Law of International Institutions*, 1982, p 187.

79 George Marshall (1880–1959) (Secretary of State 1947–49). Marshall had announced the general principles in July 1947. The objective of the United States was to promote economic growth in Western Europe and thus minimise the risk of further communist expansion. One of the tasks of the OEEC was to scrutinise national economic plans and to monitor the distribution of American help.

recovery in Europe. By 1960, that task had clearly been accomplished and so, in December 1960, the organisation was reconstituted by treaty as the Organisation for Economic Co-operation and Development (OECD). The objects of the organisation are now not to assist recovery from wartime damage but to build sustainable economic growth. Thus, Art 1 of the treaty reflects its broadly Keynesian objectives as being 'to achieve the highest sustainable economic growth and employment and a rising standard of living, in Member countries ... and, thus, to contribute to the expansion of world trade on a multilateral non discriminatory basis'. The principal organ of the organisation is the Council whose membership comprises all members; the treaty provides for decisions to be reached by unanimity save in special cases. Membership is open to any government at the invitation of the Council. In contrast to the OEEC, membership is wider and the original 20 members of 1960 included Australia, New Zealand, Canada, Japan and the United States. The Council operates through an Executive Committee and various sub-committees together with a Secretariat that is based in Paris. Although principally concerned with matters of macroeconomics, the organisation has established committees to promote co-operation in areas of agriculture and nuclear energy.

(j) The Western European Union

In March 1948, the United Kingdom, France, Belgium, Netherlands and Luxembourg signed the Brussels Treaty establishing the Western European Union as a regional treaty for self-defence under the terms of Art 51 of the United Nations Charter. With the subsequent development of NATO, the defence arrangements became obsolete although, in an attempt to limit German rearmament, West Germany was invited to join in 1954. The Western European Union operated through a Council of Foreign Ministers, which itself functioned through a committee of permanent representatives, together with a Parliamentary Assembly. After 1960, when its cultural functions were transferred to the Council of Europe it only exercised a marginal role. However, with the ending of the Cold War and the signing of the Treaty on European Union (1992), it has acquired a fresh lease of life. At the Maastricht Summit it was declared that the Western European Union would be developed as part of a reinvigorated European Defence policy and to this end it began to promote military exchanges; it acted for the European Union at various phases of the conflict in Bosnia. Such developments have attracted some criticism; it is argued that such an organisation serves only to overlap with NATO or to act as a competitor to it; at the root of such criticism lies the concern that any European defence initiatives might weaken the existing United States involvement through NATO.

4 THE PERSONALITY OF INTERNATIONAL INSTITUTIONS

If an organisation is to operate on the international plane and be subject to rights and duties, then it must be endowed with legal personality. Whether it has such personality is a question to be determined by interpreting the relevant constituent treaties. Thus, in the *Reparation for Injuries suffered in the Service of the United Nations* case[80] the International

---

80   (1949) ICJ 174.

Court of Justice was prepared to conclude that the United Nations had such legal personality by virtue of powers conferred by the Charter itself. In many instances, it will be expressly stated in the constitutional documents that the organisation is endowed with legal personality.[81] By personality it is meant that the organisation 'is a subject of international law and capable of possessing international rights and duties, and that it has capacity to maintain its rights'. It is possible to examine express powers and to reach the conclusion that the organisation enjoys legal personality. In the *Reparation* case,[82] the Court deduced legal personality from the principles and powers expressly stated in the Charter. Prominent amongst such powers was that under Art 43 allowing the United Nations to enter into agreements, as well as the provisions of Arts 104 and 105 relating to privileges and immunity. In essence, the Court concluded that legal personality must arise because of the nature and functions of the entity. Such legal personality existed on the international plane and, being objective, was effective in respect of non-members. As the Court noted:

> ... fifty States, representing the vast majority of the members of the international community, had the power, in conformity with international law, to bring into being an entity possessing objective international personality and not merely personality recognised by them alone.[83]

Whether international legal personality exists is a question of the proper interpretation to be placed on relevant documents. Thus, in *Nauru v Australia*,[84] an examination of the Trusteeship Agreement between the United Kingdom, New Zealand and Australia led the International Court of Justice to conclude that the agreement was made between member states and did not create an entity with international legal personality.

Whether an organisation has legal personality on the international plane is a distinct question from the existence of legal personality in municipal law. Some international treaties stipulate that the organisation shall have legal personality in domestic law, but whether this provision is effective will depend on the status of treaty provisions in the municipal law of the state. In states operating with a dualist tradition, this is no more than an undertaking to legislate to confer such personality.[85]

The large number of international organisations means that it will often be the case that a municipal court is confronted with a problem concerning the status of such an entity.[86] One approach might be to treat the entire matter as one of private international law and seek to apply the proper law of the corporation which would be international law. However, this has not been the approach of the United Kingdom courts where the emphasis has been on preserving traditional constitutional principles as to the status of

---

81 See Art 6 of the European Coal and Steel Community Treaty (1951, the Treaty of Paris); Art 210, European Economic Community Treaty (1957, the Treaty of Rome).

82 (1949) ICJ 174.

83 (1949) ICJ 174,179.

84 *Nauru v Australia* (1992) ICJ 240.

85 See the terms of Art 104 of the United Nations Charter (1945).

86 CW Jenks, 'The legal personality of international organisations' (1945) BYIL 270; FA Mann, 'International corporation and and national law' (1967) BYIL 145; JW Bridge, 'The United Nations and English law' (1969) 18 ICLQ 689; G Marston, 'The origin of the personality of international organisations in United Kingdom law' (1991) 40 ICLQ 403; FA Mann, 'International organisations as national corporations' (1991) 107 LQR 357. See also, JC Collier, 'The status of an international corporation', in *Festschrift für Kurt Lipstein*, 1980.

treaties. The tendency in the United Kingdom has been for separate legal personality to be created by a statutory instrument made under primary legislation.[87] In *JH Rayner (Mincing Lane) Ltd v Department of Trade and Industry*[88] the issue was whether member states could be held liable for the debts of the insolvent International Tin Council; the House of Lords in upholding the judgment of the Court of Appeal ruled that the effect of the International Tin Council (Immunities and Privileges) Order 1972 was to confer separate legal personality with the consequence that the Tin Council rather than the members were responsible for the debts. The traditional dualist view was stated by Lord Templeman when he observed:

> A treaty is a contract between the governments of two or more sovereign states. International law regulates the relations between sovereign states and determines the validity, the interpretation and the enforcement of treaties. A treaty to which Her Majesty's Government is a party does not alter the laws of the United Kingdom ... The Order of 1972 conferred on the ITC the legal capacities of a body corporate.[88a]

The English courts were confronted by the same problem, but in a different context, in the case of the *Arab Monetary Fund v Hashim (No 3)*,[89] where the plaintiffs had brought an action in the Chancery Division of the High Court for the recovery of funds allegedly misappropriated. Certain of the defendants sought to strike out the action on the grounds that the plaintiffs were not an entity recognised in English law. The relevant 1976 treaty between a number of Arab states gave the organisation 'independent juridical personality' and a decree was promulgated in Abu Dhabi giving the organisation legal personality under the law of the United Arab Emirates. At first instance, Hoffmann J held that the plaintiffs were entitled to sue in England as the rules of private international law required recognition of a corporation established under the law of a friendly foreign state. The Court of Appeal by a majority[90] reversed this decision and held that the House of Lords judgment in the *Tin Council*[91] case prevented the recognition of an international organisation arising under treaty simply because it had been constituted under some other municipal law. This narrow interpretation of the *Tin Council* judgment was then reversed by the House of Lords which held that *locus standi* could be acquired by its creation as a legal person under a foreign law. As Lord Templeman observed:[92]

---

87 The relevant legislation in the United Kingdom being the Diplomatic Privileges (Extension) Act 1944; the Diplomatic Privileges (Extension) Act 1946; the Diplomatic Privileges (Extension) Act 1950; the International Organisations (Immunities and Privileges) Act 1950; the International Organisations Act 1968. The history of the provisions in England is traced by Lord Oliver in his judgment in *JH Rayner (Mincing Lane) Ltd v Department of Trade and Industry* [1990] 2 AC 418 at 484.

88 *JH Rayner (Mincing Lane) Ltd v Department of Trade and Industry Ltd* [1990] 2 AC 418, affirming Court of Appeal judgments at [1989] Ch 72 (Kerr, Nourse and Ralph Gibson LJJ) and [1989] Ch 253 dismissing appeals from Millett J [1988] Ch 1 and (1987) BCLC 707 and Staughton J (1987) BCLC 667.

88a [1990] 2 AC 418, p 476.

89 *Arab Monetary Fund v Hashim (No 3)* [1991] 2 AC 114 (HL: Lords Bridge, Templeman, Griffiths and Ackner, Lord Lowry dissenting) on appeal from Court of Appeal (Donaldson MR, Nourse and Bingham LJJ) [1990] 3 WLR 139 reversing Hoffmann J [1990] 3 WLR 139.

90 The Court of Appeal judgment (Lord Donaldson MR, Nourse LJ, Bingham LJ dissenting) is reported at [1990] 3 WLR 139; [1990] 2 All ER 769.

91 [1990] 2 AC 418.

92 In his speech in *Arab Monetary Fund v Hashim (No 3)*, Lord Templeman observed that an international organisation might have *locus standi* in England where: (i) there had been primary legislation, eg, Bretton Woods Agreement Act 1945; (ii) by delegated legislation; (iii) by express recognition by the executive branch or as a matter of comity.

Although a treaty cannot become part of the law of the United Kingdom without the intervention of Parliament, the recognition of foreign states is a matter for the Crown to decide and by comity the courts of the United Kingdom recognise a corporate body created by the law of a foreign state recognised by the Crown.

Thus, the AMF was entitled to sue in England because its status under a foreign municipal legal system could be recognised under the rules of private international law notwithstanding the fact that it was created under a treaty to which the United Kingdom was not a party and which had itself not been followed by municipal legislation in England.[93] So, in the *Tin Council* case,[94] legal personality under municipal law arose by virtue of domestic legislation, while in *Arab Monetary Fund v Hashim (No 3)*,[95] status in English law arose following the recognition of the laws of a friendly foreign state. Where an international organisation seeks to participate in proceedings in a municipal court it will have to establish its status from the constituent treaty and where the applicable law is international law a title that depends upon ruling on the validity of the legislative acts of a foreign state will not be sufficient.[96]

To accept that an international organisation has legal personality is simply the first step. As was recognised in the *Reparation* case,[97] this does not involve an assertion that it has the same rights and obligations as a state. Once personality or legal existence has been established, it is necessary to examine the constituent documents to determine the powers or capacity of the international institution.

5 CAPACITY AND POWERS

It is accepted that, while an international organisation may have legal personality on the international plane, it is also recognised that its rights and duties are not the same as those of a state.[98] While a state has, in principle, unlimited legal capacity an international organisation is subject to the principle of specialty; it only has the express or implied powers arising from its constituent instruments.[99] In the *Reparation* case,[100] the International Court of Justice noted that an international organisation 'must be deemed to have those powers which, though not expressly provided in the Charter, are conferred upon it by necessary implication as being essential to the performance of its duties'.[101] In

---

93 Account now has to be taken of the Foreign Corporations Act 1991, which allows the courts of the United Kingdom to recognise the corporate of a company established under 'the laws of a territory which is not at the time a recognised state' so long as 'it appears that the laws of that territory are at that time applied by a settled court system in the territory'.

94 [1990] 2 AC 418.

95 [1991] 2 AC 114 .

96 *Westland Helicopters Ltd v Arab Organisation for Industrialisation* [1995] QB 283; see also *Buck v Attorney General* [1965] Ch 745; *Manuel v AG* [1982] 3 All ER 786.

97 *Reparations* case (1949) ICJ 174: '... the Court has come to the conclusion that the Organisation is an international person. That is not the same thing as saying that it is a State, which it certainly is not, or that its legal personality and rights and duties are the same as those of a State.'

98 *Reparation for Injuries Suffered in the Service of the United Nations* case (1949) ICJ 174.

99 *Legality of the Use by a State of Nuclear Weapons* (1996) ICJ 66.

100 (1949) ICJ 174.

101 *Ibid*, p 182.

reviewing constituent instruments, there has been a willingness to find implied powers where they are essential for the exercise of express duties[102] or where they arise by necessary implication;[103] the process has some similarity with the *ultra vires* doctrine in municipal company law. The matter was considered in the *Legality of the Use by a State of Nuclear Weapons* case,[104] where the World Health Organisation had sought an advisory opinion on the legality of the use of nuclear weapons. The constitution of the World Health Organisation, dating from 1946, gave the organisation jurisdiction 'to deal with the effects on health of the use of nuclear weapons'.[105] The International Court of Justice considered that competence to deal with 'effects' was distinct from the question of 'legality' and, therefore, no advisory opinion could be given under the terms of Art 96(2) of the United Nations Charter (1945).

A question that sometimes arises in respect of the competence of international organisations concerns the capacity of the organisation to enter into treaties. It does not follow that, because an organisation has international personality, it necessarily has treaty making power. Whether the entity possesses treaty making power will depend on the express powers contained in its constituent documents together with any implied powers and evidence of actual conduct.[106]

6 THE RELEVANT LAW[107]

Questions may arise as to the relevant law to be applied in respect of international organisations. As most are established by treaty, then the applicable or proper law will be the established rules of public international law. In the case of headquarters agreements, which are in effect treaties between the organisation and a specific state, it is accepted that

---

102 There seems to be two approaches in respect of implied powers. First, there is a willingness to find implied powers to ensure institutional effectiveness so, in the *Reparation* case, the International Court of Justice could observe: 'Under international law, the Organisation must be deemed to have those powers which, though not expressly provided in the Charter, are conferred upon it by necessary implication as being essential to the performance of its duties.' However, this should be contrasted with the more cautious formulation of Judge Hackworth in his dissenting opinion in the same case, where he observed: 'Powers not expressed cannot freely be implied. Implied powers flow from a grant of expressed powers and are limited to those that are "necessary" to the exercise of powers expressly granted.' Traces of this more conservative approach are to be found in the dissenting opinions in the *Expenses* case (1962) ICJ 230 and the *South West Africa (Preliminary Objections)* case (1962) ICJ 319, as well as the opinion delivered by Judge Fitzmaurice in the *Namibia* case (1971) ICJ 16.

103 The *International Status of South West Africa* (1950) ICJ 128; *Effect of Awards of Compensation Made by the United Nations Administrative Tribunal* case (1954) ICJ 47; *Certain Expenses of the United Nations* case (1962) ICJ 151.

104 (1996) ICJ 66. The actual question posed by the World Health Organisation was: 'In view of the health and environmental effects, would the use of nuclear weapons by a State in war or other armed conflict be a breach of its obligations under international law including the WHO Constitution?' For the view that questions concerning nuclear weapons were too wide to be legally meaningful, see AV Lowe [1996] CLJ 415.

105 WHO Constitution (1946), Art 2.

106 See Art 6 of the Vienna Convention on the Law of Treaties between States and International Organisations (1986); see Bowett, *The Law of International Institutions*.

107 CW Jenks, *The Proper Law of International Organisations*, 1961; FA Mann, 'International corporations and national law' (1967) 42 BYIL 145; F Seyersted, 'Applicable law in relations between intergovernmental organisations and private parties' (1967) 122 HR 427.

the relevant law will also be public international law.[108] So that questions of status constitution and succession will all normally be governed by international law.

However, where the problem concerns the operations of the organisation then the position may well be different. Where the organisation enters into contractual relations, then there may be an express choice of municipal law or such a choice as would be implied from the circumstances.[109] In litigation, it would seem that the municipal court will determine the relevant law by reference to its own rules of private international law.[110] Where the organisation is involved in tortious acts, then in principle such acts or omissions will be governed by the *lex loci delicti*;[111] in cases where agents of the state have acted against the headquarters or personnel of an international organisation, then the relevant law will be international law.

7 LIABILITY OF MEMBER STATES

Questions can arise as to whether the member states are liable for the conduct of the international organisation. In accordance with traditional principles, such a matter depends on the existence of legal personality. If the organisation lacks legal personality then, subject to any express constitutional provision, it would seem that acts and debts are the liability of member states. If, however, the international organisation possesses legal personality then, in principle, the member states will not be responsible for its debts or the conduct of the organisation on the basis that a state will not be liable for treaties or agreements to which it is not a party.

Such problems are likely to arise in the context of the operations of an international organisation in trading operations. An example is afforded by the collapse of the *International Tin Council*,[112] which announced in October 1985 that it was unable to meet its debts. After some preliminary litigation,[113] a number of creditors brought an action in the English courts[114] seeking to make the member states liable for the debts of the

---

108 The Agreement may expressly specify such and provide for arbitration; see *Applicability of the Obligation to Arbitrate* case [1988] ICJ 12.

109 The *Serbian Loans* case (1929) PCIJ, Ser A, No 20; 5 ILR 466.

110 For England, see *Vita Food Products Incorporated v Unus Shipping Co Ltd* [1939] AC 227 and now Contracts (Applicable Law) Act 1990, on which see FA Mann (1991) 107 LQR 353; FA Mann (1982) 32 ICLQ 265; A Briggs (1990) LMCLQ 192; A Jaffey (1984) 33 ICLQ 531.

111 If taking place in the state in which the headquarters is situate; if not then, in principle, such tortious acts would be governed by the relevant rules of private international law if litigated in that state.

112 I Cheyne, 'The International Tin Council' (1987) 36 ICLQ 931; (1989) 38 ICLQ 417; (1990) 39 ICLQ 945; CF Amerasinghe, 'Liability to third parties of member states of international organisations, practice, principle, and judicial precedent' (1991) 85 AJIL 259; I Seidl-Hohenveldern, 'Piercing the corporate veil of international organisations, the *International Tin Council* case in the English Court of Appeals' (1989) 32 GYIL 43.

113 *Standard Chartered Bank v ITC* [1986] 3 All ER 257; *Re International Tin Council* [1988] 3 All ER 257.

114 *JH Rayner (Mincing Lane) Ltd v Department of Trade and Industry* [1990] 2 AC 418. See the speech of Lord Templeman where the learned judge did not bother to conceal his opinion that the evidentiary material and length of the case had tended to obscure the traditional principles which, properly applied, rendered the outcome inevitable.

organisation. Although a number of arguments were advanced,[115] the action failed for the reason that one could identify 'three fundamental principles – that the capacities of a body corporate include the capacity to contract, that no one is liable on a contract save the parties to the contract and that treaty rights and obligations are not enforceable in the courts of the United Kingdom unless incorporated into law by statute'. Although the case itself reflects the dualist tradition of the United Kingdom and turned on domestic legislation, it seems correct in principle that a member state will not be liable in international law[116] for the debts of an international organisation, if that organisation has legal personality in international law, save in circumstances where there has been an express acceptance of responsibility in the constituent documents.

8 PRIVILEGES AND IMMUNITIES

It is generally accepted that an international organisation will require certain privileges and immunities so that it may properly discharge its tasks.[117] While there is an obvious analogy with diplomatic privileges and immunities, these are founded on the sovereign equality of states and the need for reciprocity. In the case of international organisations, any immunity is justified on the basis that the immunity is required in order that the work of the organisation may be properly undertaken.[118] An example is afforded by Art 105 of the United Nations Charter which reads in part:

(1) The Organisation shall enjoy in the territory of each of its Members such privileges and immunities as are necessary for the fulfilment of its purposes.

(2) Representatives of the Members of the United Nations and officials of the Organisation shall similarly enjoy such privileges and immunities as are necessary for the independent exercise of their functions in connection with the Organisation.

In the case of the United Nations, it was unrealistic to expect that detailed questions of privileges and immunities could be set out in the main Charter. The detailed provisions are thus set out in the General Convention on the Privileges and Immunities of the United Nations[119] and the Convention on the Privileges and Immunities of the Specialised Agencies.[120] However, it has been necessary to supplement these general conventions

---

115 The arguments advanced were: (i) that the ITC was but an unincorporated association; (ii) that even if the 1972 statutory instrument had conferred legal personality it did not confer the capacities of a body corporate; (iii) that as a mixed entity the member states were jointly and severally liable for its debts; (iv) that if the ITC had separate corporate personality it was acting as agent of the member states. All the submissions were rejected by the House of Lords.

116 And also in most systems of municipal law. In England, it had been established since *Salomon v A Salomon and Co Ltd* [1897] AC 22 that an independent legal person with the capacity of a body corporate was, in principle, solely responsible for its own debts and that the motives of those promoting the company were normally irrelevant. Interestingly, Lord Griffiths, who delivered a short speech, considered that member states might bear an ethical responsibility to reimburse an insolvent international organisation that they had promoted.

117 *Mendaro v World Bank* (1983) 717 F 2d 610; *Iran-US Claims Tribunal v AS* (1984) 94 ILR 321.

118 Article IV, s 14 of the United Nations General Convention (1946).

119 Approved by the General Assembly, 13 February 1946.

120 Approved 21 November 1947.

with specific headquarters agreements in respect of the state in which a relevant office is situated. Thus, headquarters agreements have been made with the United States,[121] Switzerland, Kenya and Austria. Such agreements protect the headquarters from local laws providing for search, seizure and confiscation; further, it is normally stipulated for an exemption from local taxation save in respect of specific forms of utility charges. The object of such agreements is to regulate in detailed terms the relationship between the organisation and the host state. So that, in the *Application of the Obligation to Arbitrate (PLO Observer Mission) case*[122] the United States was held by the International Court of Justice to an obligation to arbitrate arising from the headquarters agreement when it sought to close the PLO Observer Mission in New York. At present, there seems to be no general agreement on the scope of immunities, save that most accept that officials of international organisations are immune from legal action in respect of acts performed in their official capacity. The decisions in municipal courts cannot be harmoniously reconciled, save that there does seems to be a willingness to accord immunity on functional grounds rather than simply pursue analogies based on diplomatic immunity.[123]

So that in *Porru v Food and Agriculture Organisation*, an Italian court[124] was able to find that immunity arose both in customary international law and under the relevant Headquarters Agreement in respect of matters pertaining to the internal structure of the organisation. In the subsequent case of the *Food and Agriculture Organisation v INPDAI*,[125] the Italian Court of Cassation concluded that a dispute arising under a lease of premises did not relate to institutional objectives so as to attract immunity. Much will depend on how the question is characterised. In *Mukuro v European Bank for Reconstruction and Development*,[126] an individual brought a complaint alleging discrimination in the employment context. At first instance, the industrial tribunal upheld a claim for immunity. In rejecting the appeal, Mummery J ruled that the correct approach was to ask whether the activity in issue such as the selection of staff was within the official activities of the organisation and he went on to observe that 'official activities include all activities undertaken ... including its administrative activities'.[127]

Everything will depend on the relevant international agreement, any headquarters agreement, and any implementing municipal legislation. A distinction has to be drawn between privileges and immunities claimed by the organisation itself and privileges

---

121 United States (1947), Switzerland (1947), Kenya (1975), Austria (1979).

122 (1988) ICJ 12; 82 ILR 225.

123 *Porru v FAO* 71 ILR 240; *African Reinsurance Corporation v Abate Fantaye* 86 ILR 655; *FAO v INDPAI*, 87 ILR 1; *Mininni v Bari Institute* 87 ILR 28; *Iran-United States Claims Tribunal v AS* 94 ILR 321; *Mukuro v European Bank for Reconstruction and Development* (1994) ICR 897.

124 *Porru v Food and Agriculture Organisation* (1969) 71 ILR 240 (the case was brought before a Tribunal of First Instance (Labour Section)). (The case concerned a refusal to offer permanent employment and was thus categorised as a matter of staff selection and thus an internal matter).

125 *Food and Agriculture Organisation v Inpdai* (1982) 87 ILR 1 (the issue being obligations arising under a lease of premises which were viewed as not pertaining to the internal organisation of the institution).

126 *Mukuro v European Bank for Reconstruction and Development* (1994) ICR 897. (The case concerned an allegation of racial discrimination; it had been argued on appeal that the relevant activity was unlawful racial discrimination for which no immunity could be claimed. This was quite properly rejected by Mummery J in the Employment Appeal Tribunal who categorised the activity as one of staff selection and the complaint as being founded on its manner.)

127 *Mukuro v European Bank for Reconstruction and Development* (1994) ICR 896 at 906 .

claimed by state representatives attending that organisation. In respect of the latter case, the flavour is conveyed by Art IV, s 11 of the United Nations General Convention which stipulates the following privileges and immunities:

(a) immunity from personal arrest or detention and from seizure of their personal baggage, and in respect of words spoken or written and all acts done by them in their capacity as representatives, immunity from legal process of every kind;

(b) inviolability for all papers and documents;

(c) the right to use codes and to receive papers or correspondence by courier or in sealed bags;

(d) exemption in respect of themselves and their spouses from immigration restrictions, alien registration or national service obligation in the state they are visiting or through which they are passing in the exercise of their functions;

(e) the same facilities in respect of currency or exchange restrictions as are accorded to representatives of foreign governments on temporary official missions;

(f) the same immunities and facilities in respect of their personal baggage as are accorded to diplomatic envoys; and also

(g) such other privileges, immunities and facilities not inconsistent with the foregoing as diplomatic envoys enjoy, except that they shall have no right to claim exemption from customs duties on goods imported (otherwise than as part of their personal baggage) or from excise duties or sales taxes.

It is normal for the relevant headquarters agreement to deal with the question of the privileges and immunities of representatives. While these agreements vary in content, an example is afforded by Art V, s 15 of the United Nations Headquarters Agreement 1947, which provides that representatives are entitled within the United States 'to the same privileges and immunities, subject to corresponding conditions and obligations, as it accords to diplomatic envoys accredited to it'. The question of privileges and immunities is also governed by the Vienna Convention on the Representation of States in their Relations with International Organisations of a Universal Character (1975), which contains provisions similar to the Vienna Convention on Diplomatic Relations (1961). However, the Convention itself has only received a mixed reception on grounds that it pays insufficient regard to the interests of the host state.[128]

Such agreements on the international plane are normally followed by specific municipal legislation. In the United Kingdom, the principal measure was the International Organisation (Privileges and Immunities) Act 1950, which was replaced by the International Organisations Act 1968, which was itself extended by the International Organisations Act 1981. Under the 1968 legislation, provision[129] is contained for Orders

---

128 The Convention requires 35 ratifications or accessions to enter into force; some states take the view that it goes beyond existing international law.

129 See *JH Rayner (Mincing Lane) Ltd v Department of Trade* [1990] 2 AC 418, where reference is made to the relevant statutory instruments in respect of the International Tin Council, ie, the International Organisations (Immunities and Privileges of the International Tin Council) Order 1956 (SI 1956/1214) and the International Tin Council (Immunities and Privileges) Order 1972 (SI 1972/120). See also *Zoernsch v Waldock* [1964] 1 WLR 675.

in Council to be made extending immunities included within the Schedule to the Act to specific organisations.[130]

9 DISSOLUTION AND SUCCESSION[131]

Some international organisations are intended to be permanent, so it would be illogical to include express provisions as to dissolution. However, where there is express provision, such as in the case of some financial institutions, it may be stipulated that the majority vote should attain a certain percentage. Where there is express provision as to dissolution, then the tendency has been to follow the practice in municipal company law and to stipulate that any payment of creditors should take priority over distribution of assets. In the case of distribution of assets, it may be stipulated that any such distribution is proportionate to the contributions of members. As a matter of constitutional propriety, the decision to dissolve should in principle be undertaken by the supreme representative body; so that the League of Nations was dissolved by a vote taken by its Assembly although at the time of the vote a number of states were absent.

Succession may be full or partial and may be effected by absorption, merger or transfer. Normally, succession is accomplished by a detailed agreement. In principle, the original organisation must have the capacity to transfer or it may be a case of dissolution followed by a transfer of assets to a new organisation. The successor organisation can, in principle, accept only those functions that are consistent with its constitution. The new organisation may include express provision in respect of the prior organisation; thus, Arts 36(5) and 37 of the Statute of the International Court of Justice provided for the continuance of the jurisdiction of the Permanent Court of International Justice. Normally, because of the importance of the issues, questions of succession will be determined by the contents of the agreement made by the former organisation although, in principle, succession may arise by implication from the circumstances.[132]

---

130 See *JH Rayner (Mincing Lane) Ltd v Department of Trade and Industry* [1990] AC 2 AC 418 (where the relevant Headquarters Agreement was given effect to the International Tin Council (Immunities and Privileges) Order 1972 (SI 1972/120) and *Mukoro v European Bank for Reconstruction and Development* (1994) ICR 897 (where a Headquarters Agreement was followed by the European Bank for Reconstruction and Development (Immunities and Privileges) Order 1991 made under the International Organisations Act 1968).

131 CW Jenks, 'Some constitutional problems of international organisations' (1945) 22 BYIL 11; Mackinnon Wood, 'The dissolution of the League of Nations' (1946) 13 BYIL 317; PR Myers, 'Liquidation of the League of Nations' functions' (1948) 42 AJIL 320; C Parry (1949) BYIL 133; H Chiu, 'Succession in international organisations' (1965) 14 ICLQ 83.

132 *Re Status of South West Africa (Advisory Opinion)* (1950) ICJ 128; the *Namibia* case (1971) ICJ 16.

CHAPTER 24

THE LAW OF ARMED CONFLICT[1]

1 INTRODUCTION

International law has long contained rules designed to regulate the conduct of war and armed conflict. This is hardly surprising because, for the earliest writers on the law of nations, the circumstances in which force might be used by a ruler was a matter of central concern. A distinction has traditionally been drawn between those rules that regulate when and in what circumstances force may be employed (*jus ad bellum*)[2] and those rules that pertain when armed conflict has broken out (*jus in bello*). In this chapter, we are concerned with the latter situation, namely the *jus in bello*.

The *jus in bello* itself is divided into those conventions that regulate the conduct of armed conflict and those instruments that govern the treatment and protection of those *hors de combat*, civilians and other non-combatants. This division is expressed as the distinction between the 'Hague law', named after the various Hague Conventions which seek to regulate the means and methods of warfare, and the 'Geneva law' or international humanitarian law, which seeks to ensure minimum standards of treatment for the victims of armed conflict, who include the wounded, sick, prisoners of war and civilians. The division between the 'Hague law' and 'Geneva law' is not clear cut, but serves to indicate the distinction between operational matters and questions of humanitarian or human rights concerns.

At the root of the *jus in bello* is the principle of moderation in armed conflict. The principle of moderation between states does not have a precise direct equivalent in municipal law; however, on the international plane there has been a concern to limit the conduct of states. Such limitations spring partly from ethical considerations and a proper concern to limit the undue waste of human life but also from the pragmatic realisation that conflict is a temporary state and that, in the future, normal relations may have to be resumed. The content of the law is grounded in both idealism and realism. Although there has been concern with the nature of conflict, from the outset of the Law of Nations this has grown in importance in the last 500 years; in broad terms, the scientific and technological advances of the last two centuries have resulted in more and more lethal weapons systems culminating in the deployment of nuclear weapons in 1945.

---

1 See generally TE Holland, *The Laws of War on Land*, 1908; L Oppenheim, *International Law*, Vol 2, *War and Neutrality*, 1st edn, 1906; L Oppenheim, *International Law*, Vol 2, 7th edn, 1955, by H Lauterpacht; G Schwarzenberger, *International Law*, Vol 2, *The Law of Armed Conflict*, 1958; G Best, *Humanity in Warfare*, 1983; I Detter, *The Law of War*, 1st edn, 1987; H McCoubrey, *International Humanitarian Law*, 1990; H McCoubrey and N White, *International Law and Armed Conflict*, 1992; L Green, *The Contemporary Law of Armed Conflict*, 1993; A Arend and R Beck, *International Law and the Use of Force*, 1993; G Best, *War and Law since 1945*, 1994; AP Rogers, *Law on the Battlefield*, 1996; D Fleck (ed), *The Handbook of Humanitarian Law in Armed Conflicts*, 1999; A Roberts and R Guelff, *Documents on the Laws of War*, 3rd edn, 2000; I Detter, *The Law of War*, 2nd edn, 2000.

2 The question as to when force may be lawfully employed is considered in Chapter 21.

References to the treatment of prisoners of war can be traced back to at least the time of the Old Testament. The Judaeo-Christian tradition was augmented when Christianity became the religion of the Roman Empire.[3] Attempts were then made to specify the precise circumstances in which a just resort to force could be made; this was normally on the basis of some injustice that had arisen earlier. From the outset, it was recognised that there was a connection between resort to force and actual conduct, Augustine of Hippo (354–430), in discussing the question, expressed the opinion that a just cause might be negated by excessive conduct by a participant.[4] Although the doctrine of the just war was developed further by Thomas Aquinas (1225–74), this had the effect of prompting the opinion that the other side were often regarded as worthy of less consideration.

After the Treaty of Westphalia (1648) and the rise of the European state, conflicts tended to be between professional armies and were entered into for dynastic or policy reasons or to secure the balance of power so that the enemy of today might be the ally of tomorrow. In these circumstances, writers such as Grotius[5] and later Rousseau[6] began to stress the case for moderation in the conduct of conflict. Further, the development of professional armies under commanders such as the Duke of Marlborough and later Frederick II tended to act as a force for moderate conduct.

There is some evidence to indicate that this 18th century practice of restraint ended with the outbreak of the French revolutionary wars in 1792. The *levée en masse* and the mobilisation of the French state in favour of republican values tended to inject a degree of ideological fervour that had not been present in the conflicts of the previous century; this emphasis on mass armies and ideological struggle continued during the Napoleonic Wars and resulted in heavy loss of life in battles such as Austerlitz (1805) and Borodino (1807); so much so, that Karl von Clausewitz, writing in 1832, could express doubt as to whether any principle of moderation was appropriate since:

> War arises, and by it War is ... controlled and modified. But these things do not belong to War itself, they are only given conditions; and to introduce into the philosophy of War itself a principle of moderation would be an absurdity, although he further noted that 'if civilisations do not put their prisoners to death or devastate cities and countries, it is because intelligence plays a larger part in their methods of warfare ... and has taught them more effective ways of using force than the crude expression of instinct.[7]

Although 19th century Europe did not witness prolonged war, individual conflicts were such as to prompt reflection by reformers and others appalled by events. The Crimean War (1852–55) had complicated causes linked to the collapse of the Ottoman Empire and the reactionary views of Tsar Nicholas II (1825–55). However, the conflict itself indicated three clear lessons for the future: (i) the competence of military commanders would be

---

3   Usually dated at AD 313 in the form of the Edict of Milan issued by the Emperor Constantine (274–337).

4   *De Civitate Dei; Contra Faustem.*

5   H Grotius (1583–1645), *De Jure Belli et Pacis* (*On the Law of War and Peace*), 1625.

6   JJ Rousseau (1712–78), *Du Contrat Social.* See *The Social Contract and Discourses* translated and introduced by GDH Cole, 1913.

7   Karl von Clausewitz (1780–1831), *Vom Kriege* (*On War*), 1832; see translation by M Howard and P Paret, 1976.

subject to greater scrutiny;[8] (ii) in future journalists would seek to report on such conflicts;[9] (iii) improvements in medical science would enable lives to be saved if appropriate resources could be made available.[10] The efforts of Napoleon III to aid the Italian nationalists[11] would have profound effects on the law of war and the nature of losses in the American Civil War led to the first attempts to formulate precise rules for combatants. Thus, although Clausewitz could note in 1831 that the laws of war were 'almost imperceptible and hardly worth mentioning';[12] by 1860, the outlines of the modern *jus in bello* can be clearly discerned. Before turning to how the *jus in bello* developed it is important to consider matters of definition.

2 WAR AND ARMED CONFLICT

In customary international law, much attention was given to the question as to whether a state of war might be said to exist[13] and whether it was lawful. Grotius thought that for a war to be lawful[14] it had to be between competent sovereigns and be preceded by a formal declaration; in addition, for it to be lawful, it had to be in respect of a just cause. It is arguable today that little purpose is served by drawing a distinction between the concept of 'war' and that of 'armed conflict'. Secondly, Grotius held that there could be no intermediate state between war and peace;[15] this remained the general approach down until 1914, and was accepted by the House of Lords as correct in *Janson v Driefontein Consolidated Mines Ltd*.[16] Whether a state of war existed had the effect that, in principle, the laws of war applied between the parties, that the non-hostile relations between the parties would also be effected and that the relations between the belligerents and other states would be governed by the laws of neutrality.[17]

---

8   In England, this led to the military reforms undertaken by Edward Cardwell (Secretary of State for War (1868–74) in the first administration of WE Gladstone. Among the initiatives were: (i) the ending of flogging; (ii) the ending of bounty money for recruits; (iii) the subordination of the Commander in Chief to the Secretary of State; (iv) the ending of the purchase of commissions; (v) reorganisation of the regimental and battalion system. Some of these changes were precipitated by shock at the speed of German victory at Sedan and Metz during the Franco-Prussian war, Such reforms would remain in place for than a generation until Richard Haldane became Secretary of State in 1905.

9   The reports of William Howard Russell for the *TImes* are viewed as the first modern form of war reporting; see P Knightly, *The First Casualty*, 1978, London.

10 The work of Florence Nightingale (1820–1910) at Scutari during the Crimean War led to reconsideration of the role of medical services in time of conflict and, in the longer term, to a better appreciation of the role of the nursing profession.

11 As will be seen below, the modern *jus in bello* is traceable to the Battle of Solferino (1859).

12 Karl von Clausewitz, *Vom Kriege* (*On War*), 1832, Berlin.

13 G Schwarzenberger, '*Jus Pacis ac Belli*?' (1943) 37 AJIL 430; PC Jessup, 'Should international law recognise an intermediate state between war and peace?' (1954) 48 AJIL 98.

14 *De Jure Belli ac Pacis* (1625).

15 As Grotius expressed it in *De Jure Belli ac Pacis* (1625), '*inter bellum et pacem nihil est medium*'. The 20th century witnessed the rise of the intermediate status referred to by G Schwarzenberger as a '*status mixtus*' (1943) 37 AJIL 460.

16 *Janson v Driefontein Consolidated Mines Ltd* [1902] AC 484 (where this was certainly the opinion of Lord Halsbury LC); see also *Muller v Thompson* (1811) 2 Camp 610.

17 See generally, Ian Brownlie, *International Law and the Use of Force by States*.

In respect of definitions, Clauswitz observed that war 'is an act of force to compel our enemy to do our will',[18] while Oppenheim described war as 'a contention between two or more States through their armed forces, for the purpose of overpowering each other and imposing such conditions of peace as the victor pleases'.[19] When war came to be outlawed by international society, politicians became reluctant to use the expression and this can be increasingly noted after the Kellogg-Briand Pact of 1928.[20] Even if one could agree upon a definition, the question arose as to whether the matter was subjective and dependent on the actual intention of the parties[21] or was it to be objectively determined[22] on the basis not of the intention of the parties but in relation to particular criteria. In recent decades, the seeming indiscriminate nature of war, its probable incompatibility[23] with the United Nations Charter, and the obvious ethical difficulties have caused states to deny the existence of war in almost all cases of armed conflict.[24]

In the past, not all states have made formal declarations of war.[25] From the perspective of the United Kingdom courts, whether a state of war exists may be determined in part on the content of the Foreign Office certificate;[26] on the international plane, it is sensible to regard the distinction between 'war' and 'armed conflict' as one of fact and degree. On the international plane, the *jus in bello* will apply in respect of hostilities regardless of whether there is a formal declaration of war; thus, the common Art 2 of the four 1949 Geneva Conventions[27] provides that they shall apply in 'all cases of

---

18   K von Clausewitz, *Vom Kriege*, 1832; English edition *On War*, 1976(M Howard and P Paret (eds)).

19   Oppenheim, *International Law*, Vol 2, *War and Neutrality*, 7th edn, 1952, H Lauterpacht.

20   Q Wright, 'When does war exist?' (1932) 26 AJIL 362; C Eagleton, 'The form and function of the declaration of war' (1938) 32 AJIL 19.

21   A McNair, 'The legal meaning of war and the relation of war to reprisals' (1925) 11 TGS 45.

22   E Borchard, 'War and peace' (1933) 27 AJIL 114.

23   The prohibition on the use of force can be traced through the Hague Convention I (1899) on the Peaceful Settlement of Disputes; Hague Convention I (1907) on the Peaceful Settlement of Disputes; Art 10 of the Covenant of the League of Nations (1919); Kellogg-Briand Pact of 1928; United Nations Charter (1945), Art 2(4).

24   So the United States denied being at war in respect of Korea, Vietnam or Kosovo, while the United Kingdom adopted the same approach in respect of the Falkland Islands in 1982, as did India in respect of Pakistan in 1965. In recent decades, the conflict most openly described as a 'war' was the Iran-Iraq conflict of 1980–88.

25   There was no such declaration in the Russo-Japanese War of 1904–05, when the Japanese attacked the Russian fleet at Port Arthur. There was, of course, no prior warning in respect of the attack on Pearl Harbour in 1941. The absence of prior declarations of war was noted by Mellish LJ in giving judgment in *The Teutonia* (1872) LR 4 PC 171. In 1881, the English Board of Trade calculated that out of 117 conflicts between 1700 and 1870, there had been a prior declaration of war in only 10 cases. See C Greenwood (1987) 36 ICLQ 283. A requirement for prior declaration was inserted in Hague Convention III (1907) Relative to the Opening of Hostilities but this was a response to Japanese conduct in 1904 and not an attempt to codify.

26   See generally, *Ex p Weber* [1916] 1 KB 280 (CA); [1916] 1 AC 421; *R v Vine Street Police Station ex p Liebmann* [1916] 1 KB 268; *Daimler Co v Continental Tyre and Rubber Co* [1916] 2 AC 307; *Ex p Freyberger* [1917] 2 KB 129 (CA); *Kawasaki Kisen Kabushiki Kaisha v Bantham Steamship Co* [1939] 2 KB 544; *Netz v Chuter Ede* [1946] Ch 244; *R v Bottrill ex p Keuchenmeister* [1947] KB 41. See also C Parry, 'The status of Germany and German internees' (1947) 10 MLR 403; C Schmitthoff (1948) 64 LQR 484; FA Mann (1948) 64 LQR 492.

27   The four relevant conventions being: (I) For the Amelioration of the Condition of the Wounded and Sick in Armed Forces in the Field; (II) For the Amelioration of the Condition of Wounded, Sick and Shipwrecked Members of the Armed Forces at Sea; (III) Relative to the Treatment of Prisoners of War; (IV) Relative to the Protection of Civilian Persons in Time of War.

declared war or of any other armed conflict which may arise between two or more of the High Contracting Parties, even if the state of war is not recognised by one of them'. In practice, all that is required is evidence of armed conflict between states;[28] in neither the Falkland Islands conflict of 1982 or the Gulf crisis of 1990–91 was there a formal declaration of war.

However, questions of classification remain important and it would seem that one can distinguish: (i) a formally declared war between two states;[29] (ii) an international armed conflict between two states;[30] (iii) an 'internationalised' armed conflict such as a struggle for national liberation;[31] (iv) a civil war;[32] (v) cases of civil disturbance/civil disorder.[33] Such distinctions have proved important in commercial claims in municipal courts,[34] particularly in respect of actions to enforce insurance policies.[35] They are relevant in international law in determining which legal regime may apply to a particular factual situation.

3 THE EVOLUTION OF THE *JUS IN BELLO*

It is generally accepted that the *jus in bello* began to emerge in the middle of the 19th century. The first important event arose in 1859, when a Swiss businessman, Henri Dunant, observed the suffering of the wounded after the Battle of Solferino[36] and, in 1862, published his recollections entitled Souvenirs de Solferino. In this tract, he advocated a voluntary organisation to treat battlefield injured and a degree of international agreement to regulate the treatment of the sick and the wounded. Following the publication of the book, a committee was established which summoned an international conference which met in Geneva in 1863 to create the Red Cross Organisation. The second aspect of Henri Dunant's proposal was accomplished in August 1864, when representatives at an international conference drew up the first Geneva

---

28 See C Greenwood, 'The concept of war in modern international law' (1987) 36 ICLQ 283.

29 Where the full *jus in bello* will apply.

30 Where the full *jus in bello* will apply.

31 To which the *jus in bello* may be extended by Art 1(4) of Additional Protocol 1 to the 1949 Geneva Conventions.

32 A workable test for determining the existence of a civil war was set out by Mustill J (as he then was) in *Spinney's (1948) Ltd v Royal Insurance Co Ltd* [1980] 1 Lloyd's Rep 405, where the learned judge advanced three questions: (i) Can it be said that the conflict was between opposing 'sides'? (ii) What were the objectives of the 'sides' and how did they set about them? (iii) What was the scale of the conflict, and what were its effects on the life of the inhabitants? For the treatment of civil wars, see below.

33 Where the *jus in bello* probably will not apply but the obligation to respect human rights obtains.

34 See *Curtis and Sons v Mathews* [1918] 2 KB 825.

35 As in *Janson v Driefontein Consolidated Mines Limited* [1902] AC 484.

36 The Battle of Soferino (20 June 1859) was an indecisive battle in the Franco-Piedmontese War against Austria. However, the casualty figures were so high that Napoleon III offered an armistice to Austria. It is worth noting that the battle followed shortly after the Battle of Magenta (4 June 1859) in which, although France triumphed, the casualty figures also had been high. The level of casualties and the summer heat caused Napoleon III to become discouraged and to conclude the Peace of Villefranche with Austria, whereby Lombardy was ceded to France who then passed it to Piedmont. See H Hearder and DP Waley (eds), *A Short History of Italy*, 1966.

Convention for the Amelioration of the Condition of the Wounded in Armies in the Field (1864). Although these developments stemmed from the conflict between France and Austria, the ground had already been laid during the Crimean War where the efforts of Florence Nightingale at Scutari to lower the mortality rate had attracted widespread attention. At the same time, in the United States the heavy losses in the battles of the Civil War (1861–65) served to indicate the urgency of the task. In the United States, the administration of President Lincoln requested Dr Francis Lieber[37] of Columbia University to draw up 'Instructions for the Government of Armies of the United States in the Field'. Once a start had been made, then progress was rapid. In 1868, a conference meeting at Geneva proposed extending the 1864 Geneva Convention to maritime affairs.

However, at the same time concern was growing at the nature expense and power of modern armaments. As early as 1868, Tsar Alexander II[38] called a military conference in St Petersburg which resulted in a Declaration which included a call for restraint in the manufacture of armaments.[39] The same sovereign was responsible for summoning the 1874 Brussels Conference which drew up the Brussels Declaration Concerning the Laws of Land Warfare; this document was not itself a treaty but was followed by the Institute of International Law in 1880 which produced its own Manual of the Laws and Customs of War at its meeting in Oxford.

It was the growing tension in Europe and the power of armaments that persuaded Tsar Nicholas II to call an international conference on the subject at the Hague in 1899. The first Hague Conference of 1899 resulted in three Conventions[40] and three Declarations[41] although the Convention on the Peaceful Settlement of Disputes was not strictly part of the laws of war. Of particular interest was Hague Convention II (1899) which included in its preamble the so called Martens clause which read:[42]

> Until a more complete code of the laws of war is issued, the high contracting Parties think it right to declare that, in cases not included in the Regulations adopted by them, populations and belligerents remain under the protection and empire of the principles of international

---

37 Francis Lieber (1800–72), Professor of Political Science and Jurisprudence at Columbia University.

38 Alexander II (1818–81) after succeeding Nicholas II terminated the Crimean War by The Treaty of Paris (1856). Best known for his emancipation of the serfs, he had a reputation as a reformer. There are indications that, later in the century, Russia as an economically backward state was concerned that it could not compete in any arms race.

39 The actual purpose of the St Petersburg Declaration (1868) was to certain calibres of fragmenting bullets.

40 The three Conventions being: (i) on the Pacific Settlement of Disputes; (ii) on the Regulations and Customs of War on Land; and (iii) on Maritime War (Protection of Wounded, Sick and Shipwrecked).

41 The three Declarations relating to (i) Balloons; (ii) Asphyxiating Gases; and (iii) Expanding Bullets. The second Declaration in respect of Gas was seen to be wanting in World War I and was replaced by the 1925 Geneva Protocol .

42 Later included in the preamble to Hague Convention (IV) (1907) Respecting the Laws and Customs of War on Land. Named after Fyodor Fyodorovich Martens (1845–1909) who served as the delegate of Tsar Nicholas II at the conference.

law, as they result from the usages established between civilised nations, from the laws of humanity and the requirements of public conscience.[43]

Annexed to Hague Convention II (1899) were a set of regulations[44] seeking to amplify the rules of war in respect of warfare on land; the content of these regulations drew upon the earlier drafts of 1874 and 1880.

One of the recommendations of the Hague Conference of 1899 was that an international conference should be summoned to revise the 1864 Geneva Convention;[45] the conference which was convened in Geneva in 1906 resulted in the Geneva Convention for the Amelioration of the Condition of the Wounded and Sick in Armies in the Field (1906) which applied in this form throughout the First World War (1914–18).

The next significant step was the summoning of the second Hague Conference in 1907; although formally convened by Tsar Nicholas II it owed much to the efforts of President Theodore Roosevelt.[46] By this stage, the pattern of alliances and the build up of arms in Europe was beginning to give cause for concern. The Conference resulted in a number of Conventions which for the most part were regarded as declaratory of customary international law. The relevant Conventions were as follows:

Hague Convention I (1907)	On the Peaceful Settlement of Disputes[47]
Hague Convention II (1907)	On Limitation of Force in Recovering Contract Debts
Hague Convention III (1907)	On the Opening of Hostilities[48]
Hague Convention IV (1907)	Respecting the Laws and Customs of War on Land[49]
Hague Convention V (1907)	On Neutrality in Land War
Hague Convention VI (1907)	On Enemy Merchant Ships[50]
Hague Convention VII (1907)	On the Conversion of Merchant Ships into Warships
Hague Convention VIII (1907)	On Automatic Submarine Contact Mines
Hague Convention IX (1907)	On Naval Bombardment

43 This was repeated with slightly different wording in the preamble to 1907 Hague Convention IV. Provisions to like effect appear in 1949 Geneva Convention I, Art 63; Convention II, Art 62; Convention III, Art 142; Convention IV, Art 158. The same principle is stated in 1977 Geneva Protocol I, Art 1; 1977 Geneva Protocol II, Preamble; 1980 UN Conventional Weapons Convention, Preamble.

44 The Regulations were later annexed to Hague Convention IV (1907).

45 The 1864 Convention being followed by those in 1906, 1929 and forming the basis of Geneva Convention I (1949).

46 Who had played a role in the ending of the Russo-Japanese War (1904–05) for which he won the Nobel Peace Prize in 1906.

47 Strictly speaking Hague Conventions (I, II, III) do not relate to the law of war.

48 Hague Convention III (1907) contained a requirement that a state should make a declaration of war. This had been included because of the conduct of Japan in mounting a surprise attack on Russian vessels at Port Arthur in 1904.

49 Representing a continuance of the 1899 Hague Convention II. As with Hague Convention II (1899) it was supplemented by a detailed Annex of Regulations Respecting the Laws and Customs of War on Land which covered subject such as: (a) belligerents; (b) prisoners of war; (c) hostilities; (d) spying; (e) flags of truce.

50 See generally *The Blonde* [1922] 1 AC 313; *The Mowe* [1951] P 1.

Hague Convention X (1907)	On Maritime Warfare (Protection of Wounded, Sick and Shipwrecked)[51]
Hague Convention XI (1907)	On Capture in Naval Warfare
Hague Convention XII (1907)	On International Prize Court
Hague Convention XIII (1907)	On the Rights and Duties of Neutral Powers in Naval War

Although the Conventions only strictly bound those states who were a party to them it was clear that many were declaratory of customary international or constitutive of it. There was, thus, a considerable corpus of the law which had emerged in half century prior to 1914. The Hague Conventions were intended to remain in force until the summoning of a third conference but that was frustrated by the outbreak of the First World War (1914–18). So that, during the First World War, the relevant law was comprised in the 1907 Hague Conventions together with the 1909 London Declaration on the Rules of Naval Warfare.[52] The unprecedented loss of human life during the First World War and the pace of technological advance prompted thought as to how the *jus in bello* might be strengthened. Particular incidents such as the sinking of the Lusitania in 1915[53] or the commencement of aerial bombing[54] gave specific cause for concern.

The development of aerial power prompted international action. The Washington Conference of 1920–21 failed to produce any agreement on the sensitive subject of the limitation of armaments, but the following year a committee of jurists under John Bassett Moore produced the 1923 Hague Rules of Aerial Warfare designed to place some restrictions the new technology.[55] A second cause for concern in the First World War had been the employment of gas on the Western Front to break the seeming impasse. An International Conference meeting at Geneva produced the 1925 Geneva Protocol for the Prohibition of the Use in War of Asphyxiating, Poisonous or Other Gases and of Bacteriological Methods of Warfare.[56] This Protocol has attracted a high number of ratifications and secured a good level of observance.

---

51 Now superseded by 1949 Geneva Convention (II).

52 Which was not itself ratified by any state.

53 The sinking of the Cunard Liner *The Lusitania* in May 1915 raised the question of the nature of submarine operations; the exact nature of the cargo has remained a question of controversy since. The death of 100 American passengers resulted in an official protest by President Wilson. For an individual case history, see *Re Jones Estate* (1921) 192 Iowa 78; 182 NW 227 (Iowa Supreme Court).

54 In actual fact, only 1,117 civilians were killed by aerial bombing in England during World War I. This contrasts with a figure of over 60,000 civilian deaths in England in World War II. It is calculated that over 500,000 German civilians died in aerial bombing in World War II (see AJP Taylor, *English History (1914–45)*, 1965; Ingrid Detter, *The Law of War*, 2nd edn, 2000.

55 Prior to World War II, concern was raised by the Italian conduct in Ethiopia in 1936 and by the German conduct in Spain (1936–39). The nature of aerial bombardment was to be one of the most difficult issues of World War II. In 1938, Prime Minister Chamberlain asserted three principles: (i) direct attack against civilian populations was unlawful; (ii) targets for aerial bombardment must be legitimate, identifiable military objectives; (iii) reasonable care must be taken in attacking a military objective so as to avoid the civilian population in the neighbourhood.

56 The main complaints since have concerned Italy in Ethiopia (1935–36); Japan in China (1937–45) and in respect of both sides during the Iran-Iraq War (1980–88). See Security Council Resolution 1988/620.

The experience of the First World War as regards prisoners of war had been broadly in conformity with the content of the 1907 Hague Regulations; however, in 1929 an International Conference decided upon revision and the 1929 Geneva Convention on Prisoners of War[57] and the 1929 Geneva Convention on Wounded and Sick served to extend the corpus of the *jus in bello*. These latter two Conventions remained in force during the Second World War. The gradual development of the law during the inter war period was completed by London Treaty of 1930 and the London Protocol of 1936 which sought to restrict the use of submarines; however, these documents did not prevent unrestricted submarine warfare in the Second World War. In looking at the evolution of the law from the 1860s, it is clear that the legal framework was struggling to keep up with advances in military, naval and aviation technology.

The Second World War included mass brutality against civilians and non-combatants on an unprecedented scale. After the conclusion of the conflict a certain number of persons stood trial at Nurmeburg and the principle of individual responsibility was upheld. The worst abuses were outlawed in the Genocide Convention (1948) and a process of revision of humanitarian law resulted in the four Geneva Conventions[58] of 1949. The relevant Conventions are:

Geneva Convention I (1949)	Geneva Convention for the Amelioration of the Condition of the Wounded and Sick in Armed Forces in the Field[59]
Geneva Convention II (1949)	For the Amelioration of the Condition of Wounded, Sick and Shipwrecked Members of Armed Forces at Sea[60]
Geneva Convention III (1949)	On the Treatment of Prisoners of War[61]
Geneva Convention IV (1949)	On the Protection of Civilian Persons in Time of War[62]

The developments in the inter-war years had been precipitated by technological change; this remained an impetus after 1945, but it was allied to the changing forms of conflict. The conventional scenario in which state A invaded state B had largely been outlawed and ended by the United Nations Charter. The *jus in bello* was now required to adapt to more complex situations of conflict, such as internal wars and struggles for self-determination. One lamentable feature of the Second World War had been the theft, looting and destruction of cultural and art works by German forces. Under the Initiative

---

57 The 1929 Geneva Convention on Prisoners of War supplemented the earlier 1899 and 1907 Hague Regulations on the same subject.

58 Given effect to in the United Kingdom in the Geneva Conventions Act 1957.

59 The Geneva Convention I 1949 represents the continuation of the earlier 1864, 1906 and 1929 Conventions. It is a revised and enlarged version of the 1929 Geneva Convention.

60 The Geneva Convention II 1949 can be traced back to the Additional Articles of 1868 which did not enter into force. These were then taken up in Hague Convention III 1899 which was then replaced by Hague Convention X 1907. Article 58 of the 1949 Convention provides that the present Convention replaces Hague Convention X 1907.

61 Prisoners of War were provided for in the Regulations Annexed to both 1899 Hague Convention II and 1907 Hague Convention IV. These regulations were supplemented by the 1929 Geneva Convention on Prisoners of War. The Geneva Convention III (1949) complements the 1899 and 1907 regulations and expands the 1929 Geneva Convention (Art 135).

62 Geneva Convention IV (1949) represents the first convention exclusively devoted to civilians.

of UNESCO, the existing law was extended and clarified in the 1954 Hague Convention for the Protection of Cultural Property in the Event of Armed Conflict.[63]

The Second World War had concluded with the use of nuclear weapons. One of the legacies of the conflict was that concerted action needed to be taken to restrain weapon systems that caused environmental damage. This was effected in the 1972 Convention on the Prohibition of the Development, Production and Stockpiling of Bacteriological (Biological) and Toxin Weapons and on their Destruction. Any attempt to manipulate the weather for military purposes was outlawed by the 1976 United Nations Convention on the Prohibition of Military or Any Other Hostile Use of Environmental Modification Techniques (known as the ENMOD Convention). By the end of the decade the human rights consequences of certain weapons systems resulted in the 1980 United Nations Convention[64] on Prohibitions or Restrictions on the Use of Certain Conventional Weapons and later in the 1997 Convention on the Prohibition of the Use, Stockpiling Production and Transfer of Anti Personnel Mines and on their Destruction.

The possession of nuclear weapons in the 1950s tended to act as a restraint on all out conflict in Europe even though at times the atmosphere was tense. Instead, the post-war period was characterised by new and more intractable forms of armed conflict; some were civil wars, others might be classified as wars of liberation, colonial struggles, guerrillas wars or secessionist wars. The basic question arose as to whether these were to be categorised as internal struggles or international conflicts. In particular, the question arose as to whether the *jus in bello* applied and whether the 1949 Geneva Conventions should be extended to apply in a wider variety of circumstances. Although common, Art 3 of the 1949 Geneva Conventions had been intended to confer a minimum degree of protection in the context of civil wars there was a general view that more specific provision needed to be made. A conference of experts met under the auspices of the ICRC between 1971–72 and this was followed by the convening in Geneva in February 1974 of the Diplomatic Conference on the Reaffirmation and Development of International Humanitarian Law Applicable to Armed Conflicts.[65] On 8 June 1977, the Conference formally adopted two Protocols Additional to the Geneva Conventions of 12 August 1949. The two Additional Protocols[66] referred to international and non-international armed conflicts.

---

63 The 1954 Hague Convention has been followed by two Protocols: (i) The 1954 First Hague Protocol for the Protection of Cultural Property in the Event of Armed Conflict – which is concerned with the export of cultural property from occupied territory; and (ii) the 1999 Second Hague Protocol for the Protection of Cultural Property in the Event of Armed Conflict. Protection under the 1954 Convention did not deter Yugoslav forces from shelling Dubrovnik in 1991.

64 To give it the full title, the United Nations Convention on Prohibitions or Restrictions on the Use of Certain Conventional Weapons which may be deemed to be Excessively Injurious or to Have Indiscriminate Effects (1980). This was accompanied by a number of Protocols: (i) 1980 Protocol I on Non Detectable Fragments; (ii) 1980 Protocol II on Prohibitions or Restrictions on the Use of Mines, Booby Traps and Other Devices; (iii) 1980 Protocol III on Prohibitions or Restrictions on the Use of Incendiary Weapons. The first review conference in 1995 resulted in: (i) Protocol on Blinding Laser Weapons; (ii) Amended Protocol on Prohibitions or Restrictions on the Use of Mines, Booby Traps and Other Devices.

65 The Conference met in a number of sessions being February to March 1974; February to April 1975; April to June 1976 and March to June 1977. Some national liberation movements were invited to attend but only states were entitled to vote.

66 For implementing legislation in the United Kingdom, see Geneva Conventions (Amendment) Act 1995.

Additional Protocol I[67] concerns the protection of the victims of international armed conflicts and expands the law previously contained in the 1949 Geneva Conventions and the Regulations annexed to the 1907 Hague Convention IV. There are a number of features that are worthy of comment. First, the category of lawful belligerents as stipulated in the 1907 Hague Convention IV and the 1949 Geneva Conventions I, II and III is expanded to include guerrilla movements.[68] Secondly, it is provided that mercenaries will not be entitled to the status of lawful combatants.[69] Thirdly, the scope of the Protocol is expanded beyond those situations set out in common Art 2 of the 1949 Geneva Conventions by Art 1(4) which provides that the instrument shall extend to 'armed conflicts in which peoples are fighting against colonial domination and alien occupation and against racist regimes in the exercise of their right of self-determination'. The effect of this provision is to reclassify 'wars of national liberation' as 'international armed conflicts'. Fourthly, Part IV, s 1 (Arts 48–67) contains detailed provisions designed to protect civilian populations against military operations.[70] This constitutes an extension of 1949 Geneva Convention IV which was restricted to protecting civilians in enemy territory at the outbreak of a war or those in territory subsequently occupied by an enemy.

Additional Geneva Protocol II (1977) is designed to afford protection to the victims of 'internal' or 'civil wars'. Since 1945, these have proved the most intractable and thus the most difficult for United Nations agencies to resolve. Such conflicts are of course not new; since the Russian Revolution of 1917 the Red Cross has been active in helping victims of such conflicts. However, the actual state of the law was very confused; in customary international law there was some doubt as to whether the laws of war applied in the absence of an express recognition of belligerency. Conferences held by the Red Cross failed to carry the matter forward; this was perhaps not surprising given that prior to 1945 there was a greater readiness to regard some matters as within the domestic jurisdiction of a state. However, particular events in the Spanish Civil War (1936–39) prompted popular revulsion and precipitated demands for further action. In 1948, Art 1 of the Genocide Convention provided for its application in the context of a civil war. At

---

67 See generally GH Aldrich, 'Prospects for United States ratification of Additional Protocol I to the 1949 Geneva Conventions' (1991) 85 AJIL 1; T Meron, 'The time has come for the United States to ratify Geneva Protocol I' (1994) 85 AJIL 678; AP Rubin 'Correspondence on United States ratification of Geneva Protocol 1' (1995) 89 AJIL 363.

68 See Additional Protocol 1 (1977), Art 44.

69 See *ibid,* Art 47. This matter was of particular concern to African States; the Portuguese Revolution of 1974 had stimulated liberation struggles in Africa in which mercenaries participated on different sides. The subject was at the time of the 1977 conference very topical; Frederick Forsyth's best selling novel *The Dogs of War,* set in Africa, was published in 1974 and was then followed by the Angolan trials of mercenaries in 1976. The trials resulted in convictions and in some cases capital sentences. For the United Kingdom, see the Foreign Enlistment Act 1870 passed in the aftermath of the Franco Prussian War and the Alabama claims incident. See *R v Sandoval and others* (1886) 3 TLR 411 (AL Smith J); 3 TLR 436 (Day J, Wills J); 3 TLR 498 (AL Smith J, Grantham J) (failed attempt to incite rebellion in Venezuela). For the prosecution under the 1870 Act arising out of the Jameson Raid of 1895 see *R v Jameson* [1896] 2 QB 425.

70 Particularly relevant in the light of the the area or 'carpet' bombing of Germany from 1942–45 and some of the bombing undertaken during the Vietnam War. In more recent years, the problem has surfaced again with the bombing of Iraq in 1991 and the campaign in respect of Kosovo in spring 1999.

the 1949 Diplomatic Conference, charged with drawing up the 1949 Geneva Conventions, there was some reluctance[71] to extending the full laws of war to situations of internal conflict so that a compromise was drafted with a common Art 3 stipulating for minimum humanitarian obligations. However, the provision was limited and vague and some governments sought to disavow it on the basis that the situation within their state did not constitute an 'armed conflict not of an international character'.

The purpose of Additional Protocol II (1977) is to afford additional protection to the victims of 'internal wars' or 'civil wars'. These constitute a majority of the conflicts in the modern world. In broad terms Additional Protocol II is designed to build upon the common cl 3 in the 1949 Geneva Conventions. In effect, it applies to all armed conflicts which do not fall within Additional Protocol I and which take place on a state's territory and between its forces and organised armed groups. In particular Art 1(1) applies to armed conflicts:

> ... which take place in the territory of a High Contracting Party between its armed forces and dissident armed forces or other organised armed groups which, under responsible command, exercise such control over a part of its territory as to enable them to carry out sustained and concerted military operations and to implement this Protocol.

To ensure that the provisions are not extended to mere internal disturbances Art 1(2) provides:

> This Protocol shall not apply to situations of internal disturbances and tensions, such as riots, isolated and sporadic acts of violence and other acts of a similar nature, as not being armed conflicts.

The 1974 Diplomatic Conference which drew up Additional Protocol II was meeting against a background of liberation struggles in Africa, the recent memory of the Nigerian civil war and the on going conflict in Vietnam. In these circumstances, it is perhaps not surprising that the contents of Additional Protocol II impose much more limited obligations than Additional Protocol I. Both Protocols were a response to contemporary events and the tendency in this area has been for the law to respond to specific and publicised events. Thus, in respect of land mines the 1980 Convention[72] was in 1996 expanded in the Amended Protocol on Prohibitions or Restrictions on the Use of Mines, Booby Traps and Other Devices. However, this was an issue that attracted considerable public attention; in 1992 a non-governmental organisation known as the International Campaign to Ban Landmines (ICBL) was formed and its work was sustained by a number of General Assembly Resolutions[73] pointing out the inadequacy of the law. This

---

71 Not least by those states seeking to resolve colonial conflicts. In 1949, this concerned the United Kingdom in Malaysia, France in Indo China and the Netherlands in Indonesia. The proposal to deal with internal wars separately by a common Art 3 was made by France. See Geoffrey Best, *War and Law since 1945*, 1994, pp 168–79.

72 United Nations Convention on Prohibitions or Restrictions on the Use of Certain Conventional Weapons which May be Deemed to be Excessively Injurious or to Have Indiscriminate Effects. (1980). The Convention had been followed by a number of Protocols: (i) Protocol I on Non Detectable Fragments (1980); (ii) Protocol II on Prohibitions or Restrictions on the Use of Mines, booby Traps and Other Devices (1980); (iii) Protocol III on Prohibitions or Restrictions on the Use of Incendiary Weapons (1980); (iv) Protocol IV on Blinding Laser Weapons (1995); (v) Amended Protocol II on Prohibitions or Restrictions on the Use of Mines, Booby Traps and Other Devices (1996).

73 Resolutions 48/75 (16 December 1993); 49/75 (15 November 1994); 50/70 and 50/74 (12 December 1995); and 51/45 (10 December 1996).

problem was perceived as a very serious matter by many.[74] A number of states convened a diplomatic conference in Ottawa in October 1996 followed by a second meeting in Brussels in June 1997. A treaty was prepared in Oslo in September 1997 and opened for signature in December 1997. The 1997 Ottawa Convention on the Prohibition of the Use, Stockpiling, Production and Transfer of Anti-Personnel Mines and on their Destruction having secured the necessary ratifications came into effect on 1 March 1999.

In reviewing the evolution of the *jus in bello* a number of general conclusions can be drawn. First, the subject itself remains closely linked with the *jus ad bellum*; the evolution in methods of peaceful resolution of disputes has lead to the view that war is obsolete and in most cases unlawful. Secondly, the *jus in bello* itself has since 1864 normally been in the position of trying to regulate use of armaments following changes in weapons technology that have already taken place. Thirdly, since 1945 the conventional war where state A invades state B has been a rarity and most conflicts tend to focus on some form of internal or ethnic conflict. Fourthly, it has proved difficult to enforce the rules of the *jus in bello* in the absence of serious attempts to impose personal responsibility on those guilty of grave breaches. Fifthly, under pressure from developments in general human rights law there has been an increasing emphasis on seeking to impose personal responsibility for breaches of the laws of war.

4 THE INSTITUTIONAL STRUCTURE

As indicated above, the publication of *Souvenirs de Solferino* in 1862 resulted in the establishment of a committee of five which supervised the calling of the first international conference on humanitarian law in 1863. The conference agreed in 1863 to the establishment of the Red Cross as an international humanitarian organisation. In essence, the Red Cross has four distinct elements namely the International Committee of the Red Cross (ICRC), the national Red Cross and Red Crescent Societies, the League of Red Cross and Red Crescent Societies and the International Red Cross Conference.

The International Committee of the Red Cross[75] developed from the original committee of five and being composed of Swiss nationals is concerned with the development of international humanitarian law. After the conference of 1864, those states that were parties to the Geneva Convention began to establish national Red Cross Societies. In the case of the United Kingdom, the British Red Cross Society began life as the National Society for Aid to the Sick and Wounded in War;[76] within two decades, national societies had been established in many countries.[77] Such societies are co-ordinated at the international level by the League of Red Cross and Red Crescent Societies. Every four years, representatives of the three elements of the Red Cross and

---

74 By 1999, there were calculated to be 110 million landmines in 63 countries killing or maiming nearly 26,000 persons a year, most of whom are civilians. See I Detter, *The Law of War*, 2000, p 227.

75 It became known as the International Committee of the Red Cross.

76 The British Red Cross Society secured a Royal Charter in 1908 and is a registered charity.

77 The Franco Prussian War acted as a stimulus and societies were formed in Turkey (1876), Peru (1879), United States (1881) and Japan (1879).

representatives from signatories to the Geneva Conventions meet in the International Red Cross Conference which is concerned to promote developments in international humanitarian law.

In order for the organisation to operate in situations of conflict it is necessary for it to have a distinctive emblem. The traditional emblem formed by reversing the Federal colours of Switzerland is protected under Art 38 of 1949 Geneva Convention I which also extends to the red crescent;[78] writers are unanimous in condemning attempts to introduce other emblems that may serve only to confuse. Arts 53 and 54 provide for the legal protection of the emblem against use by others and this is effected in the United Kingdom by s 6 of the Geneva Conventions Act 1957.

The International Committee of the Red Cross is funded by contributions from both National Societies and by individuals. Operating with an Assembly and an Executive Board it is concerned with the development of international humanitarian law. Moreover, in times of conflict, it is responsible for organising relief and for visiting prisoners of war to ensure that the jus in bello is being observed. Additionally, through its Central Tracing Agency (CTA) it is concerned to keep records of persons killed injured or detained and to transmit such information to family members.

5 THE CONDUCT OF CIVIL WARS[79]

Civil wars have justifiably acquired a reputation of being difficult to control and such conflicts have often been characterised by primitive acts of brutality. In the narrow sense a civil war or internal war is an intra state conflict with no external involvement. From early in the 20th century, the Red Cross[80] had sought to bring such conflicts expressly within the laws of war; however, many argued that internal wars in customary international law were outside the scope of the laws of war and within the domestic domain. The Spanish Civil War (1936–39) was marked by publicised incidents of brutality and lead to a reassessment of the position. At the Diplomatic Conference in 1949, a number of colonial powers were unwilling to extend the full laws of war to internal conflicts so a compromise was arrived at by stating certain minimum duties in common Art 3 to the 1949 Geneva Conventions and these basic requirements have been subsequently accepted as representing customary international law.[81]

When the Diplomatic Conference of 1974 was charged with drawing up Additional Protocol II in respect of non-international conflicts there were complaints from some

---

78 The first Red Crescent Society being set up by the Ottomann Empire in 1876 and the red crescent emblem being used to reflect Islamic feeling. However, the late Shah of Iran tried to introduce the Red lion and sun and Israel has used the red star of David. Any attempt to undermine the universality of the emblem has been subject to criticism. See Jean Pictet, 'Development and principles of international humanitarian law', 1985.

79 E Luard (ed), *International Regulation of Civil Wars*, 1972; DP Forsythe, 'Legal management of internal war, the 1977 Protocol on Non-International Armed Conflict' (1978) 78 AJIL 272.

80 At the 9th International Conference of the Red Cross in Washington 1912, which was followed in 1921 at the 10th International Conference of the Red Cross in Geneva and restated at the 1938 16th International Conference of the Red Cross in London.

81 *Nicaragua v The United States (The Merits)* (1986) ICJ 14.

world countries that extensive provisions would interfere with matters within their domestic sphere. Thus, there is a high threshold for the application of Additional Protocol II[82] and some doubts as to how it can encompass guerrillas forces. In terms of actual content Additional Protocol II (1977) requires humane treatment of belligerents,[83] the safeguarding of the wounded, sick and shipwrecked[84] and the protection of the civilian population.[85]

In respect of civil wars a common problem concerns the intervention of outside parties.[86] As indicated elsewhere, it is commonly stated that it is unlawful to aid insurgents against an established government[87] and that the general principle should be one of non-intervention and compliance with any resolutions made by the Security Council.[88] However, past history indicates that states are often minded to intervene if they perceive important interests are at stake;[89] it has become common to seek to justify support for an existing regime by alleging that the insurgents are receiving external support of a subversive nature. In some circumstances, this is simply factually incorrect[90] and used as a justification for expansionist designs. Difficulties can arise in respect of the supply of arms;[91] in some cases a Security Council resolution[92] will forbid all arms sales in other situations outsiders may continue to supply arms to an established government.[93]

It has to be admitted that the record is mixed; the last two decades have seen internal wars in states such as Columbia, Nicaragua, El Salvador, Liberia, Guatemala, Rwanda, Sierra Leone and Afghanistan and many of these conflicts have witnessed abusive acts that have been recorded by journalists and other independent observers. Overshadowing such conflicts has been the civil war that arose on the disintegration of the Socialist Federal Republic of Yugoslavia and the irrefutable evidence of serious abuses of humanitarian law. The pressure of public opinion or fear of war crimes trials may act as some restraint but there is no ground for complacency.

---

82 Additional Protocol II (1977), Art 1(2).

83 *Ibid*, Arts 4–6.

84 *Ibid*, Arts 7–12.

85 *Ibid*, Arts 13–18.

86 The classic example being the Spanish Civil War (1936–39). It is often argued that the involvement of outsiders may make direct negotiations less likely.

87 See generally TJ Farer, 'The regulation of foreign intervention in civil armed conflict' (1974) 142 HR 291; L Doswald-Beck, 'The legal validity of military intervention by invitation of the government' (1985) 56 BYIL 189.

88 Although in some cases the United Nations or a regional organisation may request specific help for a government, as has been the case in Sierra Leone (1997–2000).

89 See United States interventions in Lebanon (1958) and the Dominican Republic (1965) and its increasing involvement in the Vietnam conflict (1965–75).

90 As indicated by the conduct of the Soviet Union is respect of Hungary (1956), Czechoslovakia (1968) and Afghanistan (1979).

91 This was not, of course, the main issue in *Nicaragua v United States* (1986) ICJ 14; in that case, the question was whether the United States was entitled to aid insurgents (the *contras*) in Nicaragua as a form of collective self defence on the basis that Nicaragua had been assisting insurgents in El Salvador. This, of course, raised the issues: (i) Had an armed attack been made on El Salvador? (ii) Had any such armed attack been followed by a request to the United States to assist in self-defence?

92 As was the case in Sierra Leone (1997–2000).

93 As was the case during the Nigerian civil war (1967–70).

6 INTERNATIONALISED CONFLICTS AND LIBERATION WARS

Between international armed conflicts to which the full laws of war apply and internal or civil wars to which a reduced regime applies there exists an intermediate category of conflicts to which some of the laws of war apply.[94] This category has arisen only recently arisen and not without a degree of controversy. Such conflicts are described as 'internationalised conflicts' and arise by operation of Additional Protocol I (1977)[95] which provides in Art 1(4) that the Protocol shall apply to 'armed conflicts in which people are fighting against colonial domination and alien occupation and against racist regimes in the exercise of their right to self determination'.

The background to such a provision lies in the steady evolution of three principles of international law; the first the principle of self-determination is traceable back to 1919. The second principle of decolonisation began to emerge after 1945 and the third principle of non-discrimination has grown in the years since 1960. Thus, many Third World countries sought to give liberation struggles the status of 'international armed conflicts';[96] in contrast many developed counties were fearful that such an approach might be seen as aiding terrorism.[97] Additional Protocol I will apply to wars of liberation by the operation of Art 1(4)and 1(3) together with common Art 2 of the 1949 Geneva Convention but only if the movement itself has adhered to Protocol II under Art 96(3). The general principle of liberation from alien or racist rule had already attracted support in the International Court of Justice in the *Namibia*[98] and the *Western Sahara* cases.[99] The draftsmen of Additional Protocol I were principally concerned with liberation struggles in Africa many of which were at their height in the 1970s. Today it is arguable that the heightened language of Art 1(4) will mean that Additional Protocol I will only apply in very limited circumstances[100] which itself reflects the limited intentions of the draftsmen.

---

94 See generally D Schindler, 'The different types of armed conflict according to the Geneva Conventions and Protocols' (1979) HR 117.

95 See GH Aldrich, 'New life for the laws of war' (1981) 75 AJIL 764.

96 They were joined in this by some communist states; but it is noticeable that neither showed equal enthusiasm for Additional Protocol II.

97 This was particularly the view of the United States. The Carter Administration had broadly welcomed Protocol I but after January 1981 the Reagan Administration exhibited growing scepticism. See GH Aldrich, 'Prospects for United States ratification of Additional Protocol I of the 1949 Geneva Conventions' (1991) 85 AJIL 1. The case for the Reagan Administration being put by Abraham Sofaer in 'The rationale for the United States decision' (1988) 82 AJIL 784. One of the principal objections of the United States concerned whether irregular combatants might be entitled to prisoner of war status under Arts 43 and 44 of the Protocol.

98 The *Namibia* case (1971) ICJ 16.

99 The *Western Sahara* case (1975) ICJ 12.

100 Such a problem was presented by the situation in Kosovo prior to NATO intervention; was the conflict waged by the Kosovo Liberation Army (KLA) against Belgrade a conflict within Art 1(4) even though the object appeared to be a restoration of autonomy?

7 NUCLEAR WEAPONS[101]

The precise status of nuclear weapons is a matter of considerable legal debate and the possession and use of such weapons continue to pose ethical dilemmas.[102] Such weapons derive from the Second World War when the United States Manhattan Project conducted at the Los Alamos Science Laboratory[103] succeeded in the production of an atomic bomb.[104] In August 1945, President Truman authorised the dropping of the atomic bomb on Hiroshima and Nagasaki[105] with the express intention of bringing the conflict with Japan to an early conclusion. The arguments for and against that decision have been debated ever since.[106] Thereafter, Western powers justified the possession of such weapons on the basis of resisting the numerical superiority of Warsaw Pact and Soviet Union forces in Europe and deterring aggression. Since 1945, nuclear weapons have not been used in conflict but their use was contemplated in the Korean War and the issue was raised in the Gulf War in 1991, when it appeared that chemical and biological weapons might be employed by Iraq.

The widespread desire to curtail the possession of such weapons is reflected in the constitution of a number regional treaties whereby states agree not to deploy such weapons; examples are afforded by the Treaty of Tlatelolco (1967)[107] and the Treaty of Rarotonga (1985). The practical problem that has faced international society since 1945 is that nuclear weapons may be destroyed but they cannot be dis-invented. In these circumstances, questions arise as to: (i) the acquisition of nuclear technology; (ii) the use of nuclear weapons; (iii) the possession or proliferation of nuclear weapons; (iv) the testing of such weapons. In principle, these are distinct questions but they tend to be

---

101 See generally L Oppenheim, *International Law*, Vol 2, 7th edn, 1952, by H Lauterpacht; H Lauterpacht, 'Rules of warfare in an unlawful war', in GA Lipinsky (ed), *Law and Politics in the World Community*, 1953; G Schwarzenberger, *The Legality of Nuclear Weapons*, 1958; N Singh, *Nuclear Weapons and International Law*, 1959; R Rhodes, *The Making of the Atomic Bomb*, 1988; EC Stowell, 'The laws of war and the atomic bomb' (1945) 39 AJIL 784; I Brownlie, 'Some legal aspects of nuclear weapons' (1965) 14 ICLQ 437; LC Green, 'Nuclear weapons and the law of armed conflict' (1988) 17 Denver Journal of International Law 1.

102 The ethical arguments about use centre around three points: (i) the state has a right to order the killing of those threatening its own people or causing injustice; (ii) aerial bombing of military targets which entails unintended but foreseeable civilian death is not murder; (iii) however, the intentional killing of innocent persons as a means to an end is murder. It is argued that the use of nuclear weapons involves accepting that innocent persons can be killed as a means to an end. The ethical arguments discussed by GE Anscombe in *Ethics, Religion and Politics: Collected Philosophical Papers*, 3 vols, 1981.

103 Directed by J Robert Oppenheimer (1904–67) in the years 1943–45.

104 For the German efforts, see M Walker, *German National Socialism and the Quest for Nuclear Power 1938–49*, 1989.

105 See *Memoirs of Harry S Truman*, Vol 1, Year of Decisions, 1955, New York.

106 Particularly since there is now a greater volume of knowledge about the long term environmental and health effects of such weapons.

107 There are now a growing number of regional treaties which place restrictions on the possession of nuclear weapons. Examples are afforded by the Antarctic Treaty (1959); Treaty for Prohibition of Nuclear Weapons in Latin America and the Caribbean (Treaty of Tlatelolco) (1967); South Pacific Nuclear Free Zone Treaty (Treaty of Rarotonga) (1985); Treaty on the South East Asia Nuclear Weapon Free Zone (Bangkok Agreement) (1995); African Nuclear Weapon Free Zone Treaty (Pelindaba/Cairo Agreement) (1996).

merged. Indeed on this emotionally charged topic some writers sometime seem unable to distinguish between *de lege lata* and *de lege ferenda*.

Many writers today[108] proceed from the presumption that the first use of nuclear weapons is in principle unlawful because of their indiscriminate nature, disproportionate effect and incalculable environmental and health consequences. In the years since 1945, the General Assembly has repeatedly condemned the use of nuclear weapons[109] and weapons of mass destruction[110] and has expressly warned against any doctrine of partial or limited use.[111] In these circumstances it might be said that the disproportionate and indiscriminate nature of such weapons make any first use contrary to customary international law. Others have argued that the use of such weapons would violate the 1907 Hague Regulations,[112] or the 1925 Geneva Protocol for the Prohibition of the Use in War of Asphyxiating, Poisonous or Other Gases and indeed some consider that such a use would violate the 1948 Genocide Convention.[113] It strongly arguable that the indiscriminate nature of nuclear weapons is such as to violate Arts 48–60 of Geneva Additional Protocol I (1977) save that the nuclear powers comprising the United States, France and the United Kingdom entered qualifying declarations before signing the Protocol.

The legality of the use of such weapons was considered by the International Court of Justice in 1996 following requests for advisory opinions by the World Health Organisation and the General Assembly in 1993 and 1994.[114] The actual requests were posed in slightly different terms. In the case of the General Assembly, the question posed was: 'Is the threat or use of nuclear weapons in any circumstance permitted under international law?' Following oral hearings in 1995, the full Court delivered an advisory opinion in 1996. The Court dismissed the request by WHO for an advisory opinion[115] on the legality of use of such weapons arguing that under the WHO constitution the organisation lacked the jurisdiction or competence to consider the legality of the use of nuclear weapons notwithstanding the environmental and health consequences. Such a conclusion was reached by applying traditional concepts of specialty or *ultra vires*. In respect of the answer to the request made by the General Assembly the opinion was not conspicuous by its clarity;[116] however a number of general points can be isolated which at the risk of oversimplification might be summarised as follows:

---

108 For an early view, see EC Stowell, 'The laws of war and the atomic bomb' (1945) 39 AJIL 784.

109 See GA Res1653 (XVI) (1961) 'On the Prohibition of Nuclear Weapons for War Purposes', where use was described as not only a violation of the United Nations Charter but also contrary to 'laws of humanity and constituting a crime against mankind and civilisation'. See also GA Res 2936(XXVII) (1972) to the same effect.

110 See GA Resolutions 3479(XXX) (1975); 31/74, 1976; 35/149, 1980; 36/89, 1981; 37/77, 1982.

111 GA Res 35/152 B 1980.

112 In particular, Art 23(a) 1907 Hague Regulations.

113 See I Brownlie, 'Some legal aspects of the use of nuclear weapons' (1965) 14 ICLQ 437.

114 *Legality of the Threat or Use of Nuclear Weapons* (1996) ICJ 66, p 226.

115 The actual question posed by the WHO Assembly was 'In view of the health and environmental effects, would the use of nuclear weapons by a State in war or other armed conflict be a breach of its obligations under international law including the WHO constitution?' (1996) ICJ 66, p 226.

116 Not least because of the failure to obtain unanimity on the central question.

(i) There is a duty on all states to pursue in good faith and to bring to conclusions negotiations both for nuclear disarmament and to promote the establishment of effective international control mechanisms.[117]

(ii) There is nothing in customary international law or conventional law authorising the threat or use of nuclear weapons.[118]

(iii) However, neither customary international law nor conventional law contains expressly any comprehensive or universal prohibition.

(iv) In principle any threat or use of nuclear weapons violating Art 2 (4)of the United Nations Charter and not justified under Art 51 would be unlawful.[119]

(v) Any threat or use of nuclear weapons would in general be incompatible with the international law of armed conflict and in particular the requirements of international humanitarian law.[120]

(vi) Any threat or use of nuclear weapons must pay regard to any specific treaty obligations.

(vii) However, the Court was unable to state whether there might be a threat or use of nuclear weapons that might be lawful in extreme circumstances of self-defence where the very survival of the state was in issue.[121]

It must be open to question as to whether the advisory opinion has made matters any clearer[122] or whether it constitutes a *non liquet* in respect of the central matter before the court. Certainly, the ruling is at best inconclusive on the main question as to whether in certain circumstances there might be a lawful threat or use of nuclear weapons and it affords no practical guidance. The clearest aspect is the duty on all states to co-operate in matters of disarmament and inspection. In the circumstances, this is hardly surprising; the wisdom of the requests is certainly open to question and no judicial body[123] could contemplate all possible situations in which all possible types of nuclear weapons might be threatened or employed.

After 1945, when it became clear that nuclear weapons could not be disinvented the international community became concerned to restrain the spread of nuclear technology; this is sometime referred to as the problem of nuclear proliferation. The five original nuclear powers were anxious to ensure that nuclear weapons did not fall into the hands of politically unstable states. However, while proliferation was the immediate concern as the possible environmental damage became better known the international community

---

117 Although listed last in the Advisory Opinion, this holding was unanimous and, in some respects, the most useful and practical of the findings.

118 This holding was unanimous.

119 This finding was unanimous nd might be said to constitute a narrow ratio.

120 By 7:7 and carried on the casting vote of the President.

121 By 7:7 and on the casting vote of the President.

122 There is much force in the dissenting opinion of Judge Higgins who considered the eventual conclusion as to border on the meaningless. It was very difficult to envisage the possible factual situations in which a threat of use might be made; with the facts and the law both based on speculation, it is difficult to imagine what practical value such an advisory opinion might have. The problem faced by the court raised issues of justiciability. See generally, I Brownlie 'The justiciability of disputes and issues in international relations' (1967) 42 BYIL 123.

123 See AV Lowe, 'Shock verdict, nuclear war may or may not be unlawful' (1996) 55 CLJ 415.

became equally perturbed about methods of testing. Negotiations on these matters have been progressing for 40 years either on a bilateral basis between the United States and the then Soviet Union or on a multilateral basis. The first concrete agreement was concluded in 1963 in the form of the Partial Test Ban Treaty of 1963[124] and this was followed by the Non Proliferation Treaty of 1968. The latter treaty imposes restrictions on non-nuclear states acquiring nuclear weapons and it imposes duties on nuclear states to engage in good faith in negotiations for nuclear disarmament. These attempts to restrict testing and to curtail proliferation were accompanied by treaties directed to regional restriction. The Antarctic Treaty of 1959[125] and the Outer Space Treaty of 1967[126] both outlawed nuclear weapons and this principle was followed in the Seabed and Ocean Floor Treaty of 1971.[127]

As relations between the superpowers began to improve after 1972, bilateral agreements were the vehicle for arms limitation. The Anti Ballistic Missile Agreement of 1972[128] was followed by the SALT (Strategic Arms Limitation) Interim Agreement of the same year.[129] The subsequent changes in the Soviet Union permitted progress to be made in securing agreements on the Reduction and Limitation of Strategic Offensive Arms (START). START I (1991)[130] was negotiated between 1981 and 1991 and was followed by the Lisbon Protocol (1992), which extended its geographical ambit to Belarus, Kazakhstan and the Ukraine. In broad terms, the treaty required phased reductions in strategic nuclear offensive capabilities over a period of seven years. START II, concluded in 1993, represents a continuance of the process and stipulates that by 2003 not more than 3,500 nuclear warheads will be held by the parties.

The general reduction in international tension since 1985, and the progress on superpower arms reduction talks, is to be contrasted with the seeming lack of progress on matters of nuclear testing;[131] this has coincided with the rise in international environmental law and increased scientific knowledge about the consequences of nuclear testing. From the early 1960s, some progress had been made in drawing up treaties to control testing culminating in the Threshold Test Ban Treaty (TTBT) but much depended on the goodwill of existing nuclear states. In the 1973 *Nuclear Tests* case,[132] the International Court of Justice was prepared to indicate certain provisional measures in respect of the atmospheric nuclear testing by France[133] in the South Pacific although the

---

124 Treaty Banning Nuclear Weapon Tests in the Atmosphere, in Outer Space and Under Water (1963).

125 See Antarctic Treaty (1959) Art 5; in force from 1961.

126 See Art 4, Outer Space Treaty (1967); in force from 1967. See D Goedhuis (1968) 15 NILR 17 .

127 Treaty on the Prohibition of the Emplacement of Nuclear Weapons and other Weapons of Mass Destruction on the Sea Bed and Ocean Floor and in the Subsoil Thereof (1971), in force 1972; it had acquired 100 ratifications by 1997.

128 The Anti-Ballistic Missile Agreement (1972) restricted missile defences to two sites with 100 permitted at each site.

129 The Interim Agreement on Certain Measures with Respect to the Limitation of Strategic Offensive Weapons (1972) 11 ILM 897 The Agreement limited the number of inter continental ballistic missile launchers (ICBMs) and submarine launched ballistic missiles (SLBMs).

130 The Agreement on the Reduction and Limitation of Strategic Offensive Arms (START I; 1991 START II 1993).

131 For subsequent consideration in a municipal court, see *Pearce v Secretary of State for Defence* [1988] AC 755.

132 *Nuclear Tests* cases (*Interim Protection*) (1973) ICJ 99.

133 The Nuclear Test Ban Treaty of 1963 did prohibit testing on the high seas, but France was not a party to the treaty.

subsequent unilateral declaration by France meant that the matter did not proceed to a full hearing on the merits.[134] When France began underground testing in the South Pacific in the summer of 1995, New Zealand and Australia filed an application for reconsideration of the matter under Arts 62 and 63 of the Statute of the International Court of Justice. However, in the request for an examination of the situation in accordance with para 63 of the Court's Judgment of 20 December 1974,[135] the Court concluded that the application did not fall within the said paragraph and the application was dismissed. The justification was that the 1973 and 1974 proceedings had concerned atmospheric nuclear testing while the activities in 1995 related to underground nuclear testing.

8 REPRISALS AND COUNTERMEASURES

A reprisal is an act which would normally be unlawful but which is considered lawful by virtue of the prior unlawful act initiated by the state against which the reprisal is directed. In essence a reprisal is an illegal act in response to a illegal act with the objective of securing termination of the prior illegal act.[136] Often such reprisals are referred to as 'countermeasures'. Reprisals may be non-forcible[137] or they may be of a forcible[138] or belligerent nature.[139] Reprisals may be exercised by an individual state or they may be undertaken collectively. The justification for this branch of the Law of Nations was that the reprisal was a method of ensuring that a particular state observed the Law of Nations in the future. The evidence must indicate that the act is capable of constituting a reprisal. For this to be the case there must be both an 'unsatisfied demand' and an intention 'to effect reparation from the offending state for the offence or a return to legality by the avoidance of further offences'; it therefore follows that the act of reprisal must be proportionate.[140] It was therefore said that the three requirements were: (i) a prior violation of international law; (ii) an unsuccessful demand for redress; and (iii) the reprisal must be proportionate to the injury suffered.[141]

---

134 *Nuclear Test* cases (*Australia v France; New Zealand v France*) (1974) ICJ 253, 457; France terminated its declaration under the Optional clause in 1974 so that in 1995 the ICJ would not have had jurisdiction in respect of action by Australia and New Zealand.

135 (1995) ICJ 288; see MC Craven (1996) 45 ICLQ 725.

136 LC Green, *The Contemporary Law of Armed Conflict*, 1993, Manchester, p 80.

137 Such as a boycott of goods or an mass expulsion of aliens. An example is afforded by the decision in 1935 by Yugoslavia to order the mass expulsion of Hungarians following the assassination of King Alexander of Yugoslavia in Marseilles in December 1934. The act was motivated by a suspicion of Hungarian involvement; in the event; the act had been undertaken by an individual acting for a Croatian nationalist group.

138 In 1937, German warships bombarded the Spanish port of Almeira as a reprisal following the bombing of the German warship *Deutschland* by aircraft under the control of Republican forces.

139 The best known incident in recent years being the decision of the administration of President Reagan (1981–89) on 14 April 1986 to launch a bombing raid on targets in Tripoli and Benghazi. The raid was launched following allegations of Libya's involvement in terrorist incidents directed against United States personnel abroad. A subsequent draft Security Council resolution was vetoed by the United States, France and the United Kingdom.

140 The *Naulilaa* Claim (*Portugal v Germany*) (1928) 2 RIAA 1012; *I'm Alone* case (*Canada v United States*) (1935) 3 RIAA 1609; *Re Air Services Agreement case* (*France v United States*) (1978) 18 RIAA 416; see also *The Zamora* (1916) 2 AC 77.

141 The *Naulilaa* Claim (1928) 2 RIAA 1012.

Old learning on the law of reprisals has now to be read in the light of the United Nations Charter (1945) under which the Security Council may take action to restrain persistent breaches of international law. Secondly, it is generally accepted that reprisals should not be resorted to until all proper methods for peaceful resolution of the dispute have been exhausted,[142] particularly having regard to the investigatory powers of the Security Council under Arts 34 and 35 of the United Nations Charter. This principle was restated in the Declaration on Principles of International Law Concerning Friendly Relations and Co-operation among States in Accordance with The Charter of the United Nations[143] (1970) which stated: 'States have a duty to refrain from acts of reprisal involving the use of force.'

Because of revulsion at reprisals undertaken in German occupied territory during the Second World War, the 1949 Geneva Conventions sought to outlaw specific forms of conduct. Thus reprisals are prohibited against prisoners of war,[144] the wounded, sick and shipwrecked[145] and civilians.[146] These prohibitions were strengthened in Geneva Additional Protocol I[147] in Arts 51(6), 53 and 75; particular note should be taken of Art 51(6) which reads 'attacks against the civilian population or civilians by way of reprisals are prohibited'. In practice, it is sometimes difficult to draw a distinction between self-defence and reprisals;[148] traditionally, self-defence is action to repel or prevent an attack while reprisals normally comprise punitive acts in respect of past unlawful conduct.[149]

9 RETORSION

Retorsion is the term employed for the unfriendly but legal act of state A taken in retaliation for the previous illegal or unfriendly act of state B; the act of state B, therefore, need not be illegal and it is sufficient for it to be discourteous, unfriendly, unfair or otherwise inequitable. The essence of retorsion is that the retaliation by state A should be a legitimate act within the competence of the offended state; examples would be the severance of diplomatic relations, the removal of tariff concessions or the termination of economic aid. Retorsion has some similarity with acts of reprisal in that its effectiveness may depend on the relative strength of the two states.

While retorsion has an accepted place in customary international law it cannot be said that such acts increase the level of international harmony. Thus it is sometimes argued that such acts might in extreme cases infringe Arts 2(3) and 33 of the United Nations Charter (1945).

---

142 In particular, having regard to the duty to settle disputes peacefully arising under Art 33 of the Charter. In 1986, the United States argued that the sustained conduct of Libya constituted an armed attack so that its subsequent action represented an exercise of rights under Art 51.

143 As set out in the Annex to General Assembly Resolution 2625 (XXV) (24 October 1970).

144 1949 Geneva Convention (III), Art 13.

145 1949 Geneva Convention (I), Art 46; 1949 Geneva Convention (II), Art 47.

146 1949 Geneva Convention (IV), Art 33.

147 See generally, FJ Hampson, 'Belligerent reprisals and the 1977 Protcols to the Geneva Conventions of 1949' (1988) 37 ICLQ 818.

148 See generally RW Tucker, 'Reprisals and self defence, the customary law' (1972) 66 AJIL 586.

149 See Oppenheim, *International Law*, Vol 1, 1992, p 419; on the subject generally, see M Akehurst (1970) 44 BYIL 1; DW Bowett (1972) 66 AJIL 1; Tucker (1972) 66 AJIL 586.

10 NEUTRALITY

A state not militarily engaged in armed conflict may be considered as a neutral. Such neutrality may arise by declaration, by constitutional provision[150] or treaty Article.[151] A neutral state may not engage in the conflict itself although the pattern of its trading and diplomatic links may indicate where its sympathies lie.[152] Prior to 1945, the law of neutrality occupied a central position in the corpus of international law. Since that date the near universal participation in the United Nations Charter (1945) and the outlawing of the use of armed force has tended to lead to a situation that when a conflict does break out one state is adjudged the aggressor and the other a victim. The Security Council may take some form of action against the aggressor and other states do not lose their status of neutrality by aiding the victim or taking action against the aggressor in a manner consistent with their obligations under Art 2(5) or Art 25 of the United Nations Charter. In the 18th and 19th century, the rules of neutrality allowed state C to pursue its own affairs and stand aside while states A and B were engaged in conflict. Today, that is far less likely to be the case with the 'aggressor state' being subject to condemnation by the Security Council and other states being obliged to respect any relevant Security Council resolution. In an era of collective security the concept of absolute neutrality probably has to be modified.

The basic duty of the neutral state is to abstain from intervention; two of the relevant 1907 Hague Conventions set out the operative duties and both are considered declaratory of customary international law. The two conventions are 1907 Hague Convention V Respecting the Rights and Duties of Neutral Powers and persons in Case of War on Land and 1907 Hague Convention XIII Concerning the Rights and Duties of Neutral Powers in Naval War. This division reflected the fact that the laws of neutrality operated differently in respect of land and maritime warfare.

In respect of maritime warfare the object was to sever the trading links of the enemy. To this end the belligerent state would seek to intercept and seize both enemy merchant vessels as well as warships.[153] In respect of neutral merchant vessels the traditional view in the 19th century was that such vessels might be intercepted and seized if they were carrying contraband or trying to break through a blockade.[154] The enemy character of a vessel was determined in the common law world by domicile[155] and in the civil law states by nationality.[156] In the case of companies the emphasis might be on the place of

---

150 As in the case of Switzerland or Sweden.

151 As in the case of Belgium in 1914.

152 As was the case with the United States in the period 1939–41.

153 The enemy warship may be seized and the enemy merchant vessel may be taken as prize. See A Pearce Higgins, 'Ships of war as prize' (1925) 6 BYIL 103.

154 This was referred to as seeking to 'run' a blockade.

155 The *Anglo-Mexican* [1918] AC 422; see also *The Hyptia* [1917] P 36; *The Manningtry* [1916] P 329; *The Lutzow* [1918] AC 435. The case law in England during World War I on the subject of enemy domicile is reviewed by M Lewis in 'Domicile as a test of enemy character' (1924) 4 BYIL 60 .

156 The private international law of most Western European states provide for nationality as the connecting factor. This is because nationality was taken as the connecting factor in the Code Napoleon of 1804 and followed then in Belgium, Luxembourg, Austria and The Netherlands. In some cases, nationality was taken as the connecting factor to assert national identity; see Art 6 of the Italian Civil Code (1865). States such as the United Kingdom, United States Canada and Australia which embody a number of legal systems employ domicile rather than nationality.

registration or the degree of enemy control[157] while in the case of vessels particular reliance would be placed on the flag;[158] in the case of cargo character is *prima facie* determined by the domicile of the owner.[159]

An enemy warship may be seized outright and an enemy merchant ship may be taken as prize.[160] In most states there will be a well established code on prize proceedings[161] and settled rules of international law are applied.[162] Prizes may be taken on the high seas or in enemy waters, but not in the territorial waters of a neutral state. In principle, enemy cargo could always be taken as prize; however, cargo on a neutral ship could only be taken as prize if it constituted contraband. A neutral vessel is not liable to prize unless it can be shown to be carrying contraband to an enemy destination or in some other manner assisting the enemy. In respect of private goods, a distinction was drawn between 'absolute contraband',[163] 'conditional contraband'[164] and 'free goods'.[165] These distinctions, which derived from the 1856 Paris Declaration Respecting Maritime Law,[166] the 1907 Hague Conference and the 1909 London Declaration on Naval War proved difficult to maintain in practice and in the First World War much depended on individual interpretation. In theory, a neutral vessel carrying absolute contraband was liable to seizure[167] while a neutral vessel carrying free goods was not; in many cases it was a question of the proportion of the contraband to the entire cargo.[168] Thus, where the proportion of contraband exceeded 50% then the vessel was liable to seizure. Difficulties could arise about the destination of the goods; particularly where the goods are to be acquired by citizens in a neutral state for sale to an enemy. The law of contraband looked to the ultimate destination[169] by preying in aide the doctrine of continuous voyage.[170]

Thus the law of contraband was far from straightforward; it involved judgments on: (i) the nature of the vessel; (ii) the place of seizure; (iii) the nature and destination of the cargo; (iv) the proportion of contraband in the cargo; (v) the genuineness of the documentation. In the First World War, under pressure to secure victory, the emphasis was on extending the powers of seizure to anything of potential value to the enemy.

---

157 *The Tommi* [1914] P 251; *Continental Tyre & Rubber Co Ltd v Daimler Co Ltd* [1916] 2 AC 307.

158 *The Unitas* [1950] AC 536 (PC).

159 *The William Bagaley* (1866) 5 Wall 377.

160 A Pearce Higgins, 'Ships of war as prize' (1925) 6 BYIL 103.

161 In England, the role of the Prize Court was developed during the Napoleonic wars under the direction of Sir William Scott (1745–1836) (Lord Stowell) who served as an admiralty judge from 1798–1827; he did much to formulate the relevant principles on the law of the sea, the nature of contraband and the requirements for a blockade. See, eg, *The Anna* (1805) 5 Ch Rob 373; *The Harmony* (1802) 2 C Rob 220; *The Indian Prince* (1804) 3 C Rob 20; *The Yonge Klassina* (1804) 5 C Rob 297.

162 *The Zamora* [1916] 2 AC 77.

163 Good capable of direct military use.

164 Sometimes described as relative contraband it covered dual use goods such as food, fuel, optical equipment.

165 Luxury goods, chinaware, silk, glass, etc.

166 HA Smith, 'The Declaration of Paris in modern war' (1939) 55 LQR 237.

167 Ie, the cargo would be liable to seizure and so would the vessel if the overall proportion of exceeded 50% of the cargo.

168 *Prins der Nederlanden* [1921] 1 AC 564 .

169 *The Maria* (1805) 5 Ch Rob 365.

170 *The Kim* [1915] P 215; *The Balto* [1917] P 79.

There was also a willingness to presume a hostile destination if the bill of lading was made out to order or where the consignee was not named. To enforce the system of checks in the First World War, a procedure of advance notification of non-hostile intention was introduced in 1916 in the form of a 'navicert' certificate; thus, in the Second World War when the rules were applied even more rigorously the absence of such a certificate was taken as evidence of a hostile destination.

The second doctrine that restricted a neutral trading with a belligerent was that of the blockade. The naval blockade was in principle an act of war and is effected by restricting the egress and ingress of vessels in respect of an enemy port. The object is to limit the trading links of the enemy. In the 19th century, certain requirements came to be accepted as needing to be present before a blockade could be said to exist. In principle, the blockade had to be: (i) effective;[171] (ii) declared by a belligerent; (iii) notified to neutrals; and (iv) specified as to geographical limits; there was some doubt as to whether a blockade could only arise when a war had been declared. In principle, the blockade must be restricted to the coast of the enemy. International waterways and canals subject to treaty may not be subject to a blockade.[172] A blockade is distinct from an attempt to patrol the coasts of the enemy or simply to close its ports.

Ships that seek to break the blockade are likely to be seized and will be taken to a port for adjudication by a Prize Court. The vessel and its cargo are likely to be confiscated as a prize unless it can be shown that those shipping the goods had no knowledge of the blockade. It seems that liability can be established on the basis of actual or constructive knowledge.

In the 19th century, a blockade could be effected close to the enemy coast however such a practice had to be modified after 1900 with the development both of mining and submarines. Thus, after 1915, the British conducted a long distance blockade of Germany's coasts which had an effect on the entry to neutral ports; vessels were taken to British ports to be searched. Such conduct went beyond 19th century precedents and attracted some complaint from neutrals but was justified by the need to undermine the economic strength of the enemy. A similar policy was followed in the Second World War.[173]

There is no doubt that the use of the blockade has declined since 1945; in some cases something approaching a blockade has been applied but not described as such. In 1962 in the Cuban Missile crisis the United States described the exclusion zone around Cuba as a 'a quarantine zone';[174] a form of blockade was enforced in the India Pakistan War in 1971 while, in 1972, the United States effected a blockade of the port of Hai-Phong in Vietnam to deter the flow of arms. After 1982, an exclusion zone was enforced around the Falkland Islands.

---

171 *The Betsey* (1798) 1 C Rob 93; *The Franciska* (1855) 2 Ecc & Ad 113; *Geipel v Smith* (1872) 7 QB 404. See also 1856 Paris Declaration Respecting Maritime Law; 1909 Declaration of London on the Laws of Naval War.

172 1888 Constantinople Convention of 1888 on the Suez Canal.

173 See G Fitzmaurice, 'Some aspects of modern contraband control and the law of prize' (1945) 22 BYIL 173; S Rowson, 'Modern blockade, some legal aspects' (1946) 23 BYIL 346.

174 CQ Christol and CR Davies, 'Maritime quarantine, the naval interdiction of offensive weapons and associated materials to Cuba' (1963) 57 AJIL 525; Q Wright, 'The Cuban quarantine' (1963) 57 AJIL 546; M McDougal, 'The Soviet Cuban quarantine and self defence' (1963) 57 AJIL 597.

A matter that has attracted some attention and given rise to several incidents concerns the extent to which a belligerent warship may seek to use the port of a neutral state. Under the terms of Arts 12 and 13 of 1907 Hague Convention XIII Concerning the Rights and Duties of Neutral Persons in Naval War the neutral state is entitled to give the belligerent warship notice to leave after 24 hours.[175] It is further provided that vessels from opposing belligerents shall not leave port within a period of 24 hours of each other. It is to be noted that Art 15 of the 1907 Hague Convention XIII requires that at no time shall more than three warships of a belligerent be present in a neutral port.[176]

Associated with the question of the blockade was the status of merchant ships; before 1914 there was no general consensus about whether a merchant ship could be lawfully sunk however it was assumed that there was a duty to rescue survivors. After 1914, the use of submarines meant that such vessels were attacked and often the crew were not rescued. The employment of unrestricted submarine warfare by Germany in 1915 attracted an official protest from the United States after the sinking of the *Lusitania* in May 1915; the resumption of such conduct in 1917 played a role in the entry of America into the war.[177] The short cruising range of submarines and their limited size had the consequence that they could not rescue survivors.[178] In the inter-war years,[179] an attempt was made to introduce a duty to rescue survivors but this was ignored in the Second World War and the acquittal of Grand Admiral Doenitz at Nuremberg on charges arising out of the submarine war indicated that the traditional rules no longer applied.

11 WAR CRIMES AND INDIVIDUAL RESPONSIBILITY

In the time of John Westlake and Lassa Oppenheim the traditional view of Public International Law was that it was concerned to regulate the relations between states and

175 These provisions formed the basis for the decision of the Uruguayan authorities to request the German warship the *Graf Spee* to leave the port of Montevideo after the Battle of the River Plate in December 1939. The subsequent scuttling of the vessel attracting much attention in the early months of World War II. The timing of the departure of the *Graf Spee* being dictated by the departure of a prior French cargo ship .

176 The operation of the rule was illustrated in the early months of World War I when the German Asian fleet under Count Maximilian von Spee (1861–1914) defeated a British force at the Battle of Coronel (3 November 1914) and then split with three vessels going to Valpariso with the *Dresden* and *Leipzig* proceeding to Masa Fuera. The subsequent attack on the *Dresden* by *HMS Glasgow* while in Chilean waters would appear to have been a clear breach of Art 1 1907 Hague Convention XIII. The remainder of the force was sunk at the Battle of the Falkland Islands in December 1914 with Admiral von Spee going down with his flagship.

177 Unrestricted submarine warfare was announced in January 1917 and in April 1917 the United States entered the war. In that same month, Prime Minister Lloyd George forced a reluctant Board of Admiralty to institute a convoy system. Thereafter, such a system enabled the threat of submarine warfare to be surmounted; the scale of the problem being indicated by the fact that in April 1917 alone 700,000 tons of British shipping had been lost. Although the principal object of the convoy system was to safeguard shipping, it did allow for the possibility that survivors of a sunken vessel might be picked up by other members of the convoy. See AJP Taylor, *The First World War* (1965); *English History (1914–45)* (1965).

178 It is very difficult to reconcile the *modus operandi* of the submarine with the *jus in bello*. It is noticeable that the most controversial incident of the Falkland Islands conflict (1982) concerned sinking by a submarine of the Argentinian vessel *General Belgrano*.

179 1930 International Treaty for the Limitation and Reduction of Naval Armament, Part IV, Art 22; 1936 *Procès Verbal Relating to the Rules of Submarine Warfare Set Forth in Part IV of the Treaty of London* (1930).

that the interests of individuals were at best marginal. However, states operate through governments and governments comprise individuals. As the 20th century too often testified, if a government was comprised of individuals contemptuous of the rule of law then breaches of international law and abuses of human rights are likely to ensue. However, it has been long recognised that one of the most effective methods of enforcing the *jus in bello* is to focus upon the principle of individual responsibility. Some writers assert that this principle was not firmly established until 1945, but the precedents are in fact much older. The first recorded trial might be said to be that in *Hagenbach's* case in 1474, where a tribunal not only convicted Peter von Hagenbach for atrocities committed as Governor of Breisach but also rejected a defence of superior orders. Over a century later, and conscious of the turmoil of the Thirty Years' War (1618–48), Grotius was concerned to limit the circumstances in which the use of force might be employed and to outline the dangers posed by unprovoked aggression.[180] This view, being reliant on natural law thinking, had less influence in the 18th century when ambitious monarchs such as Frederick II of Prussia were willing to use force to secure territorial gains.

The first concrete evidence that the international community disapproved of the ready use of force is to be found in the condemnation of Napoleon as an outlaw by the Congress of Vienna in 1815 after he had escaped from Elba and re-entered France with an armed force. This change in approach is not surprising as the 18th century wars were often conducted by mercenaries and had little direct effect on the social order while the revolutionary and Napoleonic wars had lead to the toppling of monarchs and the disturbance of the established order; this fact was not lost on Count Metternich and those seeking to establish a framework for inter state relations in Europe after 1815.

However, the treatment of Napoleon served as a precedent when in 1919 European powers sought to examine responsibility for the outbreak of the conflict. The nature of the war and the scale of the losses made it inevitable that some attempt would be made to affix personal responsibility. The conflict had been the first example of 'total war' in which economies had been mobilised, taxes imposed and men conscripted by elected governments; in circumstances where sacrifices had been called for it was logical that the victors would seek to hold the vanquished to account. Moreover, the resort to aerial bombing of civilians and unrestricted submarine warfare served to require that aggression should not go unpunished. The Commission established by the Preliminary Peace Conference was under no doubt that there should be individual responsibility and Art 227 of the Treaty of Versailles did envisage the trial of Kaiser Wilhelm II. Article 228 compelled the German government to accept the principle of war crimes trials and, under the terms of Art 229, individuals were to be handed over for prosecution. In the event, Holland refused to extradite the Kaiser and Germany rejected requests to hand over named persons. A small number of individuals were tried before the German Supreme Court in Leipzig, but only very limited terms of imprisonment were imposed. The failure to pursue the matter was due to divisions on the part of the allies. The United State was anxious not to isolate Germany from post-war European society while France was more interested in securing an appropriate level of agreed reparations. Prime Minister Lloyd George had been anxious for trials but was unable to persuade his partners. However, a

---

180 *De Jure Belli ac Pacis* (1625).

precedent had been set in that the original list of persons requested by the Allies included the names Bethmann Hollweg,[181] Hindenburg[182] and Ludendorf.

The background to the Second World War was entirely different and the losses caused considerably greater. While it was arguable that the First World War had been caused by a breakdown in the traditional balance of power the causes of the Second World War[183] owed much to a disregard not only of the Covenant of the League of Nations but also of the Kellogg-Briand Pact. By the closing years of the conflict it was clear that German personnel had been guilty of the execution of regular forces, and the killing of civilians and prisoners of war as well as sustained campaigns against particular groups such as homosexuals, gypsies and the mentally ill. In addition the sustained and organised murder of Jewish citizens was without precedent in modern European history.[184]

At first, President Roosevelt and Prime Minister Churchill were not minded to hold a trial.[185] It was felt that a trial might be used as a propaganda exercise[186] and so the initial view was that as the guilt of certain Nazi leaders was so obvious they should simply be executed when captured. However, President Roosevelt was influenced by a number of individuals that a trial would provide a basis for explaining[187] the purpose of the conflict and setting out a marker for the future; it was argued that if the post-war world was to be built around the rule of law then this could not be done at the same time as sanctioning summary executions. By 1 November 1943 at the Moscow Conference the allied leaders were prepared to commit themselves to 'the punishment' of major war criminals.

On 8 August 1945, the United States, France, the United Kingdom and the Soviet Union concluded the London Agreement which provided for the establishment of an international military tribunal. Annexed to the Agreement was the Charter of the Nuremberg Tribunal.

The trial[188] lasted from 14 November 1945 until 1 October 1946 and 24 defendants were indicted. The indictment comprised four charges, namely: (i) conspiracy or common plan;[189] (ii) crimes against peace;[190] (iii) war crimes;[191] (iv) crimes against humanity.[192]

---

181 Theobald von Bethmann Hollweg (1856–1921) (Chancellor 1909–17).

182 Paul von Hindenburg (1847–1934); Victor of Tannenberg (1914), Field Marshall and Supreme Commander (1915–18); he would later serve as President of Germany (1925–33).

183 *The Origins of the Second World War*, 1961.

184 Which, in planning, extended also to territories not under German rule. See the Protocol of the Wansee Conference (20 January 1942) International Military Tribunal, Nuremberg NG 2586 F (6). See generally, M Gilbert, *The Holocaust*, 1986.

185 This had been the provisional agreement at Quebec in September 1942.

186 This was the view of the British Foreign Office as late as February 1944.

187 President Roosevelt was influenced by the American constitutional tradition and the representations made by Cordell Hull and Henry Stimson as well as by Felix Frankfurter (whom Roosevelt had appointed to the United States Supreme Court).

188 See generally, A Tusa and J Tusa, *The Nuremberg Trial*, 1983; T Taylor, *The Anatomy of the Nuremberg Trials*, 1992; H Shawcross, *Life Sentence*, 1992.

189 This gave rise to some discussion. It was urged by the United States and intended to cover conspiracies in respect of the other three charges.

190 Ie, planning, preparing or waging a war of aggression and included violations of the 1899 and 1907 Hague Conventions as well as the Treaty of Versailles (1919) and the Kellogg-Briand Pact (1928).

191 This embraced breaches of 1907 Hague Convention (IV) and the 1929 Geneva Convention (II).

192 This embraced murder and extermination of civilians before or during the conflict.

The convictions and sentences at Nuremberg represented a watershed. The judgment of the tribunal established: (i) that senior officials within a state would be answerable for breaches of international law; (ii) that high office would not confer immunity; (iii) that there would be no general defence of superior orders. The Nuremberg Trial was followed by the Tokyo Trial where an International Military Tribunal sat hearing evidence from May 1946 until November 1948; the charges were similar but not identical to those at Nuremberg and the trial resulted in the conviction of two former Prime Ministers of Japan and five senior generals.

Although the Tokyo Trial did not pass off without incident[193] there is no doubt that the decision hold trials was justified; the subsequent judgment of objective historians has been that the trials represented an attempt to build a new international community by revealing the consequences of aggression[194] and a disregard of the rule of law in international affairs. It was perhaps unfortunate that the judges had to be supplied by the victorious states but in the case of Nuremberg the German judiciary was so compromised that participation was not practical. Some argued that the Nuremberg process included a retrospective element but while aggression may not have been expressly specified as a crime entailing individual responsibility in the Kellogg-Briand Pact (1928)[195] it had been expressly condemned in a number of League of Nations resolutions.[196] In any event the judgment of the Nuremberg court was subsequently approved by the General Assembly.[197]

The concept of individual responsibility was in accord with the democratic spirit of the post-war world. Thus, at the height of the Vietnam War (1965–75) the elderly philosopher Bertrand Russell[198] helped establish an 'International War Crimes Tribunal' which met in 1967 and proceeded to hear charges of aggression and bombardment of civilians arising from United States actions in the Vietnam War. This was not an official body and thus did not have the legitimacy arising form being established by government but it did indicate that the concept of answerability was beginning to develop a momentum of its own. However, much depended on the proximity of the conflict; thus no official international tribunal was set up to bring to justice the leaders of the Khmer Rouge in respect of the campaign of genocide undertaken in Cambodia in the years 1975–79.[199]

---

193 The judges having reservations about imposing the death penalty when immunity had been accorded to the Emperor of Japan; the verdicts were by a majority of eight to three (see Y Beigbeder, *Judging War Criminals – The Politics of International Justice*, 1999.

194 According to Robert H Jackson (Chief Prosecutor) the principal purpose was to demonstrate the criminality of aggressive war under international law.

195 The tribunal pointed out: (i) that the Kellogg-Briand pact had been ratified by most states prior to 1939; (ii) the treaty had been ratified by Germany, Italy and Japan; (iii) the terms of the treaty expressly stated that disputes were to be resolved by peaceful means.

196 The specific resolutions are referred to in the judgment of the tribunal; see (1947) 41 AJIL 172.

197 GA Resolution (1946) 95 (1).

198 By this stage Bertrand Russell (1872–1970) was elderly and subject to the influence of others; however, the family had a long interest in international affairs. In 1871, in the aftermath of the Franco Prussian War, his father Lord Amberley had written an article in the *Fortnightly Review* arguing that war should give way to the resolution of disputes by an authoritative international body. For Russell's interest in international affairs see Ray Monk, *Bertrand Russell*, Volume 1, 1996; Volume 2, 2000.

199 Although following the Vietnamese invasion in December 1978, a People's Revolutionary Tribunal convened in Phnom Penh in August 1979 did convict Pol Pot of the crime of Genocide and condemn him to death *in absentia*.

(a) The International Criminal Tribunal for the former Yugoslavia

It was the later conflict in Yugoslavia that prompted the next steps in the process. The disintegration of the Socialist Federal Republic of Yugoslavia after 1991 resulted in a violent struggle for territory and the perpetration of acts of genocide and 'ethnic cleansing' the likes of which had not been seen in Europe since 1945. As early as October 1992, the Security Council had established a Committee of Experts[200] to investigate and collect evidence of grave breaches of the 1949 Geneva Conventions; these were confirmed in its final report of May 1994. The European location of the conflict had the consequence that it was widely reported and public opinion in a number of European states began to press governments to act. The practical response of the Security Council was to establish an international criminal tribunal[201] to investigate and try breaches of international humanitarian law.[202] The jurisdiction of the tribunal was restricted to the territory of Yugoslavia[203] and concerned events after 1 January 1991.[204] The Tribunal itself was established under Chapter VII of the United Nations Charter[205] and marked the first time that these powers had been used to establish a judicial body;[206] the decision to do so was subsequently welcomed by the General Assembly.[207]

Unlike the Nuremberg trials there is an international panel of judges headed by a President;[208] the structure of the court comprises two trial chambers[209] (three Judges) and an Appeals Chamber (five judges).[210] The rules of procedure adopted on 11 February 1994 favour an adversarial rather than an inquisitorial approach. The Prosecutor[211] is appointed by the Security Council upon nomination by the Secretary General.[212] The Prosecutor investigates and formulates indictments;[213] before being issued such an indictment it has to be confirmed by a judge.[214] The Tribunal has jurisdiction over natural

---

200 SC Res 780 (6 October 1992) .

201 There was room for debate as to whether the Tribunal was independent of the Security Council and whether the Security Council could delegate judicial functions which, as a body, it did not itself possess. These, however, were the practical imperative was that there was a demand for immediate action and a court established by treaty would have taken too long.

202 See SC Res 808, 22 February 1993; SC Res 827, 25 May 1993.

203 Article 1 of the Statute of the Tribunal.

204 *Ibid*, Art 8.

205 See SC Res 827 of 25 May 1993 with Annex containing Statute of Tribunal.

206 In the subsequent case of *Dusan Tadic*, the defence made a number of jurisdictional objections, including a submission that act of establishing the tribunal was outside the terms of Art 41 of the Charter of the United Nations. This was rejected by the tribunal at a pre trial hearing in June 1995. See 35 ILM 32 (Appeal on Jurisdiction). For a general discussion, see C Warbrick and P Rowe, 'The International Criminal Tribunal for Yugoslavia, the decision of the Appeals Chamber on the interlocutory appeal on jurisdiction in the *Tadic* case' (1996) 45 ICLQ 691.

207 GA Res 48/88 (December 1993).

208 Professor Antonio Cassese was elected as the first President on 18 November 1993.

209 Article 11 of the Statute of the Tribunal.

210 *Ibid*.

211 The office having been held by Judge Richard Goldstone (South Africa) (1994–96) and Judge Louise Arbour (Canada) from February 1996.

212 Article 16 of the Statute of the Tribunal.

213 *Ibid*, Art 18.

214 *Ibid*, Art 19.

persons but not organisations;[215] the jurisdiction of the tribunal takes precedence over national courts.[216]

In respect of responsibility, the statute provides for liability as a principal or accomplice[217] and excludes claims based on immunity[218] or indeed any defence based upon superior orders.[219] Jurisdiction[220] is founded on 'serious violations of international humanitarian law committed in the territory of the former Yugoslavia';[221] in particular the Tribunal has jurisdiction in respect of: (i) grave breaches of the 1949 Geneva Conventions;[222] (ii) violations of the laws and customs of war;[223] (iii) Genocide;[224] (iv) crimes against humanity.[225] Unlike the Nuremberg and Tokyo precedents, the tribunal cannot impose the death penalty and is limited to imprisonment and orders for the return of property.[226]

The tribunal held its first plenary session in November 1993; it began operating as a judicial body in November 1994. By November 1996, 75 persons had been indicted. Where there has been a refusal to hand over indicted persons, the Tribunal may adopt a special procedure and issue an international arrest warrant;[227] the matter will then be reported to the Security Council who will decide on measures of enforcement.

It is probably too early to form a judgment as to the success of the tribunal; however an encouraging start has been made. However, much will depend on whether the tribunal can secure the attendance of all those for whom warrants have been issued.[228]

(b) The International Criminal Tribunal for Rwanda[229]

Tension between the Hutus and Tutsi people had been a permanent feature of life in the territory of Burundi and Rwanda from at least the time of German colonisation at the end of the 19th century. After the First World War, the territories passed to Belgium and were administered as a League of Nations Mandate and later as a United Nations Trust

---

215 *Ibid*, Art 6.
216 A challenge to this principle in the *Tadic* case was rejected (1996) 35 ILM 32.
217 Article 7(1) of the Statute of the Tribunal.
218 *Ibid*, Art 7(2).
219 *Ibid*, Art 7(4).
220 See generally, G Aldrich, 'Jurisdiction of the International Criminal Tribunal for the former Yugoslavia' (1996) 90 AJIL 64.
221 This is designed to prevent the type of argument that was raised and rejected in the *Tadic* case, namely that the obligations arise only in an international armed conflict and not an internal armed conflict such as that pertaining in Yugoslavia after 1991.
222 See Art 2 of the Statute of the Tribunal.
223 Defined in Art 3 but drawing upon 1907 Hague Convention (IV) on Land Warfare and Annex thereto.
224 Article 4 of the Statute of the Tribunal.
225 Defined in Art 5 but drawing upon the Nuremberg Judgment of October 1946.
226 Article 24 of the Statute of the Tribunal.
227 See procedure stipulated in Rules 50–61 of the Rules of Procedure and Evidence.
228 By July 2001, 105 persons had been indicted and 27 remained at large. The Dayton Peace Agreement made on 21 November 1995 and signed in Paris on 14 December 1995 established a rather fragile peace. The support of certain individuals was needed to ensure that the agreements were carried out.
229 P Akhavan, 'The International Tribunal for Rwanda; the politics and pragmatics of punishment' (1996) 90 AJIL 501.

Territory. In general, the minority Tutsis had exercised control at the expense of the majority of Hutus people. The problem of ethnic tension increased when both territories became independent in 1962. In 1972, the Tutsi government of Burundi engaged in open conflict against the Hutus majority. Refugees tended to flee across the borders to Uganda. In 1973, a Hutu General Habyarimana seized power in Rwanda. A one party state was established and Tutsi leaders fled to adjoining states. The opposition Tutsis organised themselves in the Rwandan Patriotic Front (RPF) based in Uganda. An invasion of Rwanda in 1990 failed, but in August 1993 the Arusha Peace Agreement was negotiated which provided for power sharing between Tutsi and Hutu in Rwanda subject to a peacekeeping mission – the United Nations Assistance Mission for Rwanda (UNAMIR).

However, on 6 April 1994 the President Habyarimana of Rwanda and President Ntaryamira of Burundi were killed when their aircraft was shot down. This event precipitated an uprising by the Hutus majority in Rwanda against the Tutsi minority. In the period April–July 1994, nearly 250,000 persons were killed[230] and over 1 million fled as refugees. The Rwandan Patriotic Front (RPF) then launched an invasion to end the genocide and, at the end of June 1994, were able to seize Kigali and establish a government of national unity. This resulted in nearly 2 million Hutus fleeing to Zaire and other adjacent countries.

In the face of a violent uprising that may have been planned in advance, the Security Council was uncertain how to proceed. On 17 May 1994, they reaffirmed the traditional condemnation of genocide in international law;[231] as with Yugoslavia they appointed a Commission of Experts to investigate the facts.[232] Following the report, they decided to establish a second *ad hoc* international criminal court[233] on 8 November 1994. It has to be recognised that there was some criticism about whether action had been taken quickly enough to restrain the actual conflict; be that as it may, the purpose of the tribunal was to punish the guilty and to assist in the process of national reconciliation. The statute of the tribunal is similar to that of the Yugoslav tribunal but modified to account for specific needs. The list of crimes against humanity remains the same for both tribunals and the internal nature of the conflict is recognised by asserting jurisdiction in respect of 'violations of Art 3 common to the Geneva Conventions and Additional Protocol II'.

As is the case with Yugoslavia, the Tribunal is to have jurisdiction in priority to national courts. It shares a Prosecutor and an Appeals Chamber with the Yugoslav tribunal. In February 1995, the Security Council decided that the seat of the tribunal should be in Arusha, Tanzania.[234] The Rules of Procedure adopted were modelled on those of the Yugoslav tribunal.

---

230 The figure may well have been higher; the majority of the victims were Tutsi but those killed included those Hutus who favoured power sharing and accommodation between the two ethnic groupings.

231 SC Res 918, 17 May 1994.

232 SC Res 935, 1 July 1994.

233 SC Res 955, 8 November 1994. The official title was the International Tribunal for the Prosecution of Persons Responsible for Genocide or Other Serious Violations of International Humanitarian Law Committed in the Territory of Rwanda and Rwandan Citizens Responsible for Genocide and other Such Violations Committed in the Territory of Neighbouring States between 1 January 1994 and 31 December 1994.

234 SC Res 977, 22 February 1995. The Rwandan government itself objected to (i) the tribunal not being situate in Rwanda; and (ii) the fact that the Statute of the Tribunal did not permit the imposition of the death penalty.

The early years of the tribunal have been marked by a shortage of administrative and judicial resources and progress has been slow although, by the end of 1997, 21 defendants had been detained in the Arusha jail. Some states, such as the United States, Denmark and The Netherlands, have assisted with personnel but some neighbouring states such as Kenya and Zaire have been reluctant to extradite suspects. At the same time, the national legal system has been reconstituted in Rwanda and, by the end of 1996, 50,000 persons had been detained in overcrowded jails. The subsequent difficulties of the tribunal owed much to the shortage of administrative and legal resources in contrast to the Yugoslav tribunal in the Hague.

12 THE INTERNATIONAL CRIMINAL COURT[235]

The concept of an international criminal court has a long history. As early as 1927, at the Paris Congress of the Fédération internationale des ligues des droits de l'homme (FIDH), the Austrian League of Human Rights proposed the creation of a 'Permanent International Court of Moral Justice'. With the benefit of hindsight, it is clear that the atmosphere of the Cold War was such as to prevent a permanent court after Nuremberg. However, at the time of the adoption of the Genocide Convention, the General Assembly called upon the International Law Commission to study the possibility of a Criminal Chamber within the International Court of Justice; this initiative came to nothing.

The General Assembly set up a Special Committee to prepare a Draft Statute for an International Criminal Court which produced a provisional text in 1951, which was revised in 1953. However, the entire project was set aside in 1957 following opposition from the Soviet Union and states of Eastern Europe who, being nominally Marxist, were ideologically opposed to 'bourgeois' justice. The issue was raised again in relation to the problems of transboundary drug related offences. In 1990 the General Assembly invited the International Law Commission to undertake a second investigation of the issue.

By the early 1990s, the omens were indeed more propitious. The end of the Cold War had removed any ideological objections. In the 1970s and 1980s, human rights groups had drawn attention to the fact that there were a large number of abuses that were likely to go unpunished in the absence of a permanent tribunal. As the decade progressed, it was clear that there was no diminution in cases of serious abuse and, in some cases, the perpetrators had indeed gone unpunished. To some extent, this was remedied by the ad hoc tribunals for Yugoslavia and Rwanda established under Chapter VII of the United Nations Charter however it was assumed that these tribunals would be of limited duration.

The International Law Commission established a working group which produced a draft statute in 1993; in that same year, the ILC at its 45th session took note of the report

---

235 J Crawford, 'The ILC's Draft Statute for an International Criminal Court' (1994) 88 AJIL 140; J Crawford, 'The ILC adopts a Statute for an International Criminal Court' (1995) 89 AJIL 404; J Crawford, 'Prospects for an International Criminal Court' (1995) 48 CLP 303; P Marquandt, 'Law without borders: the constitutionality of an International Criminal Court' (1995) 33 Columbia Journal of Transnational Law; K Ambos, 'Establishing an International Criminal Court and an International Criminal Code' (1996) 7 EJIL 519; J Dugard, 'Obstacles in the way of an International Criminal Court' (1997) 56 CLJ 329.

and passed it to the General Assembly for comment. The General Assembly noted the draft statute and, in 1994, the ILC, after reflecting on various comments, adopted a Draft Statute for an International Criminal Court (that is, the 1994 Draft Statute). By 1994, the *ad hoc* Yugoslav and Rwanda tribunals had been established and the seeming impasse in the *Lockerbie* case appeared to point to the need for a permanent international criminal tribunal.

The 1994 ILC Draft Statute was grounded in five principles, namely: (i) that the ICC should be established by treaty rather then Security Council Resolution; (ii) the ICC should exercise jurisdiction over persons rather than states; (iii) the jurisdiction of the Court should be specified by reference to limited crimes of an international character; (iv) the jurisdiction of the court should be consensual; (v) the Court should not be a full time body but should be established under treaty in a manner so as to be available when required. In the course of subsequent discussion, principles (iii) and (iv) were subject to some modification. In December 1994, the ILC declined to hold an immediate international conference but submitted the entire question to an *Ad Hoc* Committee which, in December 1995, was replaced by a Preparatory Commission. This latter body meeting in 1996 and 1997 considered a number of difficult questions including the jurisdiction of the Court, its relationship with the United Nations and the problem of finance. Following this detailed work, an international conference met in Rome in June 1998 and, after five weeks of intensive negotiations, the text of Statute of an International Criminal Court was adopted on 17 July 1998 by a vote of 120 in favour and 7 against, with 21 abstentions.

The broad division was between those states and NGOs who wanted a strong court with clear powers and those states, such as France and the United States,[236] who were concerned about the effect on peacekeeping duties.

Under the terms of Art 126, the Statute will enter into force one month after the 60th day after the receipt of the 60th document of ratification or accession. The Statute itself will be subject to review after a period of seven years.[237] The International Criminal Court is to be a permanent institution[238] based in the Hague;[239] it will not be part of the United Nations but will be brought into relationship by a subsequent agreement.[240] It will have jurisdiction over four crimes,[241] namely genocide,[242] crimes against humanity,[243] war crimes,[244] and the crime of aggression.[245] The national court will have primacy[246] of investigation and prosecution unless that state is unwilling or unable to

---

236 The particular concerns of the United States are: (i) that the present statute might jeopardise its role in peacemaking; (ii) the prosecutor's power to initiate investigations; (iii) jurisdiction over the conduct of citizens of non signatory countries.
237 Statute of the International Criminal Court (1998), Art 123.
238 *Ibid*, Art 1.
239 *Ibid*, Art 3.
240 *Ibid*, Art 2.
241 *Ibid*, Art 5.
242 *Ibid*, Art 6.
243 *Ibid*, Art 7.
244 *Ibid*, Art 8.
245 *Ibid*, Art 5(d).
246 See *ibid*, Preamble and Art 17.

carry out the investigation or prosecution. Investigations are commenced by the prosecutor[247] but, beyond the preliminary stage, has such an investigation to be authorised by the Court.[248] An investigation or prosecution may be deferred for a period of 12 months following a vote by the Security Council.[249]

The Statute embraces the general principles of criminal law: *ne bis in idem*,[250] *nullum crimen sine lege*,[251] *nulla poena sine lege*[252] and non-retroactivity *ratione personae*.[253] The Court operates on the basis of the presumption of innocence[254] and convictions require proof beyond a reasonable doubt.[255] There is no defence of superior orders,[256] and no immunity arising from office.[257] Jurisdiction rises where the relevant crime is committed on the territory of a state that is a party to the Statute or of a state which has accepted the jurisdiction of the Court, or in respect of crimes committed by a person who is a national of such a state.[258] The Court itself is divided into a number of organs: the Presidency, an Appeals Division, a Trial Division, and a Pre Trial Division together with the Office of Prosecutor and the Registry. In respect of penalties and orders, the Court may make an order specifying reparations;[259] it may impose sentences of imprisonment up to a maximum of 30 years,[260] but in exceptional cases it may make an order of life imprisonment.[261] In addition to imprisonment, the Court may order fines[262] or the forfeiture of property, proceeds or assets derived directly or indirectly from crime.[263]

In respect of the United Kingdom, the International Criminal Court Act 2001 has been enacted to make the requisite changes in domestic law. In broad terms the legislation incorporates the offences in the ICC Statue into United Kingdom law. Further, it allows the United Kingdom to meet its obligations under the ICC Statute and thus enable ratification to take place. Provision is made in the legislation to enable the United Kingdom to reach agreement with the ICC so that persons convicted can serve prison sentences in the United Kingdom.

However, it is unlikely that the ICC Statute will be in force for some time. Article 28 of the Statute requires 60 ratifications before it comes into force. As at May 2001, only 32 instruments of ratification had been received.

---

247 Statute of the International Criminal Court (1998), Art 15.
248 *Ibid*, Art 15.3.
249 *Ibid*, Art 16.
250 *Ibid*, Art 20.
251 *Ibid*, Art 22.
252 *Ibid*, Art 23.
253 *Ibid*, Art 24.
254 *Ibid*, Art 66.1.
255 *Ibid*, Art 66.3.
256 *Ibid*, Art 33.
257 *Ibid*, Art 27.
258 *Ibid*, Art 12.
259 *Ibid*, Art 75.
260 *Ibid*, Art 77.1(a).
261 *Ibid*, Art 77.1(b).
262 *Ibid*, Art 77.2(a).
263 *Ibid*, Art 77.2(b).

13 CONCLUDING OBSERVATIONS

The period since 1945 has witnessed the adoption of a considerable number of international conventions designed to promote minimum standards of conduct, either in the sphere of humanitarian law or in the related field of human rights law. It is not in dispute that the period has witnessed a decline in conventional forms of aggression: that is, where state A would attack state B; to this extent the system of collective security put in place by the United Nations Charter (1945) has worked. This may also be influenced by the realisation that, in an interdependent world, most states have concluded that the cost of conflict is too high and that it is sensible to resolve disputes in a peaceful and orderly manner. Among the majority of states the concept of the rule of law in international affairs enjoys a greater degree of prominence than it did 100 years ago.

However, the period since 1945 has witnessed a considerable increase in internal conflicts where the belligerents are sometimes aided by other states. To a significant extent these conflicts are concentrated in the poorer economic regions of the world. In many instances, such internal conflicts have been accompanied by serious breaches of humanitarian law and grave abuses of human rights. In some instances also, the international community has had to grapple with the problem of abuses committed within a totalitarian state. In recent years, the civil conflicts in Yugoslavia and Rwanda have indicated that there is no room for complacency.

In these circumstances, there has been a natural tendency to examine how methods of observance might be improved. In municipal systems, laws that are broken with impunity are liable to be the subject of contempt. In these circumstances, writers and practitioners have in recent years searched for mechanisms to ensure better enforcement of humanitarian standards. One school sees the problem as likely to be resolved by an extension of democratic government and improved trading links.[264] A second school of thought places emphasis on the need to minimise the economic differences between states.[265] A third school, while not disagreeing with these approaches, is anxious to ensure that the principle of international criminal responsibility is upheld; this may be done through the speedy establishment of an International Criminal Court, but it is also to be achieved by withdrawing immunity in criminal proceedings before municipal courts.[266]

A fourth approach can be detected in the writings of those who believe that the need is to ensure that dangerous weapons are not passed to politically immature and unstable regimes.[267] A further influence that should not be discounted is the ease with which the television news media can now report far away conflicts and thus generate pressure on

---

264 The argument that there is a natural evolution to the Western liberal democratic state was advanced by F Fukuyama in *The End of History and the Last Man*, 1992; see also T Franck, 'The emerging right to democratic governance' (1992) 82 AJIL 46.

265 See T Franck, *Fairness in International Law and Institutions*, 1995; S Marks, *The Riddle of all Constitutions, International Law, Democracy and the Critique of Ideology*, 2000.

266 See G Robertson, *Crimes Against Humanity: The Struggle for Global Justice*, 1999.

267 See M Kaldor and B Vashee (eds), *Restructuring the Global Military Sector*, Vol 1, *New Wars*, 1997.

policy makers that 'something' should be done; the Vietnam war (1965–1975), the Falklands conflict (1982) and the Gulf conflict (1990/1991) were all the subject of detailed contemporaneous coverage and, in all three, the need to secure the support of domestic public opinion was crucial.

It may be that the end of the Cold War produced unrealistic demands about what the international community in general and the United Nations in particular could accomplish. The United Nations has a proud record in the development of international law and the promotion of the peaceful settlement of disputes; there is every reason to believe that, with the good will and co-operation of states, an International Criminal Court can come into operation and act as an effective deterrent against gross breaches of humanitarian law. A much more difficult question is likely to be how international action can reduce the inequalities in income, literacy and health care that exist between the developed and the underdeveloped worlds. International law will continue to occupy a central role if only because it provides a mechanism for co-operation between states.

BIBLIOGRAPHY

Addo, M, 'Interim measures of protection for rights under the Vienna Convention on Consular Relations' (1999) 10 EJIL 713

Addo, M, 'Vienna Convention on Diplomatic Relations: application for provisional measures' (1999) 48 ICLQ 673

Adede, AO, 'Law of the sea – the Integration of the system of settlement of disputes under the Draft Convention as a whole' (1978) 72 AJIL 84

Adede, AO, 'Settlement of disputes arising under the Law of the Sea Convention' (1975) 69 AJIL 798

Adler, M, 'The exhaustion of the local remedies rule after the International Court of Justice's Decision in *ELSI*' (1990) 39 ICLQ 641

Ago, R, '"Binding" advisory opinions of the International Court of Justice' (1991) 85 AJIL 439

Akehurst, M, *A Modern Introduction to International Law*, 6th edn, 1987, London: Routledge

Akehurst, M, 'The application of general principles of law by the Court of Justice of the European Communities' (1981) 52 BYIL 29

Akehurst, M, *A Modern Introduction to International Law*, 3rd edn, 1977, London: Allen and Unwin

Akehurst M, 'The use of force to protect nationals abroad' (1977) 5 International Relations 3

Akehurst, M, 'Equity and general principles of law' (1975) 25 ICLQ 801

Akehurst, M, 'Uganda Asians and the *Thakrar* case' (1975) 38 MLR 72

Akehurst, M, 'Custom as a source of international law' (1974-75) 47 BYIL 1

Akehurst M, 'The hierarchy of the sources of international law' (1974-75) 47 BYIL 273

Akehurst, M, 'Jurisdiction in international law' (1972–73) 46 BYIL 145

Akehurst, M, 'Reprisals by third states' (1970) 44 BYIL 1

Akhaven, P, 'The International Tribunal for Rwanda: the politics and pragmatics of punishment' (1990) 90 AJIL 501

Akinsanya, A, 'The Dikko affair and Anglo Nigerian relations' (1985) 34 ICLQ 602

Aldrich, GH, *The Jurisprudence of the Iran-United States Claims Tribunal*, 1996, Oxford: OUP

Aldrich, GH, 'Prospects for United States ratification of Additional Protocol I to the 1949 Geneva Conventions' (1991) 85 AJIL 1

Aldrich, GH, 'New life for the laws of war' (1981) 75 AJIL 764

Allott, P, 'The concept of international law' (1999) 10 EJIL 31

Allott, P, '"*Mare nostrum*": a new international law of the sea' (1992) 86 AJIL 764

Allott, P, 'Reconstituting humanity: new international law' (1992) 3 EJIL 219

Allott, P, *Eunomia: New Order for a New World*, 1990, Oxford: OUP

Allott, P, 'Language, method and the nature of international law' (1971) 45 BYIL 79

Alston, P, *The United Nations and Human Rights: A Critical Appraisal*, 1992, Oxford: Clarendon

Alston, P, 'Revitalising United Nations work on human tights and development' (1991) 18 Melb UL Rev 216

Alston, P, 'United States ratification of the Covenant on Economic and Social Rights: the need for an entirely new strategy' (1990) 84 AJIL 365

Alston, P and Simma, B, 'The second session of the United Nations Committee on Economic, Social and Cultural Rights' (1988) 82 AJIL 603

Alston, P and Simma, B, 'The first session of the United Nations Committee on Economic, Social and Cultural Rights' (1987) 81 AJIL 747

Alverez, J, 'Judging the Security Council' (1996) 90 AJIL 1

D'Amato, A, 'Peace v accountability in Bosnia' (1994) 88 AJIL 500

D'Amato, A, 'Nicaragua and international law: the "academic" and the real' (1985) 79 AJIL 657

D'Amato, A, *The Concept of Custom*, 1971, Ithaca: Cornell UP

D'Amato, A, 'The concept of special custom in international law' (1969) 63 AJIL 211

Ambos, K, 'Establishing an International Criminal Court and an International Criminal Code' (1996) 7 EJIL 519

Amerasinghe, CF, 'Issues of compensation for the taking of alien property in the light of recent cases and practice' (1992) 41 ICLQ 22

Amerasinghe, CF, 'Liability to third parties of member states of international organisations: practice, principle and judicial precedent' (1991) 85 AJIL 259

Amerasinghe, CF, 'The problem of archipelagos in the international law of the sea' (1974) 23 AJIL 539

Amin, SH, 'Iran-United States claims settlement' (1983) 32 ICLQ 750

Anand, RP, 'Sovereign equality of states in international law' (1986) 197 HR 9

Anand, RP, 'Attitude of the Asian-African states to certain problems of international law' (1966) 15 ICLQ 55

Anaya SJ, *Indigeneous Peoples in International Law*, 1996, Oxford: OUP

Anderson, DH, 'British accession to the United Nations Convention on the Law of the Sea' (1997) 46 ICLQ 761

Anderson, DH, 'The straddling stocks agreement of 1995 – an initial assessment' (1996) 45 ICLQ 463

Anderson, DH, 'Further efforts to ensure universal participation in the United Nations Convention on the Law of the Sea' (1994) 43 ICLQ 886

Anderson, DH, 'Efforts to ensure universal participation in the United Nations Convention on the Law of the Sea' (1993) 42 ICLQ 654

Andrews, J, 'The concept of statehood and the acquisition of territory in the nineteenth century' (1978) 94 LQR 408

Anscombe, GE, *Ethics, Religion and Politics: Collected Philosophical Papers,* 1981, Oxford: OUP, 3 vols

Arangio-Ruiz, G, 'The normative role of the General Assembly of the United Nations and the Declaration of Principles of Friendly Relations' (1972) 137 HR 419

Archer, C, *International Organisations,* 2nd edn, 1992, London: Routledge

de Arechega, EJ, 'Treaty stipulations in favour of third states' (1956) 50 AJIL 338

Arendt, H, *Eichmann in Jerusalem,* 1963, New York: Viking

Arnull, A, 'The scope of Article 177' (1988) 13 ELR 40

Arnull, A, 'The uses and abuses of Article 177 EEC' (1989) 52 MLR 622

Atiyah, P, *The Rise and Fall of Freedom of Contract,* 1979, Oxford: OUP

Attard, D, *The Exclusive Economic Zone in International Law,* 1987, Oxford: OUP

Aust, A, *Modern Treaty Law and Practice,* 2000, Cambridge: CUP

Aust, A, 'The theory and practice of informal international instruments' (1986) 35 ICLQ 787

Austin, J, *The Province of Jurisprudence Determined* (1832), 1954, London: Weidenfeld & Nicholson

Ayer, AJ, *Thomas Paine,* 1989, London: Faber & Faber

Ayer, AJ, *Voltaire,* 1988, London: Faber & Faber

Barnes, J, *Aristotle,* 1982, Oxford: OUP

Barsh, R, 'Indigenous peoples in the 1990s: from object to subjects of international law' (1994) 7 Harv Hum Rts J 33

Barsh, R, 'The right to development as a human right' (1991) 13 HRQ 322

Barsh, R, 'Indigeneous peoples: an emerging object of international law' (1986) 80 AJIL 369

Bartlett, CJ, *The Global Conflict – The International Rivalry of the Great Powers (1880–1990)* 2nd edn, 1994, London: Longman

Bartlett, K, 'Feminist legal methods' (1990) 103 HLR 829

Baty, T, 'The three mile limit' (1928) 22 AJIL 503

Beck, A, 'A South African homeland appears in the English Courts: legitimation of the illegitimate?' (1987) 36 ICLQ 350

Becker J, *Hitler's Children: The Story of the Baader Meinhof Gang*, 1978, London: Granada

Beckett, F, *Clem Attlee: A Biography*, 1997, London: Richard Cohen

Beckett, WE, 'Human rights' (1949) 34 TGS 69

Beckett, WE, 'International law in England' (1939) 55 LQR 257

Beckett, WE, '*Les questions d'intérêt général au point de vue juridique dans la jurisprudence de la Cour Permanente de Justice Internationale*' (1932) 39 HR 131; (1934) 50 HR 189

Beckett, WE, 'Diplomatic claims in respect of injuries to companies' (1931) 17 TGS 175

Beckett, WE, 'Criminal jurisdiction over foreigners, the *Franconia* and the *Lotus* (1927) 8 BYIL 108

Beckett, WE, 'Exercise of criminal jurisdiction over foreigners' (1925) 6 BYIL 44

Beddard, R, *Human Rights in Europe*, 3rd edn, 1993, Cambridge: CUP

Bekker, P, 'Note on *Portugal v Australia* (1995) ICJ Rep 90' (1996) 90 AJIL 94

Berlin I, *Karl Marx: His Life and Environment*, 2nd edn, 1978, Oxford: Clarendon

Bernhardt, R, 'Reform of the control machinery under the European Convention on Rights: Protocol No 11' (1995) 89 AJIL 145

Best, G, *War and Law since 1945*, 1994, Oxford: OUP

Best, G, *Humanity in Warfare*, 1983, London: Methuen

Beveridge, F, 'The *Lockerbie* affair' (1992) 41 ICLQ 907

Bianchi, A, 'Immunity versus human rights: the *Pinochet* case' (1999) 10 EJIL 237

Bindschelder, RL, '*La protéction de la propriété privée en droit international public*' (1956) 90 HR 173

Birnie, P and Boyle, A, *International Law and the Environment*, 1992, Oxford: OUP

Blackman, A, *Seasons of Her Life: A Biography of Madeleine Korbal Albright*, 1998, New York: Scribner

Blake, R, *Disraeli*, 1966, London: Eyre & Spottiswoode

Blishenko, I, 'International treaties and their application in the territory of the USSR' (1975) 69 AJIL 819

Blum, Y, 'Russia takes over the Soviet Union seat at the United Nations' (1992) 3 EJIL 354

Blum, Y, 'United Nations membership of the "new" Yugoslavia: continuity or break?' (1992) 86 AJIL 830

Blum, Y, 'The Beirut raid and and the international double standard' (1970) 64 AJIL 73

Bonwick, C, *The American Revolution*, 1991, London: Macmillan

Borchard, E, 'War and peace' (1933) 27 AJIL 114

Bossouyt, M, *'La distinction entre les droits civils et politiques et les droits économiques, sociaux et culturels'* (1975) 8 HRJ 783

Boutros Ghali, B, *Unvanquished: A US-UN Saga*, 1999, New York: Random House

Boutros Ghali, B, *'La Ligue des Etats arabes'* (1972) 137 HR 1

Boutros Ghali, B, 'The Arab league (1945–1970)' (1969) 25 Revue Egyptiènne de Droit International 67

Bowett, DW, 'State contracts with aliens: contemporary developments on compensation for termination or breach' (1988) 59 BYIL 49

Bowett, DW, 'Contemporary developments in legal techniques in the settlement of disputes' (1983) 180 HR 169

Bowett, DW, 'Jurisdiction: changing patterns of authority over activities and resources' (1982) 53 BYIL 1

Bowett, DW, *The Law of International Institutions*, 4th edn, 1982, London, Sweet & Maxwell

Bowett, DW, 'Reservations to non-restricted multilateral treaties' (1978) 48 BYIL 67

Bowett DW, 'The *Arbitration Between the United Kingdom and France Concerning the Continental Shelf Boundary in the English Channel'* (1978) 49 BYIL 1

Bowett, DW, 'The State Immunity Act 1978' (1978) 37 CLJ 193

Bowett, DW, 'Reprisals involving recourse to armed force' (1972) 66 AJIL 1

Bowett, DW, *Self-Defence in International Law*, 1958, Manchester: Manchester UP

Bowett, DW, 'Estoppel before international tribunals and its relation to acquiesence' (1957) 33 BYIL 176

Boyle, A, 'Nuclear energy and international law: an environmental perspective' (1989) 60 BYIL 257

Brandon, M, 'The legal status of the premises of the United Nations' (1951) 28 BYIL 100

Bridge JW, 'The law and politics of United States foreign policy export controls' (1984) 4 LS 2

Bridge, JW, 'The United Nations and English law' (1969) 18 ICLQ 689

Brierly, JL, *The Outlook for International Law*, 1944, Oxford: OUP

Brierly, JL, 'The basis of obligation in international law', in Hersch Lauterpacht and Humphrey Waldock (eds), *The Basis of Obligation in International and Other Papers by the Late James Leslie Brierly*, 1958, Oxford: Clarendon (the original appearing as *'Le fondement du caractère obligatoire du droit international'* (1928) 23 HR 463)

Brierly, JL, 'The *Lotus* case' (1928) 44 LQR 154

Brierly, JL, 'Some consideration on the obsolesence of treaties' (1925) 11 TGS 11

Brierly, JL, 'The shortcomings of international law' (1924) 5 BYIL 4

Briggs, A, *Victorian Cities*, 1968, London: Penguin

Briggs, HW, '*Barcelona Traction*: the *jus standi* of Belgium' (1971) 65 AJIL 327

Briggs, HW, 'The *Columbian Peruvian Asylum* case and proof of customary international law' (1951) 45 AJIL 728

Brodie, F, *Thomas Jefferson: An Intimate History*, 1974, London: Methuen

Brown, EH, *The International Law of the Sea*, 1994, Aldershot: Dartmouth, Vols 1 and 2

Brown, J, 'Diplomatic immunity: state practice under the Vienna Convention on Diplomatic Relations' (1988) 37 ICLQ 53

Brownlie, I, *Principles of Public International Law*, 5th edn, 1998, Oxford, Clarendon (4th edn, 1990)

Brownlie, I, 'The justiciability of disputes and Issues in international relations' (1967) 42 BYIL 123

Brownlie, I, 'Some legal aspects of the use of nuclear weapons' (1965) 14 ICLQ 437

Brownlie, I, *International Law and the Use of Force by States*, 1963, Oxford: OUP

Brownlie, I, 'The individual before tribunals exercising international jurisdiction' (1962) 11 ICLQ 701

Van Bueren, G, *The International Law on the Rights of the Child*, 1995, Dordrecht: Martinus Nijhoff

Van Bueren, G, 'The international legal protection of children in armed conflicts' (1994) 43 ICLQ 809

Buergenthal, T, 'The Inter-American Court, human rights and the OAS' (1986) 7 HRLJ 157

Buergenthal, T, 'The advisory practice of the Inter-American Court' (1985) 79 AJIL 1

Buergenthal, T, 'The Inter-American Court of Human Rights' (1982) 76 AJIL 231

Buergenthal, T, 'The revised OAS Charter and the protection of human rights' (1975) 69 AJIL 828

Buergenthal, T, 'The American Convention on Human Rights: illusions and hopes' (1971) 21 Buffalo Law Review 121

Bunch, C, 'Women's rights as human rights: towards a revision of human rights' (1990) 12 HRQ 486

Bundu, AC, 'Recognition of revolutionary authorities: law and practice of states' (1978) 27 ICLQ 18

de Burca, G, 'Fundamental human rights and the breach of EC Law' (1993) 13 OJLS 283

Burgers, J, 'The road to San Francisco' (1992) 14 HRQ 447

Burrows, N, 'The 1979 Convention on the Elimination of All Forms of Discrimination against Women' (1985) 32 NILR 419

Bushe Fox, P, 'Unrecognised states: cases in the Admiralty and common law courts (1805–1826)' (1932) 13 BYIL 39

Bushe Fox, P, 'The Court of Chancery and recognition' (1931) 12 BYIL 63

Byers, M, *The Role of Law in International Politics*, M Byers (ed), 2000, Oxford: OUP

Byers, M, *Custom, Power and the Power of Rules: International Relations and Customary International Law*, 1999

Byers, M, 'Decisions of British courts during 1999 involving questions of public international law' (1999) 70 BYIL 277

Byers, M, 'State immunity: Article 18 of the International Law Commission's Draft' (1995) 44 ICLQ 882

Byrnes, A, 'The other human rights treaty body: the work of the Committee on the Elimination of Discrimination against Women' (1989) 14 YJIL 1

Caflisch, L, 'Land-locked states and their access to and from the sea' (1978) 49 BYIL 71

Cameron, I, 'The First Report of the Foreign Affairs Committee of the House of Commons' (1985) 34 ICLQ 610

Camins, H, 'The legal regime of Straits in the 1982 United Nations Convention on the Law of the Sea' (1987) 205 HR 9

Caron, DD, 'The nature of of the Iran-US Claims Tribunal and the evolving structure of international law' (1990) 84 AJIL 104

Carr, EH, *The Twenty Years' Crisis (1919-1939)*, 1939, London: Macmillan

Carter, PB, 'Decisions on private international law: 1984' (1984) 55 BYIL 358

Carty, A, 'Critical international law: recent trends in the theory of international law' (1991) 2 EJIL 66

Carty, A, *The Decay of International Law? A Reappraisal of the Limits of Legal Imagination in International Affairs*, 1986, Manchester: Manchester UP

Cassesse, A, 'The Martens Clause: half a loaf or simply pie in the sky?' (2000) 11 EJIL 187

Cassesse, A, 'The structure of the International Criminal Court: some preliminary reflections' (1999) 10 EJIL 144

Cassesse, A, *Self Determination of Peoples: A Legal Reappraisal*, 1995, Cambridge: CUP

Cassesse, A, 'A new approach to human rights: the European Convention for the Prevention of Torture' (1989) 83 AJIL 128

Charlesworth, H, Chinkin, C and Wright, S, 'Feminist approaches to international law' (1991) 85 AJIL 613

Charney, J, 'United States Provisional Application of the 1994 Deep Seabed Agreement' (1994) 88 AJIL 705

Charney, J, 'Universal international law' (1993) 87 AJIL 529

Charney, J, 'Judicial deference in foreign relations' (1989) 83 AJIL 805

Charney, J, 'The persistent objector rule and the development of customary international law' (1985) 56 BYIL

Charteris, A, 'The legal position of merchantmen in foreign ports and national waters' (1920) 1 BYIL 45

Chatterjee, SK, 'The Convention establishing the Multilateral Investment Guarantee Agency' (1987) 36 ICLQ 76

Cheng, B, *Studies in International Law*, 1997, Oxford: Clarendon

Cheng, B, 'The Moon Treaty' (1980) 33 CLP 213

Cheng, B, 'The 1966 South West Africa Judgment of the World Court' (1967) CLP 181

Cheng, B, 'The extraterrestial application of international law' (1965) 18 CLP 132

Cheng, B, 'United Nations resolutions on outer space: "instant" customary international law?' (1965) 5 IJIL 23

Cheng, B, *The Law of International Air Transport*, 1962, London: Stevens

Cheng, B, 'The United Nations and outer space' (1961) 14 CLP 247

Cheng, B, 'From air law to space law' (1960) 10 CLP 228

Cheng, B, 'Recent developments in air law' (1956) 9 CLP 208

Cheng, B, 'Justice and equity in international law' (1955) 8 CLP 185

Cheyne, I, 'The International Tin Council' (1989) 38 ICLQ 417

Cheyne, I, 'The International Tin Council (III)' (1990) 39 ICLQ 945

Chinkin, C, 'The challenge of soft law: development and change in international law' (1989) 38 ICLQ 850

Chinkin, C, 'Third party intervention before the International Court of Justice' (1986) 80 AJIL 495

Chiu, H, 'Succession in international organisations' (1965) 14 ICLQ 83

Christenson, G, 'The World Court and *jus cogens*' (1987) 81 AJIL 93

Christol, C, 'The Moon Treaty enters into force' (1985) 79 AJIL 163

Christol, C, 'International liability for damage caused by space objects' (1980) 74 AJIL 346

Christol, C, 'Maritime quarantine: the naval interdiction of offensive weapons and associated material to Cuba' (1963) 57 AJIL 525

Christopher, W, *In the Stream of History*, 1998, Stanford: Stanford UP

Chui, H, 'Succession in international organisations' (1965) 14 ICLQ 83

Churchill, R and Lowe, AV, *The Law of the Sea*, 3rd edn, 1999, Manchester: MUP

Churchill, R and Lowe, AV, *The Law of the Sea*, 2nd edn, 1988, Manchester: Manchester UP

Clapham, A, 'Creating the High Commissioner for Human Rights: the outside story' (1994) 5 EJIL 556

Clark, G and Sohn, LB, *World Peace through World Law: Two Alternative Plans*, 3rd edn, 1966, Cambridge, Mass: Harvard UP

Claude, I, *National Minorities: An International Problem*, 1955, Cambridge: CUP

von Clausewitz, K, *Vom Kriege* (1832: Berlin), Howard, M and Paret, P (trans), 1976, London: Penguin

Cobbah, JAM, 'African values and the human rights debate: an African perspective' (1987) 9 HRQ 309

Cobban, A, *Nation State and National Self Determination*, 1969, London: Penguin

Cobban, A, *A History of Modern France*, 1961, London: Penguin, Vol 1 (1715–1799)

Cohen, AF, 'Cosmos 954 and the international law of satellite accidents' (1984) 10 YJIL 78

Cohn, EJ, 'Book review of H Lauterpacht's *Recognition in International Law*' (1948) 64 LQR 404

Collier, JG and Lowe, AV, *The Settlement of Disputes in International Law*, 1999, Cambridge: CUP

Collier, JG, *Conflict of Laws*, 2nd edn, 1994, Cambridge: CUP

Collier, JG, 'Is international law really part of the law of England?' (1989) 38 ICLQ 924

Collier, JG, 'Conflict of laws – restraining foreign proceedings – private rights and public policy' (1984) 43 CLJ 253

Cook, R (ed), *Human Rights of Women: National and International Perspectives*, 1994, Philadelphia: University of Philadelphia Press

Cook, R, 'Women's international human rights law: the way forward' (1993) 15 HRQ 230

Cook, R, 'Reservations to the Convention on the Elimination of all Forms of Discrimination Against Women' (1990) 30 Va JIL 643

Cordingly, D, *Life Among the Pirates: The Romance and the Reality*, 1995, New York: Little, Brown

Coulter, RT, 'The Draft United Nations Declaration on the Rights of Indigenous Peoples' (1995) 13 NQHR 123

Craven, M, *The International Covenant on Economic, Social and Cultural Rights*, 1995, Oxford: OUP

Crawford, J, 'Prospects for an International Criminal Court' (1995) 48 CLP 303

Crawford, J, 'The ILC adopts a statute for an International Criminal Court' (1995) 89 AJIL 404

Crawford, J, 'The ILC's Draft Statute for an International Criminal Tribunal' (1994) 88 AJIL 140

Crawford, J, 'Democracy and international law' (1993) 64 BYIL 113

Crawford, J, 'Decisions of British courts during 1985–1986 involving questions of public international law' (1986) 57 BYIL 405

Crawford, J, 'The execution of judgments and foreign sovereign immunity' (1981) 75 AJIL 820

Crawford, J, *The Creation of States in International Law*, 1979, Oxford: OUP

Crawford, J, 'The criteria for statehood in international law' (1976–77) 48 BYIL 93

Crena, C, 'The structure and functioning of the Inter-American Court of Human Rights (1979–1992)' (1992) 63 BYIL 135

Crosland, CAR, *Socialism Now*, 1974, London: Jonathan Cape

Crosland, CAR, *The Future of Socialism*, 1956, London: Jonathan Cape

Czaplinski, W, 'Sources of law in the *Nicaragua* case' (1989) 38 ICLQ 151

Dallen, R, 'An overview of EEC protection of human rights' [1990] 27 CMLR 761

Dannilenko, G, 'Implementation of international law in CIS states: theory and practice' (1999) 10 EJIL 51

Dannilenko, G, 'The new Russian constitution and international law' (1994) 88 AJIL 451

Dannilenko, G, 'International *jus cogens*: issues of law making' (1991) 2 EJIL 42

Darwin, HG, 'The Outer Space Treaty' (1967) 42 BYIL 278

Davidson, S, 'Remedies for violations of the American Convention on Human Rights' (1995) 44 ICLQ 405

Davidson, S, *Human Rights*, 1st edn, 1992, Buckingham: OUP

Davidson, S, *The Inter-American Court of Human Rights*, 1992, Aldershot: Dartmouth

Davies, PG and C Redgwell, 'The international regulation of straddling fish stocks' (1996) 67 BYIL 199

Davies, PG, 'The EC/Canadian Fisheries dispute in the North West Atlantic' (1995) 44 ICLQ 927

Delaume, G, 'ICSID arbitration and the courts' (1983) 77 AJIL 784

Delaume, G, 'The State Immunity Act 1978 of the United Kingdom' (1979) 73 AJIL 185

Dencho, G, 'Politics or rule of law: deconstruction and legitimacy in international law' (1993) 4 EJIL 1

Detter, I, *The Law of War*, 2nd edn, 2000, Cambridge: CUP

Detter, I, *The International Legal Order*, 1994, Aldershot: Dartmouth

Detter, I, *The Law of War*, 1st edn, 1987, Cambridge: CUP

Detter, I, 'The problem of unequal treaties' (1966) 15 ICLQ 1069

Dicey, AV, *The Conflict of Laws*, 1st edn, 1896, London: Stevens

Dickstein, HL, 'National environmental hazards and international law' (1974) 23 ICLQ 426

Dinstein, Y, *War, Aggression and Self Defence*, 2nd edn, 1994, Cambridge: CUP

Dinstein, Y, 'Collective human rights of peoples and minorities' (1976) 25 ICLQ 102

Dinstein, Y, 'Diplomatic immunity from jurisdiction: *ratione materiae*' (1966) 15 ICLQ 76

Dinwiddy, J, *Bentham*, 1989, Oxford: OUP

Dixon, M, *Textbook on International Law*, 4th edn, 2000, London: Blackstone

Dixon, M, 'The *Danube Dams* and international law' (1998) 57 CLJ 1

Dixon, M, 'The *ELSI* case' (1992) 41 ICLQ 701

Donnelly, J, *Universal Human Rights in Theory and Practice*, 1989, New York: Cornell UP

Donnelly, J, 'In search of the unicorn: the jurisprudence and politics of the right to development' (1985) 15 Calif WILJ 473

Dormenval, A, 'United Nations Committee Against Torture: practice and perspectives' (1990) 8 NQHR 26

Doswald Beck, L, 'The legal validity of military intervention by invitation of the Government' (1985) 56 BYIL 189

Dremczewski, A, 'The domestic application of the European Human Rights Convention as European Community law' (1981) 30 ICLQ 118

Duclos, N, 'Lessons of difference: feminist theory on cultural diversity' (1990) 38 Buff L Rev 36

Duffy, P, 'Article 3 ECHR' (1983) 32 ICLQ 316

Dugard, J, 'Obstacles in the way of an International Criminal Court' (1997) 56 CLJ 329

Dutton, D, *Simon: A Political Biography of Sir John Simon*, 1992, London: Arum

Dworkin, R, *A Matter of Principle*, 1986, Oxford: Clarendon

Dworkin, R, *Taking Rights Seriously*, 1977, London: Duckworth

Eagleton C, 'The form and function of the declaration of war' (1938) 32 AJIL 19

Edwards, S, *Rebel: A Biography of Thomas Paine*, 1974, New York: Praeger

Elbareidi, M, 'The Eygptian-Israeli Peace Treaty and access to the Gulf of Aqaba: a new legal regime' (1982) 76 AJIL 532

van Elbe, J, 'The evolution of the concept of the just war in international law' (1939) 33 AJIL 665

El Chiati, AZ, 'Protection of investment in the context of petroleum agreements' (1987) 204 HR 9

Elias, TO, 'The nature of the subjective element in international law' (1995) 44 ICLQ 501

Elias, TO, 'The doctrine of intertemporal law' (1980) 74 AJIL 285

Elias, TO, *The Modern Law of Treaties*, 1974, Dobbs Ferry: Oceana

Elias, TO, 'The Charter of the Organisation of African Unity' (1965) 59 AJIL 243

Elias, TO, 'The Commission of Mediation, Concilliation and Arbitration of the Organisation of African Unity' (1964) 40 BYIL 336

Engels, F, *The Origins of the Family, Private Property and the State* (1884), 1940 London: Lawrence & Wishart

Ensor, RK, *England, 1870–1914*, 1936, Oxford: OUP

d'Entreves, AP, *Natural Law*, 2nd edn, 1970, London: Hutchinson

Ermacora, F, 'The protection of minorities before the United Nations' (1983) 182 HR 251

van Essen, JLF, 'Some reflections on the judgments of the International Court of Justice in the *Asylum* and *Haya de la Torre* cases (1952) 1 ICLQ 533

Evans JM, *Immigration Law*, 1983, London: Sweet & Maxwell

Evans, MD and Morgan, R, 'The European Convention for the Prevention of Torture (1992–1997)' (1997) 46 ICLQ 663

Evans, MD, '*Case concerning Maritime Delimitation and Territorial Questions Between Qatar and Bahrain (Jurisdiction and Admissibility)*' (1995) 44 ICLQ 691

Evans, MD, '*Case concerning Maritime Delimitation in the Area between Greenland and Jan Mayen (Denmark v Norway)*' (1994) 43 ICLQ 697

Evans, MD, 'Delimitation and the common maritime boundary' (1994) 64 BYIL 283

Evans, MD, 'Less than an ocean apart: the St Pierre and Miquelon and Jan Mayen Islands and the delimitation of maritime zones' (1994) 43 ICLQ 678

Evans, MD and Morgan, R, 'The European Torture Committee: membership issues' (1994) 5 EJIL 249

Evans, MD and Morgan, R, 'The European Convention for the Protection of Torture: operational practice' (1991) 41 ICLQ 590

Evenson, J, 'The *Anglo Norwegian Fisheries* case and its legal consequences' (1952) 46 AJIL 609

Falk, RA, *The Status of Law in International Society*, 1970, Ewing, New Jersey: Princeton UP

Falk, R, 'The Beirut raid and the international law of retaliation' (1969) 63 AJIL 415

Falk, R, 'On the quasi legislative competence of the General Assembly' (1966) 60 AJIL 782 4

Farer, TJ, 'The regulation of foreign intervention in civil armed conflict' (1974) 142 HR 291

Farrer, T, 'Human rights in law's empire: the jurisprudence war' (1991) 85 AJIL 117

Fatouros, A, 'International law and the internationalised contract' (1980) 74 AJIL 134

Fawcett, JES, *The Application of the European Convention on Human Rights*, 2nd edn, 1987, Oxford: OUP

Fawcett, JES, *Outer Space: New Challenges to Law and Policy*, 1984, Oxford: OUP

Fawcett, JES, *The Law of Nations*, 2nd edn, 1971, London: Penguin

Fawcett, JES, *International Law and the Uses of Outer Space*, 1968, Manchester: Manchester UP

Feldman, D, *Civil Liberties and Human Rights in England and Wales*, 1993, Oxford: OUP

Fellmeth, A, 'Feminism and international law: theory, methodology and substantive reform' (2000) 22 HRQ 658

Fenn, P, 'Origins of the theory of territorial waters' (1926) 20 AJIL 465

Fenn, P, 'Justinian and freedom of the seas' (1925) 19 AJIL 716

Fennessy, JG, 'The 1975 Vienna Convention on the Representation of States in their Relations with International Organisations of a Universal Character' (1976) 70 AJIL 62

Fentiman, R, *Foreign Law in English Courts*, 1998, Oxford: OUP

Fentiman, R, 'Foreign law in English courts' (1992) 108 LQR 142

Fenwick, CG, 'The Honduras-Nicaragua Boundary dispute' (1957) 51 AJIL 761

Finnis, J, *Natural Law and Natural Rights*, 1980, Oxford: Clarendon

Fischer, D, 'Reporting under the Covenant on Civil and Political Rights: the first five years of the Human Rights Committee' (1982) 76 AJIL 142

Fischer Williams, J, 'International law and the property of aliens' (1928) 9 BYIL 1

Fitzmaurice, GG, 'The problem of the "non-appearing" defendant Government' (1980) 51 BYIL 89

Fitzmaurice, GG, 'The general principles of international law considered from the standpoint of the rule of law' (1957) 92 HR 1

Fitzmaurice, GG, 'The foundations of the authority of international law and the problem of enforcement' (1956) 19 MLR 1

Fitzmaurice, GG, 'Reservations to multilateral conventions' (1953) 2 ICLQ 1

Fitzmaurice, GG, 'The law and procedure of the ICJ: treaty interpretation' (1951) 28 BYIL 1

Fitzmaurice, GG, 'Some aspects of modern contraband control and the law of prize' (1945) 22 BYIL 173

Fleck, D (ed), *The Handbook of Humanitarian Law in Armed Conflicts*, 1999, Oxford: OUP

Forrest, RM, 'Carriage by air: the Hague Convention' (1961) 10 ICLQ 726

Forsyth, F, *The Biafra Story*, 1969, London: Penguin

Forsythe, DP, 'Legal management of internal war: the 1977 Protocol on Non-International Armed Conflict' (1978) 72 AJIL 272

Fox, H, 'The *Pinochet* case' (1999) 48 ICLQ 687

Fox, H, 'The *Pinochet* case' (1999) 48 ICLQ 207

Fox, H, 'Employment contracts as an exception to state immunity' (1995) 66 BYIL 97

Fox, H, 'State immunity: the House of Lords decision in *I Congresso del Partido*' (1982) 98 LQR 94

Franck, TM, *Fairness in International Law and Institutions*, 1995, Oxford: Clarendon

Franck, TM, 'Fairness in the international legal and institutional system' (1993) 240 HR 9

Franck, TM, 'The emerging right to democratic governance' (1992) 86 AJIL 46

Franck, TM, 'The "powers of appreciation": who is the ultimate guardian of United Nations legality?' (1992) 86 AJIL 519

Franck, TM, *The Power of Legitimacy Among Nations*, 1990, New York: OUP

Franck, TM, 'Legitimacy in the international system' (1988) 82 AJIL 705

Franck, TM and Rodley, N, 'After Bangladesh: the law of humanitarian intervention by military force' (1973) 67 AJIL 287

Franck, TM, 'Who killed Article 2(4)?' (1970) 64 AJIL 809

Franck, TM, *The Structure of Impartiality*, 1968, New York: Macmillan

Franconi, F, 'The Gulf of Sidra incident and international law' (1980) 5 Italian Yearbook of International Law

French, D, 'Developing states and international environmental law' (2000) 49 ICLQ 35

Friedmann, W (ed) (with Henkin L and Lissityn O), *Transnational Law in a Changing Society: Essays in Honour of PC Jessup*, 1972, New York: Columbia UP

Friedmann, W, *The Changing Structure of International Law*, 1964, London: Stevens

Frowein, JA, 'The reunification of Germany' (1992) 86 AJIL 152

Frowein, JA, 'Germany reunited' (1991) 51 Zao RV 331

Fukuyama, F, *The End of History and the Last Man*, 1992, New York: Free Press

Fung, D, 'The basic law of the Hong Kong special administrative region of the People's Republic of China' (1988) 37 ICLQ 701

Gaer, F, 'First fruits: reporting by states under the African Charter on Human and Peoples' Rights' (1992) 10 NQHR 29

Gaja, G, 'A "new" Vienna Convention on Treaties between States and International Organisations or between International Organisations: a critical commentary' (1987) 58 BYIL 253

Galey, M, 'International enforcement of women's rights' (1984) 6 HRQ 463

Gamble, JK, 'Reservations to multilateral treaties: a macroscopic view of state practice' (1980) 74 AJIL 372

Garner, J, 'The doctrine of *rebus sic stantibus* and the termination of treaties' (1927) 21 AJIL 409

Garnett, R, 'State immunity in employment matters' (1997) 46 ICLQ 81

Gearty, G, 'The European Court of Human Rights and the protection of civil liberties' (1993) 52 CLJ 90

Geny, F, *Méthode d'interprétation et sources en droit privé positif*, 2nd edn, 1919, Paris: Librairie Générale de Droit et de Jurisprudence

Ghai, Y, 'Human rights and governance' (1994) 15 AYIL 5

Ghandi, P, 'The Human Rights Committee and the right of individual communication' (1986) 57 BYIL 201

Gidel, GC, '*La mer territoriale et la zone contigue*' (1934) 48 HR 133

Gilbert, G, 'Crimes *sans frontières*: jurisdictional problems in English law' (1992) 63 BYIL 415

Gilbert, G, *Aspects of Extradition Law*, 1991, The Hague: Martinus Nijhoff

Gilbert, G, 'The criminal responsibility of states' (1990) 39 ICLQ 345

Gilbert, M, *The Holocaust: The Jewish Tragedy*, 1986, London: William Collins

Gioia, A, 'The law of multinational bays and the case of the *Gulf of Fonseca*' (1993) NYIL 81

Gittleman, R, 'The African Charter on Human and Peoples' Rights: a legal analysis' (1982) 22 Va JIL 667

Glennon, MJ, 'State sponsored abduction: a comment on *United States v Alvarez- Machain*' (1992) 86 AJIL 736

Glover, J, *Humanity: A Moral History of the Twentieth Century*, 1999, London: Jonathan Cape

Goedhuis, D, 'Questions of public international air law' (1952) 81 HR 201

Goedhuis, D, 'Conflicts of law and divergencies in the legal regimes of air space and outer space' (1963) 109 HR 257

Goedhuis, D, 'The changing legal regime of air and outer space' (1978) 27 ICLQ 576

Goedhuis, D, 'The problems of the frontiers of outer space and air space' (1982) 174 HR 367

Gold, J, *Interpretation: The IMF and International Law*, 1996, The Hague: Kluwer

Gordon, E, 'The World Court and the interpretation of constitutive treaties' (1965) 59 AJIL 794

Gowlland Debbas, V, 'The relationship between the International Court of Justice and the Security Council in the light of the *Lockerbie* case' (1994) 88 AJIL 643

Graeforth, B, 'The International Law Commission tomorrow: improving its organisation and methods of work' (1991) 85 AJIL 597

Gray, C, *Judicial Remedies in International Law*, 1987, Oxford: OUP

Gray, C, 'Is there an international law of remedies?' (1985) 56 BYIL 25

Gray, C, 'After the ceasefire: Iraq, the Security Council and the use of force' (1994) 65 BYIL 135

Gray, C, 'Legality of the threat or use of nuclear weapons' (1997) 46 ICLQ 68

Gray, C, 'The *Lockerbie* Case continues' (1998) 57 CLJ 433

Green, LC, *The Contemporary Law of Armed Conflict*, 1993, Manchester: Manchester UP

Green, LC, 'Nuclear weapons and the law of armed conflict' (1988) 17 Denver J Int Law 1

Green, LC, 'Self-determination and the settlement of the Arab Israeli Conflict' (1971) 65 AJIL 40

Green, LC, 'The *Eichmann* case' (1960) 23 MLR 507

Green, LC, 'Recent practice in the law of extradition' (1953) 6 CLP 274

Greenwood, C, 'The concept of war in modern international law' (1987) 36 ICLQ 283

Greenwood, C, 'State contracts in international law – the *Libyan Oil Arbitrations*' (1982) 53 BYIL 27

Greig, DW, 'Self-defence and the Security Council: what does Article 51 require?' (1991) 40 ICLQ 366

Greig, DW, 'The *Carl Zeiss* case and the position of an unrecognised government in English law' (1967) 87 LQR 96

Greig, DW, 'The advisory jurisdiction of the International Court and the settlement of disputes between states' (1966) 15 ICLQ 325

Gribben, J, *The Hole in the Sky: Man's Threat to the Ozone Layer*, 1988, London: Corgi

Guggenheim, P, *Traité de droit international public*, 2nd edn, 1967, Geneva: Librairie de l'Université

Gutteridge, H, 'The meaning of the scope of Article 38(1)(c) of the Statute of the International Court of Justice' (1952) 38 TGS 125

Halberstam, M, 'In defence of the Supreme Court decision in *Alvarez-Machain*' (1992) 86 AJIL 746

Halberstam, M, '*Sabbatino* resurrected: the act of state doctrine in the revised restatement of United States foreign relations law' (1985) 79 AJIL 68

Halderman, JW, 'Some legal aspects of sanctions in the *Rhodesian* case' (1968) 17 ICLQ 672

Hale, JR, *Machiavelli and Renaissance Italy*, 1961, London: HUP

Hambro, E, 'The authority of the advisory opinions of the International Court of Justice' (1954) 3 ICLQ 2

Hampson, FJ, 'Belligerent reprisals and the 1977 Protocols to the Geneva Conventions of 1949' (1988) 37 ICLQ 818

Hampson, N, *The Enlightenment*, 1968, London: Pelican

Hargrove, J, 'The *Nicaragua* judgment and the future of the law of force and self-defence' (1987) 81 AJIL 135

Harris, DJ, O'Boyle, M and Warbrick, C, *Law of the European Convention on Human Rights*, 1st edn, 1995, London: Butterworths

Harris, DJ, 'A fresh impetus for the European Social Charter' (1992) 41 ICLQ 660

Hart, HLA, *The Concept of Law*, 2nd edn, 1994, Oxford: OUP (1st edn, 1961)

Hart, HLA, 'Positivism and the separation of law and morals' (1958) 71 HLR 593

Hassan, F, 'The shooting down of Korean Airlines Flight 007 by the USSR and the furtherance of air safety for passengers' (1984) 33 ICLQ 712

Hastings, M and Jenkins, S, *The Battle for the Falklands*, 1983, London: Penguin

Hazard, J, 'Codifying peaceful co-existence' (1961) 55 AJIL 111

Hearder, H and Waley, DP, *A Short History of Italy*, 1966, Cambridge: CUP

Heilbronner, K, 'Legal aspects of the unification of the two German states' (1991) 2 EJIL 18

Heintze, HJ, '*Volkerrecht* und indigenous peoples' (1990) 50 Zao RV 39

Hendry, I and Wood, M, *The Legal Status of Berlin*, 1987, Cambridge: CUP

Henkin, L, 'US ratification of Human Rights Conventions: the ghost of Senator Bricker' (1995) 89 AJIL 341

Henkin, L, 'International law: politics, values and functions. General course on public international law' (1989) 216 HR 9

Henkin L, *How Nations Behave*, 2nd edn, 1979, New York: Columbia UP

Henkin, L, 'The Connally Reservation revisited and, hopefully contained' (1971) 65 AJIL 374

Henkin, L, 'The reports of the death of Article 2(4) are greatly exaggerated' (1971) 65 AJIL 544

Hevener, NA and Mosher, SA, 'General principles of law and the United Nations Covenant on Civil and Political Rights' (1978) 27 ICLQ 596

Van Der Heydte, FA, 'Discovery, symbolic annexation and virtual effectiveness in international law' (1935) 29 AJIL 448

Heyking, A (Baron), 'The international protection of minorities: the Achilles' heel of the League of Nations' (1928) 13 TGS 31

Higgins, R, 'International law in a changing international system' (1999) 58 CLJ 78

Higgins, R, *Problems and Process: International Law and How We Use It*, 1994, Oxford: OUP

Higgins, R, 'International law and the avoidance, containment and resolution of disputes' (1991) 230 HR 9

Higgins, R, 'The taking of property by the state: recent developments in international law' (1982) 176 HR 259

Higgins, R, 'Derogations under human rights treaties' (1976-1977) BYIL 281

Higgins, R, 'The advisory opinion on Namibia. Which United Nations Resolutions are binding under Article 25 of the Charter?' (1972) 21 ICLQ 270

Highet, K, 'Delimitation of the maritime areas between Canada and France' (1993) AJIL 452

Highet, K, 'Evidence, the Court and the *Nicaragua* case' (1987) 81 AJIL 1

Hirst, M, 'Jurisdiction over cross frontier offences' (1981) 97 LQR 80

Hobbes, T, *The Leviathan* (1651), 1973, London: JM Dent

Holland, TE, *The Laws of War on Land*, 1908, Oxford: Clarendon

Hopkins, J, 'Former Head of Foreign State – note on *Re Pinochet*' (1999) 58 CLJ 461

Hopkins, J, 'Government of Foreign State – proof of existence' (1998) 57 CLJ 436

Hopkins, J, 'Immunity – Head of Foreign State'(1998) 57 CLJ 4

Hoskova, M, *'Die Selbstauflosung der CSFR – Ausgewahlte rechtliche Aspekte'* (1993) 53 ZaoRV 697

Hudec, R, *The GATT Legal System and World Trade Diplomacy*, 1975, New York: Praeger

Hudson, M, 'Integrity of international instruments' (1948) 42 AJIL 105

Hune, S and Niessen, J, 'Ratifying the United Nations Migrant Workers Convention: current difficulties and prospects' (1994) 12 NQHR 393

Hune, S and Niessen J, 'The First United Nations Convention on Migrant Workers' (1991) 9 NQHR 133

Hurst, CJ, 'Whose is the bed of the sea ?' (1924) 4 BYIL 34

Hurst, CJ, 'The effect of war on treaties' (1922) 3 BYIL 37

Hutchinson, D, 'The significance of the registration or non-registration of an international agreement in determining whether or not it is a treaty' (1993) CLP 257

Hutchinson, D, 'Solidarity and breaches of multilateral treaties' (1988) 59 BYIL 151

Hyde, CC, 'The interpretation of treaties by the Permanent Court of International Justice' (1930) 24 AJIL 1

Ijalaye, D, 'Was Biafra at any time a state in international law?' (1971) 65 AJIL 51

Ignatieff, M, *Isaiah Berlin: A Life*, 1998, London: Chatto and Windus

Imbert, PH, 'Reservations to the European Convention on Human Rights before the Strasbourg Commission' (1984) 33 ICLQ 558

Iwasawa, Y, 'The relationship between international law and national law: Japanese experiences' (1993) 64 BYIL 333

Jackson, JH, *The Jurisprudence of GATT and the WTO*, 2000, Cambridge: CUP

Jackson, JH, *World Trade Law and the Law of GATT*, 1969, New York: Bobbs Merrill

Jacobs, F and White, R, *The European Convention on Human Rights*, 2nd edn, 1996, Oxford: Clarendon

Jacque, JP, 'German reunification and the European Community' (1991) 2 EJIL 1

James, H, *International Monetary Co-operation since Bretton Woods*, 1996, Oxford: OUP

Janis, M, Kay, R and Bradley A, *European Human Rights Law: Text and Materials*, 1st edn, 1995, Oxford: OUP

Jenks, CW, *Space Law*, 1965, London: Stevens

Jenks, CW, 'State succession in respect of law making treaties' (1952) 29 BYIL 105

Jenks, CW, 'Some constitutional problems of international organisations' (1945) 22 BYIL 11

Jenks, CW, 'The legal personality of international organisations' (1945) 22 BYIL 267

Jennings, RY, 'The judiciary, international and national, and the development of international law' (1996) 45 ICLQ 1

Jennings, RY and Watts, AD, *Oppenheim's International Law*, 9th edn, 1992, London: Longmans

Jennings, RY, 'Equity and equitable principles' (1986) 42 SYBIL 27

Jennings, RY, 'A changing international law of the sea' (1972) 31 CLJ 32

Jennings, RY, 'The limits of the *Continental Shelf* jurisdiction: some possible implications of the *North Sea* case judgment' (1969) 18 ICLQ 819

Jennings, RY, 'Recent developments in the International Law Commission' (1964) 13 ICLQ 385

Jennings, RY, 'Recent cases on "automatic" reservations to the optional clause' (1958) 7 ICLQ 349

Jennings, RY, 'Extra-territorial jurisdiction and the United States anti-trust laws' (1957) 33 BYIL 146

Jennings, RY, 'Some aspects of the international law of the air' (1949) 75 HR 509

Jennings, RY, 'The progressive development of international law and its codification' (1947) 24 BYIL 301

Jennings, RY, 'International civil aviation and the law' (1945) 23 BYIL 191

Jennings, RY, 'The *Caroline* and *McLeod* cases' (1938) 32 AJIL 82

Jessup, P, 'Should international law recognise an intermediate state between war and peace?' (1954) 48 AJIL 98

Jessup, P, *A Modern Law of Nations*, 1948, New York: Macmillan

Jessup, P, 'The *Estrada* doctrine' (1931) 25 AJIL 719

Jessup, P, 'The *Palmas Island* arbitration' (1928) 22 AJIL 735

Jessup, P, *The Law of Territorial Waters and Maritime Jurisdiction*, 1927, New York: Jennings

Johnson, D, 'Consolidation as a root of title in international law' (1955) CLJ 215

Johnson, D, 'The *Minquiers and Ecrehos* case' (1954) 3 ICLQ 14

Johnson, DH, 'The case concerning the *Temple of Preah Vihear*' (1962) 11 ICLQ 1183

Johnson, DH, 'Piracy in modern international law' (1957) 43 TGS 63

Johnson, DH, 'The effect of resolutions of the General Assembly of the United Nations' (1955-56) 32 BYIL 97

Johnson-Odim, C, 'Common themes, different contexts', in Mohanty, C, Russo, A and Torres, L (eds), *Third World Women and the Politics of Feminism*, 1991, Bloomington: Indiana UP

Jolliffe, J, *Raymond Asquith: Life and Letters*, 1980, London: William Collins

Jones, A, *Jones on Extradition*, 1989, London: Sweet & Maxwell

Jones, JM, 'The *Nottebohm* case' (1956) 5 ICLQ 230

Jones, JW, 'Leibniz as international lawyer' (1945) 22 BYIL 1

Jones, JW, 'The "pure" theory of international law' (1935) 16 BYIL 5

Joyner, C (ed), *The United Nations and International Law*, 1997, Cambridge: CUP

Kearney, R and Dalton, R, 'The treaty on treaties' (1970) 64 AJIL 495

Kelsen, H, *Pure Theory of Law,* Knight, M (trans), 1967, California, University of California Press

Kelsen, H, *General Theory of Law and State,* Wedberg, A (trans), 1949, Cambridge: Harvard UP

Kelsen, H, 'Recognition in international law: theoretical observations' (1941) 35 AJIL 605

Kelsen, H, 'The pure theory of law: Part II' (1935) 51 LQR 517

Kelsen, H, 'The pure theory of law: its method and fundamental concepts' (1934) 50 LQR 474

Kelsen, H, '*Les rapports de système entre le droit interne et le droit international public*' (1926) 14 HR 227

Kennedy, D, 'A new stream of international law scholarship' (1988) 7 Wis ILJ 6

Kenny, A, *Aquinas,* 1979, Oxford: OUP

Kent, H, 'Historical origins of the three mile limit' (1954) 48 AJIL 537

Kikwanuku, R, 'The meaning of "people" in the African Charter on Human and Peoples' Rights' (1988) 82 AJIL 80

Kissinger, H, *Diplomacy,* 1994, New York: Simon and Schuster

Klabbers, J, *The Concept of the Treaty in International Law,* 1996, The Hague: Kluwer

Klepcki, ZL, *The Organs of International Organisations,* 1973, Alphen aan den Rijn: Sijhoff und Noordhoff

Kochan, L, *The Making of Modern Russia,* 1962, London: Jonathan Cape

Kodjo, E, 'African Charter on Human and Peoples' Rights' (1990) HRLJ 272

Koskenniemi, M, 'National self-determination today: problems of theory and practice' (1994) 43 ICLQ 241

Koskenniemi, M, 'The politics of international law' (1990) 1 EJIL 4

Koskenniemi, M, *From Apology to Utopia: The Structure of International Legal Argument,* 1989, Helsinki: Finnish Lawyer's Publishing

Kritsiotis, D, 'The Kosovo crisis and NATO's application of armed force against the Federal Republic of Yugoslavia' (2000) 49 ICLQ 330

Kummer, K, *The International Management of Hazardous Wastes,* 2nd edn, 2000, Oxford: OUP

Kummer, K, 'The international regulation of transboundary traffic in hazardous waste: the 1989 Basel Convention' (1992) 41 ICLQ 530

Kunz, JL, 'The *Nottebohm* case' (1960) 54 AJIL 558

Kunz, JL, 'Chapter XI of the United Nations Charter in action' (1954) 48 AJIL 103

Kunz, JL, 'The nature of customary international law' (1953) 47 AJIL 662

Kunz, JL, 'The chaotic status of the laws of war and the urgent necessity for their revision' (1951) 45 AJIL 37

Kunz, JL, 'Review of Lauterpacht's recognition in international law' (1950) 44 AJIL 713

Kunz, JL, 'Privileges and immunities of international organisations' (1947) 41 AJIL 828

Lacey, N, 'Legislation against sex discrimination: questions from a feminist perspective' (1987) 14 Journal of Law and Society 411

Lachs, M, 'The challenge of the environment' (1990) 39 ICLQ 663

Lachs, M, 'The international law of outer space' (1964) 113 HR 1

Lamb, R, *Promising the Earth*, 1996, London: Routledge

Lapidoth, R, 'The Strait of Tiran, the Gulf of Aqaba and the 1979 Treaty of Peace between Eygpt and Israel' (1983) 77 AJIL 84

Lasok, DP and Lasok, KP, *Lasok and Bridge's Law and Institutions of the European Community*, 6th edn, 1998, London: Butterworths

Lauterpacht, E, '*Case concerning Rights of Passage over Indian Territory*' (1958) 7 ICLQ 593

Lauterpacht, E, 'Freedom of transit in international law' (1958) 44 TGS 313

Lauterpacht, H, *The Function of Law in the International Community*, 1933, Oxford: Clarendon

Lauterpacht, H, *The Development of International Law by the Permanent Court of International Justice*, 1934, London: Stevens

Lauterpacht, H, *Recognition in International Law*, 1948, Cambridge: CUP

Lauterpacht, H, *International Law and Human Rights*, 1950, London: Stevens

Lauterpacht, H, *The Development of International Law by the International Court*, 1958, London: Stevens

Lauterpacht, H, '*The Cristina*' (1938) 53 LQR 339

Lauterpacht, H, 'Recognition of insurgents as *de facto* government' (1939) 3 MLR 1

Lauterpacht, H, 'Is international law part of the law of England?' (1939) 25 TGS 51

Lauterpacht , H, 'The Grotian tradition in international law' (1946) 23 BYIL 1

Lauterpacht, H, 'Allegiance, diplomatic protection and criminal jurisdiction over aliens' (1947) 9 CLJ 330

Lauterpacht, H, 'The subjects of the Law of Nations' (1947) 63 LQR 460

Lauterpacht, H, 'The subjects of the Law of Nations' (1948) 64 LQR 97

Lauterpacht, H, 'Restrictive interpretation and the principle of effectiveness in the interpretation of treaties' (1949) 26 BYIL 48

Lauterpacht, H, 'Sovereignty over submarine areas' (1950) 27 BYIL 395

Lauterpacht, H, 'The problem of jurisdictional immunities of foreign states' (1951) 28 BYIL 220

Lauterpacht, H, 'The problem of the revision of the laws of war' (1952) 29 BYIL 366

Lauterpacht, H, 'The limits of the operation of the laws of war' (1953) 30 BYIL

Lauterpacht, H, 'Codification and development of international law' (1955) 49 AJIL 16

Lavalle, RL, 'Dispute settlement under the Vienna Convention on succession of states in respect of treaties' (1979) 73 AJIL 407

Lee, RW, 'Hugo Grotius' (1946) 62 LQR 53

Leich, M, 'Destruction of Korean Airliner: action by international organisations' (1984) 78 AJIL 244

Lester, A, 'Government compliance with international human rights law' [1996] PL 187

Lim, R, 'EEZ legislation of ASEAN states' (1991) 40 ICLQ 170

Lissitzyn, O, 'The treatment of aerial intruders in recent practice in international law' (1953) 47 AJIL 554

Lissitzyn, O, 'Some implications of the U2 and RB 47 incidents' (1962) 56 AJIL 135

Lipinsky, GA (ed), *Law and Politics in the World Community*, 1953, Berkeley: California UP

Llewelyn, K, 'Some realism about realism' (1931) 44 HLR 1222

Lloyd, GER, *Aristotle: The Growth and Structure of his Thought*, 1968, Cambridge: CUP

Lloyd Jones, D, 'The Iran-United States Claims Tribunal: private rights and state responsibility' (1984) 24 Va JIL 259

Locke, J, *Two Treatises of Government* (1690), 1977, London: JM Dent

Locke, J, *Essay Concerning Human Understanding* (1690) 1990, Oxford: Clarendon

Lofgren, C, *The Plessy Case*, 1987, Oxford: OUP

Lowe, AV and Fitzmaurice, M, *Fifty Years of the International Court of Justice*, 1996, Cambridge: CUP

Lowe, AV, 'The development of the concept of the contiguous zone' (1981) 52 BYIL 109

Lowe, AV, 'The problems of extra-territorial jurisdiction: economic sovereignty and the search for a solution' (1985) 34 ICLQ 724

Lowe, AV, 'The role of equity in international law' (1992) 12 AYIL 54

Lowe, AV, '*Lockerbie* – changing the rules during the game' (1992) 51 CLJ 408

Lowe, AV, 'The International Court in a timorous mood' (1995) 54 CLJ 484

Lowe, AV, 'Shock verdict: nuclear war may or may not be unlawful' (1996) 55 CLJ 415

Lowe, AV, 'The *M/V Saiga*: the first case in the International Tribunal of the Law of the Sea' (1999) 48 ICLQ 187

Lowenfeld, A, 'US enforcement abroad: the constitution of international law' (1989) 83 AJIL 880

Lowenfeld, A, 'The constitution and international law continued' (1990) 84 AJIL 444

Lowenfeld, A, 'Kidnapping by government order: a follow up' (1990) 84 AJIL 712

Lowenfeld, A, 'Still more on kidnapping' (1991) 85 AJIL 655

Lyster, S, *International Wildlife Law*, 1985, Cambridge: CUP

Mackinnon, C, *Towards a Feminist Theory of the State*, 1989, Cambridge, Mass: Harvard UP

Macgibbon, I, 'Some observations on the part of protest in international law' (1953) 29 BYIL 119

Macgibbon, I, 'Customary international law and acquiesence' (1957) 33 BYIL 115

Maier, H, '*Ex gratia* payments and the Iranian Airline tragedy' (1989) 83 AJIL 325

Malanczuk, P, *Akehurst's Modern Introduction to International Law*, 7th edn, 1997, London: Routledge

Mann, FA, *The Legal Aspect of Money*, 1982, Oxford: OUP

Mann, FA, 'The sacrosanctity of foreign acts of state' (1943) 59 LQR 43

Mann, FA, 'Recognition of sovereignty' (1958) 16 MLR 226

Mann, FA, 'The doctrine of jurisdiction in international law' (1964) 111 HR 1

Mann, FA, 'International co-operation and national law' (1967) 42 BYIL 145

Mann, FA, 'The effect of state succession upon corporations' (1972) 88 LQR 57

Mann, FA, 'A new aspect of the restrictive theory of sovereign immunity' (1982) 31 ICLQ 573

Mann, FA, 'The doctrine of international jurisdiction revisited after twenty years' (1984) 186 HR 9

Mann, FA, 'International organisations as national corporations' (1991) 107 LQR 357

Marks, S, *The Riddle of All Constitutions: International Law, Democracy and the Critique of Ideology*, 2000, Oxford: OUP

Marks, S, 'Reservations unhinged' (1990) 39 ICLQ 300

Marquandt, P, 'Law without borders: the constitutionality of International Criminal Court' (1995) 33 Columbia Journal of Transnational Law

Marston, G, 'Low tide elevations and straight baselines' (1972) 46 BYIL 405

Marston, G, 'The origin of the personality of international organisations in United Kingdom law' (1990) 40 ICLQ 403

Marston, G, 'The incorporation of continental shelf rights into United Kingdom law' (1996) 45 ICLQ 13

Marston, G, 'The personality of the foreign state in English law' (1997) 56 CLJ 374

Massie, RK, *Dreadnought: Britain, Germany and the Coming of the Great War*, 1991, New York: Random House

Matheson, MJ, 'The opinions of the International Court of Justice on the threat or use of nuclear weapons' (1997) 91 AJIL 419

Mapp, W, *The Iran-United States Claims Tribunal: The First Ten Years 1981–1991*, 1993, Manchester: Manchester UP

Marks, S, 'Reservations unhinged: the *Belilos* case before the European Court of Human Rights' (1990) 39 ICLQ 300

Marks, S, 'The roots of the Universal Declaration of Human Rights in the French Revolution' (1998) 20 HRQ 483

Mavroidis, PV, 'Surveillance schemes: the GATT's new trade policy review mechanism' (1992) 13 Michigan Journal of International Law 374

McCorquodale, R, 'Self-determination: a human rights approach' (1994) 43 ICLQ 857

McCoubrey, H, *International Humanitarian Law*, 1990, Aldershot: Dartmouth

McCoubrey, H and White, N, *International Law and Armed Conflict*, 1992, Aldershot: Dartmouth

McDonald, R and Johnston, D (eds), *The Structure and Process of International Law: Essays in Legal Philosophy, Doctrine and Theory*, 1983, Dordrecht: Martinus Nijhoff

McDougal, M, Laswell, H and Chen, I, *Human Rights and World Public Order*, 1980, New Haven: Yale UP

McDougall, M, 'The Soviet Cuban quarantine and self-defence' (1963) 57 AJIL 597

McDougall, M, Laswell, H and Chen, I, 'Human rights for Women and world public order: the outlawing of sex based discrimination' (1975) 69 AJIL 497

McGoldrick, D, *The Human Rights Committee*, 1991, Oxford: OUP

McGoldrick, D, 'Sustainable development and human rights: an integrated conception' (1996) 45 ICLQ 796

McLellan, D, *Karl Marx: His Life and Thought*, 1973, London: Macmillan

McMahon, J, 'Legal aspects of outer space' (1962) 38 BYIL 339

McNair, A, *The Law of Treaties*, 1961, Oxford: Clarendon

McNair, A, *The Law of the Air*, Michael Kerr and Anthony Evans (eds), 3rd edn, 1964, London: Stevens

McNair, A, 'The legal meaning of war and the relation of war to reprisals' (1925) 11 TGS 45

McNair, A, 'The present position of the codification of international law' (1928) 13 TGS 120

McNair, A, 'The functions and differing legal character of treaties' (1930) 11 BYIL 101

McNair, A, 'The law relating to the Civil War in Spain' (1937) 53 LQR 471

McNair, A, 'Problems connected with the position of the merchant vessel in private international law with particular reference to the power of requisition' (1946) 31 TGS 30

McWhinney, E and Grzybowski, K, 'Soviet theory of international law for the seventies' (1983) 77 AJIL 862

Meeker, L, 'Defensive quarantine and the law' (1963) 57 AJIL 515

Mendelsohn, M, 'The European Court of Justice and Human Rights' (1981) 1 YEL 126

Mendelsohn, M, 'Practice, propaganda and principle in international law' (1990) CLP 3

Meron, T, 'Enhancing the effectiveness of the prohibition of discrimination against women' (1990) 84 AJIL 213

Meron, T, 'The time has come for the United States to ratify Geneva Protocol I' (1995) 89 AJIL 678

Meron, T, 'Common rights of mankind in Gentili, Grotius and Suarez' (1991) 85 AJIL 110

Merrills, J, International Dispute Settlement, 3rd edn, 1998, Cambridge: CUP

Merrills, J, 'The Land and Maritime Boundary case' (1997) 46 ICLQ 676

Merrills, J, International Dispute Settlement, 2nd edn, 1991, Cambridge: CUP

Merrills, J, Anatomy of International Law, 2nd edn, 1981, London: Sweet & Maxwell

Merrills, J, 'The International Court of Justice and the General Act of 1928' (1980) CLJ 137

Merrills, J, 'Recognition and construction' (1971) 20 ICLQ 476

Merrills, J, 'Morality and the international legal order' (1968) 31 MLR 520

Monk, R, Bertrand Russell: The Spirit of Solitude, 1996, London: Jonathan Cape

Moore, JN (ed), Law and Civil War in the Modern World, 1974, Ewing, New Jersey: Princeton UP

Moore, M (ed), National Self-Determination and Secession, 1998, Oxford: OUP

Moggridge, DE, Maynard Keynes: An Economist's Biography, 1992, London: Routledge

Morgenstern, F, 'Jurisdiction in seizures effected in violation of international law' (1952) 29 BYIL 256

Morgenthau, H, Politics Among Nations, 2nd edn, 1954, New York: Alfred Knopf

Morison, WL, 'Some myths about positivism' (1960) YLJ 212

Morsink, J, 'World War Two and the Universal Declaration' (1993) 15 HRQ 357

Mulgan, RG, *Aristotle's Political Theory: An Introduction for Students of Political Theory*, 1977, Oxford: OUP

Mullerson, R, 'Sources of international law: new tendencies in Soviet thinking' (1989) 83 AJIL 494

Mullerson, R, 'The continuity and succession of states by reference to the former USSR and Yugoslavia' (1993) 42 ICLQ 473

Mullerson, R, 'NATO enlargement and Russia' (1998) 47 ICLQ 172

Muluwa, T, 'The peaceful settlement of disputes among African states 1963–1983: some conceptual issues and practical trends' (1989) 38 ICLQ 299

Murdoch, J, 'The work of the Council of Europe's Torture Committee' (1994) 5 EJIL 220

Mutua, M, 'The African Human Rights Court: a two legged school?' (1999) 21 HRQ 342

Myers, P, 'Liquidation of the League of Nations functions' (1948) 42 AJIL 380

Naldi, G, 'Peace-keeping attempts by the Organisation of African Unity' (1985) 34 ICLQ 593

Ndulo, M, 'Harmonisation of trade laws in the African Economic Community' (1993) 42 ICLQ 101

Neff, S, 'Human Rights in Africa: thoughts on the African Charter on Human and Peoples' rights in the light of case law from Botswana, Lesotho and Swaziland' (1984) 33 ICLQ 331

Nelson, L, 'The patrimonial sea' (1974) 22 ICLQ 668

Nicholas, HG, *The United Nations as a Political Institution*, 1959, Oxford: OUP

Niebuhr, R, 'The illusion of world government' (1948) 27 Foreign Affairs 379

Northedge, FS, *The League of Nations*, 1986, Leicester: Leicester UP

Norton, P, 'A law of the future or a law of the past? Modern tribunals and the international law of expropriation' (1991) 85 AJIL 474

Nussbaum, A, *A Concise History of the Law of Nations*, 2nd edn, 1962, New York: Macmillan

O'Brien, CC, *To Katanga and Back: A United Nations Case History*, 1962, London: Chatto and Windus

O'Brien, CC, *Writers and Politics*, 1965, London: Chatto and Windus

O'Brien, J, *Smith's Conflict of Laws*, 2nd edn, 1999, London: Cavendish Publishing

O'Connell, DP, *State Succession in Municipal and International Law*, 1967, Cambridge: CUP

O'Connell, DP, 'Recent problems of state succession in relation to new states' (1970) 130 HR 95

O'Connell, DP, 'Mid ocean archipelagos in the international law of the sea' (1971) 45 BYIL 1

O'Connell, DP, 'The juridical status of the territorial sea' (1971) 45 BYIL 303

O'Connell, DP, 'The condominium of the New Hebrides' (1972) 43 BYIL 71

Oda, S, 'The concept of the contiguous zone' (1962) 11 ICLQ 131

Oda, S, 'Further thoughts on the Chambers Procedure of the International Court of Justice' (1988) 82 AJIL 556

Oeter, S, 'German unification and state succession' (1991) 51 Zao RV 349

O'Higgins, P, 'Unlawful seizure and irregular extradition' (1960) 36 BYIL 279

O'Keefe, R, 'Palm-fringed benefits: island dependencies in the new law of the sea' (1996) 45 ICLQ 408

Okere, O, 'The protection of human rights in Africa and the African Charter on Human and Peoples' Rights: a comparative analysis with the European and American Systems' (1984) 6 HRQ 141

Okowa, PN, 'Procedural obligations in international environmental agreements' (1996) 67 BYIL 275

Onuf, N, '*Civitas Maxima*: Wolff, Vattel and the fate of Republicanism' (1994) 88 AJIL 280

Oppenheim, LH, *International Law: A Treatise* (2 Vols) 1905, 1906 (2nd edn, 1912), London: Longman

Osieke, E, 'Majority voting systems in the International Labour Organisation and the International Monetary Fund' (1984) 33 ICLQ 381

Ostrihansky, R, 'Chambers of the International Court of Justice' (1988) 37 ICLQ 30

Oxman, B, 'The 1994 Agreement on the Implementation of the Seabed Provisions of the Convention on the Law of the Sea' (1994) 88 AJIL 687

Parry, C, 'The status of Germany and German internees' (1947) 10 MLR 403

Parry, C, *The Sources and Evidences of International Law*, 1965, Manchester: Manchester UP

Parry, JH, *The Age of Reconaissance*, 1963, New York: Mentor

Pearce Higgins, A, 'Ships of war as prize' (1925) 6 BYIL 103

Pepin, E, '*Le droit aerien*' (1947) 71 HR 477

Petersen, MJ, 'Recognition of governments should not be abolished' (1983) 77 AJIL 31

Petersmann, EU, 'The dispute system of the World Trade Organisation and the evolution of the GATT dispute system since 1948' [1994] 31 CMLR 1157

Phillimore, W (Lord), 'Scheme for the Permanent Court of International Justice' (1920) 6 TGS 89

Pinto, R, *'Les règles du droit international concernant la guerre civile'* (1965) 114 HR 451

Plant, G, 'The Convention for the Suppression of Unlawful Acts against the Safety of Maritime Navigation' (1990) 39 ICLQ 27

Plant, G, 'Safer ships, cleaner seas: Lord Donaldson's inquiry' (1995) 44 ICLQ 939

Plender, R, 'The role of consent in the termination of treaties' (1986) 57 BYIL 133

Pole, JR, *The Pursuit of Equality in American Life*, 1978, Berkley: Berkley UP

Pollock, E, 'The International Court of the League of Nations' (1921) 1 CLJ 29

Pomerance, M, 'The United Nations and self-determination' (1976) 70 AJIL 1

Pound, R, 'A survey of social interests' (1944) 57 HLR 1

Poulantzas, NM, *The Right of Hot Pursuit in International Law*, 1969, Leyden: Sijhoff

Priest, S, *The British Empiricists*, 1990, London: Penguin

Quane, H, 'The United States and the evolving right to self-determination' (1998) 47 ICLQ 537

Quigley, R, 'Perestroika and international law' (1988) 82 AJIL 788

Rayfuse, R, 'International abduction and the United States Supreme Court: the law of the jungle reigns' (1993) 42 ICLQ 882

Ratner, SR, 'Image and reality in the United Nation's peaceful settlement of disputes' (1995) 6 EJIL 426

Rawlings, R, 'Legal politics: the United Kingdom and the ratification of the TEU' [1994] PL 254

Reeves, J, 'The Hague Conference on the Codification of International Law' (1930) 24 AJIL 52

Reisman, WM, 'The regime of Straits and national security: an appraisal of international law making' (1980) 74 AJIL 48

Reisman, WM, 'The breakdown of the control mechanism in ICSID arbitration' (1989) 4 Duke LJ 739

Reisman, WM, 'International law after the Cold War' (1990) 84 AJIL 859

Reisman, WM, 'The constitutional crisis in the United Nations' (1993) 87 AJIL 83

Reisman, WM, 'Preparing to wage peace: toward the creation of an international peacemaking command and staff college' (1994) 88 AJIL 76

Reisman, WM, 'Protecting indigenous rights in international adjudication' (1995) 89 AJIL 350

Ress, G, 'The legal status of Hong Kong after 1997' (1986) 46 Zao RV 647

Reynolds, PA, *An Introduction to International Relations*, 3rd edn, 1994, London: Longman

Rhodes ,R, *The Making of the Atomic Bomb*, 1988, Harmondsworth: Penguin

Rich, R, 'The right to development as an emerging human right' (1983) 23 Va JIL 287

Righter R, *Utopia Lost: The United Nations and World Order*, 1995, New York: Twentieth Century Fund

Roberts, A and Guelff, R, *Documents on the Laws of War*, 3rd edn, 2000, Oxford: OUP

Roberts, A and Kingsbury, B (eds), *United Nations, Divided World*, 2nd edn, 1993, Oxford: OUP

Robertson, AH and Merrills, J, *Human Rights in the World*, 4th edn, 1996, Manchester: Manchester UP

Robertson, G, *Crimes Against Humanity: The Struggle for Global Justice*, 1999, London: Penguin

Rodley, N, 'Conceptual problems in the protection of minorities' international legal developments' (1995) 17 HRQ 48

Rogers, AP, *Law on the Battlefield*, 1996, Manchester: Manchester UP

Rosencranz, A, 'The ECE Convention of 1979 on Long Range Transboundary Air Pollution' (1981) 75 AJIL 975

Rosenne, S, 'The International Law Commission (1949–1959)' (1960) 36 BYIL 104

Rosenne, S, *Breach of Treaty*, 1985, Cambridge: CUP

Roth, P, 'Reasonable extraterritriality' (1992) 41 ICLQ 245

Rousseau, C, *Droit International Public*, 1953, Paris: Sirey

Rousseau, C, *Principes de Droit International Public* (1958) 93 HR 369

Rousseau, JJ, *Du Contrat Social* (1762) (*The Social Contract and Discourses*, Cole, GDH (trans), 1913, London: Everyman's Library)

Rowlands, I, *The Politics of Global Atmospheric Change*, 1995, Manchester: Manchester UP

Rowson, S, 'Modern blockade: some legal aspects' (1946) 23 BYIL 346

Rubin, AP, 'Correspondence on United States ratification of Geneva Protocol I' (1995) 89 AJIL 363

Sands, P and Boisson de Chazournes, L (ed), *International Law, the International Court of Justice and Nuclear Weapons*, 1997, Cambridge: CUP

Sands, P, *Principles of International Environmental Law*, 1995, Manchester: Manchester UP

Sands, P, 'International law in the field of sustainable development' (1994) 65 BYIL 303

Sanders, D, 'Collective rights' (1991) 13 HRQ 368

Sarooshi, D, *The United Nations and the Development of Collective Security*, 1999, Oxford: Clarendon

Schachter, O, 'Dag Hammarskjold and the relation of law to politics' (1962) 56 AJIL 1

Schachter, O, 'The emerging international law of development' (1976) 15 Columbia Journal of Transnational Law 1

Schachter, O, 'The twilight existence of non binding international agreements' (1977) 71 AJIL 296

Schachter, O, 'Human dignity as a normative concept' (1983) 77 AJIL 848

Schachter, O, 'Compensation for expropriation' (1984) 78 AJIL 121

Scheman, LR, 'The Inter American Commission on Human Rights' (1965) 59 AJIL 335

Schermers, H, 'The scales in the balance: National Constitutional Court v Court of Justice' [1990] 27 CMLR 97

Schermers, H, 'The European Community bound by Fundamental Human Rights' [1990] 27 CMLR 249

Schermers, HG, 'The Eleventh Protocol to the European Convention on Human Rights' (1994) 17 ELR 367

Schindler, D, 'The different types of armed conflict according to the Geneva Conventions and Protocols' (1979) 163 HR 117

Schoenbaum, TJ, 'WTO dispute settlement: praise and suggestions for reform' (1998) 47 ICLQ 647

Schwarzenberger, G, *Power Politics*, 1941, London: Stevens

Schwarzenberger, G, *International Law*, 3rd edn, 1957, London: Stevens

Schwarzenberger, G, *International Law*, Volume 2, *The Law of Armed Conflict*, 1958, London: Stevens

Schwarzenberger, G, '*Jus pacis ac belli?*' (1943) 37 AJIL 430

Schwarzenberger, G, 'Title to territory: response to a challenge' (1957) 57 AJIL 308

Schwarzenberger, G, 'The *Eichmann* judgment' [1962] CLP 248

Schwebel, S, *The Secretary General of the United Nations*, 1952, Cambridge, Mass: Harvard UP

Schwebel, S, '*Ad hoc* Chambers of the International Court of Justice' (1987) 81 AJIL 831

Schwebel, S, 'Was the capacity to request an advisory opinion wider in the Permanent Court of International Justice in the International Court of Justice?' (1991) 62 BYIL 77

Schwelb, E, 'The International Court of Justice and the human rights clauses of the Charter' (1972) 66 AJIL 337

Scobie, I, 'Towards the elimination of international law: some radical scepticism about sceptical radicalism' (1990) 61 BYIL 339

Scott, JB, 'The legal nature of international law' (1907) 1 AJIL 831

Seidl-Hohenveldern, I, *International Economic Law*, 2nd edn, 1992, The Hague: Kluwer

Seidl-Hohenveldern, I, 'Piercing the corporate veil of international organisations: the International Tin Council in the English Court of Appeals' (1989) 32 GYIL 43

Seyersted, F, 'Applicable law in relations between intergovernmental organisations and private parties' (1967) 122 HR 427

Sharpe, AW, 'The first three years of WTO dispute settlement: observation and comment' (1998) 1 Journal of International Economic Law 277

Sharpston, E, 'Legitimate expectations and economic reality' (1990) 15 ELR 103

Shaw, M, *International Law*, 4th edn, 1997, Cambridge: CUP

Shaw, M, '*Case concerning the Land, Island and Maritime Frontier Dispute*' (1993) 42 ICLQ 929

Shaw, M, *Title to Territory in Africa: International Legal Issues*, 1986, Oxford: OUP

Shaw, M, 'Legal acts of an unrecognised entity' (1978) 94 LQR 500

Shawcross, C and Beaumont, P, *Air Law*, 4th edn, 1977, London: Sweet & Maxwell

Shearer, I, 'The internationalisation of Australian law' (1995) 17 Sydney L Rev 121

Shearer, IA, *Starke's International Law*, 11th edn, 1994, London: Butterworths

Shihata, IF, 'The Multilateral Investment Guarantee Agency and the legal treatment of foreign investment' (1987) 203 HR 95

Sieghart, P, *The International Law of Human Rights*, 1983, Oxford: Clarendon

Sinclair, I, *The International Law Commission*, 1967, Manchester: Manchester UP

Sinclair, I, *The Vienna Convention on the Law of Treaties*, 1984, 2nd edn, Manchester: Manchester UP

Sinclair, I, 'Nationality of claims: British practice' (1950) 27 BYIL 125

Sinclair, I, 'The principles of treaty interpretation' (1963) 12 ICLQ 508

Sinclair, I, 'Some procedural aspects of recent international litigation' (1981) 30 ICLQ 338

Simpson, FD, 'How far does the Law of England forbid Monopoly ?' (1925) 41 LQR 393

Singer, M, 'The United Kingdom act of state doctrine' (1981) 75 AJIL 283

Singer, P, *Marx*, 1980, Oxford: OUP

Singer, P, *Hegel,* 1983, Oxford: OUP

Singh, N, *Nuclear Weapons and International Law,* 1959

Skidelsky, R, *John Maynard Keynes Vol 1 – Hopes Betrayed,* 1983, London: Macmillan

Skidelsky, R, *John Maynard Keynes Vol 2 – The Economist as Saviour,* 1991, London: Macmillan

Skidelsky, R, *John Maynard Keynes Vol 3 – Fighting for Britain,* 2000, London: Macmillan

Sloan, B, 'The binding force of a 'recommendation' of the General Assembly of the United Nations' (1948) 25 BYIL 1

Sloan, B, 'General Assembly Resolutions (revisited)' (1988) 58 BYIL 41

Smith, HA, 'The Declaration of Paris in modern war' (1939) 55 LQR 237

Sofaer, A, 'The rationale for the United States decision' (1988) 82 AJIL 784

Sohn, L, 'International law implications of the 1994 Agreement' (1994) 88 AJIL 696

Sornarajah, M, *The International Law of Foreign Investment,* 1994, Cambridge: CUP

Sornarajah, M, 'Problems in applying the restrictive theory of sovereign immunity' (1982) 31 ICLQ 661

Springer, A, 'Towards a meaningful concept of pollution in international law' (1977) 26 ICLQ 531

Stallybrass, W, 'Dangerous things and the non natural user of land' (1929) 3 CLJ 376

Stamatopoulu, E, 'Indigenous peoples and the United Nations' (1994) 16 HRQ 58

Stein, L, 'Jurisprudence and jurists' prudence: the Iranian forum clause decisions of the Iran-US Claims Tribunal' (1984) 78 AJIL 1

Steiner, H and Alston, P, *International Human Rights in Context,* 1996, Oxford: OUP

Steiner, J, *Enforcing EC Law,* 1995, London: Blackstone

Steiner, J, *Textbook on EEC Law,* 5th edn, 1996, London: Blackstone

Stowell, EC, 'The laws of war and the atomic bomb' (1945) 39 AJIL 784

Strupp, K, *'Le droit du juge international de statuer selon l'équité'* (1930) 33 HR 3515

Sunga, L, 'The Commission of Experts on Rwanda and the creation of the International Tribunal for Rwanda' (1995) 16 HRLJ 121

Sullivan, D, 'Gender equality and religious freedom: toward a framework for conflict resolution' (1992) 24 NYU J Int Law & Politics 795

Symmons, C, *The Maritime Zones of Islands in International Law,* 1979, The Hague: Martinus Nijhoff

Symmons, C, 'United Kingdom abolition of the doctrine of recognition of governments' [1981] PL 249

Symmons, C, 'The Rockall dispute deepens: an analysis of recent Danish and Icelandic actions' (1986) 35 ICLQ 344

Taylor, AJP, *The Hapsburg Monarchy*, 1948, London: Hamish Hamilton

Taylor, AJP, *The Struggle for Mastery in Europe*, 1954, Oxford: OUP

Taylor, AJP, *English History (1914–1945)*, 1965, Oxford: Clarendon

Taylor, AJP, *The First World War*, 1965, London: Hamish Hamilton

Taylor, C, *Hegel*, 1975, Oxford: OUP

Thirlway, H, *International Customary Law and Codification*, 1972, Leiden: Sijthoff

Thornberry, P, *International Law and Minorities*, 1991, Oxford: OUP

Thornberry, P, 'Is there a phoenix in the ashes? International law and minority rights' (1980) 15 Texas Int LJ 421

Thornberry, P, 'Self determination, minorities, human rights, a review of international instruments' (1989) 38 ICLQ 867

Tridmans, T, *The General Principles of EC Law*, 2000, Oxford: OUP

Triepel, H, *Volkerrecht und Landesrecht* (1899), 1958, Aalen: Scientia Antiquariat

Tucker, RW, 'Reprisals and self defence: the customary law' (1972) 66 AJIL 586

Tunkin, GI, 'Co-existence and international law' (1958) 95 HR 1

Tunkin, GI, 'The legal nature of the United Nations' (1966) 119 HR 1

Tunkin, GI, 'International law in the international system' (1975) 147 HR 1

Tunkin, GI, 'Politics, law and force in the interstate system' (1989) 219 HR 227

Tunkin, GI, 'The contemporary Soviet theory in international law' (1978) CLP 177

Twining, W, *Karl Llewelyn and the Realist Movement*, 1973, London, Weidenfeld & Nicholson

Umbricht, VH, *Multilateral Mediation: Practical Experiences and Lessons*, 1989, Dordrecht: Kluwer

Umzurike, U, 'The African Charter on Human and Peoples' Rights' (1983) 77 AJIL 902

Unger, R, *The Critical Legal Studies Movement*, 1983, Cambridge, Mass: Harvard UP

Unger, R, 'Legal analysis as institutional imagination' (1996) 59 MLR 11

Urquhart, B, *Hammarskjold*, 1973, New York: Simon and Schuster

Vamvoukis, A, *Termination of Treaties in International Law: The Doctrines of* Rebus Sic Stantibus *and Desuetude*, 1985, Oxford: OUP

Vasquez, CM, 'The Four Doctrines of Self Executing Treaties' (1995) 89 AJIL 695

de Vattel, E, *Le Droit des Gens ou Principes de la loi naturelle appliqés a la conduite et aux affaires des nations et des souverains* (1758), de Lapradelle, A (trans), Washington DC: Carnegie Institution

Vierdag, E, 'The legal nature of the rights granted by the International Covenant on Economic, Social and Cultural Rights' (1978) 9 NYIL 69

de Visscher, C, *Theory and Reality in Public International Law*, Corbett, P (trans), 1957, Princeton: Princeton UP

Voitovich, SA, 'The commonwealth of independent states: an emerging institutional model' (1992) 3 EJIL 403

Volterra, R, 'The *Nuclear Tests* case: avoiding the meta juridical' (1996) 55 CLJ 3

Von Verdross, A, *'Les principes généraux du droit dans la jurisprudence internationale'* (1935) 52 HR 191

Watson, JS, 'Auto interpretation, competence and the continuing validity of Article 2(7) of the United Nations Charter' (1977) 71 AJIL 60

Waldock, CHM, *'Forum prorogatum* or acceptance of a unilateral summons to appear before the International Court' (1948) 2 ILQ 377

Waldock, CHM, 'The *Anglo Norwegian Fisheries* case' (1951) 28 BYIL 114

Walker, M, *German National Socialism and the Quest for Nuclear Power (1938–1949)*, 1989, Cambridge: CUP

Walker, W, 'Territorial waters: the canon shot rule' (1945) 22 BYIL 210

Wallace, R, *International Human Rights*, 1997, London: Sweet & Maxwell

Warbrick, C, 'Kampuchea: representation and recognition' (1981) 31 ICLQ 234

Warbrick, C, 'Executive certificates in foreign affairs: prospects for review and control' (1986) 35 ICLQ 138

Warbrick, C, 'The invasion of Kuwait by Iraq' (1991) 40 ICLQ 482

Warbrick, C, 'Recent developments in the recognition of states' (1992) 41 ICLQ 473

Warbrick, C, 'Recognition of governments' (1993) 56 MLR 92

Warbrick, C and Rowe, P, 'The International Criminal Tribunal for Yugoslavia: the decision of the Appeals Chamber on the *Interlocutory Appeal on Jurisdiction in the Tadic* case (1996) 45 ICLQ 691

Wasserman, G, *The Juridical Bay*, 1987, Oxford: OUP

Weatherill, S and Beaumont, P, *EC Law*, 2nd edn, 1995, London: Penguin

Weeramantry, C, 'The right to development' (1985) 25 IJIL 482

Wegen, G, 'Discontinuance of international proceedings: the *Hostages* case' (1982) 76 AJIL 717

Weller, M, 'The international response to the dissolution of the Socialist Federal Republic of Yugoslavia' (1992) 86 AJIL 569

Weller, M, 'Peacekeeping and peace enforcement in the Republic of Bosnia-Herzegovina' (1996) 56 Zao RV 70

West, R, 'Jurisprudence and gender' (1988) 55 University of Chicago L Rev 1

G Westerman, *The Juridical Bay*, 1987, Oxford: OUP

Wetter, JG, 'The *Rann of Kutch* Arbitration' (1971) 65 AJIL 346

Whelan, A, 'Wilsonian self determination and the Versailles Settlement' (1994) 43 ICLQ 99

White, G, *Nationalisation of Foreign Property*, 1961, Manchester: Manchester UP

White, GE, 'The Marshall Court and international law: the *Piracy* cases' (1989) 83 AJIL 727

White, N, *Keeping the Peace: The United Nations and The Maintenance of International Peace and Security*, 1990, Manchester: Manchester UP

Wilmhurst, E, 'Executive certificates in foreign affairs: the United Kingdom' (1986) 35 ICLQ 157

Wood, M, 'The dissolution of the League of Nations' (1946) 13 BYIL 317

Woodliffe, J, 'Chernobyl: four years on' (1990) 39 ICLQ 461

Woolf, C, *Bartolus of Sassoferrato: His Position in the History of Medieval Political Thought*, 1913, Cambridge: CUP

Woolsey, L, 'Commissions of inquiry and concilliation, Bolivia and Paraguay' (1929) 23 AJIL 110; (1930) 24 AJIL 122

Wortley, B, *Expropriation in Public International Law*, 1959, Manchester: Manchester UP

Wright, Q, 'The legal nature of treaties' (1916) 10 AJIL 706

Wright, Q, 'When does war exist?' (1932) 26 AJIL 362

Wright, Q, 'Legal aspects of the U2 incident' (1960) 54 AJIL 836

Wright, Q, 'The Cuban quarantine' (1963) 57 AJIL 546

Wyatt, D and Dashwood, A, *European Community Law*, 3rd edn, 1993, London: Sweet & Maxwell

Yolton, JW, *Locke: An Introduction*, 1985, Oxford: Basil Blackwell

Zander, M, 'The act of state doctrine' (1959) 53 AJIL 826

Zemanek, K, 'State succession after decolonisation' (1965) 116 HR 181

Zoglin, K, 'United Nations action against slavery: a critical evaluation' (1986) 8 HRQ 306

Zoller, E, 'The Second Session of the United Nations Committee against Torture' (1989) 7 NQHR 250